Index of American Periodical Verse: 1991

Rafael Catalá

and

James D. Anderson

assisted by

Martha Park Sollberger

The Scarecrow Press, Inc.
Metuchen, N.J., & London
1993

Library of Congress Catalog Card No. 73-3060
ISBN 0-8108-2724-7
Copyright © 1993 by Rafael Catalá and James D. Anderson
Manufactured in the United States of America
Printed on acid-free paper

Contents

Contents

Preface

This volume of the *Index* was produced with the cooperation of 287 participating periodicals from Canada, the United States, and the Caribbean. More than 6,900 entries for individual poets and translators are included, with more than 18,000 entries for individual poems. A separate index provides access by title or first line.

The importance of the *Index* continues to grow as its necessity becomes more apparent in circles of contemporary poetry research. The increasing demand for inclusion corroborates this fact. The *Index* constitutes an objective measure of poetry in North America, recording not only the publication of our own poets in Canada, the U.S. and the Caribbean, but also those from other lands and cultures and from other times. Of course, the *Index*'s primary purpose is to show what poems have been published by particular poets, what poems have been translated by particular translators, and who wrote poems with particular titles or first lines. But taken together, the *Index* reveals trends and influences: the ebb and flow of particular poets, as well as the influence of cultures of other lands and times as represented by their poets published in North American journals.

James D. Anderson has made a major contribution to the *Index* by designing and refining computer programs that have greatly facilitated the indexing process, proof-reading and error-checking, control of cross references and consistency in names, sorting, formatting and typesetting. To him also goes credit for managing relations with participating journals and seeing that all indexing gets done in a timely and accurate manner. Also, I want to express my sincere appreciation to Martha Park Sollberger, librarian *emerita*, for her valuable assistance.

Rafael Catalá
Co-Editor

Introduction

Scope

The *Index of American Periodical Verse* indexes poems published in a broad cross-section of poetry, literary, scholarly, popular, general, and "little" magazines, journals and reviews published in the United States, Canada, and the Caribbean. These periodicals are listed in the "Periodicals Indexed" section, together with name of editor(s), address, issues indexed in this volume, and subscription information. Selection of periodicals to index is the responsibility of the editors, based on recommendations of poets, librarians, literary scholars and publishers. Publishers participate by supplying copies of all issues to the editors. Criteria for inclusion include the quality of poems and their presentation and the status or reputation of poets. Within these very broad and subjective guidelines, the editors attempt to include a cross-section of periodicals by type of publisher and/or publication, place of publication, language, and type of poetry. Periodicals published outside of North America are included only if they have North American editors.

Compilation

Citation data are compiled using the WordStar word-processing program, version 4, on a 286 MS/DOS computer. "Shorthand" macro programs are used to repeat author headings for multiple poems by the same poet, create translator entries from author entries for translated poems, and transform complex author names into cross-reference entries. Sorting is done by "IOTA Big Sort," a fast program for sorting very large files written by Fred A. Rowley. Title entries were extracted from the original author entries and sorted. Formatted author and title entries were transferred to a Macintosh computer with laser printer for typesetting and page formatting using MacWrite and PageMaker programs.

Persons interested in the precise details of compilation, including the computer programs used for error checking, sorting and formatting, should write to the editors at P.O. Box 38, New Brunswick, NJ 08903-0038. The *Indexes* for 1982 through 1991 are available from the editors on micro-computer disks.

Names and Cross References

Because many poets have compound surnames and surnames containing various prefixes, we recognize the need for systematic provision of cross references from alternative forms of name to the form chosen for entry in the *Index*. We have included cross references whenever the form used for entry does not fall under the last part or element of the name. In addition, many poets publish under different forms of the same name, for example, with or without a middle initial. When poets are known to use different forms of the same name, alternative forms may be indicated using the format authorized by the *Anglo-American Cataloguing Rules*, Second Edition. For example:

WHEATLEY, Pat (Patience)

This heading indicates that this poet has poems published under two forms of name: Pat Wheatley and Patience Wheatley.

When two or more different names refer to the same poet, one name will be chosen, with "see" references to the chosen name from other names. When it is not possible to determine with assurance whether a single poet is using variant forms of name or different poets have similar names, both names will be used. In such cases, "see also" references may be added to headings to remind users to check the variant name forms which might possibly refer to the same poet.

Format and Arrangement of Entries

The basic format and style of the *Index* remain unchanged. Poets are arranged alphabetically first by surname, then by forenames. In creating this alphabetical sequence, we have adopted principles of the filing rules issued in 1980 by the American Library Association and the Library of Congress. Names are arranged on the basis of their spelling, rather than their pronunciation, so that, for example, names beginning with "Mac" and "Mc" are no longer interfiled. Similarly, the space consistently counts as a filing element, so that similar compound and prefixed surnames are often separated by some distance, as illustrated in the following examples. Note that "De BOLT" precedes "DeBEVOISE" by a considerable number of entries.

De ANGELIS	Van BRUNT
De BOLT	Van DUYN
De GRAVELLES	Van HALTEREN
De LOACH	Van TOORN
De PALCHI	Van TROYER
De RONSARD	Van WERT
De VAUL	Van WINCKEL
DEAL	VANCE
DeBEVOISE	Vander DOES
DeFOE	VANDERBEEK
DEGUY	VanDEVENTER
Del VECCHIO	
DeLISLE	
DeMOTT	
DENNISON	
Der HOVANESSIAN	
DESY	
DeYOUNG	

Abbreviations are also arranged on the basis of spelling, rather than pronunciation, so that "ST. JOHN" is *not* filed as "SAINT JOHN", but as "ST+space+JOHN". Punctuation, signs and symbols other than alphabetic letters and numerals are not considered; a hyphen is filed as if it were a space and apostrophes and accents are ignored for purposes of filing. In title entries, initial articles are also ignored. Numerals are arranged in numerical order preceding alphabetical letters rather than as if they were spelled out.

Under each poet's name, poems are arranged alphabetically by title or, if there is no title, by first line. Poems with only "Untitled" printed as if it were the title are entered as "Untitled" followed by the first line of the poem. In the title index, two entries are provided, one under "Untitled" followed by the first line, and one directly under the first line. Numbered poems are handled in the same way. Under poets, initial numbers are treated as the first part of titles, and they are so entered. In the title index, they are entered both under their initial numbers and under the part following the number, if any.

Poem titles and first lines are placed within quotation marks. All significant words of titles are capitalized, but in first lines, only the first word and proper nouns are capitalized. Incomplete excerpts from larger works are followed by the note "Excerpt" or "Excerpts", or, if they are presented as complete sections, by "Selection" or "Selections". The title, first line or number of excerpts or selections may follow if given in the publication. For example:

WALCOTT, Derek
"Midsummer" (Selections: XXXIV-XXXVI). [Agni] (18) 83, p. 5-7.

WEBB, Phyllis
"The Vision Tree" (Selection: "I Daniel"). [PoetryCR] (5:2) Wint 83-84, p. 11.

WAINWRIGHT, Jeffrey
"Heart's Desire" (Excerpt: "Some Propositions and Part of a Narrative"). [Agni] (18) 83, p. 37.

WATTEN, Barret
"One Half" (Excerpts). [ParisR] (24:86) Wint 82, p. 112-113.

If an excerpt is treated as a complete "sub-work", it receives an independent entry, with reference to the larger work in a note. For example:

ANDERSON, Jack
"Magnets" (from "The Clouds of That Country"). [PoNow] (7:2, #38) 83, p. 23.

Notes about dedications, joint authors, translators, and sources follow the title, enclosed in parentheses. A poem with more than one author is entered under each author. Likewise, a translated poem is entered under each translator, as well as its author(s). Each entry includes the names of all authors and all translators. Multiple authors or translators are indicated by the abbreviation "w.", standing for "with". Translators are indicated by the abbreviation "tr. by", standing for "translated by", and original authors are indicated by the abbreviation "tr. of", standing for "translation of". For example:

AGGESTAM, Rolf
"Old Basho" (tr. by Erland Anderson and Lars Nordström).
[NewRena] (16) Spr 83, p. 25.

ANDERSON, Erland
"Old Basho" (tr. of Rolf Aggestam, w. Lars Nordström).
[NewRena] (16) Spr 83, p. 25.

NORDSTRÖM, Lars
"Old Basho" (tr. of Rolf Aggestam, w. Erland Anderson).
[NewRena] (16) Spr 83, p. 25.

The periodical citation includes an abbreviation standing for the periodical title, followed by volume and issue numbers, date, and page or pages on which the poem appears. The periodical abbreviation is enclosed in square brackets. An alphabetical list of these periodical abbreviations is included at the front of the volume, followed by the full periodical title, name of editor(s), address, the numbers of the issues indexed for this volume of the *Index*, and subscription information. A separate list of indexed periodicals is arranged by full periodical title, with a reference to the abbreviated title. Volume and issue numbers are included within parentheses, e.g., (16:5) stands for volume 16, number 5; (21) refers to issue 21 for a periodical which does not use volume numbers. Dates are given using abbreviations for months and seasons. Year of publication is indicated by the last two digits of the year, e.g., 90. There is a list of abbreviations at the front of the volume.

Compiling this year's *Index* has been an adventure into the wealth and variety of poetry published in U. S., Caribbean and Canadian periodicals as well as the intricacies of bringing this richness together and organizing it into a consistent index. The world of poetry publication is a dynamic one, with new periodicals appearing, older periodicals declining, dying, reviving and thriving. This year saw the loss of 15 periodicals and the addition of 13 new ones. Both deleted and newly added periodicals are listed at the front of the volume. Keeping up with these changes is a big job, and we solicit suggestions as to periodicals which should be included in future volumes of the *Index*, and also, periodicals which could be dropped. Editors who would like their periodicals considered for inclusion in future volumes should send sample issues to:

Rafael Catalá, Editor
Index of American Periodical Verse
P.O. Box 38
New Brunswick, NJ 08903-0038

Although indexing is indispensable for the organization of any literature so that particular works can be found when needed and scholarship and research facilitated, it is a tedious business. I know that we have made mistakes. We solicit your corrections and suggestions, which you may send to me at the above address.

James D. Anderson
Co-Editor

Abbreviations

dir., dirs.	director, directors
ed., eds.	editor, editors
(for.)	price for foreign countries
(ind.)	price for individuals
(inst.)	price for institutions
(lib.)	price for libraries
NS	new series
p.	page, pages
po. ed.	poetry editor
pub.	publisher
(stud.)	price for students
tr. by	translated by
tr. of	translation of
U.	University
w.	with

Months

Ja	January	Jl	July
F	February	Ag	August
Mr	March	S	September
Ap	April	O	October
My	May	N	November
Je	June	D	December

Seasons

Aut	Autumn	Spr	Spring
Wint	Winter	Sum	Summer

Years

87	1987	90	1990
88	1988	91	1991
89	1989	92	1992

Periodicals Added

Periodical acronyms are followed by titles. Full information may be found in the list of periodicals indexed.

13thMoon: 13TH MOON: A Feminist Literary Magazine

Archae: ARCHAE

Elf: ELF: Eclectic Literary Forum

HopewellR: ARTS INDIANA LITERARY SUPPLEMENT

LouisL : LOUISIANA LITERATURE

Nuez: LA NUEZ: Revista Internacional de Arte y Literatura

PaintedHR: PAINTED HILLS REVIEW

PlumR: THE PLUM REVIEW

Sidewalks: SIDEWALKS: An Anthology of Poetry, Short Prose, & Art

SnailPR: THE SNAIL'S PACE REVIEW: A Biannual Little Magazine of Contemporary Poetry

Spitball: SPITBALL: The Literary Baseball Magazine

TickleAce: TICKLEACE

WorldL: WORLD LETTER

Periodicals Deleted

Acts: ACTS: A Journal of New Writing, David Levi Strauss, ed. & pub., 514 Guerrero St., San Francisco, CA 94110. No 1990 or 1991 issues received. Letters not answered.

AlphaBS: ALPHA BEAT SOUP, Dave Christy, ed., 68 Winter Ave., Scarborough, Ont. M1K 4M3 Canada. No 1990 or 1991 issues received. Ceased publication.

BallSUF: BALL STATE UNIVERSITY FORUM, Bruce W. Hozeski, ed., Darlene Mathis-Eddy, po. ed., Ball State U., Muncie, IN 47306. Ceased publication.

Cond: CONDITIONS: A Feminist Magazine of Writing by Women with an Emphasis on Writing by Lesbians, Cheryl Clarke, Melinda Goodman, Paula Martinac, Mariana Romo-Carmona, P. Mikie Sugino, eds., P.O. Box 159046, Van Brunt Station, Brooklyn, NY 11215-9046. Ceased publication in journal form. "Conditions will appear from now on as an anthology, . . . and will be published less frequently."

CrossC: CROSS-CANADA WRITERS' MAGAZINE, Ted Plantos, ed., George Swede, po. ed., 137 Birmingham St., Stratford, Ontario N5A 2T1 Canada. Superseded by "Paragraph: The Fiction Magazine."

FiveFR: FIVE FINGERS REVIEW, Aleka Chase, Elizabeth Claman, Marsha Drummond, J. Malcolm Garcia, John High, eds., 553 - 25th Ave., San Francisco, CA 94121. No 1990 or 1991 issues received. Letter returned by postal service.

Gargoyle: GARGOYLE MAGAZINE, Richard Peabody, Peggy Pfeiffer, eds., Paycock Press, P.O. Box 30906, Bethesda, MD 20814. Ceased publication.

HeliconN: HELICON NINE: The Journal of Women's Arts & Letters, Gloria Vando Hickok, ed., P.O. Box 22412, Kansas City, MO 64113. Ceased publication.

KeyWR: KEY WEST REVIEW, William J. Schlicht, Jr., ed., 9 Ave. G, Key West, FL 33040. Ceased publication.

LightY: LIGHT YEAR: The Biennial of Light Verse & Witty Poems, Robert Wallace, ed., Bits Press, Dept. of English, Case Western Reserve U., Cleveland, OH 44106. Ceased publication.

Lyra: LYRA, Lourdes Gil, Iraida Iturralde, eds., P.O. Box 3188, Guttenberg, NJ 07093. No 1990 or 1991 issues received. Letters not answered.

PaperAir: PAPER AIR, Gil Ott, ed. and pub., Singing Horse Press, P.O. Box 40034, Philadelphia, PA 19106. Ceased publication.

Rampike: RAMPIKE, Karl Jirgens, Jim Francis, James Gray, eds., 95 Rivercrest Road, Toronto, Ontario M6S 4H7 Canada. No 1990 or 1991 issues received. Letters not answered.

Screens: SCREENS AND TASTED PARALLELS, Terrel Hale, ed. & pub., 3032 Emerson St., Palo Alto, CA 94306. Letter returned by postal service.

Temblor: TEMBLOR, Contemporary Poets, Leland Hickman, ed., 4624 Cahuenga Blvd., #307, North Hollywood, CA 91602. No 1990 or 1991 issues received. Letters not answered.

Periodicals Indexed

Arranged by acronym, with names of editors, addresses, issues indexed, and subscription information. New titles added to the *Index* in 1991 are marked with an asterisk (*).

*13thMoon: 13TH MOON : A Feminist Literary Magazine, Judith Emlyn Johnson, ed., Judith Johnson, Mary Ann Murray, Miranda Sherwin, po. eds., Dept. of English, State U. of NY, Albany, NY 12222. Issues indexed: (9:1/2). Subscriptions: $8/1 vol., $15/2 vols., $21.50/3 vols.

Abraxas: ABRAXAS, Ingrid Swanberg, ed., 2518 Gregory St., Madison, WI 53711. Issues indexed: (40/41). Subscriptions: $12/4 issues; Single issues: $3; Double issues: $6.

Aerial: AERIAL, Rod Smith, ed., P.O. Box 25642, Washington, DC 20007. Issues indexed: (6/7). Subscriptions: $20/3 issues; Single issues: $7.50; Double issues: $15.

Agni: AGNI, Askold Melnyczuk, ed., Creative Writing Program, Boston U., 236 Bay State Rd., Boston, MA 02115. Issues indexed: (33-34). Subscriptions: $12/yr., $23/2 yrs., $34/3 yrs.; $24/yr. (inst.); plus $5/yr. (for.); Single issues: $7.

Amelia: AMELIA, Frederick A. Raborg, Jr., ed., 329 "E" St., Bakersfield, CA 93304. Issues indexed: No 1991 issues received. Subscriptions: $20/yr. (4 issues), $38/2 yrs., $56/3 yrs.; $22/yr., $42/2 yrs., $62/3 yrs. (Canada, Mexico); $36/yr., $70/2 yrs., $104/3 yrs. (for. air mail); Single issues: $6.50, $7 (Canada & Mexico), $10 (for. air mail).

Americas: THE AMERICAS REVIEW, A Review of Hispanic Literature and Art of the USA, Julián Olivares, ed., U. of Houston, Houston, TX 77204-2090. Issues indexed: (19:1). Subscriptions: $15/yr. (ind.), $20/yr. (inst.); Single issues: $5; Double issues. $10.

AmerPoR: THE AMERICAN POETRY REVIEW, Stephen Berg, David Bonanno, Arthur Vogelsang, eds., 1721 Walnut St., Philadelphia, PA 19103. Issues indexed: (20:1-6). Subscriptions: $13/yr., $23/2 yrs., $32/3 yrs.; $16/yr., $29/2 yrs., $41/3 yrs. (for.); classroom rate $6.50/yr. per student; Single issues: $2.75. PA residents add 6% sales tax.

AmerS: THE AMERICAN SCHOLAR, Joseph Epstein, ed., The Phi Beta Kappa Society, 1811 Q St. NW, Washington, DC 20009. Issues indexed: (60:1-4). Subscriptions: $21/yr., $38/2 yrs., $57/3 yrs.; $25/yr., $46/2 yrs., $69/3 yrs. (inst.); plus $3/yr. (for.); Single issues: $5.75; $7 (inst.).

AmerV: THE AMERICAN VOICE, Frederick Smock, eds., The Kentucky Foundation for Women, Inc., 332 West Broadway, Suite 1215, Louisville, KY 40202. Issues indexed: (22-25). Subscriptions: $12/yr.; Back issues: $5; Single issues: $4.

AnotherCM: ANOTHER CHICAGO MAGAZINE, Lee Webster, Barry Silesky, eds. & pubs., Box 11223, Chicago, IL 60611. Issues indexed: No 1991 issues published. Subscriptions: $15/yr., $60/5 yrs., $199.95/lifetime; Single issues: $8.

Antaeus: ANTAEUS, Daniel Halpern, ed., The Ecco Press, 100 W. Broad St., Hopewell, NJ 08525. Issues indexed: (66-67). Subscriptions: $30/4 issues; Single issues: $10; Double issues: $15.

AnthNEW: THE ANTHOLOGY OF NEW ENGLAND WRITERS, Frank Anthony, ed., New England Writers/Vermont Poets Association, P.O. Box 483, Windsor, VT 05089. Issues indexed: (3).

AntigR: THE ANTIGONISH REVIEW, George Sanderson, ed., St. Francis Xavier U., Antigonish, Nova Scotia B2G 1C0 Canada. Issues indexed: (84, 85/86, 87/88). Subscriptions: $18/4 issues; Single issues: $5.

Periodicals Indexed

AntR: THE ANTIOCH REVIEW, Robert S. Fogarty, ed., David St. John, po. ed., P.O. Box 148, Yellow Springs, OH 45387. Issues indexed: (49:1-4). Subscriptions: $25/yr. (4 issues), $44/2 yrs., $62/3 yrs. (ind.); $36/yr., $66/2 yrs., $96/3 yrs. (inst.); $44/yr. (for.); Single issues: $5.50. Subscription address: P.O. Box 626, Dayton, OH 45459-0626.

ApalQ: APALACHEE QUARTERLY, Barbara Hamby, Pam Ball, Bruce Boehrer, Claudia Johnson, Paul McCall, eds., P.O. Box 20106, Tallahassee, FL 32316. Issues indexed: No 1991 issues received. Subscriptions: $12/yr. (2 issues, ind.), $15/yr. (inst.), $20/yr. (for.); Single issues: $5; Double issues: $7./50.

Arc: ARC, John Barton, Nadine McInnis, eds., P.O. Box 7368, Ottawa, Ont. K1L 8E4 Canada. Issues indexed: (26-27). Subscriptions: $18/4 issues (2 years, USA and Canada); $22/yr. (for.); Single issues: $6 (USA and Canada), $7 (for.); Back issues: $2-$3.

*Archae: ARCHAE, Alan Davis Drake, ed., 10 Troilus, Old Bridge, NJ 08857-2724. Issues indexed: (1-2). Subscriptions: $13/yr. (2 issues); $17/yr. (for.); Single issues: $7, $9 (for.).

Areíto: AREITO, Andrés Gómez, Director, P.O. Box 44-1803, Miami, FL 33144. Issues indexed: Segunda Epoca (3:9). Subscriptions: $12/yr. (ind.), $20/yr. (inst.), $18/yr. (for. ind.), $30/yr. (for. inst.).

ArtfulD: ARTFUL DODGE, Daniel Bourne, Karen Kovacik, eds., Dept. of English, College of Wooster, Wooster, OH 44691. Issues indexed: (20/21). Subscriptions: $10/2 double issues (ind.), $16/2 double issues (inst.); Single issues: $5.

Ascent: ASCENT, Audrey Curley, Mark Costello, Paul Friedman, Rocco Fumento, Philip Graham, Carol LeSeure, Jerry Mirskin, Nancy Roberts, George Scouffas, Jean Thompson, Michael Van Walleghen, Kirsten Wasson, eds., P.O. Box 967, Urbana, IL 61801. Issues indexed: (15:2-3, 16:1). Subscriptions: $3/yr. (3 issues), $4.50/yr. (for.); Single issues: $1 (bookstore), $1.50 (mail).

Asylum: ASYLUM, Greg Boyd, ed., P.O. Box 6203, Santa Maria, CA 93456. Issues indexed: (6:3/4). Subscriptions: $10/yr. (ind.), $15/yr. (inst.), plus $2/yr. (for.).

Atlantic: THE ATLANTIC, William Whitworth, ed., Peter Davison, po. ed., 745 Boylston St., Boston, MA 02116-2603. Issues indexed: (267:1-6, 268:1-6). Subscriptions: $15.94/yr., $27.95/2 yrs., $39.95/3 yrs., plus $6/yr. (Canada), $10/yr. (for.); Single issues: $2.95. Subscription address: Atlantic Subscription Processing Center, Box 52661, Boulder, CO 80322.

Avec: AVEC: A Journal of Writing, Cydney Chadwick, ed., P.O. Box 1059, Penngrove, CA 94951. Issues indexed: (4:1). Subscriptions: $12/2 issues; $15/issue (inst.); Single issue: $7.50.

BambooR: BAMBOO RIDGE: The Hawaii Writers' Quarterly, Eric Chock, Darrell H. Y Lum, eds., P.O. Box 61781, Honolulu, HI 96839-1781. Issues indexed: (50/51, 52, 53/54). Subscriptions: $12/yr. (4 issues), $16/yr. (inst.).; Single issues, $4; Double issues: $8.

BellArk: BELLOWING ARK, Robert R. Ward, ed., P.O. Box 45637, Seattle, WA 98145. Issues indexed: (7:1-6). Subscriptions: $12/yr. (6 issues), $20/2 yrs.; Single issues: $2.

BellR: THE BELLINGHAM REVIEW, Susan E. Hilton, ed., 1007 Queen St., Bellingham, WA 98226. Issues indexed: (14:1-2, #29-30). Subscriptions: $5/yr. (2 issues), $9.50/2 yrs., $12.50/3 yrs.; plus $1/yr. (for.); through agencies, $6/yr.; Single issues: $2.50.

BelPoJ: THE BELOIT POETRY JOURNAL, Marion K. Stocking, ed., RR 2, Box 154, Ellsworth, ME 04605. Issues indexed: (41:3-4, 42:1-2). Subscriptions: $8/yr. (4 issues, ind.), $22/3 yrs.; $12/yr., $33/3 yrs. (inst.); plus $3.20/yr. (Canada), $3.70/yr. (for.); Single issues: $2.

BilingR: THE BILINGUAL REVIEW / LA REVISTA BILINGÜE, Gary D. Keller, ed., Hispanic Research Center, Arizona State U., Tempe, AZ 85287-2702. Issues indexed: (15:1-3, 16:1-2/3) 1989-1990, 1991. Subscriptions: $16/yr., $30/2 yrs., $42/3 yrs. (ind.); $28/yr. (inst.).

BlackALF: BLACK AMERICAN LITERATURE FORUM, Division on Black American Literature and Culture, Modern Language Association, Joe Weixlmann, ed., Thadious Davis, Pinkie Gordon Lane, E. Ethelbert Miller, Sterling Plumpp, po. eds., Dept. of English, Indiana State U., Terre Haute, IN 47809. Issues indexed: (25:1-4). Subscriptions: $20/yr. (ind.), $32/yr. (inst.), $25/yr. (for.), $37/yr. (for. inst.). Single issues: $8.50.

BlackBR: BLACK BEAR REVIEW, Ave Jeanne, po. ed., 1916 Lincoln St., Croydon, PA 19021. Issues indexed: (13-14). Subscriptions: $10/yr. (2 issues); Single issues: $5.

BlackWR: BLACK WARRIOR REVIEW, Glenn Mott, ed., James H. N. Martin, po. ed., U. of Alabama, P.O. Box 2936, Tuscaloosa, AL 35487-2936. Issues indexed: (17:2, 18:1). Subscriptions: $9/yr. (ind.), $14/yr. (inst.); Single issues: $5.

BlueBldgs: BLUE BUILDINGS: An International Magazine of Poetry, Translations and Art, Guillaume Williams, ed., Dept. of English, Drake U., Des Moines, IA 50311. Issues indexed: No 1991 issues received. Subscriptions: $20/2 issyus; $12/1 issue; Back issues: $4.

Blueline: BLUELINE, Anthony Tyler, ed., Stephanie Coyne DeGhett, John W. Cross, Richard Londraville, Alan Steinberg, po. eds., English Dept., Potsdam College, SUNY, Potsdam, NY 13676. Issues indexed: (12). Single issues: $6.

Bogg: BOGG, John Elsberg, ed., 422 N. Cleveland St., Arlington, VA 22201. Issues indexed: (64). Subscriptions: $12/3 issues; Single issues: $4.50.

Bomb: BOMB MAGAZINE, Betsy Sussler, ed. & pub., Roland Legiardi-Laura, po. ed., New Art Publications, P.O. Box 2003, Canal Station, New York, NY 10013. Issues indexed: (34, 36); No. 35 not received. Subscriptions: $16/yr., $30/2 yrs.; $26/yr. (for.); Single issues: $4.

BostonR: BOSTON REVIEW, Sophie Glazer, managing ed., Sean Broderick, po. ed., 33 Harrison Ave., Boston, MA 02111. Issues indexed: (16:1-2, 3/4, 5-6). Subscriptions: $15/yr., $30/2 yrs. (ind.); $18/yr., $36/2 yrs. (inst.); plus $6/yr. (Canada, Mexico); plus $12/yr. (for.); Single issues: $4.

Boulevard: BOULEVARD, Richard Burgin, ed., Drexel U., 2400 Chestnut St., No. 2208, Philadelphia, PA 19103. Issues indexed: (5:3/6:1, 6:2/3, #15/16, 17/18). Subscriptions: $12/3 issues, $20/6 issues, $25/9 issues; Single issues: $6.

BrooklynR: BROOKLYN REVIEW, Jeffery Conway, Joe L. Woodward, po. eds., Dept. of English, Brooklyn College, Brooklyn, NY 11210. Issues indexed: (8). Subscriptions: $5/issue.

Caliban: CALIBAN, Lawrence R. Smith, ed., P.O. Box 4321, Ann Arbor, MI 48106. Issues indexed: (10). Subscriptions: $10/yr. (2 issues), $18/2 yrs. (ind.); $17/yr. (inst.); plus $2/yr. (for.); Single issues: $6.

Callaloo: CALLALOO: A Journal of Afro-American and African Arts and Letters, Charles H. Rowell, ed., Dept. of English, Wilson Hall, U. of Virginia, Charlottesville, VA 22903. Issues indexed: (14:1-4). Subscriptions: $21/yr. (ind.), $45/yr. (inst.); plus $6 (Canada, Mexico); plus $18 (outside North America, airfreight); Subscription address: The Johns Hopkins University Press, Journals Publishing Division, 701 W. 40th St., Suite 275, Baltimore, MD 21211-2190.

CalQ: CALIFORNIA QUARTERLY, Jack Hicks, ed., Jordan Jones, po. ed., 100 Sproul Hall, U. of California, Davis, CA 95616. Issues indexed: (31, 32/33, 35/36); No. 34 was indexed in 1990 volume. Subscriptions: $14/yr. (4 issues); Single issues: $4.

Periodicals Indexed

Calyx: CALYX: A Journal of Art and Literature by Women, Margarita Donnelly, Managing ed., Catherine Holdorf, Beverly McFarland, Linda Varsell Smith, eds, P.O. Box B, Corvallis, OR 97339-0539. Issues indexed: (13:2-3). Subscriptions: $18/yr. (3 issues), $32/2 yrs., $42/3 yrs.; $22.50/yr. (inst.); for. postage billed; $15/yr. (low income individual); Single issues: $8 plus $1.25 postage.

CanLit: CANADIAN LITERATURE, W. H. New, ed., U. of British Columbia, 2029 West Mall, Vancouver, B.C. V6T 1W5 Canada. Issues indexed: (128-131). Subscriptions: $30/yr. (ind.), $45/yr. (inst.) plus $5/yr. outside Canada; Single issues: $15.

CapeR: THE CAPE ROCK, Harvey Hecht, ed., Southeast Missouri State U., Cape Girardeau, MO 63701. Issues indexed: (26:2). Subscriptions: $5/yr. (2 issues); Single issues: $3.

CapilR: THE CAPILANO REVIEW, Robert Sherrin, ed., Capilano College, 2055 Purcell Way, North Vancouver, B.C. V7J 3H5 Canada. Issues indexed: (Series 2:5-6/7). Subscriptions: $20/yr. (3 issues), plus $5/yr. (USA, for.); Single issues: $8; Double issues: $14.

CarolQ: CAROLINA QUARTERLY, David Kellogg, ed., Barnsley Brown, po. ed., Greenlaw Hall CB#3520, U. of North Carolina, Chapel Hill, NC 27599-3520. Issues indexed: (43:2-3, 44:1). Subscriptions: $10/yr. (ind.), $12/yr. (3 issues) (inst.), $11/yr. (for.); Single issues: $5.

CentR: THE CENTENNIAL REVIEW, R. K. Meiners, ed., College of Arts and Letters, 312 Linton Hall, Michigan State U., East Lansing, MI 48824-1044. Issues indexed: (35:1-3). Subscriptions: $10/yr., $15/2 yrs., plus $3/yr. (for.); Single issues: $5.

CentralP: CENTRAL PARK, Stephen-Paul Martin, Eve Ensler, eds., Box 1446, New York, NY 10023. Issues indexed: (19/20). Subscriptions: $15/yr., 2 issues (ind.), $20/yr. (inst.); Single issues: $9 (ind), $10 (inst).

ChamLR: CHAMINADE LITERARY REVIEW, Loretta Petrie, ed., Chaminade U. of Honolulu, 3140 Waialae Ave., Honolulu, HI 96816. Issues indexed: (8-9). Subscriptions: $10/yr. (2 issues); $18/2 yrs.; plus $2 (for.).; Single issues: $5.

ChangingM: CHANGING MEN: Issues in Gender, Sex and Politics, Michael Biernbaum, Rick Cote, managing eds., 306 N. Brooks St., Madison, WI 53715; Bob Vance, po. ed., 1024 Emmet St., Petosky, MI 49770. Issues indexed: (22-23). Subscriptions: $24/4 issues, $40/4 issues (inst.); $16/4 issues (limited income); $27/4 issues (Canada & Mexico); $40/4 issues (for., air mail); Single issues: $6.

CharR: THE CHARITON REVIEW, Jim Barnes, ed., Northeast Missouri State U., Kirksville, MO 63501. Issues indexed: (17:1-2). Subscriptions: $9/4 issues; Single issues: $2.50.

ChatR: THE CHATTAHOOCHEE REVIEW, Lamar York, ed., Collie Owens, po. ed., DeKalb College, 2101 Womack Road, Dunwoody, GA 30338-4497. Issues indexed: (11:2-4, 12:1). Subscriptions: $15/yr. (4 issues), $25/2 yrs.; Single issues: $4.

Chelsea: CHELSEA, Sonia Raiziss, ed., P.O. Box 5880, Grand Central Station, New York, NY 10163. Issues indexed: (50-52). Subscriptions: $11/yr. (2 issues or 1 double issue), $20/2 yrs.; $14/yr., $27/2 yrs. (for.); Single issues: $6, $7 (for.).

ChiR: CHICAGO REVIEW, Andy Winston, ed., Anne Myles, po. ed., 5801 South Kenwood, Chicago, IL 60637. Issues indexed: (37:2/3). Subscriptions: $20/ yr. (ind.), $40/2 yrs., $60/3 yrs., plus $6/yr. (for.); $30/yr. (inst.); Single issues: $5.

ChironR: CHIRON REVIEW, Michael Hathaway, ed., 1514 Stone, Great Bend, KS 67530-4027. Issues indexed: (10:1-4). Subscriptions: $8/yr. (4 issues); $16/yr. (for.); $20/yr. (inst.); Single issues: $2; $4. (for.).

ChrC: THE CHRISTIAN CENTURY, James M. Wall, ed., 407 S. Dearborn St., Chicago, IL 60605. Issues indexed: (108:1-37). Subscriptions: $30/yr.; Single issues: $1.50. Christian Century Subscription Service, 5615 W. Cermak, Cicero, IL 60650.

CimR: CIMARRON REVIEW, Gordon Weaver, ed., Thomas Reiter, Randy Phillis, Sally Shigley, po. eds., 205 Morrill Hall, Oklahoma State U., Stillwater, OK 74078-0135. Issues indexed: (94-97). Subscriptions: $12/yr., $15 (Canada); $30/3 yrs., $40 (Canada); plus $2.50/yr. (for.); Single issues: $3.

CinPR: CINCINNATI POETRY REVIEW, Dallas Wiebe, ed., Dept. of English, ML 069, U. of Cincinnati, Cincinnati, OH 45221. Issues indexed: (21-22). Subscriptions: $9/4 issues; Single issues: $3; Sample copies: $2.

CityLR: CITY LIGHTS REVIEW, Nancy J. Peters, ed., Lawrence Ferlinghetti, pub., City Lights Bookstore, 261 Columbus Ave., San Francisco, CA 94133. Issues indexed: No 1991 issues published. Single issues: $11.95.

ClockR: CLOCKWATCH REVIEW: A Journal of the Arts, James Plath, ed., Dept. of English, Illinois Wesleyan Univ., Bloomington, IL 61702. Issues indexed: (7:1/2), c1991, 1992. Subscriptions: $8/yr. (2 issues); Single issues: $4.

CoalC: COAL CITY REVIEW, Brian Daldorph, Sandra Tompson, eds., U. of Kansas, English Dept., Lawrence, KS 66045. Issues indexed: (3-4). Subscriptions: $6/2 issues; Single issues: $4.

ColEng: COLLEGE ENGLISH, National Council of Teachers of English, James C. Raymond, ed., Dara Wier, po. ed., P.O. Drawer AL, Tuscaloosa, AL 35487. Issues indexed: (53:1-4). Subscriptions: $35/yr. (ind.), $40/yr. (inst.), plus $4/yr. (for.); Single issues: $5.; NCTE, 1111 Kenyon Rd., Urbana, IL 61801.

ColR: COLORADO REVIEW, Bill Tremblay, ed., Dept. of English, Colorado State U., 360 Eddy Bldg., Fort Collins, CO 80523. Issues indexed: (NS 17:1, 18:1-2). Subscriptions: $12.50/yr. (2 issues), $25/2 yrs.; Single issues: $7.

Colum: COLUMBIA: A Magazine of Poetry & Prose, Paul Gediman, David Elliott Kidd, eds., Richard Dock, Sarah Kennedy, po. eds., Graduate Writing Division, 404 Dodge Hall, Columbia Univ., New York, NY 10027. Issues indexed: (15-17). Subscriptions: $11/yr. (2 issues).

Comm: COMMONWEAL, Margaret O'Brien Steinfels, ed., Rosemary Deen, po. ed., 15 Dutch St., New York, NY 10038. Issues indexed: (118:1-22). Subscriptions: $36/yr., $39/yr. (Canada), $41/yr. (for.); $62/2 yrs., $66/2 yrs. (Canada), $72/2 yrs. (for.), ; Single issues: $2.

Confr: CONFRONTATION, Martin Tucker, ed., Katherine Hill-Miller, po. ed., English Dept., C. W. Post Campus of Long Island U., Brookville, NY 11548. Issues indexed: (46/47). Subscriptions: $10/yr., $20/2 yrs., $30/3 yrs.; plus $5/yr. (for.).; Single issues: $7.

Conjunc: CONJUNCTIONS: Bi-Annual Volumes of New Writing, Bard College, Bradford Morrow, ed., 33 W. 9th St., New York, NY 10011. Issues indexed: (16-17). Subscriptions: P.O. Box 115, Bard College, Annandale-on-Hudson, NY 12504; $18/yr. (2 issues), $32/2 yrs. (ind.); $25/yr., $45/2 yrs. (inst., for.); Back and single issues: $10.

ConnPR: THE CONNECTICUT POETRY REVIEW, J. Claire White, James Wm. Chichetto, eds., P.O. Box 3783, Amity Station, New Haven, CT 06525. Issues indexed: (10:1). Single issues: $3 (including postage).

Contact: CONTACT II: A Poetry Review, Maurice Kenny, J. G. Gosciak, eds., P.O. Box 451, Bowling Green, New York, NY 10004. Issues indexed: (10:59/60/61). Subscriptions: $10/yr. (ind.); $16/yr. (inst.); Single issues: $6.

ContextS: CONTEXT SOUTH, David Breeden, po. ed., pub., Box 4504, Schreiner College, 2100 Memorial Blvd., Kerrville, TX 78028-5697. Issues indexed: (2:1-2). Subscriptions: $10/3 issues; Single issues: $3.

CrabCR: CRAB CREEK REVIEW, Linda Clifton, ed., 4462 Whitman Ave. N., Seattle WA 98103. Issues indexed: (7:2-3). Subscriptions: $8/yr. (3 issues), $15/2 yrs.; Single issues: $3.

Periodicals Indexed

Crazy: CRAZYHORSE, Zabelle Stodola, managing ed., Ralph Burns, po. ed., Dept. of English, U. of Arkansas, 2801 S. University, Little Rock, AR 72204. Issues indexed: (40-41). Subscriptions: $10/yr. (2 issues), $18/2 yrs., $27/3 yrs. Single issues: $5.

CreamCR: CREAM CITY REVIEW, Kit Pancoast, Linda Geimer, eds., Aedan Hanley, Monroe Lerner, Marilyn Taylor, po. eds., English Dept., U. of Wisconsin, P.O. Box 413, Milwaukee, WI 53201. Issues indexed: (14:2, 15:1-2). Subscriptions: $10/yr. (2 issues), $14/2 yrs.; Single issues: $6; Sample & back issues: $4.50.

CrossCur: CROSSCURRENTS, Linda Brown Michelson, ed., 2200 Glastonbury Road, Westlake Village, CA 91361. Issues indexed: (9:4, 10:1). Subscriptions: $18/yr. (4 issues), $25/2 yrs.; Single issues: $6.

Crucible: CRUCIBLE, Terrence L. Grimes, ed., Barton College, College Station, Wilson, NC 27893. Issues indexed: (27). Subscriptions: $4/yr. (1 issue), $8/2 yrs; Back issues: $3.

CuadP: CUADERNOS DE POÉTICA, Diógenes Céspedes, Director, Apartado Postal 1736, Santo Domingo, República Dominicana; US Editors: Kate Nickel, 1111 Oldfather Hall, U. of Nebraska, Lincoln, NE 68588-0315, Rafael Catalá, P.O. Box 450, Corrales, NM 87048. Issues indexed: No 1991 issues received. Subscriptions: America & Europe, $25/yr. (ind.), $30/yr. (inst.); Africa, Asia & Oceania, $30/yr. (ind.), $40/yr. (inst).

CumbPR: CUMBERLAND POETRY REVIEW, Ingram Bloch, Bob Darrell, Malcolm Glass, Jeanne Gore, Thomas Heine, Laurence Lerner, Anthony Lombardy, Alison Touster-Reed, Eva Touster, eds., Poetics, Inc., P.O. Box 120128, Acklen Station, Nashville, TN 37212. Issues indexed: (10:2, 11:1). Subscriptions: $14/yr, $26/2 yrs. (ind.); $17/yr., $31/2 yrs. (inst.); $23/yr., $37/2 yrs. (for.); Single issue: $7; $10 (for.).

CutB: CUTBANK, Peter Fong, Dennis Held, ed., Marnie Bullock, po. ed., Jocelyn Siler, faculty advisor, Dept. of English, U. of Montana, Missoula, MT 59812. Issues indexed: (35-36). Subscriptions: $12/yr., $22/2 yrs.; Single issues: $6.95-$9.95; Sample copies: $4.

Dandel: DANDELION, Chris Horgan, managing ed., Deborah Miller, Allan Serafino, po eds., Alexandra Centre, 922 - 9th Ave., S.E., Calgary, Alberta T2G 0S4 Canada. Issues indexed: (18:1-2). Subscriptions: $10/yr. (2 issues), $18/2 yrs.; $15/yr. (inst.); Single issues: $6.

DenQ: DENVER QUARTERLY, Donald Revell, ed., U. of Denver, Denver, CO 80208. Issues indexed: (25:3-4, 26:1-2). Subscriptions: $15/yr., $18/yr. (inst.); $28/2 yrs.; plus $1/yr. (for.); Single issues: $5.

Descant: DESCANT, Karen Mulhallen, ed., P.O. Box 314, Station P, Toronto, Ontario M5S 2S8 Canada. Issues indexed: (22:2-4, #73-75). Subscriptions: $22.47/yr., $40.66/2 yrs., $58.85/3 yrs. (ind.); $31.03/yr., $62.06/2 yrs., $88.81/3 yrs. (inst.); plus $6/yr. (for.); Single issues: $13.91.

DogRR: DOG RIVER REVIEW, Laurence F. Hawkins, Jr., Allove DeVito, eds., Trout Creek Press, 5976 Billings Road, Parkdale, OR 97041. Issues indexed: (10:1-2). Subscriptions: $7/yr.; Single issues: $3.50; Sample copy: $3.

DustyD: DUSTY DOG, John Pierce, ed. & pub., P.O. Box 1103, Zuni, NM 87327. Issues indexed: (2:1 plus 2 unnumbered issues): Ja, Ap, Je 91; Chapbooks 1-2. Subscriptions: $8/yr. (3 chapbooks plus annual issues); Single issues: $3-4.

*Elf: ELF: Eclectic Literary Forum, C. K. Erbes, ed., P. O. Box 392, Tonawanda, NY 14150. Issues indexed: (1:1-4). Subscriptions: $12/yr. (4 issues), $24/yr. (inst.), plus $6/yr. (for.); Single issues: $4.50.

EmeraldCR: EMERALD COAST REVIEW: West Florida Authors and Artists, Ellen G. Peppler, Charmaine Wellington, eds., West Florida Literary Federation, P.O. Box 1644, Pensacola, FL 32597-1644. Issues indexed: (3-4). Single issues: $9.95.

EngJ: ENGLISH JOURNAL, National Council of Teachers of English, Ben F. Nelms, ed., 200 Norman Hall, U. of Florida, Gainesville, FL 32611; Paul Janeczko, po. ed., P.O. Box 1079, Gray, ME 04039. Issues indexed: (80:1-4). Subscriptions: $40/yr. (inst.), $35/yr. (ind.), plus $4/yr. (for.); Single issues: $5; Subscription address: 1111 Kenyon Rd., Urbana, IL 61801.

Epoch: EPOCH, Michael Koch, ed., 251 Goldwin Smith Hall, Cornell U., Ithaca, NY 14853-3201. Issues indexed: (40:1//2-3). Subscriptions: $11/yr.; Single issues: $4.

Event: EVENT: The Douglas College Review, Dale Zieroth, ed., Gillian Harding-Russell, po. ed., Douglas College, P.O. Box 2503, New Westminster, B.C. V3L 5B2 Canada. Issues indexed: (20:1-3). Subscriptions: $13/yr., $22/2 yrs.; Single issue: $5.

EvergreenC: THE EVERGREEN CHRONICLES: A Journal of Gay and Lesbian Writers, Randy Beard, Jim Berg, Sima Rabinowitz, Betsy Rivers, eds., P.O. Box 8939, Minneapolis, MN 55408. Issues indexed: (6:2). Subscriptions: $15/yr. (2 issues); Single issues: $8.

Farm: FARMER'S MARKET, Jean C. Lee, John E. Hughes, Jim McCurry, Lisa Ress, Tracey Rose, eds., Midwest Farmer's Market, Inc., P.O. Box 1272, Galesburg, IL 61402. Issues indexed: (8:1-2). Subscriptions: $8/yr. (2 issues); Single issues: $4.50.

Field: FIELD: Contemporary Poetry and Poetics, Stuart Friebert, David Young, eds., Rice Hall, Oberlin College, Oberlin, OH 44074. Issues indexed: (44-45). Subscriptions: $12/yr., $20/2 yrs.; Single issues: $6; Back issues: $12.

FloridaR: THE FLORIDA REVIEW, Russ Kesler, ed., Dept. of English, U. of Central Florida, Orlando, FL 32816. Issues indexed: No 1991 issues received. Subscriptions: $7/yr., $11/2 yrs.; Single issues: $4.50.

Footwork: FOOTWORK: The Paterson Literary Review, A Literary Collection of Contemporary Poetry, Short Fiction, and Art, Maria Mazziotti Gillan, ed., Passaic County Community College, College Boulevard, Paterson, NJ 07509. Issues indexed: No 1991 issues received. Subscriptions: $5/issue + $1 for postage and handling.

FourQ: FOUR QUARTERS, John J. Keenan, ed., La Salle U., 1900 W. Olney, Philadelphia, PA 19141. Issues indexed: (4:2, 5:1-2). Subscriptions: $8/yr. (2 issues), $13/2 yrs.; Single issues: $4.

FreeL: FREE LUNCH: A Poetry Journal, Free Lunch Arts Alliance, Ron Offen, ed., P.O. Box 7647, Laguna Niguel, CA 92607-7647. Issues indexed: (7-8). Subscriptions: $10/3 issues; $13/3 issues (for.); Single issues: $4, $5 (for.).

GeoR: GEORGIA REVIEW, Stanley W. Lindberg, ed., U. of Georgia, Athens, GA 30602. Issues indexed: (45:1-4). Subscriptions: $12/ yr., $20/2 yrs., plus $3/yr. (for.); Single issues: $5; Back issues: $5.

GettyR: GETTYSBURG REVIEW, Peter Stitt, ed., Gettysburg College, Gettysburg, PA 17325-1491. Issues indexed: (4:1-4). Subscriptions: $15/yr., $27/2 yrs., $36/3 yrs., plus $5 (for.); Single issues: $6.

GrahamHR: GRAHAM HOUSE REVIEW, Peter Balakian & Bruce Smith, eds., Colgate U. Press, Box 5000, Colgate U., Hamilton, NY 13346; Issues indexed: (14-15); #13 not received. Subscriptions: $15/2 yrs. (2 issues); Single issues: $7.50.

Grain: GRAIN, Saskatchewan Writers Guild, Geoffrey Ursell, ed., Lorna Crozier, Elizabeth Philips, po. eds., Box 1154, Regina, Saskatchewan S4P 3B4 Canada. Issues indexed: (19:1-4). Subscriptions: $15/yr., $28/2 yrs. (ind.); Single issues: $5.

GrandS: GRAND STREET, Jean Stein, ed., Erik Rieselbach, po. ed., 131 Varick St. #906, New York, NY 10013. Issues indexed: (10:1-4, #37-40). Subscriptions: $24/yr. (4 issues), $34/yr. (for.); Single issues: $8.50; Subscription address: Dept. GRS, PO Box 3000, Denville, NJ 07834..

Periodicals Indexed

GreenMR: GREEN MOUNTAINS REVIEW, Jane E. Jeffrey, Daniel Towner, po. ed., Donna Stewart, managing ed., Box A58, Johnson State College, Johnson, VT 05656. Issues indexed: (NS 4:2, 5:1). Single issues: $4.

GreensboroR: THE GREENSBORO REVIEW, Jim Clark, ed., Mark Caskie, po. eds., Dept. of English, U. of North Carolina, Greensboro, NC 27412. Issues indexed: (50-51). Subscriptions: $8/yr. (2 issues), $20/3 yrs.; Single issues: $4.

Gypsy: GYPSY LITERARY MAGAZINE, Belinda Subraman, S. Ramnath, eds, 10708 Gay Brewer Dr., El Paso, TX 79935. Issues indexed: (17); No. 16 was a cassette and was not indexed. Subscriptions: $12/2 issues; Single issues: $7.

HampSPR: THE HAMPDEN-SYDNEY POETRY REVIEW, Tom O'Grady, ed., P.O. Box 126, Hampden-Sydney, VA 23943. Issues indexed: Wint 1991. Subscriptions: $5/single issue; 1990 Anthology, $12.95.

HangL: HANGING LOOSE, Robert Hershon, Dick Lourie, Mark Pawlak, Ron Schreiber, eds., 231 Wyckoff St., Brooklyn, NY 11217. Issues indexed: (58-59). Subscriptions: $12.50/3 issues, $24/6 issues, $35/9 issues (ind.); $15/3 issues, $30/6 issues, $45/9 issues (inst.); $22/3 issues, $42/6 issues, $62/9 issues (for.); Sample issues: $5 plus $1.50 postage and handling.

Harp: HARPER'S MAGAZINE, Lewis H. Lapham, ed., 666 Broadway, New York, NY 10012. Issues indexed: (282:1688-1693, 283:1694-1699). Subscriptions: $18/yr., plus $2/yr. (USA possessions, Canada), plus $20/yr. (for.); Single issues: $2; Subscription address: P.O. Box 7511, Red Oak, IA 51591-0511.

HarvardA: THE HARVARD ADVOCATE, David Lehrer, Managing ed., Peter Nohrnberg, po. ed., 21 South St., Cambridge, MA 02138. Issues indexed: (125:3-5, 126:1); 125:3, Ja 91 is incorrectly numbered 127:3. Subscriptions: $15/yr. (ind.), $17/yr. (inst.), $20/yr. (for.); Single issues: $4.

HawaiiR: HAWAI'I REVIEW, Jeanne K. Tsutsui, ed., Megan Thompson, po. ed., Dept. of English, U. of Hawai'i, 1733 Donaghho Rd., Honolulu, HI 96822. Issues indexed: (15:2-3, 16:1, #32-334). Subscriptions: $15/yr. (3 issues), $25/2 yrs.; Single issue: $5.

HayF: HAYDEN'S FERRY REVIEW, Salima Keegan, Managing ed., Deirdre McDonough, Kelleen Zubick, po. eds., Matthews Center, Arizona State U., Tempe, AZ 85287-1502. Issues indexed: (8-9). Subscriptions: $10/yr. (2 issues), $18/2 yrs.; $13/yr., $26/2 yrs. (inst.); Single issues: $5 plus $1 postage.

HeavenB: HEAVEN BONE, Steven Hirsch, ed., pub., P.O. Box 486, Chester, NY 10918. Issues indexed: (9). Subscriptions: $14.95/4 issues; Single issue: $5.

Hellas: HELLAS: A Journal of Poetry and the Humanities, Gerald Harnett, ed., 304 S. Tyson Ave., Glenside, PA 19038. Issues indexed: (2:1-2); vol. 1, nos. 1-2 were indexed in the 1990 volume. Subscriptions: $12/yr. (2 issues), $22/2 yrs.; plus $4/yr. (for.); Single issues: $6.50.

HighP: HIGH PLAINS LITERARY REVIEW, Robert O. Greer, Jr., ed., Joy Harjo, po. ed., 180 Adams St., Suite 250, Denver, CO 80206. Issues indexed: (6:1-3). Subscriptions: $20/yr. (3 issues), $38/2 yrs., plus $5/yr. (for.); Single issues: $7.

HiramPoR: HIRAM POETRY REVIEW, English Dept., Hiram College, Hale Chatfield & Carol Donley, eds., P.O. Box 162, Hiram, OH 44234. Issues indexed: (50) plus supplement #12. Subscriptions: $4/yr. (2 issues); Single issues: $2; Supplements, $6.

HolCrit: THE HOLLINS CRITIC, John Rees Moore, ed., Hollins College, VA 24020. Issues indexed: (28:1-5). Subscriptions: $6/yr., $10/2 yrs., $14/3 yrs.; $7.50/yr., $11.50/2 yrs., $15.50/3 yrs. (for.).

*HopewellR: ARTS INDIANA LITERARY SUPPLEMENT (beginning 1992: Hopewell Review), Alison Jester, ed., Arts Indiana, Inc., 27 S. Pennsylvania St., Suite 701, Indianapolis, IN 46204-3622. Issues indexed: (1991). Subscriptions: $4.95/issue incl. postage, handling and tax.

Hudson: THE HUDSON REVIEW, Paula Deitz, Frederick Morgan, eds., 684 Park Ave., New York, NY 10021. Issues indexed: (43:4, 44:1-3). Subscriptions: $20/yr., $38/2 yrs., $56/3 yrs., plus $4/yr. (for.); Single issues: $6.

Imagine: IMAGINE: International Chicano Poetry Journal, Tino Villanueva, ed., 89 Mass. Ave., Suite 270, Boston, MA 02115. Issues indexed: No 1991 issues received. Subscriptions: $8/yr. (2 issues), $14/2 yrs. (ind.); $12/yr., $18/2 yrs. (inst.); plus $1/yr. (for.); Single issues: $6.50-8.00.

IndR: INDIANA REVIEW, Allison Joseph, ed., Bret Flournoy, Gretchen Knapp, po. eds., 316 N. Jordan Ave., Bloomington, IN 47405. Issues indexed: (14:2-3). Subscriptions: $12/3 issues, $15/3 issues (inst.); $22/6 issues (ind.), $25/6 issues (inst.); plus $5/3 issues (for.). Single issues: $5.

Interim: INTERIM, A. Wilber Stevens, ed., Dept. of English, U. of Nevada, 4505 Maryland Parkway, Las Vegas, NV 89154-5011. Issues indexed: (10:1-2). Subscriptions: $8/yr. (2 issues), $13/2 yrs., $16/3 yrs. (ind.); $14/yr. (lib.), $16/yr. (for.); Single issues: $5, $8 (for.).

InterPR: INTERNATIONAL POETRY REVIEW, Dept. of Romance Languages, U. of North Carolina, Greensboro, NC 27412-5001. Issues indexed: (15:1, 17:1-2); vol. 15, no. 1 had not been received for the 1989 volume. Subscriptions: $10/yr. (2 issues, ind.), $15/yr. (inst.); Single issues: $5.

Inti: INTI, Revista de Literatura Hispanica, Roger B. Carmosino, ed., Dept. of Modern Languages, Providence College, Providence, RI 02918. Issues indexed: (34/35); numbers 31 and 32/33 were indexed in the 1990 volume; the 1990 listing "(31-32)" was in error. Subscriptions: $25/yr. (2 issues, ind.), $40/yr. (inst.); Single issues: $20, $30 (double issues).

Iowa: IOWA REVIEW, David Hamilton, ed., 308 EPB, U. of Iowa, Iowa City, IA 52242. Issues indexed: (21:1-3). Subscriptions: $15/yr. (3 issues, ind.), $20/yr. (inst.), plus $3/yr. (for.); Single issues: $6.95.

Jacaranda: THE JACARANDA REVIEW, Bruce Kijewski, Katherine Swiggart, eds., Gregory Castle, po. ed., Dept. of English, U. of California, Los Angeles, CA 90024. Issues indexed: No 1990 or 1991 issues received. Subscriptions: $10/yr. (2 issues, ind.), $14/yr. (inst.); Sample issues: $6.

JamesWR: THE JAMES WHITE REVIEW, A Gay Men's Literary Journal, Greg Baysans, ed., P.O. Box 3356, Traffic Station, Minneapolis, MN 55403. Issues indexed: (8:2-4, 9:1). Subscriptions: $12/yr., $20/2 yrs.; $14/yr. (Canada); $17/yr. (other for.); Single issues: $3; Back issues: $1 (for minimum order of $10).

JlNJPo: THE JOURNAL OF NEW JERSEY POETS, Sander Zulauf, ed., English Dept., Division of Humanities, County College of Morris, 214 Center Grove Rd., Randolph, NJ 07869-2086. Issues indexed: (13:1-2). Subscriptions: $7/yr. (2 issues), $12/2 yrs.; Single issues: $4.

Journal: THE JOURNAL, Kathy Fagan, po. ed., The Ohio State U., Dept. of English, 164 W. 17th Ave., Columbus, OH 43210. Issues indexed: (14:2, 15:1-2). Subscriptions: $8/yr. (2 issues), $16/2 yrs., $24/3 yrs.; Single issues: $5.

Kaleid: KALEIDOSCOPE, International Magazine of Literature, Fine Arts, and Disability, Darshan Perusek, ed., Chris Hewitt, po. ed. (51 W. 86th ST., #404, New York, NY 10024), United Cerebral Palsy and Services for the Handicapped, 326 Locust St., Akron, OH 44302. Issues indexed: (22-23). Subscriptions: $9/yr. (2 issues, ind.), $12/yr. (inst.), plus $5/yr. (Canada); plus $8/yr. (other for.); Single issues: $4.50, $7 (for.); Sample issue: $2.

Kalliope: KALLIOPE: A Journal of Women's Art, Mary Sue Koeppel, ed., Florida Community College at Jacksonville, 3939 Roosevelt Blvd., Jacksonville, FL 32205. Issues indexed: (13:1-3). Subscriptions: $10.50/1 yr. (3 issues), $20/2 yrs. (ind.); $18/yr. (inst.); plus $6/yr. (for.); free to women in prison; Single issues: $7; Back issues: $4-8.

Periodicals Indexed

KanQ: KANSAS QUARTERLY, Harold Schneider, Ben Nyberg, W. R. Moses, John Rees, eds., Dept. of English, Denison Hall, Kansas State U., Manhattan, KS 66506-0703. Issues indexed: No 1991 issues received. Subscriptions: $20/yr., $35/2 yrs. (USA, Canada, Latin America); $21/yr., $37/2 yrs. (other countries); Single issues: $6; Double issues: $8.

KenR: KENYON REVIEW, Marilyn Hacker, ed., David Baker, po. ed., Kenyon College, Gambier, OH 43022. Issues indexed: (NS 13:1-4). Subscriptions: Kenyon Review, P.O. Box 837, Farmingdale, NY 11735; $20/yr., $35/2 yrs., $45/3 yrs. (ind.); $23/yr. (inst.); plus $5 (for.); Single issues: $7, including postage; Back issues: $10.

Lactuca: LACTUCA, Mike Selender, ed., P.O. Box 621, Suffern, NY 10901. Issues indexed: (14). Subscriptions: $10/yr. (3 issues), $13/yr. (for.); Single issues: $4, plus $2 (for.).

LakeSR: THE LAKE STREET REVIEW, Kevin FitzPatrick, ed., Box 7188, Minneapolis, MN 55407. Issues indexed: (25). Subscriptions: Single issues: $2. "This is the final issue."

LaurelR: LAUREL REVIEW, Craig Goad, David Slater, William Trowbridge, eds., Green Tower Press, Dept. of English, Northwest Missouri State U., Maryville, MO 64468. Issues indexed: (25:1-2). Subscriptions: $8/yr. (2 issues), $14/2 yrs.; $11/yr., $20/2 yrs. (for.); Single issues: $5; Back issues: $4.50.

LindLM: LINDEN LANE MAGAZINE, Belkis Cuza Malé, ed., P.O. Box 2384, Princeton, NJ 08543-2384. Issues indexed: (10:1-4). Subscriptions: $12/yr. (ind.), $22/yr. (inst.), $22/yr. (Latin America, Europe); Single issues: $2.

LitR: THE LITERARY REVIEW: An International Journal of Contemporary Writing, Walter Cummins, ed., Fairleigh Dickinson U., 285 Madison Ave., Madison, NJ 07940. Issues indexed: (34:2-4, 35:1). Subscriptions: $18/yr., $21/yr. (for.); $30/2 yrs., $36/2 yrs. (for.); Single issues: $5, $6 (for.).

*LouisL : LOUISIANA LITERATURE: A Review of Literature and Humanities, Tim Gautreaux, ed., Dept. of English, Southeastern Louisiana Univ., Box 792, Hammond, LA 70402. Issues indexed: (8:1-2). Subscriptions: $10/yr. (2 issues, ind.); $12.50/yr. (inst.).

LullwaterR: LULLWATER REVIEW, William P. Eiselstein, ed., Box 22036, Emory Univ., Atlanta, GA 30322. Issues indexed: (2:2, 3:1). Subscriptions: $10/yr. (2 issues), plus $3 (for.); Single issues: $5.

MalR: THE MALAHAT REVIEW, Constance Rooke, ed., P.O. Box 3045, Victoria, BC, Canada V8W 3P4. Issues indexed: (94-97). Subscriptions: $15 plus $1.05 GST/yr. (4 issues), $40 plus $2.80/3 yrs., (ind., USA, Canada); $25 plus $1.75 GST/yr. (inst., USA, Canada); Single issues: $6.

ManhatPR: MANHATTAN POETRY REVIEW, Elaine Reiman-Fenton, ed., P.O. Box 8207, New York, NY 10150. Issues indexed: (13); nos. 11 & 12 were indexed in the 1990 volume, not nos. 10 & 11 as listed; no. 10 was indexed in the 1988 volume. Subscriptions: $12/yr. (2 issues); Single issues: $7; plus $5 per item (for.).

ManhatR: THE MANHATTAN REVIEW, Philip Fried, ed., 440 Riverside Dr., #45, New York, NY 10027. (6:1). Subscriptions: $8/2 issues (ind.), $12/2 issues (inst.), plus $2.50/2 issues (outside USA & Canada); Back issues: $4 (ind.), $6 (inst); include 6" x 9" envelope and $1.25 for postage.

Manoa: MANOA: A Pacific Journal of International Writing, Robert Shapard, ed., English Dept., U. of Hawaii, Honolulu, HI 96822. Issues indexed: (3:1-2). Subscriptions: $15/yr. (2 issues), $27/2 yrs. (ind.); $18/yr., $32.40/2 yrs. (inst.); $18/yr., $32.40/2 yrs. (for. ind.); $22/yr., $39.60/2 yrs. (for. inst.); plus $12/yr. (for. airmail); subscription address: Univ. of Hawaii Press, 2840 Kolowalu St., Honolulu, HI 96822.

MassR: THE MASSACHUSETTS REVIEW, Jules Chametzky, Mary Heath, Paul Jenkins, eds., Anne Halley, Paul Jenkins, po. eds., Memorial Hall, U. of Massachusetts, Amherst, MA 01003. Issues indexed: (32:1-4). Subscriptions: $14/yr. (4 issues, ind.), $17/yr. (lib.), $20/yr. (for.); Single issues: $5.

MemphisSR: MEMPHIS STATE REVIEW: *name changed to* RiverC: RIVER CITY.

Mester: MESTER, Jacqueline Cruz, ed., Dept. of Spanish and Portuguese, U. of California, Los Angeles, CA 90024-1532. Issues indexed: (20:1-2); 19:1-2 were indexed in the 1990 volume; 18:1-2 were indexed in the 1989 volume; the 1990 listing was incorrect. Subscriptions: $12/yr. (2 issues, ind.), $20/yr. (inst.), $8/yr. (stud.), plus $4/yr. outside U.S., Canada, Mexico.

MichQR: MICHIGAN QUARTERLY REVIEW, Laurence Goldstein, ed., 3032 Rackham Bldg., U. of Michigan, Ann Arbor, MI 48109. Issues indexed: (30:1-4). Subscriptions: $13/yr., $24/2 yrs. (ind.), $15/yr. (inst.); Single issues: $3.50; Back issues: $2.

MidAR: MID-AMERICAN REVIEW, Ken Letko, ed., John Bradley, po. ed., 106 Hanna Hall, Dept. of English, Bowling Green State U., Bowling Green, OH 43403. Issues indexed: (11:1-2. 12:1). Subscriptions: $8/yr. (2 issues), $15/2 yrs., $20/3 yrs; Single issues: $5; Sample issue: $4.

MidwQ: THE MIDWEST QUARTERLY: A Journal of Contemporary Thought, James B. M. Schick, ed., Stephen E. Meats, po. ed., Pittsburg State U., Pittsburg, KS 66762-5889. Issues indexed: (32:2-4, 33:1). Subscriptions: $10/yr. plus $3 (for.); Single issues: $3.

Mildred: MILDRED, Ellen Biss, Kathryn Poppino, eds., 961 Birchwood Lane, Schenectady, NY 12309. Issues indexed: (4:2/5:1). Subscriptions: $12/yr. (2 issues), $20/2 yrs., $28/3 yrs.; $14/yr., $24/2 yrs., $30/3 yrs. (inst.); Single issues: $6; Double issues: $8.

MinnR: THE MINNESOTA REVIEW, Jeffrey Williams, ed, Dept. of English, East Carolina Univ., Greenville, NC 27858-4353. Issues Indexed: (NS 36-37). Subscriptions: $8/yr. (2 issues), $14/2 yrs. (ind.); $16/yr., $28/2 yrs. (inst. & for.); Single issues: $4.50.

MissouriR: THE MISSOURI REVIEW, Speer Morgan, ed., College of Arts & Science, 1507 Hillcrest Hall, U. of Missouri, Columbia, MO 65211. Issues indexed: (13:3, 14:1-3). Subscriptions: $15/yr. (3 issues), $27/2 yrs., $36/3 yrs.; Single issues: $6.

MissR: MISSISSIPPI REVIEW, Frederick Barthelme, ed., The Center for Writers, U. of Southern Mississippi, Southern Station, Box 5144, Hattiesburg, MS 39406-5144. Issues indexed: (19:3, 20:1/2, #[57], 58/59). Subscriptions: $15/yr. (2 issues), $28/2 yrs., $40/3 yrs., plus $2/yr. (for.); Single issues: usually $8; double issues: $12.

MoodySI: MOODY STREET IRREGULARS, Joy Walsh, ed., P.O. Box 157, Clarence Center, NY 14032. Issues indexed: (24/25/26). Subscriptions: $20/4 single, 2 double issues (ind.), $30/4 single, 2 double issues (lib.); Single issues: $5, double issues: $10.

MSS: *superseded by* New Myths.

Nat: THE NATION, Victor Navasky, ed., Grace Schulman, po. ed., 72 Fifth Ave., New York, NY 10011. Issues indexed: (252:1-24, 253:1-23). Subscriptions: $44/yr., $75/2 yrs., plus $18/yr. (for.); Single issues: $1.75; Back issues: $3, $4 (for.). Send subscription correspondence to: P.O. Box 10763, Des Moines, IA 50340-0763.

NegC: NEGATIVE CAPABILITY, Sue Walker, ed., 62 Ridgelawn Dr. East, Mobile, AL 36608. Issues indexed: (11:1-3). Subscriptions: $12/yr. (3 issues, ind.), $16/yr. (inst., for.); Single issues: $5.

NewAW: NEW AMERICAN WRITING, Maxine Chernoff, Paul Hoover, eds., OINK! Press, 2920 West Pratt, Chicago, IL 60645. Issues indexed: (7, 8/9). Subscriptions: $12/yr. (2 issues); $16/yr. (lib.).; $18/yr. (for.); Single issues: $6.

NewDeltaR: NEW DELTA REVIEW, Kathleen Fitzpatrick, ed., David Starkey, po. ed., English Dept., Louisiana State U., Baton Rouge, LA 70803. Issues indexed: No 1991 issues received. Subscriptions: $7/yr. (2 issues); Single issues: $4.

Periodicals Indexed

NewEngR: NEW ENGLAND REVIEW, Middlebury Series, T. R. Hummer, ed, Middlebury College, Middlebury, VT 05753. Issues indexed: (13:3/4, 14:1). Subscriptions: $18/yr. (4 issues), $33/2 yrs., $50/3 yrs. (ind.); $30/yr., $55/2 yrs., $83/3 yrs. (lib., inst.); plus $6/yr. (for. surface) or $15/yr. (for. airmail); Single issues: $6, $7 (for. surface), $9.50 (for. airmail); subscription address: University Press of New England, 17 1/2 Lebanon St., Hanover, NH 03755.

NewL: NEW LETTERS, James McKinley, ed., U. of Missouri-Kansas City, 5100 Rockhill Rd., Kansas City, MO 64110. Issues indexed: (57:3-4, 58:1). Subscriptions: $17/yr. (4 issues), $28/2 yrs., $55/5 yrs. (ind.); $20/yr., $34/2 yrs., $65/5 yrs. (lib.); Single issues: $5.

NewMyths: NEW MYTHS, Robert Mooney, ed., State U. of New York, P.O. Box 6000, Binghamton, NY 13902-6000. Issues indexed: No 1991 issues received. Subscriptions: $8.50/yr. (2 issues), $15/2 yrs. (ind.); $13/yr., $23/2 yrs. (libs.); Single issues: $5.

NewOR: NEW ORLEANS REVIEW, John Biguenet, John Mosier, eds., Box 195, Loyola U., New Orleans, LA 70118. Issues indexed: (18:1-4). Subscriptions: $25/yr. (ind.), $30/yr. (inst.), $35/yr. (for.); Single issues: $9.

NewRena: THE NEW RENAISSANCE, Louise T. Reynolds, ed., James E. A. Woodbury, po. ed., 9 Heath Road, Arlington, MA 02174. Issues indexed: (8:2, #25). Subscriptions: $14/3 issues, $26/6 issues; $16.50/3 issues, $29.50/6 issues (for.); Single issues: $9, $9.50 (for.).

NewRep: THE NEW REPUBLIC, Andrew Sullivan, ed., Richard Howard, po. ed., 1220 19th St. NW, Washington, DC 20036. Issues indexed: (204:1/2-25, 205:1-26/27). Subscriptions: $69.97/yr., $84.97/yr. (Canada), $99.97/yr. (elsewhere). Back issues: $3.50. Single issues: $2.95. Subscription Service Dept., The New Republic, P.O. Box 56515, Boulder, CO 80322.

NewYorker: THE NEW YORKER, 25 W. 43rd St., New York, NY 10036. Issues indexed: (66:47-53, 67:1-45). Subscriptions: $32/yr., $52/2 yrs.; $56/yr. (Canada); $66/yr. (other for.); Single issues: $1.75; Subscription correspondence to: Box 56447, Boulder, CO 80322.

NewYorkQ: THE NEW YORK QUARTERLY, William Packard, ed., P.O. Box 693, Old Chelsea Station, New York, NY 10113. Issues indexed: (44-46). Subscriptions: $15/yr., $30/2 yrs., $45/3 yrs.; $25/yr. (lib.); plus $5/yr. (for.); Single issues: $6; subscription address: 302 Neville Hall, U. of Maine, Orono, ME 04469.

NewYRB: THE NEW YORK REVIEW OF BOOKS, Robert B. Silvers, Barbara Epstein, eds., 250 W. 57th St., New York, NY 10107. Issues indexed: (38:1/2-21). Subscriptions: $39/yr.; Single issues: $2.50; NY Review of Books, Subscription Service Dept., P.O. Box 2094, Knoxville, IA 50197-2094.

Nimrod: NIMROD, Francine Ringold, ed., Manly Johnson, po. ed., Arts and Humanities Council of Tulsa, 2210 S. Main St., Tulsa, OK 74114. Issues indexed: (34:2, 35:1). Subscriptions: $10/yr. (2 issues), $18/2 yrs., $26/3 yrs.; $13/yr. (for.); Single issues: $6.95.

NoAmR: THE NORTH AMERICAN REVIEW, Robley Wilson, ed., Peter Cooley, po. ed., U. of Northern Iowa, Cedar Falls, IA 50614-0516. Issues indexed: (276:1-4). Subscriptions: $18/yr., $22/yr. (Canada, Latin America), $24/yr. (elsewhere); Single issues: $4, $5 (Canada).

NoDaQ: NORTH DAKOTA QUARTERLY, Robert W. Lewis, ed., Jay Meek, po. ed., U. of North Dakota, Grand Forks, ND 58202-8237. Issues indexed: (59:1-4). Subscriptions: $15/yr., $20/yr. (inst.); $23/yr. (for. ind.), $28/yr. (for. inst.); Single issues: $5 (ind.), $7 (for.).

Northeast: NORTHEAST, John Judson, ed., Juniper Press, 1310 Shorewood Dr., La Crosse, WI 54601. Issues indexed: (Ser. 5:4-5). Subscriptions: $33 (2 issues, ind.), $38 (inst.), includes "books and gifts of the press" in addition to NORTHEAST; Single issues: $4.

NorthStoneR: THE NORTH STONE REVIEW, James Naiden, ed., D Station, Box 14098, Minneapolis, MN 55414. Issues indexed: (10). Subscriptions: $15/yr. (2 issues); Single issues: $7.

Notus: NOTUS, New Writing, Pat Smith, ed., 2420 Walter Dr., Ann Arbor, MI 48103. Issues indexed: (9). Subscriptions: $12/yr. (2 issues, U.S. & Canada, ind.), $15/yr. (elsewhere), $15/yr. (inst.).

NowestR: NORTHWEST REVIEW, John Witte, ed. & po. ed., 369 PLC, U. of Oregon, Eugene, OR 97403. Issues indexed: (29:2-3). Subscriptions: $14/yr. (3 issues), $26/2 yrs., $35/3 yrs.; $12/yr., $22/2 yrs. (stud.); plus $2/yr. (for.); Single issues: $5.

*Nuez: LA NUEZ: Revista Internacional de Arte y Literatura, Rafael Bordao, ed., P.O. Box 023617, Brooklyn, NY 11202. Issues indexed: (3:7-8/9). Subscriptions: $12/yr. (ind.), $15/yr. (inst.), $18/yr. (for.).

Obs: OBSIDIAN II: Black Literature in Review, Gerald Barrax, ed. & po. ed., Dept. of English, Box 8105, North Carolina State U., Raleigh, NC 27695-8105. Issues indexed: (6:1-3). Subscriptions: $12/yr. (3 issues), $20/2 yrs.; $13/yr. (Canada), $15/yr. (other for.); Single issues: $5; Double issues: $10.

OhioR: THE OHIO REVIEW, Wayne Dodd, ed., Ellis Hall, Ohio U., Athens, OH 45701-2979. Issues indexed: (46-47). Subscriptions: $12/yr. (3 issues), $30/3 yrs.; Single issues: $4.25.

Ometeca: OMETECA: Ciencia y Literatura, Science & Literature, Ciéncia e literatura, Rafael Catalá, ed., P.O. Box 450, Corrales, NM 87048. Issues Indexed: No 1991 issues published. Subscriptions: $20/yr. (2 issues) (ind.), $30/yr. (inst.) (USA, Canada, Mexico); $33/yr. (elsewhere).

OnTheBus: ONTHEBUS: A New Literary Magazine, Jack Grapes, ed., Bombshelter Press, 6421-1/2 Orange St., Los Angeles, CA 90048. Issues indexed: (8/9). Subscriptions: $24/3 issues (ind.), $27/3 issues (inst.); Single issues: $9, plus $1 postage.

OntR: ONTARIO REVIEW, Raymond J. Smith, ed., 9 Honey Brook Dr., Princeton, NJ 08540. Issues indexed: (34-35). Subscriptions: $10/yr. (2 issues), $18/2 yrs., $24/3 yrs., plus $2/yr. (for.); Single issues: $4.95.

Os: OSIRIS, Andrea Moorhead, ed., P.O. Box 297, Deerfield, MA 01342. Issues indexed: (32-33). Subscriptions: $8/2 issues (ind.), $10/2 issues (inst.). Single issues: $4.

Outbr: OUTERBRIDGE, Charlotte Alexander, ed., English Dept. (A323), College of Staten Island, 715 Ocean Terrace, Staten Island, NY 10301. Issues indexed: (22). Subscriptions: $5/yr. (1 issue).

OxfordM: OXFORD MAGAZINE, Constance Pierce, editorial advisor, Bachelor Hall, Miami U., Oxford, OH 45056. Issues indexed: No 1991 issues received. Single issues: $4.

PacificR: THE PACIFIC REVIEW: A Magazine of Poetry and Prose, James Brown, faculty ed., Dept. of English, California State U., 5500 University Parkway, San Bernardino, CA 92407-2397. Issues indexed: (9-10). Subscriptions: $6.50/yr. (1 issue), $12/2 yrs.; Sample issue: $2.50.

Paint: PAINTBRUSH: A Journal of Poetry, Translations, and Letters, Ben Bennani, ed., Northeast Missouri State U., Kirksville, MO 63501. Issues indexed: (18:35-36). Subscriptions: $9/yr. (2 issues, ind.), $12/yr. (inst.); Single & back issues: $7.

PaintedB: PAINTED BRIDE QUARTERLY, Lee W. Potts, Teresa Leo, eds., Painted Bride Arts Center, 230 Vine St., Philadelphia, PA 19106. Issues indexed: (42-43). Subscriptions: $16/yr. (4 issues), $28/2 yrs., $20/yr. (lib, inst.); Single issues: $5. Distributed free to inmates.

*PaintedHR: PAINTED HILLS REVIEW, Michael Ishii, Kara D. Kosmatka, eds., P.O. Box 494, Davis, CA 95617-0494. Issues indexed: (1-4). Subscriptions: $12/yr. (4 issues); $14/yr. (inst., Canada); $16/yr. (other for.); Single issues: $3.50.

Periodicals Indexed

ParisR: THE PARIS REVIEW, George A. Plimpton, Peter Matthiessen, Donald Hall, Robert B. Silvers, Blair Fuller, Maxine Groffsky, eds., Patricia Storace, po. ed., 541 East 72nd St., New York, NY 10021. Issues indexed: (33:118-121). Subscriptions: $24/4 issues, $48/8 issues, $1000/life, plus $7/4 issues (for.); Single issues: $7; Subscription address: 45-39 171st Place, Flushing, NY 11358.

Parting: PARTING GIFTS, Robert Bixby, ed., 3413 Wilshire Dr., Greensboro, NC 27408-2923. Issues indexed: (4:1-2). Subscriptions: $5/yr. (2 issues), $9/2 yrs., $13/3 yrs.; Single issues: $3.

PartR: PARTISAN REVIEW, William Phillips, ed., Boston U., 236 Bay State Rd., Boston, MA 02215. Issues indexed: (58:1-4). Subscriptions: $18/yr. (4 issues), $33/2 yrs., $47/3 yrs.; $21/yr., $36/2 yrs. (for.); $28/yr. (inst.); Single issues: $5 plus $1 per issue postage and handling.

PassN: PASSAGES NORTH, Ben Mitchell, ed., Mark Cox, po. ed., Kalamazoo College, 1200 Academy St., Kalamazoo, MI 49007. Issues indexed: (12:1-2). Subscriptions: $5/yr., $8/2 yrs; Single issues: $3.

Pearl: PEARL, Joan Jobe Smith, Marilyn Johnson, Barbara Hauk, eds., 3030 E. 2nd St., Long Beach, CA 90803. Issues indexed: (13-14). Subscriptions: $10/yr. (ind.); $15/yr. (lib.); $25/yr. (patrons); Single issues: $5.

Pembroke: PEMBROKE MAGAZINE, Shelby Stephenson, ed., Box 60, Pembroke State U., Pembroke, NC 28372. Issues indexed: (23). Subscriptions: $5/issue (USA, Canada, Mexico), $5.50/issue (other for.).

PennR: THE PENNSYLVANIA REVIEW, Ed Ochester, executive ed., Deborah Pursifull, Lori Jakiela, eds., Leasa Burton, Jan Beatty, po. eds., 526 Cathedral of Learning, U. of Pittsburgh, Pittsburgh, PA 15260. Issues indexed: (5:1). Subscriptions: $10/yr. (2 issues), $18/2 yrs.; Single issues: $5.

Pequod: PEQUOD, Mark Rudman, ed., Dept. of English, Room 200, New York U., 19 University Place, New York, NY 10003. Issues indexed: (32). Subscriptions: $12/yr. (2 issues), $20/2 yrs. (ind.); $18/yr., $34/2 yrs. (inst).; plus $3/yr. (for.); Single issues: $7.50.

Pig: PIG IRON, Jim Villani, Naton Leslie, eds., Pig Iron Press, P.O. Box 237, Youngstown, OH 44501. Issues indexed: (17). Single issues: $9.95.

PikeF: THE PIKESTAFF FORUM, Robert D. Sutherland, James R. Scrimgeour, eds./pubs., P.O. Box 127, Normal, IL 61761. Issues indexed: 10. Subscriptions: $10/6 issues; Single issues: $2.

Plain: PLAINSONGS, Dwight Marsh, ed., Dept. of English, Hastings College, Hastings, NE 68902. Issues indexed: (11:2-3, 12:1-2). Subscriptions: $9/yr. (3 issues).

Ploughs: PLOUGHSHARES, DeWitt Henry, executive director, Joyce Peseroff, po. ed., Emerson College, 100 Beacon St., Boston, MA 02116. Issues indexed: (17:1, 2/3, 4). Subscriptions: $19/yr. (ind.), $24/yr. (for. ind.); $22/yr. (inst.), $27/yr. (for. inst.). Single issues: $8.95.

*PlumR: THE PLUM REVIEW, M. Hammer, Christina Daub, eds., 1654a Avon Pl. NW, Washington, DC 20007. Issues indexed: (1). Subscriptions: $10/yr. (2 issues), $18/2 yrs.; plus $2/yr. (for.); Single issues: $5.

Poem: POEM, Huntsville Literary Association, Nancy Frey Dillard, ed., c/o English Dept., U. of Alabama, Huntsville, AL 35899. Issues indexed: (65-66). Subscriptions: $10/yr.; Back issues: $5; subscription address: Huntsville Literary Association, P.O. Box 919, Huntsville, AL 35804.

PoetC: POET AND CRITIC, Neal Bowers, ed., 203 Ross Hall, Iowa State U., Ames, IA 50011. Issues indexed: (22:2-4, 23:1); 21:4 is a special issue: "Five Years of Iowa Literary Awards." Subscriptions: Iowa State U. Press, South State St., Ames, IA 50010, $16/yr. (3 issues), plus $3/yr. (for.); Single issues: $6.

Periodicals Indexed

PoetL: POET LORE, Philip K. Jason, Roland Flint, Barbara Goldberg, executive eds., The Writer's Center, 7815 Old Georgetown Rd., Bethesda, MD 20814. Issues Indexed: (86:1-4). Subscriptions: $10/yr. (Writer's Center members); $15/yr. (ind.); $24/yr. (inst.), plus $5/yr. (for.); Single issues: $4.50, plus $1 postage and handling; Samples: $4.

Poetry: POETRY, Joseph Parisi, ed., 60 W. Walton St., Chicago, IL 60610. Issues indexed: (157:4-6, 158:1-6, 159:1-3). Subscriptions: $25/yr. (ind.); $31/yr. (for.); $27/yr. (inst.); $33/yr. (for. inst.); Single issues: $2.50 plus $1 postage; Back issues: $3 plus $1 postage.

PoetryC: POETRY CANADA, Barry Dempster, po. ed., P.O. Box 1061, Kingston, Ont. K7L 4Y5 Canada. Issues indexed: 12:1. Subscriptions: $16.05/4 issues (ind.); $32.10/4 issues (inst.); Back issues: $5; Single issues: $3.95.

PoetryE: POETRY EAST, Richard Jones, ed., Dept. of English, 802 W. Belden Ave., DePaul Univ., Chicago, IL 60614. Issues indexed: (31-32). Subscriptions: $12/yr.; Single issues: $7.

PoetryNW: POETRY NORTHWEST, David Wagoner, ed., U. of Washington, 4045 Brooklyn Ave. NE, Seattle, WA 98105. Issues indexed: (32:1-4). Subscriptions: $10/yr., $12/yr. (for.); Single issues: $3, $3.50 (for.).

PoetryUSA: POETRY USA, National Poetry Association, Jack Foley, ed., 2569 Maxwell Ave., Oakland, CA 94601. Issues indexed: (22-23). Subscriptions: $7.50/yr.; Single issues: $1.

PottPort: THE POTTERSFIELD PORTFOLIO, Shari Andrews, Joe Blades, Jo-Anne Elder, Raymond Fraser, Carlos Gomes, Margaret McLeod, eds., Wild East Publishing Co-operative Ltd., PO Box 1135, Stn. A/CP 1135, Succ. A, Fredericton, NB, Canada E3B 5C2. Issues indexed: (13:1-2). Subscriptions: $12/yr. (2 issues, ind.), $15/yr. (inst.); $15/yr. (USA, for.); Single issues: $6.

PraF: PRAIRIE FIRE: A Canadian Magazine of New Writing, Andris Taskans, managing ed., Di Brandt, po. ed., 423-100 Arthur Street, Winnipeg, Manitoba R3B 1H3 Canada. Issues indexed: (12:1-4, #54-57). Subscriptions: $24/yr., $44/2 yrs. (ind.); $32/yr. (inst.), plus $4 (USA), plus $6 (for.); Single issues: $6.95-7.95.

PraS: PRAIRIE SCHOONER, Hilda Raz, ed., 201 Andrews Hall, U. of Nebraska, Lincoln, NE 68588-0334. Issues indexed: (65:1-4). Subscriptions: $15/yr., $28/2 yrs., $39/3 yrs. (ind.); $19/yr. (lib.); Single issues: $4.

Prima: PRIMAVERA, Lisa Grayson, Elizabeth Harter, Ruth Young, eds., 700 E. 61st St, Box 37-7547, Chicago, IL 60637. Issues indexed: (14/15). Single issues: $7; Back issues: $5-6.

Quarry: QUARRY, Steven Heighton, ed., P.O. Box 1061, Kingston, Ontario K7L 4Y5 Canada. Issues indexed: (40:1/2-4). Subscriptions: $20.33/yr. (4 issues), $36.38/2 yrs. (8 issues); Single issues: $5.95.

QRL: QUARTERLY REVIEW OF LITERATURE, T. & R. Weiss, 26 Haslet Ave., Princeton, NJ 08540. Issues indexed: (Poetry series 10, vol. 30). Subscriptions: $20/2 volumes (paper), $20/volume (cloth, inst.).

QW: QUARTERLY WEST, Regina Oost, Tom Hazuka, eds., C. F. Pinkerton, Janet Bianchi, po. eds., 317 Olpin Union, U. of Utah, Salt Lake City, UT 84112. Issues indexed: (32-33). Subscriptions: $8.50/yr. (2 issues), $16/2 yrs.; $12.50/yr., $24/2 yrs. (for.); Single issues: $4.50.

RagMag: RAG MAG, Beverly Voldseth, ed. & pub., Black Hat Press, Box 12, Goodhue, MN 55027. Issues indexed: (9:1-2). Subscriptions: $10/yr. (2 issues), $15/yr. (inst.); Single issues: $5.50.

Raritan: RARITAN: A Quarterly Review, Richard Poirier, ed., Rutgers U., 31 Mine St., New Brunswick, NJ 08903. Issues indexed: (10:3-4, 11:1-2). Subscriptions: $16/yr., $26/2 yrs.; $20/yr., $30/2 yrs. (inst.); plus $5.50/yr (for.); Single issues: $5; Back issues: $6.

Periodicals Indexed

RedBass: RED BASS, Jay Murphy, ed., 216, New Chartres St., New Orleans, LA 70130; 105 W. 28th St., New York, NY 10001. Issues indexed: (15). Subscriptions: $20/2 issues (ind.), $35 (inst., for.); Single issues: $8.50; Back issues: $5.

RiverC: RIVER CITY, Sharon Bryan, ed., Dept. of English, Memphis State U., Memphis, TN 38152. Issues indexed: (11:2, 12:1). Subscriptions: $9/yr. (ind., 2 issues), $10/yr. (inst.); Single issues: $5.

RiverS: RIVER STYX, Lee Fournier, ed., 14 South Euclid, St. Louis, MO 63108. Issues indexed: (33-35). Subscriptions: $20/yr. (3 issues, ind.); $38/yr. (inst.); Single issues: $7.

Rohwedder: ROHWEDDER, Nancy Antell, Robert Dassanowsky-Harris, Hans Jurgen Schacht, eds., P.O. Box 29490, Los Angeles, CA 90029. Issues indexed: (6). Subscriptions: $12/4 issues (USA, Canada, Mexico, ind.); $18/4 issues (inst.); $16/4 issues (other for., surface mail, plus $1/copy airmail); Single issues: $4.

Salm: SALMAGUNDI, Robert Boyers, ed., Skidmore College, Saratoga Springs, NY 12866. Issues indexed: (90/91, 92). Subscriptions: $12/yr., $20/2 yrs. (ind.); $16/yr., $25/2 yrs. (inst.); plus $2/yr. (for.); Sample issues: $4; Single issues: $6.

SenR: SENECA REVIEW, Deborah Tall, ed., Hobart & William Smith Colleges, Geneva, NY 14456. Issues indexed: (21:1). Subscriptions: $8/yr. (2 issues), $15/2 yrs.; Single issues: $5.

Sequoia: SEQUOIA: The Stanford Literary Journal, Marion Rust, managing ed., Annie Finch, Carlos Rodriguez, po. eds., Storke Publications Building, Stanford U., Stanford, CA 94305. Issues indexed: (34:1). Subscriptions: $10/yr. (2 issues), $11/yr. (for.), $15/yr. (inst.); Single issues: $5.

SewanR: THE SEWANEE REVIEW, George Core, ed., U. of the South, Sewanee, TN 37375. Issues indexed: (98:3-4, 99:1-4). Subscriptions: $15/yr., $27/2 yrs., $38/3 yrs. (ind.); $20/yr., $37/2 yrs., $54/3 yrs. (inst.); plus $5/yr. (for.); Single issues: $5; Back issues: $7-10.

ShadowP: SHADOW PLAY, Jan Bender and Joe Zanoni, eds., Landside Press, 99 Reynolds Rd., Grand Isle, VT 05458. Issues indexed: (2). Single issues: $3.

Shen: SHENANDOAH, Dabney Stuart, ed., Washington and Lee U., Box 722, Lexington, VA 24450. Issues indexed: (41:1-4). Subscriptions: $11/yr., $18/2 yrs., $25/3 yrs.; $14/yr., $24/2 yrs., $33/3 yrs. (for.); Single issues: $3.50; Back issues: $6.

Shiny: SHINY: The Magazine of the Future, Michael Friedman, ed. & pub., 39 E. 12th St., Suite 603, New York, NY 10003. Issues indexed: (6). Subscriptions: $18/4 issues; Single issues: $5.

*Sidewalks: SIDEWALKS: An Anthology of Poetry, Short Prose, & Art, Tome Heie, ed., P.O. Box 321, Champlin, MN 55316. Issues indexed: (1). Subscriptions: $8/yr. (2 issues), $12/yr. (inst.); Single issues: $5.

SilverFR: SILVERFISH REVIEW, Rodger Moody, ed., P.O. Box 3541, Eugene, OR 97403. Issues indexed: (20-21). Subscriptions: $9/3 issues (ind.), $12/3 issues (inst.), Single issues: $3-5.

SingHM: SING HEAVENLY MUSE!: Women's Poetry and Prose, Ruth Berman, Sheila Burns, Joline Gitis, Karen Karsten, Carol Masters, Sue Ann Martinson, Corinna Nelson, Kathleen Todd, Rafael Tilton, Linda Webster, eds, P.O. Box 13320, Minneapolis, MN 55414. Issues indexed: (19). Subscriptions: $14/2 issues, $19/3 issues, $36/6 issues (ind.); $21/3 issues, $40/6 issues (inst.); $16/3 issues (low income); Single issues: $7.

SinW: SINISTER WISDOM: A Journal for the Lesbian Imagination in the Arts and Politics, Elana Dykewomon, ed. & pub., P.O. Box 3252, Berkeley, CA 94703. Issues indexed: (43/44-45). Subscriptions: $17/yr. (4 issues), $30/2 yrs. (ind.); $30/yr. (inst.); $22/yr. (for.); $8-15/yr. (hardship); Free on request to women in prisons and mental institutions; Single issues: $5.

SlipS: SLIPSTREAM, Robert Borgatti, Livio Farallo, Dan Sicoli, eds., Box 2071, New Market Station, Niagara Falls, NY 14301. Issues indexed: (11) plus chapbook supplement. Subscriptions: $8.50/2 issues; Single issues: $5.

SmPd: THE SMALL POND MAGAZINE OF LITERATURE, Napoleon St. Cyr, ed., pub., P.O. Box 664, Stratford, CT 06497. Issues indexed: (28:1-3, #81-83). Subscriptions: $7.50/yr. (3 issues), $13/2 yrs., $19/3 yrs.; Single issues: $3.

*SnailPR: THE SNAIL'S PACE REVIEW: A Biannual Little Magazine of Contemporary Poetry, Ken Denberg, Darby Penney, eds., RR 2 Box 363 Brownell Rd., Cambridge, NY 12816. Issues indexed: (1:1-2). Subscriptions: $6/yr. (ind.), $10/yr. (inst.); Single issues: $3.50.

Sonora: SONORA REVIEW, Joan Marcus, ed, Jennifer Rocco, Andrea Werblin, po. eds., Dept. of English, U. of Arizona, Tucson, AZ 85721. Issues indexed: (20-21). Subscriptions: $10/yr. (2 issues); Single issues: $5.

SoCaR: SOUTH CAROLINA REVIEW, Richard J. Calhoun, executive ed., Dept. of English, Clemson U., Clemson, SC 29634-1503. Issues indexed: (23:2, 24:1). Subscriptions: $7/yr., $13/2 yrs. (USA, Canada, Mexico); $8/yr., $15/2 yrs. (inst.); plus $.50/yr. (other for.); Back issues: $5.

SoCoast: SOUTH COAST POETRY JOURNAL, John J. Brugaletta, ed., English Dept., California State U., Fullerton, CA 92634. Issues indexed: (10-11). Subscriptions: $9/yr. (2 issues), $17/2 yrs. (ind.); $10/yr. (inst.); Single issues: $5.

SoDakR: SOUTH DAKOTA REVIEW, John R. Milton, ed., Dept. of English, U. of South Dakota, Box 111, U. Exchange, Vermillion, SD 57069. Issues indexed: (29:1-4); No. 3 has 2 parts. Subscriptions: $15/yr., $25/2 yrs. (USA, Canada); plus $1/yr. elsewhere; Single issues: $5.

SouthernHR: SOUTHERN HUMANITIES REVIEW, Dan R. Latimer, Thomas L. Wright, eds., R. T. Smith, po. ed., 9088 Haley Center, Auburn U., AL 36849. Issues indexed: (25:1-4). Subscriptions: $12/yr.; Single issues: $4.

SouthernPR: SOUTHERN POETRY REVIEW, Lucinda Grey, Ken McLaurin, eds., English Dept., U. of North Carolina, Charlotte, NC 28223. Issues indexed: (31:1-2). Subscriptions: $8 yr.

SouthernR: SOUTHERN REVIEW, James Olney, Dave Smith, eds., Louisiana State U., 43 Allen Hall, Baton Rouge, LA 70803. Issues indexed: (27:1-4). Subscriptions: $15/yr., $27/2 yrs., $38/3 yrs.; $30/yr., $52/2 yrs., $75/3 yrs. (inst.); Single issues: $5, $10 (inst.).

SouthwR: SOUTHWEST REVIEW, Willard Spiegelman, ed., Southern Methodist U., Dallas, TX 75275. Issues indexed: (76:1-4). Subscriptions: $20/yr., $40/2 yrs., $50/3 yrs. (ind.); $25/yr. (inst.); Single issues: $5.

Sparrow: SPARROW: The Politically Incorrect Verse Magazine, Felix Stefanile, ed./pub., Sparrow Press, 103 Waldron St., West Lafayette, IN 47906. Issues indexed: (58). Subscriptions: $7.50/3 issues; Single issues: $3.

Spirit: THE SPIRIT THAT MOVES US, Morty Sklar, ed., pub., P.O. Box 820, Jackson Heights, NY 11372. Issues indexed: (11). Also published as monograph, "Editor's Choice III: Fiction, Poetry & Art from the U.S. Small Press" (1991, $12.50 paper, $18.50 cloth).

SpiritSH: SPIRIT, David Rogers, ed., Dept. of English, Seton Hall U., South Orange, NJ 07079. Issues indexed: (56). Subscriptions: $4/yr. (2 issues); Single issues: $2.

*Spitball: SPITBALL: The Literary Baseball Magazine, Mike Shannon, pub. & ed., 6224 Collegevue Pl., Cincinnati, OH 45224. Issues indexed: (36-39). Subscriptions: $12/yr. (4 issues); $16/yr. (Canada, U.S. funds); Single issues: $4.

Periodicals Indexed

SpoonRQ: THE SPOON RIVER QUARTERLY, Lucia Cordell Getsi, ed., English Dept., Illinois State U., Normal, IL 61761. Issues indexed: (16:1/2-3/4). Subscriptions: $12/yr. (2 double issues); $15/yr. (inst.); Single issues: $6.

Stand: STAND, Jessie Emerson, U.S.A. ed., P.O. Box 5923, Huntsville, AL 35814. Issues indexed: (32:1-4, 33:1). Subscriptions: $22/yr., $40/2 yrs.; $18/yr. (students, unwaged); Single issues: $6.50; U.S.A. distributor: Anton J. Mikovsky, 57 West 84th St., #1-C, New York, NY 10024.

Sulfur: SULFUR: A Literary Bi-Annual of the Whole Art, Clayton Eshleman, ed., English Dept., Eastern Michigan U., Ypsilanti, MI 48197. Issues indexed: (11:1-2, #28-29). Subscriptions: $13/2 issues (ind.), $19/2 issues (inst.), plus $4 (for.) or $10 for airmail postage; Single issues: $8.

SwampR: SWAMP ROOT, Al Masarik, ed., Route 2, Box 1098, Hiwassee One, Jacksboro, TN 37757. Issues indexed: (7/8). Subscriptions: $12/3 issues; $15/3 issues (inst.); Single issues: $8.

SycamoreR: SYCAMORE REVIEW, Henry Hughes, ed., Pamela Proffitt, po. ed., Dept. of English, Heavilon Hall, Purdue U., West Lafayette, IN 47907. Issues indexed: (3:1-2). Subscriptions: $9/yr., $16/2 yrs.; Single issues: $5.

Talisman: TALISMAN: A Journal of Contemporary Poetry and Poetics, Edward Foster, ed., Box 1117, Hoboken, NJ 07030. Issues indexed: (6-7). Subscriptions: $9/yr. (2 issues); $13/yr. (inst.); plus $2/yr. (for.); Single issues: $5.

TampaR: TAMPA REVIEW: Literary Journal of the University of Tampa, Richard Mathews, ed., Donald Morrill, Kathryn Van Spanckeren, po. eds., Box 19F, U. of Tampa, 401 W. Kennedy Blvd., Tampa, FL 33606-1490. Issues indexed: (3). Subscriptions: $7.50/yr. (1 issue); plus $2.50/yr. (for.); Single issues: $7.95 plus $1 postage.

TarRP: TAR RIVER POETRY, Peter Makuck, ed., Dept. of English, General Classroom Bldg., East Carolina U., Greenville, NC 27858-4353. Issues indexed: (29:2, 230:1); "230:1" in the 1990 index volume should have been "30:1". Subscriptions: $8/yr (2 issues), $14/2 yrs.; Single issues: $4.50.

TexasR: TEXAS REVIEW, Paul Ruffin, ed., Division of English and Foreign Languages, Sam Houston State U., Huntsville, TX 77341. Issues indexed: (11:1/2, 12:1/2-3/4); 11:3/4 was included in 1990 index volume. Subscriptions: $10/yr., $18/2 yrs., $26/3 yrs.; $10.50/yr. (Canada), $11/yr. (for.); Single issues: $5.

Thirteenth Moon: *See* 13thMoon *at beginning of file.*

ThRiPo: THREE RIVERS POETRY JOURNAL, Gerald Costanzo, ed., Three Rivers Press, P.O. Box 21, Carnegie-Mellon U., Pittsburgh, PA 15213. Issues indexed: (37/38). Subscriptions: $10/4 issues; Single issues: $2.50; Double issues: $5.

Thrpny: THE THREEPENNY REVIEW, Wendy Lesser, ed., pub., P.O. Box 9131, Berkeley, CA 94709. Issues indexed: (44-45). Subscriptions: $12/yr., $20/2 yrs., $24/yr. (for.); Single issues: $3.

*TickleAce: TICKLEACE, Pamela Hodgson, Lawrence Mathews, Bruce Porter, Michael Winter, eds., P.O. Box 5353, St. John's, Nfld. A1C 5W2 Canada. Issues indexed: (21-22). Subscriptions: $9/yr. (2 issues), $11/yr. (inst.), plus $3/yr. (for.); Single issues: $4.95.

Timbuktu: TIMBUKTU, Molly Turner, ed., pub., RR 1, Box 758, Scottsville, VA 24590. Issues indexed: (6); "last issue"; No. 5 not received.

Trans: TRANSLATION, The Journal of Literary Translation, Frank MacShane, Lori M. Carlson, eds., The Translation Center, 412 Dodge Hall, Columbia U., New York, NY 10027. Issues indexed: (25). Subscriptions: $17/yr. (2 issues), $30/2 yrs.; Single issues: $9.

Tribe: TRIBE: An American Gay Journal, Bernard Rabb, ed., Columbia Publishing Co., 234 E. 25th St., Baltimore, MD 21218. Issues indexed: (1:2-4). Subscriptions: $22/yr. (4 issues), $40/2 yrs., $58/3 yrs.; $26/yr., $48/2 yrs., $70/3 yrs. (for.); Single issues: $6 plus $1.50 postage and handling, $2.50 (for.).

TriQ: TRIQUARTERLY, Reginald Gibbons, ed., Northwestern U., 2020 Ridge Ave., Evanston, IL 60208. Issues indexed: (81-83). Subscriptions: $18/yr. (3 issues), $32/2 yrs., $250/life (ind.); $26/yr., $44/2 yrs., $300/life (inst.), plus $4/yr. (for.); Single issues: cost varies; Sample copies: $4.

Turnstile: TURNSTILE, Jill Benz, Lindsey Crittenden, Ann Biester Deane, Twisne Fan, Sara Gordonson, John Paul Jones, Philip Metcalf, Mitchell Nauffts, Paolo Pepe, George Witte, eds., 175 Fifth Avenue, Suite 2348, New York, NY 10010. Issues indexed: (3:1). Subscriptions: $12/2 issues, $22/4 issues; Single issues: $6.50.

US1: US 1 WORKSHEETS, Sondra Gash, ed., Jean Hollander, Frederick Tibbetts, po eds., US 1 Poets' Cooperative, P.O. Box 1, Ringoes, NJ 08551. Issues indexed: (24/25). Subscriptions: $8/2 double issues; Single issues: $5.

Verse: VERSE, Henry Hart, U. S. ed., Dept. of English, College of William and Mary, Williamsburg, VA 23185. Issues indexed: (8:1-2). Subscriptions: $15/yr. (3 issues); Single issues: $5.

VirQR: THE VIRGINIA QUARTERLY REVIEW: A National Journal of Literature and Discussion, Staige D. Blackford, ed., Gregory Orr, po. consultant, One West Range, Charlottesville, VA 22903. Issues indexed: (67:1-4). Subscriptions: $15/yr., $22/2 yrs., $30/3 yrs. (ind.); $22/yr., $30/2 yrs., $50/3 yrs. (inst.); plus $3/yr. (for.); Single issues: $5.

Vis: VISIONS INTERNATIONAL, Bradley R. Strahan, po. ed., pub., Black Buzzard Press, 1110 Seaton Lane, Falls Church, VA 22046. Issues indexed: (35-37). Subscriptions: $14/yr., $27/2 yrs. (ind.); $42/3 yrs. (lib.); Single issues: $5.

WashR: WASHINGTON REVIEW, Clarissa K. Wittenberg, ed., P.O. Box 50132, Washington, DC 20091. Issues indexed: (16:5-6; 17:1-4). Subscriptions: $12/yr. (6 issues), $20/2 yrs.; Single issues: $3.

WeberS: WEBER STUDIES: An Interdisciplinary Humanities Journal, Neila C. Seshachari, ed., Weber State College, Ogden, UT 84408-1214. Issues indexed: (8:1-2). Subscriptions: $10/yr. (3 issues), $20/yr. (inst.); plus actual extra postage costs per year (for.); Back issues: $7; Single issues: $2.75.

WebR: WEBSTER REVIEW, Nancy Schapiro, ed., Pamela White Hadas, Jerred Metz, po. eds., Webster U., 470 E. Lockwood, Webster Groves, MO 63119. Issues indexed: (15). Subscriptions: $5/yr. (1 issue).

WestB: WEST BRANCH, Karl Patten, Robert Taylor, eds., Bucknell Hall, Bucknell U., Lewisburg, PA 17837. Issues indexed: (28-29). Subscriptions: $7/yr. (2 issues), $11/2 yrs.; Single issues: $4.

WestCL: WEST COAST LINE: A Journal of Contemporary Writing and Criticism (formerly West Coast Review), Roy Miki, ed., English Dept., Simon Fraser U., Burnaby, B.C. V5A 1S6 Canada. Issues indexed: (25:1-2, #5-6). Subscriptions: $18/yr. (ind., 3 issues), $24/yr. (inst.); Single issues: $8.

WestHR: WESTERN HUMANITIES REVIEW, Barry Weller, ed., Richard Howard, po. ed., U. of Utah, Salt Lake City, UT 84112. Issues indexed: (45:1-4). Subscriptions: $18/yr. (4 issues, ind.), $24/yr. (inst.); Single issues: $5.

WilliamMR: THE WILLIAM AND MARY REVIEW, Christopher Vitiello, ed., Paula Hopping, po. ed., College of William and Mary, Williamsburg, VA 23185. Issues indexed: (29). Subscriptions: $4.50/single issue, plus $1.50 (for.); Single issues: $5.

WillowR: WILLOW REVIEW, Paulette Roeske, Kathee Szaksztylo, Michael Daish, Iris Martin, eds., College of Lake County, 19351 W. Washington St., Grayslake, IL 60030-1198. Issues indexed: Sping 1991.

WillowS: WILLOW SPRINGS, Nance Van Winckel, ed., Scott Starbuck, po. ed., Eastern Washington U., MS-1, Cheney, WA 99004-2496. Issues Indexed: (27-28). Subscriptions: $7/yr. (2 issues), $13/2 yrs.; Single issues: $4.

Wind: WIND, Quentin R. Howard, ed., RFD Route 1, Box 809K, Pikeville, KY 41501. Issues indexed: No 1991 issues received. Subscriptions: $7/3 issues (ind.), $8/3 issues (inst.), $12/3 issues (for.); Single issues: $2.50; $5 (for.).

WindO: THE WINDLESS ORCHARD, Robert Novak, ed., English Dept., Indiana-Purdue U., Fort Wayne, IN 46805. Issues indexed: (54-55). Subscriptions: $10/3 issues; Single issues: $4.

Witness: WITNESS, Peter Stine, ed., 31000 Northwestern Highway, Suite 200, Farmington Hills, MI 48018. Issues indexed: No 1991 issues received. Subscriptions: $15/yr. (4 issues), $28/2 yrs.; $20/yr., $38/2 yrs. (inst.); plus $4/yr. (for.); Single copies: $6.

*WorldL: WORLD LETTER, Jon Cone, ed., 2726 E. Court St., Iowa City, IA 52245. Issues indexed: (1:1, 2). Subscriptions: $7/2 issues (U.S.), $8/2 issues (Canada); Single issues: $4 (U.S.), $5 (Canada).

WorldO: WORLD ORDER, Firuz Kazemzadeh, Betty J. Fisher, Howard Garey, Robert H. Stockman, James D. Stokes, eds., National Spiritual Assembly of the Bahá'ís of the United States, 415 Linden Ave., Wilmette, IL 60091. Issues indexed: (24:1/2, 2/3 [sic]). Subscriptions: $10/yr., $18/2 yrs. (USA, Canada, Mexico); $15/yr., $28/2 yrs. (elsewhere); $20/yr., $38/2 yrs. (for. airmail); Single issues: $3.

WormR: THE WORMWOOD REVIEW, Marvin Malone, ed., P.O. Box 4698, Stockton, CA 95204-0698. Issues indexed: (31:1, 2/3, 4; #121, 122/123, 124). Subscriptions: $8/4 issues (ind.), $10/4 issues (inst.); Single issues: $4.

Writ: WRIT, Roger Greenwald, ed., Innis College, U. of Toronto, 2 Sussex Ave., Toronto, Canada M5S 1J5. Issues indexed: 23/24. Subscriptions: $15/2 issues (ind.), $18/2 issues (inst.); same amount in U.S. funds outside Canada; Back issues: $7.50-15.

Writer: THE WRITER, Sylvia K. Burack, ed., pub., 120 Boylston St., Boston, MA 02116-4615. Issues indexed: (104:1-12). Subscriptions: $27/yr., $50/2 yrs., $74/3 yrs.; plus $8/yr. (for.); $10/5 issues for new subscribers; Single issues: $2.

WritersF: WRITERS' FORUM, Alexander Blackburn, Victoria McCabe, Craig Lesley, Bret Lott, eds., P.O. Box 7150, U. of Colorado, Colorado Springs, CO 80933-7150. Issues indexed: (17). Subscriptions: $8.95/yr. (1 issues) plus $1.05 postage and handling; Back issue sample: $5.95 plus $1.05 postage and handling.

YaleR: THE YALE REVIEW, J. D. McClatchy, ed., Yale U., 1902A Yale Station, New Haven, CT 06520. Issues indexed: No 1991 issues published. Resumes with volume 80 in 1992. Subscriptions: $20/yr., $36/2 yrs., $54/3 yrs.; $30/yr., $54/2 yrs., $81/3 yrs. (for.); $40/yr. (inst.), $45/yr. (for. inst.)

YellowS: YELLOW SILK, Journal of Erotic Arts, Lily Pond, ed., pub., P.O. Box 6374, Albany, CA 94706. Issues indexed: (36-38). Subscriptions: $30/yr. (ind.), $38/yr. (lib., inst.), plus $6/yr. (for. surface) or $20/yr. (for. air). Single issues: $6.

Zyzzyva: ZYZZYVA: The Last Word, West Coast Writers & Artists, Howard Junker, ed, 41 Sutter St., Suite 1400, San Francisco, CA 94104. Issues indexed: (7:1-4, #25-28); 7:4, #28 is an unnumbered special issue: "Roots and Branches: Contemporary Essays by West Coast Writers," collected from Zyzzyva, ed. by Howard Junker (San Francisco: Mercury House, 1991, 286 p.); in the 1990 index volume "#17-20" should have been "#21-24". Subscriptions: $20/yr. (4 issues), $32/2 yrs. (ind.); $28/yr. (inst.); $30/yr. (for.); Single copies: $8 post paid.

Alphabetical List of Journals Indexed, with Acronyms

13th Moon: A Feminist Literary Magazine : 13th Moon

Abraxas : Abraxas
Aerial : Aerial
Agni : Agni
Amelia : Amelia
The American Poetry Review : AmerPoR
The American Scholar : AmerS
The American Voice : AmerV
The Americas Review : Americas
Another Chicago Magazine : AnotherCM
Antaeus : Antaeus
The Anthology of New England Writers : AnthNEW
The Antigonish Review : AntigR
The Antioch Review : AntR
Apalachee Quarterly : ApalQ
Arc : Arc
Archae : Archae
Areíto : Areíto
Artful Dodge : ArtfulD
Arts Indiana Literary Supplement : HopewellR
Ascent : Ascent
Asylum : Asylum
The Atlantic : Atlantic
Avec : Avec

Bamboo Ridge : BambooR
The Bellingham Review : BellR
Bellowing Ark : BellArk
The Beloit Poetry Journal : BelPoJ
The Bilingual Review/La Revista Bilingüe : BilingR
Black American Literature Forum : BlackALF
Black Bear Review : BlackBR
Black Warrior Review : BlackWR
Blue Buildings : BlueBldgs
Blueline : Blueline
Bogg : Bogg
Bomb Magazine : Bomb
Boston Review : BostonR
Boulevard : Boulevard
Brooklyn Review : BrooklynR

Caliban : Caliban
California Quarterly : CalQ
Callaloo : Callaloo
Calyx : Calyx
Canadian Literature : CanLit
The Cape Rock : CapeR
The Capilano Review : CapilR
Carolina Quarterly : CarolQ
The Centennial Review : CentR
Central Park : CentralP
Chaminade Literary Review : ChamLR
Changing Men : ChangingM
The Chariton Review : CharR
The Chattahoochee Review : ChatR

Alphabetical List of Journals

Chelsea : Chelsea
Chicago Review : ChiR
Chiron Review : ChironR
The Christian Century : ChrC
Cimarron Review : CimR
Cincinnati Poetry Review : CinPR
City Lights Review : CityLR
Clockwatch Review : ClockR
Coal City Review : CoalC
College English : ColEng
Colorado Review : ColR
Columbia : Colum
Commonweal : Comm
Confrontation : Confr
Conjunctions : Conjunc
The Connecticut Poetry Review : ConnPR
Contact II : Contact
Context South : ContextS
Crab Creek Review : CrabCR
Crazyhorse : Crazy
Cream City Review : CreamCR
Crosscurrents : CrossCur
Crucible : Crucible
Cuadernos de Poética : CuadP
Cumberland Poetry Review : CumbPR
Cutbank : CutB

Dandelion : Dandel
Denver Quarterly : DenQ
Descant : Descant
Dog River Review : DogRR
Dusty Dog : DustyD

Elf: Eclectic Literary Forum : Elf
Emerald Coast Review : EmeraldCR
English Journal : EngJ
Epoch : Epoch
Event: The Douglas College Review : Event
The Evergreen Chronicles : EvergreenC

Farmer's Market : Farm
Field: Contemporary Poetry and Poetics : Field
The Florida Review : FloridaR
Footwork : Footwork
Four Quarters : FourQ
Free Lunch : FreeL

Georgia Review : GeoR
Gettysburg Review : GettyR
Graham House Review : GrahamHR
Grain : Grain
Grand Street : GrandS
Green Mountains Review : GreenMR
The Greensboro Review : GreensboroR
Gypsy Literary Magazine : Gypsy

The Hampden-Sydney Poetry Reivew : HampSPR
Hanging Loose : HangL
Harper's Magazine : Harp
The Harvard Advocate : HarvardA
Hawaii Review : HawaiiR
Hayden's Ferry Review : HayF
Heaven Bone : HeavenB
Hellas : Hellas
High Plains Literary Review : HighP

Hiram Poetry Review : HiramPoR
The Hollins Critic : HolCrit
The Hudson Review : Hudson

Imagine : Imagine
Indiana Review : IndR
Interim : Interim
International Poetry Review : InterPR
Inti : Inti
Iowa Review : Iowa

The Jacaranda Review : Jacaranda
The James White Review : JamesWR
The Journal : Journal
The Journal of New Jersey Poets : JlNJPo

Kaleidoscope : Kaleid
Kalliope : Kalliope
Kansas Quarterly : KanQ
Kenyon Review : KenR

Lactuca : Lactuca
The Lake Street Review : LakeSR
Laurel Review : LaurelR
Linden Lane Magazine : LindLM
The Literary Review : LitR
Louisiana Literature : LouisL
Lullwater Review : LullwaterR

The Malahat Review : MalR
Manhattan Poetry Review : ManhatPR
The Manhattan Review : ManhatR
Manoa : Manoa
The Massachusetts Review : MassR
Memphis State Review : *Name changed to* River City : RiverC
Mester : Mester
Michigan Quarterly Review : MichQR
Mid-American Review : MidAR
The Midwest Quarterly : MidwQ
Mildred : Mildred
The Minnesota Review : MinnR
Mississippi Review : MissR
The Missouri Review : MissouriR
Moody Street Irregulars : MoodySI
Mss : *superseded by* New Myths

The Nation : Nat
Negative Capability : NegC
New American Writing : NewAW
New Delta Review : NewDeltaR
New England Review : NewEngR
New Letters : NewL
New Myths : NewMyths
New Orleans Review : NewOR
The New Renaissance : NewRena
The New Republic : NewRep
The New York Quarterly : NewYorkQ
The New York Review of Books : NewYRB
The New Yorker : NewYorker
Nimrod : Nimrod
The North American Review : NoAmR
North Dakota Quarterly : NoDaQ
The North Stone Review : NorthStoneR
Northeast : Northeast
Northwest Review : NowestR

Alphabetical List of Journals

Notus : Notus
La Nuez: Revista Internacional de Arte y Literatura : Nuez

Obsidian II : Obs
The Ohio Reivew : OhioR
Ometeca : Ometeca
Ontario Review : OntR
OnTheBus : OnTheBus
Osiris : Os
Outerbridge : Outbr
Oxford Magazine : OxfordM

Pacific Review : PacificR
Paintbrush : Paint
Painted Bride Quarterly : PaintedB
Painted Hills Review : PaintedHR
The Paris Review : ParisR
Parting Gifts : Parting
Partisan Review : PartR
Passages North : PassN
Pearl : Pearl
Pembroke Magazine : Pembroke
The Pennsylvania Review : PennR
Pequod : Pequod
Pig Iron : Pig
The Pikestaff Forum : PikeF
Plainsongs : Plain
Ploughshares : Ploughs
The Plum Review : PlumR
Poem : Poem
Poet And Critic : PoetC
Poet Lore : PoetL
Poetry : Poetry
Poetry Canada : PoetryC
Poetry East : PoetryE
Poetry Northwest : PoetryNW
Poetry USA : PoetryUSA
The Pottersfield Portfolio : PottPort
Prairie Fire : PraF
Prairie Schooner : PraS
Primavera : Prima

Quarry : Quarry
Quarterly Review of Literature : QRL
Quarterly West : QW

Rag Mag : RagMag
Raritan: A Quarterly Review : Raritan
Red Bass : RedBass
River City : RiverC
River Styx : RiverS
Rohwedder : Rohwedder

Salmagundi : Salm
Seneca Review : SenR
Sequoia : Sequoia
The Sewanee Review : SewanR
Shadow Play : ShadowP
Shenandoah : Shen
Shiny : Shiny
Sidewalks: An Anthology of Poetry, Short Prose, & Art : Sidewalks
Silverfish Review : SilverFR
Sing Heavenly Muse! : SingHM
Sinister Wisdom : SinW
Slipstream : SlipS

The Small Pond Magazine of Literature : SmPd
The Snail's Pace Review: A Biannual Little Magazine of Contemporary Poetry : SnailPR
Sonora Review : Sonora
South Carolina Review : SoCaR
South Coast Poetry Journal : SoCoast
South Dakota Review : SoDakR
Southern Humanities Review : SouthernHR
Southern Poetry Review : SouthernPR
Southern Review : SouthernR
Southwest Review : SouthwR
Sparrow Poverty Pamphlets : Sparrow
Spirit : SpiritSH
The Spirit That Moves Us : Spirit
Spitball: The Literary Baseball Magazine : Spitball
The Spoon River Quarterly : SpoonRQ
Stand : Stand
Sulfur : Sulfur
Swamp Root : SwampR
Sycamore Review : SycamoreR

Talisman : Talisman
Tampa Review : TampaR
Tar River Poetry : TarRP
Texas Review : TexasR
Thirteenth Moon: *See* 13th Moon *at beginning of file*
Three Rivers Poetry Journal : ThRiPo
The Threepenny Review : Thrpny
TickleAce : TickleAce
Timbuktu : Timbuktu
Translation : Translation
Tribe : Tribe
Triquarterly : TriQ
Turnstile : Turnstile

US 1 Worksheets : US1

Verse : Verse
The Virginia Quarterly Review : VirQR
Visions International : Vis

Washington Review : Wash
Weber Studies : WeberS
Webster Review : WebR
West Branch : WestB
West Coast Line (*formerly* West Coast Review) : WestCL
Western Humanities Review : WestHR
The William and Mary Review : WilliamMR
Willow Review : WillowR
Willow Springs : WillowS
Wind : Wind
The Windless Orchard : WindO
Witness : Witness
World Letter : WorldL
World Order : WorldO
The Wormwood Review : WormR
Writ : Writ
The Writer : Writer
Writers' Forum : WritersF

The Yale Review : YaleR
Yellow Silk : YellowS

Zyzzyva : Zyzzyva

The Author Index

"The Prophetic Phrase." [Boulevard] (6:2/3, #17/18) Fall 91, p. 196.
20. ACUFF, Gale G.
"Remembering Mr. Gott, Who Died of the Cure" (to Robert Bly). [LullwaterR] (3:1) Fall 91, p. 52-53.
"Vacation Accident." [Parting] (4:2) Wint 91-92, p. 18-19.
ACUNTO, Sabino d'
See D'ACUNTO, Sabino
21. ACZEL, Tamas
"Requiem." [AmerPoR] (20:5) S-O 91, p. 36.
22. ADAMS, Anna
"The Ballad of Jack Maclacuddy." [NewYorkQ] (45) 91, p. 49.
"The Gravedigger's Nightmare." [NewYorkQ] (46) 91, p. 25-25.
"I Told My Old Great Winter Coat." [NewYorkQ] (44) 91, p. 53.
23. ADAMS, Barbara
"Going Through My Pockets." [ChironR] (10:3) Aut 91, p. 44.
"Old Red Eye." [ChironR] (10:3) Aut 91, p. 12.
"The Turtle and *Henry IV*." [ChironR] (10:3) Aut 91, p. 12.
24. ADAMS, Jane Southwell
"The Limoges Tea Set." [EmeraldCR] (3) 91, c1990, p. 31.
25. ADAMS, Jefferson
"Apology From a Small Garden Beside Railroad Tracks." [HayF] (8) Spr-Sum 91, p. 74.
"Farewell." [Caliban] (10) 91, p. 136.
26. ADAMS, LaVerne
"Finished Business." [Grain] (19:4) Wint 91, p. 112.
"For Evangeline." [Grain] (19:4) Wint 91, p. 111.
"History Lesson." [AntigR] (84) Wint 91, p. 20.
27. ADAMS, Mary
"Flying Down to Rio." [NoAmR] (276:1) Mr 91, p. 66.
"The Sphere of Influence." [BlackWR] (18:1) Fall-Wint 91, p. 170.
28. ADAMS, Mary Roche
"Education." [Farm] (8:2) Fall-Wint 91-92, p. 42.
29. ADAMS, Maureen
"Coming Through Getting." [CentralP] (19/20) Spr-Fall 91, p. 240-242.
30. ADAMS, Monica
"December." [TarRP] (31:1) Fall 91, p. 24.
31. ADAMS, Phillip
"Chill." [PoetryUSA] (22) Spr 91, p. 19.
32. ADAMS, Sylvia
"O's." [Arc] (27) Aut 91, p. 9.
"Small Deaths, Sad Interludes." [Arc] (27) Aut 91, p. 12.
"Trebinje." [Arc] (27) Aut 91, p. 10-11.
33. ADAMS, Terry
"I Believe in All Things Visible and Invisible." [ManhatPR] (13) [91?], p. 37.
"Pietà." [Poetry] (158:6) S 91, p. 315.
"The Touching." [Poetry] (157:5) F 91, p. 264.
34. ADCOCK, Betty
"Dear Fred." [Pembroke] (23) 91, p. 79-80.
35. ADDERLEY, Carol
"Soldier's Song." [WorldL] (2) 91, p. 16.
36. ADDINGTON, Jennifer
"Being Stone." [Nimrod] (35:1) Fall-Wint 91, p. 62.
37. ADDINGTON, Rosa Lea
"Leonardo's Notebooks." [WindO] (55) Wint 91-92, p. 15-16.
"Our Fathers." [WindO] (55) Wint 91-92, p. 17-18.
"There Were Neighborhoods." [WindO] (55) Wint 91-92, p. 14-15.
"Transference." [WindO] (55) Wint 91-92, p. 16-17.
38. ADDONIZIO, Kim
"China Camp, California." [PraS] (65:3) Fall 91, p. 28.
"The Concept of God." [NewEngR] (13:3/4) Spr-Sum 91, p. 168-169.
"Explication." [Agni] (34) 91, p. 106-108.
"His Ghost, Again." [Thrpny] (47) Fall 91, p. 16.
"In Late Summer." [PraS] (65:3) Fall 91, p. 27.
"The Sound." [NewEngR] (13:3/4) Spr-Sum 91, p. 168.
"The Taste of Apples." [NewEngR] (13:3/4) Spr-Sum 91, p. 167.
"Them." [PraS] (65:3) Fall 91, p. 26.

39. ADEWALE, Toyin
    "Trial." [LitR] (34:4) Sum 91, p. 432.
    "You Cannot Avoid Me." [LitR] (34:4) Sum 91, p. 433.
40. ADILMAN, Mona Elaine
    "The Lobbyist." [CanLit] (128) Spr 91, p. 9-10.
41. ADKINS, Keith Joseph
    "GreatBrownPrince." [ChangingM] (23) Fall-Wint 91, p. 25.
    "This Is My Manhood." [ChangingM] (23) Fall-Wint 91, p. 24.
42. ADKINS, Paul David
    "Cousteau in Normandy." [CapeR] (26:1) Spr 91, p. 7.
    "The World Before the Story of Jonah." [Elf] (1:1) Spr 91, p. 37.
43. ADONIS
    "This Is My Name" (tr. by Kamal Abu-Deeb). [GrandS] (10:4, #40) 91, p. 151-163.
44. AESCHYLUS
    "Sisyphus" (fragments: 121-127, tr. by John Taggart). [Talisman] (6) Spr 91, p. 26.
    "The Wool-Carders" (fragments: 84-87, tr. by John Taggart). [Talisman] (6) Spr 91, p.
        25.
45. AGARD, John
    "Anancy's Thoughts on Love." [GrahamHR] (14) Spr 91, p. 22-23.
    "Come from That Window Child" (for Pat Rodney & her children and the other
        thousands in whom Walter Rodney lives on). [GrahamHR] (14) Spr 91, p. 26.
    "Cowtalk." [GrahamHR] (14) Spr 91, p. 24-25.
46. AGARWAL, Bina
    "Jealousy." [Agni] (33) 91, p. 48.
    "On the Passing of Age." [Ploughs] (17:2/3) Fall 91, p. 126.
AGHA SHAHID ALI
    See ALI, Agha Shahid
47. AGOSIN, Marjorie
    "Ports" (tr. by Cola Franzen). [Agni] (34) 91, p. 162.
    "When the evening light burns" (tr. by Celeste Kostopulus-Cooperman). [Agni] (33)
        91, p. 41.
48. AGOSTINO, Paul
    "Blank Screens." [WormR] (31:4, #124) 91, p. 101.
    "Institutional Cooking." [WormR] (31:4, #124) 91, p. 100-101.
    "Luminaries." [WormR] (31:4, #124) 91, p. 100.
    "Prose Writing." [ChironR] (10:2) Sum 91, p. 45.
    "Shadow Seeds." [WormR] (31:4, #124) 91, p. 102.
AGUIAR, Fred d'
    See D'AGUIAR, Fred
49. AGUSTINI, Delmira
    "Vision." [Agni] (34) 91, p. 193-194.
50. AHARONI, Ada
    "A Bridge of Peace Above the Intefada." [InterPR] (15:1) Spr 89, p. 98.
    "The Bus Station" (tr. of Yehuda Amichai). [InterPR] (15:1) Spr 89, p. 101.
    "Israel at Forty." [InterPR] (15:1) Spr 89, p. 99.
    "A Jewish Woman's Poem: Not in Your Museum Anymore." [InterPR] (15:1) Spr 89,
        p. 100.
51. AHO, Margaret
    "Dreaming the Sound of Yellow." [BelPoJ] (41:4) Sum 91, p. 12-13.
52. AI
    "Oedipus." [OnTheBus] (8/9) 91, p. 15-16.
53. AIDOO, Ama Ata
    "Modern African Stories 1." [LitR] (34:4) Sum 91, p. 434.
    "A Path in the Sky or 7 A.M. and Airborne." [LitR] (34:4) Sum 91, p. 435-436.
54. AISENBERG, Katy
    "The Night Under Glass." [MissR] (19:3) 91, p. 136-137.
    "Out of the Element." [MissR] (19:3) 91, p. 134-135.
    "Street Construction." [MissR] (19:3) 91, p. 133.
55. AIZENBERG, Mikhail
    "Untitled: Be careful: You mustn't get mixed up with that fellow" (tr. by J. Kates).
        [OnTheBus] (8/9) 91, p. 199.
    "Untitled: The life of the soul. The soul trembles like foliage" (tr. by J. Kates).
        [OnTheBus] (8/9) 91, p. 199.
    "Untitled: Who now remembers what kind of animal" (tr. by J. Kates). [GreenMR]
        (NS 5:1) Sum-Fall 91, p. 31.

56. AIZENBERG, Susan
"The Life You Really Have." [Journal] (15:2) Fall 91, p. 15-16.
57. AKERS, Ellery
"Letters to Anna, 1846-54: A Pioneer Woman's Journey." [CalQ] (32/33) Spr 90, p. 34-41.
58. AKHMATOVA, Anna
"Answer" (tr. by Jean Murphy). [WebR] (15) Spr 91, p. 27.
"Falling" (tr. by Julia V. Ostashchenko). [Kalliope] (13:1) 91, p. 42.
AKIMINE, Ki no
See KI no AKIMINE
59. AKMAKJIAN, Alan P.
"Addicts." [BlackBR] (13) Spr-Sum 91, p. 13.
"August Moon in Harlem, NY." [BlackBR] (14) Fall-Wint 91, p. 20.
"Grounded Angels." [BlackBR] (13) Spr-Sum 91, p. 13.
"Moonlighting at McDonald's." [BlackBR] (14) Fall-Wint 91, p. 21.
"Runaway in Washington, DC." [BlackBR] (14) Fall-Wint 91, p. 20.
"Street Window a Cappella." [BlackBR] (13) Spr-Sum 91, p. 13.
AL-QASTALLI, Ibn Darraj
See IBN DARRAJ AL-QASTALLI
60. ALARCON, Diana
"Memories." [Mildred] (4:2/5:1) 91, p. 98.
61. ALARCON, Francisco X.
"Dialectica del Amor" (Selections: 4 poems). [JamesWR] (8:3) Spr 91, p. 1.
"Dialectics of Love" (Selections: 4 poems). [JamesWR] (8:3) Spr 91, p. 1.
"Grandson's Rage." [PoetryUSA] (23) Sum 91, p. 15.
"Mestizo." [Zyzzyva] (7:2) Sum 91, p. 101-102.
"Ode to Tomatoes." [Zyzzyva] (7:2) Sum 91, p. 104.
"*Ollin:* Movement." [Zyzzyva] (7:2) Sum 91, p. 103.
"Visions." [PoetryUSA] (22) Spr 91, p. 13.
62. ALBERT, Sam
"Layers." [Agni] (34) 91, p. 230-231.
63. ALBERTS, Mick
"Ode to a Lady Standing on a Dead Cat After the Greyhound Broke Down." [SycamoreR] (3:2) Sum 91, p. 29.
"Reunion at Kittyhawk." [SycamoreR] (3:2) Sum 91, p. 30-32.
64. ALBO, Elisa
"Knowledge." [PoetryE] (32) Fall 91, p. 123-124.
65. ALBRECHT, Laura
"Folding Flowers." [CoalC] (4) S 91, p. 5.
"Her Summer." [Parting] (4:1) Sum 91, p. 8.
"Nasturtiums." [WestB] (29) 91, p. 63.
"Quarter after Midnight." [TexasR] (12:3/4) Fall-Wint 91, p. 68-69.
"Shoe Poem." [SmPd] (28:2, #82) Spr 91, p. 31.
"Tied." [WestB] (29) 91, p. 62.
66. ALCAEUS
"Drinking Song" (tr. by Jane Stuart). [GrahamHR] (15) Fall 91, p. 88.
"Hebrus" (tr. by Jane Stuart). [GrahamHR] (15) Fall 91, p. 87.
67. ALCOSSER, Sandra
"Music for the Dark Earth / Fiddling for Worms." [Colum] (15) 90, p. 173-174.
"Pole Boat at Honey Island." [Colum] (15) 90, p. 172.
68. ALDRIDGE, Richard
"Alice Packard" (b. 1896, d. 1988). [CapeR] (26:1) Spr 91, p. 32-33.
"Her Note to Him, Slid Under the Door." [BellArk] (7:2) Mr-Ap 91, p. 11.
"The Rock." [BellArk] (7:6) N-D 91, p. 24.
"Why We Went That Far." [BellArk] (7:1) Ja-F 91, p. 7.
"The Youth of America Meet Nonook of the North." [BellArk] (7:1) Ja-F 91, p. 12.
69. ALEJANDRE, Rich
"Rhythm." [PacificR] (10) 91-92, p. 79.
70. ALESHIRE, Joan
"Top of the World." [Poetry] (158:6) S 91, p. 330-331.
ALEX I
See I., Alex
71. ALEXANDER, Elizabeth
"After." [ParisR] (33:121) Wint 91, p. 49.
"Blackwater River." [ManhatPR] (13) [91?], p. 36.
"Butter." [Callaloo] (14:4) Fall 91, p. 909.

"Dream # 3." [ParisR] (33:121) Wint 91, p. 48.
"Family Stone." [Callaloo] (14:4) Fall 91, p. 910.
"Passage." [Callaloo] (14:4) Fall 91, p. 912-913.
"What I'm Telling You." [Callaloo] (14:4) Fall 91, p. 911.

72. ALEXANDER, Francis W.
"Near the atomic plant." [BlackBR] (13) Spr-Sum 91, p. 19.
"Veteran bugler." [BlackBR] (13) Spr-Sum 91, p. 19.

73. ALEXANDER, Hannah (Hanna)
"Ballerina." [DustyD] Ap 91, p. 3.
"For a Son Who Died." [DustyD] Je 91, p. 40.
"Madame Bovary of Levittown." [Vis] (36) 91, p. 34.

74. ALEXANDER, Lynn
"The One Without an Umbrella." [LullwaterR] (2:2) Spr 91, p. 8.

75. ALEXANDER, Meena
"Paper Filled with Light" (In memory of Uma Shankar Joshi, 1911-1988). [GrandS]
(10:3, #39) 91, p. 99-101.

76. ALEXANDER, Ronald
"Fifth Period Study Hall." [OnTheBus] (8/9) 91, p. 17.

77. ALEXANDER, Will
"A National Day in Bangladesh." [Caliban] (10) 91, p. 74-77.
"Utopian Stellar Concentrations." [Caliban] (10) 91, p. 78-83.

78. ALEXANDRE, António Franco
"Don't Come Back to Me. Don't Look for Me" (tr. by Alexis Levitin). [Trans] (25) Spr
91, p. 145.
"Might We, One Day, Love These Store Windows" (tr. by Alexis Levitin). [Trans] (25)
Spr 91, p. 142.
"There Are So Many Reasons" (tr. by Alexis Levitin). [Trans] (25) Spr 91, p. 144.
"Your Love, I Well Know, Is a Musical Word" (tr. by Alexis Levitin). [Trans] (25) Spr
91, p. 143.

79. ALEXIE, Sherman
"Breakaway Bar #1." [SlipS] (11) 91, p. 10.
"Breakaway Bar #3." [SlipS] (11) 91, p. 10.
"Breakaway Bar #4." [SlipS] (11) 91, p. 11.
"Breaking Out the Shovel" (for Spike). [BelPoJ] (42:2) Wint 91-92, p. 28-29.
"Ceremonies." [HangL] (58) 91, p. 5.
"Horses" (For John & Alex). [BelPoJ] (41:4) Sum 91, p. 16-18.
"If You're an Indian, Why Don't You Write Nature Poetry?" [BlackBR] (14) Fall-Wint
91, p. 6.
"Introduction to Native American Literature." [Caliban] (10) 91, p. 55-57.
"Lottery." [Caliban] (10) 91, p. 54.
"Misdemeanors." [Caliban] (10) 91, p. 54.
"No Drugs or Alcohol Allowed." [HangL] (58) 91, p. 6.
"Reservation Graffiti." [Caliban] (10) 91, p. 59-60.
"Shoes." [BelPoJ] (42:2) Wint 91-92, p. 26-27.
"Songs from the Film." [Caliban] (10) 91, p. 58.
"Tattoo Tears" (for Joy Harjo). [Caliban] (10) 91, p. 51-53.
"War All the Time." [HangL] (58) 91, p. 7.

80. ALEY, Elizabeth
"Batik." [HawaiiR] (16:1, #34) Wint 91-92, p. 77.

81. ALFARO, Luis
"True Stories from the Corner of Pico & Union." [Rohwedder] (6) Sum-Fall 91, p.
3-7.

82. ALFERI, Pierre
"Les Allures Naturelles" (P.O.L. 1991, selections: 8-9, tr. by Cole Swensen). [Avec]
(4:1) 91, p. 82-84.

83. ALI, Agha Shahid
"From Another Desert." [Bomb] (36) Sum 91, p. 86-87.
"Ghazal." [GrandS] (10:3, #39) 91, p. 97-98.
"I See Chile in My Rearview Mirror." [Field] (44) Spr 91, p. 47-49.
"A Nostalgist's Map of America" (for Philip Paul Orlando). [ParisR] (33:120) Fall 91,
p. 118-120.
"The Rain of Stones Is Finished" (Elegy for Hassan Nasir, tortured to death in the
Labore [sic] Fort, 1959, tr. of Faiz Ahmed Faiz). [Spirit] (11) 91, p. 23.

84. ALKAIOS
Excerpts (tr. by Sam Hamill). [WillowS] (28) Sum 91, p. 66-69.

85. ALKALAY-GUT, Karen
    "Lovers." [AmerV] (23) Sum 91, p. 63-64.
86. ALLARDT, Linda
    "The Quarry." [CinPR] (22) Spr 91, p. 29.
87. ALLEN, Annette
    "The Apple." [SouthernPR] (31:2) Fall 91, p. 13.
    "Lineage." [SouthernPR] (31:2) Fall 91, p. 12.
88. ALLEN, Blair H.
    "Graveyard Shift." [Gypsy] (17) 91, p. 61.
89. ALLEN, Deborah
    "Fishing for Bass." [SoDakR] (29:3 part 2) Aut 91, p. 89.
90. ALLEN, Gilbert
    "Cecilia." [Pembroke] (23) 91, p. 35.
    "Mist and Fire." [Pembroke] (23) 91, p. 34.
    "Professor of the Mall." [CumbPR] (11:1) Fall 91, p. 68-69.
91. ALLEN, Heather
    "The Country of Childhood." [Poetry] (158:2) My 91, p. 69-71.
92. ALLEN, Jeffery Renard
    "The American Graveyard" (for George Romero). [Contact] (10:59/60/61) Spr 91, p. 35.
    "Erzulie-Red Eyes." [Obs] (6:2) Sum 91, p. 18-19.
    "Eyes in the Water." [Obs] (6:2) Sum 91, p. 20-21.
    "Harbors and Spirits" (for Alice Allen, Mom). [Obs] (6:2) Sum 91, p. 21-29.
    "He Was Like Us" (for Steve Biko). [Contact] (10:59/60/61) Spr 91, p. 32-34.
    "Kaabaa" (for Muhammad Ali). [Caliban] (10) 91, p. 46-50.
    "Mawu-Lisa." [Obs] (6:2) Sum 91, p. 19.
    "Petro." [Obs] (6:2) Sum 91, p. 20.
93. ALLEN, Paul
    "Attack." [CharR] (17:1) Spr 91, p. 100-102.
94. ALLEN, Paula Gunn
    "Perhaps Somebody Dreams" (for John Coltrane). [PoetryE] (32) Fall 91, p. 36-39.
95. ALLIN, Louise
    "Blueberries" (tr. of Thérèse Desrosiers). [WebR] (15) Spr 91, p. 38.
    "She Cannot Fade." [Vis] (35) 91, p. 41.
    "Transubstantiation" (tr. of Thérèse Desrosiers). [WebR] (15) Spr 91, p. 38.
96. ALLMAN, John
    "Refigurations" (after an exhibit of recent painting from Germany). [AntR] (49:2) Spr 91, p. 238-239.
    "Taking the 9:26 Out of Katonah" (for Steven). [PoetryNW] (32:2) Sum 91, p. 16-17.
97. ALMON, Bert
    "Bon Appetit." [AntigR] (85/86) Spr-Sum 91, p. 11.
    "Complaint to Miles Francis Stapleton Fitzalan-Howard, K. G., 17th Duke of Norfolk and Earl Marshal of England." [AntigR] (85/86) Spr-Sum 91, p. 12.
    "Grand Texas Minuet" (for Nancy Mattson). [Arc] (27) Aut 91, p. 30.
    "Timekeepers." [AntigR] (85/86) Spr-Sum 91, p. 9-10.
98. ALMON, Margaret
    "Love at the Five and Dime" (for Nanci Griffith). [MalR] (96) Fall 91, p. 75.
99. ALMY, Kathryn
    "Orientation." [WillowR] Spr 91, p. 34.
ALONSO, Jose ("Chien") Garcia
    See GARCIA-ALONSO, Jose ("Chien")
100. ALPERT, Cathryn
    "Zen Dog Tricks." [Parting] (4:1) Sum 91, p. 33.
101. ALTHAUS, Keith
    "Letter to M." [Agni] (34) 91, p. 221-222.
102. ALTIZER, Nell
    "The Churching of Women." [13thMoon] (9:1/2) 91, p. 12.
    "The Churching of Women." [BambooR] (50/51) Spr-Sum 91, p. 111.
    "Night Music." [13thMoon] (9:1/2) 91, p. 13.
    "Pantoum." [13thMoon] (9:1/2) 91, p. 11.
    "Pantoum." [BambooR] (50/51) Spr-Sum 91, p. 106-107.
    "Pearl." [BambooR] (50/51) Spr-Sum 91, p. 105.
    "Runes for the Stepmother." [BambooR] (50/51) Spr-Sum 91, p. 108-110.
103. ALVELO, Wilfredo
    "Punto y Coma." [Nuez] (3:8/9) 91, p. 21.

104. ALYN, Marc
"A la Gare" (French tr. of Srecko Kosovel). [InterPR] (17:1) Spr 91, p. 72.
"Ce N'Est Pas Toi" (French tr. of Srecko Kosovel). [InterPR] (17:1) Spr 91, p. 76.
"Le Chant des Humiliés" (French tr. of Srecko Kosovel). [InterPR] (17:1) Spr 91, p. 72.
"Le Village Karstique" (French tr. of Srecko Kosovel). [InterPR] (17:1) Spr 91, p. 74, 76.

105. AMATUZIO, Anna
"Does Air Need Earth or Does Earth Need Air?" [Event] (20:2) Sum 91, p. 105.

106. AMEN, Grover
"On the Runway." [GrandS] (10:2, #38) 91, p. 204-205.

107. AMICHAI, Yehuda
"The Bus Station" (tr. by Ada Aharoni). [InterPR] (15:1) Spr 89, p. 101.

108. AMICOST, Chele
"Civil War Immortality." [EmeraldCR] (3) 91, c1990, p. 124-125.
"Since You Cared Enough to Ask" (Inspired by and dedicated to Leonard Temme). [EmeraldCR] (3) 91, c1990, p. 81-82.

109. AMIDON, Richard
"Things You Almost Had Before You Lost Them." [CutB] (35) Wint-Spr 91, p. 82-83.

110. AMIRTHANAYAGAM, Indran
"Beating the Drum." [HangL] (59) 91, p. 11.
"Dim Sum." [HangL] (59) 91, p. 12.
"There Are Many Things I Want to Tell You." [KenR] (NS 13:4) Fall 91, p. 57-59.
"The White Piano." [KenR] (NS 13:4) Fall 91, p. 60.

111. AMMANN, Alan
"The World Famous Davenport Brothers." [LullwaterR] (3:1) Fall 91, p. 23-25.

112. AMMONS, A. R.
"Cracking a Few Hundred Million Years." [Spirit] (11) 91, p. 279.
"An Improvisation for Angular Momentum." [Poetry] (159:1) O 91, p. 2-3.
"An Improvisation for Soot and Suet." [Poetry] (159:1) O 91, p. 4.
"An Improvisation for the Pieties of Modernism." [Poetry] (159:1) O 91, p. 1-2.
"Museums." [PartR] (58:1) Wint 91, p. 118.
"Religious Matters." [SouthernR] (27:1) Ja 91, p. 49-50.
"Time Being." [PartR] (58:1) Wint 91, p. 118-119.

113. ANDAY, Melih Cevdet
"Are We Going to Live Without Aging?" (tr. by Talat Halman). [Talisman] (6) Spr 91, p. 105-106.
"Barefoot" (tr. by Talat Halman). [Talisman] (6) Spr 91, p. 106.
"The Battle of Kadesh" (tr. by Talat Halman). [Talisman] (6) Spr 91, p. 104.
"The Future" (tr. by Talat Halman). [Talisman] (6) Spr 91, p. 105.
"Gypsies" (tr. by Talat Halman). [Talisman] (6) Spr 91, p. 106.
"I Became a Tree" (tr. by Talat Halman). [Talisman] (6) Spr 91, p. 105.
"Vertigo" (tr. by Talat Halman). [Talisman] (6) Spr 91, p. 104.

114. ANDERSEN, Benny
"The Last Poem in the World" (tr. by Alex Taylor). [Vis] (37) 91, p. 14.

115. ANDERSEN, Steen
"Closer" (tr. by the author). [Vis] (37) 91, p. 11.

116. ANDERSON, Barbara
"Dorothy: 11:21 PM." [Crazy] (40) Spr 91, p. 25-28.
"Melinda: Dawn." [Sonora] (20) Wint 91, p. 109-115.

117. ANDERSON, Chester G.
"2 x 7" (for John, Henry, Sir Bones). [NorthStoneR] (10) Fall 91-Wint 92, p. 85-99.

118. ANDERSON, Cynthia
"New Adirondacks." [SoCoast] (11) Wint 91, p. 57.

119. ANDERSON, Daniel
"Buddy Check." [NewRep] (205:26/27) 23-30 D 91, p. 45.

120. ANDERSON, David
"Oriental Song" (tr. of Federico García Lorca, w. Linda C. Ehrlich). [CumbPR] (11:1) Fall 91, p. 37-43.

121. ANDERSON, Doug
"Corso." [MoodySI] (24/25/26) Spr 91, p. 50.
"Los Desastres de la Guerre." [SouthernR] (27:4) O 91, p. 924-928.
"Jones / Baraka." [MoodySI] (24/25/26) Spr 91, p. 20.
"Night Ambush" (Quang Nam Province, 1967). [PoetC] (22:2) Wint 91, p. 45.
"Prisoner's Song." [SouthernR] (27:4) O 91, p. 928-929.

122. ANDERSON, Elaine
  "Oklahoma." [HayF] (9) Fall-Wint 91, p. 61.
123. ANDERSON, Emily F.
  "Haiku." [Bogg] (64) 91, p. 18.
124. ANDERSON, Jack
  "Callings." [WashR] (16:6) Ap-My 91, p. 13.
  "The Cities You Fly Over." [Chelsea] (50) 91, p. 37.
  "Complaints." [HangL] (58) 91, p. 10-11.
  "Golden Moment." [HangL] (58) 91, p. 9.
  "The San Andreas Fault." [Chelsea] (50) 91, p. 36.
  "Sleeping Together." [HangL] (58) 91, p. 8.
125. ANDERSON, James C. (James Clark)
  "The Dark Bedroom." [YellowS] (37) Fall-Wint 91, p. 8.
  "The Look Back." [YellowS] (38) Wint-Spr 91-92, p. 28-29.
  "Tarragon." [YellowS] (37) Fall-Wint 91, p. 10.
  "Waking Up Twice." [YellowS] (37) Fall-Wint 91, p. 9.
126. ANDERSON, Janet
  "Alone in the golden grasss, under the sky" (grasss [sic]). [US1] (24/25) Spr 91, p.
     5.
127. ANDERSON, Jon
  "35 Years Before Christ." [Sonora] (20) Wint 91, p. 43-46.
  "The Cure." [Sonora] (20) Wint 91, p. 45.
128. ANDERSON, Kathy Elaine
  "Ember." [IndR] (14:3) Fall 91, p. 24-27.
129. ANDERSON, Ken
  "The Christmas Tree." [InterPR] (17:2) Fall 91, p. 122.
  "Little Miss Lazarus" (to Lara). [LullwaterR] (2:2) Spr 91, p. 50-51.
130. ANDERSON, Lori
  "Adding to My Angel-Hair Collection." [13thMoon] (9:1/2) 91, p. 15.
  "Autobiography." [13thMoon] (9:1/2) 91, p. 17.
  "If This Quilt of Names Were Made of Fire." [13thMoon] (9:1/2) 91, p. 16.
  "I'm Talking Fast to My Sister on How to Sharpen an Axe." [13thMoon] (9:1/2) 91,
     p. 18-20.
  "Ode." [13thMoon] (9:1/2) 91, p. 14.
  "What If I Write a Poem in Which a Mammiform Situla Speaks." [13thMoon] (9:1/2)
     91, p. 21.
  "What Then." [13thMoon] (9:1/2) 91, p. 22.
131. ANDERSON, Maggie
  "End of Summer in a Small Garden." [AmerV] (24) Fall 91, p. 12.
132. ANDERSON, Marilyn
  "On Being Asked What I Would Save If My House Caught Fire." [Sidewalks] (1)
     Aug 91, p. 28.
133. ANDERSON, Mark
  "The Light in Hell's Canyon." [SouthernPR] (31:1) Spr 91, p. 3536.
  "Possession." [Parting] (4:2) Wint 91-92, p. 34.
  "Remains." [SouthernPR] (31:2) Fall 91, p. 36.
134. ANDERSON, Marlene
  "Butter Flies." [PacificR] (10) 91-92, p. 91.
135. ANDERSON, Michael
  "Deuteronomy, a little torque of extruded plastic." [WashR] (17:3) O-N 91, p. 12.
  "Men begin to resemble the idealogical [sic] constructs." [WashR] (17:3) O-N 91, p.
     12.
  "Patio de los Naranjos." [Aerial] (6/7) 91, p. 76.
  "Prate City." [Aerial] (6/7) 91, p. 76.
  "Prate City." [WashR] (17:3) O-N 91, p. 12.
136. ANDERSON, Peter
  "Key to the Kingdom" (For Phoenix Quin). [AnthNEW] (3) 91, p. 14.
137. ANDERSON, Phil
  "For Soyo — Remembering Her a Manzanar." [BambooR] (52) Fall 91, p. 13-14.
  "Portrait of My Father and Me." [BambooR] (52) Fall 91, p. 15-16.
138. ANDERSON, Robert
  "G.I. Joe." [Thrpny] (45) Spr 91, p. 20.
139. ANDERSON, Susan
  "The Butterfly." [CarolQ] (44:1) Fall 91, p. 51.
  "O.K., Who Gets to be Jim Morrison?" [Caliban] (10) 91, p. 121.

140. ANDERSON, Warwick
     "The Dalang." [Caliban] (10) 91, p. 111.
     "Unit." [Caliban] (10) 91, p. 110.
141. ANDERSON-POLK, Lara
     "The 2nd Husband." [PacificR] (9) 91, p. 27.
     "Bad Apple." [PacificR] (9) 91, p. 26.
     "Lost Identity." [PacificR] (9) 91, p. 25.
142. ANDRADE, Eugénio de
     "Again" (tr. by Alexis Levitin). [Vis] (36) 91, p. 24.
     "Ainda Espero." [HawaiiR] (15:2, #32) Spr 91, p. 26.
     "The Bitter Taste of an Orange" (tr. by Alexis Levitin). [Chelsea] (50) 91, p. 69.
     "Body" (tr. by Alexis Levitin). [Trans] (25) Spr 91, p. 82.
     "The Body Knows" (tr. by Alexis Levitin). [Chelsea] (50) 91, p. 69.
     "By the Fire" (tr. by Alexis Levitin). [GrahamHR] (15) Fall 91, p. 102.
     "Com as sete cores desenhas uma criança." [SouthernHR] (25:4) Fall 91, p. 369.
     "Home" (tr. by Alexis Levitin). [Trans] (25) Spr 91, p. 80.
     "I Hear You As If Hearing Summer Come" (tr. by Alexis Levitin). [ColR] (NS 17:2)
          Fall-Wint 90, p. 103.
     "I Leave to Miguel the Things of Morning" (tr. by Alexis Levitin). [Chelsea] (50) 91,
          p. 69.
     "Jacarandas" (tr. by Alexis Levitin). [NewOR] (18:4) Wint 91, p. 45.
     "The lamp lit" (tr. by Alexis Levitin). [SouthernHR] (25:4) Fall 91, p. 370.
     "A Lâmpada acesa." [SouthernHR] (25:4) Fall 91, p. 370.
     "The Patio Light" (tr. by Alexis Levitin). [GrahamHR] (15) Fall 91, p. 103.
     "Peaches" (tr. by Alexis Levitin). [Trans] (25) Spr 91, p. 81.
     "Short Subject" (tr. by Alexis Levitin). [NewOR] (18:4) Wint 91, p. 64.
     "South" (tr. by Alexis Levitin). [HawaiiR] (15:2, #32) Spr 91, p. 27.
     "Still I Hope" (tr. by Alexis Levitin). [HawaiiR] (15:2, #32) Spr 91, p. 26.
     "Still on Purity" (tr. by Alexis Levitin). [Trans] (25) Spr 91, p. 81.
     "Sul." [HawaiiR] (15:2, #32) Spr 91, p. 27.
     "To Follow Still Those Signs" (tr. by Alexis Levitin). [Trans] (25) Spr 91, p. 80.
     "With the seven colors you draw a child" (tr. by Alexis Levitin). [SouthernHR] (25:4)
          Fall 91, p. 369.
     "You Speak of Sun" (tr. by Alexis Levitin). [Trans] (25) Spr 91, p. 82.
143. ANDRASICK, Kathleen Dudden
     "Sea Dream." [ChamLR] (8-9) Spr-Fall 91, p. 102-103.
     "Temptation at Mid-ocean." [ChamLR] (8-9) Spr-Fall 91, p. 104.
144. ANDRE, Jean
     "The Dream-Maker." [Elf] (1:2) Sum 91, p. 24-25.
145. ANDRESEN, Sophia de Mello Breyner
     "The Navigators" (tr. by Alexis Levitin). [Trans] (25) Spr 91, p. 91.
     "Olympus" (tr. by Richard Zenith). [Trans] (25) Spr 91, p. 92.
     "Penelope" (tr. by Alexis Levitin). [Trans] (25) Spr 91, p. 91.
     "Portrait of an Unknown Princess" (tr. by Alexis Levitin). [Trans] (25) Spr 91, p. 90.
     "We Will Recognize" (tr. by Alexis Levitin). [Trans] (25) Spr 91, p. 91.
     "Writing II" (tr. by Richard Zenith). [Trans] (25) Spr 91, p. 93.
146. ANDREWS, Allison L.
     "Out of the Manics." [MoodySI] (24/25/26) Spr 91, p. 49.
147. ANDREWS, Bruce
     "Divestiture — E." [WestCL] (25:2, #5) Fall 91, p. 74-82.
     "Drug/Hysteria." [Caliban] (10) 91, p. 13.
     "Who Shouted?" [Sulfur] (11:1, #28) Spr 91, p. 40-49.
148. ANDREWS, Claudia Emerson
     "Abandoned Farm Grave." [TriQ] (83) Wint 91-92, p. 115.
     "Dry Spell." [SouthernPR] (31:2) Fall 91, p. 36-37.
     "The Moon Is Made." [TriQ] (83) Wint 91-92, p. 116.
     "Preserves." [SouthernPR] (31:2) Fall 91, p. 38.
     "Romantic Fever." [TriQ] (83) Wint 91-92, p. 118.
     "Stable." [SouthernPR] (31:2) Fall 91, p. 37-38.
     "The Taxidermist." [TriQ] (83) Wint 91-92, p. 117.
149. ANDREWS, Cynthia
     "Birch Leaves on the Placement." [DogRR] (10:2) Fall-Wint 91, p. 34.
150. ANDREWS, Linda
     "Greuor Farm, North Wales." [MidwQ] (32:2) Wint 91, p. 181-182.
     "Only Men Go to Garnet." [CutB] (36) Sum 91, p. 40.
     "The True Story of the Bird Women." [WillowS] (28) Sum 91, p. 11.

151. ANDREWS, Michael
"Cao Dai Temple, 1969, the Nam." [OnTheBus] (8/9) 91, p. 18.
"Old Woman in the Tehran Post Office." [OnTheBus] (8/9) 91, p. 22.
"Serapes, La Paz, Bolivia, 1976." [OnTheBus] (8/9) 91, p. 23-24.
"She Broke the Rules." [OnTheBus] (8/9) 91, p. 20-22.
152. ANDREWS, Nin
"The Artichoke." [ParisR] (33:120) Fall 91, p. 203.
153. ANDREYEVA, Victoria
"The Half-Faded Day" (tr. by Thomas Epstein). [LitR] (34:3) Spr 91, p. 372-374.
"Summer in Mr. Thompson's House in Sussex" (tr. by Thomas Epstein). [LitR]
(34:3) Spr 91, p. 375.
"Wandering in Parallel Dreams" (tr. by Thomas Epstein). [LitR] (34:3) Spr 91, p.
375.
154. ANDROLA, Ron
"Duke Tang." [Gypsy] (17) 91, p. 67.
"Worm Becomes Bird." [Bogg] (64) 91, p. 15.
155. ANGEL, Ralph
"At the Seams." [Crazy] (40) Spr 91, p. 7.
"From Goya's Room." [Crazy] (40) Spr 91, p. 8.
"In Every Direction." [Poetry] (158:4) Jl 91, p. 197.
"Leaving One." [Crazy] (40) Spr 91, p. 9-10.
"Like Land Crabs." [CimR] (97) O 91, p. 45.
ANGELLE, Lesli l'
See L'ANGELLE, Lesli
ANGELO, G. Pearce de
See DeANGELO, G. Pearce
156. ANGIOLIERI, Cecco
"If I Were Fire" (tr. by Felix Stefanile). [Hellas] (2:1) Spr 91, p. 65.
157. ANGST, Bim
"Backwater, March." [WestB] (29) 91, p. 5.
"Fishing the Allegheny Mountains" (for my father). [WestB] (29) 91, p. 7.
"Sounding the Drawn Dirt Circle" (for Addie). [WestB] (29) 91, p. 6.
158. ANHALT, Nedda G. de
"La Risa." [Nuez] (3:7) 91, p. 24.
159. ANI, Friedrich
"In the Eighty-Fifth Century" (tr. by Renata Cinti). [ArtfulD] (20/21) 91, p. 38-39.
160. ANNANDALE, David
"Dismemberment." [PraF] (12:1 #54) Spr 91, p. 18-23.
161. ANNENSKY, Innokenty
"First Fortepiano Sonnet" (tr. by Nancy Tittler and Devon Miller-Duggan).
[SpoonRQ] (16:3/4) Sum-Fall 91, p. 41.
"The Second Fortepiano Sonnet" (tr. by Nancy Tittler and Devon Miller-Duggan).
[SpoonRQ] (16:3/4) Sum-Fall 91, p. 42.
162. ANONYMOUS
"Although spring returns" (tr. by Sam Hamill). [ColR] (NS 17:2) Fall-Wint 90, p. 20.
"An Answer to Lord Byron's Lines to the Governess." [KenR] (NS 13:3) Sum 91, p.
79-80.
"Autumn has returned" (tr. by Sam Hamill). [ColR] (NS 17:2) Fall-Wint 90, p. 19.
"Autumn's consequence" (tr. by Sam Hamill). [ColR] (NS 17:2) Fall-Wint 90, p. 21.
"Cicadas sing" (tr. by Sam Hamill). [ColR] (NS 17:2) Fall-Wint 90, p. 22.
"Don't let that cold wind" (tr. by Sam Hamill). [ColR] (NS 17:2) Fall-Wint 90, p. 19.
"Epic of Gilgamesh" (Selections, tr. by David Ferry). [TriQ] (83) Wint 91-92, p.
135-155.
"Four Nahautl Poems [sic, i.e. Nahuatl]" (tr. from the Spanish by Michael Dunev).
[Zyzzyva] (7:2) Sum 91, p. 59-62.
"From an Ancient Monastic Customary: Rules for Novices" (fragment found in a
ruined library somewhere in France, tr. from the Frankish by Benedict Auer).
[CrabCR] (7:3) 91, p. 27.
"Hearing cicadas" (tr. by Sam Hamill). [ColR] (NS 17:2) Fall-Wint 90, p. 22.
"In bare autumn fields" (tr. by Sam Hamill). [ColR] (NS 17:2) Fall-Wint 90, p. 22.
"In the high bare limbs" (tr. by Sam Hamill). [ColR] (NS 17:2) Fall-Wint 90, p. 21.
"Mr. Sununu" (Response to "Save the Clerihew" appeal). [BostonR] (16:3/4) Je-Ag
91, p. 33.
"No one ever traced" (tr. by Sam Hamill). [ColR] (NS 17:2) Fall-Wint 90, p. 21.
"Nostalgia." [HarvardA] (127 [i.e. 125]:3) Ja 91, p. 37.

"The Relationship Is in the Mail (II)" (messages taken from a series of "non-occasion" greeting cards by Hallmark). [Harp] (282:1692) My 91, p. 28, 30.
"The Ruin" (tr. from the Old Englilsh by Gwendolyn Morgan and Brian McAllister). [NowestR] (29:3) 91, p. 107-108.
"So high in the mountains" (tr. by Sam Hamill). [ColR] (NS 17:2) Fall-Wint 90, p. 20.

163. ANONYMOUS (/Xam, Southern Cape Bushmen)
"Rain in a Dead Man's Footsteps" (tr. by Stephen Watson). [PartR] (58:1) Wint 91, p. 123-124.

164. ANONYMOUS (Man 'yoshu, 1165)
"My rocky journey" (tr. by Sam Hamill). [ColR] (NS 17:2) Fall-Wint 90, p. 16.

165. ANONYMOUS (New Mexican Folk Poetry)
"A Santa Fé." [BilingR] (16:2/3) My-D 91, p. 146-148.
"A Una Niña de Este País." [BilingR] (16:2/3) My-D 91, p. 141-142.
"La Americanita." [BilingR] (16:2/3) My-D 91, p. 142-143.
"Los Americanos." [BilingR] (16:2/3) My-D 91, p. 140-141.
"El Contrabando." [BilingR] (16:2/3) My-D 91, p. 134-135.
"Los Dos Soldatos." [BilingR] (16:2/3) My-D 91, p. 136-137.
"La Guerra Mundial." [BilingR] (16:2/3) My-D 91, p. 138-140.
"El Guerrero Enamorado." [BilingR] (16:2/3) My-D 91, p. 135-136.
"Lo de Siempre." [BilingR] (16:2/3) My-D 91, p. 145-146.
"Mi Gusto." [BilingR] (16:2/3) My-D 91, p. 142.
"The Night Before Christmas." [BilingR] (16:2/3) My-D 91, p. 148.
"Un Picnic." [BilingR] (16:2/3) My-D 91, p. 143-145.
"Los Presos." [BilingR] (16:2/3) My-D 91, p. 133-134.

166. ANOS, Joanna
"Astronomy Lesson." [SouthwR] (76:2) Spr 91, p. 295-296.

167. ANTHONY, Ellen
"Black Eggs." [PoetryE] (31) Spr 91, p. 108-109.
"Boy and Dog." [PoetryE] (31) Spr 91, p. 1o7.

168. ANTHONY, Frank
"Whiskey and Cigars." [NegC] (11:1) 91, p. 16.

169. ANTHONY, Pat
"Legacy." [Farm] (8:2) Fall-Wint 91-92, p. 40.
"Ode to a Migrating Monarch." [HolCrit] (28:1) F 91, p. 18.

170. ANTLER
"Atheist Conches." [Talisman] (7) Fall 91, p. 140.
"Everything Is Different Now." [JamesWR] (8:4) Sum 91, p. 12.
"Factory Sacrifice." [HeavenB] (9) Wint-Spr 91-92, p. 20.
"From Twilight to Twilight." [RiverS] (35) 91, p. 51.
"Home, Home on the Harangue." [NewYorkQ] (45) 91, p. 50.
"Lucky Trees." [NewYorkQ] (46) 91, p. 31-32.
"Proposal." [RiverS] (35) 91, p. 50.
"Pussysmell Candlelight." [JamesWR] (8:4) Sum 91, p. 12.
"River Anatomy." [ChironR] (10:3) Aut 91, p. 13.
"Solace My Soul with a Whiff." [Gypsy] (17) 91, p. 42.
"What Every Boy Knows." [ChironR] (10:3) Aut 91, p. 13.
"A Whole Lake to Yourself." [NewYorkQ] (44) 91, p. 50.

171. ANTRIM, Kathy
"Recircuits" (w. Richard Kostelanetz). [WilliamMR] (29) 91, p. 73-81.

172. APOLLINAIRE, Guillaume
"The New Spirit and the Poets (1918)" (Excerpt). [PassN] (12:2) Wint 91, p. 17.

173. APOLLONIUS OF RHODES
"Jason and Medeia" (The Argonautica, Book III, lines 744-1407, tr. by Peter Green). [SouthernHR] (25:3) Sum 91, p. 217-233.

174. APPLEWHITE, James
"Among Names of My Fathers." [SewanR] (99:3) Sum 91, p. 434-435.
"The Autumn Potato." [SewanR] (99:3) Sum 91, p. 435-436.
"Fields' Scroll." [NewEngR] (13:3/4) Spr-Sum 91, p. 251.
"Imaginary Photograph." [NewEngR] (13:3/4) Spr-Sum 91, p. 252.
"Making Tobacco Money." [Turnstile] (3:1) 91, p. 93-94.
"Slender Pines in Smoky Light." [NewEngR] (13:3/4) Spr-Sum 91, p. 250.
"Storm in the Briar Patch." [Poetry] (158:5) Ag 91, p. 272.

175. APTER, Ronnie
"The Answer" (tr. of Anna Rupertina Fuchsin). [NewOR] (18:4) Wint 91, p. 12-14.

176. ARANGO, Guillermo
"El Gato Barcino" (A Belkis Cuza-Malé y sus gatos de Princeton). [LindLM] (10:4)
O-D 91, p. 17.
"Mis Tias se Despiden." [LindLM] (10:4) O-D 91, p. 17.
177. ARBOLAY, Dominick
"Observador." [Nuez] (3:8/9) 91, p. 20.
178. ARENAS, Marion
"Laughing Cathy's Reversal." [ChironR] (10:4) Wint 91, p. 37.
179. ARENAS, Rosa Maria
"Mother of Revelations." [Calyx] (13:2) Sum 91, p. 56.
"Mother of Shrines." [KenR] (NS 13:4) Fall 91, p. 89.
"Mother of the Historical Tree." [KenR] (NS 13:4) Fall 91, p. 89.
"Mother of the Long Good-Bye." [KenR] (NS 13:4) Fall 91, p. 90.
180. ARENDS, Cheryl
"Ice Cream Won't Freeze Without Rock Salt." [Plain] (11:3) Spr 91, p. 27.
"In Anna's Attic." [Plain] (12:1) Fall 91, p. 32.
181. ARENDT, Mark
"Travis Loves Darcy." [PoetryE] (31) Spr 91, p. 67.
ARGEL, Gail D. Mac
See Mac ARGEL, Gail D.
182. ARGÜELLES, Ivan
"Atropos." [Os] (33) Fall 91, p. 35.
"Feed Your Angel the Exploration of Your Despair." [ColR] (NS 18:1) Spr-Sum 91,
p. 114-115.
"Library of Congress." [SilverFR] (20) Spr 91, p. 22-23.
"Memento Mori" (for Sarah). [ColR] (NS 18:1) Spr-Sum 91, p. 112-113.
"(No Thanks, Larry)" (pp. 1069-1071 of the 10th book of "Pantograph," called
"Ulysses a Companion Guide"). [PoetryUSA] (23) Sum 91, p. 8.
"Pan's Music." [Abraxas] (40/41) 91, p. 125.
"Pantograph, Book I: Canto the Tenth" (Excerpt). [Caliban] (10) 91, p. 130-135.
"Proserpina" (for sarah cahill). [YellowS] (38) Wint-Spr 91-92, p. 24-25.
183. ARJONILLA, Christian
"Dans l'Ombre de l'Ombre" (extraits). [Os] (32) Spr 91, p. 30-31.
"Dans l'Ombre de l'Ombre" (extraits). [Os] (33) Fall 91, p. 12-14.
"Soudain le guépard s'agite dans la cage du rêve" (poème inédit). [Os] (32) Spr 91, p.
29.
184. ARMANTROUT, Rae
"Mapping." [Conjunc] (17) 91, p. 270.
"Turn of Events." [Conjunc] (17) 91, p. 269.
185. ARMENGOL, Alejandro A.
"Elogio de la Astucia." [Nuez] (3:8/9) 91, p. 7.
"Jóvenes Poetas." [Nuez] (3:8/9) 91, p. 7.
"Murallas del Kremlin." [LindLM] (10:4) O-D 91, p. 22.
186. ARMITAGE, Barri
"After Words." [OhioR] (46) 91, p. 32.
"And a Time to Keep." [SouthernPR] (31:1) Spr 91, p. 60-61.
"Seven Loaves and a Few Small Fish." [WashR] (17:1) Je-Jl 91, p. 10.
187. ARMITAGE, Simon
"Not the Furniture Game." [Verse] (8:1) Spr 91, p. 9091.
188. ARMSTRONG, Diana
"Women Waiting." [Vis] (36) 91, p. 28-29.
189. ARMSTRONG, Gene
"Afterword to a Teacher." [BellArk] (7:4) Jl-Ag 91, p. 11.
"Alchemy." [BellArk] (7:5) S-O 91, p. 7.
"Art Store." [BellArk] (7:5) S-O 91, p. 7.
"Dance Lesson." [BellArk] (7:5) S-O 91, p. 7.
"Kern River Canyon." [BellArk] (7:4) Jl-Ag 91, p. 12.
"Revision" (after Paul Klee's "Memory of a Bird"). [BellArk] (7:5) S-O 91, p. 7.
190. ARMSTRONG, Glen
"Benjamin Franklin's Other Penis." [FreeL] (7) Spr 91, p. 24.
"A City of Hats." [PoetryNW] (32:3) Aut 91, p. 25.
"Painting the Saint Jockeys." [PoetryNW] (32:3) Aut 91, p. 24-25.
"The Price of California" (After John Woods). [FreeL] (7) Spr 91, p. 23.
"The Simplified Dogs of October." [Plain] (12:1) Fall 91, p. 38.
"To the Level Poets of Iowa" (for John Woods). [ChironR] (10:4) Wint 91, p. 37.

191. ARMSTRONG, Kate
    "Removed" (from "Stilleben," 1983, tr. of Günter Kunert). [Verse] (8:1) Spr 91, p. 104.
192. ARMSTRONG, Patricia Mees
    "Matinada Sth Kphth (Song from Crete)." [Writer] (104:3) Mr 91, p. 20.
193. ARNDT, Rolf
    "First Illness." [OnTheBus] (8/9) 91, p. 25.
    "Harley-Davidson." [OnTheBus] (8/9) 91, p. 25.
194. ARNETT, H.
    "Weeds." [CapeR] (26:2) Fall 91, p. 41.
195. ARNEY, Robert
    "A Fiction About the Woman I Loved." [PoetryE] (32) Fall 91, p. 107.
    "Window." [PoetryE] (32) Fall 91, p. 106.
196. ARNOLD, Bob
    "Disciplines." [PoetryE] (32) Fall 91, p. 108.
    "Flea Market." [PoetryE] (32) Fall 91, p. 109.
    "Here & Gone." [PoetryE] (32) Fall 91, p. 110.
197. ARNOLD, Kevin
    "Notes in the Margin." [Vis] (35) 91, p. 45.
198. ARONZON, Leonid
    "Beginning of a Long Poem" (tr. by Richard McKane). [LitR] (34:3) Spr 91, p. 333-334.
    "I Turn My Face to the River" (tr. by Richard McKane). [LitR] (34:3) Spr 91, p. 334.
    "Sonnet to Igarka" (For Altshuler, tr. by Richard McKane). [LitR] (34:3) Spr 91, p. 336.
    "What Does the Lead Reveal" (tr. by Richard McKane). [LitR] (34:3) Spr 91, p. 335.
    "With a Scented Eruption" (tr. by Richard McKane). [LitR] (34:3) Spr 91, p. 336.
    "Young Skies in the Sky" (tr. by Richard McKane). [LitR] (34:3) Spr 91, p. 333.
199. ARRIETA, Marcia
    "I Need to Iron." [RagMag] (9:2) 91, p. 40.
200. ARROWSMITH, William
    "Backwards" (tr. of Eugenio Montale). [Ploughs] (17:1) Spr 91, p. 12-13.
    "Easter Evening" (tr. of Eugenio Montale). [Ploughs] (17:1) Spr 91, p. 15.
    "Intellectual Education" (tr. of Eugenio Montale). [Ploughs] (17:1) Spr 91, p. 9-10.
    "Literary Histories." (tr. of Eugenio Montale). [Ploughs] (17:1) Spr 91, p. 14.
    "Once" (tr. of Eugenio Montale). [Ploughs] (17:1) Spr 91, p. 11-12.
    "A Poet" (tr. of Eugenio Montale). [Ploughs] (17:1) Spr 91, p. 13.
    "Xenia I" (tr. of Eugenio Montale). [Agni] (34) 91, p. 277-290.
201. ARROYO, Rane
    "Dream Bed of Light." [HeavenB] (9) Wint-Spr 91-92, p. 35.
    "My Long Life." [HeavenB] (9) Wint-Spr 91-92, p. 4.
202. ARSENYEV, Gleb
    "My Dog" (tr. by Thomas Epstein). [LitR] (34:3) Spr 91, p. 317.
    "The Runway" (tr. by Thomas Epstein). [LitR] (34:3) Spr 91, p. 317-320.
    "The Soul" (tr. by Thomas Epstein). [LitR] (34:3) Spr 91, p. 315-316.
    "A Vision" (tr. by Thomas Epstein). [LitR] (34:3) Spr 91, p. 321-322.
    "Why Stars Fall" (tr. by Thomas Epstein). [LitR] (34:3) Spr 91, p. 316.
203. ARTMANN, H. C.
    "The Inventor of Tarot Cards" (tr. by Derk Wynand). [Event] (20:2) Sum 91, p. 62-63.
    "Teacher and Janitor" (tr. by Derk Wynand). [Event] (20:2) Sum 91, p. 60-61.
204. ARURI, Naseer H.
    "The Children of Stone" (tr. of Nizar Qabbani). [InterPR] (17:1) Spr 91, p. 15.
    "Diaries of a Woman Who Does Not Care" (tr. of Nizar Qabbani). [InterPR] (17:1) Spr 91, p. 11.
    "Honorary Doctorate in Stone Chemistry" (tr. of Nizar Qabbani). [InterPR] (17:1) Spr 91, p. 13.
    "My Friend, I Am Tired of Being an Arab" (tr. of Nizar Qabbani). [InterPR] (17:1) Spr 91, p. 6-9.
205. ASAPH, Philip
    "How Town's Changed." [HampSPR] Wint 91, p. 19.
    "Marriage." [Hellas] (2:1) Spr 91, p. 71.
206. ASEKOFF, L. S.
    "Film Noir." [Poetry] (157:5) F 91, p. 280-281.
    "On Certainty" (After Wittgenstein). [Poetry] (157:5) F 91, p. 282.
    "The Seaward Skerries." [BrooklynR] (8) 91, p. 53.

"Skywriters over Tokyo." [Poetry] (157:4) Ja 91, p. 216.
207. ASH, John
"The Seventeenth Sermon." [ParisR] (33:120) Fall 91, p. 198-200.
"Twentieth Century." [NewYorker] (67:23) 29 Jl 91, p. 26.
"The Ungrateful Citizens." [ParisR] (33:120) Fall 91, p. 194-197.
208. ASHBERY, John
"Black Diamond" (tr. of Pierre Martory). [NewYorker] (67:16) 10 Je 91, p. 46.
"Erebus." [NewYRB] (38:7) 11 Ap 91, p. 6.
"Una Existencia Sedentaria" (tr. by Harry Morales). [Nuez] (3:8/9) 91, p. 2.
"Flow Chart" (). [ParisR] (33:118) Spr 91, p. 16-23.
"Flow Chart" (2 selections: "Double Sestina," "Girls, I Don't Know"). [AmerPoR]
    (20:2) Mr-Ap 91, p. 21-27.
"Frontispiece." [Verse] (8:1) Spr 91, p. 14.
"Love's Old Sweet Song." [NewYorker] (67:36) 28 O 91, p. 42.
"A Maple Leaf" (tr. of Piotr Sommer, w. the author). [Ploughs] (17:2/3) Fall 91, p.
    228.
"Poem at the New Year." [NewYorker] (66:52) 11 F 91, p. 46.
"A Sedentary Existence." [NewYRB] (38:5) 7 Mr 91, p. 18.
209. ASHBURY, Susan
"Cemetery." [LaurelR] (25:1) Wint 91, p. 94-95.
210. ASHLEY, Renée A.
"The Generosity of Souls." [NewEngR] (13:3/4) Spr-Sum 91, p. 165-166.
"How I Would Steal the Child." [NewEngR] (13:3/4) Spr-Sum 91, p. 166.
"The Hyacinth Bowl." [SouthernPR] (31:1) Spr 91, p. 58-60.
"The Language of Sirens" (To a Father). [SouthernPR] (31:2) Fall 91, p. 28-30.
211. ASPENSTRÖM, Werner
"After the Storm" (tr. by Robin Fulton). [KenR] (NS 13:3) Sum 91, p. 126.
"Great, Marvelous Structures" (tr. by Stephen Klass and Leif Sjoberg). [Vis] (37) 91,
    p. 50.
"Icarus and the Lad Graystone" (tr. by Stephen Klass and Leif Sjoberg). [Vis] (37)
    91, p. 49.
"Mining Country IV" (tr. by Stephen Klass and Leif Sjoberg). [Vis] (37) 91, p. 49.
"The Position (Version II)" (tr. by Stephen Klass and Leif Sjoberg). [Vis] (37) 91, p.
    50.
"Revisiting" (tr. by Robin Fulton). [KenR] (NS 13:3) Sum 91, p. 127.
"Rousseau the Painter's Departure from Life" (tr. by Stephen Klass and Leif Sjoberg).
    [Vis] (37) 91, p. 48.
"The Rower" (tr. by Stephen Klass and Leif Sjoberg). [Vis] (37) 91, p. 50.
212. ASPINWALL, Dorothy
"Holiday" (tr. of Gilbert Baque). [WebR] (15) Spr 91, p. 39.
"Twilight" (tr. of Pierre Béarn). [CrabCR] (7:2) Sum 91, p. 12.
213. ASSIS, Luiza
"Vagabond" (tr. by the author). [Vis] (35) 91, p. 33.
214. ATCHLEY, Amy
"The Altar Boy." [WindO] (54) Sum 91, p. 16.
"Bed Time." [WindO] (54) Sum 91, p. 14.
"Cigar Rings." [WindO] (54) Sum 91, p. 15.
215. ATKINS, Cynthia
"Driving All Night." [DenQ] (26:2) Fall 91, p. 5.
"Vermeer, A Meditation." [CreamCR] (14:2) Wint 91, p. 153.
216. ATKINS, Daniel A.
"'I Thought About You' (Miles Davis)." [LullwaterR] (3:1) Fall 91, p. 76-77.
217. ATKINS, Priscilla
"The Amish Girl." [BambooR] (50/51) Spr-Sum 91, p. 53.
218. ATKINSON, Alan
"Tea for Two." [SoCoast] (11) Wint 91, p. 58-59.
219. ATKINSON, Jennifer
"Beside the Connecticut River." [BlackWR] (17:2) Spr-Sum 91, p. 23.
220. ATKINSON, Michael
"Awakening." [MinnR] (NS 37) Fall 91, p. 23-25.
"Falling in Love with Women Poets." [NewYorkQ] (45) 91, p. 64.
"Film School." [MassR] (32:2) Sum 91, p. 316-317.
"Highway." [MinnR] (NS 37) Fall 91, p. 22-23.
"In His Mother's House." [MinnR] (NS 37) Fall 91, p. 25-26.
"Lineage." [ChironR] (10:2) Sum 91, p. 10.
"On Entropy." [ChatR] (11:3) Spr 91, p. 27.

"One Second of 'Frankenstein' (1931)." [ChironR] (10:2) Sum 91, p. 10.
"Sayville, New York." [Interim] (10:1) Spr-Sum 91, p. 43-44.
"Teaching Pigs to Pray." [WillowS] (27) Wint 91, p. 30-31.
"Wild Fields." [Interim] (10:1) Spr-Sum 91, p. 42-43.
"Wild Fields." [MinnR] (NS 37) Fall 91, p. 27-28.
221. ATWOOD, Calvin
    "They Blow Brass Real Good." [Pembroke] (23) 91, p. 72.
222. ATWOOD, Laurence
    "Angel" (tr. of Heinrich Böll). [InterPR] (17:2) Fall 91, p. 45.
    "Angel" (tr. of Heinrich Böll). [LitR] (34:2) Wint 91, p. 228.
    "Cologne I" (tr. of Heinrich Böll). [InterPR] (17:2) Fall 91, p. 43.
    "My Muse" (tr. of Heinrich Böll). [InterPR] (17:2) Fall 91, p. 41, 43.
223. AUBREY, Keith
    "Long Distance." [SnailPR] (1:2) Fall 91-Wint 92, p. 21.
224. AUBRY, C.
    "Stubble." [US1] (24/25) Spr 91, p. 17.
225. AUER, Benedict
    "From an Ancient Monastic Customary: Rules for Novices" (tr. of Frankish fragment
        found in a ruined library somewhere in France). [CrabCR] (7:3) 91, p. 27.
    "A Mantra Unknown." [NewRena] (8:2, #25) Fall 91, p. 75.
    "A Poet in Puris Naturalibus." [NewRena] (8:2, #25) Fall 91, p. 76.
    "Steadfastness." [Pembroke] (23) 91, p. 161.
    "A Visit to the Venetian Ghetto." [ManhatPR] (13) [91?], p. 31.
226. AUGUSTINI, Delmira
    "Lo Inefable" (From "Cantos de la Mañana, 1910). [ChiR] (37:2/3) 91, p. 88.
    "Unspeakable" (tr. by David Johnson). [ChiR] (37:2/3) 91, p. 89.
227. AUNKST, Beverly
    "Land of the Free: Home of the Homeless." [BlackBR] (14) Fall-Wint 91, p. 34-35.
228. AUSLANDER, Bonnie
    "Already West." [SpoonRQ] (16:3/4) Sum-Fall 91, p. 100.
    "Solomon's Wife in Bed with Animals." [PoetL] (86:4) Wint 91-92, p. 12.
229. AUSTIN, Annemarie
    "Green Belt." [SoCoast] (11) Wint 91, p. 39.
230. AUSTIN, Dave
    "Tattoos." [MinnR] (NS 37) Fall 91, p. 40.
231. AUSTIN, David Craig
    "An Absolute." [Journal] (14:2) Wint 91, p. 16-17.
    "Advent." [Antaeus] (67) Fall 91, p. 209.
    "The Given Names." [Journal] (14:2) Wint 91, p. 13-15.
    "The Long Night Through." [Colum] (17) Fall 91, p. 231-232.
    "A Mild Winter." [Journal] (14:2) Wint 91, p. 12.
    "North." [Journal] (14:2) Wint 91, p. 10.
    "A Pathetic Fallacy." [Journal] (14:2) Wint 91, p. 11.
    "Small Brazilian Geode." [Colum] (17) Fall 91, p. 233.
    "Some Houses." [Journal] (14:2) Wint 91, p. 8-9.
232. AUSTIN, Jerry
    "How and Why." [BellArk] (7:2) Mr-Ap 91, p. 3.
    "Nelson Bentley." [BellArk] (7:1) Ja-F 91, p. 4.
    "Skagit Flats." [BellArk] (7:6) N-D 91, p. 12.
233. AUSTIN, Penelope
    "Aubade" (For Chris). [MissouriR] (14:1) 91, p. 61.
    "Azaleas, 1989." [MissouriR] (14:1) 91, p. 68-69.
    "Bringing in the Child." [MissouriR] (14:1) 91, p. 66-67.
    "Clandestine." [MissouriR] (14:1) 91, p. 70.
    "Club HTRC Presents Bobby Benton, Jan. 24, 1942: My Mother Sells Tickets" (For
        my mother). [MissouriR] (14:1) 91, p. 65.
    "Dancing After Oswiecim." [KenR] (NS 13:1) Wint 91, p. 33.
    "Distillation" (for Ann and Fred Blumer). [Journal] (15:1) Spr 91, p. 53-54.
    "Memory and Imagination." [HighP] (6:2) Fall 91, p. 21-23.
    "Moon Above the Twenties." [MissouriR] (14:1) 91, p. 62-63.
234. AUTREY, Ken
    "My Daughter Rowing." [Poem] (66) N 91, p. 24.
    "To Build a Wall." [Plain] (12:1) Fall 91, p. 37.
235. AVERILL, Diane
    "A 1950's Duel." [CarolQ] (43:3) Spr 91, p. 31.

236. AVERY, Brian C.
    "Knocking on Doors, Taking Census." [PoetL] (86:2) Sum 91, p. 37.
    "To Those Who Read by the Light of the Page." [PoetL] (86:2) Sum 91, p. 36.
237. AVICOLLI, Tommi
    "For Joe Beam." [Tribe] (1:4) Spr-Sum 91, p. 35-36.
238. AWAD, Joseph
    "Dies Irae." [Paint] (18:35) Spr 91, p. 20.
    "On the Commissioning of My Son Tim." [Paint] (18:35) Spr 91, p. 19.
239. AWOONOR, Kofi
    "A Death Foretold." [LitR] (34:4) Sum 91, p. 445-446.
    "In Memoriam: Return to Kingston" (For Neville Dawes, 1926-1984). [LitR] (34:4)
        Sum 91, p. 441-444.
    "Light Hours in Verse." [LitR] (34:4) Sum 91, p. 447-448.
    "Readings and Musings." [LitR] (34:4) Sum 91, p. 437.
    "Rio De Janeiro: Fearful & Lovely City." [LitR] (34:4) Sum 91, p. 438-440.
240. AXELROD, David
    "Skill of the Heart." [MalR] (94) Spr 91, p. 91-92.
    "Third Shift." [MalR] (94) Spr 91, p. 89-90.
241. AZEVEDO, Kathleen de
    "Yemanja." [Vis] (35) 91, p. 34-35.
242. AZRAEL, Mary
    "Indian Summer." [ChatR] (11:2) Wint 91, p. 33.
    "Night Singer." [ChatR] (11:2) Wint 91, p. 32.
AZUCENA TORRES, Alba
    See TORRES, Alba Azucena
243. AZZOPARDI, Mario
    "Teleisthai." [InterPR] (17:2) Fall 91, p. 84.
    "Teleisthai" (tr. by Grazio Falzon). [InterPR] (17:2) Fall 91, p. 85.
244. AZZOUNI, Jody
    "Odin Gets to See It All." [CalQ] (35/36) 91, p. 75.
245. BAAFOUR, Richard Afari
    "Fictive or Nameless One." [LitR] (34:4) Sum 91, p. 449-450.
    "Growing Up." [Harp] (283:1697) O 91, p. 44.
    "Growing Up." [LitR] (34:4) Sum 91, p. 451.
    "A Page Crossed by a Tide" (Extract). [LitR] (34:4) Sum 91, p. 452-453.
    "They and Us." [LitR] (34:4) Sum 91, p. 455-456.
    "Trade Winds." [LitR] (34:4) Sum 91, p. 454.
246. BAATZ, Ronald
    "Damp After Evening." [WormR] (31:4, #124) 91, p. 112-113.
    "Dawn Wine." [WormR] (31:4, #124) 91, p. 113.
    "Late in the Night." [WormR] (31:4, #124) 91, p. 111.
    "On the Edge." [WormR] (31:4, #124) 91, p. 114.
247. BABB, Nancy
    "Travels." [Prima] (14/15) 91, p. 75.
BACA, Jimmy Santiago
    See SANTIAGO-BACA, Jimmy
248. BACCHILEGA, Cristina
    "Bonsai." [BambooR] (50/51) Spr-Sum 91, p. 225.
249. BACHARACH, Deborah
    "Alan and His Mother." [Kalliope] (13:2) 91, p. 20.
250. BACHHUBER, Daniel
    "For Willie Kince, in Prison." [LakeSR] (25) 91, p. 15.
251. BACHMANN, Evelyn
    "Images Re-Visited." [Nimrod] (34:2) Spr-Sum 91, p. 27.
252. BACHMANN, Ingeborg
    "Miriam" (tr. by James Reidel). [Vis] (35) 91, p. 11.
    "Paris" (tr. by Peter Filkins). [Vis] (35) 91, p. 18.
    "Roman Night Scene" (tr. by James Reidel). [ArtfulD] (20/21) 91, p. 40.
253. BACHNER, Jane
    "Dinner at Patsy's." [Paint] (18:36) Aut 91, p. 29.
    "Tom Learns to Drive." [Paint] (18:36) Aut 91, p. 30.
254. BACON, Crystal (Crystal V.)
    "At the Academy Street School." [JINJPo] (13:1) Spr 91, p. 2.
    "Picture" (after Auden). [BlackBR] (14) Fall-Wint 91, p. 33.
    "Torch Song." [JINJPo] (13:1) Spr 91, p. 3.

255. BADDOUR, Margaret Boothe
   "The Day Dorothy and I Picked Up Pine Cones Because Women Have Always Borne
      the Burden." [Pembroke] (23) 91, p. 73.
   "The Mystery of the Sweater Trunk." [Crucible] (27) Fall 91, p. 16-17.
   "Sailing." [Pembroke] (23) 91, p. 74.
256. BAECHLER, Lea
   "A Flat Dark Sky." [SouthernR] (27:3) Jl 91, p. 652-654.
   "Healing." [SouthernR] (27:3) Jl 91, p. 654-656.
257. BAER, Tamara
   "Thinking the Wrong Things." [BostonR] (16:6) D 91, p. 28.
258. BAER, William
   "Fever-Struck, in the Carolina Woods." [NewYorkQ] (44) 91, p. 61.
259. BAEZ, Pedro F.
   "Claro Enigma" (A la partida de Reinaldo Arenas). [Nuez] (3:7) 91, p. 20.
260. BAGGETT, Rebecca
   "Adultery Discovered in a Letter." [Calyx] (13:3) Wint 91-92, p. 52.
   "Change of Perspective" (for S.). [RiverC] (11:2) Spr 91, p. 32.
   "The Children I Will Not Bear." [BostonR] (16:6) D 91, p. 32.
   "Teeth" (for Emma at 18 months). [RiverC] (11:2) Spr 91, p. 30-31.
   "When Your Child Dies." [Kalliope] (13:2) 91, p. 14.
261. BAHAN, Lee Harlin
   "Best Ladies' Room on U.S. 50." [CinPR] (21) Spr 90, p. 14-15.
   "Drilling the Troops." [KenR] (NS 13:2) Spr 91, p. 160.
   "Hope." [KenR] (NS 13:2) Spr 91, p. 162.
   "Last Bard in Wales" (after a painting in the exhibit, "Wordsworth and the age of
      English Romanticism"). [KenR] (NS 13:2) Spr 91, p. 161.
   "Sonnet 75, from Petrarch" (Francesco Petrarca, "Rerum Vulgarium Fragmenta").
      [Hellas] (2:1) Spr 91, p. 73.
   "Two, After Petrarch" ("Vaucluse," "Words, Between Us"). [CrabCR] (7:2) Sum 91,
      p. 6.
   "The Women and the Good News." [CinPR] (21) Spr 90, p. 16.
262. BAHLINGER, Lisa (Lisa Liehe)
   "Traced in Water." [CimR] (97) O 91, p. 46.
   "Vertigo." [GreenMR] (NS 5:1) Sum-Fall 91, p. 58-60.
263. BAHORSKY, Russell
   "Green Age" (for Dave Smith). [HayF] (8) Spr-Sum 91, p. 81.
264. BAI, Juyi
   "Li Po's Grave" (tr. by C. H. Kwock and Vincent McHugh). [PoetryUSA] (22) Spr
      91, p. 21.
BAI, Li
      See LI, Po
265. BAIDAO
   "Let's Go" (tr. by Wang Jun Ru). [Vis] (35) 91, p. 5.
266. BAILEY, Sallie N.
   "Dumb Bird." [Writer] (104:9) S 91, p. 23.
267. BAILLIE, Martha
   "Stone Forest" (From "Poems of Distance and Desire"). [AntigR] (85/86) Spr-Sum
      91, p. 57.
   "Travel #1" (From "Poems of Distance and Desire"). [AntigR] (85/86) Spr-Sum 91,
      p. 55.
   "Xian #3" (From "Poems of Distance and Desire"). [AntigR] (85/86) Spr-Sum 91, p.
      56.
   "Xian #4" (From "Poems of Distance and Desire"). [AntigR] (85/86) Spr-Sum 91, p.
      54.
268. BAIOCCO, Robert
   "Retired." [MoodySI] (24/25/26) Spr 91, p. 23.
269. BAIOCCO, Sharon
   "To Lose a Mother." [Elf] (1:1) Spr 91, p. 28-29.
270. BAKER, Alison
   "Winter." [RiverC] (11:2) Spr 91, p. 66.
271. BAKER, David
   "The Afterlife." [Manoa] (3:1) Spr 91, p. 125.
   "Among Men." [NewEngR] (13:3/4) Spr-Sum 91, p. 105.
   "Cotton." [RiverS] (33) 91, p. 64.
   "The Couple." [Atlantic] (268:1) Jl 91, p. 50.
   "The Deer." [Boulevard] (5:3/6:1, #15/16) Spr 91, p. 191.

"Determinism." [PoetryNW] (32:3) Aut 91, p. 46-47.
"The Future." [OhioR] (46) 91, p. 7-8.
"Missouri." [NewEngR] (13:3/4) Spr-Sum 91, p. 106-109.
"More Rain." [NewEngR] (13:3/4) Spr-Sum 91, p. 110-112.
"Piano Music." [Crazy] (40) Spr 91, p. 38.
"The Plain Style." [GettyR] (4:1) Wint 91, p. 128.
"The Principle of Uncertainty." [Manoa] (3:1) Spr 91, p. 125.
"Sex." [PoetryNW] (32:3) Aut 91, p. 45.
"Snow Figure." [OhioR] (46) 91, p. 5-6.
"Still Life with Jacket." [PoetryNW] (32:3) Aut 91, p. 43-44.
"Stroke." [SouthwR] (76:2) Spr 91, p. 251.
"Taxi After an Evening Shower." [Poetry] (158:1) Ap 91, p. 21.
"Two Signatures." [RiverS] (33) 91, p. 65.
"The Yard." [GettyR] (4:1) Wint 91, p. 129.

272. BAKER, Devreaux
"Reunion with Katya." [HighP] (6:2) Fall 91, p. 100-101.

273. BAKER, Donald W.
"And Now, Interrogation, Merely Routine." [Parting] (4:2) Wint 91-92, p. 13.
"Auntie Ellen." [Thrpny] (47) Fall 91, p. 33.
"Dust." [Interim] (10:1) Spr-Sum 91, p. 12.
"Lines Written in Dejection a Few Miles Above the Early Warning Installations at North Truro." [Parting] (4:2) Wint 91-92, p. 14.
"The Neighborhood." [Interim] (10:1) Spr-Sum 91, p. 13.

274. BAKER, Jason
"Juan." [Dandel] (18:1) Spr-Sum 91, p. 16.

275. BAKER, June Frankland
"After Finding a Photo of Kensett's *Lake George, 1858* in the Paper." [Blueline] (12) 91, p. 77.
"Infection." [SouthernPR] (31:1) Spr 91, p. 52-53.
"Upon Hearing the Elgar Cello Concerto" (for Jacqueline DuPré). [Kaleid] (23) Sum-Fall 91, p. 32.

276. BAKER, Tony
"A Neckeverse" (for Guy Birchard). [NewAW] (8/9) Fall 91, p. 63.
"Postcards Written at the Places in Question." [NewAW] (8/9) Fall 91, p. 59-60.
"The Roots." [NewAW] (8/9) Fall 91, p. 62.
"A Threesome." [NewAW] (8/9) Fall 91, p. 64-65.
"Valdeez" (Yuman song, after Frances Densmore). [NewAW] (8/9) Fall 91, p. 61-62.
"Yellow Blue Tibia." [NewAW] (8/9) Fall 91, p. 64.

277. BAKER, Winona
"Raincoast." [PoetryUSA] (22) Spr 91, p. 11.

278. BAKOWSKI, Peter
"12 Miles Short of Mexico." [WormR] (31:1, #121) 91, p. 37.
"The Artists." [WormR] (31:1, #121) 91, p. 35.
"The Beautiful Girl." [WormR] (31:1, #121) 91, p. 35.
"Night and Heart." [HangL] (59) 91, p. 13.
"The Old Women of Bulgaria." [ChironR] (10:3) Aut 91, p. 45.
"The Perfume of Question Marks" (for Simon Killen). [WormR] (31:1, #121) 91, p. 36.
"Walking the Streets of Paris (December 1985)." [WormR] (31:1, #121) 91, p. 36-37.
"The Wounds of Life and the Glass Heart of Love" (for Frida Kahlo). [MoodySI] (24/25/26) Spr 91, p. 32-33.

279. BALAKIAN, Peter
"III. The News" (from "An Armenian Journal"). [Agni] (33) 91, p. 92-93.
"The History of Armenia." [CentR] (35:3) Fall 91, p. 529-530.
"Home." [Ploughs] (17:4) Wint 91-92, p. 138.
"Wallace Stevens's America, or Three Places in New England." [Ploughs] (17:4) Wint 91-92, p. 136-137.

280. BALASHOVA, Elena
"Xenia" (Excerpt, tr. of Arkadii Dragomoshchenko, w. Lyn Hejinian). [GrandS] (10:4, #40) 91, p. 82-87.

281. BALAZ, Joe
"Ku'u Momi Makamae." [HawaiiR] (16:1, #34) Wint 91-92, p. 1.
"My Precious Pearl" (for Eunice K. Balaz). [HawaiiR] (16:1, #34) Wint 91-92, p. 2.
"Tings Change Wit Da Wise Ass Young." [ChamLR] (8-9) Spr-Fall 91, p. 16.

282. BALAZS, Mary
"On the College Soccer Field." [Crucible] (27) Fall 91, p. 45.
283. BALDVINSSON, Sveinbjorn I.
"Before Daybreak" (tr. by the author). [Vis] (37) 91, p. 34.
284. BALDWIN, Tama
"No Innocence, No Mercy." [SouthernPR] (31:2) Fall 91, p. 50-51.
"Questions Raised As He Enters the Room to Pray." [SouthernPR] (31:2) Fall 91, p. 49-50.
285. BALK, Christianne
"Kantishna Terns." [PoetryNW] (32:4) Wint 91-92, p. 29-30.
"Storm." [PoetryNW] (32:4) Wint 91-92, p. 28-29.
286. BALKITS, Ivars
"Revenge Comedy." [NewYorkQ] (46) 91, p. 77.
287. BALL, Angela
"The Artist's Wife" (for Maureen Tower). [MalR] (95) Sum 91, p. 50-53.
"Charm." [SouthernPR] (31:2) Fall 91, p. 35.
"Cover." [Field] (45) Fall 91, p. 66.
"Double Take." [MalR] (95) Sum 91, p. 56-57.
"Flash." [Field] (45) Fall 91, p. 67.
"Gender Specific." [MalR] (95) Sum 91, p. 55.
"Keats in Rome." [WillowS] (27) Wint 91, p. 12-13.
"A New Exile Talks of His Country." [WillowS] (27) Wint 91, p. 14.
"Reflex." [MalR] (95) Sum 91, p. 54.
"Sky." [KenR] (NS 13:1) Wint 91, p. 96-97.
"Text." [KenR] (NS 13:1) Wint 91, p. 97-98.
"Theater." [SouthernPR] (31:1) Spr 91, p. 44.
"Towns." [Stand] (33:1) Wint 91, p. 64.
288. BALL, Roger A.
"Mid-day Dream." [CoalC] (3) My 91, p. 9.
289. BALOIAN
"Morning." [Gypsy] (17) 91, p. 37.
290. BALTATZI, Adamantia
"First Series" (10 selections, tr. of Yannis Ritsos, w. José García). [OnTheBus] (8/9) 91, p. 222-223.
291. BANDER, Elaine
"Top Withens." [Grain] (19:3) Fall 91, p. 130-131.
292. BANERJEE, Paramita
"The Blood-Mark" (tr. of Mallika Sengupta, w. Carolyne Wright). [MichQR] (30:1) Wint 91, p. 210.
"Business Woman's Story" (tr. of Anuradha Mahapatra, w. Carolyne Wright). [TriQ] (81) Spr-Sum 91, p. 229.
"Girl Before Her Marriage" (tr. of Anuradha Mahapatra, w. Carolyne Wright). [TriQ] (81) Spr-Sum 91, p. 230-231.
293. BANGS, Carol Jane
"An Essay on the Nature of Water." [ColR] (NS 17:2) Fall-Wint 90, p. 53.
"She Waits for Him to Call." [ColR] (NS 17:2) Fall-Wint 90, p. 54.
294. BANKSTON, Carl L., III
"The Castle at Santorini." [Comm] (118:13) 12 Jl 91, p. 436.
"Light Along the Erie Canal." [Comm] (118:13) 12 Jl 91, p. 436.
"A Phenomenology of Fog." [Comm] (118:12) 14 Je 91, p. 402.
295. BANUS, Marìa
"Autumn" (tr. by Mary Mattfield). [Paint] (18:36) Aut 91, p. 52.
"Fayum Portrait" (tr. by Mary Mattfield). [Vis] (36) 91, p. 32.
"Hunger" (tr. by Marguerite Dorian and Elliott B. Urdang). [MidAR] (11:1) 91, p. 131.
"The Shivering" (tr. by Mary Mattfield). [Paint] (18:36) Aut 91, p. 53.
"Spyglass" (tr. by Mary Mattfield). [Vis] (35) 91, p. 9.
"Through Bucharest, After the Rain" (tr. by Marguerite Dorian and Elliott B. Urdang). [MidAR] (11:1) 91, p. 130.
296. BAPST, Don
"With Gino at a Village Cafe." [ChangingM] (23) Fall-Wint 91, p. 18.
297. BAQUE, Gilbert
"Holiday" (tr. by Dorothy Aspinwall). [WebR] (15) Spr 91, p. 39.
298. BARAKA, Amiri
"The City of New Ark: Wave Beats." [GrandS] (10:3, #39) 91, p. 125-133.

"Masked Angel Costume: The Sayings of Mantan Moreland." [Spirit] (11) 91, p. 72-74.
"A Meditation on Bob Kaufman." [Sulfer] (11:2, #29) Fall 91, p. 61-66.
299. BARANCZAK, Stanislaw
"Home" (tr. by Joanna Warwick). [OnTheBus] (8/9) 91, p. 202.
"If Porcelain, Then Only the Kind" (tr. by Joanna Warwick). [OnTheBus] (8/9) 91, p. 201.
"If You Must Scream, Do It Quietly" (tr. by Joanna Warwick). [OnTheBus] (8/9) 91, p. 202-203.
"It Was His Own Fault" (tr. by Joanna Warwick). [OnTheBus] (8/9) 91, p. 202.
"Out of Thin Mud and Clay" (tr. by Joanna Warwick). [OnTheBus] (8/9) 91, p. 203.
"We Can't Get It" (tr. by Joanna Warwick). [OnTheBus] (8/9) 91, p. 203.
300. BARANOW, Joan
"In Memory of Lisa Vogel." [US1] (24/25) Spr 91, p. 7.
301. BARATTA, Edward
"The Freeway to Boston." [SouthernPR] (31:2) Fall 91, p. 64.
"Light Seekers." [Ascent] (15:3) Spr 91, p. 15.
302. BARBACHANO, Lilia
"Aldebarán" (In memory of Howard Phillips Lovecraft, tr. by Thomas Hoeksema). [Paint] (18:36) Aut 91, p. 62.
303. BARBARESE, J. T.
"Photo of Pebbles Beside a Bomb Crater." [DenQ] (26:1) Sum 91, p. 7.
"The Young Wife Counts Her Kids on the Beach." [DenQ] (26:1) Sum 91, p. 8.
304. BARBEE, Sam
"Resolution." [Elf] (1:4) Wint 91, p. 31.
"Tomato." [Elf] (1:4) Wint 91, p. 31.
305. BARBOUR, Douglas
"Bird of Paradise" (Excerpts). [WestCL] (25:2, #5) Fall 91, p. 39-40.
"Breath Ghazal 23." [PraF] (12:3 #56) Aut 91, p. 35.
"Breath Ghazal 6." [PraF] (12:3 #56) Aut 91, p. 35.
"Concerning Dr Ewan Cameron." [PraF] (12:3 #56) Aut 91, p. 36-37.
"For Fred." [WestCL] (25:2, #5) Fall 91, p. 41.
"I watch her thru a window." [PraF] (12:3 #56) Aut 91, p. 37-38.
"Lee Konitz at the Yardbird Suite." [WestCL] (25:2, #5) Fall 91, p. 40.
"Tom Thompson: 'The Jack Pine' 1916 1917'" (The National Gallery, Ottawa). [WestCL] (25:2, #5) Fall 91, p. 41.
306. BARCIA, Elena
"Mexico." [OnTheBus] (8/9) 91, p. 26.
307. BARCLAY, Heather
"Hmong People at the Holloween Play" (Short Grain Contest Winners: Prose Poem Winners: Third Prize). [Grain] (19:4) Wint 91, p. 71-72.
308. BARDEN, Louise
"Evolution." [GreensboroR] (50) Sum 91, p. 104.
309. BARGEN, Walter
"At a Glance." [MissouriR] (14:2) 91, p. 180-181.
"Birding in Costa Rica." [MissouriR] (14:2) 91, p. 186-187.
"Cap Size." [Ascent] (15:2) Wint 91, p. 40.
"Car Deals." [CharR] (17:1) Spr 91, p. 89-90.
"Crystal Collecting" (Old Joe, Arkansas). [WebR] (15) Spr 91, p. 87.
"Father in the New World." [DenQ] (26:2) Fall 91, p. 6.
"Festering." [Farm] (8:1) Spr-Sum 91, p. 65.
"Hunting Trophy." [WebR] (15) Spr 91, p. 85.
"Reading." [CharR] (17:1) Spr 91, p. 91-92.
"Reporting in the Off Season." [MissouriR] (14:2) 91, p. 182-183.
"Sadhu, Mahamakham Festival." [SpoonRQ] (16:1/2) Wint-Spr 91, p. 106.
"Sirocco Heart." [PoetryNW] (32:1) Spr 91, p. 43-44.
"They Shoot Don't They." [WebR] (15) Spr 91, p. 86.
"This, That, or the Other." [Farm] (8:1) Spr-Sum 91, p. 66-68.
"Transmissions." [MissouriR] (14:2) 91, p. 185.
"Walking on Air." [MissouriR] (14:2) 91, p. 184.
"The Western Front." [PoetryNW] (32:3) Aut 91, p. 26-27.
"Zeno's Cinema." [MissouriR] (14:2) 91, p. 188.
310. BARHAM, Wayne
"Aslant from the Poet's Mouth (a Dialogue)" (to Ted Enslin). [MidAR] (11:1) 91, p. 230-233.

311. BARKAN, Stanley H.
     "The Cracked Planet" (after Alfred Van Loen's sculpture). [Confr] (46/47) Fall
          91-Wint 92, p. 276.
312. BARKER, Wendy
     "14th Spring." [PraS] (65:1) Spr 91, p. 28-30.
     "For Want of Dolls" (The Mary Elinore Smith Poetry Prize). [AmerS] (60:3) Sum 91,
          p. 414-416.
     "The Freezer in the House." [CalQ] (35/36) 91, p. 125-126.
     "Playing the Game of Statues." [CalQ] (35/36) 91, p. 124-125.
313. BARLOW, John
     "Run." [Event] (20:1) Spr 91, p. 84.
314. BARNARD, Anita M.
     "Idyll Worship." [HawaiiR] (16:1, #34) Wint 91-92, p. 80.
315. BARNATO, Joseph
     "Libagioni." [Os] (32) Spr 91, p. 33.
316. BARNES, Jim
     "After the Great Plains." [KenR] (NS 13:1) Wint 91, p. 55.
     "The Cabin on Nanny Ridge." [PoetryE] (32) Fall 91, p. 48.
     "Duel" (tr. of Dagmar Nick). [SycamoreR] (3:1) Wint 91, p. 41.
     "Flying Weather" (tr. of Dagmar Nick). [SycamoreR] (3:1) Wint 91, p. 42.
     "Military Burial, Summerfield Cemetery: A Late Eulogy." [PraS] (65:1) Spr 91, p.
          88-89.
     "Near the Top." [PoetryE] (32) Fall 91, p. 49-50.
     "Night Flight." [KenR] (NS 13:1) Wint 91, p. 54.
     "Remembering Hiroshima and Propaganda." [PraS] (65:1) Spr 91, p. 89-90.
     "Snowbound at the Bar 2, Below Winding Stair Mountain, 1943." [Nat] (252:2) 21 Ja
          91, p. 60.
     "Tracking Rabbits: Night." [SoDakR] (29:3 part 2) Aut 91, p. 35.
317. BARNES, Kate
     "The Old Lady's Story." [BelPoJ] (42:1) Fall 91, p. 20-21.
318. BARNES, Kim
     "Blue Ice." [CutB] (36) Sum 91, p. 23-24.
     "Circle of Women." [GeoR] (45:2) Sum 91, p. 330-331.
     "Puzzle." [CutB] (36) Sum 91, p. 22.
319. BARNES, Rita
     "Woman with Headache in the National Gallery." [CapeR] (26:2) Fall 91, p. 43.
320. BARNES, W. J.
     "Ex Cathedra." [Quarry] (40:1/2) Wint-Spr 91, p. 12.
     "Leaving Damascus." [Quarry] (40:1/2) Wint-Spr 91, p. 13.
321. BARNETT, Ruth Anderson
     "Annie Parker." [BelPoJ] (42:2) Wint 91-92, p. 17-19.
     "The Anorexic." [BelPoJ] (42:2) Wint 91-92, p. 14-16.
322. BARNETT, S. L.
     "Sisters — Manele Beach." [ChamLR] (8-9) Spr-Fall 91, p. 58.
     "Sisters." [ChamLR] (8-9) Spr-Fall 91, p. 56-57.
323. BARNETT, Susan
     "Mary's Special Child." [BambooR] (50/51) Spr-Sum 91, p. 119.
     "Pagoda." [BambooR] (50/51) Spr-Sum 91, p. 120.
324. BARNHILL, Anne C.
     "Sylvanus and His Big City Woman." [Crucible] (27) Fall 91, p. 23.
325. BARNSTONE, Tony
     "Black Desert" (suite, tr. of Tang Ya Ping, w. Newton Liu). [LitR] (34:2) Wint 91, p.
          214-215.
     "Window Onto a Cliff" (tr. of Bei Dao, w. Newton Liu). [Thrpny] (46) Sum 91, p.
          16.
326. BARNSTONE, Willis
     "Gospel of Declarations by John the Theologian." [NewRep] (204:7) 18 F 91, p. 62.
     "Gospel of the Mountain." [SouthernR] (27:3) Jl 91, p. 708.
     "On the Floor of the Creation." [PartR] (58:4) Fall 91, p. 691-692.
327. BARON, Enid L.
     "After Chernobyl." [SingHM] (19) 91, p. 50-51.
328. BARONE, Frank
     "Driven." [EngJ] (80:2) F 91, p. 97.
329. BARQUET, Jesús J.
     "Revenges." [PoetryUSA] (22) Spr 91, p. 11.
     "Sima." [LindLM] (10:1) Ja-Mr 91, p. 24.

330. BARR, Burlin
   "Lake." [NowestR] (29:3) 91, p. 26.
   "Seven Thursdays." [NowestR] (29:3) 91, p. 27-29.
331. BARR, Tina
   "Antique Shop." [Spirit] (11) 91, p. 182.
   "Blue Rotunda." [Chelsea] (50) 91, p. 31-33.
   "Bull Pasture." [Boulevard] (6:2/3, #17/18) Fall 91, p. 164-165.
   "Fool's Gold." [Crazy] (40) Spr 91, p. 55-57.
   "The Gatekeepers." [Chelsea] (50) 91, p. 34-35.
   "Twelve Dancing Princesses" (for Henri). [ParisR] (33:119) Sum 91, p. 246-248.
332. BARRACK, Jack
   "Beached Whales." [Poetry] (158:2) My 91, p. 89.
333. BARRAGAN, Nina
   "Descendant Patterns." [WorldL] (2) 91, p. 42-46.
334. BARRESI, Dorothy
   "Live Remote, Puritan Road, November 24, 1963." [PennR] (5:1) Spr 91, p. 1-3.
   "Some Questions We Might Ask." [IndR] (14:2) Spr 91, p. 71-73.
335. BARRETT, Carol
   "Approach." [SoCoast] (10) Fall 91, p. 26-27.
   "Drawing a Garden." [Kalliope] (13:1) 91, p. 14.
   "Drawing a Milk Bottle." [Kalliope] (13:1) 91, p. 14.
   "Hemisphere." [WestB] (28) 91, p. 16.
   "Why I Can't Send a Cover Photo." [SwampR] (7/8) Spr-Sum 91, p. 92-94.
336. BARRETT, Joseph
   "John Berryman's Bridge." [Bogg] (64) 91, p. 56.
   "A Winter Baptism." [RiverS] (33) 91, p. 55.
337. BARRIE, Brenda
   "Faigie's Song." [PraF] (12:1 #54) Spr 91, p. 11.
   "Long Distance." [PraF] (12:1 #54) Spr 91, p. 12.
338. BARRINGER, Margaret C.
   "New England Nights." [Boulevard] (5:3/6:1, #15/16) Spr 91, p. 150.
339. BARROWS, Anita
   "What World" (for Nora). [Journal] (15:2) Fall 91, p. 63-66.
340. BARRY, Sandra
   "A Whisper in the Autumn Wind" (October 14, 1990, for Elizabeth Bishop). [AntigR]
      (85/86) Spr-Sum 91, p. 76-78.
341. BARSOTTI, Richard
   "River Snails." [CalQ] (32/33) Spr 90, p. 148.
342. BARST, Fran
   "Altar of the Dead." [SoCaR] (24:1) Fall 91, p. 156-157.
   "Passage." [ContextS] (2:2) 91, p. 3-4.
   "Ruins Outside Rome." [ContextS] (2:2) 91, p. 4-5.
343. BART, Jill
   "Body-Speak." [PoetryE] (31) Spr 91, p. 83.
344. BARTHELME, Steven
   "She Cares. Aria Blattaria." [SouthernPR] (31:1) Spr 91, p. 5-6.
345. BARTLETT, Brian
   "Cousin Gifts." [CanLit] (131) Wint 91, p. 6.
   "Feast." [CanLit] (131) Wint 91, p. 99.
   "The Hands That Soap the Old Russian's Back." [Arc] (27) Aut 91, p. 8.
   "Museum Radiance" ("man's hat, ca. 1740"). [Arc] (27) Aut 91, p. 6-7.
   "Underwater Carpentry." [MalR] (96) Fall 91, p. 15-25.
346. BARTLETT, Elizabeth
   "After Ravilious." [Verse] (8:2) Sum 91, p. 101.
347. BARTLETT, Lee
   "Paris Notebook." [CalQ] (31) Fall 88, p. 34-35.
348. BARTON, John
   "13047 Sherbrooke Avenue." [PraF] (12:3 #56) Aut 91, p. 70-71.
   "Cave." [PraF] (12:3 #56) Aut 91, p. 72-73.
   "Delivery." [TickleAce] (22) Fall-Wint 91, p. 5-6.
   "Vancouver Gothic." [Grain] (19:4) Wint 91, p. 102-103.
   "Who Is This" (after a painting by Rachel Hesse). [Grain] (19:4) Wint 91, p. 104.
349. BASINSKI, Michael
   "Do Not Go Gentle." [PoetryUSA] (23) Sum 91, p. 6.
350. BASNEY, Lionel
   "Lessons." [Shen] (41:1) Spr 91, p. 70.

"The Morning." [Shen] (41:1) Spr 91, p. 68-69.
351. BASSETT, Lawrence F.
    "One Red Tree Does Not." [Hellas] (2:2) Fall 91, p. 274.
    "The Walnuts First." [Hellas] (2:2) Fall 91, p. 274.
352. BASSO, Eric
    "The Red Tree." [Asylum] (6:3/4) 91, p. 5.
353. BAT-YISRAEL, Shulamith
    "Indifference." [BlackBR] (13) Spr-Sum 91, p. 9.
    "Peace Now" (In memory of the beloved poet of Lebanon . . .). [JINJPo] (13:2) Aut
        91, p. 28-36.
354. BATEMAN, Claire
    "A Day Without the Car." [SoCaR] (24:1) Fall 91, p. 127.
    "Explicit." [SoCaR] (23:2) Spr 91, p. 14.
355. BATES, Kyle Anne
    "Basketball Tryouts." [JamesWR] (9:1) Fall 91, p. 10.
356. BATES, Ralph
    "So They Say." [NewYorkQ] (46) 91, p. 27.
357. BATHANTI, Joseph
    "I Will Mark the Tattler." [CalQ] (32/33) Spr 90, p. 144.
358. BATKI, John
    "As in a Field" (tr. of Attila József). [Talisman] (6) Spr 91, p. 12.
    "The Bell" (tr. of Attila József). [Talisman] (6) Spr 91, p. 11.
    "Only Those Should Read My Poems" (tr. of Attila József). [Talisman] (6) Spr 91, p.
        11.
359. BATTIN, Wendy
    "Diana." [GettyR] (4:1) Wint 91, p. 70.
    "Eastpoint." [RiverC] (11:2) Spr 91, p. 20.
    "Five O Five." [RiverC] (11:2) Spr 91, p. 18-19.
    "Invocation." [GettyR] (4:1) Wint 91, p. 71.
    "Saguaro National Forest." [RiverC] (11:2) Spr 91, p. 21.
360. BATTRAM, Michael R.
    "The Night of the First Spring Storm." [ChironR] (10:2) Sum 91, p. 48.
    "Now, If They Call You an Asshole, What Should You Say?" [ChironR] (10:3) Aut
        91, p. 45.
361. BAUDELAIRE, Charles (Pierre Charles)
    "The Blind People" (tr. by David Ferry). [PartR] (58:4) Fall 91, p. 692.
    "The Jewels" (tr. by James McGowan). [SpoonRQ] (16:3/4) Sum-Fall 91, p. 44-45.
    "Misty Sky" (tr. by Rachel Hadas). [Raritan] (11:1) Sum 91, p. 13.
    "Music" (tr. by James McGowan). [SpoonRQ] (16:3/4) Sum-Fall 91, p. 43.
    "The Promises of a Face" (tr. by Rachel Hadas). [Raritan] (11:1) Sum 91, p. 15.
    "Retreat" (tr. by Rachel Hadas). [Raritan] (11:1) Sum 91, p. 14.
    "Sonnet in Autumn" (tr. by Rachel Hadas). [Raritan] (11:1) Sum 91, p. 16.
    "La Voix" (tr. by Rachel Hadas). [NewYRB] (38:4) 14 F 91, p. 24.
362. BAUER, Bill
    "Children of the Dust." [NewL] (58:1) Fall 91, p. 38-39.
363. BAUER, Bruce
    "ASPCA" (for Sari). [ParisR] (33:121) Wint 91, p. 138-139.
364. BAUER, Grace
    "Conundrum." [SwampR] (7/8) Spr-Sum 91, p. 34.
    "The Eye of the Beholder" (After Diane Arbus). [Poetry] (158:6) S 91, p. 334-335.
    "Poem in December" (for my father & brothers). [SwampR] (7/8) Spr-Sum 91, p.
        35-36.
    "She Thinks She Smells a Bad Metaphor." [MichQR] (30:1) Wint 91, p. 82-83.
365. BAUER, Steven
    "Gleaning." [HopewellR] (1991) 91, p. 14.
    "Harvest." [HopewellR] (1991) 91, p. 8.
366. BAUGH, Edward
    "Old Talk, or West Indian History." [GrahamHR] (14) Spr 91, p. 49-50.
367. BAUM, Betsy
    "Only Yesterday." [PikeF] (10) Spr 91, p. 18.
368. BAUMEL, Judith
    "Outside, in Fact, There Wasn't Any Change" (tr. of Patrizia Cavalli). [NewYorker]
        (66:49) 21 Ja 91, p. 56.
    "Thumbs Up." [Thrpny] (46) Sum 91, p. 14.
    "You Weren't Crazy and You Weren't Dead." [NewYorker] (67:14) 27 My 91, p. 40.

369. BAUMGAERTNER, Jill P.
    "Story." [ChrC] (108:26) 18-25 S 91, p. 838.
370. BAUTISTA, Ramón C.
    "The Inauguration." [Zyzzyva] (7:1) Spr 91, p. 126-127.
    "The Night of the Glowworms." [Zyzzyva] (7:1) Spr 91, p. 130-131.
    "The Trap." [Zyzzyva] (7:1) Spr 91, p. 128.
371. BAWER, Bruce
    "Lenox Hill." [Agni] (34) 91, p. 206-207.
372. BAYER, Deanne
    "Barnacles." [Elf] (1:1) Spr 91, p. 38.
    "Ladies of the Club." [Elf] (1:2) Sum 91, p. 39.
    "Reprise." [Elf] (1:1) Spr 91, p. 38.
    "Tivoli." [Elf] (1:4) Wint 91, p. 25.
    "To Matthew Arnold." [Elf] (1:4) Wint 91, p. 24.
373. BAYLEY, Edgar
    "Like the Rivers, Clouds, and Roses" (tr. by Thorpe Running). [ColR] (NS 18:1)
        Spr-Sum 91, p. 86-87.
374. BEACH, Jack
    "Bruegel Country." [EmeraldCR] (3) 91, c1990, p. 135-136.
    "Masks." [EmeraldCR] (4) 91, p. 67-68.
    "Save the Seals." [EmeraldCR] (3) 91, c1990, p. 23-25.
    "The Winter of '48." [EmeraldCR] (3) 91, c1990, p. 140-142.
375. BEAKE, Fred
    "Midsummer" (Excerpt). [Stand] (33:1) Wint 91, p. 58.
376. BEAM, Jeffery
    "The Beautiful Tendons" (Selections: 5, 11-12). [JamesWR] (8:3) Spr 91, p. 1.
BEAR, Ray Young (Ray A. Young)
    See YOUNG BEAR, Ray (Ray A.)
377. BEAR WITH TWO CUBS
    "The Woman on the White Buffalo Turns." [SingHM] (19) 91, p. 69.
378. BEARD, David
    "Old Woman." [Gypsy] (17) 91, p. 32.
    "Poem: The radio is on." [RagMag] (9:1) 91, p. 25.
379. BEARDSLEY, Jene Erick
    "The New Testament." [ChrC] (108:15) 1 My 91, p. 486.
380. BÉARN, Pierre
    "Twilight" (tr. by Dorothy Aspinwall). [CrabCR] (7:2) Sum 91, p. 12.
381. BEASLEY, Bruce
    "The Instrument and Proper Corps of the Soule." [NewEngR] (14:1) Fall 91, p.
        82-83.
    "Sacrifice." [OntR] (35) Fall-Wint 91-92, p. 85-87.
    "Zeta Hercules." [AntR] (49:2) Spr 91, p. 252.
382. BEASLEY, Conger, Jr.
    "Letter to a Friend from a Man in the Hills" (after Wang Wei). [Interim] (10:1)
        Spr-Sum 91, p. 38-39.
    "We Are All Immortal in August." [Interim] (10:1) Spr-Sum 91, p. 39.
383. BEATTY, Brian
    "Diner." [SycamoreR] (3:1) Wint 91, p. 23.
384. BEAUMONT, Jeanne
    "Annunciation: Three Views." [Sonora] (21) Sum 91, p. 77-78.
    "Arrangement." [Nat] (253:12) 14 O 91, p. 459.
    "The Greening of the Fire Escape." [Nat] (253:6) 26 Ag-2 S 91, p. 243.
    "Journey." [QW] (32) Wint-Spr 91, p. 100.
    "Judging the Book by Its Cover." [Poetry] (158:5) Ag 91, p. 278.
    "My Demure." [Poetry] (157:5) F 91, p. 263.
    "Pearl Hour." [Poetry] (158:2) My 91, p. 99.
    "Reliquary." [QW] (32) Wint-Spr 91, p. 99.
    "Suspicion." [Kalliope] (13:2) 91, p. 40-41.
385. BEAUTIFUL WILLOW, Ana
    "Eight long legs." [PoetryUSA] (23) Sum 91, p. 12.
386. BEAUVAIS, Phyllis
    "My Father Will Die." [Poetry] (158:1) Ap 91, p. 35.
387. BECK, Art
    "The Grace to Be Free" (Selections: 8 poems). [SwampR] (7/8) Spr-Sum 91, p.
        107-117.

388. BECK, Marion
      "Dolls" (Short Grain Contest Winners: Prose Poem Winners: First Prize). [Grain]
            (19:4) Wint 91, p. 66.
389. BECKER, Carol
      "Titwillow." [US1] (24/25) Spr 91, p. 19.
390. BECKER, Robin
      "From Taos to Santa Fe" (for Nora Ryerson). [13thMoon] (9:1/2) 91, p. 23-25.
      "On the Mesa." [ColR] (NS 18:2) Fall-Wint 91, p. 120-121.
      "The Star Show." [Ploughs] (17:2/3) Fall 91, p. 29-30.
391. BECKETT, Larry
      "I'm glad I'm at Green Bank, where I map neutral." [PoetL] (86:2) Sum 91, p. 42.
      "It's just heaven, this country theater, the actors." [PoetL] (86:2) Sum 91, p. 43.
      "To the Virginia Girl" (after Li Po). [CrabCR] (7:2) Sum 91, p. 25.
392. BEDARD, Brian
      "The Assiniboin Hear about a Speech Clinic." [CharR] (17:1) Spr 91, p. 69.
      "The Kiowa Hear about a School of Modern Dance." [CharR] (17:1) Spr 91, p. 71.
      "The Navajo Hear about a U.F.O." [CharR] (17:1) Spr 91, p. 69.
      "The Utes Hear about Some Stolen Furs." [CharR] (17:1) Spr 91, p. 70.
393. BÉDARD, Nicole
      "In Harmony." [TickleAce] (22) Fall-Wint 91, p. 35-38.
      "Withinness." [TickleAce] (22) Fall-Wint 91, p. 34.
394. BEDELL, Jack B.
      "The Maker in the Sky." [LaurelR] (25:2) Sum 91, p. 75.
395. BEDIENT, Cal
      "Julius T. and the Melancholie of God Avec Stupeur" (after K. L. Kahlbaum's
            Catatonia, 1874). [Ploughs] (17:4) Wint 91-92, p. 49-50.
396. BEGGS-UEMA, Marck (Marck L.)
      "Appreciation Is Twenty-seven Thirtieths of the Art." [LaurelR] (25:1) Wint 91, p.
            96.
      "Wine." [LaurelR] (25:1) Wint 91, p. 97.
397. BEHN, Robin
      "Five O'Clock in Your Childhood." [AmerV] (23) Sum 91, p. 88-90.
      "The House in the Clearing." [OhioR] (47) 91, p. 38-39.
      "Slow Movement in G" (for H.). [DenQ] (26:1) Sum 91, p. 9-10.
398. BEHRENDT, Stephen C.
      "Beggar Girl at Dupont Circle, Washington." [SouthernR] (27:4) O 91, p. 930-931.
      "Cornfields." [HighP] (6:3) Wint 91, p. 64-65.
      "Hidden Cares." [HighP] (6:1) Spr 91, p. 68-69.
      "The Tower." [SouthernR] (27:4) O 91, p. 931-932.
      "Wordsworth's Daffodils." [SouthernR] (27:4) O 91, p. 932-33.
399. BEI, Dao
      "The Accomplices" (tr. by Xiaofei Tian). [PraS] (65:2) Sum 91, p. 101.
      "Ars Poetica" (tr. by Xiaofei Tian). [PraS] (65:2) Sum 91, p. 104.
      "Boundaries" (tr. by Xiaofei Tian). [PraS] (65:2) Sum 91, p. 103.
      "Country Night." [LitR] (34:2) Wint 91, p. 211.
      "An Elegy." [LitR] (34:2) Wint 91, p. 211.
      "The Host" (tr. by Xiaofei Tian). [PraS] (65:2) Sum 91, p. 102.
      "A Local Accent" (tr. by Bonnie S. McDougall and Chen Maiping). [ManhatR] (6:1)
            Fall 91, p. 8.
      "My Country" (tr. by Bonnie S. McDougall and Chen Maiping). [ManhatR] (6:1) Fall
            91, p. 11.
      "Old Snow" (tr. by Bonnie S. McDougall and Chen Maiping). [ManhatR] (6:1) Fall
            91, p. 6.
      "Ordinary Days." [LitR] (34:2) Wint 91, p. 212.
      "A Picture" (for Tiantian's fifth birthday, tr. by Bonnie S. McDougall and Chen
            Maiping). [ManhatR] (6:1) Fall 91, p. 9.
      "Prague" (tr. by Bonnie S. McDougall and Chen Maiping). [ManhatR] (6:1) Fall 91,
            p. 4.
      "Rebel" (tr. by Bonnie S. McDougall and Chen Maiping). [ManhatR] (6:1) Fall 91, p.
            12.
      "The Space" (tr. by Xiaofei Tian). [PraS] (65:2) Sum 91, p. 102-103.
      "A Step." [LitR] (34:2) Wint 91, p. 212.
      "Temptation" (tr. by Xiaofei Tian). [PraS] (65:2) Sum 91, p. 103-104.
      "Terminal Illness" (tr. by Bonnie S. McDougall and Chen Maiping). [ManhatR] (6:1)
            Fall 91, p. 7.

"To Memory" (tr. by Bonnie S. McDougall and Chen Maiping). [ManhatR] (6:1) Fall 91, p. 10.
"Untitled: He opens wide a third eye" (tr. by Bonnie S. McDougall and Chen Maiping). [ManhatR] (6:1) Fall 91, p. 5.
"Window Onto a Cliff" (tr. by Tony Barnstone and Newton Liu). [Thrpny] (46) Sum 91, p. 16.

400. BELEV, Georgi
"Clay and Star" (tr. of Ivan Davidkov, w. Lisa Sapinkopf). [CarolQ] (44:1) Fall 91, p. 44.
"The Forest Comes Down at Night" (tr. by Lisa Sapinkopf, w. the author). [ParisR] (33:121) Wint 91, p. 119.
"Lake" (tr. by Lisa Sapinkopf, w. the author). [Agni] (34) 91, p. 179.
"Love" (tr. by Lisa Sapinkopf, w. the author). [Agni] (34) 91, p. 180-181.
"Museum" (tr. by Lisa Sapinkopf, w. the author). [BostonR] (16:1) F 91, p. 28.
"Perhaps" (tr. by Roumen Mitkov and Ron Butlin). [Verse] (8:2) Sum 91, p. 117.
"Tale" (tr. by Lisa Sapinkopf, w. the author). [Poetry] (159:1) O 91, p. 21.
"Train" (tr. by Lisa Sapinkopf, w. the author). [Poetry] (159:1) O 91, p. 20.
"Villages Like Ghosts" (tr. of Ivan Davidkov, w. Lisa Sapinkopf). [CarolQ] (44:1) Fall 91, p. 43.

401. BELGUM, Erik
"I Am a Bit Breathless, But Ordinary." [Caliban] (10) 91, p. 116-120.

402. BELL, Jill C.
"L'Hiver." [SoCoast] (11) Wint 91, p. 42.
"Winter." [SoCoast] (11) Wint 91, p. 43.

403. BELL, Marguerite
"Paying for the Wine." [OxfordM] (7:2) Fall-Wint 91, p. 70.

404. BELL, Marvin
"American Children of the Fifties." [ThRiPo] (37/38) 91, p. 89.
"At the Writers' Conference." [NewEngR] (14:1) Fall 91, p. 195-204.
"Poem in Orange Tones." [GeoR] (45:1) Spr 91, p. 73-74.
"Rows of Apartments." [Nat] (252:7) 25 F 91, p. 247.
"Snake River Seminars." [ThRiPo] (37/38) 91, p. 88.

405. BELL, Sydney
"The God Who Says My Name." [PoetryUSA] (23) Sum 91, p. 17.

406. BELLEN, Martine
"Cistern." [NewAW] (7) Spr 91, p. 32-33.

407. BELLIN, Steven G.
"Breakings." [CumbPR] (11:1) Fall 91, p. 29-30.
"The Others" (Rt. 16, Harmony, Maryland). [CumbPR] (11:1) Fall 91, p. 28.

408. BELLOWS, Timothy Parker
"Wolf's Dusk." [MidwQ] (32:3) Spr 91, p. 288.

409. BELO, Roy
"Muriel" (from "Toda a Terra," 1976, tr. by William Jay Smith). [Trans] (25) Spr 91, p. 76-79.

410. BENBOW-NIEMIER, Glynis
"Vigia." [CinPR] (21) Spr 90, p. 24-25.

411. BENDALL, Molly
"Ballad of Peaches." [Journal] (15:2) Fall 91, p. 57-60.
"Invitations to Spring: Letters with Elizabeth." [CarolQ] (43:3) Spr 91, p. 32-34.
"The Visitation." [AmerPoR] (20:2) Mr-Ap 91, p. 19.

412. BENEDETTI, Mario
"Typist" (tr. by Harry Morales). [Vis] (36) 91, p. 10.

413. BENEDETTO, Judith
"Curse of the Cat Woman." [Crucible] (27) Fall 91, p. 53.

414. BENEDIKT, Michael
"True Misery (Report from Ancient Asia Minor)." [AntR] (49:3) Sum 91, p. 434.
"Up Late Writing." [ColR] (NS 18:1) Spr-Sum 91, p. 110-111.

415. BENEVENTO, Joe
"Not Sleeping with You." [SlipS] (11) 91, p. 66.
"Returning the Favor: Sympathy for a Fallen Hero." [SlipS] (11) 91, p. 65.

416. BENFEY, Christopher
"Something Like a Rainbow." [ParisR] (33:121) Wint 91, p. 187.
"Two Typos." [ParisR] (33:121) Wint 91, p. 188.

417. BENJAMIN, Jerry
"Dancing into the Air" (for Freddie Herko). [Abraxas] (40/41) 91, p. 132-133.

418. BENJAMIN, Ruth
   "You Must Go to the Moon." [ChironR] (10:2) Sum 91, p. 42.
419. BENNANI, Ben
   "American Jihad" (Editorial). [Paint] (18:35) Spr 91, p. 5-6.
420. BENNETT, Bruce
   "Alternative Advice to a Friend Whose Work Has Come to Nothing." [TarRP] (31:1)
      Fall 91, p. 35.
   "Summer's Day." [TarRP] (31:1) Fall 91, p. 34-35.
421. BENNETT, John (John M.)
   "Bye Bying." [CrabCR] (7:2) Sum 91, p. 29.
   "Chance Mutterance." [Caliban] (10) 91, p. 66.
   "Château" (tr. into French by Philippe Billé). [WorldL] (2) 91, p. 49.
   "Fold." [PoetryUSA] (22) Spr 91, p. 11.
   "Ici" (tr. into French by Philippe Billé). [WorldL] (2) 91, p. 50.
   "Lagrimation." [DustyD] (2:1) Ja 91, p. 25.
   "El Ninguneo." [ContextS] (2:2) 91, p. 31.
   "Poche" (tr. into French by Philippe Billé). [WorldL] (2) 91, p. 49.
   "Small Pancakes." [SoDakR] (29:3 part 2) Aut 91, p. 30-31.
   "The Story." [Caliban] (10) 91, p. 66.
   "Transubstantiation." [Bogg] (64) 91, p. 5.
422. BENNETT, Maria
   "And" (tr. of Carlos Edmundo de Ory). [SnailPR] (1:2) Fall 91-Wint 92, p. 9.
   "Permit Me to Speak of Love" (tr. of Carlos Edmundo de Ory). [SnailPR] (1:2) Fall
      91-Wint 92, p. 8.
   "Persistence of Memory." [CrabCR] (7:2) Sum 91, p. 7.
423. BENNETT, Paul
   "On Newfoundland Rocks" (To the memory of Charles Kirby Potter, 1918-1942).
      [Agni] (34) 91, p. 109-115.
424. BENSE, Robert
   "Contra August." [Poetry] (158:5) Ag 91, p. 276.
425. BENSKO, Rosemary
   "The Lateness of the Night Lies Dreaming." [ColR] (NS 18:1) Spr-Sum 91, p. 31-32.
426. BENSON, Dominique
   "A Black Man Told Me" (for David Diop, tr. of Chiekh Ahmadou Dieng, w. Peter
      Benson). [LitR] (34:4) Sum 91, p. 459.
   "Lice" (tr. of Chiekh Ahmadou Dieng, w. Peter Benson). [LitR] (34:4) Sum 91, p.
      458.
   "Passion of a Vulture" (tr. of Chiekh Ahmadou Dieng, w. Peter Benson). [LitR]
      (34:4) Sum 91, p. 458.
427. BENSON, Joan
   "Aged Woman Looking at a Man." [Nimrod] (34:2) Spr-Sum 91, p. 8.
   "Antichrist 1986." [Nimrod] (34:2) Spr-Sum 91, p. 10.
   "Barren." [Nimrod] (34:2) Spr-Sum 91, p. 9.
428. BENSON, Peter
   "A Black Man Told Me" (for David Diop, tr. of Chiekh Ahmadou Dieng, w.
      Dominique Benson). [LitR] (34:4) Sum 91, p. 459.
   "Lice" (tr. of Chiekh Ahmadou Dieng, w. Dominique Benson). [LitR] (34:4) Sum 91,
      p. 458.
   "Passion of a Vulture" (tr. of Chiekh Ahmadou Dieng, w. Dominique Benson). [LitR]
      (34:4) Sum 91, p. 458.
429. BENSON, Robert
   "Grandfather." [SewanR] (99:3) Sum 91, p. 364-365.
430. BENSYL, Stacia
   "Equinox." [CapeR] (26:1) Spr 91, p. 11.
431. BENTLEY, Beth
   "Suspense at Meran." [Pig] (17) 91, p. 79.
432. BENTLEY, Roy
   "Dizzy Gillespie at the Blue Note." [MidAR] (11:2) 91, p. 115-116.
433. BENTLEY, Sean
   "Hymns Against Our Silences." [PaintedB] (44) 91, p. 38-39.
   "Ravine." [PoetL] (86:1) Spr 91, p. 23-24.
434. BENTON, Keith G.
   "Scarecrow." [CoalC] (4) S 91, p. 8.
435. BENVENUTO, Richard
   "Incident at the Lake." [SoDakR] (29:3 part 2) Aut 91, p. 44-45.

436. BERDESHEVSKY, Margo
"A Day in the Life." [Vis] (35) 91, p. 10-11.
437. BERG, Stephen
"17 from Sappho: You Burn Me" (tr. of Sappho). [TriQ] (81) Spr-Sum 91, p.
246-249.
"Oblivion" (Excerpt). [DenQ] (25:4) Spr 91, p. 6-13.
"Unfinished Double Sonnet." [DenQ] (26:1) Sum 91, p. 11-12.
438. BERGAMINO, Gina
"December Blackout." [HawaiiR] (15:3, #33) Fall 91, p. 12.
"Double Talk." [Plain] (11:2) Wint 91, p. 16.
"In Munich's City Square." [BlackBR] (13) Spr-Sum 91, p. 36.
"Invisible." [HawaiiR] (15:2, #32) Spr 91, p. 106.
"The Man from Auschwitz." [BlackBR] (13) Spr-Sum 91, p. 36.
"Mehinaku Indian." [HawaiiR] (15:3, #33) Fall 91, p. 11.
"Not Far Away, the Bridge." [HawaiiR] (15:2, #32) Spr 91, p. 107.
"Poem Fragment." [BlackBR] (13) Spr-Sum 91, p. 36.
439. BERGER, Bruce
"The Misconstrued." [Poetry] (158:3) Je 91, p. 147.
"Of Joe." [NewL] (58:1) Fall 91, p. 113.
"Opus Posthumous." [NewL] (58:1) Fall 91, p. 112.
440. BERGMAN, David
"David to the Harpist." [Tribe] (1:2) Spr 90, p. 27-29.
"Goya's Enlightenment." [NewRep] (205:19) 4 N 91, p. 35.
"The Wrath of Medea." [JamesWR] (8:3) Spr 91, p. 18.
441. BERGMAN, Susan
"First Things: A Source Study." [Ploughs] (17:4) Wint 91-92, p. 32-36.
442. BERKE, Judith
"Alicia (Poland, 1942)" (for Alicia Appleman-Jurman). [MassR] (32:3) Fall 91, p.
358.
"Dorothy Day" (American, d. 1980. Being considered for sainthood). [MassR] (32:4)
Wint 91-92, p. 543.
"Freedom." [MassR] (32:4) Wint 91-92, p. 544.
"Glass-Bottom Boat." [IndR] (14:3) Fall 91, p. 65-66.
"The Myth." [DenQ] (26:2) Fall 91, p. 7.
"The Old Child" (Progyria). [Field] (44) Spr 91, p. 9.
"Tinnitus" (for John B.). [Field] (44) Spr 91, p. 10-11.
443. BERLANDT, Herman
"Concert." [PoetryUSA] (23) Sum 91, p. 14.
"People Who Have Stuck." [PoetryUSA] (22) Spr 91, p. 15.
"Toss the Bums Out!" [PoetryUSA] (23) Sum 91, p. 18.
444. BERLIND, Bruce
"After a Long Journey" (tr. of Imre Oravecz, w. Mária Körösy). [HampSPR] Wint
91, p. 64.
"America" ("Dear Dr. Orbán — a letter from Washington D.C., February 1987, tr. of
Ottó Orbán, w. Mária Körösy). [OnTheBus] (8/9) 91, p. 218.
"And Sometimes It's the Cities" (tr. of Ottó Orbán, w. Mária Körösy). [Agni] (34)
91, p. 223.
"De Profundis" (tr. of Georg Trakl). [Chelsea] (51) 91, p. 58.
"Dust" (tr. of Imre Oravecz, w. Mária Körösy). [GrandS] (10:1, #37) 91, p.
197-198.
"Europe" (tr. of Ottó Orbán, w. Mária Körösy). [Agni] (34) 91, p. 224.
"The Hole" (tr. of Imre Oravecz, w. Mária Körösy). [GrandS] (10:1, #37) 91, p.
199.
"Hope in the Air" (tr. of Gyula Illyés, w. Mária Körösy). [Os] (33) Fall 91, p. 3.
"I Couldn't Tell You Back Then" (tr. of Imre Oravecz, w. Mária Körösy). [Stand]
(32:4) Aut 91, p. 24.
"I Have a Recurring" (tr. of Imre Oravecz, w. Mária Körösy). [InterPR] (17:2) Fall
91, p. 32.
"In the Beginning There Was" (tr. of Imre Oravecz, w. Mária Körösy). [ColR] (NS
17:2) Fall-Wint 90, p. 104.
"In the East" (tr. of Georg Trakl). [Chelsea] (51) 91, p. 59.
"In Theodore Roosevelt Park" (New York Columbus Avenue, tr.tr. of Ottó Orbán, w.
Mária Körösy). [OnTheBus] (8/9) 91, p. 219.
"The Landscape Unfolding Before Us" (American Automobile Association Road
Atlas, 1987 Edition, tr. of Ottó Orbán, w. Mária Körösy). [ColR] (NS 18:2)
Fall-Wint 91, p. 78.

55

"Last Year in Jerusalem." [Agni] (34) 91, p. 241-243.
"Nine A.M." (tr. of Imre Oravecz, w. Mária Körösy). [InterPR] (17:2) Fall 91, p. 33.
"Sinking" (To Karl Borromaus Heinrich, tr. of Georg Trakl). [Chelsea] (51) 91, p. 57.
"Sleep" (tr. of Georg Trakl). [Chelsea] (51) 91, p. 61.
"There I Stood" (tr. of Imre Oravecz, w. Mária Körösy). [InterPR] (17:2) Fall 91, p. 35.
"To the Boy Elis" (tr. of Georg Trakl). [Chelsea] (51) 91, p. 60.
"Under the Thundering Ceiling" (Hamline University, St. Paul, Minnesota, tr. of Ottó Orbán, w. Mária Körösy). [OnTheBus] (8/9) 91, p. 219.
"When We Resolved" (tr. of Imre Oravecz, w. Mária Körösy). [InterPR] (17:2) Fall 91, p. 34.
"The Year Drops Anchor, Tihany" (tr. of Gyula Illés, w. Mária Körösy). [Vis] (36) 91, p. 21.
445. BERLOSO CANDELARIO, Ginetta E.
"In My Country." [BilingR] (16:2/3) My-D 91, p. 220.
"Untitled: I'm not sure." [BilingR] (16:2/3) My-D 91, p. 218-219.
446. BERMAN, Ruth
"And Sought to Kill Him (Ex. 4.24)." [Poem] (66) N 91, p. 26.
"Double Planet Night." [Poem] (66) N 91, p. 25.
"Wordplay." [NegC] (11:1) 91, p. 61.
447. BERN, Dan
"The Ballad of Dave and Eddie." [Zyzzyva] (7:2) Sum 91, p. 127-135.
448. BERNARD, April
"Psalm: Cris de Coeur." [ParisR] (33:121) Wint 91, p. 120-121.
"Psalm: It Must Be the Medication." [ParisR] (33:121) Wint 91, p. 120.
449. BERNHARD, Jim
"The Boxer" (8 poems). [BellArk] (7:1) Ja-F 91, p. 8-9.
"Footsteps." [BellArk] (7:6) N-D 91, p. 8.
450. BERNSTEIN, Carole
"The Common Atlantic Moon Snail Conceives of Herself." [Chelsea] (51) 91, p. 28.
"Montauk." [Chelsea] (51) 91, p. 26-27.
"Three-Toed Sloth." [Poetry] (158:2) My 91, p. 91-92.
451. BERNSTEIN, Charles
"At the Reading (3)." [Aerial] (6/7) 91, p. 87.
"Ballad of Blue Green Plates." [Aerial] (6/7) 91, p. 86.
"Blind Witness News" (An Opera in Four Parts). [Ploughs] (17:1) Spr 91, p. 21-34.
"A Defence of Poetry" (for Brian McHale). [Aerial] (6/7) 91, p. 83-84.
"Disordering" (tr. of Dubravka Djuric, w. the author). [Sulfer] (11:2, #29) Fall 91, p. 23-24.
"Emotions of Normal People." [Pequod] (32) 91, p. 33-44.
"The Influence of Kinship Patterns upon Perception of an Ambiguous Stimulus." [Verse] (8:1) Spr 91, p. 73-77.
"No Tieing Up." [Aerial] (6/7) 91, p. 85.
"Red, Green and Black" (Potes and Poets 1990. Selection: 4, tr. of Olivier Cadiot, w. the author). [Avec] (4:1) 91, p. 61-64.
"Searchless Warrant." [WorldL] (1:1) 91, p. 26.
452. BERRY, D. C.
"I'm Going Where the Women Point." [MassR] (32:3) Fall 91, p. 402.
"Insomnia." [NewEngR] (13:3/4) Spr-Sum 91, p. 68.
"Ten-Pound Bible." [MassR] (32:3) Fall 91, p. 401.
453. BERRY, David
"Fishing." [TexasR] (11:1/2) Spr-Sum 90, p. 14-15.
"The Italy Not in the Travel Brochures" (for Mernie King). [NewOR] (18:2) Sum 91, p. 29.
"Knee Caps." [TexasR] (11:1/2) Spr-Sum 90, p. 16.
454. BERRY, Jake
"1991." [PoetryUSA] (22) Spr 91, p. 5.
"Keep him out of the box." [PoetryUSA] (23) Sum 91, p. 27.
"When I open my eyes beneath the river." [PoetryUSA] (22) Spr 91, p. 11.
455. BERRY, John
"Zenobia of Palmyra." [ManhatPR] (13) [91?], p. 38.
456. BERRY, Robert
"Cars and Planes." [DogRR] (10:2) Fall-Wint 91, p. 7.
457. BERRY, Thomas
"Dark Curve." [InterPR] (17:2) Fall 91, p. 104.

"The Garden Walk." [InterPR] (17:2) Fall 91, p. 104.
"Riverdale December." [InterPR] (17:2) Fall 91, p. 103-104.
"Seagull." [InterPR] (17:2) Fall 91, p. 102-103.
"Valentine Season: Riverdale." [InterPR] (17:2) Fall 91, p. 101.
"A Wedding Ode" (For the Mountain Wedding of a Cellist and His Bride, Summer 1990). [InterPR] (17:2) Fall 91, p. 101-102.
458. BERRY, Wendell
"The Barn." [SouthernR] (27:3) Jl 91, p. 535.
"Duality." [Hudson] (44:1) Spr 91, p. 91-94.
459. BERRYMAN, John
"Gislebertus' Eve." [DenQ] (25:3) Wint 91, p. 87-88.
"A Glory There Is Over Ireland Now." [GettyR] (4:4) Aut 91, p. 555.
"Of Poets — to Richard Wilbur." [GettyR] (4:4) Aut 91, p. 562.
"On the Death of Yeats." [GettyR] (4:4) Aut 91, p. 557.
"Professional Notes." [GettyR] (4:4) Aut 91, p. 556.
"Roethke's Yule" (Jarrell stone sober in obligato). [GettyR] (4:4) Aut 91, p. 559.
"Slattery's, in Ballsbridge." [DenQ] (25:3) Wint 91, p. 87.
"To Dylan Thomas." [GettyR] (4:4) Aut 91, p. 558.
"To His Ghost." [GettyR] (4:4) Aut 91, p. 560.
"Yes, Yes, I Offered Him a Cigarette." [GettyR] (4:4) Aut 91, p. 561.
460. BERSSENBRUGGE, Mei-mei
"Experience." [Sulfur] (11:2 #29) Fall 91, p. 159-162.
"Size." [Conjunc] (16) 91, p. 260-261.
461. BERTHELOT, Dolly
"T.P. 101." [EmeraldCR] (3) 91, c1990, p. 52-53.
462. BETANZOS PALACIOS, Odón
"Del Hombre Desolado Que Ni Vio a Dios." [Nuez] (3:7) 91, p. 3.
"Del Tiempo en Muerte y del Ceño que Tenía la Muerte." [Nuez] (3:7) 91, p. 2.
"Mi Madre." [Nuez] (3:7) 91, p. 2.
463. BETTS, Gregory
"Dedications." [PraF] (12:4) Wint 91-92, p. 13.
"Midnight Vow." [PraF] (12:4) Wint 91-92, p. 12.
"Two Weeks in a Suspense Movie." [Grain] (19:1) Spr 91, p. 46.
464. BEUM, Robert
"Cornflowers." [ChrC] (108:17) 15-22 My 91, p. 559.
465. BEVERIDGE, Robert P.
"The Land of Rape and Honey." [Gypsy] (17) 91, p. 16.
466. BEYERS, Joanna
"Every Morning Peter Gzowski." [CapilR] (2:6/7) Fall 91, p. 160-161.
"Joy Kogawa at La Quena" (April 24, 1986). [CapilR] (2:6/7) Fall 91, p. 163.
"Re: The Green River Murders" (Based on Pacific Report, CBC-TV, Jan. 19, 1987). [CapilR] (2:6/7) Fall 91, p. 162.
467. BEYNON, B. W.
"Brynmawr." [Stand] (32:4) Aut 91, p. 9.
468. BEZNER, Kevin
"Going to the Cemetery." [OnTheBus] (8/9) 91, p. 27.
"To Have Knowledge." [OnTheBus] (8/9) 91, p. 27.
469. BHASIN, Mohit
"On the Mammoth, 1975." [Callaloo] (14:3) Sum 91, p. 665-666.
470. BHATT, Sujata
"What Does One Write When the World Starts to Disappear?" (for Eleanor and Bob). [Calyx] (13:2) Sum 91, p. 37-38.
471. BIALOSKY, Jill
"Ave Marie." [Agni] (34) 91, p. 225-226.
472. BIASOTTI, Raymond
"Diamonds." [SmPd] (28:3, #83) Fall 91, p. 19.
473. BIBLE
"Psalms" (Selections: 19, 23, 126, 137, tr. by Jacob Rabinowitz). [WorldL] (1:1) 91, p. 27-30.
474. BICHET, Yves
"The Spring on the Lance" (tr. by Mark Treharne). [Verse] (8:2) Sum 91, p. 121-122.
475. BIENEN, Leslie
"American Dreams." [PoetL] (86:3) Fall 91, p. 8.
"Living in Your New Country." [PoetL] (86:3) Fall 91, p. 7.
"Love Poem." [PoetL] (86:3) Fall 91, p. 5.
"Traveler's Advisory." [PoetL] (86:3) Fall 91, p. 6.

476. BIERDS, Linda
    "Abundance" (Tom Thumb, circa 1880). [PoetryNW] (32:1) Spr 91, p. 8-9.
    "Audubon's Border Boy." [KenR] (NS 13:3) Sum 91, p. 33-34.
    "From Blakesware: Mary Lamb." [KenR] (NS 13:3) Sum 91, p. 34-36.
    "The Grandsire Bells." [NewYorker] (67:9) 22 Ap 91, p. 40.
    "Halley's Bell" (from the diary of Marc Brunel). [PoetryNW] (32:1) Spr 91, p. 9-10.
    "The Running-Machines." [Journal] (15:1) Spr 91, p. 7-8.
    "Träumerei." [NewYorker] (66:49) 21 Ja 91, p. 36.
    "Wanting Color" (Sergei Prokudin-Gorskii). [PoetryNW] (32:1) Spr 91, p. 11-12.
    "Winterreise, for Three Voices" (homage to Hawthrone Gray, b. 1889, d.
        stratosphere balloon flight, 1927). [Journal] (15:1) Spr 91, p. 9-12.
477. BIERNBAUM, Michael
    "On the Road to the Men's Gathering." [ChangingM] (22) Wint-Spr 91, p. 13.
478. BIESPIEL, David
    "All the Amenities of Modern Life." [PlumR] (1) Spr-Sum 91, p. 21.
    "At Twenty-Eight Thousand Feet." [PoetryNW] (32:4) Wint 91-92, p. 21.
    "Gusts of Stillness Still Deep in the Trees." [GreenMR] (NS 5:1) Sum-Fall 91, p.
        102105.
    "The Idea of What's Here." [PoetryNW] (32:4) Wint 91-92, p. 19-20.
    "There Were No Deer in the Thicket." [OhioR] (46) 91, p. 73.
    "What Gifts of Love or Quiet Joy." [Journal] (15:2) Fall 91, p. 18-19.
479. BIGEAGLE, Duane
    "Islands of Light." [Zyzzyva] (7:3) Fall 91, p. 47.
480. BIGGINS, Michael
    "The Burning Bush" (tr. of Tomaz Salamun). [MissR] (19:3) 91, p. 185.
    "The Color of Morning" (tr. of Ales Debeljak). [PassN] (12:2) Wint 91, p. 23.
    "Distant Voices II" (tr. of Ales Debeljak, w. the author). [LitR] (35:1) Fall 91, p. 70.
    "Distant Voices III" (tr. of Ales Debeljak, w. the author). [LitR] (35:1) Fall 91, p. 70.
    "Elegy" (tr. of Ales Debeljak). [GrandS] (10:3, #39) 91, p. 209.
    "Fiery Night" (tr. of Edvard Kocbek). [CimR] (96) Jl 91, p. 21.
    "Litmus" (tr. of Tomaz Salamun). [CimR] (96) Jl 91, p. 28.
    "Marko" (tr. of Tomaz Salamun). [Agni] (33) 91, p. 98.
    "Melancholy of the Second Echelon" (In memory of my father, killed in 1943, tr. of
        Veno Taufer). [CimR] (96) Jl 91, p. 31-33.
    "Moonlight" (tr. of Edvard Kocbek). [CimR] (96) Jl 91, p. 22.
    "Of Fate" (tr. of Tomaz Salamun). [CimR] (96) Jl 91, p. 29.
    "Our Faith" (tr. of Tomaz Salamun). [NewL] (58:1) Fall 91, p. 36-37.
    "Outline of History" (from "Dictionary of Silence," tr. of Ales Debeljak). [Boulevard]
        (5:3/6:1, #15/16) Spr 91, p. 57-58.
    "Paris, 1978" (tr. of Tomaz Salamun). [Agni] (33) 91, p. 99.
    "The Past in My Mind" (tr. of Ales Debeljak). [Agni] (34) 91, p. 245.
    "Pour un Jeune Chalamoun Qui Se Vend dans la Rue" (tr. of Tomaz Salamun). [Agni]
        (33) 91, p. 100.
    "The Power of the *Oeuvre*" (tr. of Tomaz Salamun). [CimR] (96) Jl 91, p. 30.
    "Radio: Night Program" (tr. of Ales Debeljak). [PassN] (12:2) Wint 91, p. 23.
    "Under Eastern Eyes" (tr. of Ales Debeljak). [Shen] (41:2) Sum 91, p. 90.
    "Walls" (tr. of Tomaz Salamun). [NewL] (58:1) Fall 91, p. 35.
    "Woman on the Border" (tr. of Ales Debeljak). [PassN] (12:2) Wint 91, p. 23.
481. BILGERE, George
    "Alert." [Iowa] (21:2) Spr-Sum 91, p. 94.
    "Another Anniversary." [CimR] (94) Ja 91, p. 109.
    "The Bull." [CumbPR] (10:2) Spr 91, p. 24-25.
    "Ceremony." [Iowa] (21:2) Spr-Sum 91, p. 94.
    "Childhood." [SewanR] (99:1) Wint 91, p. 24.
    "Exiles." [Shen] (41:4) Wint 91, p. 23.
    "Healing." [Iowa] (21:2) Spr-Sum 91, p. 95-97.
    "Long Distance." [Shen] (41:4) Wint 91, p. 22.
    "Nine Months." [SewanR] (99:1) Wint 91, p. 23.
    "Physical Education." [CimR] (94) Ja 91, p. 108.
    "Snapshot, 1934." [SewanR] (99:1) Wint 91, p. 25.
    "The Taxidermist's Wife." [SewanR] (99:1) Wint 91, p. 22.
482. BILLÉ, Philippe
    "Château" (French tr. of John M. Bennett). [WorldL] (2) 91, p. 49.
    "Ici" (French tr. of John M. Bennett). [WorldL] (2) 91, p. 50.
    "Poche" (French tr. of John M. Bennett). [WorldL] (2) 91, p. 49.

483. BILOFSKY, Ellen
"Ride Back from Town." [MinnR] (NS 37) Fall 91, p. 21.
484. BILOTSERKIVETS, Natalka
"May" (tr. by Virlana Tkacz and Wanda Phipps). [Agni] (34) 91, p. 51-54.
BING, Liang Xiao
See LIANG, Xiao Bing
485. BIRCHARD, Guy
"Returning to Verwood from Thousands of Miles." [PraF] (12:2 #55) Sum 91, p. 19.
"Town Without Elevators." [PraF] (12:2 #55) Sum 91, p. 18.
486. BIRNEY, Dion
"Son Keeps Dead Mom in Chair 8 Months." [NewYorkQ] (45) 91, p. 62.
487. BIRNEY, Earle
"Caribbean Kingdoms." [Quarry] (40:1/2) Wint-Spr 91, p. 14-15.
488. BIRSE, Penny
"The Dogs." [Verse] (8:2) Sum 91, p. 103.
489. BISCHMANN, Paul
"Order." [CoalC] (4) S 91, p. 8.
490. BISHOP, Elizabeth
"The Armadillo." [AmerPoR] (20:5) S-O 91, p. 32.
"The Ballad of the Subway Train." [WestHR] (45:1) Spr 91, p. 25-26.
"In the Waiting Room." [TriQ] (81) Spr-Sum 91, p. 146-148.
491. BISHOP, Wendy
"Centers of Gravity: For Summer and Winter Solstice." [HighP] (6:2) Fall 91, p.
96-97.
"Moving Into Light" (for Tait, Fairbanks, 1987). [HiramPoR] (50) Spr-Sum 91, p. 3-
4.
"Painting: The Raven" (Honorable Mention, 5th Annual Contest). [SoCoast] (11)
Wint 91, p. 6.
"Still Life in Grays and Blues." [Vis] (35) 91, p. 49.
"Time in the Southwest." [CreamCR] (14:2) Wint 91, p. 149-151.
"Touching Liliana." [AmerPoR] (20:1) Ja-F 91, p. 31-32.
492. BISSETT, Bill
"I Was Dewing a Reeding." [Quarry] (40:1/2) Wint-Spr 91, p. 19.
"Th Fevr Peopul." [CanLit] (131) Wint 91, p. 83.
"Th Undrtakrs uv Democrasee." [Quarry] (40:1/2) Wint-Spr 91, p. 16.
"Wer Yu Falling Down." [Quarry] (40:1/2) Wint-Spr 91, p. 18.
"What Amazd th Cab Drivr." [Quarry] (40:1/2) Wint-Spr 91, p. 17.
493. BITAR, Walid
"Ciao, Johnny Medici!" [NewAW] (7) Spr 91, p. 65-67.
"For Walter, a Dog Who Fell on His Head." [DenQ] (26:1) Sum 91, p. 13.
"A Northern Reply to Vallejo's Twilight." [BlackWR] (18:1) Fall-Wint 91, p. 95.
494. BITTNER, Richard
"Warning Signs." [BlackBR] (14) Fall-Wint 91, p. 26-27.
495. BIZZARO, Patrick
"Your Cold Dream" (for my mother). [RiverC] (11:2) Spr 91, p. 68-69.
496. BJORNDOTTIR, Anna S.
"And the Night Laughed" (tr. by the author). [Vis] (37) 91, p. 34.
"Tango" (tr. by the author). [Vis] (37) 91, p. 34.
497. BLACK, Candace
"Letter in Spring." [SoDakR] (29:3 part 2) Aut 91, p. 84.
"Talisman" (after a photograph by John Cohen). [Vis] (36) 91, p. 29.
"The Volunteer." [PennR] (5:1) Spr 91, p. 24.
498. BLACK, David
"For Plato and My Mother." [DogRR] (10:2) Fall-Wint 91, p. 10.
"Lightning." [HampSPR] Wint 91, p. 29.
"A Matter of Some Concern." [DogRR] (10:1) Sum 91, p. 11.
"My Father at Christmas." [DogRR] (10:2) Fall-Wint 91, p. 10.
"Pitchfork." [HampSPR] Wint 91, p. 29.
"Summer Wheatfields." [BellArk] (7:6) N-D 91, p. 10.
499. BLACK, Patricia
"Water's Edge." [EmeraldCR] (3) 91, c1990, p. 63-64.
500. BLACK, R. D.
"Jeweler's Hammer." [CapeR] (26:2) Fall 91, p. 22.
"Spanish Dance." [OxfordM] (7:2) Fall-Wint 91, p. 66.
501. BLACK, Ralph (Ralph W.)
"Birds of Prayer." [Chelsea] (52) 91, p. 135-137.

"A City Letter to the Country." [PoetL] (86:1) Spr 91, p. 15-16.
"Last Will." [Chelsea] (52) 91, p. 143.
"Letter to Hugo from the Upper West Side." [Chelsea] (52) 91, p. 138-139.
"A Moment with Apples." [CarolQ] (43:2) Wint 91, p. 42.
"Parable of Brother Sorrow." [Chelsea] (52) 91, p. 140-142.
"Slicing Ginger." [Colum] (15) 90, p. 175.
"Triangulating Home." [Chelsea] (52) 91, p. 134.
502. BLACK, Sophie Cabot
"Higher Ground." [Antaeus] (67) Fall 91, p. 210.
"The Island." [Field] (45) Fall 91, p. 46.
"Next." [KenR] (NS 13:3) Sum 91, p. 128.
"Sometimes a Refusal to Heal." [PraS] (65:1) Spr 91, p. 27-28.
"Tonight." [KenR] (NS 13:3) Sum 91, p. 129.
"The Visitations." [PraS] (65:1) Spr 91, p. 24-26.
"The Woman at the Other Grave." [PraS] (65:1) Spr 91, p. 26-27.
503. BLACK-OLIVE, Charmaine
"Birthday Party in El Salvador." [NewYorkQ] (46) 91, p. 74.
"Fucking Genius." [HawaiiR] (15:2, #32) Spr 91, p. 28-30.
504. BLACKWELL, Ronnie
"Go to the Window." [CrabCR] (7:2) Sum 91, p. 14.
505. BLACKWOOD, Margaret
"Miss Calculation Learns the Facts." [CanLit] (129) Sum 91, p. 27.
"The Quilt-Maker's Dream." [CanLit] (129) Sum 91, p. 86-88.
506. BLADES, Joe
"Awake: Still." [PottPort] (13:2) Fall-Wint 91, p. 64-65.
"Flat Grey Morning." [TickleAce] (21) Spr-Sum 91, p. 59.
"Gather." [PottPort] (13:2) Fall-Wint 91, p. 68-70.
"Stones of My Flesh." [PottPort] (13:2) Fall-Wint 91, p. 66-67.
507. BLAICH, Beryl
"Season Transiting Light." [ChamLR] (8-9) Spr-Fall 91, p. 49.
"Sleep Returning." [ChamLR] (8-9) Spr-Fall 91, p. 50-51.
508. BLAIR, John
"Breath." [SewanR] (99:1) Wint 91, p. 27.
"Madness and Love." [SewanR] (99:1) Wint 91, p. 26.
509. BLAIR, Peter
"New Year's Eve." [DogRR] (10:2) Fall-Wint 91, p. 15.
"Uniform." [WestB] (29) 91, p. 89.
510. BLAKE, Jonathan
"'K' Car After Midnight." [Mildred] (4:2/5:1) 91, p. 65.
511. BLAKE, Sarah
"A Catch of Air." [Sequoia] (34:1) Spr 91, p. 4.
"Cutting Peonies." [CumbPR] (11:1) Fall 91, p. 64.
"Helen's Song." [CumbPR] (11:1) Fall 91, p. 63.
"The Throwers." [Thrpny] (47) Fall 91, p. 4.
"White as the Color of Lies." [CumbPR] (11:1) Fall 91, p. 61-62.
512. BLAKER, Margaret
"D.H. Lawrence Writes to Katherine Mansfield." [Pig] (17) 91, p. 75.
BLANC, Diane Le
See LeBLANC, Diane
513. BLANCHARD, Maryann
"The Silent Screamer." [MinnR] (NS 36) Spr 91, p. 23.
514. BLANCHARD, Sarah
"North of Here." [Calyx] (13:2) Sum 91, p. 68-69.
515. BLAND, James
"The Big Sea" (for the young Langston Hughes). [Callaloo] (14:3) Sum 91, p. 688.
516. BLAND, Peter
"Seeing" (For Allen Curnow on his 80th birthday). [Verse] (8:2) Sum 91, p. 36.
517. BLANDIANA, Ana
"About the Country We Come From" (tr. by Chrisula Stefanescu and Inta
Moriss-Wiest). [Iowa] (21:2) Spr-Sum 91, p. 41.
"The Children's Crusade" (tr. by Chrisula Stefanescu and Inta Moriss-Wiest). [Iowa]
(21:2) Spr-Sum 91, p. 41.
"Everything" (tr. by Chrisula Stefanescu and Inta Moriss-Wiest). [Iowa] (21:2)
Spr-Sum 91, p. 42.
"Humility" (tr. by Chrisula Stefanescu and Inta Moriss-Wiest). [Iowa] (21:2)
Spr-Sum 91, p. 40.

"Links" (tr. by Chrisula Stefanescu and Inta Moriss-Wiest). [Iowa] (21:2) Spr-Sum 91, p. 40.

"Magic Spell of Rain" (tr. by Chrisula Stefanescu and Inta Moriss-Wiest). [Iowa] (21:2) Spr-Sum 91, p. 39.

518. BLASING, Randy
"Color Values." [PoetC] (23:1) Fall 91, p. 7.
"Hymn to the Sun" (for Mutlu). [ParisR] (33:118) Spr 91, p. 122-134.
"Second Language." [LitR] (34:2) Wint 91, p. 198.
"Setting Out" (for my son). [PoetC] (23:1) Fall 91, p. 8.

519. BLASKI, Steven (Steve)
"The Crossing Over." [CreamCR] (15:2) Fall 91, p. 65-69.
"Into Capricorn." [Vis] (36) 91, p. 14.
"May 6." [PoetC] (22:3) Spr 91, p. 28-29.

520. BLATNER, Barbara
"Edge." [Gypsy] (17) 91, p. 27.

521. BLAUNER, Laurie
"Blood Thicker Than Water." [IndR] (14:2) Spr 91, p. 70.

522. BLAZEK, Douglas
"At Night, When We Can Hear Ourselves." [SoDakR] (29:3 part 2) Aut 91, p. 28.

523. BLAZEVIC, Neda Miranda
"Female / Male" (tr. by Dasha Culic Nisula). [ColR] (NS 18:2) Fall-Wint 91, p. 79.

524. BLESSINGTON, Francis
"The Cellar." [FourQ] (5:2) Fall 91, p. 48.

525. BLEWETT, Peter
"The Butcher." [PoetryE] (31) Spr 91, p. 135.

526. BLIZNETSOVA, Ina
"The Garden of the 9th of January" (tr. of Victor Krivulin, w. Leonard Schwartz). [LitR] (34:3) Spr 91, p. 387.
"The Idea of Russia" (tr. of Victor Krivulin, w. Leonard Schwartz). [LitR] (34:3) Spr 91, p. 387.
"Main Line" (tr. of Victor Krivulin, w. Leonard Schwartz). [LitR] (34:3) Spr 91, p. 389.
"Mountain Ode" (tr. of Olga Sedakova, w. Leonard Schwartz). [LitR] (34:3) Spr 91, p. 329-332.
"The Road Home" (tr. of Victor Krivulin, w. Leonard Schwartz). [LitR] (34:3) Spr 91, p. 388.

527. BLOCH, Chana
"Anniversary." [Iowa] (21:3) Fall 91, p. 91.
"The Captive" (After Michelangelo). [Poetry] (157:4) Ja 91, p. 213.
"Crossing the Table." [Iowa] (21:3) Fall 91, p. 90.
"Listening." [Field] (45) Fall 91, p. 73.
"Milkweed." [SouthernR] (27:2) Ap 91, p. 338.
"Primer." [Field] (45) Fall 91, p. 71-72.
"Thirteen." [Iowa] (21:3) Fall 91, p. 89.

528. BLOCK, Jonathan
"October at the War Memorial." [ChironR] (10:1) Spr 91, p. 20.

529. BLOK, Alexander
"At the Storms' Summons" (tr. by Stephen Unsino). [CrabCR] (7:3) 91, p. 6.
"Day's Shadows" (tr. by R. H. Morrison). [LitR] (34:2) Wint 91, p. 231.
"Night, Street, Lamp" (tr. by R. H. Morrison). [LitR] (34:2) Wint 91, p. 231.
"Wings" (tr. by Stephen Unsino). [CrabCR] (7:3) 91, p. 7.

530. BLOMAIN, Karen
"In This Stone" (tr. of Myriam Diaz Diocaretz). [Vis] (36) 91, p. 41.

531. BLOMQUIST, Eric
"We Handle Air." [ChatR] (11:4) Sum 91, p. 32.

532. BLONSTEIN, Anne
"Footnote." [DogRR] (10:1) Sum 91, p. 6-7.
"Is This a Manifestation of." [Prima] (14/15) 91, p. 97.
"On Being Alone on New Year's Eve." [GreenMR] (NS 5:1) Sum-Fall 91, p. 135-136.
"Tango for Three Women." [DogRR] (10:1) Sum 91, p. 6.

533. BLUE, Jane
"Springtime Dreams." [CalQ] (31) Fall 88, p. 62-63.

534. BLUESTONE, Stephen
"Three Anatomists" (Second Prize, Robert Penn Warren Poetry Prize Competition). [CumbPR] (11:1) Fall 91, p. 11-14.

535. BLUMBERG, Michele
  "The Love of Small Cold Towns." [Arc] (27) Aut 91, p. 13.
536. BLUMENTHAL, Jay A.
  "Amphibian at Midday" (Waldenbooks, 1990). [GrahamHR] (15) Fall 91, p. 65-70.
  "Brief Encounter." [GreenMR] (NS 5:1) Sum-Fall 91, p. 133.
  "The Canonization: August 16, 1948." [CalQ] (32/33) Spr 90, p. 130-131.
  "The Frontier of Hindsight." [CalQ] (32/33) Spr 90, p. 131.
  "Half-Baked Alaska." [GreenMR] (NS 5:1) Sum-Fall 91, p. 134.
  "Houston Peterson." [SoCaR] (23:2) Spr 91, p. 37.
  "January 1, 1965." [SlipS] (11) 91, p. 49.
537. BLUMENTHAL, Michael
  "And the Wages of Goodness Are Not Assured." [Poetry] (159:2) N 91, p. 95-96.
  "The Apprentice." [ColR] (NS 17:2) Fall-Wint 90, p. 122.
  "Letters Floating Around Ellis Island." [ColR] (NS 17:2) Fall-Wint 90, p. 120.
  "Ordinary Heartbreaks." [Poetry] (159:2) N 91, p. 96.
  "Pineapples." [ColR] (NS 17:2) Fall-Wint 90, p. 123.
  "The Wall." [ColR] (NS 17:2) Fall-Wint 90, p. 121.
538. BLUNK, Jonathan
  "Near Charles Olson's Home in Worcester." [Nat] (253:13) 21 O 91, p. 494.
539. BLY, Robert
  "The Crippled Godwit." [Ploughs] (17:2/3) Fall 91, p. 185.
  "Fall Poem." [NorthStoneR] (10) Fall 91-Wint 92, p. 279.
  "Night of New Snow." [Mildred] (4:2/5:1) 91, p. 86.
  "October Frost." [NorthStoneR] (10) Fall 91-Wint 92, p. 279.
  "Passing an Orchard by Train." [NorthStoneR] (10) Fall 91-Wint 92, p. 281-282.
  "To Live." [NorthStoneR] (10) Fall 91-Wint 92, p. 280.
540. BLYLER, Diane
  "Another Country." [Calyx] (13:2) Sum 91, p. 60-61.
541. BLYTHE, Randy
  "Black Birds." [SouthernHR] (25:3) Sum 91, p. 266.
  "Past Due." [CinPR] (21) Spr 90, p. 40-41.
542. BOB, Indiana
  "Disc Jocky Poem." [WindO] (55) Wint 91-92, p. 47.
543. BOBYSHEV, Dmitry
  "The Octaves of Mourning" (Selection: "Her Glance," tr. by Judith Hemschemeyer).
      [Agni] (33) 91, p. 49.
544. BOCOCK, Maclin
  "On Standing Outside Villa Robermund, March 2, 1968." [SouthernR] (27:4) O 91,
      p. 935-936.
  "Song." [SouthernR] (27:4) O 91, p. 934-935.
545. BODO, Murray
  "No Light Apart." [CinPR] (21) Spr 90, p. 8-9.
546. BOE, Marilyn J.
  "Aunt Millie's Money." [RagMag] (9:1) 91, p. 33.
  "In Exchange." [Sidewalks] (1) Aug 91, p. 57.
  "Naked Women in the Locker Room." [Sidewalks] (1) Aug 91, p. 56.
  "Pencil Boxes." [SoCoast] (10) Fall 91, p. 3.
  "Seagulls Near Haugesund, Norway." [RagMag] (9:1) 91, p. 32.
547. BOEHRER, Bruce Thomas
  "Help Help Me Rondeau." [FourQ] (5:1) Spr 91, p. 24.
548. BOERST, William J.
  "Prophecy." [Writer] (104:3) Mr 91, p. 22.
549. BOESE, Christine
  "Alone." [PaintedHR] (3) Sum 92, p. 11.
550. BOGAN, Louise
  "Cassandra." [SouthwR] (76:4) Aut 91, p. 463.
  "The Daemon." [SouthwR] (76:4) Aut 91, p. 478.
551. BOGDANOVIC, Simha Levi
  "And While the Watch Hands of the Blue Clock Still Melt" (tr. of Zvonimir Kostic).
      [InterPR] (15:1) Spr 89, p. 63.
  "Black Flour" (tr. of Stevan Tontic). [InterPR] (15:1) Spr 89, p. 31.
  "A Bloody Wedding in Brzava" (tr. of Dragomir Brajkovic). [InterPR] (15:1) Spr 89,
      p. 47.
  "Going Away" (tr. of Stevan Tontic). [InterPR] (15:1) Spr 89, p. 33.
  "Sometimes, in a Deserted Street" (tr. of Zvonimir Kostic). [InterPR] (15:1) Spr 89,
      p. 59.

"They Will Lock You in a Room" (tr. of Zvonimir Kostic). [InterPR] (15:1) Spr 89,
    p. 61.
552. BOGEN, Don
"The Palace at Granada." [WestHR] (45:3) Aut 91, p. 226-227.
"Salver." [NewRep] (205:24) 9 D 91, p. 42.
"Thoroughbreds." [ParisR] (33:118) Spr 91, p. 173.
"A Waiting Room in Vienna." [WestHR] (45:3) Aut 91, p. 228-229.
553. BOGEN, Laurel Ann
"A Little Death." [Rohwedder] (6) Sum-Fall 91, p. 21.
"Nothing Breaks But the Resilient Heart" (poem on a line by Anne Pitkin). [Pearl]
    (13) Spr-Sum 91, p. 21.
554. BOGUS, S. Diane
"How Does You Love Me, Sweet Baby?" (For Dori). [SinW] (43/44) Sum 91, p.
    239.
555. BOHORQUEZ, Eduardo
"Last Goodbye" (tr. of José Rizal, w. Naomi Lazard and Bettina Escudero). [Trans]
    (25) Spr 91, p. 209-211.
556. BOISSEAU, Michelle
"Your Nightmares." [CalQ] (32/33) Spr 90, p. 135.
557. BOLAND, Eavan
"The Achill Woman." [Field] (44) Spr 91, p. 100-101.
"At the Glass Factory in Cavan Town." [ParisR] (33:118) Spr 91, p. 253-256.
"The Black Lace Fan My Mother Gave Me." [Field] (44) Spr 91, p. 97-98.
"In a Dublin Suburb, I Revise the Fate of the Heroine." [Ploughs] (17:1) Spr 91, p.
    35-37.
"Inscriptions." [ParisR] (33:118) Spr 91, p. 257-258.
"Midnight Flowers." [Field] (44) Spr 91, p. 95-96.
"Nocturne." [Field] (44) Spr 91, p. 94-95.
"A Sparrow Hawk in the Suburbs." [NewYorker] (67:7) 8 Ap 91, p. 40.
"The Women." [Field] (44) Spr 91, p. 92-93.
558. BOLDT, Christine A.
"Initial Faith." [WorldO] (24:1/2) Fall 89-Wint 89-90, c1991, p. 5.
559. BÖLL, Heinrich
"Angel" (tr. by Laurence Atwood). [InterPR] (17:2) Fall 91, p. 45.
"Angel" (tr. by Laurence Atwood). [LitR] (34:2) Wint 91, p. 228.
"Cologne I." [InterPR] (17:2) Fall 91, p. 42.
"Cologne I" (tr. by Laurence Atwood). [InterPR] (17:2) Fall 91, p. 43.
"Engel." [InterPR] (17:2) Fall 91, p. 44.
"Meine Muse." [InterPR] (17:2) Fall 91, p. 40, 42.
"My Muse" (tr. by Laurence Atwood). [InterPR] (17:2) Fall 91, p. 41, 43.
560. BOLLING, Madelon
"Cherry Tree." [BellArk] (7:3) My-Je 91, p. 5-7.
"Red Runners, Green Runners." [BellArk] (7:5) S-O 91, p. 6-7.
"Whelming Tree." [BellArk] (7:6) N-D 91, p. 6.
"Wildflower." [BellArk] (7:4) Jl-Ag 91, p. 3.
561. BOLLING, R. Stepp
"Fireflies Among the Coffins." [DustyD] (2:1) Ja 91, p. 9.
562. BOLLS, Imogene (Imogene L.)
"Briefly, on the Balcony at Deer Creek Lodge." [OhioR] (47) 91, p. 48.
"Conglomerate." [SoDakR] (29:4) Wint 91, p. 169.
"Listening for Coyotes." [SoDakR] (29:4) Wint 91, p. 170.
"Obligation." [CinPR] (22) Spr 91, p. 17.
"On a Two Gray Hills Rug." [SoDakR] (29:3 part 2) Aut 91, p. 115.
563. BOLSTER, Stephanie
"Either Way." [Grain] (19:2) Sum 91, p. 36.
"Is This Okay." [PraF] (12:3 #56) Aut 91, p. 86.
"Occasional Slips." [PraF] (12:3 #56) Aut 91, p. 87.
564. BOLTON, Joe
"The Circumstances." [Crazy] (40) Spr 91, p. 47.
"Death in Orange County." [Crazy] (40) Spr 91, p. 48-49.
"Metropolitan Twilight." [SouthernR] (27:3) Jl 91, p. 694-696.
"Near" (for Little Johnny Cosco, San Francisco). [DenQ] (25:3) Wint 91, p. 6-7.
"Style." [Crazy] (40) Spr 91, p. 45-46.
"Watching Bergman Films with My Father." [SouthernR] (27:3) Jl 91, p. 697-698.
565. BOMBA, Bernard
"Father and Son." [CalQ] (31) Fall 88, p. 36-37.

"In Dogwood Bloom." [AmerPoR] (20:2) Mr-Ap 91, p. 16.

BOMBARD, Joan La
    See LaBOMBARD, Joan

566. BONAFFINI, Luigi
    "The Gamekeeper" (tr. of Sabino D'Acunto). [InterPR] (17:2) Fall 91, p. 17.
    "Molisan Elegy" (tr. of Sabino D'Acunto). [InterPR] (17:2) Fall 91, p. 11-15.
    "September" (tr. of Giose Rimanelli). [Vis] (36) 91, p. 22-23.

567. BOND, Bruce
    "Acoustic Shadows." [MissouriR] (14:3) 91, p. 161.
    "The Anteroom of Paradise" (for Nicki and my good friend Ken Shedd. 34 poems).
        [QRL] (Poetry ser. 10, vol. 30) 91, 55 p.
    "Book of the Living." [MissouriR] (14:3) 91, p. 166-167.
    "Chinatown." [MissouriR] (14:3) 91, p. 164-165.
    "Emigrant's Song." [MissR] (19:3) 91, p. 168-169.
    "Gallery of Rivers." [MissouriR] (14:1) 91, p. 150.
    "Guido's Hand." [PacificR] (9) 91, p. 51.
    "The Last Great Flood." [MissouriR] (14:3) 91, p. 160.
    "Legacy." [MissouriR] (14:3) 91, p. 162-163.
    "Medals: A Processional of Rooms." [Agni] (34) 91, p. 103-104.
    "Naked Guest." [PoetC] (22:3) Spr 91, p. 25.
    "On Certainty." [Poetry] (158:5) Ag 91, p. 268-269.
    "Still Life with Lemons." [Salm] (90/91) Spr-Sum 91, p. 206-207.
    "Visitation." [Agni] (34) 91, p. 105.

568. BOND, David
    "Metaphysical Mining." [DustyD] Je 91, p. 22.

569. BOND, Joan
    "For the Record" (to Christ in the desert). [PraF] (12:4) Wint 91-92, p. 93.

570. BONDS, Diane
    "The Lawrence Tree." [Poem] (66) N 91, p. 10.
    "Persimmons." [Poem] (66) N 91, p. 9.

571. BONINA, Mary
    "37 Bennett Street." [HangL] (59) 91, p. 15.
    "English Lesson Plan: Present Perfect." [HangL] (59) 91, p. 14-15.
    "Examples." [HangL] (59) 91, p. 16.

572. BONNEFOY, Yves
    "Dedham, Seen from Langham" (title of several paintings by John Constable, tr. by
        Lisa Sapinkopf). [SouthernR] (27:4) O 91, p. 917-923.
    "Dedham, Vu de Langham" (From "Ce qui fut sans lumière"). [SouthernR] (27:4) O
        91, p. 916-922.
    "A Summer's Night" (tr. by Lisa Sapinkopf). [ParisR] (33:119) Sum 91, p. 255-257.
    "The Task of Hope" (tr. by Lisa Sapinkopf). [ParisR] (33:119) Sum 91, p. 258.

573. BOOKER, Stephen
    "About the Size of It." [CreamCR] (15:1) Spr 91, p. 1-2.
    "Requiem." [Timbuktu] (6) Spr 91, p. 64-65.

574. BOOKER, Stephen Todd
    "Escape to Kismet." [SenR] (21:1) Spr 91, p. 49-51.

575. BOOTH, Philip
    "After the Exhibition." [BostonR] (16:1) F 91, p. 27.
    "Fragments" (Selections). [Ploughs] (17:1) Spr 91, p. 38-42.
    "Jazz in the Garden." [SouthernR] (27:2) Ap 91, p. 268.

576. BORAN, Pat
    "A Diary of Water" (Excerpt, For Georg Gräwe). [Interim] (10:1) Spr-Sum 91, p. 22.
    "The Sun Comes Up." [Interim] (10:1) Spr-Sum 91, p. 22.

BORDA, Juan Gustavo Cobo
    See COBO BORDA, Juan Gustavo

577. BORDEN, Jonathan
    "March Moon." [LakeSR] (25) 91, p. 12.

578. BORDERS, Andrew
    "Beautiful Girl Photograph." [Poem] (65) My 91, p. 39.
    "Breath of the Moon." [Poem] (65) My 91, p. 38.

579. BORDERS, J. B.
    "Clio Street Song." [IndR] (14:3) Fall 91, p. 46-48.

580. BORGATTI, Robert
    "Garbage Day." [SlipS] (11) 91, p. 80.

581. BORGES, Guillermo
    "El Mar." [LindLM] (10:3) Jl-S 91, p. 13.

"Noble Amiga." [LindLM] (10:3) Jl-S 91, p. 13.
"Pensativo Es." [LindLM] (10:3) Jl-S 91, p. 13.
"Voz y Silencio." [LindLM] (10:3) Jl-S 91, p. 13.
582. BORGES, Jorge Luis
"Elegy" (tr. by Robert Mezey). [Hudson] (44:3) Aut 91, p. 417-418.
"Elegy for the Impossible Memory" (tr. by Robert Mezey). [Hudson] (44:3) Aut 91, p. 415-416.
"Happiness" (tr. by Roberta Balstad Miller). [PoetL] (86:3) Fall 91, p. 49.
"My Books" (tr. by Robert Mezey). [Hudson] (44:3) Aut 91, p. 411.
"One of Lee's Soldiers (1962)" (tr. by Robert Mezey). [Hudson] (44:3) Aut 91, p. 414-415.
"Poem of the Gifts" (tr. by Robert Mezey). [Hudson] (44:3) Aut 91, p. 410-411.
"Relics" (tr. by Robert Mezey). [Hudson] (44:3) Aut 91, p. 417.
"Simón Carbajal" (tr. by Robert Mezey). [Hudson] (44:3) Aut 91, p. 412.
"Temptation" (tr. by Robert Mezey). [Hudson] (44:3) Aut 91, p. 413-141.
"To One No Longer Young" (tr. by Robert Mezey). [Hudson] (44:3) Aut 91, p. 418.
"The White Hind" (tr. by Robert Mezey). [Hudson] (44:3) Aut 91, p. 415.
583. BORICH, Barrie Jean
"The Disappeared." [SinW] (43/44) Sum 91, p. 254-256.
584. BORKHUIS, Charles
"Quartet." [CentralP] (19/20) Spr-Fall 91, p. 244-247.
"The Surgeon's Glove." [Avec] (4:1) 91, p. 143-150.
585. BORN, Anne
"Always Now" (tr. of Pia Tafdrup). [Vis] (37) 91, p. 9.
"Dark Brightness" (tr. of Pia Tafdrup). [Vis] (37) 91, p. 8.
"Keep on Driving" (tr. of Pia Tafdrup). [Vis] (37) 91, p. 8.
586. BORROFF, Marie
"John Hollander" (Corrected reprint. Response to "Save the Clerihew" appeal). [BostonR] (16:5) O 91, p. 24.
"John Hollander" (Response to "Save the Clerihew" appeal). [BostonR] (16:3/4) Je-Ag 91, p. 33.
"Sight." [QW] (32) Wint-Spr 91, p. 101.
587. BORSON, Roo
"My Lover and I Have a." [Quarry] (40:1/2) Wint-Spr 91, p. 20.
"That You." [Quarry] (40:1/2) Wint-Spr 91, p. 21.
588. BORST, Steve
"The Blue Rooster." [Abraxas] (40/41) 91, p. 139-140.
"In Our doorway the Sand Was Drifting." [Abraxas] (40/41) 91, p. 139.
589. BORUCH, Marianne
"The Berlin Wall, 1966." [MassR] (32:2) Sum 91, p. 195.
"Driving After Supper." [Poetry] (158:3) Je 91, p. 128.
"The Luxor Baths." [MassR] (32:2) Sum 91, p. 196-198.
590. BORUN-JAGODZINSKA, Katarzyna
"Babes in the Woods" (tr. by Karen Kovacik). [ArtfulD] (20/21) 91, p. 15.
"Exorcist" (tr. by the author and Lia Purpura). [Agni] (34) 91, p. 195.
"A Few Years After Nero" (tr. by the author and Lia Purpura). [Agni] (34) 91, p. 197-198.
"The Match" (tr. by Karen Kovacik). [AmerPoR] (20:4) Jl-Ag 91, p. 33.
"Medea Has Forgotten How to Cry" (tr. by Karen Kovacik). [ArtfulD] (20/21) 91, p. 13.
"On Manet's 'Olympia'" (tr. by the author and Lia Purpura). [Agni] (34) 91, p. 196.
"Tenant" (tr. by Karen Kovacik). [ArtfulD] (20/21) 91, p. 14.
"Today Twilight Comes More Quickly to Our Summer Kitchens" (tr. by Karen Kovacik). [AmerPoR] (20:4) Jl-Ag 91, p. 33.
591. BOSCH, Daniel
"The Anger That Breaks the Man" (tr. of César Vallejo). [Agni] (33) 91, p. 239.
"In English." [DenQ] (26:1) Sum 91, p. 14-15.
"Paris, October 1936" (tr. of César Vallejo). [Agni] (33) 91, p. 240.
"Until the Day of My Return" (tr. of César Vallejo). [Agni] (33) 91, p. 241.
592. BOSQUET, Alain
"I. Rumors" (tr. by Edouard Roditi). [Talisman] (6) Spr 91, p. 107.
"II. By night the young mare" (tr. by Edouard Roditi). [Talisman] (6) Spr 91, p. 107.
"III. Every morning I shrink" (tr. by Edouard Roditi). [Talisman] (6) Spr 91, p. 107.
593. BOSTRUM, Annette
"Muhammad Ali." [TexasR] (12:3/4) Fall-Wint 91, p. 70.

594. BOTHWELL, Roberta
    "Hawk." [Elf] (1:2) Sum 91, p. 44.
595. BOTKIN, Nancy
    "Fertility Dance." [MidwQ] (32:3) Spr 91, p. 289.
596. BOTTELLI, Suzanne
    "Promise" (with a line from Beckett). [PlumR] (1) Spr-Sum 91, p. 17.
    "Wafers." [PlumR] (1) Spr-Sum 91, p. 18-19.
597. BOTTOMS, David
    "Living Lingerie: In the Modeling Parlor." [ParisR] (33:119) Sum 91, p. 245.
    "Snake on the Etowah." [ParisR] (33:119) Sum 91, p. 244.
598. BOUCHER, Alan
    "Winter Past" (tr. of Olafur Johann Sigurdsson). [Vis] (37) 91, p. 38.
599. BOUCHERON, Robert
    "Catullus 11." [Hellas] (2:1) Spr 91, p. 57.
600. BOURASSA, Alan
    "Landscape." [Grain] (19:1) Spr 91, p. 31.
    "Pentecost Service — Christmas Eve 1989." [Grain] (19:1) Spr 91, p. 28.
    "Poem for My Uncle." [Grain] (19:1) Spr 91, p. 29.
    "The Rain Boys." [Grain] (19:1) Spr 91, p. 30.
601. BOURNE, Daniel
    "After Visiting Lewiston Graveyard." [PraS] (65:4) Wint 91, p. 48-49.
    "Aunt Linda Speaks." [PoetryNW] (32:3) Aut 91, p. 14-15.
    "The Bald Mountains." [GrahamHR] (15) Fall 91, p. 25-26.
    "Bus Stop, the Outskirts of Warsaw, Martial Law." [GrahamHR] (15) Fall 91, p. 24.
    "Cancer and the Alien." [SpoonRQ] (16:1/2) Wint-Spr 91, p. 27.
    "Cancer Clears Out a Fencerow." [SpoonRQ] (16:1/2) Wint-Spr 91, p. 26.
    "Cancer in Rio." [SpoonRQ] (16:1/2) Wint-Spr 91, p. 29.
    "The Country Doctor." [Confr] (46/47) Fall 91-Wint 92, p. 278-281.
    "A Day in Which to Save the Orchard." [PraS] (65:4) Wint 91, p. 49.
    "Distance" (tr. of Bronislaw Maj). [WebR] (15) Spr 91, p. 46.
    "Gleaning the Field (1973)." [CinPR] (21) Spr 90, p. 19.
    "Icon." [CinPR] (21) Spr 90, p. 18.
    "Illinois Primer." [WebR] (15) Spr 91, p. 48.
    "No One, Everyone" (tr. of Bronislaw Maj). [WebR] (15) Spr 91, p. 47.
    "Not Again" (tr. of Bronislaw Maj). [WebR] (15) Spr 91, p. 47.
    "November Evening" (to Adam Zagajewski, tr. of Ryszard Holzer). [CharR] (17:1)
        Spr 91, p. 86.
    "The Poet of the Antipodes." [PraS] (65:4) Wint 91, p. 47.
    "Quiet Apartment in Which Someone Lies Dying" (tr. of Bronislaw Maj). [SenR]
        (21:1) Spr 91, p. 25.
    "Stony Brook on Long Island" (tr. of Tomasz Jastrun). [NewOR] (18:2) Sum 91, p.
        52-53.
    "The Talk Show Cancer." [SpoonRQ] (16:1/2) Wint-Spr 91, p. 28.
    "This Day" (tr. of Bronislaw Maj). [WebR] (15) Spr 91, p. 46.
    "To a Woman Mauled in Yellowstone." [Confr] (46/47) Fall 91-Wint 92, p. 278.
    "Why Is It That in My World" (tr. of Bronislaw Maj). [SenR] (21:1) Spr 91, p. 24.
    "Without Pathos or Metaphysics" (tr. of Bronislaw Maj). [WebR] (15) Spr 91, p. 46.
    "The World Is a Still Life" (tr. of Bronislaw Maj). [SenR] (21:1) Spr 91, p. 23.
602. BOURNE, Louis
    "Destello." [Nuez] (3:8/9) 91, p. 27.
    "Espuela." [Nuez] (3:8/9) 91, p. 27.
603. BOUVARD, Marguerite (Marguerite Guzman)
    "Etiquette" (for Hebe de Bonafini). [SouthernHR] (25:1) Wint 91, p. 50.
    "The Fathers." [Event] (20:1) Spr 91, p. 89.
    "The Mothers of the Plaza de Mayo: Pieta" (for Susannah). [Event] (20:1) Spr 91, p.
        88.
    "Power." [PartR] (58:4) Fall 91, p. 686-687.
    "The White Shawl." [Event] (20:1) Spr 91, p. 90.
    "With Giacometti." [LitR] (34:2) Wint 91, p. 173.
604. BOUZANE, Lillian
    "The Birth." [TickleAce] (22) Fall-Wint 91, p. 47-49.
605. BOVE, Robert
    "An Urban Tradition." [JINJPo] (13:1) Spr 91, p. 28.
606. BOWDAN, Janet
    "Applauds the Falling of Towers." [RiverS] (34) 91, p. 70.
    "Writing Back." [MissouriR] (14:1) 91, p. 156-157.

607. BOWEN, Kevin
"Danang." [ChironR] (10:1) Spr 91, p. 13.
"Drive-in." [PoetL] (86:3) Fall 91, p. 10.
"Nui Ba Den: Black Virgin Mountain" (for J.C., killed in action May 13, 1969,
Mother's Day). [ChironR] (10:1) Spr 91, p. 13.
"Playing Basketball with the Viet Cong" (for Nguyen Quang Sang). [PoetL] (86:3)
Fall 91, p. 9.
608. BOWERING, George
"On the Picadilly Tube." [Quarry] (40:1/2) Wint-Spr 91, p. 22-23.
"Play & Work & Art." [Spitball] (39) Wint 91, p. 19.
609. BOWERS, Andrea L.
"Dreaming It Right." [Sequoia] (34:1) Spr 91, p. 27.
BOWERS, Cathy Smith
See SMITH-BOWERS, Cathy
610. BOWERS, Edgar
"Breakages." [Thrpny] (45) Spr 91, p. 13.
611. BOWERS, Neal
"Adonis at the Throttle." [VirQR] (67:2) Spr 91, p. 266-267.
"Afternoon Nap." [VirQR] (67:2) Spr 91, p. 267-268.
"Being Philosophical." [SoDakR] (29:3 part 2) Aut 91, p. 94.
"Buying Dirt." [HighP] (6:2) Fall 91, p. 17.
"The Call." [SewanR] (99:4) Fall 91, p. 526-527.
"A Cure." [CreamCR] (15:2) Fall 91, p. 53.
"Dead Man Interview." [Poetry] (158:1) Ap 91, p. 11-12.
"Essences." [CreamCR] (15:2) Fall 91, p. 52.
"Everything." [SewanR] (98:4) Fall 90, p. 601.
"Exotic Places." [SewanR] (98:4) Fall 90, p. 603.
"Faith." [SouthernPR] (31:2) Fall 91, p. 20-21.
"For Personal Enjoyment." [HighP] (6:2) Fall 91, p. 16.
"The Garden at the Edge of the World." [LaurelR] (25:1) Wint 91, p. 114-115.
"The Hades Cinema Club." [LaurelR] (25:1) Wint 91, p. 115.
"Hymns." [Poetry] (158:1) Ap 91, p. 10-11.
"Indian Fever." [SewanR] (99:4) Fall 91, p. 528.
"Laps after Hours." [Hudson] (44:3) Aut 91, p. 430.
"A Legacy." [SouthernPR] (31:2) Fall 91, p. 18-19.
"The Man Who Courted Disaster." [SewanR] (98:4) Fall 90, p. 602.
"Night Shift." [SewanR] (99:2) Spr 91, p. 184-185.
"Tenth-Year Elegy" (Editors note: "an apparently plagiarized poem under the supposed
authorship of David Sumner . . . printed as 'Someone Forgotten' was in fact the
work of Neal Bowers"). [Poem] (66) N 91, p. 3.
612. BOWERS, Star
"In This Dark Pond." [Abraxas] (40/41) 91, p. 146.
613. BOWIE, Robert
"With A Whimper and a Bang." [LitR] (35:1) Fall 91, p. 52.
614. BOWLING, Sam
"Some Rules of Winter Baseball." [PoetC] (22:3) Spr 91, p. 39.
615. BOWLING, Tim
"Moving." [Event] (20:2) Sum 91, p. 91.
616. BOWMAN, P. C.
"Northern Blues." [LitR] (35:1) Fall 91, p. 58.
617. BOWMAN, William R., Sr.
"America." [EmeraldCR] (3) 91, c1990, p. 114-116.
"The Game of War." [EmeraldCR] (4) 91, p. 41.
"Layout." [EmeraldCR] (3) 91, c1990, p. 97.
"Songs of Earth." [EmeraldCR] (3) 91, c1990, p. 70-72.
"Winter's Snow." [EmeraldCR] (4) 91, p. 42.
618. BOYCHUK, Bohdan
"Highest Sickness" (tr. of Boris Pasternak, w. Mark Rudman). [Pequod] (32) 91, p.
45-53.
"Prayers" (Selections: 1, 9, 13, 24, tr. by Askold Melnyczuk). [Agni] (33) 91, p.
118-121.
619. BOYD, Gerald
"Shopping with Cecile." [US1] (24/25) Spr 91, p. 10.

620. BOYD, Robert
"Let Us Suppose That That Red Truck — A Narrative of the Romantic South" (Guy
Owen Poetry Prize Winner, Susan Ludvigson, Judge). [SouthernPR] (31:2)
Fall 91, p. 5-7.
621. BOYD, Scott
"Oxygen Tent Variations." [PraF] (12:1 #54) Spr 91, p. 26-33.
622. BOYER, Gloria
"Apostrophe to the Heart." [PoetryNW] (32:2) Sum 91, p. 46.
"Big Laughing Gymnopilus." [PoetryNW] (32:2) Sum 91, p. 47.
"Cane Toad Wars." [PoetryNW] (32:4) Wint 91-92, p. 22.
"The Place Where Lost Things Are Found." [PoetryNW] (32:2) Sum 91, p. 45-46.
623. BOYLAN, Matthew
"Fix." [WormR] (31:1, #121) 91, p. 16.
"Seems to Me." [WormR] (31:1, #121) 91, p. 16.
624. BOYLE, Kevin
"Oneness." [NoAmR] (276:4) D 91, p. 52.
"Unhitched." [NoAmR] (276:3) S 91, p. 33.
625. BOZANIC, Nick
"Above Ibiza, Mid-Afternoon." [Manoa] (3:2) Fall 91, p. 119.
"Ecce Homo." [Manoa] (3:2) Fall 91, p. 118.
"Muse." [Manoa] (3:2) Fall 91, p. 117-118.
626. BRACKENBURY, Alison
"I Go to the Room." [Verse] (8:2) Sum 91, p. 100.
"May." [Verse] (8:2) Sum 91, p. 100.
627. BRACKENRIDGE, Valery
"The Breaking of Leaves." [JINJPo] (13:1) Spr 91, p. 14-15.
"Want to Write." [ChironR] (10:2) Sum 91, p. 45.
628. BRACKER, Jonathan
"Trees." [NewYorker] (67:12) 13 My 91, p. 78.
629. BRADBURY, Steven
"The Fish" (tr. of Yuan Ch'iung-Ch'iung). [BambooR] (52) Fall 91, p. 160.
630. BRADFORD, Harold
"Earthworms." [Writer] (104:9) S 91, p. 23.
631. BRADLEY, George
"The New Sentimentality." [Boulevard] (5:3/6:1, #15/16) Spr 91, p. 224.
"A Short Article or Poem in Response to the Work." [Verse] (8:1) Spr 91, p. 4.
"Very Large Array." [WestHR] (45:4) Wint 91, p. 274.
"Waiting for Gloria" (for my mother and father). [SouthwR] (76:1) Wint 91, p.
23-28.
632. BRADLEY, Jerry
"Nighttime in the House of God." [WeberS] (8:1) Spr 91, p. 94.
"Yacht Brokers." [WeberS] (8:1) Spr 91, p. j94.
633. BRADLEY, John
"The Moon Does Not Exist." [Caliban] (10) 91, p. 98-101.
634. BRADY, Stephen
"Judith II." [BellArk] (7:6) N-D 91, p. 1.
635. BRAID, Kate
"Metamorphosis." [CapilR] (2:6/7) Fall 91, p. 41.
"Woman's Touch." [CapilR] (2:6/7) Fall 91, p. 39-40.
636. BRAJKOVIC, Dragomir
"A Bloody Wedding in Brzava" (tr. by Simha Levi Bogdanovic). [InterPR] (15:1) Spr
89, p. 47.
"Budim Jutro." [InterPR] (15:1) Spr 89, p. 40.
"I Wake Up the Morning" (tr. by Vasa D. Mihailovich). [InterPR] (15:1) Spr 89, p.
41.
"Icy Mountains, South Seas" (tr. by Vasa D. Mihailovich). [InterPR] (15:1) Spr 89,
p. 43, 45.
"Krvana Svadba U Brzavi." [InterPR] (15:1) Spr 89, p. 46.
"Ledene Gore, Juzna Mora." [InterPR] (15:1) Spr 89, p. 42, 44.
"Prolece U Teheranu" (xii). [InterPR] (15:1) Spr 89, p. 44.
"The Spring in Teheran" (xii, tr. by Vasa D. Mihailovich). [InterPR] (15:1) Spr 89, p.
45.
"Trace" (tr. by Vasa D. Mihailovich). [InterPR] (15:1) Spr 89, p. 39.
"Trag." [InterPR] (15:1) Spr 89, p. 38.

637. BRAMBACH, Rainer
"Portrait of a Young Man" (tr. by Sammy McClean). [SnailPR] (1:2) Fall 91-Wint 92,
p. 13.
638. BRAME, Gloria Glickstein
"Desire." [PlumR] (1) Spr-Sum 91, p. 38.
639. BRANDEL, Christine
"14 Race Street." [FreeL] (7) Spr 91, p. 13.
640. BRANDI, John
"At Wovoka's Ghostdance Place." [RiverS] (35) 91, p. 14.
641. BRANDON, Sherry
"Snapshots of Tripoli, Libya" (9 poems). [BellArk] (7:2) Mr-Ap 91, p. 4-6.
642. BRANDONISIO, Michael
"Widow." [SlipS] (11) 91, p. 55.
643. BRANDT, Di
"crossing the bridge over the Mosel River." [Quarry] (40:4) Fall 91, p. 53-54.
"from now on, i will call you." [Quarry] (40:4) Fall 91, p. 50-51.
"how close i was to being born in Barcelona" (for Eugenia Iborra). [Quarry] (40:4)
Fall 91, p. 51-52.
"Mother, No Mother" (Selections). [PoetryC] (12:1) D 91, p. 18-19.
644. BRANDT, Jorgen Gustava
"Sound of the Bell" (tr. by the author and Alex Taylor). [Vis] (37) 91, p. 10.
645. BRANDWEIN, Nancy J.
"The Giraffe." [VirQR] (67:2) Spr 91, p. 260-261.
646. BRANT, Beth
"Her Name Is Helen." [SinW] (43/44) Sum 91, p. 221-223.
647. BRASK, Per
"E. Munch: Self portrait, 1895, exhibited at Nasjonalgalleriet, Oslo." [PraF] (12:4)
Wint 91-92, p. 59.
"E. Munch: Skrik, 1893, exhibited at Nasjonalgalleriet, Oslo." [PraF] (12:4) Wint
91-92, p. 59.
"'Loddeallmai ja alla albmi' [The Birdman under High Sky], a drawing by the Sami
artist Inguun Utsi, exhibited at the Arctic Gallery, Tromsø." [PraF] (12:4) Wint
91-92, p. 58.
648. BRAVERMAN, Kate
"Kauai." [OnTheBus] (8/9) 91, p. 28-29.
649. BRAVERMAN, Melanie
"Because We Must and Still Love." [CarolQ] (44:1) Fall 91, p. 47.
"Lucky." [Caliban] (10) 91, p. 150.
"Remedy (Perspicacity)." [Caliban] (10) 91, p. 151.
650. BRAY, John
"Reflections of a Pious Convalescent" (from "Tobacco: A Valedictory"). [PoetryUSA]
(23) Sum 91, p. 22.
651. BRAY, Pat
"Registered Trademark." [Contact] (10:59/60/61) Spr 91, p. 47.
652. BRAYBROOKE, Neville
"A Christmas Alphabet." [Comm] (118:22) 20 D 91, p. 752-753.
653. BREBNER, Diana
"Black Wall." [Event] (20:1) Spr 91, p. 83.
"Eastern Massasauga Rattlesnake." [Quarry] (40:4) Fall 91, p. 10.
"Fall." [Quarry] (40:4) Fall 91, p. 7.
"Hallucigenia." [Quarry] (40:4) Fall 91, p. 11.
"Snake Bodies." [Quarry] (40:4) Fall 91, p. 9.
"Speed of Traffic." [Event] (20:1) Spr 91, p. 82.
"Yellow." [Quarry] (40:4) Fall 91, p. 8.
654. BRECHT, Bertolt
"The Drowned Girl" (tr. by Richard Moore). [AmerPoR] (20:2) Mr-Ap 91, p. 9.
"Memories of Marie" (tr. by Richard Moore). [AmerPoR] (20:2) Mr-Ap 91, p. 9.
"War Primer" (Selections: 1, 20, 22, 29, 37, 40, 45, 66, 69, tr. by Warren Hope).
[LullwaterR] (2:2) Spr 91, p. 27-32.
655. BREDIMUS, Bitsy
"The Woman in My Bed." [EvergreenC] (6:2) Sum-Fall 91, p. 29.
656. BREEDEN, David
"Giving." [CalQ] (35/36) 91, p. 47.
"Velvet Drapes." [LitR] (35:1) Fall 91, p. 85.
657. BREINER, Laurence
"Scholar." [Agni] (34) 91, p. 140-141.

658. BRENNAN, Carl
    "Another Morning." [DustyD] Ap 91, p. 7.
    "Sojourns." [DustyD] Je 91, p. 39.
    "Souvenir." [DustyD] Ap 91, p. 6.
    "Twenty-Five Years." [DustyD] Je 91, p. 28.
    "Vague Citizen." [DustyD] Je 91, p. 1.
659. BRENNAN, Karen
    "Ego Scriptor." [CentralP] (19/20) Spr-Fall 91, p. 168.
    "Not Nearly Enough." [OhioR] (47) 91, p. 115.
    "Psalm Whoever." [CentralP] (19/20) Spr-Fall 91, p. 167.
660. BRENNAN, Matthew
    "Clear Winter Nights." [ContextS] (2:1) 91, p. 10.
    "Driving Home Alone, Before Twilight, on Highway 41" (for Richard). [HopewellR]
        (1991) 91, p. 18.
    "A Ghost." [Mildred] (4:2/5:1) 91, p. 95.
    "Homesick." [Mildred] (4:2/5:1) 91, p. 96.
    "November Dusk." [Mildred] (4:2/5:1) 91, p. 95.
    "White." [Mildred] (4:2/5:1) 91, p. 97.
661. BRENTLINGER, Richard G.
    "Fear." [EmeraldCR] (3) 91, c1990, p. 105-108.
662. BRESKIN, David
    "Billy Joel." [NewAW] (7) Spr 91, p. 64.
    "Nothing on TV (Tonight)." [NewAW] (7) Spr 91, p. 62-63.
663. BRESLIN, Julia Galligan
    "Discovery." [Boulevard] (5:3/6:1, #15/16) Spr 91, p. 207.
664. BRESLIN, Paul
    "Elijah" (Selection: 5). [TriQ] (83) Wint 91-92, p. 121-122.
    "Late Arrival." [TriQ] (83) Wint 91-92, p. 119-120.
665. BRETON, André
    "Slow Down Construction" (with René Char and Paul Éluard, tr. by Jeanie Puleston
        Fleming and Christopher Merrill). [AmerPoR] (20:3) My-Je 91, p. 25-30.
666. BREWER, Gay
    "Luck." [SlipS] (11) 91, p. 69.
    "Making Tracks." [ChamLR] (8-9) Spr-Fall 91, p. 139.
    "The Man." [LullwaterR] (3:1) Fall 91, p. 20.
    "Me and Paul Newman." [NewYorkQ] (45) 91, p. 63.
    "November." [ChironR] (10:2) Sum 91, p. 44.
    "Stealth." [SlipS] (11) 91, p. 68.
    "These Woods." [ChamLR] (8-9) Spr-Fall 91, p. 140.
667. BREWER, Jack
    "Solicitors." [Pearl] (14) Fall-Wint 91, p. 61.
668. BREWSTER, Elizabeth
    "Drums in Fredericton." [Grain] (19:3) Fall 91, p. 52-53.
    "First of July." [Grain] (19:3) Fall 91, p. 51-52.
    "In October." [Grain] (19:3) Fall 91, p. 54-56.
    "John the Baptist Day." [Grain] (19:3) Fall 91, p. 49-50.
    "Standing on Guard." [CanLit] (129) Sum 91, p. 128.
    "What Is My Country?" [CanLit] (129) Sum 91, p. 128-129.
    "Wheel of Change" (Selections: 2 poems). [Quarry] (40:1/2) Wint-Spr 91, p. 24-25.
BREYNER ANDRESEN, Sophia de Mello
    See ANDRESEN, Sophia de Mello Breyner
669. BRICE-MEANS, B. J.
    "Ghosts." [Obs] (6:2) Sum 91, p. 90-91.
    "Sea Salt." [Obs] (6:2) Sum 91, p. 91-92.
670. BRIDEWELL, Leslie
    "Locked in Light." [NewYorkQ] (46) 91, p. 86.
    "Long Winter, Warm Barn." [ChironR] (10:2) Sum 91, p. 38.
671. BRIDGES, William
    "Silkby to Kelby." [BelPoJ] (42:2) Wint 91-92, p. 32.
672. BRIDGFORD, Kim
    "At the Zoo." [LaurelR] (25:2) Sum 91, p. 72.
    "The Call." [NoDaQ] (59:1) Wint 91, p. 5.
    "Earthly Things." [NoDaQ] (59:1) Wint 91, p. 3-4.
    "Fire." [SpoonRQ] (16:3/4) Sum-Fall 91, p. 97.
    "The Garden." [BellR] (14:1) Spr 91, p. 26.
    "Messages." [LaurelR] (25:2) Sum 91, p. 73-74.

70

"Saying Good-bye." [NoDaQ] (59:1) Wint 91, p. 6-7.
"The Storyteller." [SpoonRQ] (16:3/4) Sum-Fall 91, p. 98-99.
"Tea." [CreamCR] (15:2) Fall 91, p. 58.
"Words." [CapeR] (26:1) Spr 91, p. 42-43.
673. BRIEGER, Randy
"The Lump." [WestHR] (45:1) Spr 91, p. 47-50.
"Pig 311." [HawaiiR] (15:3, #33) Fall 91, p. 51-52.
674. BRITO, Manuel
"Palms on the Cold Flagstone" (part I, tr. of Andrés Sánchez Robayna, w. Fernando
Galván). [Talisman] (6) Spr 91, p. 71.
"Spout" (part III, tr. of Andrés Sánchez Robayna, w. Fernando Galván). [Talisman]
(6) Spr 91, p. 70-71.
"To a Rock" (tr. of Andrés Sánchez Robayna, w. Fernando Galván). [Talisman] (6)
Spr 91, p. 69.
675. BRIXIUS, Liz
"Labor Day Dusk at the Fairgrounds, Minnesota." [PoetryE] (32) Fall 91, p. 102.
"The Neighborhood Speaks." [PoetryE] (32) Fall 91, p. 101.
"Salvation Jamboree." [Shen] (41:4) Wint 91, p. 106.
"Swaggers into Sound of Mind." [GeoR] (45:1) Spr 91, p. 124.
676. BROCK, Van K.
"Chagall Among Developers." [AmerV] (25) Wint 91, p. 67-68.
677. BROCK-BROIDO, Lucie
"Bodhisattva." [AmerPoR] (20:5) S-O 91, p. 47.
"Carnivorous." [AmerPoR] (20:5) S-O 91, p. 46.
"An Egotistical Sublime." [WestHR] (45:2) Sum 91, p. 83-84.
"Haute Couture Vulgarity." [ParisR] (33:118) Spr 91, p. 138-139.
"Her Habit." [AmerPoR] (20:5) S-O 91, p. 47.
"In Medias Res." [AmerPoR] (20:5) S-O 91, p. 47.
"Inevitably, She Declined." [MichQR] (30:1) Wint 91, p. 172.
"Into Those Great Countries of the Blue Sky of Which We Don't Know Anything."
[ParisR] (33:118) Spr 91, p. 140-141.
"The Last Passenger Pigeon in the Cincinnati Zoo." [AmerPoR] (20:5) S-O 91, p. 46.
"Obsession, Compulsion." [AmerPoR] (20:5) S-O 91, p. 47.
"Queen Recluse." [NewRep] (205:18) 28 O 91, p. 38.
"The Supernatural Is Only the Natural, Disclosed." [Ploughs] (17:2/3) Fall 91, p.
137-138.
"When the Gods Go, Half-Gods Arrive." [AmerPoR] (20:5) S-O 91, p. 46.
"Work." [AmerPoR] (20:5) S-O 91, p. 45.
678. BROCKI, A. C.
"Question." [Poem] (65) My 91, p. 6.
"Reminders." [Poem] (65) My 91, p. 8.
"Withholding." [Poem] (65) My 91, p. 7.
679. BRODERSON, Lucille
"Diminished." [Nimrod] (35:1) Fall-Wint 91, p. 69.
"Exits." [Nimrod] (35:1) Fall-Wint 91, p. 70.
"Last Look." [Nimrod] (35:1) Fall-Wint 91, p. 71.
"Requiem." [Poetry] (159:3) D 91, p. 144.
"September Sunday." [Poetry] (159:3) D 91, p. 142.
"This Is Your Old Age, Lucy." [Poetry] (159:3) D 91, p. 143.
680. BRODSKY, Joseph
"Homage to Gerolamo Marcello" (tr. by the author). [NewYorker] (66:49) 21 Ja 91,
p. 30.
"Odysseus to Telemachus" (tr. by Harry Thomas). [PartR] (58:4) Fall 91, p.
680-681.
"Six Years Later" (tr. by Richard Wilbur). [Shen] (41:4) Wint 91, p. 79-80.
681. BRODSKY, Louis Daniel
"The Ghosts of Rowan Oak" (For Eva Miller). [SoCaR] (23:2) Spr 91, p. 52.
"Gowan's Enchantment." [HampSPR] Wint 91, p. 4.
"Lipizzaner Fantasies of an SS Officer." [FourQ] (5:2) Fall 91, p. 11-12.
682. BRODY, Deborah
"Home Ownership" (Honorable Mention). [GreensboroR] (51) Wint 91-92, p. 166.
683. BRODY, Harry
"The Halfway House." [Lactuca] (14) My 91, p. 58.
"It's '68 and You're 18." [DustyD] (2:1) Ja 91, p. 25.
"The Return: Easter '89." [CinPR] (22) Spr 91, p. 35.
"Soft Goods for Sale '63." [DustyD] Ap 91, p. 11.

"Two Nights in 1956." [DustyD] Ap 91, p. 11.
684. BRODY, Polly
       "Mimbres." [SingHM] (19) 91, p. 104.
685. BROGAN, Jacque Vaught
       "Before the Fire." [ConnPR] (10:1) 91, p. 23-24.
       "The Bond." [Kalliope] (13:2) 91, p. 32.
       "Chaos Theory." [BellR] (14:1) Spr 91, p. 18.
       "Freya." [BellR] (14:2) Fall 91, p. 41.
       "Sometimes." [ConnPR] (10:1) 91, p. 25.
686. BROGAN, Sharon
       "A Journey Woman's Travel Log." [Calyx] (13:2) Sum 91, p. 32-36.
BROIDO, Lucie Brock
       See BROCK-BROIDO, Lucie
687. BROMIGE, David
       "Couplets." [WestCL] (25:1) Spr 91, p. 74.
       "The Edible World." [WestCL] (25:1) Spr 91, p. 75-76.
       "On a Hundred-Block Walk." [Sulfur] (11:1, #28) Spr 91, p. 84-88.
       "With Each Step Down, the Air Grows Cooler." [WestCL] (25:1) Spr 91, p. 77-79.
688. BROMLEY, Anne (Anne C.)
       "Before the Hurricane: Flight of the Dead." [ColR] (NS 18:1) Spr-Sum 91, p.
             102-103.
       "Dusk Clouds." [DenQ] (26:1) Sum 91, p. 16-17.
       "Timberline, Mt. Agassiz." [ColR] (NS 18:1) Spr-Sum 91, p. 100-101.
689. BROOK, Donna
       "The Cure" (for George and Jack). [HangL] (58) 91, p. 13-14.
       "The New York Hospital Poem." [HangL] (59) 91, p. 17-20.
BROOK, Kimball MacKay
       See MacKAY-BROOK, Kimball
690. BROOKHOUSE, Christopher
       "The Reverend B. E. Palmer Considers His Harvest." [SewanR] (99:4) Fall 91, p.
             530-531.
       "When Someone in Our Country Parish Died." [SewanR] (99:4) Fall 91, p. 529-530.
691. BROOKS, Gwendolyn
       "Brelve. A Battered Woman." [Elf] (1:3) Fall 91, p. 25.
       "Jack Conroy." [NewL] (57:4) Sum 91, p. 3.
692. BROOKS, James
       "Stopping by Woods to Find My Golf Ball" (with all due respect to Robert Frost).
             [EngJ] (80:1) Ja 91, p. 93.
693. BROOKS, Julie A.
       "Painted Faces." [Crucible] (27) Fall 91, p. 18.
694. BROUGHTON, James
       "Having Come This Far." [NewYorkQ] (45) 91, p. 52.
       "A Laud for a Brother" (To William Everson in his Seventy-fifth Year). [NewYorkQ]
             (44) 91, p. 44.
       "Remembering a Great Bear" (A Star Turn for Robert Duncan, 1919-1988).
             [NewYorkQ] (46) 91, p. 26.
       "They Are Bombing the Garden of Eden." [PoetryUSA] (22) Spr 91, p. 14.
695. BROUGHTON, T. Alan
       "After the Funeral." [Northeast] (5:4) Sum 91, p. 6.
       "Aroma of Thyme." [Agni] (34) 91, p. 229.
       "Break-Out." [PraS] (65:1) Spr 91, p. 60.
       "Homecoming." [PraS] (65:1) Spr 91, p. 61.
       "The Idea Who Dreamed Plato." [Northeast] (5:4) Sum 91, p. 5.
       "Improvisation." [KenR] (NS 13:1) Wint 91, p. 124.
       "Invitation Poems." [SenR] (21:1) Spr 91, p. 62-68.
       "Local Habitation." [Chelsea] (51) 91, p. 22.
       "Lyric." [Poetry] (159:1) O 91, p. 24.
       "Minor Earthquake." [TexasR] (11:1/2) Spr-Sum 90, p. 63.
       "On the Way to School" (Rome, 1950). [AntR] (49:4) Fall 91, p. 557.
       "A Prayer." [FourQ] (4:2) Fall 90, p. 56.
       "Serenade for Winds." [Writer] (104:1) Ja 91, p. 18.
       "Stillwater Canticles" (for Anne Harris). [PraS] (65:1) Spr 91, p. 57-59.
       "Where Home Was." [TexasR] (11:1/2) Spr-Sum 90, p. 62.
696. BROUMAS, Olga
       "Offertory." [AmerV] (24) Fall 91, p. 40-41.

697. BROWDER, Clifford
    "Nerve Gas." [HawaiiR] (15:2, #32) Spr 91, p. 122-124.
698. BROWN, Allan
    "Le Gouffre." [Quarry] (40:1/2) Wint-Spr 91, p. 27.
    "Lemoine Point." [Quarry] (40:1/2) Wint-Spr 91, p. 26.
699. BROWN, Amy Benson
    "The Permanent Wave." [LullwaterR] (2:2) Spr 91, p. 37.
700. BROWN, Barnsley
    "Medusa's Dread Locks." [ChironR] (10:4) Wint 91, p. 6.
    "Mother." [ChironR] (10:4) Wint 91, p. 6.
    "Wings." [ChironR] (10:4) Wint 91, p. 6.
701. BROWN, Bill
    "My Lost Child." [WestB] (28) 91, p. 92.
    "Planting." [WestB] (28) 91, p. 93.
702. BROWN, Chocolate
    "El Quinto Sol." [BilingR] (16:2/3) My-D 91, p. 225.
703. BROWN, Christopher (Christopher Nicholas)
    "Prelude to Thanksgiving." [NewYorkQ] (44) 91, p. 62.
704. BROWN, Christopher, I
    "More Death." [PoetryUSA] (22) Spr 91, p. 18.
705. BROWN, Clarence
    "The Age" (tr. of Osip Mandelstam, w. W. S. Merwin). [Field] (45) Fall 91, p. 29-30.
    "Black Earth" (tr. of Osip Mandelstam, w. W. S. Merwin). [Field] (45) Fall 91, p. 35.
    "I was washing outside in the darkness" (tr. of Osip Mandelstam, w. W. S. Merwin). [Field] (45) Fall 91, p. 24.
    "Take from my palms, to soothe your heart" (tr. of Osip Mandelstam, w. W. S. Merwin). [Field] (45) Fall 91, p. 8.
    "We shall meet again, in Petersburg" (tr. of Osip Mandelstam, w. W. S. Merwin). [Field] (45) Fall 91, p. 16.
706. BROWN, Cory
    "Animation." [ChatR] (11:4) Sum 91, p. 35.
    "Cicadas on a Gray Day." [WestB] (28) 91, p. 65.
    "Deep Fog and Rain." [WestB] (29) 91, p. 65.
    "Philosophic Pain" (for Colleen Brown). [ChatR] (11:3) Spr 91, p. 16.
    "Summercoming." [Farm] (8:1) Spr-Sum 91, p. 82-86.
    "Threshold." [ChatR] (11:3) Spr 91, p. 15.
707. BROWN, Dan
    "Facing It." [TarRP] (31:1) Fall 91, p. 27-28.
    "Where I Was." [CreamCR] (15:2) Fall 91, p. 56-57.
    "A Wreck." [PoetC] (22:3) Spr 91, p. 11-14.
708. BROWN, Dorothy Hanson
    "Sunday Drive." [Elf] (1:3) Fall 91, p. 36.
BROWN, Dorothy (Dorothy Brown (Howe))
    See BROWN (HOWE), Dorothy
709. BROWN, George
    "While You Work." [JamesWR] (8:4) Sum 91, p. 13.
710. BROWN, Glen
    "Double Vision." [WillowR] Spr 91, p. 32.
711. BROWN, Harriet
    "The Frivolousness of Intention." [PraS] (65:4) Wint 91, p. 92.
    "Mirage." [ManhatPR] (13) [91?], p. 12.
    "My Mother Bends Her Head." [PraS] (65:4) Wint 91, p. 91.
    "Prowler." [PraS] (65:4) Wint 91, p. 89-90.
    "Symbiosis." [PraS] (65:4) Wint 91, p. 90.
712. BROWN, Jane Relaford
    "With Open Eyes." [MinnR] (NS 36) Spr 91, p. 7-9.
713. BROWN, Kurt
    "Cartology." [IndR] (14:3) Fall 91, p. 69-70.
    "The Dace." [IndR] (14:3) Fall 91, p. 67-68.
714. BROWN, Pat
    "Beholden." [WillowR] Spr 91, p. 18.
715. BROWN, Robert
    "The Gardener." [Elf] (1:1) Spr 91, p. 31.
    "Morphology." [LitR] (34:2) Wint 91, p. 256-257.

"The Taken Measure." [QW] (32) Wint-Spr 91, p. 135.
"When Things Dream." [Elf] (1:1) Spr 91, p. 30-31.
"Widow in a Violin Coat" (tr. of Jean Tardieu). [ArtfulD] (20/21) 91, p. 41.
716. BROWN, Ronnie R.
"Background Shadow." [Arc] (26) Spr 91, p. 44.
717. BROWN, Steven Ford
"Birthday" (tr. of Angel Gonzalez). [Paint] (18:36) Aut 91, p. 49.
"The Days Were Like That" (tr. of Angel Gonzalez, w. Gutierrez Revuelta).
[WillowS] (28) Sum 91, p. 18.
"The Defeated One" (tr. of Angel Gonzalez, w. Gutierrez Revuelta). [WillowS] (28)
Sum 91, p. 17.
"The Future" (tr. of Angel González, w. Pedro Gutirrez Revuelta). [WebR] (15) Spr
91, p. 34.
"Human Geography" (tr. of Angel Gonzalez, w. Gutierrez Revuelta). [WillowS] (28)
Sum 91, p. 16.
"I Know What It's Like to Wait" (tr. of Angel Gonzalez). [Paint] (18:36) Aut 91, p.
50.
"I Myself" (tr. of Angel Gonzalez, w. Gutierrez Revuelta). [Paint] (18:36) Aut 91, p.
43.
"Inventory of Places Propitious for Love" (tr. of Angel Gonzalez). [Paint] (18:36) Aut
91, p. 51.
"The Least Corpse" (tr. of Angel González, w. Pedro Gutirrez Revuelta). [WebR]
(15) Spr 91, p. 33-34.
"Love Dressed in White" (tr. of Angel Gonzalez). [Paint] (18:36) Aut 91, p. 48.
"Preamble to Silence" (tr. of Angel Gonzalez). [Paint] (18:36) Aut 91, p. 44.
"The Scandalous Rose" (tr. of Angel Gonzalez, w. Gutierrez Revuelta). [TexasR]
(12:1/2) Spr-Sum 91, p. 103.
"Sinestesia" (tr. of Angel Gonzalez, w. Gutierrez Revuelta). [Paint] (18:36) Aut 91,
p. 47.
"The So-Called Twilight" (tr. of Angel Gonzalez, w. Gutierrez Revuelta). [TexasR]
(12:1/2) Spr-Sum 91, p. 104.
"So It Seems" (tr. of Angel Gonzalez, w. Gutierrez Revuelta). [Paint] (18:36) Aut 91,
p. 45-46.
"Square with Towers and Palaces" (tr. of Angel Gonzalez). [HayF] (9) Fall-Wint 91,
p. 45.
"Sunday" (tr. of Angel Gonzalez). [ColR] (NS 18:2) Fall-Wint 91, p. 86-87.
"That River Ran Backwards" (tr. of Angel González, w. Pedro Gutirrez Revuelta).
[WebR] (15) Spr 91, p. 32.
"Through Here a River Passes" (tr. of Angel Gonzalez). [HayF] (9) Fall-Wint 91, p.
43.
"Twilight, Albuquerque, Summer" (tr. of Angel Gonzalez, w. Gutierrez Revuelta).
[TexasR] (12:1/2) Spr-Sum 91, p. 105.
718. BROWN, Susan M.
"The Keeper of Sheep" (Selections: VII, XI, XIII, XXIX, tr. of Fernando Pessoa
(Alberto Caeiro), w. Edwin Honig). [Trans] (25) Spr 91, p. 14-16.
719. BROWN-DAVIDSON, Terri
"In the Greenhouse." [NewYorkQ] (45) 91, p. 76.
"The Loch Ness Monster" (For my mother). [Prima] (14/15) 91, p. 82-85.
720. BROWN (HOWE), Dorothy
"A Gathering of Men" (for Robert Bly). [MalR] (96) Fall 91, p. 69-70.
721. BROWNE, Michael Dennis
"AIDS Patient." [AmerPoR] (20:6) N-D 91, p. 25.
"Biking About in the Hot Dark." [AmerPoR] (20:6) N-D 91, p. 26.
"Breech." [AmerPoR] (20:6) N-D 91, p. 25.
"Driving South, Sunset, February." [AmerPoR] (20:6) N-D 91, p. 25.
"Primitive." [AmerPoR] (20:6) N-D 91, p. 25.
"Telepathy." [Sidewalks] (1) Aug 91, p. 5.
"A Visit." [AmerPoR] (20:6) N-D 91, p. 25.
"Watering." [Sidewalks] (1) Aug 91, p. 6.
722. BROWNING, Deborah
"The Brown Thing." [Poem] (66) N 91, p. 41.
"Elephants." [Poem] (66) N 91, p. 42.
"Hurricane: Bath, England." [Poem] (66) N 91, p. 43.
723. BROWNING, Janisse
"Race to Culture." [CapilR] (2:6/7) Fall 91, p. 12-13.
"Sunday Morning Jingoism." [CapilR] (2:6/7) Fall 91, p. 14-15.

724. BRUCATO, Lisa
    "Meeting with Mary Magdalene." [MoodySI] (24/25/26) Spr 91, p. 30.
725. BRUCE, Debra
    "Beauty on the Beach." [MichQR] (30:1) Wint 91, p. 42-43.
    "Breakfast in Wyoming." [NewOR] (18:4) Wint 91, p. 28.
726. BRUCE, George
    "The Chair: Poet's and Painter's." [Interim] (10:2) Fall-Wint 91-92, p. 3-7.
    "Departure and Departure and." [Interim] (10:1) Spr-Sum 91, p. 32.
    "Soup and Sherry." [Interim] (10:1) Spr-Sum 91, p. 31.
727. BRUCE, Marge
    "Double Vision." [ChrC] (108:31) 30 O 91, p. 1006.
728. BRUCE, Todd
    "Jiggers" (Excerpt). [PraF] (12:1 #54) Spr 91, p. 13-17.
729. BRUCHAC, Joseph (Joseph, III)
    "At Ex Libris Bookstore" (Nuremberg, Germany). [RiverS] (33) 91, p. 48.
    "The Baux" (Provence, France). [SnailPR] (1:1) Spr 91, p. 7.
    "Drum at 31,000 Feet." [MidAR] (11:1) 91, p. 32.
    "East Berlin Woods." [RiverS] (33) 91, p. 47.
    "Seeing the Whales." [BambooR] (52) Fall 91, p. 17-20.
    "Skamonkas Kisos / Corn Moon." [PoetryE] (32) Fall 91, p. 45-46.
    "Snapping Turtle on the Expressway" (for Ron Welburn). [MidAR] (11:1) 91, p.
        33-34.
    "Song for the Elk" (from "The Songs of Tatan'ka Iyota'ke," tr. of Tatan'ka Iyota'ke).
        [MidAR] (11:1) 91, p. 2.
    "Steel" (For Rick Hill, Buster Mitchell and my students at Akwesasne). [MidAR]
        (11:1) 91, p. 35-37.
    "Tatan'ka Iyota'ke's Vision" (from "The Songs of Tatan'ka Iyota'ke," tr. of Tatan'ka
        Iyota'ke). [MidAR] (11:1) 91, p. 4.
    "Tatan'ka Iyota'ke's Warning to His People" (from "The Songs of Tatan'ka
        Iyota'ke," tr. of Tatan'ka Iyota'ke). [MidAR] (11:1) 91, p. 4.
    "While Walking Barefoot at Dawn" (from "The Songs of Tatan'ka Iyota'ke," tr. of
        Tatan'ka Iyota'ke). [MidAR] (11:1) 91, p. 2.
730. BRUCHANSKI, Rhonda
    "The Antidyke." [PraF] (12:1 #54) Spr 91, p. 87.
731. BRUNK, Juanita
    "Flood." [PassN] (12:1) Sum 91, p. 7.
    "Infidelity." [PassN] (12:1) Sum 91, p. 7.
BRUNO, Carmen Michael la
    See LaBRUNO, Carmen Michael
BRUNO, Michael la
    See LaBRUNO, Carmen Michael
BRUNT, H. L. van
    See Van BRUNT, Lloyd
BRUNT, Lloyd van
    See Van BRUNT, Lloyd
732. BRUNTY, C. Payne
    "Art Imitates Life at the Throbbing Opera." [WindO] (55) Wint 91-92, p. 32-34.
733. BRUSH, Thomas
    "Lines on a Postcard of Lombard Street, San Francisco" (From Dick Hamby).
        [Poetry] (158:4) Jl 91, p. 212-213.
    "Small Town." [Poetry] (158:4) Jl 91, p. 210-211.
    "Stars." [Poetry] (159:3) D 91, p. 145.
734. BRUTON, Heidi
    "Looking Upon Open Fields." [Nimrod] (35:1) Fall-Wint 91, p. 61.
735. BRYAN, Sharon
    "Bonne Chance." [Crazy] (40) Spr 91, p. 39.
    "Housing." [PoetryNW] (32:2) Sum 91, p. 34.
    "Synecdoche." [Crazy] (40) Spr 91, p. 40-41.
736. BRYANT, Anne
    "For Allegra." [NewYorkQ] (44) 91, p. 58.
737. BUCHANAN, Carl
    "Nick Adams and the Swamp." [SoDakR] (29:1) Spr 91, p. 50.
    "Sacred Moons." [SoDakR] (29:1) Spr 91, p. 49.
738. BUCHMAN, Ruth
    "Going Back." [SingHM] (19) 91, p. 106.

739. BUCKHOLTS, Claudia
"Hawks Above the Porch." [ConnPR] (10:1) 91, p. 16.
"Instrument." [ConnPR] (10:1) 91, p. 17.
740. BUCKLEY, Christopher
"Cruising State" (Santa Barbara, California, 1964). [CimR] (97) O 91, p. 54-57.
"Early Morning — Ucross, Wyoming." [CumbPR] (11:1) Fall 91, p. 70-71.
"Father, 1952." [Crazy] (41) Wint 91, p. 61-62.
"Graffiti: Ellis Island" (for the opening of the restored Main Building and Immigration
Museum, 1990). [SewanR] (99:4) Fall 91, p. 532-534.
"Isotropic" (After the launching of the Hubble Space Telescope, April 25, 1990).
[Poetry] (159:2) N 91, p. 85-86.
"Meditation on Ambition at Triple Creek — Ucross, Wyoming." [CumbPR] (11:1)
Fall 91, p. 72.
"Morning Journal" (Ucross, Wyoming). [GreenMR] (NS 5:1) Sum-Fall 91, p. 27-28.
"Perseid Meteor Shower" (Ucross, Wyoming). [Poetry] (158:3) Je 91, p. 133-134.
"Perspective from the School House Porch" (Ucross, Wyoming). [GreenMR] (NS
5:1) Sum-Fall 91, p. 29.
"Reincarnation." [Poetry] (159:2) N 91, p. 82-83.
"Thursday Evening BBC Mystery." [PoetL] (86:3) Fall 91, p. 11-12.
741. BUCKLEY, Joy
"Changing Styles." [Asylum] (6:3/4) 91, p. 59.
742. BUCKLEY, Patricia
"Guise a la Lettre." [Pig] (17) 91, p. 57.
743. BUCKNER, Sally
"Mid-Fest." [Pembroke] (23) 91, p. 86-88.
744. BUDDE, Robert
"Flicker." [PraF] (12:1 #54) Spr 91, p. 25.
"Loom." [PraF] (12:1 #54) Spr 91, p. 24.
745. BUDEK, Michael H.
"An Epileptic." [SpiritSH] (56) Spr-Sum 91, p. 29.
"Tour, Yggdrasil." [SpiritSH] (56) Spr-Sum 91, p. 28.
746. BUDY, Andrea Hollander
"Choice." [Shen] (41:1) Spr 91, p. 59.
"Gretel." [ContextS] (2:2) 91, p. 35-36.
"Hansel." [ContextS] (2:2) 91, p. 35.
"Just." [KenR] (NS 13:1) Wint 91, p. 34.
"A Way of Speaking." [Shen] (41:1) Spr 91, p. 58.
747. BUGEJA, Michael J.
"The Abduction." [PraS] (65:1) Spr 91, p. 31-33.
"An American Buddha." [PraS] (65:1) Spr 91, p. 35-37.
"Ars Poetica: The Tree Parables." [LaurelR] (25:1) Wint 91, p. 60-65.
"Aunt Melita Takes Another Captive." [Sparrow] (58) Jl 91, p. 6.
"Bats." [PraS] (65:1) Spr 91, p. 33-35.
"Day Moon." [HampSPR] Wint 91, p. 58.
"How to Hate Hitler." [GrahamHR] (15) Fall 91, p. 20-21.
"The Hutch." [Sparrow] (58) Jl 91, p. 9.
"The New Dress." [Sparrow] (58) Jl 91, p. 8.
"Prognosis of the Pupa." [SouthernHR] (25:3) Sum 91, p. 234.
"Reconstructing Herr Schicklgruber." [GrahamHR] (15) Fall 91, p. 18-19.
"Snow in the Tropics." [Sparrow] (58) Jl 91, p. 7.
"Trakl / Hitler." [GrahamHR] (15) Fall 91, p. 15-17.
"Triolet." [HampSPR] Wint 91, p. 58.
"We Plot While My Lame Uncle Prays." [Sparrow] (58) Jl 91, p. 10.
"What Poets Want II." [HampSPR] Wint 91, p. 60.
"White Noise." [SouthernHR] (25:3) Sum 91, p. 216.
748. BUGGÉ, Carol
"A Mother Speaks of Boston" (Second Place Winner, Eve of St. Agnes Poery
Awards). [NegC] (11:3) 91, p. 14-15.
749. BUISSON, Justine
"Like Roethke, For Instance." [ChironR] (10:3) Aut 91, p. 44.
750. BUKER, Russel
"Father of the Light." [AntigR] (87/88) Fall 91-Wint 92, p. 264.
751. BUKOWSKI, Charles
"6:30 a.m." [ColR] (NS 17:2) Fall-Wint 90, p. 46.
"An Answer." [Pearl] (14) Fall-Wint 91, p. 6.
"Anyhow." [SlipS] (11) 91, p. 17-18.

"Batting Order." [CharR] (17:1) Spr 91, p. 48-49.
"Bent." [PaintedB] (43) 91, p. 38.
"Betting on the Muse." [HeavenB] (9) Wint-Spr 91-92, p. 3.
"Chinaski: Skewered." [NewYorkQ] (44) 91, p. 43.
"Corsage." [CalQ] (35/36) 91, p. 101-106.
"Displaced." [Boulevard] (5:3/6:1, #15/16) Spr 91, p. 205-206.
"For a Man Who Walks Around My Typewriter Very Often." [WormR] (31:1, #121) 91, p. 42.
"Ginsberg?" [WormR] (31:4, #124) 91, p. 141-142.
"The Glory Days." [SycamoreR] (3:1) Wint 91, p. 28-30.
"I'll Have It to Go." [OnTheBus] (8/9) 91, p. 30-35.
"I'm Flattered." [SlipS] (11) 91, p. 18-19.
"The Inspection." [Pearl] (14) Fall-Wint 91, p. 7.
"The Last Salamander." [ColR] (NS 17:2) Fall-Wint 90, p. 45.
"Living in a Great Big Way." [NewYorkQ] (46) 91, p. 28.
"Look Back, Look Up." [GreenMR] (NS 5:1) Sum-Fall 91, p. 49-51.
"Luck Was Not a Lady for Me." [SycamoreR] (3:1) Wint 91, p. 31-33.
"A Mention of Some Lucky Pay-Offs." [WormR] (31:1, #121) 91, p. 40-41.
"Met a Man on the Street." [PaintedB] (43) 91, p. 37.
"No Sale." [ColR] (NS 17:2) Fall-Wint 90, p. 42-44.
"Note in and from a Bottle." [SlipS] (11) 91, p. 13-14.
"Now." [PaintedB] (43) 91, p. 39-40.
"On the Bum." [Pearl] (14) Fall-Wint 91, p. 8.
"One More Day." [SycamoreR] (3:2) Sum 91, p. 46-47.
"People Poems: 1982-1991" (A Wormwood Chapbook). [WormR] (31:2/3, #122-123) 91, p. 49-96.
"Perfect." [SlipS] (11) 91, p. 14.
"The Player." [WorldL] (2) 91, p. 1-2.
"Putting It to Bed." [GreenMR] (NS 5:1) Sum-Fall 91, p. 54-55.
"A Quick One." [GreenMR] (NS 5:1) Sum-Fall 91, p. 56-57.
"The Secret." [PaintedB] (43) 91, p. 45.
"See Here You." [SlipS] (11) 91, p. 15-16.
"A Sickness." [NewYorkQ] (45) 91, p. 36-43.
"Skinny-Dipping." [SlipS] (11) 91, p. 12.
"Storm." [BelPoJ] (42:1) Fall 91, p. 8-9.
"They Need What They Need." [WormR] (31:4, #124) 91, p. 142-143.
"Think of It." [GreenMR] (NS 5:1) Sum-Fall 91, p. 52-53.
"This Rejoinder." [WorldL] (2) 91, p. 3.
"The Train Station." [WormR] (31:4, #124) 91, p. 139-141.
"A Visitation." [CharR] (17:1) Spr 91, p. 50.
"Within the Dense Overhang." [CalQ] (35/36) 91, p. 98-101.
"The World War One Movies." [PaintedB] (43) 91, p. 41-44.
"You Gotta Get Down." [HeavenB] (9) Wint-Spr 91-92, p. 51.
752. BULLOCK, Donald B.
"Biak 1944." [EmeraldCR] (3) 91, c1990, p. 113-114.
753. BULMER, April
"Angels." [MalR] (96) Fall 91, p. 77.
"Cow." [MalR] (96) Fall 91, p. 78-79.
"Tooth." [MalR] (96) Fall 91, p. 80.
754. BUNDE, Gary
"The Bug Man of Alcatraz." [EmeraldCR] (3) 91, c1990, p. 126-128.
755. BUNDY, Alison
"Restrained Theory on the Disappearance of Women." [Ploughs] (17:4) Wint 91-92, p. 73-75.
756. BUNDY, Gary
"Black Jack." [ChironR] (10:4) Wint 91, p. 23.
757. BUNSE, Lois
"Chicken Poem." [CalQ] (31) Fall 88, p. 55.
"Escher Paints Flight." [CalQ] (31) Fall 88, p. 55.
"Exactly Like a Woman from Toronto." [CalQ] (31) Fall 88, p. 56.
"The Parlor." [CalQ] (31) Fall 88, p. 57.
"This Marriage." [CalQ] (31) Fall 88, p. 58.
758. BURKARD, Michael
"Before the Dark." [ParisR] (33:121) Wint 91, p. 180-185.
759. BURKE, Kelley Jo
"Fat Girls Love to Swim." [Grain] (19:2) Sum 91, p. 31.

"Fat Girl's Rhapsody." [Grain] (19:2) Sum 91, p. 32.
"Metamorphosis 1." [Grain] (19:2) Sum 91, p. 33.
760. BURKE, Marianne
"Funeral Home." [NewYorker] (67:44) 23 D 91, p. 62.
"Our Daily Bread." [Boulevard] (5:3/6:1, #15/16) Spr 91, p. 176.
761. BURKE, Raymond W.
"The Emperor Is Dead." [DustyD] Ap 91, p. 21.
"Magnolier's Child" (In Special Memory of Tennessee Williams." [DustyD] Ap 91, p. 24-25.
"Il Vicolo Stanza del Santo Spirito" (aka The Dead Room of Santo Spirito). [DustyD] Ap 91, p. 16.
762. BURLESON, Derick
"After This." [Poetry] (158:2) My 91, p. 66.
"Skipping School." [Poetry] (158:2) My 91, p. 67-68.
763. BURLESON, Jim
"A Report to the Dean." [ContextS] (2:1) 91, p. 12.
764. BURNABY, Frank
"I Don't Get Enough Sex." [OnTheBus] (8/9) 91, p. 38-39.
"Passion." [OnTheBus] (8/9) 91, p. 36-37.
765. BURNEY, Jeanette (Jeannette)
"Introduction to the Kitchen." [MinnR] (NS 36) Spr 91, p. 15-16.
"The Opening" (for Les Miller). [MinnR] (NS 37) Fall 91, p. 30-31.
"Unemployment Office — Right." [MinnR] (NS 36) Spr 91, p. 16.
766. BURNHAM, Deborah
"Losing a Wallet." [Prima] (14/15) 91, p. 45.
767. BURNS, Gerald
"Artist's Studios." [NewAW] (8/9) Fall 91, p. 25-26.
768. BURNS, Michael
"After Ten Years." [PoetC] (23:1) Fall 91, p. 34.
"Beginnings" (for Dakotah). [KenR] (NS 13:1) Wint 91, p. 156.
"The First Time." [LaurelR] (25:1) Wint 91, p. 84.
"For What It's Worth." [LaurelR] (25:1) Wint 91, p. 84-85.
"I Said It Could Have Been." [Poetry] (158:1) Ap 91, p. 13.
"Matriarchs." [PoetC] (23:1) Fall 91, p. 33.
"My Handle." [SouthernR] (27:2) Ap 91, p. 322-323.
"The Teacher." [NewOR] (18:3) Fall 91, p. 33.
"Why the Poet Wanted to Write a Novel." [PoetC] (23:1) Fall 91, p. 32.
769. BURNS, Ralph
"Try." [Crazy] (40) Spr 91, p. 42-44.
770. BURNS, Richard
"Aubade" (tr. of Aleksandar Petrov, w. the author). [NewOR] (18:2) Sum 91, p. 88.
"I Have No More Time" (tr. of Desanka Maksimovic, w. Jasna Misic). [NewOR] (18:2) Sum 91, p. 66.
"When a Child Dies" (For Nikola, tr. of Duska Vrhovac, w. Vera Radojevic). [NewOR] (18:2) Sum 91, p. 83.
771. BURNS, Robert
"Let Us Now Praise the Cultured Poor" (from "Epistle to John Lapraik," an old Scottish bard). [PoetryUSA] (22) Spr 91, p. 3.
772. BURNS, Suzanne
"Blackberries Are Green When They Are Red." [Sonora] (21) Sum 91, p. 30.
"Drawing in the Orchard." [Sonora] (21) Sum 91, p. 31.
"Trying to Understand My Brother Later." [HayF] (9) Fall-Wint 91, p. 88.
773. BURNSIDE, John
"Aphasia in Childhood." [Verse] (8:2) Sum 91, p. 47.
"Between Dorking and Shalford." [Verse] (8:2) Sum 91, p. 49.
"Chlorpromazine." [Verse] (8:2) Sum 91, p. 48.
"Folk Story." [Verse] (8:2) Sum 91, p. 49.
"The Noli me Tangere Incident." [Verse] (8:2) Sum 91, p. 48.
774. BURRELL, Clarice A.
"The Sand Dollar Legend." [EmeraldCR] (3) 91, c1990, p. 68-70.
775. BURRELL, Todd
"The Arts of Fire" (to Mariacristina Bethencourt, tr. of Maira Delmar). [WebR] (15) Spr 91, p. 36.
"Melody" (tr. of Maira Delmar). [WebR] (15) Spr 91, p. 37.
"Radiance" (tr. of Maira Delmar). [WebR] (15) Spr 91, p. 37.
"This Love" (tr. of Maira Delmar). [WebR] (15) Spr 91, p. 35.

BURROWS, D. G.
   See BURROWS, E. G.
776. BURROWS, E. G.
   "Hard Maple." [Vis] (35) 91, p. 30.
   "Limits." [Poetry] (157:5) F 91, p. 260.
   "The Statue." [Poetry] (157:5) F 91, p. 261.
777. BURSK, Christopher
   "Abbondonza." [ManhatR] (6:1) Fall 91, p. 77-78.
   "Air." [ManhatR] (6:1) Fall 91, p. 80.
   "A Thousand Points of Light." [ManhatR] (6:1) Fall 91, p. 81-82.
   "Words Said in the Dark." [ManhatR] (6:1) Fall 91, p. 79.
778. BURSKY, Rick
   "The Frigid Wind." [OnTheBus] (8/9) 91, p. 41.
   "Past the Yellow Walls." [OnTheBus] (8/9) 91, p. 41.
   "War Watch." [OnTheBus] (8/9) 91, p. 40.
779. BURTON, Leasa
   "Lessons from Her Belly." [QW] (32) Wint-Spr 91, p. 136.
780. BURTON, Scott
   "Carrie Ann — 1967." [RagMag] (9:2) 91, p. 59-60.
   "I Remember Mama." [RagMag] (9:2) 91, p. 58-59.
781. BUSAILAH, R. (Reja-e)
   "Children of the Stones" (tr. of Nizar Qabbani). [InterPR] (17:2) Fall 91, p. 83.
   "Her Temper." [NewRena] (8:2, #25) Fall 91, p. 153.
   "The Old Man." [Elf] (1:3) Fall 91, p. 41.
   "One Life at a Time." [SnailPR] (1:2) Fall 91-Wint 92, p. 17.
   "A Slice of Palestine." [NewRena] (8:2, #25) Fall 91, p. 155.
   "Something's the Matter." [NewRena] (8:2, #25) Fall 91, p. 154.
   "The Students of Gaza" (Arabic title: "The Angry Ones," tr. of Nizar Qabbani).
      [InterPR] (17:2) Fall 91, p. 82-83.
782. BUSCH, Trent
   "The Clay." [PoetC] (22:2) Wint 91, p. 9-10.
   "Dorothy's Room." [LullwaterR] (2:2) Spr 91, p. 66-67.
   "House of Breaking Hearts." [PoetC] (22:2) Wint 91, p. 7-8.
783. BUSH, Barney
   "Dreamfast." [MidAR] (11:1) 91, p. 24-29.
784. BUSHROWSKY, Aaron
   "Another Quasar (Red Shift)." [Dandel] (18:2) Wint 91, p. 63.
785. BUTCHER, Grace
   "Child, House, World" (44 poems). [HiramPoR] (Suppl. No. 12) 91, 82 p.
   "Here I Am." [ManhatPR] (13) [91?], p. 16.
   "Learning from Trees." [Poetry] (158:1) Ap 91, p. 32.
   "Lost Letter." [Pig] (17) 91, p. 78.
   "Motel." [LitR] (35:1) Fall 91, p. 123.
   "One Sorcerer to Another." [ManhatPR] (13) [91?], p. 15.
   "Poem I Didn't Want." [BellR] (14:1) Spr 91, p. 53.
   "Reading the X-Ray: A Modern Mythology." [Poetry] (158:1) Ap 91, p. 31.
   "Riders Must Be in Control of Their Animals at All Times." [WestB] (29) 91, p. 31.
   "The Sound of Sleeping." [WestB] (29) 91, p. 29.
   "Thanksgiving, Christmas, Easter and All the Rest." [CinPR] (22) Spr 91, p. 34.
   "Whatever Has Always Been in Darkness Is Still There." [WestB] (29) 91, p. 30.
786. BUTLER, Carolyne J.
   "Remembering Pensacola, 1945." [EmeraldCR] (3) 91, c1990, p. 3.
787. BUTLER, Jack
   "Gyro Gearloose." [NewOR] (18:3) Fall 91, p. 48-53.
788. BUTLER, Lynne B.
   "Reading the Poem." [CimR] (97) O 91, p. 48.
   "Trouble." [CimR] (97) O 91, p. 47.
789. BUTLIN, Ron
   "Perhaps" (tr. of Georgi Belev, w. Roumen Mitkov). [Verse] (8:2) Sum 91, p. 117.
790. BUTSCHER, Edward
   "Wake." [ConnPR] (10:1) 91, p. 29-30.
791. BUTTS, W. E.
   "Day Labor" (for James Haug). [MidAR] (11:2) 91, p. 110.
   "Sterling Diner." [SoCoast] (10) Fall 91, p. 16-17.
792. BYRD, Sigman
   "Faith." [Sonora] (21) Sum 91, p. 32.

793. BYRD, Stephanie
   "A Birthday Deserves a Handsome Surprise." [KenR] (NS 13:4) Fall 91, p. 190.
   "War and Eggs." [KenR] (NS 13:4) Fall 91, p. 189.
794. BYRNE, Donald E., Jr.
   "Carpenter Bee." [WindO] (54) Sum 91, p. 7.
   "Compost Heap." [WindO] (54) Sum 91, p. 3-6.
   "I Will Never Again Curse the Ground Because of Man" (Genesis 8:21). [CreamCR]
      (15:1) Spr 91, p. 44-46.
   "Murph." [WestB] (28) 91, p. 44-46.
   "Under the Marble Arch." [WindO] (54) Sum 91, p. 8-9.
795. BYRNE, Edward
   "Driving North at Nightfall" (for Pam). [RiverC] (12:1) Fall 91, p. 56.
796. BYRNE, Elena Karina
   "In Particular." [Poetry] (158:1) Ap 91, p. 30.
797. BYRNES, Fred
   "Apple Pie à la Mode" (for Jack Kerouac). [MoodySI] (24/25/26) Spr 91, p. 30.
798. BYRON, Arthur
   "Recueillement" (Rumination, after Baudelaire). [PoetryUSA] (23) Sum 91, p. 14.
799. BYRUM, John
   "Deforming." [CentralP] (19/20) Spr-Fall 91, p. 181.
   "Explement." [CentralP] (19/20) Spr-Fall 91, p. 208.
   "Insurgent." [CentralP] (19/20) Spr-Fall 91, p. 243.
   "Post-Oblique Works, 1990" (Exceprts). [Aerial] (6/7) 91, p. 36-40.
800. CABACUNGAN, Darryl Keola
   "November Wind Song" (in response to John Corigliano's Sympony #1). [ChamLR]
      (8-9) Spr-Fall 91, p. 144-145.
801. CABLE, Gerald
   "Axle." [PennR] (5:1) Spr 91, p. 37.
   "Home Movie." [Abraxas] (40/41) 91, p. 151.
   "Trouble." [PennR] (5:1) Spr 91, p. 37.
802. CABRAL, Olga
   "The Breathing Night." [SingHM] (19) 91, p. 73.
   "The Horses of Your Childhood" (for Aaron). [Vis] (35) 91, p. 12-13.
   "An Interior." [CreamCR] (15:2) Fall 91, p. 82-83.
   "Woman Ironing." [AmerV] (22) Spr 91, p. 72.
803. CABRI, Louis
   "Ante." [Avec] (4:1) 91, p. 161-162.
804. CADDEL, Richard
   "Rigmarole: Night-Driving in Correze." [NewAW] (8/9) Fall 91, p. 66-69.
805. CADDELL, Marsha
   "Grocery Shopping, St. Petersburg, Florida." [ManhatPR] (13) [91?], p. 35.
806. CADDY, David
   "Letter to Andy Jordan." [Stand] (32:1) Wint 90-91, p. 73.
   "Picking Sloes." [Stand] (32:1) Wint 90-91, p. 74.
807. CADER, Teresa
   "At the Trenton State Hospital." [TriQ] (81) Spr-Sum 91, p. 212-214.
808. CADIOT, Olivier
   "Corriere della Sera" (from "L'Art Poetic," P.O.L. 1988, tr. by Cole Swensen).
      [Avec] (4:1) 91, p. 65-67.
   "Red, Green and Black" (Potes and Poets 1990. Selection: 4, tr. by Charles Bernstein
      and the author). [Avec] (4:1) 91, p. 61-64.
809. CADNUM, Michael
   "Blackberries." [Comm] (118:15) 13 S 91, p. 518.
   "The Cities We Will Never See." [CreamCR] (14:2) Wint 91, p. 144.
   "Dragonfly." [SoDakR] (29:4) Wint 91, p. 26.
   "Drought Burn." [Comm] (118:15) 13 S 91, p. 518.
   "Faith." [NoDaQ] (59:1) Wint 91, p. 176.
   "Glass Eye." [CinPR] (21) Spr 90, p. 48.
   "Mine Shaft." [Comm] (118:15) 13 S 91, p. 518.
   "Nine-Month Drought." [WillowS] (27) Wint 91, p. 11.
   "Planting in August." [WindO] (55) Wint 91-92, p. 22.
   "Plaster Gnome." [CinPR] (22) Spr 91, p. 61.
   "Saving *Beowulf*." [DustyD] Je 91, p. 4.
   "To Not Believe in Miracles." [LitR] (34:2) Wint 91, p. 270.
   "Web." [WillowS] (27) Wint 91, p. 10.
   "What the Nights Are Like." [LitR] (34:2) Wint 91, p. 269.

"Why It Never Snows." [PoetryNW] (32:1) Spr 91, p. 41-42.
CAEIRO, Alberto
    See PESSOA, Fernando
810. CAFAGNA, Marcus
    "Cracking Eggs." [CinPR] (22) Spr 91, p. 30.
    "Little Dogs." [SlipS] (11) 91, p. 46-47.
    "My Omen." [SlipS] (11) 91, p. 47.
    "Pink Cadillac." [HangL] (58) 91, p. 16-17.
    "Suits." [WestB] (28) 91, p. 70-71.
811. CAFFERTY, Candace
    "Two Months Before Getting My Master's Degree." [Pearl] (14) Fall-Wint 91, p. 23.
812. CAGE, John
    "Art Is Either a Complaint or Do Something Else." [Aerial] (6/7) 91, p. 1-35.
813. CAHEN, Alfred
    "Hart Crane: Townsman." [HiramPoR] (50) Spr-Sum 91, p. 5.
814. CAI, Qi-jiao
    "Still Praying" (tr. by Edward Morin and Fang Dai). [NewOR] (18:2) Sum 91, p. 41.
815. CAIN, Kathleen
    "Wild Onions." [SingHM] (19) 91, p. 7-8.
816. CAINE, Shulamith W. (Shulamith Wechter)
    "Craniology." [AmerS] (60:4) Aut 91, p. 504.
    "She." [Kalliope] (13:2) 91, p. 33.
CAIRNES, Scott
    See CAIRNS, Scott
817. CAIRNS, Scott
    "Herod." [NewRep] (205:15) 7 O 91, p. 44.
    "In the General Area of North Texas." [TexasR] (12:3/4) Fall-Wint 91, p. 71.
    "Serenade." [TampaR] (4) 91, p. 73.
818. CALBERT, Cathleen
    "Fainting." [Nat] (252:18) 13 My 91, p. 639.
819. CALDARA, Anna Maria
    "Men Waiting in a Gynecologist's Office." [NewYorkQ] (46) 91, p. 48.
820. CALDAS, Renalto
    "Agitation" (tr. by Gerald Standley). [InterPR] (17:1) Spr 91, p. 39.
    "Arvorada Matuta." [InterPR] (17:1) Spr 91, p. 36.
    "Confession" (tr. by Gerald Standley). [InterPR] (17:1) Spr 91, p. 41.
    "Cunfissão." [InterPR] (17:1) Spr 91, p. 40.
    "Dawn in the Backlands" (tr. by Gerald Standley). [InterPR] (17:1) Spr 91, p. 37.
    "Flower of the Mato" (tr. by Gerald Standley). [InterPR] (17:1) Spr 91, p. 37.
    "Fulô do Mato." [InterPR] (17:1) Spr 91, p. 26.
    "Juramento." [InterPR] (17:1) Spr 91, p. 42, 44.
    "Minha Casinha." [InterPR] (17:1) Spr 91, p. 44.
    "My Little House" (tr. by Gerald Standley). [InterPR] (17:1) Spr 91, p. 45.
    "The Oath" (tr. by Gerald Standley). [InterPR] (17:1) Spr 91, p. 43, 45.
    "Rebulico." [InterPR] (17:1) Spr 91, p. 38.
821. CALDERON, Roberto R.
    "American Queque" (a papácuya frase fue y a mamá quien lo acompañó). [KenR] (NS 13:4) Fall 91, p. 170-171.
822. CALDWELL, Andrew
    "The Anarchist Goes to Albertsons" (A Stunt Poem to Andy Warhol). [SycamoreR] (3:1) Wint 91, p. 24-27.
823. CALHOUN, E. Frank
    "The Loss." [EmeraldCR] (3) 91, c1990, p. 64-65.
824. CALHOUN, Harry
    "A Tropical Depression" (To a memory). [ChironR] (10:2) Sum 91, p. 46.
825. CALHOUN, Tara
    "The Writer." [EmeraldCR] (3) 91, c1990, p. 80.
826. CALISCH, Richard
    "Bird Song" (From the Secret Files of the International Audubon Society). [Elf] (1:1) Spr 91, p. 24.
    "Father After Curfew." [Elf] (1:3) Fall 91, p. 34.
    "In the Pazzi Chapel" (Florence). [WillowR] Spr 91, p. 16.
    "Riff for a Summer Evening." [Elf] (1:1) Spr 91, p. 22-23.
CALISH, Richard
    See CALISCH, Richard

827. CALLAHAN, Jean
"Centenarian, 1958." [EmeraldCR] (4) 91, p. 6.
828. CALLANAN, Deirdre G.
"Camilla, Georgia." [YellowS] (36) Spr 91, p. 12.
"The Last Dance at the Last Chance Saloon." [YellowS] (36) Spr 91, p. 13.
"What Sort of Question Is This" (for Selma). [ColR] (NS 17:2) Fall-Wint 90, p. 52.
829. CALVILLO-CRAIG, Lorenza
"Untitled: On the way to tomorrow." [BilingR] (16:1) Ja-Ap 91, p. 60-61.
"Vietnam Memorial." [BilingR] (16:1) Ja-Ap 91, p. 59.
830. CAMACHO-GINGERICH, Alina (Alma?)
"La Creacion" (A Tanya y Daniel). [LindLM] (10:1) Ja-Mr 91, p. 15.
831. CAMERON, Mary
"Deer." [AntigR] (85/86) Spr-Sum 91, p. 95.
"Night Shift." [Grain] (19:4) Wint 91, p. 113.
"Power." [Grain] (19:4) Wint 91, p. 114.
"Silence." [AntigR] (85/86) Spr-Sum 91, p. 94.
832. CAMP, James
"Amor in Inferno" (After Ransom). [Pembroke] (23) 91, p. 57.
833. CAMPBELL, Barbara
"Jimmy." [NewAW] (8/9) Fall 91, p. 53.-54.
834. CAMPBELL, John
"Learning to Ski." [NowestR] (29:2) 91, p. 90.
"The Poetic Moment." [NowestR] (29:2) 91, p. 89.
"A Speech to the Calm and Formal." [NowestR] (29:2) 91, p. 91.
835. CAMPBELL, Mary Belle
"Reflections — To End Is to Make a Beginning" (postscript from the book "Light
from Dark Tombs: A Traveller's Map to Mysteries of the Ancient Maya").
[Crucible] (27) Fall 91, p. 6.
836. CAMPBELL, P. Michael
"Astronauts." [Thrpny] (45) Spr 91, p. 29.
837. CAMPIGLIO, Stephen
"Untimely Schedules." [Mildred] (4:2/5:1) 91, p. 54.
"Where You Are." [Mildred] (4:2/5:1) 91, p. 53.
838. CAMPION, Dan
"A Bowl of Fruit." [Ascent] (16:1) Fall 91, p. 9.
"The Exile of Glass." [Ascent] (16:1) Fall 91, p. 9.
839. CAMPO, Rafael
"El Curandero." [KenR] (NS 13:3) Sum 91, p. 5-6.
"Finally." [Ploughs] (17:2/3) Fall 91, p. 201.
"The Love of Someone." [KenR] (NS 13:3) Sum 91, p. 6.
"La Madre Patria." [GrahamHR] (15) Fall 91, p. 80.
"Sonnets for My Grandfather" (Selections: II, IV, VIII). [Agni] (33) 91, p. 145-147.
CAMPOS, Alvaro de
See PESSOA, Fernando
840. CANAN, Janine
"Bentley's Is Going Out of Business." [PoetryUSA] (23) Sum 91, p. 13.
CANDELARIO, Ginetta E. Berloso
See BERLOSO CANDELARIO, Ginetta E.
841. CANNON, Cynthia
"Turning Toward Egypt." [ChrC] (108:9) 13 Mr 91, p. 296.
842. CANTALUPO, Charles
"Gestation." [Sulfer] (11:2, #29) Fall 91, p. 59-60.
843. CANTELON, C. N.
"Lessons." [BellArk] (7:5) S-O 91, p. 1.
844. CANTON y CANTON, Juan
"Qué Sé Yo Si Son Mis Ojos." [Nuez] (3:7) 91, p. 14.
845. CANTRELL, Charles
"From Fat to Happy." [Ascent] (16:1) Fall 91, p. 18-19.
"Poem: It's your old obsession with snow." [CrabCR] (7:3) 91, p. 20.
846. CANTWELL, Kevin
"Inscription" (for Mike White). [Journal] (15:1) Spr 91, p. 51-52.
"Land Surveyor's Office." [Journal] (15:1) Spr 91, p. 50.
"Small Boy at a Window Sill." [NewRep] (204:9) 4 Mr 91, p. 36.
847. CAO, Wei
"Death" (tr. of Chen Ming Hua). [GreenMR] (NS 4:2) Wint-Spr 91, p. 28.
"Metal" (tr. of Chen Ming Hua). [GreenMR] (NS 4:2) Wint-Spr 91, p. 26.

"Reading Aloud" (tr. of Wang Yan). [GreenMR] (NS 4:2) Wint-Spr 91, p. 8.
"River" (tr. of Yu Jian). [GreenMR] (NS 4:2) Wint-Spr 91, p. 36.
"Standing on the Veranda Watching the Polluted River." [GreenMR] (NS 4:2)
    Wint-Spr 91, p. 62.
"The Ward" (tr. of Chen Ming Hua). [GreenMR] (NS 4:2) Wint-Spr 91, p. 27.
CAPO, Marylín Diaz
    See DIAZ CAPO, Marylín
848. CAPRONI, Giorgio
    "Prayer" (tr. by Erasmo G. Gerato). [AnthNEW] (3) 91, p. 7.
    "Preghiera." [AnthNEW] (3) 91, p. 6.
849. CARBAUGH, Amie
    "The Father Mask." [BellR] (14:2) Fall 91, p. 5.
CARBEAU, Mitchell Les
    See LesCARBEAU, Mitchell
850. CARDEA, Caryatis
    "Class" (to white feminists of class privilege). [SinW] (43/44) Sum 91, p. 293-294.
851. CARDENAL, Ernesto
    "The Parrots." [NoDaQ] (59:4) Fall 91, p. 80.
    "Somoza Watching the Statue of Somoza in Somoza Stadium" (tr. by Rob Mitchell
        Moore). [MidAR] (12:1) 91, p. 160.
852. CARDENAS, Esteban L.
    "Vigia." [LindLM] (10:1) Ja-Mr 91, p. 6.
853. CARDENAS, Rene F.
    "Everywhere Blooms." [CapeR] (26:2) Fall 91, p. 50.
854. CARDIFF, Gladys
    "Beautiful Zombies." [PoetryE] (32) Fall 91, p. 55-56.
855. CARDILLO, Joe
    "Brook." [Lactuca] (14) My 91, p. 16.
    "Distances." [Lactuca] (14) My 91, p. 13.
    "Lake." [Lactuca] (14) My 91, p. 17-18.
    "Pond." [Lactuca] (14) My 91, p. 14-15.
856. CARDONA, Jacinto Jesús
    "Pan Dulce." [MidAR] (12:1) 91, p. 21-22.
857. CAREY, Barbara
    "Out There." [MalR] (95) Sum 91, p. 24-25.
    "The Power of Memory." [MalR] (95) Sum 91, p. 26-27.
    "A Wire Kiss." [MalR] (95) Sum 91, p. 28-29.
858. CAREY, Michael
    "Ashes." [LaurelR] (25:1) Wint 91, p. 92.
    "Aunt Fannie" (for Ellen West). [Plain] (12:1) Fall 91, p. 34-35.
    "By the Rising Waters" (for Sharon and Toby Parriott). [OnTheBus] (8/9) 91, p.
        42-43.
    "The Crazy Quilt of Spoons" (for Kenneth Gee). [LaurelR] (25:1) Wint 91, p. 93.
    "Daredevil" (for Jim Skahill). [Plain] (12:2) Wint 91, p. 14.
    "The Graves of the Old French Settlement Near Hamburg" (for Faye Brown). [PoetC]
        (22:3) Spr 91, p. 30-31.
    "The Home Place" (for Helen, Maeve, Andrew and Fionnuala). [PoetC] (22:3) Spr
        91, p. 32-33.
    "The Music of Icicles" (for Frosty and Mary Lou Foster). [LaurelR] (25:1) Wint 91,
        p. 90-91.
    "The Poet in Nature." [OnTheBus] (8/9) 91, p. 42.
859. CAREY, Sarah
    "Trespass." [ContextS] (2:2) 91, p. 19.
860. CAREY, Tom
    "World Without End." [NewAW] (7) Spr 91, p. 60-61.
861. CARLILE, Henry
    "Dead Reckoning." [OhioR] (47) 91, p. 104-105.
    "The Death of Casanova." [Shen] (41:2) Sum 91, p. 45-46.
    "Train Whistles in the Wind and Rain." [Shen] (41:2) Sum 91, p. 43-45.
862. CARLISLE, Jim
    "Aviary." [Writer] (104:3) Mr 91, p. 20.
    "December Leaf Burning." [Writer] (104:6) Je 91, p. 26.
863. CARLISLE, Thomas John
    "To Spangle Our Darkness." [ChrC] (108:35) 4 D 91, p. 1138.
864. CARLSEN, Ioanna
    "Fat." [Poetry] (157:6) Mr 91, p. 319.

"Mornings, Writing." [PoetryE] (32) Fall 91, p. 131-132.
"Nothing" (Excerpt). [Nimrod] (35:1) Fall-Wint 91, p. 72.
"On a Dead Dog." [Chelsea] (51) 91, p. 20-21.
"Two Songs from a Car." [Poetry] (159:3) D 91, p. 135.

865. CARLSON, Barbara Siegel
"At the Train Station" (tr. of the French tr. by Marc Alyn of Srecko Kosovel).
        [InterPR] (17:1) Spr 91, p. 73.
"Coral." [MidwQ] (33:1) Aut 91, p. 53.
"For Michael." [SpoonRQ] (16:3/4) Sum-Fall 91, p. 94-95.
"For the Undying" (in memory of Fred Diengott d. 1989). [Poem] (65) My 91, p.
        4-5.
"It's Not You" (tr. of the French tr. by Marc Alyn of Srecko Kosovel). [InterPR]
        (17:1) Spr 91, p. 77.
"The Karstic Village" (tr. of the French tr. by Marc Alyn of Srecko Kosovel).
        [InterPR] (17:1) Spr 91, p. 75, 77.
"Our Hunchback." [Poem] (65) My 91, p. 3.
"Song of the Humble" (tr. of the French tr. by Marc Alyn of Srecko Kosovel).
        [InterPR] (17:1) Spr 91, p. 73.
"Standing in the Falls." [Poem] (65) My 91, p. 1-2.
"Visiting the Toledo Zoo." [MidwQ] (33:1) Aut 91, p. 54-55.

866. CARLSON, Paula
"When I Get to Be a Teacher." [PikeF] (10) Spr 91, p. 20.

867. CARLSON, R. S.
"Awash." [HolCrit] (28:1) F 91, p. 19.
"Cove." [CapeR] (26:1) Spr 91, p. 18.
"Emergency Room." [HawaiiR] (16:1, #34) Wint 91-92, p. 79.
"Love Artist." [HawaiiR] (16:1, #34) Wint 91-92, p. 78.
"Shelter Cove." [TexasR] (11:1/2) Spr-Sum 90, p. 38-39.
"Waiting to Say Amen." [CapeR] (26:1) Spr 91, p. 16-17.

CARLTON, R. S.
        See CARLSON, R. S.

868. CARMAN, Bliss
"Low Tide on Avon" ("Avon" Version: June 1886). [CanLit] (129) Sum 91, p. 134,
        136.
"Low Tide on Grand-Pré" ("Grand-Pré" Version: March 1887). [CanLit] (129) Sum
        91, p. 135, 137.

869. CARMELL, Pamela
"Amnesia" (tr. of Gloria Fuertes). [AmerPoR] (20:2) Mr-Ap 91, p. 4.
"The Beggar with Those Eyes" (tr. of Gloria Fuertes). [AmerPoR] (20:2) Mr-Ap 91,
        p. 3.
"Circus" (tr. of Gloria Fuertes). [AmerPoR] (20:2) Mr-Ap 91, p. 3.
"Doves" (tr. of Gloria Fuertes). [AmerPoR] (20:2) Mr-Ap 91, p. 4.
"Every Night I Kill Myself a Little" (tr. of Gloria Fuertes). [AmerPoR] (20:2) Mr-Ap
        91, p. 4.
"Here I Am Exposed Like Everyone" (tr. of Gloria Fuertes). [AmerPoR] (20:2)
        Mr-Ap 91, p. 4.
"Notice" (tr. of Gloria Fuertes). [AmerPoR] (20:2) Mr-Ap 91, p. 4.
"Our Chains Wear Us Down" (tr. of Gloria Fuertes). [AmerPoR] (20:2) Mr-Ap 91, p.
        4.
"Profession: Ghost" (tr. of Gloria Fuertes). [AmerPoR] (20:2) Mr-Ap 91, p. 3.
"Pyramid of Enmity" (tr. of Gloria Fuertes). [AmerPoR] (20:2) Mr-Ap 91, p. 3.
"We Must Try Not to Lie" (tr. of Gloria Fuertes). [AmerPoR] (20:2) Mr-Ap 91, p. 3.

870. CARMONA, José A.
"Salvacion." [LindLM] (10:1) Ja-Mr 91, p. 6.

871. CARNEY, Belinda
"The Gift: for Robert and Gregory." [PottPort] (13:1) Spr 91, p. 43-45.
"Halifax and the White Whale." [PottPort] (13:1) Spr 91, p. 46-47.
"The Swim (Augustine's Mound, Red Bank, N.B.)" (for Julia). [PottPort] (13:1) Spr
        91, p. 41-42.

872. CARNEY, Jeanne
"Return to Bedrock." [SingHM] (19) 91, p. 9.

873. CARNEY, Rob
"April." [BellArk] (7:2) Mr-Ap 91, p. 1.
"I Saw the Weather Laughing." [BellArk] (7:2) Mr-Ap 91, p. 11.
"The Shoes of the Fisherman's Wife Are Some Jive-Ass Slippers." [BellArk] (7:3)
        My-Je 91, p. 11.

"Summer." [BellArk] (7:4) Jl-Ag 91, p. 1.
874. CAROLINE (Homeless author, Berkeley, CA, Submitted by Sydney Bell)
"Close to My Heart." [PoetryUSA] (23) Sum 91, p. 20.
"Lillian." [PoetryUSA] (23) Sum 91, p. 20.
CAROLIS, Cristen di
    See DiCAROLIS, Cristen
875. CARPELAN, Bo
"Like Sitting" (tr. by Thomas and Vera Vance). [Vis] (37) 91, p. 28.
"The Storytellers" (tr. by Thomas and Vera Vance). [Vis] (37) 91, p. 28.
876. CARPENTER, Bogdana
"The Abyss of Mr. Cogito" (tr. of Zbigniew Herbert, w. John Carpenter).
    [NewYorker] (67:1) 25 F 91, p. 36.
"Hakeldama" (tr. of Zbigniew Herbert, w. John Carpenter). [ParisR] (33:121) Wint
    91, p. 38-39.
"Meditations of Mr. Cogito on Redemption" (tr. of Zbigniew Herbert, w. John
    Carpenter). [ParisR] (33:121) Wint 91, p. 40.
"Mr. Cogito and Pop" (tr. of Zbigniew Herbert, w. John Carpenter). [ParisR]
    (33:121) Wint 91, p. 41-42.
"Mr. Cogito Laments the Pettiness of Dreams" (tr. of Zbigniew Herbert, w. John
    Carpenter). [NewYorker] (67:9) 22 Ap 91, p. 34.
"Mr. Cogito Looks at a Deceased Friend" (tr. of Zbigniew Herbert, w. John
    Carpenter). [NewYorker] (67:24) 5 Ag 91, p. 38.
"Mr. Cogito Thinks of Returning to the City Where He Was Born" (tr. of Zbigniew
    Herbert, w. John Carpenter). [NewYorker] (67:1) 25 F 91, p. 36.
"Ordinariness of the Soul" (tr. of Zbigniew Herbert, w. John Carpenter). [ParisR]
    (33:121) Wint 91, p. 37.
"Sometimes Mr. Cogito Receives Strange Letters" (tr. of Zbigniew Herbert, w. John
    Carpenter). [NewYorker] (67:1) 25 F 91, p. 36.
877. CARPENTER, J. D.
"Corn Road." [CanLit] (130) Aut 91, p. 105.
878. CARPENTER, John
"The Abyss of Mr. Cogito" (tr. of Zbigniew Herbert, w. Bogdana Carpenter).
    [NewYorker] (67:1) 25 F 91, p. 36.
"Hakeldama" (tr. of Zbigniew Herbert, w. Bogdana Carpenter). [ParisR] (33:121)
    Wint 91, p. 38-39.
"Meditations of Mr. Cogito on Redemption" (tr. of Zbigniew Herbert, w. Bogdana
    Carpenter). [ParisR] (33:121) Wint 91, p. 40.
"Mr. Cogito and Pop" (tr. of Zbigniew Herbert, w. Bogdana Carpenter). [ParisR]
    (33:121) Wint 91, p. 41-42.
"Mr. Cogito Laments the Pettiness of Dreams" (tr. of Zbigniew Herbert, w. Bogdana
    Carpenter). [NewYorker] (67:9) 22 Ap 91, p. 34.
"Mr. Cogito Looks at a Deceased Friend" (tr. of Zbigniew Herbert, w. Bogdana
    Carpenter). [NewYorker] (67:24) 5 Ag 91, p. 38.
"Mr. Cogito Thinks of Returning to the City Where He Was Born" (tr. of Zbigniew
    Herbert, w. Bogdana Carpenter). [NewYorker] (67:1) 25 F 91, p. 36.
"Ordinariness of the Soul" (tr. of Zbigniew Herbert, w. Bogdana Carpenter). [ParisR]
    (33:121) Wint 91, p. 37.
"Sometimes Mr. Cogito Receives Strange Letters" (tr. of Zbigniew Herbert, w.
    Bogdana Carpenter). [NewYorker] (67:1) 25 F 91, p. 36.
879. CARPENTER, Linda
"Borrowed Sight." [Event] (20:2) Sum 91, p. 42-43.
"Dog." [Event] (20:2) Sum 91, p. 40.
"Food Bank of the Gods." [Event] (20:2) Sum 91, p. 38-39.
"The Locked Ward." [Event] (20:2) Sum 91, p. 41.
"The Pictures of Blue Women." [Event] (20:2) Sum 91, p. 44.
"Skeletons." [Event] (20:2) Sum 91, p. 43.
880. CARPENTER, Sandra
"Frisco, 1899." [Writer] (104:6) Je 91, p. 26.
881. CARPER, Thomas
"Even the Weariest River" (Recollecting Swinburne's "Garden of Proserpine").
    [Poetry] (158:1) Ap 91, p. 14.
882. CARR, Dan
"The Ox Coming Out of the Sea." [ConnPR] (10:1) 91, p. 35-36.
"Standing in the Trees." [ConnPR] (10:1) 91, p. 31-32.
883. CARR, Mary Jo
"Dear Lawrence Ferlinghetti." [EmeraldCR] (4) 91, p. 72.

884. CARRASCO, Jennifer McCabe
"Glass Heart." [Vis] (35) 91, p. 46.
885. CARRINO, Michael
"New York Movie — 1939." [PoetryE] (31) Spr 91, p. 139.
886. CARROLL, Paul
"Psalm 11." [AmerPoR] (20:5) S-O 91, p. 42.
"Psalm 13." [AmerPoR] (20:5) S-O 91, p. 42.
887. CARROLL, Rhoda
"Those Christmas Lights, That Trompe L'Oeil Ridge." [GreenMR] (NS 5:1) Sum-Fall
91, p. 118-119.
888. CARRUTH, Hayden
"At His Last Gig." [OhioR] (47) 91, p. 22.
"None." [AmerPoR] (20:4) Jl-Ag 91, p. 18.
"Questions." [AmerPoR] (20:4) Jl-Ag 91, p. 18.
"Ray." [AmerPoR] (20:4) Jl-Ag 91, p. 19.
"Sex." [SewanR] (99:4) Fall 91, p. 535-536.
"Woodsmoke at 68." [AmerPoR] (20:4) Jl-Ag 91, p. 18.
889. CARRUTH, Joe-Anne
"Half Note for Hayden." [Poetry] (157:5) F 91, p. 265.
"Muse Tune." [Poetry] (157:5) F 91, p. 266.
"To the Tune of Fats Waller's 'Rockin' Chair'." [Poetry] (157:5) F 91, p. 267.
890. CARSON, Anne
"Short Talks." [Descant] (22:3, #74) Fall 91, p. 12-22.
891. CARSON, Jeffrey
"Good Friday" (tr. of Odysseus Elytis). [ConnPR] (10:1) 91, p. 9.
"Holy Thursday" (tr. of Odysseus Elytis). [ConnPR] (10:1) 91, p. 8.
"In Place of a Dream" (tr. of Odysseus Elytis). [ConnPR] (10:1) 91, p. 7.
"Variations on a Sunbeam" (a 7-poem sequence: selections: I-II, VII, tr. of Odysseus
Elytis, w. Nikos Sarris). [ConnPR] (10:1) 91, p. .10-13.
892. CARSON, Jo
"I Am Asking You to Come Back Home." [Spirit] (11) 91, p. 277.
893. CARSON, Josephine
"Old Sweetness." [PoetryUSA] (22) Spr 91, p. 14.
894. CARSON, Meredith
"Beach Bottles." [ChamLR] (8-9) Spr-Fall 91, p. 55.
"Dusting Books." [BambooR] (50/51) Spr-Sum 91, p. 316-317.
"Light." [BambooR] (50/51) Spr-Sum 91, p. 315.
"Maribou Stork." [BambooR] (52) Fall 91, p. 21.
"Shipwrecks." [BambooR] (52) Fall 91, p. 22.
895. CARTAGENA, Julio
"Betrayal." [Americas] (19:1) Spr 91, p. 61.
"Welcome." [Americas] (19:1) Spr 91, p. 60.
896. CARTER, Anne Babson
"Domov." [Nat] (253:1) 1 Jl 91, p. 26.
"A Killing Frost." [Nat] (252:17) 6 My 91, p. 604.
897. CARTER, David
"Fried Diamondback." [CinPR] (21) Spr 90, p. 35.
"Letter from Cincinnati" (for A.C.). [CinPR] (22) Spr 91, p. 32.
"The Unbroken Wood" (Selection: "The Star"). [CinPR] (22) Spr 91, p. 33.
898. CARTER, Ellin
"Poem for Woodville, Mississippi." [Kalliope] (13:3) 91, p. 13-14.
"Talisman." [Kalliope] (13:3) 91, p. 15.
899. CARTER, Jared
"Between." [SoDakR] (29:4) Wint 91, p. 69.
"Cistern." [SoDakR] (29:4) Wint 91, p. 66-68.
"The Mummers." [Vis] (36) 91, p. 42-43.
"Portrait Studio." [NewL] (58:1) Fall 91, p. 104.
"Train Station." [SoDakR] (29:4) Wint 91, p. 64-65.
"Transmigration." [Farm] (8:2) Fall-Wint 91-92, p. 18-21.
900. CARTER, Jefferson
"Bodysurfing (Puerto Vallarta)." [CarolQ] (43:2) Wint 91, p. 30.
901. CARTER, John
"This Poem Takes No Prisoners." [PoetryUSA] (23) Sum 91, p. 10.
902. CARTER, Martin
"Bitter Wood." [GrahamHR] (14) Spr 91, p. 45.
"The Great Dark." [GrahamHR] (14) Spr 91, p. 44.

"Our Number." [GrahamHR] (14) Spr 91, p. 46.
903. CARTER, Michael
"Locker Room." [JamesWR] (9:1) Fall 91, p. 6.
CARTER, Roberta Rennert
See RENNERT-CARTER, Roberta
CARTERET, Mark de
See DeCARTERET, Mark
904. CARVER, Robert
"Plums." [PlumR] (1) Spr-Sum 91, p. 5-8.
"She." [PlumR] (1) Spr-Sum 91, p. 10.
"Untitled: At the end, there is always a street, blocked off." [PlumR] (1) Spr-Sum 91,
p. 9.
905. CASAL, Victor del
"Emotions." [NegC] (11:3) 91, p. 18-19.
"Lovers." [NegC] (11:3) 91, p. 20.
906. CASAS, Walter de las
"La Caridad del Cobre." [LindLM] (10:3) Jl-S 91, p. 8.
907. CASE, Sandra
"First Affair." [NorthStoneR] (10) Fall 91-Wint 92, p. 127.
"Remnants." [NorthStoneR] (10) Fall 91-Wint 92, p. 127.
908. CASELLA, Robert Rantes
"My Barber." [OnTheBus] (8/9) 91, p. 49-50.
"Poem: I am hardly a poet, but." [OnTheBus] (8/9) 91, p. 47-49.
"So Much American Poetry Is Just Pure Shit." [OnTheBus] (8/9) 91, p. 44, 47.
909. CASEY, Brenda
"Death" (tr. of Gisèle Prassinos, w. Elizabeth Hahn). [Vis] (36) 91, p. 49.
"Hélène" (tr. of Pierre Morency, w. Elizabeth Hahn). [Vis] (36) 91, p. 12.
910. CASEY, Crysta
"Loneliness." [BellArk] (7:6) N-D 91, p. 6.
"Prayer." [BellArk] (7:5) S-O 91, p. 5.
"Questions to Be Asked and Answered." [BellArk] (7:5) S-O 91, p. 5.
CASEY, David Lahoma
See LAHOMA-CASEY, David
911. CASEY, Deb
"To Let the Morning In" (for rs and her parents). [Calyx] (13:2) Sum 91, p. 117.
912. CASEY, Susan M.
"Celebration." [EmeraldCR] (3) 91, c1990, p. 37.
"Summer Job Syndrome." [EmeraldCR] (3) 91, c1990, p. 102-103.
913. CASKIE, Mark
"At the Hatchery." [GreensboroR] (50) Sum 91, p. 60-61.
914. CASSELLS, Cyrus
"Hoop Dance." [Ploughs] (17:2/3) Fall 91, p. 229-231.
"Hummingbird Medicine." [JamesWR] (8:3) Spr 91, p. 11.
"Life Indestructible" (for Etty Hillesum, 1914-1943). [KenR] (NS 13:4) Fall 91, p.
32-39.
"Sethe's Poem" (for Toni Morrison, in homage to *Beloved*). [IndR] (14:3) Fall 91, p.
28.
"Soul, Make a Path Through Shouting" (Little Rock, Arkansas, 1957). [IndR] (14:3)
Fall 91, p. 29-30.
915. CASSELMAN, Barry
"You and I Received a Grievance Early." [NorthStoneR] (10) Fall 91-Wint 92, p.
131.
916. CASSIAN, Nina
"Parallel Destinies" (tr. by Naomi Lazard). [Trans] (25) Spr 91, p. 204-208.
917. CASSIDY, Tom
"Ride the Bus in Fur." [Sidewalks] (1) Aug 91, p. 50-51.
918. CASSITY, Turner
"L'Alba Separà dalla Luce L'Ombra." [Salm] (90/91) Spr-Sum 91, p. 78-79.
"But Will the Uniforms Be Pretty?" [Salm] (90/91) Spr-Sum 91, p. 80-81.
"It Wasn't God Who Made Honky Tonk Angels, It Was Henrik Ibsen." [LullwaterR]
(3:1) Fall 91, p. 8-9.
"Là-bas on Russian Hill." [LullwaterR] (3:1) Fall 91, p. 14.
"Rondo on the Rio Negro." [MassR] (32:1) Spr 91, p. 98-99.
919. CASSUTT, Glenda
"Firstborn." [SingHM] (19) 91, p. 34.
"From the Cloister." [BellR] (14:2) Fall 91, p. 17.

920. CASTAÑARES, Tony
    "At the Buffalo Jump Museum." [OnTheBus] (8/9) 91, p. 52.
    "Situation Ethics." [OnTheBus] (8/9) 91, p. 51-52.
    "Syllogistic Reflection on the Poet's Mortality." [OnTheBus] (8/9) 91, p. 51.
921. CASTILLO, Amelia del
    "Promesa." [LindLM] (10:1) Ja-Mr 91, p. 15.
922. CASTLEBURY, John
    "Yankee Doodle Dharma." [HeavenB] (9) Wint-Spr 91-92, p. 38.
923. CASTON, Anne
    "Codicil" (for my children). [FreeL] (8) Aut 91, p. 19.
    "Stumbling into a Pecan Grove at Midnight Just After the Lynching." [FreeL] (8) Aut
        91, p. 18.
    "Survivors." [FreeL] (8) Aut 91, p. 16.
    "Untitled: In the end, she welcomed death." [FreeL] (8) Aut 91, p. 17.
924. CATINA, Ray
    "Fire." [FreeL] (7) Spr 91, p. 30.
    "Too Late." [FreeL] (7) Spr 91, p. 31.
925. CATLETT, Greg
    "New Birth." [PoetryUSA] (22) Spr 91, p. 18.
926. CATLIN, Alan
    "Another Woman on the Edge of the Time." [Mildred] (4:2/5:1) 91, p. 57.
    "By the Numbers." [Mildred] (4:2/5:1) 91, p. 59.
    "The End." [Mildred] (4:2/5:1) 91, p. 60.
    "He Was Like" (from "Bar Wars"). [Bogg] (64) 91, p. 53.
    "Holidays Suck." [SlipS] (11) 91, p. 41.
    "A Phoenix Rising from the Ashes." [Mildred] (4:2/5:1) 91, p. 58.
    "True Confessions Time after Last Call" (from "Bar Wars"). [Bogg] (64) 91, p. 53.
    "Uneasy Riders." [SlipS] (11) 91, p. 41-42.
927. CATRON, Douglas M.
    "The Better Gardener." [OxfordM] (7:2) Fall-Wint 91, p. 22.
    "The Mountain Kami." [OxfordM] (7:2) Fall-Wint 91, p. 20.
    "The Physician Reflects on Bones and Hearts." [OxfordM] (7:2) Fall-Wint 91, p. 21.
928. CAUDILL, Carla
    "The Air Hangs Full and Expectant on Harvest Moon Morning." [HopewellR] (1991)
        91, p. 13.
    "Climbing Ring Mountain." [DogRR] (10:2) Fall-Wint 91, p. 18.
929. CAUFIELD, Tom
    "Butter-Scotch." [WormR] (31:4, #124) 91, p. 118.
    "Danny." [WormR] (31:4, #124) 91, p. 116-117.
    "Downtown, Memphis." [ChironR] (10:3) Aut 91, p. 7.
    "Going Down to a Gay Bar, Honey." [ChironR] (10:3) Aut 91, p. 7.
    "I Used to Drink Mad Dog Twentytwenty." [WormR] (31:4, #124) 91, p. 116.
    "Larry." [WormR] (31:4, #124) 91, p. 119-120.
    "Last Night." [WormR] (31:4, #124) 91, p. 118-119.
    "Our Cat." [WormR] (31:4, #124) 91, p. 120.
    "Star Dog." [WormR] (31:4, #124) 91, p. 115.
    "Washington Story." [WormR] (31:4, #124) 91, p. 117-118.
930. CAULFIELD, Carlota
    "Limbo." [LindLM] (10:1) Ja-Mr 91, p. 5.
931. CAVADINI, John
    "In August on Atlantic Street." [Comm] (118:14) 9 Ag 91, p. 460.
    "May Is the Military Month." [Comm] (118:11) 1 Je 91, p. 362.
    "Rio Grande." [Comm] (118:18) 25 O 91, p. 612.
932. CAVAFY, Constantine
    "Nero's Warning" (tr. by Edouard Roditi). [Talisman] (6) Spr 91, p. 132.
    "The Tomb of the Grammarian Lysias" (tr. by Edouard Roditi). [Talisman] (6) Spr
        91, p. 132.
933. CAVALCANTI, Guido
    "Rima IV" (tr. into Spanish by Juan Gelman). [Inti] (34/35) Otoño 91-Primavera 92,
        p. 252.
    "Rima XVIII" (tr. into Spanish by Juan Gelman). [Inti] (34/35) Otoño 91-Primavera
        92, p. 252.
    "Rima XXII" (tr. into Spanish by Juan Gelman). [Inti] (34/35) Otoño 91-Primavera
        92, p. 253.
    "Rima LXII" (tr. into Spanish by Juan Gelman). [Inti] (34/35) Otoño 91-Primavera
        92, p. 253.

934. CAVALIERI, Grace
   "The Devoted Dead." [EmeraldCR] (3) 91, c1990, p. 14-15.
   "For Our Readers." [US1] (24/25) Spr 91, p. 15.
935. CAVALLI, Patrizia
   "Outside, in Fact, There Wasn't Any Change" (tr. by Judith Baumel). [NewYorker]
      (66:49) 21 Ja 91, p. 56.
936. CAVERLY, Dan
   "A View from Signal Hill." [PacificR] (10) 91-92, p. 33-34.
937. CAYLOR, Duane K.
   "The Way of Geese." [Hellas] (2:2) Fall 91, p. 272.
   "What Ptolemy Knew." [SoCoast] (10) Fall 91, p. 41.
938. CEA, Jose Roberto
   "Instructions for Interpreting a Stela" (tr. by Ann Neelon). [MidAR] (12:1) 91, p.
      163.
939. CECCHINI, Yvonne
   "The Shaft." [Sidewalks] (1) Aug 91, p. 54.
940. CECIL, Richard
   "Concerto for Voice, Guitar and Darkness." [ColR] (NS 17:2) Fall-Wint 90, p.
      124-125.
   "Fame." [ColR] (NS 17:2) Fall-Wint 90, p. 126-127.
   "Homage to Benvenuto Cellini." [Crazy] (40) Spr 91, p. 15-17.
   "Metro Tire" (After refusing to attend my eighth-grade reunion). [Crazy] (40) Spr 91,
      p. 18-20.
941. CEDRINS, Peteris
   "Ponck Hockie." [Sulfur] (11:2 #29) Fall 91, p. 141.
   "Three TVs ablaze in a single unveiled body at Margaret & Tower" (for Jeffra, 1991.
      12. May, reading Trakl). [Sulfur] (11:2 #29) Fall 91, p. 142-143.
942. CELAC, Sergiu
   "Breath" (tr. of Daniela Crasnaru, w. Adam J. Sorkin). [Poetry] (159:1) O 91, p. 28.
   "Certainty" (tr. of Ioana Ieronim, w. Adam J. Sorkin). [LitR] (35:1) Fall 91, p. 34.
   "The Ironical Poet" (tr. of Nicolae Prelipceanu, w. Adam J. Sorkin). [LitR] (35:1)
      Fall 91, p. 35-36.
   "Lethal Dose" (tr. of Daniela Crasnaru, w. Adam J. Sorkin). [Poetry] (159:1) O 91,
      p. 28.
   "Oath of Allegiance" (tr. of Ioana Ieronim, w. Adam J. Sorkin). [LitR] (35:1) Fall 91,
      p. 34.
   "So?!" (tr. of Mircea Dinescu, w. Adam J. Sorkin). [LitR] (35:1) Fall 91, p. 36.
   "To Her Highness Our Landlady for a More Just Apportioning of the Body" (tr. of
      Mircea Dinescu, w. Adam J. Sorkin). [LitR] (35:1) Fall 91, p. 36.
943. CELAN, Paul
   "Fugue of Death." [Crazy] (41) Wint 91, p. 86-87.
944. CELL, Kate
   "The History of Women in Space." [MidAR] (12:1) 91, p. 109-110.
945. CENDRARS, Blaise
   "The Prose of the Trans-Siberian and of Little Jeanne of France" (tr. by Ron Padgett).
      [Sulfur] (11:1, #28) Spr 91, p. 15-29.
   "Unnatural Sonnets" (tr. by Ron Padgett). [Sulfur] (11:1, #28) Spr 91, p. 30-32.
946. CERDA, Susana
   "Patrimonies" (tr. by Ernesto Livon Grosman and Molly Weigel). [AmerPoR] (20:5)
      S-O 91, p. 37-38.
947. CERRO, Emeterio
   "Risa Noche Despierta Electra." [Nuez] (3:7) 91, p. 24.
CERTAIN, Miguel Falquez
   See FALQUEZ-CERTAIN, Miguel
948. CERVANTES, Pedro
   "Dignity." [PikeF] (10) Spr 91, p. 18.
949. CERVO, Nathan
   "The Beast." [SpiritSH] (56) Spr-Sum 91, p. 11.
   "Dolphin." [SpiritSH] (56) Spr-Sum 91, p. 8.
   "Hair Too Scant to Be Braided." [SpiritSH] (56) Spr-Sum 91, p. 9.
   "Opposite the Bananas." [SpiritSH] (56) Spr-Sum 91, p. 10.
   "The Sublime." [SpiritSH] (56) Spr-Sum 91, p. 5.
950. CÉSPEDES, Jorge Enrique de
   "Laberinto." [Nuez] (3:8/9) 91, p. 20.
951. CHABEREK, Ed
   "Dependency (A Rambler's Story)." [Plain] (12:2) Wint 91, p. 9.

"A Revelation." [Plain] (12:1) Fall 91, p. 13.
952. CHABROWSKI, Tadeusz
"Instead of a Sonnet" (tr. by Basia and Grazyna Drabik). [HeavenB] (9) Wint-Spr
91-92, p. 8.
"A Letter from a Grandmother in Greenpoint to Her Granddaughter in Poland" (tr. by
Basia and Grazyna Drabik). [HeavenB] (9) Wint-Spr 91-92, p. 8.
953. CHACE, Joel
"Swimmers." [Pembroke] (23) 91, p. 68.
954. CHADWICK, Jerah
"The Butcher Tree." [BellR] (14:1) Spr 91, p. 19.
"The Life to Come." [NewYorkQ] (46) 91, p. 82.
955. CHALLENDER, Craig
"Bill." [HampSPR] Wint 91, p. 54-55.
"Continental Drift" (for Michael Waters). [SycamoreR] (3:1) Wint 91, p. 16-17.
956. CHALMER, Judith (Judy)
"Brooding Over My Breasts." [PassN] (12:2) Wint 91, p. 28.
"Personal to Kaplan." [CimR] (97) O 91, p. 49-50.
"Spider Stalking." [SpoonRQ] (16:3/4) Sum-Fall 91, p. 17-18.
957. CHALMERS, Emily
"Vanity" (tr. of Chrisula Stefanescu, w. the author). [Iowa] (21:2) Spr-Sum 91, p.
43.
958. CHAMBERLAIN, Cara
"A Trip Through the West." [VirQR] (67:1) Wint 91, p. 57-60.
959. CHAMBERS, John Allan
"Disenchantment." [NegC] (11:1) 91, p. 88.
960. CHAMLEE, Ken
"Renaissance." [Crucible] (27) Fall 91, p. 48.
961. CHAMP, Robert
"Going Down to Die" (A "found" poem, from an interview with William Rose, 80, an
ex-slave of Edisto Island, South Carolina). [Callaloo] (14:3) Sum 91, p.
686-687.
962. CHAMPAGNE, John
"Three Married Men." [ChironR] (10:3) Aut 91, p. 46.
963. CHAN, Brian
"Pegasus." [GrahamHR] (14) Spr 91, p. 41.
964. CHANDLER, Joyce A.
"Abuse of Substance." [ChironR] (10:3) Aut 91, p. 16.
"Alcoholics Anonymous: Poodles & Noodles." [ChironR] (10:3) Aut 91, p. 16.
"Awareness." [ChironR] (10:3) Aut 91, p. 16.
"Brooklyn Beat." [ChironR] (10:3) Aut 91, p. 16.
"Catching Cockroaches." [ChironR] (10:3) Aut 91, p. 16.
"Epitaph-Like" (In Color). [HawaiiR] (15:3, #33) Fall 91, p. 45.
"Nuclear Fission." [HawaiiR] (15:3, #33) Fall 91, p. 44.
965. CHANDLER, Tom
"And Even the Dead Shall See." [InterPR] (15:1) Spr 89, p. 111.
"Artemus Bailey." [HawaiiR] (15:2, #32) Spr 91, p. 35.
"Climbing Through the Night." [InterPR] (15:1) Spr 89, p. 110.
"For No Reason." [HawaiiR] (15:2, #32) Spr 91, p. 36.
"James Madison Chandler, 1962." [CapeR] (26:1) Spr 91, p. 21.
"Monkey on the Ceiling." [HawaiiR] (15:2, #32) Spr 91, p. 39-40.
"Photos of the Dead." [InterPR] (15:1) Spr 89, p. 112.
"Watching the Wings." [CapeR] (26:1) Spr 91, p. 22.
966. CHANDONNET, Ann Fox
"In Velvet." [Spirit] (11) 91, p. 143-148.
"Quirks, Quarks." [Elf] (1:4) Wint 91, p. 42.
967. CHANDRA, G. S. Sharat
"Identities." [PoetC] (22:2) Wint 91, p. 40.
"The Swedish Embassy, Bangladesh." [MissouriR] (14:1) 91, p. 153.
968. CHANEY, Joseph
"Orange." [BlackWR] (18:1) Fall-Wint 91, p. 96.
969. CHANG, Ana
"Untitled: Who is your mother?" [CapilR] (2:6/7) Fall 91, p. 66-67.
970. CHANG, David
"Prediction" (Winner, Michael Jasper Gioia Award). [Sequoia] (34:1) Spr 91, p. 101.
971. CHANG, Diana
"A Way of the Withdrawn." [ChamLR] (8-9) Spr-Fall 91, p. 119.

972. CHANG, Janice M.
  "These Street." [PacificR] (9) 91, p. 24.
973. CHANG, Lisbeth
  "Belated Autumn, the Remains of Roanoke." [HarvardA] (125:5) My 91, p. 15.
  "Ingonish." [HarvardA] (126:1) Fall 91, p. 19.
  "Postcard from a False Sense of Arrival." [HarvardA] (126:1) Fall 91, p. 31.
  "Thaumaturgy." [HarvardA] (126:1) Fall 91, p. 26.
CHANG, Soo Ko
  See KO, Chang Soo
974. CHAPMAN, Robin S.
  "Portuguese Men-of-War." [PassN] (12:1) Sum 91, p. 30.
  "Some Kind of Meeting." [SouthernPR] (31:1) Spr 91, p. 39-40.
  "Where Did We Come From? What Are We? Where Are We Going?" (— Gauguin
      painting, 1898). [PoetL] (86:3) Fall 91, p. 13.
975. CHAPPELL, Fred
  "The Small Goodbye." [SnailPR] (1:1) Spr 91, p. 1.
976. CHAR, René
  "The Black Stags" (from "Lascaux," tr. by Gustaf Sobin). [Talisman] (6) Spr 91, p.
      8.
  "Invitation" (tr. by Gustaf Sobin). [Talisman] (6) Spr 91, p. 10.
  "One and the Other" (tr. by Gustaf Sobin). [Talisman] (6) Spr 91, p. 8.
  "Slow Down Construction" (with André Breton and Paul Éluard, tr. by Jeanie
      Puleston Fleming and Christopher Merrill). [AmerPoR] (20:3) My-Je 91, p.
      25-30.
  "That It Resume" (tr. by Gustaf Sobin). [Talisman] (6) Spr 91, p. 9.
  "The Trout" (from "Four Fascinators," tr. by Gustaf Sobin). [Talisman] (6) Spr 91,
      p. 8.
977. CHARACH, Ron
  "Brenda, It's OK!" [Grain] (19:1) Spr 91, p. 52-53.
  "A Cosmology for Captive Elephants." [Arc] (27) Aut 91, p. 54.
  "Hellen on Fire." [PraF] (12:3 #56) Aut 91, p. 84-85.
  "Lal Bahadur Shastri" (Response to "Save the Clerihew" appeal). [BostonR] (16:5) O
      91, p. 24.
  "What did George Bush intendo" (Response to "Save the Clerihew" appeal).
      [BostonR] (16:5) O 91, p. 24.
978. CHARLES, Clayton E. (Clayton Edward)
  "Clown and Fox Dream Together (#3)." [SmPd] (28:3, #83) Fall 91, p. 7.
  "Clown and Fox Dream Together (#7)." [SmPd] (28:3, #83) Fall 91, p. 8.
  "Clown Hears the Joking." [SoCoast] (11) Wint 91, p. 10.
979. CHARLES, Faustin
  "The Red Robber." [GrahamHR] (14) Spr 91, p. 83.
980. CHARLO, Victor
  "Sky e Me, Eagle." [PoetryE] (32) Fall 91, p. 44.
981. CHARLTON, Elizabeth
  "Campo de Confianza (Field of Faith)." [SoCoast] (11) Wint 91, p. 44-45.
982. CHARNEY, Lena L. (Lena London)
  "Dry Spell." [Elf] (1:3) Fall 91, p. 39.
  "The Flamenco Dancers." [Gypsy] (17) 91, p. 13.
983. CHASE, Alfonso
  "Raison d'Etre" (tr. by John Oliver Simon). [ArtfulD] (20/21) 91, p. 59.
984. CHASE, Jeanne
  "I Saw My Parents Dance." [WillowR] Spr 91, p. 22-23.
985. CHASE, Naomi Feigelson
  "Red July" (3rd Prize, 5th Annual Contest). [SoCoast] (10) Fall 91, p. 28.
  "Venus Rising." [SouthernPR] (31:2) Fall 91, p. 57-58.
986. CHATTMAN, Elmo
  "Beads of Wax." [Sequoia] (34:1) Spr 91, p. 10.
987. CHAVEZ, Lisa D.
  "In a Motel in Anchorage." [SingHM] (19) 91, p. 30-31.
988. CHAZAL, Malcolm de
  "Transformations of Water" (from "Sens-Plastique," tr. by Irving Weiss). [Archae]
      (1) Fall 90, p. 43-45.
989. CHEN, Maiping
  "A Local Accent" (tr. of Bei Dao, w. Bonnie S. McDougall). [ManhatR] (6:1) Fall 91,
      p. 8.

"My Country" (tr. of Bei Dao, w. Bonnie S. McDougall). [ManhatR] (6:1) Fall 91, p. 11.
"Old Snow" (tr. of Bei Dao, w. Bonnie S. McDougall). [ManhatR] (6:1) Fall 91, p. 6.
"A Picture" (for Tiantian's fifth birthday, tr. of Bei Dao, w. Bonnie S. McDougall). [ManhatR] (6:1) Fall 91, p. 9.
"Prague" (tr. of Bei Dao, w. Bonnie S. McDougall). [ManhatR] (6:1) Fall 91, p. 4.
"Rebel" (tr. of Bei Dao, w. Bonnie S. McDougall). [ManhatR] (6:1) Fall 91, p. 12.
"Terminal Illness" (tr. of Bei Dao, w. Bonnie S. McDougall). [ManhatR] (6:1) Fall 91, p. 7.
"To Memory" (tr. of Bei Dao, w. Bonnie S. McDougall). [ManhatR] (6:1) Fall 91, p. 10.
"Untitled: He opens wide a third eye" (tr. of Bei Dao, w. Bonnie S. McDougall). [ManhatR] (6:1) Fall 91, p. 5.

990. CHEN, Ming Hua
"Death" (tr. by Cao Wei). [GreenMR] (NS 4:2) Wint-Spr 91, p. 28.
"Departure" (tr. by Hua Fengmao). [GreenMR] (NS 4:2) Wint-Spr 91, p. 29.
"Metal" (tr. by Cao Wei). [GreenMR] (NS 4:2) Wint-Spr 91, p. 26.
"The Ward." [AmerPoR] (20:5) S-O 91, p. 21.
"The Ward" (tr. by Cao Wei). [GreenMR] (NS 4:2) Wint-Spr 91, p. 27.

CHEN, Rajandaye Ramkissoon
See RAMKISSOON-CHEN, Rajandaye

991. CHEN, Willie
"San Fernando, South Coast City." [GrahamHR] (14) Spr 91, p. 82.

CHENG, Gu
See GU, Cheng

992. CHERKOVSKI, Neeli
"Fire." [PoetryUSA] (22) Spr 91, p. 7.

993. CHERNOFF, Maxine
"Breasts" (from "Leap Year Day," Another Chicago Press, 1990). [ClockR] (7:1/2) 91-92, p. 116-117.
"The Shoe and the City." [DenQ] (25:4) Spr 91, p. 14.
"Subtraction." [DenQ] (25:4) Spr 91, p. 16.
"Token." [AntR] (49:2) Spr 91, p. 250-251.
"Wash." [AntR] (49:2) Spr 91, p. 249.
"The Woman Who Straddled the Globe." [DenQ] (25:4) Spr 91, p. 15.

994. CHERNOW, Ann
"Fortune." [NewYorkQ] (45) 91, p. 77.

995. CHERRY, Kelly
"Alzheimer's." [Colum] (15) 90, p. 40.
"At a Resort by the Black Sea." [LullwaterR] (3:1) Fall 91, p. 60.
"Between Earth and Sky." [LaurelR] (25:1) Wint 91, p. 99.
"The Blossoming" (the centurion speaks). [LullwaterR] (2:2) Spr 91, p. 7.
"Bubbling." [Colum] (15) 90, p. 41-42.
"Crackers." [LaurelR] (25:1) Wint 91, p. 98.
"Glasnost." [Boulevard] (5:3/6:1, #15/16) Spr 91, p. 177.
"In the End." [MidwQ] (32:2) Wint 91, p. 183.
"Nobody's Fool." [FourQ] (5:1) Spr 91, p. 10.
"Prayer." [AmerS] (60:4) Aut 91, p. 588.

996. CHESS, Richard
"The Idea of the Holy." [TampaR] (4) 91, p. 54.
"Nothing But Pleasure." [TampaR] (4) 91, p. 53.
"The Story Goes On." [AmerPoR] (20:1) Ja-F 91, p. 6.

997. CHETWYND, Richard
"Drought." [CapeR] (26:2) Fall 91, p. 24.

998. CHI, Moku
"Desert Sesshin 1990." [HawaiiR] (15:3, #33) Fall 91, p. 33.

999. CHICHETTO, J. Wm.
"To a Poet with Writer's Block." [Poem] (66) N 91, p. 50.

CH'IEN, T'ao
See T'AO, Ch'ien

1000. CHILDERS, Henry
"Selling the Farm" (near Linden, Indiana). [NorthStoneR] (10) Fall 91-Wint 92, p. 71.

1001. CHILDERS, Joanne
"The Butterfly Fishermen of Janitzia." [Kalliope] (13:3) 91, p. 33.

"The Coastal Clouds." [Kalliope] (13:3) 91, p. 32-33.
1002. CHILDRESS, Jesse
"Babe." [PoetryUSA] (22) Spr 91, p. 17.
1003. CHILDRESS, William
"The Jack and Jill Affair." [CharR] (17:1) Spr 91, p. 41.
1004. CHIN, Justin
"Tied." [BambooR] (52) Fall 91, p. 23-25.
1005. CHIN, Marilyn
"Tienanmen, the Aftermath" (for the Chinese Democratic Movement). [KenR] (NS
    13:4) Fall 91, p. 191.
"Turtle Soup" (for Ben Huang). [KenR] (NS 13:4) Fall 91, p. 192.
CHIN, Yung
    See YUNG, Chin
1006. CHING, Laureen
"China Song." [SoDakR] (29:3 part 2) Aut 91, p. 33.
CHISATO, Oe no
    See OE no CHISATO (ca. 825)
1007. CHITTICK, William C.
"The Lovers' Tailor's Shop" (tr. of Jalaloddin Rumi, w. Peter Lamborn Wilson).
    [Talisman] (6) Spr 91, p. 30.
1008. CHITWOOD, Michael
"Dogwood." [SouthernPR] (31:1) Spr 91, p. 73-74.
"Grease." [MissR] (19:3) 91, p. 166-167.
"Juke." [OhioR] (46) 91, p. 48-56.
"Photographs from the Mountain Empire." [VirQR] (67:3) Sum 91, p. 490-493.
"Shenandoah Valley Triptych." [MalR] (94) Spr 91, p. 83-85.
"Singing Hymns to Go to Sleep." [SouthernPR] (31:2) Fall 91, p. 22-23.
"The Story As Told by Ice." [Thrpny] (44) Wint 91, p. 17.
"Weave Room." [PoetryE] (32) Fall 91, p. 105.
"When Country People Come In." [PoetryE] (32) Fall 91, p. 103-104.
CH'IUNG-CH'IUNG, Yuan
    See YUAN, Ch'iung-Ch'iung
1009. CHOE, Wolhee
"A Lullaby — at Night with Insomnia" (tr. of Hyon-Jong Chong, w. Peter Fusco).
    [ArtfulD] (20/21) 91, p. 63.
1010. CHOI, Kathleen T.
"City Sermon." [Comm] (118:8) 19 Ap 91, p. 254.
"A Firm Hand." [HawaiiR] (15:2, #32) Spr 91, p. 156.
1011. CHONG, Hyon-Jong
"A Lullaby — at Night with Insomnia" (tr. by Wolhee Choe and Peter Fusco).
    [ArtfulD] (20/21) 91, p. 63.
1012. CHOO, Mary E.
"Amulets." [PraF] (12:4) Wint 91-92, p. 74-75.
1013. CHORLTON, David
"Architecture." [DogRR] (10:1) Sum 91, p. 26.
"Correspondences." [WebR] (15) Spr 91, p. 10-12.
"Followed." [Lactuca] (14) My 91, p. 49.
"Leaving the City." [Contact] (10:59/60/61) Spr 91, p. 40.
"Marcos de Niza." [DustyD] Je 91, p. 4.
"El Mirage." [Pembroke] (23) 91, p. 110.
"A Notice to Aliens Preparing to Cross the Desert, As Posted by U.S. Authorities at
    the Border." [Lactuca] (14) My 91, p. 50.
"The Picture Postcards." [FreeL] (7) Spr 91, p. 29.
"The Road." [Lactuca] (14) My 91, p. 49.
"Second Lives" (for Philip C. Curtis). [PoetL] (86:4) Wint 91-92, p. 9-11.
1014. CHOU, Ping
"Ways of Looking at a Poet." [LitR] (34:2) Wint 91, p. 216-217.
1015. CHOUDHURI, Pradip
"Gol Park." [MoodySI] (24/25/26) Spr 91, p. 24.
"Gol Park." [RedBass] (15) 91, p. 45-47.
1016. CHOYCE, Lesley
"August 5: Three Fathom Harbour to Hockey Island." [JINJPo] (13:2) Aut 91, p.
    6-7.
"Beauty." [JINJPo] (13:2) Aut 91, p. 4.
"Left Hand in the Pocket." [JINJPo] (13:2) Aut 91, p. 5.
"Wordsworth's Socks" (Grasmere, May 14, 1983). [JINJPo] (13:2) Aut 91, p. 3.

1017. CHRISTAKOS, Margaret
    "Flushing." [PoetryC] (12:1) D 91, p. 10.
    "Superstar." [PoetryC] (12:1) D 91, p. 10.
1018. CHRISTENSEN, Donna
    "I'm Falling Out of Love With You." [JamesWR] (9:1) Fall 91, p. 10.
1019. CHRISTENSEN, Faye D.
    "Shadowed Thoughts." [EngJ] (80:1) Ja 91, p. 92.
1020. CHRISTGAU, John
    "Reading the Bible at Supper." [RagMag] (9:2) 91, p. 57.
1021. CHRISTIANSON, Kevin
    "Blizzard." [CrabCR] (7:3) 91, p. 25.
1022. CHRISTIE, A. V.
    "Mute Poet." [PlumR] (1) Spr-Sum 91, p. 27.
1023. CHRISTINA, Martha
    "Bird in My Hand." [PassN] (12:1) Sum 91, p. 6.
CHRISTINA, S. J. di
    See DiCHRISTINA, S. J.
1024. CHRISTOPHER, Nicholas
    "Cancer Ward." [NewRep] (205:11) 9 S 91, p. 41.
    "Drinking Cold Water on the Acropolis at Lindos." [NewRep] (204:8) 25 F 91, p.
        34.
    "The First Day of Spring." [WestHR] (45:3) Aut 91, p. 253.
    "Green Chair on a Fire Escape in Autumn." [NewRep] (205:23) 2 D 91, p. 38.
    "In the Year of the Comet." [GrandS] (10:4, #40) 91, p. 116-117.
    "The Morning of the Funeral." [Colum] (17) Fall 91, p. 51-52.
    "On the Peninsula." [NewYorker] (67:30) 16 S 91, p. 88.
    "The Pocketwatch." [Nat] (252:11) 25 Mr 91, p. 392.
    "Reading the Sunday Comics, Summer, 1963." [NewYorker] (67:44) 23 D 91, p.
        36-37.
    "Xanía, 1983." [WestHR] (45:2) Sum 91, p. 89.
1025. CHRYSTOS
    "I Am Not Your Princess" (especially for Dee Johnson). [SinW] (43/44) Sum 91, p.
        273-274.
1026. CHUN, Jacqueline
    "An Art Student's Attempt to Recreate the Egg Tempera Wood Panel of St. Anthony
        Tempted by a Heap of Gold." [HawaiiR] (16:1, #34) Wint 91-92, p. 111-112.
    "Baisan." [HawaiiR] (16:1, #34) Wint 91-92, p. 113.
1027. CHURCH, Todd
    "Anatomical Specimen." [Contact] (10:59/60/61) Spr 91, p. 49.
1028. CHURCHILL, Charlotte
    "Poetry in Plastic." [MoodySI] (24/25/26) Spr 91, p. 46.
1029. CHUTE, Robert (Robert M.)
    "At the Theater in Athens." [LitR] (34:2) Wint 91, p. 253.
    "Aunt Anne Puts the Cat Out for the Last Time." [BelPoJ] (42:2) Wint 91-92, p. 30.
    "Casting Off." [CapeR] (26:1) Spr 91, p. 15.
    "Moonlighting." [BelPoJ] (42:2) Wint 91-92, p. 31.
    "Near Ice-out." [LitR] (35:1) Fall 91, p. 88.
    "The View at Drummore Bay: Phippsburg, Me." [Ascent] (15:3) Spr 91, p. 34.
1030. CIAVONNE, Carol
    "Main Street Saloon." [BellR] (14:1) Spr 91, p. 57.
1031. CIMON, Anne
    "Waiting in the Cabane for the Schoolbus." [AntigR] (85/86) Spr-Sum 91, p. 188.
1032. CINTI, Renata
    "In the Eighty-Fifth Century" (tr. of Friedrich Ani). [ArtfulD] (20/21) 91, p. 38-39.
1033. CIRINO, Leonard (Leonard J.)
    "Little Powers." [Paint] (18:36) Aut 91, p. 31.
    "An Old Loneliness." [Sparrow] (58) Jl 91, p. 15.
    "The Poet." [Sparrow] (58) Jl 91, p. 14.
    "Scrimshaw for the Stone Carver." [DustyD] (2:1) Ja 91, p. 8.
    "White Stone Boat." [Sparrow] (58) Jl 91, p. 13.
1034. CITINO, David
    "Air Raid Over Bari." [NewEngR] (13:3/4) Spr-Sum 91, p. 119-121.
    "The Art of Hummingbirds." [RiverS] (33) 91, p. 17.
    "The History of Facial Expressions." [PoetC] (22:3) Spr 91, p. 23-24.
    "Homage to Our Lady of the Strays." [LaurelR] (25:1) Wint 91, p. 10-11.
    "Homage to the Corn." [MidAR] (11:1) 91, p. 97-98.

"Homage to the Undertaker." [TexasR] (11:1/2) Spr-Sum 90, p. 17.
"In a Clearing Hacked Out of the Rain Forest, Sister Mary Appassionata Lectures the Young Cannibals." [SouthwR] (76:4) Aut 91, p. 496-497.
"Just Before Dawn I Greet the Paperboy, Who Brings News of the World" (For the students of Beijing, June 1989). [SoDakR] (29:1) Spr 91, p. 157-160.
"Meditation on the Three Forms of Tongue Protrusion" (after Desmond Morris). [CinPR] (22) Spr 91, p. 56-57.
"New Poem." [WestB] (29) 91, p. 12.
"On the Whiteness of Cocaine." [NewEngR] (13:3/4) Spr-Sum 91, p. 118-119.
"Painting the Stars." [SoDakR] (29:3 part 2) Aut 91, p. 77.
"The Reckoning." [PoetC] (22:3) Spr 91, p. 20-22.
"Returning to the Field." [ColR] (NS 18:1) Spr-Sum 91, p. 58-59.
"The Revolt." [LaurelR] (25:1) Wint 91, p. 6.
"Salt." [Poetry] (157:6) Mr 91, p. 320-321.
"Senior Class Play: A Man for All Seasons." [CentR] (35:1) Wint 91, p. 79-80.
"Sister Mary Appassionata Announces the Winning Project in the Eighth-Grade Science Fair: 'Our Good Friends the Insects'." [CreamCR] (15:1) Spr 91, p. 61-62.
"Sister Mary Appassionata, On Hearing that Kant Disregarded the Sense of Smell Purely on Aesthetic Grounds." [OhioR] (47) 91, p. 110-111.
"Sister Mary Appassionata to the Chamber of Commerce: Remains of Earliest Female Hominid Discovered in Ruins of Atlantis under Lake Erie." [LaurelR] (25:1) Wint 91, p. 8-9.
"Sister Mary Appassionata to the Eighth Grade Boys and Girls on the First Degree of Lust: *Visus*, Sight." [LaurelR] (25:1) Wint 91, p. 7.
"Those Old Songs." [CharR] (17:1) Spr 91, p. 76.
"The Threat of Allergies in the Afterlife." [CentR] (35:1) Wint 91, p. 78-79.
"U2 Concert, Cleveland Municipal Stadium." [ColR] (NS 18:1) Spr-Sum 91, p. 60-61.
"Winter." [Poetry] (159:3) D 91, p. 125-126.
CLAIR, Richard J. la
    See LaCLAIR, Richard J.
1035. CLAIRMAN, Gary Phillip
    "For Lynn MacGillivray." [Dandel] (18:1) Spr-Sum 91, p. 17.
1036. CLAMAN, Elizabeth
    "A Nightmare for Every Day of the Month of My Birth." [PoetryUSA] (23) Sum 91, p. 5.
1037. CLAMPITT, Amy
    "'Eighty-Nine'" (In memory of Andrew Meyers). [NewEngR] (13:3/4) Spr-Sum 91, p. 212-215.
    "Green." [Nimrod] (34:2) Spr-Sum 91, p. 40.
    "Inferno" (Canto IX-X, tr. of Dante). [Antaeus] (67) Fall 91, p. 51-60.
    "North Fork." [NewYorker] (67:22) 22 Jl 91, p. 26.
1038. CLARK, Donna
    "Noises from Quiet Rooms." [CapilR] (2:6/7) Fall 91, p. 174-178.
1039. CLARK, Jeanne E.
    "That Summer, Joe, and Prison" (Prison officials assign hostage value numbers to employees). [Vis] (35) 91, p. 20, 22.
1040. CLARK, Jenny
    "Remembrance." [HiramPoR] (50) Spr-Sum 91, p. 6.
1041. CLARK, Jim
    "Harvest Moon." [Poem] (65) My 91, p. 42.
    "Last Summer When the Moon." [Poem] (65) My 91, p. 40.
    "Letter." [Pig] (17) 91, p. 53.
    "Letter to Ciardi: April 3, 1986." [Pig] (17) 91, p. 75.
    "The Life You've Led." [Poem] (65) My 91, p. 41.
    "Lights." [Poem] (65) My 91, p. 44.
    "The Man Who Walks Out" (for Mark Shearon). [NegC] (11:1) 91, p. 101-102.
    "Moonrise at Dale Hollow Lake." [SouthernPR] (31:1) Spr 91, p. 20.
    "My Father, Singing." [Poem] (65) My 91, p. 43.
    "No Love Lost" (for J.D.). [NegC] (11:1) 91, p. 103-104.
    "Once More, the Night." [NegC] (11:1) 91, p. 99-100.
1042. CLARK, Mary
    "Our Philosophy Professor Used the Table as an Example of the Physical World." [PassN] (12:1) Sum 91, p. 4.

"The Small, Black Velvet Purse with the Rhinestone Clasp." [PassN] (12:1) Sum
   91, p. 4.
1043. CLARK, Michael
   "Sleep." [DustyD] Ap 91, p. 8.
1044. CLARK, Naomi
   "Birder." [GreensboroR] (51) Wint 91-92, p. 22-23.
   "The Cave." [IndR] (14:2) Spr 91, p. 32-33.
   "The Comics." [PoetryNW] (32:4) Wint 91-92, p. 10-11.
   "Dreams of Places Briefly Known." [Interim] (10:1) Spr-Sum 91, p. 14.
   "The Fourth Eye." [ColR] (NS 18:1) Spr-Sum 91, p. 56-57.
   "The Glass Eye." [NoDaQ] (59:3) Sum 91, p. 139-140.
   "Needle's Eye." [NoDaQ] (59:3) Sum 91, p. 141.
   "Omens." [PoetryNW] (32:4) Wint 91-92, p. 6-9.
   "Potato, Grandmother, & Bear." [PoetryNW] (32:4) Wint 91-92, p. 9-10.
   "The Rose-Tree." [SoDakR] (29:2) Sum 91, p. 49.
   "Sisters." [Timbuktu] (6) Spr 91, p. 40.
   "The Turtle Queen." [LaurelR] (25:2) Sum 91, p. 32-33.
   "The Weasel." [Timbuktu] (6) Spr 91, p. 39.
1045. CLARK, Ron
   "Frogs and Wasps." [PraF] (12:2 #55) Sum 91, p. 35.
   "Oregon Rain." [PraF] (12:2 #55) Sum 91, p. 33.
   "So Frigging Blue." [PraF] (12:2 #55) Sum 91, p. 34.
1046. CLARK, Suzanne Underwood
   "What Did You Find in the Sea?" [LullwaterR] (3:1) Fall 91, p. 27.
1047. CLARK, Tom
   "Baby Book Fate Dream." [NewAW] (8/9) Fall 91, p. 13.
1048. CLARK, William
   "Horus" (tr. of Gérard de Nerval). [WilliamMR] (29) 91, p. 19.
1049. CLARKE, Duncan
   "Fish." [US1] (24/25) Spr 91, p. 14.
1050. CLARKE, George Elliott
   "Valliere's Les Negres Blancs de l'Amerique du Nord." [Quarry] (40:1/2) Wint-Spr
      91, p. 28.
   "War Measures." [Quarry] (40:1/2) Wint-Spr 91, p. 29.
   "The Wisdom of Shelley." [PottPort] (13:1) Spr 91, p. 29.
1051. CLARKE, Katharine
   "Dead Fish." [AntigR] (84) Wint 91, p. 10.
1052. CLARKE, Peter E.
   "The Letter to Halfon." [Pig] (17) 91, p. 55.
1053. CLARVOE, Jennifer
   "Thou Art Translated" (For Anthony). [Pequod] (32) 91, p. 68-72.
1054. CLARY, Killarney
   "All day I felt like saying goodbye." [Ploughs] (17:4) Wint 91-92, p. 91.
   "For every demon thrown out, seven return calling me home." [Ploughs] (17:4) Wint
      91-92, p. 92.
   "I've had a number of rosy days, desert-cloud sunrises, windy dusks." [Ploughs]
      (17:4) Wint 91-92, p. 93.
   "The sound was not unlike a drum." [Ploughs] (17:4) Wint 91-92, p. 90.
   "There's no song strained enough tonight." [Shiny] (6) Spr-Sum 91, p. 63-67.
   "An unlikely one will guide me, I won't know I'm being helped." [Ploughs] (17:4)
      Wint 91-92, p. 94.
1055. CLAUSEN, Jan
   "Critical Habitat." [Contact] (10:59/60/61) Spr 91, p. 25.
   "Gusher." [Contact] (10:59/60/61) Spr 91, p. 24.
1056. CLEARY, Michael
   "Aunt Sara and the 4-Letter Word." [TexasR] (12:1/2) Spr-Sum 91, p. 92.
   "Aunt Sara and the Tattoo." [TexasR] (12:1/2) Spr-Sum 91, p. 93.
1057. CLEARY, Suzanne
   "Acting." [PoetryNW] (32:1) Spr 91, p. 34-35.
   "The Docks of New York" (After the film by Josef von Sternberg, 1928). [BelPoJ]
      (41:4) Sum 91, p. 2-3.
   "Friday Meditation." [OhioR] (47) 91, p. 18-19.
   "Looking at the Pictures." [NoDaQ] (59:3) Sum 91, p. 135-136.
   "Madame Beaumont." [PoetryNW] (32:1) Spr 91, p. 33-34.
   "Summary of 15 Years" (for Mark Hurlbert). [OhioR] (47) 91, p. 20-21.

1058. CLEAVELAND, Ruzha
  "After the Exhibit About Jews in Yugoslavia We Went to Dinner" (tr. of Josip Osti).
    [CimR] (96) Jl 91, p. 23.
  "Aha" (tr. of Josip Osti). [CimR] (96) Jl 91, p. 24.
  "'At Nightfall' — Wine Gurgles, Soup Steams, White Salvos Float Up or Down"
    (tr. of Josip Osti). [CimR] (96) Jl 91, p. 24.
  "First We Fed the Pigeons Around Preseran Memorial, Afterwards Fish Under the
    Triple Bridge" (tr. of Josip Osti). [InterPR] (17:2) Fall 91, p. 78.
  "I Kissed Your Brow as We Looked at an Exhibit About Jews on Yugoslavian Soil"
    (tr. of Josip Osti). [CimR] (96) Jl 91, p. 23.
  "We Resurrected the Dead in Family Albums" (tr. of Josip Osti). [InterPR] (17:2)
    Fall 91, p. 79.
  "We Sleep Shoulders into Each Other, So Gazing at the Same View" (tr. of Josip
    Osti). [InterPR] (17:2) Fall 91, p. 79.
  "When Grandpa Disappeared During the War, Grandma Fell in Love with Jesus" (tr.
    of Josip Osti). [InterPR] (17:2) Fall 91, p. 78.
1059. CLEMENTS, Susan
  "Deer." [MidAR] (11:1) 91, p. 55-56.
  "Discovering Columbus." [NoDaQ] (59:4) Fall 91, p. 21.
  "Guadirikiri." [MidAR] (11:1) 91, p. 51-52.
  "Otsiningo Powwow." [MidAR] (11:1) 91, p. 49-50.
  "Panther." [MidAR] (11:1) 91, p. 53-54.
  "Wooden Indian." [MidAR] (11:1) 91, p. 48.
1060. CLEVE, Emerald
  "Midnight Hill." [SpiritSH] (56) Spr-Sum 91, p. 27.
  "Old Man." [SpiritSH] (56) Spr-Sum 91, p. 26.
  "Voices." [SpiritSH] (56) Spr-Sum 91, p. 28.
1061. CLEVER, Bertolt
  "Halftime." [FourQ] (4:2) Fall 90, p. 45.
  "My Gods." [ChangingM] (23) Fall-Wint 91, p. 13.
1062. CLEWELL, David
  "Do Not Disturb." [NewEngR] (14:1) Fall 91, p. 134-136.
1063. CLIFF, Michelle
  "Down the Shore." [AmerV] (25) Wint 91, p. 28-30.
1064. CLIFTON, Harry
  "Crossing the Appenines." [Stand] (33:1) Wint 91, p. 37.
1065. CLIFTON, Lucille
  "Tree of Life" (10 poems) [AmerPoR] (20:2) Mr-Ap 91, p. 28-29.
1066. CLINE, Ed
  "On Juli's Jeans" (With apologies to R.H.). [Northeast] (5:4) Sum 91, p. 19.
1067. CLINE, Helen
  "Determinate Flaws." [Nimrod] (34:2) Spr-Sum 91, p. 24.
  "Goatpoem." [Nimrod] (34:2) Spr-Sum 91, p. 23.
  "Graphics." [Nimrod] (34:2) Spr-Sum 91, p. 25.
1068. CLINTON, Michelle T.
  "Don't Wanna Lose Your Love." [Rohwedder] (6) Sum-Fall 91, p. 26.
  "I'm Dating." [OnTheBus] (8/9) 91, p. 53.
  "It's them flat flat flat freeways." [Rohwedder] (6) Sum-Fall 91, p. 26.
1069. CLINTON, Robert
  "The Corn Doll." [WillowS] (28) Sum 91, p. 9.
  "A Pattern of Authority." [WillowS] (28) Sum 91, p. 10.
  "The Tithe." [WillowS] (28) Sum 91, p. 8.
  "The Two Birds." [WillowS] (28) Sum 91, p. 7.
1070. CLOVER, Joshua
  "Blue Louise." [AmerPoR] (20:5) S-O 91, p. 28.
  "Photograph: 'Two Black Musicians'." [DenQ] (26:2) Fall 91, p. 8-9.
CLUE, Charlotte de
  See DeCLUE, Charlotte
1071. CLUFF, Mike
  "Innocent Repetition." [BlackBR] (13) Spr-Sum 91, p. 12.
1072. CLUNY, Claude Michel
  "Le Bal a la Mer." [SoCoast] (10) Fall 91, p. 7.
  "The Sea Ball" (tr. by Frederick Lowe). [SoCoast] (10) Fall 91, p. 6.
1073. CLUTE, Mitchell
  "Fringe on the Coat, Coat on the Fringe." [SouthernPR] (31:1) Spr 91, p. 38-39.

1074. COATES, Chris
 "My Favorite Words from James Merrill's *New Yorker* Poem October 23, 1989,
 Page 50." [FreeL] (8) Aut 91, p. 8.
 "Peep Show." [Parting] (4:1) Sum 91, p. 28.
1075. COBERLY, Lenore McComas
 "I Thought." [Nimrod] (34:2) Spr-Sum 91, p. 26.
 "We Stand." [Nimrod] (34:2) Spr-Sum 91, p. 26.
1076. COBIN, Susan
 "For Marie." [SilverFR] (20) Spr 91, p. 14-15.
 "November in California." [SilverFR] (20) Spr 91, p. 13.
1077. COBO BORDA, Juan Gustavo
 "Epilogue" (tr. by Garry Emmons). [Agni] (33) 91, p. 217.
 "Henry James" (tr. by Garry Emmons). [Agni] (33) 91, p. 213.
 "In Nerval's Pocket" (tr. by Garry Emmons). [Agni] (33) 91, p. 215.
 "A Little Pregnant Woman Walks in the Park" (tr. by Garry Emmons). [Agni] (33)
 91, p. 216.
 "Self-criticism" (tr. by Garry Emmons). [Agni] (33) 91, p. 214.
1078. COCHRAN, Brian
 "The Man at the Door." [LaurelR] (25:2) Sum 91, p. 76-77.
1079. COCHRAN, Jo Whitehorse
 "Suka Wakan: Holy Dog Horse." [PoetryE] (32) Fall 91, p. 9-10.
 "Tundra Dream" (for Collette). [PoetryE] (32) Fall 91, p. 11-12.
1080. COCHRAN, Leonard
 "Bonsai." [Atlantic] (267:5) My 91, p. 78.
1081. COCHRANE, Guy R.
 "A Pass." [WormR] (31:4, #124) 91, p. 134.
 "Possessive." [WormR] (31:4, #124) 91, p. 134.
 "Your Static." [WormR] (31:4, #124) 91, p. 134.
1082. COCHRANE, Mark
 "The Bean Is a Girl." [PraF] (12:4) Wint 91-92, p. 29-30.
 "I Prefer the Talk of Women." [PraF] (12:4) Wint 91-92, p. 28-29.
 "The Wood Louse." [Grain] (19:1) Spr 91, p. 108.
 "Work." [AntigR] (84) Wint 91, p. 7.
1083. COCHRANE, Shirley G.
 "In the Bishop's Garden." [PoetL] (86:3) Fall 91, p. 14.
1084. COCTEAU, Jean
 "Alchemists" (tr. by Charles Guenther). [AmerPoR] (20:5) S-O 91, p. 24.
 "Angel Back" (tr. by Charles Guenther). [AmerPoR] (20:5) S-O 91, p. 26.
 "Broken Poem for Picasso" (tr. by Charles Guenther). [AmerPoR] (20:5) S-O 91, p.
 26.
 "He Slew" (tr. by Charles Guenther). [AmerPoR] (20:5) S-O 91, p. 25.
 "Heart's Gravity" (tr. by Charles Guenther). [AmerPoR] (20:5) S-O 91, p. 25.
 "Homage to Goya" (tr. by Charles Guenther). [AmerPoR] (20:5) S-O 91, p. 24.
 "Homage to Velasquez" (tr. by Charles Guenther). [AmerPoR] (20:5) S-O 91, p. 24.
 "I Must" (tr. by Charles Guenther). [AmerPoR] (20:5) S-O 91, p. 25.
 "In Prison" (tr. by Charles Guenther). [AmerPoR] (20:5) S-O 91, p. 25.
 "The King of the World" (tr. by Charles Guenther). [AmerPoR] (20:5) S-O 91, p.
 24.
 "A Living Body" (tr. by Charles Guenther). [AmerPoR] (20:5) S-O 91, p. 26.
 "Malaga" (tr. by Charles Guenther). [AmerPoR] (20:5) S-O 91, p. 26.
 "Noël" (tr. by Charles Guenther). [AmerPoR] (20:5) S-O 91, p. 25.
 "Noon" (tr. by Charles Guenther). [AmerPoR] (20:5) S-O 91, p. 26.
 "Romance" (tr. by Charles Guenther). [AmerPoR] (20:5) S-O 91, p. 26.
 "Sometimes Cruel Time" (tr. by Charles Guenther). [AmerPoR] (20:5) S-O 91, p.
 24.
1085. COE, Dina
 "Approach." [US1] (24/25) Spr 91, p. 6.
1086. COFER, Judith Ortiz
 "An Early Mystery." [KenR] (NS 13:4) Fall 91, p. 19-20.
 "The Game." [IndR] (14:3) Fall 91, p. 42-43.
 "The Latin Deli." [Americas] (19:1) Spr 91, p. 70-71.
 "A Legion of Dark Angels." [KenR] (NS 13:4) Fall 91, p. 20-21.
 "The Lesson of the Tongue." [KenR] (NS 13:4) Fall 91, p. 21-22.
 "Lessons of the Past." [IndR] (14:3) Fall 91, p. 44-45.
 "That Old Time." [Americas] (19:1) Spr 91, p. 72.

1087. COFFEY, Kathy
"Poetry Reading Signed for the Imaginatively Impaired." [ChrC] (108:24) 21-28 Ag
91, p. 776.
1088. COFFMAN, Lisa
"The Products of Hog" (Based on "Sketches and Statistics of Cincinnati," 1851).
[RiverC] (12:1) Fall 91, p. 53.
"The Simple Day." [RiverC] (12:1) Fall 91, p. 54-55.
1089. COGGESHALL, Rosanne
"Harmonies." [Shen] (41:4) Wint 91, p. 90.
1090. COGSWELL, Fred
"Entente Cordiale." [Quarry] (40:1/2) Wint-Spr 91, p. 30-31.
"G17024." [CanLit] (128) Spr 91, p. 28.
1091. COHEN, Andrea
"Ode to the Noodle." [Ploughs] (17:2/3) Fall 91, p. 232-233.
1092. COHEN, Bruce
"New Grass." [Elf] (1:2) Sum 91, p. 31.
"The Wrong Coat Home." [GreensboroR] (51) Wint 91-92, p. 64.
1093. COHEN, Elizabeth
"Articulating the Paw." [HopewellR] (1991) 91, p. 8.
"Ice Storm." [HopewellR] (1991) 91, p. 17.
"There Is Still Some Doubt But." [HopewellR] (1991) 91, p. 19.
1094. COHEN, Marc
"Bald Eagle." [HangL] (58) 91, p. 18-20.
1095. COHEN, Miriam A.
"Peace." [ChironR] (10:4) Wint 91, p. 22.
1096. COHEN, Phoebe
"Pamela Smart" (Response to "Save the Clerihew" appeal). [BostonR] (16:3/4)
Je-Ag 91, p. 33.
1097. COHEN, Robert
"Sleep." [PaintedHR] (1) Ja 91, p. 20.
1098. COHN, Jim
"Arches." [HeavenB] (9) Wint-Spr 91-92, p. 32-33.
"George Washington Bridge, Lower Level, Clear Day." [HangL] (59) 91, p. 21-25.
1099. COKINOS, Christopher
"Tradition." [AntigR] (85/86) Spr-Sum 91, p. 85-86.
1100. COLE, Henri
"40 Days and 40 Nights." [NewYorker] (67:38) 11 N 91, p. 44.
"Horoscope." [PlumR] (1) Spr-Sum 91, p. 65-66.
"The Look of Things." [Antaeus] (67) Fall 91, p. 170.
"Tarantula." [Colum] (17) Fall 91, p. 176-177.
1101. COLE, Norma
"The Icelandic Consul" (fig. 3, Paris, 1990, tr. of Emmanuel Hocquard). [Avec]
(4:1) 91, p. 68-69.
"M.S. 1544" (tr. of Jacqueline Risset). [Talisman] (6) Spr 91, p. 40-41.
"Theater" (Editions Unes 1990, excerpts, tr. of Jean Frémon). [Avec] (4:1) 91, p.
85-92.
"La Traduition Commence" (Christian Bourgois, Paris, 1978. Selection: "Bite," tr.
of Jacqueline Risset). [Avec] (4:1) 91, p. 78-79.
"Y K 61" (tr. of Jacqueline Risset). [Talisman] (6) Spr 91, p. 41.
1102. COLE, Peter
"Love" (Selections: 20-21, 26, tr. of Aharon Shabtai). [Agni] (33) 91, p. 42-44.
"Lowell" (Selections: 6, 9, 86, tr. of Harold Schimmel). [Talisman] (6) Spr 91, p.
133-134.
"On the Death and Existence of Isaac His Brother" (after the Hebrew of Samuel
Hanagid, also known as Ismail Ibn Nagrela, 993-1056 CE). [Conjunc] (17)
91, p. 310-318.
"Pacific Jam." [Talisman] (7) Fall 91, p. 36-37.
"Stocks and Bonds." [Talisman] (7) Fall 91, p. 37-38.
1103. COLE, Robert
"Firelighter." [SoCoast] (10) Fall 91, p. 46.
"Headlines: Husband killed in Falkland's campaign." [Verse] (8:1) Spr 91, p. 102.
1104. COLEMAN, Alexander
"Puerta de Golpe, Cuba" (tr. of Heberto Padilla, w. Alastair Reid). [NewYRB]
(38:13) 18 Jl 91, p. 39.
"The Rose, Its Specter" (*Rilke*, from "A Fountain, A House of Stone," tr. of
Heberto Padilla, w. Alastair Reid). [PartR] (58:4) Fall 91, p. 690.

1105. COLEMAN, John
　　　"Exodus." [SouthernPR] (31:2) Fall 91, p. 62-63.
　　　"The Myth of Embracing." [HampSPR] Wint 91, p. 48.
　　　"The Rushing of Sundays." [LitR] (35:1) Fall 91, p. 91.
1106. COLEMAN, Mary Ann
　　　"Driving to Your House on a Spring Night in Indiana." [LullwaterR] (2:2) Spr 91, p.
　　　　68-69.
　　　"Fishing in Sequins" (for Judi). [EngJ] (80:1) Ja 91, p. 92.
　　　"On Watching the Martian Chronicles." [LullwaterR] (2:2) Spr 91, p. 56.
1107. COLEMAN, Victor
　　　"Going Home" (for Mari-Lou). [Quarry] (40:1/2) Wint-Spr 91, p. 40-41.
　　　"Nostalgia for the Sixties." [Quarry] (40:1/2) Wint-Spr 91, p. 38-39.
1108. COLEMAN, Wanda
　　　"American Sonnet (2)" (for Robert Mezey). [NewAW] (7) Spr 91, p. 7.
　　　"Black Madonna." [Rohwedder] (6) Sum-Fall 91, p. 8.
　　　"Chuck Man." [Rohwedder] (6) Sum-Fall 91, p. 9.
　　　"Confessions Noir." [Rohwedder] (6) Sum-Fall 91, p. 9.
　　　"Unfinished Ghost Story (3)." [NewAW] (7) Spr 91, p. 8.
　　　"The Waif of Echo Park." [Spirit] (11) 91, p. 164-165.
1109. COLES, Katharine
　　　"Drought Year." [NewRep] (205:25) 16 D 91, p. 46.
　　　"Sex as a Trope." [WeberS] (8:1) Spr 91, p. 49-53.
1110. COLGIN, Paul David
　　　"Arms of Eve." [OxfordM] (7:2) Fall-Wint 91, p. 51.
COLLADO, Alfredo Villanueva
　　　See VILLANUEVA-COLLADO, Alfredo
1111. COLLIER, Michael
　　　"Mission Boulevard." [Atlantic] (268:5) N 91, p. 84.
　　　"Parents" (after William Meredith). [PlumR] (1) Spr-Sum 91, p. 26.
　　　"The Parish Fiesta" (For William Maxwell). [Sonora] (20) Wint 91, p. 47-48.
　　　"Ricordo: Città Del Vaticano." [Sonora] (20) Wint 91, p. 46.
1112. COLLIER, Phyllis K.
　　　"A Fusing of Diverse Waters." [GreenMR] (NS 5:1) Sum-Fall 91, p. 131-132.
　　　"International Women's Day Poem." [CapeR] (26:2) Fall 91, p. 15.
　　　"The Last Bus to Ephesus: Wings of Horses." [GreenMR] (NS 5:1) Sum-Fall 91, p.
　　　　130.
　　　"May Night." [CapeR] (26:2) Fall 91, p. 16.
1113. COLLIN, Thomas B.
　　　"What? Back?" [CreamCR] (14:2) Wint 91, p. 152.
1114. COLLINS, Andrea V.
　　　"Ode to the Future." [Nimrod] (35:1) Fall-Wint 91, p. 115.
1115. COLLINS, Billy
　　　"The Art of Drowning." [Poetry] (159:1) O 91, p. 19.
　　　"Consolation." [Poetry] (158:4) Jl 91, p. 189.
　　　"Dancing Toward Bethlehem." [Poetry] (159:3) D 91, p. 138.
　　　"The Dead." [Spirit] (11) 91, p. 250.
　　　"Earthquake." [Pearl] (13) Spr-Sum 91, p. 37.
　　　"Embrace." [NewYorkQ] (46) 91, p. 96-97.
　　　"Fiftieth Birthday Eve." [Poetry] (159:3) D 91, p. 137-138.
　　　"Inside Outside." [Pearl] (13) Spr-Sum 91, p. 37.
　　　"Nostalgia." [GeoR] (45:1) Spr 91, p. 24-25.
　　　"One Life to Live." [Boulevard] (5:3/6:1, #15/16) Spr 91, p. 59.
　　　"Saturday Morning." [Pearl] (13) Spr-Sum 91, p. 37.
　　　"The Wires of the Night." [Boulevard] (5:3/6:1, #15/16) Spr 91, p. 60.
1116. COLLINS, Caroline
　　　"The Atlantic Pilot's Bride." [TexasR] (12:1/2) Spr-Sum 91, p. 94.
1117. COLLINS, Floyd
　　　"The Blue Coat." [SouthernPR] (31:2) Fall 91, p. 14.
　　　"The Death of Georg Trakl (1887-1914)." [SouthernPR] (31:2) Fall 91, p. 15-16.
COLLINS, Kate Reider
　　　See REIDER-COLLINS, Kate
1118. COLLINS, Martha
　　　"And Also to My Wife." [SnailPR] (1:1) Spr 91, p. 30.
　　　"Door." [PraS] (65:1) Spr 91, p. 51-52.
　　　"Exposure." [KenR] (NS 13:3) Sum 91, p. 84.
　　　"Field." [Field] (44) Spr 91, p. 8.

"Hair." [SnailPR] (1:2) Fall 91-Wint 92, p. 6-7.
"Hammers." [WestB] (29) 91, p. 8-9.
"Her Mother Said." [KenR] (NS 13:3) Sum 91, p. 85.
"A History of Small Life on a Windy Planet." [Agni] (34) 91, p. 214-215.
"Home Fires." [Field] (44) Spr 91, p. 7.
"Little Boy." [Field] (44) Spr 91, p. 5-6.
"News of the World." [DenQ] (26:1) Sum 91, p. 18-19.
"Open." [PraS] (65:1) Spr 91, p. 50-51.
"Them." [Agni] (34) 91, p. 216.
"Wet." [SnailPR] (1:1) Spr 91, p. 28-29.
"Wrapped." [SouthernR] (27:3) Jl 91, p. 662-664.

1119. COLLINS, Michael
"A Bellhop Looks at a Tourist (1987)." [Callaloo] (14:4) Fall 91, p. 780-785.
"Ise's Iron (1986)." [Callaloo] (14:4) Fall 91, p. 786.

1120. COLLINS, Richard
"Linoleum Light." [ChironR] (10:2) Sum 91, p. 6.
"Rearranging Things You Said." [ChironR] (10:2) Sum 91, p. 6.

1121. COLMAN, Cathy A.
"An Order." [Rohwedder] (6) Sum-Fall 91, p. 22.

1122. COLONNESE, Michael
"After the Acceptance of Gifts." [ChatR] (11:2) Wint 91, p. 67.
"Lessons from Survival School." [AnthNEW] (3) 91, p. 18.

1123. COLTER, Cyrus
"Imogene Poems" (Selections: 4 poems). [TriQ] (82) Fall 91, p. 9-13.

1124. COLTMAN, Paul
"Soul." [CumbPR] (10:2) Spr 91, p. 36.
"Winspit." [CumbPR] (10:2) Spr 91, p. 35.

1125. COMANN, Brad
"Sentences." [GreensboroR] (51) Wint 91-92, p. 110-111.

1126. COMBELLICK, Henry
"Not Constantinople." [Epoch] (40:2) 91, p. 191-196.

1127. COMISKEY, Patrick
"Afterword Without Forethought." [NewAW] (8/9) Fall 91, p. 36-37.

1128. COMPTON, Cathleen
"Arctic Spring" (for Charlie Baxter). [BellR] (14:1) Spr 91, p. 55.
"The Little Lady Gets Prudent." [SoDakR] (29:2) Sum 91, p. 124.
"Memory of the Oregon Trail." [SoDakR] (29:2) Sum 91, p. 122.
"Still Life, 1933." [SoDakR] (29:2) Sum 91, p. 123.

1129. CONE, Jon
"The Box Maker" (for Vasko Popa 1922-1991). [WorldL] (2) 91, p. 47.
"Burning in Céline." [WorldL] (1:1) 91, p. 42.
"Fragment." [WorldL] (2) 91, p. 48.
"The Right Hand Searching." [WorldL] (2) 91, p. 48.

1130. CONN, Jan
"Between the Golfo de Ancud and the Golfo Corcovado." [PraF] (12:4) Wint 91-92,
      p. 60.
"The Long Blue Shadows of Sea Oats." [PraF] (12:4) Wint 91-92, p. 61.

1131. CONNELLAN, Leo
"The $100 Street Person." [NewYorkQ] (44) 91, p. 42.
"Hot Day in New York." [NewYorkQ] (45) 91, p. 45.
"Stockbridge, Massachusetts." [NewYorkQ] (46) 91, p. 24.

1132. CONNELLY, Karen
"I Return to the Farm." [Grain] (19:2) Sum 91, p. 53.
"The Word Is Absurd." [Grain] (19:2) Sum 91, p. 54-55.

1133. CONNOLLY, Carol
"Distance at Close Range." [LakeSR] (25) 91, p. 26.

1134. CONNOLLY, David
"A Goodbye" (for the Bac Se, the Medics). [ChironR] (10:1) Spr 91, p. 7.
"On Security for a Medcap to the Montagnards." [ChironR] (10:1) Spr 91, p. 7.
"Thach, First NVA Confirmed." [ChironR] (10:1) Spr 91, p. 7.

1135. CONNOLLY, Geraldine
"All Saints' Day." [WestB] (29) 91, p. 67.
"Dream of the Past." [CreamCR] (14:2) Wint 91, p. 148.
"Face Lift." [Poetry] (158:6) S 91, p. 333.
"The Lake of the Unconscious." [Shen] (41:1) Spr 91, p. 55.
"Trapeze." [WestB] (29) 91, p. 66-67.

1136. CONNOR, Jean L.
    "Remembrance." [ManhatPR] (13) [91?], p. 40.
1137. CONNORS, Diana Jean
    "Sugar Cookies Obsession." [OnTheBus] (8/9) 91, p. 54.
1138. CONOLEY, Gillian
    "Beauty Queen." [KenR] (NS 13:3) Sum 91, p. 91-92.
    "Bedrock." [KenR] (NS 13:3) Sum 91, p. 93.
    "The Birth of a Nation." [KenR] (NS 13:3) Sum 91, p. 92-93.
    "The Birth of Beauty." [DenQ] (25:4) Spr 91, p. 17.
    "White on White." [ThRiPo] (37/38) 91, p. 87.
1139. CONOVER, Carl
    "After Degas." [NewRep] (204:6) 11 F 91, p. 38.
    "Caliban to Prospero." [InterPR] (15:1) Spr 89, p. 87-88.
    "Transience" (After the Impressionists). [InterPR] (15:1) Spr 89, p. 89.
1140. CONOVER, Roger
    "Cornering." [NorthStoneR] (10) Fall 91-Wint 92, p. 21-22.
    "Laws of the Lawn." [NorthStoneR] (10) Fall 91-Wint 92, p. 22.
    "Ruffian." [NorthStoneR] (10) Fall 91-Wint 92, p. 23.
1141. CONOVER, Steve
    "February's Monkey." [Caliban] (10) 91, p. 32-34.
1142. CONRAD, James
    "Dress-Up." [JamesWR] (9:1) Fall 91, p. 6.
1143. CONROY, Lynn
    "Game." [SoCoast] (10) Fall 91, p. 10-11.
1144. CONTI, Edmund
    "Bang!" [ChironR] (10:4) Wint 91, p. 35.
    "Haiku." [Bogg] (64) 91, p. 67.
    "One Day at a Time." [ChironR] (10:4) Wint 91, p. 35.
1145. CONVERY, Ann
    "Untitled: I have loved, hard." [DustyD] Ap 91, p. 28.
1146. CONWAY, Jeffery (Jeffrey)
    "Blood." [JamesWR] (8:3) Spr 91, p. 7.
    "Photo." [JamesWR] (9:1) Fall 91, p. 15.
    "Tuesday Night." [BrooklynR] (8) 91, p. 28-29.
1147. COOK, Jonathan Thomas
    "Melted Crayons." [CapeR] (26:1) Spr 91, p. 37.
1148. COOK, R. L.
    "Prothalamion." [DogRR] (10:1) Sum 91, p. 27.
1149. COOK, Willard
    "Desire." [Gypsy] (17) 91, p. 6.
1150. COOKE, Robert P.
    "Back in Oregon" (Greensboro Review Literary Award Poem). [GreensboroR] (51)
        Wint 91-92, p. 153.
    "Sitting Outside, at the Cabin, Nightfall." [GreensboroR] (50) Sum 91, p. 105.
1151. COOLEY, Mason
    "City Aphorisms." [Outbr] (22) 91, p. 22-23.
1152. COOLEY, Nicole
    "Rio de Janeiro." [AntR] (49:2) Spr 91, p. 242-243.
1153. COOLEY, Peter
    "Alba with Spider." [PoetryNW] (32:3) Aut 91, p. 19-20.
    "An Ecstasy." [NewEngR] (14:1) Fall 91, p. 147.
    "The Intercession." [CalQ] (32/33) Spr 90, p. 140.
    "Macular Degeneration." [Iowa] (21:3) Fall 91, p. 193.
    "Prayer for My Son." [CalQ] (32/33) Spr 90, p. 141.
    "Rhapsode." [VirQR] (67:3) Sum 91, p. 482-483.
    "The Roach." [PoetryNW] (32:3) Aut 91, p. 19.
    "Round and Round." [NewRep] (204:20) 20 My 91, p. 38.
    "The Sea Birds." [NewEngR] (14:1) Fall 91, p. 147-148.
    "The Sleep of Beasts." [CimR] (97) O 91, p. 41-42.
    "To Emily Dickinson in New Orleans." [Iowa] (21:3) Fall 91, p. 192.
1154. COOLIDGE, Clark
    "Comes Through in the Call Hold" (Excerpt. Improvisations on Cecil Taylor).
        [Conjunc] (16) 91, p. 102-106.
    "Copper Plate Back Tonight." [Pequod] (32) 91, p. 125-129.
    "The Dream's Green Deceits." [GrandS] (10:1, #37) 91, p. 23-25.
    "The Gallery" (Selections: IV-VI). [Avec] (4:1) 91, p. 15-18.

"Supernatural Overtones" (w. Ron Padgett, 10 selections). [Shiny] (6) Spr-Sum 91, p. 27-36.
1155. COON, Jeanette
"Rainbow on My Ceiling." [BrooklynR] (8) 91, p. 13-14.
"Senior Yearbook." [JamesWR] (9:1) Fall 91, p. 10.
1156. COONEY, Ellen
"During the Quarrel." [PaintedHR] (2) Spr 91, p. 33.
"Eggstone Goddess Image, Glastonbury Abbey." [Bogg] (64) 91, p. 48.
1157. COOPER, Allan
"The Buttercup Squash." [MidAR] (11:2) 91, p. 53.
1158. COOPER, David
"Cinderella in Afghanistan." [Outbr] (22) 91, p. 50-52.
1159. COOPER, Jane
"The Calling." [AmerPoR] (20:1) Ja-F 91, p. 5.
"The Green Notebook" (for May Stevens and Rudolf Baranik). [AmerPoR] (20:1) Ja-F 91, p. 5.
"My Friend." [Nimrod] (34:2) Spr-Sum 91, p. 29.
"My Mother in Three Acts." [Nimrod] (34:2) Spr-Sum 91, p. 28.
"Ordinary Detail." [AmerPoR] (20:1) Ja-F 91, p. 5.
"What the Seer Said." [NewYorker] (66:47) 7 Ja 91, p. 28.
1160. COOPER, Jane Todd
"On Sundays That June." [US1] (24/25) Spr 91, p. 18.
1161. COOPER, M. Truman
"How the Grandmother Died." [SoDakR] (29:1) Spr 91, p. 106.
"I'm Married and My Daddy's Rich Too." [PraS] (65:3) Fall 91, p. 30-31.
"The Jar's Story." [SoDakR] (29:1) Spr 91, p. 107.
"Pearl." [PraS] (65:3) Fall 91, p. 31-33.
"Ruby." [SoDakR] (29:1) Spr 91, p. 108-109.
"She Said She Had Ants." [PraS] (65:3) Fall 91, p. 29.
1162. COOPER, Manuel
"The Old Grad." [LullwaterR] (2:2) Spr 91, p. 70-71.
1163. COOPER, William E.
"How It Will End." [TexasR] (12:3/4) Fall-Wint 91, p. 72.
1164. COOPER-FRATRIK, Julie
"Arbeit Macht Frei." [HayF] (9) Fall-Wint 91, p. 39.
"Dog Days." [CapeR] (26:2) Fall 91, p. 14.
"Rumors of Christopher." [SouthernPR] (31:2) Fall 91, p. 45-47.
COOPERMAN, Celeste Kostopulus
See KOSTOPULUS-COOPERMAN, Celeste
1165. COOPERMAN, Matthew
"Cicadas." [GrahamHR] (15) Fall 91, p. 62-64.
1166. COOPERMAN, Robert
"Adamant as Michaelangelo." [MinnR] (NS 36) Spr 91, p. 24.
"The Apocrypha — Lot Mourns His Wife." [SoCaR] (23:2) Spr 91, p. 38.
"Beatrice Murphy, Nurse at the Murray Hospital: Butte, Montana, 1909." [CoalC] (3) My 91, p. 3.
"Claudia Gets By." [Outbr] (22) 91, p. 49.
"Dancing with My Brother to a Recording by the Chieftains." [SmPd] (28:3, #83) Fall 91, p. 17.
"Don't." [ChironR] (10:3) Aut 91, p. 18.
"Edith Dyer Climbs Pike's Peak, July 3, 1930." [ChironR] (10:3) Aut 91, p. 18.
"From *The Death of a Badman*, a New Dime Novel by Percy Gilmore, 1876." [SoCoast] (10) Fall 91, p. 54-55.
"From the Sierra Trail Calendar, 1983" (October — Aspen Avenue in the San Juan Mountains). [WebR] (15) Spr 91, p. 112.
"The General on the Eve of His Military Parade." [Plain] (12:2) Wint 91, p. 11.
"Geoffrey Chaucer Recants on His Death Bed." [WebR] (15) Spr 91, p. 113.
"George Keats Sets Sail for America, 1818." [DustyD] Ap 91, p. 26.
"The Hangman Retires." [ChamLR] (8-9) Spr-Fall 91, p. 132-133.
"The Hero." [HampSPR] Wint 91, p. 10-11.
"If He'd Listen." [Plain] (12:1) Fall 91, p. 14.
"Keats Gives Up on *The Fall of Hyperion*, 21 September 1819." [DustyD] Ap 91, p. 27.
"Klytemnestra After Killing Agamemnon." [WebR] (15) Spr 91, p. 111-112.
"A Military Gentlemen Accosts Percy Bysshe Shelley in the Rome Poste Restante." [CoalC] (4) S 91, p. 2.

"Mysteries." [SoDakR] (29:3 part 2) Aut 91, p. 87-88.
"Nero's Last Word." [Northeast] (5:4) Sum 91, p. 4.
"On the Night of 3 February 1820, Keats Suffers His First Hemorrhage." [DogRR] (10:1) Sum 91, p. 36.
"On the Ransoming of Chaucer by King Edward III, 1630." [ChironR] (10:3) Aut 91, p. 18.
"Percy Bysshe Shelley Considers His Father-in-law William Godwin's Demands for More Money." [OxfordM] (7:2) Fall-Wint 91, p. 47.
"The Sad Morning." [ChatR] (11:3) Spr 91, p. 58-59.
"Simone Weil Starves Herself to Death, 1943." [TickleAce] (22) Fall-Wint 91, p. 59-60.
"Some of That Gift." [SmPd] (28:1, #81) Wint 91, p. 25.
"Tall Tales." [CoalC] (3) My 91, p. 10.
"The Taste of Fear." [HampSPR] Wint 91, p. 12.
"We Must Leave Tomorrow." [SwampR] (7/8) Spr-Sum 91, p. 19.
"Wordsworth's Dog, His Poetry Critic." [WindO] (55) Wint 91-92, p. 20-21.
"Yom Kippur Feast." [HiramPoR] (50) Spr-Sum 91, p. 7.
1167. COOPERMAN, Stanley
"The Engraver." [SoDakR] (29:3 part 2) Aut 91, p. 18.
1168. COPE, Dave
"A Young Healthy Doe." [HeavenB] (9) Wint-Spr 91-92, p. 23.
1169. COPE, Steven R.
"Aesop Come to Perch." [InterPR] (15:1) Spr 89, p. 115.
"At Kensington Showers." [InterPR] (15:1) Spr 89, p. 114-115.
"Hunting with Professors." [HolCrit] (28:1) F 91, p. 17.
1170. COPIOLI, Rosita
"Repose of the Green" (tr. by Renata Treitel). [Paint] (18:36) Aut 91, p. 54.
"White" (tr. by Renata Treitel). [Paint] (18:36) Aut 91, p. 55.
1171. CORBETT, William
"Collarbone." [Sulfur] (11:1, #28) Spr 91, p. 81-83.
1172. CORBUS, Patricia
"Carmen Miranda's Hat." [SoCaR] (24:1) Fall 91, p. 140.
1173. CORCORAN, Kelvin
"I could write through the table, cursively gouge down." [NewAW] (8/9) Fall 91, p. 72.
"I live above the shop. I see things." [NewAW] (8/9) Fall 91, p. 72.
"I ride big letters across the map." [NewAW] (8/9) Fall 91, p. 70.
"John, that passionate man, in his action tower." [NewAW] (8/9) Fall 91, p. 71.
"So you can travel to one place and think of another." [NewAW] (8/9) Fall 91, p. 71.
"Tony and Liz." [NewAW] (8/9) Fall 91, p. 70.
1174. CORDING, Robert
"Circles." [SewanR] (99:4) Fall 91, p. 537-540.
"Hummingbirds." [KenR] (NS 13:2) Spr 91, p. 133-135.
"Instinct." [GeoR] (45:3) Fall 91, p. 505-506.
"Niagara Falls." [CimR] (95) Ap 91, p. 43-46.
"Squirrels." [SewanR] (99:4) Fall 91, p. 540-541.
1175. COREY, Chet
"The Separateness of Joy." [RagMag] (9:2) 91, p. 47.
"Sweet Sound in a Sow's Ear." [Plain] (11:2) Wint 91, p. 10.
1176. COREY, Stephen
"Redundancies." [YellowS] (38) Wint-Spr 91-92, p. 5.
1177. CORKERY, Caleb
"Sit Down Meals." [BellR] (14:1) Spr 91, p. 23.
CORMACK, Karen Mac
See Mac CORMACK, Karen
1178. CORMAN, Cid
"A Suite of Six" (for Greg). [WillowS] (28) Sum 91, p. 12-13.
"To the extent this is poetry." [Talisman] (6) Spr 91, p. 140.
CORMIER-SHEKERJIAN, Regina de
See DeCORMIER-SHEKERJIAN, Regina
1179. CORN, Alfred
"Coventry." [NewYorker] (67:42) 9 D 91, p. 52.
"La Madeleine." [ParisR] (33:120) Fall 91, p. 106-115.
"Message to Tim." [WashR] (16:6) Ap-My 91, p. 13.

1180. CORNING, Howard McKinley
"Footprints on Memaloose." [SoDakR] (29:3 part 2) Aut 91, p. 22.
CORNIS, Marcel Pop
See CORNIS-POP, Marcel
1181. CORNIS-POP, Marcel
"Landscape in White" (tr. of Anghel Dumbraveanu, w. Robert J. Ward). [Talisman]
(6) Spr 91, p. 138.
"Magic Words for the One Confined in Silence" (tr. of Anghel Dumbraveanu, w.
Robert J. Ward). [Talisman] (6) Spr 91, p. 138.
1182. CORNISH, Sam
"Horseface." [Ploughs] (17:2/3) Fall 91, p. 73-74.
1183. CORRALES, José
"Muerte de un Personaje Famoso del Pueblo." [LindLM] (10:1) Ja-Mr 91, p. 8.
1184. CORRIE, Daniel
"The Big Bang." [LullwaterR] (2:2) Spr 91, p. 64-65.
"Little World." [SouthwR] (76:4) Aut 91, p. 592.
"The Skunk." [GreensboroR] (50) Sum 91, p. 116.
1185. CORRIE-COZART, Virginia
"The Women's Dance." [Calyx] (13:3) Wint 91-92, p. 38-39.
1186. CORSO, Gregory
"Hi." [Spirit] (11) 91, p. 204-205.
1187. CORT, John E.
"The Moon, 1" (tr. of Yogeshvara). [Abraxas] (40/41) 91, p. 159.
"The Moon, 2" (tr. of Yogeshvara). [Abraxas] (40/41) 91, p. 159.
"Sunrise, 1" (tr. of Yogeshvara). [Abraxas] (40/41) 91, p. 157.
"Sunrise, 2" (tr. of Yogeshvara). [Abraxas] (40/41) 91, p. 157.
1188. CORTAZAR, Mercedes
"Albergue de hojas." [LindLM] (10:1) Ja-Mr 91, p. 22.
1189. CORTRIGHT, Risa
"China: A Photograph." [PoetryUSA] (22) Spr 91, p. 12.
1190. CORWIN, Chris
"In Rain." [HawaiiR] (16:1, #34) Wint 91-92, p. 104.
1191. CORWIN, Phillip
"Airborne Students in Search of a Navigator." [Pembroke] (23) 91, p. 140.
1192. CORY, Cynthia Jay
"Fishing." [IndR] (14:2) Spr 91, p. 25-26.
1193. CORY, Jim
"1st Love." [Pearl] (13) Spr-Sum 91, p. 63.
"Kept." [Contact] (10:59/60/61) Spr 91, p. 48.
1194. CORY, P.
"Desert Solitude." [DogRR] (10:2) Fall-Wint 91, p. 11.
1195. COSBY, Nancy
"Welcome." [NegC] (11:3) 91, p. 17.
1196. COSIER, Tony
"Finding the Church." [AntigR] (85/86) Spr-Sum 91, p. 88.
"Running the Klondike Road." [AntigR] (85/86) Spr-Sum 91, p. 87.
"Summering North." [Farm] (8:2) Fall-Wint 91-92, p. 70-72.
1197. COSTANZO, Gerald
"American River." [NoDaQ] (59:3) Sum 91, p. 98.
"Bournehurst-on-the-Canal." [Ploughs] (17:2/3) Fall 91, p. 118-119.
"Provincetown." [NoDaQ] (59:3) Sum 91, p. 97.
1198. COSTOPOULOS, Olga
"The Muskox Poems." [Event] (20:3) Fall 91, p. 58-61.
1199. COTTINGHAM, Dave
"Bye-word." [AntigR] (85/86) Spr-Sum 91, p. 70.
"Conference." [AntigR] (85/86) Spr-Sum 91, p. 68.
"Mon Semblable, Mon Frère." [AntigR] (85/86) Spr-Sum 91, p. 69.
"Raven." [AntigR] (85/86) Spr-Sum 91, p. 67.
1200. COULEHAN, Jack
"Medicine Stone." [SoCoast] (11) Wint 91, p. 46-47.
1201. COUNCILMAN, Emily Sargent
"Light Touch." [InterPR] (15:1) Spr 89, p. 113.
"Shape of Change." [InterPR] (15:1) Spr 89, p. 113.
1202. COUNSIL, Wendy
"On the Mine Ride." [HawaiiR] (15:2, #32) Spr 91, p. 165.

COURCY, Lynne H. de
 See DeCOURCY, Lynne H.
1203. COURSEN, H. R.
 "18 August, 1985." [LitR] (34:2) Wint 91, p. 174.
 "Blues in the Day: May, 1989." [LitR] (34:2) Wint 91, p. 174.
 "The Fourteenth." [SmPd] (28:2, #82) Spr 91, p. 24.
1204. COUTURIER, John
 "I shave in the dark." [NewYorkQ] (45) 91, p. 63.
1205. COUTURIER, Michel
 "L'Ablatif Absolu" (Maeght editeur 1976, excerpts, tr. by Robert Kocik). [Avec]
  (4:1) 91, p. 70-77.
1206. COWEE, Bill
 "More Than Worms Slip Through Wormholes." [SoDakR] (29:4) Wint 91, p. 62.
 "Offerings to the Late Days of Autumn." [SoDakR] (29:4) Wint 91, p. 63.
1207. COWING, Sue
 "Barbara." [BambooR] (50/51) Spr-Sum 91, p. 183-187.
 "City Apples." [HawaiiR] (15:3, #33) Fall 91, p. 85.
 "A Letter from Worpswede" (Paula Modersohn-Becker). [BambooR] (50/51)
  Spr-Sum 91, p. 188-189.
 "My Breathing." [BambooR] (50/51) Spr-Sum 91, p. 192-193.
 "Rivers." [HawaiiR] (15:3, #33) Fall 91, p. 86.
 "To Clara Rilke-Westhoff, February 1902." [BambooR] (50/51) Spr-Sum 91, p.
  191.
 "Young Girl with Flower Vases" (Painting by Paula Modersohn-Becker).
  [BambooR] (50/51) Spr-Sum 91, p. 190.
1208. COWSER, Robert
 "Upon Reading That an Emperor Had Bought Acres of Timber in a Texas County."
  [CapeR] (26:2) Fall 91, p. 17.
1209. COX, Carol
 "Cleaning Out the House." [HangL] (59) 91, p. 25.
1210. COX, Ed
 "In the Before." [WashR] (16:6) Ap-My 91, p. 6.
1211. COX, Kathleen Lawless
 "Feathers & Iced Tea." [NorthStoneR] (10) Fall 91-Wint 92, p. 172.
 "An Onion, a Poem, a Conjunction of Motes." [NorthStoneR] (10) Fall 91-Wint 92,
  p. 174.
 "Sudek: Czech Photographer" (for Jessie). [NorthStoneR] (10) Fall 91-Wint 92, p.
  173.
1212. COX, Wayne
 "City Storm." [ChatR] (11:3) Spr 91, p. 57.
 "The Shadow Field" (For James Dickey, East Falkland Island, 14 June 1990).
  [SouthernPR] (31:1) Spr 91, p. 27-30.
1213. COY, David
 "His Brooding." [AntR] (49:4) Fall 91, p. 562.
1214. COYLE, Charles
 "Turkish Quarter." [LullwaterR] (2:2) Spr 91, p. 33.
COYLE, Don Winter
 See WINTER-COYLE, Don
1215. COYLE, William
 "Fairies, Fairy Tales." [ChangingM] (23) Fall-Wint 91, p. 25.
COZART, Virginia Corrie
 See CORRIE-COZART, Virginia
CRABBE, Chris Wallace
 See WALLACE-CRABBE, Chris
1216. CRAGO, Louise
 "Baglady." [WritersF] (17) Fall 91, p. 209.
 "Denial, Anger, Bargaining, Et Cetera." [WeberS] (8:1) Spr 91, p. 98.
 "Frequent Flier." [WeberS] (8:1) Spr 91, p. 97.
 "The Talking Cure." [PaintedHR] (3) Sum 92, p. 5.
1217. CRAIG, Christine
 "St. Ann Saturday." [GrahamHR] (14) Spr 91, p. 56-57.
1218. CRAIG, Linda-Robin
 "The Scenic View." [PacificR] (9) 91, p. 48-49.
CRAIG, Lorenza Calvillo
 See CALVILLO-CRAIG, Lorenza

1219. CRAMER, Steven
        "After the Miracle" (for my brother-in-law, Phil). [IndR] (14:3) Fall 91, p. 78-80.
        "Constellations." [Boulevard] (5:3/6:1, #15/16) Spr 91, p. 178-179.
        "Eclogue." [AntR] (49:1) Wint 91, p. 92-93.
        "The Game." [Poetry] (159:1) O 91, p. 22-23.
        "Jacuzzi." [ParisR] (33:119) Sum 91, p. 185-186.
        "The Marriage of Heaven and Hell." [Agni] (34) 91, p. 99-100.
        "Mother Conjuring in Hondo, Texas, 1945." [Ploughs] (17:2/3) Fall 91, p. 112.
        "Nineteen Sixty-Three." [Agni] (34) 91, p. 101-102.
        "Nocturne." [ParisR] (33:119) Sum 91, p. 187-188.
        "What We Didn't Risk." [Agni] (34) 91, p. 97-98.
1220. CRANFIELD, Steve
        "Bargain Hunters." [JamesWR] (8:2) Wint 91, p. 7.
1221. CRASNARU, Daniela
        "Breath" (tr. by Adam J. Sorkin and Sergiu Celac). [Poetry] (159:1) O 91, p. 28.
        "Lethal Dose" (tr. by Adam J. Sorkin and Sergiu Celac). [Poetry] (159:1) O 91, p.
            28.
1222. CRATE, Joan
        "Eating a Pomegranate in the Bath." [Dandel] (18:1) Spr-Sum 91, p. 6.
        "Our Fathers." [Dandel] (18:1) Spr-Sum 91, p. 5.
1223. CRAWFORD, Charles Slade
        "The Morning Glories" (for Zia). [EmeraldCR] (3) 91, c1990, p. 65-66.
1224. CRAWFORD, Lynn
        "Just That Would Be Enough." [SinW] (43/44) Sum 91, p. 257-258.
1225. CRAWFORD, Tom
        "Gretel." [MalR] (95) Sum 91, p. 94.
        "Gretel II." [MalR] (95) Sum 91, p. 95.
        "Gretel III" (for Thomas McGrath, Some Recent Criticism). [MalR] (95) Sum 91, p.
            96-97.
CRAY, Sharon de
        See DeCRAY, Sharon
1226. CREAGER, Alfred L.
        "Haiku." [Nimrod] (34:2) Spr-Sum 91, p. 30.
        "The Wrens Are Back." [Nimrod] (34:2) Spr-Sum 91, p. 30.
1227. CREED, Lynda Futch
        "Sunflowers." [EmeraldCR] (4) 91, p. 43.
1228. CREEL, Heather Noel
        "Swingset." [EmeraldCR] (4) 91, p. 37.
        "To Cry." [EmeraldCR] (3) 91, c1990, p. 92.
1229. CREEL, Melanie
        "A Month from Your Birthday, Again." [EmeraldCR] (4) 91, p. 58.
        "Shadings." [EmeraldCR] (4) 91, p. 57-58.
1230. CREELEY, Robert
        "Other." [GrandS] (10:1, #37) 91, p. 91.
1231. CRESPO, Eugenio
        "Dos." [Nuez] (3:7) 91, p. 8.
        "Tres." [Nuez] (3:7) 91, p. 8.
        "Uno." [Nuez] (3:7) 91, p. 8.
CREW, Louie
        See LI, Min Hua
1232. CREWS, Judson
        "Embroidered or Perchance Tattooed" (Special Section: 19 poems). [WormR] (31:4,
            #124) 91, p. 121-130.
        "Her Cunt Had More in Common With." [Pearl] (13) Spr-Sum 91, p. 58.
        "The Home Again of Noname Beginning." [Pearl] (14) Fall-Wint 91, p. 30.
        "How Exquisite I thought Ed Corbet's." [Lactuca] (14) My 91, p. 37.
        "How Much the World Has Changed." [DogRR] (10:2) Fall-Wint 91, p. 25.
        "The Idea." [Lactuca] (14) My 91, p. 38.
        "If One Should Be Thought a Freak Because Of." [Lactuca] (14) My 91, p. 38.
        "If Those Bodies Are Only Objects." [Lactuca] (14) My 91, p. 38.
        "The Meld, or Eclat of Your Pillow-Talk." [NewYorkQ] (45) 91, p. 51.
        "She Said She Thought She Saw Me." [CrabCR] (7:2) Sum 91, p. 28.
        "The Stones and the Stars I Have Often." [DogRR] (10:2) Fall-Wint 91, p. 24.
        "This Guarded Epiphany That Grabbed Me." [Lactuca] (14) My 91, p. 36.
        "This Old Stallion Is Restless, Pacing." [CrabCR] (7:2) Sum 91, p. 28.
        "To Follow a Fugue Tenuously Dancing Beyond." [CrabCR] (7:2) Sum 91, p. 28.

"To Make Judgments of a Less Judgmental." [NewYorkQ] (44) 91, p. 49.
"Your Platinum Eyes and Bronze." [Lactuca] (14) My 91, p. 37.
1233. CREWS, Mary
"Breaking Silence." [Crucible] (27) Fall 91, p. 35-36.
"Dawn Drifting." [Crucible] (27) Fall 91, p. 37.
1234. CRICHTON, Juliet
"The Gracious Prelude." [Mildred] (4:2/5:1) 91, p. 79.
"Mom's Thunderbird." [Mildred] (4:2/5:1) 91, p. 80.
"Psalm: The Sax." [Sequoia] (34:1) Spr 91, p. 44.
"Pursuance." [Sequoia] (34:1) Spr 91, p. 43.
"To Smolder Forever." [Mildred] (4:2/5:1) 91, p. 81-82.
1235. CRILL, Hildred
"For Jane Who Also Rejoices." [Kalliope] (13:1) 91, p. 51.
1236. CRISICK, Maureen Micus
"Jingsheng Does Not Regret His Crime." [CapeR] (26:2) Fall 91, p. 12.
1237. CROCKETT, Andy
"The Grand Canyon: Hiking Out." [CalQ] (35/36) 91, p. 132.
1238. CRONWALL, Brian
"At the Cemetery" (for Martha Cronwall Johnson). [RagMag] (9:2) 91, p. 38-39.
"Morning in Malta" (A Plainsongs Award Poem). [Plain] (11:2) Wint 91, p. 20.
"Peace Garden, Lake Harriet" (Minneapolis, August 6, 1990). [RagMag] (9:2) 91,
p. 37.
1239. CROOKER, Barbara
"The Cancer Letters" (from Anne Zellars). [WestB] (28) 91, p. 115-122.
"Grating Parmesan." [DenQ] (26:2) Fall 91, p. 10-11.
"The Mother of a Handicapped Child Dreams of Respite." [PennR] (5:1) Spr 91, p.
28.
"Writers' Colony." [FourQ] (5:1) Spr 91, p. 52.
1240. CROSS, Elsa
"Bacchantes (VIII)" (tr. by John Oliver Simon). [ArtfulD] (20/21) 91, p. 60.
1241. CROSS, Mary
"The Archives of a Saturday." [Journal] (15:1) Spr 91, p. 75-76.
"At a Distance." [Journal] (15:1) Spr 91, p. 78-79.
"Fait Accompli." [Journal] (15:1) Spr 91, p. 77.
"This Is the Sound I Make." [Journal] (15:1) Spr 91, p. 81.
1242. CROSSMAN, Charles
"In Search of a Burial Ground." [PottPort] (13:2) Fall-Wint 91, p. 61.
1243. CROW, Mary
"IV.8. Eleventh Vertical Poetry" (tr. of Roberto Juarroz). [QW] (33) Sum-Fall 91, p.
170.
"Animal Catechism" (tr. of Olga Orozco). [AmerV] (24) Fall 91, p. 68-69.
"Christ Appeared in Ahumada Mall Where He Was Thoroughly Screwed Over" (tr.
of Enrique Lihn). [AmerPoR] (20:4) Jl-Ag 91, p. 24.
"Cows." [HighP] (6:1) Spr 91, p. 42-43.
"Cultivation." [ArtfulD] (20/21) 91, p. 6.
"Eleventh II.6" (tr. of Roberto Juarroz). [Sonora] (20) Wint 91, p. 107.
"Eleventh IV.14" (tr. of Roberto Juarroz). [Sonora] (20) Wint 91, p. 108.
"Eleventh IV.23" (tr. of Roberto Juarroz). [QW] (33) Sum-Fall 91, p. 169.
"Finding Wild Bees on My Sister's Farm Near Baltimore, Ohio." [ArtfulD] (20/21)
91, p. 5.
"Flaubert's Egypt." [ArtfulD] (20/21) 91, p. 4.
"Future?" (tr. of Bogomil Gjuzel, w. the author). [CimR] (96) Jl 91, p. 20.
"Future Prehistory of Chile" (tr. of Enrique Lihn). [AmerPoR] (20:4) Jl-Ag 91, p.
24.
"Games" (tr. of Jorge Teillier). [ArtfulD] (20/21) 91, p. 8.
"Green Wine" (Tomislav dom, near Zagreb). [PoetryE] (32) Fall 91, p. 92-93.
"News of the Future from an Astronaut, Candidate for the Presidency of the World"
(tr. of Enrique Lihn). [AmerPoR] (20:4) Jl-Ag 91, p. 25.
"Omen" (tr. of Olga Orozco). [ArtfulD] (20/21) 91, p. 9.
"Pandora" (tr. of Bogomil Gjuzel, w. the author). [NewOR] (18:2) Sum 91, p. 80.
"Quest: In Search of My Genes" (tr. of Bogomil Gjuzel, w. the author). [CimR] (96)
Jl 91, p. 18-19.
"A Reception for Exiles Will be Held in Ahumada Mall" (tr. of Enrique Lihn).
[AmerPoR] (20:4) Jl-Ag 91, p. 24.
"Shadows" (Sarajevo). [ChatR] (11:2) Wint 91, p. 41.

"Short Course on How to Shoot and Drive at the Same Time" (tr. of Enrique Lihn).
[AmerPoR] (20:4) Jl-Ag 91, p. 26.
"Strip Tease of the Recession" (tr. of Enrique Lihn). [AmerPoR] (20:4) Jl-Ag 91, p.
25.
"Tenth . 12" (tr. of Robert Juarroz). [ConnPR] (10:1) 91, p. 43.
"Tenth . 19" (tr. of Robert Juarroz). [ConnPR] (10:1) 91, p. 44.
"The Threshold of Other Sound" (A Selection from "Vertical Poetry," 12 poems, tr.
of Roberto Juarroz. Translation Chapbook Series, Number 17). [MidAR]
(12:1) 91, p. 77-105.
"Torture Chamber" (tr. of Enrique Lihn). [AmerPoR] (20:4) Jl-Ag 91, p. 26.
"Vampire Continent" (tr. of Olga Orozco). [GrahamHR] (15) Fall 91, p. 104-105.
"Vertical Poetry" (Selections: Eighth.50, Eighth.76, tr. of Roberto Juarroz).
[GrahamHR] (15) Fall 91, p. 99-101.
"Vertical Poetry: Eleventh I 3" (tr. of Robert Juarroz). [ArtfulD] (20/21) 91, p. 7.
"Vertical Poetry, Eleventh I. 8" (tr. of Roberto Juarroz). [Ploughs] (17:4) Wint
91-92, p. 51.
"Vertical Poetry, Eleventh II. 1" (for Jean Paul Neveu, tr. of Roberto Juarroz).
[Ploughs] (17:4) Wint 91-92, p. 52-53.
"Vertical Poetry: Eleventh.II.25" (tr. of Robert Juarroz). [Agni] (34) 91, p. 160-161.
1244. CROW, Pamela
"Fathers." [Northeast] (5:5) Wint 91-92, p. 5.
1245. CROZIER, Lorna
"Against Ars Poetica." [Descant] (22:4, #75) Wint 91-92, p. 8-9.
"Angel of Salamanders." [Quarry] (40:1/2) Wint-Spr 91, p. 43.
"Angel of Tigers." [Quarry] (40:1/2) Wint-Spr 91, p. 43.
"Birds and Mustard Field." [PraF] (12:3 #56) Aut 91, p. 23.
"Hemingway in Nerja." [PraF] (12:3 #56) Aut 91, p. 24-25.
"Mid-Summer Morning Run." [PraF] (12:3 #56) Aut 91, p. 26.
"Moving Toward Speech." [Quarry] (40:1/2) Wint-Spr 91, p. 44-45.
"Sperm Whales Washed Ashore on the Coast of Oregon." [Quarry] (40:1/2)
Wint-Spr 91, p. 42.
1246. CRUMMEY, Michael
"Balcony Poem #11." [TickleAce] (22) Fall-Wint 91, p. 32.
"Harvest." [TickleAce] (22) Fall-Wint 91, p. 33.
"In Canada There Is Already Snow." [Event] (20:2) Sum 91, p. 92-93.
1247. CRUNK, T.
"Earthly Garments." [HighP] (6:3) Wint 91, p. 66-68.
"Redemption." [ParisR] (33:119) Sum 91, p. 135-137.
1248. CRUZ, Victor Hernandez
"Agriculture." [RiverS] (34) 91, p. 21.
"Problems with Hurricanes." [RiverS] (34) 91, p. 20.
1249. CRUZ VARELA, Maria Elena
"Conversacion a Solas con Isadora Duncan." [LindLM] (10:2) Ap-Je 91, p. 3.
"Ora pro Nobis." [LindLM] (10:2) Ap-Je 91, p. 3.
"Plegaria congra el Miedo." [LindLM] (10:2) Ap-Je 91, p. 3.
"La Trampa." [LindLM] (10:2) Ap-Je 91, p. 3.
1250. CSAMER, M. E. (Mary Ellen)
"Angel." [Event] (20:3) Fall 91, p. 64.
"How It Began." [PraF] (12:3 #56) Aut 91, p. 63.
"In the Painful Light." [AntigR] (84) Wint 91, p. 58-59.
"Pattern #7." [Grain] (19:3) Fall 91, p. 107.
"Pieces, Pieces." [Grain] (19:3) Fall 91, p. 108-109.
"Testament." [Grain] (19:3) Fall 91, p. 110.
1251. CSOORI, Sándor
"A Drop of Blood on the Ground" (tr. by Len Roberts). [LitR] (34:2) Wint 91, p.
227.
"Ez a Nap. This Day" (tr. by Len Roberts). [DenQ] (26:2) Fall 91, p. 12-13.
"I Have to Look Long" (Hosszan kell nezllem, tr. by Len Roberts and Gabor Toro).
[Agni] (34) 91, p. 159.
"Maple Leaf" (tr. by Len Roberts and László Vertes). [NewEngR] (13:3/4) Spr-Sum
91, p. 195-196.
"My Masters" (tr. by Len Roberts). [Trans] (25) Spr 91, p. 195.
"Questions, to Carriers of the Dead (Kérdések, halottvivokhoz)" (tr. by Len Roberts
and Laszlo Vertes). [Plain] (11:3) Spr 91, p. 24.
"Questions, to Carriers of the Dead" (tr. by Len Roberts and László Vértes). [LitR]
(34:2) Wint 91, p. 226.

"Summer, with Halo" (tr. by Len Roberts and László Vertes). [NewEngR] (13:3/4) Spr-Sum 91, p. 196.
"What Do You Envy Me" (tr. by Len Roberts). [Vis] (35) 91, p. 32.
"You, Hungry for the Sun" (tr. by Len Roberts). [Trans] (25) Spr 91, p. 193-194.
"Zörög Éjjel a Mák. The Poppy Clatters at Night" (tr. by Len Roberts and László Vértes). [DenQ] (26:2) Fall 91, p. 14.
1252. CSUKAS, Istvan
"Plaintive Song to the Members of My Generation" (tr. by Len Roberts and Marta Mezey). [TriQ] (81) Spr-Sum 91, p. 183-184.
1253. CUADRA, Angel
"Orfeo y Euridice." [LindLM] (10:3) Jl-S 91, p. 8.
1254. CUDDIHY, Michael
"Ride." [Crazy] (40) Spr 91, p. 58.
1255. CUDDY, Dan
"Swan Lake, Maine." [AntR] (49:3) Sum 91, p. 432.
1256. CULHANE, Brian
"Glossarium." [Chelsea] (50) 91, p. 78-83.
"Upstate." [Boulevard] (5:3/6:1, #15/16) Spr 91, p. 192-193.
1257. CULL, David
"15 O'clock News." [WestCL] (25:1) Spr 91, p. 64-65.
"Jaipur to Delhi." [WestCL] (25:1) Spr 91, p. 62.
"Jakarta Airport." [WestCL] (25:1) Spr 91, p. 63.
"Port Hardy to Prince Rupert." [WestCL] (25:1) Spr 91, p. 65.
"Three Songs for Taofi." [WestCL] (25:1) Spr 91, p. 61-62.
"Through a Round Gate Facing Keefer St." [WestCL] (25:1) Spr 91, p. 66.
1258. CULLY, Barbara
"Black Is a Bright Light." [AmerPoR] (20:3) My-Je 91, p. 31.
"Issue #306." [AmerPoR] (20:3) My-Je 91, p. 32.
"The New Intimacy." [AmerPoR] (20:3) My-Je 91, p. 31.
"The Thing Itself." [AmerPoR] (20:3) My-Je 91, p. 32.
"Watching Television." [Ploughs] (17:4) Wint 91-92, p. 68-69.
1259. CUMBERLAND, Sharon
"Lipstick." [Contact] (10:59/60/61) Spr 91, p. 26.
1260. CUMPIANO, Ina
"Advice." [Iowa] (21:1) Wint 91, p. 203.
"Luna Nueva." [Iowa] (21:1) Wint 91, p. 210203.
"Migraine." [Iowa] (21:1) Wint 91, p. 201.
1261. CUNNINGHAM, Brent
"The Dream of the High School Track Star." [BellR] (14:1) Spr 91, p. 27.
1262. CUNNINGHAM, Mark
"After the End." [RiverC] (11:2) Spr 91, p. 28.
"Days Without Weather." [RiverC] (12:1) Fall 91, p. 59.
"Last Visit." [RiverC] (11:2) Spr 91, p. 29.
"Missouri Summer." [CrabCR] (7:3) 91, p. 3.
"Openings." [CrabCR] (7:3) 91, p. 3.
"Swallows." [MidwQ] (33:1) Aut 91, p. 58.
1263. CURBELO, Silvia
"Bringing Her Back." [MidAR] (12:1) 91, p. 31-32.
"The Geography of Leaving" (11 poems. Winner of the 1990 Gerald Cable Poetry Chapbook Competition). [SilverFR] (21) 91, 24 p.
"The Lake Has Swallowed the Whole Sky." [MidAR] (12:1) 91, p. 35.
"Last Call." [TampaR] (4) 91, p. 10.
"Lunes de Revolucion" (for Tania Díaz Castro, under house arrest). [MidAR] (12:1) 91, p. 33-34.
"The Simple Geography of Leaving." [Shen] (41:2) Sum 91, p. 63.
1264. CURL, John
"Earthquake under the Ocean." [PoetryUSA] (22) Spr 91, p. 6.
1265. CURNOW, Allen
"A Busy Port." [Verse] (8:2) Sum 91, p. 5-6.
1266. CURRIE, Sheldon
"Our Fathers Who Are: R.J., C.C., et Al." [AntigR] (87/88) Fall 91-Wint 92, p. 265.
1267. CURRY, Elizabeth (Elizabeth R.)
"Old Still Life." [Interim] (10:2) Fall-Wint 91-92, p. 43.
"On the Eve of War" (for Walter Tonetto). [CentR] (35:3) Fall 91, p. 542-543.
"Potted Plants." [WindO] (55) Wint 91-92, p. 9.

"Writing the Day." [Interim] (10:2) Fall-Wint 91-92, p. 44.
1268. CURTIS, Carol J.
"Stigmata." [Writer] (104:6) Je 91, p. 27.
1269. CURTIS, Mary Louise
"Definition." [EmeraldCR] (4) 91, p. 74.
"Friends in the Air." [EmeraldCR] (3) 91, c1990, p. 36.
1270. CURTIS, Tony
"At the Hutterites in South Dakota." [SoDakR] (29:3 part 2) Aut 91, p. 48.
1271. CURWEN, D'Arcy
"Looking for My Own Name in Any Telephone Book." [PacificR] (10) 91-92, p. 106.
"Union Square." [PacificR] (9) 91, p. 81.
1272. CURZON, David
"The Owl: A Dream." [Confr] (46/47) Fall 91-Wint 92, p. 266.
1273. CUSCADEN, R. R.
"Sold." [SoDakR] (29:3 part 2) Aut 91, p. 15.
1274. CUSHING, James
"A Cottage for Sale." [WritersF] (17) Fall 91, p. 183.
"I Concentrate on You." [WashR] (17:1) Je-Jl 91, p. 9.
"Laura." [BellR] (14:2) Fall 91, p. 22.
"Laura." [WashR] (17:1) Je-Jl 91, p. 11.
"This Nearly Was Mine." [BellR] (14:2) Fall 91, p. 23.
"This Was Nearly Mine." [Pearl] (14) Fall-Wint 91, p. 26.
1275. CUSHMAN, Stephen
"Rapunzel." [Shen] (41:4) Wint 91, p. 107.
1276. CUSTER, Charley
"Seed." [Hellas] (2:1) Spr 91, p. 77.
1277. CUTLER, Bruce
"Sand Creek! A Burial" (Norhtern Cheyenne Reservation, Montana, August 14, 1911). [SpoonRQ] (16:3/4) Sum-Fall 91, p. 13-16.
1278. CUTULY, Joan
"Swan Dance" (for Leonora Cutuly, April 29, 1990). [Interim] (10:1) Spr-Sum 91, p. 33.
1279. CZEKANOWICZ, Anna
"Untitled: All you sad ones" (tr. by Georgia Scott and David Malcolm). [Calyx] (13:3) Wint 91-92, p. 10.
1280. DABASI, Roseann
"About Beets." [RagMag] (9:2) 91, p. 52-53.
1281. DABYDEEN, Cyril
"The Husband." [GrahamHR] (14) Spr 91, p. 35-36.
1282. DABYDEEN, David
"Coolie Mother." [GrahamHR] (14) Spr 91, p. 27.
"Turner" (Excerpt). [Callaloo] (14:3) Sum 91, p. 569-570.
1283. DACEY, Philip
"The Book of Stones" (Selections: 1-5). [SoDakR] (29:3 part 2) Aut 91, p. 29.
"The Burial." [Paint] (18:36) Aut 91, p. 17.
"Coming Attractions." [CharR] (17:1) Spr 91, p. 97.
"The Empty Room" (for Bill Holm). [PassN] (12:2) Wint 91, p. 26.
"Hands." [CharR] (17:1) Spr 91, p. 96.
"Harry Stafford: Whitman at Timber Creek." [SouthernR] (27:3) Jl 91, p. 670-673.
"He Discovers a Gravemarker in the Flower Garden of His New House." [SingHM] (19) 91, p. 5-6.
"The Ice-Cream Return." [Journal] (15:2) Fall 91, p. 6-8.
"Macaroons." [LullwaterR] (2:2) Spr 91, p. 36.
"Movie Kisses." [PoetryE] (32) Fall 91, p. 117.
"Musica." [MidAR] (11:1) 91, p. 236-237.
"Notes of the Ancient Chinese Poet." [CoalC] (3) My 91, p. 11.
"The President Saves Face." [Paint] (18:36) Aut 91, p. 16.
"The Sailor" (for Linda). [CoalC] (4) S 91, p. 6.
"She Writes Offering to Buy for Her Son, in Minnesota, an Electric Blanket." [CreamCR] (15:2) Fall 91, p. 61.
"Upon the Establishment of a Minnesota State Lottery." [CreamCR] (15:2) Fall 91, p. 62-63.
"The Wheel." [PoetC] (22:2) Wint 91, p. 5-6.
1284. D'ACUNTO, Sabino
"Elegia Molisana" (from "Ricordo è Amore"). [InterPR] (17:2) Fall 91, p. 10-14.

"The Gamekeeper" (tr. by Luigi Bonaffini). [InterPR] (17:2) Fall 91, p. 17.
"Il Guardiacaccia." [InterPR] (17:2) Fall 91, p. 16.
"Molisan Elegy" (tr. by Luigi Bonaffini). [InterPR] (17:2) Fall 91, p. 11-15.

1285. DaGAMA, Steven
"Colors." [YellowS] (36) Spr 91, p. 6.
"Damming the Flood." [YellowS] (36) Spr 91, p. 7.
"Dogs of July." [YellowS] (36) Spr 91, p. 9.
"A Greek Star." [YellowS] (36) Spr 91, p. 8.
"Green Wine." [YellowS] (36) Spr 91, p. 5.
"In the Philippines." [YellowS] (36) Spr 91, p. 4.
"Log of the Princessa." [YellowS] (36) Spr 91, p. 5.
"Telefonata." [YellowS] (36) Spr 91, p. 6.

1286. DAGGETT, Lyle
"I've Known This Dance" (for J.). [LakeSR] (25) 91, p. 16.

1287. D'AGUIAR, Fred
"A Jamaican Airman Foresees His Death" (Selections: 4 poems). [Stand] (32:2) Spr 91, p. 46-47.
"Mama Dot Warns Against an Easter Rising." [GrahamHR] (14) Spr 91, p. 52-53.
"Town-Daddy" (for Donald D'Aguiar). [GrahamHR] (14) Spr 91, p. 51.

DAI, Fang
See FANG, Dai

1288. DAIGON, Ruth
"The Messiah's Late As Usual." [Vis] (35) 91, p. 36.

1289. DAILEY, Joel
"Diagnosis, Prognosis, Psychosis." [Timbuktu] (6) Spr 91, p. 56-57.

1290. DALDORPH, Brian
"The Blood Pump." [DogRR] (10:1) Sum 91, p. 39.
"Domestic Politics" (20 poems. For Sara, Sandra, Brenna and Lucy). [DustyD] (Chapbook Series #2) 91, 24 p.
"Love Poetry." [Bogg] (64) 91, p. 11.
"Perry Kitsmiller" (1917-1990). [DogRR] (10:1) Sum 91, p. 38.

1291. DALE, David
"Deaconess Home for Children." [CutB] (36) Sum 91, p. 75-76.

1292. DALE, Jo Anna
"#11. I am not my brother's keeper." [ChironR] (10:4) Wint 91, p. 39.

1293. DALE, Karen
"Cooking Lesson." [PaintedHR] (4) Fall 92, p. 28.

1294. DALEY, Argentina
"Nelson at Lake Sammamish, 1970." [BellArk] (7:1) Ja-F 91, p. 4.

1295. DALEY, Michael
"Myrtle Lake in the Morning." [PoetryE] (31) Spr 91, p. 142.

1296. DALGON, Ruth
"Complaints." [Pearl] (13) Spr-Sum 91, p. 18.
"Eve's Legacy." [Pearl] (13) Spr-Sum 91, p. 18.

1297. DALIBARD, Jill
"The House Garden." [AntigR] (85/86) Spr-Sum 91, p. 97-98.

1298. DALLAT, Cahal
"Adelaide Park." [Verse] (8:2) Sum 91, p. 104.
"On Metaphor." [Verse] (8:2) Sum 91, p. 104.

1299. DALTON, Mary
"Bedroom Sketch." [TickleAce] (21) Spr-Sum 91, p. 86.
"Buttercup Poem." [TickleAce] (21) Spr-Sum 91, p. 87.
"The Comfort of Images." [TickleAce] (21) Spr-Sum 91, p. 88.
"Song for Dandelion." [Arc] (27) Aut 91, p. 71.
"Thirst." [TickleAce] (21) Spr-Sum 91, p. 85.

1300. DALTON, Roque
"Poema de Amor." [Areíto] (3:9) Je 91, p. 22.

1301. DALY, Daniel
"Camping in Northern Woods." [FourQ] (5:1) Spr 91, p. 36.

1302. DALY, M. A.
"Three Geraniums." [Vis] (36) 91, p. 35.

1303. DALY, Mary Hunter
"Skin of Glass" (Second Prize, 1991 Literary Contest). [Crucible] (27) Fall 91, p. 3.

1304. DAME, Enid
"Lilith." [Spirit] (11) 91, p. 137-138.

1305. DANA, Robert
"Five Short Complaints." [Manoa] (3:1) Spr 91, p. 44-47.
"In the Gardens of Fabulous Desire." [WestHR] (45:2) Sum 91, p. 85-86.
"Rat" (For Godwin, Vincent, Kim). [Poetry] (158:2) My 91, p. 87-88.
"Refracted Light: Life as Text" (Selections: 4 poems). [Ploughs] (17:1) Spr 91, p.
43-47.
1306. DANIEL, David
"Blue Ridge Near Dark." [PoetryE] (32) Fall 91, p. 148.
1307. DANIEL, Yuli
"Romance About My Motherland" (in Russian and English, tr. by B. Z. Niditch).
[InterPR] (17:2) Fall 91, p. 76-77.
1308. DANIELS, Barbara
"Losing the Farm." [FourQ] (5:2) Fall 91, p. 54.
1309. DANIELS, Jim
"Bedtime Story." [LitR] (35:1) Fall 91, p. 119.
"Broke." [ColR] (NS 17:2) Fall-Wint 90, p. 64-66.
"Deep Fried." [RiverS] (34) 91, p. 50-51.
"Digger Pays Off the Mortgage." [PoetryE] (31) Spr 91, p. 93.
"Faith." [ColR] (NS 17:2) Fall-Wint 90, p. 62-63.
"Ghazals" (70-75). [NoAmR] (276:1) Mr 91, p. 34-35.
"Hoagie." [WestB] (29) 91, p. 76-77.
"Ice." [RiverC] (12:1) Fall 91, p. 62-63.
"Minigolf Love, Corsica." [ArtfulD] (20/21) 91, p. 58.
"Passing." [RiverS] (34) 91, p. 52-53.
"Spell." [PraS] (65:3) Fall 91, p. 34-36.
1310. DANIELS, Kate
"Worlds" (beginning with a line from Rilke). [LouisL] (8:1) Spr 91, p. 30-31.
1311. DANIELS, Peter
"Breakfast, Palermo." [JamesWR] (8:3) Spr 91, p. 1.
1312. DANKLEFF, Richard
"The Splash." [NowestR] (29:2) 91, p. 88.
1313. DANTE
"Inferno" (Canto IX-X, tr. by Amy Clampitt). [Antaeus] (67) Fall 91, p. 51-60.
"Inferno" (Canto XV-XVI, tr. by Richard Howard). [Antaeus] (67) Fall 91, p.
61-67.
"Inferno" (Canto XXVI-XXVII, tr. by W. S. Merwin). [Antaeus] (67) Fall 91, p.
68-77.
DAO, Bei
See BEI, Dao
DAO, Jia
See JIA, Dao
1314. DARLING, Robert
"The Jape of the Mock." [Hellas] (2:1) Spr 91, p. 74-76.
1315. DARLINGTON, Andrew
"Poem Quoting Richard Mason and Henry Normal." [Bogg] (64) 91, p. 16.
1316. DARNIELLE, John
"Karen Carpenter." [SpoonRQ] (16:1/2) Wint-Spr 91, p. 35.
1317. DARR, Ann
"Five You's of February." [CreamCR] (15:2) Fall 91, p. 74-75.
DARRAJ AL-QASTALLI, Ibn
See IBN DARRAJ AL-QASTALLI
1318. DARROW, David
"Pohaku Ola." [HawaiiR] (15:3, #33) Fall 91, p. 28-29.
1319. DAS, Mahadai
"The Clown." [GrahamHR] (14) Spr 91, p. 37-38.
1320. DASSANOWSKY-HARRIS, Robert
"Album Page" (For R.J., tr. of Alexander Lernet-Holenia). [Os] (33) Fall 91, p. 18.
"Autumnal." [Abraxas] (40/41) 91, p. 142.
"Communique." [Rohwedder] (6) Sum-Fall 91, p. 23.
"Not with Hands, Erato." [Abraxas] (40/41) 91, p. 142-143.
"There Is a Rumor." [Rohwedder] (6) Sum-Fall 91, p. 23.
"Upon Seeing the Panels of Pierre Puvis de Chavannes (1824-1898)." [Abraxas]
(40/41) 91, p. 141.
"When the Wild Geese Cry" (tr. of Alexander Lernet-Holenia). [Os] (33) Fall 91, p.
16.

1321. DATTA, Jyotirmoy
"Bestial" (tr. of Anuradha Mahapatra, w. Carolyne Wright). [TriQ] (81) Spr-Sum 91, p. 223-224.
"God" (tr. of Anuradha Mahapatra, w. Carolyne Wright). [TriQ] (81) Spr-Sum 91, p. 232-233.
"To You, Mother" (tr. of Anuradha Mahapatra, w. Carolyne Wright). [TriQ] (81) Spr-Sum 91, p. 235-236.
"Wasteland Without Chariot Wheels" (tr. of Anuradha Mahapatra, w. Carolyne Wright). [TriQ] (81) Spr-Sum 91, p. 225-226.
"The Year 1984" (tr. of Anuradha Mahapatra, w. Carolyne Wright). [TriQ] (81) Spr-Sum 91, p. 222.
1322. DAUMAL, René
"The Great Day of the Dead" (tr. by Jordan Jones). [HeavenB] (9) Wint-Spr 91-92, p. 28-29.
"The Notorious Surprise" (tr. by Jordan Jones). [HeavenB] (9) Wint-Spr 91-92, p. 25.
"The Only One" (tr. by Jordan Jones). [HeavenB] (9) Wint-Spr 91-92, p. 26-27.
1323. DAUNT, Jon
"The Way Hands Move." [CalQ] (31) Fall 88, p. 38.
1324. DAVID, Gary
"Dakota Dry." [SwampR] (7/8) Spr-Sum 91, p. 10.
"A Nightmare Cafe on the High Plains." [SwampR] (7/8) Spr-Sum 91, p. 9.
1325. DAVIDKOV, Ivan
"Clay and Star" (tr. by Lisa Sapinkopf, w. Georgi Belev). [CarolQ] (44:1) Fall 91, p. 44.
"Villages Like Ghosts" (tr. by Lisa Sapinkopf, w. Georgi Belev). [CarolQ] (44:1) Fall 91, p. 43.
1326. DAVIDSON, Catherine
"The Marriage of Frida and Diego" (A Plainsongs Award Poem). [Plain] (12:2) Wint 91, p. 37.
1327. DAVIDSON, Cynthia
"Contact Sheet." [WillowR] Spr 91, p. 28-29.
1328. DAVIDSON, Daniel
"Long Division" (Excerpt). [Aerial] (6/7) 91, p. 140-142.
"Transit" (Selections: 1-10). [Avec] (4:1) 91, p. 34-41.
"Transit" (Selections: 11-1). [Talisman] (7) Fall 91, p. 132-135.
1329. DAVIDSON, K. L.
"Matter at Hand." [Grain] (19:4) Wint 91, p. 30.
1330. DAVIDSON, Karen
"Abroad." [PottPort] (13:2) Fall-Wint 91, p. 17.
"The Amaryllis." [PottPort] (13:2) Fall-Wint 91, p. 15.
"Foster Plant." [PottPort] (13:2) Fall-Wint 91, p. 15.
"New Leaf." [PottPort] (13:2) Fall-Wint 91, p. 16.
1331. DAVIDSON, Phebe
"The House As Vortex." [JINJPo] (13:1) Spr 91, p. 26.
"My Great Uncle Henry Smoked Cigars." [JINJPo] (13:1) Spr 91, p. 27.
"My Last Glad Summer." [JINJPo] (13:1) Spr 91, p. 25.
"The Road." [JINJPo] (13:1) Spr 91, p. 22-24.
DAVIDSON, Terri Brown
See BROWN-DAVIDSON, Terri
1332. DAVIDUKE, K.
"Orion's Lament." [BellArk] (7:6) N-D 91, p. 6.
1333. DAVIE, Donald
"Three Pastors in Berlin." [PartR] (58:3) Sum 91, p. 574-578.
1334. DAVIES, John
"Say Hello to Phoenix." [Stand] (33:1) Wint 91, p. 66.
1335. DAVIS, Angela J.
"Among Other Things." [OnTheBus] (8/9) 91, p. 55-56.
"Life in Progress: Page 10956/ Turning Thirty." [OnTheBus] (8/9) 91, p. 56-57.
1336. DAVIS, Barbara Rosson
"Calla Lily." [SouthernHR] (25:1) Wint 91, p. 38.
1337. DAVIS, Christopher
"Against Death." [DenQ] (26:2) Fall 91, p. 16.
"Against Shattering." [SouthernHR] (25:4) Fall 91, p. 382.
"His Prayer to Men." [JamesWR] (8:3) Spr 91, p. 11.
"In Effigy." [WillowS] (27) Wint 91, p. 15-17.

"The Patriot" (Poetry Chapbook: 13 poems). [BlackWR] (17:2) Spr-Sum 91, p. 59-80.
"Please Come Down." [Journal] (15:1) Spr 91, p. 22-23.
"Silent Hymn." [Journal] (15:1) Spr 91, p. 20-21.
"A Soaking Flag." [Journal] (15:1) Spr 91, p. 24.
"To One Dead Boy." [DenQ] (26:2) Fall 91, p. 15.

1338. DAVIS, Cortney
"Goddess" (National Geographic, 1955). [Calyx] (13:2) Sum 91, p. 54-55.
"The Smoke We Make Pictures of." [Calyx] (13:2) Sum 91, p. 52-53.

1339. DAVIS, DeeAnne
"We Come from Iowa." [SinW] (43/44) Sum 91, p. 295-298.

1340. DAVIS, Ellen
"Letter from New Hampshire." [AnthNEW] (3) 91, p. 29.

1341. DAVIS, Glover
"Bird Watcher." [Journal] (14:2) Wint 91, p. 71-72.

1342. DAVIS, Joann
"Stoking the Fire." [Parting] (4:1) Sum 91, p. 32.

1343. DAVIS, John
"Sunday Morning: Cat on My Bed." [BellR] (14:1) Spr 91, p. 20.

1344. DAVIS, Melody (Melody D.)
"Blessing." [PoetryNW] (32:4) Wint 91-92, p. 37-38.
"Cielo." [PoetryNW] (32:4) Wint 91-92, p. 36-37.
"Getting Rid of Him." [Turnstile] (3:1) 91, p. 59-61.
"Pink." [Poetry] (157:5) F 91, p. 275.
"Topos." [Poetry] (158:3) Je 91, p. 131.
"Twin." [BrooklynR] (8) 91, p. 33.

1345. DAVIS, Michael C.
"The Lover Should Not Have Returned." [PoetL] (86:3) Fall 91, p. 15.

1346. DAVIS, Owen
"Bruges Sunday Early Morning Rain." [Os] (33) Fall 91, p. 4-5.
"Rain on the Roof." [Os] (32) Spr 91, p. 8-9.
"This Rain." [Os] (32) Spr 91, p. 6-7.

1347. DAVIS, Pamela Oberon
"Prayer to Morpheus." [CapeR] (26:2) Fall 91, p. 37.
"To a Dying Planet." [NewYorkQ] (44) 91, p. 63.

1348. DAVIS, Tim
"Three Letters from Europe." [Notus] (9) Fall 91, p. 66-68.

1349. DAVIS, Whitney
"In summer I sat on my knees and the grass." [EngJ] (80:4) Ap 91, p. 36.

1350. DAVIS, William Virgil
"Driving Through Wales." [Bogg] (64) 91, p. 50.
"For My Father" (In memory). [Poetry] (158:1) Ap 91, p. 36.
"The Orchard." [Poetry] (158:1) Ap 91, p. 36.
"Signs." [NorthStoneR] (10) Fall 91-Wint 92, p. 230.
"Still Life." [NorthStoneR] (10) Fall 91-Wint 92, p. 227.
"Summer Tree." [NorthStoneR] (10) Fall 91-Wint 92, p. 228-229.
"Watercolor." [NewOR] (18:4) Wint 91, p. 33.

1351. DAVISON, Peter
"The Black Aspen" (For Robert Penn Warren). [SewanR] (99:3) Sum 91, p. 362-363.

1352. DAVISON, Steven
"The Perseids." [US1] (24/25) Spr 91, p. 23.

1353. DAWE, Gerald
"Double-Take." [Verse] (8:2) Sum 91, p. 109.

1354. DAWE, Tom
"In Hardy Country." [TickleAce] (22) Fall-Wint 91, p. 8.
"Salmon." [TickleAce] (22) Fall-Wint 91, p. 9.
"Top of the World." [TickleAce] (22) Fall-Wint 91, p. 7.

1355. DAWID, Annie
"Things We Call Home." [PaintedHR] (2) Spr 91, p. 17-18.

1356. DAWSON, David
"Moon Poem." [WestCL] (25:1) Spr 91, p. 43-46.
"Omage" (for Louis & Celia Zukofsky). [WestCL] (25:1) Spr 91, p. 41-42.
"Small Forms in a Thicket" (variations, in a progression). [WestCL] (25:1) Spr 91, p. 39-40.
"Upstream, at One Remove: 6:02 AM." [WestCL] (25:1) Spr 91, p. 47-48.

1357. DAY, Sarah
　　"Biography." [PoetryUSA] (23) Sum 91, p. 23.
1358. DAYTON, Irene G.
　　"Archaeology's Wanderings." [Elf] (1:1) Spr 91, p. 32-33.
De . . .
　　　See also names beginning with "De" without the following space, filed below in their
　　　　alphabetic positions, e.g., DeFOE.
De ANDRADE, Eugénio
　　See ANDRADE, Eugénio de
De ANHALT, Nedda G.
　　See ANHALT, Nedda G. de
De AZEVEDO, Kathleen
　　See AZEVEDO, Kathleen de
De CAMPOS, Alvaro
　　See PESSOA, Fernando
De CARTERET, Mark
　　See DeCARTERET, Mark
De CÉSPEDES, Jorge Enrique
　　See CÉSPEDES, Jorge Enrique de
De CHAZAL, Malcolm
　　See CHAZAL, Malcolm de
De COURCY, Lynne H.
　　See DeCOURCY, Lynne H.
1359. De FRATES, Steven Craig
　　"Sixth Sense." [ChironR] (10:3) Aut 91, p. 44.
1360. De GRAFT-ROSENIOR, Arthur
　　"B E (Best Effort)." [LitR] (34:4) Sum 91, p. 457.
De KAMP, Alexandra van
　　See Van de KAMP, Alexandra
1361. De la VEGA, Yvonne
　　"I Want to Be a Man." [Pearl] (14) Fall-Wint 91, p. 49.
De las CASAS, Walter
　　See CASAS, Walter de las
De LESCOET, Henri
　　See LESCOET, Henri de
1362. De MARIS, Ron
　　"False Spring." [PraS] (65:3) Fall 91, p. 25.
　　"The Man Who Dressed Well." [PraS] (65:3) Fall 91, p. 23-24.
De NERVAL, Gérard
　　See NERVAL, Gérard de
De NIORD, Chard
　　See DeNIORD, Chard
De OLIVEIRA, Carlos
　　See OLIVEIRA, Carlos de
De ORY, Carlos Edmundo
　　See ORY, Carlos Edmundo de
1363. De QUESADA, Isa
　　"Bones." [OnTheBus] (8/9) 91, p. 58.
　　"First Drink." [Pearl] (13) Spr-Sum 91, p. 38.
De UNGRIA, Ricardo M.
　　See UNGRIA, Ricardo M. de
1364. DEAN, Debi Kang
　　"Aloha, 'Aina." [Ploughs] (17:4) Wint 91-92, p. 82-83.
　　"Geophagy." [SingHM] (19) 91, p. 35.
1365. DEANE, John F.
　　"The Monastery." [Interim] (10:1) Spr-Sum 91, p. 16-17.
　　"The Museum of Cosmonautics." [Interim] (10:1) Spr-Sum 91, p. 15.
　　"The Stylized City." [Interim] (10:1) Spr-Sum 91, p. 18.
1366. DeANGELO, G. Pearce
　　"The View from an Open Window." [EmeraldCR] (3) 91, c1990, p. 138-139.
1367. DEARING, Carol
　　"Re-creation by Microwave." [OxfordM] (7:2) Fall-Wint 91, p. 64.
1368. DEBELJAK, Ales
　　"The Color of Morning" (tr. by Michael Biggins). [PassN] (12:2) Wint 91, p. 23.
　　"Distant Voices II" (tr. by the author and Michael Biggins). [LitR] (35:1) Fall 91, p.
　　　70.

"Distant Voices III" (tr. by the author and Michael Biggins). [LitR] (35:1) Fall 91, p. 70.
"Elegy" (tr. by Michael Biggins). [GrandS] (10:3, #39) 91, p. 209.
"Outline of History" (from "Dictionary of Silence," tr. by Michael Biggins). [Boulevard] (5:3/6:1, #15/16) Spr 91, p. 57-58.
"The Past in My Mind" (tr. by Michael Biggins). [Agni] (34) 91, p. 245.
"A Poem to No Avail." [PlumR] (1) Spr-Sum 91, p. 4.
"Radio: Night Program" (tr. by Michael Biggins). [PassN] (12:2) Wint 91, p. 23.
"Under Eastern Eyes" (tr. by Michael Biggins). [Shen] (41:2) Sum 91, p. 90.
"Woman on the Border" (tr. by Michael Biggins). [PassN] (12:2) Wint 91, p. 23.

1369. DEBNEY, Jack
"The Republic of Wholeness." [Stand] (33:1) Wint 91, p. 59.

DEBORAH JOY
  See JOY, Deborah

1370. DEBUT, Laurent
"Suite Silencieuse." [Os] (32) Spr 91, p. 34-35.

1371. DeCARTERET, Mark
"Deaths Behind." [DustyD] Je 91, p. 24.
"So There." [SmPd] (28:3, #83) Fall 91, p. 9.

1372. DECKER, Michael
"The Stonecutter." [NewRep] (204:5) 4 F 91, p. 38.

1373. DeCLUE, Charlotte
"Said He Was Coyote" (for Liz — you don't wanna know). [PoetryE] (32) Fall 91, p. 17-18.
"Voices" (for Joy). [PoetryE] (32) Fall 91, p. 13-16.

1374. DeCORMIER-SHEKERJIAN, Regina
"Light Etches Like Acid." [ManhatPR] (13) [91?], p. 39.
"Ritual." [Nat] (252:9) 11 Mr 91, p. 319.

1375. DeCOURCY, Lynne H.
"A Girl's Astronomy" (For Becky, her story). [Prima] (14/15) 91, p. 98-99.
"Lowcountry Portrait." [Kalliope] (13:3) 91, p. 9.
"The Task at Hand" (for David). [Calyx] (13:3) Wint 91-92, p. 57.
"Thirst" (Drought, 1988). [Prima] (14/15) 91, p. 100-101.

1376. DeCRAY, Sharon
"Neighbor." [Vis] (35) 91, p. 19.

DEEB, Kamal Abu
  See ABU-DEEB, Kamal

1377. DEES, Joe E.
"Autumn Evening." [EmeraldCR] (3) 91, c1990, p. 57.
"The Soothsmith's Song." [EmeraldCR] (3) 91, c1990, p. 82-83.

1378. DEFFEBACH, Nancy
"Cave of Bronze" (tr. of Alice Rahon, w. Vanina Deler). [OnTheBus] (8/9) 91, p. 195.
"Despair" (to Pablo Picasso, tr. of Alice Rahon, w. Vanina Deler). [OnTheBus] (8/9) 91, p. 188.
"Hourglass Lying Down" (tr. of Alice Rahon, w. Vanina Deler). [OnTheBus] (8/9) 91, p. 196.
"Pointed Out Like a Star" (to Ixtaccihuatl, tr. of Alice Rahon, w. Vanina Deler). [OnTheBus] (8/9) 91, p. 194.
"A Woman Who Was Beautiful" (tr. of Alice Rahon, w. Vanina Deler). [OnTheBus] (8/9) 91, p. 174.

1379. DeFOE, Mark
"In the Midst of a Shower, in the Middle of a Drought, a Tortoise." [WebR] (15) Spr 91, p. 66.
"Opening Day." [WebR] (15) Spr 91, p. 64-66.
"The Rehearsal." [CapeR] (26:2) Fall 91, p. 47.
"Warm Spring Night/Upscale Single's Bar." [WebR] (15) Spr 91, p. 67.

1380. DeFREES, Madeline
"Japanese Carp in the Pond: Maui." [Ploughs] (17:2/3) Fall 91, p. 186-187.
"Scarecrow Gardens." [Nimrod] (34:2) Spr-Sum 91, p. 31.

1381. DEIKE, Marta
"Clark Coolidge/Gerturde Stein" (with Gary Sullivan). [Avec] (4:1) 91, p. 135-136.

1382. DEISROTH, Nancy
"Blackberries." [NewYorkQ] (45) 91, p. 78-80.

1383. DEITCH, Robin
"Procedure." [BrooklynR] (8) 91, p. 24.

1384. DeJOHN, Paul
"I saw a tree standing alone." [PoetryE] (31) Spr 91, p. 51.

Del . . .
See also names beginning with "Del" without the following space, filed below in
their alphabetical positions, e.g., DELGADO, Juan.

Del CASAL, Victor
See CASAL, Victor del

Del CASTILLO, Amelia
See CASTILLO, Amelia del

1385. Del GUERCIO, Margaret
"Confession." [Elf] (1:3) Fall 91, p. 40-41.

Del PINO, José Manuel
See PINO, José Manuel del

1386. DELANO, Page Dougherty
"Coal Bones: R & R on Ice." [Confr] (46/47) Fall 91-Wint 92, p. 257-258.
"Death and Eros." [PoetryE] (31) Spr 91, p. 134.
"Happy Land." [RiverS] (34) 91, p. 37.
"Snake Verse: Understanding West Virginia." [Confr] (46/47) Fall 91-Wint 92, p.
257.
"We Are All Girls." [RiverS] (34) 91, p. 35-36.

1387. DELANTY, Greg
"Complaint to the Watchmaker." [SouthernR] (27:2) Ap 91, p. 341.
"On an Oil Spillage Due North." [GreenMR] (NS 5:1) Sum-Fall 91, p. 102.
"The Scarecrow." [InterPR] (17:2) Fall 91, p. 125.
"A Wake on Lake Champlain." [GreenMR] (NS 5:1) Sum-Fall 91, p. 101.

1388. DELER, Vanina
"Cave of Bronze" (tr. of Alice Rahon, w. Nancy Deffebach). [OnTheBus] (8/9) 91,
p. 195.
"Despair" (to Pablo Picasso, tr. of Alice Rahon, w. Nancy Deffebach). [OnTheBus]
(8/9) 91, p. 188.
"Hourglass Lying Down" (tr. of Alice Rahon, w. Nancy Deffebach). [OnTheBus]
(8/9) 91, p. 196.
"Pointed Out Like a Star" (to Ixtaccihuatl, tr. of Alice Rahon, w. Nancy Deffebach).
[OnTheBus] (8/9) 91, p. 194.
"To Alice" (10 February XXXVI, tr. of Pablo Picasso). [OnTheBus] (8/9) 91, p.
190-193.
"A Woman Who Was Beautiful" (tr. of Alice Rahon, w. Nancy Deffebach).
[OnTheBus] (8/9) 91, p. 174.

1389. DELGADO, Juan
"A Better View." [BilingR] (16:2/3) My-D 91, p. 215.
"The Brown Boy's Love." [BilingR] (16:2/3) My-D 91, p. 217.
"One Hundred Dollars Per Month." [BilingR] (16:2/3) My-D 91, p. 216.
"The Santa Ana Winds." [BilingR] (16:2/3) My-D 91, p. 214.

DelGUERCIO, Margaret
See Del GUERCIO, Margaret

1390. DELIGIORGIS, Stavros
"For I Will Consider Harold." [Iowa] (21:3) Fall 91, p. 84-86.

1391. DellaROCCA, L.
"Anytime in New York City (To John Lennon)" (from "Elegy for Friends and
Strangers"). [SlipS] (11) 91, p. 20-22.

1392. DELMAR, Maira
"The Arts of Fire" (to Mariacristina Bethencourt, tr. by Todd Burrell). [WebR] (15)
Spr 91, p. 36.
"Melody" (tr. by Todd Burrell). [WebR] (15) Spr 91, p. 37.
"Radiance" (tr. by Todd Burrell). [WebR] (15) Spr 91, p. 37.
"This Love" (tr. by Todd Burrell). [WebR] (15) Spr 91, p. 35.

Delos SANTOS, Pablo
See SANTOS, Pablo Delos

1393. DeLOTTO, Jeffrey
"In Traction, Basma Hospital: Irbid, Jordan, Spring, 1982." [BlackBR] (13)
Spr-Sum 91, p. 26.

1394. DELP, Michael
"River Gods." [RiverS] (35) 91, p. 34.
"Sowing Darkness." [RiverS] (35) 91, p. 35.

1395. DeMAY, Anna
"Letting Go." [Plain] (11:2) Wint 91, p. 9.

1396. DEMING, Alison
"Caffe Trieste." [Crazy] (40) Spr 91, p. 13-14.
"Shakers." [Crazy] (40) Spr 91, p. 11-12.
1397. DEMING, Barbara
"Our love, like the new moon." [SinW] (43/44) Sum 91, p. 57.
1398. DEMING, Kay
"Winter Tribute." [RagMag] (9:1) 91, p. 24.
1399. DEMPSEY, Ivy
"In New Mexico: Looking for Home." [Nimrod] (34:2) Spr-Sum 91, p. 33.
"Journey" (Variation on a theme by Transtromer). [Nimrod] (34:2) Spr-Sum 91, p. 35.
"L.A.: Night Life." [Nimrod] (34:2) Spr-Sum 91, p. 32.
"Translation." [Nimrod] (34:2) Spr-Sum 91, p. 34.
1400. DEMPSTER, Barry
"Breathless, the Sanatorium 1930." [PraF] (12:3 #56) Aut 91, p. 62.
"Del Monte Ranch, Questa, New Mexico 1924." [PraF] (12:3 #56) Aut 91, p. 61.
"Dreaming West" (National Geographic). [AntigR] (85/86) Spr-Sum 91, p. 100.
"Feeling the Heat, Ceylon 1922." [Quarry] (40:1/2) Wint-Spr 91, p. 47-48.
"Italy 1914." [PraF] (12:3 #56) Aut 91, p. 60.
"Last Lights, Vence 1930." [Grain] (19:2) Sum 91, p. 90-91.
"Letters from a Long Illness with the World, the D.H. Lawrence Poems" (Selection: "London 1912"). [Quarry] (40:1/2) Wint-Spr 91, p. 46.
"Modern Love" (Cosmopolitan). [AntigR] (85/86) Spr-Sum 91, p. 99.
"When I Close My Eyes, Vence, March 1930." [Grain] (19:2) Sum 91, p. 92.
1401. DeNIORD, Chard
"Break." [GreenMR] (NS 5:1) Sum-Fall 91, p. 139.
"The Din of Ringers." [Agni] (34) 91, p. 201.
"Our Eyes Are Sweet Obedient Dogs." [PoetryE] (32) Fall 91, p. 121.
"This Is a Blessing, This Is a Curse." [PoetryE] (32) Fall 91, p. 120.
"Time Was." [QW] (33) Sum-Fall 91, p. 171-172.
1402. DENNIS, C. J.
"The world 'as got me snouted jist a treat" (from "A Spring Song," "The Songs of a Sentimental Bloke," 1915). [PoetryUSA] (23) Sum 91, p. 22.
1403. DENNIS, Carl
"The Messiah." [AmerPoR] (20:2) Mr-Ap 91, p. 18.
"Spring Letter." [Poetry] (158:2) My 91, p. 63-64.
"Tuesday at First Presbyterian." [KenR] (NS 13:1) Wint 91, p. 90-91.
1404. DENNISON, Matt
"The Big Boys." [Spitball] (37) Sum 91, p. 40-41.
"I Believed No Machine." [WindO] (55) Wint 91-92, p. 29-30.
"Mr. Borenstein." [WindO] (55) Wint 91-92, p. 24-28.
1405. DENNISON, Michael
"Primo Levi, *The Periodic Table*, and Me." [Journal] (15:2) Fall 91, p. 37-38.
1406. DENT, Tory
"Walking Away I." [PartR] (58:4) Fall 91, p. 689.
"Walking Away II." [Talisman] (7) Fall 91, p. 90.
"Walking Away III." [Talisman] (7) Fall 91, p. 90.
1407. DEPTA, Victor M.
"The Allusion to America." [ContextS] (2:2) 91, p. 28.
"Point Reyes, California." [CapeR] (26:1) Spr 91, p. 34.
1408. DER-HOVANESSIAN, Diana
"Break-In." [AmerS] (60:4) Aut 91, p. 516-517.
"If You Are a Poet" (tr. of Gevorg Emin). [InterPR] (17:2) Fall 91, p. 81.
"My Borders" (tr. of Henrik Edoyan). [Vis] (36) 91, p. 36.
"When Your Country Is Small" (tr. of Hovhanness Grigorian). [InterPR] (17:2) Fall 91, p. 80.
1409. DERRICOTTE, Toi
"Christmas Eve: My Mother Dressing." [Callaloo] (14:3) Sum 91, p. 649-650.
"Fifty." [Callaloo] (14:3) Sum 91, p. 646.
"Holy Cross Hospital." [Callaloo] (14:3) Sum 91, p. 642-644.
"Leaving." [Callaloo] (14:3) Sum 91, p. 645.
"The Minks." [Callaloo] (14:3) Sum 91, p. 652-653.
"On Reading About Frank Purdue's Extensive and Continuing Moving Violations, Including an Accident in which an Accountant Was Killed." [US1] (24/25) Spr 91, p. 43.

"On the Turning Up of Unidentified Black Female Corpses." [Callaloo] (14:3) Sum 91, p. 647-648.
"Poem for My Father." [Callaloo] (14:3) Sum 91, p. 637-639.
"The Promise." [Callaloo] (14:3) Sum 91, p. 640-641.
"The Rice King of the South." [Callaloo] (14:3) Sum 91, p. 651.

1410. DERRY, Alice
"Bluedicks." [HighP] (6:1) Spr 91, p. 91-93.
"Montana Song." [Prima] (14/15) 91, p. 94-95.

1411. Des FORETS, Louis-René
"Poèmes de Samuel Wood" (Excerpt, tr. by Ann Smock). [Talisman] (6) Spr 91, p. 82-85.

1412. DESAI, Ravi
"The Empty Air." [HarvardA] (127 [i.e. 125]:3) Ja 91, p. 7.

1413. DESCH, Robert
"Sunday in the Suburbs." [ChrC] (108:33) 13 N 91, p. 1062.
"Teaching an Adult to Read." [ChrC] (108:24) 21-28 Ag 91, p. 773.

1414. DESEY, Peter
"Coming Home from a Long Drive on Route 23, Ohio." [Farm] (8:1) Spr-Sum 91, p. 16.

1415. DESMARAIS, Karl
"Over a Cliff in Montana." [PacificR] (10) 91-92, p. 21.
"Wetstone." [PacificR] (10) 91-92, p. 103.

1416. DESMOND, Walter
"Ancient Neighbor (A Woman Recluse)." [Writer] (104:6) Je 91, p. 26.

1417. DESNOS, Robert
"The Spaces of Sleep" (tr. by Janis Mark). [CrabCR] (7:2) Sum 91, p. 16-17.
"Under the Kindness of Night" (tr. by Keith Abbott). [Talisman] (7) Fall 91, p. 67.

1418. DESPORTE, Charles
"Lenin on a Rope." [LullwaterR] (3:1) Fall 91, p. 61.

1419. DESROCHERS, Kerry
"Dee-san" (for Deirdre Curle). [PraF] (12:1 #54) Spr 91, p. 82.

1420. DESROSIERS, Thérèse
"Blueberries" (tr. by Louise Allin). [WebR] (15) Spr 91, p. 38.
"Transubstantiation" (tr. by Louise Allin). [WebR] (15) Spr 91, p. 38.

1421. DESY, Peter
"Almost Oedipal." [WestB] (29) 91, p. 94-95.
"The Heart of It All." [PacificR] (10) 91-92, p. 71.
"Leaving Pennsylvania." [SouthernPR] (31:2) Fall 91, p. 63.
"Like Some Rivers." [FourQ] (5:1) Spr 91, p. 35.
"Losing It." [PacificR] (10) 91-92, p. 126.
"Love in the 50's." [HampSPR] Wint 91, p. 62.
"My Doctor, His Proctoscope." [CreamCR] (15:2) Fall 91, p. 76-77.
"Outrigger Fishing for Salmon." [ChironR] (10:2) Sum 91, p. 41.
"Sister Mary Lucinda." [NewEngR] (14:1) Fall 91, p. 48-49.
"TV in Their Vans." [HampSPR] Wint 91, p. 63.

1422. DETWEILER, Robert
"False Spring." [ChrC] (108:6) 20 F 91, p. 198.

1423. DEVET, Rebecca McClanahan
"Traveling." [Boulevard] (6:2/3, #17/18) Fall 91, p. 197-199.

1424. DEVINE, Nancy
"The Shape Changer." [BelPoJ] (41:3) Spr 91, p. 21-22.
"You Have the Fingers For It." [BelPoJ] (41:3) Spr 91, p. 20.

1425. DEVINE, Richard
"Blawearie." [Stand] (32:2) Spr 91, p. 34-35.

1426. DeVRIES, Rachel Guido
"Blues Bird, Darling Bird." [YellowS] (36) Spr 91, p. 24.
"Daydream / Soon." [YellowS] (36) Spr 91, p. 22.
"Hands Like Birds, Flying." [YellowS] (36) Spr 91, p. 25.

1427. DeWITT, Jim
"The Color of Cranberry." [HawaiiR] (15:2, #32) Spr 91, p. 56.
"Dry Roasted Peanuts." [ContextS] (2:2) 91, p. 25-26.

DeWITT, Susan Kelly
See KELLY-DeWITT, Susan

DHOMHNAILL, Nuala Ni
See Ni DHOMHNAILL, Nuala

Di . . .
    See also names beginning with "Di" without the following space, filed below in their
        alphabetic positions, e.g., DiPALMA
1428. Di LASSO, Orlando
    "Matona, Mia Cara" (tr. by W. D. Snodgrass). [Poetry] (157:5) F 91, p. 270-271.
1429. Di PIERO, W. S.
    "Buddy's Corner." [TriQ] (83) Wint 91-92, p. 123-124.
    "In the Driveway" (for P.K.). [Thrpny] (47) Fall 91, p. 17.
    "Reading Ovid." [TriQ] (83) Wint 91-92, p. 130-131.
    "Saturday Afternoon." [TriQ] (83) Wint 91-92, p. 125-127.
    "Self-Portrait." [TriQ] (83) Wint 91-92, p. 128-129.
    "The Sleepers." [Thrpny] (46) Sum 91, p. 22.
DIAZ, Pablo Montenegro
    See MONTENEGRO DIAZ, Pablo
1430. DIAZ CAPO, Marylín
    "Trance." [Nuez] (3:8/9) 91, p. 20.
DIAZ-DIOCARETZ, Myriam
    See DIOCARETZ, Myriam Diaz
1431. DiCAROLIS, Cristen
    "1. 4th and Orange." [ChironR] (10:2) Sum 91, p. 12.
    "2. 3121 E. Corto Place #1 (Across the Street from Taco Bell)." [ChironR] (10:2)
        Sum 91, p. 12.
    "3. Long Beach Is the Murphy Bed Capital of the World." [ChironR] (10:2) Sum 91,
        p. 12.
    "4. In the Privacy of Your Own Home." [ChironR] (10:2) Sum 91, p. 12.
    "5. It's Like Doo-wop." [ChironR] (10:2) Sum 91, p. 12.
1432. DiCHRISTINA, S. J.
    "The Poet." [Elf] (1:1) Spr 91, p. 26-27.
1433. DICKEY, William
    "Genealogy Program." [SenR] (21:1) Spr 91, p. 39-44.
    "Vigils." [Chelsea] (51) 91, p. 15-19.
1434. DICKINSON, Laura
    "Lithography Portrait." [PoetryNW] (32:1) Spr 91, p. 17-18.
1435. DICKSON, John
    "Black Watch." [Elf] (1:2) Sum 91, p. 20-21.
    "Filling in the Past." [Poetry] (158:2) My 91, p. 65.
    "The Troubadour Chronicles." [Elf] (1:2) Sum 91, p. 18-19.
1436. DICKSON, Ron
    "Hunger." [SlipS] (11) 91, p. 36.
1437. DIEHL-JONES, Charlene
    "Loving Merlin." [PraF] (12:1 #54) Spr 91, p. 35.
    "Practising Magic." [PraF] (12:1 #54) Spr 91, p. 36-37.
1438. DIEMER, Gretchen
    "The Boy Who Died Under the Ice." [PoetryNW] (32:2) Sum 91, p. 42-43.
    "Lost in the Woods." [PoetryNW] (32:2) Sum 91, p. 43-44.
    "Return from the City During Sugar Beet Harvest." [PoetryNW] (32:2) Sum 91, p.
        44-45.
1439. DIENES, Louis
    "A birth's a something out of nothing." [SmPd] (28:1, #81) Wint 91, p. 28.
    "It's drip-dry saturday and noon." [SmPd] (28:1, #81) Wint 91, p. 26.
    "To Machu Picchu." [SmPd] (28:1, #81) Wint 91, p. 27.
1440. DIENG, Chiekh Ahmadou
    "A Black Man Told Me" (for David Diop, tr. by Dominique Benson and Peter
        Benson). [LitR] (34:4) Sum 91, p. 459.
    "Lice" (tr. by Dominique Benson and Peter Benson). [LitR] (34:4) Sum 91, p. 458.
    "Passion of a Vulture" (tr. by Dominique Benson and Peter Benson). [LitR] (34:4)
        Sum 91, p. 458.
1441. DIFALCO, Sam
    "The Zoo." [Dandel] (18:1) Spr-Sum 91, p. 7.
1442. DIGGES, Deborah
    "Blue Willow." [Antaeus] (67) Fall 91, p. 140-141.
    "Cleopatra's Funeral Gown." [Colum] (17) Fall 91, p. 184.
    "In-House Harvest." [Antaeus] (67) Fall 91, p. 138-139.
    "We Are Light We Are Nothing Blessed." [Colum] (17) Fall 91, p. 183.
1443. DILLARD, Gavin
    "4/14/90." [ChironR] (10:2) Sum 91, p. 13.

"4/15/90." [ChironR] (10:2) Sum 91, p. 13.
"6/3/90." [ChironR] (10:2) Sum 91, p. 13.
"6/24/90." [ChironR] (10:2) Sum 91, p. 13.
"8/27/90." [ChironR] (10:2) Sum 91, p. 13.

1444. DILLON, Andrew
"Building a Home." [SoDakR] (29:2) Sum 91, p. 76.
"Erogenous Zone." [SoDakR] (29:4) Wint 91, p. 38.
"A Fresh Self." [SoDakR] (29:1) Spr 91, p. 52.
"Goodnight to My Son." [NoDaQ] (59:3) Sum 91, p. 170.
"Historian." [SpoonRQ] (16:3/4) Sum-Fall 91, p. 33.
"Home Galaxy — in August." [SoDakR] (29:2) Sum 91, p. 77.
"Near Rapid City." [SoDakR] (29:4) Wint 91, p. 39.
"A Ripple of Knowing." [MidwQ] (32:2) Wint 91, p. 184.
"Suicide: a Motel in the Dakotas." [SoDakR] (29:1) Spr 91, p. 51.
"To a Reader of Poems." [SoDakR] (29:2) Sum 91, p. 75.
"To a Writing Class: First Day." [SoDakR] (29:4) Wint 91, p. 40.
"What Am I Coming To?" [InterPR] (17:2) Fall 91, p. 108.

1445. DILSAVER, Paul
"New Age Rebel." [Bogg] (64) 91, p. 17.

1446. DIMITROVA, Blaga
"If" (tr. by Jascha Kessler and Alexander Shurbanov). [Vis] (36) 91, p. 16.

1447. DINE, Carol
"Going Away Without You." [BellR] (14:1) Spr 91, p. 5.
"I Decide to Make Death Subtle." [SpoonRQ] (16:1/2) Wint-Spr 91, p. 36.
"The Papermaker." [SpoonRQ] (16:1/2) Wint-Spr 91, p. 37-38.

1448. DINEEN, Thomas
"An Imagined Ending." [Writer] (104:3) Mr 91, p. 21.

1449. DINESCU, Mircea
"So?!" (tr. by Adam J. Sorkin and Sergiu Celac). [LitR] (35:1) Fall 91, p. 36.
"To Her Highness Our Landlady for a More Just Apportioning of the Body" (tr. by
   Adam J. Sorkin and Sergiu Celac). [LitR] (35:1) Fall 91, p. 36.

1450. DING, Dennis
"Cigarette Butts" (tr. of Xu Gang, w. Edward Morin and Fang Dai). [Iowa] (21:2)
   Spr-Sum 91, p. 45.
"A Figure Seen from Behind" (tr. of Xu Gang, w. Edward Morin and Fang Dai).
   [Iowa] (21:2) Spr-Sum 91, p. 45.
"Red Azalea on the Cliff" (tr. of Xu Gang, w. Edward Morin and Fang Dai). [Iowa]
   (21:2) Spr-Sum 91, p. 44.
"Summer" (tr. of Xu Gang, w. Edward Morin and Fang Dai). [Iowa] (21:2)
   Spr-Sum 91, p. 46.

1451. DINGS, Fred
"The Concession." [ContextS] (2:2) 91, p. 11.
"Old Men Fishing." [PoetL] (86:1) Spr 91, p. 22.
"Renaissance." [ContextS] (2:2) 91, p. 10.

1452. DINO
"How Quickly the Good Things Go" (Homeless Writers Coalition). [PoetryUSA]
   (23) Sum 91, p. 21.

1453. DIOCARETZ, Myriam Diaz
"In This Stone" (tr. by Karen Blomain). [Vis] (36) 91, p. 41.

1454. DIORIO, Margaret
"Holdup." [ChironR] (10:2) Sum 91, p. 45.

1455. DiPALMA, Ray
"Coconut Harry." [HangL] (59) 91, p. 26.
"The Hallways." [WashR] (16:6) Ap-My 91, p. 8.
"Rebus Tact." [NewAW] (8/9) Fall 91, p. 27-28.
"A Strange Menagerie of Golden Monsters." [HangL] (59) 91, p. 26.

1456. DIRANAS, Ahmet Muhip
"Bitmez Tükenmez Can Sikintisi." [InterPR] (17:1) Spr 91, p. 18.
"Endless Boredom" (tr. by Ozcan Yalim, William A. Fielder and Dionis Coffin
   Riggs). [InterPR] (17:1) Spr 91, p. 19.

1457. DISCH, Tom
"The Crumbling Infrastructure." [Spirit] (11) 91, p. 37-38.
"A Gravedigger's Soliloquy." [Salm] (92) Fall 91, p. 200-201.
"Not Quite a Sonnet But I Love You Just the Same." [Boulevard] (5:3/6:1, #15/16)
   Spr 91, p. 44.
"What Is Orgasm." [Boulevard] (5:3/6:1, #15/16) Spr 91, p. 42-43.

1458. DISCHELL, Stuart
"The Body Surfer." [GettyR] (4:1) Wint 91, p. 155.
"The Bulletin Board." [GettyR] (4:1) Wint 91, p. 156.
"For Robert Maurer." [AntR] (49:1) Wint 91, p. 97.
"Wishes." [Ploughs] (17:2/3) Fall 91, p. 223-224.
1459. DITSKY, John
"Shortages." [TexasR] (11:1/2) Spr-Sum 90, p. 64.
1460. DITTA, Joseph M.
"Advice to John and Henry." [WeberS] (8:2) Fall 91, p. 39-40.
"(J.D.)." [WeberS] (8:2) Fall 91, p. 38.
"On the Banks of the James." [WeberS] (8:2) Fall 91, p. 37-38.
1461. DITTBERNER-JAX, Norita
"In the Garden." [LakeSR] (25) 91, p. 24.
"The Nun's Hands." [LakeSR] (25) 91, p. 25.
1462. DIVAKARUNI, Chitra
"The Arranged Marriage." [CreamCR] (15:1) Spr 91, p. 54-55.
"At the Sati Temple, Bikaner" (after a photograph by Raghubir Singh). [CreamCR]
(15:1) Spr 91, p. 56-57.
"The First Time" (for Surjo). [Thrpny] (45) Spr 91, p. 25.
"The Quilt." [Calyx] (13:2) Sum 91, p. 4-5.
"The Snake Charmers." [Chelsea] (50) 91, p. 21-22.
"Two Women Outside a Circus, Pushkar" (after a photograph by Raghubir Singh).
[CreamCR] (15:1) Spr 91, p. 58-59.
"Villagers Visiting Jodhpur Enjoy Iced Sweets" (after a photograph by Raghubir
Singh). [Chelsea] (50) 91, p. 20.
1463. DIXON, John
"An Evening in High Bentham." [Verse] (8:2) Sum 91, p. 44.
"Lullaby." [Verse] (8:2) Sum 91, p. 44.
"Scots Baronial." [Verse] (8:2) Sum 91, p. 43.
1464. DIXON, K. Reynolds (Kent R.)
"After Words." [ChatR] (11:3) Spr 91, p. 44.
"Fallow." [Turnstile] (3:1) 91, p. 36.
"Opening the Blue Pod" (On the occasion of an open house in the neuro-muscular
ward . . .). [Turnstile] (3:1) 91, p. 34-35.
"Shadowfall." [TriQ] (83) Wint 91-92, p. 114.
"Vigil." [ChatR] (11:3) Spr 91, p. 43.
"Vigil." [TriQ] (81) Spr-Sum 91, p. 211.
"Whitsun Sounding at Holy Loch." [TriQ] (81) Spr-Sum 91, p. 209-210.
1465. DIXON, Melvin
"And These Are Just a Few." [KenR] (NS 13:2) Spr 91, p. 4-5.
"Aunt Ida Pieces a Quilt." [Spirit] (11) 91, p. 104-106.
"Camp 1940" (to Abdoulaye Ly, tr. of Léopold Sédar Senghor). [AmerPoR] (20:6)
N-D 91, p. 6.
"Elegy for the Queen of Sheba" (for two koras and a balaphon, tr. of Léopold Sédar
Senghor). [AmerPoR] (20:6) N-D 91, p. 8-10.
"The Enlisted Man's Despair" (tr. of Léopold Sédar Senghor). [AmerPoR] (20:6)
N-D 91, p. 5.
"The Falling Sky" (In memory of Chester W. Weineman). [JamesWR] (8:3) Spr 91,
p. 18.
"Governor Eboué" (to Henri and Robert Eboué, tr. of Léopold Sédar Senghor).
[AmerPoR] (20:6) N-D 91, p. 6.
"Imaginings, or Dreaming of a Young Girl" (tr. of Léopold Sédar Senghor).
[AmerPoR] (20:6) N-D 91, p. 6.
"In Memoriam" (tr. of Léopold Sédar Senghor). [AmerPoR] (20:6) N-D 91, p. 4.
"Man and Beast" (for the three tabalas or war drums, tr. of Léopold Sédar Senghor).
[AmerPoR] (20:6) N-D 91, p. 8.
Mirrors Still" (tr. of Léopold Sédar Senghor). [AmerPoR] (20:6) N-D 91, p. 7.
"My Greeting" (tr. of Léopold Sédar Senghor). [AmerPoR] (20:6) N-D 91, p. 5.
"Shadow Song" (tr. of Léopold Sédar Senghor). [AmerPoR] (20:6) N-D 91, p. 4-5.
"To Death" (tr. of Léopold Sédar Senghor). [AmerPoR] (20:6) N-D 91, p. 4.
"To New York" (for jazz orchestra and trumpet solo, tr. of Léopold Sédar Senghor).
[AmerPoR] (20:6) N-D 91, p. 7.
"Totem" (tr. of Léopold Sédar Senghor). [AmerPoR] (20:6) N-D 91, p. 4.
1466. DJANIKIAN, Gregory
"For Us." [PoetryNW] (32:4) Wint 91-92, p. 5-6.
"In Alexandria." [Poetry] (158:3) Je 91, p. 140-141.

"Mrs. Kinsey's House of Children." [PoetryNW] (32:4) Wint 91-92, p. 3-4.
"Mrs. Mitstifer." [Crazy] (40) Spr 91, p. 23-24.
"Unhappiness." [PoetryNW] (32:4) Wint 91-92, p. 4-5.
"The Visit." [Poetry] (158:1) Ap 91, p. 25-26.
"Visiting Irasburg, Vermont in July." [Crazy] (40) Spr 91, p. 21-22.

1467. DJURIC, Dubravka
"Disordering" (tr. by the author and Charles Bernstein). [Sulfer] (11:2, #29) Fall 91, p. 23-24.

1468. DLUGI-KING, Julie
"As Soon as You Step into Juarez." [ChironR] (10:4) Wint 91, p. 36.
"For One Day I Forget You Hate Green." [ChironR] (10:2) Sum 91, p. 42.

1469. DLUGOS, Tim
"D.O.A." [Spirit] (11) 91, p. 101-103.
"Etiquette in 1969." [Shiny] (6) Spr-Sum 91, p. 54.
"Friends Service." [Shiny] (6) Spr-Sum 91, p. 55-56.
"Good Morning." [BrooklynR] (8) 91, p. 2-3.
"Lagoon Capriccio." [WashR] (16:6) Ap-My 91, p. 4.
"Last Letter" (Music by Christopher Berg). [WashR] (16:6) Ap-My 91, p. 16-18.
"Not Stravinsky." [WashR] (16:6) Ap-My 91, p. 9.
"Swede." [WashR] (16:6) Ap-My 91, p. 4.
"Turandot." [Shiny] (6) Spr-Sum 91, p. 53.

1470. DOANE, R. Michael
"Burning Letters in Wintertime." [SoDakR] (29:3 part 2) Aut 91, p. 32.

1471. DOBSON, Rosemary
"The Other Eye" (from "Seeing and Believing"). [PoetryUSA] (23) Sum 91, p. 23.

1472. DOBYNS, Stephen
"Bleeder." [EngJ] (80:3) Mr 91, p. 47.

1473. DODD, Elizabeth
"Like Memory, Caverns." [VirQR] (67:3) Sum 91, p. 483-484.
"Lyric." [LaurelR] (25:1) Wint 91, p. 69.

1474. DODD, Wayne
"Before Divorce." [GeoR] (45:4) Wint 91, p. 654-655.
"On Any Given Afternoon." [GeoR] (45:1) Spr 91, p. 169.

1475. DODDS, Charles
"Drought." [PoetryUSA] (23) Sum 91, p. 26.
"Harmonica-Beaked Hummingbird Sings the Blues" (An Elegy for a Devoured Lover?). [PoetryUSA] (23) Sum 91, p. 26.

1476. DODGE, George Burton, Sr.
"Antonio." [EmeraldCR] (4) 91, p. 32-33.
"Autumn Reaper." [EmeraldCR] (3) 91, c1990, p. 58-60.

1477. DODSON, Keith A.
"Budgets Are Getting Tight." [Pearl] (14) Fall-Wint 91, p. 10.
"Every Morning." [DustyD] (2:1) Ja 91, p. 21.
"I Don't Mind." [ChironR] (10:2) Sum 91, p. 8.
"I Like Long Handled Tools." [Pearl] (14) Fall-Wint 91, p. 10.
"I Watch the Moon." [ChironR] (10:2) Sum 91, p. 8.
"In the Night." [ChironR] (10:2) Sum 91, p. 8.
"It Was an Honor." [ChironR] (10:2) Sum 91, p. 8.
"Let's Take a Walk." [ChironR] (10:2) Sum 91, p. 8.
"Maybe I Shouldn't Have Talked So Much." [ChironR] (10:2) Sum 91, p. 8.
"Men's Slow-Pitch." [Pearl] (13) Spr-Sum 91, p. 56.
"There Are Days." [Pearl] (14) Fall-Wint 91, p. 10.
"Tried." [ChironR] (10:2) Sum 91, p. 8.
"Tropical Fish." [HawaiiR] (15:3, #33) Fall 91, p. 38.
"The Undersea World of." [SlipS] (11) 91, p. 40.

1478. DOHERTY, Jim
"The Lament of Caliban." [PacificR] (10) 91-92, p. 147.

1479. DOLAN, John
"The Lecture on Scarcity." [Thrpny] (45) Spr 91, p. 16.

1480. DOLGIN, Steven
"Juarez." [CoalC] (3) My 91, p. 20.
"Michael Leaving for New Zealand to Become a Zen Cowboy." [CoalC] (3) My 91, p. 8.

1481. DOLIN, Sharon
"Reading." [Boulevard] (6:2/3, #17/18) Fall 91, p. 143-144.

1482. DOLTON, Alexia Lyn
"In Protest." [RagMag] (9:2) 91, p. 13.
"Stereotypes." [RagMag] (9:2) 91, p. 12.
1483. DOMEN, Ron
"Asphalt Man" (in memoriam, Loren Eisley). [BlackBR] (14) Fall-Wint 91, p. 9.
1484. DOMINA, Lynn
"A Shy and New Desire." [SouthernPR] (31:2) Fall 91, p. 34-35.
"White Candles." [LaurelR] (25:2) Sum 91, p. 48-49.
"A White Jug and Large White Bowl." [LaurelR] (25:2) Sum 91, p. 47.
1485. DONAGHY, Michael
"Erratum." [Poetry] (157:5) F 91, p. 278-279.
"Liverpool." [Poetry] (157:5) F 91, p. 277.
1486. DONAHUE, Joseph
"Christ Enters Manhattan II." [CentralP] (19/20) Spr-Fall 91, p. 45-46.
1487. DONALD, Pamela
"Suzi Meets a Musician Backstage at Center Stage Theatre." [SoCaR] (24:1) Fall 91,
p. 198.
"Waiting for Echo Lake." [SoCaR] (23:2) Spr 91, p. 187.
1488. DONALD, Peter Lawrence
"Margaret Thatcher" (Response to "Save the Clerihew" appeal). [BostonR] (16:3/4)
Je-Ag 91, p. 33.
1489. DONALDSON, Beth
"Fig Grip." [Poem] (66) N 91, p. 40.
"Fish Blood." [Poem] (66) N 91, p. 39.
"My Mother's Vegetable Garden." [Poem] (66) N 91, p. 38.
1490. DONALDSON, Jeffery
"Deep River, Ontario, Population 4,325" (for Jeffery Peter Haindl, Born 5 June
1988). [NewRep] (204:11) 18 Mr 91, p. 42.
"A Floating Garden at Giverny." [Salm] (92) Fall 91, p. 174-178.
"The Man Who Drew Days." [WestHR] (45:1) Spr 91, p. 23-24.
1491. DONALDSON, Lee
"Father." [ManhatPR] (13) [91?], p. 6.
1492. DONALDSON, Leigh
"Firehouse." [InterPR] (17:2) Fall 91, p. 121.
DONG, Hang
See HANG, Dong
1493. DONNELLY, Karen
"One Warm Evening." [HawaiiR] (15:2, #32) Spr 91, p. 88.
"She Lives What Others Cannot Hear." [CapeR] (26:1) Spr 91, p. 39.
1494. DONNELLY, P. N. W.
"Counting the Days." [Bogg] (64) 91, p. 52.
1495. DONOGHUE, John
"Breath." [PraS] (65:3) Fall 91, p. 55-56.
"Hometown." [PraS] (65:3) Fall 91, p. 56-57.
"Morning Walk." [GreenMR] (NS 5:1) Sum-Fall 91, p. 122.
"Reasoning with My Son." [PraS] (65:3) Fall 91, p. 55.
"Say Something Certain." [PraS] (65:3) Fall 91, p. 54.
"Siren." [GreenMR] (NS 5:1) Sum-Fall 91, p. 123.
"Stars." [CreamCR] (15:2) Fall 91, p. 64.
1496. DONOHUE, Sheila P.
"Clean and Fine." [TriQ] (81) Spr-Sum 91, p. 193-195.
"Metastasis." [TriQ] (81) Spr-Sum 91, p. 192.
"The Mirror." [TriQ] (81) Spr-Sum 91, p. 196.
1497. DONOVAN, Daria
"Between Lit and Out." [OnTheBus] (8/9) 91, p. 59-60.
1498. DONOVAN, Frances
"The angry men have come to talk." [Writer] (104:6) Je 91, p. 25.
1499. DONOVAN, Gregory
"Nietzsche in the Engadine." [PoetL] (86:4) Wint 91-92, p. 13-15.
1500. DONOVAN, Karen
"The Many Uses of Camouflage." [SouthernPR] (31:1) Spr 91, p. 37-38.
"The Scout Looks for Bee Purple." [SouthernPR] (31:1) Spr 91, p. 36.
1501. DONOVAN, Stewart
"Antigonish Landing" (In Memoriam, R.J. MacSween, 1915-1990). [AntigR]
(87/88) Fall 91-Wint 92, p. 306-309.
"Cape Breton Quarry" (Selection: I). [AntigR] (84) Wint 91, p. 151-154.

"The North West Arm" (i.m. Hugh MacLennan 1907-1990). [AntigR] (85/86)
Spr-Sum 91, p. 32.
1502. DOOLITTLE, Deborah H.
"Trees From My Windows." [MidAR] (12:1) 91, p. 110.
1503. DORAINE
"Now." [OnTheBus] (8/9) 91, p. 61.
1504. DORESKI, William
"Astronaut." [Outbr] (22) 91, p. 24.
"Dream-Lives." [Poem] (66) N 91, p. 48.
"F Alliterations." [HawaiiR] (15:3, #33) Fall 91, p. 97.
"From the Old Sewage Plant on Columbia Point." [Poem] (66) N 91, p. 50.
"My Affair with Meryl Streep." [Poem] (66) N 91, p. 49.
"The Railroad Bridge at Bellows Falls." [Poem] (66) N 91, p. 47.
1505. DORF, Marilyn
"Cranes on the Platte at Sunset." [Plain] (11:3) Spr 91, p. 38.
"Now That He Has Turned Timeless." [Plain] (12:2) Wint 91, p. 17.
"Shyness." [Northeast] (5:5) Wint 91-92, p. 10.
"Water Is Wild." [Plain] (12:1) Fall 91, p. 29.
1506. DORIAN, Marguerite
"Hunger" (tr. of Maria Banus, w. Elliott B. Urdang). [MidAR] (11:1) 91, p. 131.
"Through Bucharest, After the Rain" (tr. of Maria Banus, w. Elliott B. Urdang).
[MidAR] (11:1) 91, p. 130.
1507. DORING, Stephan
"Wind-Lament Rain-Delusion" (tr. by Agnes Stein). [QW] (32) Wint-Spr 91, p. 96.
1508. DORIS, Stacy
"Days." [CentralP] (19/20) Spr-Fall 91, p. 203-207.
"A View of Islands." [AntR] (49:3) Sum 91, p. 440.
1509. DORSETT, Robert
"For Simone Weil." [InterPR] (17:2) Fall 91, p. 113.
"Night Movements." [Paint] (18:36) Aut 91, p. 18.
"Palestinian Camp Fire." [Paint] (18:36) Aut 91, p. 19.
"Surrealist Love Poem." [InterPR] (17:2) Fall 91, p. 113.
"Three Adolescent Poems on the Mystery of Women." [InterPR] (17:2) Fall 91, p.
112-113.
1510. DORSEY, Candas Jane
"Events cloud the word field." [PraF] (12:3 #56) Aut 91, p. 40.
"(For KOB)." [PraF] (12:3 #56) Aut 91, p. 41-42.
"The Rolling Landscape." [PraF] (12:3 #56) Aut 91, p. 38.
"Until my thirty fourth year I managed to conceal my small bones." [PraF] (12:3
#56) Aut 91, p. 39.
1511. DOTY, Catherine
"Yes." [JINJPo] (13:1) Spr 91, p. 31.
1512. DOTY, Mark
"Demolition." [Poetry] (158:4) Jl 91, p. 208-209.
"Esta Noche." [JamesWR] (8:3) Spr 91, p. 10.
"Fog." [Boulevard] (5:3/6:1, #15/16) Spr 91, p. 36-39.
"Human Figures." [Boulevard] (5:3/6:1, #15/16) Spr 91, p. 40-41.
"Pharoah's Daughter" [sic: i.e. Pharaoh's]. [NewEngR] (13:3/4) Spr-Sum 91, p.
170-171.
"Roadside." [BrooklynR] (8) 91, p. 31-32.
"To Bessie Drennan." [Poetry] (159:3) D 91, p. 155-156.
1513. DOUBIAGO, Sharon
"South America Mi Hija" (2 selections). [Zyzzyva] (7:2) Sum 91, p. 114-120.
"Wrecking Yard." [Ploughs] (17:4) Wint 91-92, p. 122.
1514. DOUGHERTY, Sean Thomas
"Principle of Degrees." [OnTheBus] (8/9) 91, p. 63.
"Workdays." [MoodySI] (24/25/26) Spr 91, p. 51.
1515. DOUGLAS, Ann
"St. Vitus's Dance." [Ascent] (16:1) Fall 91, p. 32.
1516. DOUGLAS, M. Scott
"The Pittsburgh Allis Chalmers." [BlackBR] (13) Spr-Sum 91, p. 6-7.
1517. DOUSKEY, Franz
"Carl Furillo, 1922-1989." [Spitball] (36) Spr 91, p. 9.
"Is It Something I Said." [NewYorkQ] (45) 91, p. 46.
"Wasted Night." [NewYorkQ] (46) 91, p. 35.
"When the President Comes." [NewYorkQ] (44) 91, p. 47.

"White." [NorthStoneR] (10) Fall 91-Wint 92, p. 100.
1518. DOVE, Rita
"Aircraft." [Spirit] (11) 91, p. 183.
"Nike" (Berlin, Brandenburger Tor, December 1989). [Ploughs] (17:2/3) Fall 91, p.
270.
1519. DOVER, Ron
"Words to the Wise." [WindO] (55) Wint 91-92, p. 10.
1520. DOW, Mark
"On Reading Keats's Letters to Fanny Brawne." [ChiR] (37:2/3) 91, p. 106.
1521. DOWNE, Lise
"Predestined in Twelve Parts" (Selections: 1, 3, 5, 10-12). [Avec] (4:1) 91, p.
127-130.
1522. DOWNING, Kim
"The File Cabinet." [Sidewalks] (1) Aug 91, p. 33-34.
1523. DOYLE, James
"The Donkey." [CarolQ] (43:3) Spr 91, p. 44.
"The Landscape." [ChironR] (10:2) Sum 91, p. 14.
"Mr. Terence." [ChironR] (10:2) Sum 91, p. 14.
"The Pond." [Colum] (15) 90, p. 200.
"Primavera." [ChironR] (10:2) Sum 91, p. 14.
"Termites." [LullwaterR] (3:1) Fall 91, p. 55.
1524. DOYLE, Lynn
"Watching" (for J. James). [HighP] (6:3) Wint 91, p. 73-74.
1525. DOYLE, Sally
"Can you erase all traces of yourself?" [CentralP] (19/20) Spr-Fall 91, p. 66-69.
"I can't stop talking." [CentralP] (19/20) Spr-Fall 91, p. 69-70.
"Shepherding (Transporting Sheep)" (Selections: 3 poems). [Aerial] (6/7) 91, p.
167-168.
"Take a pledge to investigate Americans who are not returning their census."
[CentralP] (19/20) Spr-Fall 91, p. 70-72.
1526. DRABIK, Basia
"Instead of a Sonnet" (tr. of Tadeusz Chabrowski, w. Grazyna Drabik). [HeavenB]
(9) Wint-Spr 91-92, p. 8.
"A Letter from a Grandmother in Greenpoint to Her Granddaughter in Poland" (tr. of
Tadeusz Chabrowski, w. Grazyna Drabik). [HeavenB] (9) Wint-Spr 91-92, p.
8.
1527. DRABIK, Grazyna
"Instead of a Sonnet" (tr. of Tadeusz Chabrowski, w. Basia Drabik). [HeavenB] (9)
Wint-Spr 91-92, p. 8.
"A Letter from a Grandmother in Greenpoint to Her Granddaughter in Poland" (tr. of
Tadeusz Chabrowski, w. Basia Drabik). [HeavenB] (9) Wint-Spr 91-92, p. 8.
1528. DRAGNEA, Gabriela
"Cognition" (tr. of Marin Sorescu, w. Stuart Friebert). [Aerial] (6/7) 91, p. 82.
"Descent" (tr. of Marin Sorescu, w. Stuart Friebert). [PraF] (12:3 #56) Aut 91, p.
52.
"Getting Used to Your Name" (tr. of Marin Sorescu, w. Stuart Friebert). [PraS]
(65:3) Fall 91, p. 122.
"Miracle" (tr. of Marin Sorescu, w. Stuart Friebert). [PraF] (12:3 #56) Aut 91, p.
51.
1529. DRAGOMOSHCHENKO, Arkadii
"Xenia" (Excerpt, tr. by Lyn Hejinian and Elena Balashova). [GrandS] (10:4, #40)
91, p. 82-87.
1530. DRAGONSUN, Jabiya
"First Patrol." [ChironR] (10:1) Spr 91, p. 12.
1531. DRAKE, Alan
"To a Poet Recognizing a Pervasive Theme." [Archae] (1) Fall 90, p. 38-39.
1532. DRAKE, Albert
"Homesick." [SwampR] (7/8) Spr-Sum 91, p. 103.
"Tomato Soup." [SwampR] (7/8) Spr-Sum 91, p. 102.
1533. DRAKE, James
"Errancies, Anomalies, Promiscuities." [WritersF] (17) Fall 91, p. 59.
"Faithed — Time." [PacificR] (10) 91-92, p. 104.
"Nature on Television." [WritersF] (17) Fall 91, p. 59.
1534. DRAKE, Jim
"Not a Through Tree." [PacificR] (10) 91-92, p. 76-78.

1535. DRANOW, Ralph
    "You've Got a Long Way to Go, Baby." [PoetryUSA] (23) Sum 91, p. 14.
1536. DRECHSLER, Mark
    "Losing to Junipers." [BellR] (14:2) Fall 91, p. 18.
1537. DRENNAN, Ellen
    "Twenty Years." [CanLit] (128) Spr 91, p. 10.
DRESSAY, Anne Le
    See Le DRESSAY, Anne
1538. DREW, George
    "Back from the Vanishing Point." [SnailPR] (1:2) Fall 91-Wint 92, p. 30.
    "Directions for Obtaining Knowledge of All Dark Things" (— Ahmes Papyrus).
        [PoetryNW] (32:4) Wint 91-92, p. 13-15.
    "Matthew Brady Speaks." [PoetryNW] (32:4) Wint 91-92, p. 11-13.
    "The Scholar Skunk." [PoetryNW] (32:4) Wint 91-92, p. 15-16.
1539. DREXEL, John
    "A Last Resort." [FourQ] (5:1) Spr 91, p. 26.
    "Wholly Dedicated to a House." [Hudson] (44:3) Aut 91, p. 432.
1540. DRIEDGER, Diane
    "Bonsai." [PraF] (12:1 #54) Spr 91, p. 83.
    "The Grip." [PraF] (12:1 #54) Spr 91, p. 83.
1541. DRISKELL, Kathleen Mason
    "Leaving the Argument." [MidAR] (12:1) 91, p. 111-112.
    "Tornado, Louisville, 1974." [HayF] (9) Fall-Wint 91, p. 75.
1542. DRIZHAL, Peter
    "Exploiting Mother." [ChironR] (10:4) Wint 91, p. 14.
    "Talking." [ContextS] (2:2) 91, p. 15-16.
    "These Days." [ContextS] (2:2) 91, p. 16-18.
    "Today You Can Call Me." [ChironR] (10:4) Wint 91, p. 14.
1543. DRUMMOND, Robbie Newton
    "Egg Crate Creation Poem." [Event] (20:2) Sum 91, p. 95.
    "Flowersong of the Not Yet Alive." [Dandel] (18:2) Wint 91, p. 64.
    "Kidneys." [Event] (20:2) Sum 91, p. 94.
1544. DRURY, John
    "Hot Spell." [Journal] (14:2) Wint 91, p. 74.
    "Pursuing the Delta Blues." [WestHR] (45:4) Wint 91, p. 285.
    "Semester Abroad." [WestHR] (45:4) Wint 91, p. 286-287.
Du . . .
    See also names beginning with "Du" without the following space, filed below in their
        alphabetic positions, e.g., DuPLESSIS.
1545. DU, Fu
    "Night Thoughts When I Am Voyaging" (in Chinese and English, tr. by Fuh
        Shyh-jen). [Abraxas] (40/41) 91, p. 154-155.
1546. DUBIE, Norman
    "The Aztec Lord of the Near and Close." [SouthernR] (27:1) Ja 91, p. 38-39.
    "Bellevue Exchange." [MissR] (19:3) 91, p. 182.
    "The Blue Hog." [MissR] (19:3) 91, p. 183.
    "The Children." [SouthernR] (27:1) Ja 91, p. 40-42.
    "Confession." [SouthernR] (27:1) Ja 91, p. 42-43.
    "Revelation 20:11-15" (for Tito). [SouthernR] (27:1) Ja 91, p. 44-45.
    "A True Story of God." [SouthernR] (27:1) Ja 91, p. 43-44.
    "The White River Road." [SouthernR] (27:1) Ja 91, p. 39-40.
1547. DUCKER, Bruce
    "The Cricket in the City." [Poetry] (158:2) My 91, p. 86.
1548. DUDIS, Ellen K. (Ellen Kirvin)
    "Capuchin." [CalQ] (35/36) 91, p. 84.
    "Frog Prince." [SoCoast] (10) Fall 91, p. 8-9.
1549. DUDLEY, Betty
    "Heart Beats." [SinW] (45) Wint 91-92, p. 118-119.
1550. DUDLEY, Ellen
    "Weekend Yankees." [Blueline] (12) 91, p. 42.
1551. DUDOIT, Darlaine Mahealani Muilan
    "A Portrait of Willy." [BambooR] (50/51) Spr-Sum 91, p. 243-244.
    "Silk Dragons." [BambooR] (50/51) Spr-Sum 91, p. 242.
1552. DUECK, Lynnette
    "Daddy I." [PraF] (12:1 #54) Spr 91, p. 58-59.

1553. DUEHR, Gary
"Census." [Timbuktu] (6) Spr 91, p. 68.
"November." [WillowS] (28) Sum 91, p. 63.
"Richness, Goodness." [WillowS] (28) Sum 91, p. 62.
"To Rising and Falling." [SycamoreR] (3:1) Wint 91, p. 7-8.
1554. DUEMER, Joseph
"Dog Years." [Iowa] (21:3) Fall 91, p. 94-95.
"Mathematics of Chaotic Systems." [NewEngR] (14:1) Fall 91, p. 22-23.
"Plainsong." [NewEngR] (14:1) Fall 91, p. 23-25.
"Reader Response." [TampaR] (4) 91, p. 88-89.
"Sculpture Garden." [Iowa] (21:3) Fall 91, p. 92.
"Sketch for an Elegy." [NewEngR] (14:1) Fall 91, p. 25-26.
"Water Music." [Iowa] (21:3) Fall 91, p. 93-94.
1555. DUENAS, Warren
"Genin — Darkness Visible." [ChironR] (10:4) Wint 91, p. 21.
1556. DUENSING, Danica
"Life." [PoetryUSA] (23) Sum 91, p. 24.
"Things I Didn't Know I Loved." [PoetryUSA] (23) Sum 91, p. 24.
1557. DUER, David
"After Today" (for Emma and Jesse). [Ascent] (15:3) Spr 91, p. 9.
1558. DUFFIN, Brent
"Poetry Is a Heavenly Crime" (tr. of Vicente Huidobro, w. Astrid Lindo). [InterPR]
    (17:2) Fall 91, p. 67.
"Revisiting a Mountain Town" (tr. of Kyong-rim Sin, w. Yang Seung-Tai).
    [InterPR] (17:1) Spr 91, p. 25.
"A Traveler" (tr. of Mok-Wol Park, w. Yang Seung-Tai). [InterPR] (17:1) Spr 91,
    p. 22.
1559. DUFFY, Carol Ann
"Litany." [Verse] (8:2) Sum 91, p. 123.
"The Professor of Philosophy Attempts Prayer." [Verse] (8:2) Sum 91, p. 125.
DUGGAN, Devon Miller
    See MILLER-DUGGAN, Devon
1560. DUHAMEL, Denise
"The Lotus Position" (January 26, 1991). [WestB] (28) 91, p. 87.
"Mary Moppets Daycare Center" (Tucson, Arizona). [FreeL] (7) Spr 91, p. 9-12.
"Prayer, or Nostalgia for Heaven." [PoetryE] (31) Spr 91, p. 73-74.
"Sighs and Whistles." [CimR] (95) Ap 91, p. 47.
"Stories from the Body." [PlumR] (1) Spr-Sum 91, p. 23-25.
"That's Going to Mean Something Later On" (for Kathleen Rockwell Lawrence).
    [PoetryE] (31) Spr 91, p. 71-72.
1561. DUKE, Lee
"There Is No One Here But You." [BlackBR] (14) Fall-Wint 91, p. 16.
1562. DUMARAN, Adele
"A Blessing" (for my daughter). [DenQ] (26:1) Sum 91, p. 20.
"The Violent Pictures." [Manoa] (3:1) Spr 91, p. 208-209.
1563. DUMARS, Denise
"Questions." [Rohwedder] (6) Sum-Fall 91, p. 19.
"Urbanity." [Rohwedder] (6) Sum-Fall 91, p. 19.
1564. DUMBRAVEANU, Anghel
"Landscape in White" (tr. by Robert J. Ward and Marcel Cornis-Pop). [Talisman]
    (6) Spr 91, p. 138.
"Magic Words for the One Confined in Silence" (tr. by Robert J. Ward and Marcel
    Cornis-Pop). [Talisman] (6) Spr 91, p. 138.
1565. DUMITRU, Cyra Sweet
"Dream of the Missing Children." [SouthernPR] (31:1) Spr 91, p. 43.
1566. DUNCAN, Garth
"Little Dictators by Frankie." [Grain] (19:4) Wint 91, p. 59.
1567. DUNCAN, Graham
"Mirror Talk." [DustyD] Ap 91, p. 19.
"Porcupine." [ManhatPR] (13) [91?], p. 42.
"Rural Delivery." [DustyD] Ap 91, p. 4.
1568. DUNCAN, Julia Nunnally
"Dust." [InterPR] (15:1) Spr 89, p. 103.
"Earth." [InterPR] (15:1) Spr 89, p. 102.
"Letter to Her Sister." [Lactuca] (14) My 91, p. 46.
"Lord Only Knows." [Lactuca] (14) My 91, p. 45.

"Magic." [Lactuca] (14) My 91, p. 44.
"Mountain Boy." [InterPR] (15:1) Spr 89, p. 104.
1569. DUNCAN, Peter
"Artifacts." [JINJPo] (13:2) Aut 91, p. 12.
"Morris County Tornado." [JINJPo] (13:2) Aut 91, p. 11.
1570. DUNEV, Michael
"Four Nahautl Poems [sic, i.e. Nahuatl]" (tr. of anonymous poems, from the
Spanish). [Zyzzyva] (7:2) Sum 91, p. 59-62.
1571. DUNFORD, Mary C.
"Fire Dogs." [NorthStoneR] (10) Fall 91-Wint 92, p. 199.
"Grandmother." [NorthStoneR] (10) Fall 91-Wint 92, p. 197.
"Mother to My Mother." [NorthStoneR] (10) Fall 91-Wint 92, p. 198.
1572. DUNGEY, Christopher
"Old Story." [ChironR] (10:2) Sum 91, p. 43.
"The Sister-in-law Swimming." [SnailPR] (1:2) Fall 91-Wint 92, p. 24.
"Soaky." [SoCoast] (11) Wint 91, p. 21.
1573. DUNN, Douglas
"Spanish Oranges." [SouthernR] (27:2) Ap 91, p. 339-340.
1574. DUNN, Sharon
"Black Bananas." [Crazy] (41) Wint 91, p. 11-12.
"Blood." [Crazy] (41) Wint 91, p. 10.
"City." [Crazy] (41) Wint 91, p. 9.
"Twirling" (Sasha at twelve). [Crazy] (41) Wint 91, p. 7-8.
1575. DUNN, Stephen
"Back Then in America" (Cottonwood, 1970). [SnailPR] (1:2) Fall 91-Wint 92, p.
22-23.
"Breakfast After the Blood Test." [GeoR] (45:3) Fall 91, p. 470.
"Contrary." [ThRiPo] (37/38) 91, p. 73-74.
"Drift." [SycamoreR] (3:1) Wint 91, p. 34-35.
"The False Music." [Iowa] (21:2) Spr-Sum 91, p. 136.
"The Gentle Man." [ThRiPo] (37/38) 91, p. 72.
"Ghosts." [TampaR] (4) 91, p. 21.
"Good Talk." [ParisR] (33:119) Sum 91, p. 249.
"The Man in the Forest." [Boulevard] (5:3/6:1, #15/16) Spr 91, p. 180-181.
"Ordinary Days." [NewEngR] (13:3/4) Spr-Sum 91, p. 230-231.
"Regardless." [VirQR] (67:1) Wint 91, p. 65-66.
"Smiles." [Iowa] (21:2) Spr-Sum 91, p. 137-139.
"Stations." [Poetry] (157:5) F 91, p. 268-269.
"Update" (To Bartleby). [VirQR] (67:1) Wint 91, p. 63-65.
"White Collar." [TampaR] (4) 91, p. 22.
"The Woman on Edgehill Road." [Iowa] (21:2) Spr-Sum 91, p. 139-140.
"Working the Landscape." [NewEngR] (13:3/4) Spr-Sum 91, p. 229-230.
1576. DUNN, Susan E.
"Dusk at the Twi-lite Inn." [ChironR] (10:3) Aut 91, p. 43.
"The Railroad Engineer Paces the Kitchen, Talking of the Tragedy." [ChironR]
(10:3) Aut 91, p. 43.
"What Brought Her to This." [ChironR] (10:3) Aut 91, p. 43.
1577. DUNNING, Stephen
"A Little Request." [Nimrod] (34:2) Spr-Sum 91, p. 120.
"Mother as Tattooed Lady." [Parting] (4:2) Wint 91-92, p. 30.
"Tastes." [Nimrod] (34:2) Spr-Sum 91, p. 121.
1578. DUODUO
"Crossing the Sea" (tr. by Gregory Lee). [ManhatR] (6:1) Fall 91, p. 22.
"In England" (tr. by Gregory Lee). [ManhatR] (6:1) Fall 91, p. 20.
"Northern Earth" (tr. by Gregory Lee). [ManhatR] (6:1) Fall 91, p. 17-18.
"Residents" (tr. by Gregory L. Lee). [KenR] (NS 13:4) Fall 91, p. 105.
"Sea" (tr. by Gregory Lee). [ManhatR] (6:1) Fall 91, p. 15.
"September" (tr. by Gregory Lee). [ManhatR] (6:1) Fall 91, p. 19.
"Solicitude" (tr. by Gregory Lee). [ManhatR] (6:1) Fall 91, p. 16.
"They" (tr. by Gregory Lee). [ManhatR] (6:1) Fall 91, p. 23.
"Winter's Day" (tr. by Gregory Lee). [ManhatR] (6:1) Fall 91, p. 21.
1579. DUPIN, Jacques
"Egyptian Woman" (tr. by Elton Glaser and Janice Fritsch). [Paint] (18:36) Aut 91,
p. 60.
1580. DuPLESSIS, Rachel Blau
"Diasporas." [Sulfer] (11:2, #29) Fall 91, p. 52-58.

"Draft X: Letters" (Selections). [Aerial] (6/7) 91, p. 61-62.
"Draft 11: Schwa." [GrandS] (10:3, #39) 91, p. 26-33.
1581. DUPREE, Edison
"Fin de Siècle." [Shen] (41:2) Sum 91, p. 9.
1582. DURBIN, Libby A.
"Between Jobs." [CalQ] (32/33) Spr 90, p. 96.
"Blood Will Never Tell." [CalQ] (32/33) Spr 90, p. 97.
"January of '36." [CalQ] (32/33) Spr 90, p. 98.
"Ladies Night at the Legion." [Calyx] (13:3) Wint 91-92, p. 46.
1583. DURHAM, Daniel
"Mi amigo, the incomparable" (from "Other Figures in the Mirror"). [DustyD] Je 91,
p. 16.
1584. DUTTON, Paul
"Visionary Portraits, 6." [PraF] (12:2 #55) Sum 91, p. 59-61.
1585. DUVAL, Quinton
"Woodcutter." [CalQ] (35/36) 91, p. 85.
DUYN, Mona van
See Van DUYN, Mona
1586. DWELLER, Cliff
"Mapping the Asphalt Meadows" (chapbook supplement, 12 poems). [SlipS] (11)
91, 28 p.
1587. DYBEK, Stuart
"Breath." [Parting] (4:1) Sum 91, p. 35.
"Here." [Parting] (4:1) Sum 91, p. 1.
"Signs." [Parting] (4:1) Sum 91, p. 2.
"The Story of Mist." [MichQR] (30:4) Fall 91, p. 552.
1588. DYCK, Marje A.
"Waiting for Rain." [PraF] (12:4) Wint 91-92, p. 40.
1589. DYER, Linda
"What I Would Say." [DenQ] (25:4) Spr 91, p. 18-19.
1590. DYKEWOMON, Elana
"The Real Fat Womon Poems." [SinW] (43/44) Sum 91, p. 245-253.
1591. EADDY, Morris Lee
"I Saw You Again." [EmeraldCR] (4) 91, p. 54-55.
"Secrets." [EmeraldCR] (3) 91, c1990, p. 51.
1592. EADIE, Tom
"Salmon Spawn." [Quarry] (40:1/2) Wint-Spr 91, p. 56.
1593. EADY, Cornelius
"Alabama, c. 1963: A Ballad by John Coltrane." [RiverS] (33) 91, p. 25.
"Grace." [RiverS] (33) 91, p. 23.
"Intermission on East 7th Street." [RiverS] (33) 91, p. 26-27.
"Romare Bearden Retrospect at the Brooklyn Museum." [RiverS] (33) 91, p. 28.
"Spic" (for Cathy). [RiverS] (33) 91, p. 24.
"Why Was I Born? A Duet Between John Coltrane & Kenny Burell." [RiverS] (33)
91, p. 22.
EAGLE, Duane Big
See BIGEAGLE, Duane
1594. EARLE, Karen
"My One Good Suit." [ChamLR] (8-9) Spr-Fall 91, p. 61-62.
"Near the Hospital." [ChamLR] (8-9) Spr-Fall 91, p. 59-60.
1595. EARLY, Gerald
"Diet of Worms." [Callaloo] (14:2) Spr 91, p. 466-467.
"Teaching Contemporary African-American Literature." [Callaloo] (14:2) Spr 91, p.
464.
"When James Baldwin of the *Magpie* Interviewed Countee Cullen, Poet." [Callaloo]
(14:2) Spr 91, p. 465.
1596. EARNHART, Brady
"The Invention of the Death of Wonder." [SnailPR] (1:2) Fall 91-Wint 92, p. 28-29.
1597. EASTON, Paul
"Conversations with Brady." [Farm] (8:1) Spr-Sum 91, p. 17-22.
1598. EATON, Amy
"Headache." [ChironR] (10:2) Sum 91, p. 43.
"Memory #28." [ChironR] (10:4) Wint 91, p. 36.
1599. EATON, Charles Edward
"Ace in the Hole." [CharR] (17:1) Spr 91, p. 62-63.
"Androcles." [MidwQ] (33:1) Aut 91, p. 60-61.

131

"Arms and the Man." [Interim] (10:2) Fall-Wint 91-92, p. 42.
"Blue Blazes." [CharR] (17:1) Spr 91, p. 61-62.
"End Game." [SewanR] (99:1) Wint 91, p. 29.
"The Goblet." [Pembroke] (23) 91, p. 162.
"Jacaranda." [SewanR] (99:1) Wint 91, p. 28.
"Last Word." [HolCrit] (28:2) Ap 91, p. 18.
"The Lion." [LullwaterR] (3:1) Fall 91, p. 10.
"The Loser." [Paint] (18:36) Aut 91, p. 10-11.
"Manet Mania." [MidwQ] (33:1) Aut 91, p. 59.
"Notes of a Native." [LaurelR] (25:1) Wint 91, p. 49.
"The Periscope." [Sonora] (20) Wint 91, p. 79-80.

1600. EBERSOLE, Glenda
"At the Laundromat." [SouthernR] (27:1) Ja 91, p. 153-154.
"Racquetball." [SouthernR] (27:1) Ja 91, p. 152-153.
"Witnessing." [SouthernR] (27:1) Ja 91, p. 151-152.

1601. ECHELBERGER, M. J.
"The Player Piano." [SmPd] (28:2, #82) Spr 91, p. 35.

1602. ECONOMOU, George
"All-American." [WorldL] (2) 91, p. 18.
"Play / Fables 4" (for Lawrence Frank). [WorldL] (2) 91, p. 17.

1603. EDELMAN, Carolyn Foote
"White Cyclamen." [US1] (24/25) Spr 91, p. 16-17.

1604. EDELMAN, Elaine
"Winter Night Sound." [SoDakR] (29:3 part 2) Aut 91, p. 36.

1605. EDGECOMB, Rebecca
"Cassandra." [BellR] (14:2) Fall 91, p. 12.

1606. EDGERTON, Larry
"Sleight of Hand." [SmPd] (28:1, #81) Wint 91, p. 8.

1607. EDGU, Ferit
"In May" (tr. by Talat Halman). [Vis] (35) 91, p. 18.

1608. EDMISTEN, Patricia (Patricia Taylor)
"Aluminum Beach." [EmeraldCR] (4) 91, p. 28.
"Christmas Eve 1989." [EmeraldCR] (3) 91, c1990, p. 94.
"Summa Cum Laude." [EmeraldCR] (4) 91, p. 26-27.
"Summer's End." [EmeraldCR] (4) 91, p. 28.

1609. EDMONDSON, Richard
"Fionnuala." [PoetryUSA] (22) Spr 91, p. 16.

1610. EDMUNDS, Martin
"Moon." [ParisR] (33:121) Wint 91, p. 186.
"Nocturne." [Nat] (252:18) 13 My 91, p. 641.

1611. EDOYAN, Henrik
"My Borders" (tr. by Diana Der-Hovanessian). [Vis] (36) 91, p. 36.

1612. EDSON, Russell
"The Absorptions." [ColR] (NS 17:2) Fall-Wint 90, p. 68.
"Doing the World." [DenQ] (25:4) Spr 91, p. 21-22.
"Geography." [DenQ] (25:4) Spr 91, p. 23-24.
"An Inventory." [ColR] (NS 17:2) Fall-Wint 90, p. 67.
"The Night Invaded." [DenQ] (25:4) Spr 91, p. 20.
"Of Chickens." [ColR] (NS 17:2) Fall-Wint 90, p. 69.
"The Sad Message." [Ploughs] (17:2/3) Fall 91, p. 31.

1613. EDSTROM, Bethany
"The Forgotten One." [SmPd] (28:3, #83) Fall 91, p. 10.

1614. EDWARDS, Ken
"In the Japanese Fashion." [NewAW] (8/9) Fall 91, p. 73.
"Kinetically." [NewAW] (8/9) Fall 91, p. 73-74.
"Lexically." [NewAW] (8/9) Fall 91, p. 74-75.
"Materially." [NewAW] (8/9) Fall 91, p. 75-76.
"Narratively." [NewAW] (8/9) Fall 91, p. 76.
"Organically." [NewAW] (8/9) Fall 91, p. 77.

1615. EDWARDS, Robert
"Amazements." [Timbuktu] (6) Spr 91, p. 4-5.
"Over There." [DogRR] (10:1) Sum 91, p. 37.
"Poem in Autumn." [RagMag] (9:1) 91, p. 26.

1616. EDWARDS, Susan
"Ode for H.D." [CalQ] (32/33) Spr 90, p. 82-85.

1617. EEN, Andrea
    "Three Matrons in White Drink Sunday Coffee on Madeleine Island." [RagMag]
        (9:2) 91, p. 42-43.
1618. EGGHORN, Ylva
    "If You Could See Me" (tr. by Daniel Ogden). [Vis] (37) 91, p. 51.
    "Letters" (tr. by Daniel Ogden). [Vis] (37) 91, p. 51.
1619. EHRHART, W. D.
    "For a Coming Extinction." [ChironR] (10:1) Spr 91, p. 3.
    "The Invasion of Grenada." [ChironR] (10:1) Spr 91, p. 3.
    "The Lotus Cutters of Hô' Tây." [ChironR] (10:1) Spr 91, p. 3.
    "The Simple Lives of Cats." [PoetL] (86:4) Wint 91-92, p. 25.
    "To Those Who Have Gone Home Tired." [ChironR] (10:1) Spr 91, p. 3.
1620. EHRLICH, Linda C.
    "Oriental Song" (tr. of Federico García Lorca, w. David Anderson). [CumbPR]
        (11:1) Fall 91, p. 37-43.
1621. EHRLICH, P. S.
    "Drink to Our Dreamed-Of." [DogRR] (10:1) Sum 91, p. 40-41.
1622. EIBEL, Deborah
    "Middle Class." [CanLit] (131) Wint 91, p. 25.
1623. EICHNER, Maura
    "The Embroiderer." [ChrC] (108:22) 24-31 Jl 91, p. 717.
1624. EIMERS, Nancy
    "In the Fish Age." [IndR] (14:2) Spr 91, p. 74-75.
1625. EISELE, Thomas
    "At birth society puts the noose on." [OnTheBus] (8/9) 91, p. 64.
    "I haven't the time for your fun and games." [PoetryE] (31) Spr 91, p. 146.
    "I know who I am." [PoetryE] (31) Spr 91, p. 145.
    "I was a slender guy and started to lift weights." [PoetryE] (31) Spr 91, p. 144.
    "The people spared a thief." [PoetryE] (32) Fall 91, p. 97.
    "Today is Memorial Day and I'm pondering what Americans memorize." [PoetryE]
        (31) Spr 91, p. 143.
    "When you serve on a trial jury." [PoetryE] (32) Fall 91, p. 98.
1626. EISENHOWER, Cathy
    "Vallisneria Spiralis" (January 1991). [CarolQ] (44:1) Fall 91, p. 45.
1627. EKHOLM, John
    "I Am Colder Than I Should Be." [JamesWR] (8:4) Sum 91, p. 6.
1628. EKLUND, George
    "36. We read to each other from the Sunday paper" (from "Kissing Each Other's
        Crimes). [PoetL] (86:2) Sum 91, p. 8.
    "Dressing My Daughter." [BellR] (14:1) Spr 91, p. 28.
    "Horse of My Body." [WindO] (54) Sum 91, p. 12.
    "In Here." [CinPR] (22) Spr 91, p. 54.
    "Ready." [WindO] (54) Sum 91, p. 13.
    "Three Stones." [CreamCR] (15:2) Fall 91, p. 54.
    "The Woman Crossed Her Legs." [CinPR] (22) Spr 91, p. 55.
1629. ELDER, Karl
    "The Betrayal." [Ascent] (15:2) Wint 91, p. 10.
    "Revelation." [Ascent] (15:2) Wint 91, p. 11.
    "Walls." [PoetL] (86:3) Fall 91, p. 16.
1630. ELDRIDGE, Kevin Joe
    "Big Wind, Lost Nation." [NoDaQ] (59:1) Wint 91, p. 196-197.
1631. ELEFSON, J. C.
    "Dream of Returning to the People's Republic Photographic Studio." [GreenMR]
        (NS 4:2) Wint-Spr 91, p. 15-16.
    "Miss Zhou's Essay Concerning Solitude." [GreenMR] (NS 4:2) Wint-Spr 91, p.
        14.
    "Willie Li Speaks Only a Bit Metaphorically" (From Inside the Shadow Poems).
        [GreenMR] (NS 4:2) Wint-Spr 91, p. 17.
1632. ELEFTHERIOU, Stephanie
    "The Logger." [HighP] (6:1) Spr 91, p. 94-95.
1633. ELENBOGEN, Dina
    "Peeling Onions." [Calyx] (13:3) Wint 91-92, p. 53.
1634. ELIASSON, Gyrdir
    "The Woodcarving Demon" (tr. by Hallberg Hallmundsson). [Vis] (37) 91, p. 37.
1635. ELISE, Michelle
    "Geography of a Body." [CinPR] (21) Spr 90, p. 46-47.

1636. ELIZABETH, Martha
    "Beloved." [CalQ] (35/36) 91, p. 127.
    "Patience." [DogRR] (10:1) Sum 91, p. 9.
1637. ELKIND, Sue Saniel
    "The Book." [Elf] (1:1) Spr 91, p. 35.
    "Clothes Cemetery." [Kalliope] (13:1) 91, p. 59.
    "Feeling the Pressure." [Kalliope] (13:1) 91, p. 60.
    "History Lesson." [Kalliope] (13:1) 91, p. 58.
    "In Silence and Alone." [Elf] (1:4) Wint 91, p. 39.
    "Just Another Death." [Elf] (1:4) Wint 91, p. 39.
    "A Sign of Mourning." [Elf] (1:1) Spr 91, p. 35.
    "Too Late." [Elf] (1:3) Fall 91, p. 32.
1638. ELLEDGE, Jim
    "Blame." [Farm] (8:2) Fall-Wint 91-92, p. 58.
    "Firenze: Il Rinascimento." [TexasR] (12:1/2) Spr-Sum 91, p. 95-96.
    "Household Gods." [ParisR] (33:121) Wint 91, p. 204-205.
    "There Is the Silence." [TexasR] (12:1/2) Spr-Sum 91, p. 97.
    "Tongues: An Essay." [PoetC] (23:1) Fall 91, p. 24-25.
1639. ELLEN
    "California Poppies." [Rohwedder] (6) Sum-Fall 91, p. 16.
    "Descanso Gardens with Mother." [BellR] (14:2) Fall 91, p. 26.
    "Invisibility." [Rohwedder] (6) Sum-Fall 91, p. 16.
    "Oranges." [Rohwedder] (6) Sum-Fall 91, p. 17.
    "Symbiosis." [OnTheBus] (8/9) 91, p. 65.
    "Too Young" (for my niece). [SlipS] (11) 91, p. 53-55.
1640. ELLINGSON, Nancy
    "Independence Day" (a Warsaw square). [Northeast] (5:4) Sum 91, p. 7.
1641. ELLIOT, Alistair
    "The Love of Horses." [NoDaQ] (59:3) Sum 91, p. 7.
    "Miss Vermilion." [NoDaQ] (59:3) Sum 91, p. 6.
    "Remains of Mining in the Upper Peninsula, Michigan." [NoDaQ] (59:3) Sum 91, p.
        3-4.
    "A Workshop in Boulder, Colorado." [NoDaQ] (59:3) Sum 91, p. 5.
1642. ELLIOTT, Carmen
    "From the Dark Room." [Crucible] (27) Fall 91, p. 49-50.
1643. ELLIOTT, William I.
    "One Word." [ChrC] (108:23) 7-14 Ag 91, p. 748.
1644. ELLIS, Carol
    "Light in the Window." [SwampR] (7/8) Spr-Sum 91, p. 18.
1645. ELLIS, Mary Lynn
    "Ark." [WestB] (28) 91, p. 9.
    "Keeping Watch." [Kalliope] (13:1) 91, p. 25.
1646. ELLIS, Ron
    "Camp Song." [CreamCR] (14:2) Wint 91, p. 177.
1647. ELLIS, Scott
    "I'm Confessin' That I Love You." [PraF] (12:2 #55) Sum 91, p. 44.
    "Money's Worth." [PraF] (12:2 #55) Sum 91, p. 45-46.
1648. ELLIS, Stephen
    "Academy in the Leaves." [Notus] (9) Fall 91, p. 69.
    "Annotated Strains." [Notus] (9) Fall 91, p. 71.
    "Fruited by Function." [Notus] (9) Fall 91, p. 70.
    "In Crossflow and Forever Spent." [Notus] (9) Fall 91, p. 69.
    "To Dawning Curtains Drawn." [Notus] (9) Fall 91, p. 70.
1649. ELLIS, Thomas Sayers
    "Barracuda." [Agni] (33) 91, p. 105-106.
    "Making Ends Meet." [Agni] (33) 91, p. 107-108.
    "The Man of Numbers." [Callaloo] (14:4) Fall 91, p. 924.
    "The Roll Call." [Agni] (33) 91, p. 109.
1650. ELLISON, Julie
    "The Swiss Army Knife in the Window." [RiverS] (35) 91, p. 48-49.
1651. ELLSWORTH, Anne
    "Eden in Winter." [CumbPR] (10:2) Spr 91, p. 15.
    "Maybe." [Kalliope] (13:1) 91, p. 40.
    "Roads." [Kalliope] (13:1) 91, p. 40.
1652. ELMSLIE, Kenward
    "Area J" (Words & Music). [Conjunc] (16) 91, p. 135-146.

"Night Emerald" (a musical play: six segments). [NewAW] (8/9) Fall 91, p. 213-229.
1653. ELMUSA, Sharif S.
"Camel Fragments." [Paint] (18:35) Spr 91, p. 75.
"When Slippers Mingle." [Paint] (18:35) Spr 91, p. 76.
1654. ELSTED, Crispin
"Kenfield Variations" (for Patricia and Graeme). [MalR] (97) Wint 91, p. 57-74.
"Trillium Grandiflorum." [MalR] (95) Sum 91, p. 22-23.
1655. ÉLUARD, Paul
"Circumstantial End" (tr. by Christopher Sawyer-Lauçanno). [Talisman] (7) Fall 91, p. 65.
"Construction Set" (for Raymond Roussel, tr. by Christopher Sawyer-Lauçanno). [Talisman] (7) Fall 91, p. 64.
"First in the World" (for Pablo Picasso, tr. by Christopher Sawyer-Lauçanno). [Talisman] (7) Fall 91, p. 66.
"No Longer Shared" (tr. by Christopher Sawyer-Lauçanno). [Talisman] (7) Fall 91, p. 65.
"Paul Klee" (tr. by Christopher Sawyer-Lauçanno). [Talisman] (7) Fall 91, p. 64.
"Slow Down Construction" (with André Breton and René Char, tr. by Jeanie Puleston Fleming and Christopher Merrill). [AmerPoR] (20:3) My-Je 91, p. 25-30.
1656. ELYTIS, Odysseus
"Good Friday" (tr. by Jeffrey Carson). [ConnPR] (10:1) 91, p. 9.
"Holy Thursday" (tr. by Jeffrey Carson). [ConnPR] (10:1) 91, p. 8.
"In Place of a Dream" (tr. by Jeffrey Carson). [ConnPR] (10:1) 91, p. 7.
"Variations on a Sunbeam" (a 7-poem sequence: selections: I-II, VII, tr. by Jeffrey Carson and Nikos Sarris). [ConnPR] (10:1) 91, p. .10-13.
1657. EMANS, Elaine V.
"Father the Lignum Vitae." [TexasR] (11:1/2) Spr-Sum 90, p. 7.
1658. EMANUEL, James A.
"Deadly James" (For All the Victims of Police Brutality). [NegC] (11:3) 91, p. 270-271.
"Eric, at the Blythe Road Post Office." [NegC] (11:3) 91, p. 267-268.
"Fishermen." [NegC] (11:3) 91, p. 266.
"Haiku: Ksenia's Paintings" (for Ksenia Milicevic). [KenR] (NS 13:4) Fall 91, p. 169.
"Sittin'-Log Blues." [KenR] (NS 13:4) Fall 91, p. 168.
"To Kill a Morning Spider." [NegC] (11:3) 91, p. 269.
1659. EMANUEL, Lynn
"Big Black Car." [GeoR] (45:1) Spr 91, p. 37.
"Chinoiserie." [PraS] (65:4) Wint 91, p. 25-26.
"Far." [ThRiPo] (37/38) 91, p. 13-14.
"Heartsick." [SouthernR] (27:2) Ap 91, p. 298-300.
"Inspiration." [ThRiPo] (37/38) 91, p. 11-12.
"On Waking After Dreaming of Raoul." [SouthernR] (27:2) Ap 91, p. 297-298.
"The Poet in Heaven." [Hudson] (43:4) Wint 91, p. 620.
"A Red Kimono." [PraS] (65:4) Wint 91, p. 25.
"Riddle." [OhioR] (46) 91, p. 76.
"Self-Portrait at Eighteen." [ThRiPo] (37/38) 91, p. 16.
"Stone Soup." [GeoR] (45:1) Spr 91, p. 35.
"What Ely Was." [PraS] (65:4) Wint 91, p. 26.
"What Grieving Was Like." [ThRiPo] (37/38) 91, p. 15.
"What the Keyhole Was." [GeoR] (45:1) Spr 91, p. 36.
"Whites (Ely, Nevada, 1953)." [PraS] (65:4) Wint 91, p. 24.
"Who Is She Kidding." [OhioR] (46) 91, p. 77.
1660. EMBLEN, D. L.
"Botany: First Lesson." [BellArk] (7:3) My-Je 91, p. 3.
1661. EMERSON, Jocelyn L.
"Song." [CarolQ] (44:1) Fall 91, p. 52.
1662. EMERY, Michael
"Blackberries: July 4th." [WindO] (55) Wint 91-92, p. 41.
1663. EMERY, Thomas
"Arkadhi: Variations on a Theme (Diminuendo)." [PassN] (12:2) Wint 91, p. 10.
1664. EMIN, Gevorg
"If You Are a Poet" (tr. by Diana Der Hovanessian). [InterPR] (17:2) Fall 91, p. 81.

1665. EMIOT, Israel
"As Long As We Are Not Alone" (tr. by Leah Zazuyer and Brina Rose). [SenR]
(21:1) Spr 91, p. 30.
"Before You Extinguish Me" (tr. by Leah Zazuyer and Brina Rose). [SenR] (21:1)
Spr 91, p. 26.
"My God I Believe in You So Much" (tr. by Leah Zazuyer and Brina Rose). [SenR]
(21:1) Spr 91, p. 27.
"A Prayer in Nineteen Forty-Three" (for H. Lang, tr. by Leah Zazuyer and Brina
Rose). [SenR] (21:1) Spr 91, p. 28.
"Prayer of a Man in Snow" (tr. by Leah Zazuyer and Brina Rose). [SenR] (21:1) Spr
91, p. 29.
"With or Without Me" (tr. by Leah Zazuyer and Brina Rose). [SenR] (21:1) Spr 91,
p. 31.

1666. EMMONS, Garry
"Epilogue" (tr. of Juan Gustavo Cobo Borda). [Agni] (33) 91, p. 217.
"Henry James" (tr. of Juan Gustavo Cobo Borda). [Agni] (33) 91, p. 213.
"In Nerval's Pocket" (tr. of Juan Gustavo Cobo Borda). [Agni] (33) 91, p. 215.
"A Little Pregnant Woman Walks in the Park" (tr. of Juan Gustavo Cobo Borda).
[Agni] (33) 91, p. 216.
"Self-criticism" (tr. of Juan Gustavo Cobo Borda). [Agni] (33) 91, p. 214.
"Sorceresses" (tr. of Juan Manuel Roca). [Agni] (33) 91, p. 235.

1667. EMMOTT, Kirsten
"Jaws." [CapilR] (2:6/7) Fall 91, p. 50-54.
"On Being Reprimanded for Being 'Too Women's Libbish'." [CapilR] (2:6/7) Fall
91, p. 55.

1668. ENCARNACIÓN, Alfred
"Bulosan Listens to a Recording of Robert Johnson." [IndR] (14:2) Spr 91, p. 79.
"Threading the Miles" (In Memory of Carlos Bulosan, 1911-1956). [IndR] (14:2)
Spr 91, p. 76-78.

1669. ENDREZZE, Anita
"Cow" (From a newspaper article). [PoetryE] (32) Fall 91, p. 56.
"In the Horizontal Sky" (12 views). [Archae] (2) Spr 91, p. 5-9.
"In the House of Animals." [PoetryE] (32) Fall 91, p. 58-59.
"La Llorona, the Crying Woman." [KenR] (NS 13:4) Fall 91, p. 109-111.
"The Migration of Trees." [KenR] (NS 13:4) Fall 91, p. 108-109.
"Perceptions of Three Birches." [KenR] (NS 13:4) Fall 91, p. 106-108.

1670. ENEKWE, Onuora Ossie
"After the War." [LitR] (34:4) Sum 91, p. 460.
"Before the War." [LitR] (34:4) Sum 91, p. 460.

1671. ENGELS, John
"Details of the Frozen Man." [SouthernR] (27:1) Ja 91, p. 111-112.
"Hagfish." [SouthernR] (27:1) Ja 91, p. 110-111.
"River." [SouthernR] (27:1) Ja 91, p. 109.
"Walking to Cootehill." [AntR] (49:3) Sum 91, p. 424-425.

1672. ENGELSKIRCHEN, Howard
"I will not name this place." [HawaiiR] (15:3, #33) Fall 91, p. 81.
"Sea's Edge." [HawaiiR] (15:3, #33) Fall 91, p. 82.

1673. ENGLAND, Stephanie
"Bones." [Nimrod] (35:1) Fall-Wint 91, p. 60.

1674. ENGLER, Robert (Robert Klein)
"Del Poema Frustrado" (English version, tr. of José Gorostiza). [Colum] (16) Spr
91, p. 14-24.
"Fireflies" (tr. of José Gorostiza). [MidAR] (12:1) 91, p. 161-162.
"Ghosts." [PlumR] (1) Spr-Sum 91, p. 15.
"In Memory of All the Homosexuals Who Were Cut in Half by Saws." [Tribe] (1:2)
Spr 90, p. 63-64.
"Reruns." [EvergreenC] (6:2) Sum-Fall 91, p. 28.

1675. ENGMAN, John
"Air Guitar." [PoetryNW] (32:3) Aut 91, p. 41-43.
"The Common Expression Our Grief Leads Us To." [PassN] (12:2) Wint 91, p. 3.
"Leftover Lines from an Old Journal." [PraS] (65:4) Wint 91, p. 28-29.
"Lemon Sun." [PraS] (65:4) Wint 91, p. 27.
"On Summer Evenings Several Summers Before the Next War." [PoetryNW] (32:3)
Aut 91, p. 40-41.
"The Superstitions" (for my mother). [PraS] (65:4) Wint 91, p. 29-31.
"Think of Me in D Major." [PoetryNW] (32:3) Aut 91, p. 39-40.

1676. ENRIQUEZ, R.
"Omen" (tr. of Blanca Luz Pulido, w. Thomas Hoeksema). [Paint] (18:36) Aut 91, p. 63.
1677. ENSLER, Eve
"Dicks in the Desert" (For Richard). [CentralP] (19/20) Spr-Fall 91, p. 5-6.
"My-Flag" (He wears two little flags beind his ears. He waves one little flag. All the flags are plastic). [CentralP] (19/20) Spr-Fall 91, p. 9.
1678. ENSLIN, Theodore
"Among my own   the tangles." [Talisman] (7) Fall 91, p. 32.
"To think of things   too many." [Talisman] (7) Fall 91, p. 32.
"What Eye or Ear for It." [Talisman] (7) Fall 91, p. 33.
1679. ENSRUD, Shirley
"And Life Goes On." [Sidewalks] (1) Aug 91, p. 39-40.
"We Tend the Gardens." [Sidewalks] (1) Aug 91, p. 40.
1680. EPPSTEIN, Maureen
"Bedrock." [Kalliope] (13:2) 91, p. 29.
1681. EPSTEIN, Daniel Mark
"The Hanging Gardens." [AmerS] (60:1) Wint 91, p. 118-119.
1682. EPSTEIN, Richard
"At the Sill." [Plain] (11:2) Wint 91, p. 6.
1683. EPSTEIN, Thomas
"'Armageddon!' Hoarsely Sang the Iron Fence" (tr. of Dmitri Volchek). [LitR] (34:3) Spr 91, p. 384.
"At Last I've Renounced" (tr. of Dmitri Volchek). [LitR] (34:3) Spr 91, p. 385.
"Deceased! What Now for Empty Voids" (tr. of Dmitri Volchek). [LitR] (34:3) Spr 91, p. 384.
"Evening Song" (tr. of Igor Vishnevetsky). [LitR] (34:3) Spr 91, p. 379.
"The Half-Faded Day" (tr. of Victoria Andreyeva). [LitR] (34:3) Spr 91, p. 372-374.
"Hermit in Bathyscape Besotting Robe" (tr. of Dmitri Volchek). [LitR] (34:3) Spr 91, p. 386.
"How Andrey Bely Nearly Fell Under a Streetcar" (tr. of Yelena Shwartz). [LitR] (34:3) Spr 91, p. 326-327.
"My Dog" (tr. of Gleb Arsenyev). [LitR] (34:3) Spr 91, p. 317.
"New Jerusalem" (tr. of Yelena Shwartz). [LitR] (34:3) Spr 91, p. 325.
"No *Bool* of Holes No *Ubeshchoor* of Awls Only" (tr. of Dmitri Volchek). [LitR] (34:3) Spr 91, p. 386.
"On and On" (tr. of Lev Rubenstein, w. Alexei Pavlenko). [LitR] (34:3) Spr 91, p. 352-360.
"A Parrot at Sea" (tr. of Yelena Shwartz). [LitR] (34:3) Spr 91, p. 328.
"Perhaps I Did Come Here" (tr. of Igor Vishnevetsky). [LitR] (34:3) Spr 91, p. 378.
"The Runway" (tr. of Gleb Arsenyev). [LitR] (34:3) Spr 91, p. 317-320.
"So What? the Logpile of Culture" (tr. of Dmitri Volchek). [LitR] (34:3) Spr 91, p. 385.
"The Soul" (tr. of Gleb Arsenyev). [LitR] (34:3) Spr 91, p. 315-316.
"Summer in Mr. Thompson's House in Sussex" (tr. of Victoria Andreyeva). [LitR] (34:3) Spr 91, p. 375.
"A Vision" (tr. of Gleb Arsenyev). [LitR] (34:3) Spr 91, p. 321-322.
"Wandering in Parallel Dreams" (tr. of Victoria Andreyeva). [LitR] (34:3) Spr 91, p. 375.
"Why Stars Fall" (tr. of Gleb Arsenyev). [LitR] (34:3) Spr 91, p. 316.
1684. EQUI, Elaine
"Poem du Jour" (for Joe Brainard). [Shiny] (6) Spr-Sum 91, p. 57-62.
1685. ERB, Lisa
"At the Grave of My Mother's Mother." [BambooR] (50/51) Spr-Sum 91, p. 91.
"Four Darks." [SouthernPR] (31:1) Spr 91, p. 53-54.
"White Eclipse." [BambooR] (50/51) Spr-Sum 91, p. 92.
"Words for the Body." [SouthernPR] (31:1) Spr 91, p. 53.
1686. ERBA, Luciano
"Redblooded" (tr. by Sonia Raiziss). [Boulevard] (6:2/3, #17/18) Fall 91, p. 167.
"Sunset at Montluçon" (tr. by Sonia Raiziss). [Boulevard] (6:2/3, #17/18) Fall 91, p. 166.
1687. ERBES, C. K.
"Ancient Land." [Elf] (1:1) Spr 91, p. 36.
1688. ERDRICH, Louise
"Owls." [YellowS] (38) Wint-Spr 91-92, p. 38.

1689. EREMENKO, Aleksandr
"Philological Verse" (tr. by John High). [Talisman] (6) Spr 91, p. 101-102.
1690. ERICKSON, Ann
"Agapanthus." [PoetryUSA] (22) Spr 91, p. 10.
1691. ERKIS, Jack L.
"The Bum." [Gypsy] (17) 91, p. 64-65.
1692. ERMEY, Thomas
"What a Man Knows." [HopewellR] (1991) 91, p. 8.
1693. ERNEST, R. M.
"Hangers-On." [Verse] (8:1) Spr 91, p. 40.
1694. ERNST, Alexandra
"Deciphering Myth." [AnthNEW] (3) 91, p. 12.
1695. ERNST, Myron
"The Abiding Sadness of Handel's Oratorios: The High Slide at Coney Island."
[PoetC] (22:2) Wint 91, p. 33-34.
"The Carousel at Ross Park." [WestB] (28) 91, p. 63.
"Florida: On the Problem of Balance, Also of Majesty and Mrs. Hanna Schnur."
[OxfordM] (7:2) Fall-Wint 91, p. 69.
"In the Forests of Bydgoszcz" (Poland, 1939). [PoetL] (86:3) Fall 91, p. 20.
"The Wife in the Mural at Pompeii." [ManhatPR] (13) [91?], p. 41.
1696. EROGLU, Ebubekir
"To Die One Night" (tr. by Talat Halman). [Vis] (35) 91, p. 35.
1697. ERVIN, Cheryl
"Real Life." [SouthernPR] (31:1) Spr 91, p. 22-23.
1698. ERWIN, Wilma
"Two Haiku." [PaintedHR] (3) Sum 92, p. 34.
1699. ESCUDERO, Bettina
"Last Goodbye" (tr. of José Rizal, w. Naomi Lazard and Eduardo Bohorquez).
[Trans] (25) Spr 91, p. 209-211.
1700. ESHLEMAN, Clayton
"Trilce" (Selections: I-X, tr. of César Vallejo, w. Julio Ortega). [DenQ] (25:4) Spr
91, p. 69-89.
"Trilce" (Selections: XI-XX, tr. of César Vallejo, w. Julio Ortega. Translation
Chapbook Series, Number 16). [MidAR] (11:2) 91, p. 71-101.
"Trilce" (Selections: XXXIII, XXXV, XXXVII, tr. of César Vallejo, w. Julio
Ortega). [Antaeus] (67) Fall 91, p. 107-109.
"Trilce LX-LXIX" (tr. of Cesar Vallejo, w. Julio Ortega). [Sulfer] (11:2, #29) Fall
91, p. 4-15.
"Under World Arrest" (Selections: 21, 28, 45, 54). [DenQ] (25:4) Spr 91, p. 25-31.
"Under World Arrest" (Selections: 37-40). [WorldL] (2) 91, p. 4-6.
1701. ESOLEN, Tony
"Gardening." [HampSPR] Wint 91, p. 24.
"Grizzlies." [HampSPR] Wint 91, p. 24-25.
1702. ESPADA, Martín
"Bully" (Boston, Massachusetts, 1987). [RiverS] (33) 91, p. 31.
"City of Coughing and Dead Radiators" (Chelsea, Massachusetts). [KenR] (NS
13:4) Fall 91, p. 141-142.
"Cusin and Tata" (Rio Piedras, Puerto Rico, 1988). [IndR] (14:3) Fall 91, p. 16-17.
"Mrs. Baez Serves Coffee on the Third Floor." [Spirit] (11) 91, p. 78-80.
"The Other Alamo" (San Antonio, Texas, 1990). [Ploughs] (17:4) Wint 91-92, p.
124-125.
"Rebellion Is the Circle of a Lover's Hands" (Pellín and Nina, for the 50th
anniversary of the Ponce Massacre). [NoDaQ] (59:4) Fall 91, p. 81-82.
"The Saint Vincent de Paul Food Pantry Stomp" (Madison, Wisconsin, 1980).
[RiverS] (33) 91, p. 30.
"The Savior Is Abducted in Puerto Rico" (Adjuntas, Puerto Rico, 1985). [IndR]
(14:3) Fall 91, p. 18.
"A Taste for Silk and Black Servants." [IndR] (14:3) Fall 91, p. 19.
"To Skin the Hands of God" (for Maynard Gilbert, Rocky Hill, Connecticut). [IndR]
(14:3) Fall 91, p. 14-15.
1703. ESPAILLAT, Rhina P.
"Changeling." [Poetry] (158:5) Ag 91, p. 255.
"Cutting Bait." [Poetry] (158:5) Ag 91, p. 255-254.
1704. ESPEL, Santiago
"Abejas." [Nuez] (3:8/9) 91, p. 9.
"Bulevar." [Nuez] (3:8/9) 91, p. 9.

"Los Extraños Hombres Mudos." [Nuez] (3:8/9) 91, p. 9.
"Los Trenes Largos." [Nuez] (3:8/9) 91, p. 9.
1705. ESTABROOK, Michael
"Honking Horns." [Elf] (1:4) Wint 91, p. 23.
"Lumps." [SmPd] (28:2, #82) Spr 91, p. 23.
"My Grandfather." [Gypsy] (17) 91, p. 63.
"Waving Passers-by in for a Drink." [Interim] (10:2) Fall-Wint 91-92, p. 23.
1706. ESTABROOK, Susan
"Nap Time." [OnTheBus] (8/9) 91, p. 66-67.
1707. ESTES, Angie
"Before Surgery." [Journal] (14:2) Wint 91, p. 39.
"For My Grandmother." [NegC] (11:1) 91, p. 110-111.
"The Uses of Passion." [Journal] (14:2) Wint 91, p. 40.
1708. ETIENNE, Guy
"La Pierre du Oui / Maen Ar Ya" (Selections: 1 poem in Breton, 1 poem in French
        (tr. with the author), 10 poems in English, tr. by Alain E. Le Berre). [Sulfur]
        (11:1, #28) Spr 91, p. 157-161.
1709. ETTER, Carrie
"Lot's Wife." [Plain] (12:2) Wint 91, p. 15.
"Meeting My Birthmother" (for Nancy). [ChironR] (10:3) Aut 91, p. 17.
"Suddenly Persimmons" (for Leslie). [ChironR] (10:3) Aut 91, p. 17.
"The Woman in the Cage Remembers." [ChironR] (10:3) Aut 91, p. 17.
1710. ETTER, Dave (David Pearson)
"History." [LaurelR] (25:1) Wint 91, p. 14-15.
"Home from Work." [PoetC] (22:2) Wint 91, p. 25-26.
"Incest." [WestB] (29) 91, p. 36-37.
"The Midnight Fox." [SoDakR] (29:3 part 2) Aut 91, p. 12.
"Redball." [LaurelR] (25:1) Wint 91, p. 16-17.
"Scratch." [CoalC] (3) My 91, p. 17.
1711. EVANS, Bradford
"Weather Report." [Pig] (17) 91, p. 61.
1712. EVANS, Brett
"Nola" (Excerpts). [WashR] (17:3) O-N 91, p. 12.
1713. EVANS, David
"To an Injured Grackle" (Sunset Motel, Britton, South Dakota). [ChironR] (10:2)
        Sum 91, p. 41.
1714. EVANS, David Allan
"Poem Without a Metaphor" (for father, dead seven springs). [SoDakR] (29:3 part 2)
        Aut 91, p. 26.
"Scarecrow." [CharR] (17:1) Spr 91, p. 95.
"The Town Where Nothing Can Happen." [CharR] (17:1) Spr 91, p. 93-94.
1715. EVANS, George
"Pachinko King." [Poetry] (157:5) F 91, p. 276.
1716. EVANS, Kathy
"Psychic Healers." [SouthernPR] (31:2) Fall 91, p. 8-10.
"To Jacob." [OnTheBus] (8/9) 91, p. 68.
1717. EVANS, Kevin
"Off Peyton Bridge." [NewOR] (18:3) Fall 91, p. 94.
"Stranger." [GeoR] (45:4) Wint 91, p. 745-746.
1718. EVANS, Laurie A.
"Plums into Jam." [SpoonRQ] (16:3/4) Sum-Fall 91, p. 81-82.
1719. EVANS, Lee
"The Past." [CutB] (35) Wint-Spr 91, p. 86.
1720. EVANS, Michael
"The Glass Photograph." [SoDakR] (29:2) Sum 91, p. 158.
"Grave-Digger." [Outbr] (22) 91, p. 44.
"The Only Honeymoon Picture of My Grandmother, Sitting on the Hood of a 1926
        Ford." [SpoonRQ] (16:3/4) Sum-Fall 91, p. 38.
"Opening the West." [HighP] (6:3) Wint 91, p. 119-120.
"Remembering the Slow Boy." [HawaiiR] (15:2, #32) Spr 91, p. 57-58.
"Ways to Shell Walnuts." [WestB] (29) 91, p. 77-78.
1721. EVASCO, Marjorie M.
"Sagada Stills in a F l o a t i n g World." [TampaR] (4) 91, p. 85.
1722. EVERDING, Kelly
"Pastoral." [BlackWR] (17:2) Spr-Sum 91, p. 106.
"Rape." [Caliban] (10) 91, p. 102.

1723. EVERSAUL, Denise Spicer
"Jamy." [PaintedHR] (1) Ja 91, p. 26.
1724. EVERWINE, Peter
"Speaking of Accidents." [NewYorker] (67:45) 30 D 91, p. 32.
EVTUSHENKO, Eugenio
See YEVTUSHENKO, Yevgeny
1725. EWING, Blair
"Philadelphia." [CapeR] (26:1) Spr 91, p. 38.
1726. EXLER, Samuel
"A Changed Life." [InterPR] (17:1) Spr 91, p. 108.
"Mercy." [LitR] (35:1) Fall 91, p. 92.
"Names." [PoetryE] (31) Spr 91, p. 76.
"The Nun's Meditation." [InterPR] (17:1) Spr 91, p. 108.
1727. FABILLI, Mary
"The Lord and Shingles." [PoetryUSA] (22) Spr 91, p. 13.
1728. FAHRBACH, Helen
"Canvas." [RagMag] (9:2) 91, p. 74.
"Elizabeth Taylor Joins the Merry Maids." [RagMag] (9:2) 91, p. 75.
1729. FAINLIGHT, Ruth
"Homage." [NewYorker] (67:43) 16 D 91, p. 46.
"This Time of Year." [NewYorker] (67:38) 11 N 91, p. 38.
1730. FAIRCHILD, B. H.
"In Czechoslovakia." [PraS] (65:3) Fall 91, p. 17-19.
"Language, Nonsense, Desire." [Salm] (90/91) Spr-Sum 91, p. 200-201.
"Local Knowledge" (for Patricia Lea Fairchild. 35 poems). [QRL] (Poetry ser. 10, vol. 30) 91, 72 p.
"The Machinist, Teaching His Daughter to Play the Piano." [TriQ] (81) Spr-Sum 91, p. 217-218.
"Maize." [PraS] (65:3) Fall 91, p. 20-21.
"The March of the Suicides." [PraS] (65:3) Fall 91, p. 19-20.
1731. FAISON, Jody
"Lonesome as an Oboe." [CumbPR] (10:2) Spr 91, p. 37.
1732. FAIVRE, Rob
"Taking Out the Trash at Midnight." [AnthNEW] (3) 91, p. 8.
1733. FAIZ, Faiz Ahmed
"Let Me Think" (tr. by Naomi Lazard, w. Ahmad Hamidi). [Trans] (25) Spr 91, p. 212-213.
"The Rain of Stones Is Finished" (Elegy for Hassan Nasir, tortured to death in the Labore [sic] Fort, 1959, tr. by Agha Shahid Ali). [Spirit] (11) 91, p. 23.
1734. FALCO, Edward
"Brooklyn." [Iowa] (21:1) Wint 91, p. 179.
"Magic!" [Iowa] (21:1) Wint 91, p. 179-180.
FALCO, Sam di
See DIFALCO, Sam
FALCON, Leticia Garza
See GARZA-FALCON, Leticia
1735. FALES, Anna-Lisa
"Mantis." [Crucible] (27) Fall 91, p. 31.
1736. FALLON, A. D.
"I Was a Typical Kid." [Pearl] (14) Fall-Wint 91, p. 54.
"Rape." [Pearl] (14) Fall-Wint 91, p. 54.
1737. FALQUEZ-CERTAIN, Miguel
"Viajes" (tr. of Mark Strand). [Nuez] (3:8/9) 91, p. 34.
1738. FALUDY, György
"The 52nd" (tr. by Nicholas Kolumban). [MidAR] (11:2) 91, p. 55.
1739. FALZON, Grazio
"Teleisthai" (tr. of Mario Azzopardi). [InterPR] (17:2) Fall 91, p. 85.
1740. FAMA, Maria
"Teddy Bears for Two Voices." [Pearl] (14) Fall-Wint 91, p. 24.
1741. FANDEL, John
"Ablative Absolute." [FourQ] (5:2) Fall 91, p. 47.
"Petrarch Speaking." [FourQ] (5:2) Fall 91, p. 47.
1742. FANG, Dai
"Cigarette Butts" (tr. of Xu Gang, w. Edward Morin and Dennis Ding). [Iowa] (21:2) Spr-Sum 91, p. 45.

1778. FELTGES, Kenneth J.
    "Conspicuous Consumption." [SlipS] (11) 91, p. 68.
    "That's Amoré." [SlipS] (11) 91, p. 67-68.
FEMINA, Gerry La
    See LaFEMINA, Gerry
1779. FENG, Anita N.
    "Concerning Children." [NowestR] (29:2) 91, p. 86.
    "A Letter to Beijing." [NowestR] (29:2) 91, p. 87.
FENGMAO, Hua
    See HUA, Fengmao
1780. FENSTERMAKER, Vesle
    "January Thaw." [HopewellR] (1991) 91, p. 13.
1781. FERGUSON, Gordon
    "Hunger Striker" (for Jerry Rau). [LakeSR] (25) 91, p. 14.
1782. FERGUSON, Judith
    "Like Every Mother." [Calyx] (13:3) Wint 91-92, p. 49.
    "What's Inside." [Calyx] (13:3) Wint 91-92, p. 50-51.
    "The Woman in the Street is Still Screaming." [Calyx] (13:3) Wint 91-92, p. 48.
1783. FERGUSON, Penny L.
    "Abuse." [PottPort] (13:1) Spr 91, p. 53.
    "Grandmother." [PottPort] (13:1) Spr 91, p. 52.
    "Pup's Chocolates." [PottPort] (13:1) Spr 91, p. 53.
FERNANDES JORGE, João Miguel
    See JORGE, João Miguel Fernandes
1784. FERNANDEZ, Pablo Armando
    "Ambush" (tr. by Daniela Gioseffi, w. Enildo Garcia). [Contact] (10:59/60/61) Spr 91, p. 13.
    "Ballad of the Three Wars" (tr. by Daniela Gioseffi, w. Enildo Garcia). [Contact] (10:59/60/61) Spr 91, p. 16.
    "A Permanent Place" (tr. by Daniela Gioseffi, w. Enildo Garcia). [Contact] (10:59/60/61) Spr 91, p. 18.
    "Solitude, Cruel Season" (tr. by Daniela Gioseffi, w. Enildo Garcia). [Contact] (10:59/60/61) Spr 91, p. 14.
    "To a Young Freedom Fighter in Prison" (tr. by Daniela Gioseffi, w. Enildo Garcia). [Contact] (10:59/60/61) Spr 91, p. 15.
    "To the Great Cantor" (tr. by Daniela Gioseffi, w. Enildo Garcia). [Contact] (10:59/60/61) Spr 91, p. 17.
    "Trajan" (The Poet's Testament, tr. by Daniela Gioseffi, w. Enildo Garcia). [Contact] (10:59/60/61) Spr 91, p. 18.
1785. FERNCASE, Anne
    "Family Cycles." [TickleAce] (21) Spr-Sum 91, p. 20-22.
    "I." [TickleAce] (21) Spr-Sum 91, p. 17.
    "Love and Marriage." [TickleAce] (21) Spr-Sum 91, p. 18-19.
1786. FERRA, Lorraine
    "Evening Sky" (to my mother). [PoetC] (22:3) Spr 91, p. 27.
    "Snowshoe Hare." [PoetC] (22:3) Spr 91, p. 26.
1787. FERRY, David
    "At the Hospital." [Raritan] (11:1) Sum 91, p. 10.
    "The Blind People" (tr. of Charles Baudelaire). [PartR] (58:4) Fall 91, p. 692.
    "Epic of Gilgamesh" (Selections, tr. of Anonymous). [TriQ] (83) Wint 91-92, p. 135-155.
    "Mnemosyne" (tr. of Friedrich Hölderlin). [Raritan] (11:1) Sum 91, p. 11-12.
    "Petrarchan." [Ploughs] (17:2/3) Fall 91, p. 134.
    "Roman Elegy VIII" (tr. of Johann Wolfgang von Goethe). [Raritan] (11:1) Sum 91, p. 12.
1788. FETHERLING, Douglas
    "Dissimulation." [Quarry] (40:1/2) Wint-Spr 91, p. 57-60.
FICK, Karen Ohnesorge
    See OHNESORGE-FICK, Karen
FICK, Marlon Ohnesorge
    See OHNESORGE-FICK, Marlon
1789. FICKERT, Kurt
    "A Sepia Snapshot." [Elf] (1:1) Spr 91, p. 39.
    "Vanished Places." [Elf] (1:1) Spr 91, p. 40.
1790. FIELD, Brad
    "Cans." [Parting] (4:1) Sum 91, p. 1.

1791. FIELD, Edward
"Callas." [AmerPoR] (20:6) N-D 91, p. 28.
"The Centaur." [ColR] (NS 18:1) Spr-Sum 91, p. 34.
"Ganesh." [ColR] (NS 18:2) Fall-Wint 91, p. 102.
"The Kuntzes." [AmerPoR] (20:6) N-D 91, p. 29.
"Oh, the Gingkos." [AmerPoR] (20:6) N-D 91, p. 28.
"The Shining" (in memoriam May Swenson). [MichQR] (30:2) Spr 91, p. 275-276.
"The Stumps." [AmerPoR] (20:6) N-D 91, p. 30.
"Subsidence." [ColR] (NS 18:1) Spr-Sum 91, p. 33.
"The Time Bomb." [MichQR] (30:2) Spr 91, p. 273-274.
"Tired." [ColR] (NS 18:2) Fall-Wint 91, p. 101.
"Whatever Became of: Freud." [AmerPoR] (20:6) N-D 91, p. 27.
"The Winners and the Losers." [AmerPoR] (20:6) N-D 91, p. 29.
1792. FIELD, Julia
"Do Unto Others." [SouthernPR] (31:1) Spr 91, p. 63.
1793. FIELD, Simon
"Family Folding." [Mildred] (4:2/5:1) 91, p. 88.
"The Institute of Astronomy at Cambridge." [Mildred] (4:2/5:1) 91, p. 87.
"The Shape of Large Sounds." [Bogg] (64) 91, p. 12.
1794. FIELDER, William A.
"Endless Boredom" (tr. of Ahmet Muhip Diranas, w. Ozcan Yalim and Dionis Coffin
Riggs). [InterPR] (17:1) Spr 91, p. 19.
"In the Home for the Elderly" (tr. of Özcan Yalim, w. the author and Dionis Coffin
Riggs). [InterPR] (17:1) Spr 91, p. 20.
"Such Love" (tr. of Attila Ilhan, w. Ozcan Yalim and Dionis Coffin Riggs).
[InterPR] (17:1) Spr 91, p. 17.
"To Live" (tr. of Cahit Külebi, w. Ozcan Yalim and Dionis Coffin Riggs). [InterPR]
(17:1) Spr 91, p. 19.
1795. FIELDS, Leslie Leyland
"Mondays on this Island." [PoetL] (86:3) Fall 91, p. 48.
1796. FIFER, Ken
"In the Talmud." [US1] (24/25) Spr 91, p. 6.
1797. FIGUEROA, José A.
"Verano." [Nuez] (3:8/9) 91, p. 29.
1798. FILES, Meg
"The Widow." [BellR] (14:2) Fall 91, p. 44.
1799. FILKINS, Peter
"Another Life." [Journal] (15:2) Fall 91, p. 31.
"Paris" (tr. of Ingeborg Bachmann). [Vis] (35) 91, p. 18.
1800. FILSON, B. K.
"August." [AntigR] (84) Wint 91, p. 50.
"October." [AntigR] (84) Wint 91, p. 52.
"September." [AntigR] (84) Wint 91, p. 51.
1801. FINALE, Frank
"Salt Girl" ("When it rains, it pours"). [JINJPo] (13:2) Aut 91, p. 27.
1802. FINCH, Anna
"Grandmother's Tree." [BelPoJ] (41:3) Spr 91, p. 1.
1803. FINCH, Casey
"The Problem of Fun." [RiverS] (34) 91, p. 54-55.
"Thomas Edison." [MissR] (19:3) 91, p. 162-163.
1804. FINCH, Rebecca
"Communion." [Crucible] (27) Fall 91, p. 52.
1805. FINCH, Roger
"Home Stay." [BelPoJ] (41:4) Sum 91, p. 9.
"Through This Window." [BelPoJ] (41:4) Sum 91, p. 10.
"What Is Written on the Shore." [Sparrow] (58) Jl 91, p. 27.
"Woman Drinking with a Gentleman." [WebR] (15) Spr 91, p. 110.
1806. FINCKE, Gary
"Attack of the Fifty-foot Woman." [LaurelR] (25:1) Wint 91, p. 55-56.
"The Conversation of Elephants." [Poetry] (158:5) Ag 91, p. 264-265.
"The Durable Word for Wonder." [Boulevard] (6:2/3, #17/18) Fall 91, p. 173-174.
"The Hunza Dream." [Poetry] (158:1) Ap 91, p. 27-28.
"I Married a Monster from Outer Space." [LaurelR] (25:1) Wint 91, p. 56-57.
"Inventing Angels." [GettyR] (4:4) Aut 91, p. 655-656.
"Mesa of Lost Women." [LaurelR] (25:1) Wint 91, p. 54-55.
"The Metabolism Insight." [OxfordM] (7:2) Fall-Wint 91, p. 65.

"The Perfume Symphony." [PoetryNW] (32:3) Aut 91, p. 28-29.
"Reaching the Deaf." [Poetry] (158:5) Ag 91, p. 263-264.
"The Stuttering Cures." [Poetry] (158:5) Ag 91, p. 265-266.
"Watching the Onions." [BellR] (14:1) Spr 91, p. 56.
"The Wonder Children." [PoetryNW] (32:3) Aut 91, p. 29-30.

1807. FINK, Robert A.
"Idalou Spencer, My Eighth-Grade Teacher, Is Found Dead in the Middle of
Summer." [TexasR] (12:3/4) Fall-Wint 91, p. 75.

1808. FINKELSTEIN, Caroline
"For That Husband." [Poetry] (158:6) S 91, p. 321.
"Soup of the Evening." [ParisR] (33:121) Wint 91, p. 203.
"With Fox Eyes." [Poetry] (158:6) S 91, p. 322.

1809. FINKELSTEIN, Norman
"Elegy." [DenQ] (26:1) Sum 91, p. 26-27.
"Job's Daughters." [Salm] (90/91) Spr-Sum 91, p. 103-104.
"Lyrical Life." [DenQ] (26:1) Sum 91, p. 28-29.
"Mládi." [Salm] (90/91) Spr-Sum 91, p. 101-102.

1810. FINLAY, John
"A Prayer to the Father." [SouthernR] (27:3) Jl 91, p. 726.

1811. FINNEGAN, Brenda
"In Talia's Eyes." [TexasR] (12:3/4) Fall-Wint 91, p. 76.

1812. FINNEGAN, James
"An American Afternoon." [PoetryE] (32) Fall 91, p. 114.
"A Ghost Story." [SoDakR] (29:3 part 2) Aut 91, p. 71.
"Hard River." [WestB] (28) 91, p. 48.
"Toilet of a Dead Woman/Bride." [DenQ] (26:1) Sum 91, p. 30-31.

1813. FINNELL, Dennis
"Singing Tree." [PoetryE] (32) Fall 91, p. 149.

1814. FINNEY, Frank
"J.J. Muscles." [FreeL] (7) Spr 91, p. 14.

1815. FINNIGAN, Joan
"The Breakwater and the Web" (Excerpt). [Quarry] (40:1/2) Wint-Spr 91, p. 68.
"Untitled: The hired men on my grandfather's Valley farm." [Quarry] (40:1/2)
Wint-Spr 91, p. 69.

1816. FIREBAUGH, Joseph
"Penumbra" (St. John 1:5). [FourQ] (4:2) Fall 90, p. 36.

1817. FIREFLY, John
"Goldfish Fantail." [ClockR] (7:1/2) 91-92, p. 131.

1818. FIRER, Susan
"The Bright Waterfall of Angels." [Iowa] (21:2) Spr-Sum 91, p. 142-144.
"Michigan." [Farm] (8:1) Spr-Sum 91, p. 71-72.
"Monet's Beard" (for John Garey). [CreamCR] (15:1) Spr 91, p. 53.
"A Paper Prayer." [Iowa] (21:2) Spr-Sum 91, p. 141-142.

1819. FIRMAGE, Robert
"On Crutches of Naked Poplars" (Translation Chapbook Series, Number 15: 14
poems, tr. of Peter Huchel). [MidAR] (11:1) 91, p. 137-173.

FIRMAT, Gustavo Pérez
See PÉREZ FIRMAT, Gustavo

1820. FISCHER, Sara
"Amaryllis: Easter Prelude." [ChrC] (108:10) 20-27 Mr 91, p. 324.

1821. FISER, Karen
"Flatlanders." [HangL] (59) 91, p. 27.
"Teaching Myself to Read." [HangL] (59) 91, p. 27.

1822. FISH, Cheryl
"Pedals on a Side-Street, Swing." [Talisman] (7) Fall 91, p. 93.

1823. FISH, Karen
"The Annunciation." [IndR] (14:2) Spr 91, p. 23-24.
"December." [IndR] (14:2) Spr 91, p. 21-22.
"Egypt in Flaubert's Time" (for Molly Bendall). [HayF] (9) Fall-Wint 91, p.
101-102.
"The Fire's Hypnotic Flickering." [HayF] (9) Fall-Wint 91, p. 70-72.

1824. FISHER, Allen
"Boogie Woogie." [NewAW] (8/9) Fall 91, p. 78-81.
"Gravity As a Consequence of Shape" (2 selections). [Avec] (4:1) 91, p. 108-109.

1825. FISHER, Bill
"Math and the Wart." [PaintedB] (42) 91, p. 12-13.

1826. FISHER, David Lincoln
"The Spring." [Abraxas] (40/41) 91, p. 124.
"The Time of the Grapes." [Abraxas] (40/41) 91, p. 123.
1827. FISHER, Frances
"Ink Stains." [OnTheBus] (8/9) 91, p. 71.
1828. FISHER, Janet
"By the Pump Dry-Eyed." [SycamoreR] (3:2) Sum 91, p. 38.
"Raw." [SycamoreR] (3:2) Sum 91, p. 39.
1829. FISHER, Joan
"In Progress (We Trust)." [NewAW] (7) Spr 91, p. 36-40.
1830. FISHER, Roy
"According to Clocks." [NewAW] (8/9) Fall 91, p. 84-86.
"Every Man His Own Eyebright" (for Dr. Baker's botanisings). [NewAW] (8/9) Fall 91, p. 82-83.
"Hollywood Legend." [NewAW] (8/9) Fall 91, p. 86.
"The Mark." [NewAW] (8/9) Fall 91, p. 86-87.
"Upright Drawing." [NewAW] (8/9) Fall 91, p. 82.
1831. FISHER, Steve
"Bio on Judge Cunt." [Pearl] (13) Spr-Sum 91, p. 59.
"Responding to Prison Guards." [Pearl] (13) Spr-Sum 91, p. 59.
1832. FISHMAN, Charles
"Quiet, It's Too Quiet." [Pearl] (13) Spr-Sum 91, p. 14.
"Sentimental Journey." [Gypsy] (17) 91, p. 16.
1833. FITCH, Liz
"The Lost Room." [PaintedB] (44) 91, p. 6.
1834. FITTERMAN, Rob
"Heaven & East Houston St." (Selection: 1). [Avec] (4:1) 91, p. 131-133.
1835. FITZGIBBONS, Eleanor (Eleanor M.)
"Dream Land." [Sparrow] (58) Jl 91, p. 11.
"Little Girl, Arise!" (Mark 5:41). [ChrC] (108:21) 10-17 Jl 91, p. 693.
"October." [Sparrow] (58) Jl 91, p. 11.
"Winter Triptych: Outdoor Stations of the Cross." [Sparrow] (58) Jl 91, p. 12.
1836. FITZPATRICK, Evelyn
"Untitled: The beautiful white orchids had turned to brown." [MinnR] (NS 36) Spr 91, p. 22.
1837. FITZPATRICK, Kevin
"After the Burglary." [Sidewalks] (1) Aug 91, p. 29.
"Clearing of the Site." [NorthStoneR] (10) Fall 91-Wint 92, p. 152-153.
"Guns Don't Kill People." [NorthStoneR] (10) Fall 91-Wint 92, p. 154.
1838. FITZSIMMONS, Thomas
"Through the Gold." [Vis] (36) 91, p. 46.
1839. FIXEL, Lawrence
"The Fifth Room." [Notus] (9) Fall 91, p. 80-81.
"The Situation Room." [Notus] (9) Fall 91, p. 79.
1840. FLANAGAN, Timothy
"Private Reserve." [PoetryE] (31) Spr 91, p. 94-95.
1841. FLANDERS, Jane
"Aunt Maude's Pocketbook." [NewRep] (205:12/13) 16-23 S 91, p. 42.
"Blue Lobster." [ColR] (NS 18:2) Fall-Wint 91, p. 122-123.
"Wildlife in Indiana." [ColR] (NS 18:2) Fall-Wint 91, p. 124-125.
1842. FLANNAGAN, Beckie
"Capricious." [Plain] (12:1) Fall 91, p. 28.
1843. FLANNERY, Matthew
"Cold in the North" (for MRF, tr. of Li Ho). [LitR] (34:2) Wint 91, p. 229.
"Deer Fence" (tr. of Wang Wei, for JE). [SouthernHR] (25:2) Spr 91, p. 136.
"Drinking Poem V." (For I M, tr. of T'ao Ch'ien). [CrabCR] (7:3) 91, p. 22.
"Home to Garden and Field V" (For RRF, tr. of T'ao Ch'ien). [CrabCR] (7:3) 91, p. 22.
"Hsin-I Village" (tr. of Wang Wei, for BMW). [SouthernHR] (25:2) Spr 91, p. 124.
"In the Yueh-lu Mountains" (tr. of Hu Hsiao-shih). [LitR] (35:1) Fall 91, p. 75.
"Listening to the Singing of Tung Lien-chih" (tr. of Hu Hsiao-shih). [LitR] (35:1) Fall 91, p. 75.
"On Dead Soldiers: II" (tr. of Hu Hsiao-shih). [LitR] (35:1) Fall 91, p. 76.
"Watching a Homeless Woman Sell Her Clothing" (tr. of Hu Hsiao-shih). [LitR] (35:1) Fall 91, p. 75.

1844. FLEMING, Jack
"The Elephant." [LitR] (35:1) Fall 91, p. 122.
1845. FLEMING, Jeanie Puleston
"Slow Down Construction" (tr. of André Breton, René Char and Paul Éluard, w.
Christopher Merrill). [AmerPoR] (20:3) My-Je 91, p. 25-30.
1846. FLEMING, Ronnie, Sr.
"What Is God Like." [PoetryUSA] (22) Spr 91, p. 18.
1847. FLETCHER, Dorothy K.
"C. 1960." [InterPR] (17:2) Fall 91, p. 94.
"Duchess." [InterPR] (17:2) Fall 91, p. 96.
"Hair." [InterPR] (17:2) Fall 91, p. 95.
"My Mama's House." [InterPR] (17:2) Fall 91, p. 93.
"Two German Women." [InterPR] (17:2) Fall 91, p. 92-93.
1848. FLINT, Roland
"Blow!" [PlumR] (1) Spr-Sum 91, p. 56.
"Easy." [PlumR] (1) Spr-Sum 91, p. 58-59.
"First Poem." [NoDaQ] (59:1) Wint 91, p. 179-180.
"Shellfish." [PlumR] (1) Spr-Sum 91, p. 57.
"Skin." [PraS] (65:4) Wint 91, p. 41.
"Spilled." [NoDaQ] (59:1) Wint 91, p. 177-178.
"Writing Italian Christmas at 'The Foreigner's Desk'." [NoDaQ] (59:1) Wint 91, p.
178.
1849. FLINTOFF, Eddie
"Crossing Ross-Shire." [Bogg] (64) 91, p. 49.
"I Shall Go without Seeing You" (tr. of María Teresa Sánchez). [Stand] (32:1) Wint
90-91, p. 67.
"A Word to Maria" (tr. of Beltrán Morales). [Stand] (32:1) Wint 90-91, p. 66-67.
1850. FLOCK, Miriam
"Rough Justice." [ThRiPo] (37/38) 91, p. 90.
"The Story of Breathing." [WestHR] (45:3) Aut 91, p. 213-214.
1851. FLOREA, Ted
"The Bindweed of Love." [Plain] (11:2) Wint 91, p. 11.
"Driving to Mullen." [Plain] (12:1) Fall 91, p. 12-13.
"The Fireworks at Sumner." [Plain] (12:2) Wint 91, p. 12-13.
"Near Macpherson National Cemetery." [Plain] (11:3) Spr 91, p. 16.
"Sonnet to the Homeplace." [Plain] (12:2) Wint 91, p. 13.
"Watching the Cranes." [Plain] (11:2) Wint 91, p. 11.
1852. FLORIAN, Miguel
"Territorio Verbal, I" (Bahía del Viejo San Juan, 1989). [Nuez] (3:7) 91, p. 19.
"Territorio Verbal, II (NY)." [Nuez] (3:7) 91, p. 19.
1853. FLORIT, Eugenio
"La Ventana." [Nuez] (3:8/9) 91, p. 3.
1854. FLOTT, Phil, Jr.
"Under the Peach Tree." [Writer] (104:9) S 91, p. 24.
1855. FLOYD, Marguerite
"Brilliance." [CinPR] (21) Spr 90, p. 67.
"T.S. Eliot Is Dead." [CinPR] (21) Spr 90, p. 66.
1856. FLYNN, Kevin
"Travel and Exile." [DustyD] Je 91, p. 5-7.
1857. FLYNN, Patrick
"In My Dream Childhood." [PoetryUSA] (22) Spr 91, p. 14.
1858. FLYTHE, Starkey, Jr.
"The Moment Before the Song Begins." [GeoR] (45:1) Spr 91, p. 120-121.
FOE, Mark de
See DeFOE, Mark
1859. FOERSTER, Richard
"Disposing of His Ashes." [Poetry] (158:6) S 91, p. 319.
"Windows at the Metropolitan." [Nat] (252:21) 3 Je 91, p. 750.
1860. FOLEY, Adelle
"Early plum blossoms." [PoetryUSA] (23) Sum 91, p. 18.
1861. FOLEY, Jack
"President Bush Today Was Described As Being 'At Peace with Himself'" (a round
for three voices). [PoetryUSA] (22) Spr 91, p. 15.
"Villanelle" (for Ivan Argüelles). [PoetryUSA] (23) Sum 91, p. 9.
1862. FOLLETT, C. B.
"Wet Paint." [SoCoast] (10) Fall 91, p. 4-5.

1863. FONDA, Sheridan
"Untitled: My right hand supports." [Elf] (1:2) Sum 91, p. 40-41.
1864. FONTANA, Jennie
"Wintering the Turkoman Mare." [Stand] (32:2) Spr 91, p. 4-5.
1865. FOOTE, Leonard
"Pathways II." [AnthNEW] (3) 91, p. 28.
1866. FOOTMAN, Jennifer
"Grandpa." [Grain] (19:4) Wint 91, p. 116.
"Lucky Scheherazade." [Grain] (19:4) Wint 91, p. 115.
1867. FORBES, Jack D.
"Euro Blues." [PoetryE] (32) Fall 91, p. 22-24.
"A Pledge of Allegience." [PoetryE] (32) Fall 91, p. 19-21.
1868. FORBES, Matt
"Poetry and Alzheimer's." [Bogg] (64) 91, p. 10.
1869. FORCIER, Audrey
"Dreamsong." [BambooR] (50/51) Spr-Sum 91, p. 52.
1870. FORD, Cathy
"Faith, By Any Other Name" (for my youngest brother). [Event] (20:3) Fall 91, p.
65-69.
"Moon's Face Over the Mountains" (for my youngest brother). [Arc] (27) Aut 91, p.
49-50.
1871. FORD, Charles Henri
"The Minotaur Sutra" (Excerpt). [Bomb] (34) Wint 91, p. 90.
1872. FORD, Martyn
"After the Funeral." [CumbPR] (10:2) Spr 91, p. 46.
"Nineteen Eighty-Four." [CumbPR] (10:2) Spr 91, p. 47.
"Thrift." [CumbPR] (10:2) Spr 91, p. 48-49.
1873. FORD, Michael C.
"Acts of Contrition." [Pearl] (13) Spr-Sum 91, p. 64.
"Judy Garland." [Pearl] (14) Fall-Wint 91, p. 65.
"Renaissance Haunting at the No Hope Inn." [Pearl] (14) Fall-Wint 91, p. 65.
1874. FORD, William
"Audition." [Poetry] (158:6) S 91, p. 332.
"August Depression, Winter Dreams" (West Branch, Iowa). [Iowa] (21:2) Spr-Sum
91, p. 91-92.
"Backwoods Love." [NorthStoneR] (10) Fall 91-Wint 92, p. 163.
"From the Bedroom Window." [NorthStoneR] (10) Fall 91-Wint 92, p. 162.
"Love's Archivist." [NorthStoneR] (10) Fall 91-Wint 92, p. 164.
"Of Miles Davis" (for Paul Zimmer). [Iowa] (21:2) Spr-Sum 91, p. 92-93.
"A Quarry in Iowa." [PoetC] (22:2) Wint 91, p. 41.
"The Second Death." [Iowa] (21:2) Spr-Sum 91, p. 93.
FORETS, Louis-René des
See Des FORETS, Louis-René
1875. FORHAN, Chris
"Yes, Well." [CreamCR] (15:1) Spr 91, p. 43.
1876. FORKER, Jeffrey Armadillo
"Waiting in Ambush." [CoalC] (4) S 91, p. 16.
1877. FORSHAW, Cliff
"Sonnet to Orpheus." [HeavenB] (9) Wint-Spr 91-92, p. 31.
1878. FORSSTROM, Tua
"Until You Are Caught" (tr. by Daniel Ogden). [Vis] (37) 91, p. 31.
1879. FORTNEY, Steven (Steven D.)
"Kendall's Song" (dead, Vietnam Feb. 1968). [Vis] (35) 91, p. 15.
"Nagasaki: 9 August 45, One Bomb. 70,000 Dead." [HeavenB] (9) Wint-Spr 91-92,
p. 41.
1880. FORTUNATO, Margot
"The Last Seal in the Baltic, Summer 1988." [SingHM] (19) 91, p. 43-45.
1881. FOSS, Phillip
"The Trespass Epistles." [Notus] (9) Fall 91, p. 45-52.
1882. FOSTER, Clarise
"It has all been written." [PraF] (12:1 #54) Spr 91, p. 66.
"Klee raced across the page and dropped his pants where picasso." [PraF] (12:1 #54)
Spr 91, p. 67.
1883. FOSTER, Edward
"Blind" (tr. of Zahrad, w. the author). [Talisman] (6) Spr 91, p. 139.

"Untitled: Which of the sailors first noticed the crutches" (tr. of Zahrad, w. the author). [Talisman] (6) Spr 91, p. 139.
1884. FOSTER, Greg
"Entropy." [Timbuktu] (6) Spr 91, p. 80.
"Little Rootie Tootie." [Timbuktu] (6) Spr 91, p. 81.
1885. FOSTER, June
"Inspiration." [OnTheBus] (8/9) 91, p. 72.
1886. FOSTER, Leslie D.
"Legalities." [Northeast] (5:5) Wint 91-92, p. 9.
"Orpheus at a Fish Fry." [Northeast] (5:5) Wint 91-92, p. 8.
"The Tough Exam Paper." [ChironR] (10:2) Sum 91, p. 46.
1887. FOSTER, Linda Nemec
"Climbing Harney Peak, Black Hills, South Dakota" (for Bob and Therese). [MidAR] (11:2) 91, p. 126-127.
"Lost." [ManhatPR] (13) [91?], p. 24.
1888. FOSTER, Prescott
"Your Lovely Lovers." [ContextS] (2:2) 91, p. 37.
1889. FOSTER, Robert
"Dawn Patrol" (For Bud Weldon). [FreeL] (8) Aut 91, p. 25.
1890. FOURMYLE, Gulliver Wm.
"ColtPython Bipolarcreek." [HawaiiR] (16:1, #34) Wint 91-92, p. 17.
"In the Galaxy of Plants." [HawaiiR] (16:1, #34) Wint 91-92, p. 14.
"Mahana." [HawaiiR] (16:1, #34) Wint 91-92, p. 15.
"Thesymbolforuncertaintyislittle u." [HawaiiR] (16:1, #34) Wint 91-92, p. 16.
1891. FOWLER, Anne Carroll
"Mudtime." [TexasR] (12:1/2) Spr-Sum 91, p. 98.
"Snapshot." [CumbPR] (11:1) Fall 91, p. 25.
1892. FOWLER, Jim
"Khe Sanh Diary." [NewYorkQ] (44) 91, p. 67-68.
1893. FOX, Hugh
"Father of the Bride." [DustyD] (2:1) Ja 91, p. 10-12.
"The First Day of the Third Millenium." [DustyD] (2:1) Ja 91, p. 4-5.
1894. FOX, Kate
"Dream of Flying Horses." [BelPoJ] (41:3) Spr 91, p. 17-18.
"Love After Love." [PoetL] (86:2) Sum 91, p. 39-40.
"Shaving David." [BelPoJ] (41:3) Spr 91, p. 16.
1895. FOX, Ken
"The Tall Dark Man." [DenQ] (26:1) Sum 91, p. 32.
FOX, Sandra Inskeep
See INSKEEP-FOX, Sandra
1896. FOX, Valerie
"In a World." [WestB] (28) 91, p. 69-70.
"This Is Not My Cousin." [WestB] (28) 91, p. 68j-69.
1897. FOY, John
"The Orangutan" (in the Jardin des Plantes, Paris, in memory of Rainer Maria Rilke) [AntigR] (84) Wint 91, p. 9.
"Rue des Martyrs" (Selections from the sonnet sequence: 20, 27). [AntigR] (84) Wint 91, p. 8.
"Rue des Martyrs, 23." [GrahamHR] (15) Fall 91, p. 55.
"Rue des Martyrs, 29." [GrahamHR] (15) Fall 91, p. 56.
1898. FRAGOS, Emily
"Cello" (For Leslie Lynn, In memory of Jacqueline du Pré, 1945-1987). [PacificR] (10) 91-92, p. 63-64.
1899. FRANCE, Brandel
"The King and Queen of Cassava." [ChironR] (10:4) Wint 91, p. 33.
1900. FRANCIS, David
"Near the Supposed Gravesite of Loyalist Officers." [SouthernPR] (31:1) Spr 91, p. 26.
1901. FRANCIS, Scott
"Mr. Mu Zhang Ying (I)." [SlipS] (11) 91, p. 30-33.
"Mr. Mu Zhang Ying (II)." [SlipS] (11) 91, p. 33-36.
"A Tourist Visits a Monastery Cave." [PacificR] (9) 91, p. 47.
1902. FRANCO, Michael
"Works and Days" (2 Selections). [Agni] (33) 91, p. 220-223.
FRANCO ALEXANDRE, António
See ALEXANDRE, António Franco

1903. FRANK, Bernhard
"The Sestina of Bhopal." [InterPR] (17:1) Spr 91, p. 78-79.
1904. FRANK, David
"Memento Mori." [SlipS] (11) 91, p. 47.
1905. FRANK, Edwin
"Likeness" (for E. B.). [GrandS] (10:4, #40) 91, p. 122-125.
1906. FRANK, Robert
"One Hour" (Excerpt: New York City, July 16, 1990, 15:45-16:45, One take).
[GrandS] (10:4, #40) 91, p. 33-48.
1907. FRANKLIN, Michael K.
"1974: Me at Eight, Even Then Theatrical." [BrooklynR] (8) 91, p. 18.
"My Father's Belt." [JamesWR] (9:1) Fall 91, p. 11.
1908. FRANKLIN, Russ
"Cherry Street Pool Hall." [ChatR] (11:3) Spr 91, p. 87-88.
1909. FRANZA, A.
"All This Creation." [DustyD] Ap 91, p. 7.
1910. FRANZEN, Cola
"The Lake." [Kalliope] (13:3) 91, p. 31.
"Ports" (tr. of Marjorie Agosín). [Agni] (34) 91, p. 162.
"Visiting Granddaddy." [Kalliope] (13:3) 91, p. 30.
"We Are and We Are Not" (tr. of Saúl Yurkievich). [LitR] (34:2) Wint 91, p. 230.
1911. FRASER, Caroline
"All Bears." [NewYorker] (67:16) 10 Je 91, p. 40.
"Drowning in Grain." [NewYorker] (67:21) 15 Jl 91, p. 28.
1912. FRASER, Sanford
"From Lawn Mowers I Have Known." [Turnstile] (3:1) 91, p. 112.
"O Say Can You See." [NewYorkQ] (44) 91, p. 66.
"Sunoco Kid." [NewYorkQ] (45) 91, p. 61.
"Susan Hot Sauce." [Turnstile] (3:1) 91, p. 113.
1913. FRASER, Stephen
"Mother Flies to Brazil for Adoption." [ChatR] (11:3) Spr 91, p. 67.
FRATES, Steven Craig de
See De FRATES, Steven Craig
FRATRIK, Julie Cooper
See COOPER-FRATRIK, Julie
1914. FRATTALI, Steven
"Sonnet: Come out to meet me in the garden's close." [Hellas] (2:1) Spr 91, p. 67.
"Sonnet: Her skin, this patina or nacreous shell." [Hellas] (2:1) Spr 91, p. 66.
"Sunlight and White Curtains." [Hellas] (2:1) Spr 91, p. 66-67.
"Under the Plum Tree." [Mildred] (4:2/5:1) 91, p. 94.
1915. FRAZER, Vernon
"Pilgrimage to the Big Sur Inn." [DogRR] (10:1) Sum 91, p. 47-48.
1916. FRAZIER, Andrea
"Blue Ridge." [Crucible] (27) Fall 91, p. 19.
1917. FRAZIER, Annie
"Crossfire" (a poem written in call and response). [CapilR] (2:6/7) Fall 91, p.
181-188.
1918. FRAZIER, Jan
"Fingers." [Calyx] (13:3) Wint 91-92, p. 59.
"Let's Go Play in the Corn." [NegC] (11:1) 91, p. 64-65.
1919. FRAZIER, Mark
"Louise Declines an Invitation." [CumbPR] (10:2) Spr 91, p. 16.
"Mother, Drawing." [Prima] (14/15) 91, p. 41.
1920. FREDERICKSON, Todd
"Elegy for August Gordon." [SoDakR] (29:3 part 2) Aut 91, p. 90-91.
1921. FREDERICKSON, Yahya
"Philosophies of Mexican Trucks." [OhioR] (47) 91, p. 100-101.
1922. FREDERIKSEN, Nancy
"The Dream" (to T. A. H.). [Sidewalks] (1) Aug 91, p. 51-52.
1923. FREDLUND, Terri
"I'd Rather Have a Running Vehicle Than Therapy." [SinW] (45) Wint 91-92, p.
12-15.
1924. FREEBAIRN, Rachel
"Smoke Signal." [PikeF] (10) Spr 91, p. 18.
1925. FREEDMAN, Robert
"Colorado Ritual." [FourQ] (4:2) Fall 90, p. 55.

"Misericordia." [WestB] (28) 91, p. 11-12.
"Sunday Barber." [FourQ] (5:1) Spr 91, p. 25.
"Tongue." [NewYorkQ] (46) 91, p. 58.
"The Union Refuses to Observe Martin Luther King Day So I Perform Hambone at
My Desk." [WestB] (28) 91, p. 10-11.
1926. FREELAND, Charles
"Mother of the Pilot." [CinPR] (22) Spr 91, p. 74-75.
"Stanley's Statues." [CinPR] (22) Spr 91, p. 72-73.
1927. FREEMAN, Jan
"Hyena." [AmerV] (22) Spr 91, p. 24.
1928. FREEMAN, Jessica
"Cha-cha Congo Line." [WashR] (17:3) O-N 91, p. 13.
"David Duke Recruits." [WashR] (17:3) O-N 91, p. 13.
"Gadding About." [CoalC] (3) My 91, p. 9.
"Nearbeer & Riots." [CoalC] (3) My 91, p. 9.
"Orleans' Artiste." [WashR] (17:3) O-N 91, p. 13.
"Roll Call." [CoalC] (4) S 91, p. 1.
1929. FREEMAN, Mary
"The Dead." [ChrC] (108:32) 6 N 91, p. 1037.
FREES, Madeline de
See DeFREES, Madeline
1930. FREIDENBERG, Anita
"The Departure Into Nocturnal Enchantment: Opossum" (after Pattiann Rogers).
[BellArk] (7:5) S-O 91, p. 24.
1931. FREISINGER, Randall R.
"Stopping to Dance" (for Jim Goetz). [NewL] (58:1) Fall 91, p. 78-79.
1932. FRÉMON, Jean
"Theater" (Editions Unes 1990, excerpts, tr. by Norma Cole). [Avec] (4:1) 91, p.
85-92.
1933. FRENCH, Catherine
"1949 Marion, Ohio." [PoetL] (86:1) Spr 91, p. 12.
1934. FRIAR, Kimon
"Evening Procession" (tr. of Yannis Ritsos, w. Kostas Myrsiades). [SouthernHR]
(25:1) Wint 91, p. 94.
"Succession" (tr. of Yannis Ritsos, w. Kostas Myrsiades). [SouthernHR] (25:1)
Wint 91, p. 93.
1935. FRIEBERT, Stuart
"About You" (tr. of Marin Sorescu, w. Adriana Varga). [FourQ] (5:1) Spr 91, p. 58.
"The Ancient Tree and the Villagers" (tr. of Tang Lan, w. Tang Tao). [PraS] (65:2)
Sum 91, p. 35.
"Apparition" (tr. of Marin Sorescu, w. Adriana Varga). [NoDaQ] (59:1) Wint 91, p.
119-120.
"Arizona Tenors." [PikeF] (10) Spr 91, p. 3.
"The Awakening" (tr. of Tang Lan, w. Tang Tao). [PraS] (65:2) Sum 91, p. 29.
"Babies in Boats" (for N. W.). [NewEngR] (13:3/4) Spr-Sum 91, p. 271.
"Bee Catchers." [WestB] (29) 91, p. 13.
"Beginning's Shudder" (tr. of Marin Sorescu, w. Adriana Varge). [RiverS] (33) 91,
p. 38.
"Bells" (tr. of Judita Vaiciunaite, w. Victoria Skrupskelis). [Mildred] (4:2/5:1) 91, p.
19.
"A Big Dog Pulling an Island" (for A. B.). [NewEngR] (13:3/4) Spr-Sum 91, p.
272.
"Black Widow at the Kitchen Window." [NewEngR] (13:3/4) Spr-Sum 91, p. 273.
"Bouquet of Marigolds" (tr. of Judita Vaiciunaite, w. Victoria Skrupskelis).
[Mildred] (4:2/5:1) 91, p. 18.
"Butterfly" (tr. of Judita Vaiciunaite, w. Victoria Skrupskelis). [Mildred] (4:2/5:1)
91, p. 21.
"Cabbage Fleas and Crocodiles" (tr. of Marin Sorescu, w. Adriana Varga). [PassN]
(12:1) Sum 91, p. 27.
"Caravan" (tr. of Marin Sorescu, w. Adriana Varga). [GrahamHR] (15) Fall 91, p.
95.
"Choke Rag." [LaurelR] (25:1) Wint 91, p. 106.
"City" (tr. of Judita Vaiciunaite, w. Victoria Skrupskelis). [Mildred] (4:2/5:1) 91, p.
19.
"Cognition" (tr. of Marin Sorescu, w. Gabriela Dragnea). [Aerial] (6/7) 91, p. 82.
"The Country Preacher." [SoDakR] (29:3 part 2) Aut 91, p. 10.

"The Days Are Changing" (tr. of Karl Krolow). [MidAR] (11:2) 91, p. 59-60.
"Descent" (tr. of Marin Sorescu, w. Gabriela Dragnea). [PraF] (12:3 #56) Aut 91, p.
    52.
"The Details Get Lost" (tr. of Karl Krolow). [MidAR] (11:2) 91, p. 58.
"The Drummer" (tr. of Judita Vaiciunaite, w. Victoria Skrupskelis). [Mildred]
    (4:2/5:1) 91, p. 20.
"Early to Bed." [Iowa] (21:1) Wint 91, p. 205.
"Evening Light" (tr. of Judita Vaiciunaité, w. Victoria Skrupskelis). [Timbuktu] (6)
    Spr 91, p. 99.
"Eyelashes" (tr. of Marin Sorescu, w. Adriana Varga). [GrahamHR] (15) Fall 91, p.
    93.
"Getting Used to Your Name" (tr. of Marin Sorescu, w. Gabriela Dragnea). [PraS]
    (65:3) Fall 91, p. 122.
"Girl with Ermine" (tr. of Judita Vaiciunaité, w. Victoria Skrupskelis). [Timbuktu]
    (6) Spr 91, p. 99.
"Horizontal" (tr. of Marin Sorescu). [Field] (44) Spr 91, p. 45.
"Hospital in Winter" (tr. of Tang Lan, w. Tang Tao). [PraS] (65:2) Sum 91, p. 32.
"I Stopped Right by the Tragic" (tr. of Marin Sorescu, w. Adriana Varga).
    [GrahamHR] (15) Fall 91, p. 94.
"In Peace-Time" (tr. of Karl Krolow). [PassN] (12:1) Sum 91, p. 26.
"Inheritance" (Excerpt, tr. of Judita Vaiciunaite, w. Viktoria Skrupskelis). [Os] (32)
    Spr 91, p. 28.
"July and August" (tr. of Karl Krolow). [MidAR] (11:2) 91, p. 61-62.
"Light from an Autumn Night" (tr. of Judita Vaiciunaite, w. Viktoria Skrupskelis).
    [Os] (32) Spr 91, p. 24.
"Miracle" (tr. of Marin Sorescu, w. Gabriela Dragnea). [PraF] (12:3 #56) Aut 91, p.
    51.
"Motives." (tr. of Karl Krolow). [GrahamHR] (15) Fall 91, p. 96-98.
"My Soul, You're Good at Everything" (tr. of Marin Sorescu). [Field] (44) Spr 91,
    p. 46.
"Nature" (tr. of Tang Lan, w. Tang Tao). [PraS] (65:2) Sum 91, p. 32-33.
"Not This or That" (tr. of Tang Lan, w. Tang Tao). [PraS] (65:2) Sum 91, p. 34.
"The Owl" (tr. of Judita Vaiciunaite, w. Viktoria Skrupskelis). [Os] (32) Spr 91, p.
    26.
"The Path" (tr. of Marin Sorescu). [Field] (44) Spr 91, p. 43.
"Pavilion" (tr. of Judita Vaiciunaité, w. Victoria Skrupskelis). [Timbuktu] (6) Spr
    91, p. 100.
"Peace" (tr. of Marin Sorescu, w. Adriana Varga). [PraF] (12:3 #56) Aut 91, p. 50.
"Pedestrian" (tr. of Marin Sorescu). [Field] (44) Spr 91, p. 42.
"Poem for Literature" (tr. of Karl Krolow). [PassN] (12:1) Sum 91, p. 26.
"Rainfall" (tr. of Tang Lan, w. Tang Tao). [PraS] (65:2) Sum 91, p. 30.
"The Requiem Shark" (for Annette). [Confr] (46/47) Fall 91-Wint 92, p. 265.
"Sand Worms." [ChamLR] (8-9) Spr-Fall 91, p. 54.
"Secret Transfusion" (tr. of Marin Sorescu, w. Adriana Varga). [Os] (32) Spr 91, p.
    4.
"Seeing Clearly" (tr. of Marin Sorescu). [Field] (44) Spr 91, p. 44.
"The Silence of Cornflowers" (tr. of Judita Vaiciunaite, w. Victoria Skrupskelis).
    [Mildred] (4:2/5:1) 91, p. 18.
"Spectacle" (tr. of Judita Vaiciunaite, w. Victoria Skrupskelis). [Mildred] (4:2/5:1)
    91, p. 20.
"The Spider Arrived" (tr. of Marin Sorescu, w. Adriana Varge). [RiverS] (33) 91, p.
    42.
"Start" (tr. of Marin Sorescu). [CarolQ] (43:3) Spr 91, p. 28-29.
"Study" (tr. of Marin Sorescu, w. Adriana Varge). [RiverS] (33) 91, p. 40.
"There Is Earth" (tr. of Marin Sorescu, w. Adriana Varge). [RiverS] (33) 91, p. 44.
"Two Mutes in Love" (tr. of Judita Vaiciunaite, w. Viktoria Skrupskelis). [Os] (32)
    Spr 91, p. 27.
"Visiting Robert Francis with My Son" (for S. & R.F.). [Iowa] (21:1) Wint 91, p.
    204.
"When Wild Apple Trees Blossom" (tr. of Judita Vaiciunaite, w. Viktoria
    Skrupskelis). [Crazy] (41) Wint 91, p. 16.
"White Octaves" (tr. of Judita Vaiciunaite, w. Viktoria Skrupskelis). [Journal] (15:1)
    Spr 91, p. 13-14.
1936. FRIED, Erich
    "A Poem about Poems" (tr. by Lauren Hahn). [ColR] (NS 17:2) Fall-Wint 90, p.
        106-107.

1937. FRIED, Michael
   "Becky." [WestHR] (45:1) Spr 91, p. 22.
   "Examples." [WestHR] (45:1) Spr 91, p. 19.
   "In a New Apartment." [WestHR] (45:1) Spr 91, p. 21.
   "Pain." [WestHR] (45:1) Spr 91, p. 20.
1938. FRIED, Philip
   "As God, I Have Been Many Things." [WindO] (54) Sum 91, p. 35.
   "Catechism." [CrabCR] (7:3) 91, p. 15.
   "Koussipsky." [BelPoJ] (41:3) Spr 91, p. 14.
1939. FRIEDKIN, David
   "A Waste of Words" (Excerpt). [Caliban] (10) 91, p. 142-147.
1940. FRIEDLANDER, Benjamin
   "Aporia" (after Friedrich Hölderlin). [Talisman] (6) Spr 91, p. 93-95.
1941. FRIEDMAN, Dorothy
   "This War Never Touched Me." [Writer] (104:12) D 91, p. 26.
   "Your Father." [Writer] (104:3) Mr 91, p. 22.
1942. FRIEDMAN, Michael
   "Lester Friedman." [NewAW] (7) Spr 91, p. 70-71.
   "Love." [HangL] (59) 91, p. 28.
   "Melanie Soffa." [CalQ] (31) Fall 88, p. 60.
   "Mind." [HangL] (59) 91, p. 28.
   "On My Way to See You." [CalQ] (31) Fall 88, p. 60-61.
   "The Passing Cloud." [WashR] (16:6) Ap-My 91, p. 15.
   "Seasons." [HangL] (59) 91, p. 28.
   "Tim Dlugos." [WashR] (16:6) Ap-My 91, p. 15.
1943. FRIEDMAN, Ron
   "Cold Water Flats (305 Park Ave.)." [US1] (24/25) Spr 91, p. 27.
1944. FRIEDMAN, Stan
   "Voyager." [BelPoJ] (42:2) Wint 91-92, p. 36.
1945. FRIEL, Raymond
   "A Talking To." [Verse] (8:2) Sum 91, p. 46.
1946. FRIES, Kenny
   "Beauty and Variations." [AmerV] (25) Wint 91, p. 72-75.
   "Body Language." [JamesWR] (9:1) Fall 91, p. 6.
1947. FRIESEN, Bernice
   "First Apple." [Grain] (19:4) Wint 91, p. 131.
   "Prairie Woman." [Grain] (19:4) Wint 91, p. 130-131.
1948. FRIMAN, Alice
   "Eurydice's Lot." [WritersF] (17) Fall 91, p. 183-184.
   "Eve" (from a sculpture by Rodin). [Shen] (41:4) Wint 91, p. 85.
   "Flight to Australia, 1989." [Shen] (41:1) Spr 91, p. 90-91.
   "In This Night's Rain." [BelPoJ] (42:1) Fall 91, p. 32.
   "Introduction to April." [LaurelR] (25:2) Sum 91, p. 78.
   "Invitation to a Minor Poet" (Canadian Rockies). [Poetry] (159:1) O 91, p. 31.
   "Night Drive." [BelPoJ] (41:3) Spr 91, p. 15.
   "On Loving a Younger Man." [NoDaQ] (59:1) Wint 91, p. 198.
   "Plums" (to Bruce). [IndR] (14:2) Spr 91, p. 80.
   "Poets Manual." [HopewellR] (1991) 91, p. 19.
   "Red Bones" (Canadian Rockies). [HopewellR] (1991) 91, p. 19.
   "Schoodic Lake, Maine 1988" (for Gladys Swan). [LaurelR] (25:2) Sum 91, p.
      78-80.
   "Snake Hill" (to my mother). [PoetryNW] (32:2) Sum 91, p. 30-31.
   "Tonight." [Shen] (41:1) Spr 91, p. 92.
   "Two Poems for Paul." [LitR] (35:1) Fall 91, p. 56-57.
   "Why They Approved His Sabbatical Proposal to Join the Circus" (to Bruce). [Shen]
      (41:4) Wint 91, p. 84.
1949. FRITCHIE, Barbara
   "City Glass." [CreamCR] (14:2) Wint 91, p. 185.
   "Midsummer Love Poem." [CreamCR] (14:2) Wint 91, p. 184.
   "Tulips." [CreamCR] (14:2) Wint 91, p. 183.
1950. FRITSCH, Janice
   "Amen." (tr. of Jacques Reda, w. Elton Glaser). [Paint] (18:36) Aut 91, p. 61.
   "Egyptian Woman" (tr. of Jacques Dupin, w. Elton Glaser). [Paint] (18:36) Aut 91,
      p. 60.
1951. FROST, Carol
   "Apple Rind." [AmerPoR] (20:2) Mr-Ap 91, p. 46.

153

"C. O." [Ploughs] (17:2/3) Fall 91, p. 234.
"Modern History." [KenR] (NS 13:2) Spr 91, p. 132.
"The Torturer's Horse." [GettyR] (4:2) Spr 91, p. 198.
1952. FROST, Celestine
    "And for the homeless." [Epoch] (40:3) 91, p. 254.
    "Surrender." [Epoch] (40:3) 91, p. 255.
    "Where the Numbers Come From." [Asylum] (6:3/4) 91, p. 33.
1953. FROST, Elisabeth
    "Skating." [TexasR] (12:1/2) Spr-Sum 91, p. 99.
1954. FROST, Helen
    "Two Sides of the Horizon" (based on a story told by Barbara Nikolai, tr. by her
        son, Steven Nikolai, Telida, Alaska). [Calyx] (13:2) Sum 91, p. 70-71.
1955. FROST, Kenneth
    "The Frisbee of My Clavicle." [Salm] (90/91) Spr-Sum 91, p. 202-203.
    "Henri Poincaré." [ChamLR] (8-9) Spr-Fall 91, p. 87.
    "Loons on a Lake." [NegC] (11:1) 91, p. 91.
    "My sleep arranges hammers." [CinPR] (21) Spr 90, p. 65.
    "Standing at Attention." [PaintedB] (42) 91, p. 7.
    "Time on Its Own." [NewRena] (8:2, #25) Fall 91, p. 102.
1956. FROST, Linda A.
    "From What I've Heard about Alaska." [Colum] (15) 90, p. 185.
1957. FROST, Richard
    "The Naked Eye." [CalQ] (35/36) 91, p. 46.
    "Storm." [NewEngR] (13:3/4) Spr-Sum 91, p. 69-70.
    "The Torturer's Horse." [GettyR] (4:2) Spr 91, p. 199-200.
1958. FROST, Robert
    "Directive." [TriQ] (81) Spr-Sum 91, p. 164-166.
    "Out, Out." [Shen] (41:4) Wint 91, p. 72.
    "Spring Pools." [Shen] (41:4) Wint 91, p. 70.
1959. FRUMKIN, Gene
    "Dreaming About Kathy Acker." [Caliban] (10) 91, p. 138-139.
FU, Du
    See DU, Fu
FU, Tu
    See DU, Fu
1960. FUCHS, Barbara
    "The Night You Called Me a Shadow." [Dandel] (18:1) Spr-Sum 91, p. 36.
1961. FUCHSIN, Anna Rupertina
    "The Answer" (tr. by Ronnie Apter). [NewOR] (18:4) Wint 91, p. 12-14.
1962. FUERTES, Gloria
    "Amnesia" (tr. by Pamela Carmell). [AmerPoR] (20:2) Mr-Ap 91, p. 4.
    "The Beggar with Those Eyes" (tr. by Pamela Carmell). [AmerPoR] (20:2) Mr-Ap
        91, p. 3.
    "Circus" (tr. by Pamela Carmell). [AmerPoR] (20:2) Mr-Ap 91, p. 3.
    "Doves" (tr. by Pamela Carmell). [AmerPoR] (20:2) Mr-Ap 91, p. 4.
    "Every Night I Kill Myself a Little" (tr. by Pamela Carmell). [AmerPoR] (20:2)
        Mr-Ap 91, p. 4.
    "Here I Am Exposed Like Everyone" (tr. by Pamela Carmell). [AmerPoR] (20:2)
        Mr-Ap 91, p. 4.
    "Notice" (tr. by Pamela Carmell). [AmerPoR] (20:2) Mr-Ap 91, p. 4.
    "Our Chains Wear Us Down" (tr. by Pamela Carmell). [AmerPoR] (20:2) Mr-Ap 91,
        p. 4.
    "Profession: Ghost" (tr. by Pamela Carmell). [AmerPoR] (20:2) Mr-Ap 91, p. 3.
    "Pyramid of Enmity" (tr. by Pamela Carmell). [AmerPoR] (20:2) Mr-Ap 91, p. 3.
    "We Must Try Not to Lie" (tr. by Pamela Carmell). [AmerPoR] (20:2) Mr-Ap 91, p.
        3.
1963. FUH, Shyh-jen
    "Night Thoughts When I Am Voyaging" (tr. of Tu Fu). [Abraxas] (40/41) 91, p.
        155.
    "On the Mountain Lodge" (tr. of Wang Wei). [Abraxas] (40/41) 91, p. 155.
1964. FUHRMAN, Joanna
    "The Museum." [HangL] (58) 91, p. 83-84.
    "The Museum." [HangL] (59) 91, p. 72-73.
    "The Problem with Thirst." [HangL] (58) 91, p. 85.
    "The Swimming Monk." [HangL] (58) 91, p. 82.
    "The Swimming Monk." [HangL] (59) 91, p. 73.

1965. FUJIWARA, Naboru
"Sadness of Cool Melons" (28 Haiku, tr. of Issa, w. Lucien Stryk). [MidAR] (11:2)
91, p. 1-10.
1966. FUJIWARA, Tadafusa (d. 928)
"Lonely cricket-cries" (tr. by Sam Hamill). [ColR] (NS 17:2) Fall-Wint 90, p. 21.
FUJIWARA NO TEIKA
See TEIKA, Fujiwara No
1967. FUKE, Victor
"Fishing For." [Bogg] (64) 91, p. 13.
FUKUYABU, Kiyowara (900-930)
See KIYOWARA, Fukuyabu (900-930)
1968. FULKER, Tina
"Plastic Poem." [Vis] (36) 91, p. 50.
1969. FULLEN, George
"Music Lovers." [InterPR] (15:1) Spr 89, p. 90.
"Nocturne: White on Black." [InterPR] (15:1) Spr 89, p. 91.
1970. FULLER, William
"The Groves" (Excerpts). [Avec] (4:1) 91, p. 170-172.
"Where Everyone Walked" (Excerpt). [Aerial] (6/7) 91, p. 165-166.
1971. FULMER, Elizabeth
"Comfort Smell." [ArtfulD] (20/21) 91, p. 79.
1972. FULTON, Alice
"A Little Heart-to-Heart with the Horizon." [Ploughs] (17:2/3) Fall 91, p. 27-28.
1973. FULTON, Leah Shelleda
"Current Events." [SoDakR] (29:3 part 2) Aut 91, p. 103-104.
"A Drugstore Fable" (Age 4). [ConnPR] (10:1) 91, p. 39-40.
1974. FULTON, Robin
"After a Visit to the DDR" (November 1990, tr. of Tomas Tranströmer). [Antaeus]
(67) Fall 91, p. 104.
"After the Storm" (tr. of Werner Aspenström). [KenR] (NS 13:3) Sum 91, p. 126.
"April and Silence" (tr. of Tomas Tranströmer). [KenR] (NS 13:3) Sum 91, p. 125.
"From a History of Music." [Verse] (8:1) Spr 91, p. 102.
"National Insecurity" (tr. of Tomas Tranströmer). [Antaeus] (67) Fall 91, p. 105.
"A Page of the Night-Book" (tr. of Tomas Tranströmer). [Antaeus] (67) Fall 91, p.
106.
"Revisiting" (tr. of Werner Aspenström). [KenR] (NS 13:3) Sum 91, p. 127.
1975. FULWYLIE, Christine B. J.
"First Place City Home." [EmeraldCR] (3) 91, c1990, p. 142.
"Zaire." [EmeraldCR] (4) 91, p. 9-12.
1976. FUNGE, Robert
"Five-Finger Frannie." [Pearl] (14) Fall-Wint 91, p. 16.
"Hemingway Sitting at the Feet of Gertrude Stein." [NewYorkQ] (45) 91, p. 61.
"Henry & Ted." [SoDakR] (29:2) Sum 91, p. 93.
"Imagined Lives." [LitR] (35:1) Fall 91, p. 59.
"John / Henry" (Selection: "Sudden It Came"). [NewYorkQ] (46) 91, p. 87.
"Neither Father Nor Lover." [SoDakR] (29:2) Sum 91, p. 94.
"November Song." [PacificR] (9) 91, p. 64.
"Sunday Evening." [TexasR] (12:1/2) Spr-Sum 91, p. 100.
1977. FUNK, Allison
"Cicada." [GrahamHR] (15) Fall 91, p. 61.
1978. FUNKHOUSER, Erica
"Vagrancy." [OhioR] (47) 91, p. 102-103.
"Valentine." [Poetry] (157:5) F 91, p. 251-252.
1979. FUQUA, C. S.
"Recycling." [ChironR] (10:2) Sum 91, p. 44.
1980. FURBUSH, Matthew
"The Cathedral of the Mind" (An Elegy for Henry Adams). [Agni] (33) 91, p. 113.
"Freight Cars, Gloucester" (on the painting by Edward Hopper). [TexasR] (12:3/4)
Fall-Wint 91, p. 77.
1981. FURBUSH, Michael
"Mobil Station" (After the painting Gas, by Edward Hopper). [TexasR] (12:1/2)
Spr-Sum 91, p. 102.
"A Touch of Cain." [TexasR] (12:1/2) Spr-Sum 91, p. 101.
1982. FUREY, Leo
"Sonnet" (for R.J. MacSween). [AntigR] (87/88) Fall 91-Wint 92, p. 263.

155

FUSCO

1983. FUSCO, Peter
"A Lullaby — at Night with Insomnia" (tr. of Hyon-Jong Chong, w. Wolhee Choe). [ArtfulD] (20/21) 91, p. 63.
"Not winged like birds, but like a flock of squid." [HawaiiR] (15:2, #32) Spr 91, p. 65.
1984. FUSEK, Serena
"Roadside Mermaid." [Bogg] (64) 91, p. 11.
1985. FUSSELMAN, Amy
"American Couple." [Timbuktu] (6) Spr 91, p. 33.
"Moviegoers." [Timbuktu] (6) Spr 91, p. 32.
"Things Going into Things." [Timbuktu] (6) Spr 91, p. 32-33.
1986. GABBARD, G. N.
"Hymn and Viking Tune: Parergon to a Translation of *Beowulf*." [Hellas] (2:2) Fall 91, p. 275-277.
"Loss of Dream Sleep (Beowulf 697-836)" (Selections: 54-64). [LitR] (35:1) Fall 91, p. 103-107.
1987. GABLE, Cate
"Sadhj." [BambooR] (52) Fall 91, p. 26-27.
1988. GABO, Nuam
"Of Divers Arts (1962)" (Excerpt). [PassN] (12:2) Wint 91, p. 21.
1989. GABRIELLI, Cynthia
"Motets, Number 13" (tr. of Eugenio Montale). [SycamoreR] (3:1) Wint 91, p. 45.
"Motets, Number 15" (tr. of Eugenio Montale). [SycamoreR] (3:1) Wint 91, p. 47.
1990. GADD, Bernard
"Recension." [Bogg] (64) 91, p. 9.
1991. GADD, Maxine
"Feb. 1990." [CapilR] (2:5) Sum 91, p. 66.
"I Had to Buy a New Broom." [CapilR] (2:5) Sum 91, p. 62-63.
"Late Summer, 1990." [CapilR] (2:5) Sum 91, p. 67-70.
"Old Gothic Mar 1985." [CapilR] (2:5) Sum 91, p. 60-61.
"Riff for a Bill (19)." [CapilR] (2:5) Sum 91, p. 64-65.
1992. GAGE, Carolyn
"On Singing Women's Praises." [SinW] (43/44) Sum 91, p. 48.
1993. GAGLIONE, Jerry
"Wall Builder." [PoetryUSA] (22) Spr 91, p. 19.
1994. GALL, Sally M.
"The Singers of Lesbos" (Opera Libretto. Selections). [Ploughs] (17:1) Spr 91, p. 55-j58.
1995. GALLAGHER, Ann Maureen
"Demeter." [FourQ] (4:2) Fall 90, p. 46.
1996. GALLAGHER, M. T.
"Where?" (tr. of Heinrich Heine). [SpiritSH] (56) Spr-Sum 91, p. 46.
"You Are Like a Flower" (tr. of Heinrich Heine). [SpiritSH] (56) Spr-Sum 91, p. 46.
1997. GALLAGHER, Rhian
"Riding Pillion." [Stand] (33:1) Wint 91, p. 15.
1998. GALLAGHER, Tess
"Behind Which There Is an Expanse Past the World." [ColR] (NS 18:2) Fall-Wint 91, p. 12.
"Black Pearl." [ColR] (NS 18:2) Fall-Wint 91, p. 10-11.
"Black Pudding." [NewEngR] (14:1) Fall 91, p. 5-6.
"Blue Grapes." [NewEngR] (14:1) Fall 91, p. 7.
"Cold Crescent." [PassN] (12:2) Wint 91, p. 24.
"Deaf Poem." [PassN] (12:2) Wint 91, p. 24.
"Ebony." [NewEngR] (14:1) Fall 91, p. 6.
"Ghost-Life of a Ring." [Ploughs] (17:2/3) Fall 91, p. 124-125.
"He Would Have." [HayF] (9) Fall-Wint 91, p. 90.
"His Moment." [ColR] (NS 18:2) Fall-Wint 91, p. 8.
"I Stop Writing the Poem." [PassN] (12:2) Wint 91, p. 24.
"In the Laboratory of Kisses." [HayF] (9) Fall-Wint 91, p. 25.
"Infinite Room." [Atlantic] (268:6) D 91, p. 108.
"Letter to a Kiss That Died for Us." [ColR] (NS 18:2) Fall-Wint 91, p. 9.
"Precious." [ParisR] (33:119) Sum 91, p. 196.
"Stopping to Buy Bread on the Way to the Cemetery." [HayF] (9) Fall-Wint 91, p. 24.

"Valentine Delivered by a Raven" (for Ray and Alfredo on Valentine's Day). [CimR] (94) Ja 91, p. 93.
"The Valentine Elegies" (Selections: 7 poems). [Ploughs] (17:1) Spr 91, p. 59-64.
"We're All Pharaohs When We Die." [ParisR] (33:119) Sum 91, p. 194-195.

1999. GALLER, David
"The Abortion" (Greenwich Village, 1952). [PraS] (65:4) Wint 91, p. 52-53.
"The Cake." [PraS] (65:4) Wint 91, p. 50-52.
"For C. (of 1951)." [PraS] (65:4) Wint 91, p. 53-54.
"A Suite for R. W." [PraS] (65:4) Wint 91, p. 55-59.
"The Tapping." [HolCrit] (28:4) O 91, p. 18.

2000. GALLIANO, Alina
"La Madre de Magali Me Devuelve." [Nuez] (3:7) 91, p. 17.
"Yo Nunca Logro." [Nuez] (3:7) 91, p. 17.

2001. GALLOWAY, Elizabeth
"Ritual for Dead Land" (A Mourning for Land Contaminated by Radioactive Waste). [SingHM] (19) 91, p. 52-63.

2002. GALLOWAY, Louie
"Child in Louisiana." [Kalliope] (13:3) 91, p. 57.
"Hot Country." [Kalliope] (13:3) 91, p. 56.

2003. GALLUP, Dick
"In Fields of Longing." [Talisman] (7) Fall 91, p. 91.
"Victims of the Hearty Echo." [Talisman] (7) Fall 91, p. 91.

2004. GALVAN, Fernando
"Palms on the Cold Flagstone" (part I, tr. of Andrés Sánchez Robayna, w. Manuel Brito). [Talisman] (6) Spr 91, p. 71.
"Spout" (part III, tr. of Andrés Sánchez Robayna, w. Manuel Brito). [Talisman] (6) Spr 91, p. 70-71.
"To a Rock" (tr. of Andrés Sánchez Robayna, w. Manuel Brito). [Talisman] (6) Spr 91, p. 69.

2005. GALVIN, Brendan
"Against Genealogy." [GettyR] (4:4) Aut 91, p. 706.
"Anchorites." [ColR] (NS 18:2) Fall-Wint 91, p. 25-26.
"Below the Hill of the Three Churches." [Shen] (41:1) Spr 91, p. 29.
"Draggers." [KenR] (NS 13:2) Spr 91, p. 127-128.
"Estuary." [ColR] (NS 18:2) Fall-Wint 91, p. 21.
"Getting Through" (a little disquisition for my daughter). [GeoR] (45:4) Wint 91, p. 734-735.
"Nimblejacks." [GettyR] (4:4) Aut 91, p. 707.
"One for the Life List." [Atlantic] (267:6) Je 91, p. 72.
"Raiding the Boundary Stone." [ColR] (NS 18:2) Fall-Wint 91, p. 27-28.
"The Red Toolbox." [Shen] (41:1) Spr 91, p. 30-31.
"A Sea-Drift Monk to His Chronicler" (Ireland, 6th century). [SouthernHR] (25:2) Spr 91, p. 160-164.
"Skylights." [KenR] (NS 13:2) Spr 91, p. 128-129.
"Word Cells." [ColR] (NS 18:2) Fall-Wint 91, p. 22-24.

2006. GALVIN, James
"Book Learning." [NewYorker] (67:3) 11 Mr 91, p. 38.
"Emancipation Denunciation." [AntR] (49:1) Wint 91, p. 95.
"Expecting Company." [ColR] (NS 18:2) Fall-Wint 91, p. 42.
"Matins." [Sonora] (20) Wint 91, p. 33.
"The Other Reason It Rains, Etc." (for Ray Worster, 1918-1984 and Lyle Van Waning, 1922-1988). [ColR] (NS 18:2) Fall-Wint 91, p. 43.
"Postcard." [ColR] (NS 18:2) Fall-Wint 91, p. 41.
"The Weather Spider." [ColR] (NS 18:2) Fall-Wint 91, p. 39-40.

2007. GALVIN, Martin
"Enough." [PoetC] (22:3) Spr 91, p. 9-10.
"Hilda and Me and Hazel" (1990 John Williams Andrews Prize Winner). [PoetL] (86:1) Spr 91, p. 7-11.

GAMA, Steven da
See DaGAMA, Steven

2008. GAMACHE, Laura
"Comparative Biology." [BellArk] (7:1) Ja-F 91, p. 7.
"Love Song." [BellArk] (7:1) Ja-F 91, p. 3.

2009. GAMBLE, Marcia
"Childfilled." [SoCoast] (10) Fall 91, p. 23.

2010. GANASSI, Ian
"The Indifferent Beak." [DenQ] (25:3) Wint 91, p. 8-9.
"Lacrimae Rerum." [Boulevard] (5:3/6:1, #15/16) Spr 91, p. 194-195.
"Walter Pater's Paper Patter." [NewAW] (7) Spr 91, p. 50.
2011. GANDER, Forrest
"Amorous." [SouthernR] (27:2) Ap 91, p. 273.
"Diner, Evening." [SouthernR] (27:2) Ap 91, p. 271.
"Librettos for Eros" (Selections: 8 poems). [Sulfur] (11:1, #28) Spr 91, p. 119-125.
"The Provinces of Mars" (from "Wild Psalms"). [PartR] (58:1) Wint 91, p.
122-123.
"Red Shirt." [SouthernR] (27:2) Ap 91, p. 273-274.
"Revival." [SouthernR] (27:2) Ap 91, p. 272.
"Wisteria Blue." [SouthernR] (27:2) Ap 91, p. 272.
GANG, Li
See LI, Gang
2012. GANICK, Peter
"Ice Seed." [Talisman] (7) Fall 91, p. 126.
"Untitled (Crisp Appeal)" (for Carol). [Avec] (4:1) 91, p. 166-169.
2013. GANNON, Tom
"Bird Poem." [SoDakR] (29:3 part 2) Aut 91, p. 68.
2014. GANT, Shaun
"Poets." [CutB] (35) Wint-Spr 91, p. 32.
2015. GAO, Yu-hua
"A Farewell to Guang-Ling" (tr. of Wei Ying-wu). [GreenMR] (NS 4:2) Wint-Spr
91, p. 111.
"Fishing by an Autumn River" (tr. of Wang Shi-Zheng). [GreenMR] (NS 4:2)
Wint-Spr 91, p. 112.
"The Moon in the Mid-Autumn Night" (tr. of Wang Jian). [GreenMR] (NS 4:2)
Wint-Spr 91, p. 113.
"Mountain Village" (tr. of Jia Dao). [GreenMR] (NS 4:2) Wint-Spr 91, p. 114.
"Su Mu Zhe" (tr. of Fang Zhong-yan). [GreenMR] (NS 4:2) Wint-Spr 91, p. 110.
"Willow" (tr. of Li Shang-yin). [GreenMR] (NS 4:2) Wint-Spr 91, p. 115.
2016. GARBETT, Ann Davison
"Before Ash Wednesday." [ChrC] (108:5) 6-13 F 91, p. 136.
2017. GARCES, Michael
"In Calixto." [DogRR] (10:1) Sum 91, p. 24-25.
2018. GARCIA, Diana
"An Orchard of Figs in the Fall." [MidAR] (12:1) 91, p. 71.
2019. GARCIA, Enildo
"Ambush" (tr. of Pablo Armando Fernández, w. Daniela Gioseffi). [Contact]
(10:59/60/61) Spr 91, p. 13.
"Ballad of the Three Wars" (tr. of Pablo Armando Fernández, w. Daniela Gioseffi).
[Contact] (10:59/60/61) Spr 91, p. 16.
"A Permanent Place" (tr. of Pablo Armando Fernández, w. Daniela Gioseffi).
[Contact] (10:59/60/61) Spr 91, p. 18.
"Solitude, Cruel Season" (tr. of Pablo Armando Fernández, w. Daniela Gioseffi).
[Contact] (10:59/60/61) Spr 91, p. 14.
"To a Young Freedom Fighter in Prison" (tr. of Pablo Armando Fernández, w.
Daniela Gioseffi). [Contact] (10:59/60/61) Spr 91, p. 15.
"To the Great Cantor" (tr. of Pablo Armando Fernández, w. Daniela Gioseffi).
[Contact] (10:59/60/61) Spr 91, p. 17.
"Trajan" (The Poet's Testament, tr. of Pablo Armando Fernández, w. Daniela
Gioseffi). [Contact] (10:59/60/61) Spr 91, p. 18.
2020. GARCIA, José
"The Cost of Bread." [BlackBR] (14) Fall-Wint 91, p. 11.
"First Series" (10 selections, tr. of Yannis Ritsos, w. Adamantia Baltatzi).
[OnTheBus] (8/9) 91, p. 222-223.
"Meditation on Nietzche's Death Mask" (for Paul DuNard). [PaintedHR] (1) Ja 91,
p. 15.
"The Poet's July." [PaintedHR] (1) Ja 91, p. 14.
"Story from a Greek Island" (Third Place, 1991 Paintbrush Award in Poetry).
[PaintedHR] (3) Sum 92, p. 10-11.
"To Be." [SoCoast] (10) Fall 91, p. 40.
2021. GARCIA, Richard
"Los Amantes." [KenR] (NS 13:3) Sum 91, p. 145.
"The Book of Forgetting." [MidAR] (12:1) 91, p. 75.

"The Defiant Ones." [MidAR] (12:1) 91, p. 72-73.
"The Detective Gone Bad." [MidAR] (12:1) 91, p. 74.
"Dixit Dominus, Domino Meo." [BilingR] (16:1) Ja-Ap 91, p. 69.
"Outside Fallon." [BilingR] (16:1) Ja-Ap 91, p. 68.
"Pancho Villa in the Land of Forever." [NoDaQ] (59:4) Fall 91, p. 123.
"Pen." [SenR] (21:1) Spr 91, p. 34-35.
"Sadness and the Movies." [SenR] (21:1) Spr 91, p. 32-33.
"The Story of Keys." [KenR] (NS 13:3) Sum 91, p. 144-145.
"Swinging from the Moon on a Bosun's Chair." [YellowS] (37) Fall-Wint 91, p. 12.
2022. GARCIA ALONSO, Agustín
"A Tí, Estatua." [Nuez] (3:8/9) 91, p. 15.
"Entre el Marco" (a mi madre). [Nuez] (3:8/9) 91, p. 15.
2023. GARCIA-ALONSO, Jose ("Chien")
"El Mar." [LindLM] (10:1) Ja-Mr 91, p. 32.
2024. GARCIA-FALCON, Leticia
"The Alhambra Inscription" (tr. of Ibn Zamrak, w. Christopher Middleton). [ParisR]
(33:118) Spr 91, p. 24-25.
"Eggplant" (tr. of Ibn Sara, w. Christopher Middleton). [ParisR] (33:118) Spr 91, p.
26.
"The Lily" (tr. of Ibn Darraj al-Qastalli, w. Christopher Middleton). [ParisR]
(33:118) Spr 91, p. 26.
2025. GARCIA LORCA, Federico
"La Balada del Agua del Mar." [NewYorkQ] (45) 91, p. 74.
"Cancion Oriental" (from "Libro de Poemas" 1920). [CumbPR] (11:1) Fall 91, p.
36-42.
"Four Ballads in Yellow" (tr. by Jerome Rothenberg). [SnailPR] (1:1) Spr 91, p.
16-19.
"Oriental Song" (tr. by Linda C. Ehrlich and David Anderson). [CumbPR] (11:1)
Fall 91, p. 37-43.
"Sea Water Ballad" (tr. by Joel Zeltzer). [NewYorkQ] (45) 91, p. 74.
"Somnambulist Ballad" (tr. by W. D. Snodgrass). [Poetry] (157:5) F 91, p.
271-273.
"Three Crepuscular Poems" (for my sister Conchita, tr. by Jerome Rothenberg).
[Talisman] (6) Spr 91, p. 112-113.
2026. GARCIA RAMOS, Reinaldo
"Salvación por el Agua." [Nuez] (3:8/9) 91, p. 7.
2027. GARD, Peter
"On Hearing Bartok's Second String Quartet, 1917." [TickleAce] (21) Spr-Sum 91,
p. 66-67.
"Two Dreams" (Dreamed at Swain's Tickle, Bonavista Bay). [TickleAce] (21)
Spr-Sum 91, p. 68-69.
2028. GARDINER, Sheila
"Changes of Being." [BambooR] (50/51) Spr-Sum 91, p. 296.
"Play It with Pathos, Ruby." [BambooR] (50/51) Spr-Sum 91, p. 297-298.
2029. GARDINIER, Suzanne
"1939." [GrandS] (10:1, #37) 91, p. 109-114.
"The Admiral." [AmerV] (24) Fall 91, p. 35-36.
"The New World" (Selections: 4-5). [Pequod] (32) 91, p. 85-89.
"To Justice." [KenR] (NS 13:3) Sum 91, p. 2-3.
"To Peace." [KenR] (NS 13:3) Sum 91, p. 1-2.
"To the Strangers." [KenR] (NS 13:3) Sum 91, p. 3-4.
"To the Tribunal." [KenR] (NS 13:3) Sum 91, p. 1.
2030. GARDNER, Drew
"Practice." [Notus] (9) Fall 91, p. 72-73.
2031. GARDNER, Eric
"Dinner." [CoalC] (4) S 91, p. 8.
"Dry." [CoalC] (3) My 91, p. 1.
2032. GARDNER, Geoffrey
"The Burden of One Day's Work" (tr. of Jules Supervielle). [AmerPoR] (20:4) Jl-Ag
91, p. 37.
"The First Dog" (tr. of Jules Supervielle). [AmerPoR] (20:4) Jl-Ag 91, p. 36.
"The First Tree" (tr. of Jules Supervielle). [AmerPoR] (20:4) Jl-Ag 91, p. 35.
"Forest" (tr. of Jules Supervielle). [AmerPoR] (20:4) Jl-Ag 91, p. 36.
"God Speaks to Man" (tr. of Jules Supervielle). [AmerPoR] (20:4) Jl-Ag 91, p. 34.
"God Thinks of Man" (tr. of Jules Supervielle). [AmerPoR] (20:4) Jl-Ag 91, p. 34.
"God's Sadness" (tr. of Jules Supervielle). [AmerPoR] (20:4) Jl-Ag 91, p. 35.

"Homage to Life" (tr. of Jules Supervielle). [AmerPoR] (20:4) Jl-Ag 91, p. 36.
"Horses Without Horsemen" (tr. of Jules Supervielle). [AmerPoR] (20:4) Jl-Ag 91,
  p. 37.
"If There Weren't Any Trees" (tr. of Jules Supervielle). [AmerPoR] (20:4) Jl-Ag 91,
  p. 36.
"The Star" (tr. of Jules Supervielle). [AmerPoR] (20:4) Jl-Ag 91, p. 37.
2033. GARDNER, Isabella
  "The Moth Happened." [SoDakR] (29:3 part 2) Aut 91, p. 50.
2034. GARDNER, Melita B.
  "Faces." [EmeraldCR] (3) 91, c1990, p. 48.
2035. GARDNER, Philip
  "Agriculture." [TickleAce] (21) Spr-Sum 91, p. 84.
  "First of May." [TickleAce] (22) Fall-Wint 91, p. 16-17.
  "Ghosts." [TickleAce] (22) Fall-Wint 91, p. 18.
  "Old Haymarket, 1955." [TickleAce] (21) Spr-Sum 91, p. 82-83.
2036. GARDNER, Thomas
  "Laugh." [DenQ] (25:4) Spr 91, p. 34-35.
2037. GARLAND, Max
  "For a Johnson County Snowfall." [ChiR] (37:2/3) 91, p. 49-50.
  "Revisiting the Sistine Chapel." [Poetry] (159:2) N 91, p. 92-94.
2038. GARMON, John
  "Grandfathers." [SoDakR] (29:3 part 2) Aut 91, p. 61-62.
2039. GARREN, Christine
  "Beginnings." [TriQ] (83) Wint 91-92, p. 79.
  "The Drive." [TriQ] (83) Wint 91-92, p. 81.
  "First Magnitudes." [TriQ] (83) Wint 91-92, p. 77.
  "Homage." [TriQ] (83) Wint 91-92, p. 80.
  "The Soul." [TriQ] (83) Wint 91-92, p. 78.
2040. GARRETT, Daniel
  "Dark." [ChangingM] (23) Fall-Wint 91, p. 37.
  "Tormented Thoughts." [ChangingM] (22) Wint-Spr 91, p. 12.
2041. GARRETT, George
  "Days of Our Lives Lie in Fragments" (In Memory of O. B. Hardison, Jr.,
    1928-1990). [SewanR] (99:1) Wint 91, p. 166.
2042. GARRINGER, Jeff
  "August 8, 1986." [WindO] (54) Sum 91, p. 23.
  "Late for Work." [WindO] (54) Sum 91, p. 24.
2043. GARRISON, Deborah Gottlieb
  "3 A.M. Comedy." [NewYorker] (67:36) 28 O 91, p. 36.
  "I Answer Your Question with a Question." [NewYorker] (67:18) 24 Je 91, p. 30.
  "She Thinks of Him on Her Birthday." [NewYorker] (67:5) 25 Mr 91, p. 60.
2044. GARRISON, Jay
  "At the Hy-Vee." [Plain] (12:1) Fall 91, p. 26-27.
2045. GARTEN, Bill
  "I Have Outgrown." [DustyD] Je 91, p. 29.
  "I Sleep Here with My Wine." [DustyD] Je 91, p. 20.
2046. GARTHE, Karen
  "Toy Yacht." [BrooklynR] (8) 91, p. 11.
2047. GARTNER, Leslie
  "At the End of September" (tr. of Sándor Petöfi). [NewEngR] (13:3/4) Spr-Sum 91,
    p. 202.
2048. GARZA, José L.
  "Stone Tip the Flight of the Arrow." [PoetryE] (32) Fall 91, p. 47.
2049. GASH, Sondra
  "Late in Life a Woman Discovers Poetry." [US1] (24/25) Spr 91, p. 22.
2050. GASKIN, Bob
  "From Chagall's *Lovers in Venice*." [TexasR] (11:1/2) Spr-Sum 90, p. 28.
2051. GASPAR, Frank
  "Lookouts, Foul Weather." [Nat] (253:5) 12-19 Ag 91, p. 207.
  "Work." [MassR] (32:1) Spr 91, p. 38.
2052. GASTIGER, Joseph
  "Hollyhocks on the Alley." [Farm] (8:2) Fall-Wint 91-92, p. 37.
  "Para Mi Esposa en el Dia de las Madres." [SpoonRQ] (16:1/2) Wint-Spr 91, p.
    12-13.
  "Tainanmen Square." [Vis] (35) 91, p. 6-9.

2053. GASTON, Bill
"Sun's Toys." [Grain] (19:1) Spr 91, p. 121.
2054. GASWAY, Pamela K.
"Show and Tell." [Spitball] (39) Wint 91, p. 52.
2055. GATES, Beatrix
"One-to-One." [YellowS] (36) Spr 91, p. 20.
2056. GATES, Davida
"Creativity." [EmeraldCR] (3) 91, c1990, p. 79.
2057. GATES, Edward
"Boats." [TickleAce] (21) Spr-Sum 91, p. 36.
"Cold wind howls." [PottPort] (13:1) Spr 91, p. 15-16.
2058. GATTO, Alfonso
"A un Straniero." [Sequoia] (34:1) Spr 91, p. 30-31.
"Amore Della Vita." [Sequoia] (34:1) Spr 91, p. 28.
"Love of Life" (tr. by Phillip Parisi). [Sequoia] (34:1) Spr 91, p. 29.
"To a Stranger" (tr. by Phillip Parisi). [Sequoia] (34:1) Spr 91, p. 32-33.
2059. GAVIN, Tim
"Shadow Bird." [BlackBR] (14) Fall-Wint 91, p. 5.
2060. GAVRON, Jacquelyn
"Lifting My Skirt." [NewEngR] (13:3/4) Spr-Sum 91, p. 149-150.
"Mother's Girl." [CimR] (95) Ap 91, p. 48.
2061. GAWBOY, A.
"Alien." [SoDakR] (29:1) Spr 91, p. 148-149.
2062. GAY, Zan
"Of Light and Earth and Water." [Crucible] (27) Fall 91, p. 10.
2063. GEAREN, Ann
"Eagle Waters Resort." [Prima] (14/15) 91, p. 43-44.
2064. GEAREN, Cameron
"The People." [Prima] (14/15) 91, p. 30-31.
2065. GEBHARD, Christine
"Ambition." [Journal] (15:1) Spr 91, p. 63.
"Postscript." [GeoR] (45:1) Spr 91, p. 54.
2066. GEDDES, Gary
"Locating the Motherlode." [Quarry] (40:1/2) Wint-Spr 91, p. 70-75.
2067. GEELEGG, Arno
"Septic" (2 poems with same title). [Caliban] (10) 91, p. 122-123.
2068. GEIGER, Timothy
"Insomnia." [PaintedHR] (2) Spr 91, p. 13-16.
"Wintering." [PaintedHR] (3) Sum 92, p. 35-36.
2069. GELETA, Greg
"Anarchy Rides the Bus." [Lactuca] (14) My 91, p. 25.
"Laying Pipe in Alaska." [SlipS] (11) 91, p. 57.
"Lee Morgan's Last Words." [Pearl] (13) Spr-Sum 91, p. 61.
"Skin." [Pearl] (13) Spr-Sum 91, p. 61.
"To Have and to Hold." [FreeL] (7) Spr 91, p. 18-19.
"Translation Bee" (For James Reiss, Greg Boyd, and Silvina Ocampo). [Gypsy]
(17) 91, p. 52-53.
2070. GELINEAU, Renate
"Commuting." [AnthNEW] (3) 91, p. 28.
2071. GELMAN, Juan
"Rima IV" (Spanish tr. of Guido Cavalcanti). [Inti] (34/35) Otoño 91-Primavera 92,
p. 252.
"Rima XVIII" (Spanish tr. of Guido Cavalcanti). [Inti] (34/35) Otoño 91-Primavera
92, p. 252.
"Rima XXII" (Spanish tr. of Guido Cavalcanti). [Inti] (34/35) Otoño 91-Primavera
92, p. 253.
"Rima LXII" (Spanish tr. of Guido Cavalcanti). [Inti] (34/35) Otoño 91-Primavera
92, p. 253.
2072. GELSANLITER, David
"By the Time I Could Get There He Was Gone." [NewYorkQ] (44) 91, p. 69.
"Ready for Spring." [NewYorkQ] (46) 91, p. 55.
"Sex Between Them Was Something That Never Failed." [NewYorkQ] (45) 91, p.
81.
2073. GENEGA, Paul
"Istanbul." [WashR] (17:1) Je-Jl 91, p. 9.
"Neighbors." [Poetry] (158:1) Ap 91, p. 22.

2074. GENNETT, Len Carretta
"The Tattoo." [SingHM] (19) 91, p. 29.
2075. GENT, Andrew
"Listening in the Dark." [SouthernHR] (25:4) Fall 91, p. 383.
2076. GENTRY, Bruce
"Green and Sharp." [HopewellR] (1991) 91, p. 8.
2077. GEORGE, Anne
"My Mother Candling Eggs, 1936." [Kalliope] (13:3) 91, p. 35.
2078. GEORGE, Beth
"Cider and Salt." [PoetL] (86:3) Fall 91, p. 17-18.
2079. GEORGE, Donald
"Broken Things." [EmeraldCR] (3) 91, c1990, p. 30.
"The Kiss." [EmeraldCR] (4) 91, p. 51-52.
2080. GEORGE, Faye
"Birthday." [MidwQ] (33:1) Aut 91, p. 62.
"Blood Moon." [MidwQ] (33:1) Aut 91, p. 63.
"Kore." [Poetry] (157:4) Ja 91, p. 212.
2081. GEORGE, Gerald
"Jesus in Madrid." [ChrC] (108:16) 8 My 91, p. 521.
2082. GEORGE, Stafan
"1. [To Ida Coblenz]" (tr. by Peter Viereck). [Boulevard] (5:3/6:1, #15/16) Spr 91,
p. 172.
"2 [Year]" (tr. by Peter Viereck). [Boulevard] (5:3/6:1, #15/16) Spr 91, p. 174-175.
"Love Lyrics by Stefan George: Heterosexual and Homosexual" (tr. by Peter
Viereck). [Boulevard] (5:3/6:1, #15/16) Spr 91, p. 172-175.
"Southern Strand: Bay" (tr. by Peter Viereck). [Boulevard] (5:3/6:1, #15/16) Spr 91,
p. 173.
2083. GERATO, Erasmo G.
"Prayer" (tr. of Giorgio Caproni). [AnthNEW] (3) 91, p. 7.
2084. GERBER, Dan
"Sea Breeze." [PassN] (12:1) Sum 91, p. 30.
"Turning Fifty." [PassN] (12:1) Sum 91, p. 30.
2085. GERBER, Sabrina
"Home of the Brethren." [PacificR] (10) 91-92, p. 128.
2086. GERFEN, Henry
"Flasher." [NewYorkQ] (46) 91, p. 75.
2087. GERGELY, Agnes
"Vision" (tr. by Elizabeth Szàsz). [Interim] (10:1) Spr-Sum 91, p. 36.
2088. GERLACH, Lee
"Ghazals." [GrahamHR] (15) Fall 91, p. 43-48.
"Ghazals II." [GrahamHR] (15) Fall 91, p. 49-54.
2089. GERMAN, Norman
"Bone Mouse Sings a Skeleton Song." [BelPoJ] (42:2) Wint 91-92, p. 2-3.
"Practical Ecology." [HawaiiR] (15:3, #33) Fall 91, p. 95-96.
"The Weight of Old Coins" (for Charles Steib, numismatist). [BelPoJ] (42:2) Wint
91-92, p. 5-6.
"Whitey Goes Along." [BelPoJ] (42:2) Wint 91-92, p. 4-5.
2090. GERNEAUX, Robert
"A Mémère." [MoodySI] (24/25/26) Spr 91, p. 31.
2091. GERNER-MATHISEN, Aina
"Grass" (tr. of Rolf Jacobsen, w. Stephanie Hegstad). [Field] (44) Spr 91, p. 39.
"Refugee" (tr. of Rolf Jacobsen, w. Stephanie Hegstad). [Field] (44) Spr 91, p. 40.
"Sky Lab" (tr. of Rolf Jacobsen, w. Stephanie Hegstad). [Field] (44) Spr 91, p. 41.
"Suddenly. In December" (tr. of Rolf Jacobsen, w. Stephanie Hegstad). [Field] (44)
Spr 91, p. 38.
2092. GERNES, Sonia
"The First Year of Living Alone." [IndR] (14:3) Fall 91, p. 87.
"The Glazier's Daughter" (for Eva Mayer, 1823-1899). [IndR] (14:3) Fall 91, p. 88.
"On Refusing to Rent My House to the Calvinist Minister Who Is Convinced That It
Was Meant for Him." [HopewellR] (1991) 91, p. 13.
2093. GERSHENSON, Bernard
"This Afternoon." [OnTheBus] (8/9) 91, p. 73.
"Worship in the United States." [OnTheBus] (8/9) 91, p. 73.
2094. GERSTLER, Amy
"Consolation." [DenQ] (25:4) Spr 91, p. 36.
"Dead Hunters." [AmerPoR] (20:5) S-O 91, p. 18.

"Duration." [AmerPoR] (20:5) S-O 91, p. 18.
"The Mermaid's Purse" (a children's book). [MichQR] (30:4) Fall 91, p. 683-685.
"A Sad Women's Harvest Song." [BrooklynR] (8) 91, p. 34-35.
"A Sinking Feeling." [AmerPoR] (20:5) S-O 91, p. 18.
2095. GERVASIO, Michael
"Last Snapshot of Allende." [HawaiiR] (15:2, #32) Spr 91, p. 25.
"Tenure." [HampSPR] Wint 91, p. 57.
2096. GERY, John
"The Day after Labor Day." [CumbPR] (11:1) Fall 91, p. 51.
"Directions for Surprise." [CumbPR] (11:1) Fall 91, p. 52.
2097. GESIN, Julie
"Blue Vitriol: The Second Deviation of Labor" (tr. of Aleksei Parshchikov, w. John
High). [Avec] (4:1) 91, p. 141-142.
2098. GETSI, Lucia Cordell
"Homecoming, With Cat." [LaurelR] (25:2) Sum 91, p. 67-69.
"Living in Trees." [LaurelR] (25:2) Sum 91, p. 69-71.
2099. GETTLER, Andrew
"Bro." [ChironR] (10:1) Spr 91, p. 2.
"L.B.J." (Long Binh Jail, largest military stockade in Vietnam). [ChironR] (10:1)
Spr 91, p. 2.
"Mulier Cantat." [Vis] (35) 91, p. 37.
"Spoils of War" (for Bill Shields). [ChironR] (10:1) Spr 91, p. 2.
"TV Dinner." [ChironR] (10:1) Spr 91, p. 2.
"Waiting for Cowboy" (from junkpomes). [DogRR] (10:1) Sum 91, p. 17.
2100. GEVIRTZ, Susan
"Romansh: The Stations of Cannonization." [Avec] (4:1) 91, p. 117-126.
2101. GHIMOSOULIS, Kostís
"Ditty" (in Greek and English, tr. by Yannis Goumas). [SycamoreR] (3:2) Sum 91,
p. 54-55.
"The Malady That Is Saturday" (in Greek and English, tr. by Yannis Goumas).
[SycamoreR] (3:2) Sum 91, p. 56-57.
2102. GHITELMAN, David
"When the News Arrived in Bensonhurst That Italy Had Won the World Cup."
[AntR] (49:1) Wint 91, p. 98-99.
2103. GHOLSON, Christien
"Red Moods, Red Desire." [BlackBR] (14) Fall-Wint 91, p. 12-13.
2104. GIANFERRARI, Marie C.
"My Sister and I." [BlackBR] (13) Spr-Sum 91, p. 33.
2105. GIANNINI, David
"Pond" (for my father). [DustyD] Je 91, p. 27.
2106. GIBB, Robert
"Bartonsville" (for Andrew). [CinPR] (22) Spr 91, p. 76-77.
"Brown Bat." [Field] (44) Spr 91, p. 18-19.
"The Drought Year." [SnailPR] (1:2) Fall 91-Wint 92, p. 4-5.
"How Trees Are Known and Named." [HampSPR] Wint 91, p. 8-9.
"In the Carnegie Museum." [Antaeus] (67) Fall 91, p. 206-207.
"Jack-Lighting." [MidAR] (11:1) 91, p. 95-96.
"Landscape with Crows." [CinPR] (22) Spr 91, p. 78-79.
"Landscape with Figures." [SnailPR] (1:2) Fall 91-Wint 92, p. 3.
"Naming the Lone Bird." [LaurelR] (25:1) Wint 91, p. 28-29.
"Owls." [Field] (44) Spr 91, p. 17.
"Skunk Cabbage." [Field] (44) Spr 91, p. 20-21.
2107. GIBBLE, Melissa
"The Woods." [BellR] (14:2) Fall 91, p. 10-11.
2108. GIBBONS, Reginald
"From a Paper Boat." [PoetryE] (31) Spr 91, p. 5-16.
"Madrid." [SouthwR] (76:2) Spr 91, p. 298-299.
"My Beginning." [PoetryE] (31) Spr 91, p. 17.
"One of Cesar Vallejo's Human Poems." [PoetryE] (31) Spr 91, p. 21-22.
"Piano (and Voice)." [PoetryE] (31) Spr 91, p. 18.
"Retributions." [PoetryE] (31) Spr 91, p. 19-20.
2109. GIBBS, Robert
"Hearts Slated for Burning." [PottPort] (13:1) Spr 91, p. 70.
"So I Draw a Line." [PottPort] (13:1) Spr 91, p. 71.
"Waiting for a Window." [PottPort] (13:1) Spr 91, p. 69.
"Waiting for War." [PottPort] (13:1) Spr 91, p. 72.

"Waiting Together Through a Cold Season." [PottPort] (13:1) Spr 91, p. 73.
2110. GIBSON, Amy
"Songs from the Roof." [OhioR] (47) 91, p. 74-80.
GIBSON, Elisabeth Grant
See GRANT-GIBSON, Elisabeth
2111. GIBSON, John
"Five Scenes from Two Funerals." [WashR] (16:6) Ap-My 91, p. 14.
2112. GIBSON, Mary Milam
"Birthday." [EmeraldCR] (3) 91, c1990, p. 20-21.
"Child of Divorce." [EmeraldCR] (3) 91, c1990, p. 29-30.
2113. GIBSON, Morgan
"The Tabernacle Where My Father Preached." [Farm] (8:2) Fall-Wint 91-92, p. 73.
"Tweezers." [Farm] (8:2) Fall-Wint 91-92, p. 74.
2114. GIBSON, Stephen M.
"The Great War: A Memory." [ManhatPR] (13) [91?], p. 8.
2115. GIGANTE, Denise
"Like Ahab." [OnTheBus] (8/9) 91, p. 74.
"Soapdish." [OnTheBus] (8/9) 91, p. 75.
"Who Would Have Thought." [OnTheBus] (8/9) 91, p. 75.
2116. GIL, Lourdes
"Ana" (De "Blanca aldaba preludia," 1989). [LindLM] (10:3) Jl-S 91, p. 7.
"Niña Rota" (para Ana Maria Mendieta, de "Vencido el fuego de la especie," 1983).
[LindLM] (10:3) Jl-S 91, p. 7.
2117. GILBERT, Alan
"École Normale Supérieure." [DenQ] (26:1) Sum 91, p. 33-34.
2118. GILBERT, Celia
"Elms of the American Blue" (for Jorge Guillen, 1893-1984). [Thrpny] (46) Sum
91, p. 16.
"An Evening Meal." [Poetry] (158:3) Je 91, p. 127.
"For Anne Frank." [BostonR] (16:1) F 91, p. 21.
"The Marketplace." [NewYorker] (67:25) 12 Ag 91, p. 62.
"Our Lady of Revelation" (for Kate). [Ploughs] (17:2/3) Fall 91, p. 251-252.
2119. GILBERT, Chris (Christopher)
"The Art of Improvisers." [HangL] (59) 91, p. 31-32.
"The Atmosphere." [ColR] (NS 18:1) Spr-Sum 91, p. 27.
"An Improvisation." [HangL] (59) 91, p. 30-31.
"The Plum." [ColR] (NS 18:1) Spr-Sum 91, p. 28.
"Straight Outta Truth." [GrahamHR] (15) Fall 91, p. 13-14.
"The 'The'." [WilliamMR] (29) 91, p. 83-85.
"The Turn." [Callaloo] (14:4) Fall 91, p. 787-789.
2120. GILBERT, Marie
"Finding the Link" (Stuart, Florida). [Crucible] (27) Fall 91, p. 14-15.
"Speech Lesson from the Vegetable Man." [Crucible] (27) Fall 91, p. 13.
2121. GILBERT, Sandra M.
"About the Beginning." [Poetry] (158:3) Je 91, p. 154-155.
"Anniversary Waltz" (For E.). [CalQ] (35/36) 91, p. 16-17.
"In the Garage of the Retirement Complex." [Poetry] (159:2) N 91, p. 99.
"Indoor Camellia." [Poetry] (159:2) N 91, p. 100.
"The Magi in Florida." [Poetry] (159:2) N 91, p. 97-98.
2122. GILCREST, David
"Caveat Emptor" (for Tipper Gore). [NewYorkQ] (46) 91, p. 80.
2123. GILFOND, Henry
"Victory and Defeat." [CentR] (35:3) Fall 91, p. 541.
2124. GILGUN, John
"Bashing" (for David Lamble, film-maker). [ChironR] (10:3) Aut 91, p. 6.
"Dan Turner" (June 4, 1990). [ChironR] (10:3) Aut 91, p. 6.
"Relationship." [JamesWR] (9:1) Fall 91, p. 10.
"Sow." [Elf] (1:2) Sum 91, p. 43.
"Whitman's Hands." [ChironR] (10:3) Aut 91, p. 6.
2125. GILKES, Michael
"Littoral." [GrahamHR] (14) Spr 91, p. 19.
"Woodbine." [GrahamHR] (14) Spr 91, p. 17-18.
2126. GILL, Evalyn Pierpont
"After the Concert and 'Symphonie Fantastique'." [Crucible] (27) Fall 91, p. 32.
2127. GILL, James V. (James Vladimir)
"The Absent-Minded Inventor" (tr. of Jean Tardieu). [CimR] (94) Ja 91, p. 15-16.

"Adversity" (tr. of Jean Tardieu). [CimR] (94) Ja 91, p. 16.
"Cemeterization." [MissR] (19:3) 91, p. 174.
"The Dangers of Remembrance" (tr. of Jean Tardieu). [CimR] (94) Ja 91, p. 13.
"The Diary of a Suspicious Man" (Excerpt, tr. of Jean Tardieu). [CimR] (94) Ja 91,
    p. 15.
"Hölderlin's Grave" (tr. of Jean Tardieu). [CimR] (94) Ja 91, p. 18-19.
"Images of Time" (tr. of Jean Tardieu). [CimR] (94) Ja 91, p. 17.
"The Inanimate's Dreams" (tr. of Jean Tardieu). [CimR] (94) Ja 91, p. 14-15.
"The Secret Tribunal" (tr. of Jean Tardieu). [CimR] (94) Ja 91, p. 13-14.
2128. GILL, John
    "The Thomas Poems." [HangL] (58) 91, p. 21-25.
2129. GILL, Stephen
    "Blind and Deaf." [Gypsy] (17) 91, p. 62-63.
2130. GILLEN, Thomas
    "Blind Contour." [Chelsea] (50) 91, p. 39-40.
    "The Missing Man." [Chelsea] (50) 91, p. 38-39.
2131. GILLESPIE, Janis
    "The Bicycle Rider." [NewRena] (8:2, #25) Fall 91, p. 149.
    "Shattered Glass." [NewRena] (8:2, #25) Fall 91, p. 150.
2132. GILLESPIE, Netta
    "Preparation for Landing." [SoDakR] (29:3 part 2) Aut 91, p. 59.
2133. GILLET, Edward J.
    "The Hunters." [EmeraldCR] (4) 91, p. 40.
2134. GILLIHAN, Sean
    "Early November." [PaintedHR] (4) Fall 92, p. 9.
2135. GILLILAND, Mary
    "Expressiveness." [Mildred] (4:2/5:1) 91, p. 70.
    "Light Under Night." [Mildred] (4:2/5:1) 91, p. 71-72.
2136. GILLIS, Don
    "Danny's Return." [PottPort] (13:2) Fall-Wint 91, p. 63.
    "You Are Here" (for Krawncks). [PottPort] (13:2) Fall-Wint 91, p. 62.
2137. GILLOOLY, Sheila
    "Taking Shape." [ManhatPR] (13) [91?], p. 18.
2138. GILMARTIN, Dale Moana
    "Dolphins Dive Naked." [HawaiiR] (16:1, #34) Wint 91-92, p. 58.
    "El Nido Perdido: The Lost Nest." [HawaiiR] (16:1, #34) Wint 91-92, p. 59-60.
2139. GILMORE, John
    "Some Account of the Late Horrid Rebellion" (of the Slaves at the Barbadoes from a
        Letter supposed to be writ by a Merchant . . .). [GrahamHR] (14) Spr 91, p.
        14.
2140. GILONIS, Harry
    "Catullus Played Bach." [NewAW] (8/9) Fall 91, p. 88-90.
2141. GILSDORF, Ethan
    "According to the Campus Police (II)." [NegC] (11:1) 91, p. 84.
    "Be All That You Can Be." [NewYorkQ] (46) 91, p. 48.
    "Famous." [NewYorkQ] (45) 91, p. 47.
GINGERICH, Alina (Alma?) Camacho
    See CAMACHO-GINGERICH, Alina (Alma?)
2142. GINSBERG, Allen
    "Return of Kral Majales." [BrooklynR] (8) 91, p. 10.
2143. GINSBERG, Marla Hasten
    "Torn Pajamas." [BrooklynR] (8) 91, p. 36-37.
2144. GIOIA, Dana
    "Becoming a Redwood." [ParisR] (33:119) Sum 91, p. 138.
2145. GIOSEFFI, Daniela
    "Ambush" (tr. of Pablo Armando Fernández, w. Enildo Garcia). [Contact]
        (10:59/60/61) Spr 91, p. 13.
    "Ballad of the Three Wars" (tr. of Pablo Armando Fernández, w. Enildo Garcia).
        [Contact] (10:59/60/61) Spr 91, p. 16.
    "Blood Autumn" (Grand Prize Winner, Eve of St. Agnes Poery Awards). [NegC]
        (11:3) 91, p. 9-13.
    "A Permanent Place" (tr. of Pablo Armando Fernández, w. Enildo Garcia). [Contact]
        (10:59/60/61) Spr 91, p. 18.
    "Solitude, Cruel Season" (tr. of Pablo Armando Fernández, w. Enildo Garcia).
        [Contact] (10:59/60/61) Spr 91, p. 14.

"To a Young Freedom Fighter in Prison" (tr. of Pablo Armando Fernández, w. Enildo Garcia). [Contact] (10:59/60/61) Spr 91, p. 15.
"To the Great Cantor" (tr. of Pablo Armando Fernández, w. Enildo Garcia). [Contact] (10:59/60/61) Spr 91, p. 17.
"Trajan" (The Poet's Testament, tr. of Pablo Armando Fernández, w. Enildo Garcia). [Contact] (10:59/60/61) Spr 91, p. 18.
2146. GIOVINGO, Anne M.
"It's Only Good When You're Young." [ContextS] (2:2) 91, p. 27.
2147. GIPPS, Marina
"Hell with Three Dog Heads." [Abraxas] (40/41) 91, p. 160.
2148. GIPSON, Colin W.
"Apple Pie" (A Tribute to Andy Warhol). [Parting] (4:1) Sum 91, p. 24.
2149. GIRR, Catherine
"Dream Sequence." [PaintedHR] (3) Sum 92, p. 8.
"Watching Ducks at Putah Creek." [PaintedHR] (3) Sum 92, p. 9.
2150. GIVAN, Christopher F.
"Between Sleepers" (Hyena, tr. of Marin Sorescu). [WebR] (15) Spr 91, p. 28.
"The Eyes" (tr. of Marin Sorescu). [WebR] (15) Spr 91, p. 29.
"Holy Fire" (tr. of Marin Sorescu). [WebR] (15) Spr 91, p. 30.
2151. GIZZI, Michael
"A Load Is a Memory." [Shiny] (6) Spr-Sum 91, p. 52.
"A Penny in the Dust." [Shiny] (6) Spr-Sum 91, p. 51.
2152. GIZZI, Peter
"Blue Peter." [Conjunc] (17) 91, p. 362-363.
"News at Eleven." [NewAW] (7) Spr 91, p. 43-44.
2153. GJUZEL, Bogomil
"Future?" (tr. by Mary Crow and the author). [CimR] (96) Jl 91, p. 20.
"Pandora" (tr. by Mary Crow and the author). [NewOR] (18:2) Sum 91, p. 80.
"Quest: In Search of My Genes" (tr. by Mary Crow and the author). [CimR] (96) Jl 91, p. 18-19.
2154. GLADDING, Jody
"The Fisherman's Wife." [GreenMR] (NS 5:1) Sum-Fall 91, p. 85-86.
"Midwifery." [GreenMR] (NS 5:1) Sum-Fall 91, p. 84.
2155. GLADE, Jon Forrest
"Body Bags." [Lactuca] (14) My 91, p. 52.
"Cops." [Pearl] (14) Fall-Wint 91, p. 9.
"FNG (Fucking New Guy)." [Lactuca] (14) My 91, p. 51.
"Ladies Man." [Lactuca] (14) My 91, p. 52.
"Medical Report (Ashau Valley, 1969)." [Lactuca] (14) My 91, p. 52.
"Payday in the Jungle" (Ashau Valley, 1969). [ChironR] (10:1) Spr 91, p. 11.
"Souvenirs." [ChironR] (10:1) Spr 91, p. 11.
"Typhoon at Eagle Beach, 1969." [SlipS] (11) 91, p. 61.
"Walking Wounded" (Denver, 1969). [ChironR] (10:1) Spr 91, p. 11.
2156. GLANCY, Diane
"An Anchor in the Basis of the Mind." [WillowS] (27) Wint 91, p. 29.
"Ethnic Arts: The Cultural Bridge." [MidAR] (11:1) 91, p. 5-9.
"Female Figure, Elie Nadelman, 1855-1946, Nelson-Atkins Museum of Art, Kansas City." [Caliban] (10) 91, p. 10.
"The General Arena." [Caliban] (10) 91, p. 8-9.
"The Great Divide." [NoDaQ] (59:4) Fall 91, p. 122.
"Hard to Give Up." [WillowS] (27) Wint 91, p. 28.
"The Shadow's Horse." [Caliban] (10) 91, p. 11.
"Squaw." [Caliban] (10) 91, p. 12.
"Yeast." [MidAR] (11:1) 91, p. 13.
2157. GLANCY, Gabrielle
"Deer on the Way to Work." [ParisR] (33:120) Fall 91, p. 207.
"The Lost Boy." [HighP] (6:3) Wint 91, p. 72.
"My Innocent Shadow." [NewAW] (8/9) Fall 91, p. 41-43.
"The Point That Is This Moment." [ParisR] (33:120) Fall 91, p. 204-206.
2158. GLASER, Elton
"Amen." (tr. of Jacques Reda, w. Janice Fritsch). [Paint] (18:36) Aut 91, p. 61.
"American Flyer." [SouthernHR] (25:3) Sum 91, p. 246.
"Cafe Voltaire." [CinPR] (21) Spr 90, p. 68-69.
"Dozing through Italy." [NoDaQ] (59:1) Wint 91, p. 143.
"Egyptian Woman" (tr. of Jacques Dupin, w. Janice Fritsch). [Paint] (18:36) Aut 91, p. 60.

"Elegy for Clifton Chenier." [SouthernPR] (31:1) Spr 91, p. 71-72.
"Every Harmonica Player Needs a Train Song." [SouthernPR] (31:1) Spr 91, p. 72.
"Hymn and Harangue for Hesperus." [PoetryNW] (32:3) Aut 91, p. 38.
"In the Offing" (2nd Prize, 1st Annual Martha Scott Trimble Poetry Award). [ColR]
    (NS 18:2) Fall-Wint 91, p. 109-110.
"Nine Roses More Than Gertrude." [OxfordM] (7:2) Fall-Wint 91, p. 15.
"Patronage." [LaurelR] (25:2) Sum 91, p. 38-39.
"Regressional." [NoDaQ] (59:1) Wint 91, p. 141-142.
"Sepulchritude." [LaurelR] (25:2) Sum 91, p. 38.
"Shiftless Evenings." [Journal] (15:1) Spr 91, p. 36.
"Son et Lumiére." [LaurelR] (25:2) Sum 91, p. 39.
"White Pines." [SouthernPR] (31:2) Fall 91, p. 64-65.
2159. GLASER, Michael S.
    "Giverney: Our Children Are Lost." [HiramPoR] (50) Spr-Sum 91, p. 9.
2160. GLASS, Malcolm
    "Hawk." [SouthernHR] (25:3) Sum 91, p. 265.
2161. GLASS, Terrence
    "The Carpenter's Dream in New Burlington." [BelPoJ] (41:3) Spr 91, p. 8-9.
    "Dead Man's Float." [CinPR] (22) Spr 91, p. 12-13.
    "John Bryan in Clifton Gorge" (Second Prize, Cincinnati Poetry Review
        Competition). [CinPR] (22) Spr 91, p. 14-16.
    "Spokes in the Wheel." [MinnR] (NS 36) Spr 91, p. 13-14.
2162. GLATSHTEYN, Jacob
    "Sesame" (tr. by Dr. Ken Frieden's Yiddish 101 class at Emory University).
        [LullwaterR] (2:2) Spr 91, p. 34.
2163. GLATT, Lisa
    "Crank." [ChironR] (10:2) Sum 91, p. 5.
    "Monsters and Other Lovers." [ChironR] (10:2) Sum 91, p. 5.
    "The Threat." [Pearl] (14) Fall-Wint 91, p. 53.
    "The World in My Mother's Hair." [ChironR] (10:2) Sum 91, p. 5.
2164. GLAYSHER, Frederick
    "Basic Training." [ChamLR] (8-9) Spr-Fall 91, p. 116.
2165. GLAZE, Andrew
    "Being a Thief." [NewYorkQ] (46) 91, p. 34.
    "Courage." [NewYorkQ] (44) 91, p. 54.
    "My Nose My Needle." [NewYorkQ] (45) 91, p. 55.
2166. GLAZER, Jane
    "Final disposition" (Xela Chantry Belton 1898-1974). [Calyx] (13:2) Sum 91, p. 57.
    "To My Daughter in the Recovery Room." [Calyx] (13:2) Sum 91, p. 58-59.
2167. GLAZER, Michele
    "Sequence, Costa Rica." [Sonora] (20) Wint 91, p. 104-106.
2168. GLAZER, Sophie
    "The Boston Review" (Response to "Save the Clerihew" appeal). [BostonR] (16:3/4)
        Je-Ag 91, p. 33.
2169. GLAZNER, Greg
    "After the Night Shift." [MidAR] (11:1) 91, p. 127-129.
    "At the North Window, Instead of a Lament." [Journal] (15:2) Fall 91, p. 80.
    "The Constant Upward Spiraling, the Cost." [NewEngR] (13:3/4) Spr-Sum 91, p.
        314-316.
2170. GLEASON, Cassandra
    "Alex." [EmeraldCR] (4) 91, p. 52.
    "Memories at Times Are Solid Things." [EmeraldCR] (4) 91, p. 53.
    "Untitled. Visions stolen from the depths of time." [EmeraldCR] (3) 91, c1990, p.
        49-50.
2171. GLEN, Emilie
    "Bells of Noon." [DogRR] (10:2) Fall-Wint 91, p. 29.
    "Go Go Go Go." [SmPd] (28:2, #82) Spr 91, p. 36.
    "White As." [SoDakR] (29:3 part 2) Aut 91, p. 17.
2172. GLENDAY, John
    "The Difficult Colour." [PoetryC] (12:1) D 91, p. 21.
    "Flounder Fishing." [PoetryC] (12:1) D 91, p. 21.
    "The Rise of Icarus." [PoetryC] (12:1) D 91, p. 21.
    "Shell." [PoetryC] (12:1) D 91, p. 21.
2173. GLENN, Helen Trubek"
    "Winter Cooking Song" (1st Prize, 5th Annual Contest). [SoCoast] (10) Fall 91, p.
        18-19.

2174. GLENN, Laura
"Cicadas." [Boulevard] (6:2/3, #17/18) Fall 91, p. 200-201.
2175. GLENN, Terri
"After the Movers Left." [Pearl] (14) Fall-Wint 91, p. 54.
2176. GLOEGGLER, Tony
"Emilio." [NewYorkQ] (44) 91, p. 72.
"The lady downstairs." [SlipS] (11) 91, p. 29.
"Pirate." [SlipS] (11) 91, p. 28.
"Song of Solomon." [Bogg] (64) 91, p. 4.
2177. GLOVER, Albert
"Consciousness." [Contact] (10:59/60/61) Spr 91, p. 30.
"For a Babe in Toadland" (a prophecy for Chris, Feb. 6, 1990). [Contact]
(10:59/60/61) Spr 91, p. 31.
"A Jaguar for Jack." [Contact] (10:59/60/61) Spr 91, p. 30.
2178. GLOVER, Jon
"The Restored Canal." [Stand] (32:2) Spr 91, p. 6-7.
"The Vase." [Stand] (32:2) Spr 91, p. 7.
2179. GLÜCK, Louise
"The Silver Lily." [NewYorker] (67:43) 16 D 91, p. 94.
"Vespers." [NewYorker] (67:37) 4 N 91, p. 68.
2180. GNIATCZYNSKI, Wojciech
"Farewell" (tr. by Steven Polgar). [AmerPoR] (20:2) Mr-Ap 91, p. 30.
"There Is a Goal to Our Peregrinations" (tr. by Steven Polgar, w. the author).
[AmerPoR] (20:2) Mr-Ap 91, p. 30.
2181. GODFREY, Joyzelle
"Cowboys and Indians." [PoetryE] (32) Fall 91, p. 53.
"Haiku for Nikki." [PoetryE] (32) Fall 91, p. 53.
"Neil's View." [PoetryE] (32) Fall 91, p. 54.
2182. GODING, Cecile (Cecile Hanna)
"All the Sacred Places." [SnailPR] (1:2) Fall 91-Wint 92, p. 14-15.
"Bangalore." [PoetryNW] (32:4) Wint 91-92, p. 44-45.
"Diptera." [Journal] (14:2) Wint 91, p. 34-35.
"If the Last Words I Speak Are 'Piet Mondrian'." [PoetryNW] (32:2) Sum 91, p.
10-11.
"Naming the Stone." [GeoR] (45:2) Sum 91, p. 340-343.
"A Summer Night" (From an account of a Viking funeral by Ibn Fadlan, envoy from
Baghdad, 922 A.D.). [PoetryNW] (32:4) Wint 91-92, p. 45-47.
"To My Brother: The Boy Who Didn't Drown." [GreensboroR] (50) Sum 91, p. 74.
2183. GOEDICKE, Patricia
"Coin of the Realm." [ThRiPo] (37/38) 91, p. 66-68.
"Conquerors." [PaintedHR] (4) Fall 92, p. 10-11.
"Door / Ways." [NewEngR] (13:3/4) Spr-Sum 91, p. 172-178.
"In This Landscape." [ThRiPo] (37/38) 91, p. 69-71.
"No Hospital" (for M.G. and N.K.). [ColR] (NS 18:2) Fall-Wint 91, p. 67-68.
"On this Island." [ColR] (NS 18:2) Fall-Wint 91, p. 69-70.
"Sisters." [NewEngR] (13:3/4) Spr-Sum 91, p. 178-180.
2184. GOERNER, Leslie
"Common Experience." [BellArk] (7:3) My-Je 91, p. 1.
"Endings." [BellArk] (7:4) Jl-Ag 91, p. 11.
"Glossed Prints." [BellArk] (7:2) Mr-Ap 91, p. 8-9.
"Sanctuary." [BellArk] (7:3) My-Je 91, p. 4.
2185. GOETHE, Johann Wolfgang von
"Night" (from "Faust," tr. by Martin Greenberg). [Pequod] (32) 91, p. 111-115.
"Roman Elegy VIII" (tr. by David Ferry). [Raritan] (11:1) Sum 91, p. 12.
2186. GOETT, Lise
"Something Close." [Ploughs] (17:4) Wint 91-92, p. 86-87.
2187. GOETZ, Melody
"Facing to Winter." [PraF] (12:1 #54) Spr 91, p. 75.
"One with No Name." [Grain] (19:1) Spr 91, p. 87.
"Outside, Shovelling Snow." [PraF] (12:1 #54) Spr 91, p. 74.
"Saturday After Supper, Washing the Floor." [Grain] (19:1) Spr 91, p. 87.
"VIA Jasper." [PraF] (12:1 #54) Spr 91, p. 75.
2188. GOFF, Paula
"Virginia Street." [FreeL] (7) Spr 91, p. 16-17.

2189. GOGOL, John M.
>"The Dance" (tr. of Zbigniew Zalewski). [NorthStoneR] (10) Fall 91-Wint 92, p. 194.
>"Expectation" (tr. of Zbigniew Zalewski). [NorthStoneR] (10) Fall 91-Wint 92, p. 194.

2190. GOLDBARTH, Albert
>"12th Century Chinese Painting with a Few Dozen Seal Imprints Across It." [AmerPoR] (20:2) Mr-Ap 91, p. 45.
>"12,000 Bones of Frogs and Toads." [BelPoJ] (42:2) Wint 91-92, p. 8-11.
>"Adventures in Decipherment." [Journal] (15:2) Fall 91, p. 49-51.
>"Astounding." [LaurelR] (25:2) Sum 91, p. 13-14.
>"The Books / P, L, E." [LaurelR] (25:2) Sum 91, p. 5-12.
>"Bruno's Place." [PoetryNW] (32:2) Sum 91, p. 38-39.
>"The Candies." [Agni] (34) 91, p. 136-137.
>"Coin." [Boulevard] (5:3/6:1, #15/16) Spr 91, p. 92-93.
>"Desire Song." [Boulevard] (5:3/6:1, #15/16) Spr 91, p. 90-91.
>"Farder to Reache." [OhioR] (47) 91, p. 46-47.
>"Finely Written Labels." [Poetry] (157:6) Mr 91, p. 336-337.
>"The Flowers of Koonwarra." [OhioR] (47) 91, p. 43-45.
>"The Gold Note Lounge and Boogie Palace." [TriQ] (81) Spr-Sum 91, p. 190-191.
>"How Did They Live?" [Journal] (15:2) Fall 91, p. 54-55.
>"How Easy It Is." [OnTheBus] (8/9) 91, p. 76-77.
>"Inside." [Journal] (15:2) Fall 91, p. 52-53.
>"Lullabye." [BelPoJ] (42:2) Wint 91-92, p. 12.
>"'Protection''s." [Agni] (34) 91, p. 133-135.
>"A Refuge." [IndR] (14:2) Spr 91, p. 34-35.
>"The Saga of Stupidity and Wonder." [Agni] (34) 91, p. 132.
>"Shoyn Fergéssin: T've Forgotten' in Yiddish." [Crazy] (41) Wint 91, p. 27.
>"Sixteenth Century, Brush and Ink: A Hermit on a Riverbank." [GeoR] (45:2) Sum 91, p. 276-277.
>"Some Doors." [IndR] (14:2) Spr 91, p. 36-37.
>"Sumerian Votive Figurines." [OntR] (34) Spr-Sum 91, p. 39-40.
>"Thermodynamics / Sumer." [PoetryNW] (32:2) Sum 91, p. 41-42.
>"This and That." [PoetC] (23:1) Fall 91, p. 15.
>"A Thousand Eyes in the Darkness." [PoetryNW] (32:2) Sum 91, p. 40-41.
>"The Title for a Collection of Poems Appears from out of Nowhere." [Poetry] (157:6) Mr 91, p. 335-336.
>"To Iron." [Ploughs] (17:2/3) Fall 91, p. 227.
>"To Where." [PoetC] (23:1) Fall 91, p. 16-17.
>"The Two Parts of the Day Are." [OnTheBus] (8/9) 91, p. 77.
>"The Voices." [GeoR] (45:2) Sum 91, p. 269-273.
>"Will the Real Shakespeare Please Stand Up?" [GeoR] (45:2) Sum 91, p. 274-275.
>"Would You Know a Snook, or a Large-eyed Whiff, from a Goggle-eyed Scad, Should the Necessity Arise? I Thought So" (— Will Cuppy). [LaurelR] (25:2) Sum 91, p. 14-16.

2191. GOLDBERG, Barbara
>"Miami Vice." [ColR] (NS 18:1) Spr-Sum 91, p. 29.
>"Superego Serenade." [ColR] (NS 18:1) Spr-Sum 91, p. 30.

2192. GOLDBERG, Beckian Fritz
>"Adam." [HayF] (8) Spr-Sum 91, p. 39-40.
>"Annunciation." [Journal] (15:2) Fall 91, p. 12-13.
>"Backlight." [HayF] (8) Spr-Sum 91, p. 63.
>"Black Heart." [PoetryNW] (32:1) Spr 91, p. 38-39.
>"Eve." [HayF] (8) Spr-Sum 91, p. 41.
>"The Horse in the Cellar." [Journal] (15:2) Fall 91, p. 9.
>"In the Badlands of Desire." [PoetryNW] (32:1) Spr 91, p. 35-36.
>"The Influence of Hair." [PoetryNW] (32:1) Spr 91, p. 40-41.
>"The Lives of the Poets." [Journal] (15:2) Fall 91, p. 10-11.
>"Love, Scissor, Stone." [PoetryNW] (32:1) Spr 91, p. 36-38.
>"Resolutions." [PoetryNW] (32:1) Spr 91, p. 39-40.
>"Satan's Box." [VirQR] (67:4) Aut 91, p. 679-680.

GOLDBERG, Caryn Mirriam
>*See* MIRRIAM-GOLDBERG, Caryn

2193. GOLDBERG, Janet
>"Pruning." [BellR] (14:2) Fall 91, p. 19.

2194. GOLDBERG, Natalie
"Across Four States." [JamesWR] (8:4) Sum 91, p. 10.
2195. GOLDBERGER, Tefke
"Unanswered" (tr. of Willy Spillebeen). [Vis] (36) 91, p. 24.
2196. GOLDEMBERG, Isaac
"El Angel de los Celos." [Nuez] (3:8/9) 91, p. 16.
"Caminos del Amor." [Nuez] (3:8/9) 91, p. 16.
"Dobles." [Nuez] (3:8/9) 91, p. 16.
2197. GOLDEN, Robert
"The Affair." [DustyD] (2:1) Ja 91, p. 15.
2198. GOLDENSOHN, Barry
"Bathsheba." [Agni] (34) 91, p. 154.
"Divorce" (after Meleager). [Agni] (34) 91, p. 155.
"Fixing It." [Agni] (34) 91, p. 156.
2199. GOLDENSOHN, Lorrie
"Saratoga Ballet." [Ploughs] (17:2/3) Fall 91, p. 173-174.
2200. GOLDENSTERN, Joyce
"Open Letter to Friedrich Engels." [Pig] (17) 91, p. 76.
2201. GOLDFIELD, Bina
"Nocturnal Visit." [NegC] (11:3) 91, p. 21.
2202. GOLDIE, Matthew
"Flat Iron." [BrooklynR] (8) 91, p. 12.
2203. GOLDMAN, Judy
"Between Losses." [Crazy] (41) Wint 91, p. 26.
"Endless Odds." [Crazy] (41) Wint 91, p. 23-25.
"Hundred Happinesses" (After "Hundred Happinesses of the Hundred Beauties,"
    Japanese ink on paper by Takahisa Ryuko, 1801-1859). [Crazy] (41) Wint 91,
    p. 21-22.
"Night Sweat." [PraS] (65:4) Wint 91, p. 122.
"The Permanence of Things." [PraS] (65:4) Wint 91, p. 123-124.
"Putting Things Right." [PraS] (65:4) Wint 91, p. 123.
"We Who've Been Married So Long." [Journal] (14:2) Wint 91, p. 75.
2204. GOLDMAN, Kathleen Zeisler
"The Body of Grief." [OnTheBus] (8/9) 91, p. 78.
"The Well-Trained Ear." [OnTheBus] (8/9) 91, p. 79.
2205. GOLDMAN, Mark
"The Hunger Artist." [InterPR] (15:1) Spr 89, p. 97.
2206. GOLDMAN, Paula
"Burrowings from Joyce and Bogan: Unlikely Paris." [ClockR] (7:1/2) 91-92, p.
    118.
2207. GOLDOWSKY, Barbara
"Before." [Confr] (46/47) Fall 91-Wint 92, p. 282.
2208. GOLDSCHLAG, David
"November in Compton." [CoalC] (3) My 91, p. 5.
"November in Kingston." [CoalC] (3) My 91, p. 5.
2209. GOLDSMITH, Ellen
"Awakening." [Elf] (1:2) Sum 91, p. 41.
2210. GOLDSTEIN, Laurence
"A Broken Coriolan." [RiverS] (34) 91, p. 43-44.
"Folkestone, 1917." [Boulevard] (6:2/3, #17/18) Fall 91, p. 163.
"In Memory, J. T." [OntR] (34) Spr-Sum 91, p. 42-43.
"Is Reality One or Many?" [Salm] (92) Fall 91, p. 197-199.
"Lost Friend." [OntR] (34) Spr-Sum 91, p. 44-45.
"Summer Camp Fund." [RiverS] (34) 91, p. 42.
"An Unromantic Story." [PoetC] (22:3) Spr 91, p. 6-7.
2211. GOLDSTEIN, Niles Elliot
"The Young Knight" (for Ayden). [Elf] (1:2) Sum 91, p. 25.
2212. GOLDSWORTHY, Peter
"The Operation." [Verse] (8:2) Sum 91, p. 99.
"A Statistician to His Love." [Verse] (8:2) Sum 91, p. 100.
2213. GOLUB, Deborah
"Buenos Aires." [Salm] (90/91) Spr-Sum 91, p. 208-209.
"Confession." [Salm] (90/91) Spr-Sum 91, p. 210.
2214. GOMEZ BETTENCOURT, Eduarda Maria
"Rise and Fall." [GreenMR] (NS 5:1) Sum-Fall 91, p. 99-100.
"The Story of My Name." [GreenMR] (NS 5:1) Sum-Fall 91, p. 98.

2215. GONET, Jill
"Blessing of the Fleet." [RiverC] (12:1) Fall 91, p. 58.
"Body Will." [Zyzzyva] (7:1) Spr 91, p. 47.
"The Delivery of the Keys." [Zyzzyva] (7:1) Spr 91, p. 44.
"On the Ferry's Outer Deck." [Descant] (22:3, #74) Fall 91, p. 64.
"Perfume." [Descant] (22:3, #74) Fall 91, p. 64.
"Ties." [BlackWR] (17:2) Spr-Sum 91, p. 107.
"Venus in the Library." [RiverC] (12:1) Fall 91, p. 57.
2216. GONTAREK, Leonard
"Homage to the Square." [Parting] (4:2) Wint 91-92, p. 28-29.
"The Last Judgment." [Parting] (4:2) Wint 91-92, p. 8.
"The New Season." [HangL] (58) 91, p. 27.
2217. GONZALES, Laurence
"Egg Harbor." [NewL] (58:1) Fall 91, p. 34.
"Full Body Erection." [NewL] (58:1) Fall 91, p. 31.
"Mastectomy." [NewL] (58:1) Fall 91, p. 32-33.
"No Guitars." [NewL] (58:1) Fall 91, p. 30-31.
"Protest Movement." [NewL] (58:1) Fall 91, p. 29.
2218. GONZALEZ, Angel
"Birthday" (tr. by Steven Ford Brown). [Paint] (18:36) Aut 91, p. 49.
"The Days Were Like That" (tr. by Steven Ford Brown and Gutierrez Revuelta).
[WillowS] (28) Sum 91, p. 18.
"The Defeated One" (tr. by Steven Ford Brown and Gutierrez Revuelta). [WillowS]
(28) Sum 91, p. 17.
"The Future" (tr. by Steven Ford Brown and Pedro Gutirrez Revuelta). [WebR] (15)
Spr 91, p. 34.
"Human Geography" (tr. by Steven Ford Brown and Gutierrez Revuelta). [WillowS]
(28) Sum 91, p. 16.
"I Know What It's Like to Wait" (tr. by Steven Ford Brown). [Paint] (18:36) Aut
91, p. 50.
"I Myself" (tr. by Steven Ford Brown and Gutierrez Revuelta). [Paint] (18:36) Aut
91, p. 43.
"Inventory of Places Propitious for Love" (tr. by Steven Ford Brown). [Paint]
(18:36) Aut 91, p. 51.
"The Least Corpse" (tr. by Steven Ford Brown and Pedro Gutirrez Revuelta).
[WebR] (15) Spr 91, p. 33-34.
"Love Dressed in White" (tr. by Steven Ford Brown). [Paint] (18:36) Aut 91, p. 48.
"Plaza con Torreones y Palacios." [HayF] (9) Fall-Wint 91, p. 44.
"Por Aquí Pasa un Río." [HayF] (9) Fall-Wint 91, p. 42.
"Preamble to Silence" (tr. by Steven Ford Brown). [Paint] (18:36) Aut 91, p. 44.
"The Scandalous Rose" (tr. by Steven Ford Brown and Gutierrez Revuelta).
[TexasR] (12:1/2) Spr-Sum 91, p. 103.
"Sinestesia" (tr. by Steven Ford Brown and Gutierrez Revuelta). [Paint] (18:36) Aut
91, p. 47.
"The So-Called Twilight" (tr. by Steven Ford Brown and Gutierrez Revuelta).
[TexasR] (12:1/2) Spr-Sum 91, p. 104.
"So It Seems" (tr. by Steven Ford Brown and Gutierrez Revuelta). [Paint] (18:36)
Aut 91, p. 45-46.
"Square with Towers and Palaces" (tr. by Steven Ford Brown). [HayF] (9)
Fall-Wint 91, p. 45.
"Sunday" (tr. by Steven Ford Brown). [ColR] (NS 18:2) Fall-Wint 91, p. 86-87.
"That River Ran Backwards" (tr. by Steven Ford Brown and Pedro Gutirrez
Revuelta). [WebR] (15) Spr 91, p. 32.
"Through Here a River Passes" (tr. by Steven Ford Brown). [HayF] (9) Fall-Wint
91, p. 43.
"Twilight, Albuquerque, Summer" (tr. by Steven Ford Brown and Gutierrez
Revuelta). [TexasR] (12:1/2) Spr-Sum 91, p. 105.
2219. GONZALEZ, Anson
"Gasparillo Remembered." [GrahamHR] (14) Spr 91, p. 76-77.
2220. GONZALEZ, Rafael Jesús
"Calli: House" (Definition in the Nahua mode). [MidAR] (12:1) 91, p. 66.
2221. GONZALEZ, Ray
"The Distant Father." [ColR] (NS 18:1) Spr-Sum 91, p. 108-109.
"Fathers." [MidAR] (12:1) 91, p. 49-50.
"Memory of the Hand." [CutB] (36) Sum 91, p. 66-67.
"Old Friend." [MidAR] (12:1) 91, p. 51.

"Snakeskin (A Dream)." [ColR] (NS 18:1) Spr-Sum 91, p. 107.
2222. GOOCH, Amy Alley
"Drugged." [PoetryUSA] (23) Sum 91, p. 25.
"If I could suffocate within myself right now, I'm sure I would." [PoetryUSA] (23) Sum 91, p. 24.
2223. GOOCH, Brad
"Hudson." [Shiny] (6) Spr-Sum 91, p. 75-76.
2224. GOOD, George
"Territorial" (a love poem). [Stand] (32:3) Sum 91, p. 16.
2225. GOOD, Regan
"Peacock as Divinity." [Colum] (17) Fall 91, p. 9.
2226. GOOD, Ruth
"As Adam's Flesh Was Rent to Make Us." [HawaiiR] (15:2, #32) Spr 91, p. 120.
"The Child Who Grew Into Myself." [HawaiiR] (15:2, #32) Spr 91, p. 121.
"Hanging the Dog." [HawaiiR] (15:2, #32) Spr 91, p. 119.
2227. GOODELL, Larry
"Attraction." [Sulfur] (11:1, #28) Spr 91, p. 52.
"Gemini in the Forest." [Sulfur] (11:1, #28) Spr 91, p. 50.
"Making It Big" (for Dagoberto Gilb). [Sulfur] (11:1, #28) Spr 91, p. 51-52.
"New Mexico Style." [Sulfur] (11:1, #28) Spr 91, p. 51.
2228. GOODENOUGH, J. B.
"Flatlander." [TexasR] (11:1/2) Spr-Sum 90, p. 87.
"Sunflower." [InterPR] (15:1) Spr 89, p. 96.
2229. GOODISON, Lorna
"Birth Stone." [Hudson] (43:4) Wint 91, p. 618-619.
"On Becoming a Tiger." [MichQR] (30:4) Fall 91, p. 632-633.
"Recommendation for Amber." [Hudson] (43:4) Wint 91, p. 617-618.
2230. GOODMAN, Ryah Tumarkin
"Ancestors." [InterPR] (17:2) Fall 91, p. 118.
"A Coat Can Walk." [CumbPR] (10:2) Spr 91, p. 27.
"The End." [InterPR] (17:2) Fall 91, p. 118.
2231. GOODRICH, Charles
"Stinging Nettles." [Zyzzyva] (7:3) Fall 91, p. 69.
2232. GOODRICH, Judith N.
"They Called Her a Peacemaker." [BellArk] (7:2) Mr-Ap 91, p. 12.
2233. GOODRICH, Patricia
"Black-Out." [MinnR] (NS 37) Fall 91, p. 42.
"A Poem for All Red Riding Hoods." [MinnR] (NS 37) Fall 91, p. 41.
2234. GOODWIN, Douglas
"Peripheral View." [SlipS] (11) 91, p. 60.
2235. GOODWIN, June
"Hyacinth." [LullwaterR] (3:1) Fall 91, p. 31.
"Open and Closed: A Sonnet on Sound." [CapeR] (26:1) Spr 91, p. 49.
"'Strue." [SouthwR] (76:1) Wint 91, p. 99.
"Work." [CapeR] (26:1) Spr 91, p. 50.
2236. GOOLSBY, Hannah
"The Pen." [EngJ] (80:2) F 91, p. 97.
2237. GORCZYNSKI, Renata
"Autumn" (Excerpted from "Canvas," tr. of Adam Zagajewksi, w. Benjamin Ivry and C. K. Williams). [ManhatR] (6:1) Fall 91, p. 50.
"The Bells" (for C. K. Williams, Excerpted from "Canvas," tr. of Adam Zagajewksi, w. Benjamin Ivry and C. K. Williams). [ManhatR] (6:1) Fall 91, p. 51.
"Burgundy's Grasslands" (Excerpted from "Canvas," tr. of Adam Zagajewksi, w. Benjamin Ivry and C. K. Williams). [ManhatR] (6:1) Fall 91, p. 46.
"Canvas" (Excerpted from "Canvas," tr. of Adam Zagajewksi, w. Benjamin Ivry and C. K. Williams). [ManhatR] (6:1) Fall 91, p. 53.
"Covenant" (tr. of Adam Zagajewski, w. Benjamin Ivry). [NewYorker] (66:48) 14 Ja 91, p. 34.
"Dictionary of Wilno Streets (1967)" (from "Beginning with My Streets," tr. of Czeslaw Milosz, w. the author, Robert Hass and Robert Pinsky). [ParisR] (33:120) Fall 91, p. 261-263.
"Electric Elegy" (Excerpted from "Canvas," tr. of Adam Zagajewksi, w. Benjamin Ivry and C. K. Williams). [ManhatR] (6:1) Fall 91, p. 47.
"From the Lives of Things" (Excerpted from "Canvas," tr. of Adam Zagajewksi, w. Benjamin Ivry and C. K. Williams). [ManhatR] (6:1) Fall 91, p. 52.

"Green Linnaeus" (Excerpted from "Canvas," tr. of Adam Zagajewksi, w. Benjamin
    Ivry and C. K. Williams). [ManhatR] (6:1) Fall 91, p. 48.
"On a Side Street" (Excerpted from "Canvas," tr. of Adam Zagajewksi, w. Benjamin
    Ivry and C. K. Williams). [ManhatR] (6:1) Fall 91, p. 45.
"Spider's Song" (Excerpted from "Canvas," tr. of Adam Zagajewksi, w. Benjamin
    Ivry and C. K. Williams). [ManhatR] (6:1) Fall 91, p. 44.
"Watching *Shoah* in a Hotel Room in America" (Excerpted from "Canvas," tr. of
    Adam Zagajewksi, w. Benjamin Ivry and C. K. Williams). [ManhatR] (6:1)
    Fall 91, p. 49.
2238. GORDETT, Marea
    "The Consent of Sight and Memory." [Ploughs] (17:4) Wint 91-92, p. 61-62.
    "Vigil." [Ploughs] (17:4) Wint 91-92, p. 60.
2239. GORDON, Carol
    "Second Child." [BellR] (14:2) Fall 91, p. 27.
2240. GORDON, Kirpal
    "Don't Get Caught." [ChironR] (10:2) Sum 91, p. 4.
    "Waiting for Friends Who Do Not Arrive." [ChironR] (10:2) Sum 91, p. 4.
2241. GORDON, Laurie
    "In the Year of Our Earth 1685." [HarvardA] (127 [i.e. 125]:3) Ja 91, p. 26.
    "Maleficium." [HarvardA] (127 [i.e. 125]:3) Ja 91, p. 27.
    "The Midwife's Confession." [HarvardA] (127 [i.e. 125]:3) Ja 91, p. 26.
2242. GORDON, Robert M.
    "Manspider." [BelPoJ] (42:2) Wint 91-92, p. 13.
2243. GORDON, Sarah
    "Parity." [Calyx] (13:2) Sum 91, p. 62-63.
2244. GORHAM, Nancy Lea
    "University Ave." [NewYorkQ] (46) 91, p. 79.
2245. GORHAM, Sarah
    "1900, Peking." [CinPR] (21) Spr 90, p. 51.
    "Celestial Flowers." [AntR] (49:1) Wint 91, p. 96.
    "Hymn to the Intellect." [Poetry] (158:5) Ag 91, p. 261-262.
    "The Minor Manchu's Daughter." [GrandS] (10:2, #38) 91, p. 129.
    "Motherly and Auspicious." [CinPR] (21) Spr 90, p. 38.
    "Painting Lesson." [CinPR] (21) Spr 90, p. 50.
    "Portrait of the Last Empress." [AntR] (49:1) Wint 91, p. 96.
    "Stillshot." [SoDakR] (29:3 part 2) Aut 91, p. 79.
    "Two Sonnets for the Last Empress of China." [AmerV] (24) Fall 91, p. 55-56.
2246. GORMAN, LeRoy
    "My Dictionary Enlightenment." [Bogg] (64) 91, p. 9.
2247. GORNON, Alexander
    "Phonosematics." [LitR] (34:3) Spr 91, p. 350-351.
2248. GOROSTIZA, José
    "Del Poema Frustrado" (English version, tr. by Robert Klein Engler). [Colum] (16)
        Spr 91, p. 14-24.
    "Fireflies" (tr. by Robert Engler). [MidAR] (12:1) 91, p. 161-162.
2249. GORRELL, Nancy
    "Applesauce." [EngJ] (80:2) F 91, p. 96.
2250. GORRICK, Anne
    "Analogous Curves." [CreamCR] (14:2) Wint 91, p. 132.
    "Lions, We Are." [CreamCR] (14:2) Wint 91, p. 131.
    "Spell." [YellowS] (37) Fall-Wint 91, p. 4-5.
    "We bed at night like two river stones, erratics." [YellowS] (37) Fall-Wint 91, p. 4.
2251. GORST, Norma (Norma Wunderlich)
    "6190 Grayton Road." [BambooR] (50/51) Spr-Sum 91, p. 84-85.
    "Christmas Eve, Hawaii." [BambooR] (50/51) Spr-Sum 91, p. 78-79.
    "Hearts Beating Full Measure." [ChamLR] (8-9) Spr-Fall 91, p. 97-98.
    "Lament." [ChamLR] (8-9) Spr-Fall 91, p. 99-100.
    "Lute Player." [BambooR] (50/51) Spr-Sum 91, p. 86.
    "Northeast Wind." [ChamLR] (8-9) Spr-Fall 91, p. 96.
    "Point of Entry." [BambooR] (50/51) Spr-Sum 91, p. 81.
    "Warren Avenue Shop." [BambooR] (50/51) Spr-Sum 91, p. 82-83.
    "White Ducks." [BambooR] (50/51) Spr-Sum 91, p. 80.
2252. GOSNELL, W. C.
    "The Washing Machines." [WindO] (54) Sum 91, p. 40.
2253. GOSNELL, Will
    "Sheila's Advice." [BlackBR] (13) Spr-Sum 91, p. 10.

2254. GOTERA, Vince
"Halloween 1963." [KenR] (NS 13:4) Fall 91, p. 165-166.
"Newly Released, Papa Tells Me What It's Like Inside" (for Martin Gotera,
1921-1989). [KenR] (NS 13:4) Fall 91, p. 166-167.
2255. GOTO, Stan
"Mirror in the Men's Room" (Mapplethorpe Exhibit, March 1990). [Colum] (16) Spr
91, p. 32-33.
2256. GOTO, T. M.
"Bone White Moon." [BambooR] (50/51) Spr-Sum 91, p. 34.
"Miranda Cries, Father's Raping Me and Blaming It on Caliban." [BambooR]
(50/51) Spr-Sum 91, p. 35.
"The Music of Bombs." [HawaiiR] (15:3, #33) Fall 91, p. 136.
2257. GOTT, George
"After the Meeting." [CrabCR] (7:2) Sum 91, p. 24.
"The Fog." [RagMag] (9:2) 91, p. 36.
2258. GOTTLIEB, Art
"Vietnam Vet." [ChironR] (10:1) Spr 91, p. 20.
2259. GOUMAS, Yannis
"Ditty" (tr. of Kostís Ghimosoúlis). [SycamoreR] (3:2) Sum 91, p. 54-55.
"The Malady That Is Saturday" (tr. of Kostís Ghimosoúlis). [SycamoreR] (3:2) Sum
91, p. 56-57.
2260. GOVAN, Donald
"The Difference." [NorthStoneR] (10) Fall 91-Wint 92, p. 109.
2261. GOVE, Jim
"Dumb Deaths I." [ChironR] (10:3) Aut 91, p. 5.
"Of Cats Chickens Cows & Men" (a letter to Will Inman). [ChironR] (10:3) Aut 91,
p. 5.
"Plums & Chips." [ChironR] (10:3) Aut 91, p. 5.
"Scrap Metal." [SmPd] (28:2, #82) Spr 91, p. 23.
"A Twenty Liner Ending with an Exodus in Renaults." [ChironR] (10:3) Aut 91, p.
5.
2262. GOVER, Paula K.
"The Fat Girl Looks at Men." [Calyx] (13:3) Wint 91-92, p. 44-45.
"The Fat Girl Remembers Dancing: Part One." [Calyx] (13:3) Wint 91-92, p. 40-41.
"The Fat Girl Remembers Dancing: Part Two." [Calyx] (13:3) Wint 91-92, p. 42-43.
2263. GOYER, Gloria
"Running with the Grasshoppers." [Prima] (14/15) 91, p. 14-15.
2264. GRABILL, Jim
"Buck's Metaphysical Thinking Midwives." [Caliban] (10) 91, p. 114-115.
"The Price of Money." [Caliban] (10) 91, p. 112-113.
2265. GRADY, Carolyn Kieber
"Sweet William's Pantoum." [Blueline] (12) 91, p. 47.
2266. GRAFF, Herman
"Portrait of Clockworks." [Lactuca] (14) My 91, p. 2-10.
GRAFT-ROSENIOR, Arthur de
See De GRAFT-ROSENIOR, Arthur
2267. GRAFTON, Grace
"Ancient Bristlecone Pine, White Mountains, California" (from a series inspired by
photographer David Muench's "Nature's America"). [BellArk] (7:6) N-D 91,
p. 6.
"Classroom and Mountains." [BellArk] (7:3) My-Je 91, p. 8.
"Columbine." [Prima] (14/15) 91, p. 96.
"Little Girls." [DustyD] Je 91, p. 33.
"Paintbrush and Bluebonnet, Texas" (from a series inspired by photographer David
Muench's "Nature's America"). [BellArk] (7:3) My-Je 91, p. 4.
"Spring Break." [BellArk] (7:6) N-D 91, p. 11.
2268. GRAHAM, Jorie
"Aubade." [ColR] (NS 18:2) Fall-Wint 91, p. 33-35.
"Face It." [ColR] (NS 18:2) Fall-Wint 91, p. 36-38.
"Manifest Destiny" (F. H. 1947-1990). [MichQR] (30:2) Spr 91, p. 267-272.
"Theatre of Operations." [ColR] (NS 18:2) Fall-Wint 91, p. 29-32.
2269. GRAHAM, Loren
"Mose." [Timbuktu] (6) Spr 91, p. 83-92.
2270. GRAHAM, Martha
"Angel Mounds." [HopewellR] (1991) 91, p. 10.

2271. GRAHAM, Neile
"Four Crow Photographs" (from the photographs of Fred E. Miller). [AntigR]
(85/86) Spr-Sum 91, p. 27-29.
"The Lovers in Grey." [AntigR] (85/86) Spr-Sum 91, p. 30-31.
"Midfire." [Prima] (14/15) 91, p. 12-13.
"Postcard of O'Keeffe." [Arc] (26) Spr 91, p. 41.
"Sea Glass from Execution Rock." [Quarry] (40:4) Fall 91, p. 74-75.
"Tam Lin." [Quarry] (40:4) Fall 91, p. 76-77.
"Winter or Goodbye." [Arc] (26) Spr 91, p. 40.
2272. GRAHAM, Taylor
"Aurora Borealis." [RagMag] (9:2) 91, p. 44.
"Bats." [ConnPR] (10:1) 91, p. 14-15.
"Charlie." [RagMag] (9:2) 91, p. 45.
"Dogs, Coming Home." [CreamCR] (15:2) Fall 91, p. 80.
"Driving Country." [ContextS] (2:2) 91, p. 23.
"The Falling Edge" (for Janet, at Echo Summit). [OxfordM] (7:2) Fall-Wint 91, p. 8.
"Island of Diminishing Deer." [SouthernHR] (25:2) Spr 91, p. 123.
"Palm Reader." [CoalC] (4) S 91, p. 3.
"Rewrite." [PoetL] (86:3) Fall 91, p. 19.
"River Watch, Stockton." [CoalC] (4) S 91, p. 2.
"Sparks" (for Julie, 5). [PaintedHR] (4) Fall 92, p. 7.
"Stained Glass." [InterPR] (17:2) Fall 91, p. 107.
"Trespass." [PaintedHR] (4) Fall 92, p. 6-7.
"Uncle's Earthquake Story." [RagMag] (9:2) 91, p. 46.
"A Visit." [CumbPR] (10:2) Spr 91, p. 18.
"Wakeup Call." [Poem] (66) N 91, p. 14.
"What Drives Us." [Poem] (66) N 91, p. 13.
2273. GRANADOS, Pedro
"Amiga en America." [Inti] (34/35) Otoño 91-Primavera 92, p. 261-262.
"Cada vez me parezco más a mi hermano Germán." [Inti] (34/35) Otoño
91-Primavera 92, p. 259.
"Desde los comentarios." [Inti] (34/35) Otoño 91-Primavera 92, p. 260-261.
"Empezar a acariciar la página." [Inti] (34/35) Otoño 91-Primavera 92, p. 262-263.
"El Olor de Esta Pagina." [Inti] (34/35) Otoño 91-Primavera 92, p. 263-264.
2274. GRANT, Craig
"Big Apple Honeymoon" (Selections: 2 prose poems). [PraF] (12:2 #55) Sum 91, p.
47-51.
2275. GRANT, Paul
"Abstract." [Vis] (36) 91, p. 11.
"The Broken-Hearted." [HampSPR] Wint 91, p. 18.
"Graveyard Working." [ChironR] (10:2) Sum 91, p. 40.
"Malcolm's Reach." [HampSPR] Wint 91, p. 17.
2276. GRANT-GIBSON, Elisabeth
"In This Shovel of Compost Are." [LouisL] (8:1) Spr 91, p. 47.
2277. GRASSI, Carolyn
"The Whiteness of Franz Marc." [NegC] (11:1) 91, p. 62-63.
2278. GRAVES, Bob
"Adorned." [EmeraldCR] (3) 91, c1990, p. 17.
"Mary." [EmeraldCR] (4) 91, p. 59.
"Vagrants." [EmeraldCR] (4) 91, p. 59.
2279. GRAVES, Michael P.
"Eating the Shadow." [ChrC] (108:7) 27 F 91, p. 234.
2280. GRAVES, Paul
"At the window I watch the nocturnal clouds pass" (tr. of Aleksandr Kushner, w.
Carol Ueland). [AmerPoR] (20:1) Ja-F 91, p. 3.
"It's longer, harder saying our goodbyes" (tr. of Aleksandr Kushner, w. Carol
Ueland). [AmerPoR] (20:1) Ja-F 91, p. 4.
"Mozart's skull, from between two columns of the news" (tr. of Aleksandr Kushner,
w. Carol Ueland). [AmerPoR] (20:1) Ja-F 91, p. 4.
"No woman that I'd met before" (tr. of Aleksandr Kushner, w. Carol Ueland).
[AmerPoR] (20:1) Ja-F 91, p. 4.
"On this, the near side of the mystery line, a cloud" (tr. of Aleksandr Kushner, w.
Carol Ueland). [AmerPoR] (20:1) Ja-F 91, p. 4.
"Tragedy's easy: once onstage, men wreck or slaughter" (tr. of Aleksandr Kushner,
w. Carol Ueland). [AmerPoR] (20:1) Ja-F 91, p. 4.

"Vyritsa" (tr. of Aleksandr Kushner, w. Carol Ueland). [AmerPoR] (20:1) Ja-F 91,
p. 3.
"Your exit's into frost, and the audience exits" (tr. of Aleksandr Kushner, w. Carol
Ueland). [AmerPoR] (20:1) Ja-F 91, p. 4.
2281. GRAVES, Thomas
"Longfellow Park." [PoetryE] (31) Spr 91, p. 65-66.
2282. GRAY, Beth
"Callas." [CrabCR] (7:2) Sum 91, p. 5.
2283. GRAY, Janet
"What I Said in the Discount Department Store" (after David Budbill). [BrooklynR]
(8) 91, p. 23.
2284. GRAY, Jeffrey
"Day and Night in Nakasho." [LitR] (34:2) Wint 91, p. 251.
"First Autumn." [WebR] (15) Spr 91, p. 100.
"In Hieronymous' House (Dürer)." [LitR] (34:2) Wint 91, p. 250.
"In the North." [WebR] (15) Spr 91, p. 99.
"The Road from Koufounissi." [WebR] (15) Spr 91, p. 102.
"Vascularity." [WebR] (15) Spr 91, p. 101.
2285. GRAY, Mary
"Tests." [CreamCR] (15:1) Spr 91, p. 75.
"This Year." [SouthernPR] (31:1) Spr 91, p. 69-70.
2286. GRAY, Patrick Worth
"Gothic." [MidwQ] (32:3) Spr 91, p. 291.
"Nebraska, It Was Nebraska and I Remember What Day of the Week It Was."
[MidwQ] (32:3) Spr 91, p. 290.
"Nickels." [PoetL] (86:3) Fall 91, p. 21.
2287. GRAY, Robert
"Present Tense." [Abraxas] (40/41) 91, p. 143.
2288. GRAYSON, Lisa
"They Wash Cars in the Blood of the Lamb." [PikeF] (10) Spr 91, p. 3.
2289. GREALY, Lucy
"In the Nick of Time" (after a poem by Robert Hass). [Sonora] (21) Sum 91, p. 1-2.
"Ward 10." [ParisR] (33:121) Wint 91, p. 124-125.
GRECA, T. R. la
See LaGRECA, T. R.
2290. GRECO, Heidi
"Because." [Event] (20:3) Fall 91, p. 53.
2291. GREEAR, Mildred
"In Storage." [Nimrod] (34:2) Spr-Sum 91, p. 1.
"Remainder." [Nimrod] (34:2) Spr-Sum 91, p. 2.
2292. GREEN, Joseph
"In the Smaller Picture." [DogRR] (10:1) Sum 91, p. 20.
"Situation." [DustyD] Ap 91, p. 17.
"Some Fish Don't Even Care to Swim." [DogRR] (10:1) Sum 91, p. 21.
2293. GREEN, Maisha
"Dreaming my life away." [PoetryUSA] (22) Spr 91, p. 9.
2294. GREEN, Melissa
"Akeldama" (Excerpt). [PartR] (58:1) Wint 91, p. 121-122.
2295. GREEN, Peter
"Jason and Medeia" (The Argonautica, Book III, lines 744-1407, tr. of Apollonius
of Rhodes). [SouthernHR] (25:3) Sum 91, p. 217-233.
2296. GREENBAUM, Jessica
"After Rereading 'Notes of a Native Son'." [NewYorker] (67:27) 26 Ag 91, p. 34.
"Driving Friday Night." [Boulevard] (6:2/3, #17/18) Fall 91, p. 171-172.
"The Yellow Star That Goes with Me." [NewYorker] (67:5) 25 Mr 91, p. 36.
2297. GREENBERG, Arielle
"Babysitting." [Calyx] (13:3) Wint 91-92, p. 58.
2298. GREENBERG, Martin
"Night" (from "Faust," tr. of Johann Wolfgang von Goethe). [Pequod] (32) 91, p.
111-115.
2299. GREENBLATT, Ray
"Delft, 1945." [InterPR] (17:1) Spr 91, p. 115.
"Effects." [InterPR] (17:2) Fall 91, p. 109.
"From a Madhouse at Arles." [InterPR] (17:2) Fall 91, p. 110-111.
"Ladder Against Wall." [InterPR] (17:1) Spr 91, p. 115.
"Modern Life." [CoalC] (4) S 91, p. 3.

"Posing." [InterPR] (17:1) Spr 91, p. 114.
"A Simple Example of Relativity." [InterPR] (17:2) Fall 91, p. 111.
"Upstate." [CoalC] (3) My 91, p. 11.
2300. GREENE, Anne
"When a Man Is Dying" (July '88). [MoodySI] (24/25/26) Spr 91, p. 29.
2301. GREENE, James
"I'm in a lion's trench, plunged in a fort" (tr. of Osip Mandelstam). [Field] (45) Fall
91, p. 39.
2302. GREENE, Jeffrey
"The Design." [GreenMR] (NS 5:1) Sum-Fall 91, p. 88.
"The Octopus." [HighP] (6:3) Wint 91, p. 75.
"White Horses." [GreenMR] (NS 5:1) Sum-Fall 91, p. 89.
2303. GREENING, John
"Fall in Clinton." [Verse] (8:2) Sum 91, p. 102.
"View from the Observatory" (February 1991). [CumbPR] (11:1) Fall 91, p. 17-18.
"Wild Spiders." [CumbPR] (11:1) Fall 91, p. 15-16.
2304. GREENING, Thomas
"Phoooom." [AmerS] (60:1) Wint 91, p. 95.
2305. GREENLEE, Sonja
"Couscous." [Parting] (4:2) Wint 91-92, p. 37-38.
2306. GREENLEY, Emily
"December 26, 1988." [Agni] (33) 91, p. 46.
"Placement." [Agni] (33) 91, p. 45.
2307. GREENMUN, Linda
"Return." [Calyx] (13:2) Sum 91, p. 66-67.
2308. GREENWALD, Roger
"To You" (tr. of Rolf Jacobsen). [AmerPoR] (20:1) Ja-F 91, p. 16.
2309. GREENWAY, William
"All of Us Are Children." [LaurelR] (25:1) Wint 91, p. 13.
"Atlantis." [ManhatPR] (13) [91?], p. 5.
"F—k." [SpoonRQ] (16:1/2) Wint-Spr 91, p. 44.
"Fortified Hills." [SpoonRQ] (16:1/2) Wint-Spr 91, p. 41-42.
"Hypochondria." [Poetry] (159:1) O 91, p. 14.
"My Last Father Poem." [ManhatPR] (13) [91?], p. 4.
"Old Snow and New." [Ascent] (15:2) Wint 91, p. 9.
"The Original Adam and Eve." [LaurelR] (25:1) Wint 91, p. 12.
"Stooge." [SpoonRQ] (16:1/2) Wint-Spr 91, p. 43.
"You'll Never Get This." [ContextS] (2:1) 91, p. 36.
2310. GREGER, Debora
"The Afternoon of Rome." [NewYorker] (67:8) 15 Ap 91, p. 42.
"Air-Conditioned Air." [NewYorker] (67:26) 19 Ag 91, p. 34.
"Blue Mirrors." [Poetry] (157:6) Mr 91, p. 329-331.
"Briar Rose." [ParisR] (33:120) Fall 91, p. 201-202.
"The Flowering Crab." [GeoR] (45:1) Spr 91, p. 107-108.
"Invitation to the Past." [NewYorker] (66:48) 14 Ja 91, p. 48.
"The Later Archaic Wing." [GettyR] (4:1) Wint 91, p. 105-106.
"On the Margins." [SouthwR] (76:1) Wint 91, p. 141-142.
"The Practice Room." [Nat] (252:23) 17 Je 91, p. 824.
"The Widower, His Weeds." [Poetry] (158:4) Jl 91, p. 207.
2311. GREGERMAN, Debra
"After the Blues." [MassR] (32:2) Sum 91, p. 281.
"Baltimore." [NowestR] (29:3) 91, p. 33-34.
"Employment." [NowestR] (29:3) 91, p. 31.
"For What Remains." [PassN] (12:1) Sum 91, p. 9.
"Jealousy and the Things You Are Not." [MassR] (32:2) Sum 91, p. 282.
"Lullaby." [NowestR] (29:3) 91, p. 30.
"Strictly Speaking." [NowestR] (29:3) 91, p. 32.
"Truth or Dare." [NoAmR] (276:2) Je 91, p. 5.
"Two Love Poems Joined on a Sunday." [NewL] (58:1) Fall 91, p. 105.
2312. GREGG, Linda
"Life on the Rio Escondido." [AmerPoR] (20:4) Jl-Ag 91, p. 33.
2313. GREGOR, Arthur
"Interior." [Interim] (10:2) Fall-Wint 91-92, p. 10.
2314. GREGORY, M.
"Turning Calypso." [CrabCR] (7:2) Sum 91, p. 3.

2315. GREGSON, Ian
"The Arrival." [Verse] (8:2) Sum 91, p. 110.
2316. GRELL, Terri Lee
"Independent Measures." [BellR] (14:2) Fall 91, p. 40.
2317. GRENNAN, Eamon
"The All Clear." [SouthwR] (76:3) Sum 91, p. 356.
"Bat." [NewYorker] (67:37) 4 N 91, p. 42.
"Breakfast Room." [NewYorker] (67:25) 12 Ag 91, p. 34.
"The Cave Painters." [Poetry] (157:6) Mr 91, p. 324-325.
"Couple." [NewYorker] (67:32) 30 S 91, p. 38.
"Family Sketches." [Thrpny] (45) Spr 91, p. 32.
"A Few Last Lines of Laundry." [Poetry] (157:6) Mr 91, p. 326.
"Night Figure." [NewYorker] (67:5) 25 Mr 91, p. 32-33.
"Sitting in a Field on a Windy Day." [Poetry] (157:6) Mr 91, p. 325-326.
"Woman at Lit Window." [SouthwR] (76:3) Sum 91, p. 357.
2318. GRESSINGER, Chris
"How the Party Started." [CimR] (97) O 91, p. 53.
2319. GREY, John
"Identities." [ChironR] (10:2) Sum 91, p. 46.
"Incomplete." [Sequoia] (34:1) Spr 91, p. 97.
"News at Night." [SlipS] (11) 91, p. 11.
"The Secret Address." [HeavenB] (9) Wint-Spr 91-92, p. 9.
"The Storied Year." [Plain] (11:2) Wint 91, p. 17.
"The Third of Three." [Paint] (18:36) Aut 91, p. 25-26.
"Time Outside Mine." [DustyD] (2:1) Ja 91, p. 3.
"The Trail." [Parting] (4:1) Sum 91, p. 2.
"Waiting for Light." [ChangingM] (22) Wint-Spr 91, p. 36.
"A Walk Across." [Sidewalks] (1) Aug 91, p. 54.
"We Happen In and Around the Murder." [Parting] (4:1) Sum 91, p. 35.
"Where Battles Are Fought." [Bogg] (64) 91, p. 45.
"With Donna at the Wake." [CoalC] (3) My 91, p. 13.
2320. GREY, Lucinda
"Clearer Than Life." [SouthernHR] (25:2) Spr 91, p. 147.
"Saying Goodbye to the Animals." [Shen] (41:3) Fall 91, p. 97.
2321. GREY, Robert
"Dark Land." [Crucible] (27) Fall 91, p. 7.
2322. GRIERSON, Bruce
"Sympathy." [MalR] (96) Fall 91, p. 81.
2323. GRIERSON, Tom
"Images of Canada." [Bogg] (64) 91, p. 8.
2324. GRIFFIN, Maureen Ryan
"Southern Spring." [Crucible] (27) Fall 91, p. 20-21.
2325. GRIFFIN, Sheila
"Art." [AntR] (49:2) Spr 91, p. 235.
"Clam and Effect." [CimR] (94) Ja 91, p. 104.
"Disincarnate." [CimR] (94) Ja 91, p. 103.
"Keen." [AntR] (49:2) Spr 91, p. 236.
2326. GRIFFIN, Walter
"Body Parts." [ThRiPo] (37/38) 91, p. 51.
"The Bones of Montgomery Clift." [InterPR] (17:2) Fall 91, p. 90.
"The Bones of Montgomery Clift." [NegC] (11:1) 91, p. 86.
"The Bones of Montgomery Clift." [ParisR] (33:119) Sum 91, p. 254.
"The Bones of Montgomery Clift." [TexasR] (12:3/4) Fall-Wint 91, p. 78.
"Crazy Billy." [NegC] (11:1) 91, p. 85.
"The Crib Biter." [PacificR] (10) 91-92, p. 107.
"Day of the Soft Mouth." [ThRiPo] (37/38) 91, p. 52-53.
"Harmless Blood." [Mildred] (4:2/5:1) 91, p. 52.
"New Year's Eve." [DustyD] (2:1) Ja 91, p. 17.
"Night Trains." [DustyD] Ap 91, p. 14.
"Night Trains." [InterPR] (17:2) Fall 91, p. 89-90.
"Night Trains." [Mildred] (4:2/5:1) 91, p. 51.
"Night Trains." [PacificR] (10) 91-92, p. 13.
"Night Trains." [SycamoreR] (3:1) Wint 91, p. 6.
"Other Cities." [Poetry] (158:1) Ap 91, p. 20.
"Outlaws." [Poetry] (158:1) Ap 91, p. 19.
"The Season of the Falling Face." [Plain] (12:2) Wint 91, p. 35.

"The Secrets of Ballroom Dancing." [PacificR] (10) 91-92, p. 37.
"Sliding Home." [NegC] (11:1) 91, p. 87.
"Some Strange Place." [DustyD] (2:1) Ja 91, p. 22.
"Stanley Smith Is Dead." [DustyD] Ap 91, p. 14.
"Stanley Smith Is Dead." [InterPR] (17:2) Fall 91, p. 91.
"The Trees Are Falling." [InterPR] (17:2) Fall 91, p. 89.
"Water." [CreamCR] (15:1) Spr 91, p. 81.

2327. GRIFFITH, Kevin
"The Age of Age." [CreamCR] (15:1) Spr 91, p. 77.
"Labor." [CreamCR] (15:1) Spr 91, p. 78.
"Reef Boy" (Sulu Islands, The Philippines). [SouthernR] (27:2) Ap 91, p. 324-325.

2328. GRIFFITH, Margot
"Coming to Waha'ula." [HawaiiR] (15:3, #33) Fall 91, p. 36.

2329. GRIFFITHS, Bill
"News — Elvis Sets Sail." [NewAW] (8/9) Fall 91, p. 91-94.
"The Ship." [NewAW] (8/9) Fall 91, p. 95-96.
"South Song." [NewAW] (8/9) Fall 91, p. 96.

2330. GRIGORIAN, Hovhanness
"When Your Country Is Small" (tr. by Diana Der Hovanessian). [InterPR] (17:2)
    Fall 91, p. 80.

2331. GRILL, Andrea S.
"Loosening." [PoetL] (86:2) Sum 91, p. 34.
"Low Blood Sugar." [PoetL] (86:2) Sum 91, p. 35.

2332. GRIM, Jessica
"Untitled: Embrasure syllogies." [Aerial] (6/7) 91, p. 172.

2333. GRIMES, Susan
"Washtub Cake." [Kalliope] (13:3) 91, p. 34.

2334. GRIMM, Susan
"Living in Fear of the Venus of Willendorf." [ArtfulD] (20/21) 91, p. 56.

2335. GRINDE, Olav
"Channels" (tr. of Helge Vatsend). [Vis] (37) 91, p. 43.
"The Silence" (tr. of Helge Vatsend). [Vis] (37) 91, p. 42.

2336. GRINDLEY, Carl
"Composition #2." [CreamCR] (14:2) Wint 91, p. 135.
"Composition #16." [CreamCR] (14:2) Wint 91, p. 133-134.

2337. GRINSTEAD
"Aberrant Behavior." [DogRR] (10:2) Fall-Wint 91, p. 6.

2338. GRISWOLD, Jay
"After the Ghost Dance." [Plain] (12:2) Wint 91, p. 6.
"America." [SouthernPR] (31:1) Spr 91, p. 7.
"At the Asylum" (for Dino Campana). [Callaloo] (14:3) Sum 91, p. 691.
"Black Water" (for Phil Woods). [SouthernPR] (31:1) Spr 91, p. 8.
"Cordoba, the White Road." [InterPR] (17:1) Spr 91, p. 86-87.
"Gravity." [Plain] (12:1) Fall 91, p. 11.
"Monastery." [NegC] (11:1) 91, p. 105.
"Onions" (for Miguel Hernandez). [InterPR] (17:1) Spr 91, p. 90.
"The Prisoner's Dream." [InterPR] (17:1) Spr 91, p. 87-88.
"Respite." [Gypsy] (17) 91, p. 42.
"A Shirt Called Ghost Dancing." [InterPR] (17:1) Spr 91, p. 89.
"The Sower." [LitR] (34:2) Wint 91, p. 199.
"Unfinished Poems" (for Gaspar Garcia Laviana, killed in Nicaragua, 1978).
    [Callaloo] (14:3) Sum 91, p. 690.
"Variation on an Ancient Theme" (for Paul Nelson). [PoetL] (86:4) Wint 91-92, p.
    41-42.

2339. GRITZ, Ona
"How Your Hand Might Move." [PoetryE] (32) Fall 91, p. 84.
"Taking It In." [PoetryE] (32) Fall 91, p. 83.

2340. GROLLMES, Eugene E.
"After the Grief." [ManhatPR] (13) [91?], p. 23.
"Hardin Moore: On the Edge of Ripening Fields." [ManhatPR] (13) [91?], p. 23.

2341. GROLMES, Sam
"A Tree Frog in the Wild Preserve." [Abraxas] (40/41) 91, p. 126-127.

2342. GRONDAL, Gylfi
"On the Screen" (tr. by Kenry Kratz). [Vis] (37) 91, p. 39.

2343. GROOMS, Anthony
"Catherine." [Confr] (46/47) Fall 91-Wint 92, p. 248.

2344. GROSHOLZ, Emily
"63, Rue Mirabeau." [PraS] (65:3) Fall 91, p. 57-58.
"Commuter Marriage." [SouthernR] (27:3) Jl 91, p. 674-678.
"Life of a Salesman." [NewEngR] (13:3/4) Spr-Sum 91, p. 135-136.
"Sidonie." [PraS] (65:3) Fall 91, p. 58-59.
"Thirty-Six Weeks." [Poetry] (158:3) Je 91, p. 156-157.
2345. GROSMAN, Ernesto Livon
"Patrimonies" (tr. of Susana Cerdá, w. Molly Weigel). [AmerPoR] (20:5) S-O 91,
p. 37-38.
2346. GROSS, H. M.
"Haiku." [EmeraldCR] (3) 91, c1990, p. 86.
2347. GROSS, Judith
"Mohawk Land Dispute: Red Sanctuary." [HawaiiR] (15:3, #33) Fall 91, p. 9-10.
2348. GROSS, Pamela
"Breughel's Bird." [PoetryNW] (32:4) Wint 91-92, p. 18-19.
"Letting Go." [GeoR] (45:1) Spr 91, p. 157-158.
"Losing the Eight Colors." [Poetry] (157:6) Mr 91, p. 327-328.
2349. GROSS, Philip
"Son of Snotnose" (for J.K.G.). [Stand] (32:1) Wint 90-91, p. 22-23.
2350. GROSSMAN, Allen
"Flax" (A Ballad of Schools and Dreams). [AmerPoR] (20:5) S-O 91, p. 48.
"Poland of Death (III)." [Ploughs] (17:2/3) Fall 91, p. 92-93.
"Poland of Death (V)." [Boulevard] (6:2/3, #17/18) Fall 91, p. 84-86.
2351. GROSSMAN, Edith
"Barcelona Days" (tr. of Jaime Manrique). [Journal] (15:1) Spr 91, p. 55-56.
"Barranco de Loba, 1929" (tr. of Jaime Manrique). [GrandS] (10:4, #40) 91, p.
49-51.
2352. GROSSMAN, Florence
"Cobwebs." [Poetry] (158:2) My 91, p. 93.
2353. GROSSMAN, K. Margaret
"1922 and She's Still Considering Her Vote." [CinPR] (21) Spr 90, p. 23.
"Doubt Without Sin, Apples Without Trees." [Chelsea] (51) 91, p. 32.
"Migrating Birds." [CinPR] (21) Spr 90, p. 22.
"Mime." [Chelsea] (51) 91, p. 29.
"Some Things You Can't Avoid." [Chelsea] (51) 91, p. 30-31.
2354. GROSSMAN, Rebekah
"God on Wheels." [AntR] (49:2) Spr 91, p. 253.
2355. GROSSMAN, Richard
"Everglades." [ChiR] (37:2/3) 91, p. 90-91.
2356. GROVES, Paul
"Annus Mirabilis." [Verse] (8:2) Sum 91, p. 108.
2357. GROW, Mary
"Calathea Musaica." [Archae] (2) Spr 91, p. 12.
2358. GROWNEY, Joanne
"A Mathematician." [FourQ] (5:2) Fall 91, p. 36.
2359. GRUBB, David H. W.
"Old." [Stand] (32:4) Aut 91, p. 5.
"Two Weeks After My Father's Death We Pick the Pears." [Stand] (33:1) Wint 91,
p. 65.
2360. GRUBBS, Gerald (Gerald R.)
"At Night." [CreamCR] (15:2) Fall 91, p. 59.
"Flowers." [CinPR] (21) Spr 90, p. 32-33.
"He Climbs In." [CrabCR] (7:2) Sum 91, p. 15.
"Night." [WindO] (55) Wint 91-92, p. 7-8.
"The Storm." [WindO] (55) Wint 91-92, p. 8.
2361. GRUMMAN, Bob
"Mathemaku No. 1." [PoetryUSA] (22) Spr 91, p. 4.
2362. GRUMMER, Greg
"The Invisible Man." [Ploughs] (17:4) Wint 91-92, p. 67.
2363. GRUNBERGER, Aimée
"Glen Echo Park." [PaintedB] (42) 91, p. 30.
2364. GRUWEZ, Luuk
"Collection" (tr. by David Siefkin and Catharina Kochuyt). [Trans] (25) Spr 91, p.
233-234.
"Street" (tr. by David Siefkin and Catharina Kochuyt). [Trans] (25) Spr 91, p. 235.

2365. GRYNEWICZ, Eugene R.
"Rewriting Poe." [PennR] (5:1) Spr 91, p. 5.
2366. GRYNIEWICZ, Eugene R.
"Alchemy." [Elf] (1:4) Wint 91, p. 41.
"Poetry Is a Splinter." [BlackBR] (13) Spr-Sum 91, p. 29.
"A Victim of Cricumstance." [BlackBR] (13) Spr-Sum 91, p. 32.
2367. GU, Cheng
"Image." [VirQR] (67:3) Sum 91, p. 463.
"In This Broad and Bright World" (tr. by Zhang Yichun). [GreenMR] (NS 4:2)
Wint-Spr 91, p. 105.
2368. GUDAS, Eric
"Best Western." [AmerPoR] (20:3) My-Je 91, p. 42.
"Broke in West Berlin." [AmerPoR] (20:3) My-Je 91, p. 43.
"The Names of Cities." [AmerPoR] (20:3) My-Je 91, p. 42.
"Standing in a Field" (for Mary Clark). [AmerPoR] (20:3) My-Je 91, p. 43.
2369. GUENTHER, Charles
"Alchemists" (tr. of Jean Cocteau). [AmerPoR] (20:5) S-O 91, p. 24.
"Angel Back" (tr. of Jean Cocteau). [AmerPoR] (20:5) S-O 91, p. 26.
"Broken Poem for Picasso" (tr. of Jean Cocteau). [AmerPoR] (20:5) S-O 91, p. 26.
"He Slew" (tr. of Jean Cocteau). [AmerPoR] (20:5) S-O 91, p. 25.
"Heart's Gravity" (tr. of Jean Cocteau). [AmerPoR] (20:5) S-O 91, p. 25.
"Homage to Goya" (tr. of Jean Cocteau). [AmerPoR] (20:5) S-O 91, p. 24.
"Homage to Velasquez" (tr. of Jean Cocteau). [AmerPoR] (20:5) S-O 91, p. 24.
"I Must" (tr. of Jean Cocteau). [AmerPoR] (20:5) S-O 91, p. 25.
"In Prison" (tr. of Jean Cocteau). [AmerPoR] (20:5) S-O 91, p. 25.
"The King of the World" (tr. of Jean Cocteau). [AmerPoR] (20:5) S-O 91, p. 24.
"A Living Body" (tr. of Jean Cocteau). [AmerPoR] (20:5) S-O 91, p. 26.
"Malaga" (tr. of Jean Cocteau). [AmerPoR] (20:5) S-O 91, p. 26.
"Noël" (tr. of Jean Cocteau). [AmerPoR] (20:5) S-O 91, p. 25.
"Noon" (tr. of Jean Cocteau). [AmerPoR] (20:5) S-O 91, p. 26.
"Romance" (tr. of Jean Cocteau). [AmerPoR] (20:5) S-O 91, p. 26.
"Sometimes Cruel Time" (tr. of Jean Cocteau). [AmerPoR] (20:5) S-O 91, p. 24.
2370. GUENTHER, Gabriele
"Friday Nights, Consorting with Cards." [Dandel] (18:2) Wint 91, p. 65.
GUERCIO, Margaret del
See Del GUERCIO, Margaret
2371. GUERIN, Christopher D.
"Equals Infinity." [OxfordM] (7:2) Fall-Wint 91, p. 39.
2372. GUERNSEY, Bruce
"Cliché." [WillowR] Spr 91, p. 4.
"Poetics." [WillowR] Spr 91, p. 2-3.
2373. GUERRERO, Juan
"Escoria" (Selections: II, VI-VII, XI, XIII-XIV, XXIV, XXVI, XXVIII). [Mester]
(20:1) Spr 91, p. 81.
2374. GUEST, Barbara
"Bandusia" (from The Odes of Horace, Book III, ode xiii). [Pembroke] (23) 91, p.
10.
"Beautiful / Evil." [NewAW] (7) Spr 91, p. 12-13.
"The Borderlands." [AmerPoR] (20:2) Mr-Ap 91, p. 48.
"Dissonance Royal Traveller." [Sulfer] (11:2, #29) Fall 91, p. 16-19.
"The Pleiades." [Pembroke] (23) 91, p. 9.
"Winter Horses." [Conjunc] (17) 91, p. 329-333.
2375. GUEVARA, Maurice Kilwein
"Downswirling of the Young Beast." [CreamCR] (15:1) Spr 91, p. 65-66.
2376. GUILFORD, Chuck
"A Chinese Puzzle." [WeberS] (8:2) Fall 91, p. 82.
"For Tomorrow." [WeberS] (8:2) Fall 91, p. 81-82.
"Lochsa Morning." [WeberS] (8:2) Fall 91, p. 81.
2377. GUILLÉN, Nicolás
"Burgueses" (De: "La rueda dentada"). [Areíto] (3:9) Je 91, inside front cover.
"Responde Tú" (De "Tengo"). [Areíto] (3:9) Je 91, inside back cover.
2378. GUILLORY, Dan
"Whorehouse on the Bayou." [SpoonRQ] (16:3/4) Sum-Fall 91, p. 19-20.
2379. GUILLORY, Stella Jeng
"Father Assumes His Squatting Position." [BambooR] (50/51) Spr-Sum 91, p.
87-88.

"In the Hotel Room in Hong Kong." [BambooR] (50/51) Spr-Sum 91, p. 89-90.
2380. GUITART, Jorge
"The Milk Project." [SnailPR] (1:2) Fall 91-Wint 92, p. 10.
"The Week." [SnailPR] (1:2) Fall 91-Wint 92, p. 11.
2381. GULLETTE, David
"Orbiter Dicta." [Ploughs] (17:2/3) Fall 91, p. 116-117.
2382. GUNDERSON, Ketih
"Baja Journal" (Excerpts). [NorthStoneR] (10) Fall 91-Wint 92, p. 178-193.
2383. GUNDY, Jeff
"The Country as Old Wars and Sunshine." [ArtfulD] (20/21) 91, p. 121.
"Fish." [OhioR] (47) 91, p. 108-109.
"Inquiries into the Technology of Hell and Certain Rumors Recently Circulating."
[SpoonRQ] (16:3/4) Sum-Fall 91, p. 52-53.
"Inquiry into Faces, Light, the Guilt of Metaphor." [PikeF] (10) Spr 91, p. 6.
"Inquiry into Gifts, or The Indigo Bunting." [SpoonRQ] (16:3/4) Sum-Fall 91, p.
50-51.
"Inquiry into Simply Responding to the Negative." [CinPR] (22) Spr 91, p. 58-59.
"Inquiry into Targets of Opportunity and the Poetry of Witness." [SpoonRQ]
(16:3/4) Sum-Fall 91, p. 54-55.
"Inquiry into the Discovery of the City into Which the Saints Have Been Said to Go,
Marching." [SpoonRQ] (16:3/4) Sum-Fall 91, p. 56-57.
"Inquiry on Infections." [CinPR] (22) Spr 91, p. 60.
"Inquiry on the Fire Sermon." [SpoonRQ] (16:3/4) Sum-Fall 91, p. 58.
"Just a Dog." [SpoonRQ] (16:3/4) Sum-Fall 91, p. 49.
"Kafka in Ohio, or These Sunny Tuesdays." [OhioR] (47) 91, p. 106-107.
"On the Bluffs of Memory and the Only Blue Bird with a Rusty Breast" (for Dean).
[SpoonRQ] (16:3/4) Sum-Fall 91, p. 68-69.
"Poem at the Hypothetical End of History, or What I Want Anyhow." [SpoonRQ]
(16:3/4) Sum-Fall 91, p. 59-61.
"Three for April." [SpoonRQ] (16:3/4) Sum-Fall 91, p. 66-67.
"Where I Grew Up." [SpoonRQ] (16:3/4) Sum-Fall 91, p. 64-65.
"Where I Live." [SpoonRQ] (16:3/4) Sum-Fall 91, p. 62-63.
2384. GUNN, Thom
"The Antagonism" (to Helena Shire). [Thrpny] (44) Wint 91, p. 11.
"A Home." [NewYorker] (67:37) 4 N 91, p. 48.
"The Reassurance." [Sequoia] (34:1) Spr 91, p. 14.
2385. GUNSON, Patricia
"Give me another Bud Dan, make sure it's cold this time." [MoodySI] (24/25/26)
Spr 91, p. 49.
2386. GUO, Wei
"A Black Tunnel" (tr. of Tang Ya Ping, w. Ginny MacKenzie). [Agni] (34) 91, p.
220.
"An Old Song" (tr. of Lu Lu, w. Ginny MacKenzie). [Agni] (34) 91, p. 219.
"Saying Good-bye to a Friend Going Abroad" (tr. of Shu Ting, w. Ginny
MacKenzie). [Agni] (34) 91, p. 218.
"The Two of Us" (tr. of Meng Lang, w. Ginny MacKenzie). [Agni] (34) 91, p. 217.
2387. GURKIN, Kathryn Bright
"Even the Towers of Ilium." [Crucible] (27) Fall 91, p. 33.
2388. GURLEY, James
"Five Variations: Seattle." [Grain] (19:2) Sum 91, p. 22-24.
"Gauguin's Chair." [QW] (33) Sum-Fall 91, p. 173-175.
"A Map of the World." [PoetL] (86:2) Sum 91, p. 19-20.
"New Moon." [Grain] (19:2) Sum 91, p. 25-26.
"Night Crossing." [NoDaQ] (59:1) Wint 91, p. 199.
"Variations on a Theme by Kandinsky." [Event] (20:3) Fall 91, p. 72-73.
2389. GUSSLER, Phyllis
"Tattoo." [HawaiiR] (15:2, #32) Spr 91, p. 154-155.
2390. GUSTAFSON, Ralph
"At the Jungfrau." [CanLit] (128) Spr 91, p. 22-24.
"The House Fire." [Quarry] (40:1/2) Wint-Spr 91, p. 76.
"News of the Day." [Quarry] (40:1/2) Wint-Spr 91, p. 77.
"Winter Solstice." [Arc] (26) Spr 91, p. 71.
2391. GUSTAFSSON, Lars
"Albrecht Dürer's Rhinoceros, 1515" (tr. by Yvonne L. Sandstroem). [SouthwR]
(76:1) Wint 91, p. 139-140.

"Elegy on the Density of the World" (tr. by Yvonne L. Sandstroem). [SouthwR] (76:1) Wint 91, p. 138-139.
"For All Those Who Wait for Time to Pass" (tr. by Yvonne L. Sandstroem). [NewYorker] (67:11) 6 My 91, p. 38.
2392. GUSTAVSON, Jeffrey
"The Mink." [NewYorker] (66:47) 7 Ja 91, p. 34.
"Sequence for Detroit Red." [Agni] (34) 91, p. 67-69.
GUT, Karen Alkalay
See ALKALAY-GUT, Karen
2393. GUTIERREZ REVUELTA, Pedro
"The Days Were Like That" (tr. of Angel Gonzalez, w. Steven Ford Brown). [WillowS] (28) Sum 91, p. 18.
"The Defeated One" (tr. of Angel Gonzalez, w. Steven Ford Brown). [WillowS] (28) Sum 91, p. 17.
"The Future" (tr. of Ángel González, w. Steven Ford Brown). [WebR] (15) Spr 91, p. 34.
"Human Geography" (tr. of Angel Gonzalez, w. Steven Ford Brown). [WillowS] (28) Sum 91, p. 16.
"I Myself" (tr. of Angel Gonzalez, w. Steven Ford Brown). [Paint] (18:36) Aut 91, p. 43.
"The Least Corpse" (tr. of Angel González, w. Steven Ford Brown). [WebR] (15) Spr 91, p. 33-34.
"The Scandalous Rose" (tr. of Angel González, w. Steven Ford Brown). [TexasR] (12:1/2) Spr-Sum 91, p. 103.
"Sinestesia" (tr. of Angel Gonzalez, w. Steven Ford Brown). [Paint] (18:36) Aut 91, p. 47.
"The So-Called Twilight" (tr. of Angel Gonzalez, w. Steven Ford Brown). [TexasR] (12:1/2) Spr-Sum 91, p. 104.
"So It Seems" (tr. of Angel Gonzalez, w. Steven Ford Brown). [Paint] (18:36) Aut 91, p. 45-46.
"That River Ran Backwards" (tr. of Angel González, w. Steven Ford Brown). [WebR] (15) Spr 91, p. 32.
"Twilight, Albuquerque, Summer" (tr. of Angel Gonzalez, w. Steven Ford Brown). [TexasR] (12:1/2) Spr-Sum 91, p. 105.
GUTIRREZ REVUELTA, Pedro
See GUTIERREZ REVUELTA, Pedro
2394. GUTTMAN, Naomi
"Ginette." [Grain] (19:1) Spr 91, p. 56-57.
"He Is." [Grain] (19:1) Spr 91, p. 58.
"Shelter." [Grain] (19:1) Spr 91, p. 54-55.
2395. GUZMAN, Graciela
"Resemblances" (tr. by Sandra Gail Teichmann). [WritersF] (17) Fall 91, p. 129.
"Semejanzas." [WritersF] (17) Fall 91, p. 128.
"To Sleep Rocking in the Fear of Termination" (tr. by Sandra G. Teichmann). [Vis] (36) 91, p. 33.
HA, Jin
See JIN, Ha
2396. HABOVA, Dana
"Duties of a Train Conductor" (tr. of Miroslav Holub, w. David Young). [GrandS] (10:4, #40) 91, p. 191-192.
"The End of the Week" (tr. of Miroslav Holub, w. David Young). [Field] (45) Fall 91, p. 43.
"The Wall in the Corner by the Stairs" (tr. of Miroslav Holub, w. David Young). [Field] (45) Fall 91, p. 41-42.
2397. HACHTOUN, A.
"Havannah." [LindLM] (10:4) O-D 91, p. 16.
2398. HACKER, Marilyn
"Annunciation 8 AM." [Boulevard] (6:2/3, #17/18) Fall 91, p. 12-13.
"Cleis." [ParisR] (33:119) Sum 91, p. 133-134.
"Elysian Fields." [ParisR] (33:119) Sum 91, p. 131-132.
"Her Ring." [KenR] (NS 13:2) Spr 91, p. 98.
"Letter on June 15." [KenR] (NS 13:2) Spr 91, p. 100-101.
"Letter to a Wound." [Ploughs] (17:2/3) Fall 91, p. 139-141.
"Letter to Julie in a New Decade." [Boulevard] (6:2/3, #17/18) Fall 91, p. 8-11.
"Quai Saint-Bernard." [KenR] (NS 13:2) Spr 91, p. 98-100.

2399. HADAS, Rachel
"Fin de Siècle." [NewRep] (205:1) 1 Jl 91, p. 38.
"Frieze Advancing." [NewRep] (205:1) 1 Jl 91, p. 38.
"Less Than Kind." [DenQ] (26:1) Sum 91, p. 35-36.
"Misty Sky" (tr. of Pierre Charles Baudelaire). [Raritan] (11:1) Sum 91, p. 13.
"The Paris Health Club." [Confr] (46/47) Fall 91-Wint 92, p. 251-252.
"Passage." [NewRep] (205:1) 1 Jl 91, p. 38.
"The Promises of a Face" (tr. of Pierre Charles Baudelaire). [Raritan] (11:1) Sum
        91, p. 15.
"Restored Medieval House, Sensational Views" (Selections: I-II). [Ploughs] (17:1)
        Spr 91, p. 67-70.
"Retreat" (tr. of Pierre Charles Baudelaire). [Raritan] (11:1) Sum 91, p. 14.
"Six of One." [NewRep] (205:1) 1 Jl 91, p. 38.
"Sleepy's Entrance" (in memory of Gregory Kolovakos). [Thrpny] (44) Wint 91, p.
        35.
"Sonnet in Autumn" (tr. of Pierre Charles Baudelaire). [Raritan] (11:1) Sum 91, p.
        16.
"La Voix" (tr. of Charles Baudelaire). [NewYRB] (38:4) 14 F 91, p. 24.
2400. HADDUCK, Kevin
"A Fishing Song for My Wife." [BellArk] (7:6) N-D 91, p. 2.
"Meditations on Marie." [BellArk] (7:6) N-D 91, p. 10.
2401. HADELLA, Paul
"Directional." [Parting] (4:2) Wint 91-92, p. 5.
2402. HAHN, Elizabeth
"After the Long Translation" (In memory of Anne Hébert's "Il y a certainement
        quelqu'un"). [CapeR] (26:1) Spr 91, p. 44.
"Blind Sight." [AnthNEW] (3) 91, p. 20.
"Cow Monologue." [BellArk] (7:4) Jl-Ag 91, p. 1.
"Death" (tr. of Gisèle Prassinos, w. Brenda Casey). [Vis] (36) 91, p. 49.
"The Dogs Begin Before Dawn with Their Barking." [HolCrit] (28:4) O 91, p. 17.
"Hélène" (tr. of Pierre Morency, w. Brenda Casey). [Vis] (36) 91, p. 12.
"The Labor of Zechariah" (Of Zechariah's muteness until Elizabeth delivers John).
        [ChrC] (108:36) 11 D 91, p. 1169.
"The Leveler: My Laundromat." [BellArk] (7:4) Jl-Ag 91, p. 12.
"Vital Signs of Virgo." [BellArk] (7:4) Jl-Ag 91, p. 23.
2403. HAHN, Lauren
"A Poem about Poems" (tr. of Erich Fried). [ColR] (NS 17:2) Fall-Wint 90, p.
        106-107.
2404. HAHN, Oscar
"Spirit's Ecology" (tr. by James Hoggard). [ColR] (NS 18:1) Spr-Sum 91, p. 85.
2405. HAHN, Robert
"Maidens, Martinis, Midnight Hours." [NewRep] (204:25) 24 Je 91, p. 31.
"Venice Obscured" (Paris, July 1989). [WestHR] (45:3) Aut 91, p. 224-225.
2406. HAHN, S. C.
"The Lovers" (after Chagall's "The Lovers"). [CreamCR] (14:2) Wint 91, p.
        157-159.
"Readiness." [CreamCR] (14:2) Wint 91, p. 156.
2407. HAHN, Susan
"Between Rosh Hashanah and Yom Kippur." [Poetry] (158:6) S 91, p. 327.
"Itch" (after being bitten by a flea). [MichQR] (30:3) Sum 91, p. 413.
"Nerve." [RiverS] (35) 91, p. 57.
"Susan Hahn." [KenR] (NS 13:1) Wint 91, p. 73.
"Virgin." [MichQR] (30:3) Sum 91, p. 414.
2408. HAI-JEW, Shalin
"The Same Hand" (June 3-4, 1989, Tiananmen Square, Beijing, People's Republic
        of China). [Kalliope] (13:1) 91, p. 36-38.
2409. HAINES, Anne
"Grappling with the Cosmos." [Sidewalks] (1) Aug 91, p. 18-19.
"I Want to Learn Words." [Sidewalks] (1) Aug 91, p. 20.
2410. HAINES, John
"Head of Sorrow, Head of Thought." [Nat] (253:18) 25 N 91, p. 677-678.
"Meditation on a Skull Carved in Crystal" (Selections: I, III-V, VIII-IX). [Nat]
        (253:18) 25 N 91, p. 678-679.
2411. HAIZLIP, Dee
"Prairie." [Writer] (104:6) Je 91, p. 25.

2412. HALE, Dori
"A New Year in Vermont." [CreamCR] (14:2) Wint 91, p. 179-180.
2413. HALE, Eileen Adele
"In Wild Grass." [OnTheBus] (8/9) 91, p. 80.
2414. HALES, Corrinne
"Argument." [SouthernR] (27:1) Ja 91, p. 88-91.
"Sunday Morning." [SouthernR] (27:1) Ja 91, p. 91-92.
2415. HALIBURTON, Debora
"Spring / 89." [PraF] (12:1 #54) Spr 91, p. 84.
2416. HALL, Barry
"Vows." [Vis] (36) 91, p. 50.
2417. HALL, Daniel
"A Fifties 4th." [Poetry] (158:4) Jl 91, p. 194-196.
"Winged Torso of Eros." [Poetry] (158:4) Jl 91, p. 194.
2418. HALL, David
"Drying Out." [Lactuca] (14) My 91, p. 58.
2419. HALL, Donald
"And Now." [SycamoreR] (3:2) Sum 91, p. 21.
"The Caption." [SycamoreR] (3:2) Sum 91, p. 20.
"The Coalition." [Nat] (253:17) 18 N 91, p. 630.
"Daylilies on the Hill." [MichQR] (30:4) Fall 91, p. 535-551.
"A History of Aesthetics." [NoDaQ] (59:3) Sum 91, p. 1.
"A History of Sears Roebuck." [NoDaQ] (59:3) Sum 91, p. 1.
"My Life and Times" (Selections: 3 poems). [Ploughs] (17:1) Spr 91, p. 74-75.
"My Life and Times: First Series." [GettyR] (4:2) Spr 91, p. 257-263.
"Spring Glen Grammar School." [NewYorker] (67:30) 16 S 91, p. 32.
"A Theory of Creativity." [NoDaQ] (59:3) Sum 91, p. 2.
"The Third Inning." [ParisR] (33:120) Fall 91, p. 151-153.
"The White Closed Door." [Ploughs] (17:2/3) Fall 91, p. 94.
2420. HALL, Joan Joffe
"For the Heart." [Pig] (17) 91, p. 57.
"From a Cousin After Many Years." [Pig] (17) 91, p. 57.
"Letter from the Girl Next Door." [Pig] (17) 91, p. 57.
2421. HALL, Judith
"All We Know of Heaven." [NewRep] (204:13) 1 Ap 91, p. 38.
"Postcard of Degas' Washerwomen Carrying Washing." [NewRep] (205:5) 29 Jl
91, p. 40.
2422. HALL, Marni
"A Reason Not to Go to Work." [OnTheBus] (8/9) 91, p. 81.
2423. HALL, Phil
"Lovis Corinth (Art History Lesson)." [Event] (20:3) Fall 91, p. 76-77.
2424. HALL, Steven
"Salt Mines" (Excerpt). [Shiny] (6) Spr-Sum 91, p. 79-84.
2425. HALL, Thelma R.
"Betrayal." [ChatR] (11:2) Wint 91, p. 37.
2426. HALLAWELL, Susan (Susan W.)
"Gianna in the Bath." [PaintedHR] (2) Spr 91, p. 6.
"Life Story." [HampSPR] Wint 91, p. 49.
"Rosebush in a Tin Can" (at a Tibetan orphanage in India). [PaintedHR] (2) Spr 91,
p. 5.
2427. HALLIDAY, Mark
"Alley Sketch." [CimR] (96) Jl 91, p. 106.
"Departure." [DenQ] (25:4) Spr 91, p. 37.
"Dirt Road." [OhioR] (47) 91, p. 40.
"Graded Paper." [MichQR] (30:2) Spr 91, p. 334-335.
"Harris Lumber." [ParisR] (33:118) Spr 91, p. 27.
"He sat in a given place at a given time feeling and thinking." [OhioR] (47) 91, p.
42.
"Installment." [OhioR] (47) 91, p. 41.
"Joan Armatrading." [CimR] (96) Jl 91, p. 107.
"Lionel Trilling." [MissR] (19:3) 91, p. 170-171.
"Location." [Poetry] (158:4) Jl 91, p. 187-188.
"New New Poetics." [PassN] (12:2) Wint 91, p. 3.
"New Wife." [Agni] (33) 91, p. 57-58.
"Pasco, Barbara." [Agni] (33) 91, p. 59-61.
"Rosanna." [Ploughs] (17:2/3) Fall 91, p. 172.

"Skirt." [ParisR] (33:118) Spr 91, p. 28.
"The Turn." [DenQ] (26:2) Fall 91, p. 17-18.
2428. HALLMUNDSSON, Hallberg
"Empty Wait the Paths" (tr. of Snorri Hjartarson). [Vis] (37) 91, p. 38.
"Flotsam" (tr. of Snorri Hjartarson). [Vis] (37) 91, p. 38.
"I Am So Big" (tr. of Jon ur Vor). [Vis] (37) 91, p. 36.
"Lifelong Journey" (tr. of Hannes Sigfusson). [Vis] (37) 91, p. 40.
"Sailboats." [Vis] (37) 91, p. 39.
"What Were You Born For?" (tr. of Jon ur Vor). [Vis] (37) 91, p. 36.
"The Woodcarving Demon" (tr. of Gyrdir Eliasson). [Vis] (37) 91, p. 37.
2429. HALMAN, Talat
"Are We Going to Live Without Aging?" (tr. of Melih Cevdet Anday). [Talisman] (6)
    Spr 91, p. 105-106.
"Barefoot" (tr. of Melih Cevdet Anday). [Talisman] (6) Spr 91, p. 106.
"The Battle of Kadesh" (tr. of Melih Cevdet Anday). [Talisman] (6) Spr 91, p. 104.
"Bird's Eye View" (tr. of Ozdemir Ince). [Talisman] (6) Spr 91, p. 113.
"The Future" (tr. of Melih Cevdet Anday). [Talisman] (6) Spr 91, p. 105.
"Gypsies" (tr. of Melih Cevdet Anday). [Talisman] (6) Spr 91, p. 106.
"I Became a Tree" (tr. of Melih Cevdet Anday). [Talisman] (6) Spr 91, p. 105.
"In May" (tr. of Ferit Edgu). [Vis] (35) 91, p. 18.
"Poet's Nonalignment" (tr. of Ozdemir Ince). [Talisman] (6) Spr 91, p. 113.
"To Die One Night" (tr. of Ebubekir Eroglu). [Vis] (35) 91, p. 35.
"Vertigo" (tr. of Melih Cevdet Anday). [Talisman] (6) Spr 91, p. 104.
2430. HALME, Kathleen
"Aspirants and Postulants." [MichQR] (30:3) Sum 91, p. 481-483.
"In a Rooming House for Women Only." [BostonR] (16:5) O 91, p. 12.
"In Situ." [BostonR] (16:5) O 91, p. 12.
"A Small Red Parcel." [BostonR] (16:5) O 91, p. 12.
"Something New." [BostonR] (16:5) O 91, p. 12.
2431. HALOVANIC, Patricia
"Afternoon Delight." [Kaleid] (23) Sum-Fall 91, p. 30.
2432. HALPERIN, Joan
"Examination." [NewYorkQ] (46) 91, p. 52.
2433. HALPERIN, Mark
"Orphans." [Iowa] (21:2) Spr-Sum 91, p. 89.
"Returning Home." [Agni] (34) 91, p. 157-158.
"Time as Distance." [SenR] (21:1) Spr 91, p. 37-38.
"What Every Traveler Knows." [Iowa] (21:2) Spr-Sum 91, p. 90.
2434. HALPERN, Daniel
"Argument." [WestHR] (45:4) Wint 91, p. 278.
"Clumsy Gratitude." [SouthernR] (27:2) Ap 91, p. 301-302.
"Collectors." [GrahamHR] (15) Fall 91, p. 82-83.
"Dead Birds." [Boulevard] (6:2/3, #17/18) Fall 91, p. 138-140.
"For the Unidentified." [TriQ] (81) Spr-Sum 91, p. 185-186.
"Foreign Neon." [Boulevard] (6:2/3, #17/18) Fall 91, p. 141-142.
"Foreign Neon" (Selections: 3 poems). [OntR] (35) Fall-Wint 91-92, p. 38-48.
"Infidelities." [ParisR] (33:119) Sum 91, p. 124-130.
"Jerry." [Ploughs] (17:4) Wint 91-92, p. 130-131.
"Last Dance." [TriQ] (81) Spr-Sum 91, p. 187-189.
"Metaphysical." [NewYorker] (67:15) 3 Je 91, p. 38.
"Muriel." [Ploughs] (17:4) Wint 91-92, p. 126-127.
"The Name." [Ploughs] (17:4) Wint 91-92, p. 128-129.
"Tokens of Exchange." [GrahamHR] (15) Fall 91, p. 81.
2435. HALPERN, Reuben
"On Measure." [ChangingM] (22) Wint-Spr 91, p. 13.
2436. HALSALL, Jalaine
"Swan." [NewYorkQ] (44) 91, p. 71-72.
2437. HALSEY, Alan
"Table Talk." [NewAW] (8/9) Fall 91, p. 97-101.
2438. HAMBERGER, Robert
"The Gift." [Verse] (8:2) Sum 91, p. 101.
2439. HAMBLIN, Robert
"Farm Mother." [CapeR] (26:1) Spr 91, p. 8-9.
2440. HAMBRICK, Myra
"Directive to the Old Ones." [IndR] (14:3) Fall 91, p. 35-36.
"The Island Women." [IndR] (14:3) Fall 91, p. 37-38.

2441. HAMERSKI, Susan Thurston
"Catalpa Ghazal." [Sidewalks] (1) Aug 91, p. 7.
"Joanne's Birthday Breakfast." [RagMag] (9:2) 91, p. 17.
"My Mother's Body." [RagMag] (9:2) 91, p. 15.
"One Thing to Watch For." [RagMag] (9:2) 91, p. 16.
"Wild Bone Season." [Sidewalks] (1) Aug 91, p. 8-9.
2442. HAMIDI, Ahmad
"Let Me Think" (tr. of Faiz Ahmed Faiz, w. Naomi Lazard). [Trans] (25) Spr 91, p.
212-213.
2443. HAMILL, Janet
"Friendship with the Virign." [Abraxas] (40/41) 91, p. 138.
"Metaphysical Interior." [Abraxas] (40/41) 91, p. 137.
2444. HAMILL, Paul J.
"Triage: An Essay." [GeoR] (45:3) Fall 91, p. 463-469.
2445. HAMILL, Sam
"Although spring returns" (tr. of anonymous Japanese poem). [ColR] (NS 17:2)
Fall-Wint 90, p. 20.
"Approaching midnight" (tr. of Ki no Tsurayuki (ca., 872-945). [ColR] (NS 17:2)
Fall-Wint 90, p. 19.
"Autumn has returned" (tr. of anonymous Japanese poem). [ColR] (NS 17:2)
Fall-Wint 90, p. 19.
"Autumn's consequence" (tr. of anonymous Japanese poem). [ColR] (NS 17:2)
Fall-Wint 90, p. 21.
"Cicadas sing" (tr. of anonymous Japanese poem). [ColR] (NS 17:2) Fall-Wint 90,
p. 22.
"Crossing open fields" (tr. of Naga Okimaro, 702). [ColR] (NS 17:2) Fall-Wint 90,
p. 16.
"Dawn has almost come" (tr. of Kiyowara Fukuyabu, 900-930). [ColR] (NS 17:2)
Fall-Wint 90, p. 20.
"Don't let that cold wind" (tr. of anonymous Japanese poem). [ColR] (NS 17:2)
Fall-Wint 90, p. 19.
"Dusk, the Omi Sea" (tr. of Kakinomoto no Hitomaro, 681-729). [ColR] (NS 17:2)
Fall-Wint 90, p. 17.
"The flowers have bloomed" (tr. of Ono no Komachi, ca. 850). [ColR] (NS 17:2)
Fall-Wint 90, p. 19.
"Hearing cicadas" (tr. of anonymous Japanese poem). [ColR] (NS 17:2) Fall-Wint
90, p. 22.
"Hold on a moment" (tr. of Mikuni no Machi). [ColR] (NS 17:2) Fall-Wint 90, p.
18.
"How does it happen?" (tr. of the priest Tsukan, ca. 710). [ColR] (NS 17:2)
Fall-Wint 90, p. 17.
"How mysterious!" (tr. of the monk Henjo, 816-890). [ColR] (NS 17:2) Fall-Wint
90, p. 20.
"I pin to my sleeve" (tr. of Otomo, Tabito, ca. 730). [ColR] (NS 17:2) Fall-Wint 90,
p. 17.
"I see you only" (tr. of Otomo, Yakamochi, ca. 739). [ColR] (NS 17:2) Fall-Wint
90, p. 18.
"If pressed to compare" (tr. of the priest Mansei, ca. 730). [ColR] (NS 17:2)
Fall-Wint 90, p. 17.
"I'm wearing your robe" (tr. of Otomo, Yakamochi, ca. 739). [ColR] (NS 17:2)
Fall-Wint 90, p. 18.
"In bare autumn fields" (tr. of anonymous Japanese poem). [ColR] (NS 17:2)
Fall-Wint 90, p. 22.
"In summer mountains" (tr. of Ki no Akimine). [ColR] (NS 17:2) Fall-Wint 90, p.
19.
"In the high bare limbs" (tr. of anonymous Japanese poem). [ColR] (NS 17:2)
Fall-Wint 90, p. 21.
"Lonely cricket-cries" (tr. of Fujiwara Tadafusa, d. 928). [ColR] (NS 17:2)
Fall-Wint 90, p. 21.
"Looking at the moon" (tr. of Oe no Chisato, ca. 825). [ColR] (NS 17:2) Fall-Wint
90, p. 21.
"Mandala" (Selections: 6 poems). [Ploughs] (17:1) Spr 91, p. 76-81.
"Melancholy days" (tr. of Takayasu, Oshima, ca. 705). [ColR] (NS 17:2) Fall-Wint
90, p. 16.
"My rocky journey" (tr. of anonymous Japanese poem, Man 'yoshu 1165). [ColR]
(NS 17:2) Fall-Wint 90, p. 16.

"No one ever traced" (tr. of anonymous Japanese poem). [ColR] (NS 17:2)
    Fall-Wint 90, p. 21.
"Now that nights grow cold" (tr. of Princess Yoza, ca. 702). [ColR] (NS 17:2)
    Fall-Wint 90, p. 16.
"Poetic justice?" (tr. of the monk Sosei, ca. 890). [ColR] (NS 17:2) Fall-Wint 90,
    p. 20.
"Sappho" (tr. of Sappho). [TriQ] (81) Spr-Sum 91, p. 243-245.
"So high in the mountains" (tr. of anonymous Japanese poem). [ColR] (NS 17:2)
    Fall-Wint 90, p. 20.
"This world of exile" (tr. of Prince Omi, 676). [ColR] (NS 17:2) Fall-Wint 90, p.
    16.
"To one who wanders" (tr. of Kakinomoto no Hitomaro, 681-729). [ColR] (NS
    17:2) Fall-Wint 90, p. 18.
"Wanting to preserve" (tr. of Kyogoku Tamekane, 1254-1332). [ColR] (NS 17:2)
    Fall-Wint 90, p. 15.
"When my wife left home" (tr. of Otomo, Yakamochi, ca. 739). [ColR] (NS 17:2)
    Fall-Wint 90, p. 18.
"The white plum blossoms" (tr. of Kakinomoto no Hitomaro, 681-729). [ColR] (NS
    17:2) Fall-Wint 90, p. 17.
Excerpts (tr. of Alkaios). [WillowS] (28) Sum 91, p. 66-69.
2446. HAMILTON, Alfred Starr
    "An Apple and the Sun." [JINJPo] (13:2) Aut 91, p. 24.
    "Chimes." [JINJPo] (13:2) Aut 91, p. 23.
    "Chimpanzee." [Epoch] (40:3) 91, p. 263.
    "Daylights." [JINJPo] (13:2) Aut 91, p. 25.
    "Indelible Pencil." [Epoch] (40:1) 91, p. 5.
    "The Sixth Grade Reader." [JINJPo] (13:2) Aut 91, p. 22.
2447. HAMILTON, Fritz
    "All Over My." [GreenMR] (NS 5:1) Sum-Fall 91, p. 64-65.
    "As I See It!" [GreenMR] (NS 5:1) Sum-Fall 91, p. 63.
    "Because It's Not" (for Pamela). [MidwQ] (33:1) Aut 91, p. 64.
    "The Dark Fire of." [SmPd] (28:3, #83) Fall 91, p. 29.
    "Discovering America!" [SmPd] (28:2, #82) Spr 91, p. 17.
    "Getting My Kicks at the Newspaper Machine." [PoetryE] (32) Fall 91, p. 127.
    "I Wonder." [MidwQ] (33:1) Aut 91, p. 65-66.
    "Noble Search." [WindO] (54) Sum 91, p. 37-38.
    "Plowing." [HawaiiR] (16:1, #34) Wint 91-92, p. 105.
    "Possum Playing / No Game!" [PikeF] (10) Spr 91, p. 8.
    "Rough Descent." [GreenMR] (NS 5:1) Sum-Fall 91, p. 61-62.
    "To Help Her!" [SmPd] (28:2, #82) Spr 91, p. 18.
    "Upon Staring at Van Gogh's Wheatland with Crows" (for Pamela). [Kaleid] (22)
        Wint-Spr 91, p. 30.
    "Winos & Children." [SmPd] (28:2, #82) Spr 91, p. 17.
2448. HAMILTON, J. A.
    "Forecast" (for Brook). [AmerV] (24) Fall 91, p. 48-49.
2449. HAMILTON, Jeff
    "The Aura of Distant Objects." [RiverS] (34) 91, p. 39.
    "Broken Off Correspondence." [BlackWR] (18:1) Fall-Wint 91, p. 56.
    "Politics." [RiverS] (34) 91, p. 40.
2450. HAMILTON, Judith
    "Poem Teacha" (for Tony McNeill, Mervyn Morris & Dennis Scott). [GrahamHR]
        (14) Spr 91, p. 54-55.
2451. HAMMER, Patrick, Jr.
    "Ask a Miracle." [Vis] (35) 91, p. 29.
    "Nitrous Oxide and a Plume or Two." [JINJPo] (13:2) Aut 91, p. 20.
    "Permutations." [JINJPo] (13:2) Aut 91, p. 19.
2452. HAMMOND, Catherine
    "The Whale Hanna and the Ferry Voksa." [YellowS] (37) Fall-Wint 91, p. 7.
2453. HAMMOND, Mary Stewart
    "Canaan." [Field] (45) Fall 91, p. 80-82.
    "My Mother-in-law Sailing." [ParisR] (33:120) Fall 91, p. 208-209.
    "Positive Thinking." [Field] (45) Fall 91, p. 85.
    "Praying for Separation." [Boulevard] (6:2/3, #17/18) Fall 91, p. 204-205.
    "Second Sight." [AmerPoR] (20:6) N-D 91, p. 37.
    "Snowbound in a Summer House off the Coast of Massachusetts." [Boulevard]
        (6:2/3, #17/18) Fall 91, p. 202-203.

"Triptych with Missing Madonna." [Boulevard] (6:2/3, #17/18) Fall 91, p. 206-209.
"World Without End." [Field] (45) Fall 91, p. 83-84.
2454. HAMMOND, Terri
"Sparking on Todhunter Hill." [Writer] (104:3) Mr 91, p. 21.
2455. HANAN, Deborah
"LVI. In China, the corners of the bronze statuary lions' mouths curve upward."
[Antaeus] (67) Fall 91, p. 193.
"After Hardship." [Antaeus] (67) Fall 91, p. 198.
"Don." [Antaeus] (67) Fall 91, p. 198.
"Fragment." [Antaeus] (67) Fall 91, p. 197.
"A Girl's Sex." [Antaeus] (67) Fall 91, p. 197.
"Manchurian Fugue." [Antaeus] (67) Fall 91, p. 194.
"Slate Juncos" (For Don). [Antaeus] (67) Fall 91, p. 196.
"Unlike Anything." [Antaeus] (67) Fall 91, p. 195.
"Walking Through Rough Wall." [Antaeus] (67) Fall 91, p. 195.
2456. HANDLER, Joan Cusack
"4 A.M. Phone Call from My Father-in-Law." [US1] (24/25) Spr 91, p. 10.
2457. HANDLIN, Jim
"Father, You Learn to Die." [Spirit] (11) 91, p. 253.
2458. HANDY, Nixeon Civille
"Face Says Yes to Picasso." [DustyD] (2:1) Ja 91, p. 23.
2459. HANE, Norman
"One for *Los Caribeños* — Juan, Virgilio, Hector." [PoetC] (22:2) Wint 91, p. 18.
2460. HANEBURY, Derek
"Clues." [PraF] (12:4) Wint 91-92, p. 73.
"Heat Squeezes Landscape." [PraF] (12:4) Wint 91-92, p. 72.
HANFF, Aaron Yamada
See YAMADA-HANFF, Aaron
2461. HANG, Dong
"The Woman Strange to Me" (tr. by Zhang Yichun). [GreenMR] (NS 4:2) Wint-Spr
91, p. 104.
2462. HANIFAN, Jill
"Organum: Plainsong and Counterpoint." [HeavenB] (9) Wint-Spr 91-92, p. 34.
2463. HANKINS, Liz Porter
"Wapanocca Lake." [Vis] (35) 91, p. 23.
2464. HANKLA, Cathryn
"Morning Half-Light." [ColEng] (53:1) Ja 91, p. 35.
"A Way to Dance." [ColEng] (53:1) Ja 91, p. 36.
2465. HANLEY, Aedan Alexander
"Bullhead Fishing on Lac la Belle." [PoetC] (23:1) Fall 91, p. 14.
2466. HANLEY, Shannon
"Japanese Spring." [LullwaterR] (3:1) Fall 91, p. 28-29.
2467. HANNON, Michael
"And Angels." [Manoa] (3:2) Fall 91, p. 17-19.
2468. HANOSKI, Evelyn
"My Weird Uncle Ralph." [Dandel] (18:1) Spr-Sum 91, p. 28.
2469. HANSEN, Paul
"Out on the Lake Returning Late" (tr. of Lin Ho-ching). [LitR] (35:1) Fall 91, p. 72.
"A Recluse on Orphan Mountain" (tr. of Lin Ho-ching). [LitR] (35:1) Fall 91, p. 72.
2470. HANSEN, Tom
"Prolegomenon to Any Future Metaphysics" (drawing by Christopher, age 5).
[CrabCR] (7:2) Sum 91, p. 23.
"Variations on Kant's *Prolegomena*." [LitR] (34:2) Wint 91, p. 170-171.
2471. HANSEN, Twyla
"Garbage." [WestB] (28) 91, p. 95-96.
"The Pine Grove." [LaurelR] (25:1) Wint 91, p. 26.
"Spring." [LaurelR] (25:1) Wint 91, p. 27.
2472. HANSON, Charles
"Blond." [NorthStoneR] (10) Fall 91-Wint 92, p. 201.
"The Kiss." [NorthStoneR] (10) Fall 91-Wint 92, p. 200.
2473. HANSON, Elizabeth
"Old Mortality." [Elf] (1:3) Fall 91, p. 42.
2474. HANSON, Harold P.
"Departure" (tr. of Stein Mehren). [Vis] (37) 91, p. 46.
"In My Opinion" (tr. of Jan Erik Vold). [Vis] (37) 91, p. 44.
"Not All Caresses" (tr. of Jan Erik Vold). [Vis] (37) 91, p. 44.

"Summer-Song" (tr. of Jan Erik Vold). [Vis] (37) 91, p. 43.
"Time" (tr. of Gunvor Hofmo). [Vis] (37) 91, p. 45.
2475. HANSON, Julie (Julie Jordan)
"Evolution." [ThRiPo] (37/38) 91, p. 55.
"Hurdle." [Colum] (17) Fall 91, p. 163.
"Star Island." [ThRiPo] (37/38) 91, p. 54.
"Under Lights, Early February." [WestB] (29) 91, p. 91.
2476. HANSON, Kenneth O.
"Last Acts." [Interim] (10:1) Spr-Sum 91, p. 34-35.
"Small Ode on Greek Beans." [Interim] (10:1) Spr-Sum 91, p. 35.
2477. HANZIMANOLIS, Margaret
"By the Fountain, in the Garden." [MidAR] (11:1) 91, p. 212-213.
"Giraud, in the Meditation Cell." [MidAR] (11:1) 91, p. 211.
"I Am Further, Father, From You Now than Ever." [MidAR] (11:1) 91, p. 214-215.
2478. HARD, Rock
"Kiss in the Wind." [EmeraldCR] (3) 91, c1990, p. 130-132.
2479. HARDER, Dan
"Searching the palpable patterns." [PoetryUSA] (23) Sum 91, p. 9.
"Suddenly (Not only does it pierce) a thought." [PoetryUSA] (23) Sum 91, p. 8.
2480. HARDIN, Jeff
"Names." [PoetC] (22:2) Wint 91, p. 19-20.
2481. HARDING, Deborah
"Death in the Dressing Room Mirror." [Calyx] (13:3) Wint 91-92, p. 5.
"Late." [MichQR] (30:1) Wint 91, p. 173.
2482. HARDING-RUSSELL, Gillian
"Pink Eye and Yellow Throat" (for my husband). [Dandel] (18:2) Wint 91, p. 61-62.
2483. HARDMAN, Katherine Reeves
"Fourth of July." [EmeraldCR] (4) 91, p. 47.
"Pool of Inversion." [EmeraldCR] (3) 91, c1990, p. 89-90.
2484. HARDMAN, Thomas
"Help Wanted." [EmeraldCR] (3) 91, c1990, p. 118-119.
"This Is Costing Your Government Money." [EmeraldCR] (3) 91, c1990, p. 119-121.
2485. HARDY, Jan
"The Bath." [Calyx] (13:3) Wint 91-92, p. 14-15.
2486. HARDY, Thomas
"In Front of the Landscape." [SouthernR] (27:3) Jl 91, p. 551-553.
"In the Moonlight." [SouthernR] (27:3) Jl 91, p. 549-550.
"Where the Picnic Was." [SouthernR] (27:3) Jl 91, p. 548-549.
2487. HARER, Katharine
"After the Chiropractor." [OnTheBus] (8/9) 91, p. 82.
"Hazards" (or The Death Agony of Capitalism). [OnTheBus] (8/9) 91, p. 82-83.
2488. HARING, Cynthia
"The Kiss." [NorthStoneR] (10) Fall 91-Wint 92, p. 83.
"Thanatopsis Tells the Truth." [NorthStoneR] (10) Fall 91-Wint 92, p. 78-82.
2489. HARJO, Joy
"Heartshed" (for Lajuana). [SinW] (43/44) Sum 91, p. 209-210.
"The Myth of Blackbirds." [KenR] (NS 13:4) Fall 91, p. 134-135.
2490. HARLEY, Peter
"Be We." [TickleAce] (22) Fall-Wint 91, p. 69.
"Outside the Music Building." [TickleAce] (22) Fall-Wint 91, p. 67.
"Sketch." [TickleAce] (22) Fall-Wint 91, p. 68.
2491. HARMON, William
"Heav'n Is Musick" (Campion). [Ploughs] (17:1) Spr 91, p. 82-83.
"Prose Song: Somebody medieval — the celebrated Anonymous of Bologna."
[Ploughs] (17:1) Spr 91, p. 85.
"Prose Song: this dictionary here calls scorpions." [Ploughs] (17:1) Spr 91, p. 83-84.
2492. HARMS, James
"At the Rally to Protest." [PassN] (12:2) Wint 91, p. 4.
"Days Before Grace." [Journal] (15:1) Spr 91, p. 60-61.
"Explaining the Evening News to Corbyn" (after Ben Watt). [KenR] (NS 13:1) Wint 91, p. 49-50.
"If All of Us Worry." [PassN] (12:2) Wint 91, p. 27.
"Isabelle's Sister." [ThRiPo] (37/38) 91, p. 34-35.
"Serious Affection." [KenR] (NS 13:1) Wint 91, p. 52-53.

"So Long Lonely Avenue." [ThRiPo] (37/38) 91, p. 32-33.
"When You Wish Upon a Star That Turns into a Plane." [KenR] (NS 13:1) Wint 91, p. 51-52.
2493. HARNACK, Curtis
"Near the Mediterranean." [AmerPoR] (20:1) Ja-F 91, p. 32.
"On the Face of the Earth." [AmerPoR] (20:1) Ja-F 91, p. 32.
2494. HARNETT, Gerald
"The Lost Knight: An Idyll." [Hellas] (2:2) Fall 91, p. 193.
"The Lost Knight: an Idyll." [Sequoia] (34:1) Spr 91, p. 75.
"The Men of Mars." [Hellas] (2:2) Fall 91, p. 194.
2495. HARP, Jerry
"A Letter from the Castle." [Pig] (17) 91, p. 56.
2496. HARPER, Linda Lee
"Merline Swears." [GeoR] (45:4) Wint 91, p. 705.
2497. HARPER, Zo
"In the Valley of Shame." [DustyD] Je 91, p. 23.
2498. HARPOOTIAN, Alysia (Alysia K.)
"Blue Bead." [GrahamHR] (15) Fall 91, p. 42.
"Exchange." [ChamLR] (8-9) Spr-Fall 91, p. 121.
"How I Got to Like." [Parting] (4:2) Wint 91-92, p. 6.
"Imagine an apartment twice the size of your tool shed." [GrahamHR] (15) Fall 91, p. 41.
"It Is Easy to Get What You Did Not Ask For." [Parting] (4:2) Wint 91-92, p. 6.
"The Silence Was From What They Had Seen." [ChamLR] (8-9) Spr-Fall 91, p. 120.
"They Said Her Dress Was Red Then Pink." [Prima] (14/15) 91, p. 29.
"Using Your Word." [PoetryE] (31) Spr 91, p. 117.
"Yes I'd." [PoetryE] (31) Spr 91, p. 118.
2499. HARRIS, Gail
"An Effigy of You." (Excerpts). [CapilR] (2:6/7) Fall 91, p. 189-192.
2500. HARRIS, James
"Bristlecone at Timberline." [SouthwR] (76:4) Aut 91, p. 510.
"In Route." [Crazy] (40) Spr 91, p. 50-51.
2501. HARRIS, Jana
"The Great Mother." [SingHM] (19) 91, p. 40-42.
"The Temple of My Discontent." [OntR] (34) Spr-Sum 91, p. 21-23.
"Who Done It?" [SouthernPR] (31:1) Spr 91, p. 30-32.
2502. HARRIS, Jean
"Love and Such." [EmeraldCR] (4) 91, p. 50-51.
2503. HARRIS, John Sterling
"Desert." [TarRP] (31:1) Fall 91, p. 39.
"I Find Green." [TarRP] (31:1) Fall 91, p. 40.
"Soldiers of the Legion." [TarRP] (31:1) Fall 91, p. 41.
2504. HARRIS, Joseph
"Edward Hopper's U.S.A." [TexasR] (11:1/2) Spr-Sum 90, p. 29.
2505. HARRIS, Lynn Farmer
"Spring in Knoxville." [LullwaterR] (3:1) Fall 91, p. 65-69.
2506. HARRIS, Marie
"Peacetime." [HangL] (59) 91, p. 33.
"Physics One." [Spirit] (11) 91, p. 278.
"Standard Plumbing." [HangL] (59) 91, p. 33.
HARRIS, Robert Dassanowsky
    See DASSANOWSKY-HARRIS, Robert
2507. HARRIS, Stuart E.
"Faith's Barn." [WestB] (29) 91, p. 64-65.
2508. HARRISON, Devin
"Estate Auctions." [SoDakR] (29:3 part 2) Aut 91, p. 101-102.
"Letter." [Grain] (19:2) Sum 91, p. 119.
"X-Ray." [Grain] (19:2) Sum 91, p. 118.
2509. HARRISON, Jeffrey
"Brief History of an Atlas." [NewYorker] (67:41) 2 D 91, p. 44.
"Mycology." [Poetry] (159:1) O 91, p. 12-13.
"Poem from My Mother's Point of View." [SouthernR] (27:3) Jl 91, p. 685-686.
2510. HARRISON, Jennifer
"Railway." [Abraxas] (40/41) 91, p. 140.
"Television." [AnthNEW] (3) 91, p. 21.

2511. HARRISON, Pamela
"So, Caravaggio." [Poetry] (157:6) Mr 91, p. 322.
2512. HARRISON, Richard
"Batman." [MalR] (96) Fall 91, p. 65.
"Hysterectomy." [MalR] (96) Fall 91, p. 66-67.
"I Wanted to Be a Soldier." [Quarry] (40:4) Fall 91, p. 48-49.
"Soldiers Sleeping in One Another's Arms." [MalR] (96) Fall 91, p. 64.
"The Suicide." [Arc] (26) Spr 91, p. 63.
2513. HARRISON, Tony
"Initial Illumination." [Verse] (8:2) Sum 91, p. 94.
2514. HARROD, Lois Marie
"Artifacts." [JINJPo] (13:1) Spr 91, p. 18-19.
"Endymion." [Vis] (35) 91, p. 40.
"High Places." [US1] (24/25) Spr 91, p. 26.
"Mackinaw Wool Vest." [SnailPR] (1:2) Fall 91-Wint 92, p. 25.
"Sadness." [JINJPo] (13:1) Spr 91, p. 17.
"Whites." [CarolQ] (44:1) Fall 91, p. 48.
2515. HARROLD, William
"Jack Frost's Text." [CreamCR] (14:2) Wint 91, p. 168-170.
2516. HARRY, David
"Astoria" (tr. of Eva Runefelt). [Vis] (37) 91, p. 54.
"I Am Steinkind" (tr. of Eva Strom). [Vis] (37) 91, p. 55.
"Love Poem (Rome)" (tr. of Eva Runefelt). [Vis] (37) 91, p. 53-54.
"Summer Body" (tr. of Anna Rydstedt). [Vis] (37) 91, p. 55.
2517. HARRYMAN, Carla
"The Wide Road" (Excerpt, with Lyn Hejinian). [Aerial] (6/7) 91, p. 163-164.
2518. HARSHMAN, Marc
"Between Low Gap and Ramon" (for Jean Haley). [SycamoreR] (3:1) Wint 91, p.
18-19.
2519. HART, Barbara Fritchie
"The Legacy." [Colum] (15) 90, p. 184.
2520. HART, Henry
"The City." [Salm] (90/91) Spr-Sum 91, p. 84-85.
"Icarus on Stone Mountain." [Poetry] (158:3) Je 91, p. 135.
"Norwegian Wharf Rats." [Salm] (90/91) Spr-Sum 91, p. 82-83.
2521. HART, Jack
"Classroom Study." [Hellas] (2:1) Spr 91, p. 69.
"How to Lose Your Ass" (from Babrius). [Hellas] (2:2) Fall 91, p. 261.
"A Lesson for Us All." [Hellas] (2:2) Fall 91, p. 262.
"Mad Scientist." [Vis] (35) 91, p. 31.
"Midterm." [FourQ] (5:1) Spr 91, p. 24.
"Strap Lines." [Hellas] (2:2) Fall 91, p. 263.
"Tullia." [Hellas] (2:1) Spr 91, p. 68-69.
2522. HART, Joanne
"Ma-Ni-Do Gee-Zhi-Gance." [SoDakR] (29:1) Spr 91, p. 150-151.
2523. HART, William
"Old grave." [BlackBR] (13) Spr-Sum 91, p. 10.
2524. HARTER, Penny
"A Dream of Stars." [US1] (24/25) Spr 91, p. 3.
2525. HARTMAN, Melissa
"In the Garden of the Cathedral of St. John the Divine." [Interim] (10:1) Spr-Sum
91, p. 7.
2526. HARTOG, Diana
"Butterfly." [MalR] (94) Spr 91, p. 12.
"Dragons." [MalR] (94) Spr 91, p. 7.
"Griffin." [MalR] (94) Spr 91, p. 5.
"Mosquito." [MalR] (94) Spr 91, p. 6.
"Snake." [MalR] (94) Spr 91, p. 9-10.
"Spider." [MalR] (94) Spr 91, p. 8.
"Sturgeon." [MalR] (94) Spr 91, p. 11.
2527. HARVEY, Andrew
"About the War." [NewYorkQ] (46) 91, p. 47.
2528. HARVEY, Gayle Elen
"After Bach's 'Partita #2 for Unaccompanied Violin'" (for David). [YellowS] (38)
Wint-Spr 91-92, p. 13.
"Among All Instruments" (for David). [YellowS] (38) Wint-Spr 91-92, p. 13.

"Another Man." [ChironR] (10:3) Aut 91, p. 37.
"It Matters. September's Dalliance" (For George Mosby, Jr., 1950-1989).
    [PoetryNW] (32:3) Aut 91, p. 15-16.
"Then, As Now (after a Photograph)." [ChironR] (10:4) Wint 91, p. 34.
"Three Egrets." [SoCoast] (10) Fall 91, p. 37.
"To Exist Is to Continue." [PoetryNW] (32:3) Aut 91, p. 16.

2529. HARVEY, John
"Outside the Blaffer Gallery." [WestHR] (45:4) Wint 91, p. 335.
"Utopia." [WestHR] (45:4) Wint 91, p. 334.

2530. HARVEY, Matt
"Attic Martins." [Plain] (12:2) Wint 91, p. 26-27.

2531. HARVEY, Richard F.
"Portrait of the Dog as a Young Artist." [ChironR] (10:2) Sum 91, p. 45.

2532. HARVOR, Elisabeth
"Bloom, Rain." [Arc] (26) Spr 91, p. 37-39.
"Burning Hammock, 1917." [OntR] (34) Spr-Sum 91, p. 88-91.
"How Long Will It Last?" [MalR] (96) Fall 91, p. 72-74.
"Living with Poets." [Event] (20:1) Spr 91, p. 77.
"Madam Abundance." [Event] (20:1) Spr 91, p. 73-76.
"The Street Where We Lived." [Event] (20:1) Spr 91, p. 78-81.

2533. HARWOOD, Lee
"African Violets" (for Pansy Harwood, my grandmother, 1896-1989). [NewAW]
    (8/9) Fall 91, p. 104-106.
"The Rowan Tree" (for Rowan Harwood). [NewAW] (8/9) Fall 91, p. 102-103.
"Tao-Yun Meets Sandy Berrigan." [NewAW] (8/9) Fall 91, p. 103-104.

2534. HASA
"Dusting her body with ash from the burning ground" (from the "Sattasai," tr. by
    Andrew Schelling). [Talisman] (6) Spr 91, p. 24.

2535. HASAN, Rabiul
"Grasp." [ContextS] (2:1) 91, p. 11.
"The Mermaid." [ContextS] (2:1) 91, p. 11.

2536. HASHIMOTO, Sharon
"The Mountain Where Old People Are Abandoned." [AmerS] (60:3) Sum 91, p.
    424.

2537. HASHMI, Alamgir
"A Find from the Dead-Letter Office." [Pig] (17) 91, p. 66.
"Lines to Amir." [Pig] (17) 91, p. 66.
"The Woman at the Lahore G.P.O." [Pig] (17) 91, p. 66.

2538. HASKINS, Lola
"The Amateur." [BelPoJ] (42:1) Fall 91, p. 18.
"Bleeding Chunks." [BelPoJ] (42:1) Fall 91, p. 17.
"Camille Descending — Three Sculptures." [CreamCR] (15:1) Spr 91, p. 51-52.
"Keeping the White Hen" (for my daughter). [MidwQ] (32:2) Wint 91, p. 185.
"The Lady Plants a Tree." [LitR] (35:1) Fall 91, p. 53.
"Nocturne" (after Chopin). [BelPoJ] (42:1) Fall 91, p. 19.
"On How the Dappled Pony." [CalQ] (32/33) Spr 90, p. 143.
"Since 1970 the Vigin Mary." [NewYorkQ] (46) 91, p. 37.
"The Storm Flag." [SouthernPR] (31:2) Fall 91, p. 27-28.
"Toning the Felts." [BelPoJ] (42:1) Fall 91, p. 16.
"When Dawn Comes." [CalQ] (32/33) Spr 90, p. 142.

2539. HASLEM, John
"One Town Remains." [Sparrow] (58) Jl 91, p. 23.
"Under the Grandstands." [Sparrow] (58) Jl 91, p. 24.

2540. HASNAT, Farah
"Confusion" (tr. of Parveen Shakir). [Talisman] (6) Spr 91, p. 131.
"Welcome" (tr. of Parveen Shakir). [Vis] (35) 91, p. 42.

2541. HASS, Robert
"Dictionary of Wilno Streets (1967)" (from "Beginning with My Streets," tr. of
    Czeslaw Milosz, w. the author, Robert Pinsky and Renata Gorczynski).
    [ParisR] (33:120) Fall 91, p. 261-263.
"Far Away" (tr. of Czeslaw Milosz, w. the author). [PartR] (58:4) Fall 91, p.
    677-680.
"In Music" (tr. of Czeslaw Milosz, w. the author). [NewYorker] (67:3) 11 Mr 91, p.
    66.
"Lastingness" (tr. of Czeslaw Milosz, w. the author). [Thrpny] (47) Fall 91, p. 27.

"Mister Hanusevich" (tr. of Czeslaw Milosz, w. the author). [NewYorker] (67:34)
14 O 91, p. 62-63.
"My Mother's Nipples." [MichQR] (30:4) Fall 91, p. 573-581.
"A New Province" (tr. of Czeslaw Milosz, w. the author). [Antaeus] (67) Fall 91, p.
100-103.
"On a Beach" (tr. of Czeslaw Milosz, w. the author). [NewYorker] (67:20) 8 Jl 91,
p. 34.
"Philology" (tr. of Czeslaw Milosz, w. the author). [Zyzzyva] (7:3) Fall 91, p.
134-135.
"Reconciliation" (tr. of Czeslaw Milosz, w. the author). [NewYorker] (66:52) 11 F
91, p. 34.
"Tahoe in August." [Manoa] (3:1) Spr 91, p. 218-219.
"Youth" (tr. of Czeslaw Milosz, w. the author). [NewYorker] (67:29) 9 S 91, p. 34.
2542. HASSAN, Ihab
"The Angels." [CreamCR] (15:2) Fall 91, p. 12.
2543. HASSELSTROM, Linda M.
"Staying in One Place." [SoDakR] (29:3 part 2) Aut 91, p. 46.
"Waiting." [SwampR] (7/8) Spr-Sum 91, p. 11-12.
2544. HASSETT, Julie
"The Sacrament" (to my brother). [Pearl] (14) Fall-Wint 91, p. 60.
2545. HASTINGS, Nancy Peters (Nancy Peter)
"On the Delta Queen." [Hellas] (2:1) Spr 91, p. 46.
"Those Things We Do for Our Children." [Plain] (11:2) Wint 91, p. 6.
2546. HATHAWAY, Jeanine
"Translation of Lights" (for my sister, the artist, 1951-1973). [GreensboroR] (50)
Sum 91, p. 115.
2547. HATHAWAY, Michael
"The Feminist" (for ljz). [Pearl] (13) Spr-Sum 91, p. 58.
2548. HATHAWAY, William
"After the Beep." [LaurelR] (25:1) Wint 91, p. 44-45.
"Attention Shoppers." [Ascent] (15:2) Wint 91, p. 46.
"A Cock for Asclepius." [GettyR] (4:4) Aut 91, p. 682-683.
"Compounded Interest." [Paint] (18:36) Aut 91, p. 14-15.
"Fall Reunion." [Paint] (18:36) Aut 91, p. 12-13.
"Lost Toys of Justice." [GettyR] (4:4) Aut 91, p. 680-681.
"The Mute Gospel." [AmerPoR] (20:4) Jl-Ag 91, p. 17.
2549. HAUCK, Richard
"Killing Chickens." [EmeraldCR] (3) 91, c1990, p. 10-11.
"Sequence: In the Far Reaches of Color." [EmeraldCR] (3) 91, c1990, p. 54-55.
"Tricycles." [EmeraldCR] (3) 91, c1990, p. 11-12.
2550. HAUG, James
"In the Dream He Had." [QW] (32) Wint-Spr 91, p. 93.
"In the Town of Endless Reduction." [MassR] (32:2) Sum 91, p. 218.
2551. HAUGHN, W. Clifford
"Mercy." [HawaiiR] (16:1, #34) Wint 91-92, p. 18.
2552. HAUSER, Alisa
"Friends." [PoetryUSA] (23) Sum 91, p. 24.
"March 21, 1991." [PoetryUSA] (23) Sum 91, p. 24.
"Sagging Chests." [PoetryUSA] (23) Sum 91, p. 24.
2553. HAUSKEN, Ed
"Gray Morning." [PlumR] (1) Spr-Sum 91, p. 73.
2554. HAVEN, Stephen
"The Flounder." [RiverS] (33) 91, p. 58-59.
"Resuscitating a Fly." [RiverS] (33) 91, p. 60.
2555. HAWK, Gary W.
"Before Christmas Eve." [ChrC] (108:37) 18-25 D 91, p. 1190.
HAWK, Red
See RED HAWK
2556. HAWKER, Heather
"Are You a Boy?" [OxfordM] (7:2) Fall-Wint 91, p. 48-49.
"Ghetto Daddy Slinks Off." [OxfordM] (7:2) Fall-Wint 91, p. 50.
"Zydeco Girls." [PaintedB] (43) 91, p. 7.
2557. HAWKINS, Hunt
"The Great Depression." [GeoR] (45:2) Sum 91, p. 344.
"Pennies." [SouthernR] (27:3) Jl 91, p. 687-688.

2558. HAWKINS, Sheryl T.
        "Recess." [Callaloo] (14:2) Spr 91, p. 549.
2559. HAWKINS, Tom
        "Half a Full Moon." [InterPR] (15:1) Spr 89, p. 95.
        "Landing in the Tropics After Dark." [InterPR] (15:1) Spr 89, p. 95.
        "Owl Woman." [InterPR] (15:1) Spr 89, p. 94.
2560. HAWLEY-MEIGS, James
        "The Girls at the Language Institute: Antigua, Guatemala, July, 1976." [ClockR]
                (7:1/2) 91-92, p. 119.
2561. HAXTON, Brooks
        "Falls." [Atlantic] (268:2) Ag 91, p. 86.
2562. HAYDON, Rich
        "Small Regrets." [CrabCR] (7:3) 91, p. 4.
2563. HAYES, J. Michael
        "Nightmares, Extra, Etc." [PoetryUSA] (23) Sum 91, p. 20.
2564. HAYES, Noreen
        "Communion in the Hand." [SpiritSH] (56) Spr-Sum 91, p. 17.
        "Community." [SpiritSH] (56) Spr-Sum 91, p. 16.
2565. HAYNA, Lois Beebe
        "Afterglow" (Selections. The Pablo Neruda Prize for Poetry, Finalist). [Nimrod]
                (35:1) Fall-Wint 91, p. 116-117.
2566. HAYNES, Robert (Robert E.)
        "Dogs of Reading." [Farm] (8:2) Fall-Wint 91-92, p. 75.
        "Earth Crossers." [ChatR] (11:2) Wint 91, p. 40.
        "One the Surface of the Water" (For Voyager 2). [ChatR] (11:2) Wint 91, p. 39.
        "Thunderstorm Through the Window." [PoetL] (86:2) Sum 91, p. 16.
        "Wings" (For David Sosnowski). [PoetL] (86:2) Sum 91, p. 17.
2567. HAYNES, William P.
        "All About Estelle." [MoodySI] (24/25/26) Spr 91, p. 46.
2568. HAYS, Mary
        "Hilar Adenopathy." [CoalC] (3) My 91, p. 12.
2569. HAYWARD, Amber
        "A Real Doll." [AntigR] (84) Wint 91, p. 129.
        "Wounded Doll." [AntigR] (84) Wint 91, p. 130.
2570. HAYWARD, Camille
        "Because I Could Not Bury You." [BellArk] (7:1) Ja-F 91, p. 7.
        "Thought." [BellArk] (7:1) Ja-F 91, p. 1.
2571. HAYWARD, L. N.
        "The Kill." [DustyD] Je 91, p. 24.
2572. HAZEN, James
        "Jean Giono's *Blue Boy*." [Blueline] (12) 91, p. 58.
        "Karl Marx Greets the Spring." [SoCoast] (10) Fall 91, p. 20.
        "Spring Evening." [HampSPR] Wint 91, p. 26-27.
        "Waiting for the Zinnias" (in memory of BFH). [HampSPR] Wint 91, p. 26.
2573. HAZNERS, Dainis
        "Where the Water Goes." [CrabCR] (7:2) Sum 91, p. 18-19.
2574. HAZO, Samuel
        "All Mirrors Show the World Reversed." [SouthernR] (27:3) Jl 91, p. 679-680.
        "The Best Place in America to Be on Saturdays." [TarRP] (31:1) Fall 91, p. 47-48.
        "The Courage Not to Talk." [Paint] (18:35) Spr 91, p. 13-14.
        "If I Were a Chef, I'd Say." [AmerS] (60:2) Spr 91, p. 258-259.
        "On the Eve of the First Shot." [Paint] (18:35) Spr 91, p. 15.
        "Pipe Dream." [SouthernR] (27:3) Jl 91, p. 683-684.
        "The Real Reason for Going Is Not Just to Get There." [SouthernR] (27:3) Jl 91, p.
                681-683.
        "The Wait When the Patient Is You." [TarRP] (31:1) Fall 91, p. 49-50.
        "War News Viewed in the Tropics." [Paint] (18:35) Spr 91, p. 11-12.
2575. HAZZARD, Melvina
        "Spit of Shame." [GrahamHR] (14) Spr 91, p. 70.
HE, Jiang
        See JIANG, He
HE, Li
        See LI, He
2576. HEAD, Robert
        "Poetry is my calling." [Bogg] (64) 91, p. 54.
        "Waking up the morning after english class is over." [Bogg] (64) 91, p. 10.

"You've Heard All Those Stories About Saturday Night Well They Aren't True."
[ChironR] (10:4) Wint 91, p. 5.
2577. HEADDON, Bill
"Raid." [CoalC] (4) S 91, p. 16.
"Voyeur." [CoalC] (4) S 91, p. 12.
2578. HEANEY, Seamus
"A Basket of Chestnuts." [NewYorker] (67:14) 27 My 91, p. 36.
"Casting and Gathering" (for Ted Hughes). [Field] (44) Spr 91, p. 55.
"The Fair Hill." [NewYorker] (67:10) 29 Ap 91, p. 36.
"Field of Vision." [Field] (44) Spr 91, p. 54.
"Markings." [Field] (44) Spr 91, p. 52-53.
"Punishment." [Crazy] (41) Wint 91, p. 80-81.
"A Royal Prospect." [Thrpny] (46) Sum 91, p. 5.
2579. HEARLE, Kevin
"To Go Home." [NewOR] (18:4) Wint 91, p. 39.
2580. HEARNE, Vicki
"The American Dream" (for Jim Weaver). [BostonR] (16:2) Ap 91, p. 8.
"The Claim of Speech" (for Stanley Cavell). [BostonR] (16:2) Ap 91, p. 8.
"Comparative Enormity." [PartR] (58:1) Wint 91, p. 119-120.
"Fireplaces and Sailboats." [PartR] (58:1) Wint 91, p. 120.
"Huck Finn, Credulous at the Circus." [SouthwR] (76:3) Sum 91, p. 359.
"Intimations of Intimacy." [BostonR] (16:2) Ap 91, p. 8.
"The Moral for Us." [BostonR] (16:2) Ap 91, p. 8.
"The Runner and the Mountain." [NewRep] (204:1/2) 7-14 Ja 91, p. 48.
"St. Luke Painting the Virgin." [Raritan] (10:4) Spr 91, p. 15-17.
"To the Circus." [SouthwR] (76:3) Sum 91, p. 358.
"Touch of Class, or, View from within Any Imperial Riding Academy." [SouthwR]
(76:3) Sum 91, p. 360.
2581. HEARST, James
"What Shall We Do?" [SoDakR] (29:3 part 2) Aut 91, p. 16.
2582. HEATH-STUBBS, John
"Goyesca." [Interim] (10:2) Fall-Wint 91-92, p. 24.
2583. HECHT, Anthony
"A Hill." [GettyR] (4:4) Aut 91, p. 676-677.
2584. HECHT, Roger
"Landscape in a Sentence." [HayF] (9) Fall-Wint 91, p. 91.
2585. HECK, Bessie H.
"Finale." [Nimrod] (34:2) Spr-Sum 91, p. 48.
2586. HEDDEREL, Vance Philip
"Animal Locomotion." [Chelsea] (52) 91, p. 92.
"A Culture and Amorality: The Failure of America." [Ploughs] (17:4) Wint 91-92, p.
29-32.
"L.A.P.D. File Photo." [CapeR] (26:2) Fall 91, p. 44.
2587. HEDDERMAN, Richard
"Ophelia." [NegC] (11:3) 91, p. 22.
2588. HEDIN, Laura
"Appetites." [CoalC] (3) My 91, p. 4.
"Hard Subjects: Preparing for Radcliffe." [Kalliope] (13:2) 91, p. 24.
2589. HEDIN, Robert
"Antenna-Forest" (tr. of Rolf Jacobsen). [WillowS] (27) Wint 91, p. 58.
"Are They Waiting for a Star?" (tr. of Rolf Jacobsen). [CrabCR] (7:2) Sum 91, p.
13.
"Aviation" (tr. of Rolf Jacobsen). [WillowS] (27) Wint 91, p. 59.
"Bridge" (tr. of Rolf Jacobsen). [InterPR] (17:2) Fall 91, p. 37.
"But We Live" (tr. of Rolf Jacobsen). [ColR] (NS 17:2) Fall-Wint 90, p. 101.
"First Night of Frost" (tr. of Stein Mehren). [CrabCR] (7:2) Sum 91, p. 13.
"The May Moon" (tr. of Rolf Jacobsen). [WillowS] (27) Wint 91, p. 60.
"Metro" (tr. of Rolf Jacobsen). [WillowS] (27) Wint 91, p. 61.
"There Was an Old Night" (tr. of Rolf Jacobsen). [InterPR] (17:2) Fall 91, p. 37.
"Warm Park in August" (tr. of Stein Mehren). [InterPR] (17:2) Fall 91, p. 39.
2590. HEFFERNAN, Michael
"The Music of Forgiveness." [WillowS] (28) Sum 91, p. 57-58.
"Requiem." [WillowS] (28) Sum 91, p. 56.
"A Sign from Heaven." [SycamoreR] (3:1) Wint 91, p. 9-10.
2591. HEFFERNAN, Virginia
"Paper Anniversary" (Ars Poetica). [PraS] (65:3) Fall 91, p. 97.

"Water." [PraS] (65:3) Fall 91, p. 97-98.
2592. HEGSTAD, Stephanie
"Grass" (tr. of Rolf Jacobsen, w. Aina Gerner-Mathisen). [Field] (44) Spr 91, p.
39.
"Refugee" (tr. of Rolf Jacobsen, w. Aina Gerner-Mathisen). [Field] (44) Spr 91, p.
40.
"Sky Lab" (tr. of Rolf Jacobsen, w. Aina Gerner-Mathisen). [Field] (44) Spr 91, p.
41.
"Suddenly. In December" (tr. of Rolf Jacobsen, w. Aina Gerner-Mathisen). [Field]
(44) Spr 91, p. 38.
2593. HEIBUTZKI, Ralph
"All My Millions Die in Smithereens." [SlipS] (11) 91, p. 5.
2594. HEIGHTON, Steven
"Near Ephesus." [Arc] (26) Spr 91, p. 86-87.
"Near Ephesus." [Poem] (65) My 91, p. 9.
"Old Lies" (January 16, 1991). [Arc] (26) Spr 91, p. 85.
"Sailing, Gulf Islands." [Poem] (65).My 91, p. 10.
"Scholar As a Child." [CanLit] (129) Sum 91, p. 8.
2595. HEIM, Scott
"Brad, Bottom Drawer." [EvergreenC] (6:2) Sum-Fall 91, p. 38.
"The Day I Learned the F Word." [SpoonRQ] (16:3/4) Sum-Fall 91, p. 23.
"Extractions." [SpoonRQ] (16:3/4) Sum-Fall 91, p. 26.
"Girl No One Knew." [SpoonRQ] (16:3/4) Sum-Fall 91, p. 27.
"The Memory of Fingers." [SpoonRQ] (16:3/4) Sum-Fall 91, p. 24-25.
"Turtle." [MinnR] (NS 37) Fall 91, p. 34-35.
2596. HEINE, Heinrich
"Where?" (tr. by M. T. Gallagher). [SpiritSH] (56) Spr-Sum 91, p. 46.
"You Are Like a Flower" (tr. by M. T. Gallagher). [SpiritSH] (56) Spr-Sum 91, p.
46.
HEINE, Lala Koehn
See KOEHN-HEINE, Lala
2597. HEINE-KOEHN, Lala
"Your Shadow." [Dandel] (18:1) Spr-Sum 91, p. 32.
2598. HEINESEN, William
"Nightmare of the Unknown Soldier" (tr. by Lawrence Millman). [Vis] (37) 91, p.
17.
2599. HEINLEIN, David A.
"Thumbprint." [US1] (24/25) Spr 91, p. 5.
2600. HEINY, Katherine
"About My Mother." [HangL] (59) 91, p. 34.
"At My Grandfather's Funeral." [HangL] (59) 91, p. 34.
2601. HEITZMAN, Judith Page (Judy Page)
"Getting Over the Loss of My Lover." [SoCoast] (11) Wint 91, p. 11.
"March." [ThRiPo] (37/38) 91, p. 57.
"The Schoolroom on the Second Floor of the Knitting Mill." [NewYorker] (67:41) 2
D 91, p. 102.
"Spaces." [ThRiPo] (37/38) 91, p. 56.
2602. HEJINIAN, Lyn
"The Wide Road" (Excerpt, with Carla Harryman). [Aerial] (6/7) 91, p. 163-164.
"Xenia" (Excerpt, tr. of Arkadii Dragomoshchenko, w. Elena Balashova). [GrandS]
(10:4, #40) 91, p. 82-87.
2603. HEKKANEN, Ernest
"Ode to Dad." [Dandel] (18:1) Spr-Sum 91, p. 30.
"Veering Out of Ice." [Event] (20:1) Spr 91, p. 85.
2604. HELD, Dennis
"Impact." [TarRP] (31:1) Fall 91, p. 29-30.
2605. HELLER, Michael
"Creeks in Berkeley." [Archae] (1) Fall 90, p. 20.
"From the Notes." [Manoa] (3:2) Fall 91, p. 200.
"Homan's Etchings." [Archae] (1) Fall 90, p. 21-23.
"Report on the Dispatches." [Talisman] (7) Fall 91, p. 4-5.
"A Terror of Tonality." [Manoa] (3:2) Fall 91, p. 200-201.
2606. HELMSDAL, Gudrid
"Thaw" (tr. by Leyvoy Joensen). [Vis] (37) 91, p. 21.
"To an Old Relative" (tr. by Leyvoy Joensen). [Vis] (37) 91, p. 21.

197

2607. HEMPEL, Elise
"At Grandfather's Funeral Service." [PoetryE] (31) Spr 91, p. 138.
"Birdbath." [PoetryE] (31) Spr 91, p. 137.
"Looking at Michelangelo's St. Matthew (Unfinished)." [PoetryE] (31) Spr 91, p.
136.
2608. HEMPHILL, Essex
"American Wedding." [WashR] (16:5) F-Mr 91, p. 27.
"Family Jewells." [WashR] (16:5) F-Mr 91, p. 23.
"Heavy Breathing" (Excerpt). [WashR] (16:5) F-Mr 91, p. 25.
"To Some Supposed Brothers." [WashR] (16:5) F-Mr 91, p. 26.
"The Tomb of Sorrow" (for Wolf). [Tribe] (1:3) Wint 90, p. 27-39.
2609. HEMSCHEMEYER, Judith
"The Egg Lady." [SnailPR] (1:1) Spr 91, p. 4.
"The Gift of the Magi." [SnailPR] (1:1) Spr 91, p. 5-6.
"The Octaves of Mourning" (Selection: "Her Glance," tr. of Dmitry Bobyshev).
[Agni] (33) 91, p. 49.
2610. HENDERSHOT, Cynthia
"I Want to Play This Lust." [Vis] (36) 91, p. 44.
2611. HENDERSON, Archibald
"Taking Off." [Nimrod] (34:2) Spr-Sum 91, p. 15.
"A Touch of Santa." [Nimrod] (34:2) Spr-Sum 91, p. 16.
2612. HENDERSON, David D.
"Drawing Lightning." [YellowS] (37) Fall-Wint 91, p. 29.
"Luminaria" (For A.W.). [YellowS] (37) Fall-Wint 91, p. 28.
2613. HENDERSON, Donna
"Cataracts." [CutB] (35) Wint-Spr 91, p. 30-31.
2614. HENJO (monk, 816-890)
"How mysterious!" (tr. by Sam Hamill). [ColR] (NS 17:2) Fall-Wint 90, p. 20.
2615. HENKE, Mark
"Campania." [Poetry] (157:5) F 91, p. 285-286.
"Dentist." [CapeR] (26:2) Fall 91, p. 39.
"Grid." [MidwQ] (32:3) Spr 91, p. 292.
"Hekla." [MidAR] (11:2) 91, p. 111.
"San Tan Mountains." [CapeR] (26:2) Fall 91, p. 40.
"Serengeti Rosary." [Writer] (104:9) S 91, p. 21-22.
2616. HENN, Mary Ann
"September." [Pearl] (14) Fall-Wint 91, p. 24.
2617. HENNESSEY, Bill
"Running Shoes." [WillowR] Spr 91, p. 26.
2618. HENNING, Barbara
"Heartbreak in the Twentieth Century." [RiverS] (34) 91, p. 56.
"Occasionally Smart Off." [RiverS] (34) 91, p. 57.
2619. HENNING, Dianna
"Between Them." [SpoonRQ] (16:1/2) Wint-Spr 91, p. 97-98.
"Champian Plow." [ContextS] (2:1) 91, p. 9-10.
"Close to the House." [Pembroke] (23) 91, p. 163-164.
"Scarf." [ContextS] (2:1) 91, p. 8-9.
"Separating the Wash." [SpoonRQ] (16:1/2) Wint-Spr 91, p. 99.
"A Spy in the House of Pastures and the Green Grasses." [SouthernPR] (31:2) Fall
91, p. 66-67.
2620. HENRY, Gordon
"The Failure of Certain Charms." [MidAR] (11:1) 91, p. 22.
"A Medicine Song." [MidAR] (11:1) 91, p. 23.
2621. HENSLER, Charles
"Before." [CrabCR] (7:3) 91, p. 13.
"Story." [CrabCR] (7:3) 91, p. 12.
2622. HENSLEY, Michael C.
"Festival of Stigma Martyrs." [NegC] (11:3) 91, p. 23.
2623. HENSON, Lance
"Journal Entries." [PoetryE] (32) Fall 91, p. 51-52.
2624. HENTZ, Robert R.
"Nothing More Obvious." [SoCoast] (11) Wint 91, p. 55.
2625. HENTZE, Ebba
"Kata — a Belated Eulogy" (tr. by Leyvoy Joensen). [Vis] (37) 91, p. 23-26.
2626. HEPBURN, Peter J.
"Moon: You Are a Distant, Stately Lover." [CapeR] (26:2) Fall 91, p. 27.

2627. HERBECK, Ernest
    "The Bat" (tr. by Melissa Monroe). [OnTheBus] (8/9) 91, p. 204.
    "The Moon" (tr. by Melissa Monroe). [OnTheBus] (8/9) 91, p. 205.
    "The Snake" (tr. by Melissa Monroe). [OnTheBus] (8/9) 91, p. 205.
    "Spring" (tr. by Melissa Monroe). [OnTheBus] (8/9) 91, p. 204-205.
2628. HERBERT, Kristin
    "Burgeoning Season." [CreamCR] (15:2) Fall 91, p. 81.
    "Retrospect, Regret." [Parting] (4:2) Wint 91-92, p. 20.
2629. HERBERT, Nanette
    "Invisible Barriers." [SinW] (45) Wint 91-92, p. 30.
2630. HERBERT, W. N.
    "The Ladder of Babel." [Verse] (8:2) Sum 91, p. 82-83.
2631. HERBERT, Zbigniew
    "The Abyss of Mr. Cogito" (tr. by John and Bogdana Carpenter). [NewYorker]
        (67:1) 25 F 91, p. 36.
    "Hakeldama" (tr. by John and Bogdana Carpenter). [ParisR] (33:121) Wint 91, p.
        38-39.
    "Meditations of Mr. Cogito on Redemption" (tr. by John and Bogdana Carpenter).
        [ParisR] (33:121) Wint 91, p. 40.
    "Mr. Cogito and Pop" (tr. by John and Bogdana Carpenter). [ParisR] (33:121) Wint
        91, p. 41-42.
    "Mr. Cogito Laments the Pettiness of Dreams" (tr. by John and Bogdana Carpenter).
        [NewYorker] (67:9) 22 Ap 91, p. 34.
    "Mr. Cogito Looks at a Deceased Friend" (tr. by Bogdana and John Carpenter).
        [NewYorker] (67:24) 5 Ag 91, p. 38.
    "Mr. Cogito Thinks of Returning to the City Where He Was Born" (tr. by John and
        Bogdana Carpenter). [NewYorker] (67:1) 25 F 91, p. 36.
    "Ordinariness of the Soul" (tr. by John and Bogdana Carpenter). [ParisR] (33:121)
        Wint 91, p. 37.
    "Sometimes Mr. Cogito Receives Strange Letters" (tr. by John and Bogdana
        Carpenter). [NewYorker] (67:1) 25 F 91, p. 36.
2632. HERING, Rene
    "Genesis" (Excerpt). [PraF] (12:2 #55) Sum 91, p. 66.
    "Language Test" (Excerpt). [PraF] (12:2 #55) Sum 91, p. 67.
2633. HERMAN, Maja
    "Harbor of Salvation" (tr. of Stevan Tontic). [InterPR] (15:1) Spr 89, p. 37.
    "A Horse Ballad" (tr. of Stevan Tontic). [InterPR] (15:1) Spr 89, p. 37.
2634. HERNANDEZ, Francisco
    "Cómo Cantarte, Diótima, Sin Vino." [Nuez] (3:7) 91, p. 7.
2635. HERNANDEZ, Inés
    "Texas / Tejano Exile." [PoetryE] (32) Fall 91, p. 28-29.
    "The Trail of Tears Has Not Ended." [PoetryE] (32) Fall 91, p. 30-31.
    "Who is good with words they say." [PoetryE] (32) Fall 91, p. 27.
HERNANDEZ CRUZ, Victor
    See CRUZ, Victor Hernandez
2636. HERRERA, Juan Felipe
    "Binoculars (Manhattan, Circa 1943)." [NewEngR] (13:3/4) Spr-Sum 91, p.
        242-243.
    "Fuselage Installation." [AmerPoR] (20:1) Ja-F 91, p. 48.
    "Iowa Blues Bar Spiritual." [NewEngR] (13:3/4) Spr-Sum 91, p. 244-246.
    "Norteamérica, I Am Your Scar." [NewEngR] (13:3/4) Spr-Sum 91, p. 246-249.
    "Tatarema." [MidAR] (12:1) 91, p. 61-65.
2637. HERRSTROM, David Sten
    "White Cat & Marigolds." [US1] (24/25) Spr 91, p. 9.
2638. HERSHON, Robert
    "Like." [PoetryNW] (32:2) Sum 91, p. 29.
    "Post Card from Youngstown." [PoetryNW] (32:2) Sum 91, p. 29.
2639. HERTZ, Lou
    "Terminal Games." [Gypsy] (17) 91, p. 59.
2640. HERTZLER, Leslie
    "Alone at Last." [EmeraldCR] (3) 91, c1990, p. 33-34.
2641. HESKETH, Phoebe
    "Love Song." [Stand] (32:1) Wint 90-91, p. 33.
    "Retrospection: 1916 July 2nd." [Stand] (32:1) Wint 90-91, p. 33.
2642. HESS, Errol
    "Pushing Spring." [ContextS] (2:2) 91, p. 20.

2643. HESS, Sonya
"Angels" (2 selections: "Secret Cow," "Maureen"). [Caliban] (10) 91, p. 88-89.
"If I Hadn't Met You." [WestB] (28) 91, p. 13.
2644. HESSON, Angela
"Sisters." [CinPR] (21) Spr 90, p. 59.
2645. HETHERINGTON, Paul
"A Different Life" (from "Mapping Wildwood Road"). [PoetryUSA] (23) Sum 91,
p. 22.
2646. HETTLINGER, Graham
"On Lake Erie." [CarolQ] (43:2) Wint 91, p. 31.
"Scene." [CarolQ] (43:2) Wint 91, p. 32.
2647. HEWITT, Christopher
"A Calm Space." [Salm] (92) Fall 91, p. 195-196.
"The Defrocking of Pastor Van Dieman." [CimR] (95) Ap 91, p. 58.
"The Defrocking of Pastor Van Dieman." [JamesWR] (8:3) Spr 91, p. 10.
"For Winter." [CimR] (95) Ap 91, p. 57.
"Newly Blind." [CimR] (95) Ap 91, p. 57.
2648. HEWITT, Geof
"The Sailor." [ColR] (NS 18:1) Spr-Sum 91, p. 116.
2649. HEYEN, William
"By the Time I Loved Him." [ColR] (NS 18:1) Spr-Sum 91, p. 72-73.
"The Candle." [Ploughs] (17:1) Spr 91, p. 86-87.
"Communion Spoon." [FourQ] (5:2) Fall 91, p. 11.
"Pterodactyl Rose" (Selections: 5 poems). [Ploughs] (17:1) Spr 91, p. 87-89.
"The Scar." [ColR] (NS 18:1) Spr-Sum 91, p. 70-71.
2650. HICKERSON, Patricia
"My Mother Was Born in Westbourne, TN." [PaintedHR] (1) Ja 91, p. 37.
"The Poet in Solitary." [PaintedHR] (1) Ja 91, p. 36.
2651. HICKOFF, Stephen
"1972." [Spitball] (37) Sum 91, p. 9.
2652. HICKS, Frederick
"So." [DogRR] (10:2) Fall-Wint 91, p. 13.
2653. HICKS, Wendy
"Wounds of War." [EngJ] (80:3) Mr 91, p. 75.
2654. HICKSON, Paddy
"A Belfast Sunday." [Interim] (10:1) Spr-Sum 91, p. 23.
2655. HICOK, Bob
"Contrary Woman." [ClockR] (7:1/2) 91-92, p. 21.
"In Defense of Tourism." [SoCoast] (11) Wint 91, p. 22.
"Letter Home." [CreamCR] (15:2) Fall 91, p. 55.
2656. HIESTAND, E. (Emily)
"Becoming Earth." [SouthwR] (76:4) Aut 91, p. 563.
"Between the Snow, Crows" (for Peter Niels Dunn). [PartR] (58:4) Fall 91, p. 691.
"Chain of Species." [SouthwR] (76:4) Aut 91, p. 562-563.
"EARTH's Answer." [CarolQ] (43:3) Spr 91, p. 40.
"The Scientific Method" (Step Two: Gathering Evidence). [CarolQ] (43:3) Spr 91, p.
39.
2657. HIGGINS, Dick
"Another Gentle One." [Caliban] (10) 91, p. 87.
"Cito's Song." [WorldL] (2) 91, p. 39-41.
"A Gentle One." [Caliban] (10) 91, p. 86.
"Pink." [Talisman] (7) Fall 91, p. 122-123.
2658. HIGGINS, Joanne
"The Deaf Wife." [CrabCR] (7:2) Sum 91, p. 11.
2659. HIGGINS, Mary Rising
"Red Table." [CentralP] (19/20) Spr-Fall 91, p. 234-236.
2660. HIGGINS, Sean
"General Emotions." [PikeF] (10) Spr 91, p. 19.
2661. HIGH, John
"Blue Vitriol: The Second Deviation of Labor" (tr. of Aleksei Parshchikov, w. Julie
Gesin). [Avec] (4:1) 91, p. 141-142.
"Fugue" (tr. of Nina Iskrenko, w. Katya Olmsted). [Talisman] (6) Spr 91, p.
114-115.
"The Lives of Thomas: Episodes and Prayers" (4 selections). [Talisman] (7) Fall 91,
p. 23-25.

"Philological Verse" (tr. of Aleksandr Eremenko). [Talisman] (6) Spr 91, p. 101-102.
2662. HIGHTOWER, David
"My Cousin Came to Stay the Night." [LullwaterR] (2:2) Spr 91, p. 25-26.
2663. HIGHTOWER, Dawn A.
"The City." [HawaiiR] (15:2, #32) Spr 91, p. 64.
"A Dance." [Kalliope] (13:1) 91, p. 70.
"Shades." [Kalliope] (13:1) 91, p. 70.
2664. HIGHTOWER, Shakira
"Harlemite Easter." [HangL] (59) 91, p. 76.
"Kisses." [HangL] (59) 91, p. 77.
"Love Poem" (for JRW). [HangL] (59) 91, p. 74.
"Poem: I am (w)hol(l)y" (for ebonee s.). [HangL] (59) 91, p. 75.
2665. HILBERT, Donna
"64 Flavors." [ChironR] (10:2) Sum 91, p. 2.
"Boy with the Pee Scared Out of Him." [ChironR] (10:2) Sum 91, p. 2.
"Dear John Letter to My Uterus." [Pearl] (13) Spr-Sum 91, p. 63.
"Metaphor." [Pearl] (13) Spr-Sum 91, p. 21.
"The Penis." [ChironR] (10:2) Sum 91, p. 2.
2666. HILDRETH, Margaret (Margret)
"Three." [EmeraldCR] (3) 91, c1990, p. 40-41.
"Trees." [EmeraldCR] (4) 91, p. 35.
2667. HILL, Adam Craig
"Between Worlds." [AmerPoR] (20:3) My-Je 91, p. 43.
"Going Home Again." [CimR] (95) Ap 91, p. 49-50.
"Two Shapes in Nature" (for Stanley Plumly). [Journal] (15:1) Spr 91, p. 58.
2668. HILL, Ann
"Back Door Poets" (on the publication of Leonard Temme's book of poetry). [EmeraldCR] (4) 91, p. 63.
"The Moon Has Grown Bright." [EmeraldCR] (3) 91, c1990, p. 73.
"The Moon Is a Living Being." [EmeraldCR] (3) 91, c1990, p. 72.
"This Is for Roy." [EmeraldCR] (4) 91, p. 62.
"We Sleep With Our Eyes Open." [EmeraldCR] (3) 91, c1990, p. 73.
2669. HILL, Geoffrey
"Christmas Trees." [CentR] (35:3) Fall 91, p. 577.
"Ovid in the Third Reich." [CentR] (35:3) Fall 91, p. 580.
"September Song" (born 19.6.32 - deported 24.9.42). [CentR] (35:3) Fall 91, p. 582.
2670. HILL, Jack
"Highschool Tryouts." [Spitball] (37) Sum 91, p. 33.
2671. HILL, James J.
"The Crusts." [ChrC] (108:21) 10-17 Jl 91, p. 685.
2672. HILL, John G.
"Mother Superior." [SlipS] (11) 91, p. 51.
"An Ordinary Night at the Strip Joint." [SlipS] (11) 91, p. 50.
2673. HILL, John Meredith
"Poem Using the Word Robin." [PoetC] (23:1) Fall 91, p. 26.
2674. HILL, Rick
"Big Boy." [GeoR] (45:1) Spr 91, p. 144-145.
2675. HILLARD, Jeffrey
"Waldhoning, 1790." [CinPR] (22) Spr 91, p. 66-67.
2676. HILLES, Robert
"Canto 15: Gentle Suggestions." [Dandel] (18:1) Spr-Sum 91, p. 13-15.
"New Places to Remember." [Dandel] (18:1) Spr-Sum 91, p. 12.
"Noises Outside My Window." [Dandel] (18:1) Spr-Sum 91, p. 10-11.
"Second Nature." [Event] (20:2) Sum 91, p. 99-101.
2677. HILLHOUSE, Martha
"Commuting." [PraF] (12:4) Wint 91-92, p. 40.
"Pesto." [PraF] (12:4) Wint 91-92, p. 39.
2678. HILLMAN, Brenda
"Death Tractates" (Selection: IV. Finding Her). [Ploughs] (17:1) Spr 91, p. 90-94.
2679. HINE, Daryl
"In Place." [ParisR] (33:121) Wint 91, p. 118.
"Medea to Jason." [ParisR] (33:119) Sum 91, p. 44-51.
"Oenone to Paris." [ParisR] (33:119) Sum 91, p. 38-43.

201

2680. HINER, James
"Anthologie D'une Manière Typique." [BelPoJ] (42:2) Wint 91-92, p. 20-21.
2681. HINES, Debra
"A Letter from Margaret to Her Sister." [GeoR] (45:1) Spr 91, p. 38.
"Maximilian's Execution." [CalQ] (32/33) Spr 90, p. 126-129.
"The Monarch of Meritocracy." [KenR] (NS 13:1) Wint 91, p. 46-48.
"Sarah's Triumvirate." [MassR] (32:1) Spr 91, p. 54-60.
2682. HINRICHSEN, Dennis
"Shoulder-to-Shoulder Ode" (to M., 1952-1968). [SouthernPR] (31:1) Spr 91, p.
16-17.
2683. HINTON, Jacquelyn
"The Journal." [EngJ] (80:3) Mr 91, p. 97.
2684. HIPPOLYTE, Kendel
"Antonette's Boogie." [GrahamHR] (14) Spr 91, p. 66-67.
"I Came Upon This Town." [GrahamHR] (14) Spr 91, p. 68.
2685. HIRSCH, Edward
"At the Grave of Wallace Stevens" (Section 14, Cedar Hill Cemetery, Hartford,
Connecticut). [SouthernR] (27:3) Jl 91, p. 667-669.
"The Crying." [RiverS] (35) 91, p. 30-33.
"In the Midwest." [NewRep] (204:12) 25 Mr 91, p. 34.
"The Italian Muse" (Henry James in Rome, 1869). [Raritan] (10:3) Wint 91, p.
24-27.
"Man on a Fire Escape." [NewYorker] (67:40) 25 N 91, p. 46.
"Mergers and Acquisitions." [Chelsea] (52) 91, p. 98.
"On the Death of Hart Crane." [SouthernR] (27:3) Jl 91, p. 665-666.
"Skywriting" (Harper Grace Hospital, July 15, 1984). [MichQR] (30:2) Spr 91, p.
357-358.
"Uncertainty." [NewYorker] (67:14) 27 My 91, p. 74.
"Waiting for the Hurricane." [SouthwR] (76:2) Spr 91, p. 252-253.
2686. HIRSCH, Steve
"Oak and Blame." [HeavenB] (9) Wint-Spr 91-92, p. 55.
"Some Week." [HeavenB] (9) Wint-Spr 91-92, p. 54-55.
2687. HIRSCHMAN, Jack
"Jessie." [PoetryUSA] (22) Spr 91, p. 15.
"The Night" (In memory of Cornelius Cardew). [AmerPoR] (20:3) My-Je 91, p. 39.
"The Painting." [AmerPoR] (20:3) My-Je 91, p. 37.
"The Tremor." [AmerPoR] (20:3) My-Je 91, p. 38.
"The Weeping." [AmerPoR] (20:3) My-Je 91, p. 38.
2688. HIRSH, Lester
"In the Face of Spring." [CoalC] (4) S 91, p. 6.
2689. HIRSHFIELD, Jane
"Childhood, Horses, Rain." [SwampR] (7/8) Spr-Sum 91, p. 104.
"Completing the Weave" (for M.T.). [SwampR] (7/8) Spr-Sum 91, p. 105-106.
"Each Step." [PlumR] (1) Spr-Sum 91, p. 1.
"Floor." [PlumR] (1) Spr-Sum 91, p. 2.
"The Groundfall Pear." [YellowS] (38) Wint-Spr 91-92, p. 4.
"No idea where you are" (tr. of Izumi Shikibu). [WilliamMR] (29) 91, p. 20.
"Of the Body." [PlumR] (1) Spr-Sum 91, p. 3.
"The Wedding." [ParisR] (33:120) Fall 91, p. 42-43.
"Within This Tree." [Atlantic] (268:3) S 91, p. 66.
HITOMARO, Kakinomoto no (681-729)
See KAKINOMOTO no HITOMARO (681-729)
2690. HITTLE, Gervase
"Sioux" (tr. of Peter Pabisch). [SoDakR] (29:3 part 2) Aut 91, p. 92-93.
2691. HIX, H. Edgar
"Desert Storm / Monday Meeting." [Writer] (104:12) D 91, p. 26.
"Invitation." [Writer] (104:3) Mr 91, p. 22.
2692. HIX, H. L.
"Diary of the Departed" (After the 1916 cycle of anonymous Czechoslovakian dialect
poems, and the musical composition based on them by Leos Janacek). [Crazy]
(41) Wint 91, p. 28-30.
"Villanelle After Wittgenstein" (Philosophical Investigations 525). [Poetry] (158:6) S
91, p. 314.
2693. HJALMARSSON, Johann
"Dream, Reality" (tr. by Sverrir Holmarsson). [Vis] (37) 91, p. 40.
"Life" (tr. by Sverrir Holmarsson). [Vis] (37) 91, p. 39.

"Unknown Rooms" (tr. by Sverrir Holmarsson). [Vis] (37) 91, p. 40.
"World" (tr. by Sverrir Holmarsson). [Vis] (37) 91, p. 39.
2694. HJARTARSON, Snorri
"Empty Wait the Paths" (tr. by Hallberg Hallmundsson). [Vis] (37) 91, p. 38.
"Flotsam" (tr. by Hallberg Hallmundsson). [Vis] (37) 91, p. 38.
2695. HO, Alan
"Song." [PoetryUSA] (22) Spr 91, p. 22.
HO, Li
    See LI, Ho
HO-CHING, Lin
    See LIN, Ho-ching
2696. HOAGLAND, Tony
"Ducks." [Sonora] (20) Wint 91, p. 49-50.
"Emigration." [Poetry] (158:1) Ap 91, p. 17-18.
"Oh Mercy." [Sonora] (20) Wint 91, p. 51-52.
"Paradise." [DenQ] (26:1) Sum 91, p. 37-38.
"Safeway." [Poetry] (158:1) Ap 91, p. 15-17.
2697. HOAGLAND, William
"Admissions." [Poem] (65) My 91, p. 28.
"After the Facts." [Poem] (65) My 91, p. 27.
"Incident in a Cornfield." [Poem] (65) My 91, p. 26.
2698. HOANG, Michael
"I'm Sorry" (after William Carlos Williams). [PoetryUSA] (22) Spr 91, p. 22.
2699. HOBBS, Blair
"The Drunk's Table." [Crucible] (27) Fall 91, p. 43.
"O'Keeffe's Still Life." [TexasR] (12:1/2) Spr-Sum 91, p. 106-107.
"Painted Birds." [LaurelR] (25:1) Wint 91, p. 83.
2700. HOBBS, James
"Rivers." [Plain] (12:1) Fall 91, p. 25.
2701. HOBSON, Christopher Z.
"The Burning of McCormick Place 1967." [BlackWR] (18:1) Fall-Wint 91, p. 77.
2702. HOCKMAN, Will
"Not Always Located in Nicaragua." [DustyD] Ap 91, p. 20.
2703. HOCQUARD, Emmanuel
"The Icelandic Consul" (fig. 3, Paris, 1990, tr. by Norma Cole). [Avec] (4:1) 91, p.
    68-69.
2704. HODGE, Margaret
"How Marjorie Sweeney Went to Heaven." [BellArk] (7:1) Ja-F 91, p. 2.
"Pink Cluster for Nelson Bentley." [BellArk] (7:1) Ja-F 91, p. 5.
2705. HODGEN, John
"The Garden of the Living and the Dead." [SycamoreR] (3:1) Wint 91, p. 11.
2706. HODOR, Timothy
"The Lazarus Love." [Comm] (118:15) 13 S 91, p. 509.
"The Rag Man in the Vatican." [Comm] (118:6) 22 Mr 91, p. 190.
2707. HOEFER, David
"The Magician at 8000 Feet." [CinPR] (21) Spr 90, p. 11.
2708. HOEFLEIN, Rita
"Me and Evelyn." [HayF] (8) Spr-Sum 91, p. 29-30.
2709. HOEKSEMA, Thomas
"Aldebarán" (In memory of Howard Phillips Lovecraft, tr. of Lilia Barbachano).
    [Paint] (18:36) Aut 91, p. 62.
"Omen" (tr. of Blanca Luz Pulido, w. R. Enriquez). [Paint] (18:36) Aut 91, p. 63.
2710. HOEPPNER, Edward Haworth
"Pickets Not Chosen at Random." [ChironR] (10:2) Sum 91, p. 46.
"Shade Tree Mechanics." [ChironR] (10:4) Wint 91, p. 22.
2711. HOEY, Allen
"The Adventures of Water." [SouthernR] (27:3) Jl 91, p. 659-661.
"Cool Fire." [SouthernR] (27:3) Jl 91, p. 657-658.
"Shaping the Day." [TexasR] (11:1/2) Spr-Sum 90, p. 8.
"Wolves at the Burnett Park Zoo." [TexasR] (11:1/2) Spr-Sum 90, p. 9.
2712. HOFER, Marianna
"Cutting the Lilacs on Sunday." [Parting] (4:2) Wint 91-92, p. 24.
"Gun Shy." [ChironR] (10:2) Sum 91, p. 41.
2713. HOFFERT, Barbara
"Painting by the River." [Elf] (1:2) Sum 91, p. 27.

2714. HOFFMAN, Barbara
"The Cobalt Machine." [MinnR] (NS 36) Spr 91, p. 28-29.
"The Examination." [MinnR] (NS 36) Spr 91, p. 26.
"Field of Radiation." [MinnR] (NS 36) Spr 91, p. 33-34.
"On the Edge." [MinnR] (NS 36) Spr 91, p. 27-28.
"One-Sided" (Breast Cancer: Power vs. Prosthesis, Essay by Audre Lord). [MinnR]
    (NS 36) Spr 91, p. 29.
"Reconstruction." [MinnR] (NS 36) Spr 91, p. 30-31.
"The Second Cut." [MinnR] (NS 36) Spr 91, p. 32-33.
"Skeletons." [MinnR] (NS 36) Spr 91, p. 31-32.
"Tight White Silence." [MinnR] (NS 36) Spr 91, p. 26-27.
2715. HOFFMAN, Daniel
"Buddies." [Pequod] (32) 91, p. 54-56.
"Identities." [Boulevard] (6:2/3, #17/18) Fall 91, p. 210-211.
"A Pile of Rocks." [GettyR] (4:2) Spr 91, p. 292.
"Vane." [Boulevard] (6:2/3, #17/18) Fall 91, p. 212.
"A Wall of Stone." [GettyR] (4:2) Spr 91, p. 293.
2716. HOFFMAN, Deborah
"Mating Season." [SoCaR] (24:1) Fall 91, p. 4.
"Sanctuary." [SoCaR] (23:2) Spr 91, p. 135.
2717. HOFFMAN, Fred
"Jesus in Muncie." [MissR] (19:3) 91, p. 140.
2718. HOFFMAN, Joan
"Remembering Willie Mae" (Funeral services for Wilma Mae Kettridge were held . .
    . on Friday, December 3rd. Mrs. Kettridge owned and operated King's Hotel.
    She had no survivors). [Nimrod] (34:2) Spr-Sum 91, p. 17-18.
2719. HOFFMAN, N. M.
"Cooper Union." [Chelsea] (51) 91, p. 33.
"For the Inmate of the House on the Fontanka." [NegC] (11:1) 91, p. 59.
HOFFMAN, Roald
    See HOFFMANN, Roald
2720. HOFFMAN, Ruth
"Rue du Cherche-Midi" (for Greg). [Plain] (11:3) Spr 91, p. 36.
2721. HOFFMAN, Ruth Cassel
"In the Wyck Garden." [Plain] (11:2) Wint 91, p. 19.
2722. HOFFMANN, Roald
"Giving In." [ParisR] (33:121) Wint 91, p. 190.
"Ponder Fire." [ParisR] (33:121) Wint 91, p. 191.
"A Sunset Clause." [CarolQ] (43:2) Wint 91, p. 33.
2723. HOFMO, Gunvor
"Time" (tr. by Harold P. Hanson). [Vis] (37) 91, p. 45.
2724. HOGAN, Linda
"Carry." [Manoa] (3:1) Spr 91, p. 207.
"Drum." [AmerV] (23) Sum 91, p. 6.
"Hunger." [Manoa] (3:1) Spr 91, p. 205-206.
"Map." [MidAR] (11:1) 91, p. 57-58.
"Skin." [PlumR] (1) Spr-Sum 91, p. 49-50.
2725. HOGAN, Michael
"The Coldest Winter" (Selections: 6 poems). [SwampR] (7/8) Spr-Sum 91, p.
    96-101.
"Love." [SwampR] (7/8) Spr-Sum 91, p. 31.
"Love of the Ordinary Passing." [ColR] (NS 17:2) Fall-Wint 90, p. 70-71.
"Missing the Moon." [SwampR] (7/8) Spr-Sum 91, p. 32.
"Planting Azaleas." [ColR] (NS 17:2) Fall-Wint 90, p. 72-73.
2726. HOGG, Robert
"Becoming Night" (for Harry Flaig, artist). [WestCL] (25:1) Spr 91, p. 69-70.
"Extreme Positions" (for bp). [WestCL] (25:1) Spr 91, p. 67-68.
"Falling Through Space." [WestCL] (25:1) Spr 91, p. 72-73.
"The Present" (with thanks to Harry & Bea). [WestCL] (25:1) Spr 91, p. 71-72.
2727. HOGGARD, James
"Spirit's Ecology" (tr. of Oscar Hahn). [ColR] (NS 18:1) Spr-Sum 91, p. 85.
2728. HOGUE, Cynthia
"Lonely Hearts Club." [CentralP] (19/20) Spr-Fall 91, p. 155-158.
2729. HOH, Collin
"At the Bottom of My Heart." [PoetryUSA] (22) Spr 91, p. 22.

2730. HOHLWEIN, Laura
"In Significance." [GrahamHR] (15) Fall 91, p. 30.
"My Sister's Nightmare." [GrahamHR] (15) Fall 91, p. 32.
"The Sick Man." [GrahamHR] (15) Fall 91, p. 33.
"Sit." [GrahamHR] (15) Fall 91, p. 31.

2731. HOHN, Donovan
"Dishes." [HangL] (59) 91, p. 79.
"Family Farm." [HangL] (59) 91, p. 78.

2732. HOLAHAN, Tom
"Memo: Van Leer Containers Ltd., Lagos, Nigeria" (found in 1969 in a collection of
stamps, the text by P.T.O. as written, the lining revised). [Pig] (17) 91, p. 62.

2733. HOLBROOK, David
"In the Pyrenees." [Stand] (32:1) Wint 90-91, p. 56-57.

2734. HOLBROOK, L.
"Forms." [BelPoJ] (41:3) Spr 91, p. 36-37.
"Rites of Passage." [BelPoJ] (41:3) Spr 91, p. 38.

2735. HOLDEN, Jonathan
"Bank." [MissouriR] (13:3) 91, p. 36-37.
"The Crash" (October, 1987, Wall Street). [MissouriR] (13:3) 91, p. 42-45.
"Late November." [MissouriR] (13:3) 91, p. 41.
"The Parable of the Snow Man." [MissouriR] (13:3) 91, p. 38-39.
"The Principle of Duality." [MissouriR] (13:3) 91, p. 40.

2736. HÖLDERLIN, Friedrich
"A Map of Mnemosyne" (tr. by Richard Sieburth). [Talisman] (6) Spr 91, p. 51-64.
"Mnemosyne" (tr. by David Ferry). [Raritan] (11:1) Sum 91, p. 11-12.

2737. HOLDT, David
"Baseball Cards." [Spitball] (39) Wint 91, p. 24-25.

HOLENIA, Alexander Lernet
See LERNET-HOLENIA, Alexander

2738. HOLIHEN, Joseph Markham
"El Tormento de Perdido Amigos (The Torment of Lost Friends)." [EmeraldCR] (3)
91, c1990, p. 112-113.

2739. HOLLADAY, Hilary
"Memoir of the Magician's Girl." [WestB] (29) 91, p. 92-93.

2740. HOLLAHAN, Eugene
"Instanter." [SoDakR] (29:1) Spr 91, p. 110.
"Jefferson's Arch" (St. Louis, 1990). [LullwaterR] (3:1) Fall 91, p. 32-33.
"Last First Lady." [LullwaterR] (2:2) Spr 91, p. 24.
"Tourist in Four Landscapes." [SoDakR] (29:4) Wint 91, p. 171-172.
"War Bride, 1921." [SoDakR] (29:1) Spr 91, p. 111-112.

2741. HOLLAND, Kelvin
"The Dark Seed of Whitman." [BlackWR] (18:1) Fall-Wint 91, p. 32-34.

2742. HOLLAND, Larry
"October 12." [Plain] (11:2) Wint 91, p. 22.
"The Whisper of Bones Grating." [WestB] (28) 91, p. 8.

2743. HOLLAND, Michelle
"Fires." [JINJPo] (13:2) Aut 91, p. 1-2.
"The Summer Visit." [US1] (24/25) Spr 91, p. 8.

2744. HOLLANDER, Jean
"Fiesole." [Poem] (66) N 91, p. 19.
"The Reality of Green in Florence." [SouthernHR] (25:1) Wint 91, p. 51.
"The Sick Child. An Edvard Munch Painting." [US1] (24/25) Spr 91, p. 18.

2745. HOLLANDER, John
"Colored Illustration, Tipped-In." [NewRep] (205:10) 2 S 91, p. 34.
"Days of Autumn." [GrandS] (10:2, #38) 91, p. 178-181.
"Garden Sundial." [Poetry] (157:6) Mr 91, p. 315.
"Lazy Susan." [Poetry] (157:6) Mr 91, p. 318.
"Selected Short Subjects." [ParisR] (33:118) Spr 91, p. 243-245.
"Stable Ego." [Poetry] (157:6) Mr 91, p. 316.
"A Watched Pot" (For Paul Bertolli and Alice Waters). [Poetry] (157:6) Mr 91, p.
317.

2746. HOLLANDS, Neil
"Paradise Revisited." [Plain] (12:2) Wint 91, p. 27.

2747. HOLLEY, Margaret
"Appleflesh, This Lily." [LaurelR] (25:1) Wint 91, p. 33.
"Blue Herons." [WestB] (28) 91, p. 89.

"Brahms' *Requium*." [SouthernR] (27:3) Jl 91, p. 700-701.
"A Critique of Pure Reason." [Poetry] (157:6) Mr 91, p. 339.
"Eastering." [Poetry] (157:6) Mr 91, p. 339-340.
"The Fireflies." [LaurelR] (25:1) Wint 91, p. 34-35.
"Half-Life." [SouthernR] (27:3) Jl 91, p. 702-703.
"Its Unfathomable Largo." [WestB] (28) 91, p. 88.
"Koan." [Poetry] (157:6) Mr 91, p. 340-341.
"The Marriage of Marie Curie" (Selections: i, iv). [CarolQ] (43:3) Spr 91, p. 35-38.
"Midsummer in Manayunk." [MidwQ] (33:1) Aut 91, p. 67-68.
"Neanderthal." [SouthernR] (27:3) Jl 91, p. 701-702.
"Peepers." [LaurelR] (25:1) Wint 91, p. 31-32.
"The Perfect Transparency of the Artist." [AmerS] (60:3) Sum 91, p. 440.
"The Sink." [Sequoia] (34:1) Spr 91, p. 7-9.
"The Tree of Life." [Poetry] (157:6) Mr 91, p. 340.
"Under the Trees." [TarRP] (31:1) Fall 91, p. 33.
2748. HOLLINGER, Douglas L.
"Reflections of the Sun." [ChrC] (108:16) 8 My 91, p. 524.
2749. HOLLIS, Marnie
"Hazard." [AnthNEW] (3) 91, p. 22.
2750. HOLLO, Anselm
"Chicago." [NewAW] (8/9) Fall 91, p. 8.
"The Comparative Avec." [NewAW] (8/9) Fall 91, p. 9.
"Cripple Creek Aforismos." [NewAW] (8/9) Fall 91, p. 11-12.
"Western Thought." [NewAW] (8/9) Fall 91, p. 10.
2751. HOLLOWELL, Andrea
"Noon." [Zyzzyva] (7:1) Spr 91, p. 54-55.
2752. HOLM, Bill
"At the Rural Writers' Conference." [NorthStoneR] (10) Fall 91-Wint 92, p. 30.
"Black Duck Love Song" (for John and Lorna Rezmerski). [NorthStoneR] (10) Fall
91-Wint 92, p. 29.
"Mozart, Saskatchewan" (for Tom Sand). [Grain] (19:1) Spr 91, p. 45.
"Paranoia." [NorthStoneR] (10) Fall 91-Wint 92, p. 28.
"Snoring in the Yukon." [Grain] (19:1) Spr 91, p. 45.
"Spring Again." [NorthStoneR] (10) Fall 91-Wint 92, p. 28.
"Turtle." [NorthStoneR] (10) Fall 91-Wint 92, p. 24-27.
2753. HOLMAN, Bob
"30 Minutes." [BrooklynR] (8) 91, p. 27.
2754. HOLMAN, Karen
"Tiny Poems about the Body." [YellowS] (38) Wint-Spr 91-92, p. 6-7.
2755. HOLMARSSON, Sverrir
"Dream, Reality" (tr. of Johann Hjalmarsson). [Vis] (37) 91, p. 40.
"Life" (tr. of Johann Hjalmarsson). [Vis] (37) 91, p. 39.
"Unknown Rooms" (tr. of Johann Hjalmarsson). [Vis] (37) 91, p. 40.
"World" (tr. of Johann Hjalmarsson). [Vis] (37) 91, p. 39.
2756. HOLMES, Darryl
"Behind Closed Doors" (for Ben Shulka Williams." [Obs] (6:1) Spr 91, p. 37-39.
"Fire." [Obs] (6:1) Spr 91, p. 32-33.
"The Movement of Blood." [Obs] (6:1) Spr 91, p. 33-34.
"Oil Spills." [Obs] (6:1) Spr 91, p. 36-37.
"Standing Room" (for Art Blakey). [Obs] (6:1) Spr 91, p. 34-36.
2757. HOLMES, Elizabeth
"Four Stands." [CumbPR] (10:2) Spr 91, p. 1-14.
2758. HOLMES, Janet
"The Dog Season." [PoetryNW] (32:4) Wint 91-92, p. 23.
2759. HOLMES, Nancy
"The Body of My Garden" (Marianne North, 1830-1890). [MalR] (94) Spr 91, p.
46-54.
2760. HOLSTEIN, Michael
"Bamboo" (Concourse, Taipei Airport). [ManhatPR] (13) [91?], p. 30.
"Pine and Cranes" (Concourse, Taipei Airport). [ManhatPR] (13) [91?], p. 30.
2761. HOLT, Dawn
"Rocking" (9/15/89-11/29/89). [SoCoast] (10) Fall 91, p. 24.
2762. HOLT, Lois
"Tomatoes." [Crucible] (27) Fall 91, p. 24-25.
HOLTEN, Dan von
See Von HOLTEN, Dan

2763. HOLTEN, Knud
"And the Wind Seen As Waves." [SoDakR] (29:3 part 2) Aut 91, p. 65.
"Ocean View." [SoDakR] (29:3 part 2) Aut 91, p. 65.
2764. HOLUB, Miroslav
"Duties of a Train Conductor" (tr. by Dana Hábová and David Young). [GrandS]
(10:4, #40) 91, p. 191-192.
"The End of the Week" (tr. by Dana Hábová and David Young). [Field] (45) Fall 91,
p. 43.
"The Wall in the Corner by the Stairs" (tr. by Dana Hábová and David Young).
[Field] (45) Fall 91, p. 41-42.
2765. HOLZER, Ryszard
"November Evening" (to Adam Zagajewski, tr. by Daniel Bourne). [CharR] (17:1)
Spr 91, p. 86.
2766. HOMER
"Hektor and Andromache" (from the Illiad, tr. by Jim Powell). [TriQ] (83) Wint
91-92, p. 156-167.
"Iliad (Book III, lines 310-78)" (from "Men in Aïda," tr. by David Melnick).
[Talisman] (6) Spr 91, p. 45-46.
"To Hermes" (from the Homeric Hymn to Hermes, tr. by Jim Powell). [TriQ] (83)
Wint 91-92, p. 168-182.
2767. HOMER, Art
"After Hearing an Anonymous Singer." [CharR] (17:1) Spr 91, p. 109.
"Blowhole and Green Glass at the Apostles" (for Ken and Pat Anderson). [CharR]
(17:1) Spr 91, p. 110.
"Breaking." [ColR] (NS 17:2) Fall-Wint 90, p. 117-118.
"Driving." [ColR] (NS 17:2) Fall-Wint 90, p. 115-116.
"Homeplace." [ColR] (NS 17:2) Fall-Wint 90, p. 113.
"Walking to Work." [ColR] (NS 17:2) Fall-Wint 90, p. 119.
"A Why-Not of Stones." [ColR] (NS 17:2) Fall-Wint 90, p. 114.
2768. HONIG, Edwin
"For Abe Honig at 95 (From Edwin at 70)." [MichQR] (30:3) Sum 91, p. 458.
"God Talk." [Agni] (33) 91, p. 224-226.
"Imaginary Loves." [Agni] (33) 91, p. 227-228.
"The Keeper of Sheep" (Selections: VII, XI, XIII, XXIX, tr. of Fernando Pessoa
(Alberto Caeiro), w. Susan M. Brown). [Trans] (25) Spr 91, p. 14-16.
2769. HOOD, Mary (Mary A.)
"Alice May Durban: Barrier Island." [EmeraldCR] (4) 91, p. 14.
"Anna Bates: Molt." [EmeraldCR] (4) 91, p. 18.
"Little Things Around the House: Mrs. Jane Edwards." [EmeraldCR] (4) 91, p.
17-18.
"Mary Bordelon: Figs." [EmeraldCR] (4) 91, p. 15.
"Opatoula" (Selections: 4 poems). [EmeraldCR] (3) 91, c1990, p. 6-9.
"Train." [EmeraldCR] (3) 91, c1990, p. 132-133.
2770. HOOGLAND, Cornelia
"Angel in the Library" (for Cheryl). [Event] (20:2) Sum 91, p. 64.
"The Centre of the Universe." [PraS] (65:3) Fall 91, p. 68-69.
"The Elizabeth Smart Poems" (Selections: 2 poems). [PraF] (12:2 #55) Sum 91, p.
17.
"Love Letters: Her First, My Last." [PraS] (65:3) Fall 91, p. 65-66.
"My Mother's House." [PraS] (65:3) Fall 91, p. 66-67.
"Party." [PraS] (65:3) Fall 91, p. 67-68.
"Play." [PraF] (12:2 #55) Sum 91, p. 16.
"Tailor Shop in Cairo." [Verse] (8:2) Sum 91, p. 105.
"Young Girl's Thoughts of Birds." [PraF] (12:2 #55) Sum 91, p. 15.
2771. HOOPER, Patricia
"The Foal." [CinPR] (22) Spr 91, p. 20-21.
2772. HOOVER, Paul
"Theory." [Ploughs] (17:4) Wint 91-92, p. 132-133.
"Whitman in a Corner." [Ploughs] (17:4) Wint 91-92, p. 134-135.
2773. HOPE, Akua Lezli
"Alien Homeboy." [Obs] (6:1) Spr 91, p. 90.
"The Big Three-O." [Obs] (6:1) Spr 91, p. 92-94.
"Memorial Day." [Obs] (6:1) Spr 91, p. 90-91.
"This Mother" (for lovely Laura). [Obs] (6:1) Spr 91, p. 91-92.
2774. HOPES, David
"Asking Forgiveness of the Squirrels." [LouisL] (8:1) Spr 91, p. 39.

207

2775. HOPPEY, Tim
  "The Stone Sea." [Chelsea] (51) 91, p. 23-24.
  "Wind Buffaloes." [Chelsea] (51) 91, p. 25.
2776. HORN, Jim
  "Poem for English Journal." [EngJ] (80:3) Mr 91, p. 97.
2777. HORNE, Jennifer
  "She Wakes in a State of Elation." [SycamoreR] (3:1) Wint 91, p. 2.
2778. HORNIK, Jessica
  "9:00." [HampSPR] Wint 91, p. 32.
  "Seeing" (for Rex Wilder). [HampSPR] Wint 91, p. 31.
2779. HORNING, Ron
  "Plato: the American Years" (w. David Lehman). [NewAW] (7) Spr 91, p. 45-48.
  "Plato's Retreat" (with David Lehman). [Boulevard] (6:2/3, #17/18) Fall 91, p.
    65-70.
  "The Time at the Tone." [NewYorker] (67:21) 15 Jl 91, p. 34.
2780. HORNOSTY, Cornelia C.
  "Invasion of the Body Snatchers." [CanLit] (128) Spr 91, p. 140.
  "A Narration of Everything." [MalR] (96) Fall 91, p. 76.
2781. HORNSEY, Richard
  "No Peace or Safe Passage" (Don Polson, 1934-1989). [AntigR] (85/86) Spr-Sum
    91, p. 138.
2782. HORODYSKI, Mary
  "3 Postcards." [Grain] (19:2) Sum 91, p. 34-35.
2783. HOROWITZ, Mikhail
  "After Whalen." [Archae] (1) Fall 90, p. 15.
  "The Books." [Archae] (1) Fall 90, p. 9.
  "Cross Country Clouds." [Archae] (1) Fall 90, p. 10-13.
  "Empty Collector." [Archae] (1) Fall 90, p. 16-19.
  "Real Eyes." [Archae] (1) Fall 90, p. 14.
  "Rune" (for Jack Hirschman). [Archae] (2) Spr 91, p. 19.
  "Up All Night, I Dream of Mother Russia." [Archae] (2) Spr 91, p. 20-23.
2784. HOROWITZ, Rose
  "Hey Girl." [OnTheBus] (8/9) 91, p. 84.
2785. HORSTING, Eric
  "Eating You." [PoetryE] (32) Fall 91, p. 86.
  "Fallatio at 6 A.M." [PoetryE] (32) Fall 91, p. 87.
  "Seasoning." [Poem] (66) N 91, p. 12.
  "Vacation." [PoetryE] (32) Fall 91, p. 88.
  "Waiting on the West Coast." [Poem] (66) N 91, p. 11.
2786. HORVATH, Brooke
  "Jeu de Paume: Paris." [SycamoreR] (3:1) Wint 91, p. 36-37.
  "A Matter of Trees." [AntR] (49:2) Spr 91, p. 237.
  "My Girl" (For my daughter, Susan Alessandra). [Sparrow] (58) Jl 91, p. 4-5.
  "The Neo-Natal Intensive Care Unit" (for my daughter). [SycamoreR] (3:1) Wint 91,
    p. 38.
2787. HORVATH, Linda M.
  "Jailhouse Games." [ChironR] (10:2) Sum 91, p. 38.
2788. HOSPITAL, Carolina
  "The Edge of Dreams." [HayF] (9) Fall-Wint 91, p. 89.
  "Near Pigeon Key" (Where pigeons migrate to Florida from Cuba each spring).
    [MidAR] (12:1) 91, p. 59.
  "Scattered Wings." [MidAR] (12:1) 91, p. 60.
  "Sunday Afternoon." [BilingR] (16:1) Ja-Ap 91, p. 62.
  "La vida de la polilla." [LindLM] (10:1) Ja-Mr 91, p. 32.
2789. HOTHAM, Gary
  "Fogged up." [Northeast] (5:5) Wint 91-92, p. 36.
  "Picking up the shells." [Northeast] (5:4) Sum 91, p. 16.
  "Shadow." [Northeast] (5:5) Wint 91-92, p. 36.
2790. HOUCHIN, Ron
  "The Deadly Mantis." [WillowS] (28) Sum 91, p. 59.
2791. HOUSE, Tom
  "The Cutesy-Pie Poetry Review." [ChironR] (10:4) Wint 91, p. 8.
  "The Next New Bukowski." [ChironR] (10:4) Wint 91, p. 8.
  "S & M Commentary." [ChironR] (10:4) Wint 91, p. 8.
2792. HOUSTMAN, Dale M.
  "The Radiant Kingdom." [Caliban] (10) 91, p. 137.

2793. HOUSTON, Beth
"Ars Poetica." [CalQ] (35/36) 91, p. 91-92.
"August." [CapeR] (26:2) Fall 91, p. 18.
"Dirge." [LaurelR] (25:1) Wint 91, p. 46-48.
"Looking Up into a Tree in Late Spring." [CapeR] (26:2) Fall 91, p. 19.
"Passion." [BellR] (14:1) Spr 91, p. 17.
HOUTEN, Lois van
See Van HOUTEN, Lois
HOVANESSIAN, Diana Der
See DER-HOVANESSIAN, Diana
2794. HOWARD, Ben
"Arteries." [SewanR] (98:4) Fall 90, p. 608.
"Articulation." [SewanR] (98:4) Fall 90, p. 607.
"Dublin in July." [SewanR] (98:4) Fall 90, p. 605.
"Letter from Ireland." [SewanR] (98:4) Fall 90, p. 604.
"Old Men of Monaghan." [SewanR] (98:4) Fall 90, p. 606.
2795. HOWARD, Cynthia Anne
"On the Porch Before Church." [EmeraldCR] (3) 91, c1990, p. 66-67.
2796. HOWARD, David
"In the Mean Time." [PoetL] (86:4) Wint 91-92, p. 40.
2797. HOWARD, Jake
"A Homeless Woman's Civic Center Plaza Prayer." [PoetryUSA] (22) Spr 91, p.
17.
2798. HOWARD, Joy
"Terms of Trade." [LullwaterR] (3:1) Fall 91, p. 57-59.
2799. HOWARD, Justice
"Black Garters, Marilyn Dreams." [ChironR] (10:2) Sum 91, p. 11.
"Maybe If the Moon Turns Opaque." [ChironR] (10:2) Sum 91, p. 11.
"Maybe If the Moon Turns Opaque." [Pearl] (13) Spr-Sum 91, p. 50.
2800. HOWARD, Richard
"After K. 452." [NewYorker] (67:19) 1 Jl 91, p. 28.
"Beating About Executive Privilege." [Nat] (252:7) 25 F 91, p. 240.
"Centenary Peripeteia and Anagnorisis Beginning with a Line by Henry James."
[Chelsea] (52) 91, p. 94-95.
"Executive Pursuits." [Nat] (253:7) 9 S 91, p. 278.
"For Matthew Ward, 1951-1990" (who stipulated that I speak, at a memorial service,
of his "professional development," halted by AIDS). [KenR] (NS 13:2) Spr
91, p. 1-3.
"The Given Case" (For David Kalstone, 1932-1986). [Raritan] (10:4) Spr 91, p.
10-14.
"Inferno" (Canto XV-XVI, tr. of Dante). [Antaeus] (67) Fall 91, p. 61-67.
"To the Tenth Muse: A Recommendation." [SouthwR] (76:4) Aut 91, p. 492-495.
"Writing Off." [PartR] (58:4) Fall 91, p. 681-685.
2801. HOWARD, Roger
"Abernethy." [Stand] (32:1) Wint 90-91, p. 55.
2802. HOWARD, Sherwin W.
"From the Diaries of Emily Winthrop" (Excerpts from a poetic narrative). [WeberS]
(8:2) Fall 91, p. 59-63.
2803. HOWD, Eric Stephen Machan
"When Father and Son Blow 'Taps'." [ChamLR] (8-9) Spr-Fall 91, p. 122.
2804. HOWE, Fanny
"Areas." [Ploughs] (17:4) Wint 91-92, p. 27-28.
"Banking." [Agni] (33) 91, p. 47.
"Conclusively." [Ploughs] (17:2/3) Fall 91, p. 225-226.
"The Domestic." [Ploughs] (17:4) Wint 91-92, p. 26.
"Good Friday Night." [GrandS] (10:4, #40) 91, p. 30-31.
"It Was No Dream." [Zyzzyva] (7:2) Sum 91, p. 74.
"Looking Up." [Zyzzyva] (7:2) Sum 91, p. 73.
2805. HOWE, Susan
"Silence Wager Stories." [AmerPoR] (20:2) Mr-Ap 91, p. 14-15.
2806. HOWE, Susan Elizabeth
"Mantis." [SouthwR] (76:4) Aut 91, p. 550.
"Telephoning China." [RiverS] (34) 91, p. 26.
2807. HOWELL, Christopher
"Alienation." [PoetryNW] (32:2) Sum 91, p. 24.
"Everyday Dramatics: An Historical Tale." [WillowS] (27) Wint 91, p. 37-38.

"Out of the Body." [WillowS] (27) Wint 91, p. 39.
"Refusing to Rhyme." [WillowS] (27) Wint 91, p. 35-36.
"You Sailed Away, Oh Yes You Did" (for Adam Hammer, 1949-1984). [NoAmR] (276:4) D 91, p. 15.

2808. HOWELL, D. A.
"The End of October." [BellR] (14:2) Fall 91, p. 32.

2809. HOWELL, David
"Trees on the Slough." [HawaiiR] (15:2, #32) Spr 91, p. 164.

2810. HOWER, Mary
"Blue Cows" (After Franz Marc's "The Dream"). [CalQ] (32/33) Spr 90, p. 87.
"Field Mice." [CalQ] (32/33) Spr 90, p. 88.

2811. HOYDAL, Gunnar
"Greeting to a Paper Star Cutter" (to William Heinesen on his 85th birthday, tr. by George Johnston). [Vis] (37) 91, p. 16-17.

2812. HOYLMAN, Loana
"A Silly, Smiling Poem." [HawaiiR] (15:2, #32) Spr 91, p. 108.

2813. HRISTOV, Boris
"Solitary Man" (tr. by Lisa Sapinkopf). [BlackWR] (18:1) Fall-Wint 91, p. 99.

HSIAO-SHIH, Hu
    See HU, Hsiao-shih

2814. HU, Hsiao-shih
"In the Yueh-lu Mountains" (tr. by Matthew Flannery). [LitR] (35:1) Fall 91, p. 75.
"Listening to the Singing of Tung Lien-chih" (tr. by Matthew Flannery). [LitR] (35:1) Fall 91, p. 75.
"On Dead Soldiers: II" (tr. by Matthew Flannery). [LitR] (35:1) Fall 91, p. 76.
"Watching a Homeless Woman Sell Her Clothing" (tr. by Matthew Flannery). [LitR] (35:1) Fall 91, p. 75.

HUA, Chen Ming
    See CHEN, Ming Hua

2815. HUA, Fengmao
"Assembly Line" (tr. of Shu Ting). [GreenMR] (NS 4:2) Wint-Spr 91, p. 24.
"Departure" (tr. of Chen Ming Hua). [GreenMR] (NS 4:2) Wint-Spr 91, p. 29.
"I Can Recognize" (tr. of Liang Xiao Bing). [GreenMR] (NS 4:2) Wint-Spr 91, p. 44.

HUA, Li Min
    See LI, Min Hua

2816. HUCHEL, Peter
"The Garden of Theophrastus" (to my son, tr. by Daniel Simko). [Ploughs] (17:4) Wint 91-92, p. 17.
"Landscape Beyond Warsaw" (tr. by Daniel Simko). [Ploughs] (17:4) Wint 91-92, p. 15.
"On Crutches of Naked Poplars" (Translation Chapbook Series, Number 15: 14 poems in German and English, tr. by Robert Firmage). [MidAR] (11:1) 91, p. 137-173.
"Psalm" (tr. by Daniel Simko). [Ploughs] (17:4) Wint 91-92, p. 18.
"Roads" (tr. by Daniel Simko). [Ploughs] (17:4) Wint 91-92, p. 16.

2817. HUDDLE, David
"At the Desert Museum." [GettyR] (4:3) Sum 91, p. 460-461.
"Creation Myth." [Journal] (15:1) Spr 91, p. 18-19.
"Local Metaphysics." [GettyR] (4:3) Sum 91, p. 463-464.
"Love and Art." [AntR] (49:3) Sum 91, p. 427.
"Quiet Hour." [Journal] (15:1) Spr 91, p. 16-17.
"The Swimmer." [Boulevard] (5:3/6:1, #15/16) Spr 91, p. 210-213.
"Upstairs Hallway, 5 A.M." [Journal] (15:1) Spr 91, p. 15.

2818. HUDGINS, Andrew
"Aunt Mary Jean." [ParisR] (33:121) Wint 91, p. 189.
"Begotten." [Shen] (41:1) Spr 91, p. 56.
"Beneath Searchlights." [NewRep] (204:17) 29 Ap 91, p. 38.
"Childhood of the Ancients." [WestHR] (45:4) Wint 91, p. 324.
"Dead Christ." [NewRep] (204:14) 8 Ap 91, p. 32.
"In the Game." [Atlantic] (267:3) Mr 91, p. 96.
"Mending Socks." [WestHR] (45:4) Wint 91, p. 323.
"Salt." [KenR] (NS 13:3) Sum 91, p. 60.
"Tree." [KenR] (NS 13:3) Sum 91, p. 59.
"What a Grand World It Would Be!" [WestHR] (45:2) Sum 91, p. 111.
"When I Was Saved." [Shen] (41:1) Spr 91, p. 57.

2819. HUDSON, Marc
"Franz Marc." [CrabCR] (7:2) Sum 91, p. 4.
"Muskeg." [HopewellR] (1991) 91, p. 22.
"Query." [HopewellR] (1991) 91, p. 13.
"Remembering Nespelem." [HopewellR] (1991) 91, p. 14.
2820. HUDZIK, Robert
"The Luck of Creatures." [Poetry] (158:2) My 91, p. 90.
2821. HUERTA, Joel
"Cuauhtemoc Calendar, and Cubism." [Colum] (16) Spr 91, p. 119-120.
"The Flower Cutters." [CutB] (36) Sum 91, p. 18-19.
2822. HUESGEN, Jan
"Living with What Belongs to Us." [SoDakR] (29:3 part 2) Aut 91, p. 108-109.
2823. HUFFAKER, Phil
"Deep Chested and Pale." [OnTheBus] (8/9) 91, p. 85-86.
"Pipe Fitting." [OnTheBus] (8/9) 91, p. 87-88.
"Weenies." [OnTheBus] (8/9) 91, p. 88.
2824. HUFFSTICKLER, Albert
"Del Rio : Stars." [PaintedHR] (1) Ja 91, p. 6.
"Markings" (Joanna Nelson was here, Aug. 18, 1985 — Sept. 14, 1985 at the
Highland Mall Bus Stop, Austin, TX). [SlipS] (11) 91, p. 45.
"Sense of Place." [CoalC] (3) My 91, p. 19.
"Waiting for Margaret" (Municipal Airport, Austin, Texas, April 30, 1988). [CoalC]
(4) S 91, p. 7.
2825. HUGGINS, Peter
"The Anesthetist Dreams of Paradise." [CapeR] (26:2) Fall 91, p. 11.
"The Dead Shall Be Raised Indestructible." [CumbPR] (11:1) Fall 91, p. 59-60.
"For the Man Who Struck a Small Boy One Wednesday Afternoon in Auburn"
(Honorable Mention, Robert Penn Warren Poetry Prize Competition).
[CumbPR] (11:1) Fall 91, p. 57-58.
2826. HUGHES, Carolyn Fairweather
"Deacon Jones and the Honkytonk Hideaway." [Lactuca] (14) My 91, p. 34.
2827. HUGHES, Charlie G.
"Hearing the Owl." [InterPR] (17:2) Fall 91, p. 142.
"Storm." [InterPR] (17:2) Fall 91, p. 143.
2828. HUGHES, Henry J.
"Men Holding Eggs." [SoCoast] (10) Fall 91, p. 12.
2829. HUGHES, Peter
"Out of Europe" (Selections: I, X). [Ploughs] (17:1) Spr 91, p. 95-j99.
2830. HUGHES, Philip
"Mirror, Mirror." [Pearl] (13) Spr-Sum 91, p. 47.
2831. HUGHES, Ron
"My Brother Sleeps." [Elf] (1:2) Sum 91, p. 32.
"Ravaged Garden." [Elf] (1:2) Sum 91, p. 33.
2832. HUGHES, Stephen
"The Night I Pulled a Jesse James." [NewYorkQ] (46) 91, p. 83.
2833. HUIDOBRO, Vicente
"La Poesía Es un Atentado Celeste." [InterPR] (17:2) Fall 91, p. 64.
"Poetry Is a Heavenly Crime" (tr. by Brent Duffin and Astrid Lindo). [InterPR]
(17:2) Fall 91, p. 67.
2834. HULETT, Jon
"White Roses with Skull" (In Memory of Georgia O'Keeffe)." [FreeL] (8) Aut 91,
p. 13.
2835. HULL, Lynda
"Abacus." [GreenMR] (NS 4:2) Wint-Spr 91, p. 87-89.
"Carnival" (Barcelona). [KenR] (NS 13:1) Wint 91, p. 125-126.
"Counting in Chinese." [GreenMR] (NS 4:2) Wint-Spr 91, p. 85-86.
"Gateway to Manhattan." [Boulevard] (5:3/6:1, #15/16) Spr 91, p. 121-122.
"Lost Fugue for Chet" (Chet Baker, Amsterdam, 1988). [KenR] (NS 13:1) Wint 91,
p. 127-128.
"Ornithology." [Ploughs] (17:2/3) Fall 91, p. 198-200.
"Utopia Parkway" (After Joseph Cornell's "Penny Arcade Portrait of Lauren Bacall,
1945-46"). [Poetry] (157:4) Ja 91, p. 207-208.
2836. HULL, Robert
"Dear Parents" (for introducing a reading of poems by children writer-readers).
[CumbPR] (10:2) Spr 91, p. 44-45.
"Nearly Working." [CumbPR] (10:2) Spr 91, p. 42-43.

"Rewind." [CumbPR] (10:2) Spr 91, p. 40-41.
2837. HULSE, Michael
"Celebration." [AntigR] (87/88) Fall 91-Wint 92, p. 260.
"Eating Strawberries in the Necropolis" (Carmona, Spain). [AntigR] (84) Wint 91,
p. 77.
"Snakes." [AntigR] (84) Wint 91, p. 78-79.
"The Train Set." [AntigR] (84) Wint 91, p. 80.
2838. HUMES, Harry
"The Day Oompano Left the Surf." [CinPR] (22) Spr 91, p. 19.
"Four Entered the Heavenly Orchard" (Babylonian Talmud, Hagigah 14b).
[SnailPR] (1:1) Spr 91, p. 13.
"Hand Dancing." [PoetryNW] (32:2) Sum 91, p. 6-7.
"Horseshoe Crab Shell." [PoetC] (23:1) Fall 91, p. 10.
"It Could Almost Stop a Heart." [CinPR] (22) Spr 91, p. 18.
"My Father's Mine." [WestB] (29) 91, p. 11.
"One August I Walked." [WestB] (29) 91, p. 10.
"The Rescue Squad." [SnailPR] (1:1) Spr 91, p. 10-11.
"Yesterday I Scattered Lime." [PoetC] (23:1) Fall 91, p. 9.
2839. HUMMER, T. R.
"Confusion in the Drought Years." [KenR] (NS 13:2) Spr 91, p. 72-73.
"Greek." [KenR] (NS 13:2) Spr 91, p. 71-72.
"Philadelphia Sentimental." [KenR] (NS 13:2) Spr 91, p. 70-71.
"Plate Glass" (for Edward Hirsch, and after Barthelme). [SouthernR] (27:1) Ja 91,
p. 51-53.
2840. HUMPHREY, Katherine
"Autumn." [CapeR] (26:1) Spr 91, p. 30.
"View from Milsons Point Station: Night." [CapeR] (26:1) Spr 91, p. 29.
2841. HUMPHRIES, Jefferson (Jeff)
"Giant Clam." [SouthernPR] (31:1) Spr 91, p. 42-43.
"Southern Aphrodite." [MichQR] (30:1) Wint 91, p. 96-97.
2842. HUNGTINGTON, Elizabeth
"Fidelity." [SilverFR] (20) Spr 91, p. 20.
2843. HUNTER, Donnell
"An Accounting." [QW] (32) Wint-Spr 91, p. 97.
"Backstage." [QW] (32) Wint-Spr 91, p. 98.
"The Doe." [PoetryE] (31) Spr 91, p. 147.
2844. HUNTER, Terrell
"Jack Shack Blues." [NewYorkQ] (44) 91, p. 81-82.
2845. HURFORD, Chris
"Greek." [Verse] (8:2) Sum 91, p. 42.
"The Querist." [Verse] (8:2) Sum 91, p. 40.
"The Weatherman." [Verse] (8:2) Sum 91, p. 41.
"XXX" (3 poems, tr. of Artur Przystupa, w. Tomek Kitlinski and Góska A.
Staniewska). [Verse] (8:2) Sum 91, p. 119-120.
"Young Love." [Verse] (8:2) Sum 91, p. 42.
2846. HURLEY, Maureen
"Country of Origin." [SingHM] (19) 91, p. 65-68.
2847. HURLOW, Marcia L.
"Appointment with Ellen J., 3 P.M." [SycamoreR] (3:1) Wint 91, p. 12-15.
"The Bhagi (Mauritania)" (for Bruce Chatwin). [PoetryE] (32) Fall 91, p. 95.
"C'Hoantenn." [SpoonRQ] (16:3/4) Sum-Fall 91, p. 79.
"Dangers of Travel." [PoetryE] (32) Fall 91, p. 96.
"Dangers of Travel." [SpoonRQ] (16:3/4) Sum-Fall 91, p. 80.
2848. HURT, Lana
"Standing at the Fence." [Kalliope] (13:2) 91, p. 25-26.
2849. HURWITZ, Seth
"Whales." [PacificR] (10) 91-92, p. 60-61.
2850. HUTCHESON, Robert J., Jr.
"An Encounter with an Order Form." [EngJ] (80:3) Mr 91, p. 97.
2851. HUTCHISON, Joseph
"At the Arts Fundraiser" (For David Guerrero). [Vis] (36) 91, p. 47.
"Children's Hospital, 1959" (for Melody). [WritersF] (17) Fall 91, p. 105-106.
"Shadowy Trees." [Poetry] (157:5) F 91, p. 288.
"The Wound." [Poetry] (157:5) F 91, p. 288.
2852. HUTCHISON, S. T. (Scott Travis)
"Outer Space." [PoetL] (86:4) Wint 91-92, p. 31-32.

"Restraint." [ChatR] (11:4) Sum 91, p. 36-37.
"The Rockinghorse Winners." [PoetL] (86:4) Wint 91-92, p. 33-34.
2853. HUTH, Geof A.
"A Stone of the First Water." [Archae] (1) Fall 90, p. 36-37.
2854. HWANG, Yunte
"Flight" (tr. by Xiaofei Tian). [PraS] (65:2) Sum 91, p. 105.
2855. HYETT, Barbara Helfgott
"Columbus and the Branch of Fire." [BellR] (14:2) Fall 91, p. 20.
"The Double Reckoning of Christopher Columbus" (3 selections). [Kalliope] (13:2)
    91, p. 10-13.
"The Frigate Bird." [Agni] (34) 91, p. 139.
"Rain." [Agni] (34) 91, p. 138.
"The Widow." [SingHM] (19) 91, p. 70-71.
2856. HYKIN, Susan
"The Book." [Event] (20:3) Fall 91, p. 52.
HYON, Jong Chong
    See CHONG, Hyon-Jong
HYON-JONG, Chong
    See CHONG, Hyon-Jong
2857. I., Alex
"In a Dream." [EmeraldCR] (3) 91, c1990, p. 43-44.
2858. IBAÑEZ ROSAZZA, Mercedes
"El Autobus." [Inti] (34/35) Otoño 91-Primavera 92, p. 267-268.
"Buenas Noches Gato." [Inti] (34/35) Otoño 91-Primavera 92, p. 268.
"Sigismundo en el Sueño." [Inti] (34/35) Otoño 91-Primavera 92, p. 267.
2859. IBN DARRAJ AL-QASTALLI
"The Lily" (tr. by Christopher Middleton and Leticia Garcia-Falcón). [ParisR]
    (33:118) Spr 91, p. 26.
2860. IBN SARA
"Eggplant" (tr. by Christopher Middleton and Leticia Garcia-Falcón). [ParisR]
    (33:118) Spr 91, p. 26.
2861. IBN ZAMRAK
"The Alhambra Inscription" (tr. by Christopher Middleton and Leticia
    Garcia-Falcón). [ParisR] (33:118) Spr 91, p. 24-25.
2862. IDDINGS, Kathleen
"Catch of the Day." [Pearl] (13) Spr-Sum 91, p. 49.
"My Body Starts Remembering." [Pearl] (13) Spr-Sum 91, p. 49.
2863. IERONIM, Ioana
"Certainty" (tr. by Adam J. Sorkin and Sergiu Celac). [LitR] (35:1) Fall 91, p. 34.
"Oath of Allegiance" (tr. by Adam J. Sorkin and Sergiu Celac). [LitR] (35:1) Fall 91,
    p. 34.
2864. IGNATOW, David
"10. When I was a tiny mouselike creature." [Boulevard] (5:3/6:1, #15/16) Spr 91,
    p. 97.
"43. I don't know which to mourn." [Boulevard] (5:3/6:1, #15/16) Spr 91, p. 98.
"Armor." [NorthStoneR] (10) Fall 91-Wint 92, p. 12.
"An Autumn Tale." [FourQ] (5:2) Fall 91, p. 27.
"The Chipmunk." [ArtfulD] (20/21) 91, p. 65.
"The Chipmunk." [NorthStoneR] (10) Fall 91-Wint 92, p. 12.
"In Passing." [FourQ] (5:2) Fall 91, p. 28.
"In place of you." [SpoonRQ] (16:1/2) Wint-Spr 91, p. 100.
"Love." [ArtfulD] (20/21) 91, p. 65.
"Peace." [ArtfulD] (20/21) 91, p. 64.
"Shadowing the Ground: Untitled Poems" (Selections: 3, 24, 31, 39).
    [NorthStoneR] (10) Fall 91-Wint 92, p. 14-15.
"Signs." [ArtfulD] (20/21) 91, p. 65.
"Story." [ArtfulD] (20/21) 91, p. 65.
"Today." [NorthStoneR] (10) Fall 91-Wint 92, p. 13.
"Your body is not mine." [SpoonRQ] (16:1/2) Wint-Spr 91, p. 100.
2865. IKINS, Rachael K.
"Dinner Hour." [Writer] (104:12) D 91, p. 25.
2866. ILHAN, Attila
"Byle Bir Sevmek." [InterPR] (17:1) Spr 91, p. 16.
"Such Love" (tr. by Ozcan Yalim, William A. Fielder and Dionis Coffin Riggs).
    [InterPR] (17:1) Spr 91, p. 17.

ILLÉS, Gyula
    See ILLYÉS, Gyula
2867. ILLESCAS, Carlos
    "If You Wish" (tr. by Victor Valle). [OnTheBus] (8/9) 91, p. 207.
    "Invocation" (tr. by Victor Valle). [OnTheBus] (8/9) 91, p. 206.
    "Let's Bite His Hand" (tr. by Victor Valle). [OnTheBus] (8/9) 91, p. 207.
2868. ILLICK, Peter
    "Borrow Cars." [HighP] (6:1) Spr 91, p. 25-26.
    "Degree of Certainty." [HampSPR] Wint 91, p. 21.
    "The Farm Stand." [PlumR] (1) Spr-Sum 91, p. 36.
    "Salmon Fishing." [HampSPR] Wint 91, p. 21.
2869. ILLYÉS, Gyula
    "Hope in the Air" (tr. by Bruce Berlind, w. Mária Körösy). [Os] (33) Fall 91, p. 3.
    "Remény a Légben." [Os] (33) Fall 91, p. 2.
    "The Year Drops Anchor, Tihany" (tr. by Bruce Berlind, w. Mária Körösy). [Vis]
            (36) 91, p. 20.
2870. IMBRIGLIO, Catherine
    "Aubade." [Caliban] (10) 91, p. 27.
    "Season." [Caliban] (10) 91, p. 26.
2871. IMHOF, Susan
    "Barnswallows." [Timbuktu] (6) Spr 91, p. 21.
    "Fear." [Timbuktu] (6) Spr 91, p. 21.
2872. INADA, Lawson Fusao
    "California Vision." [PaintedHR] (2) Spr 91, p. 18.
    "Legends from Camp." [NowestR] (29:3) 91, p. 83-101.
2873. INBAR, Tomer
    "Among the Rags and Cloth." [ChangingM] (23) Fall-Wint 91, p. 13.
    "Camellia." [ChangingM] (23) Fall-Wint 91, p. 18.
2874. INCE, Ozdemir
    "Bird's Eye View" (tr. by Talat Halman). [Talisman] (6) Spr 91, p. 113.
    "Poet's Nonalignment" (tr. by Talat Halman). [Talisman] (6) Spr 91, p. 113.
INDIANA BOB
    See BOB, Indiana
2875. INDREEIDE, Erling
    "The Deer Runs Fast Through the Forest" (tr. by the author and Deborah Tannen).
            [Vis] (37) 91, p. 44.
2876. INEZ, Colette
    "The Abduction." [LitR] (35:1) Fall 91, p. 54.
    "Assault." [NewYorkQ] (46) 91, p. 22.
    "Getting Under Way." [ThRiPo] (37/38) 91, p. 18-19.
    "Guarding the Unrevealed." [ThRiPo] (37/38) 91, p. 17.
    "Hands." [SingHM] (19) 91, p. 102-103.
    "Journeys." [NewYorkQ] (45) 91, p. 47.
    "Kinderszenen Fantasy." [CalQ] (32/33) Spr 90, p. 136.
    "The Mad Shepherd." [CalQ] (32/33) Spr 90, p. 137.
    "The Maze." [LitR] (35:1) Fall 91, p. 55.
    "Ohio Letters." [PoetryNW] (32:4) Wint 91-92, p. 26-27.
    "Our Guardians in Belgium." [GrahamHR] (15) Fall 91, p. 59-60.
    "Route One's Purgatory in New Jersey." [Ploughs] (17:4) Wint 91-92, p. 123.
    "Santa Cruz Idyll." [AmerV] (23) Sum 91, p. 22-23.
2877. ING, Jason
    "Memo." [HawaiiR] (15:3, #33) Fall 91, p. 76.
2878. INGEBRETSEN, Mark
    "The Lesson." [NegC] (11:1) 91, p. 13-15.
2879. INGERSON, Martin I.
    "A Fragment of Ancient Knowledge." [BellArk] (7:4) Jl-Ag 91, p. 22.
    "Ingrid at Eighteen: November 1991." [BellArk] (7:6) N-D 91, p. 1.
    "Nelson Bentley, Poet: 1918-1990." [BellArk] (7:1) Ja-F 91, p. 4.
    "Sapphics Remembered: What Are They?" [BellArk] (7:3) My-Je 91, p. 10.
2880. INMAN, P.
    "Plainsong." [Aerial] (6/7) 91, p. 65-68.
    "Subtracted Words." [Aerial] (6/7) 91, p. 72-75.
2881. INMAN, Will
    "Essay Written on 4th of July Eve, 1990." [ChironR] (10:4) Wint 91, p. 36.
    "Geldings Restored." [NewYorkQ] (45) 91, p. 56.

2882. INSKEEP-FOX, Sandra
"Two of Us Dancing." [Comm] (118:11) 1 Je 91, p. 374.
2883. INVERARITY, Geoffrey
"In a Place of Many Paths" (Drogheda, Ireland, September 21, 1649). [AntigR] (84)
Wint 91, p. 53.
"The Inspector's Last Report" (Drogheda, Ireland, September 21, 1649). [AntigR]
(84) Wint 91, p. 56-57.
"Paths Meet in the Place of Death" (Drogheda, Ireland, September 21, 1649).
[AntigR] (84) Wint 91, p. 54.
"Sum Over Histories" (Drogheda, Ireland, September 21, 1649). [AntigR] (84) Wint
91, p. 55.
IOANNA-VERONIKA
  See WARWICK, Ioanna-Veronika
2884. IOANNOU, Susan
"At War: Winter Night, Parliament Hill." [PraF] (12:4) Wint 91-92, p. 92.
"Watching CNN: Iraq, the Aftermath." [PraF] (12:4) Wint 91-92, p. 93.
2885. IRA
"Sunbow." [PoetryUSA] (23) Sum 91, p. 21.
2886. IRBY, Kenneth
"Late, and nothing finished again, the Fratres play." [Notus] (9) Fall 91, p. 55.
"The referential is the clear telling" (After a gift of poems from Roy Gridley).
[Notus] (9) Fall 91, p. 57.
"There we have gone off along the railroad tracks into, to school." [Notus] (9) Fall
91, p. 57.
"To come to midnight writing and thinking about coming to midnight." [Notus] (9)
Fall 91, p. 56.
"To look into the pits of." [Notus] (9) Fall 91, p. 54.
2887. IRIE, Kevin
"The Exceptional Student." [AntigR] (84) Wint 91, p. 81-82.
2888. IRION, Mary Jean
"Double Rainbow" (Over a Walking Safari in Kenya). [ChrC] (108:3) 23 Ja 91, p.
71.
2889. IRWIN, Joe
"The Domestication of Language." [FreeL] (8) Aut 91, p. 20.
2890. IRWIN, Mark
"Bucharest, 1981" (for Mihai Iordache). [Agni] (33) 91, p. 238.
"For Jackson Pollock (1912-1956)." [NewEngR] (13:3/4) Spr-Sum 91, p. 253.
"Motion." [DenQ] (25:3) Wint 91, p. 12.
"On Language." [Agni] (33) 91, p. 236-237.
"Rumors of Civilization and History." [DenQ] (25:3) Wint 91, p. 10-11.
ISAAC, Robert Mac
  See Mac ISAAC, Robert
2891. ISAACS, Jennifer
"Air and Water" (8 a.m. Saturday). [PaintedB] (44) 91, p. 7.
2892. ISAACSON, Bruce
"For Barbara." [BrooklynR] (8) 91, p. 44.
2893. ISAACSON, Lisa
"The Anorexic Town." [Poem] (65) My 91, p. 35.
"The Marriage of Reina." [Poem] (65) My 91, p. 32-33.
"Town of the Twin Spires." [Poem] (65) My 91, p. 34.
2894. ISERMAN, Bruce
"The Fire Eater." [CanLit] (130) Aut 91, p. 106.
"True Heart, Two A.M." [PraF] (12:2 #55) Sum 91, p. 63.
2895. ISHIGAKI, Rin
"Lie" (tr. by John Solt). [Manoa] (3:2) Fall 91, p. 32.
2896. ISKRENKO, Nina
"Fugue" (tr. by John High and Katya Olmsted). [Talisman] (6) Spr 91, p. 114-115.
2897. ISMAIL, Jam.
"Scared Texts" (Excerpt). [CapilR] (2:6/7) Fall 91, p. 20-32.
2898. ISMAILI, Rashidah
"Reflections of Gorée." [CentralP] (19/20) Spr-Fall 91, p. 255-263.
2899. ISOLOMON, Marvin
"Emily's Room." [Poetry] (159:3) D 91, p. 136.
2900. ISRAEL, Jack
"Future Physicians' Club Field Trip, 1964." [AmerPoR] (20:2) Mr-Ap 91, p. 20.
"The Liar." [AmerPoR] (20:2) Mr-Ap 91, p. 20.

"Startled by the 'I's" (for Elaine Terranova). [CreamCR] (15:2) Fall 91, p. 71.
"Sunday Dinner." [AmerPoR] (20:2) Mr-Ap 91, p. 20.
2901. ISSA
"Sadness of Cool Melons" (28 Haiku, tr. by Lucien Stryk and Naboru Fujiwara).
[MidAR] (11:2) 91, p. 1-10.
2902. ITWARU, Arnold
"Chant Two." [GrahamHR] (14) Spr 91, p. 34.
2903. IUPPA, M. J.
"Balance." [Blueline] (12) 91, p. 85.
"Temptation: The Nest." [CalQ] (31) Fall 88, p. 39.
2904. IVEREM, Esther
"Murmur." [Nat] (253:1) 1 Jl 91, p. 26.
2905. IVERSEN, Carol Diane
"Mallard." [Writer] (104:9) S 91, p. 24.
2906. IVERSON, Carrie
"Hall of Mirrors." [Pearl] (13) Spr-Sum 91, p. 18.
2907. IVRY, Benjamin
"Autumn" (Excerpted from "Canvas," tr. of Adam Zagajewksi, w. Renata
Gorczynski and C. K. Williams). [ManhatR] (6:1) Fall 91, p. 50.
"The Bells" (for C. K. Williams, Excerpted from "Canvas," tr. of Adam Zagajewksi,
w. Renata Gorczynski and C. K. Williams). [ManhatR] (6:1) Fall 91, p. 51.
"Burgundy's Grasslands" (Excerpted from "Canvas," tr. of Adam Zagajewksi, w.
Renata Gorczynski and C. K. Williams). [ManhatR] (6:1) Fall 91, p. 46.
"Canvas" (Excerpted from "Canvas," tr. of Adam Zagajewksi, w. Renata
Gorczynski and C. K. Williams). [ManhatR] (6:1) Fall 91, p. 53.
"Covenant" (tr. of Adam Zagajewski, w. Renata Gorczynski). [NewYorker] (66:48)
14 Ja 91, p. 34.
"Electric Elegy" (Excerpted from "Canvas," tr. of Adam Zagajewksi, w. Renata
Gorczynski and C. K. Williams). [ManhatR] (6:1) Fall 91, p. 47.
"From the Lives of Things" (Excerpted from "Canvas," tr. of Adam Zagajewksi, w.
Renata Gorczynski and C. K. Williams). [ManhatR] (6:1) Fall 91, p. 52.
"Green Linnaeus" (Excerpted from "Canvas," tr. of Adam Zagajewksi, w. Renata
Gorczynski and C. K. Williams). [ManhatR] (6:1) Fall 91, p. 48.
"On a Side Street" (Excerpted from "Canvas," tr. of Adam Zagajewksi, w. Renata
Gorczynski and C. K. Williams). [ManhatR] (6:1) Fall 91, p. 45.
"Spider's Song" (Excerpted from "Canvas," tr. of Adam Zagajewksi, w. Renata
Gorczynski and C. K. Williams). [ManhatR] (6:1) Fall 91, p. 44.
"Watching *Shoah* in a Hotel Room in America" (Excerpted from "Canvas," tr. of
Adam Zagajewksi, w. Renata Gorczynski and C. K. Williams). [ManhatR]
(6:1) Fall 91, p. 49.
2908. IZENBERG, Oren
"Libertad" (Second Prize). [HarvardA] (125:4) Mr 91, p. 17.
"Olive Street, October 1990." [HarvardA] (127 [i.e. 125]:3) Ja 91, p. 18.
"On Fish, Metaphors." [HarvardA] (127 [i.e. 125]:3) Ja 91, p. 23.
"You Return." [NewYorkQ] (46) 91, p. 84.
IZUMI, Shikibu
See SHIKIBU, Izumi
2909. JABES, Edmond
"Method" (from "The Book of Resemblances III: The Ineffaceable, The
Unperceived," tr. by Rosmarie Waldrop). [ManhatR] (6:1) Fall 91, p. 40-43.
"Of Absent Mind, Of Whiteness" (from "The Book of Resemblances III: The
Ineffaceable, The Unperceived," tr. by Rosmarie Waldrop). [ManhatR] (6:1)
Fall 91, p. 34-39.
2910. JACKSON, Dan
"Annuncio." [InterPR] (17:1) Spr 91, p. 85.
"Just a Note." [InterPR] (17:1) Spr 91, p. 84.
"Lent." [InterPR] (17:1) Spr 91, p. 83.
"Spiritus Mundi." [InterPR] (17:1) Spr 91, p. 85.
2911. JACKSON, Donna
"Dreams of Red Riding." [Prima] (14/15) 91, p. 10-11.
"Rerooting." [Prima] (14/15) 91, p. 9.
2912. JACKSON, Fleda Brown
"Ballroom Dancing." [Iowa] (21:1) Wint 91, p. 102.
"Birth Facts." [SycamoreR] (3:1) Wint 91, p. 3.
"Bombay Hook." [SouthernHR] (25:1) Wint 91, p. 22.
"Burdett Palmer's Foot." [MidAR] (11:2) 91, p. 129-130.

"Cedar River." [MidAR] (11:2) 91, p. 131-132.
"The Farthest-North Southern Town." [BelPoJ] (41:4) Sum 91, p. 1.
"Flashlight Tag." [Iowa] (21:1) Wint 91, p. 103-104.
"If I Were a Swan." [Iowa] (21:1) Wint 91, p. 104-105.
"An Introduction." [Iowa] (21:1) Wint 91, p. 105-106.
"The Islanders." [WestB] (28) 91, p. 14.
"Learning to Dance." [Iowa] (21:1) Wint 91, p. 101.
"The Lost Colony." [MidwQ] (32:2) Wint 91, p. 186-187.
"Minnow." [SycamoreR] (3:2) Sum 91, p. 22.
"Mrs. Williams." [SycamoreR] (3:1) Wint 91, p. 4-5.
"Two Writers Discuss Their Work." [WestB] (28) 91, p. 15.

2913. JACKSON, Laura (Riding)
"Across a Hedge." [Chelsea] (52) 91, p. 38.
"Another apple." [Chelsea] (52) 91, p. 17.
"Appearances." [Chelsea] (52) 91, p. 19-21.
"Ars Mortis." [Chelsea] (52) 91, p. 28-29.
"Bereavement." [Chelsea] (52) 91, p. 32-33.
"Can Lips Be Laid Aside?" [Chelsea] (52) 91, p. 27.
"Dimensions." [Chelsea] (52) 91, p. 34-35.
"The Dissolution of One." [Chelsea] (52) 91, p. 31.
"Divestment." [Chelsea] (52) 91, p. 16.
"Evasions." [Chelsea] (52) 91, p. 18.
"Heed." [Chelsea] (52) 91, p. 26.
"Improprieties." [Chelsea] (52) 91, p. 36-37.
"Lines in Farewell." [Chelsea] (52) 91, p. 30.
"Makeshift." [Chelsea] (52) 91, p. 22-23.
"Notwithstanding Love." [Chelsea] (52) 91, p. 13.
"Presences." [Chelsea] (52) 91, p. 24.
"Tears Are a Celebration." [Chelsea] (52) 91, p. 25.
"To a Broken Statue." [Chelsea] (52) 91, p. 39.
"To a Proud Lover." [Chelsea] (52) 91, p. 14-15.

2914. JACKSON, Lorri
"Angelica." [NewAW] (7) Spr 91, p. 72.
"Mythmaking: I Am All" (for Lydia Lunch). [NewAW] (7) Spr 91, p. 73.
"A Prima Donna Poet Replies." [Spirit] (11) 91, p. 134-135.

2915. JACKSON, Richard
"Haydn's Head." [NoAmR] (276:2) Je 91, p. 30-31.
"The Head of the Devil." [GeoR] (45:2) Sum 91, p. 290-292.
"A Letter from the Outdoor Cafe at the Lippanzer Stud Farm, Vilenica, Yugoslavia."
       [PassN] (12:2) Wint 91, p. 25.
"A Violation." [Crazy] (40) Spr 91, p. 29-32.

2916. JACKSON, Steve
"Iron Mask." [Hellas] (2:2) Fall 91, p. 271.
"Light and Water." [Hellas] (2:2) Fall 91, p. 270.

2917. JACOB, Bob
"This Beach" (Sanibel / 1987). [US1] (24/25) Spr 91, p. 36.

2918. JACOB, Sheila
"Undercover." [CoalC] (3) My 91, p. 19.

2919. JACOBIK, Gray
"The Laughing Buddha." [ClockR] (7:1/2) 91-92, p. 32.
"Marriage Counseling." [ClockR] (7:1/2) 91-92, p. 33.

2920. JACOBOWITZ, Judah
"Immortality." [Plain] (11:2) Wint 91, p. 28.
"Madame B." [JINJPo] (13:2) Aut 91, p. 21.

2921. JACOBSEN, Josephine
"The Gathering." [13thMoon] (9:1/2) 91, p. 30-31.
"I Have Something to Declare." [KenR] (NS 13:2) Spr 91, p. 136.
"The Letters." [Nimrod] (34:2) Spr-Sum 91, p. 41.
"The Limbo Dancer." [GrandS] (10:1, #37) 91, p. 166-167.
"The Minor Poet." [KenR] (NS 13:2) Spr 91, p. 136-137.
"Survivor's Ballad." [KenR] (NS 13:2) Spr 91, p. 138.
"The Thing About Crows." [KenR] (NS 13:2) Spr 91, p. 137.

2922. JACOBSEN, Rolf
"Antenna-Forest" (tr. by Robert Hedin). [WillowS] (27) Wint 91, p. 58.
"Are They Waiting for a Star?" (tr. by Robert Hedin). [CrabCR] (7:2) Sum 91, p.
       13.

217

"Aviation" (tr. by Robert Hedin). [WillowS] (27) Wint 91, p. 59.
"Bridge" (tr. by Robert Hedin). [InterPR] (17:2) Fall 91, p. 37.
"Broen." [InterPR] (17:2) Fall 91, p. 36.
"But We Live" (tr. by Robert Hedin). [ColR] (NS 17:2) Fall-Wint 90, p. 101.
"Det Var en Gammel Natt." [InterPR] (17:2) Fall 91, p. 36.
"Grass" (tr. by Stephanie Hegstad and Aina Gerner-Mathisen). [Field] (44) Spr 91,
    p. 39.
"Green Light." [Spirit] (11) 91, p. 77.
"The May Moon" (tr. by Robert Hedin). [WillowS] (27) Wint 91, p. 60.
"Metro" (tr. by Robert Hedin). [WillowS] (27) Wint 91, p. 61.
"Refugee" (tr. by Stephanie Hegstad and Aina Gerner-Mathisen). [Field] (44) Spr
    91, p. 40.
"Sky Lab" (tr. by Stephanie Hegstad and Aina Gerner-Mathisen). [Field] (44) Spr
    91, p. 41.
"Suddenly. In December" (tr. by Stephanie Hegstad and Aina Gerner-Mathisen).
    [Field] (44) Spr 91, p. 38.
"There Was an Old Night" (tr. by Robert Hedin). [InterPR] (17:2) Fall 91, p. 37.
"To You" (tr. by Roger Greenwald). [AmerPoR] (20:1) Ja-F 91, p. 16.
2923. JACOBSEN, Steinbjørn B.
"Your Landscape and Ours" (tr. by George Johnston). [Vis] (37) 91, p. 18.
2924. JACOBSEN, Steven
"Post Marked." [SlipS] (11) 91, p. 60.
2925. JACOBSON, Dale
"Country of Lost Inventions." [AmerPoR] (20:1) Ja-F 91, p. 36.
"Faces of the Tyrant." [NorthStoneR] (10) Fall 91-Wint 92, p. 31.
2926. JACOBSON, Jean Alice
"In Stillness." [NewYorker] (67:22) 22 Jl 91, p. 56.
"Skater." [NewRep] (205:16) 14 O 91, p. 50.
2927. JACOBWITZ, Judah
"Nudes in a Warsaw Gallery (Bare Poles)." [Plain] (11:3) Spr 91, p. 31.
2928. JAEGER, Brenda
"Why We Stay." [Calyx] (13:2) Sum 91, p. 6.
2929. JAEGER, Lowell
"All I Have Learned." [PoetL] (86:1) Spr 91, p. 29-30.
"First Time." [CutB] (36) Sum 91, p. 64-65.
"Gone Fishin'." [PoetryE] (32) Fall 91, p. 99.
"How Many Horses." [HighP] (6:1) Spr 91, p. 49-50.
"Prelapsarian." [PoetL] (86:1) Spr 91, p. 27-28.
"Rainy Afternoon." [CutB] (36) Sum 91, p. 63.
"The Shelter." [PaintedHR] (2) Spr 91, p. 8.
"The Shelter." [WeberS] (8:1) Spr 91, p. 81.
"A Small Prayer." [SoCoast] (11) Wint 91, p. 51.
"Things My Children Will Never Know." [CreamCR] (14:2) Wint 91, p. 136-138.
"Transplanting the Lady Slippers." [HighP] (6:1) Spr 91, p. 47-48.
"Transplanting the Lady Slippers." [WeberS] (8:1) Spr 91, p. 79.
"Traveling Back." [WeberS] (8:1) Spr 91, p. 81.
"Vision." [PoetryE] (32) Fall 91, p. 100.
"Voices." [WeberS] (8:1) Spr 91, p. 80-81.
"What the Stones Know." [MidAR] (11:2) 91, p. 124-125.
"Wish I Could Shake Them Up." [HighP] (6:1) Spr 91, p. 44-46.
2930. JAFFE, Harold
"Vanilla Ice." [CentralP] (19/20) Spr-Fall 91, p. 248-250.
2931. JAFFE, Maggie
"Emily Dickinson." [Vis] (36) 91, p. 44.
"Henrich Heine." [FreeL] (8) Aut 91, p. 6.
"Oppie." [FreeL] (8) Aut 91, p. 7.
2932. JAFFE, Martha
"New Orleans." [Writer] (104:6) Je 91, p. 24.
2933. JAFFE, Sue
"The Biopsy." [Pearl] (13) Spr-Sum 91, p. 22.
JAGODZINSKA, Katarzyna Borun
    See BORUN-JAGODZINSKA, Katarzyna
2934. JAHN, Delila Ruth
"Future Realism." [Grain] (19:1) Spr 91, p. 44.

2935. JAKOPIN, Gitica
"5. Enough for you to simply look at me" (tr. by the author and Bruce Weigl).
[OhioR] (47) 91, p. 13.
"7. My door groans this summer night" (tr. by the author and Bruce Weigl). [ColR]
(NS 18:2) Fall-Wint 91, p. 84.
"13. All the woods smell of pitch" (tr. by the author and Bruce Weigl). [OhioR] (47)
91, p. 12.
"Peacocks" (tr. by the author and Bruce Weigl). [OhioR] (47) 91, p. 11.

2936. JAMES, Cynthia
"An Immigrant's Welcome" (Temple at Orange Valley). [GrahamHR] (14) Spr 91,
p. 75.

2937. JAMES, David
"Have You Heard the One?" [CapeR] (26:2) Fall 91, p. 21.
"No Return." [LitR] (35:1) Fall 91, p. 89.
"The Writing Workshop." [NewYorkQ] (45) 91, p. 88-89.

2938. JAMES, Frederick Bobor
"The Break of Dawn." [LitR] (34:4) Sum 91, p. 505-506.
"The Important People." [LitR] (34:4) Sum 91, p. 507.
"Ode to Gbomba." [LitR] (34:4) Sum 91, p. 506-507.

2939. JAMES, Sibyl
"Death Mama." [SwampR] (7/8) Spr-Sum 91, p. 6.
"In My Country." [SwampR] (7/8) Spr-Sum 91, p. 7-8.

2940. JAMES, Susan
"Shadows" (Prompted by the painting by J.W. Schofield). [Pembroke] (23) 91, p.
165.

2941. JAMES, Sydney
"Holiday in Yuma." [PaintedB] (44) 91, p. 8-9.
"The Untaken." (For Rockie). [NegC] (11:3) 91, p. 24-26.

2942. JAMIE, Kathleen
"Stone & Carver." [Verse] (8:2) Sum 91, p. 45.

2943. JAMISON, Barbara
"Ask This of a Mother Whose Daughter Has Been Tortured." [Spirit] (11) 91, p.
21-22.

2944. JAMMES, Francis
"Some Sunday Afternoon" (tr. by Antony Oldknow). [PoetryE] (32) Fall 91, p. 118.
"Water Trickles" (tr. by Antony Oldknow). [CalQ] (32/33) Spr 90, p. 132.
"Wet Clothes Slap" (tr. by Antony Oldknow). [CalQ] (32/33) Spr 90, p. 133.
"You'd Be Naked in the Pink" (tr. by Antony Oldknow). [CalQ] (32/33) Spr 90, p.
134.

2945. JANAS, Marci (Mari-Marcelle)
"Christmas 1961." [Timbuktu] (6) Spr 91, p. 98.
"Correlatives of Pain." [Field] (45) Fall 91, p. 47-51.
"Dreaming of Weddings." [Timbuktu] (6) Spr 91, p. 97.

2946. JANJETOVIC, Dragutin
"I Am There Where You Will Never Be" (tr. of Aleksander Ristovic). [CimR] (96) Jl
91, p. 26.
"Touches from Everywhere" (tr. of Aleksander Ristovic). [CimR] (96) Jl 91, p. 27.

2947. JANKO, Anna
"Reflection of an Old Woman in a Mirror" (Odbicie Starej w Lustrze, tr. by Georgia
Scott and David Malcolm). [Calyx] (13:3) Wint 91-92, p. 11.

2948. JANOWITZ, Phyllis
"The Saints of Leisure." [SouthwR] (76:1) Wint 91, p. 143-144.

2949. JANSMA, Esther
"Florence" (tr. by Steve Orlen). [PassN] (12:2) Wint 91, p. 27.
"Tucson, Arizona" (tr. by Steve Orlen). [PassN] (12:2) Wint 91, p. 27.

2950. JANZEN, Jean
"Chicago, 1954." [Journal] (15:2) Fall 91, p. 29-30.
"The Cousins." [PraS] (65:4) Wint 91, p. 109-110.
"Flash Flood." [PraS] (65:4) Wint 91, p. 108-109.
"Identifying the Fire." [Poetry] (158:5) Ag 91, p. 274-275.
"St. Basil's Cathedral." [Poetry] (159:3) D 91, p. 148.

2951. JANZEN, Rhoda
"Chartreuse." [CumbPR] (10:2) Spr 91, p. 34.
"Palm Jungle." [CumbPR] (10:2) Spr 91, p. 32-33.
"Pharaoh's Daughter." [ChrC] (108:12) 10 Ap 91, p. 404.
"Redbud." [InterPR] (17:2) Fall 91, p. 130.

219

JAQUISH

2952. JAQUISH, Karen I.
		"Song for Mischa." [Nat] (252:18) 13 My 91, p. 640.
2953. JARMAN, Mark
		"Chimney Swifts." [Crazy] (41) Wint 91, p. 70.
		"Cloud Sketch." [NewEngR] (13:3/4) Spr-Sum 91, p. 216.
		"Grid." [PoetryNW] (32:1) Spr 91, p. 15-16.
		"Iris." [Hudson] (44:2) Sum 91, p. 203-233.
		"Last Suppers." [Shen] (41:4) Wint 91, p. 51-55.
		"A Line of Eucalyptus." [PoetryNW] (32:1) Spr 91, p. 16.
		"Northern Insomnia." [NewEngR] (13:3/4) Spr-Sum 91, p. 217.
		"Pampocalia." [Crazy] (41) Wint 91, p. 69.
		"Patience." [Crazy] (41) Wint 91, p. 65-66.
		"Stratford-upon-Avon Butterfly Farm and Jungle Safari." [Crazy] (41) Wint 91, p.
			67-68.
		"Upwelling." [Crazy] (41) Wint 91, p. 63-64.
		"A Voice Tries Whispering." [PoetryNW] (32:1) Spr 91, p. 17.
2954. JARRELL, Randall
		"Protocols." [Crazy] (41) Wint 91, p. 84-85.
2955. JARVENPA, Diane
		"Thinking of Children." [LakeSR] (25) 91, p. 34.
2956. JARVIS, Edward
		"Punta Chueca." [Contact] (10:59/60/61) Spr 91, p. 29.
2957. JASON, Kathrine
		"The Cloister at Quattro Santi Coronati." [SoCoast] (11) Wint 91, p. 48-49.
		"Finding the Idea of Order in Vermeer" (From "Young Woman With a Water Jug").
			[Elf] (1:3) Fall 91, p. 38-39.
2958. JASPER, Pat
		"Trick or Treat." [Event] (20:2) Sum 91, p. 96-97.
2959. JASTRUN, Tomasz
		"Stony Brook on Long Island" (tr. by Daniel Bourne). [NewOR] (18:2) Sum 91, p.
			52-53.
2960. JAUSS, David
		"Elk-Hair Caddis." [Nat] (253:16) 11 N 91, p. 603.
		"The First Day" (for J.D.). [NoDaQ] (59:1) Wint 91, p. 71.
		"The Shirt" (for my son). [NoDaQ] (59:1) Wint 91, p. 72.
		"Slow River." [Nat] (253:1) 1 Jl 91, p. 27.
		"Smile." [Poetry] (157:6) Mr 91, p. 334.
JAX, Norita Dittberner
		See DITTBERNER-JAX, Norita
2961. JAY, Cellan
		"The Brain and the Body." [Grain] (19:2) Sum 91, p. 55.
		"They Hardly Know." [Grain] (19:2) Sum 91, p. 56.
2962. JAYE, Grace A.
		"At First Light." [EmeraldCR] (3) 91, c1990, p. 62-63.
2963. JECH, Jon
		"Meditation from a Beer Joint" (after a bad night). [BellArk] (7:1) Ja-F 91, p. 5.
2964. JEFFREY, Susu
		"Dancing with Tecumseh." [SingHM] (19) 91, p. 64.
2965. JENKINS, Louis
		"Adam." [PoetryE] (31) Spr 91, p. 112.
		"North Dakota." [PoetryE] (31) Spr 91, p. 110.
		"Soup." [PoetryE] (31) Spr 91, p. 111.
		"Wind Chime." [HawaiiR] (15:3, #33) Fall 91, p. 123.
2966. JENNERMANN, Donald L.
		"Calculating the Nearing Winter Solstice." [SoDakR] (29:4) Wint 91, p. 91.
		"Il Penseroso." [SoDakR] (29:4) Wint 91, p. 92.
2967. JENNESS, Rosemarie K.
		"A Conversation on the Soul: A One-Act Play" (tr. of Alexei Khvostenko). [LitR]
			(34:3) Spr 91, p. 361-362.
2968. JENNINGS, Michael
		"Green." [GrahamHR] (15) Fall 91, p. 77.
		"Hawk." [BelPoJ] (41:4) Sum 91, p. 19.
		"Mother of Angels." [GrahamHR] (15) Fall 91, p. 76.
		"Nightwood." [GrahamHR] (15) Fall 91, p. 75.
		"Tiger Dance." [ChatR] (11:4) Sum 91, p. 33.

2969. JENSEN, Carl Johan
"Early Morning Vigil" (tr. by Cathryn J. Sanderson). [Vis] (37) 91, p. 19.
2970. JENSEN, Doreen
"The Last Acre." [Plain] (12:1) Fall 91, p. 22.
2971. JENSEN, Jim
"Gomer." [NewYorkQ] (46) 91, p. 73.
2972. JENSEN, Laura
"A Didactic Poem" (After Michael Burkard). [CalQ] (32/33) Spr 90, p. 146-147.
"I Stood by the Table." [CalQ] (32/33) Spr 90, p. 145-146.
2973. JERMYN, Scott
"A Subtle Frame." [FourQ] (5:2) Fall 91, p. 46.
2974. JEROME, Judson
"3 A.M. (Más o Menos) Cadiz." [Elf] (1:1) Spr 91, p. 18-19.
"78. What I have done, first one and then another" (from "Time's Fool: A Story in
Sonnets Based on Those of Shakespeare"). [Elf] (1:3) Fall 91, p. 27.
"79. I thought this was our franchise: I alone" (from "Time's Fool: A Story in
Sonnets Based on Those of Shakespeare"). [Elf] (1:3) Fall 91, p. 28.
"80. My English skiff, that scarcely weighs a ton" (from "Time's Fool: A Story in
Sonnets Based on Those of Shakespeare"). [Elf] (1:3) Fall 91, p. 29.
"81. You will outlive me, one way or another" (from "Time's Fool: A Story in
Sonnets Based on Those of Shakespeare"). [Elf] (1:4) Wint 91, p. 21.
"82. Among females of my acquaintance, my" (from "Time's Fool: A Story in
Sonnets Based on Those of Shakespeare"). [Elf] (1:4) Wint 91, p. 22.
"Fool and Clown." [HampSPR] Wint 91, p. 56.
"Gregory of Bath on the Silk Road — a Fragment." [Pembroke] (23) 91, p.
119-129.
"Tinking Bout de Dog." [WilliamMR] (29) 91, p. 86.
"Training Flight, 1946." [CapeR] (26:1) Spr 91, p. 46.
2975. JEROZAL, Gregory
"Bannerman's Island." [InterPR] (17:2) Fall 91, p. 131.
"Ivy." [InterPR] (17:2) Fall 91, p. 132.
2976. JESS
"The Call of the Hermetic Nightjar." [PoetryUSA] (22) Spr 91, p. 5.
"A Little Ptarrydactyllic." [PoetryUSA] (22) Spr 91, p. 4.
"Song of the Little Chilldwren." [PoetryUSA] (22) Spr 91, p. 4.
"Whence Upon a Time." [PoetryUSA] (22) Spr 91, p. 8.
"Who Caught Queen Kore?" [PoetryUSA] (23) Sum 91, p. 9.
2977. JESSEAU, Ardessa-Nica
"Walking with the Samurai." [CapilR] (2:5) Sum 91, p. 56-57.
"Wood Charm." [CapilR] (2:5) Sum 91, p. 58-59.
JEW, Shalin Hai
See HAI-JEW, Shalin
2978. JEWELL, Terri (Terri L.)
"Basketeer." [SingHM] (19) 91, p. 97.
"Marking Time." [SlipS] (11) 91, p. 26.
2979. JIA, Dao
"Mountain Village" (tr. by Gao Yu-hua). [GreenMR] (NS 4:2) Wint-Spr 91, p. 114.
JIAN, Wang
See WANG, Jian
JIAN, Yu
See YU, Jian
2980. JIANG, He
"Filling the Sea" (tr. by Zhang Yichun). [GreenMR] (NS 4:2) Wint-Spr 91, p. 37.
2981. JIMENEZ, Juan Ramon
"The Jump" (tr. by Dennis Maloney). [YellowS] (36) Spr 91, p. 45.
"Return" (tr. by Dennis Maloney). [YellowS] (36) Spr 91, p. 43.
"Second Dawn" (tr. by Dennis Maloney). [YellowS] (36) Spr 91, p. 43.
"Serenade of the White Women" (Chopin, tr. by Dennis Maloney). [YellowS] (36)
Spr 91, p. 45.
"Sun" (tr. by Dennis Maloney). [YellowS] (36) Spr 91, p. 42.
"Sun in the Fragrant Spikes" (tr. by Dennis Maloney). [YellowS] (36) Spr 91, p. 42.
"To the Bread and Water of Light" (tr. by Dennis Maloney). [YellowS] (36) Spr 91,
p. 46.
"Whiteness" (tr. by Dennis Maloney). [YellowS] (36) Spr 91, p. 46.
2982. JIN, Ha
"A Child's Nature." [Ploughs] (17:2/3) Fall 91, p. 78-80.

221

JOACHIMIAK

2983. JOACHIMIAK, Zbigniew
"LVIII. A Letter to My Mother Among Things" (tr. of Tadeusz Zukowski, w. David
Malcolm and Georgia Scott). [WebR] (15) Spr 91, p. 41.
"All Souls'" (tr. of Krzysztof Lisowski, w. David Malcolm and Georgia Scott).
[WebR] (15) Spr 91, p. 44-45.
"Cell: one plank bed" (tr. of Bronislaw Maj, w. David Malcolm and Georgia Scott).
[WebR] (15) Spr 91, p. 45.
"Dice" (tr. by Georgia Scott, David Malcolm and the author). [WebR] (15) Spr 91,
p. 42.
"Whenever the conversation turned to the issue of dignity" (tr. of Andrzej Szuba, w.
David Malcolm and Georgia Scott). [WebR] (15) Spr 91, p. 42.
"Winter Time" (tr. of Jerzy Suchanek, w. David Malcolm and Georgia Scott).
[WebR] (15) Spr 91, p. 43.
2984. JOENSEN, Leyvoy
"Kata — a Belated Eulogy" (tr. of Ebba Hentze). [Vis] (37) 91, p. 23-26.
"Longing" (tr. of Roi Patursson). [Vis] (37) 91, p. 20.
"Poem About the Moon and Earth" (tr. of Roi Patursson). [Vis] (37) 91, p. 20.
"Soul" (tr. of Malan Poulsen). [Vis] (37) 91, p. 22.
"Thaw" (tr. of Gudrid Helmsdal). [Vis] (37) 91, p. 21.
"To an Old Relative" (tr. of Gudrid Helmsdal). [Vis] (37) 91, p. 21.
JOHN, Paul de
See DeJOHN, Paul
2985. JOHN, Roland
"Firelight." [SoCoast] (11) Wint 91, p. 16.
2986. JOHNSON, Adam
"The Gift" (for Don Bachardy on the Last Drawings of Christopher Isherwood).
[Interim] (10:1) Spr-Sum 91, p. 8.
2987. JOHNSON, Cary Alan
"The Piercing." [JamesWR] (8:4) Sum 91, p. 13.
"Protection: For Jay at the Big Three-O." [Agni] (33) 91, p. 70-71.
2988. JOHNSON, Corrine
"Right Out of Themselves." [OnTheBus] (8/9) 91, p. 90.
"Taking a Drink." [OnTheBus] (8/9) 91, p. 89.
2989. JOHNSON, Dan
"Attempting Magic." [LullwaterR] (2:2) Spr 91, p. 49.
"Maybe Desdemona." [LullwaterR] (2:2) Spr 91, p. 88.
2990. JOHNSON, David
"Unspeakable" (tr. of Delmira Augustini). [ChiR] (37:2/3) 91, p. 89.
2991. JOHNSON, Deborah Ann
"An Engram." [PacificR] (10) 91-92, p. 19.
2992. JOHNSON, Dick
"The Sleepwalker's Ballad" (After Garcia Lorca). [InterPR] (17:1) Spr 91, p.
102-104.
2993. JOHNSON, Doug
"After the Brief, Red Evening." [Sidewalks] (1) Aug 91, p. 35.
"Owl." [Sidewalks] (1) Aug 91, p. 34.
2994. JOHNSON, Greg
"Disease Without a Name." [MalR] (96) Fall 91, p. 68.
"Insomnia." [Poetry] (158:5) Ag 91, p. 253.
"Withholding the Last Word." [Poetry] (158:5) Ag 91, p. 253.
2995. JOHNSON, Henry
"In Memory of Charles Mingus." [RiverS] (33) 91, p. 29.
"Robins" (for William Butch Harvey). [SpoonRQ] (16:1/2) Wint-Spr 91, p.
110-111.
"White Cranes" (Hiroshima, 6 August 1945). [CimR] (95) Ap 91, p. 59-60.
2996. JOHNSON, Jacqueline
"Geechie Women." [Obs] (6:1) Spr 91, p. 73-74.
"Passionfruit." [Obs] (6:1) Spr 91, p. 74-75.
2997. JOHNSON, Jim
"Wolves" (Selections). [Nimrod] (35:1) Fall-Wint 91, p. 73-75.
2998. JOHNSON, Linnea
"Like a Monster." [ManhatPR] (13) [91?], p. 14.
"Old Women." [PraS] (65:3) Fall 91, p. 61.
"On the Return of Your Letters." [PraS] (65:3) Fall 91, p. 63-64.
"Singing with the Radio." [PraS] (65:3) Fall 91, p. 59-60.
"Upfreezing." [PraS] (65:3) Fall 91, p. 62-63.

2999. JOHNSON, M. Paula
        "Talking to Myself." [PaintedHR] (1) Ja 91, p. 25.
3000. JOHNSON, Manly
        "After Your Poems: To Astrid." [Nimrod] (34:2) Spr-Sum 91, p. 68-69.
        "Gardens." [Nimrod] (34:2) Spr-Sum 91, p. 70.
        "Transfiguration." [Nimrod] (34:2) Spr-Sum 91, p. 67.
3001. JOHNSON, Marael
        "Nut Cracker." [DustyD] (2:1) Ja 91, p. 14.
3002. JOHNSON, Margot
        "Our Lady, Krishna's Daughter." [Pearl] (13) Spr-Sum 91, p. 9.
3003. JOHNSON, Mark Allan
        "Credibility Gap." [BellArk] (7:2) Mr-Ap 91, p. 11.
        "Elegy for Nelson Bentley." [BellArk] (7:3) My-Je 91, p. 12.
        "The Man Who Came to Dinner." [BellArk] (7:6) N-D 91, p. 10.
        "The Name Game." [BellArk] (7:2) Mr-Ap 91, p. 10.
        "Poem on My Birthday." [BellArk] (7:1) Ja-F 91, p. 3.
        "Tom Corbett and Me." [BellArk] (7:2) Mr-Ap 91, p. 19.
3004. JOHNSON, Michael (Michael L.)
        "Chemistry Class" (tr. of Carlos Sahagun). [CharR] (17:1) Spr 91, p. 59-60.
        "Haruspicy: A Get-Well Card." [DustyD] Je 91, p. 28.
        "Honey." [TexasR] (12:1/2) Spr-Sum 91, p. 108.
        "Jack-o'-Lantern Carved in a Time of Stress." [CoalC] (3) My 91, p. 12.
        "Lauren in the Highchair." [CoalC] (3) My 91, p. 11.
        "Philip Kimball Pinpoints the Main Aesthetic Problem Involved in Judging Rural Art
            Fairs." [SnailPR] (1:2) Fall 91-Wint 92, back cover.
        "The Prisoner" (To the Memory of M.H., tr. of Carlos Sahagun). [CharR] (17:1)
            Spr 91, p. 57-58.
        "Rain at Night" (tr. of Carlos Sahagun). [CharR] (17:1) Spr 91, p. 58-59.
        "Softnesses" (tr. of Gabriela Mistral). [ArtfulD] (20/21) 91, p. 62.
        "Some Ruins" (tr. of Marcelin Pleynet). [WebR] (15) Spr 91, p. 40.
        "Stellar Vision." [DogRR] (10:2) Fall-Wint 91, p. 12.
3005. JOHNSON, Nicholas
        "Looking Out." [Journal] (15:1) Spr 91, p. 37-38.
3006. JOHNSON, Ron Netherton
        "Emily, It Is Not the Mail from Tunis." [Vis] (35) 91, p. 42.
3007. JOHNSON, Sandi
        "A Domestic Quarrel." [AntigR] (85/86) Spr-Sum 91, p. 182.
3008. JOHNSON, Sheila Golburgh
        "Chicken Love." [SoCoast] (10) Fall 91, p. 48.
3009. JOHNSON, Stacey Land
        "Pornography." [GrandS] (10:3, #39) 91, p. 155-157.
3010. JOHNSON, Susie Paul
        "Return, Return." [Kalliope] (13:3) 91, p. 28-29.
        "Some Girls and Their Shoes." [Kalliope] (13:3) 91, p. 29.
3011. JOHNSON, Tom
        "Apology in Second Person." [SewanR] (98:4) Fall 90, p. 612.
        "George Rogers Clark (1752-1818)." [SewanR] (98:4) Fall 90, p. 613.
        "El Mundo Es Ancho y Ajeno." [SewanR] (98:4) Fall 90, p. 609-611.
        "Ship." [SewanR] (98:4) Fall 90, p. 614.
3012. JOHNSON, Allan
        "The Tasks of Survival" (After Van Gogh). [CalQ] (32/33) Spr 90, p. 94.
3013. JOHNSTON, Arnold
        "Sestina: His Own Bright Music (1952)." [Outbr] (22) 91, p. 61-62.
3014. JOHNSTON, Fred
        "Seasonal Man" (for John Hogan). [NewL] (58:1) Fall 91, p. 27.
        "Song of the Untilled Field." [AntigR] (85/86) Spr-Sum 91, p. 49.
        "Time." [AntigR] (85/86) Spr-Sum 91, p. 50.
3015. JOHNSTON, George
        "Art May Be" (tr. of Hedin M. Klein). [Vis] (37) 91, p. 18.
        "An Epistle in Verse to Robert Melançon." [MalR] (95) Sum 91, p. 114-122.
        "Greeting to a Paper Star Cutter" (to William Heinesen on his 85th birthday, tr. of
            Gunnar Hoydal). [Vis] (37) 91, p. 16-17.
        "Lulls and Chances" (tr. of Hedin M. Klein). [Vis] (37) 91, p. 19.
        "Your Landscape and Ours" (tr. of Steinbjørn B. Jacobsen). [Vis] (37) 91, p. 18.
3016. JOHNSTON, Mark
        "Kafka for Children: 'A Hunger Artist'." [WebR] (15) Spr 91, p. 61.

"The Piano in the Alps." [CumbPR] (10:2) Spr 91, p. 21.
"The Planet of Black Clothes and White Skin" (for my daughter Emily). [SwampR]
        (7/8) Spr-Sum 91, p. 40-41.
"Scaring Mother." [CumbPR] (10:2) Spr 91, p. 20.
"The Sirens." [WebR] (15) Spr 91, p. 61.
"Snellen Chart." [WebR] (15) Spr 91, p. 60.
3017. JOHNSTON, Sean
"Garden." [Grain] (19:4) Wint 91, p. 96.
3018. JOHNSTON, Sue Ann
"The Bird of Greediness." [CanLit] (131) Wint 91, p. 35-36.
3019. JOLLIFF, William
"Burning for Spring." [CinPR] (22) Spr 91, p. 25.
"The Chaste Walker." [Poem] (65) My 91, p. 45.
"Crossing Kansas in the Dark, 1977." [LullwaterR] (3:1) Fall 91, p. 30.
"Luckies." [WindO] (54) Sum 91, p. 11.
"Mennonite Funeral on the Olentangy." [NegC] (11:1) 91, p. 25.
"My Amish Wife Is Sullen." [Poem] (65) My 91, p. 46.
"Pastor Cheney's Funeral, All Fulton County Welcomed." [BellR] (14:2) Fall 91, p.
        25.
"The Red Letting." [Poem] (65) My 91, p. 47.
"Transmigration." [PaintedB] (44) 91, p. 5.
"What the Sky Holds." [LullwaterR] (3:1) Fall 91, p. 26.
3020. JONES, Alice
"Anorexia." [CreamCR] (15:1) Spr 91, p. 68-69.
"Look Here." [LaurelR] (25:2) Sum 91, p. 54.
"Orbit." [Chelsea] (51) 91, p. 72-73.
"Prayer." [Poetry] (158:2) My 91, p. 78.
"Where the Music Comes From." [GettyR] (4:3) Sum 91, p. 407-408.
JONES, Charlene Diehl
        See DIEHL-JONES, Charlene
JONES, Claudia Novack
        See NOVACK-JONES, Claudia
3021. JONES, D. G.
"Ode on a Piece of Cast Concrete" (for Northrop Frye). [Quarry] (40:1/2) Wint-Spr
        91, p. 90.
3022. JONES, David
"China." [WillowR] Spr 91, p. 27.
3023. JONES, Elizabeth
"The Dandelion Children." [Gypsy] (17) 91, p. 54.
3024. JONES, Jamey
"Behind the Night." [EmeraldCR] (4) 91, p. 70.
"Green." [EmeraldCR] (3) 91, c1990, p. 96.
"Ted (Me and Of)" (for the poet Ted Berrigan). [EmeraldCR] (4) 91, p. 71.
3025. JONES, Jill
"Afraid to Steal Honey." [AntigR] (85/86) Spr-Sum 91, p. 114.
"The New Laws of Contracts." [AntigR] (85/86) Spr-Sum 91, p. 113.
3026. JONES, Jordan
"The Great Day of the Dead" (tr. of René Daumal). [HeavenB] (9) Wint-Spr 91-92,
        p. 28-29.
"The Notorious Surprise" (tr. of René Daumal). [HeavenB] (9) Wint-Spr 91-92, p.
        25.
"The Only One" (tr. of René Daumal). [HeavenB] (9) Wint-Spr 91-92, p. 26-27.
3027. JONES, Llisa
"Haikus for Vince Concerning Sleep." [EmeraldCR] (3) 91, c1990, p. 85.
3028. JONES, Patricia Spears
"In My Father's House." [HangL] (59) 91, p. 35-36.
3029. JONES, Renee
"I'm leaving you for another man." [SlipS] (11) 91, p. 23.
3030. JONES, Richard
"The Abandoned House." [SilverFR] (20) Spr 91, p. 18.
"After Surviving the Accident." [AmerPoR] (20:6) N-D 91, p. 44.
"Alienated." [AmerPoR] (20:6) N-D 91, p. 44.
"Back Then." [Pequod] (32) 91, p. 102-104.
"The Captain." [CimR] (94) Ja 91, p. 100.
"The Dead Calf." [SilverFR] (20) Spr 91, p. 19.
"The Happy Ending." [CimR] (94) Ja 91, p. 98-99.

"The Loft." [AmerPoR] (20:6) N-D 91, p. 44.
"The Lullaby." [AmerPoR] (20:6) N-D 91, p. 44.
"My Father's Buddha." [AmerPoR] (20:6) N-D 91, p. 45.
"The Shadow." [AmerPoR] (20:6) N-D 91, p. 44.
"The Wall." [AmerPoR] (20:6) N-D 91, p. 44.
"Wild Guesses." [Manoa] (3:2) Fall 91, p. 171-172.
3031. JONES, Roger
"Death Rattle." [PoetL] (86:3) Fall 91, p. 22.
"Stratas." [HawaiiR] (15:3, #33) Fall 91, p. 114-115.
3032. JONES, Seaborn
"Lenny Bruce." [NewYorkQ] (46) 91, p. 38.
"Telephoning Ginsberg" (for Charles Plymell). [Bogg] (64) 91, p. 44-45.
3033. JONES, Tom
"Bird Sanctuary." [InterPR] (17:2) Fall 91, p. 138.
"The Maidan." [InterPR] (15:1) Spr 89, p. 93.
"Siberian Tiger." [InterPR] (17:2) Fall 91, p. 138.
"Sketches of Mysore City." [InterPR] (15:1) Spr 89, p. 93.
3034. JORDAN, Barbara
"Meander." [Notus] (9) Fall 91, p. 34-37.
3035. JORDAN, Joanna
"Her Brightness." [BellArk] (7:5) S-O 91, p. 9.
"Inventory." [BellArk] (7:5) S-O 91, p. 9.
"Mountain Stream." [BellArk] (7:5) S-O 91, p. 9.
3036. JORDAN, Reetika Vazirani
"Lying Positions." [Vis] (35) 91, p. 23.
3037. JORDAN, Richard
"A Box of Fresh Rats for the Lab." [Obs] (6:1) Spr 91, p. 77.
"Gullah Sundown." [Obs] (6:1) Spr 91, p. 76-77.
"I Can't Believe He Had the Nerve." [Obs] (6:3) Wint 91, p. 66.
3038. JORGE, João Miguel Fernandes
"And the Floor Were My Heart" (tr. by Richard Zenith). [Trans] (25) Spr 91, p. 141.
"Ida Lupino by Carla Bley (13)" (Excerpt, tr. by Richard Zenith). [Trans] (25) Spr 91, p. 139.
"Twelve Nocturnes of Ceuta (3)" (Excerpt, tr. by Richard Zenith). [Trans] (25) Spr 91, p. 140.
3039. JORIS, Pierre
"And If They Have Not Died" (for H.B., tr. of Unica Zürn). [Sulfer] (11:2, #29) Fall 91, p. 81.
"Dans l'Attelage d'un Autre Age" (Line from a poem by Henri Michaux, tr. of Unica Zürn). [Sulfer] (11:2, #29) Fall 91, p. 81.
"Green Child: Poem 1" (tr. of Kurt Schwitters). [Sulfur] (11:1, #28) Spr 91, p. 109-110.
"In the Dust of This Life" (tr. of Unica Zürn). [Sulfer] (11:2, #29) Fall 91, p. 80.
"The Lonesome Table" (tr. of Unica Zürn). [Sulfer] (11:2, #29) Fall 91, p. 83-84.
"Nine Anagrammatic Poems" (tr. of Unica Zürn). [Sulfer] (11:2, #29) Fall 91, p. 80-84.
"Once Upon a Time a Small" (tr. of Unica Zürn). [Sulfer] (11:2, #29) Fall 91, p. 80-81.
"Revving Charon's Outboard Engine." [Notus] (9) Fall 91, p. 82-83.
"The Strange Adventures of Mr K" (tr. of Unica Zürn). [Sulfer] (11:2, #29) Fall 91, p. 82.
"Uncas, the Last of the Mohicans" (tr. of Unica Zürn). [Sulfer] (11:2, #29) Fall 91, p. 84.
"Will I Meet You Sometime?" (tr. of Unica Zürn). [Sulfer] (11:2, #29) Fall 91, p. 82.
"You'll Find the Secret in a Young City" (tr. of Unica Zürn). [Sulfer] (11:2, #29) Fall 91, p. 83.
3040. JORN, Susanne
"An apple, red" (tr. of Maj-Britt Willumsen). [AmerPoR] (20:1) Ja-F 91, p. 30.
"You meet the city and the human beings" (tr. of Maj-Britt Willumsen). [AmerPoR] (20:1) Ja-F 91, p. 30.
"Your room gets carried away" (tr. of Maj-Britt Willumsen). [AmerPoR] (20:1) Ja-F 91, p. 30.
3041. JORON, Andrew
"The Impossible Room." [Caliban] (10) 91, p. 129.

"Smart Bomb." [Caliban] (10) 91, p. 128.
3042. JOSELOW, Beth
"Line Break" (for Tim Dlugos). [WashR] (16:6) Ap-My 91, p. 3.
3043. JOSEPH, Allison
"Accomplices." [OnTheBus] (8/9) 91, p. 91-92.
"At the Island." [Plain] (12:2) Wint 91, p. 25.
"Current Affair." [ClockR] (7:1/2) 91-92, p. 19-20.
"Dolls" (for Charmaine). [KenR] (NS 13:4) Fall 91, p. 24-26.
"Endurance." [NewL] (58:1) Fall 91, p. 110-111.
"The Idiot Box." [KenR] (NS 13:4) Fall 91, p. 23-24.
"The Sales Pitch" (for my father). [CreamCR] (14:2) Wint 91, p. 175-176.
"Years." [OxfordM] (7:2) Fall-Wint 91, p. 16-17.
3044. JOSEPH, Lawrence
"Admission Against Interest." [Ploughs] (17:4) Wint 91-92, p. 101-104.
"Brooding." [Ploughs] (17:4) Wint 91-92, p. 107-109.
"Generation" (after Akhmatova). [KenR] (NS 13:4) Fall 91, p. 4-5.
"Material Facts." [Ploughs] (17:4) Wint 91-92, p. 105-106.
"Some Sort of Chronicler I Am." [KenR] (NS 13:4) Fall 91, p. 1-3.
3045. JOSEPHS, Laurence
"Fahy Swisher." [Salm] (92) Fall 91, p. 151.
"Poem: Everyone has it for someone" (For G. C.). [Salm] (92) Fall 91, p. 150.
3046. JOY, Deborah
"Vacuums into Which Fantasies Flow." [EmeraldCR] (3) 91, c1990, p. 90.
3047. JOYCE, William
"My Daughter's Pundalunda." [Spirit] (11) 91, p. 209-210.
3048. JOZSEF, Attila
"As in a Field" (tr. by John Bátki). [Talisman] (6) Spr 91, p. 12.
"The Bell" (tr. by John Bátki). [Talisman] (6) Spr 91, p. 11.
"Only Those Should Read My Poems" (tr. by John Bátki). [Talisman] (6) Spr 91, p.
11.
3049. JUARROZ, Roberto (Robert)
"IV.8. Eleventh Vertical Poetry" (tr. by Mary Crow). [QW] (33) Sum-Fall 91, p.
170.
"Eleventh II.6" (tr. by Mary Crow). [Sonora] (20) Wint 91, p. 107.
"Eleventh IV.14" (tr. by Mary Crow). [Sonora] (20) Wint 91, p. 108.
"Eleventh IV.23" (tr. by Mary Crow). [QW] (33) Sum-Fall 91, p. 169.
"Tenth . 12" (tr. by Mary Crow). [ConnPR] (10:1) 91, p. 43.
"Tenth . 19" (tr. by Mary Crow). [ConnPR] (10:1) 91, p. 44.
"The Threshold of Other Sound" (A Selection from "Vertical Poetry," 12 poems in
Spanish and English, tr. by Mary Crow. Translation Chapbook Series,
Number 17). [MidAR] (12:1) 91, p. 77-105.
"Vertical Poetry" (Selections: Eighth.50, Eighth.76, tr. by Mary Crow).
[GrahamHR] (15) Fall 91, p. 99-101.
"Vertical Poetry: Eleventh I 3" (tr. by Mary Crow). [ArtfulD] (20/21) 91, p. 7.
"Vertical Poetry, Eleventh I. 8" (tr. by Mary Crow). [Ploughs] (17:4) Wint 91-92, p.
51.
"Vertical Poetry, Eleventh II. 1" (for Jean Paul Neveu, tr. by Mary Crow).
[Ploughs] (17:4) Wint 91-92, p. 52-53.
"Vertical Poetry: Eleventh.II.25" (tr. by Mary Crow). [Agni] (34) 91, p. 160-161.
3050. JUDICE, Nuno
"Psalm" (tr. by Alexis Levitin). [Trans] (25) Spr 91, p. 148.
"Refuge" (tr. by Alexis Levitin). [Trans] (25) Spr 91, p. 146.
"Summer" (tr. by Alexis Levitin). [Trans] (25) Spr 91, p. 147.
3051. JUDY, Judi Lynne
"In Four Movements." [ChamLR] (8-9) Spr-Fall 91, p. 36-38.
3052. JUNKINS, Donald
"After the Evening Meal with Jiang Hua's Family in Shanghai." [GreensboroR] (51)
Wint 91-92, p. 154.
"Reed Flute Cave, Guilin." [GreensboroR] (51) Wint 91-92, p. 155.
3053. JUSTICE, Donald
"Sonnet." [GettyR] (4:4) Aut 91, p. 539.
3054. JUSTICE, Jack
"Watching Mama Die." [HampSPR] Wint 91, p. 50.
3055. KACHUR, Stephen Patrick
"Abiku." [HiramPoR] (50) Spr-Sum 91, p. 10.

"On Leaving Nigeria" (for the people of Ilorin and for Olisa's hand). [HiramPoR]
(50) Spr-Sum 91, p. 11-12.

3056. KADANE, Matt
"Anima." [CimR] (97) O 91, p. 52.

3057. KAGDA, Roshan
"9:31 A.M." [HangL] (59) 91, p. 81.
"Good Sweet." [HangL] (59) 91, p. 80.

3058. KAHANU, Diane
"When I Was Young on an Island." [BambooR] (50/51) Spr-Sum 91, p. 18-19.

3059. KAINWO, Moses
"Battle Talk." [LitR] (34:4) Sum 91, p. 520.
"Don't Be an Amber Gambler." [LitR] (34:4) Sum 91, p. 520.
"The Eyeless God." [LitR] (34:4) Sum 91, p. 519-520.

3060. KAKINOMOTO no HITOMARO (681-729)
"Dusk, the Omi Sea" (tr. by Sam Hamill). [ColR] (NS 17:2) Fall-Wint 90, p. 17.
"To one who wanders" (tr. by Sam Hamill). [ColR] (NS 17:2) Fall-Wint 90, p. 18.
"The white plum blossoms" (tr. by Sam Hamill). [ColR] (NS 17:2) Fall-Wint 90, p. 17.

3061. KALAMARAS, George
"Elegy for Miguel." [Abraxas] (40/41) 91, p. 134-135.

3062. KALDA, Rebecca
"An Arab Old Wives' Tale About How to Make Your Husband Obey." [PaintedHR]
(2) Spr 91, p. 36-37.

3063. KALINSKI, Todd
"Green Is the Color of Blind Horses." [BlackBR] (13) Spr-Sum 91, p. 20-21.
"Lady Lazarus." [Gypsy] (17) 91, p. 60-61.
"The Procession Marches On." [BlackBR] (13) Spr-Sum 91, p. 21-22.

3064. KALZ, Jill Kristin
"Off Monks Avenue." [CapeR] (26:1) Spr 91, p. 3.

3065. KAMAL, Daud
"Rough-Hewn Beams." [Vis] (36) 91, p. 14.

3066. KAMAUU, Mahealani
"Little Runaway." [BambooR] (50/51) Spr-Sum 91, p. 16-17.
"What I Wanted to Say to My Mother." [BambooR] (50/51) Spr-Sum 91, p. 15.

3067. KAMENETZ, Rodger
"Eucalyptus" (for D.). [RiverS] (35) 91, p. 24.
"Las Haricots Sont Pas Salés." [RiverS] (35) 91, p. 23.
"Howard and Jack at Table, What's at Stake" (1959). [CimR] (94) Ja 91, p. 97.
"Jack Conceives His Father on the Day of His Birth" (1950). [CimR] (94) Ja 91, p. 96.
"A 'Property of Blood'" (1983). [CimR] (94) Ja 91, p. 94-95.
"Stuck." [NewRep] (205:2) 8 Jl 91, p. 38.
"Turtle Soup at Mandina's." [LouisL] (8:1) Spr 91, p. 43.

3068. KAMINSKI, Helena
"Face." [ParisR] (33:118) Spr 91, p. 168-170.
"Who We Are." [ParisR] (33:118) Spr 91, p. 171-172.

KAMP, Alexandra van de
See Van de KAMP, Alexandra

3069. KANGAS, J. R.
"Slow Freight." [WestB] (28) 91, p. 64-65.

3070. KANIK, Orhan Veli
"Fine Weather" (tr. by Richard Schwarzenberger and Grace Smith). [Agni] (33) 91, p. 97.
"For the Homeland" (tr. by Richard Schwarzenberger and Grace Smith). [Agni] (33) 91, p. 94.
"Illusion" (tr. by Richard Schwarzenberger and Grace Smith). [Agni] (33) 91, p. 95.
"Stretched Out" (tr. by Richard Schwarzenberger and Grace Smith). [Agni] (33) 91, p. 96.

3071. KANTARIS, Sylvia
"Yellow Slips into White." [Stand] (32:4) Aut 91, p. 21.

3072. KAPELYAN, Gregory
"A Meditation on Chopin" (tr. by Claudia Novack-Jones). [LitR] (34:3) Spr 91, p. 369.
"A Meditation on Death" (tr. by Claudia Novack-Jones). [LitR] (34:3) Spr 91, p. 370.

3073. KAPLAN, Allan
"Chagall's The Lovers." [Vis] (35) 91, p. 43.
"Spring Rite." [HeavenB] (9) Wint-Spr 91-92, p. 40.
3074. KAPLAN, Cheryl
"Webster Hunches in the Corner." [DenQ] (26:1) Sum 91, p. 39-41.
3075. KAPLAN, Howard
"Canning." [AmerV] (24) Fall 91, p. 16-17.
3076. KAPLAN, Jonathan
"Springtime Concupiscence." [AntigR] (85/86) Spr-Sum 91, p. 115.
"Ten-Line Encounter." [AntigR] (85/86) Spr-Sum 91, p. 116.
3077. KAPLAN, Saul
"The Machine Maker." [ManhatPR] (13) [91?], p. 47.
3078. KARAWAN, Tania
"Dearest Jamie." [PikeF] (10) Spr 91, p. 20.
3079. KARR, Mary
"Parents Taking Shape." [Ploughs] (17:2/3) Fall 91, p. 113-114.
3080. KARR, Muriel (Muriel DeStaffany)
"An Awkwardness, As If Translated." [BellArk] (7:2) Mr-Ap 91, p. 12.
"Cakes, Smaller Cakes, Bells." [BellArk] (7:5) S-O 91, p. 2.
"Concurrently." [BellArk] (7:4) Jl-Ag 91, p. 22.
"His Curly Head." [YellowS] (38) Wint-Spr 91-92, p. 18.
"Once in Italy." [BellArk] (7:2) Mr-Ap 91, p. 7.
"Spring, Night, Sky." [YellowS] (38) Wint-Spr 91-92, p. 19.
"Summer Sunroom Story." [BellArk] (7:5) S-O 91, p. 2.
"Twigs and Sand." [BellArk] (7:5) S-O 91, p. 2.
"Wanting It Again." [BellArk] (7:3) My-Je 91, p. 11.
3081. KARSTEN, Karen
"Life Span." [Sidewalks] (1) Aug 91, p. 15.
"Mother Never Told Me." [Sidewalks] (1) Aug 91, p. 13-14.
3082. KASDORF, Julia
"August." [WestB] (28) 91, p. 47.
"Cousins" (Pennsylvania, 1987). [CinPR] (22) Spr 91, p. 31.
"First TV in a Mennonite Family" (1968). [SpoonRQ] (16:1/2) Wint-Spr 91, p. 95.
"It Runs in Our Family." [SpoonRQ] (16:1/2) Wint-Spr 91, p. 93.
"Uncle." [SpoonRQ] (16:1/2) Wint-Spr 91, p. 94.
3083. KASHNER, Sam
"Epithalamium" (after Robert Desnos). [WilliamMR] (29) 91, p. 37.
"The Water Lily Is Doomed." [WilliamMR] (29) 91, p. 63.
3084. KASISCHKE, Laura
"After My Little Light, I Sat in the Dark." [BelPoJ] (41:3) Spr 91, p. 32-35.
"The Driver's Lullaby" (For Cary, who slept at the wheel). [Poetry] (158:3) Je 91,
p. 129-130.
"Godmother's Advice." [BelPoJ] (41:3) Spr 91, p. 31-32.
"Godmother's Advice." [CutB] (35) Wint-Spr 91, p. 15-16.
"Hot Spell." [SoCoast] (10) Fall 91, p. 33.
"Palm." [Poetry] (157:5) F 91, p. 262.
"Porch." [PaintedB] (42) 91, p. 26-27.
"Rosebush." [RiverC] (11:2) Spr 91, p. 70-71.
3085. KASPRYK, Andrew
"A Ballad for the Passerby" (tr. of Ihor Rymaruk). [InterPR] (17:2) Fall 91, p. 75.
"Untitled: The calm mouth of the letters' breath" (tr. of Ihor Rymaruk). [InterPR]
(17:2) Fall 91, p. 69.
"Untitled: There are untold numbers. They march" (tr. of Ihor Rymaruk). [InterPR]
(17:2) Fall 91, p. 71, 73.
KASTEN, Alfonso Larrahona
See LARRAHONA KASTEN, Alfonso
3086. KASZUBA, Sophia
"Blood Is a Picture Book." [Writ] (23/24) 91-92, p. 44.
"For My Sister." [Writ] (23/24) 91-92, p. 45.
"He Walks Out of the Photograph." [Quarry] (40:4) Fall 91, p. 71.
"I Took It." [Writ] (23/24) 91-92, p. 43.
"Looking Up at a Window in Beijing." [Quarry] (40:4) Fall 91, p. 70.
"The Love Tree." [Quarry] (40:4) Fall 91, p. 69.
"Prince Edward County, It Is So Lit Up." [Writ] (23/24) 91-92, p. 46.
"They Whisper Very Low." [Writ] (23/24) 91-92, p. 42.

3087. KATES, J.
"Age" (tr. of Ricardo Feierstein, w. Stephen A. Sadow). [InterPR] (17:1) Spr 91, p. 63.
"Eros Poesis" (tr. of Tatyana Shcherbina). [Agni] (34) 91, p. 227-228.
"From Italy Near Naples" (tr. of Jean-Pierre Rosnay). [MidAR] (11:2) 91, p. 113-114.
"Full Name" (tr. of Ricardo Feierstein, w. Stephen A. Sadow). [InterPR] (17:1) Spr 91, p. 59.
"The Music Box." [MissR] (19:3) 91, p. 175.
"Place of Residence" (tr. of Ricardo Feierstein, w. Stephen A. Sadow). [InterPR] (17:1) Spr 91, p. 61.
"The Poet and the Tsar" (tr. of Tatyana Shcherbina). [OnTheBus] (8/9) 91, p. 227-228.
"Profession" (tr. of Ricardo Feierstein, w. Stephen A. Sadow). [InterPR] (17:1) Spr 91, p. 67, 69.
"Sex" (tr. of Ricardo Feierstein, w. Stephen A. Sadow). [InterPR] (17:1) Spr 91, p. 65.
"So-So" (tr. of Jean-Pierre Rosnay). [MidAR] (11:2) 91, p. 112.
"Untitled: Be careful: You mustn't get mixed up with that fellow" (tr. of Mikhail Aizenberg). [OnTheBus] (8/9) 91, p. 199.
"Untitled: The life of the soul. The soul trembles like foliage" (tr. of Mikhail Aizenberg). [OnTheBus] (8/9) 91, p. 199.
"Untitled: Who now remembers what kind of animal" (tr. of Mikhail Aizenberg). [GreenMR] (NS 5:1) Sum-Fall 91, p. 31.
"You can threaten" (tr. of Tatyana Shcherbina). [MissR] (19:3) 91, p. 176.
3088. KATES, Ron
"Raping Eva Braun." [HiramPoR] (50) Spr-Sum 91, p. 13.
3089. KATROVAS, Richard
"The Book of Complaints" (for Pavel Srut). [Crazy] (41) Wint 91, p. 31-38.
"The Bridge of Intellectuals." [Crazy] (41) Wint 91, p. 39-40.
"Eating the Kennedys." [DenQ] (26:2) Fall 91, p. 19.
"The Stones" (Prague, August 18, 1990). [Crazy] (41) Wint 91, p. 41-44.
3090. KATZ, David M.
"Collected Shorter Poems of W.H. Auden." [NewRep] (205:14) 30 S 91, p. 31.
3091. KATZ, Jeffrey
"Keeping Promises." [Journal] (14:2) Wint 91, p. 73.
3092. KATZ-LEVINE, Judy
"Woman in the Night / Women in the Night" (improvisation on Miro paintings). [US1] (24/25) Spr 91, p. 36.
3093. KAUCHER, Candace
"If It Isn't Something It's the Fucking Phone." [NewYorkQ] (44) 91, p. 86-87.
3094. KAUFFMAN, Elizabeth Doonan
"Boyacá" (for Olinda Morales and Antonio García, tr. of Luis Rebaza-Soraluz). [PlumR] (1) Spr-Sum 91, p. 68.
3095. KAUFFMAN, Steven
"Days of Nocturnal Wanderings." [PoetryUSA] (22) Spr 91, p. 10.
"January 1991 at Langley/Porter Psychiatric Institute." [PoetryUSA] (23) Sum 91, p. 16-17.
3096. KAUFMAN, Andrew
"Air." [BrooklynR] (8) 91, p. 4.
3097. KAUFMAN, Debra
"Aunt Margaret's Garden." [PoetC] (23:1) Fall 91, p. 18-19.
"Heading West." [Lactuca] (14) My 91, p. 69.
3098. KAUFMAN, James
"Heat." [PacificR] (9) 91, p. 13.
3099. KAUFMAN, Shirley
"The Core." [Atlantic] (267:1) Ja 91, p. 60.
"For Dear Life." [Nimrod] (35:1) Fall-Wint 91, p. 76.
"Gratitude." [SnailPR] (1:1) Spr 91, p. 12.
"Politics." [PoetryE] (31) Spr 91, p. 105.
3100. KAVEN, Bob
"Gone." [PraS] (65:4) Wint 91, p. 80.
"Somebody Wanders Out." [PraS] (65:4) Wint 91, p. 82.
"Things Change at Night" (for Jeannie Marcuse). [PraS] (65:4) Wint 91, p. 81-82.
3101. KAVOUNAS, Alice
"Home Ground" (For Fred). [NewEngR] (14:1) Fall 91, p. 132.

"Instinct." [NewEngR] (14:1) Fall 91, p. 133.
3102. KAZANTZIS, Judith
"A Custom." [Verse] (8:2) Sum 91, p. 105.
KAZUKO, Shiraishi
See SHIRAISHI, Kazuko
KE, Mang
See MANG, Ke
3103. KEARNEY, Barbara
"To an Unborn Child." [Kalliope] (13:1) 91, p. 23.
3104. KEARNEY, Larry
"Sleepwalk" (Excerpt). [Zyzzyva] (7:1) Spr 91, p. 97-100.
3105. KEARNS, Lionel
"The Arrow of Time." [WestCL] (25:1) Spr 91, p. 60.
"Family." [WestCL] (25:1) Spr 91, p. 118-119.
3106. KEARNS, Rick
"Check 'Other'." [PaintedB] (44) 91, p. 14-15.
3107. KEEFE, Jack
"The Vastness of the Stillness." [PottPort] (13:1) Spr 91, p. 19.
3108. KEEFER, Janice Kulyk
"Isle of Demons." [MalR] (96) Fall 91, p. 34-50.
3109. KEEGAN, Linda
"As Autumn Comes." [Plain] (11:3) Spr 91, p. 12.
"At the Polls." [Plain] (12:2) Wint 91, p. 10.
"The Braided Rug." [BellArk] (7:3) My-Je 91, p. 8.
"Leaving Home." [BellArk] (7:3) My-Je 91, p. 4.
"Never Say Die." [Plain] (12:1) Fall 91, p. 6.
"Reunification." [Plain] (11:2) Wint 91, p. 29.
"Watching the Gulls Go." [BellArk] (7:1) Ja-F 91, p. 7.
3110. KEELAN, Claudia
"The Equator." [BlackWR] (17:2) Spr-Sum 91, p. 20.
"If Not in the Field Then Where." [DenQ] (25:4) Spr 91, p. 38.
"Lines Where the Fence Is Crossed" (for Sarah). [DenQ] (26:1) Sum 91, p. 42-46.
"No Excuses." [SouthernPR] (31:1) Spr 91, p. 32-33.
"Parable 2." [NewAW] (8/9) Fall 91, p. 51.
3111. KEELER, Greg
"Grandma Wulz." [RiverS] (33) 91, p. 69.
"Telling Grandma to Shut Up." [RiverS] (33) 91, p. 68.
3112. KEELEY, Edmund
"And Recounting Them" (tr. of Yannis Ritsos). [Salm] (92) Fall 91, p. 145-146.
"Danaë" (tr. of Yannos Ritsos). [ColR] (NS 17:2) Fall-Wint 90, p. 98.
"Niobe" (tr. of Yannos Ritsos). [ColR] (NS 17:2) Fall-Wint 90, p. 100.
"Repetitions" (Selections: 3 poems, tr. of Yannis Ritsos). [Colum] (15) 90, p.
    50-52.
"Talos" (tr. of Yannis Ritsos). [NewRep] (204:3) 21 Ja 91, p. 28.
"Then and Now" (tr. of Yannos Ritsos). [ColR] (NS 17:2) Fall-Wint 90, p. 99.
3113. KEEN, Suzanne
"A Psalter" (Selections: ps. 1-3). [Agni] (34) 91, p. 189-192.
3114. KEENAN, Gary
"A Common End." [BrooklynR] (8) 91, p. 48.
3115. KEENAN, K. J.
"Charity." [Poem] (65) My 91, p. 30.
"Fertility." [Poem] (65) My 91, p. 31.
3116. KEENER, LuAnn
"Sumeria." [LouisL] (8:1) Spr 91, p. 36.
3117. KEENEY, Will
"The Apprentice Trapeze." [Outbr] (22) 91, p. 3.
"Tamer." [Outbr] (22) 91, p. 4.
3118. KEITH, Greg
"An Ethological View of the Love Song." [Chelsea] (51) 91, p. 64-65.
"I, Declared." [Chelsea] (51) 91, p. 66-67.
3119. KEITHLEY, George
"The Fourth Day of the Flood." [Spirit] (11) 91, p. 259-262.
3120. KELLER, David
"The Bad Word." [PraS] (65:4) Wint 91, p. 131-133.
"Comedy." [US1] (24/25) Spr 91, p. 16.

"Hannibal Crossed the Alps, But I Can't Get Over You." [PraS] (65:4) Wint 91, p. 136-137.
"Natural History." [NoAmR] (276:2) Je 91, p. 14-15.
"Outline for a Thank-You Note." [PraS] (65:4) Wint 91, p. 133-134.
"Solo for Tam Tam." [TarRP] (31:1) Fall 91, p. 25-26.
"The World They Went Into." [PraS] (65:4) Wint 91, p. 134-136.

3121. KELLER, Tsipi (Tsipi E., Tsipi Edith)
"The Justice of the Sting" (tr. of Dan Pagis). [Vis] (36) 91, p. 17-18.
"Mother." [ManhatPR] (13) [91?], p. 9.
"A Western" (tr. of Dan Pagis). [ColR] (NS 18:1) Spr-Sum 91, p. 88.
"You Arrive" (tr. of Dan Pagis). [Vis] (36) 91, p. 17.

3122. KELLEY, Tina
"The Only Things We Know About in Space Are Those That Shine." [ManhatPR] (13) [91?], p. 45.
"Preliminary Written Sketch of a Day and a Half" (before your first cell's first division). [LitR] (34:2) Wint 91, p. 267-268.

3123. KELLMAN, Anthony
"Isle-Man." [GrahamHR] (14) Spr 91, p. 15-16.

3124. KELLOGG, David
"Six Sonnets for Leigh." [OhioR] (46) 91, p. 70-72.

3125. KELLY, Angela
"Being the Camel." [Pearl] (13) Spr-Sum 91, p. 48.

3126. KELLY, Anne M.
"At the Subway Station." [Grain] (19:2) Sum 91, p. 87.
"Neighbour." [Grain] (19:2) Sum 91, p. 85.
"Vignette." [Grain] (19:2) Sum 91, p. 86.
"What She's Really Thinking When He Tells Her She's Well-Preserved & She Gives Him an Enigmatic Smile." [Grain] (19:2) Sum 91, p. 88-89.

3127. KELLY, Brigit Pegeen
"Dead Doe: I" (for Huck). [KenR] (NS 13:3) Sum 91, p. 14-16.
"A Live Dog Being Better Than a Dead Lion." [PoetryNW] (32:2) Sum 91, p. 21-22.
"Petition." [RiverS] (34) 91, p. 14.
"Silver Lake." [NewEngR] (14:1) Fall 91, p. 162-163.
"Wild Turkeys: The Dignity of the Damned." [RiverS] (34) 91, p. 12-13.
"The Witnesses." [PoetryNW] (32:2) Sum 91, p. 20-21.

3128. KELLY, Robert
"Against Music." [Conjunc] (16) 91, p. 66-70.
"Ensor." [Notus] (9) Fall 91, p. 40-41.
"Patmos." [Notus] (9) Fall 91, p. 38-39.
"Reading Li Shang-yin: Falling Flowers" (for Charlotte). [Conjunc] (17) 91, p. 271-276.

3129. KELLY, Robert A.
"From Purgatory Mary Flannery Reflects on Peacocks." [AntigR] (85/86) Spr-Sum 91, p. 202.
"Stanislaus Circle" (Macon, Ga.). [AntigR] (85/86) Spr-Sum 91, p. 200-201.

3130. KELLY, William
"Safe Distance." [AnthNEW] (3) 91, p. 23.

3131. KELLY-DeWITT, Susan
"Apparition." [SpoonRQ] (16:3/4) Sum-Fall 91, p. 73.
"A Boy, Almost a Man Now." [SpoonRQ] (16:3/4) Sum-Fall 91, p. 74-75.
"Francis in Ecstasy" (After Bellini). [Poetry] (159:2) N 91, p. 91.
"Haze." [SpoonRQ] (16:3/4) Sum-Fall 91, p. 72.
"The Old Sacramento Cemetery." [HawaiiR] (15:2, #32) Spr 91, p. 89-90.

3132. KEMMETT, Bill
"The End Is Come." [CimR] (95) Ap 91, p. 56.

3133. KEMP, Carolyn
"A Warm Blow." [CentralP] (19/20) Spr-Fall 91, p. 225.

3134. KEMPHER, Ruth Moon
"Bird." [WindO] (55) Wint 91-92, p. 40.
"The Chased, a Re-Vision." [Kalliope] (13:1) 91, p. 48-49.

3135. KEMPNER, Robert D.
"Lines Written After Reading the Winter 1990 Issue of *Poetry USA*" (to the Tune of "Mine Eyes Have Seen the Glory of the Coming of the Lord," aka "Solidarity Forever"). [PoetryUSA] (22) Spr 91, p. 7.

3136. KENDALL, Robert
        "Just Ahead of the Morning." [NewRena] (8:2, #25) Fall 91, p. 151.
3137. KENDIG, Diane
        "Double Exposure." [PaintedB] (43) 91, p. 14.
        "Marie Laveau at the Prison, 1850's." [Kalliope] (13:3) 91, p. 64.
        "Yoffe." [PikeF] (10) Spr 91, p. 3.
3138. KENDRICK, Dolores
        "The Ingestion of Birds (for Davis Hammond)." [Colum] (17) Fall 91, p. 59-61.
3139. KENISTON, Ann
        "What Reason." [Colum] (15) 90, p. 198.
3140. KENNEDY, Alexandra
        "The Animal Lover." [ColEng] (53:4) Ap 91, p. 430.
        "Carhart Ballroom, 1954." [ColEng] (53:4) Ap 91, p. 428.
        "January Thaw." [ColEng] (53:4) Ap 91, p. 429.
3141. KENNEDY, Chris
        "James Dean's Jacket." [TampaR] (4) 91, p. 12.
        "Modern Poetry." [TampaR] (4) 91, p. 13.
        "The Pure Acceleration of Love." [CimR] (97) O 91, p. 43-44.
3142. KENNEDY, David
        "Holyrood Beach." [TickleAce] (21) Spr-Sum 91, p. 34-35.
3143. KENNEDY, Susan
        "Sometimes It Gets Cold in This Cave." [Zyzzyva] (7:1) Spr 91, p. 73-74.
        "Wintering." [Zyzzyva] (7:1) Spr 91, p. 92.
3144. KENNEDY, X. J.
        "Aurora, New York" (for Bruce Bennett). [Interim] (10:1) Spr-Sum 91, p. 5.
        "Death of a Window Washer." [OntR] (35) Fall-Wint 91-92, p. 82.
        "Destroying Old Loveletters." [SoCoast] (11) Wint 91, p. 15.
        "Dump." [OntR] (35) Fall-Wint 91-92, p. 80.
        "The Fatted Calf Views the Prodigal Son's Return." [Interim] (10:1) Spr-Sum 91, p.
                6.
        "The Ghost of My Unfinished Ph.D." [OntR] (35) Fall-Wint 91-92, p. 81.
        "Love: A Neoplatonist View." [Paint] (18:36) Aut 91, p. 9.
        "A Minnesota Norseman Asks for a Viking Funeral." [NewYorkQ] (46) 91, p. 23.
        "On the Liquidation of the Mustang Ranch by the Internal Revenue Service."
                [Atlantic] (268:6) D 91, p. 62.
        "On the Square." [OntR] (35) Fall-Wint 91-92, p. 83.
        "The Poetry Mafia." [Paint] (18:36) Aut 91, p. 8.
        "Rat." [OntR] (35) Fall-Wint 91-92, p. 79.
        "To a Friend Whom a Literary Prize Passed Over." [SoCoast] (11) Wint 91, p. 60.
        "Veterinarian." [Paint] (18:36) Aut 91, p. 7.
        "War Newscast in St. Thomas." [OntR] (35) Fall-Wint 91-92, p. 78.
        "The Waterbury Cross." [OntR] (35) Fall-Wint 91-92, p. 84.
3145. KENNEY, Richard
        "Lucifer." [Poetry] (159:2) N 91, p. 63-82.
3146. KENNY, Maurice
        "Carleton Island." [MidAR] (11:1) 91, p. 38-39.
        "Garden." [PoetryE] (32) Fall 91, p. 64.
        "Icarus." [SnailPR] (1:1) Spr 91, p. 14.
        "Listening to Leslie Silko Telling Stories, NYC 2/8/79." [MidAR] (11:1) 91, p. 72.
        "Molly." [PoetryE] (32) Fall 91, p. 62-63.
        "Winter Forms 1990." [PoetryE] (32) Fall 91, p. 60-61.
3147. KENT, Richard
        "Ice Carver" (After a Photograph by Emmet Gowin: Dalton Dishman, ice carver.
                Danville, Va., 1970). [AntR] (49:4) Fall 91, p. 559.
3148. KENYON, Jane
        "The Argument." [Ploughs] (17:2/3) Fall 91, p. 88.
        "Back." [NewYorker] (67:31) 23 S 91, p. 82.
        "Chrysanthemums." [Iowa] (21:1) Wint 91, p. 112-114.
        "Climb." [Iowa] (21:1) Wint 91, p. 114-115.
3149. KEON, Wayne
        "Down to Agawa." [CanLit] (130) Aut 91, p. 59-61.
3150. KEOWN-BOYD, Alex
        "One More Last Crusade." [PacificR] (10) 91-92, p. 65-70.
3151. KEPHART, Ann M.
        "Hung Deer." [SoDakR] (29:1) Spr 91, p. 152.
        "Hung Deer." [SoDakR] (29:3 part 2) Aut 91, p. 113.

3152. KERIM, Ussin
"I Long for a Horse" (tr. by William Matthews). [ColR] (NS 18:2) Fall-Wint 91, p. 75.
"Recollections" (tr. by William Matthews). [ColR] (NS 18:2) Fall-Wint 91, p. 76.
"Untitled Poem: There's a slow fire in my eyes" (tr. by William Matthews). [ColR] (NS 18:2) Fall-Wint 91, p. 74.
3153. KERLEY, Gary
"Hansel and Gretel Seek Therapy." [LullwaterR] (3:1) Fall 91, p. 22.
3154. KERLIKOWSKE, Elizabeth
"Why I Will Never Be a Supreme Court Justice." [Parting] (4:1) Sum 91, p. 29.
3155. KEROUAC, Jack
"Goofing at the Table." [AmerPoR] (20:4) Jl-Ag 91, p. 31.
"Haiku" (3 poems). [AmerPoR] (20:4) Jl-Ag 91, p. 31.
3156. KERRIGAN, T. S.
"Hollywood Boulevard: Christmas Eve." [PacificR] (10) 91-92, p. 39.
3157. KERRIGAN, William
"His Mistress Compared to Jalapeños." [Hellas] (2:1) Spr 91, p. 125-126.
3158. KERSTEN, Paul
"Another Autumn Poem" (tr. by Lee Rossi). [OnTheBus] (8/9) 91, p. 208.
"Cala Muerta" (tr. by Lee Rossi). [OnTheBus] (8/9) 91, p. 209.
"Dead Child" (tr. by Lee Rossi). [OnTheBus] (8/9) 91, p. 209-211.
"Rainbow" (tr. by Lee Rossi). [OnTheBus] (8/9) 91, p. 213-214.
"The Rose" (tr. by Lee Rossi). [OnTheBus] (8/9) 91, p. 214-215.
"With Colored Pencils" (for Ina, tr. by Lee Rossi). [OnTheBus] (8/9) 91, p. 211-212.
"With the Camera" (for Peter, tr. by Lee Rossi). [OnTheBus] (8/9) 91, p. 212-213.
3159. KESSLER, Jascha
"The Birth of Tragedy" (tr. of Kirsti Simonsuuri, w. the author). [Vis] (37) 91, p. 32.
"Concert" (tr. of Ottó Orbán, w. Mária Körösy). [Vis] (36) 91, p. 19.
"The Garlic: An Aetiological Tale" (tr. from the Finnish w. Kirsti Simonsuuri). [Hellas] (2:1) Spr 91, p. 50-53.
"If" (tr. of Blaga Dimitrova, w. Alexander Shurbanov). [Vis] (36) 91, p. 16.
"Jotting" (tr. of Ottó Orbán, w. Mária Körösy). [Vis] (36) 91, p. 19.
"A Memorable Fancy" (tr. of Ottó Orbán, w. Mária Körösy). [Vis] (36) 91, p. 18.
"Morning, Evening" (tr. of Kirsti Simonsuuri, w. the author). [Vis] (37) 91, p. 31.
"Never at the Horse at Two" (tr. of Milan Richter). [MassR] (32:3) Fall 91, p. 333.
"Roots in the Air" (tr. of Milan Richter, w. the author). [ParisR] (33:119) Sum 91, p. 140.
"Spoiled Poem" (tr. of Milan Richter). [MassR] (32:3) Fall 91, p. 334.
"Spoiled Poem" (tr. of Milan Richter, w. the author). [ParisR] (33:119) Sum 91, p. 139.
"Travelling Light" (tr. of Kirsti Simonsuuri, w. the author). [Vis] (37) 91, p. 32.
3160. KESSLER, Mary
"Hello, Justine." [WorldL] (1:1) 91, p. 37-39.
"Legacies." [WorldL] (1:1) 91, p. 41.
"Yard Sailing in San Francisco." [WorldL] (1:1) 91, p. 40.
3161. KESSLER, Milton
"1988." [ThRiPo] (37/38) 91, p. 8.
"Aways." [ThRiPo] (37/38) 91, p. 8.
"Shoppers." [ThRiPo] (37/38) 91, p. 7.
3162. KESSLER, Miriam
"When My Belly Was Round." [Kalliope] (13:1) 91, p. 13.
3163. KESSLER, Sidney (*See also* KESSLER, Sydney)
"An After Word." [PaintedB] (42) 91, p. 13.
3164. KESSLER, Sydney (*See also* KESSLER, Sidney)
"Article of Faith." [CarolQ] (43:2) Wint 91, p. 41.
"Dawn, After All" (Summer, 1947). [LitR] (35:1) Fall 91, p. 50-51.
"Mobley" (November 1944). [Nimrod] (34:2) Spr-Sum 91, p. 50.
"Remembering a Ride on the Vincent Black Shadow" (for Pat). [Nimrod] (34:2) Spr-Sum 91, p. 51-52.
"Right Now, Amid This Factory Clamor." [Nimrod] (34:2) Spr-Sum 91, p. 53.
"Sing." [Nimrod] (34:2) Spr-Sum 91, p. 49.
"True Love, Stricken." [LitR] (35:1) Fall 91, p. 50.
3165. KETCHEK, Michael
"Untitled: There are only two things." [ChironR] (10:2) Sum 91, p. 39.

"With my father and brother and I it was." [Spitball] (39) Wint 91, p. 8.
3166. KEYISHIAN, Marjorie
"Slow Runner." [MassR] (32:2) Sum 91, p. 318.
3167. KHOSLA, Gouri
"And Life Goes On." [InterPR] (15:1) Spr 89, p. 92.
"A Historic Day." [InterPR] (15:1) Spr 89, p. 92.
3168. KHOSLA, Maya
"Running from Bhopal." [SenR] (21:1) Spr 91, p. 55.
3169. KHVOSTENKO, Alexei
"A Conversation on the Soul: A One-Act Play" (tr. by Rosemarie K. Jenness). [LitR] (34:3) Spr 91, p. 361-362.
3170. KI no AKIMINE
"In summer mountains" (tr. by Sam Hamill). [ColR] (NS 17:2) Fall-Wint 90, p. 19.
3171. KI no TSURAYUKI (ca. 872-945)
"Approaching midnight" (tr. by Sam Hamill). [ColR] (NS 17:2) Fall-Wint 90, p. 19.
3172. KIBBEE, Carol
"I Don't Remember." [OnTheBus] (8/9) 91, p. 93.
3173. KICKNOSWAY, Faye
"Houdini." [RiverS] (34) 91, p. 73-74.
"Mother." [BambooR] (50/51) Spr-Sum 91, p. 20-22.
"Neighbor." [RiverS] (34) 91, p. 75.
"Untitled: Can there be another I, another wall, snow." [BambooR] (50/51) Spr-Sum 91, p. 23-25.
3174. KIEFFER, Rita
"Desert Quatrains." [InterPR] (17:1) Spr 91, p. 100.
"It Would Be Best" (tr. of Jacques Roubaud). [InterPR] (17:1) Spr 91, p. 71.
3175. KIERNAN, Phyllis
"Jade Plant." [CinPR] (21) Spr 90, p. 34.
3176. KIJEWSKI, Bruce
"Bird Man." [AntR] (49:4) Fall 91, p. 563.
"Piss on Earth, Goodwill to Men" (Resolution 660). [OnTheBus] (8/9) 91, p. 95.
"The Unpronounceable Face of God." [BelPoJ] (41:3) Spr 91, p. 19.
3177. KIKEL, Rudy
"6. 107 Richards Hall, 1966-67" (from "Erogenous Zones"). [JamesWR] (8:3) Spr 91, p. 18.
3178. KIKUCHI, Carl
"Watercolor." [Poetry] (157:6) Mr 91, p. 333.
3179. KILCZEWSKI, Lisa
"Lamb Time." [IndR] (14:3) Fall 91, p. 138-139.
3180. KILDARE, D.
"Dawn." [CalQ] (35/36) 91, p. 120.
"The Full Moon Heron." [CalQ] (35/36) 91, p. 120.
3181. KILDUFF, Mike
"The Pathetic Fallacy." [CoalC] (4) S 91, p. 18.
"Poem in Time of War." [CoalC] (4) S 91, p. 16.
3182. KILIANSKI, Brenda
"Ride Forward, Race Backwards." [OnTheBus] (8/9) 91, p. 96-97.
3183. KILLIAN, Sean
"All These Scaffolds." [NewAW] (8/9) Fall 91, p. 29-30.
3184. KIM, Aegina
"Lot's Wife." [PaintedB] (44) 91, p. 36.
3185. KIM, Myung Mi
"Food, Shelter, Clothing." [Zyzzyva] (7:3) Fall 91, p. 122-124.
3186. KIM, Yoon Sik
"I, the Interpreter." [NewYorkQ] (44) 91, p. 59.
3187. KIMBALL, Cristen
"And a Jazz Iris." [WilliamMR] (29) 91, p. 51.
"Cocteau in Gold." [WilliamMR] (29) 91, p. 24.
3188. KIMBALL, Michael
"Lineage." [FreeL] (8) Aut 91, p. 28-29.
"Pretense." [FreeL] (8) Aut 91, p. 29.
3189. KIMMET, Gene F.
"Soaring." [SpoonRQ] (16:1/2) Wint-Spr 91, p. 14.
3190. KINCAID, Joan Payne
"First Letter Orbit." [ContextS] (2:1) 91, p. 18.
"Goya." [Parting] (4:1) Sum 91, p. 4.

"It Turns Some Women On." [Parting] (4:2) Wint 91-92, p. 35-36.
3191. KING, Jane
"Fellow Traveller." [GrahamHR] (14) Spr 91, p. 64-65.
"Intercity Dub for Jean." [GrahamHR] (14) Spr 91, p. 61-63.
KING, Julie Dlugi
See DLUGI-KING, Julie
3192. KING, Lyn
"All Night the Sound." [Dandel] (18:2) Wint 91, p. 59.
"Just After." [Event] (20:3) Fall 91, p. 56-57.
"Storm." [Dandel] (18:2) Wint 91, p. 58.
3193. KING, Martha
"And Perhaps Titian." [NewAW] (7) Spr 91, p. 56-57.
"From an Old Notebook." [NewAW] (7) Spr 91, p. 58-59.
3194. KINGSOLVER, Barbara
"Deadline." [AmerV] (25) Wint 91, p. 12-13.
3195. KINGSTON, Katie
"Airlines." [Plain] (11:2) Wint 91, p. 12.
3196. KINKEAD, Michaelene
"Bus Trip to Martinsville." [WillowR] Spr 91, p. 7.
3197. KINNELL, Galway
"The Auction." [KenR] (NS 13:1) Wint 91, p. 92-95.
"The Room." [SouthernR] (27:1) Ja 91, p. 101-102.
"Sheffield Pastorals" (Selections: 1-6). [Ploughs] (17:1) Spr 91, p. 100-102.
"Shooting Stars." [SouthernR] (27:1) Ja 91, p. 102-104.
3198. KINSELLA, Thomas
"At a Well Beside the Way." [Ploughs] (17:1) Spr 91, p. 106.
"Her Heels Tapped on the Tiles." [Ploughs] (17:1) Spr 91, p. 105-106.
"I Left the Road." [Ploughs] (17:1) Spr 91, p. 105.
"My Senses Tired." [Ploughs] (17:1) Spr 91, p. 105.
"Visiting Hour." [Ploughs] (17:1) Spr 91, p. 104-105.
3199. KINZIE, Mary
"Boy." [Thrpny] (47) Fall 91, p. 29.
"Circadian." [SouthwR] (76:2) Spr 91, p. 240-241.
"Ghost Ship" (for Zivile Bilaisis). [TriQ] (83) Wint 91-92, p. 107-113.
"Learning the World." [Thrpny] (45) Spr 91, p. 14.
"Old Flame." [Salm] (92) Fall 91, p. 147-149.
"Palazzo." [SouthwR] (76:2) Spr 91, p. 241-242.
"Pine." [Salm] (90/91) Spr-Sum 91, p. 92-94.
"Sound Waves." [TriQ] (81) Spr-Sum 91, p. 219-220.
"Sun and Moon." [Salm] (90/91) Spr-Sum 91, p. 90-91.
3200. KIPP, Karen
"The Dead Watching." [GrandS] (10:1, #37) 91, p. 131-133.
3201. KIRBY, Barney
"Lee, New Hampshire" (for Dom Leone). [HayF] (9) Fall-Wint 91, p. 77.
"Philadelphia" (after Norman Dubie's "Thomas Hardy"). [AmerPoR] (20:4) Jl-Ag
91, p. 37.
3202. KIRBY, David
"The Friendship of Dogs." [LaurelR] (25:2) Sum 91, p. 50.
"The Museum of Desire." [Chelsea] (50) 91, p. 75.
"The Physics of Heaven." [ClockR] (7:1/2) 91-92, p. 66.
"The Physics of Hell." [ClockR] (7:1/2) 91-92, p. 67.
"A Poor Unhappy Wretched Sick Miserable Little French Boy." [ChatR] (11:2) Wint
91, p. 73.
"Soft Black Hat." [ClockR] (7:1/2) 91-92, p. 64-65.
"The Thane of Cawdor." [ClockR] (7:1/2) 91-92, p. 53.
"Viginia Rilke." [Chelsea] (50) 91, p. 76-77.
3203. KIRCHWEY, Karl
"Buoy 32A." [PraS] (65:4) Wint 91, p. 113-114.
"Decline and Fall" (Lausanne, June 1987). [SouthwR] (76:4) Aut 91, p. 545-546.
"For the Assassins" (Air-India Flight 182, June 23, 1985). [KenR] (NS 13:3) Sum
91, p. 37-38.
"Moonrise, Indian Wells Beach, Amagansett." [PraS] (65:4) Wint 91, p. 114.
"Murray Hill Barbershop." [Nat] (252:19) 20 My 91, p. 678.
"Rhône Valley, After Rain." [Nat] (253:4) 29 Jl-5 Ag 91, p. 170.
"Stanzas from the Life of George Fox, 1651-57" (for Roberta Capers). [KenR] (NS
13:3) Sum 91, p. 39-41.

3204. KIRK, Laurie
"Union Rep." [Lactuca] (14) My 91, p. 59.

3205. KIRK, Norman Andrew
"Carolina?" [Poem] (66) N 91, p. 16.
"How Sweetly the Dawn." [Poem] (66) N 91, p. 15.

3206. KIRKLAND, Leigh
"The Matter at Issue Is an Old One." [HawaiiR] (15:2, #32) Spr 91, p. 4.

3207. KIRKPATRICK, Kathryn
"Flight." [Poem] (65) My 91, p. 19.
"The Garden." [Poem] (65) My 91, p. 18.
"Reliving the Myths." [Poem] (65) My 91, p. 20-21.
"Temperance" (for my brother). [Poem] (65) My 91, p. 22.

3208. KIRMAYER, Laurence J.
"Essay on Guernica." [Mildred] (4:2/5:1) 91, p. 75.
"Two Mothers Earth to Earth." [Mildred] (4:2/5:1) 91, p. 74-75.

3209. KIRSCH, Sarah
"Limited Light" (tr. by Agnes Stein). [Verse] (8:2) Sum 91, p. 119.
"Warmth of Snow" (tr. by Agnes Stein). [Verse] (8:2) Sum 91, p. 118.

3210. KIRSCHNER, Elizabeth
"At Gilson Pond." [GreensboroR] (51) Wint 91-92, p. 5.
"Life in the Orphanage." [MassR] (32:2) Sum 91, p. 194.

3211. KIRSTEN-MARTIN, Diane
"Heresy 2." [YellowS] (38) Wint-Spr 91-92, p. 9.

3212. KISER, Margie
"If We Should Meet." [EmeraldCR] (3) 91, c1990, p. 48-49.

3213. KISHKAN, Theresa
"I Thought I Could See Africa." [Event] (20:1) Spr 91, p. 87.

3214. KISSICK, Gary
"Coeuriers." [NorthStoneR] (10) Fall 91-Wint 92, p. 128.
"Sometimes." [NorthStoneR] (10) Fall 91-Wint 92, p. 129.

3215. KITLINSKI, Tomek
"XXX" (3 poems, tr. of Artur Przystupa, w. Chris Hurford and Góska A.
Staniewska). [Verse] (8:2) Sum 91, p. 119-120.

3216. KITSON, Herb
"Waking Up to War" (for my students at Pitt-Titusville). [Pearl] (14) Fall-Wint 91,
p. 57.

3217. KITTELL, Ronald Edward
"The Mind." [DustyD] (2:1) Ja 91, p. 24.

3218. KIYOWARA, Fukuyabu (900-930)
"Dawn has almost come" (tr. by Sam Hamill). [ColR] (NS 17:2) Fall-Wint 90, p.
20.

3219. KIZER, Carolyn
"Gifts" (tr. of Shu Ting). [WillowS] (27) Wint 91, p. 32.

3220. KLANDER, Sharon
"Memorial Weekend, Sargent's Beach." [Kalliope] (13:1) 91, p. 27.
"Stealing Peaches." [Kalliope] (13:1) 91, p. 28.
"What Becomes of the Child." [Kalliope] (13:1) 91, p. 26.

3221. KLAPPERT, Peter
"The Prime of Life." [Ploughs] (17:4) Wint 91-92, p. 139-153.

3222. KLASS, Stephen
"Great, Marvelous Structures" (tr. of Werner Aspenstrom, w. Leif Sjoberg). [Vis]
(37) 91, p. 50.
"Icarus and the Lad Graystone" (tr. of Werner Aspenstrom, w. Leif Sjoberg). [Vis]
(37) 91, p. 49.
"Mining Country IV" (tr. of Werner Aspenstrom, w. Leif Sjoberg). [Vis] (37) 91, p.
49.
"The Position (Version II)" (tr. of Werner Aspenstrom, w. Leif Sjoberg). [Vis] (37)
91, p. 50.
"Rousseau the Painter's Departure from Life" (tr. of Werner Aspenstrom, w. Leif
Sjoberg). [Vis] (37) 91, p. 48.
"The Rower" (tr. of Werner Aspenstrom, w. Leif Sjoberg). [Vis] (37) 91, p. 50.

3223. KLASSEN, Pamela
"Family Reunion." [PraF] (12:4) Wint 91-92, p. 37.
"oh i don't think i should see you for a while." [PraF] (12:4) Wint 91-92, p. 38-39.

3224. KLASSEN, Sarah
"How to Treat Hostages." [CanLit] (129) Sum 91, p. 38-39.

"Impressions." [Dandel] (18:2) Wint 91, p. 72.
"Jael." [CanLit] (129) Sum 91, p. 39.
"A Question of Space" (Short Grain Contest Winners: Prose Poem Winners: Honourable Mention). [Grain] (19:4) Wint 91, p. 74.
"Room 117, Concordia." [Dandel] (18:2) Wint 91, p. 71.
3225. KLEIN, Hedin M.
"Art May Be" (tr. by George Johnston). [Vis] (37) 91, p. 18.
"Lulls and Chances" (tr. by George Johnston). [Vis] (37) 91, p. 19.
3226. KLEIN, Melanie
"Home." [DustyD] (2:1) Ja 91, p. 3.
"In *The Dead Pool*." [DustyD] (2:1) Ja 91, p. 17.
3227. KLEIN, Michael
"Calling It By Name." [GreenMR] (NS 5:1) Sum-Fall 91, p. 120.
"Housework." [NewEngR] (13:3/4) Spr-Sum 91, p. 153-155.
"Models." [BrooklynR] (8) 91, p. 49-50.
"Scenes for an Elegy." [NewEngR] (13:3/4) Spr-Sum 91, p. 155-156.
"Scouts" (for R.B.). [JamesWR] (8:3) Spr 91, p. 11.
3228. KLEIN, Rosemary
"On Reading Some Contemporary Poetry." [ManhatR] (6:1) Fall 91, p. 71.
3229. KLEINSCHMIDT, Edward
"Accident." [NewEngR] (13:3/4) Spr-Sum 91, p. 274-275.
"Anonymous Love." [AntR] (49:4) Fall 91, p. 570.
"The Death of Literature." [Poetry] (158:5) Ag 91, p. 273.
"Depth Perception." [VirQR] (67:4) Aut 91, p. 684-685.
"Jackpot." [NewEngR] (13:3/4) Spr-Sum 91, p. 276-277.
"Just Now." [VirQR] (67:4) Aut 91, p. 682-683.
"Lead-Time." [NewEngR] (13:3/4) Spr-Sum 91, p. 273-274.
"No for an Answer." [SouthwR] (76:1) Wint 91, p. 98.
"Planes Landing and Planes Taking Off." [MissR] (19:3) 91, p. 184.
"Why Is There Something Rather Than Nothing." [NewEngR] (13:3/4) Spr-Sum 91, p. 277-278.
3230. KLEINZAHLER, August
"Afternoon in the Middle Kingdom." [NorthStoneR] (10) Fall 91-Wint 92, p. 18.
"Art & Youth." [NorthStoneR] (10) Fall 91-Wint 92, p. 18.
"As the World Turns." [Thrpny] (45) Spr 91, p. 4.
"A Case in Point." [NewAW] (7) Spr 91, p. 1.
"Crunching Numbers." [Sulfur] (11:2 #29) Fall 91, p. 110-111.
"Dream Juice." [Epoch] (40:2) 91, p. 190.
"The Festival." [Thrpny] (44) Wint 91, p. 29.
"A Glass of Claret on a Difficult Morning." [Epoch] (40:2) 91, p. 188-189.
"Heebie-Jeebies." [NewAW] (7) Spr 91, p. 2.
"The Park." [Sulfur] (11:2 #29) Fall 91, p. 109-110.
"Peaches in November." [NewYorker] (67:39) 18 N 91, p. 78.
"Poem: She's flipping like a marlin." [Sulfur] (11:2 #29) Fall 91, p. 108.
"Show Business." [NorthStoneR] (10) Fall 91-Wint 92, p. 20.
"Staying Home from Work." [NorthStoneR] (10) Fall 91-Wint 92, p. 17.
"Where Souls Go." [NorthStoneR] (10) Fall 91-Wint 92, p. 19.
"Who Stole the Horses from the Indians." [Zyzzyva] (7:3) Fall 91, p. 64-65.
3231. KLEPFISZ, Irena
"Bashert" (Selection: introductory section). [SinW] (43/44) Sum 91, p. 202-203.
3232. KLIPSCHUTZ
"Confessions of a Made Man." [PoetC] (22:2) Wint 91, p. 28-29.
"Welcome to L.A." [PoetC] (22:2) Wint 91, p. 27.
3233. KLOEFKORN, William
"Dragging Sand Creek for Minnows." [MidwQ] (32:2) Wint 91, p. 188-189.
"Drifting." [SoDakR] (29:3 part 2) Aut 91, p. 98-99.
"In a Pumpkin Patch Near Roca, Nebraska, Early Evening." [NoDaQ] (59:1) Wint 91, p. 1-2.
3234. KNAVE, Brian
"Buzzard and Salmon" (For Winfried Schleiner). [CalQ] (32/33) Spr 90, p. 69-71.
"Fifth Brian Body: a Self Portrait." [HiramPoR] (50) Spr-Sum 91, p. 14-16.
3235. KNIGHT, Arthur Winfield
"Cynthia Ann Parker: Rescued." [Parting] (4:1) Sum 91, p. 38.
"The Defeat of Jesse James Days." [Parting] (4:1) Sum 91, p. 36-37.
"Pat Garrett: Apples." [NewYorkQ] (46) 91, p. 81.
"A Soft Place." [Pearl] (14) Fall-Wint 91, p. 15.

"The Stripper." [Pearl] (14) Fall-Wint 91, p. 15.
3236. KNIGHT, Lynne
"Bright Combs." [TexasR] (12:3/4) Fall-Wint 91, p. 79.
"Clearing Acanthus." [BelPoJ] (42:1) Fall 91, p. 12-13.
"Hairpins." [NowestR] (29:3) 91, p. 41.
"Holding Patterns." [BelPoJ] (42:1) Fall 91, p. 13-14.
"Remembering the Names." [NowestR] (29:3) 91, p. 40.
"The Story." [BelPoJ] (42:1) Fall 91, p. 10-11.
3237. KNIGHT, Sondra
"Sable." [SinW] (43/44) Sum 91, p. 48.
3238. KNIGHTEN, Merrell
"A Grammar." [PoetryE] (31) Spr 91, p. 50.
"Moby II." [Plain] (11:3) Spr 91, p. 8.
"Negotiable Demands." [ChironR] (10:4) Wint 91, p. 37.
"Post-Transplantal." [Plain] (12:2) Wint 91, p. 38.
3239. KNOEPFLE, John
"Lounge Car." [RiverS] (33) 91, p. 35.
"Naming the Trees." [RiverS] (33) 91, p. 36.
"Once When We Were All the Same." [Nimrod] (34:2) Spr-Sum 91, p. 54-55.
"Poem Adrift in a Prairie Autumn." [RiverS] (33) 91, p. 33.
"Spring Tokens." [RiverS] (33) 91, p. 37.
"Voices at Breakfast." [RiverS] (33) 91, p. 34.
3240. KNOTT, Kip
"Exile" (for Yannis Ritsos). [Os] (33) Fall 91, p. 8.
"Hide and Seek." [CreamCR] (15:2) Fall 91, p. 60.
"Inheriting Sunday Creek" (for Tod Knott). [TexasR] (12:1/2) Spr-Sum 91, p.
109-110.
"Lying in a Mound of Leaves." [MidwQ] (32:3) Spr 91, p. 293.
"Rust Belt Night." [BlackBR] (14) Fall-Wint 91, p. 17.
3241. KNOWLES, Anne
"Alzheimer's 1." [Plain] (11:2) Wint 91, p. 30.
3242. KNOX, Ann (Ann B.)
"Anna." [Nimrod] (34:2) Spr-Sum 91, p. 60-61.
"The Crone Sings to the Bear." [Vis] (36) 91, p. 8.
"A Friend Leaves." [PlumR] (1) Spr-Sum 91, p. 51.
"I Divorce You, Said the Crone." [NewYorkQ] (45) 91, p. 80.
"Rooms." [Nimrod] (34:2) Spr-Sum 91, p. 59.
"She Warns Her Dog." [Nimrod] (34:2) Spr-Sum 91, p. 58.
3243. KNUTSON, John
"Untitled: On this damp deserted street." [Elf] (1:2) Sum 91, p. 26.
3244. KO, Chang Soo
"The Man and the Sea" (tr. by the author). [Vis] (35) 91, p. 17.
"The Man in the Field" (tr. by the author). [Vis] (36) 91, p. 16.
"Silence" (tr. by the author). [Vis] (35) 91, p. 17.
3245. KOCBEK, Edvard
"Fiery Night" (tr. by Michael Biggins). [CimR] (96) Jl 91, p. 21.
"Hands" (tr. by Michael Scammell and Veno Taufer). [NewYRB] (38:17) 24 O 91,
p. 61.
"Moonlight" (tr. by Michael Biggins). [CimR] (96) Jl 91, p. 22.
"Now" (tr. by Michael Scammell and Veno Taufer). [NewYRB] (38:17) 24 O 91, p.
61.
"On Freedom of Mind" (tr. by Michael Scammell and Veno Taufer). [NewYRB]
(38:17) 24 O 91, p. 61.
"Parrots" (tr. by Michael Scammell and Veno Taufer). [NewYRB] (38:17) 24 O 91,
p. 61.
3246. KOCH, Kenneth
"On Aesthetics." [ParisR] (33:120) Fall 91, p. 231-260.
3247. KOCH, Timothy D.
"Golf Course." [EngJ] (80:1) Ja 91, p. 93.
3248. KOCHER, Ruth Ellen
"Laydown Lilies." [PoetL] (86:1) Spr 91, p. 14.
"Poem to a Jazz Man." [PoetL] (86:1) Spr 91, p. 13.
3249. KOCHUYT, Catharina
"Collection" (tr. of Luuk Gruwez, w. David Siefkin). [Trans] (25) Spr 91, p.
233-234.
"Street" (tr. of Luuk Gruwez, w. David Siefkin). [Trans] (25) Spr 91, p. 235.

3250. KOCIK, Robert
"L'Ablatif Absolu" (Maeght editeur 1976, excerpts, tr. of Michel Couturier). [Avec]
(4:1) 91, p. 70-77.

3251. KOEHLER, Ron
"Pushing Up Daisies." [PoetryUSA] (22) Spr 91, p. 19.

3252. KOEHN, David
"Cockeyed Oscars." [PaintedB] (42) 91, p. 15.

3253. KOEHN, Lala-Heine
"No, He Was Not a Man of Clay." [Arc] (26) Spr 91, p. 59-60.

3254. KOEHN-HEINE, Lala
"Don't Bury Your Dead on a Sunday." [Grain] (19:4) Wint 91, p. 24-25.
"Pray, Where Do You Belong." [Grain] (19:4) Wint 91, p. 26.

3255. KOENIG, Michael
"Clouds on a Sunny Afternoon." [Spitball] (38) Fall 91, p. 25.
"Life is too long too long too long." [PoetryUSA] (23) Sum 91, p. 14.
"Pete Rose." [Spitball] (39) Wint 91, p. 23.

3256. KOENINGER, Anthony Sean
"Canto CIV." [Pearl] (14) Fall-Wint 91, p. 57.

3257. KOERNER, Edgar
"Dad's Shiny Black Wing Tips, Mother's Brown and White Pumps." [SouthernR]
(27:3) Jl 91, p. 709-710.
"Having You Both." [SouthernR] (27:3) Jl 91, p. 711-712.

3258. KOERTGE, Ron
"As Men in Gabardine Uniforms Rush Past a Tourist Talks Things Over with
Himself." [Pearl] (13) Spr-Sum 91, p. 19.
"Now & Then." [SycamoreR] (3:2) Sum 91, p. 40.
"What She Wanted." [NewYorkQ] (46) 91, p. 98.

3259. KOESTENBAUM, Phyllis
"Admission of Failure." [Epoch] (40:1) 91, p. 19.
"The Library." [Epoch] (40:1) 91, p. 18.

3260. KOESTER, Rohn
"Folk Stories from the Little Wabash." [ContextS] (2:1) 91, p. 3-6.

3261. KOHLER, Sandra
"Mountains" (for Barbara Moore and Roseann Waldstein). [AmerPoR] (20:5) S-O
91, p. 29.
"Stubborn Weed." [MassR] (32:4) Wint 91-92, p. 507-509.

3262. KOHN, Victoria
"Melancholy Waltz." [RiverS] (35) 91, p. 20-21.

3263. KOLIN, Philip C.
"The Gulls' Confirmation." [SoCaR] (23:2) Spr 91, p. 157.

3264. KOLLAR, Sybil
"In Rooms We Come and Go." [13thMoon] (9:1/2) 91, p. 34-35.
"Late Arrivals." [13thMoon] (9:1/2) 91, p. 33.
"Letter from Goldie." [13thMoon] (9:1/2) 91, p. 32.

3265. KOLODINSKY, Alison
"The Family Foundation of America." [SingHM] (19) 91, p. 32-33.
"Kari at the Pool." [CreamCR] (15:1) Spr 91, p. 76.

3266. KOLODNY, Susan
"Crisis Clinic." [BelPoJ] (42:1) Fall 91, p. 25-28.
"Six Goodbyes." [BelPoJ] (42:1) Fall 91, p. 29-30.

3267. KOLUMBAN, Nicholas
"The 52nd" (tr. of György Faludy). [MidAR] (11:2) 91, p. 55.
"A Citizen of Summer." [LindLM] (10:4) O-D 91, p. 14.
"Dark-Side Up" (tr. of György Petri). [SenR] (21:1) Spr 91, p. 19-20.
"Fall Cleaning" (tr. of Béla Markó). [MassR] (32:4) Wint 91-92, p. 489-490.
"The Huge, Dead Eye" (tr. of Ottó Tolnai). [MassR] (32:4) Wint 91-92, p. 491.
"In the Horatian Mode" (tr. of György Petri). [SenR] (21:1) Spr 91, p. 18.
"Near the Danube." [CharR] (17:1) Spr 91, p. 79.
"An Old Workshop" (tr. of János Oláh). [MassR] (32:4) Wint 91-92, p. 492.
"A Spectacle, an Opinion" (For Sz. V., tr. of György Petri). [SenR] (21:1) Spr 91,
p. 21-22.
"To My Son" (For Jean Cocteau, who, when asked what he would rescue from a
burning house, said: "The flames"). [PoetryE] (31) Spr 91, p. 132.
"A Vague Feeling Grips Me" (tr. of Zsuzsa Takács). [MassR] (32:4) Wint 91-92, p.
493.
"Watching My Own Face" (tr. of Otto Tolnai). [MidAR] (11:2) 91, p. 54.

"The Yanks" (from Germany, 1945). [LindLM] (10:4) O-D 91, p. 14.
"You Were Impersonal Like the Others" (for Imre Nagy, tr. of György Petri).
[NoDaQ] (59:1) Wint 91, p. 118.
KOMACHI, Ono no
    See ONO no KOMACHI (ca. 850)
3268. KOMATSU, Joan M.
    "Wao Kele O Puna." [HawaiiR] (15:3, #33) Fall 91, p. 31-32.
3269. KOMUNYAKAA, Yusef
    "April's Anarchy." [GeoR] (45:1) Spr 91, p. 96.
    "Fleshing-Out the Season." [KenR] (NS 13:2) Spr 91, p. 95-96.
    "Happiness." [HopewellR] (1991) 91, p. 9.
    "History Lessons." [KenR] (NS 13:2) Spr 91, p. 94-95.
    "Immolatus." [Ploughs] (17:4) Wint 91-92, p. 63-64.
    "Knights of the White Camellia & Deacons of Defense." [KenR] (NS 13:2) Spr 91,
        p. 96-97.
    "Little Man Around the House" (for Ladarius). [Ploughs] (17:4) Wint 91-92, p. 66.
    "Meat." [HopewellR] (1991) 91, p. 14.
    "Seasons Between Yes & No." [Ploughs] (17:4) Wint 91-92, p. 65.
    "Slam, Dunk, & Hook." [Callaloo] (14:3) Sum 91, p. 631-632.
    "Slam, Dunk, & Hook." [HopewellR] (1991) 91, p. 18.
3270. KONCEL, Mary A.
    "The Lake Shore Limited." [DenQ] (25:4) Spr 91, p. 39.
3271. KONG, Ann
    "Day Forty-Six." [BellR] (14:1) Spr 91, p. 25.
3272. KONKLE, Lincoln
    "Knowing No No in the Biblical Sense." [HeavenB] (9) Wint-Spr 91-92, p. 53.
    "The World According to Bird." [HeavenB] (9) Wint-Spr 91-92, p. 15.
KOON, Woon
    See WOON, Koon
3273. KOONS, Barbara
    "Wedding Ghost." [HopewellR] (1991) 91, p. 22.
3274. KOONTZ, Haven
    "The Configuration of Small Deaths" (for Rai Peterson). [HopewellR] (1991) 91, p.
        22.
3275. KOONTZ, Tom
    "The Smell of Our Sex." [HopewellR] (1991) 91, p. 17.
3276. KOOSER, Ted
    "A Finding." [ThRiPo] (37/38) 91, p. 30.
    "For My Son." [ThRiPo] (37/38) 91, p. 28-29.
    "The Gilbert Stuart Portrait of Washington." [ThRiPo] (37/38) 91, p. 26-27.
3277. KOPACKI, Paul
    "September 30, 1990, the Alcohol Rehab Center, Oka, Quebec." [BrooklynR] (8)
        91, p. 22.
3278. KOPELKE, Kendra
    "Dad's Heart." [FreeL] (7) Spr 91, p. 7.
    "Miscarriage." [FreeL] (7) Spr 91, p. 6.
3279. KOREMAN, Paul
    "Gestures." [ArtfulD] (20/21) 91, p. 67.
    "Reading Naomi Shihab Nye." [ArtfulD] (20/21) 91, p. 68.
    "Walking Backwards Through the House with a Mirror." [ArtfulD] (20/21) 91, p.
        66.
3280. KÖRÖSY, Mária
    "After a Long Journey" (tr. of Imre Oravecz, w. Bruce Berlind). [HampSPR] Wint
        91, p. 64.
    "America" ("Dear Dr. Orbán — a letter from Washington D.C., February 1987, tr.
        of Ottó Orbán, w. Bruce Berlind). [OnTheBus] (8/9) 91, p. 218.
    "And Sometimes It's the Cities" (tr. of Ottó Orbán, w. Bruce Berlind). [Agni] (34)
        91, p. 223.
    "Concert" (tr. of Ottó Orbán, w. Jascka Kessler). [Vis] (36) 91, p. 19.
    "Dust" (tr. of Imre Oravecz, w. Bruce Berlind). [GrandS] (10:1, #37) 91, p.
        197-198.
    "Europe" (tr. of Ottó Orbán, w. Bruce Berlind). [Agni] (34) 91, p. 224.
    "The Hole" (tr. of Imre Oravecz, w. Bruce Berlind). [GrandS] (10:1, #37) 91, p.
        199.
    "Hope in the Air" (tr. of Gyula Illyés, w. Bruce Berlind). [Os] (33) Fall 91, p. 3.

"I Couldn't Tell You Back Then" (tr. of Imre Oravecz, w. Bruce Berlind). [Stand] (32:4) Aut 91, p. 24.
"I Have a Recurring" (tr. of Imre Oravecz, w. Bruce Berlind). [InterPR] (17:2) Fall 91, p. 32.
"In the Beginning There Was" (tr. of Imre Oravecz, w. Bruce Berlind). [ColR] (NS 17:2) Fall-Wint 90, p. 104.
"In Theodore Roosevelt Park" (New York Columbus Avenue, tr.tr. of Ottó Orbán, w. Bruce Berlind). [OnTheBus] (8/9) 91, p. 219.
"Jotting" (tr. of Ottó Orbán, w. Jascka Kessler). [Vis] (36) 91, p. 19.
"The Landscape Unfolding Before Us" (American Automobile Association Road Atlas, 1987 Edition, tr. of Ottó Orbán, w. Bruce Berlind). [ColR] (NS 18:2) Fall-Wint 91, p. 78.
"A Memorable Fancy" (tr. of Ottó Orbán, w. Jascka Kessler). [Vis] (36) 91, p. 18.
"Nine A.M." (tr. of Imre Oravecz, w. Bruce Berlind). [InterPR] (17:2) Fall 91, p. 33.
"There I Stood" (tr. of Imre Oravecz, w. Bruce Berlind). [InterPR] (17:2) Fall 91, p. 35.
"Under the Thundering Ceiling" (Hamline University, St. Paul, Minnesota, tr. of Ottó Orbán, w. Bruce Berlind). [OnTheBus] (8/9) 91, p. 219.
"When We Resolved" (tr. of Imre Oravecz, w. Bruce Berlind). [InterPR] (17:2) Fall 91, p. 34.
"The Year Drops Anchor, Tihany" (tr. of Gyula Illés, w. Bruce Berlind). [Vis] (36) 91, p. 21.

3281. KORSON, Michael
"Courtship." [CalQ] (31) Fall 88, p. 66.
"Fidelity." [CalQ] (31) Fall 88, p. 67.
"Thanksgiving." [CalQ] (31) Fall 88, p. 65.

3282. KORT, Susanne
"Eddie." [Kalliope] (13:1) 91, p. 29.

3283. KORUSIEVIC, Maria
"XLIII. Once in a while." [Sequoia] (34:1) Spr 91, p. 59.

3284. KOSOVEL, Srecko
"A la Gare" (French tr. by Marc Alyn). [InterPR] (17:1) Spr 91, p. 72.
"At the Train Station" (tr. from the French of Marc Alyn by Barbara Siegel Carlson). [InterPR] (17:1) Spr 91, p. 73.
"Ce N'Est Pas Toi" (French tr. by Marc Alyn). [InterPR] (17:1) Spr 91, p. 76.
"Le Chant des Humiliés" (French tr. by Marc Alyn). [InterPR] (17:1) Spr 91, p. 72.
"It's Not You" (tr. from the French of Marc Alyn by Barbara Siegel Carlson). [InterPR] (17:1) Spr 91, p. 77.
"The Karstic Village" (tr. from the French of Marc Alyn by Barbara Siegel Carlson). [InterPR] (17:1) Spr 91, p. 75, 77.
"Song of the Humble" (tr. from the French of Marc Alyn by Barbara Siegel Carlson). [InterPR] (17:1) Spr 91, p. 73.
"Le Village Karstique" (French tr. by Marc Alyn). [InterPR] (17:1) Spr 91, p. 74, 76.

3285. KOSSMAN, Nina
"The Book of Air" (tr. of Igor Vishnevetsky). [LitR] (34:3) Spr 91, p. 376-377.
"Daphne and Apollo." [NewRena] (8:2, #25) Fall 91, p. 60.
"In Winter" (tr. of Valery Shubinsky). [LitR] (34:3) Spr 91, p. 382.
"Odysseus's Temptation" (tr. of Igor Vishnevetsky). [LitR] (34:3) Spr 91, p. 378.
"Spectrum" (tr. of Valery Shubinsky). [LitR] (34:3) Spr 91, p. 383.
"Teach Me to See the Star in the Deadly Pale Water" (tr. of Igor Vishnevetsky). [LitR] (34:3) Spr 91, p. 377.

3286. KOSTELANETZ, Richard
"(Complete) Shorter Stories (1990)" (Excerpt). [PaintedHR] (1) Ja 91, p. 21.
"(Complete) Shorter Stories (1990A)" (Excerpt). [ContextS] (2:1) 91, p. 35.
"Minimal Audio Plays." [CreamCR] (14:2) Wint 91, p. 41-46.
"More or Less." [Asylum] (6:3/4) 91, p. 34-49.
"Openings: After twenty years together, they were finally completing the project they began when first they met." [Parting] (4:1) Sum 91, p. 33.
"Openings: Called a 'fascist' behind his back, he couldn't prove his accusers wrong or right." [Parting] (4:1) Sum 91, p. 30.
"Openings: He died falling down a mountain he had scaled several times before." [Parting] (4:1) Sum 91, p. 26.
"Openings: He had seventeen healthy sons, all but one of whom knew how to bear his name." [Parting] (4:1) Sum 91, p. 12.

"Openings: I gave my house away to a relative I'd long detested, whose family I
wanted to ruin." [Parting] (4:1) Sum 91, p. 25.
"Openings: Our police force exits not to protect us people but mostly to protect our
police force." [Parting] (4:1) Sum 91, p. 37.
"Openings: To us her husband was a famously benevolent man." [Parting] (4:1) Sum
91, p. 4.
"Openings: When my father died suddenly, a business I knew almost nothing about
was deposited on my cluttered desk." [Parting] (4:1) Sum 91, p. 16.
"Recircuits" (w. Kathy Antrim). [WilliamMR] (29) 91, p. 73-81.
"Repartitions-III." [ChamLR] (8-9) Spr-Fall 91, p. 40-43.
"String-Two" (2 excerpts, 1989). [Caliban] (10) 91, p. 140-141.
3287. KOSTIC, Zvonimir
"Ali." [InterPR] (15:1) Spr 89, p. 64.
"And While the Watch Hands of the Blue Clock Still Melt" (tr. by Simha Levi
Bogdanovic). [InterPR] (15:1) Spr 89, p. 63.
"Bajka O Kuci." [InterPR] (15:1) Spr 89, p. 66.
"But" (tr. by Vasa D. Mihailovich). [InterPR] (15:1) Spr 89, p. 65.
"A Fairy Tale About the House" (tr. by Vasa D. Mihailovich). [InterPR] (15:1) Spr
89, p. 67.
"From a Terrible Fire an Escaped Flame" (tr. by Vasa D. Mihailovich). [InterPR]
(15:1) Spr 89, p. 67.
"I Jos Dok Se Tope Kazaljke Plavog Sata." [InterPR] (15:1) Spr 89, p. 62.
"Iz Strasnog Ognja Izbegli Plamen." [InterPR] (15:1) Spr 89, p. 66.
"Kad Ostarim Kao Prst Na Ruci Moga Dede." [InterPR] (15:1) Spr 89, p. 68.
"Ponekad, Pustom Ulicom." [InterPR] (15:1) Spr 89, p. 58.
"Sometimes, in a Deserted Street" (tr. by Simha Levi Bogdanovic). [InterPR] (15:1)
Spr 89, p. 59.
"They Will Lock You in a Room" (tr. by Simha Levi Bogdanovic). [InterPR] (15:1)
Spr 89, p. 61.
"When I Age Like the Finger on My Grandfather's Hand" (tr. by Vasa D.
Mihailovich). [InterPR] (15:1) Spr 89, p. 69.
"Zakljucace Te U Sobu." [InterPR] (15:1) Spr 89, p. 60.
3288. KOSTOLEFSKY, Joseph
"Two Harangues by the Old Boy." [Sequoia] (34:1) Spr 91, p. 46-47.
3289. KOSTOPULUS-COOPERMAN, Celeste
"When the evening light burns" (tr. of Marjorie Agosín). [Agni] (33) 91, p. 41.
3290. KOSTOS, Dean
"I Loved Spring." [ChironR] (10:2) Sum 91, p. 42.
3291. KOUMJIAN, Vaughn
"Passion." [GrahamHR] (15) Fall 91, p. 74.
3292. KOUROUS, Sharon
"Hardly." [Outbr] (22) 91, p. 46.
3293. KOVACIK, Karen
"Babes in the Woods" (tr. of Katarzyna Borun-Jagodzinska). [ArtfulD] (20/21) 91,
p. 15.
"The Bird People" (After Goya's "Disparate ridículo"). [ArtfulD] (20/21) 91, p. 10.
"Breslau." [LaurelR] (25:1) Wint 91, p. 58-59.
"Citoyen." [Salm] (90/91) Spr-Sum 91, p. 196-197.
"Drought." [CinPR] (21) Spr 90, p. 17.
"During the Sorties over Baghdad." [ArtfulD] (20/21) 91, p. 12.
"Dust Devils." [Salm] (90/91) Spr-Sum 91, p. 198.
"The Match" (tr. of Katarzyna Borun-Jagodzinska). [AmerPoR] (20:4) Jl-Ag 91, p.
33.
"Means of Flight" (After Goya's "Modo de volar"). [ArtfulD] (20/21) 91, p. 11.
"Medea Has Forgotten How to Cry" (tr. of Katarzyna Borun-Jagodzinska).
[ArtfulD] (20/21) 91, p. 13.
"Return of the Prodigal." [Salm] (90/91) Spr-Sum 91, p. 199.
"Tenant" (tr. of Katarzyna Borun-Jagodzinska). [ArtfulD] (20/21) 91, p. 14.
"Today Twilight Comes More Quickly to Our Summer Kitchens" (tr. of Katarzyna
Borun-Jagodzinska). [AmerPoR] (20:4) Jl-Ag 91, p. 33.
"WCW on Marsden Hartley." [Salm] (90/91) Spr-Sum 91, p. 194-195.
3294. KOVACS, Edna
"Avowal." [BellArk] (7:3) My-Je 91, p. 9.
"Lachrymae ('Flow My Tears')." [PaintedHR] (4) Fall 92, p. 30-31.
3295. KRAMER, Aaron
"Apollo at Gate 17." [Confr] (46/47) Fall 91-Wint 92, p. 255.

"Emily's Day." [Vis] (35) 91, p. 36.
"Glaucoma." [Confr] (46/47) Fall 91-Wint 92, p. 255-256.
"My Son" (tr. of Rajzel Zychlinska). [Vis] (36) 91, p. 49.
"Night Thoughts." [PikeF] (10) Spr 91, p. 15.

3296. KRAMER, K. L.
"Transplants." [HawaiiR] (15:3, #33) Fall 91, p. 75.

3297. KRAMER, Larry
"Wild Onions" (A Memoir of West Texas and St. Mary's Academy." [Poetry]
(159:3) D 91, p. 149-150.

3298. KRATT, Mary
"Dear Harvey." [Pembroke] (23) 91, p. 53-54.
"On Deep River." [Pembroke] (23) 91, p. 54.

3299. KRATZ, Kenry
"On the Screen" (tr. of Gylfi Grondal). [Vis] (37) 91, p. 39.

3300. KRAUSHAAR, Mark
"I Controlled Paul Molitor's Hitting Streak." [PoetryNW] (32:2) Sum 91, p. 37-38.
"The Neighbors." [PoetryNW] (32:2) Sum 91, p. 37.
"We Choose Our Parents" (— Buddhist doctrine). [SouthernPR] (31:1) Spr 91, p.
64-65.

3301. KRAVANJA, Sonja
"I Do Not Want" (tr. of Tomaz Salamun). [OnTheBus] (8/9) 91, p. 225.
"My Glass, My Flour" (tr. of Tomaz Salamun). [OnTheBus] (8/9) 91, p. 225-226.
"The Right of the Strong" (tr. of Tomaz Salamun). [OnTheBus] (8/9) 91, p. 224.
"The Sea Lasts" (tr. of Tomaz Salamun). [PraF] (12:3 #56) Aut 91, p. 29.
"Seed" (tr. of Tomaz Salamun). [OnTheBus] (8/9) 91, p. 224-225.
"Things" (VII, tr. of Tomaz Salamun). [PraF] (12:3 #56) Aut 91, p. 28.
"Turtle" (tr. of Tomaz Salamun). [PraF] (12:3 #56) Aut 91, p. 27.

3302. KRAWIEC, Richard
"The Birth." [ArtfulD] (20/21) 91, p. 55.
"Class War." [BlackBR] (13) Spr-Sum 91, p. 8-9.
"Taking to a Deaf Man." [BlackBR] (13) Spr-Sum 91, p. 11.
"Wrestling with the Angel." [BlackBR] (13) Spr-Sum 91, p. 38-39.

3303. KRESH, David
"For Léon Damas." [BelPoJ] (42:2) Wint 91-92, p. 22-23.
"Getting Mighty Crowded." [CutB] (35) Wint-Spr 91, p. 78-79.
"Little Waltz." [HighP] (6:1) Spr 91, p. 96-98.
"Secret Famous Names." [BelPoJ] (42:2) Wint 91-92, p. 24-25.

3304. KRETZ, T. (Thomas)
"Effect of." [OxfordM] (7:2) Fall-Wint 91, p. 1.
"General and Nofret Rahotep." [CoalC] (4) S 91, p. 11.
"Memories Are Made Of." [HolCrit] (28:5) D 91, p. 18.
"Pre-Pueblo Rain." [BlackBR] (14) Fall-Wint 91, p. 24-25.

3305. KRICH, A. M.
"At the Freud Museum." [ParisR] (33:118) Spr 91, p. 29.

3306. KRICORIAN, Nancy
"The Artist As the Queen of Peas." [MissR] (19:3) 91, p. 148-149.
"Letter to James." [MissR] (19:3) 91, p. 150.
"The Orphanage." [SenR] (21:1) Spr 91, p. 58-59.

3307. KRINSKY, Sharon
"Mystery Stories" (Selections). [BrooklynR] (8) 91, p. 40-42.

3308. KRIVULIN, Victor
"The Garden of the 9th of January" (tr. by Leonard Schwartz and Ina Bliznetsova).
[LitR] (34:3) Spr 91, p. 387.
"The Idea of Russia" (tr. by Leonard Schwartz and Ina Bliznetsova). [LitR] (34:3)
Spr 91, p. 387.
"Main Line" (tr. by Leonard Schwartz and Ina Bliznetsova). [LitR] (34:3) Spr 91, p.
389.
"The Road Home" (tr. by Leonard Schwartz and Ina Bliznetsova). [LitR] (34:3) Spr
91, p. 388.

3309. KRMPOTIC, Vesna
"Drum" (tr. by Dasha Culic Nisula). [ColR] (NS 17:2) Fall-Wint 90, p. 102.

3310. KROEKER, G. W.
"Dust Bowl Legacy." [Pearl] (14) Fall-Wint 91, p. 27.
"Nightmare Comforts." [BlackBR] (14) Fall-Wint 91, p. 38-39.

3311. KROETSCH, Robert
"Poem for My Dead Sister." [WestCL] (25:2, #5) Fall 91, p. 105-112.

243

3312. KROK, Peter
"Constance Adams." [NegC] (11:1) 91, p. 23-24.
3313. KROLL, Ernest
"Air Quality Index." [Comm] (118:17) 11 O 91, p. 565.
"Counterpoint in Oxford" (1870s). [WebR] (15) Spr 91, p. 114.
"James Gutmann Greets Mark Van Doren" (Hamilton Hall). [WebR] (15) Spr 91, p. 116.
"Nathaniel Hawthorne." [WebR] (15) Spr 91, p. 116.
"New England Primer" (revised). [SmPd] (28:1, #81) Wint 91, p. 11.
"Ruskin After Sunset." [WebR] (15) Spr 91, p. 115.
"Turgenev." [HolCrit] (28:1) F 91, p. 18.
3314. KROLL, Judith
"Buying the Dildo." [SouthernR] (27:3) Jl 91, p. 691-692.
"Our Elephant & That Child" (for Rafil. 33 poems). [QRL] (Poetry ser. 10, vol. 30) 91, 72 p.
"That Child." [SouthernR] (27:3) Jl 91, p. 689-691.
3315. KROLOW, Karl
"The Days Are Changing" (tr. by Stuart Friebert). [MidAR] (11:2) 91, p. 59-60.
"The Details Get Lost" (tr. by Stuart Friebert). [MidAR] (11:2) 91, p. 58.
"In Peace-Time" (tr. by Stuart Friebert). [PassN] (12:1) Sum 91, p. 26.
"July and August" (tr. by Stuart Friebert). [MidAR] (11:2) 91, p. 61-62.
"Motives." (tr. by Stuart Friebert). [GrahamHR] (15) Fall 91, p. 96-98.
"Poem for Literature" (tr. by Stuart Friebert). [PassN] (12:1) Sum 91, p. 26.
3316. KRONEN, Steve
"Owl and Mouse in a Cage." [GeoR] (45:1) Spr 91, p. 122-123.
"Tolstoy on the Train to Astapovo." [MassR] (32:3) Fall 91, p. 357.
3317. KRONENBERG, Mindy
"Witness." [Confr] (46/47) Fall 91-Wint 92, p. 277.
3318. KRONENBERG, Susan
"Hudson River Valley Poem." [ManhatPR] (13) [91?], p. 34.
3319. KRUGER, Lee
"August." [CapeR] (26:1) Spr 91, p. 36.
"A Hesitance." [CapeR] (26:1) Spr 91, p. 35.
3320. KRUK, Laurie
"Reruns." [PraF] (12:4) Wint 91-92, p. 71.
"To the end of her street and back." [PraF] (12:4) Wint 91-92, p. 70.
3321. KRUMBERGER, John
"Believing in Uncles." [LakeSR] (25) 91, p. 35.
"Olley's Farm." [Sidewalks] (1) Aug 91, p. 1.
"Sleepwalker." [ArtfulD] (20/21) 91, p. 86.
3322. KRYGOWSKI, Nancy
"Frogs." [PassN] (12:2) Wint 91, p. 4.
"Once." [PassN] (12:2) Wint 91, p. 4.
3323. KRYSL, Marilyn
"The Great Leap Forward: Cost Assessment, April, '82." [CalQ] (32/33) Spr 90, p. 138-139.
3324. KUBACH, David
"An Invitation." [Vis] (35) 91, p. 28-29.
3325. KUBO, Mari
"Winter 1989." [BambooR] (50/51) Spr-Sum 91, p. 288.
3326. KUCHARSKI, Lisa
"The Way You React to What I Say." [Lactuca] (14) My 91, p. 53.
3327. KUCHINSKY, Walter
"Well." [SmPd] (28:3, #83) Fall 91, p. 22.
3328. KUDERKA, Michael S.
"Quincy Station." [Pembroke] (23) 91, p. 69-70.
3329. KUDERKO, Lynne M.
"Willows." [CimR] (94) Ja 91, p. 101-102.
3330. KUECHLE, Lynne Maker
"Sidewalks." [Sidewalks] (1) Aug 91, p. 12.
3331. KUFFEL, Frances
"The Late Snow." [Colum] (15) 90, p. 171.
"The Visible Woman." [PlumR] (1) Spr-Sum 91, p. 62-63.
3332. KÜLEBI, Cahit
"To Live" (tr. by Ozcan Yalim, William A. Fielder and Dionis Coffin Riggs). [InterPR] (17:1) Spr 91, p. 19.

"Yasamak." [InterPR] (17:1) Spr 91, p. 18.
3333. KUMIN, Maxine
"A Brief History of Passion." [Nimrod] (34:2) Spr-Sum 91, p. 64-65.
"The Geographic Center." [Poetry] (157:4) Ja 91, p. 202-203.
"A Morning on the Hill." [Journal] (15:1) Spr 91, p. 62.
"Of Wings." [Nimrod] (34:2) Spr-Sum 91, p. 62-63.
"The Poets' Garden." [Poetry] (157:4) Ja 91, p. 201-202.
"Progress." [Poetry] (157:4) Ja 91, p. 204.
"The Rendezvous." [NewYorker] (67:8) 15 Ap 91, p. 84.
"Saga: Four Variations on the Sonnet." [Ploughs] (17:2/3) Fall 91, p. 135-136.
3334. KUNERT, Gunter
"Elegy" (tr. by Agnes Stein). [ColR] (NS 18:2) Fall-Wint 91, p. 89.
3335. KUNERT, Günter
"Removed" (from "Stilleben," 1983, tr. by Kate Armstrong). [Verse] (8:1) Spr 91,
p. 104.
3336. KUPER, Joel
"Blue and Green and Everything Before Unseen." [WindO] (55) Wint 91-92, p. 23.
3337. KURDI, Mária
"In the End" (tr. of Ida Makay, w. Len Roberts). [WebR] (15) Spr 91, p. 31.
3338. KURIBAYASHI, Tomoko
"Etrangere." [Sidewalks] (1) Aug 91, p. 10.
3339. KURITSKY, Joel
"The Infirmary." [Vis] (36) 91, p. 48-49.
3340. KURODA, Saburo
"Evening Glow" (tr. by Bruno Peter Navasky). [ParisR] (33:121) Wint 91, p. 209.
"Laundry" (tr. by Bruno Peter Navasky). [ParisR] (33:121) Wint 91, p. 208-209.
"Three O'clock Autumn Afternoon" (tr. by Bruno Peter Navasky). [ParisR] (33:121)
Wint 91, p. 210.
3341. KURZWEIL, Paul
"Ayling." [HangL] (59) 91, p. 82.
3342. KUSCH, Robert
"The Field." [CalQ] (35/36) 91, p. 128-129.
3343. KUSHNER, Aleksandr
"At the window I watch the nocturnal clouds pass" (tr. by Paul Graves and Carol
Ueland). [AmerPoR] (20:1) Ja-F 91, p. 3.
"Cypress." [PartR] (58:1) Wint 91, p. 117.
"It's longer, harder saying our goodbyes" (tr. by Paul Graves and Carol Ueland).
[AmerPoR] (20:1) Ja-F 91, p. 4.
"Mozart's skull, from between two columns of the news" (tr. by Paul Graves and
Carol Ueland). [AmerPoR] (20:1) Ja-F 91, p. 4.
"No woman that I'd met before" (tr. by Paul Graves and Carol Ueland). [AmerPoR]
(20:1) Ja-F 91, p. 4.
"On this, the near side of the mystery line, a cloud" (tr. by Paul Graves and Carol
Ueland). [AmerPoR] (20:1) Ja-F 91, p. 4.
"Tragedy's easy: once onstage, men wreck or slaughter" (tr. by Paul Graves and
Carol Ueland). [AmerPoR] (20:1) Ja-F 91, p. 4.
"Vyritsa" (tr. by Paul Graves and Carol Ueland). [AmerPoR] (20:1) Ja-F 91, p. 3.
"Your exit's into frost, and the audience exits" (tr. by Paul Graves and Carol
Ueland). [AmerPoR] (20:1) Ja-F 91, p. 4.
3344. KUSHNER, Dale
"On Skyros, the Moon." [PoetryE] (32) Fall 91, p. 94.
3345. KUSNETZ, Ilyse M.
"In Suffolk, a Grandmother Has Just Died." [BellR] (14:2) Fall 91, p. 24.
3346. KUZMA, Greg
"Auction." [PoetryE] (32) Fall 91, p. 162-163.
"Letter from a Bright Sunday." [SoDakR] (29:3 part 2) Aut 91, p. 19-20.
"My Life." [PoetryE] (32) Fall 91, p. 164-170.
"The Week." [MidwQ] (32:2) Wint 91, p. 190-191.
3347. KVASNICKA, Mellanee
"Dream State." [Plain] (11:2) Wint 91, p. 8.
3348. KWA, Lydia
"Subject to Desire." [Descant] (22:3, #74) Fall 91, p. 58-63.
3349. KWASNY, Melissa
"Presence of Birds / Absence of Birds: A Song Cycle" (Selections. The Pablo
Neruda Prize for Poetry, Honorable Mention). [Nimrod] (35:1) Fall-Wint 91,
p. 33-34.

3350. KWELISMITH
"Journal 7/22/90: The Feminist Writers Workshop." [WashR] (16:5) F-Mr 91, p. 9.
3351. KWOCK, C. H.
"Answering the Hu-chou Magistrate of Hindu Ancestry Who Asked Who I Was" (tr.
of Li Po, w. Vincent McHugh). [PoetryUSA] (22) Spr 91, p. 21.
"Li Po's Grave" (tr. of Po Chu-i, w. Vincent McHugh). [PoetryUSA] (22) Spr 91,
p. 21.
"The War Year" (tr. of Ts'ao Sung, w. Vincent McHugh). [PoetryUSA] (22) Spr
91, p. 21.
3352. KYOGOKU, Tamekane (1254-1332)
"Wanting to preserve" (tr. by Sam Hamill). [ColR] (NS 17:2) Fall-Wint 90, p. 15.
KYOKO, Mori
See MORI, Kyoko
KYONG-RIM, Sin
See SIN, Kyong-rim
3353. KYSELKA, Lee
"His Eye Is on the Sparrow." [BambooR] (50/51) Spr-Sum 91, p. 311-313.
"Secrets." [BambooR] (50/51) Spr-Sum 91, p. 309-310.
"A Wailing Wall." [BambooR] (50/51) Spr-Sum 91, p. 314.
La . . .
See also names beginning with "La" without the following space, filed below in their
alphabetic positions, e.g., LaSALLE.
La BRUNO, Carmen Michael
See LaBRUNO, Carmen Michael
La BRUNO, Michael
See LaBRUNO, Carmen Michael
3354. La LOCA
"Still Life with Women." [SycamoreR] (3:2) Sum 91, p. 27-28.
3355. La ROCCA, Lynda
"The Wall." [AnthNEW] (3) 91, p. 24.
La VEGA, Yvonne de
See De la VEGA, Yvonne
3356. LAABI, Abdellatif
"Soleils aux Arrets" (à Nelson Mandela et Abraham Serfaty, from "Tous les
Déchirements"). [InterPR] (17:2) Fall 91, p. 18-30.
"Suns under Arrest" (for Nelson Mandela and Abraham Serfaty, tr. by Victor
Reinking and Jean-Jacques Malo). [InterPR] (17:2) Fall 91, p. 19-31.
3357. LaBOMBARD, Joan
"Snapshots." [ColR] (NS 17:2) Fall-Wint 90, p. 74-75.
"Transformations." [ColR] (NS 17:2) Fall-Wint 90, p. 76-80.
3358. LaBRUNO, Carmen Michael
"Contaminated Fill W/ a Pinch of Political Mix." [Chelsea] (51) 91, p. 62-63.
"He's on TV Now. Do You Get Howard Stern in Canada. Saturdays at Eleven."
[ChiR] (37:2/3) 91, p. 23-25.
"Keeper of the Keys." [JINJPo] (13:1) Spr 91, p. 11-13.
"Pro Choice / Pro Life Gentlemen: Stay Out of Abortion Issues." [NegC] (11:1) 91,
p. 20-21.
LaBRUNO, Michael
See LaBRUNO, Carmen Michael
3359. LACHOWSKI, Cheryl
"Three Women." [PraS] (65:4) Wint 91, p. 83-85.
"Wanting to Talk." [PraS] (65:4) Wint 91, p. 85.
3360. LACKEY, Joe
"The Tattered Trade Paperback." [NewYorkQ] (46) 91, p. 66.
3361. LaCLAIR, Richard J.
"Balance in Winter." [Elf] (1:3) Fall 91, p. 35.
3362. LADIN, Jay
"Childhood." [BellR] (14:1) Spr 91, p. 22.
"The Wheel." [Sequoia] (34:1) Spr 91, p. 12-13.
3363. LADUE, Susan
"Homesick for Spring." [Kalliope] (13:1) 91, p. 39.
3364. LaFEMINA, Gerry
"Action Figures." [WestB] (29) 91, p. 32-33.
3365. LaGRECA, T. R.
"Escaping." [JINJPo] (13:1) Spr 91, p. 16.

3366. LAHOMA-CASEY, David
    "Madame Sosostris." [Boulevard] (5:3/6:1, #15/16) Spr 91, p. 196.
3367. LAI, Larissa
    "Arrangements." [CapilR] (2:6/7) Fall 91, p. 16.
    "Glory." [CapilR] (2:6/7) Fall 91, p. 17.
    "Shade." [BambooR] (52) Fall 91, p. 63-64.
3368. LAINO, E. J. Miller
    "High Relief." [Mildred] (4:2/5:1) 91, p. 69.
    "Mother's Bedroom." [Mildred] (4:2/5:1) 91, p. 68.
3369. LAINSBURY, G. P.
    "The Museum of Exotic Travel." [Dandel] (18:1) Spr-Sum 91, p. 18.
3370. LAIWAN
    "Savage" (Photo collaboration: Netsayi Chigwendere / Laiwan). [CapilR] (2:6/7) Fall
       91, p. 112-119.
3371. LAKE, Paul
    "Epitaph for a Draft Dodger." [TexasR] (12:3/4) Fall-Wint 91, p. 80.
    "Interrogations." [Pequod] (32) 91, p. 98-101.
    "Walking Backward." [Pequod] (32) 91, p. 94-97.
3372. LALLY, Michael
    "I Remember Tim." [WashR] (16:6) Ap-My 91, p. 5-6.
3373. LAMANTIA, Philip
    "Passionate Ornithology Is Another Kind of Yoga." [Sulfer] (11:2, #29) Fall 91, p.
       25-26.
3374. LAMB, Jessica
    "The Opening Question." [Poetry] (158:5) Ag 91, p. 277.
3375. LAMBERT, Nancy
    "Choice." [ChironR] (10:2) Sum 91, p. 48.
3376. LAMMON, Martin
    "From a Small Town." [SouthernPR] (31:2) Fall 91, p. 16-17.
    "Where the Children Go." [SouthernPR] (31:2) Fall 91, p. 17-18.
LAN, Tang
    See TANG, Lan
3377. LANCASTER, Robert S.
    "A House for All Living." [SewanR] (99:4) Fall 91, p. 542-544.
3378. LAND, E. Waverly
    "Lines and Curves." [WashR] (16:6) Ap-My 91, p. 14.
    "My Love Is Like." [WashR] (16:6) Ap-My 91, p. 14.
    "Sheets and Pillows." [WashR] (16:6) Ap-My 91, p. 14.
3379. LANDALE, Zoe
    "No Commercial Value." [CapilR] (2:6/7) Fall 91, p. 37.
    "There's Something You Should Know." [CapilR] (2:6/7) Fall 91, p. 38.
    "The Vasectomy." [CapilR] (2:6/7) Fall 91, p. 36.
3380. LANDAU, Julie
    "Hsiang Sze Ling" (tr. of Lin Pu). [Trans] (25) Spr 91, p. 227.
    "Shuang Tien Hsiao Chueh" (tr. of Lin Pu). [Trans] (25) Spr 91, p. 227.
    "Tien Chiang Ch'un " (tr. of Lin Pu). [Trans] (25) Spr 91, p. 226.
3381. LANDAVERDE, Mary Lee
    "Mr. Letterman." [PacificR] (9) 91, p. 67.
    "The Sun in My Mind." [PacificR] (9) 91, p. 65-66.
3382. LANDER, Jane Birdsall
    "Baptism." [WebR] (15) Spr 91, p. 81.
    "Beauty and Sorrow of an Unmade Bed." [Ascent] (15:2) Wint 91, p. 20.
    "Mask." [WebR] (15) Spr 91, p. 83.
    "My Mother's Ghost." [WebR] (15) Spr 91, p. 84.
    "Willows." [WebR] (15) Spr 91, p. 82.
3383. LANDGRAF, Susan
    "About War: A Short History of Sound." [DustyD] Je 91, p. 26.
    "Remembering the Egg." [DustyD] Je 91, p. 26.
3384. LANDRUM, Rodney
    "City Stock." [EmeraldCR] (3) 91, c1990, p. 77-78.
    "Dead in a Truckstop." [EmeraldCR] (3) 91, c1990, p. 77.
3385. LANDRUS, Matt
    "Early each morning." [NegC] (11:1) 91, p. 96.
3386. LANE, Donna M.
    "The Border." [SwampR] (7/8) Spr-Sum 91, p. 39.

3387. LANE, M. Travis
"Everything Co-Relates." [AntigR] (85/86) Spr-Sum 91, p. 204.
"Strive for a Deep Stillness." [AntigR] (85/86) Spr-Sum 91, p. 203.
3388. LANE, Michael R.
"Suicide." [Writer] (104:12) D 91, p. 27.
3389. LANE, Peter
"Branch." [Bogg] (64) 91, p. 54.
3390. LANE, Pinkie Gordon
"Girl at the Window." [LouisL] (8:1) Spr 91, p. 38.
3391. LANE, Susan
"Legger, Harecastle Tunnel" (England, 1824). [Bogg] (64) 91, p. 47.
3392. LANE, W.
"Eisenhower." [MinnR] (NS 37) Fall 91, p. 19-20.
3393. LANG, Doug
"Horror Vacui" (Excerpts. To Corinna Heumann). [Aerial] (6/7) 91, p. 158-162.
LANG, Meng
See MENG, Lang
3394. LANGAN, Steve
"Poem Against Color." [Plain] (11:3) Spr 91, p. 18.
"Sonnet" (for Don Welch). [Plain] (12:1) Fall 91, p. 30.
3395. LANGE, Jennifer
"The Berlin Symphony." [PoetC] (22:2) Wint 91, p. 35-36.
"Luck." [PoetC] (22:2) Wint 91, p. 37-38.
"The Orange Oscar." [AnthNEW] (3) 91, p. 9.
3396. L'ANGELLE, Lesli
"Flirtation." [Pearl] (13) Spr-Sum 91, p. 52.
3397. LANGEVIN, Donna
"Beginning Spanish." [Writ] (23/24) 91-92, p. 47.
"Facts." [Grain] (19:3) Fall 91, p. 96.
"How It Is with Us." [Writ] (23/24) 91-92, p. 50.
"I Wouldn't Want to Live Next Door to a Funeral Home." [Writ] (23/24) 91-92, p.
49.
"Old People at Sword Practice in Grange Park." [Writ] (23/24) 91-92, p. 51.
"Pretending I Am You." [Writ] (23/24) 91-92, p. 48.
"Stones." [Grain] (19:3) Fall 91, p. 97.
"The Vacation." [Grain] (19:3) Fall 91, p. 98.
"Writing Down the Holes." [Grain] (19:3) Fall 91, p. 97.
3398. LANGHORNE, Henry
"Bridges." [EmeraldCR] (4) 91, p. 20-21.
"Harvest." [EmeraldCR] (4) 91, p. 20.
"Home Again." [EmeraldCR] (3) 91, c1990, p. 22.
"Michael's Gift." [EmeraldCR] (4) 91, p. 19.
"When the Dove Calls." [EmeraldCR] (3) 91, c1990, p. 56.
3399. LANGLAS, James
"The First Signs of Spring." [AmerS] (60:2) Spr 91, p. 234.
"The Problem with Fathering." [IndR] (14:2) Spr 91, p. 81.
"Reminders." [ContextS] (2:2) 91, p. 14.
"The Truth About Drowning." [BlackWR] (17:2) Spr-Sum 91, p. 33.
3400. LANGTON, Daniel J.
"Everything Is Clear Except Events." [Poetry] (159:1) O 91, p. 30.
3401. LANSDOWN, Andrew
"The Colour of Life." [Verse] (8:1) Spr 91, p. 103.
3402. LANSING, Gerrit
"3 Poems of the Underworld(s)." [Notus] (9) Fall 91, p. 16-17.
"Analytic Psychology" (Selections: III-V, XV). [Notus] (9) Fall 91, p. 18-21.
"The Bereft." [Notus] (9) Fall 91, p. 8.
"Conventicle." [Notus] (9) Fall 91, p. 14.
"A Far Memory of Lazy Spring." [Notus] (9) Fall 91, p. 26.
"Graffiti, Ancient and Modern." [Notus] (9) Fall 91, p. 9.
"The Heavenly Tree Grows Downward." [Notus] (9) Fall 91, p. 7.
"In Erasmus Darwin's Generous Light" (for Thorpe Feidt). [Notus] (9) Fall 91, p.
22-25.
"Stanzas of Hyparxis." [Notus] (9) Fall 91, p. 10-12.
"Tabernacles." [Notus] (9) Fall 91, p. 15.
"The Undertaking." [Notus] (9) Fall 91, p. 13.

3403. LAO, Linette
"Untitled: I can see it clearly now." [Caliban] (10) 91, p. 90.
3404. LAO, Tzu
"Tao Te Ching" (Chapter 31, tr. by Ngawang Nyima). [Archae] (2) Spr 91, p. 49.
3405. LaPALMA, Marina
"Idiot / M." [Rohwedder] (6) Sum-Fall 91, p. 20.
3406. LAPE, Sue
"Computer Passion." [PoetC] (23:1) Fall 91, p. 28.
3407. LAPPIN, T. J.
"Before Going" (a note on the death of John Berryman). [NorthStoneR] (10) Fall
91-Wint 92, p. 175.
"Pound Refracted" (portrait by Avedon, 6-30-58). [NorthStoneR] (10) Fall 91-Wint
92, p. 76.
"Solace Broken by Migratory Birds." [NorthStoneR] (10) Fall 91-Wint 92, p. 175.
3408. LARA, Jesús
"Testament: Fragments" (Quechua People's Poetry, tr. of the Spanish of Jesús Lara
by Maria A. Proser and James Scully). [NoDaQ] (59:4) Fall 91, p. 78.
"What Cloud Is That Cloud" (Quechua People's Poetry, tr. of the Spanish of Jesús
Lara by Maria A. Proser and James Scully). [NoDaQ] (59:4) Fall 91, p. 78-79.
3409. LARCADA, Jose Ignacio
"Una Sola Hoja de Naranjo." [LindLM] (10:1) Ja-Mr 91, p. 11.
3410. LARDNER, Ted
"For Mrs. Aldous Huxley." [ColR] (NS 18:1) Spr-Sum 91, p. 53-55.
3411. LARKIN, Joan
"Interval." [BrooklynR] (8) 91, p. 26.
3412. LARKIN, Maryrose
"Helix." [HeavenB] (9) Wint-Spr 91-92, p. 36.
3413. LARRAHONA KASTEN, Alfonso
"Los Dos." [Nuez] (3:7) 91, p. 14.
"Perdido." [Nuez] (3:7) 91, p. 14.
"Temo." [Nuez] (3:7) 91, p. 14.
3414. LARS, Krystyna
"It Was Me" (To Bylam Ja, tr. by Georgia Scott and David Malcolm). [Calyx] (13:3)
Wint 91-92, p. 12-13.
3415. LARSEN, Lance
"Bathhouse Overlooking Family Cemetery." [WestHR] (45:4) Wint 91, p. 352.
"The Corner House." [WestHR] (45:4) Wint 91, p. 351.
"Elegy for Donald Pugmire, Photographer." [Shen] (41:4) Wint 91, p. 112-113.
3416. LARSON, Allen
"Of Quite the Same Earth." [JamesWR] (8:2) Wint 91, p. 8.
"Self Help." [JamesWR] (8:2) Wint 91, p. 8.
"Trains." [JamesWR] (8:2) Wint 91, p. 8.
3417. LARSON, Jacqueline
"Begining Pome." [WestCL] (25:2, #5) Fall 91, p. 98.
"Siserary." [WestCL] (25:2, #5) Fall 91, p. 97.
3418. LARSON, Michael
"My Wife, Teaching Me about Birds." [TexasR] (11:1/2) Spr-Sum 90, p. 88-89.
3419. LARSON, Rustin
"Harry James." [CimR] (97) O 91, p. 61.
"Teacher" (To David Wojahn). [Poem] (65) My 91, p. 51.
"Windfalls." [Poem] (65) My 91, p. 52.
3420. LARSSON, Janis
"The Garden." [DogRR] (10:1) Sum 91, p. 10.
3421. LaRUE, Dorie
"The Water Witch." [LouisL] (8:1) Spr 91, p. 48-49.
Las CASAS, Walter de
See CASAS, Walter de las
3422. LASDUN, James
"Baroque" (Borromini, 1599-1667). [ParisR] (33:120) Fall 91, p. 44.
"First Bodies." [ParisR] (33:120) Fall 91, p. 44-45.
"The Plague Years." [Boulevard] (5:3/6:1, #15/16) Spr 91, p. 223.
"The Revenant." [NewYorker] (67:17) 17 Je 91, p. 66.
3423. LASHER, Susan
"Is It Hot in Here or Am I Crazy." [SouthwR] (76:4) Aut 91, p. 547-550.
3424. LASSELL, Michael
"Making a Mark." [JamesWR] (8:2) Wint 91, p. 7.

3425. LASSEN, Sandra Lake
"Death by Flamingo." [ChironR] (10:3) Aut 91, p. 42.
"Lunch with Ginsberg." [ChironR] (10:3) Aut 91, p. 42.
"Rag Doll." [ChironR] (10:3) Aut 91, p. 42.
"Secrets, 1953." [ChironR] (10:3) Aut 91, p. 42.
3426. LAU, Carolyn
"All the Times I Failed the Sexual Exams." [YellowS] (38) Wint-Spr 91-92, p. 26.
"The Difference Between Self-Abuse & Self-Destruction" (A Footnote to Xunzi).
[Zyzzyva] (7:2) Sum 91, p. 56-57.
"For Uncle Huang from Shanghai." [YellowS] (38) Wint-Spr 91-92, p. 26-27.
"From the Diary of Courtesan Yang." [YellowS] (38) Wint-Spr 91-92, p. 27.
"New Year Away from Tianjin, 1990." [Zyzzyva] (7:2) Sum 91, p. 58.
"Peach God of Longevity." [YellowS] (38) Wint-Spr 91-92, p. 26.
"Post-Modern Han." [YellowS] (38) Wint-Spr 91-92, p. 26.
3427. LAU, Evelyn
"Green." [MichQR] (30:4) Fall 91, p. 606-607.
"Half." [HawaiiR] (15:2, #32) Spr 91, p. 37-38.
"Nineteen." [PraF] (12:3 #56) Aut 91, p. 59.
3428. LAUBY, Adrienne
"Denial" (from "Disability Series 1"). [SinW] (45) Wint 91-92, p. 40.
"Ulcer Surgery." [SinW] (45) Wint 91-92, p. 41.
LAUÇANNO, Christopher Sawyer
See SAWYER-LAUÇANNO, Christopher
3429. LAUCHLAN, Michael
"Water Heater, 18th St." [VirQR] (67:2) Spr 91, p. 263-264.
"What You Hadn't." [VirQR] (67:2) Spr 91, p. 262-263.
3430. LAUE, John
"The High School Dance." [Pearl] (14) Fall-Wint 91, p. 59.
3431. LAUGHLIN, J. (James)
"At the Circus." [WorldL] (2) 91, p. 19.
"The Borders of the Heart." [WorldL] (2) 91, p. 20.
"The Darkened Room." [WestCL] (25:2, #5) Fall 91, p. 37.
"It Is So Easy." [Os] (33) Fall 91, p. 38.
"Layers." [Poetry] (157:6) Mr 91, p. 342.
"Lines to Be Put into Latin." [ParisR] (33:119) Sum 91, p. 141.
"The Lost Secrets." [Chelsea] (52) 91, p. 96.
"My Cousin Alexander." [WestCL] (25:2, #5) Fall 91, p. 37.
"The Other One." [WestCL] (25:2, #5) Fall 91, p. 38.
"The Private Language." [Chelsea] (52) 91, p. 97.
"The Wristwatch." [WestCL] (25:2, #5) Fall 91, p. 38.
3432. LAURENCE, Larry
"Bus Ride to the Coast: San Blas, Mexico." [SouthernPR] (31:2) Fall 91, p. 32-33.
"By the Lake." [SouthernPR] (31:2) Fall 91, p. 31-32.
3433. LAURO, Alberto
"Boceto de Figurin para 'Las Miniaturas' de Sholem Aleichen." [LindLM] (10:3)
Jl-S 91, p. 3.
"Poema de la Extranjera" (A Maya Islas). [LindLM] (10:3) Jl-S 91, p. 3.
3434. LAUTEN, Elodie
"The Four Stages of Manifestation" (Excerpt). [Shiny] (6) Spr-Sum 91, p. 89.
3435. LAUTERBACH, Ann
"Opening Day" (for Charles Bernstein). [Talisman] (7) Fall 91, p. 108-110.
"Song of the Already Sung." [Ploughs] (17:4) Wint 91-92, p. 54-59.
"Tangled Reliquary." [Conjunc] (17) 91, p. 195-198.
3436. LAUTERMILCH, Steve
"On a greeting Card from a Friend Living in China" (Beijing, 1989). [Shen] (41:3)
Fall 91, p. 69-70.
"Plato Contemplating the Death of Socrates." [Shen] (41:3) Fall 91, p. 66-69.
3437. LAUX, Dorianne
"Drive-In." [Pearl] (14) Fall-Wint 91, p. 26.
"Ghosts." [Spirit] (11) 91, p. 53-55.
"In the room where we lie." [YellowS] (38) Wint-Spr 91-92, p. 15.
"The Job" (for T.K.). [NewEngR] (13:3/4) Spr-Sum 91, p. 67.
3438. LAWDER, Doug
"Absences: Negative Space." [BellR] (14:1) Spr 91, p. 16.
3439. LAWRENCE, Burgess
"Harbinger." [Blueline] (12) 91, p. 40.

3440. LAWRENCE, Karen
"Rooster" (Short Grain Contest Winners: Prose Poem Winners: Second Prize).
[Grain] (19:4) Wint 91, p. 68.
3441. LAWRENCE, Valerie
"Requiem for a Sister." [PennR] (5:1) Spr 91, p. 15.
3442. LAWSON, David
"Human Ties." [GreenMR] (NS 4:2) Wint-Spr 91, p. 64-65.
"Lu Xun Museum, Hongkau Park, Shanghai." [GreenMR] (NS 4:2) Wint-Spr 91,
p. 63.
3443. LAWTON, L. A.
"Fairy Tales in War Time." [EmeraldCR] (4) 91, p. 36-37.
"Frederic" (Pensacola, 1979). [EmeraldCR] (4) 91, p. 36.
3444. LAX, Robert
"Ap proach ing the is land." [WorldL] (2) 91, p. 34.
"Black and White." [PassN] (12:2) Wint 91, p. 15.
"A black door." [WorldL] (2) 91, p. 35.
"I Don't Say." [NewYorkQ] (46) 91, p. 33.
"Wind less." [WorldL] (2) 91, p. 35.
3445. LAYTON, Irving
"End of Summer." [Quarry] (40:1/2) Wint-Spr 91, p. 106.
3446. LAYTON, Peter
"Businessman's Lunch." [HawaiiR] (16:1, #34) Wint 91-92, p. 103.
"Etiquette." [HawaiiR] (16:1, #34) Wint 91-92, p. 102.
"Uncle Mays Was Slow." [DogRR] (10:2) Fall-Wint 91, p. 34.
3447. LAZARD, Naomi
"Last Goodbye" (tr. of José Rizal, w. Bettina Escudero and Eduardo Bohorquez).
[Trans] (25) Spr 91, p. 209-211.
"Let Me Think" (tr. of Faiz Ahmed Faiz, w. Ahmad Hamidi). [Trans] (25) Spr 91,
p. 212-213.
"Parallel Destinies" (tr. of Nina Cassian). [Trans] (25) Spr 91, p. 204-208.
3448. LAZER, Hank
"Displayspace 10." [CentralP] (19/20) Spr-Fall 91, p. 209-213.
Le . . .
    See also names beginning with "Le" without the following space, filed below in their
        alphabetic positions, e.g., LeFEVRE.
3449. Le BERRE, Alain E.
"La Pierre du Oui / Maen Ar Ya" (Selections: 1 poem in French (tr. with the author),
10 poems in English, tr. of Guy Etienne). [Sulfur] (11:1, #28) Spr 91, p.
157-161.
3450. Le DRESSAY, Anne
"Emploi du Temps." [Arc] (27) Aut 91, p. 18.
"The Grey Breath." [Arc] (27) Aut 91, p. 14-16.
3451. Le PERA, George
"My Favorite Thing." [Nimrod] (35:1) Fall-Wint 91, p. 63.
3452. Le RIVEREND, Pablo
"Por la Paz" (para Alina Galliano, para Pepe Corrales). [Nuez] (3:7) 91, p. 15.
3453. LEA, Sydney
"Wedding Anniversary" (for MRB). [NewEngR] (13:3/4) Spr-Sum 91, p. 289-291.
3454. LEADER, Mary
"Album of Eight Landscapes and Eight Poems." [BelPoJ] (41:4) Sum 91, p. 22-29.
3455. LEAHY, Anna
"The Bridge" (for D.D.). [Farm] (8:1) Spr-Sum 91, p. 64.
3456. LEASE, Joseph
"Higher Ground." [Agni] (33) 91, p. 149-152.
"Words Like Rain." [Agni] (33) 91, p. 148.
3457. LeBLANC, Diane
"Words for My Father." [AnthNEW] (3) 91, p. 15.
3458. LEBLANC, Gérald
"Message" (à Marc Arseneau). [PottPort] (13:2) Fall-Wint 91, p. 18.
"Strange Days." [PottPort] (13:2) Fall-Wint 91, p. 19.
"Voyage dans le Temps d'un Poème" (á France Daigle). [PottPort] (13:2) Fall-Wint
91, p. 18.
3459. LEBLANC, Raymond Guy
"Danseuse." [PottPort] (13:2) Fall-Wint 91, p. 57.
"Mystère." [PottPort] (13:2) Fall-Wint 91, p. 59.
"Sagesse du Temps." [PottPort] (13:2) Fall-Wint 91, p. 59.

"Son Regard." [PottPort] (13:2) Fall-Wint 91, p. 60.
"Le Temps de l'Arbre." [PottPort] (13:2) Fall-Wint 91, p. 58.
3460. LECKIE, Ross
"The Wheelchair" (for Liz Socolow). [US1] (24/25) Spr 91, p. 3.
3461. LECLERC, Félix
"Rêves à Vendre" (Excerpt). [AntigR] (85/86) Spr-Sum 91, p. 238.
"Rêves à Vendre" (Excerpt, tr. by John Palander). [AntigR] (85/86) Spr-Sum 91, p. 239.
3462. LECOMTE, Serge
"Halloween Night." [Mildred] (4:2/5:1) 91, p. 14-15.
"Harvesting." [Mildred] (4:2/5:1) 91, p. 13.
"My Little Helper." [Mildred] (4:2/5:1) 91, p. 12-13.
"Our Walks." [Mildred] (4:2/5:1) 91, p. 16-17.
"The Sound Barrier." [Mildred] (4:2/5:1) 91, p. 10.
"Space Voyager." [Mildred] (4:2/5:1) 91, p. 11.
"They're Forecasting Snow." [Mildred] (4:2/5:1) 91, p. 15-16.
3463. LEDBETTER, J. T.
"After the Funeral." [Journal] (15:2) Fall 91, p. 17.
3464. LEE, Alice
"Dream of a Child." [Grain] (19:3) Fall 91, p. 89.
"Grandmother's Dance." [Grain] (19:3) Fall 91, p. 87.
"Trip." [Grain] (19:3) Fall 91, p. 88-89.
3465. LEE, Candace
"Nuances." [Vis] (35) 91, p. 16.
3466. LEE, David
"Lazy." [PoetryE] (32) Fall 91, p. 152-157.
3467. LEE, Dennis
"Coming Becomes You." [Quarry] (40:1/2) Wint-Spr 91, p. 107.
3468. LEE, Gregory (Gregory L.)
"Crossing the Sea" (tr. of Duoduo). [ManhatR] (6:1) Fall 91, p. 22.
"In England" (tr. of Duoduo). [ManhatR] (6:1) Fall 91, p. 20.
"Northern Earth" (tr. of Duoduo). [ManhatR] (6:1) Fall 91, p. 17-18.
"Residents" (tr. of Duoduo). [KenR] (NS 13:4) Fall 91, p. 105.
"Sea" (tr. of Duoduo). [ManhatR] (6:1) Fall 91, p. 15.
"September" (tr. of Duoduo). [ManhatR] (6:1) Fall 91, p. 19.
"Solicitude" (tr. of Duoduo). [ManhatR] (6:1) Fall 91, p. 16.
"They" (tr. of Duoduo). [ManhatR] (6:1) Fall 91, p. 23.
"Winter's Day" (tr. of Duoduo). [ManhatR] (6:1) Fall 91, p. 21.
3469. LEE, John B.
"Ernie's a Hell of a Cat." [Grain] (19:4) Wint 91, p. 129.
"In the Name of Otherwise Precious Things." [AntigR] (85/86) Spr-Sum 91, p. 150.
"To Make the World I See." [AntigR] (85/86) Spr-Sum 91, p. 149.
"To See the Cat Dead on the Road." [Grain] (19:4) Wint 91, p. 128.
3470. LEE, Lanning
"Too Smart to Slow Down" (A one-roach play in one act). [BambooR] (52) Fall 91, p. 65-71.
3471. LEE, Pete
"In Memory of My Face." [HawaiiR] (15:2, #32) Spr 91, p. 141.
"The Kid II." [Parting] (4:1) Sum 91, p. 27.
"Last Night." [Parting] (4:1) Sum 91, p. 26.
3472. LEE, Richard E.
"Everyone Knows Me as Me" (20 poems). [Pearl] (14) Fall-Wint 91, p. 31-47.
3473. LEE, Robert
"The Catch." [CutB] (36) Sum 91, p. 20-21.
3474. LEE, Stellasue
"Rules." [OnTheBus] (8/9) 91, p. 99.
"South." [OnTheBus] (8/9) 91, p. 98-99.
3475. LEE, Steve
"Encore!" [Bogg] (64) 91, p. 68.
3476. LEEDAHL, Shelley
"Forever: A Retrospective." [Dandel] (18:2) Wint 91, p. 60.
3477. LEEN, Mary
"The Things We Do for Love." [BellArk] (7:1) Ja-F 91, p. 3.
"Women Are Born Twice" (— Anne Sexton). [BellArk] (7:1) Ja-F 91, p. 1.
3478. LEER, Jane
"When It's Too Cold to Bury the Dead." [SingHM] (19) 91, p. 105.

3479. LEER, Norman
"Remembering Robert Lowell in New England." [WillowR] Spr 91, p. 15.
3480. LeFAVOUR, Nicole
"Winter froze one breast." [Bogg] (64) 91, p. 50.
3481. LEFCOWITZ, Barbara F.
"Cleanliness." [PlumR] (1) Spr-Sum 91, p. 34-35.
"Freud's Couch." [PoetL] (86:4) Wint 91-92, p. 5-6.
3482. LEGGO, Carl
"Anthony's Nose." [TickleAce] (22) Fall-Wint 91, p. 63-64.
"Blue Star." [TickleAce] (21) Spr-Sum 91, p. 49-50.
"Blueberries." [TickleAce] (21) Spr-Sum 91, p. 46-47.
"Daisy Whiffen." [PottPort] (13:2) Fall-Wint 91, p. 45.
"Fire." [PottPort] (13:2) Fall-Wint 91, p. 46-47.
"Iceberg." [TickleAce] (21) Spr-Sum 91, p. 47-48.
"July Patchwork Quilt." [TickleAce] (21) Spr-Sum 91, p. 37-45.
"Neighbours." [AntigR] (84) Wint 91, p. 108-110.
"Pencils." [Grain] (19:3) Fall 91, p. 77.
"Red Buttons." [TickleAce] (22) Fall-Wint 91, p. 61-62.
"Rosalie Pollett." [AntigR] (84) Wint 91, p. 111.
3483. LEHMAN, David
"At LaGuardia." [ParisR] (33:119) Sum 91, p. 180-181.
"Greenhouses and Gardens" (for Marjorie Welish). [MichQR] (30:4) Fall 91, p.
604-605.
"Job and His Accusers." [SouthwR] (76:3) Sum 91, p. 416-417.
"On the Run." [NewYorker] (67:15) 3 Je 91, p. 72.
"Plato: the American Years" (w. Ron Horning). [NewAW] (7) Spr 91, p. 45-48.
"Plato's Retreat" (with Ron Horning). [Boulevard] (6:2/3, #17/18) Fall 91, p.
65-70.
"The Shield of a Greeting" (for J.A.). [Verse] (8:1) Spr 91, p. 41.
"Stages on Life's Way." [NewYorker] (67:31) 23 S 91, p. 36-37.
"The Theory of the Leisure Classes." [Boulevard] (5:3/6:1, #15/16) Spr 91, p.
94-96.
"Under the Influence." [NewRep] (204:15) 15 Ap 91, p. 34.
3484. LEIBLEIN, Adelle
"Calling to the Soul of My Unborn Child" (The Pablo Neruda Prize for Poetry, First
Honorable Mention). [Nimrod] (35:1) Fall-Wint 91, p. 31-32.
3485. LEINART, Virginia
"I Watched the Fire." [CrabCR] (7:3) 91, p. 21.
3486. LEIRIS, Michel
"Inert" (tr. by Richard Sieburth). [Sulfur] (11:2 #29) Fall 91, p. 187.
"Last Writings" (tr. by Richard Sieburth). [Sulfur] (11:2 #29) Fall 91, p. 184-188.
"Trademarks" (tr. by Richard Sieburth). [Sulfur] (11:2 #29) Fall 91, p. 184-186.
"Twigs" (tr. by Richard Sieburth). [Sulfur] (11:2 #29) Fall 91, p. 187-188.
3487. LELAND, Blake
"The Big Fish." [NewYorker] (67:25) 12 Ag 91, p. 28-29.
3488. LEMM, Richard
"Fantasy." [Arc] (26) Spr 91, p. 61-62.
3489. LEMOINE, Kris
"Ariadne." [FreeL] (8) Aut 91, p. 22-23.
"Baby Talk." [FreeL] (7) Spr 91, p. 26-27.
3490. LEMOS, Carla
"At Crossroads: Hermes Psychopomp." [Conjunc] (17) 91, p. 75-77.
"Kore." [Conjunc] (17) 91, p. 73-74.
"Through Crossroads: Hermes Trickster." [Conjunc] (17) 91, p. 78-81.
3491. LENFESTEY, Jim
"Death by War Is Finally the Same." [RagMag] (9:1) 91, p. 27.
"Nuclear Weapons." [RagMag] (9:1) 91, p. 28.
"Prayer." [RagMag] (9:1) 91, p. 29-30.
3492. LENHART, Michael
"The Lost Dutchman." [FreeL] (8) Aut 91, p. 24.
"Mundane." [Bogg] (64) 91, p. 52.
3493. LENIHAN, Dan
"Abuse." [NewYorkQ] (45) 91, p. 82.
"Airplane Rides." [ChironR] (10:3) Aut 91, p. 19.
3494. LENNON, Frank
"Mrs. Charles Sanders Pierce." [ChironR] (10:3) Aut 91, p. 19.

"Those Brilliant Ideas." [ChironR] (10:4) Wint 91, p. 33.
"Wallace Stevens Poem." [FreeL] (7) Spr 91, p. 25.
"You: An Introduction." [PoetC] (23:1) Fall 91, p. 27.
3495. LENT, John
"L'Oeil de Dieu au Quai de la Bruche" (for Jude). [MalR] (94) Spr 91, p. 86-88.
3496. LEONARD, Tom
"Scenes from Scottish Literary Life" (Selections: 1-3, 8). [NewAW] (8/9) Fall 91, p. 107-109.
"Situations Theoretical and Contemporary" (Selections: 2, 11). [NewAW] (8/9) Fall 91, p. 109.
3497. LEOPOLD, Joseph
"The Power of Ceaseless Motion." [MidAR] (11:1) 91, p. 125-126.
3498. LEPOVETSKY, Lisa
"Florida Land Scam — 1925" (for Ella Fisher). [Kalliope] (13:3) 91, p. 54-55.
"Target Shoot." [CrabCR] (7:2) Sum 91, p. 27.
3499. LERCHER, Ruth
"9:28 A.M. May 23, 1991." [OnTheBus] (8/9) 91, p. 100-101.
"Green." [OnTheBus] (8/9) 91, p. 100.
3500. LERNER, Laurence
"A Happy New Year" (to my great-great-great-grandfather, Thomas Taylor: 31 December 1800). [SewanR] (99:1) Wint 91, p. 30-31.
"The Lifeboat." [SewanR] (99:1) Wint 91, p. 32.
3501. LERNER, Linda
"Old People at the Bank." [SlipS] (11) 91, p. 44.
"Risking." [NewYorkQ] (46) 91, p. 54.
"Woman in a Beer Poster, 1907." [NorthStoneR] (10) Fall 91-Wint 92, p. 126.
3502. LERNET-HOLENIA, Alexander
"Album Page" (For R.J., tr. by Robert Dassanowsky-Harris). [Os] (33) Fall 91, p. 18.
"Albumblatt" (Für R.J.). [Os] (33) Fall 91, p. 17.
"Wenn die Wildgänse Schreien." [Os] (33) Fall 91, p. 15.
"When the Wild Geese Cry" (tr. by Robert Dassanowsky-Harris). [Os] (33) Fall 91, p. 16.
3503. LesCARBEAU, Mitchell
"The Birth of Writing." [Interim] (10:2) Fall-Wint 91-92, p. 11.
"The Comedy of Memory." [PoetL] (86:4) Wint 91-92, p. 19-20.
3504. LESCOET, Henri de
"No Desaparece la Frontera." [Nuez] (3:7) 91, p. 23.
"Yo Siento un Vaivén." [Nuez] (3:7) 91, p. 23.
3505. LESLIE, A. Michele
"Anxiety." [CapeR] (26:2) Fall 91, p. 7.
3506. LESLIE, Naton
"The Best of Angel Alley." [CinPR] (22) Spr 91, p. 43.
"Intent Upon the Grim Work" (First Prize, Cincinnati Poetry Review Competition). [CinPR] (21) Spr 90, p. 12-13.
"Noble Paraphrase." [CinPR] (22) Spr 91, p. 44-45.
3507. LESSEN, Laurie
"On Coming to the End of the 'Selected Poems of Salvador Espriu'." [Plain] (11:3) Spr 91, p. 34.
"Pandora." [Plain] (11:3) Spr 91, p. 23.
3508. LESSEN, Laurie Suzanne
"Eight Years Old Listening to Classical Music and Because I Believed in God When I Was Young." [Gypsy] (17) 91, p. 48.
"Orphan." [Abraxas] (40/41) 91, p. 133.
3509. LESSER, Rika
"Blue" (tr. of Goran Sonnevi). [Vis] (37) 91, p. 48.
3510. LESTER, Valerie
"After the Cloudburst." [Hellas] (2:2) Fall 91, p. 260.
"Came an Angel." [Hellas] (2:2) Fall 91, p. 259-260.
3511. LESTER-MASSMAN, Gordon
"Lay a Sheet of Light over a Sheet of Dark." [GeoR] (45:4) Wint 91, p. 723-724.
3512. LeSUEUR, Meridel
"Rites of Ancient Ripening." [Kaleid] (22) Wint-Spr 91, p. 21.
3513. LEV, Donald
"Communion." [NewYorkQ] (46) 91, p. 34.
"Fiesta." [NewYorkQ] (45) 91, p. 57.

"The Tasting." [NewYorkQ] (44) 91, p. 52.
3514. LEVANT, Howard
"The Last Resort." [SewanR] (98:3) Sum 90, p. 504-505.
3515. LEVANT, Jonathan
"Explaining Everything to Sandi Tan Again." [WindO] (55) Wint 91-92, p. 11.
"I Am Falstaff to Your Henna Haired Hal." [WindO] (55) Wint 91-92, p. 12.
"Narcissus Saw Himself Best in Ice." [WindO] (55) Wint 91-92, p. 13.
3516. LEVCHEV, Vladimir
"Athens" (tr. by Lisa Sapinkopf). [BlackWR] (18:1) Fall-Wint 91, p. 100.
3517. LEVENSON, Christopher
"The Ex." [Quarry] (40:1/2) Wint-Spr 91, p. 109.
"State Visit." [Quarry] (40:1/2) Wint-Spr 91, p. 108.
3518. LEVERING, Donald
"The Trench." [Contact] (10:59/60/61) Spr 91, p. 41.
3519. LEVERTOV, Denise
"The Mutes." [AmerPoR] (20:6) N-D 91, p. 41-42.
"To Rilke." [AmerPoR] (20:6) N-D 91, p. 39.
"Two Threnodies and a Psalm." [MidAR] (11:1) 91, p. 244.
3520. LEVI, Toni Mergentime
"The Late Ice Age at the Museum of Natural History." [CalQ] (35/36) 91, p. 89-90.
3521. LEVIN, John
"Aboard the Admiral Bragueton" (Special Section: 35 poems). [WormR] (31:1,
#121) 91, p. 17-34.
3522. LEVIN, Lynn E.
"Boy with a Pomegranate in Philadelphia." [BlackBR] (13) Spr-Sum 91, p. 4.
"Man Versus Lepidoptera." [BlackBR] (13) Spr-Sum 91, p. 40-41.
LEVINE, Judy Katz
    See KATZ-LEVINE, Judy
3523. LEVINE, Julia B.
"Spring Comes After the Rape." [Calyx] (13:3) Wint 91-92, p. 16.
3524. LEVINE, Mark
"At the Experimental Farm." [ParisR] (33:118) Spr 91, p. 246-247.
"Battle Hymn." [BostonR] (16:6) D 91, p. 13.
"Currency Exchange." [BostonR] (16:6) D 91, p. 14.
"Debt." [BostonR] (16:6) D 91, p. 12.
"Disposal." [BostonR] (16:6) D 91, p. 14.
"Morning Song." [BostonR] (16:6) D 91, p. 12.
"Occupied Territory." [Thrpny] (46) Sum 91, p. 27.
"Poem for the Left Hand." [AntR] (49:4) Fall 91, p. 553.
"The Polish Shoemaker." [BostonR] (16:6) D 91, p. 13.
"The Screen." [BostonR] (16:6) D 91, p. 13.
"Self Portrait." [BostonR] (16:6) D 91, p. 13.
"Triage." [DenQ] (26:1) Sum 91, p. 47-48.
3525. LEVINE, Philip
"February 14th." [NewYorker] (66:53) 18 F 91, p. 28.
"First Letter from a Vanished Uncle." [GettyR] (4:1) Wint 91, p. 17.
"Gin." [Zyzzyva] (7:1) Spr 91, p. 50-52.
"Going Back." [GettyR] (4:1) Wint 91, p. 20.
"Peter's Gift." [CreamCR] (15:2) Fall 91, p. 70.
"The Seventh Summer." [GettyR] (4:1) Wint 91, p. 18-19.
3526. LEVIS, Larry
"As It Begins with A Brush Stroke on a Snare Drum." [MissouriR] (13:3) 91, p.
178-182.
"The Clearing of the Land." [MissouriR] (13:3) 91, p. 176-177.
"Labyrinth As the Erasure of Cries Heard Once Within It or: (Mr. Bones I Succeeded
— 'Later)." [MissouriR] (13:3) 91, p. (for John Berryman). [MissouriR]
(13:3) 91, p. 174-175.
"To a Wren on Calvary." [MissouriR] (13:3) 91, p. 171-173.
3527. LEVITIN, Alexis
"Again" (tr. of Eugenio de Andrade). [Vis] (36) 91, p. 24.
"The Bitter Taste of an Orange" (tr. of Eugenio de Andrade). [Chelsea] (50) 91, p.
69.
"Body" (tr. of Eugnio de Andrade). [Trans] (25) Spr 91, p. 82.
"The Body Knows" (tr. of Eugenio de Andrade). [Chelsea] (50) 91, p. 69.
"By the Fire" (tr. of Eugenio de Andrade). [GrahamHR] (15) Fall 91, p. 102.

"Don't Come Back to Me. Don't Look for Me" (tr. of António Franco Alexandre).
    [Trans] (25) Spr 91, p. 145.
"Home" (tr. of Eugénio de Andrade). [Trans] (25) Spr 91, p. 80.
"I Hear You As If Hearing Summer Come" (tr. of Eugenio de Andrade). [ColR] (NS
    17:2) Fall-Wint 90, p. 103.
"I Leave to Miguel the Things of Morning" (tr. of Eugenio de Andrade). [Chelsea]
    (50) 91, p. 69.
"Jacarandas" (tr. of Eugenio de Andrade). [NewOR] (18:4) Wint 91, p. 45.
"The lamp lit" (tr. of Eugenio de Andrade). [SouthernHR] (25:4) Fall 91, p. 370.
"Might We, One Day, Love These Store Windows" (tr. of António Franco
    Alexandre). [Trans] (25) Spr 91, p. 142.
"The Navigators" (tr. of Sophia de Mello Breyner Andresen). [Trans] (25) Spr 91,
    p. 91.
"The Patio Light" (tr. of Eugenio de Andrade). [GrahamHR] (15) Fall 91, p. 103.
"Peaches" (tr. of Eugénio de Andrade). [Trans] (25) Spr 91, p. 81.
"Penelope" (tr. of Sophia de Mello Breyner Andresen). [Trans] (25) Spr 91, p. 91.
"Portrait of an Unknown Princess" (tr. of Sophia de Mello Breyner Andresen).
    [Trans] (25) Spr 91, p. 90.
"Psalm" (tr. of Nuno Júdice). [Trans] (25) Spr 91, p. 148.
"Refuge" (tr. of Nuno Júdice). [Trans] (25) Spr 91, p. 146.
"Short Subject" (tr. of Eugenio de Andrade). [NewOR] (18:4) Wint 91, p. 64.
"South" (tr. of Eugenio de Andrade). [HawaiiR] (15:2, #32) Spr 91, p. 27.
"Still I Hope" (tr. of Eugenio de Andrade). [HawaiiR] (15:2, #32) Spr 91, p. 26.
"Still on Purity" (tr. of Eugénio de Andrade). [Trans] (25) Spr 91, p. 81.
"Summer" (tr. of Nuno Júdice). [Trans] (25) Spr 91, p. 147.
"There Are So Many Reasons" (tr. of António Franco Alexandre). [Trans] (25) Spr
    91, p. 144.
"To Follow Still Those Signs" (tr. of Eugénio de Andrade). [Trans] (25) Spr 91, p.
    80.
"We Will Recognize" (tr. of Sophia de Mello Breyner Andresen). [Trans] (25) Spr
    91, p. 91.
"With the seven colors you draw a child" (tr. of Eugenio de Andrade). [SouthernHR]
    (25:4) Fall 91, p. 369.
"You Speak of Sun" (tr. of Eugénio de Andrade). [Trans] (25) Spr 91, p. 82.
"Your Love, I Well Know, Is a Musical Word" (tr. of António Franco Alexandre).
    [Trans] (25) Spr 91, p. 143.
3528. LEVITT, Barbara
    "Sunday Snow." [SmPd] (28:1, #81) Wint 91, p. 24.
3529. LEVY, Howard
    "Island Days" (for Herbert Chasis and Barbara Parker). [PaintedB] (44) 91, p.
        12-13.
    "Sagaponack." [Colum] (15) 90, p. 212.
3530. LEVY, Robert J.
    "Beyond Recipes." [Poetry] (159:3) D 91, p. 129-130.
    "On Looking at a Photo of Myself, Age 10, After a Tonsillectomy." [Poetry] (159:1)
        O 91, p. 15-16.
    "Paradise Fish." [SouthwR] (76:2) Spr 91, p. 253-254.
    "The Parents." [Poetry] (159:3) D 91, p. 127-128.
    "Sleeping Together." [KenR] (NS 13:1) Wint 91, p. 71-72.
3531. LEVY, Ronna J.
    "Jan." [BrooklynR] (8) 91, p. 47.
3532. LEWANDOWSKI, S.
    "Looks in His Salad Bowl." [HangL] (58) 91, p. 46.
3533. LEWIS, Caroline C.
    "Clarkia." [QW] (32) Wint-Spr 91, p. 142.
3534. LEWIS, Graham
    "The Baths of St. Marjorie." [Farm] (8:2) Fall-Wint 91-92, p. 55.
3535. LEWIS, J. Patrick
    "Amish Couple at Sugar Creek." [SycamoreR] (3:1) Wint 91, p. 20.
    "Gulls Hold Up the Sky." [GrahamHR] (15) Fall 91, p. 57-58.
    "Psalm for Enoch Powell." [WestB] (29) 91, p. 16.
3536. LEWIS, Jim
    "Epiphany." [SpoonRQ] (16:1/2) Wint-Spr 91, p. 45-46.
    "Family Suite." [SpoonRQ] (16:1/2) Wint-Spr 91, p. 47-48.

3537. LEWIS, Joel
"At the Melville Room" (for C. C.'s *Solution Passage*). [NewAW] (7) Spr 91, p. 54.
"At the Poetry Stacks of the Engineering College Library." [NewAW] (7) Spr 91, p. 51-52.
"Auspicious Clouds at the Wilderness Pavilion." [AmerPoR] (20:2) Mr-Ap 91, p. 41.
"It Came from Knowhere." [AmerPoR] (20:2) Mr-Ap 91, p. 42.
"Light Reflected Off the Oceans of the Moon." [CreamCR] (14:2) Wint 91, p. 172-174.
"North of the Sunset." [NewAW] (7) Spr 91, p. 53.
"Pethro Visits the Abyss." [Archae] (1) Fall 90, p. 40.
"The Piano on Canal Street." [Talisman] (7) Fall 91, p. 95.
"Then Let Fall." [NewAW] (7) Spr 91, p. 55.
"Yes, We Have No Nirvanas." [HeavenB] (9) Wint-Spr 91-92, p. 39-40.
3538. LEWIS, John
"Newfoundland Museum." [TickleAce] (22) Fall-Wint 91, p. 84.
3539. LEWIS, Katherine
"All Moony and Sweet, the River and the Canyon and the People." [BellArk] (7:6) N-D 91, p. 2.
"Complicated." [BellArk] (7:6) N-D 91, p. 8.
"The Horse Is Pounding Her Heart Out Below the Silver Sky." [BellArk] (7:5) S-O 91, p. 5.
"If There Is a Hell, It Is the Threat of Hell." [BellArk] (7:5) S-O 91, p. 3.
"It Has to Have Rules." [BellArk] (7:5) S-O 91, p. 4.
"It Is Very Loud Here, Really." [BellArk] (7:5) S-O 91, p. 5.
"My Heart Is Improving, and I Set Out to Ride My Horse Today." [BellArk] (7:5) S-O 91, p. 4.
"Signature Rocks." [BellArk] (7:5) S-O 91, p. 3.
"Sometimes She Protects Herself From Her Great Attraction to Him." [BellArk] (7:5) S-O 91, p. 3.
"We All Have and I Have." [BellArk] (7:5) S-O 91, p. 3.
"We Don't Know What Will Happen Now." [BellArk] (7:5) S-O 91, p. 4.
"What Deal Do I Make to Keep This Soul Free?" [BellArk] (7:5) S-O 91, p. 3.
"You've Moved Again Slightly, Shifting." [BellArk] (7:5) S-O 91, p. 4.
3540. LEWIS, Lesle
"Letters from Japan." [Pig] (17) 91, p. 68-72.
"Tulip." [AnthNEW] (3) 91, p. 25.
3541. LEWIS, Lisa
"Eclipse." [Pequod] (32) 91, p. 105-107.
"True Confessions." [Agni] (34) 91, p. 182-184.
3542. LEWIS, Mark
"Father Knows Best." [BrooklynR] (8) 91, p. 20-21.
3543. LEWIS, Melvin
"Doors 20." [WillowR] Spr 91, p. 30-31.
3544. LEXIE, Sherman
"Postcards to Columbus." [NoDaQ] (59:4) Fall 91, p. 22.
"Vision (2)." [NoDaQ] (59:4) Fall 91, p. 23.
LI, Bai
See LI, Po
3545. LI, Gang
"Spring in the Old Country" (tr. by Zhang Yichun). [GreenMR] (NS 4:2) Wint-Spr 91, p. 39.
3546. LI, He
"Tai-Hang Mountain Dawn" (tr. by Jodi Varon). [Sequoia] (34:1) Spr 91, p. 60.
"Wild Song" (tr. by Jodi Varon). [Sequoia] (34:1) Spr 91, p. 61.
3547. LI, Ho
"Cold in the North" (for MRF, tr. by Matthew Flannery). [LitR] (34:2) Wint 91, p. 229.
3548. LI, Min Hua (Louie Crew)
"When Culture Revolts" (for Lu Quofei). [RiverS] (33) 91, p. 46.
3549. LI, Po
"Answering the Hu-chou Magistrate of Hindu Ancestry Who Asked Who I Was" (tr. by C. H. Kwock and Vincent McHugh). [PoetryUSA] (22) Spr 91, p. 21.

3550. LI, Qing
"Yearning for the Red Leaves of Xiang Shan" (tr. by Emily Yau). [PoetryUSA] (22) Spr 91, p. 20.
3551. LI, Shang-yin
"Willow" (tr. by Gao Yu-hua). [GreenMR] (NS 4:2) Wint-Spr 91, p. 115.
LI, T'ai-po
See LI, Po
3552. LI, Wen
"Grandma and Buddha." [GreenMR] (NS 4:2) Wint-Spr 91, p. 48-49.
"School and Cricket." [GreenMR] (NS 4:2) Wint-Spr 91, p. 45-47.
3553. LI, Xijian
"Anthem" (tr. of Yang Lian, w. James Newcomb). [PraS] (65:2) Sum 91, p. 80.
"Dusk" (tr. of Shu Ting, w. Gordon Osing). [PraS] (65:2) Sum 91, p. 58.
"Girls Drum Corps" (tr. of Liang Xiaobin, w. James Newcomb). [PraS] (65:2) Sum 91, p. 36-37.
"Rose on the Forehead" (tr. of Liang Xiaobin, w. James Newcomb). [PraS] (65:2) Sum 91, p. 38.
"Shoes at the Edge of the Fields" (tr. of Wang Xiaoni, w. James Newcomb). [PraS] (65:2) Sum 91, p. 100.
"Smoke from the White House" (tr. of Mang Ke, w. James Newcomb). [PraS] (65:2) Sum 91, p. 56.
"Spring" (tr. of Mang Ke, w. James Newcomb). [PraS] (65:2) Sum 91, p. 56.
"To the Oak Tree" (tr. of Shu Ting, w. Gordon Osing). [PraS] (65:2) Sum 91, p. 57-58.
"The Wide Road, Free as a Lyric" (tr. of Liang Xiaobin, w. James Newcomb). [PraS] (65:2) Sum 91, p. 39.
LIAN, Yang
See YANG, Lian
3554. LIANG, Xiao Bing
"I Can Recognize" (tr. by Hua Fengmao). [GreenMR] (NS 4:2) Wint-Spr 91, p. 44.
3555. LIANG, Xiaobin
"Girls Drum Corps" (tr. by Li Xijian and James Newcomb). [PraS] (65:2) Sum 91, p. 36-37.
"Rose on the Forehead" (tr. by Li Xijian and James Newcomb). [PraS] (65:2) Sum 91, p. 38.
"The Wide Road, Free as a Lyric" (tr. by Li Xijian and James Newcomb). [PraS] (65:2) Sum 91, p. 39.
3556. LIATSOS, Sandra
"Childless" (2 poems). [Mildred] (4:2/5:1) 91, p. 85.
"Easter Eggs." [CalQ] (35/36) 91, p. 137.
"Picnic." [Prima] (14/15) 91, p. 42.
"Sunday School Picture." [SoCaR] (24:1) Fall 91, p. 73.
3557. LIBBEY, Elizabeth
"At the North Cemetery." [PraS] (65:4) Wint 91, p. 44-45.
"Dressing for Cold Weather." [NoDaQ] (59:3) Sum 91, p. 33.
"Keening" (for Pamela Painter). [PraS] (65:4) Wint 91, p. 46-47.
"Today's Chevrolet." [MinnR] (NS 37) Fall 91, p. 39.
"Winter Sunrise in the Berkshires." [PraS] (65:4) Wint 91, p. 43-44.
3558. LIBBY, Anthony
"Dorothea Lange Takes a Picture, 1936." [MidAR] (11:1) 91, p. 132-133.
3559. LICHTENSTEIN, Bernie
"On Becoming Your Job Security." [PoetryUSA] (23) Sum 91, p. 26.
3560. LIEBERMAN, Laurence
"I.V. Runaway." [Hudson] (43:4) Wint 91, p. 563-570.
"Tartine, for All Her Bulk." [CharR] (17:1) Spr 91, p. 103-105.
"Wharf Angel." [GettyR] (4:1) Wint 91, p. 83-87.
3561. LIEBLER, M. L.
"When the Mentally Retarded Live in Your Neighborhood." [RiverS] (35) 91, p. 64.
3562. LIEBMANN, Judith K.
"Aubade." [CreamCR] (14:2) Wint 91, p. 171.
"One Touch Zoom." [SmPd] (28:2, #82) Spr 91, p. 22.
3563. LIECHTY, John
"Crossing." [BellArk] (7:2) Mr-Ap 91, p. 22.
"Thoughts at the Bar." [BellArk] (7:2) Mr-Ap 91, p. 12.
"To a Student." [ChamLR] (8-9) Spr-Fall 91, p. 117-118.

3564. LIETZ, Robert
"A Dream of Islands." [CharR] (17:1) Spr 91, p. 77-78.
3565. LIFSHIN, Lyn
"7:30 A.M. Waikiki a Thursday Surfside." [NegC] (11:1) 91, p. 12.
"Afterward." [MinnR] (NS 36) Spr 91, p. 10-12.
"Afterward." [PraF] (12:4) Wint 91-92, p. 8.
"All Night Reaching Out." [Farm] (8:1) Spr-Sum 91, p. 54.
"At Emerald Lake." [HawaiiR] (15:3, #33) Fall 91, p. 64.
"Blue Ice." [HawaiiR] (16:1, #34) Wint 91-92, p. 91.
"Bone Marrow Donor Meets the Teenage Boy She's Saved." [NewYorkQ] (45) 91,
    p. 48.
"The Bowls from Bavaria." [ChironR] (10:2) Sum 91, p. 19.
"Dial a Date." [MinnR] (NS 36) Spr 91, p. 10.
"Dried Roses." [BlackBR] (14) Fall-Wint 91, p. 40.
"Elizabeth Taylor and I Are Dying." [ChironR] (10:2) Sum 91, p. 19.
"Fear." [Bogg] (64) 91, p. 57.
"Fourth of July." [PaintedB] (44) 91, p. 10.
"Georgia O'Keeffe." [13thMoon] (9:1/2) 91, p. 36.
"Hart Island Potter's Field." [DogRR] (10:2) Fall-Wint 91, p. 30.
"He Pulls the Sheets." [BlackBR] (14) Fall-Wint 91, p. 41.
"Helen Marie." [PraF] (12:4) Wint 91-92, p. 7.
"His Back Rubs Near the Lady in the Glass Case." [BellR] (14:2) Fall 91, p. 36-37.
"I Can Not Forget." [NewYorkQ] (46) 91, p. 30.
"In the House of the Dying." [WindO] (54) Sum 91, p. 10.
"In the Musk of the Bathhouse." [SwampR] (7/8) Spr-Sum 91, p. 28.
"It Starts With." [HawaiiR] (16:1, #34) Wint 91-92, p. 92.
"It Was the Asparagus." [NewYorkQ] (46) 91, p. 30.
"January." [WorldL] (2) 91, p. 7.
"July 7." [PaintedB] (44) 91, p. 11.
"Losing Even the Memory of Losing the Memory." [PraF] (12:4) Wint 91-92, p. 9.
"The Mad Girl Dreams of a Verandah." [OnTheBus] (8/9) 91, p. 102.
"The Mad Girl Frowns at the One Pewter Phrase in the Letter." [DustyD] (2:1) Ja 91,
    p. 22.
"Madonna of the Changes." [Gypsy] (17) 91, p. 31.
"Madonna Who Leaves a Blue." [ChironR] (10:2) Sum 91, p. 19.
"The Man Coming Out of Darkness." [NewYorkQ] (44) 91, p. 45.
"Men Like That Are Great." [Plain] (11:2) Wint 91, p. 19.
"Missing the Mulberries, Missing the Black Caps." [SwampR] (7/8) Spr-Sum 91, p.
    29.
"Musky Nights after Rain Rose." [PraF] (12:4) Wint 91-92, p. 6.
"My Mother and the Tweezers." [SwampR] (7/8) Spr-Sum 91, p. 27.
"My Mother Wants Lamb Chops, Steaks, Lobster, Roast Beef." [Ploughs] (17:4)
    Wint 91-92, p. 85.
"My Mother Wants Lamb Chops, Steak, Roast Beef." [Ploughs] (17:4) Wint 91-92,
    p. 84.
"My Mother Won't See the Ocean, or Maine." [BellR] (14:2) Fall 91, p. 38.
"Nichols Lodge in the Rain, on the Night Before My Mother and I Take the
    Ambulance Back to my house . . ." [Farm] (8:2) Fall-Wint 91-92, p. 38-39.
"Nicola." [PraF] (12:4) Wint 91-92, p. 10.
"November, Record Warm." [HawaiiR] (15:3, #33) Fall 91, p. 65.
"Now She Knows." [HawaiiR] (15:2, #32) Spr 91, p. 82.
"Nurses in Vietnam Twenty Years Later." [ChamLR] (8-9) Spr-Fall 91, p. 129.
"Nurses Vietnam." [ChamLR] (8-9) Spr-Fall 91, p. 127.
"On the Night of the Ironweed Performance." [US1] (24/25) Spr 91, p. 37.
"The Radio Shrink to the Woman Caller Who Says She Is 47 and Her Mother
    Disowns Each of the Children If They Do Anything to Displease Her."
    [NewYorkQ] (46) 91, p. 29.
"Rage." [BlackBR] (14) Fall-Wint 91, p. 41.
"Rage." [PoetryUSA] (23) Sum 91, p. 5.
"The Rose Window." [Bogg] (64) 91, p. 57.
"Tadoussac." [DogRR] (10:2) Fall-Wint 91, p. 31.
"The Unwritten Novel Pain." [WorldL] (2) 91, p. 9.
"Vietnam Nurses, 20 Years Later." [ChamLR] (8-9) Spr-Fall 91, p. 123-124.
"Vietnam Nurses Twenty Years Later." [ChamLR] (8-9) Spr-Fall 91, p. 125-126.
"Vietnam Nurses Twenty Years Later." [ChamLR] (8-9) Spr-Fall 91, p. 128.

"Wondering About Secrets My Mother Will Be Buried With." [ChironR] (10:2) Sum 91, p. 19.
"World War 2." [WorldL] (2) 91, p. 8.
"You Could Be Eating Frozen Yogurt." [SlipS] (11) 91, p. 79.

3566. LIGHTFOOT, Judy
"Absolutes." [CrabCR] (7:3) 91, p. 5.

3567. LIHN, Enrique
"Christ Appeared in Ahumada Mall Where He Was Thoroughly Screwed Over" (tr. by Mary Crow). [AmerPoR] (20:4) Jl-Ag 91, p. 24.
"A Diary of Dying" (tr. by Alastair Reid). [NewYorker] (67:45) 30 D 91, p. 38-39.
"Future Prehistory of Chile" (tr. by Mary Crow). [AmerPoR] (20:4) Jl-Ag 91, p. 24.
"News of the Future from an Astronaut, Candidate for the Presidency of the World" (tr. by Mary Crow). [AmerPoR] (20:4) Jl-Ag 91, p. 25.
"A Reception for Exiles Will be Held in Ahumada Mall" (tr. by Mary Crow). [AmerPoR] (20:4) Jl-Ag 91, p. 24.
"Short Course on How to Shoot and Drive at the Same Time" (tr. by Mary Crow). [AmerPoR] (20:4) Jl-Ag 91, p. 26.
"Strip Tease of the Recession" (tr. by Mary Crow). [AmerPoR] (20:4) Jl-Ag 91, p. 25.
"Torture Chamber" (tr. by Mary Crow). [AmerPoR] (20:4) Jl-Ag 91, p. 26.

3568. LIKE, Joseph
"Healing." [PikeF] (10) Spr 91, p. 5.

3569. LILLY, Rebecca (Rebecca A.)
"Irises." [WilliamMR] (29) 91, p. 49.
"The Locations of Questions We Pose About Ourselves." [WilliamMR] (29) 91, p. 99.
"Watching the Train Go By." [Plain] (11:2) Wint 91, p. 31.

3570. LIM, Shirley Geok-lin
"Unmarried Nonya." [TampaR] (4) 91, p. 32.

3571. LIMA, Lazaro
"Purgation 1 (On the Lip of Summer)." [PlumR] (1) Spr-Sum 91, p. 60-61.

3572. LIN, Ho-ching
"Out on the Lake Returning Late" (tr. by Paul Hansen). [LitR] (35:1) Fall 91, p. 72.
"A Recluse on Orphan Mountain" (tr. by Paul Hansen). [LitR] (35:1) Fall 91, p. 72.

3573. LIN, Peggy
"Dear Ian, I Don't Marry Actors." [Interim] (10:2) Fall-Wint 91-92, p. 22.
"A Place of One's Own." [WillowR] Spr 91, p. 13.

3574. LIN, Pu
"Hsiang Sze Ling" (tr. by Julie Landau). [Trans] (25) Spr 91, p. 227.
"Shuang Tien Hsiao Chueh" (tr. by Julie Landau). [Trans] (25) Spr 91, p. 227.
"Tien Chiang Ch'un " (tr. by Julie Landau). [Trans] (25) Spr 91, p. 226.

3575. LIN, Tan
"Morning Paper." [CentralP] (19/20) Spr-Fall 91, p. 192-193.
"The Nightly News." [CentralP] (19/20) Spr-Fall 91, p. 194-196.

3576. LINDBLAD, Erik
"One." [AntigR] (84) Wint 91, p. 112.

3577. LINDEMAN, Jack
"Aftermath." [CalQ] (35/36) 91, p. 138.

3578. LINDER, Richard
"Poetry Class" (Honorable Mention, 5th Annual Contest). [SoCoast] (11) Wint 91, p. 32-33.

3579. LINDGREN, Allana
"Allana." [PraF] (12:4) Wint 91-92, p. 91-92.
"Beneath this ocean." [PraF] (12:4) Wint 91-92, p. 90.
"Only a Poet." [PraF] (12:4) Wint 91-92, p. 89.

3580. LINDGREN, Esten
"Defenseless." [PoetryUSA] (23) Sum 91, p. 25.
"Protector." [PoetryUSA] (23) Sum 91, p. 25.

3581. LINDGREN, John
"Bird in the Hand." [CarolQ] (44:1) Fall 91, p. 42.
"Door" (for Charles Simic). [Chelsea] (51) 91, p. 91-92.
"Life Casts a Shadow." [Chelsea] (51) 91, p. 90.
"Three Views of an Iris." [ParisR] (33:120) Fall 91, p. 210.
"The Years." [SenR] (21:1) Spr 91, p. 73.

3582. LINDHOLDT, Paul
"Barnyard Artist." [PoetL] (86:2) Sum 91, p. 27-28.

3583. LINDNER, April
"Desks." [SpoonRQ] (16:3/4) Sum-Fall 91, p. 29-30.
"A Simple Kitchen Hymn" (for Virginia Andros). [SpoonRQ] (16:3/4) Sum-Fall 91,
p. 31-32.
3584. LINDNER, Carl
"Losing the Light." [LitR] (34:2) Wint 91, p. 257.
3585. LINDO, Astrid
"Poetry Is a Heavenly Crime" (tr. of Vicente Huidobro, w. Brent Duffin). [InterPR]
(17:2) Fall 91, p. 67.
3586. LINDOW, Sandra
"Of Wood and Will." [Kaleid] (22) Wint-Spr 91, p. 27.
"William Gustav Lindow: Testament." [Kaleid] (22) Wint-Spr 91, p. 28-29.
3587. LINDSAY, Frannie
"Cider." [PaintedB] (42) 91, p. 9.
"Whole-Body Immersion." [Prima] (14/15) 91, p. 40.
3588. LINDSAY, Maurice
"Mocking Bird Again." [Interim] (10:2) Fall-Wint 91-92, p. 9.
"Revisiting Glendaruel (1930-1990)." [Interim] (10:2) Fall-Wint 91-92, p. 8.
3589. LINDSAY, Sarah
"Ellipses." [InterPR] (15:1) Spr 89, p. 109.
"The Frightful Gila Monster." [Crucible] (27) Fall 91, p. 11.
"Gloves without Mates." [Crucible] (27) Fall 91, p. 12.
"Moving Targets." [TexasR] (12:3/4) Fall-Wint 91, p. 81.
"Muskoxen Do Not Run Away." [PlumR] (1) Spr-Sum 91, p. 20.
"The Property of Density." [Spirit] (11) 91, p. 296.
3590. LINDSEY, Kay
"Accident." [HawaiiR] (15:2, #32) Spr 91, p. 23-24.
3591. LINDSEY, Michael N.
"Robert Frost in the 21st Century." [SmPd] (28:2, #82) Spr 91, p. 21.
3592. LINEBARGER, Jim
"After School, Walking Home." [WormR] (31:4, #124) 91, p. 99.
"At Last, a True Fable." [TexasR] (12:3/4) Fall-Wint 91, p. 82.
"Man with a Gun." [WormR] (31:4, #124) 91, p. 97.
"The Salesman and the College Boy." [WormR] (31:4, #124) 91, p. 98-99.
"Semi-Formal, 1948." [WormR] (31:4, #124) 91, p. 98.
3593. LINEHAN, Don
"Woodstock House." [AntigR] (85/86) Spr-Sum 91, p. 192.
3594. LINETT, Deena
"Geysers, Light Planes" (for Don Thomas, Honorable Mention, 5th Annual
Contest). [SoCoast] (11) Wint 91, p. 52.
"Much Less." [Kalliope] (13:3) 91, p. 47.
LING-YÜN, Hsieh
See XIE, Ling-Yun
LING-YUN, Xie
See XIE, Ling-Yun
3595. LINGEMAN, Richard
"How the Bush Jump-Started Christmas." [Nat] (253:23) 30 D 91, p. 833.
3596. LINKER, Richard
"Argument and Brains." [JamesWR] (8:4) Sum 91, p. 7.
"Tea and Salt." [JamesWR] (8:4) Sum 91, p. 7.
3597. LINTHICUM, Jon
"My Son, My Stranger." [Stand] (32:2) Spr 91, p. 71.
3598. LINTON, David
"Reading and Performance Behind Ski's Chili Stand." [PoetC] (22:3) Spr 91, p. 37.
3599. LIOTTA, Christine
"Toward Avenue D." [HangL] (58) 91, p. 47.
3600. LIOTTA, P. H.
"A Children's Crusade." [HighP] (6:3) Wint 91, p. 76.
"The Hagfish." [WritersF] (17) Fall 91, p. 106.
3601. LIPFORD, Dan
"Imagine" (for R. W.). [Hellas] (2:2) Fall 91, p. 248-250.
3602. LIPKIND, A.
"The Fat Man" (2 selections). [Bogg] (64) 91, p. 55.
3603. LIPPO, Mariette
"No Second Guessing" (for Sandy). [IndR] (14:3) Fall 91, p. 137.
"Saint Francis." [PoetryE] (32) Fall 91, p. 82.

3604. LIPSCOMB, J. I.
  "Faulkner County." [CoalC] (4) S 91, p. 4.
  "Tinted Glass." [CoalC] (4) S 91, p. 4.
3605. LIPSON, Marcia
  "First Palette." [PlumR] (1) Spr-Sum 91, p. 11.
3606. LISKER, Roy
  "To fight effectively pursue imperatives." [PoetryUSA] (23) Sum 91, p. 12.
3607. LISOWSKI, Krzysztof
  "All Souls'" (tr. by Georgia Scott, David Malcolm and Zbigniew Joachimiak).
      [WebR] (15) Spr 91, p. 44-45.
3608. LISS, Andrew
  "When the Dead Are Yours." [NewYorkQ] (46) 91, p. 85.
3609. LISTON, L. K.
  "Starvation in the Sudan." [Writer] (104:12) D 91, p. 24.
3610. LITTAUER, Andrew
  "Crane and Chancellorsville." [SewanR] (99:3) Sum 91, p. 438.
  "Melville and His 'Battle-Pieces'." [SewanR] (99:3) Sum 91, p. 437.
3611. LITTLE, Geraldine C.
  "All in the Hearing." [PraS] (65:3) Fall 91, p. 127-129.
  "Fillerman of the Pine Barrens." [JINJPo] (13:1) Spr 91, p. 33-34.
  "Vision: Mary Cassatt in Her Last Years." [US1] (24/25) Spr 91, p. 38-39.
  "Women: In the Mask and Beyond" (For all women, sung and unsung. 34 poems).
      [QRL] (Poetry ser. 10, vol. 30) 91, 80 p.
3612. LITWACK, Susan
  "Double Play." [CinPR] (21) Spr 90, p. 54-55.
  "Looking for Lorca." [CinPR] (21) Spr 90, p. 56-57.
3613. LIU, Newton
  "Black Desert" (suite, tr. of Tang Ya Ping, w. Tony Barnstone). [LitR] (34:2) Wint
      91, p. 214-215.
  "Window Onto a Cliff" (tr. of Bei Dao, w. Tony Barnstone). [Thrpny] (46) Sum 91,
      p. 16.
3614. LIU, Timothy
  "Cradle." [JamesWR] (8:3) Spr 91, p. 7.
  "His Body Like Christ Passed In and Out of My Life." [AntR] (49:4) Fall 91, p.
      551.
  "Last Christmas." [NewRep] (205:21) 18 N 91, p. 46.
  "Notes Against His Absence." [RiverS] (34) 91, p. 19.
  "One Night Performance." [RiverS] (34) 91, p. 17-18.
  "The Quilt." [NewEngR] (13:3/4) Spr-Sum 91, p. 151-152.
3615. LIU, Zhan Qiu
  "Chatting About Summer" (tr. by Xiaofei Tian). [PraS] (65:2) Sum 91, p. 59.
3616. LIVESAY, Dorothy
  "Book Review" (for Pat Lowther, found drowned). [Quarry] (40:1/2) Wint-Spr 91,
      p. 110.
3617. LIYONG, Taban Lo
  "The Cows of Shambat." [LitR] (34:4) Sum 91, p. 521.
  "From Where Did God Get the Clay for Making Things?" (tr. of Okot P'Bitek).
      [LitR] (34:4) Sum 91, p. 559-566.
  "See Me Lakayana — Again." [LitR] (34:4) Sum 91, p. 522.
  "Then She Said Dont Write About Me." [LitR] (34:4) Sum 91, p. 523-524.
  "Typing Lessons." [LitR] (34:4) Sum 91, p. 524.
3618. LLEWELLYN, Chris
  "The Naphtha." [Nat] (253:1) 1 Jl 91, p. 27.
LLOSA, Ricardo Pau
  See PAU-LLOSA, Ricardo
3619. LLOYD, D. H.
  "In-Laws." [ChironR] (10:4) Wint 91, p. 13.
LOCA, La
  See La LOCA
3620. LOCHER, Edward
  "Narcissus Tankas." [BlackBR] (14) Fall-Wint 91, p. 32.
3621. LOCHHEAD, Douglas
  "Elegies 1-10." [AntigR] (85/86) Spr-Sum 91, p. 44-48.
3622. LOCKE, Duane
  "The End of Something." [MidwQ] (32:4) Sum 91, p. 434-435.
  "Fences." [MidwQ] (32:4) Sum 91, p. 433.

"Love in the 'Eighties." [MidwQ] (32:4) Sum 91, p. 430.
"A Neoteric, the Nemesis." [MidwQ] (32:4) Sum 91, p. 438.
"Out in a Pasture." [MidwQ] (32:4) Sum 91, p. 432.
"A Philosopher Eating a Lobster." [MidwQ] (32:4) Sum 91, p. 431.
"Repainted for Quick Sale." [MidwQ] (32:4) Sum 91, p. 436.
"The Repaired Venus." [MidwQ] (32:4) Sum 91, p. 439.
"A Return in the 'Eighties." [MidwQ] (32:4) Sum 91, p. 437.
"Sparse Nakedness." [MidwQ] (32:2) Wint 91, p. 192.
"Venus." [MidwQ] (32:4) Sum 91, p. 429.

3623. LOCKE, Edward
"Nueva York." [SmPd] (28:1, #81) Wint 91, p. 33-35.
"A Voice from Pork Chop Hill." [BelPoJ] (41:3) Spr 91, p. 11-13.

3624. LOCKLIN, Gerald
"A Brilliant Diagnostician Would Have Said, 'Aha, My Dear Man, So You Drive a Toyota?'." [WormR] (31:1, #121) 91, p. 40.
"Dada Dentistry." [WormR] (31:1, #121) 91, p. 28.
"Do You Remember the Scene in *The Godfather* Where James Caan Says . . . ." [WormR] (31:4, #124) 91, p. 136.
"An Early Exploiter Goes for the Whole Enchilada." [Pearl] (14) Fall-Wint 91, p. 63.
"Even Bureaucrats Are Educable." [WorldL] (2) 91, p. 33.
"The Everlasting 'Right On!'." [WormR] (31:4, #124) 91, p. 136-137.
"The Family Man." [WormR] (31:4, #124) 91, p. 134-135.
"Fifty Million Americans *Can* Be Wrong." [WormR] (31:4, #124) 91, p. 138.
"I Caught Myself About Ten Hours Too Late." [WormR] (31:4, #124) 91, p. 136.
"In Answer to More Than One Inquiry." [WormR] (31:4, #124) 91, p. 135.
"In the Article on Pain." [Pearl] (13) Spr-Sum 91, p. 40.
"Life Is a Trade-Off." [WormR] (31:4, #124) 91, p. 135.
"Life Is Hard." [WormR] (31:1, #121) 91, p. 29.
"Life Is So Dramatic So Dramatic So Dramatic So Dramatic." [WormR] (31:1, #121) 91, p. 29.
"Low-Rider Country." [Pearl] (14) Fall-Wint 91, p. 63.
"Matisse: Casbah Gate." [DustyD] Je 91, p. 38.
"Maybe Her Teacher Has Read Some of My Stuff." [WorldL] (2) 91, p. 28.
"Mrs. Edouard Manet and Eugene Manet, Wife and Brother of the Artist." [DustyD] Je 91, p. 38.
"Paul Gauguin: *The Siesta*." [DustyD] Je 91, p. 38.
"Pigeonholed." [WormR] (31:4, #124) 91, p. 137-138.
"The Recovering Alcohlic." [Pearl] (13) Spr-Sum 91, p. 40.
"Sketches of Spain." [WorldL] (2) 91, p. 29-33.
"What We Talk About When We Talk About Literature." [WormR] (31:4, #124) 91, p. 137.

3625. LOCKWOOD, Margo
"Wedding: Roslindale, Mass." [Ploughs] (17:2/3) Fall 91, p. 249-250.

3626. LOCKWOOD, Virginia C.
"Movers." [US1] (24/25) Spr 91, p. 20.

3627. LODEN, Rachel
"Nocturne for Sleepers." [CalQ] (35/36) 91, p. 45.

3628. LOEB, Nancy (Nancy K.)
"The Closer I Get to Home." [SwampR] (7/8) Spr-Sum 91, p. 20.
"Late Night at the Hamburg Inn Diner." [AnthNEW] (3) 91, p. 13.

3629. LOGAN, Erika D.
"Hail." [PacificR] (10) 91-92, p. 74.

3630. LOGAN, William
"Bad Dream." [ParisR] (33:121) Wint 91, p. 202.
"The Burning Man." [SewanR] (99:1) Wint 91, p. 33-35.
"Joachim of Fiore." [SewanR] (99:1) Wint 91, p. 36.
"Nothing." [NewYorker] (67:32) 30 S 91, p. 32.
"The Rising Sun." [ParisR] (33:118) Spr 91, p. 142-143.

3631. LOGGINS, Vernon Porter
"For Robert Penn Warren." [SouthernR] (27:3) Jl 91, p. 699.

3632. LOGSDON, Lucy (Lucy M.)
"Finding Horace." [SpoonRQ] (16:1/2) Wint-Spr 91, p. 51-53.
"Harvesting." [SpoonRQ] (16:1/2) Wint-Spr 91, p. 49-50.
"Midwest Pastoral." [Nimrod] (34:2) Spr-Sum 91, p. 102.
"The Reel." [Kalliope] (13:2) 91, p. 30.

3633. LOGUE, Mary
"Sweet Oranges" (for Yasunari Kawabata). [Spirit] (11) 91, p. 139-140.
3634. LOHMANN, Jeanne
"August Orchard at Chico." [CalQ] (35/36) 91, p. 134.
"The Bridge." [Shen] (41:1) Spr 91, p. 46.
"Frequenty a Letter." [CalQ] (35/36) 91, p. 135.
"The Headlands." [Shen] (41:1) Spr 91, p. 45.
"Winter Meditation." [CalQ] (35/36) 91, p. 136.
3635. LoLORDO, Ann
"Haleakala Light" (for Marie). [SouthernPR] (31:1) Spr 91, p. 10-11.
3636. LOMBARDO, Gian
"The Last Cleaning Before Spring." [DenQ] (25:4) Spr 91, p. 40.
"Satisfaction Not Required." [DenQ] (25:4) Spr 91, p. 41.
3637. LOMINAC, Gene
"Trusting." [Writer] (104:12) D 91, p. 25-26.
3638. LONDON, Sara
"Trespassing." [Hudson] (44:3) Aut 91, p. 429-430.
3639. LONG, Joel
"Below the Water" (for the Wedding of Jeff and Rachel). [CapeR] (26:2) Fall 91, p.
20.
"The Springs." [MidAR] (11:1) 91, p. 209-210.
3640. LONG, Richard
"Prayer for My Nieces." [ContextS] (2:1) 91, p. 17.
3641. LONG, Virginia Love
"Walnut Grove Madonna." [Crucible] (27) Fall 91, p. 51.
3642. LONGENBACH, James
"Bacco Adolescente" (after Caravaggio). [WestHR] (45:4) Wint 91, p. 338-339.
"Pinnacle Hill." [WestHR] (45:4) Wint 91, p. 336-337.
3643. LONGLEY, Judy
"Count Only Sunny Hours / Garden Tour at Dusk." [LouisL] (8:2) Fall 91, p.
48-49.
"Rainy Days Deer Come Out." [LouisL] (8:2) Fall 91, p. 49-50.
"Wintering Alone." [VirQR] (67:1) Wint 91, p. 66-67.
3644. LONGLEY, Michael
"In a Mississauga Garden." [NewYorker] (66:53) 18 F 91, p. 56.
3645. LOOMIS, Jeff
"Among Hiving Missioners." [Outbr] (22) 91, p. 20-21.
"Jillian am Klavier." [Outbr] (22) 91, p. 19.
"Visitation, Diamonded." [CoalC] (3) My 91, p. 18.
3646. LOOMIS, Jon
"The Psychic." [HiramPoR] (50) Spr-Sum 91, p. 17-18.
3647. LOONEY, Clifton Steve
"Poison." [EmeraldCR] (4) 91, p. 35.
3648. LOONEY, George
"Breaking the Surface." [Spirit] (11) 91, p. 161-162.
"Carbon Cycle." [BlackWR] (17:2) Spr-Sum 91, p. 34-36.
"One Form Love Takes" (for Jordan Douglas Smith). [TexasR] (11:1/2) Spr-Sum
90, p. 60-61.
"Snow Through Our Bodies." [PikeF] (10) Spr 91, p. 15.
"Storms We Can't Name." [OxfordM] (7:2) Fall-Wint 91, p. 40.
3649. LOOTS, Barbara
"Letter from the Far Country." [ChrC] (108:17) 15-22 My 91, p. 540.
"On the Backside of the Hill." [SoCoast] (10) Fall 91, p. 49.
3650. LOPERA, José María
"Querencia." [Nuez] (3:8/9) 91, p. 39.
"Soneto para Ser Escuchado por la Oreja Truncada de Van Gogh." [Nuez] (3:8/9)
91, p. 39.
3651. LOPEZ MEJIA, Adelaida
"Stones" (tr. by Elizabeth Macklin). [NewYorker] (67:33) 7 O 91, p. 70.
LORANT, Laurie Robertson
See ROBERTSON-LORANT, Laurie
LORCA, Federico García
See GARCIA LORCA, Federico
3652. LORDE, Audre
"Blackstudies." [Callaloo] (14:1) Wint 91, p. 49-53.
"Dear Joe" (for Joe Beam). [Callaloo] (14:1) Wint 91, p. 47-48.

"Fishing the White Water." [Callaloo] (14:1) Wint 91, p. 57-58.
"Jessehelms." [Callaloo] (14:1) Wint 91, p. 60-61.
"Making Love to Concrete." [Callaloo] (14:1) Wint 91, p. 41-42.
"Meet." [SinW] (43/44) Sum 91, p. 15-16.
"Out to the Hard Road." [Callaloo] (14:1) Wint 91, p. 59.
"A Poem for Women in Rage." [Callaloo] (14:1) Wint 91, p. 62-64.
"The Politics of Addiction." [Callaloo] (14:1) Wint 91, p. 45-46.
"A Song for Many Movements." [SinW] (43/44) Sum 91, p. 40-41.
"This Urn Contains Earth from German Concentration Camps" (Plotzensee
        Memorial, West Berlin, 1984). [Callaloo] (14:1) Wint 91, p. 43-44.
"To the Poet Who Happens to Be Black and the Black Poet Who Happens to Be a
        Woman." [Callaloo] (14:1) Wint 91, p. 39-40.
"Women on Trains." [Callaloo] (14:1) Wint 91, p. 54-56.
LORDO, Ann Lo
        See LoLORDO, Ann
LORENZA
        See CALVILLO-CRAIG, Lorenza
3653. LORENZINI, James M.
        "The Lead Cow." [EmeraldCR] (3) 91, c1990, p. 104-105.
        "Morning of the Marigolds." [EmeraldCR] (3) 91, c1990, p. 62.
3654. LORENZINI, Jim
        "At Sea." [EmeraldCR] (4) 91, p. 29-32.
3655. LOTT, Rick
        "Exile." [Poetry] (158:2) My 91, p. 85.
        "Playing in Harvest Time." [Colum] (16) Spr 91, p. 146-147.
LOTTO, Jeffrey de
        See DeLOTTO, Jeffrey
3656. LOUDIN, Robert
        "Dream Invaders." [DogRR] (10:2) Fall-Wint 91, p. 34.
3657. LOUIS, Adrian (Adrian C.)
        "After Long Silence Marilyn Returns." [KenR] (NS 13:4) Fall 91, p. 66-68.
        "Burning Trash One Sober Night" (Selection: Part III, for Pat Janis). [Mildred]
                (4:2/5:1) 91, p. 84.
        "Coyote Night." [ChironR] (10:3) Aut 91, p. 4.
        "The Last Song of the Owl." [Mildred] (4:2/5:1) 91, p. 83.
        "Palm Sunday in Pine Ridge." [ChironR] (10:3) Aut 91, p. 4.
        "Sometimes a Warrior Comes Tired." [KenR] (NS 13:4) Fall 91, p. 64-65.
        "Sunset at Pine Ridge Agency." [KenR] (NS 13:4) Fall 91, p. 65-66.
        "Verdell Reports on His Trip." [ChironR] (10:3) Aut 91, p. 4.
3658. LOURIE, Richard
        "To Robinson Jeffers" (tr. of Czeslaw Milosz, w. the author). [Spirit] (11) 91, p.
                232-233.
3659. LOUTER, David
        "Cheyenne: Home, Home on the Plains." [CutB] (35) Wint-Spr 91, p. 80-81.
3660. LOVELACE, Skyler
        "Epithalamion." [LaurelR] (25:2) Sum 91, p. 81.
        "Gyroscope." [Poetry] (158:3) Je 91, p. 132.
        "Rock, Scissors, Paper." [Poetry] (158:2) My 91, p. 84.
        "Vacuuming Kansas." [CutB] (36) Sum 91, p. 90-91.
LOW, Jackson Mac
        See Mac LOW, Jackson
3661. LOWE, Frederick
        "The Sea Ball" (tr. of Claude Michel Cluny). [SoCoast] (10) Fall 91, p. 6.
3662. LOWELL, Robert
        "Skunk Hour" (for Elizabeth Bishop). [AmerPoR] (20:5) S-O 91, p. 33.
3663. LOWENSTEIN, Robert
        "Diogenes." [DogRR] (10:1) Sum 91, p. 8.
3664. LOWERY, Janet (Jan)
        "The Dead Girl." [GreensboroR] (50) Sum 91, p. 19-20.
        "Fish." [CalQ] (35/36) 91, p. 83.
        "Married." [CalQ] (35/36) 91, p. 81-82.
3665. LOWERY, Joanne
        "Buying the Violin." [DustyD] (2:1) Ja 91, p. 6.
        "Glass Man." [LaurelR] (25:1) Wint 91, p. 86-87.
        "I Imagine a Lady." [WillowS] (27) Wint 91, p. 8.
        "It's Obvious." [WillowS] (27) Wint 91, p. 9.

"Ms. Scarecrow." [OxfordM] (7:2) Fall-Wint 91, p. 68.
"Nachusa Grasslands Two." [TexasR] (12:1/2) Spr-Sum 91, p. 111.
"Ode to Bones." [DustyD] (2:1) Ja 91, p. 7.
"Once I Thought of Rain Twice." [WillowS] (27) Wint 91, p. 7.
"Wooing." [DustyD] (2:1) Ja 91, p. 8.
3666. LOWTHER, Pat
"Growing the Season" (for Dorothy Livesay). [Quarry] (40:1/2) Wint-Spr 91, p. 111-112.
3667. LOYDELL, Rupert M.
"Nobody. The Speeches Must Wait." [SoCoast] (10) Fall 91, p. 38-39.
3668. LU, Lu
"An Old Song" (tr. by Ginny MacKenzie and Wei Guo). [Agni] (34) 91, p. 219.
3669. LUCAS, Lawrence A.
"Things Ordinary." [ChrC] (108:30) 23 O 91, p. 968.
3670. LUCIA, Joseph P.
"Climatology." [DenQ] (25:3) Wint 91, p. 13.
"Move Toward Me." [Poetry] (158:3) Je 91, p. 146.
3671. LUDOWESE, Egon
"My Grandson, Michael Jerome." [RagMag] (9:1) 91, p. 23.
3672. LUDVIGSON, Susan
"The Difficult Life of Ideas." [CharR] (17:1) Spr 91, p. 44.
"Happiness: The Forbidden Subject." [Poetry] (157:4) Ja 91, p. 209-210.
"New Orleans Feather Sculptor Dies of Knife Wounds." [Poetry] (157:4) Ja 91, p. 210-211.
"October in the Aude." [SnailPR] (1:1) Spr 91, p. 26-27.
"The Poet Takes His Leave." [SnailPR] (1:1) Spr 91, p. 25.
3673. LUEDERS, Edward
"Elegy for Terry Tempest Williams on the Passing of Her Mother." [Nimrod] (34:2) Spr-Sum 91, p. 103-104.
3674. LUKASIK, Gail
"Alyssum" (for Madame X, from "Vantage Point"). [Abraxas] (40/41) 91, p. 152.
"Trillium" (for Allie Mae Burroughs, from "Vantage Point"). [Abraxas] (40/41) 91, p. 152-153.
3675. LUKIANOV, Germann
"Jazz." [MassR] (32:3) Fall 91, p. 374.
3676. LUM, Wing Tek
"The Butcher." [BambooR] (52) Fall 91, p. 83-86.
3677. LUNCH, Lydia
"Capital Punishment for Petty Crimes." [RedBass] (15) 91, p. 48-53.
3678. LUND, Elizabeth
"At the Dairy Queen, in June." [PaintedHR] (2) Spr 91, p. 32.
"Counterfeit" (for Ruth Lund). [PaintedHR] (4) Fall 92, p. 29.
3679. LUNDE, David
"Because You Knock." [PoetL] (86:3) Fall 91, p. 23.
3680. LUNDE, Diane
"Ballade." [Mildred] (4:2/5:1) 91, p. 99.
3681. LUO, Yihe
"Chimes" (tr. by Xiaofei Tian). [PraS] (65:2) Sum 91, p. 54-55.
"The Forerunner" (tr. by Xiaofei Tian). [PraS] (65:2) Sum 91, p. 55.
"The Homing Birds" (tr. by Xiaofei Tian). [PraS] (65:2) Sum 91, p. 53.
3682. LUSH, Richard
"Reading the Map." [Arc] (26) Spr 91, p. 90.
3683. LUSK, Daniel
"Election Year." [US1] (24/25) Spr 91, p. 4.
"Fish Kill." [NewRena] (8:2, #25) Fall 91, p. 158.
"Ugarov's Daughter." [IndR] (14:2) Spr 91, p. 40-41.
3684. LUX, Thomas
"Amiel's Leg." [ThRiPo] (37/38) 91, p. 25.
"Frankly, I Don't Care." [Ploughs] (17:2/3) Fall 91, p. 179-180.
"On Matter Ontological and Eschatological." [PassN] (12:1) Sum 91, p. 27.
3685. LUZZI, Joyce K.
"Another Spring." [WritersF] (17) Fall 91, p. 199.
"Autumn, 1." [InterPR] (17:2) Fall 91, p. 133.
"Lies I Told My Chidren, 1." [InterPR] (17:2) Fall 91, p. 134.
"New Lady." [Interim] (10:2) Fall-Wint 91-92, p. 35.
"Nights, 3." [PoetL] (86:4) Wint 91-92, p. 16.

LUZZI

"Tuesday Morning." [MidwQ] (32:3) Spr 91, p. 294.
3686. LYNCH, Michael
"Late May. Toronto." [Tribe] (1:2) Spr 90, p. 43-46.
"What Scenery Looks Like from a Helicopter." [NewRep] (204:16) 22 Ap 91, p. 44.
3687. LYNN, Catherine
"And Justice Has Been Served." [Gypsy] (17) 91, p. 30-31.
"For Bill Shields." [Pearl] (14) Fall-Wint 91, p. 56.
"You Do the Best You Can." [Pearl] (13) Spr-Sum 91, p. 57.
3688. LYNN, William Kelley
"Kissing the Dark." [Journal] (14:2) Wint 91, p. 85-86.
3689. LYNSKEY, Edward (Edward C.)
"The Lame Shall Enter First." [Plain] (11:2) Wint 91, p. 13.
"Mississippi Gothic." [HiramPoR] (50) Spr-Sum 91, p. 19.
"Sculling on the Schuylkill." [Pembroke] (23) 91, p. 142.
"Water Cress." [Pembroke] (23) 91, p. 141.
3690. LYON, Hillary
"New Music." [MidwQ] (32:2) Wint 91, p. 193.
3691. LYON, Rick
"The Broom." [GrahamHR] (15) Fall 91, p. 78.
"Buttercups." [Agni] (34) 91, p. 200.
"Confession." [MassR] (32:4) Wint 91-92, p. 494.
"The Point." [Agni] (34) 91, p. 199.
3692. LYONS, Richard
"Jon Olson" (from "Tenth Street Bucolics"). [SoDakR] (29:3 part 2) Aut 91, p. 9.
"The Thousands of Little Fires." [GettyR] (4:2) Spr 91, p. 276-282.
3693. LYONS, Stephen
"Aneurysm." [SwampR] (7/8) Spr-Sum 91, p. 16-17.
"Hometown." [SwampR] (7/8) Spr-Sum 91, p. 15.
"Slow Dancing by Blue Neon." [SpoonRQ] (16:3/4) Sum-Fall 91, p. 36.
"Song of Steel." [SpoonRQ] (16:3/4) Sum-Fall 91, p. 34.
"Swimming with My Daughter." [SpoonRQ] (16:3/4) Sum-Fall 91, p. 35.
3694. LYSAGHT, Séan
"Gannet." [SpiritSH] (56) Spr-Sum 91, p. 14.
"Lapwing." [SpiritSH] (56) Spr-Sum 91, p. 12.
"Manx Shearwater." [SpiritSH] (56) Spr-Sum 91, p. 13.
"Red Grouse." [SpiritSH] (56) Spr-Sum 91, p. 15.
3695. MAASSEN, Ruth
"Dulie's Dory." [WestB] (28) 91, p. 72.
"If I Could Play the Cello." [SwampR] (7/8) Spr-Sum 91, p. 13.
"July 4, 1967." [SwampR] (7/8) Spr-Sum 91, p. 14.
Mac . . .
    See also names beginning with Mc . . .
3696. Mac ARGEL, Gail D.
"Toad Water." [SmPd] (28:3, #83) Fall 91, p. 26-28.
3697. Mac CORMACK, Karen
"The Dark Doesn't Congeal Speed." [Avec] (4:1) 91, p. 115.
"Out of Doors." [Avec] (4:1) 91, p. 113-114.
"Placard." [Avec] (4:1) 91, p. 116.
3698. Mac ISAAC, Robert
"If I Hold This Pen." [SmPd] (28:1, #81) Wint 91, p. 7.
3699. Mac LOW, Jackson
"And Other Land." [Conjunc] (17) 91, p. 309.
"Merzgedicht in Memoriam Kurt Schwitters" (38th-41st). [Aerial] (6/7) 91, p.
    88-91.
"Net Murder at Sea." [Conjunc] (17) 91, p. 307-308.
"Twenties" (52-56). [Aerial] (6/7) 91, p. 92-96.
"Twenties" (67-70). [NewAW] (7) Spr 91, p. 20-23.
MacARGEL, Gail D.
    See Mac ARGEL, Gail D.
3700. MacBRYDE, Brendon
"Abuelo." [WilliamMR] (29) 91, p. 53.
"Vladimir." [LullwaterR] (3:1) Fall 91, p. 72.
MacCORMACK, Karen
    See Mac CORMACK, Karen
3701. MACDIARMID, Leigh
"Daily I examine the scar." [BellR] (14:2) Fall 91, p. 8.

"In This World, It Is the Predator Who Moves Freely, Safely, Unconcerned."
[BellR] (14:2) Fall 91, p. 9.
3702. MacDONALD, Kathryn
"Road Kill." [RiverC] (12:1) Fall 91, p. 60-61.
3703. MacDONALD, Ranald
"Man of Snow." [Stand] (32:4) Aut 91, p. 74.
"My Continued Sound." [Stand] (32:4) Aut 91, p. 74.
3704. MacDOUGALL, Joan
"Recognition." [AntigR] (84) Wint 91, p. 119-120.
3705. MacDUNCAN, Malcolm
"Poems." [Nimrod] (35:1) Fall-Wint 91, p. 80-82.
3706. MacEWEN, Gwendolyn
"This Northern Mouth." [Quarry] (40:1/2) Wint-Spr 91, p. 113.
3707. MacFADYEN, Janet
"I Am Thirteen." [SouthernPR] (31:1) Spr 91, p. 70-71.
3708. MACH, Jean
"Anaheim." [DustyD] Je 91, p. 25.
3709. MACHAN, Katharyn Howd
"After." [Gypsy] (17) 91, p. 6.
"Call." [Blueline] (12) 91, p. 86.
"Dreaming How the House of Love Begins." [SoCoast] (10) Fall 91, p. 36.
"Lake." [Blueline] (12) 91, p. 87.
"Origami." [ArtfulD] (20/21) 91, p. 57.
"Waiting." [SwampR] (7/8) Spr-Sum 91, p. 30.
MACHI, Mikuni no
See MIKUNI no MACHI
3710. MACHMILLER, Patricia
"Tangent." [NowestR] (29:2) 91, p. 113-114.
3711. MACIOCI, R. Nikolas
"Neighbors Near the Fence." [WritersF] (17) Fall 91, p. 182.
"Rita Reclaims Ash Wednesday." [TampaR] (4) 91, p. 44-45.
"Southside Summer Errand." [SoCoast] (11) Wint 91, p. 24-25.
MacISAAC, Robert
See Mac ISAAC, Robert
3712. MACK, Jennifer Eileen
"A Purple Man." [EmeraldCR] (3) 91, c1990, p. 95-96.
3713. MACK, Lucy
"Encounter." [Sidewalks] (1) Aug 91, p. 22.
3714. MacKAY-BROOK, Kimball
"The Distance." [Journal] (15:2) Fall 91, p. 34-36.
"Field Study." [SpoonRQ] (16:3/4) Sum-Fall 91, p. 90-91.
"Reading the Mail." [Journal] (15:2) Fall 91, p. 32-33.
"Wild." [GreenMR] (NS 5:1) Sum-Fall 91, p. 108-111.
3715. MacKENZIE, F. W.
"Father MacSween: In Remembrance." [AntigR] (87/88) Fall 91-Wint 92, p.
261-262.
3716. MacKENZIE, Ginny
"A Black Tunnel" (tr. of Tang Ya Ping, w. Wei Guo). [Agni] (34) 91, p. 220.
"An Old Song" (tr. of Lu Lu, w. Wei Guo). [Agni] (34) 91, p. 219.
"Saying Good-bye to a Friend Going Abroad" (tr. of Shu Ting, w. Wei Guo).
[Agni] (34) 91, p. 218.
"There, Where the Grass Breaks." [Agni] (34) 91, p. 153.
"The Two of Us" (tr. of Meng Lang, w. Wei Guo). [Agni] (34) 91, p. 217.
3717. MACKEY, Nathaniel
"Tonu Soy" (for Jay Wright). [NewAW] (7) Spr 91, p. 14-19.
3718. MACKIE, James
"August Letter." [Poem] (66) N 91, p. 54-55.
"Indian Blanket." [Poem] (66) N 91, p. 56.
"Letter to a Poet Living in Amsterdam in Agony" (for Soren). [Poem] (66) N 91, p.
52-53.
"Moving into Harmony." [Poem] (66) N 91, p. 57.
3719. MACKIERNAN, Elizabeth Joyce
"The Autobiographies of Parallel Children." [MalR] (97) Wint 91, p. 87-88.
3720. MacKINNON, Bruce
"From a Buick Electra." [IndR] (14:3) Fall 91, p. 140-141.

3721. MacKINTOSH, Paul
"Wayfarers' Song." [Verse] (8:2) Sum 91, p. 50.
"Ziggurat." [Verse] (8:2) Sum 91, p. 50.
3722. MACKLIN, Elizabeth
"A Confession of Lies." [SouthwR] (76:4) Aut 91, p. 495.
"For Chéri." [NewYorker] (67:19 [i.e. 67:13]) 20 My 91, p. 86.
"I Fail to Speak to My Earth, My Desire." [NewYorker] (66:52) 11 F 91, p. 40.
"Interpreters in One Language." [Nat] (252:2) 21 Ja 91, p. 68.
"Proofreading My Father's Retina." [NewYorker] (67:23) 29 Jl 91, p. 36.
"Stones" (tr. of Adelaida López Mejía). [NewYorker] (67:33) 7 O 91, p. 70.
"A Walk with an Abstract Expressionist." [NewYorker] (67:7) 8 Ap 91, p. 46.
"When They Work Late." [NewYorker] (67:28) 2 S 91, p. 38.
3723. MACKOWSKI, Joanie
"The Cleaning." [PoetryNW] (32:4) Wint 91-92, p. 38-41.
"The Reception." [PoetryNW] (32:4) Wint 91-92, p. 41-42.
"Through the Ravine." [PoetryNW] (32:4) Wint 91-92, p. 42-43.
3724. MacLEOD, Kathryn
"The Infatuation." [CapilR] (2:6/7) Fall 91, p. 151-154.
MacLOW, Jackson
        See Mac LOW, Jackson
3725. MacMANUS, Mariquita
"Connections." [WebR] (15) Spr 91, p. 69.
"Rules for Living." [WebR] (15) Spr 91, p. 68.
3726. MacNEIL, Jean
"North America." [AntigR] (85/86) Spr-Sum 91, p. 145-148.
3727. MacQUEEN, Don
"Hunting." [Bogg] (64) 91, p. 18.
3728. MacSWEEN, R. J.
"Angel Wings." [AntigR] (87/88) Fall 91-Wint 92, p. 125-126.
"Called from Darkness" (1984, selections: 13 poems). [AntigR] (87/88) Fall 91-Wint 92, p. 106-119.
"Crime." [AntigR] (87/88) Fall 91-Wint 92, p. 123.
"Critic." [AntigR] (87/88) Fall 91-Wint 92, p. 281-282.
"A Door Closes." [AntigR] (87/88) Fall 91-Wint 92, p. 275.
"Double Shadows" (1973, selections: 7 poems). [AntigR] (87/88) Fall 91-Wint 92, p. 84-93.
"The Forgotten World" (1971, selections: 11 poems). [AntigR] (87/88) Fall 91-Wint 92, p. 67-83.
"Jerome." [AntigR] (87/88) Fall 91-Wint 92, p. 121-122.
"The Secret City" (1977, selections: 8 poems). [AntigR] (87/88) Fall 91-Wint 92, p. 94-105.
"That Country." [AntigR] (87/88) Fall 91-Wint 92, p. 127.
"Waiting." [AntigR] (87/88) Fall 91-Wint 92, p. 124.
"The Waters of Stillness." [AntigR] (87/88) Fall 91-Wint 92, p. 120.
"Where Are They Gone." [AntigR] (87/88) Fall 91-Wint 92, p. 277.
3729. MADDEN, David
"In Memory of Thomas Wolfe." [Pembroke] (23) 91, p. 19.
3730. MADDEN, Ed
"Yolks" (for Jim Peacock). [Farm] (8:1) Spr-Sum 91, p. 80-81.
3731. MADDOX, Marjorie
"Chiromancy." [PaintedB] (42) 91, p. 28.
"Impotence." [PaintedB] (44) 91, p. 40.
3732. MADDUX, Carolyn
"Deer Mouse." [BellArk] (7:3) My-Je 91, p. 8.
"I Protest." [BellArk] (7:4) Jl-Ag 91, p. 2.
"The Long Drive Home." [BellArk] (7:6) N-D 91, p. 4.
3733. MADIGAN, Rick
"Murals." [Crazy] (40) Spr 91, p. 33-36.
"Sacraments." [Poetry] (159:3) D 91, p. 146-147.
3734. MADISON, Patricia J.
"A Warm Picnic." [EmeraldCR] (4) 91, p. 44-45.
"Women at Thirty" (modeled after Donald Justice's poem "Men at Forty").
        [EmeraldCR] (4) 91, p. 45.
3735. MADONICK, Michael
"Innocence." [RiverS] (35) 91, p. 56.

3736. MADSEN, Janet
"Deep from the Belly of Sunday." [PoetryC] (12:1) D 91, p. 16.
"An Impression of It." [PoetryC] (12:1) D 91, p. 16.
"A Potter's Field of Forms." [PoetryC] (12:1) D 91, p. 16.
3737. MADSON, Arthur
"Glacieration." [WindO] (54) Sum 91, p. 34.
"In Thick Woods." [Nimrod] (34:2) Spr-Sum 91, p. 66.
3738. MAECK, Alexandra
"Untitled: Chant of damage *abuso, verdad*?" [OnTheBus] (8/9) 91, p. 103-104.
3739. MAGARRELL, Elaine
"Eula Banks at Sixty." [HolCrit] (28:2) Ap 91, p. 17.
3740. MAGEE, Kevin
"Happy Face" (Excerpts). [Epoch] (40:3) 91, p. 260-262.
3741. MAGER, Donald
"#9. Few of my dreams do I remember" (3/19/89-7/3/89). [RiverS] (35) 91, p.
59-60.
"#33. I am the man with the bovine legs" (3/2/89, one night). [RiverS] (35) 91, p.
61-62.
3742. MAGGIO, Mike
"That Day on the Gaza." [Gypsy] (17) 91, p. 38.
3743. MAGINNES, Al
"Earworm." [Poetry] (158:5) Ag 91, p. 267.
3744. MAGNUSSON, Sigurdur A.
"?" (tr. by the author). [Vis] (37) 91, p. 38.
3745. MAGORIAN, James
"Pond in Kansas." [Plain] (12:2) Wint 91, p. 19.
3746. MAHAPATRA, Anuradha
"Bestial" (tr. by Jyotirmoy Datta and Carolyne Wright). [TriQ] (81) Spr-Sum 91, p.
223-224.
"Business Woman's Story" (tr. by Paramita Banerjee and Carolyne Wright). [TriQ]
(81) Spr-Sum 91, p. 229.
"Girl Before Her Marriage" (tr. by Paramita Banerjee and Carolyne Wright). [TriQ]
(81) Spr-Sum 91, p. 230-231.
"God" (tr. by Jyotirmoy Datta and Carolyne Wright). [TriQ] (81) Spr-Sum 91, p.
232-233.
"To You, Mother" (tr. by Jyotirmoy Datta and Carolyne Wright). [TriQ] (81)
Spr-Sum 91, p. 235-236.
"Wasteland Without Chariot Wheels" (tr. by Jyotirmoy Datta and Carolyne Wright).
[TriQ] (81) Spr-Sum 91, p. 225-226.
"The Year 1984" (tr. by Jyotirmoy Datta and Carolyne Wright). [TriQ] (81) Spr-Sum
91, p. 222.
3747. MAHAPATRA, Jayanta
"Another Love Poem." [KenR] (NS 13:2) Spr 91, p. 74-75.
"Farewell." [Poetry] (159:1) O 91, p. 17.
"In God's Night." [KenR] (NS 13:2) Spr 91, p. 74.
"Silent in the Valleys." [KenR] (NS 13:2) Spr 91, p. 75.
3748. MAHLE, Benjamin
"Mengele's Bones." [Sidewalks] (1) Aug 91, p. 55.
3749. MAHON, Jeanne
"The Fetal Position." [CapeR] (26:2) Fall 91, p. 42.
3750. MAHONEY, MaryJo
"Wrapping the Body." [Nat] (253:1) 1 Jl 91, p. 27-28.
3751. MAIA
"The Umbrellas of Costa Rica." [Pig] (17) 91, p. 73.
3752. MAIDEN, Jennifer
"Doing a Geographical" (from "Bastille Day"). [PoetryUSA] (23) Sum 91, p. 22.
3753. MAIER, Birgit Marguerita
"I Love You Best When You're Asleep." [EmeraldCR] (3) 91, c1990, p. 41.
3754. MAILMAN, Leo
"Saint Leo" (to gerry and ray and the spirit of the 49'er tavern, 1971-82). [WormR]
(31:1, #121) 91, p. 8.
3755. MAIO, Samuel
"6th Avenue, L.A." [SoDakR] (29:3 part 2) Aut 91, p. 111.
"Had I Had Had Shakespeare As a Student." [NewYorkQ] (45) 91, p. 67.
"The Order of Insignificance." [SoDakR] (29:1) Spr 91, p. 155-156.
"Peering in Her Lover's Bedroom Window." [SoDakR] (29:1) Spr 91, p. 153-154.

MAIPING, Chen
    See CHEN, Maiping
3756. MAJ, Bronislaw
    "Cell: one plank bed" (tr. by Georgia Scott, David Malcolm and Zbigniew
        Joachimiak). [WebR] (15) Spr 91, p. 45.
    "Distance" (tr. by Daniel Bourne). [WebR] (15) Spr 91, p. 46.
    "No One, Everyone" (tr. by Daniel Bourne). [WebR] (15) Spr 91, p. 47.
    "Not Again" (tr. by Daniel Bourne). [WebR] (15) Spr 91, p. 47.
    "Quiet Apartment in Which Someone Lies Dying" (tr. by Daniel Bourne). [SenR]
        (21:1) Spr 91, p. 25.
    "This Day" (tr. by Daniel Bourne). [WebR] (15) Spr 91, p. 46.
    "Why Is It That in My World" (tr. by Daniel Bourne). [SenR] (21:1) Spr 91, p. 24.
    "Without Pathos or Metaphysics" (tr. by Daniel Bourne). [WebR] (15) Spr 91, p.
        46.
    "The World Is a Still Life" (tr. by Daniel Bourne). [SenR] (21:1) Spr 91, p. 23.
3757. MAJOR, Alice
    "Transits of Venus." [AntigR] (84) Wint 91, p. 60.
3758. MAJOR, Clarence
    "France in Five Movements." [Obs] (6:2) Sum 91, p. 46-48.
    "Train Stop." [KenR] (NS 13:4) Fall 91, p. 132-133.
3759. MAKARA, Leslie
    "Going Away." [Elf] (1:1) Spr 91, p. 29.
3760. MAKAY, Ida
    "In the End" (tr. by Mária Kurdi and Len Roberts). [WebR] (15) Spr 91, p. 31.
3761. MAKELA, JoAnne
    "Backtrack." [RagMag] (9:2) 91, p. 62.
    "Marital Insomnia." [RagMag] (9:2) 91, p. 63.
3762. MAKOFSKE, Mary
    "Absolving the Myths." [Calyx] (13:2) Sum 91, p. 14-15.
    "Doing the Nasty." [Calyx] (13:2) Sum 91, p. 12-13.
    "The Wound-Dresser" (First Prize, Robert Penn Warren Poetry Prize Competition).
        [CumbPR] (11:1) Fall 91, p. 46-50.
3763. MAKSIMOVIC, Desanka
    "I Have No More Time" (tr. by Richard Burns and Jasna Misic). [NewOR] (18:2)
        Sum 91, p. 66.
3764. MAKSIMOVIC, Miroslav
    "Banovo Brdo." [InterPR] (15:1) Spr 89, p. 14.
    "Banovo Brdo" (tr. by Aleksandar Nejgebauer). [InterPR] (15:1) Spr 89, p. 15.
    "Common Apartment Lights" (tr. by Aleksandar Nejgebauer). [InterPR] (15:1) Spr
        89, p. 17.
    "The Exchange Office" (tr. by Vasa D. Mihailovich). [InterPR] (15:1) Spr 89, p. 11.
    "I Travel, But I Have Not Seen the Absent Plain" (tr. by Vasa D. Mihailovich).
        [InterPR] (15:1) Spr 89, p. 9.
    "Inventing Happiness" (tr. by Vasa D. Mihailovich). [InterPR] (15:1) Spr 89, p. 10.
    "Izmisljanje Srece." [InterPR] (15:1) Spr 89, p. 12.
    "Menjacnica." [InterPR] (15:1) Spr 89, p. 12.
    "Prolecna Kisa." [InterPR] (15:1) Spr 89, p. 8.
    "Putujem, Ali Nisam Video Odsutnu Ravnicu." [InterPR] (15:1) Spr 89, p. 8.
    "The Spring Rain" (tr. by Vasa D. Mihailovich). [InterPR] (15:1) Spr 89, p. 9.
    "Svetlost Iz Opstih Stanova." [InterPR] (15:1) Spr 89, p. 16.
3765. MAKUCK, Peter
    "Listen." [TexasR] (12:1/2) Spr-Sum 91, p. 113.
    "Out and Back." [ChatR] (11:4) Sum 91, p. 26.
    "Out and Back." [TexasR] (12:1/2) Spr-Sum 91, p. 114.
3766. MALANGA, Gerard
    "Claire's Knee." [RiverS] (33) 91, p. 74-77.
3767. MALCOLM, David
    "LVIII. A Letter to My Mother Among Things" (tr. of Tadeusz Zukowski, w.
        Georgia Scott and Zbigniew Joachimiak). [WebR] (15) Spr 91, p. 41.
    "All Souls'" (tr. of Krzysztof Lisowski, w. Georgia Scott and Zbigniew
        Joachimiak). [WebR] (15) Spr 91, p. 44-45.
    "Cell: one plank bed" (tr. of Bronislaw Maj, w. Georgia Scott and Zbigniew
        Joachimiak). [WebR] (15) Spr 91, p. 45.
    "Dice" (tr. of Zbigniew Joachimiak, w. Georgia Scott and the author). [WebR] (15)
        Spr 91, p. 42.

"It Was Me" (To Bylam Ja, tr. of Krystyna Lars, w. Georgia Scott). [Calyx] (13:3)
Wint 91-92, p. 12-13.
"Reflection of an Old Woman in a Mirror" (Odbicie Starej w Lustrze, tr. of Anna
Janko, w. Georgia Scott). [Calyx] (13:3) Wint 91-92, p. 11.
"Untitled: All you sad ones" (tr. of Anna Czekanowicz, w. Georgia Scott). [Calyx]
(13:3) Wint 91-92, p. 10.
"Whenever the conversation turned to the issue of dignity" (tr. of Andrzej Szuba, w.
Georgia Scott and Zbigniew Joachimiak). [WebR] (15) Spr 91, p. 42.
"Winter Time" (tr. of Jerzy Suchanek, w. Georgia Scott and Zbigniew Joachimiak).
[WebR] (15) Spr 91, p. 43.
3768. MALDONADO, Fátima
"Twilight" (tr. by Richard Zenith). [Trans] (25) Spr 91, p. 110.
"When Over the Water" (tr. by Richard Zenith). [Trans] (25) Spr 91, p. 109.
3769. MALINOWITZ, Michael
"Part of a New Cold Piece." [BrooklynR] (8) 91, p. 19.
3770. MALLARMÉE, Stéphane
"The Afternoon of a Faun" (tr. by Henry Weinfield). [Talisman] (6) Spr 91, p.
75-77.
3771. MALO, Abraham Serfaty, tr. of Abdellatif Laâbi, w. Victor Reinking and Jean-Jacques
"Suns under Arrest" (for Nelson Mandela). [InterPR] (17:2) Fall 91, p. 19-31.
3772. MALONE, Gina
"Encroachment." [Kalliope] (13:1) 91, p. 24.
3773. MALONE, Joe
"Marlaine." [JlNJPo] (13:1) Spr 91, p. 10.
3774. MALONEY, Dennis
"The Jump" (tr. of Juan Ramon Jimenez). [YellowS] (36) Spr 91, p. 45.
"Return" (tr. of Juan Ramon Jimenez). [YellowS] (36) Spr 91, p. 43.
"Second Dawn" (tr. of Juan Ramon Jimenez). [YellowS] (36) Spr 91, p. 43.
"Serenade of the White Women" (Chopin, tr. of Juan Ramon Jimenez). [YellowS]
(36) Spr 91, p. 45.
"Sun" (tr. of Juan Ramon Jimenez). [YellowS] (36) Spr 91, p. 42.
"Sun in the Fragrant Spikes" (tr. of Juan Ramon Jimenez). [YellowS] (36) Spr 91,
p. 42.
"To the Bread and Water of Light" (tr. of Juan Ramon Jimenez). [YellowS] (36) Spr
91, p. 46.
"Whiteness" (tr. of Juan Ramon Jimenez). [YellowS] (36) Spr 91, p. 46.
3775. MALRAUX, André
"The Imaginary Museum (1953)" (Excerpt). [PassN] (12:2) Wint 91, p. 18.
3776. MALTMAN, Kim
"Installation #42 (Stella in Red)." [Quarry] (40:1/2) Wint-Spr 91, p. 115.
"The Technology of Alchemy." [CanLit] (129) Sum 91, p. 114-115.
"The Technology of the Secret Technology of Armaments." [Quarry] (40:1/2)
Wint-Spr 91, p. 114.
3777. MALYON, Carol
"Moon & Cow." [Arc] (27) Aut 91, p. 66.
3778. MANDEL, Charlotte
"Bellagio Grace (Studio, Villa 5)." [US1] (24/25) Spr 91, p. 27.
"Cocoon: The Movie." [Nimrod] (34:2) Spr-Sum 91, p. 79.
"Loving a Sick Man." [Nimrod] (34:2) Spr-Sum 91, p. 80.
"To Pass the Time." [Nimrod] (34:2) Spr-Sum 91, p. 81.
3779. MANDEL, Tom
"Foreign Gender." (for Susan Howe). [NewAW] (8/9) Fall 91, p. 22-24.
"Furnishings." [Aerial] (6/7) 91, p. 183-184.
"The Man Who Shot the Other Man." [Aerial] (6/7) 91, p. 185-187.
"The Prospect of Release" (Selections: 1, 3-5, 7, 10). [Talisman] (7) Fall 91, p.
56-59.
"Timestead" (for 'that one,' after "Zeitgehöft" by Paul Celan). [Talisman] (6) Spr 91,
p. 96.
"To the Cognoscenti." [NewAW] (8/9) Fall 91, p. 18-21.
3780. MANDELL, Arlene L.
"Family Fragments." [JlNJPo] (13:2) Aut 91, p. 8.
"Who's Kerouac?" [MoodySI] (24/25/26) Spr 91, p. 52.
3781. MANDELSTAM, Osip
"The Age" (tr. by Clarence Brown and W. S. Merwin). [Field] (45) Fall 91, p.
29-30.

"Black Earth" (tr. by Clarence Brown and W. S. Merwin). [Field] (45) Fall 91, p. 35.
"I was washing outside in the darkness" (tr. by Clarence Brown and W. S. Merwin). [Field] (45) Fall 91, p. 24.
"I'm in a lion's trench, plunged in a fort" (tr. by James Greene). [Field] (45) Fall 91, p. 39.
"O This Air" (tr. by Robert Tracy). [NewYRB] (38:15 [i.e. 38:16]) 10 O 91, p. 8.
"Take from my palms, to soothe your heart" (tr. by Clarence Brown and W. S. Merwin). [Field] (45) Fall 91, p. 8.
"To Cassandra" (tr. by Robert Tracy). [NewYRB] (38:15 [i.e. 38:16]) 10 O 91, p. 8.
"To some, winter is arak and blue-eyed punch" (tr. by David Young). [Field] (45) Fall 91, p. 22.
"We shall meet again, in Petersburg" (tr. by Clarence Brown and W. S. Merwin). [Field] (45) Fall 91, p. 16.

3782. MANDIELA, Ahdri Zhina
"For My Sister Whose/Heart/Broke Aginst a Poem." [Arc] (26) Spr 91, p. 27.

3783. MANEY, Christy Dowden
"State Schools in the 1970's" (for Erin). [EmeraldCR] (3) 91, c1990, p. 100.

3784. MANG, Ke
"Smoke from the White House" (tr. by Li Xijian and James Newcomb). [PraS] (65:2) Sum 91, p. 56.
"Spring" (tr. by Li Xijian and James Newcomb). [PraS] (65:2) Sum 91, p. 56.

3785. MANGER, Itzhik
"I Wandered for Years" (tr. by Fannie Peczenik). [Agni] (33) 91, p. 153.

3786. MANHIRE, Bill
"Allen Curnow Meets Judge Dredd." [Verse] (8:2) Sum 91, p. 25-26.
"Blade & Swing." [Verse] (8:2) Sum 91, p. 24.

3787. MANICKAM, S.
"Crossing the Bosphorus." [InterPR] (15:1) Spr 89, p. 105-106.
"Monsters." [InterPR] (15:1) Spr 89, p. 106.

3788. MANICOM, David
"Spilled Banks." [Arc] (26) Spr 91, p. 69-70.

3789. MANIFOLD, John
"The Sirens." [GettyR] (4:4) Aut 91, p. 538.

3790. MANKIEWICZ, Angela Consolo
"State of the Art." [HawaiiR] (15:2, #32) Spr 91, p. 1.

3791. MANN, Barbara
"Jericho." [SingHM] (19) 91, p. 72.

3792. MANN, Charles Edward
"The Guide" (after Winslow Homer). [GreensboroR] (51) Wint 91-92, p. 120.

3793. MANN, Jules
"Mènage." [PoetryUSA] (23) Sum 91, p. 5.

3794. MANN, Lisa
"Breath and Vapor." [Calyx] (13:2) Sum 91, p. 48-49.
"Enunciation." [Calyx] (13:2) Sum 91, p. 50.
"Enunciation." [PoetryUSA] (23) Sum 91, p. 13.

3795. MANNING, Kim
"The Professor." [PacificR] (10) 91-92, p. 73.

3796. MANNING, Linda
"Dementia Days" (Short Grain Contest Winners: Prose Poem Winners: Honourable Mention). [Grain] (19:4) Wint 91, p. 76-77.

3797. MANNINO, Mary Ann
"All the Rage in '65." [LitR] (35:1) Fall 91, p. 90.
"The Windrift Bar and Grill." [LitR] (35:1) Fall 91, p. 90.

3798. MANOS, Kenna Creer
"Florence Nightingale in Egypt." [CanLit] (130) Aut 91, p. 106.

3799. MANRIQUE, Jaime
"Barcelona Days" (tr. by Edith Grossman). [Journal] (15:1) Spr 91, p. 55-56.
"Barranco de Loba, 1929" (tr. by Edith Grossman). [GrandS] (10:4, #40) 91, p. 49-51.
"Metamorphosis" (tr. by Eugene Richie). [Ploughs] (17:4) Wint 91-92, p. 110.

3800. MANROE, Candace Ord
"A Corporate Fable." [TexasR] (12:1/2) Spr-Sum 91, p. 115.

3801. MANSEI (priest, ca. 730)
"If pressed to compare" (tr. by Sam Hamill). [ColR] (NS 17:2) Fall-Wint 90, p. 17.

273

3802. MANSELL, Chris
    "Angles." [Descant] (22:3, #74) Fall 91, p. 10.
    "Guitar." [HolCrit] (28:4) O 91, p. 16.
    "Koori." [Descant] (22:3, #74) Fall 91, p. 11.
3803. MANUEL, Vera
    "Dancers in a Nightclub." [CapilR] (2:6/7) Fall 91, p. 173.
    "Locked Doors." [CapilR] (2:6/7) Fall 91, p. 171-172.
3804. MAOLI, Cesare
    "Night Hearing" (tr. by John Satriano). [InterPR] (17:2) Fall 91, p. 7, 9.
    "Notte di Udienza" (from "Piccola Antologia di Poeti"). [InterPR] (17:2) Fall 91, p. 6, 8.
3805. MARABLE, Manning
    "Original Sin." [SoDakR] (29:3 part 2) Aut 91, p. 41-42.
3806. MARCACCI, Robert T., Jr.
    "The Day I Found God." [Pearl] (14) Fall-Wint 91, p. 61.
    "Of Impressions." [Pearl] (14) Fall-Wint 91, p. 26.
3807. MARCHAND, Blaine
    "The boy's eyes caught." [PraF] (12:4) Wint 91-92, p. 31.
    "Passé Composé" (for Randell Stanton). [Arc] (26) Spr 91, p. 30-31.
    "Silent Partners." [PraF] (12:4) Wint 91-92, p. 33.
    "The Story of a Soul." [PraF] (12:4) Wint 91-92, p. 32.
3808. MARCHANT, David W.
    "The Love Song of Richard Smith." [WashR] (17:1) Je-Jl 91, p. 10.
3809. MARCHANT, Fred (Frederick J.)
    "C. O." (To Robert Lowell). [TampaR] (4) 91, p. 46-47.
    "Wartime" (Feature Poet). [Agni] (34) 91, p. 79-87.
3810. MARCOU, Daniel
    "A Poem for My Father." [Northeast] (5:4) Sum 91, p. 14.
3811. MARCUS, Jacqueline
    "At the End of the Day I Listen to Bach." [AntR] (49:3) Sum 91, p. 428-429.
    "Waters of the Sun." [BellR] (14:2) Fall 91, p. 21.
3812. MARCUS, Mordecai
    "A Choice of Tailors." [SnailPR] (1:2) Fall 91-Wint 92, p. 20.
    "Return from the Desert." [SoDakR] (29:3 part 2) Aut 91, p. 72.
    "Teepee." [Ascent] (16:1) Fall 91, p. 42.
3813. MARGOLIS, Gary
    "Get-Away." [ColEng] (53:2) F 91, p. 168.
    "Shovel and Rake." [SenR] (21:1) Spr 91, p. 76.
3814. MARGOSHES, Dave
    "Changed Title." [Dandel] (18:1) Spr-Sum 91, p. 34.
    "Game 6, World Series, Bottom of the 10th, 2 Outs." [PraF] (12:4) Wint 91-92, p. 86-87.
3815. MARGRAFF, Ruth
    "Carrying a Picnic." [Epoch] (40:2) 91, p. 200-201.
    "Shortcake." [Epoch] (40:2) 91, p. 197-199.
3816. MARGULIES, Stephen
    "Aerobiology." [Timbuktu] (6) Spr 91, p. 13-15.
    "Exorcism." [Timbuktu] (6) Spr 91, p. 11-12.
MARI, Kubo
    See KUBO, Mari
3817. MARIANI, Paul
    "Duet." [RiverC] (12:1) Fall 91, p. 48.
3818. MARIN, Peter
    "'Tis of thee, of thee I sing a song of six." [Nat] (253:3) 15-22 Jl 91, p. 110.
3819. MARINELLI, Joanne M.
    "Dirty Cups." [Parting] (4:1) Sum 91, p. 10.
3820. MARINO, Gigi
    "Poetry-in-the-Schools: Harmony, Pennsylvania." [GrahamHR] (15) Fall 91, p. 79.
3821. MARINOFF, Mark
    "Powertool." [HeavenB] (9) Wint-Spr 91-92, p. 22.
3822. MARIO, José
    "Dual." [LindLM] (10:1) Ja-Mr 91, p. 18.
MARIS, Ron de
    See De MARIS, Ron
3823. MARK, Janis
    "The Spaces of Sleep" (tr. of Robert Desnos). [CrabCR] (7:2) Sum 91, p. 16-17.

3824. MARKHAM, E. A.
    "A Life." [Verse] (8:2) Sum 91, p. 107.
    "Maurice V.'s Dido." [Stand] (33:1) Wint 91, p. 31-36.
3825. MARKHAM, Jacquelyn
    "Unsheltered Garden." [LullwaterR] (3:1) Fall 91, p. 7.
3826. MARKLEY, Laura
    "Solder Lover 3." [PoetryUSA] (23) Sum 91, p. 15.
    "Soldier Lover." [PoetryUSA] (22) Spr 91, p. 13.
3827. MARKO, Béla
    "Fall Cleaning" (tr. by Nicholas Kolumban). [MassR] (32:4) Wint 91-92, p.
        489-490.
3828. MARKS, Christina
    "Black Box." [NewAW] (8/9) Fall 91, p. 55-56.
3829. MARKS, Gigi
    "Breaking Through." [SoCaR] (24:1) Fall 91, p. 30.
3830. MARKS, S. J.
    "Late at Night." [AmerPoR] (20:2) Mr-Ap 91, p. 42-43.
    "Near McNeil Point" (for Bill Kulik). [AmerPoR] (20:2) Mr-Ap 91, p. 43.
    "Zen Sequence." [AmerPoR] (20:2) Mr-Ap 91, p. 44.
3831. MARLATT, Daphne
    "The Difference Three Makes: A Narrative" (for Mary S.). [WestCL] (25:1) Spr 91,
        p. 53-54.
    "Instrument for Branding" (tr. by Florinda Mintz). [OnTheBus] (8/9) 91, p. 216.
    "A Mark" (tr. by Florinda Mintz). [OnTheBus] (8/9) 91, p. 216.
    "Pointed Stake" (tr. by Florinda Mintz). [OnTheBus] (8/9) 91, p. 217.
3832. MARLATT, Dave
    "Horse Hair Mattress." [Nimrod] (35:1) Fall-Wint 91, p. 77-78.
3833. MARLIS, Stefanie
    "Let Night Fall" (for E.R.). [MassR] (32:4) Wint 91-92, p. 639.
    "Sheet of Glass." [MassR] (32:4) Wint 91-92, p. 638.
3834. MARQUARDT, Randall
    "Bancroft." [Plain] (11:2) Wint 91, p. 26.
    "Newborn." [Hellas] (2:2) Fall 91, p. 272.
3835. MARQUART, Debra
    "Everythings a Verb." [CumbPR] (11:1) Fall 91, p. 22-23.
    "Speaking the Language" (Third Prize, Robert Penn Warren Poetry Prize
        Competition). [CumbPR] (11:1) Fall 91, p. 20-21.
    "The Weaver." [CumbPR] (11:1) Fall 91, p. 24.
3836. MARRS, John
    "Beneath What Lies." [DustyD] Je 91, p. 22.
3837. MARSDEN, Michael T.
    "Reflections at Rancho Encantado." [WeberS] (8:2) Fall 91, p. 40.
3838. MARSH, Margaret
    "Cosmic Rodeo Cowboy." [Plain] (11:3) Spr 91, p. 30.
    "Iran Airflight 655." [Plain] (11:2) Wint 91, p. 32.
3839. MARSH, Sherrie
    "Gregory." [PoetryUSA] (22) Spr 91, p. 16.
    "Ralph." [PoetryUSA] (23) Sum 91, p. 20.
3840. MARSH, Tracy
    "Let/ter Rip!" [HawaiiR] (15:2, #32) Spr 91, p. 80-81.
    "Tremors." [HawaiiR] (15:2, #32) Spr 91, p. 142.
3841. MARSHALL, Jack
    "What Took Place There." [Talisman] (7) Fall 91, p. 98-101.
3842. MARSHALL, John
    "Harewood" (for Ken Cathers). [CanLit] (129) Sum 91, p. 54-56.
    "Sargo, Talking." [CanLit] (128) Spr 91, p. 51-52.
    "Southend." [CanLit] (128) Spr 91, p. 53.
    "The Weight." [Grain] (19:4) Wint 91, p. 60-61.
3843. MARSHALL, Tom
    "Ghost Safari" (Selection: i. For Bronwen). [Quarry] (40:1/2) Wint-Spr 91, p. 116.
    "Norway" (Selections: i-iv). [Quarry] (40:1/2) Wint-Spr 91, p. 117-118.
    "Reflections (i)." [Quarry] (40:1/2) Wint-Spr 91, p. 116.
    "Sommernatt: Oslo" (after a painting by Harald Sohlberg, for Michaele and Bjørn).
        [CanLit] (129) Sum 91, p. 56.
3844. MARSHBURN, Sandra
    "Canis Major." [WestB] (28) 91, p. 67.

"Clock." [MidwQ] (33:1) Aut 91, p. 69.
"In Retreat." [MidwQ] (33:1) Aut 91, p. 70.
"Nights When I Was Nine." [WestB] (28) 91, p. 66.
3845. MARTEAU, Robert
"Les arbres nous purifient des rêves, éloignent." [Os] (32) Spr 91, p. 21.
"At the Pond's Edge" (tr. by Andrea Moorhead). [Paint] (18:36) Aut 91, p. 58.
"Le forsythia fleurit. A cru, le noroît." [Os] (32) Spr 91, p. 11.
"Le geai ébouriffe au bord de la forêt l'encre." [Os] (32) Spr 91, p. 10.
"Il avance invisible, avec la terre il joue." [Os] (32) Spr 91, p. 19.
"Lisse comme un coquillage, un bateau descend." [Os] (32) Spr 91, p. 18.
"Paris Sparkles" (tr. by Andrea Moorhead). [Paint] (18:36) Aut 91, p. 59.
MARTHA CHRISTINA
See CHRISTINA, Martha
MARTHA ELIZABETH
See ELIZABETH, Martha
3846. MARTIAL
"I, iv. Suppose the stern gaze that rules the world" (tr. by William Matthews).
[IndR] (14:2) Spr 91, p. 27.
"V, xviii. Because in December when the gifts fly" (tr. by William Matthews).
[IndR] (14:2) Spr 91, p. 29.
"V, xxxvi. Someone I flattered in a book pretends" (tr. by William Matthews).
[GrahamHR] (15) Fall 91, p. 89.
"V, xlv. You announce that you are beautiful" (tr. by William Matthews).
[GrahamHR] (15) Fall 91, p. 91.
"V, ixxvi [i.e. lxxvi?]. A little poison every day and soon" (tr. by William
Matthews). [GrahamHR] (15) Fall 91, p. 92.
"V, lxxxiii. You're hot to trot? Well then I'm not" (tr. by William Matthews).
[GrahamHR] (15) Fall 91, p. 92.
"VI, v. I've bought a country place, not cheap" (tr. by William Matthews).
[GrahamHR] (15) Fall 91, p. 90.
"VI, xx. A hundred thousand, Phoebus" (tr. by William Matthews). [GrahamHR]
(15) Fall 91, p. 90.
"VI, xxxvi. Papylus had a dong so long" (tr. by William Matthews). [GrahamHR]
(15) Fall 91, p. 91.
"VII, xxv. Well, yes, your epigrams are elegant" (tr. by William Matthews).
[GrahamHR] (15) Fall 91, p. 89.
"IX, lvii. Nothing is worn smoother than Hedylus's cloak?" (tr. by William
Matthews). [IndR] (14:2) Spr 91, p. 28.
"X, xliii. Phileros, that makes seven" (tr. by Bill Matthews). [Crazy] (41) Wint 91,
p. 14.
"X, lxx. The long year I squeezed out a tiny book" (tr. by Bill Matthews). [Crazy]
(41) Wint 91, p. 13.
"Epigrams" (Selections: I, x, xxxviii, xvi, xxiii, cx, tr. by William Matthews).
[OhioR] (46) 91, p. 33-37.
"Epigrams" (Selections: V. x, VII. xlvi, XII. xl, tr. by William Matthews). [Poetry]
(159:1) O 91, p. 28-29.
"Here Is Vesuvius" (IV, xliv, tr. by William Matthews). [SenR] (21:1) Spr 91, p.
45.
"Is This Lawyering, Cinna" (VIII, vii, tr. by William Matthews). [SenR] (21:1) Spr
91, p. 46.
"She's Half a Mind to Sleep with Me" (III, xc, tr. by William Matthews). [SenR]
(21:1) Spr 91, p. 48.
"Tell Me the Truth, Mark" (VIII, lxxvi, tr. by William Matthews). [SenR] (21:1) Spr
91, p. 47.
MARTIN, Diane Kirsten
See KIRSTEN-MARTIN, Diane
3847. MARTIN, Herbert Woodward
"Appropriate Words for Mourning" (for: Pablo Neruda). [Stand] (33:1) Wint 91, p.
63.
"The Washerwoman's Fire." [GrandS] (10:2, #38) 91, p. 73.
3848. MARTIN, Iris
"Women in Cave Paintings." [WillowR] Spr 91, p. 11.
3849. MARTIN, Leslie
"Watching Robins, Still." [BellR] (14:2) Fall 91, p. 13.
3850. MARTIN, Lynn
"Tenth Elegy." [BrooklynR] (8) 91, p. 30.

"Where Everything Is Red." [PoetryNW] (32:3) Aut 91, p. 34.
3851. MARTIN, Mary E.
"Supper." [LaurelR] (25:1) Wint 91, p. 53.
3852. MARTIN, Paul
"Into Flesh" (For Kevin). [SouthernPR] (31:2) Fall 91, p. 30-31.
3853. MARTIN, Richard
"The Philosopher." [Timbuktu] (6) Spr 91, p. 57.
"Something to Do with Quiet." [ChironR] (10:2) Sum 91, p. 39.
"Something to Do with Quiet." [ChironR] (10:3) Aut 91, p. 48.
3854. MARTIN, Sharon
"Necessity, Certainty, Questions to Ask." [QW] (32) Wint-Spr 91, p. 137-140.
3855. MARTINEZ, Demetria
"Discovering America." [RiverS] (34) 91, p. 46-47.
"Hunger." [ChrC] (108:11) 3 Ap 91, p. 372.
"Only So Long" (Old Town Plaza, Albq.). [RiverS] (34) 91, p. 45.
"War." [ChrC] (108:8) 6 Mr 91, p. 264.
3856. MARTINEZ, Dionisio (Dionisio D.)
"Ash Wednesday." [SenR] (21:1) Spr 91, p. 36.
"Charlie Parker: Almost Like Being in Love." [MidAR] (12:1) 91, p. 12.
"Charlie Parker with Strings." [MidAR] (12:1) 91, p. 13-14.
"Crimes Attempted in Daylight." [MidwQ] (33:1) Aut 91, p. 71-73.
"Each Mirror Has Its History" (tr. by the author). [TampaR] (4) 91, p. 64-65.
"Fugitives." [Turnstile] (3:1) 91, p. 91-92.
"Hopalong Cassidy" (for my mother). [MidAR] (12:1) 91, p. 10-11.
"Me Aproximo a la Realidad Subterranea." [LindLM] (10:1) Ja-Mr 91, p. 28.
"Natural Selection." [CalQ] (35/36) 91, p. 80.
"Pavane for Daddy Longlegs." [SycamoreR] (3:2) Sum 91, p. 24-26.
"Standard Time: Novena for My Father." [MidAR] (12:1) 91, p. 15-16.
"The Wind Chill Factor." [PassN] (12:1) Sum 91, p. 3.
3857. MARTINEZ, Victoriano
"Don't Forget." [PacificR] (9) 91, p. 89.
"Mistakes." [HighP] (6:2) Fall 91, p. 98-99.
"The Tumors of Night." [PacificR] (9) 91, p. 87.
"What We Find." [PacificR] (9) 91, p. 86.
3858. MARTINSON, Sue Ann
"Intermezzo." [NorthStoneR] (10) Fall 91-Wint 92, p. 165.
"London and Rain." [NorthStoneR] (10) Fall 91-Wint 92, p. 166.
"Moon." [NorthStoneR] (10) Fall 91-Wint 92, p. 166.
3859. MARTINUIK, Lorraine
"Work in Progress" (Selection: 8). [CapilR] (2:6/7) Fall 91, p. 33-35.
3860. MARTORY, Pierre
"Black Diamond" (tr. by John Ashbery). [NewYorker] (67:16) 10 Je 91, p. 46.
3861. MARVIN, John
"Swimming Off the Lighthouse Rocks." [Elf] (1:4) Wint 91, p. 28-30.
3862. MASARIK, Al
"Elevator." [Pearl] (13) Spr-Sum 91, p. 16.
"How It Will Be When the Music Begins." [Pearl] (13) Spr-Sum 91, p. 16.
"Migration." [SpoonRQ] (16:1/2) Wint-Spr 91, p. 107.
"October Light." [HighP] (6:2) Fall 91, p. 20.
"Prairie Spring." [Pearl] (13) Spr-Sum 91, p. 16.
"Rosebud Drugs." [HighP] (6:2) Fall 91, p. 18.
"South Dakota Coffee Break." [HighP] (6:2) Fall 91, p. 19.
3863. MASINI, Donna
"Nights My Father." [SouthernPR] (31:1) Spr 91, p. 67-69.
3864. MASLOWSKI, Jackie
"Tomato Angel-Bound." [PoetL] (86:3) Fall 91, p. 25-26.
3865. MASON, Cliff (Clif)
"On a Piece of Obsidian." [Hellas] (2:2) Fall 91, p. 245.
"White Tiger, White Death." [Plain] (12:2) Wint 91, p. 22-23.
3866. MASON, David
"History Lesson." [CumbPR] (11:1) Fall 91, p. 26-27.
"In the Islands." [Poetry] (158:3) Je 91, p. 139.
"A Map of Scotland." [SouthwR] (76:1) Wint 91, p. 158.
"Spooning." [Hudson] (43:4) Wint 91, p. 601-606.
3867. MASON, Jerry
"Meeting." [SoCoast] (11) Wint 91, p. 30.

3868. MASON, Kathryn E.
"Evening God." [EmeraldCR] (3) 91, c1990, p. 67-68.
"Picture This." [EmeraldCR] (4) 91, p. 74-75.
"Re-Vision." [EmeraldCR] (4) 91, p. 75.
3869. MASON, Lavonne
"Back Seat Driver." [PacificR] (9) 91, p. 45.
"I'll Make a Good Wife." [PacificR] (9) 91, p. 46.
3870. MASON, Lucinda
"Jade." [NewYorkQ] (44) 91, p. 60.
"Tell Me." [ChangingM] (23) Fall-Wint 91, p. 18.
3871. MASON, Matt
"Passion on Ice." [Plain] (11:3) Spr 91, p. 14.
3872. MASON, Steve
"After the Reading of the Names" (Shared at the Peace Memorial, Old Town, San
Diego, Memorial Day, 1984). [ChironR] (10:1) Spr 91, p. 4.
"This Time, A Warrior for Peace" (From "Warrior for Peace," 1988). [ChironR]
(10:1) Spr 91, p. 5.
"Uncle Ho." [ChironR] (10:1) Spr 91, p. 4.
MASSMAN, Gordon Lester
See LESTER-MASSMAN, Gordon
3873. MASTERS, Janelle
"Journey to Orchard House." [SmPd] (28:1, #81) Wint 91, p. 23.
"Sunflowers." [NorthStoneR] (10) Fall 91-Wint 92, p. 130.
3874. MASTERS, Marcia Lee
"Four a.m." [NewL] (58:1) Fall 91, p. 114-115.
3875. MASTERSON, Dan
"Loon." [Blueline] (12) 91, p. 65.
"Rudy." [GettyR] (4:1) Wint 91, p. 166-167.
"She Wanted to Know." [SoCaR] (23:2) Spr 91, p. 51.
"Sudden Encounter." [Archae] (1) Fall 90, p. 46-47.
MATFIELD, Mary
See MATTFIELD, Mary
3876. MATHENEY, Barbara K.
"Old Woman Chewing on the Night." [Vis] (35) 91, p. 38.
MATHEWS, William
See MATTHEWS, William
MATHISEN, Aina Gerner
See GERNER-MATHISEN, Aina
3877. MATLOCK, Wendy
"Sat." [PikeF] (10) Spr 91, p. 18.
3878. MATOVICH, Judy J.
"The Last Empty Seat on the Bus." [CutB] (35) Wint-Spr 91, p. 90-91.
3879. MATSAKIS, Cynthia
"There Have Always Been Women." [SouthernPR] (31:1) Spr 91, p. 55-56.
3880. MATSON, Clive
"Attack Virus." [Nimrod] (35:1) Fall-Wint 91, p. 93-94.
"Barrage Photons." [HawaiiR] (15:2, #32) Spr 91, p. 126-128.
"Molecule Daisies." [HangL] (59) 91, p. 37-38.
"Motion Grasshoppers." [HangL] (59) 91, p. 39-40.
3881. MATSUEDA, Pat
"Animation of Fire" (After a detail from an illuminated manuscript in the Austrian
National Library). [Manoa] (3:1) Spr 91, p. 124.
"Fiction." [Manoa] (3:1) Spr 91, p. 123.
"Two Japanese Prints." [Spirit] (11) 91, p. 142.
3882. MATTAWA, Khaled
"For Al-Tayib Salih." [Poetry] (158:3) Je 91, p. 142-143.
"Sa'doon" (Colonial Libya, 1924). [LaurelR] (25:1) Wint 91, p. 116.
3883. MATTFIELD, Mary
"Autumn" (tr. of Marìa Banus). [Paint] (18:36) Aut 91, p. 52.
"Fayum Portrait" (tr. of Maria Banus). [Vis] (36) 91, p. 32.
"The Shivering" (tr. of Marìa Banus). [Paint] (18:36) Aut 91, p. 53.
"Spyglass" (tr. of Maria Banus). [Vis] (35) 91, p. 9.
3884. MATTHEWS, Marc
"Come Come." [GrahamHR] (14) Spr 91, p. 42-43.

3885. MATTHEWS, William (Bill)
>"I, iv. Suppose the stern gaze that rules the world" (tr. of Martial). [IndR] (14:2) Spr 91, p. 27.
>"V, xviii. Because in December when the gifts fly" (tr. of Martial). [IndR] (14:2) Spr 91, p. 29.
>"V, xxxvi. Someone I flattered in a book pretends" (tr. of Martial). [GrahamHR] (15) Fall 91, p. 89.
>"V, xlv. You announce that you are beautiful" (tr. of Martial). [GrahamHR] (15) Fall 91, p. 91.
>"V, ixxvi [i.e. lxxvi?]. A little poison every day and soon" (tr. of Martial). [GrahamHR] (15) Fall 91, p. 92.
>"V, lxxxiii. You're hot to trot? Well then I'm not" (tr. of Martial). [GrahamHR] (15) Fall 91, p. 92.
>"VI, v. I've bought a country place, not cheap" (tr. of Martial). [GrahamHR] (15) Fall 91, p. 90.
>"VI, xx. A hundred thousand, Phoebus" (tr. of Martial). [GrahamHR] (15) Fall 91, p. 90.
>"VI, xxxvi. Papylus had a dong so long" (tr. of Martial). [GrahamHR] (15) Fall 91, p. 91.
>"VII, xxv. Well, yes, your epigrams are elegant" (tr. of Martial). [GrahamHR] (15) Fall 91, p. 89.
>"IX, lvii. Nothing is worn smoother than Hedylus's cloak?" (tr. of Martial). [IndR] (14:2) Spr 91, p. 28.
>"X, xliii. Phileros, that makes seven" (tr. of Martial). [Crazy] (41) Wint 91, p. 14.
>"X, lxx. The long year I squeezed out a tiny book" (tr. of Martial). [Crazy] (41) Wint 91, p. 13.
>"Babe Ruth at the End." [Colum] (17) Fall 91, p. 35-36.
>"The Buddy Bolden Cylinder." [Poetry] (159:1) O 91, p. 26.
>"Cellini's Chicken." [Antaeus] (67) Fall 91, p. 119.
>"The Dogs of Montone." [VirQR] (67:4) Aut 91, p. 685.
>"Driven." [Colum] (17) Fall 91, p. 37-38.
>"Epigrams" (Selections: I, x, xxxviii, xvi, xxiii, cx, tr. of Martial). [OhioR] (46) 91, p. 33-37.
>"Epigrams" (Selections: V. x, VII. xlvi, XII. xl, tr. of Martial). [Poetry] (159:1) O 91, p. 28-29.
>"Here Is Vesuvius" (IV, xliv, tr. of Martial). [SenR] (21:1) Spr 91, p. 45.
>"I Long for a Horse" (tr. of Ussin Kerim). [ColR] (NS 18:2) Fall-Wint 91, p. 75.
>"Is This Lawyering, Cinna" (VIII, vii, tr. of Martial). [SenR] (21:1) Spr 91, p. 46.
>"Keep a-Knockin'." [MichQR] (30:4) Fall 91, p. 665.
>"Landscape with Onlooker." [NewYorker] (67:35) 21 O 91, p. 36.
>"Loss?" [TarRP] (31:1) Fall 91, p. 24.
>"Men at My Father's Funeral." [OhioR] (47) 91, p. 17.
>"Mingus at the Half Note." [TarRP] (31:1) Fall 91, p. 23.
>"Mingus at the Showplace." [Poetry] (159:1) O 91, p. 27.
>"Mingus in Diaspora." [Antaeus] (67) Fall 91, p. 118.
>"My Father's Body." [GettyR] (4:3) Sum 91, p. 436-437.
>"No." [TarRP] (31:1) Fall 91, p. 22-23.
>"The Phrase Book Emergency." [ColR] (NS 18:1) Spr-Sum 91, p. 82.
>"The Radio Announcer." [ColR] (NS 18:1) Spr-Sum 91, p. 81.
>"Real Estate." [MichQR] (30:4) Fall 91, p. 666.
>"Recollections" (tr. of Ussin Kerim). [ColR] (NS 18:2) Fall-Wint 91, p. 76.
>"Reticence." [Poetry] (159:1) O 91, p. 25.
>"Sad Stories Told in Bars: The 'Reader's Digest' Version." [NewYorker] (67:4) 18 Mr 91, p. 66.
>"She's Half a Mind to Sleep with Me" (III, xc, tr. of Martial). [SenR] (21:1) Spr 91, p. 48.
>"Slow Work." [VirQR] (67:4) Aut 91, p. 686.
>"Tell Me the Truth, Mark" (VIII, lxxvi, tr. of Martial). [SenR] (21:1) Spr 91, p. 47.
>"A Tour of the Gardens." [OhioR] (47) 91, p. 16.
>"Untitled Poem: There's a slow fire in my eyes" (tr. of Ussin Kerim). [ColR] (NS 18:2) Fall-Wint 91, p. 74.
>"Well, You Needn't." [OhioR] (47) 91, p. 14-15.
>"The Wolf of Gubbio." [GettyR] (4:3) Sum 91, p. 438.
>"You Dance Up There" (tr. of Vasil Sotirov). [ColR] (NS 18:2) Fall-Wint 91, p. 77.
3886. MATTISON, Alice
>"A Letter to a Friend." [Ploughs] (17:2/3) Fall 91, p. 181-182.

3887. MATUZAK, Joseph
"Surface." [GeoR] (45:4) Wint 91, p. 736.
3888. MATZ, Mark
"Seduction." [PraF] (12:1 #54) Spr 91, p. 59.
3889. MAULPOIX, Jean-Michel
"Petite Suite Mélancolique." [Os] (33) Fall 91, p. 31-34.
3890. MAURER, Bonnie
"Wrecks." [HopewellR] (1991) 91, p. 9.
3891. MAURICE, Carlotta
"Auvers-sur-Oise." [ManhatPR] (13) [91?], p. 46.
"Jardin du Luxembourg." [Chelsea] (50) 91, p. 23.
"Letter from Berlin, 10 November." [Chelsea] (50) 91, p. 23.
3892. MAX, Lin
"Straight-Pins" (Honorable Mention, 5th Annual Contest). [SoCoast] (11) Wint 91,
p. 23.
3893. MAXAM, Vernard
"Delay." [OnTheBus] (8/9) 91, p. 106.
"Visit." [OnTheBus] (8/9) 91, p. 107.
3894. MAXWELL, Glyn
"Ending Equaling." [MassR] (32:1) Spr 91, p. 76.
"Poem in Blank Rhyme." [Atlantic] (268:1) Jl 91, p. 64.
"The Second Son's Escape." [MassR] (32:1) Spr 91, p. 77-78.
3895. MAY, Doug
"Circumcision." [BelPoJ] (41:4) Sum 91, p. 32-33.
"Octaroon." [BelPoJ] (41:4) Sum 91, p. 30-31.
3896. MAY, Eleanor Rodman
"Surrendering." [Crucible] (27) Fall 91, p. 30.
3897. MAYER, Barbara J.
"In the Death Seat." [SpoonRQ] (16:3/4) Sum-Fall 91, p. 37.
"Love Valley." [Pearl] (13) Spr-Sum 91, p. 53.
3898. MAYES, Frances
"In Benito Juárez's Park." [NoDaQ] (59:4) Fall 91, p. 155.
"Lullaby." [IndR] (14:2) Spr 91, p. 82-83.
"Rivera." [AntR] (49:4) Fall 91, p. 566-567.
"Rocky Streets That Made Their Feet." [NoDaQ] (59:4) Fall 91, p. 156.
"The Sacramento Street Wash-n-Dry." [Atlantic] (267:4) Ap 91, p. 64.
3899. MAYEUX, Louis T.
"Sestina for the Day of Souls." [LullwaterR] (2:2) Spr 91, p. 53-54.
3900. MAYHAR, Ardath
"East Texas June, 1939." [TexasR] (12:3/4) Fall-Wint 91, p. 83.
3901. MAYHEW, Lenore
"Beijing Morning" (tr. of Yang Liu Hong). [PraS] (65:2) Sum 91, p. 69.
"Empty Seat" (tr. of Yang Liu Hong). [PraS] (65:2) Sum 91, p. 71.
"My Way with Kites" (tr. of Yang Liu Hong). [PraS] (65:2) Sum 91, p. 71.
"Seeing the Sea Again" (tr. of Yang Liu Hong). [PraS] (65:2) Sum 91, p. 72.
"Unexpected" (tr. of Yang Liu Hong). [PraS] (65:2) Sum 91, p. 70.
"Unrealized Omen" (tr. of Yang Liu Hong). [PraS] (65:2) Sum 91, p. 73.
3902. MAYNE, Seymour
"Deathbed." [PoetL] (86:2) Sum 91, p. 46.
"Sentinel Sisters." [PoetL] (86:2) Sum 91, p. 45.
3903. MAZUR, Gail
"Another Tree." [Poetry] (158:1) Ap 91, p. 33-34.
"At Boston Garden, the First Night of War, 1991." [Agni] (34) 91, p. 7-8.
"Bedroom at Arles." [MissR] (19:3) 91, p. 146-147.
"Poem for Christian, My Student." [BostonR] (16:3/4) Je-Ag 91, p. 8.
"Whatever They Want." [Ploughs] (17:2/3) Fall 91, p. 170-171.
3904. MAZZARO, Jerome
"Ellicott Creek Park." [ColR] (NS 18:1) Spr-Sum 91, p. 123.
"Prospect: Loon Lake." [ColR] (NS 18:1) Spr-Sum 91, p. 122.
3905. MAZZOCCO, Robert
"Aftermaths." [NewYorker] (67:39) 18 N 91, p. 50-51.
Mc . . .
See also names beginning with Mac . . .
3906. McADAM, Rhona
"Epistle" (for Paul). [Pig] (17) 91, p. 54.
"Letters in Translation." [Pig] (17) 91, p. 54.

3907. McALEAVEY, David
"Cosmological." [WindO] (54) Sum 91, p. 30-32.
"The Entropic Curriculum." [WindO] (54) Sum 91, p. 28.
"February Arlington." [PoetC] (22:3) Spr 91, p. 17.
"Messages from the Children." [WindO] (54) Sum 91, p. 27.
"Near Eldorado." [RiverC] (11:2) Spr 91, p. 33-36.
"Sunset View." [SouthernPR] (31:1) Spr 91, p. 19.
"True Story." [PoetC] (22:3) Spr 91, p. 15-16.
"Vigil." [WindO] (54) Sum 91, p. 29-30.

3908. McALLISTER, Brian
"The Ruin" (tr. from the Old Englilsh, w. Gwendolyn Morgan). [NowestR] (29:3)
91, p. 107-108.

3909. McALPINE, Katherine
"SOS from an Upstate Farmhouse." [SlipS] (11) 91, p. 38.
"Uncle Jimmy." [SlipS] (11) 91, p. 39.

3910. McBREEN, Joan
"Lettergesh." [Grain] (19:2) Sum 91, p. 121.
"Moore Hall in September." [Grain] (19:2) Sum 91, p. 120.
"Woman Herding Cattle in a Field near Kilcolgan." [Grain] (19:2) Sum 91, p. 122.

3911. McBRIDE, Mekeel
"All Hallow's Eve." [NoAmR] (276:3) S 91, p. 55.
"Contents of a Breath About to Be Exhaled as 'I Love You'." [BostonR] (16:2) Ap
91, p. 21.
"The Ghost That Every Night Gives Birth To." [CalQ] (35/36) 91, p. 76-77.
"Morning, Though Still Darker Than a Bruise." [PassN] (12:1) Sum 91, p. 5.
"My Friend, Lost to Me in the World, Returns in a Dream." [PassN] (12:1) Sum 91,
p. 5.
"On the Ground, Ladies." [CalQ] (35/36) 91, p. 77-79.
"A Reminder." [ThRiPo] (37/38) 91, p. 37.
"The Tree of Life." [SenR] (21:1) Spr 91, p. 11-17.
"Why I No Longer Need to Eat." [PassN] (12:2) Wint 91, p. 8.

3912. McBRIDE, Regina
"The Talking Doll." [DenQ] (26:1) Sum 91, p. 49-50.

3913. McBRIDE, Tom
"Listening" (For William Stafford). [Interim] (10:2) Fall-Wint 91-92, p. 16.
"The Old Man with the Cat upon his Lap." [Interim] (10:2) Fall-Wint 91-92, p. 15.
"Warm November." [Interim] (10:2) Fall-Wint 91-92, p. 17.

3914. McCABE, Victoria
"Desperate Pioneers, the Toes." [CinPR] (21) Spr 90, p. 37.
"Epistle: Across Blazing Heavens." [CinPR] (21) Spr 90, p. 60-61.
"Gifted." [NewYorkQ] (46) 91, p. 53.
"If It Were Human, the Ear Would Look Like a Banker." [RiverC] (11:2) Spr 91, p.
62-63.
"Imaginary Letter to the Victim, in Multiple Voices, None Spoken." [Pig] (17) 91, p.
55.
"In the Throat." [CinPR] (21) Spr 90, p. 43.
"A Legal, Moral, Medical, Temporary Cure for Living in the World, from the Family
of Drugs: The Anti-Depressants: A Report." [NewYorkQ] (45) 91, p. 83-84.
"Needy Relatives." [RiverC] (11:2) Spr 91, p. 60-61.
"Post Traumatic Stress." [NewYorkQ] (44) 91, p. 73-74.
"The Woman Who Wished to Forget Her Throat." [HighP] (6:3) Wint 91, p. 115.

3915. McCAFFREY, Daniel J.
"Knowing the News." [BlackBR] (13) Spr-Sum 91, p. 17.
"Paper Doll." [BlackBR] (13) Spr-Sum 91, p. 17.
"The Sound We Everywhere Heard." [BlackBR] (13) Spr-Sum 91, p. 15-16.

3916. McCANN, David R.
"Daybreak Moon" (tr. of Yo Yongt'aek). [ManhatR] (6:1) Fall 91, p. 33.
"Elephant Rock" (tr. of Yo Yongt'aek). [ManhatR] (6:1) Fall 91, p. 28.
"Fairy Village" (tr. of Yo Yongt'aek). [ManhatR] (6:1) Fall 91, p. 31.
"Flocks of Gulls" (tr. of Yo Yongt'aek). [ManhatR] (6:1) Fall 91, p. 27.
"Lily Valley" (tr. of Yo Yongt'aek). [ManhatR] (6:1) Fall 91, p. 29.
"Preface to Ullung Island" (tr. of Yo Yongt'aek). [ManhatR] (6:1) Fall 91, p. 24.
"Ritual of the Sea God" (tr. of Yo Yongt'aek). [ManhatR] (6:1) Fall 91, p. 30.
"Trying for Land" (tr. of Yo Yongt'aek). [ManhatR] (6:1) Fall 91, p. 25.
"Ullung-Island" (tr. of Yo Yongt'aek). [ManhatR] (6:1) Fall 91, p. 32.
"Ullung Sunset" (tr. of Yo Yongt'aek). [ManhatR] (6:1) Fall 91, p. 26.

3917. McCANN, Janet
"The Arguments I Lose." [Kalliope] (13:2) 91, p. 27.
"Music After Midnight." [NewYorkQ] (46) 91, p. 63.
"Pepsi." [ManhatPR] (13) [91?], p. 21.
3918. McCANN, Margaret
"In My Hands." [Prima] (14/15) 91, p. 87.
3919. McCANN, Richard
"Nights of 1990" (for Stanley Garth and Jean Valentine). [Ploughs] (17:4) Wint
91-92, p. 95-100.
3920. McCARRELL, Stuart
"Frost." [NewYorkQ] (45) 91, p. 85.
"On Thompson" (His chosen biographer who turned on him). [NewYorkQ] (45) 91,
p. 85.
3921. McCARRISTON, Linda
"Answer." [TriQ] (81) Spr-Sum 91, p. 202-203.
"The Apple Tree" (for my mother). [TriQ] (81) Spr-Sum 91, p. 201.
"Bad Lay." [GeoR] (45:1) Spr 91, p. 52-53.
"Grateful" (to my brother). [SenR] (21:1) Spr 91, p. 9-10.
"A Thousand Genuflections." [TriQ] (81) Spr-Sum 91, p. 204.
"Victorian." [SenR] (21:1) Spr 91, p. 8.
3922. McCART, Lola
"A Man and a Woman." [EmeraldCR] (3) 91, c1990, p. 23.
3923. McCARTHY, Catherine Phil
"Going to Knock." [Field] (45) Fall 91, p. 79.
3924. McCARTHY, Gerald
"The Arc Welder" (for John Kellog). [PoetL] (86:2) Sum 91, p. 10.
3925. McCARTHY, Julia
"Facing North" (after David Whyte). [Event] (20:2) Sum 91, p. 110-111.
3926. McCARTHY, Mark
"I finally met my grandmother last night." [PoetryE] (31) Spr 91, p. 140.
"A Winter Dawn." [PoetryE] (31) Spr 91, p. 141.
3927. McCARTHY, Thomas
"Campaign Trail." [NorthStoneR] (10) Fall 91-Wint 92, p. 32.
"Florence Nightingale." [NorthStoneR] (10) Fall 91-Wint 92, p. 34-35.
"Historian" (for Donncha O'Corrain). [NorthStoneR] (10) Fall 91-Wint 92, p. 33.
"Power Play." [NorthStoneR] (10) Fall 91-Wint 92, p. 33.
"Spring Break at Augsburg College" (for John Mitchell). [NorthStoneR] (10) Fall
91-Wint 92, p. 35.
3928. McCASLIN, Susan
"A Mother's Prayer." [BellArk] (7:4) Jl-Ag 91, p. 12.
"My Angels Are Back." [BellArk] (7:2) Mr-Ap 91, p. 11.
"Timedreams." [BellArk] (7:2) Mr-Ap 91, p. 1.
"To Mary, Mother, Virgin of the Soul." [BellArk] (7:2) Mr-Ap 91, p. 10.
"Writing on Silence." [BellArk] (7:4) Jl-Ag 91, p. 3.
3929. McCAUGHEY, Kevin
"Boys." [CreamCR] (15:1) Spr 91, p. 64.
3930. McCAULEY, Nora
"The Pleasures of the Bath." [HarvardA] (126:1) Fall 91, p. 8.
3931. McCLANAHAN, Bill
"Stopping on Two Photographs in the University of Nevada at Reno Athletic Hall of
Fame Catalog." [CalQ] (32/33) Spr 90, p. 95.
3932. McCLANAHAN, Cia
"Invitation." [AmerV] (23) Sum 91, p. 15-17.
3933. McCLANAHAN, Rebecca
"After the Miracle." [MalR] (95) Sum 91, p. 58-59.
"Interstate." [MalR] (95) Sum 91, p. 61.
"Thirteen." [MalR] (95) Sum 91, p. 60.
3934. McCLATCHY, J. D.
"Late Night Ode" (Horace IV.i). [NewYorker] (67:6) 1 Ap 91, p. 62.
"Three Dreams About Elizabeth Bishop." [Poetry] (158:5) Ag 91, p. 249-252.
3935. McCLEAN, Sammy
"Gray Owl" (tr. of Helga M. Novak). [SnailPR] (1:2) Fall 91-Wint 92, p. 12.
"Portrait of a Young Man" (tr. of Rainer Brambach). [SnailPR] (1:2) Fall 91-Wint
92, p. 13.
3936. McCLELLAN, Christine
"Untitled: I have no money." [PaintedHR] (1) Ja 91, p. 26.

3937. McCLELLAND, Bruce
"Adam Kadmon Passes Out Thru Himself, Arrives in Malkuth." [Notus] (9) Fall 91,
p. 32-33.
3938. McCLELLAND, Neil
"Slave Ships." [Arc] (27) Aut 91, p. 31.
3939. McCLOSKEY, Mark
"The Biography of Death." [PoetryNW] (32:2) Sum 91, p. 26-28.
"The Smell." [PoetryNW] (32:2) Sum 91, p. 28.
3940. McCLUNEY, Miriam
"Fat Lady." [Kalliope] (13:2) 91, p. 31.
"Horror Film." [WritersF] (17) Fall 91, p. 198.
"Killing the Chickens, 1942." [NegC] (11:3) 91, p. 27.
3941. McCLURE, Michael
"Disturbed by Freedom." [GrandS] (10:2, #38) 91, p. 216-218.
"Spirit's Desperado." [Conjunc] (17) 91, p. 364.
3942. McCOMBS, Judith
"Interrogation." [RiverS] (35) 91, p. 47.
3943. McCONNEL, Frances Ruhlen
"What the Wolves Taught Us." [MassR] (32:1) Spr 91, p. 109-114.
3944. McCORD, Sandy
"Between Monterey Tides." [Plain] (12:2) Wint 91, p. 24.
"Boning Chicken." [CapeR] (26:2) Fall 91, p. 8.
"Earth to Earth." [ArtfulD] (20/21) 91, p. 52.
"Nefertiti in Berlin" (A Plainsongs Award Poem). [Plain] (12:1) Fall 91, p. 20.
3945. McCORKLE, James
"Alibi." [Verse] (8:1) Spr 91, p. 39.
"The Raft." [PlumR] (1) Spr-Sum 91, p. 13-14.
"Syrinx." [OntR] (35) Fall-Wint 91-92, p. 102-104.
"'The Storm Is Passing Over,' She Sang." [Verse] (8:1) Spr 91, p. 38.
3946. McCORMICK, Brian
"Inside the Inside of the Moon." [ChangingM] (23) Fall-Wint 91, p. 64.
3947. McCOY, Jenifer Sue
"Firstborn." [EmeraldCR] (3) 91, c1990, p. 34-35.
3948. McCOY, Valerie Stevens
"Whiteout." [BlackWR] (18:1) Fall-Wint 91, p. 176.
3949. McCRACKEN, Cathryn
"Skink." [Chelsea] (51) 91, p. 76-77.
3950. McCRACKEN, Kathleen
"Blue Light, Bay and College." [MalR] (95) Sum 91, p. 69.
"Date of Departure." [MalR] (95) Sum 91, p. 70.
"March." [MalR] (95) Sum 91, p. 68.
"Severance." [MalR] (95) Sum 91, p. 71-72.
3951. McCRARY, David B.
"Stone Rose: a Letter from the Eocene." [BellArk] (7:6) N-D 91, p. 3-4.
3952. McCRAY, Jane
"The Vessel." [FreeL] (8) Aut 91, p. 11.
3953. McCUE, Duncan
"Dusk in the Boathouse" (in memory of Jim). [PottPort] (13:2) Fall-Wint 91, p. 24.
"Images of the Reserve." [PottPort] (13:2) Fall-Wint 91, p. 22-23.
3954. McCUE, Frances
"Personal Progress." [CrabCR] (7:3) 91, p. 26.
3955. McCUEN, Heather C.
"Corpses Always Leave Skeletons." [BlackBR] (14) Fall-Wint 91, p. 28.
"Opossum." [BlackBR] (14) Fall-Wint 91, p. 28-29.
3956. McCULLOGH, L. E.
"Club Lido, Kansas City, 1944." [CapeR] (26:2) Fall 91, p. 13.
3957. McCULLOUGH, Ken
"For Darrell Gray" (1945-1985). [Abraxas] (40/41) 91, p. 145.
3958. McCULLOUGH, L. E.
"Club Lido, Kansas City, 1944." [PacificR] (10) 91-92, p. 35.
"Cumbia." [PacificR] (10) 91-92, p. 41.
3959. McCURRY, Jim
"Dogwag Shops at Giants." [Farm] (8:1) Spr-Sum 91, p. 35.
3960. McDADE, Jim
"Untitled: After I met my mother, my father, and God." [EmeraldCR] (4) 91, p. 38.

3961. McDADE, Linda
  "Naughty." [EmeraldCR] (3) 91, c1990, p. 20.
3962. McDADE, Thomas Michael
  "Hood." [BellArk] (7:2) Mr-Ap 91, p. 11.
  "Protection." [ChironR] (10:3) Aut 91, p. 48.
3963. McDANIEL, Debra Bokur
  "In Offering." [Kalliope] (13:2) 91, p. 56.
3964. McDANIEL, Judith
  "Raspberries." [SinW] (43/44) Sum 91, p. 22.
3965. McDANIEL, Mary
  "Nothing About This Season Is New" (Selections. The Pablo Neruda Prize for
    Poetry, Second Prize). [Nimrod] (35:1) Fall-Wint 91, p. 25-29.
3966. McDANIEL, Wilma Elizabeth
  "Alias." [HangL] (58) 91, p. 51.
  "Changing Employment." [HangL] (58) 91, p. 50.
  "Class." [WormR] (31:4, #124) 91, p. 107.
  "Funeral of a Portuguese Milker." [HangL] (58) 91, p. 48.
  "Nine-Year-Old Oklahoman Addicted to Writing Poetry." [HangL] (58) 91, p.
    48-49.
  "Percy Monette." [WormR] (31:4, #124) 91, p. 107.
  "Remembering Mama While Washing Gift Cups." [HangL] (58) 91, p. 51.
  "Unmatched." [HangL] (58) 91, p. 50.
  "A Woman Disappears." [HangL] (58) 91, p. 49.
3967. McDERMOTT, John H.
  "White shirts, blue suits, ties." [US1] (24/25) Spr 91, p. 22.
3968. McDONALD, Ian
  "The Fix." [GrahamHR] (14) Spr 91, p. 39-40.
3969. McDONALD, Robert
  "Susan's Rules for the Gigolo She Took into Her Home." [NewYorkQ] (46) 91, p.
    64-65.
3970. McDONALD, Walter
  "After a Year in Korea." [OntR] (35) Fall-Wint 91-92, p. 63.
  "After the Fall of Saigon." [HolCrit] (28:4) O 91, p. 16.
  "Boys and the Friends They Own." [AntigR] (85/86) Spr-Sum 91, p. 58.
  "Deductions from the Laws of Motion." [PraS] (65:1) Spr 91, p. 78-79.
  "Dogs in the World They Own." [GrandS] (10:1, #37) 91, p. 35.
  "Father's Wild Pheasants." [HampSPR] Wint 91, p. 47.
  "For Friends Missing in Action." [PoetC] (23:1) Fall 91, p. 3.
  "Hawks in August." [MissouriR] (14:3) 91, p. 138-139.
  "In a Cave Near Pecos." [Event] (20:3) Fall 91, p. 74-75.
  "In Green Pastures." [PoetL] (86:4) Wint 91-92, p. 29.
  "Leaving the Middle Years." [NoDaQ] (59:3) Sum 91, p. 64-65.
  "Living on Hardscrabble." [NewEngR] (13:3/4) Spr-Sum 91, p. 145.
  "Living on Open Plains." [OhioR] (47) 91, p. 112.
  "The Lookout at Wolf Creek Pass." [ManhatPR] (13) [91?], p. 27.
  "Mercy and the Brazos River." [PraS] (65:1) Spr 91, p. 77-78.
  "The Middle Years." [LullwaterR] (2:2) Spr 91, p. 76.
  "The Middle Years." [PacificR] (10) 91-92, p. 89.
  "The Middle Years." [Thrpny] (44) Wint 91, p. 19.
  "The Middle Years." [WestB] (28) 91, p. 43.
  "Mounds at Estacado." [MissouriR] (14:3) 91, p. 133.
  "Provender." [PacificR] (10) 91-92, p. 125.
  "Regular Programming on the Eve of War." [PoetC] (23:1) Fall 91, p. 4.
  "Riding on Hardscrabble." [SoCoast] (10) Fall 91, p. 47.
  "Rigging the Windmill." [MissouriR] (14:3) 91, p. 136.
  "Rigging the Windmill." [OntR] (35) Fall-Wint 91-92, p. 61-62.
  "The Risk of Open Fields." [ColR] (NS 18:1) Spr-Sum 91, p. 106.
  "The Same Old Words That Haunt Us." [WestB] (28) 91, p. 42.
  "The Signs of Prairie Rattlers." [MissouriR] (14:3) 91, p. 134-135.
  "The Songs of Corner Cowboys." [CimR] (95) Ap 91, p. 55.
  "Uncle Philip and the Endless Names." [MissouriR] (14:3) 91, p. 137.
  "Uncle Rollie and the Laws of Water." [GettyR] (4:1) Wint 91, p. 144.
  "Uncle Roy's Pearl Harbor Hot Dogs." [MissouriR] (14:3) 91, p. 132.
  "War in the Persian Gulf." [ColR] (NS 18:1) Spr-Sum 91, p. 104-105.
  "When It Seemed Easy." [MissR] (19:3) 91, p. 139.

3971. McDONOUGH, Tracy Lee
"The Dim Light of Waking." [RagMag] (9:1) 91, p. 38-39.
"The Only Man I Have Ever Known Is My Husband." [RagMag] (9:1) 91, p. 35.
"A Rainy Day, a Window." [RagMag] (9:1) 91, p. 37.
"When You Ask Me How I Know." [RagMag] (9:1) 91, p. 36.
3972. McDOUGALL, Bonnie S.
"A Local Accent" (tr. of Bei Dao, w. Chen Maiping). [ManhatR] (6:1) Fall 91, p. 8.
"My Country" (tr. of Bei Dao, w. Chen Maiping). [ManhatR] (6:1) Fall 91, p. 11.
"Old Snow" (tr. of Bei Dao, w. Chen Maiping). [ManhatR] (6:1) Fall 91, p. 6.
"A Picture" (for Tiantian's fifth birthday, tr. of Bei Dao, w. Chen Maiping).
    [ManhatR] (6:1) Fall 91, p. 9.
"Prague" (tr. of Bei Dao, w. Chen Maiping). [ManhatR] (6:1) Fall 91, p. 4.
"Rebel" (tr. of Bei Dao, w. Chen Maiping). [ManhatR] (6:1) Fall 91, p. 12.
"Terminal Illness" (tr. of Bei Dao, w. Chen Maiping). [ManhatR] (6:1) Fall 91, p. 7.
"To Memory" (tr. of Bei Dao, w. Chen Maiping). [ManhatR] (6:1) Fall 91, p. 10.
"Untitled: He opens wide a third eye" (tr. of Bei Dao, w. Chen Maiping). [ManhatR]
    (6:1) Fall 91, p. 5.
3973. McDOUGALL, Jo
"Talking with You." [PoetryE] (31) Spr 91, p. 133.
3974. McDOWELL, Robert
"The Neighborhood." [Hudson] (44:1) Spr 91, p. 74-90.
3975. McDUFFIE, Carrington
"Body of Water." [CrabCR] (7:2) Sum 91, p. 12.
3976. McELROY, Colleen J.
"Heavy in the S Curves." [KenR] (NS 13:4) Fall 91, p. 85-86.
"Lifting the Morning" (for Sally and Salvatore). [KenR] (NS 13:2) Spr 91, p. 68-69.
"Light: Reflecting Glass in the Evelyn Room." [ManhatR] (6:1) Fall 91, p. 69-70.
"A Little Traveling Music." [KenR] (NS 13:4) Fall 91, p. 86-87.
"Trompe L'Oeil: Slovenia." [KenR] (NS 13:4) Fall 91, p. 87-88.
3977. McELROY, Misty
"Untitled: The billboards would scream." [EmeraldCR] (3) 91, c1990, p. 75.
"Untitled: The ivory family has left me a widow." [EmeraldCR] (3) 91, c1990, p.
    44.
3978. McERLEAN, Toby
"Tomato Perfume." [EmeraldCR] (3) 91, c1990, p. 63.
3979. McEVILY, Mary Ellen
"Unsettled." [CapeR] (26:1) Spr 91, p. 28.
3980. McEWEN, Christian
"Obsession." [Mildred] (4:2/5:1) 91, p. 62.
3981. McEWEN, R. F.
"Lost Keys." [PraS] (65:1) Spr 91, p. 82-83.
"Tuckered In, Tuckered Out." [PraS] (65:1) Spr 91, p. 80-81.
"Wings." [PraS] (65:1) Spr 91, p. 81-82.
3982. McFARLAND, Beverly
"A Bit of Genesis." [PoetL] (86:1) Spr 91, p. 21.
3983. McFARLAND, Ron
"What My Old Maid Aunt Thought about Life." [PaintedHR] (2) Spr 91, p. 37.
3984. McFEE, Michael
"Address Book." [SouthernPR] (31:1) Spr 91, p. 50-52.
"Coronach" (in memory of John Longley). [VirQR] (67:4) Aut 91, p. 676-678.
"Funeral Home." [HampSPR] Wint 91, p. 53.
"Multi-Purpose Protractor." [Poetry] (158:6) S 91, p. 329.
"Old Baseball Found under a Bush." [VirQR] (67:4) Aut 91, p. 678-679.
"Paper." [Poetry] (158:6) S 91, p. 328.
"Scanning the Poetry Shelves in Heaven." [Poetry] (157:4) Ja 91, p. 218.
"There's Nothing Finer than a Boy!" [Shen] (41:1) Spr 91, p. 31-32.
"Venus and Mars." [SouthernHR] (25:2) Spr 91, p. 159.
"When I Read to My Son." [Nat] (252:14) 15 Ap 91, p. 499.
3985. McFERREN, Martha
"Exercise" (for Dennis). [Shen] (41:4) Wint 91, p. 86-87.
3986. McGIMPSEY, David
"Just Another Expoem, July 1990." [Spitball] (36) Spr 91, p. 46-47.
3987. McGLYNN, Brian (Brian J.)
"Cultural History." [CrabCR] (7:2) Sum 91, p. 29.
"Pachyderms." [DustyD] Je 91, p. 7.

3988. McGLYNN, Paul D.
    "And No Birds Sing." [Hellas] (2:2) Fall 91, p. 273.
    "Sunday, Sunday Night." [Hellas] (2:2) Fall 91, p. 273.
3989. McGOWAN, James
    "The Jewels" (tr. of Charles Baudelaire). [SpoonRQ] (16:3/4) Sum-Fall 91, p.
        44-45.
    "Music" (tr. of Charles Baudelaire). [SpoonRQ] (16:3/4) Sum-Fall 91, p. 43.
3990. McGOWAN, Whitman
    "God Is Gone." [PoetryUSA] (22) Spr 91, p. 23.
3991. McGRADY, Nell
    "Prayer, September 29." [PoetL] (86:3) Fall 91, p. 27.
3992. McGRATH, Beth
    "Easter at Cassis." [AnthNEW] (3) 91, p. 10.
3993. McGRATH, Campbell
    "Almond Blossoms, Rock and Roll, the Past Seen as Burning Fields." [Antaeus]
        (67) Fall 91, p. 199-201.
    "At the Freud Hilton." [Antaeus] (67) Fall 91, p. 202-203.
    "Hemingway Dines on Boiled Shrimp and Beer." [ParisR] (33:119) Sum 91, p. 243.
    "James Wright, Richard Hugo, the Vanishing Forests of the Pacific Northwest."
        [Antaeus] (67) Fall 91, p. 204-205.
    "Wheatfield Under Clouded Sky." [ParisR] (33:119) Sum 91, p. 241-242.
3994. McGRATH, Carmelita
    "Independence." [TickleAce] (21) Spr-Sum 91, p. 1-2.
    "Nightmare House." [TickleAce] (22) Fall-Wint 91, p. 53-54.
    "Wallpapering the Crooked Room." [TickleAce] (21) Spr-Sum 91, p. 3-4.
    "Yule." [TickleAce] (22) Fall-Wint 91, p. 50-52.
3995. McGRATH, Donald
    "The Old Hag." [TickleAce] (22) Fall-Wint 91, p. 55.
3996. McGRATH, Patrick
    "Clothes from a Former Life." [JamesWR] (8:4) Sum 91, p. 9.
3997. McGRATH, Thomas
    "Ah." [ColR] (NS 18:2) Fall-Wint 91, p. 73.
    "Green Kindness." [ColR] (NS 18:2) Fall-Wint 91, p. 72.
    "Housecleaning." [ColR] (NS 18:2) Fall-Wint 91, p. 73.
    "Newtonian Law." [ColR] (NS 18:2) Fall-Wint 91, p. 73.
    "Proclamation." [ColR] (NS 18:2) Fall-Wint 91, p. 72.
    "Ratios." [ColR] (NS 18:2) Fall-Wint 91, p. 73.
    "Starting Over." [ColR] (NS 18:2) Fall-Wint 91, p. 72.
    "Strange Country." [ColR] (NS 18:2) Fall-Wint 91, p. 72.
    "Underground Activities." [ColR] (NS 18:2) Fall-Wint 91, p. 71.
3998. McGUIRE, Catherine
    "Ice Fog." [Vis] (35) 91, p. 26.
3999. McGUIRE, Jerry
    "Climber." [Callaloo] (14:2) Spr 91, p. 442.
    "I Know Different." [Callaloo] (14:2) Spr 91, p. 441.
    "Terminal." [Callaloo] (14:2) Spr 91, p. 443.
4000. McGUIRE, Michael
    "Tail End: Rain" (for David Rivard). [AntR] (49:4) Fall 91, p. 568-569.
4001. McGUIRE, Shannon Marquez
    "Nuns Skating at the Comet." [LouisL] (8:2) Fall 91, p. 51-53.
4002. McHUGH, Heather
    "Everything a Hill Inherits." [Journal] (14:2) Wint 91, p. 38.
    "Intensive Care." [BostonR] (16:1) F 91, p. 11.
    "The Mirror." [Journal] (14:2) Wint 91, p. 36-37.
    "Scenes from a Death." [WestHR] (45:1) Spr 91, p. 34-38.
    "Tornado Survivor." [Spirit] (11) 91, p. 263.
4003. McHUGH, Vincent
    "Answering the Hu-chou Magistrate of Hindu Ancestry Who Asked Who I Was" (tr.
        of Li Po, w. C. H. Kwock). [PoetryUSA] (22) Spr 91, p. 21.
    "Li Po's Grave" (tr. of Po Chu-i, w. C. H. Kwock). [PoetryUSA] (22) Spr 91, p.
        21.
    "The War Year" (tr. of Ts'ao Sung, w. C. H. Kwock). [PoetryUSA] (22) Spr 91, p.
        21.
4004. McINNIS, Nadine
    "The Bitches." [PraF] (12:2 #55) Sum 91, p. 32-33.
    "The Healer" (from "retracing steps"). [PraF] (12:2 #55) Sum 91, p. 31.

"What Befalls Us." [PraF] (12:2 #55) Sum 91, p. 30.
4005. McIRVIN, Michael
"Drunk and Reeling." [DogRR] (10:1) Sum 91, p. 13.
4006. McISAAC, Claudia MonPere
"Saturdays." [CentR] (35:1) Wint 91, p. 185.
4007. McKANE, Richard
"Beginning of a Long Poem" (tr. of Leonid Aronzon). [LitR] (34:3) Spr 91, p. 333-334.
"I Turn My Face to the River" (tr. of Leonid Aronzon). [LitR] (34:3) Spr 91, p. 334.
"Sonnet to Igarka" (For Altshuler, tr. of Leonid Aronzon). [LitR] (34:3) Spr 91, p. 336.
"What Does the Lead Reveal" (tr. of Leonid Aronzon). [LitR] (34:3) Spr 91, p. 335.
"With a Scented Eruption" (tr. of Leonid Aronzon). [LitR] (34:3) Spr 91, p. 336.
"Young Skies in the Sky" (tr. of Leonid Aronzon). [LitR] (34:3) Spr 91, p. 333.
4008. McKAY, Linda Back
"Sudden Storm in Filmore County." [Farm] (8:2) Fall-Wint 91-92, p. 69.
4009. McKAY, Matthew
"Switchbacks" (For Martha). [LitR] (35:1) Fall 91, p. 121.
4010. McKEAN, James
"Les Grues." [AntR] (49:3) Sum 91, p. 430.
"House Wrens" (Troglodytes aedon). [KenR] (NS 13:2) Spr 91, p. 124-125.
"Silence Beneath the Voices in the Air." [PaintedB] (43) 91, p. 6.
4011. McKEE, Glenn
"Flashback to Fences." [Pembroke] (23) 91, p. 109.
4012. McKEE, Louis
"The Bomb." [CoalC] (4) S 91, p. 12.
"Night Music." [CoalC] (4) S 91, p. 9.
4013. McKELVEY, Barbara
"Birds." [TickleAce] (21) Spr-Sum 91, p. 60.
4014. McKELVEY, Robert S.
"Separation." [TexasR] (12:1/2) Spr-Sum 91, p. 112.
4015. McKERNAN, John
"Old Photograph." [WindO] (55) Wint 91-92, p. 42-44.
4016. McKERNAN, Llewellyn
"First Draft." [EngJ] (80:2) F 91, p. 97.
4017. McKIERNAN, Ethna
"Artifacts." [NorthStoneR] (10) Fall 91-Wint 92, p. 8.
"Breaking." [NorthStoneR] (10) Fall 91-Wint 92, p. 7.
"Heat." [NorthStoneR] (10) Fall 91-Wint 92, p. 9.
"Karen Ann Quinlan." [NorthStoneR] (10) Fall 91-Wint 92, p. 11.
"Living in the House of Lies." [NorthStoneR] (10) Fall 91-Wint 92, p. 10-11.
4018. McKINLEY, John
"The Tonsilectomy." [SlipS] (11) 91, p. 62.
4019. McKINLEY, Scott
"The State of Things" (for Tim Dlugos). [WashR] (16:6) Ap-My 91, p. 9.
4020. McKINNEY, Joshua
"The Language of Ice." [Sonora] (21) Sum 91, p. 64-66.
4021. McKINNON, Barry
"Pulp Log" (Selections: 12, 17-19, 22-24, 40, 50, 55, 59). [CapilR] (2:5) Sum 91, p. 80-90.
"Pulp Log" (Selections: thirty two - thirty seven). [PoetryC] (12:1) D 91, p. 7.
4022. McKINNON, Patrick (Pat)
"My Life As a Car." [WormR] (31:1, #121) 91, p. 9.
"Poem for a Cocktail Waitress at the Imperial Lounge, Findlay, Ohio, 1985." [WormR] (31:1, #121) 91, p. 10.
"Poem for Steve." [ChironR] (10:2) Sum 91, p. 14.
"Poem for the Workers." [WormR] (31:1, #121) 91, p. 9.
4023. McKINSEY, Martin
"Attenuation" (tr. of Yannis Ritsos). [Poetry] (158:4) Jl 91, p. 204.
"Pro Forma" (tr. of Yannis Ritsos). [Poetry] (158:4) Jl 91, p. 204.
4024. McKOWN, Derek
"Falling." [PacificR] (9) 91, p. 10.
"Following Apollo's Refrain." [PacificR] (9) 91, p. 8-9.
"Parity." [PacificR] (9) 91, p. 7.
4025. McLEOD, Donald
"Europe and Beyond." [Pearl] (14) Fall-Wint 91, p. 68.

"Sunbathing with Dog." [Pearl] (14) Fall-Wint 91, p. 67.
4026. McLEOD, Milt
"The Croaker and Other Fish Who Try to Speak." [Parting] (4:2) Wint 91-92, p.
22-23.
"Now and Then a Woman Steps Out of the Crowd." [SouthernPR] (31:1) Spr 91, p.
56-57.
4027. McMAHAN, Florence Myers
"Archaeologists." [Nimrod] (34:2) Spr-Sum 91, p. 82.
4028. McMAHON, Lynne
"Conversion." [SouthernR] (27:2) Ap 91, p. 256.
"I'm Always Coming Across the South." [SouthernR] (27:2) Ap 91, p. 253-255.
4029. McMANIMIE, H.
"Bituen." [BambooR] (50/51) Spr-Sum 91, p. 245-246.
4030. McMANUS, James
"2 Live Soul." [ClockR] (7:1/2) 91-92, p. 113-115.
"Slash Art." [NewAW] (7) Spr 91, p. 74-79.
"Triptych." [AmerPoR] (20:3) My-Je 91, p. 40-41.
4031. McMICHAEL, James
"The Longed-For" (Excerpt, from an Uncompleted Sequence). [TriQ] (83) Wint
91-92, p. 97-100.
4032. McMILLAN, James A.
"The Flying Lesson." [JINJPo] (13:1) Spr 91, p. 32.
4033. McMINN, Sheila Crocker
"My daddy never heard of Jack Kerouac." [MoodySI] (24/25/26) Spr 91, p. 53.
4034. McMURRAY, Eddie R.
"Enigma." [CapeR] (26:1) Spr 91, p. 48.
"Moss." [DustyD] Je 91, p. 41.
4035. McNAIL, Stanley
"You That Mingle May." [PoetryUSA] (22) Spr 91, p. 10.
4036. McNAIR, Wesley
"First Class in Night School." [BostonR] (16:6) D 91, p. 31.
"House in Spring." [ThRiPo] (37/38) 91, p. 79.
"Walking in Dark Town." [ThRiPo] (37/38) 91, p. 80.
4037. McNALL, Sally Allen
"Everything." [CutB] (35) Wint-Spr 91, p. 59-60.
4038. McNALLY, John
"Custom" (opening sections). [Talisman] (7) Fall 91, p. 124-125.
"Exes" (Selections: 5 poems). [WashR] (17:4) D 91-Ja 92, p. 26.
4039. McNALLY, Stephen
"The Coffin Maker." [CimR] (97) O 91, p. 51.
4040. McNAMARA, Eugene
"Destinations." [OntR] (34) Spr-Sum 91, p. 80-83.
"Peoria, 1927." [OntR] (34) Spr-Sum 91, p. 83-84.
4041. McNAMARA, Robert
"At the Edge of the Dunes" (for David York). [GettyR] (4:3) Sum 91, p. 512-514.
"Divorce Court." [Agni] (34) 91, p. 185-186.
"Doing Melaka." [Field] (45) Fall 91, p. 78.
"The End of Strife." [GettyR] (4:3) Sum 91, p. 511.
"In Ape Caves." [OhioR] (47) 91, p. 86-87.
4042. McNAMEE, Gregory
"Confesión a J. Edgar Hoover" (tr. of James Wright). [Nuez] (3:7) 91, p. 15.
"Light of the Moon" (tr. of Paul Verlaine). [WebR] (15) Spr 91, p. 40.
4043. McNARIE, Alan Decker
"Disappearing Mountain" (On judging a children's writing contest). [ChamLR] (8-9)
Spr-Fall 91, p. 4-8.
4044. McNAUGHTON, Duncan
"It's Quite Late." [CapilR] (2:5) Sum 91, p. 26.
"Lucky at Cards." [CapilR] (2:5) Sum 91, p. 24.
"Untitled: Whitman sojourned in New Orleans long enough." [CapilR] (2:5) Sum
91, p. 25.
4045. McNEIL, Elizabeth
"Circe's Pig Ship." [ChironR] (10:4) Wint 91, p. 4.
"Incident at Santa Cruz Harbor." [ChamLR] (8-9) Spr-Fall 91, p. 101.
"Myth-Mouth Deluded." [ChironR] (10:4) Wint 91, p. 4.
4046. McNEILL, Christine
"Realpolitik." [SoCoast] (10) Fall 91, p. 21.

4047. McNERNEY, Joan
"Electric Pearls." [DustyD] (2:1) Ja 91, p. 13.
4048. McNULTY, Ted
"Antietam." [Poetry] (158:6) S 91, p. 320.
"Doolin." [Vis] (36) 91, p. 27.
"White Star Liner." [Stand] (32:3) Sum 91, p. 38.
"The Wink." [SouthernPR] (31:2) Fall 91, p. 7.
4049. McPHERSON, D. Jayne
"Cavern." [ChamLR] (8-9) Spr-Fall 91, p. 105.
4050. McPHERSON, Sandra
"Anonymous Kentucky Quilter." [SouthernR] (27:2) Ap 91, p. 249.
"Artists." [Iowa] (21:3) Fall 91, p. 7-10.
"A Change of Place." [SoDakR] (29:3 part 2) Aut 91, p. 21.
"Choosing an Author for Assurance in the Night." [Field] (45) Fall 91, p. 44-45.
"Genius of Fog at Ecola Creek Mouth." [Poetry] (159:1) O 91, p. 5-6.
"Great Art, Great Criticism" (—Mattie Pickett, Quilter). [SouthernR] (27:2) Ap 91,
    p. 247.
"Illusion from a Quilt by Louise Williams." [SouthernR] (27:2) Ap 91, p. 248.
"In Memory of the Surprised" (7.1, October 17, 1989). [AmerPoR] (20:4) Jl-Ag 91,
    p. 16.
"Memento Mori: Pajamas He Fell Away from Us In." [AmerPoR] (20:4) Jl-Ag 91,
    p. 16.
"Postmark February 21, 1989: He Has Just Pulled the Hammer Back." [AmerPoR]
    (20:4) Jl-Ag 91, p. 17.
"Precipice, Rush, Sheath" (on a cliff at Yachats, central Oregon Coast). [ParisR]
    (33:120) Fall 91, p. 211.
"Three Purses of a Nomadic Woman" (for Jean Valentine). [AmerPoR] (20:4) Jl-Ag
    91, p. 14-15.
"Waiting for Lesser Duckweed: On a Proposal of Issa's" (with thanks to Lucien
    Stryk, who translated). [Iowa] (21:3) Fall 91, p. 4-7.
"Women and Objects." [TriQ] (81) Spr-Sum 91, p. 197-200.
4051. McPHILEMY, Kathleen
"Interned." [Verse] (8:1) Spr 91, p. 103.
4052. McQUEEN, Mark
"N + 21: Sermon from a Mall." [ChironR] (10:3) Aut 91, p. 37.
"N + 45, the Hippy Graveyard." [ChironR] (10:4) Wint 91, p. 35.
4053. McQUILKIN, Rennie
"Archibald as Bottom Feeder." [CinPR] (21) Spr 90, p. 26-27.
"Archibald with Sally in the Sticks." [CinPR] (21) Spr 90, p. 28-29.
4054. McRAY, Paul
"Always Very Well, As Though Traveling Backwards Were Natural." [HampSPR]
    Wint 91, p. 7.
"Bar Dog." [Blueline] (12) 91, p. 68-69.
"In Your Sailing Dream" (after Richard Hugo). [BellR] (14:1) Spr 91, p. 10.
"Picture the Significance of Anticipation" (an hour with Pattiann Rogers).
    [HampSPR] Wint 91, p. 6.
"White and Sky-Blue" (for my grandmother Harriet). [HampSPR] Wint 91, p. 5.
4055. McROBBIE, Kenneth
"Case Histories under Glass, in Our Literary Museum from East to West." [CanLit]
    (129) Sum 91, p. 88-89.
4056. McVEAY, Dale
"Life's Looking Up." [EmeraldCR] (3) 91, c1990, p. 27-28.
4057. McWATT, Mark
"Fairy Tale Blues." [GrahamHR] (14) Spr 91, p. 33.
"Penelope." [GrahamHR] (14) Spr 91, p. 32.
4058. McWHIRTER, George
"Leopard." [Chelsea] (51) 91, p. 71.
"The Ox and the Axe, and the Legions Asleep." [Chelsea] (51) 91, p. 69-70.
4059. MEAD, Jane
"Begin Where We All Know Which and Where We Are." [Pequod] (32) 91, p.
    130-133.
"For Alex at the Gladman Memorial Hospital." [Iowa] (21:3) Fall 91, p. 151-153.
"In Need of a World." [AntR] (49:4) Fall 91, p. 564-565.
"To the Body." [Iowa] (21:3) Fall 91, p. 150.
4060. MEAD, S. E.
"Amputations." [Comm] (118:12) 14 Je 91, p. 406.

"Anticipating Easter (Gethsemane)." [SmPd] (28:3, #83) Fall 91, p. 16.
"Christmas Card from your Neighbor." [Pig] (17) 91, p. 58.
"Letter from Anywhere." [Pig] (17) 91, p. 58.
"Summer Vacation." [Comm] (118:13) 12 Jl 91, p. 436.
"The Topography of Touch." [BellArk] (7:3) My-Je 91, p. 11.
MEANS, B. J. Brice
    See BRICE-MEANS, B. J.
4061. MECKLENBURG, Mervin (Mervin Mecklenberg)
    "Evening Encounter" (Sacrifice Cliff, above Billings, Montana). [CutB] (35)
        Wint-Spr 91, p. 47.
    "Recollections of a Photograph." [CutB] (35) Wint-Spr 91, p. 49.
    "Roadkill at Willowcreek Bridge." [CutB] (35) Wint-Spr 91, p. 48.
    "The Words I'd Carried." [PaintedHR] (2) Spr 91, p. 29.
4062. MEDINA, Pablo
    "El Nuevo Circo." [LindLM] (10:1) Ja-Mr 91, p. 32.
4063. MEEK, Jay
    "Hotel Ballroom." [ThRiPo] (37/38) 91, p. 10.
    "Ice Boats." [ThRiPo] (37/38) 91, p. 9.
4064. MEGAW, Neill
    "As Good As Ever." [Sequoia] (34:1) Spr 91, p. 42.
    "An Essay on the Great Food Chain of Being." [Hellas] (2:1) Spr 91, p. 60.
    "Far South of Tahiti." [Hellas] (2:1) Spr 91, p. 60-62.
    "Heaven Before My Time." [Hellas] (2:2) Fall 91, p. 224-225.
    "If You Can't Stand the Heat." [Hellas] (2:1) Spr 91, p. 62.
    "Long-run Play." [Hellas] (2:2) Fall 91, p. 226.
    "Masks." [Hellas] (2:2) Fall 91, p. 223.
    "Something Said in Passing." [Hellas] (2:1) Spr 91, p. 63.
    "Summer Fling." [Hellas] (2:2) Fall 91, p. 226.
    "Time-warp, of a Quiet Afternoon." [Hellas] (2:2) Fall 91, p. 221, 223.
    "Zero-Sum Game." [Hellas] (2:2) Fall 91, p. 225.
4065. MEHREN, Stein
    "Departure" (tr. by Harold P. Hanson). [Vis] (37) 91, p. 46.
    "First Night of Frost" (tr. by Robert Hedin). [CrabCR] (7:2) Sum 91, p. 13.
    "Varm Park i August." [InterPR] (17:2) Fall 91, p. 38.
    "Warm Park in August" (tr. by Robert Hedin). [InterPR] (17:2) Fall 91, p. 39.
4066. MEHRHOFF, Charlie
    "Christmas Tree." [DogRR] (10:1) Sum 91, p. 16.
    "Fool's Shadow." [HeavenB] (9) Wint-Spr 91-92, p. 17-18.
    "Mammoth Bones." [DogRR] (10:1) Sum 91, p. 15.
    "Not Lonely Death." [DogRR] (10:2) Fall-Wint 91, p. 19.
    "An Old Wound Remembered." [Asylum] (6:3/4) 91, p. 32.
    "Peacemaker" (for Peter Magliocco). [DogRR] (10:1) Sum 91, p. 14.
    "Prayer Flags." [DogRR] (10:1) Sum 91, p. 16.
    "Smoke." [DogRR] (10:2) Fall-Wint 91, p. 22.
    "Temporary Resurrection #408." [DogRR] (10:2) Fall-Wint 91, p. 20-21.
    "We Wintered on the High Plains." [DogRR] (10:2) Fall-Wint 91, p. 21.
    "Who." [DogRR] (10:1) Sum 91, p. 16.
MEHROFF, Charlie
    See MEHRHOFF, Charlie
4067. MEHROTRA, Arvind Krishna
    "The Inheritance." [GettyR] (4:3) Sum 91, p. 415-416.
MEI, Yuan
    See YUAN, Mei
4068. MEIER, Kay
    "African Tourist." [WillowR] Spr 91, p. 17.
4069. MEIER, Richard
    "The Headless Statue in the Roman Museum." [PraS] (65:1) Spr 91, p. 48.
    "January Rain." [PraS] (65:1) Spr 91, p. 48-49.
4070. MEINHOFF, Michael
    "Mountain Wave." [ChamLR] (8-9) Spr-Fall 91, p. 10.
    "Shave Ice." [ChamLR] (8-9) Spr-Fall 91, p. 9.
4071. MEINKE, Peter
    "Arms and the Man." [TampaR] (4) 91, p. 55.
    "Country Vacation." [ClockR] (7:1/2) 91-92, p. 88.
    "Minuet in G." [TampaR] (4) 91, p. 56.
    "Shears." [ClockR] (7:1/2) 91-92, p. 87.

"The Square Root of Love." [HighP] (6:1) Spr 91, p. 85-88.
"The True UFO Story." [ClockR] (7:1/2) 91-92, p. 4-6.
"Warpath." [GeoR] (45:1) Spr 91, p. 22-23.
4072. MEISSNER, Bill
"The Home Town Boys Mark Their Calendars." [Spitball] (39) Wint 91, p. 9.
"Laundromat Music, June Bug Rain." [ThRiPo] (37/38) 91, p. 47-48.
"Ode to a Baseball Wound." [Northeast] (5:4) Sum 91, p. 13.
"The Old Men of Summer." [ThRiPo] (37/38) 91, p. 45-46.
"Returning to Find It." [Sidewalks] (1) Aug 91, p. 21.
4073. MELCHER, Michael
"Light Seeks." [Talisman] (7) Fall 91, p. 28.
4074. MELHEM, D. H.
"Boy in a Hospital." [Paint] (18:35) Spr 91, p. 9-10.
4075. MELNICK, David
"Iliad (Book III, lines 310-78)" (from "Men in Aïda," tr. of Homer). [Talisman] (6)
Spr 91, p. 45-46.
4076. MELNICK, Patrice
"Sabine the Cook Warns Me." [PaintedHR] (2) Spr 91, p. 7.
4077. MELNYCZUK, Askold
"Alley Cat" (for TS). [SnailPR] (1:1) Spr 91, p. 21-22.
"Prayers" (Selections: 1, 9, 13, 24, tr. of Bohdan Boychuk). [Agni] (33) 91, p.
118-121.
"Vermont." [AntR] (49:1) Wint 91, p. 104.
"Young Woman in the Prado." [Nat] (252:23) 17 Je 91, p. 826.
4078. MELTON, Kathleen
"Some people choose to stay in the dark." [PoetryUSA] (22) Spr 91, p. 12.
4079. MELVIN, John
"Leaving Romey's Garden." [CinPR] (22) Spr 91, p. 26-27.
4080. MENCHING, Steffen
"Under the Linden" (tr. by William Sweet). [AntigR] (84) Wint 91, p. 143.
"Unter den Linden." [AntigR] (84) Wint 91, p. 142.
4081. MENDELL, Olga
"884-8623." [Elf] (1:1) Spr 91, p. 20.
4082. MENEFEE, Maynard
"As I savor the smell of my own rotting flesh." [PoetryUSA] (23) Sum 91, p. 20.
4083. MENEFEE, Sarah
"January 13, 1991." [PoetryUSA] (22) Spr 91, p. 15.
4084. MENG, Lang
"The Two of Us" (tr. by Ginny MacKenzie and Wei Guo). [Agni] (34) 91, p. 217.
4085. MENGES, Margaret
"Ides of March." [Blueline] (12) 91, p. 41.
MENOZZI, Wallis Wilde
See WILDE-MENOZZI, Wallis
4086. MENZIES, Ian
"Approaching Universal Comprehension." [Grain] (19:4) Wint 91, p. 55.
"Co-op Catalogue." [Grain] (19:4) Wint 91, p. 56.
"On My Way to the Neighbour's Barn Fire." [Grain] (19:4) Wint 91, p. 54-55.
4087. MER, Maggie
"Rundle Thoughts" (at the new moon). [Sequoia] (34:1) Spr 91, p. 94.
4088. MEREDITH, Joseph
"The Teacher" (for RSM). [FourQ] (4:2) Fall 90, p. 14.
4089. MEREDITH, William
"A Major Work." [PoetL] (86:4) Wint 91-92, p. 48.
"A Mild-Spoken Citizen Finally Writes to the White House." [Crazy] (41) Wint 91,
p. 76-78.
4090. MERRIAM, Eve
"Knowledge." [FreeL] (7) Spr 91, p. 5.
"Landscape." [FreeL] (7) Spr 91, p. 4.
"Morning in Bellagio." [Nimrod] (34:2) Spr-Sum 91, p. 86.
"Packing My Bags." [Nimrod] (34:2) Spr-Sum 91, p. 83-85.
"The Plague of Painlessness." [Confr] (46/47) Fall 91-Wint 92, p. 259.
"The Plague of Sweetening." [Confr] (46/47) Fall 91-Wint 92, p. 259-260.
"Prodigy." [FreeL] (7) Spr 91, p. 4.
4091. MERRICK, Beverly G.
"Walk in Cornrow Rhythm." [SmPd] (28:2, #82) Spr 91, p. 37.

291

MERRICLE

4092. MERRICLE, William
"For Reasons Unexplained." [SlipS] (11) 91, p. 28.
"If the Truth Hurts, Wear It." [SlipS] (11) 91, p. 26-27.
4093. MERRILL, Christopher
"Coastlines" (Excerpt). [Journal] (15:2) Fall 91, p. 22.
"Luck" (Excerpt). [Colum] (15) 90, p. 213-215.
"Rosehips." [Colum] (16) Spr 91, p. 5.
"The Sirens" (In memory of Elizabeth Bishop and Carlos Drummond de Andrade).
[PraS] (65:1) Spr 91, p. 53-56.
"Slow Down Construction" (tr. of André Breton, René Char and Paul Éluard, w.
Jeanie Puleston Fleming). [AmerPoR] (20:3) My-Je 91, p. 25-30.
4094. MERRILL, James
"Snow Jobs." [NewYRB] (38:20) 5 D 91, p. 15.
4095. MERRITT, Constance
"Avant Garde." [Callaloo] (14:3) Sum 91, p. 689.
4096. MERTON, Vikki
"Voices." [PennR] (5:1) Spr 91, p. 25.
4097. MERWIN, W. S.
"After Douglas." [AmerPoR] (20:1) Ja-F 91, p. 21.
"The Age" (tr. of Osip Mandelstam, w. Clarence Brown). [Field] (45) Fall 91, p.
29-30.
"Black Earth" (tr. of Osip Mandelstam, w. Clarence Brown). [Field] (45) Fall 91, p.
35.
"Cover Note." [Atlantic] (267:3) Mr 91, p. 86.
"Fulfillment." [AmerPoR] (20:1) Ja-F 91, p. 26.
"Getting Around at Last." [AmerPoR] (20:1) Ja-F 91, p. 25.
"I was washing outside in the darkness" (tr. of Osip Mandelstam, w. Clarence
Brown). [Field] (45) Fall 91, p. 24.
"Inferno" (Canto XXVI-XXVII, tr. of Dante). [Antaeus] (67) Fall 91, p. 68-77.
"Left Open." [NewYorker] (67:29) 9 S 91, p. 30.
"Lives of the Artists." [AmerPoR] (20:1) Ja-F 91, p. 23-25.
"The Moment of Green." [AmerPoR] (20:1) Ja-F 91, p. 26-28.
"On the Back of the Boarding Pass." [NewYorker] (67:19) 1 Jl 91, p. 34.
"On the Old Way." [NewYorker] (67:1) 25 F 91, p. 62.
"Paul." [AmerPoR] (20:1) Ja-F 91, p. 25.
"A Short Nap on the Way." [AmerPoR] (20:1) Ja-F 91, p. 22.
"Stone Village." [NewYorker] (67:24) 5 Ag 91, p. 30.
"Take from my palms, to soothe your heart" (tr. of Osip Mandelstam, w. Clarence
Brown). [Field] (45) Fall 91, p. 8.
"Turning." [NewYorker] (67:32) 30 S 91, p. 68.
"We shall meet again, in Petersburg" (tr. of Osip Mandelstam, w. Clarence Brown).
[Field] (45) Fall 91, p. 16.
4098. MERZLAK, Regina
"Angel." [SpiritSH] (56) Spr-Sum 91, p. 31.
"Angel" (March 22, 1990). [SpiritSH] (56) Spr-Sum 91, p. 32.
"Apsaras (Buddhist Angels)" (For James Winfield). [SpiritSH] (56) Spr-Sum 91, p.
30.
4099. MESA, Lauren
"Great-Uncles." [SilverFR] (20) Spr 91, p. 16-17.
4100. MESMER, Sharon
"Beauty." [BrooklynR] (8) 91, p. 51.
"Cafe Ennui." [HangL] (59) 91, p. 41-43.
"Death." [BrooklynR] (8) 91, p. 51.
"Love." [BrooklynR] (8) 91, p. 51.
4101. MESSINA, Frank
"A Brief Holiday with the Jazz Heroine." [OxfordM] (7:2) Fall-Wint 91, p. 2.
"Father and Son in July." [OxfordM] (7:2) Fall-Wint 91, p. 3.
METER, Frankie van
See Van METER, Frankie
4102. METEYARD, Diane
"Let This Day Begin." [Blueline] (12) 91, p. 39.
4103. METRAS, Gary
"The Last Lighthouse." [ConnPR] (10:1) 91, p. 18.
4104. METZ, Robin
"The Pummeling" (for Jean). [Vis] (35) 91, p. 50-51.

4105. MEYER, David C.
"Diamond." [CapeR] (26:1) Spr 91, p. 47.
4106. MEYER, Doering S.
"Insight." [Sidewalks] (1) Aug 91, p. 11.
"Since We Slept Together." [RagMag] (9:2) 91, p. 61.
4107. MEYER, Thomas
"A Blood Relation." [Notus] (9) Fall 91, p. 62-65.
4108. MEYERS, Linda Curtis
"Her Alarm Clock." [BellR] (14:2) Fall 91, p. 34.
"A Night on the Moon." [CrabCR] (7:3) 91, p. 24.
"Swimming at Longboat Key" (for Elizabeth Bishop). [Kalliope] (13:3) 91, p. 11.
4109. MEYN, Barbara
"At the Planning Commission." [Spirit] (11) 91, p. 330-331.
4110. MEZEY, Marta
"Plaintive Song to the Members of My Generation" (tr. of Istvan Csukas, w. Len
Roberts). [TriQ] (81) Spr-Sum 91, p. 183-184.
4111. MEZEY, Robert
"Elegy" (tr. of Jorge Luis Borges). [Hudson] (44:3) Aut 91, p. 417-418.
"Elegy for the Impossible Memory" (tr. of Jorge Luis Borges). [Hudson] (44:3) Aut
91, p. 415-416.
"My Books" (tr. of Jorge Luis Borges). [Hudson] (44:3) Aut 91, p. 411.
"One of Lee's Soldiers (1962)" (tr. of Jorge Luis Borges). [Hudson] (44:3) Aut 91,
p. 414-415.
"Poem of the Gifts" (tr. of Jorge Luis Borges). [Hudson] (44:3) Aut 91, p. 410-411.
"Relics" (tr. of Jorge Luis Borges). [Hudson] (44:3) Aut 91, p. 417.
"Simón Carbajal" (tr. of Jorge Luis Borges). [Hudson] (44:3) Aut 91, p. 412.
"Temptation" (tr. of Jorge Luis Borges). [Hudson] (44:3) Aut 91, p. 413-414.
"To One No Longer Young" (tr. of Jorge Luis Borges). [Hudson] (44:3) Aut 91, p.
418.
"The White Hind" (tr. of Jorge Luis Borges). [Hudson] (44:3) Aut 91, p. 415.
4112. MIANAKOPOUCE, Thomas
"For My Father." [DogRR] (10:1) Sum 91, p. 34-35.
"A Slight Chill." [DogRR] (10:1) Sum 91, p. 34.
4113. MICHAELS, Anne
"A Lesson from the Earth." [MalR] (94) Spr 91, p. 39-45.
4114. MICHAUD, Michael Gregg
"January 22, 1990." [JamesWR] (8:4) Sum 91, p. 13.
4115. MICHEAELS, Cathleen
"Near the End of the Twentieth Century, Brighton Beach." [SwampR] (7/8)
Spr-Sum 91, p. 44.
4116. MICUS, Edward
"Crows." [Poetry] (158:2) My 91, p. 83.
4117. MIDDLETON, Christopher
"The Alhambra Inscription" (tr. of Ibn Zamrak, w. Leticia Garcia-Falcón). [ParisR]
(33:118) Spr 91, p. 24-25.
"Eggplant" (tr. of Ibn Sara, w. Leticia Garcia-Falcón). [ParisR] (33:118) Spr 91, p.
26.
"The Lily" (tr. of Ibn Darraj al-Qastalli, w. Leticia Garcia-Falcón). [ParisR] (33:118)
Spr 91, p. 26.
4118. MIDDLETON, David
"Emerson, at Belsen." [SewanR] (98:3) Sum 90, p. 503.
"The South" (for Andrew Lytle). [SewanR] (98:4) Fall 90, p. 615.
"The Vision" (for my maternal grandmother, d. 1962). [SewanR] (98:3) Sum 90, p.
331-332.
4119. MIELE, Frank
"Prayer for Tight Rein." [HeavenB] (9) Wint-Spr 91-92, p. 14.
"A Trucker Takes His Fill." [HeavenB] (9) Wint-Spr 91-92, p. 5.
4120. MIHAILOVICH, Vasa D.
"An Actor" (tr. of Novica Tadic). [InterPR] (15:1) Spr 89, p. 57.
"Again the Morning" (tr. of Slobodan Zubanovic). [InterPR] (15:1) Spr 89, p. 27.
"Bar 'Planik'" (tr. of Slobodan Zubanovic). [InterPR] (15:1) Spr 89, p. 19.
"A Blind Man" (tr. of Novica Tadic). [InterPR] (15:1) Spr 89, p. 57.
"But" (tr. of Zvonimir Kostic). [InterPR] (15:1) Spr 89, p. 65.
"The Butterfly" (tr. of Tiodor Rosic). [InterPR] (15:1) Spr 89, p. 79.
"The Cage" (tr. of Tiodor Rosic). [InterPR] (15:1) Spr 89, p. 71.
"The Crazy Landlord" (tr. of Novica Tadic). [InterPR] (15:1) Spr 89, p. 51.

"The Crazy Tenant" (tr. of Novica Tadic). [InterPR] (15:1) Spr 89, p. 53.
"Destruction" (tr. of Slobodan Zubanovic). [InterPR] (15:1) Spr 89, p. 19.
"Dice" (tr. of Novica Tadic). [InterPR] (15:1) Spr 89, p. 49.
"Exact Outcome" (tr. of Slobodan Zubanovic). [InterPR] (15:1) Spr 89, p. 23.
"The Exchange Office" (tr. of Miroslav Maksimovic). [InterPR] (15:1) Spr 89, p. 11.
"A Fairy Tale About the House" (tr. of Zvonimir Kostic). [InterPR] (15:1) Spr 89, p. 67.
"A Fig" (tr. of Tiodor Rosic). [InterPR] (15:1) Spr 89, p. 75.
"From a Terrible Fire an Escaped Flame" (tr. of Zvonimir Kostic). [InterPR] (15:1) Spr 89, p. 67.
"A Fur-Cap, Pigeons" (tr. of Novica Tadic). [InterPR] (15:1) Spr 89, p. 55.
"The Gardener" (tr. of Novica Tadic). [InterPR] (15:1) Spr 89, p. 49.
"The House in the Sky" (tr. of Stevan Tontic). [InterPR] (15:1) Spr 89, p. 35.
"I Travel, But I Have Not Seen the Absent Plain" (tr. of Miroslav Maksimovic). [InterPR] (15:1) Spr 89, p. 9.
"I Wake Up the Morning" (tr. of Dragomir Brajkovic). [InterPR] (15:1) Spr 89, p. 41.
"Icy Mountains, South Seas" (tr. of Dragomir Brajkovic). [InterPR] (15:1) Spr 89, p. 43, 45.
"In My Workshop" (tr. of Stevan Tontic). [InterPR] (15:1) Spr 89, p. 29.
"Inventing Happiness" (tr. of Miroslav Maksimovic). [InterPR] (15:1) Spr 89, p. 10.
"A Magpie" (tr. of Tiodor Rosic). [InterPR] (15:1) Spr 89, p. 73.
"Mushrooms" (tr. of Novica Tadic). [InterPR] (15:1) Spr 89, p. 55.
"News" (tr. of Stevan Tontic). [InterPR] (15:1) Spr 89, p. 31.
"The Spring in Teheran" (xii, tr. of Dragomir Brajkovic). [InterPR] (15:1) Spr 89, p. 45.
"The Spring Rain" (tr. of Miroslav Maksimovic). [InterPR] (15:1) Spr 89, p. 9.
"Tamburitza" (tr. of Tiodor Rosic). [InterPR] (15:1) Spr 89, p. 77.
"Trace" (tr. of Dragomir Brajkovic). [InterPR] (15:1) Spr 89, p. 39.
"A Visit with an Open Dialogue" (tr. of Slobodan Zubanovic). [InterPR] (15:1) Spr 89, p. 21.
"What Did I Speak" (tr. of Slobodan Zubanovic). [InterPR] (15:1) Spr 89, p. 25.
"When I Age Like the Finger on My Grandfather's Hand" (tr. of Zvonimir Kostic). [InterPR] (15:1) Spr 89, p. 69.

4121. MIHOPOULOS, Effie
"Stage Whispers." [Pembroke] (23) 91, p. 58.

4122. MIKITA, Nancy
"Profit Margins." [HampSPR] Wint 91, p. 38.

4123. MIKULEC, Patrick B.
"Outside the Ishi Wilderness." [HawaiiR] (15:3, #33) Fall 91, p. 35.
"Separations." [Paint] (18:36) Aut 91, p. 24.

4124. MIKUNI no MACHI
"Hold on a moment" (tr. by Sam Hamill). [ColR] (NS 17:2) Fall-Wint 90, p. 18.

4125. MILBURN, Michael
"Toothbrush Time." [Ploughs] (17:2/3) Fall 91, p. 75-76.

4126. MILBURN, Suzan
"Temporary Work in a Disabled Adult Workshop." [Grain] (19:3) Fall 91, p. 78-80.

4127. MILES, Judi Kiefer
"Hiding Place." [US1] (24/25) Spr 91, p. 5.
"The Pumpkin Man." [CapeR] (26:1) Spr 91, p. 14.

4128. MILES, Louis
"The Shaker Village at Sabbath-day Lake, Maine Summer, with Light Rising." [ChrC] (108:25) 4-11 S 91, p. 808.

4129. MILES, Ron
"Managing." [CanLit] (130) Aut 91, p. 68.

4130. MILES, Steve
"Faith as I Remember It." [ColR] (NS 18:2) Fall-Wint 91, p. 130-131.
"Magpie." [ColR] (NS 18:2) Fall-Wint 91, p. 129.

4131. MILEY, Jerry
"I am going to leave as winter's first leaf." [PoetryUSA] (22) Spr 91, p. 16.

4132. MILLER, Aíne
"Ever Such." [Interim] (10:1) Spr-Sum 91, p. 20-21.
"Seventeen." [Interim] (10:1) Spr-Sum 91, p. 19.
"Woman and Haystack" (— Marc Chagall). [Interim] (10:1) Spr-Sum 91, p. 21.

4133. MILLER, B. J.
"Fiber." [EmeraldCR] (3) 91, c1990, p. 52.
"The Path Is New." [EmeraldCR] (4) 91, p. 75-76.
"Song of October." [EmeraldCR] (3) 91, c1990, p. 58.
"Tycoon." [EmeraldCR] (3) 91, c1990, p. 118.
4134. MILLER, Carolyn Reynolds
"The Curved Lens of Forgetting." [MalR] (94) Spr 91, p. 26.
"The Last Rites of Love and Disconnection." [MalR] (94) Spr 91, p. 27-31.
4135. MILLER, Ceci
"Abandoning the Well-Remembered Year." [PoetL] (86:1) Spr 91, p. 25-26.
4136. MILLER, Charles
"Gramp." [NewL] (58:1) Fall 91, p. 107.
4137. MILLER, Chuck
"Dislocado." [WorldL] (1:1) 91, p. 11.
"Dusk in the Woods." [WorldL] (1:1) 91, p. 12-13.
"For Those Who Pray for the Souls of Broken Dolls." [WorldL] (1:1) 91, p. 10.
4138. MILLER, D. C.
"Speculation, Prompted by Emptiness and Regret." [MissR] (19:3) 91, p. 173.
4139. MILLER, Deborah
"Bed Time" (for Lisa). [Grain] (19:2) Sum 91, p. 74.
"Habit." [Dandel] (18:1) Spr-Sum 91, p. 24.
"Help." [Dandel] (18:1) Spr-Sum 91, p. 23.
"Linda Loveless What Is Your Name?" [Dandel] (18:1) Spr-Sum 91, p. 21-22.
4140. MILLER, Derek
"The Coast." [HangL] (58) 91, p. 52-53.
4141. MILLER, E. Ethelbert
"Departures & Arrivals." [WilliamMR] (29) 91, p. 35.
"Elizabeth Keckley: Thirty Years a Slave and Four Years in the White House."
[WashR] (16:5) F-Mr 91, p. 11.
4142. MILLER, Ed
"Aspects of a Small Town." [PacificR] (9) 91, p. 85.
4143. MILLER, Errol
"Another Masterpiece for Judith." [Quarry] (40:4) Fall 91, p. 78.
"As for Miracle-Wings." [RagMag] (9:2) 91, p. 34.
"The Bacteria of Poems." [DustyD] Je 91, p. 34.
"But Nothing Ever Happens." [Elf] (1:1) Spr 91, p. 33.
"Crossroads." [Plain] (12:2) Wint 91, p. 18.
"Dust to Dust." [Parting] (4:1) Sum 91, p. 3.
"For Bread Loaf." [SmPd] (28:2, #82) Spr 91, p. 35.
"For California and the World." [Lactuca] (14) My 91, p. 24-25.
"The Limitations Upon the Land." [Elf] (1:1) Spr 91, p. 34.
"The Maid" (for Sylvia Plath). [Northeast] (5:4) Sum 91, p. 8-9.
"On the Lives of the Poet." [DustyD] Je 91, p. 35.
"Outside the City." [Quarry] (40:4) Fall 91, p. 79.
"Passage into Southern Night." [Crucible] (27) Fall 91, p. 46-47.
"Repleting Towards Motiff." [DustyD] Je 91, p. 34.
"Slow Train." [Caliban] (10) 91, p. 29.
"Solitary Art." [Elf] (1:4) Wint 91, p. 36.
"Some Nothern Shores Are Calling." [WebR] (15) Spr 91, p. 88.
"There Is But One Dusk at the Burying Ground." [BlackBR] (14) Fall-Wint 91, p.
7.
"This Side of Chicago." [PaintedHR] (3) Sum 92, p. 20-21.
"Valedictory." [ChamLR] (8-9) Spr-Fall 91, p. 52.
"Whatever Things They Mean." [CoalC] (4) S 91, p. 7.
"When Winter Comes." [Lactuca] (14) My 91, p. 23-24.
"Woodland Patterns." [Elf] (1:4) Wint 91, p. 37-38.
"The Writers Ancestral Sense of Place." [DustyD] Je 91, p. 36.
"The Writer's Carousel." [DustyD] Je 91, p. 37.
MILLER, Erroll
See MILLER, Errol
4144. MILLER, Heather Ross
"The Care and Feeding of Infants." [SouthernR] (27:1) Ja 91, p. 47-48.
"Cloudless Sulfur, Swallowtail, Great Spangled Fritillary." [SouthernR] (27:1) Ja
91, p. 46-47.
"Hiking the Narrows." [Shen] (41:4) Wint 91, p. 56-57.
"Inventory." [CharR] (17:1) Spr 91, p. 114.

295

MILLER

4145. MILLER, Hugh
    "Satori at 'The Cedars'" (for William (Red Pine) Porter). [AntigR] (85/86) Spr-Sum
        91, p. 190-191.
    "*Weltanschauungen* from the Foothills of the Sierra" (Ethnoherpetological Politics,
        for Gregory Warren Ramirez). [AntigR] (84) Wint 91, p. 144. Reprinted in
        [AntigR] (85/86) Spr-Sum 91, p. 189.
4146. MILLER, Jane
    "The General's Briefing." [Ploughs] (17:4) Wint 91-92, p. 114-116.
4147. MILLER, John N.
    "Breaking and Entering." [Journal] (15:1) Spr 91, p. 59.
    "Saving the Whales." [CharR] (17:1) Spr 91, p. 113.
4148. MILLER, Leslie Adrienne
    "Bliss." [NewEngR] (13:3/4) Spr-Sum 91, p. 220-221.
    "The Driving Range." [ThRiPo] (37/38) 91, p. 83-84.
    "Family Portrait, Florida." [TampaR] (4) 91, p. 74-75.
    "Holy Water." [Ploughs] (17:2/3) Fall 91, p. 49-50.
    "The Romantics." [NewEngR] (13:3/4) Spr-Sum 91, p. 221-222.
    "A Shooting." [TampaR] (4) 91, p. 76-77.
    "The Substitute." [ThRiPo] (37/38) 91, p. 81-82.
4149. MILLER, Matthew W.
    "Him." [Plain] (12:1) Fall 91, p. 36.
4150. MILLER, Melissa C.
    "The Mamo." [ChamLR] (8-9) Spr-Fall 91, p. 14.
4151. MILLER, Pamela
    "After Five Years, Linda Finally Gives Up on Trying to Get Charles to Leave His
        Wife for Her." [Prima] (14/15) 91, p. 77.
    "Instructions to an Avant-Garde Musician" (For Brian Eno). [FreeL] (8) Aut 91, p.
        32.
    "Living at the Movies." [Prima] (14/15) 91, p. 78-81.
    "Lullaby" (For Rich and the guys). [Prima] (14/15) 91, p. 76.
    "The Next Time." [FreeL] (8) Aut 91, p. 30-31.
4152. MILLER, Philip
    "Inertia." [Plain] (11:3) Spr 91, p. 17.
    "Keys." [Poem] (66) N 91, p. 6-7.
    "Like a Book." [Poem] (66) N 91, p. 5.
    "Our Positions Redefined." [Poem] (66) N 91, p. 8.
    "What Can They Say?" [PoetL] (86:4) Wint 91-92, p. 27-28.
4153. MILLER, Richard
    "Remembering Rimbaud" (For Charles Bukowski). [ChironR] (10:3) Aut 91, p. 41.
4154. MILLER, Roberta Balstad
    "Happiness" (tr. of Jorge Luis Borges). [PoetL] (86:3) Fall 91, p. 49.
4155. MILLER, Theresa W.
    "Baby Needs New Shoes." [GreensboroR] (50) Sum 91, p. 89-90.
    "There Is Wonderment in Watermelon." [GreensboroR] (50) Sum 91, p. 91.
4156. MILLER, Timothy
    "On Columbus Day." [Hellas] (2:2) Fall 91, p. 239-240.
4157. MILLER, Tyrus
    "Mimed." [Aerial] (6/7) 91, p. 60.
4158. MILLER, William
    "The Distressed Poet" (after Hogarth). [Poem] (66) N 91, p. 69.
    "For Diane Arbus." [Poem] (66) N 91, p. 72.
    "For Edvard Munch." [Poem] (66) N 91, p. 70.
    "Isis Remembered." [Poem] (66) N 91, p. 68.
    "Leopard Boy." [TampaR] (4) 91, p. 33.
    "Old Buildings." [Poem] (66) N 91, p. 71.
4159. MILLER-DUGGAN, Devon
    "First Fortepiano Sonnet" (tr. of Innokenty Annensky, w. Nancy Tittler).
        [SpoonRQ] (16:3/4) Sum-Fall 91, p. 41.
    "The Second Fortepiano Sonnet" (tr. of Innokenty Annensky, w. Nancy Tittler).
        [SpoonRQ] (16:3/4) Sum-Fall 91, p. 42.
MILLER LAINO, E. J.
    See LAINO, E. J. Miller
4160. MILLETT, John
    "Deep Song for Lydia Callaghan Dying." [Vis] (35) 91, p. 39.
4161. MILLIGAN, Paula
    "Before Science Were Light and Sound." [BellArk] (7:4) Jl-Ag 91, p. 24.

"Dare." [BellArk] (7:6) N-D 91, p. 5.
"The Eloquence of What Will Remain." [BellArk] (7:5) S-O 91, p. 12.
"Learning the Imperfect Tense." [BellArk] (7:5) S-O 91, p. 1.
"Panama Village Revisited." [BellArk] (7:5) S-O 91, p. 12.
4162. MILLIS, Christopher
"Feet." [ConnPR] (10:1) 91, p. 37.
"Lot's Wife" (for Karen). [ConnPR] (10:1) 91, p. 38.
"Winter" (tr. of Umberto Saba). [ColR] (NS 17:2) Fall-Wint 90, p. 105.
4163. MILLMAN, Lawrence
"Nightmare of the Unknown Soldier" (tr. of William Heinesen). [Vis] (37) 91, p. 17.
4164. MILLS, Billy
"Basalt." [NewAW] (8/9) Fall 91, p. 110.
"Emerald." [NewAW] (8/9) Fall 91, p. 112-113.
"Flint" (for Catherine). [NewAW] (8/9) Fall 91, p. 113.
"Quartz." [NewAW] (8/9) Fall 91, p. 111.
4165. MILLS, George
"Hello." [BostonR] (16:3/4) Je-Ag 91, p. 22.
"In the Box Car." [BostonR] (16:3/4) Je-Ag 91, p. 22.
"Lincoln." [BostonR] (16:3/4) Je-Ag 91, p. 22.
"My Hometown." [BostonR] (16:3/4) Je-Ag 91, p. 22.
"Rapture of the Depths." [BostonR] (16:3/4) Je-Ag 91, p. 22.
4166. MILLS, J. I.
"Light." [Vis] (35) 91, p. 30.
4167. MILLS, Laurel
"Biking with Beth." [Plain] (11:3) Spr 91, p. 26.
"The Cast-Iron Pot." [RagMag] (9:2) 91, p. 66.
"Daughters Need Their Mothers." [RagMag] (9:2) 91, p. 64-65.
"Waiting for Beth's Surgery." [Plain] (11:2) Wint 91, p. 33.
4168. MILLS, Ralph J., Jr.
"2/25." [NorthStoneR] (10) Fall 91-Wint 92, p. 171.
"10/29." [NorthStoneR] (10) Fall 91-Wint 92, p. 169.
"A Day Rain." [Northeast] (5:4) Sum 91, p. 15.
"Seemingly / Tangled." [NorthStoneR] (10) Fall 91-Wint 92, p. 170.
"Unexpectedly, / Clouds." [NorthStoneR] (10) Fall 91-Wint 92, p. 167.
"Whatever / Air." [NorthStoneR] (10) Fall 91-Wint 92, p. 168.
4169. MILLS, Robert
"Baseball at Summer's End." [Nimrod] (34:2) Spr-Sum 91, p. 78.
4170. MILLS, Ron
"The Happy Mistakes." [RiverC] (11:2) Spr 91, p. 64-65.
4171. MILLS, Wilmer Hastings
"Crossings." [LullwaterR] (3:1) Fall 91, p. 70-71.
"Insomnia in a Strange House." [LullwaterR] (2:2) Spr 91, p. 10.
"The Iron Bed." [LullwaterR] (2:2) Spr 91, p. 74-75.
4172. MILNER, Ian
"Circus" (tr. of Jana Stroblová, w. Jarmila Milner). [HampSPR] Wint 91, p. 65.
"The Slaughterhouse" (tr. of Jana Stroblová, w. Jarmila Milner). [HampSPR] Wint 91, p. 66.
4173. MILNER, Jarmila
"Circus" (tr. of Jana Stroblová, w. Ian Milner). [HampSPR] Wint 91, p. 65.
"The Slaughterhouse" (tr. of Jana Stroblová, w. Ian Milner). [HampSPR] Wint 91, p. 66.
4174. MILOSZ, Czeslaw
"Dictionary of Wilno Streets (1967)" (from "Beginning with My Streets," tr. by the author, Robert Hass, Robert Pinsky and Renata Gorczynski). [ParisR] (33:120) Fall 91, p. 261-263.
"Far Away" (tr. by the author and Robert Hass). [PartR] (58:4) Fall 91, p. 677-680.
"In Music" (tr. by the author and Robert Hass). [NewYorker] (67:3) 11 Mr 91, p. 66.
"Lastingness" (tr. by the author and Robert Hass). [Thrpny] (47) Fall 91, p. 27.
"Mister Hanusevich" (tr. by the author and Robert Hass). [NewYorker] (67:34) 14 O 91, p. 62-63.
"A New Province" (tr. by the author and Robert Hass). [Antaeus] (67) Fall 91, p. 100-103.
"On a Beach" (tr. by the author and Robert Hass). [NewYorker] (67:20) 8 Jl 91, p. 34.

"Philology" (tr. w. Robert Hass). [Zyzzyva] (7:3) Fall 91, p. 134-135.
"Reconciliation" (tr. by the author and Robert Hass). [NewYorker] (66:52) 11 F 91,
    p. 34.
"To Robinson Jeffers" (tr. by Richard Lourie and the author). [Spirit] (11) 91, p.
    232-233.
"Youth" (tr. by the author and Robert Hass). [NewYorker] (67:29) 9 S 91, p. 34.
4175. MILTON, John R.
"The Non-Logic of Summer Grass." [SoDakR] (29:3 part 2) Aut 91, p. 7.
4176. MINCZESKI, John
"Thumb." [Sidewalks] (1) Aug 91, p. 26.
"Water Striders." [Farm] (8:1) Spr-Sum 91, p. 34.
4177. MINDOCK, Gloria
"Barrier." [ContextS] (2:1) 91, p. 18.
"Cut." [ContextS] (2:2) 91, p. 7.
4178. MINET, Lawrence
"Sorrow Found in Unexpected Places." [Poem] (65) My 91, p. 29.
4179. MINETT, Amy (Amy J.)
"Evening in Ireland, 1985." [PoetryE] (32) Fall 91, p. 90.
"For Thomas." [PoetryE] (32) Fall 91, p. 91.
"The Immigrant." [PoetryE] (32) Fall 91, p. 89.
"Sonnet for the Widows of Niagara Street." [PoetryNW] (32:1) Spr 91, p. 26.
4180. MINTON, Helena
"Lessons" (1961). [PoetL] (86:1) Spr 91, p. 18.
"Visit." [PoetL] (86:1) Spr 91, p. 17.
4181. MINTZ, Florinda
"Instrument for Branding" (tr. of Daphne Marlatt). [OnTheBus] (8/9) 91, p. 216.
"A Mark" (tr. of Daphne Marlatt). [OnTheBus] (8/9) 91, p. 216.
"Pointed Stake" (tr. of Daphne Marlatt). [OnTheBus] (8/9) 91, p. 217.
4182. MINTZER, Elaine
"Surgical Strike." [OnTheBus] (8/9) 91, p. 108-109.
4183. MINUS, Ed
"At David's Farm." [Vis] (36) 91, p. 12.
4184. MIRRIAM-GOLDBERG, Caryn
"Aborigine on the Phone" (First Prize, Cincinnati Poetry Review Competition).
    [CinPR] (22) Spr 91, p. 11.
"Fishing." [MinnR] (NS 37) Fall 91, p. 36-37.
"In What Do You Put Your Faith?" [BelPoJ] (42:1) Fall 91, p. 35.
"Jonah and the Whale" (First Prize, Cincinnati Poetry Review Competition).
    [CinPR] (22) Spr 91, p. 8-10.
"Lullaby." [BelPoJ] (42:1) Fall 91, p. 34.
"News." [RiverC] (11:2) Spr 91, p. 27.
"Rapunzel in the Desert" (First Prize, Cincinnati Poetry Review Competition).
    [CinPR] (22) Spr 91, p. 7.
"Telling My Son About His Birth." [MinnR] (NS 37) Fall 91, p. 37-38.
"Train." [MinnR] (NS 37) Fall 91, p. 38.
"Walking the Dog." [RiverC] (11:2) Spr 91, p. 24-26.
4185. MISHKIN, Julia
"Maurice Ravel at the Piano." [AntR] (49:1) Wint 91, p. 100-101.
4186. MISIC, Jasna
"I Have No More Time" (tr. of Desanka Maksimovic, w. Richard Burns). [NewOR]
    (18:2) Sum 91, p. 66.
4187. MISTRAL, Gabriela
"Softnesses" (tr. by Michael L. Johnson). [ArtfulD] (20/21) 91, p. 62.
4188. MITCHAM, Judson
"Homage." [NewEngR] (13:3/4) Spr-Sum 91, p. 132-133.
"Last Words." [NewEngR] (13:3/4) Spr-Sum 91, p. 134.
"Nature." [GeoR] (45:2) Sum 91, p. 246-248.
"Writing." [NewEngR] (13:3/4) Spr-Sum 91, p. 133-134.
4189. MITCHELL, Adrian
"Douglas." [Stand] (33:1) Wint 91, p. 14.
4190. MITCHELL, John
"Brute Fandango." [NorthStoneR] (10) Fall 91-Wint 92, p. 232.
"Clouds at 50." [NorthStoneR] (10) Fall 91-Wint 92, p. 232.
"Sometimes I Think." [NorthStoneR] (10) Fall 91-Wint 92, p. 231.
4191. MITCHELL, Karen
"Country After Country." [Callaloo] (14:2) Spr 91, p. 336-337.

MITCHELL

  "Forgiveness." [Callaloo] (14:2) Spr 91, p. 339.
  "Frugal." [Callaloo] (14:2) Spr 91, p. 338.
4192. MITCHELL, Roger
  "Aunt Em." [SpoonRQ] (16:1/2) Wint-Spr 91, p. 9-10.
  "Between." [OhioR] (47) 91, p. 71.
  "Endangered Species." [PoetryNW] (32:3) Aut 91, p. 5-6.
  "Glacial Melt." [PoetryNW] (32:3) Aut 91, p. 6-8.
  "Looking at Recent Pictures of Ourselves." [SpoonRQ] (16:1/2) Wint-Spr 91, p. 11.
  "Music I Knew." [SpoonRQ] (16:1/2) Wint-Spr 91, p. 7-8.
  "Rather Than Crow." [NewAW] (8/9) Fall 91, p. 52.
  "The Water Poem." [SpoonRQ] (16:1/2) Wint-Spr 91, p. 6.
4193. MITCHELL, Stephen
  "Endlessly I gaze at you in wonder, blessed ones, at your composure" (tr. of Rainer
    Maria Rilke). [Talisman] (6) Spr 91, p. 103.
  "Haiku" (tr. of Rainer Maria Rilke). [Talisman] (6) Spr 91, p. 103.
  "Startle me, Music, with rhythmical fury!" (tr. of Rainer Maria Rilke). [Talisman] (6)
    Spr 91, p. 103.
4194. MITKOV, Roumen
  "Perhaps" (tr. of Georgi Belev, w. Ron Butlin). [Verse] (8:2) Sum 91, p. 117.
4195. MITTON, Jennifer
  "With a Mother in Such Pain." [MalR] (97) Wint 91, p. 28-51.
MIYOKO, Sugano
  See SUGANO, Miyoko
4196. MIZER, Ray
  "Ars Longa, Vita Brevis." [SmPd] (28:3, #83) Fall 91, p. 22.
  "Cairn." [InterPR] (17:1) Spr 91, p. 98.
  "The Halls of I.V." [InterPR] (17:1) Spr 91, p. 99.
  "Old Prayer (Revised Version)." [Pearl] (14) Fall-Wint 91, p. 62.
  "Spoon River Revisited." [BellArk] (7:4) Jl-Ag 91, p. 4-6.
4197. MNOOKIN, Wendy (Wendy M.)
  "Carefully." [OxfordM] (7:2) Fall-Wint 91, p. 5.
  "Country Music Blues." [BelPoJ] (41:4) Sum 91, p. 11.
  "Not Me." [CimR] (97) O 91, p. 58-59.
  "Seductions." [PassN] (12:2) Wint 91, p. 9.
  "Seeing in the Dark." [OxfordM] (7:2) Fall-Wint 91, p. 4.
  "Summer Camp." [OxfordM] (7:2) Fall-Wint 91, p. 6-7.
4198. MOBILIO, Albert
  "Arrival." [BrooklynR] (8) 91, p. 15.
4199. MOCARSKI, Tim
  "Comiskey Memory." [ChironR] (10:2) Sum 91, p. 44.
  "First Bike Ride." [ChironR] (10:4) Wint 91, p. 38.
4200. MOCK, Jeff
  "The Body of Losses and Lives" (3 August — for my mother). [BelPoJ] (41:3) Spr
    91, p. 23-27.
  "The Difficulty of Walking Through Walls." [HawaiiR] (15:3, #33) Fall 91, p.
    133-135.
  "Epithalamium for Colleen and Tim." [PoetryNW] (32:2) Sum 91, p. 32-33.
  "Out-of-Body Wandering." [DenQ] (26:1) Sum 91, p. 51-52.
  "Season of an Almost-Child, Almost Thirteen Years Old." [PoetryNW] (32:2) Sum
    91, p. 33.
4201. MOE, Frederick
  "Circulation." [CoalC] (4) S 91, p. 3.
  "The Pigeon Dilemma." [CoalC] (3) My 91, p. 18.
4202. MOE, H. D.
  "Ideas." [RedBass] (15) 91, p. 15.
  "Quit That Monkey Business Upstairs" (Elegy for Gary Johnston). [RedBass] (15)
    91, p. 14.
4203. MOE, Rita
  "In a Field in Joplin, Missouri." [SingHM] (19) 91, p. 3-4.
  "Nightblind." [RagMag] (9:2) 91, p. 71.
  "Wintergreen." [Sidewalks] (1) Aug 91, p. 16-17.
4204. MOEN, Irvin
  "Earth." [CrabCR] (7:3) 91, p. 14.
4205. MOFFEIT, Tony
  "Billy the Kid" ("Garrett said he mostly wore black"). [ChironR] (10:3) Aut 91, p.
    8.

"Billy the Kid" ("His gunhand his grin his will to never back down"). [ChironR] (10:3) Aut 91, p. 8.
"Gypsy Night." [ChironR] (10:3) Aut 91, p. 8.
"The Kid." [ChironR] (10:3) Aut 91, p. 8.
"Knives of Lightning." [ChironR] (10:3) Aut 91, p. 8.
"The Night Singing in Her Nerves." [ChironR] (10:3) Aut 91, p. 8.

4206. MOFFET, Penelope
"Descending Squaw Mountain" (for Meryl Natchez). [PaintedHR] (2) Spr 91, p. 28.

4207. MOFFETT, Judith
"Sympathy Card, One Year Later" (For Ronna). [Poetry] (158:1) Ap 91, p. 40.

4208. MOFFI, Larry
"Late Weeding." [PoetL] (86:3) Fall 91, p. 28.
"Yahrzeit." [Spirit] (11) 91, p. 251-252.

4209. MOHLER, Kathryn
"Getting Away." [MalR] (94) Spr 91, p. 81-82.

4210. MOIR, James M.
"Loneliness the Sharpshooter Waits." [Dandel] (18:1) Spr-Sum 91, p. 29.

4211. MOIRAI, Catherine Risingflame
"Taking Back My Night." [SinW] (43/44) Sum 91, p. 171-175.

MOK-WOL, Park
See PARK, Mok-Wol

4212. MOLDAW, Carol
"The Nest." [Agni] (33) 91, p. 64-66.
"The Window Box." [Agni] (33) 91, p. 62-63.

MOLEN, Robert vander
See VanderMOLEN, Robert

4213. MOLLENKOTT, Virginia Ramey
"Winter Solstice." [ChrC] (108:37) 18-25 D 91, p. 1197.

4214. MONACO, Cory
"Acted Like Curly." [WormR] (31:4, #124) 91, p. 133.
"& Vice Versa." [WormR] (31:4, #124) 91, p. 132.
"The Antichristmobile." [WormR] (31:4, #124) 91, p. 133.
"Makes Me Even More Jealous of My Time." [WormR] (31:4, #124) 91, p. 132.
"N.Y.C. Earthquake (1985)." [WormR] (31:4, #124) 91, p. 132.
"Notes from the Anti-Intellectual Revolution." [WormR] (31:4, #124) 91, p. 132.
"Now, You Can Set S. Vodka." [WormR] (31:4, #124) 91, p. 133.
"Our Parents Didn't Quite Get It." [WormR] (31:4, #124) 91, p. 132.
"The Patriot." [WormR] (31:4, #124) 91, p. 132.
"Searching for Insights into Sado-Masochistic Sex." [WormR] (31:4, #124) 91, p. 134.
"Uneducated Working Class." [WormR] (31:4, #124) 91, p. 132.

4215. MONAGHAN, Timothy
"After Hours." [CapeR] (26:1) Spr 91, p. 41.

4216. MONETTE, Paul
"Ed Dying." [Tribe] (1:2) Spr 90, p. 7-9.

4217. MONK, Aviva
"The Latest Rage." [WillowR] Spr 91, p. 5-6.
"Transparent As Wind." [WillowR] Spr 91, p. 6.

4218. MONK, Geraldine
"AC." [NewAW] (8/9) Fall 91, p. 116-117.
"AS." [NewAW] (8/9) Fall 91, p. 116.
"An Elegy in an Unmarked Southern County Pub." [NewAW] (8/9) Fall 91, p. 115.
"South Bound : Facing North." [NewAW] (8/9) Fall 91, p. 114.

4219. MONROE, Melissa
"The Bat" (tr. of Ernest Herbeck). [OnTheBus] (8/9) 91, p. 204.
"The Moon" (tr. of Ernest Herbeck). [OnTheBus] (8/9) 91, p. 205.
"The Snake" (tr. of Ernest Herbeck). [OnTheBus] (8/9) 91, p. 205.
"Spring" (tr. of Ernest Herbeck). [OnTheBus] (8/9) 91, p. 204-205.

4220. MONSOUR, Leslie
"An Atmosphere of Heat." [ChironR] (10:4) Wint 91, p. 38.
"The Hammock Ride." [Hellas] (2:2) Fall 91, p. 242.
"Looking for Alligators." [Hellas] (2:2) Fall 91, p. 241.

4221. MONTAGUE, Aubrey
"The American Troops." [ChironR] (10:1) Spr 91, p. 24.

4222. MONTAGUE, John
"Time in Armagh." [Ploughs] (17:1) Spr 91, p. 108-110.

4223. MONTALE, Eugenio
"A Ritroso." [Ploughs] (17:1) Spr 91, p. 12.
"Arremba." [InterPR] (17:1) Spr 91, p. 55, 57.
"At the Threshold" (tr. by Antony Oldknow). [InterPR] (17:1) Spr 91, p. 47.
"Backwards" (tr. by William Arrowsmith). [Ploughs] (17:1) Spr 91, p. 12-13.
"Debole Sistro." [InterPR] (17:1) Spr 91, p. 55.
"Easter Evening" (tr. by William Arrowsmith). [Ploughs] (17:1) Spr 91, p. 15.
"L'Educazione Intellettuale." [Ploughs] (17:1) Spr 91, p. 8-9.
"Epigram" (tr. by Antony Oldknow). [InterPR] (17:1) Spr 91, p. 47.
"Epigramma" (from "Ossi di Seppia," 1927). [InterPR] (17:1) Spr 91, p. 46.
"Felicita Raggiunta." [InterPR] (17:1) Spr 91, p. 53.
"Having Reached a Point of Happiness" (tr. by Antony Oldknow). [InterPR] (17:1)
        Spr 91, p. 54.
"In Limine." [InterPR] (17:1) Spr 91, p. 46.
"Intellectual Education" (tr. by William Arrowsmith). [Ploughs] (17:1) Spr 91, p.
        9-10.
"Literary Histories." (tr. by William Arrowsmith). [Ploughs] (17:1) Spr 91, p. 14.
"Motets, Number 13" (tr. by Cynthia Gabrielli). [SycamoreR] (3:1) Wint 91, p. 45.
"Motets, Number 15" (tr. by Cynthia Gabrielli). [SycamoreR] (3:1) Wint 91, p. 47.
"I Mottetti, 13." [SycamoreR] (3:1) Wint 91, p. 44.
"I Mottetti, 15." [SycamoreR] (3:1) Wint 91, p. 46.
"Once" (tr. by William Arrowsmith). [Ploughs] (17:1) Spr 91, p. 11-12.
"A Poet" (tr. by William Arrowsmith). [Ploughs] (17:1) Spr 91, p. 13.
"Un Poeta." [Ploughs] (17:1) Spr 91, p. 13.
"Portovenere." [InterPR] (17:1) Spr 91, p. 53.
"Portovenere" (tr. by Antony Oldknow). [InterPR] (17:1) Spr 91, p. 54.
"Sarcofaghi I-IV." [InterPR] (17:1) Spr 91, p. 48-52.
"Sarcophagi I-IV" (tr. by Antony Oldknow). [InterPR] (17:1) Spr 91, p. 49-52.
"Sera di Pasqua." [Ploughs] (17:1) Spr 91, p. 14-15.
"Ship-Owner" (tr. by Antony Oldknow). [InterPR] (17:1) Spr 91, p. 56-57.
"Sistrum" (tr. by Antony Oldknow). [InterPR] (17:1) Spr 91, p. 56.
"Le Storie Letterarie." [Ploughs] (17:1) Spr 91, p. 13-14.
"Un Tempo." [Ploughs] (17:1) Spr 91, p. 10-11.
"Valmorbia." [InterPR] (17:1) Spr 91, p. 53, 55.
"Valmorbia" (tr. by Antony Oldknow). [InterPR] (17:1) Spr 91, p. 54, 56.
"Xenia I" (tr. by William Arrowsmith). [Agni] (34) 91, p. 277-290.
4224. MONTALVO, Berta G.
"Ana Rosa Núñez está" (Imitando a J.R.J.). [Nuez] (3:8/9) 91, p. 21.
4225. MONTEJO, Eugenio
"Lo Nuestro." [Inti] (34/35) Otoño 91-Primavera 92, p. 270.
"Pasaporte de Otoño." [Inti] (34/35) Otoño 91-Primavera 92, p. 269.
"Tiempo Transfigurado" (a António Ramos Rosa). [Inti] (34/35) Otoño
        91-Primavera 92, p. 271.
4226. MONTENEGRO DIAZ, Pablo
"Los Cisnes Plateados (II)." [Nuez] (3:8/9) 91, p. 40.
"Los Cisnes Plateados (IV)." [Nuez] (3:8/9) 91, p. 40.
4227. MONTGOMERY, M. S.
"I. Apologia pro Coniugio Suo." [ChangingM] (22) Wint-Spr 91, p. 32.
"II. Apologia pro Amoris Suis." [ChangingM] (22) Wint-Spr 91, p. 32.
4228. MONTGOMERY, Nan
"At Suppertime." [RagMag] (9:2) 91, p. 55.
"Common Blue." [RagMag] (9:2) 91, p. 56-57.
"The Hopi Potter Nampeyo." [RagMag] (9:2) 91, p. 54.
4229. MOODIE, Susanna
"The Nameless Grave" (Written in Cove Church-Yard, and Occasioned by
        Observing My Own Shadow Thrown Across a Grave). [CanLit] (130) Aut 91,
        p. 12.
4230. MOODY, Rodger
"Untitled: I can't erase Interstate 80 from memory." [Caliban] (10) 91, p. 91.
4231. MOOERS, Vernon
"Down in Point May." [TickleAce] (21) Spr-Sum 91, p. 16.
"Satter's Scrapyard." [TickleAce] (21) Spr-Sum 91, p. 15.
4232. MOOLTEN, David
"Balance of Power." [Shen] (41:4) Wint 91, p. 108-109.
"Brandy Station, Virginia." [Shen] (41:4) Wint 91, p. 111.
"Flying." [Shen] (41:4) Wint 91, p. 109-110.

4233. MOONEY, Kathleen Guedry
"A Lesson Learned." [EmeraldCR] (3) 91, c1990, p. 50.
4234. MOORE, Barbara
"Setting Forth." [PoetL] (86:3) Fall 91, p. 24.
4235. MOORE, Berwyn J.
"What I Want to Tell You." [NegC] (11:3) 91, p. 28-30.
4236. MOORE, Carolyn
"Searching Tucson for Words to Say Goodbye." [LouisL] (8:1) Spr 91, p. 44-46.
4237. MOORE, Frank D.
"The Hard Bright Images of Your Passing." [LitR] (35:1) Fall 91, p. 84.
4238. MOORE, Gary
"Beijing Sing, 1991." [GreenMR] (NS 5:1) Sum-Fall 91, p. 30.
4239. MOORE, Honor
"New Haven, 1969." [Colum] (15) 90, p. 66-69.
"Sleeping Gypsy." [Ploughs] (17:4) Wint 91-92, p. 76-77.
4240. MOORE, Jacqueline
"Chasing the Dog Star." [PennR] (5:1) Spr 91, p. 24.
4241. MOORE, Lenard D.
"After desert sortie." [BlackBR] (14) Fall-Wint 91, p. 36.
"A Bluesman's Blues." [Callaloo] (14:4) Fall 91, p. 925.
"Cicada-shrilled-heat." [BlackBR] (14) Fall-Wint 91, p. 19.
"Dusty sunrise." [BlackBR] (14) Fall-Wint 91, p. 36.
"Mountain hunter." [BlackBR] (14) Fall-Wint 91, p. 19.
"Nightfall." [BlackBR] (14) Fall-Wint 91, p. 36.
"Speaking of the Spirit" (for Fred Chappell). [Pembroke] (23) 91, p. 90.
"Starless dark." [BlackBR] (14) Fall-Wint 91, p. 19.
"Why Grandpa Speaks with Dignity." [Obs] (6:1) Spr 91, p. 40-41.
4242. MOORE, Mack
"Every Mother's Son." [ChironR] (10:1) Spr 91, p. 20.
4243. MOORE, Madeline Carole
"The Boy Next Door." [Pearl] (14) Fall-Wint 91, p. 53.
4244. MOORE, Rachel
"The Surgery." [HawaiiR] (16:1, #34) Wint 91-92, p. 89.
"Wet Spot." [HawaiiR] (16:1, #34) Wint 91-92, p. 90.
4245. MOORE, Richard
"Bird in a Cage." [AntigR] (85/86) Spr-Sum 91, p. 170.
"A Consummation." [PoetC] (22:3) Spr 91, p. 38.
"The Dangerous Corner." [PoetryE] (31) Spr 91, p. 48.
"Distraction on the Platform." [NegC] (11:1) 91, p. 108.
"The Drowned Girl" (tr. of Bertolt Brecht). [AmerPoR] (20:2) Mr-Ap 91, p. 9.
"Excess Vitality" (Whose wiggling toe? It's the poet's). [NegC] (11:1) 91, p. 109.
"Golfballs." [Hellas] (2:2) Fall 91, p. 243.
"The Heap." [Salm] (92) Fall 91, p. 193-194.
"Last Day." [AntigR] (85/86) Spr-Sum 91, p. 173.
"Memories of Marie" (tr. of Bertolt Brecht). [AmerPoR] (20:2) Mr-Ap 91, p. 9.
"Old Fools" (Selection: Part III. For Knick: A Festschrift). [Agni] (34) 91, p.
    232-235.
"Planets." [CumbPR] (10:2) Spr 91, p. 31.
"Rings." [AntigR] (85/86) Spr-Sum 91, p. 171.
"Snaps." [AntigR] (85/86) Spr-Sum 91, p. 172.
"Swallows." [PoetryE] (31) Spr 91, p. 49.
"The Veil." [Hellas] (2:2) Fall 91, p. 244.
4246. MOORE, Richard C.
"Past Memory — Please Don't Serve — I'm Full." [Pearl] (13) Spr-Sum 91, p. 39.
4247. MOORE, Richard O.
"Whale Watching." [PoetryUSA] (23) Sum 91, p. 9.
"Who." [PoetryUSA] (23) Sum 91, p. 9.
4248. MOORE, Rob Mitchell
"Somoza Watching the Statue of Somoza in Somoza Stadium" (tr. of Ernesto
    Cardenal). [MidAR] (12:1) 91, p. 160.
4249. MOORE, Todd
"Blowing up Phil's." [ChironR] (10:3) Aut 91, p. 9.
"Brenda Dreams." [ChironR] (10:3) Aut 91, p. 9.
"Burning My Name" (Chapbook: 19 poems). [Bogg] (64) 91, p. 23-42.
"Every." [ChironR] (10:3) Aut 91, p. 9.
"The Girl Coming." [ChironR] (10:3) Aut 91, p. 9.

"Took a." [ChironR] (10:3) Aut 91, p. 9.
"When His Mother." [ChironR] (10:3) Aut 91, p. 9.

4250. MOORE, Wendy
"Spring Daydream" (Short Grain Contest Winners: Prose Poem Winners:
    Honourable Mention). [Grain] (19:4) Wint 91, p. 79.

4251. MOORHEAD, Andrea
"As Aachen Burns." [Abraxas] (40/41) 91, p. 118.
"At the Pond's Edge" (tr. of Robert Marteau). [Paint] (18:36) Aut 91, p. 58.
"Erie in a Trance of Light." [Abraxas] (40/41) 91, p. 119.
"A Field of Chicory." [Os] (32) Spr 91, p. 22.
"Fire Where Peach Blooms." [Abraxas] (40/41) 91, p. 118.
"Hands Cannot Hold This Light." [Os] (32) Spr 91, p. 14.
"The Heart Has Slept in Thunder." [Os] (33) Fall 91, p. 24-27.
"I'll Take You There When Spring Returns." [Os] (33) Fall 91, p. 22-23.
"Lilac Blooms." [Sequoia] (34:1) Spr 91, p. 100.
"Niagara in My Blood As a Gold Light." [Os] (32) Spr 91, p. 15.
"Paris III." [ManhatPR] (13) [91?], p. 29.
"Paris IV." [ManhatPR] (13) [91?], p. 29.
"Paris Sparkles" (tr. of Robert Marteau). [Paint] (18:36) Aut 91, p. 59.
"Snow Across Groningen." [Os] (32) Spr 91, p. 23.

4252. MOOS, Michael
"Biology." [NoDaQ] (59:3) Sum 91, p. 111.
"Confessions." [NoDaQ] (59:3) Sum 91, p. 113.
"Falling Dog." [NoDaQ] (59:3) Sum 91, p. 112.

4253. MOOSE, Ruth
"Blackberry Wine." [ChrC] (108:24) 21-28 Ag 91, p. 768.
"Homeless." [ChrC] (108:1) 2-9 Ja 91, p. 14.

4254. MOR, Barbara
"Oil" (Excerpt). [Sulfur] (11:1, #28) Spr 91, p. 4-8.
"Robbed / and When You Come Home You Find That Everything Is Gone." [Sulfur]
    (11:2 #29) Fall 91, p. 105-106.
"Untitled: It enters a mouth thrusts is chewed and suck comes it." [Sulfur] (11:2 #29)
    Fall 91, p. 107.

4255. MORA, Pat
"Dear Frida." [MidAR] (12:1) 91, p. 17-20.
"Rituals." [CinPR] (21) Spr 90, p. 39.

4256. MORAFF, Barbara
"Ahh." [ShadowP] (2) Wint 91, p. 11.
"Ahh #1." [ShadowP] (2) Wint 91, p. 14.
"Ahh #2." [ShadowP] (2) Wint 91, p. 15-16.
"Ahh #3." [ShadowP] (2) Wint 91, p. 17.
"American Dream." [ShadowP] (2) Wint 91, p. 43.
"August Full Moon of No Human Concern Iraq Invaded Kuwait." [ShadowP] (2)
    Wint 91, p. 29.
"The Breath Idea" (for Tashi). [ShadowP] (2) Wint 91, p. 18-20.
"Cutting Through." [ShadowP] (2) Wint 91, p. 27.
"Does Whatever It Imagines." [ShadowP] (2) Wint 91, p. 46.
"Everyday." [ShadowP] (2) Wint 91, p. 45.
"Feeling/Writing." [ShadowP] (2) Wint 91, p. 36-37.
"Female Flesh Fading to Pale Dawn." [ShadowP] (2) Wint 91, p. 23.
"Hokusai in the Light of Print." [ShadowP] (2) Wint 91, p. 54-64.
"July." [ShadowP] (2) Wint 91, p. 24.
"The Knife." [ShadowP] (2) Wint 91, p. 28.
"Love Poem." [ShadowP] (2) Wint 91, p. 25-26.
"Meditation #1." [ShadowP] (2) Wint 91, p. 30.
"Meditation #3, and When Asked." [ShadowP] (2) Wint 91, p. 31-32.
"Meditation #4." [ShadowP] (2) Wint 91, p. 33.
"Meditation #8, the Emotions." [ShadowP] (2) Wint 91, p. 34-35.
"Meta-Physical." [ShadowP] (2) Wint 91, p. 47.
"Mole." [ShadowP] (2) Wint 91, p. 13.
"Moonbelly." [ShadowP] (2) Wint 91, p. 39-40.
"Moonbellys' Found Poem #1." [ShadowP] (2) Wint 91, p. 38.
"Oh Owls." [ShadowP] (2) Wint 91, p. 21.
"Photo of Mind-born Painting Poem." [ShadowP] (2) Wint 91, p. 41-42.
"Poem for My Daughter." [ShadowP] (2) Wint 91, p. 6-7.
"Poem: Poetry rises early in the a.m." [ShadowP] (2) Wint 91, p. 12.

"Poets' Truth." [ShadowP] (2) Wint 91, p. 44.
"Set Fire to the Myth." [ShadowP] (2) Wint 91, p. 48-53.
"Small Is." [ShadowP] (2) Wint 91, p. 28.
"Time." [ShadowP] (2) Wint 91, p. 22.
4257. MORAGA, Cherríe
"It's the Poverty" (for Kim). [SinW] (43/44) Sum 91, p. 112-113.
4258. MORALES, Beltrán
"A Word to Maria" (tr. by Eddie Flintoff). [Stand] (32:1) Wint 90-91, p. 66-67.
4259. MORALES, Harry
"Una Existencia Sedentaria" (tr. of John Ashbery). [Nuez] (3:8/9) 91, p. 2.
"Typist" (tr. of Mario Benedetti). [Vis] (36) 91, p. 10.
4260. MORAMARCO, Fred
"Creation" (tr. of Cesare Pavese). [OnTheBus] (8/9) 91, p. 220-221.
"Fortune Cookies." [PoetryE] (31) Spr 91, p. 86-87.
"Generic Love Poem." [HawaiiR] (15:2, #32) Spr 91, p. 67.
"Heart in a Box." [HawaiiR] (15:2, #32) Spr 91, p. 68.
"Planting the Cosmos." [PoetryE] (31) Spr 91, p. 85.
"Sad Wine" (tr. of Cesare Pavese). [OnTheBus] (8/9) 91, p. 221.
"Sleeping Alone, Sleeping Together." [PoetryE] (31) Spr 91, p. 84.
4261. MORAN, Kevin
"Grudge Match." [Pearl] (13) Spr-Sum 91, p. 54.
"Health Food Breakfast with an Optimist." [Pearl] (13) Spr-Sum 91, p. 54.
"Lassie Come Home." [Pearl] (13) Spr-Sum 91, p. 54.
"One Day at the Library." [SlipS] (11) 91, p. 49-50.
4262. MORAN, Patrick
"Heads and Legs." [CreamCR] (15:1) Spr 91, p. 63.
4263. MORAN, Ronald
"Fish Out of Water." [Northeast] (5:5) Wint 91-92, p. 37.
"Golf Packages South." [Northeast] (5:4) Sum 91, p. 17.
"Lucky." [ChironR] (10:4) Wint 91, p. 32.
"Mr. Harper's Cow." [ChironR] (10:2) Sum 91, p. 43.
4264. MORDECAI, Pamela
"Dog's Other Face." [GrahamHR] (14) Spr 91, p. 58.
"Dust." [GrahamHR] (14) Spr 91, p. 59-60.
4265. MOREHEAD, Maureen
"A Chorus." [GreensboroR] (50) Sum 91, p. 34-35.
4266. MORELLI, Rolando D. H.
"Nieve." [Nuez] (3:8/9) 91, p. 21.
4267. MORENCY, Pierre
"Hélène" (tr. by Elizabeth Hahn and Brenda Casey). [Vis] (36) 91, p. 12.
4268. MORGAN, David
"Almost Not Singing." [LaurelR] (25:2) Sum 91, p. 29-30.
"A Box of Tongues." [LaurelR] (25:2) Sum 91, p. 28-29.
4269. MORGAN, Elizabeth Seydel
"Enough." [PlumR] (1) Spr-Sum 91, p. 71.
"The Uninvestigated Stanza" (— Helen Vendler). [PlumR] (1) Spr-Sum 91, p.
69-70.
"What Is the Most Elvis Ever Weighed?" [SouthernR] (27:1) Ja 91, p. 113-114.
4270. MORGAN, Gwendolyn
"The Ruin" (tr. from the Old Englilsh, w. Brian McAllister). [NowestR] (29:3) 91,
p. 107-108.
4271. MORGAN, John
"Above the Tanana: For Jerry Cable" (d. January 24, 1988). [Manoa] (3:1) Spr 91,
p. 185-189.
"Analects of the Red Canoe" (3rd Prize, 1st Annual Martha Scott Trimble Poetry
Award). [ColR] (NS 18:2) Fall-Wint 91, p. 113-119.
4272. MORGAN, Robert
"Arrowheads." [Blueline] (12) 91, p. 1.
"Besom." [SouthernR] (27:1) Ja 91, p. 150.
"Companions." [SouthernR] (27:1) Ja 91, p. 147-148.
"Crow String." [GrahamHR] (15) Fall 91, p. 35.
"Flywheel." [Blueline] (12) 91, p. 3.
"Green River." [Shen] (41:3) Fall 91, p. 31.
"Honey." [Atlantic] (268:3) S 91, p. 94.
"Junkyard." [GrahamHR] (15) Fall 91, p. 34.
"Manifest." [SouthernR] (27:1) Ja 91, p. 149-150.

"Slag." [GrahamHR] (15) Fall 91, p. 36.
"Slant Acres." [Blueline] (12) 91, p. 4.
"Sloughter." [Turnstile] (3:1) 91, p. 30.
"Speed of Time." [Blueline] (12) 91, p. 2.
"Spring Turning." [Turnstile] (3:1) 91, p. 29.
"Sundial." [Shen] (41:3) Fall 91, p. 30.
"Sunspots." [Blueline] (12) 91, p. 2.
"Weaving Drafts." [SouthernR] (27:1) Ja 91, p. 148.
"Wind Shaken." [Shen] (41:3) Fall 91, p. 30.
4273. MORGAN, Veronica
"Asylum." [ThRiPo] (37/38) 91, p. 49-50.
4274. MORI, Kyoko
"In Defense of Beauty: Weaving Federation Exhibit, Milwaukee." [PaintedHR] (2)
Spr 91, p. 30-32.
"Uncles." [AmerS] (60:1) Wint 91, p. 31-32.
4275. MORIARTY, Laura
"Laura" (Excerpt). [Avec] (4:1) 91, p. 1-5.
"Symmetry" (Selections: 16 poems. Poetry Chapbook). [BlackWR] (18:1) Fall-Wint
91, p. 57-74.
4276. MORIARTY, Michael
"Bartok." [NewYorkQ] (45) 91, p. 60.
"Rachmaninoff" (For Mel Torme). [NewYorkQ] (44) 91, p. 56.
4277. MORIN, Edward
"Cigarette Butts" (tr. of Xu Gang, w. Dennis Ding and Fang Dai). [Iowa] (21:2)
Spr-Sum 91, p. 45.
"A Figure Seen from Behind" (tr. of Xu Gang, w. Dennis Ding and Fang Dai).
[Iowa] (21:2) Spr-Sum 91, p. 45.
"Red Azalea on the Cliff" (tr. of Xu Gang, w. Dennis Ding and Fang Dai). [Iowa]
(21:2) Spr-Sum 91, p. 44.
"Still Praying" (tr. of Cai Qi-jiao, w. Fang Dai). [NewOR] (18:2) Sum 91, p. 41.
"Summer" (tr. of Xu Gang, w. Dennis Ding and Fang Dai). [Iowa] (21:2) Spr-Sum
91, p. 46.
4278. MORISS-WIEST, Inta
"About the Country We Come From" (tr. of Ana Blandiana, w. Chrisula
Stefanescu). [Iowa] (21:2) Spr-Sum 91, p. 41.
"The Children's Crusade" (tr. of Ana Blandiana, w. Chrisula Stefanescu). [Iowa]
(21:2) Spr-Sum 91, p. 41.
"Everything" (tr. of Ana Blandiana, w. Chrisula Stefanescu). [Iowa] (21:2) Spr-Sum
91, p. 42.
"Humility" (tr. of Ana Blandiana, w. Chrisula Stefanescu). [Iowa] (21:2) Spr-Sum
91, p. 40.
"Links" (tr. of Ana Blandiana, w. Chrisula Stefanescu). [Iowa] (21:2) Spr-Sum 91,
p. 40.
"Magic Spell of Rain" (tr. of Ana Blandiana, w. Chrisula Stefanescu). [Iowa] (21:2)
Spr-Sum 91, p. 39.
4279. MORITZ, A. F.
"Results of One's Research." [CanLit] (131) Wint 91, p. 72.
"What Luck, You Said." [FourQ] (5:1) Spr 91, p. 44.
4280. MORITZ, Ruth
"Winesaps." [Ploughs] (17:2/3) Fall 91, p. 115.
4281. MORLEY, David
"I Am Teaching Leviathan to Swim." [Verse] (8:2) Sum 91, p. 30.
"Mandelstam" (5 selections from a poem written to celebrate the life of Osip
Mandelstam). [AntigR] (85/86) Spr-Sum 91, p. 129-137.
"The New Technology." [Verse] (8:2) Sum 91, p. 30.
"Three Variations After Lines from Allen Curnow" (For Allen Curnow). [Verse]
(8:2) Sum 91, p. 29.
4282. MORLEY, Hilda
"Cornwall." [Antaeus] (67) Fall 91, p. 146-147.
4283. MORLEY, Marjorie
"Patriot" (for Robert R. Ward). [BellArk] (7:4) Jl-Ag 91, p. 11.
"The Second Childhood Is Better Than the First" (The Faye Connection). [BellArk]
(7:1) Ja-F 91, p. 12.
4284. MORPHEW, Melissa
"Fear." [SpoonRQ] (16:3/4) Sum-Fall 91, p. 39.
"Next to Godliness." [PoetL] (86:2) Sum 91, p. 32.

4285. MORRILL, Donald
    "The Feast." [KenR] (NS 13:1) Wint 91, p. 74-75.
    "The Taken: A Letter." [NewEngR] (14:1) Fall 91, p. 116-119.
4286. MORRIS, Bernard E.
    "Assault Weapons Are on the Front Lines of Crime." [SmPd] (28:2, #82) Spr 91, p.
        33.
4287. MORRIS, Carol
    "Home Movies." [ManhatPR] (13) [91?], p. 13.
4288. MORRIS, Herbert
    "Felice Before the Lighting of the Lamps." [Pequod] (32) 91, p. 73-j83.
    "House of Words" (Henry James, Rye, 1906). [DenQ] (26:2) Fall 91, p. 20-39.
    "Joyce on the French Coast Waiting for the Dark." [KenR] (NS 13:3) Sum 91, p.
        98-102.
    "Monkey Fur." [Salm] (92) Fall 91, p. 155-159.
    "On Cornell." [Crazy] (40) Spr 91, p. 59-72.
    "The Passion, Night to Night, of the Ringmaster." [GreenMR] (NS 5:1) Sum-Fall
        91, p. 14-26.
4289. MORRIS, Jim
    "On the Outskirts of Town." [GreensboroR] (51) Wint 91-92, p. 142.
4290. MORRIS, Mervyn
    "Writing" (after Octavio Paz). [GrahamHR] (14) Spr 91, p. 48.
    "Young Widow, Grave." [GrahamHR] (14) Spr 91, p. 47.
4291. MORRIS, Peter
    "Bulimia." [ChironR] (10:2) Sum 91, p. 9.
    "Genuflecting." [PoetryE] (32) Fall 91, p. 136.
    "Hydraulic Lift." [PoetryE] (32) Fall 91, p. 134.
    "The Mailroom." [PoetryE] (32) Fall 91, p. 133.
    "Omerta." [ChironR] (10:2) Sum 91, p. 9.
    "Scrap Metal." [ChironR] (10:2) Sum 91, p. 9.
    "The Texas School Book Depository." [ChironR] (10:2) Sum 91, p. 9.
    "Trail Mix." [PoetryE] (32) Fall 91, p. 135.
    "West Point." [NewYorkQ] (44) 91, p. 90.
4292. MORRIS, Robin Amelia
    "Thoughts of a Sun Bather." [Elf] (1:2) Sum 91, p. 26.
4293. MORRIS, Sawnie
    "We Begin Again." [Calyx] (13:2) Sum 91, p. 51.
4294. MORRISON, John C.
    "My Neighbor's Dog." [CimR] (95) Ap 91, p. 51-52.
    "The Night Before." [CimR] (95) Ap 91, p. 53.
4295. MORRISON, Kathi
    "Angels and the Real Thing." [SouthernPR] (31:1) Spr 91, p. 57-58.
4296. MORRISON, R. H.
    "Chess-Men." [Hellas] (2:1) Spr 91, p. 48.
    "Day's Shadows" (tr. of Alexander Blok). [LitR] (34:2) Wint 91, p. 231.
    "Dying in New York Is Prohibited" (tr. of Joaquín Antonio Peñalosa). [AntigR]
        (85/86) Spr-Sum 91, p. 177.
    "The Golden Rose." [Hellas] (2:1) Spr 91, p. 47.
    "Night, Street, Lamp" (tr. of Alexander Blok). [LitR] (34:2) Wint 91, p. 231.
    "Order of the Day" (tr. of Joaquín Antonio Peñalosa). [ColR] (NS 18:2) Fall-Wint
        91, p. 88.
    "Orpheus." [Hellas] (2:1) Spr 91, p. 47.
    "Recipe for Making an Orange" (tr. of Joaquín Antonio Peñalosa). [AntigR] (85/86)
        Spr-Sum 91, p. 179.
    "Short Poem Forswearing the Clock" (tr. of Joaquín Antonio Peñalosa). [AntigR]
        (85/86) Spr-Sum 91, p. 181.
    "Theory of the Ugly" (tr. of Joaquín Antonio Peñalosa). [AntigR] (85/86) Spr-Sum
        91, p. 175.
    "The Wider Mourning." [Hellas] (2:1) Spr 91, p. 49.
4297. MORRISON, Rusane
    "How to Find a Poem." [DustyD] Je 91, p. 32.
MORRISON, Tamara Wong
    See WONG-MORRISON, Tamara
4298. MORRISSEY, Kim
    "I want to shake you." [PoetryC] (12:1) D 91, p. 15.
    "July 4th, 1949." [PoetryC] (12:1) D 91, p. 15.
    "Parlour Tricks." [PoetryC] (12:1) D 91, p. 15.

"Saturday, June 3." [PoetryC] (12:1) D 91, p. 15.
"Saturday Matinee." [PoetryC] (12:1) D 91, p. 15.
"Valentine's." [PoetryC] (12:1) D 91, p. 15.
4299. MORRISSEY, Thomas
"Elements." [Blueline] (12) 91, p. 79.
"The Rock." [Blueline] (12) 91, p. 78.
4300. MORRO, Henry J. (Henry Jeronimo)
"Marilyn Monroe Is Dead." [PacificR] (10) 91-92, p. 143-144.
"Somoza's Teeth." [BlackWR] (18:1) Fall-Wint 91, p. 97.
"Winter, Los Angeles." [SenR] (21:1) Spr 91, p. 52.
4301. MORSE, Michael
"Three Walks of Near Suicide with Trakl." [Field] (45) Fall 91, p. 55-57.
"Trakl, in Charge of Wounded" (Grodek, August 1914). [Field] (45) Fall 91, p.
58-60.
4302. MORT, Graham
"Family Reunion." [Stand] (33:1) Wint 91, p. 60-61.
4303. MORTIMER, Ian
"Frailty." [Stand] (32:4) Aut 91, p. 5.
4304. MORTON, Bruce
"Lake Superior: North Shore at Night." [NorthStoneR] (10) Fall 91-Wint 92, p.
177.
4305. MORTON, Colin
"Waking Up in Guatemala." [PraF] (12:3 #56) Aut 91, p. 42-43.
4306. MOSER, Kathleen
"Nativity." [FourQ] (4:2) Fall 90, p. 22.
4307. MOSES, Daniel David
"A Farmer's Lament." [Quarry] (40:1/2) Wint-Spr 91, p. 119.
"Offhand Song." [Arc] (26) Spr 91, p. 26.
4308. MOSKOVIT, Leonard
"Theodicy." [Hellas] (2:1) Spr 91, p. 71.
4309. MOSS, Donald
"Good Boys Win Prizes." [Ascent] (15:3) Spr 91, p. 25-33.
4310. MOSS, Melissa
"Home Life." [BrooklynR] (8) 91, p. 46.
4311. MOSS, Peyton H., Jr.
"A Fox in Blood." [Journal] (15:2) Fall 91, p. 14.
4312. MOSS, Stanley
"Stations." [Poetry] (159:3) D 91, p. 151-152.
4313. MOTION, Andrew
"A Dream of Peace." [Harp] (282:1690) Mr 91, p. 42-43.
4314. MOTT, Glenn
"Precipitation." [MissouriR] (14:1) 91, p. 155.
4315. MOTT, Michael
"Birds" (for Margaret). [GeoR] (45:1) Spr 91, p. 94-95.
"Evening in Ferrara." [LullwaterR] (2:2) Spr 91, p. 35.
"Flatlands." [TarRP] (31:1) Fall 91, p. 37.
"Harlyn House, North Cornwall." [SewanR] (99:4) Fall 91, p. 547.
"In the Prague Botanical Gardens" (May 1988). [SewanR] (99:4) Fall 91, p.
545-546.
"Letter to Mistress Eleanor Gwyn." [SewanR] (98:4) Fall 90, p. 664-665.
"Loredo." [LullwaterR] (2:2) Spr 91, p. 11-13.
"On Botticelli's Drawings for *The Divine Comedy*." [TarRP] (31:1) Fall 91, p. 38.
4316. MOURÉ, Erin
"Afterthought 1." [Quarry] (40:1/2) Wint-Spr 91, p. 125.
"Afterthought 2." [Quarry] (40:1/2) Wint-Spr 91, p. 125.
"The Health of Poetry" (The poll tax riots, London, winter 1990). [Arc] (26) Spr 91,
p. 17-20.
"Photon Scanner (Blue Spruce)." [MalR] (95) Sum 91, p. 84-93.
"A Real Motorcycle." [Quarry] (40:1/2) Wint-Spr 91, p. 122-124.
"The Restoration of a Kingdom of Rain." [Quarry] (40:1/2) Wint-Spr 91, p.
120-121.
4317. MOVIUS, Geoffrey
"Closing Down in Connecticut." [ChiR] (37:2/3) 91, p. 48.
4318. MROUE, Haas H.
"Beirut." [GrahamHR] (15) Fall 91, p. 27.
"They Shot the Piano Player." [GrahamHR] (15) Fall 91, p. 28-29.

"A Tyre Ghazal." [MinnR] (NS 37) Fall 91, p. 18.
4319. MUELLER, Lisel
"Insomnia." [WillowS] (28) Sum 91, p. 14.
"Losing My Sight." [PoetryNW] (32:2) Sum 91, p. 15.
"Statues." [WillowS] (28) Sum 91, p. 15.
4320. MUHLHAUSEN, Linda
"Porcupine." [Writer] (104:9) S 91, p. 22.
4321. MUIN, Glynna
"Lightning." [EmeraldCR] (3) 91, c1990, p. 46.
4322. MULCAHY, Barbara
"Hoarfrost. The branches." [AntigR] (85/86) Spr-Sum 91, p. 96.
4323. MULKEY, F. Gordon
"Last Call." [DustyD] Ap 91, p. 23.
"Modern Western Romance." [DustyD] Ap 91, p. 28.
4324. MULKEY, Richard
"Communion." [WestB] (29) 91, p. 74-76.
"Migration." [WestB] (29) 91, p. 73-74.
4325. MULLEN, Laura
"House." [NewYorker] (67:6) 1 Ap 91, p. 38.
"A Pretty Girl Is Like a Melody." [DenQ] (26:2) Fall 91, p. 40-43.
4326. MULLEN, Michael
"Missing Mom." [HampSPR] Wint 91, p. 28.
4327. MULLER, Erik
"A Resident's Painting." [PaintedHR] (1) Ja 91, p. 8-9.
4328. MULLIGAN, J. B.
"Frastus Buys a Round." [ChironR] (10:2) Sum 91, p. 16.
"The Price." [ChironR] (10:2) Sum 91, p. 16.
"The Sanitation Department." [ChironR] (10:2) Sum 91, p. 16.
"Various Rites of Life and Death." [ChironR] (10:2) Sum 91, p. 16.
4329. MULLIN, Bob
"The View from Cape Blanco." [WorldO] (24:1/2) Fall 89-Wint 89-90, c1991, p. 20.
4330. MULLINS, Barbara
"Wild Geese." [Elf] (1:1) Spr 91, p. 40.
4331. MULLINS, Cecil J.
"The Circle." [CapeR] (26:1) Spr 91, p. 19.
4332. MULLINS, Debbie
"Crimson Cavity." [EmeraldCR] (4) 91, p. 76-77.
"First Grade." [EmeraldCR] (4) 91, p. 77.
"Quarters." [EmeraldCR] (4) 91, p. 78-79.
4333. MULRANE, Scott
"Although You Owe Nothing, You Are Owed Less." [OxfordM] (7:2) Fall-Wint 91, p. 41.
"At Büyükada." [CinPR] (22) Spr 91, p. 70.
4334. MULVEY, Bern
"His Lonely Place." [PacificR] (10) 91-92, p. 95-96.
"My Girlfriend's Son." [PacificR] (10) 91-92, p. 62.
"Words to Wear." [PacificR] (10) 91-92, p. 108.
4335. MUMM, Carl
"There It Goes, Goodbye." [HawaiiR] (15:2, #32) Spr 91, p. 59-63.
4336. MUNDEN, Susan
"Winter, 1967." [GreensboroR] (51) Wint 91-92, p. 94-95.
4337. MUNDER, Barbara
"Weed." [WillowR] Spr 91, p. 25.
4338. MUNRO, Donna
"The John Ball Park Zoo" (à la Henri Rousseau). [PassN] (12:1) Sum 91, p. 25.
"My Love as a Fruit." [PassN] (12:1) Sum 91, p. 25.
4339. MURA, David
"The Colors of Desire" (1st Prize, 1st Annual Martha Scott Trimble Poetry Award). [ColR] (NS 18:2) Fall-Wint 91, p. 104-108.
"Issei: Song of the First Years in America." [IndR] (14:3) Fall 91, p. 81-83.
"Notes on Pornography Abandoned." [IndR] (14:3) Fall 91, p. 84-86.
4340. MURAWSKI, Elisabeth (Elisabeth A.)
"Migrant." [PacificR] (9) 91, p. 83.
"Night Thoughts." [Shen] (41:2) Sum 91, p. 76.
"On a 7th-Century Couple of Painted Clay." [PoetryNW] (32:3) Aut 91, p. 3-4.

"The Other Son." [CrabCR] (7:3) 91, p. 9.
4341. MURILLO, Charles
  "Dear Babe." [PacificR] (10) 91-92, p. 90.
  "The Hood." [PacificR] (10) 91-92, p. 58.
4342. MURPHY, Barbara E.
  "Heat." [MichQR] (30:1) Wint 91, p. 84.
4343. MURPHY, Carol
  "Considerably Later, Something You Read." [MissouriR] (14:1) 91, p. 154.
  "The Yellow Sky Mentions Tornadoes." [Prima] (14/15) 91, p. 102.
4344. MURPHY, Erin
  "Science of Desire." [GeoR] (45:4) Wint 91, p. 706-707.
4345. MURPHY, Frank
  "Paper Clip, Historian, Coathanger." [Spirit] (11) 91, p. 111.
4346. MURPHY, J. K.
  "Ferret." [PoetC] (22:2) Wint 91, p. 44.
  "Water." [PoetC] (22:2) Wint 91, p. 43.
4347. MURPHY, Jean
  "Answer" (tr. of Anna Akhmatova). [WebR] (15) Spr 91, p. 27.
  "She planted apples" (tr. of Marina Tvetaeva). [WebR] (15) Spr 91, p. 27.
4348. MURPHY, Katherine
  "Miss Intensity Meets the Holy Ghost." [ArtfulD] (20/21) 91, p. 88-89.
4349. MURPHY, Kay
  "Betrayals." [SpoonRQ] (16:1/2) Wint-Spr 91, p. 57.
  "Cezanne and the Body." [SpoonRQ] (16:1/2) Wint-Spr 91, p. 58-60.
  "Thinking Woman's Blues." [NewYorkQ] (45) 91, p. 86.
  "World Sadness." [SpoonRQ] (16:1/2) Wint-Spr 91, p. 61-62.
4350. MURPHY, Peter
  "Sequence." [NewYorkQ] (46) 91, p. 62.
4351. MURPHY, Peter E.
  "Stone." [US1] (24/25) Spr 91, p. 37.
4352. MURPHY, Sheila (Sheila E.)
  "Blackberries very slanted the addition mode (desire." [Talisman] (7) Fall 91, p. 34.
  "Calendula 101." [Avec] (4:1) 91, p. 134.
  "Comprehend means to me luxury (a sample dry breeze in her silk scarf." [Talisman]
      (7) Fall 91, p. 35.
  "Every Power." [FreeL] (7) Spr 91, p. 15.
  "For Will." [ChironR] (10:2) Sum 91, p. 15.
  "Hyphen." [ChironR] (10:2) Sum 91, p. 15.
  "I Disappear." [ChironR] (10:2) Sum 91, p. 15.
  "I want to be athletic with you." [Talisman] (7) Fall 91, p. 34.
  "Mass at the Crypt." [Pembroke] (23) 91, p. 51.
  "The Money I Am Worth Is Singing." [RedBass] (15) 91, p. 24.
  "Muscle Required for Framing." [Avec] (4:1) 91, p. 134.
  "Offspring." [ChironR] (10:2) Sum 91, p. 15.
  "Unlovely Yellow Tie with Black Dots." [FreeL] (7) Spr 91, p. 15.
4353. MURRAY, Donald M.
  "August Is the Month of Leaving." [Writer] (104:8) Ag 91, p. 18.
4354. MURRAY, G. E.
  "The Amsterdam Suite (Adventures in the Art Trade)." [SewanR] (99:4) Fall 91, p.
      548-550.
  "At the Lifeboat Races" (Jersey, Channel Islands). [NewAW] (8/9) Fall 91, p. 49.
  "Northern Exposures" (for Richard Hugo). [NoAmR] (276:4) D 91, p. 23.
  "Scenes from the Finale." [NewAW] (8/9) Fall 91, p. 48.
4355. MURRAY, Joan
  "Her Head." [Nat] (253:15) 4 N 91, p. 567.
4356. MURRAY, Keith S.
  "Gravities." [BelPoJ] (41:4) Sum 91, p. 37.
4357. MURRAY, Steven T.
  "Olof Palme" (tr. of Klaus Rifbjerg). [Vis] (37) 91, p. 12-13.
4358. MURREY, Matthew
  "Nailed to the Door." [PoetryE] (31) Spr 91, p. 33.
  "The News." [PoetryE] (31) Spr 91, p. 42.
  "Toulouse-Lautrec's Laugh." [ClockR] (7:1/2) 91-92, p. 47.
  "Vincent's Father." [PoetryE] (31) Spr 91, p. 43.
  "X." [PoetC] (22:3) Spr 91, p. 8.

4359. MUSE, Charlotte
"How to Swallow a Frog." [SouthernPR] (31:1) Spr 91, p. 34-35.
4360. MUSGRAVE, John
"Horse-shoe Ambush." [CoalC] (3) My 91, p. 16.
"I knelt before my friend — unable." [CoalC] (3) My 91, p. 15.
"Of Snipers, Laughter and Death." [CoalC] (3) My 91, p. 14.
"Pucker-Factor" (2 August 1978). [CoalC] (3) My 91, p. 15.
"Suicide." [CoalC] (4) S 91, p. 13.
"There's no getting away." [CoalC] (3) My 91, p. 28.
4361. MUSGRAVE, Susan
"My Girl Is Entering the First Grade." [Quarry] (40:1/2) Wint-Spr 91, p. 127.
"Then Think of It As Gone." [Quarry] (40:1/2) Wint-Spr 91, p. 128.
"When the World Is Not Our Home." [Quarry] (40:1/2) Wint-Spr 91, p. 126.
4362. MUSKE, Carol
"Alchemy, She Said." [AmerPoR] (20:4) Jl-Ag 91, p. 7.
"Insomnia." [AmerPoR] (20:4) Jl-Ag 91, p. 5.
"Lucifer." [AmerPoR] (20:4) Jl-Ag 91, p. 5.
"My Sister Not Painting, 1990." [AmerPoR] (20:4) Jl-Ag 91, p. 4-5.
"Red Trousseau." [AmerPoR] (20:4) Jl-Ag 91, p. 3.
"Stage & Screen, 1989." [AmerPoR] (20:4) Jl-Ag 91, p. 6.
"Theories of Education." [SnailPR] (1:2) Fall 91-Wint 92, p. 1.
"To the Muse: New Year's Eve, 1990." [AmerPoR] (20:4) Jl-Ag 91, p. 6.
4363. MUTH, Parke
"The Tide As Told" (for Greg Orr). [Timbuktu] (6) Spr 91, p. 82.
4364. MUTIS, Alvaro
"Un Bel Morir" (tr. by Alastair Reid). [NewEngR] (13:3/4) Spr-Sum 91, p. 205.
"A Street in Cordoba" (tr. by Alastair Reid). [NewEngR] (13:3/4) Spr-Sum 91, p.
203-205.
"The Wanderer's Accounting" (tr. by Alastair Reid). [NewEngR] (13:3/4) Spr-Sum
91, p. 206.
4365. MYCUE, Edward
"'Down There' on a Visit Rubato." [PoetryUSA] (22) Spr 91, p. 9.
"Five-Petaled Regular Corolla Rose." [HeavenB] (9) Wint-Spr 91-92, p. 64.
4366. MYERS, Douglas
"Shooting Midnight Baskets in the Driveway" (for Dave Hall). [PennR] (5:1) Spr
91, p. 4.
4367. MYERS, Joan Rohr
"Any News." [ChrC] (108:18) 29 My-5 Je 91, p. 589.
4368. MYERS, Margaret A.
"Picking a Ten Flat Day." [CimR] (96) Jl 91, p. 123-124.
4369. MYLES, Eileen
"Maxfield Parrish." [Shiny] (6) Spr-Sum 91, p. 43-46.
4370. MYRSIADES, Kostas
"Evening Procession" (tr. of Yannis Ritsos, w. Kimon Friar). [SouthernHR] (25:1)
Wint 91, p. 94.
"Succession" (tr. of Yannis Ritsos, w. Kimon Friar). [SouthernHR] (25:1) Wint 91,
p. 93.
MYUNG, Mi Kim
See KIM, Myung Mi
4371. NAAMI, Jeffrey D.
"Tim's Toes (Sorry Bro)." [PikeF] (10) Spr 91, p. 20.
4372. NADAL, Bobbie Su
"Moving On." [HawaiiR] (15:2, #32) Spr 91, p. 105.
4373. NADELMAN, Cynthia
"Louis al Fresco." [GettyR] (4:1) Wint 91, p. 140-141.
"Naming the Birds." [ParisR] (33:120) Fall 91, p. 116-117.
"Renoir on Versailles." [GettyR] (4:1) Wint 91, p. 142-143.
4374. NAGA, Okimaro (702)
"Crossing open fields" (tr. by Sam Hamill). [ColR] (NS 17:2) Fall-Wint 90, p. 16.
4375. NAGLER, Robert
"The Angle of Repose." [TampaR] (4) 91, p. 11.
"Casserole." [SmPd] (28:2, #82) Spr 91, p. 20.
"Gene Pool." [WormR] (31:1, #121) 91, p. 1-2.
"'Kalashnikov' Street." [WormR] (31:1, #121) 91, p. 2-3.
"M.I.A., II." [CreamCR] (14:2) Wint 91, p. 154.

"The Martyrdom of Saint Julita, a Catalonian Fresco, c. 1100." [CreamCR] (14:2)
    Wint 91, p. 155.
"The Martyrdom of Saint Julita, a Catalonian Fresco, c. 1100." [Event] (20:1) Spr
    91, p. 86.
"Morte ala Dittore Borghese (Rome, 1990)." [PaintedB] (43) 91, p. 15.
"Perspective." [WormR] (31:1, #121) 91, p. 3-4.
"True West." [Bogg] (64) 91, p. 19.
"Two Stories." [BrooklynR] (8) 91, p. 45.
"The Ward." [SmPd] (28:1, #81) Wint 91, p. 9.

4376. NAJARIAN, Pete
"Talking Is Good for Us." [Zyzzyva] (7:4) Roots and Branches (San Francisco:
    Mercury House) 91, p. 61-66.

4377. NAJERA, Joseph E.
"Eugene Martinez." [BilingR] (16:2/3) My-D 91, p. 221-222.
"Las Fuerzas de Indio." [BilingR] (16:2/3) My-D 91, p. 226.
"Holland Avenue." [BilingR] (16:2/3) My-D 91, p. 224.
"Tom T. Hall on the Radio." [BilingR] (16:2/3) My-D 91, p. 223.

4378. NAMEROFF, Rochelle
"Just Before." [PoetC] (22:4) Sum 91, p. 10-11.
"Parents." [Iowa] (21:2) Spr-Sum 91, p. 158.

4379. NAPIER, Alan
"Animals in Me." [Chelsea] (50) 91, p. 24-25.
"Elephant Tears." [Chelsea] (50) 91, p. 26.
"Orpheus Remembers Why." [Chelsea] (52) 91, p. 93.

4380. NAPPER, J. David
"The Poem I Read Was Ice and Snow." [FreeL] (8) Aut 91, p. 5.

4381. NASH, Mildred J.
"Correspondence." [Pig] (17) 91, p. 53.

4382. NASH, Roger
"Means and Ends." [MalR] (97) Wint 91, p. 80.
"Parting." [MalR] (97) Wint 91, p. 81.
"Vinnie." [CanLit] (128) Spr 91, p. 89.

NATALE, Nanci Roth
See ROTH-NATALE, Nanci

4383. NATHAN, Leonard
"If." [CalQ] (31) Fall 88, p. 32.
"Models." [CalQ] (31) Fall 88, p. 27-31.
"Prelude." [PraS] (65:4) Wint 91, p. 88.
"Ragged Sonnets" (Selection: LXXXI). [KenR] (NS 13:1) Wint 91, p. 155.
"Ragged Sonnets" (Selection: LXXXVIII). [PraS] (65:4) Wint 91, p. 87-88.
"Ragged Sonnets" (Selections: XXXXV, XXXX, XXXXIV). [ColR] (NS 18:1)
    Spr-Sum 91, p. 119-121.
"Ragged Sonnets" (Two Poems). [Salm] (90/91) Spr-Sum 91, p. 98-99.

4384. NATHAN, Norman
"Communicating." [Event] (20:2) Sum 91, p. 98.
"Fire from Nostrils of Dragons." [ChamLR] (8-9) Spr-Fall 91, p. 154.
"The Lake Is Fleece." [ChamLR] (8-9) Spr-Fall 91, p. 153.

4385. NATHANIEL, Isabel
"The Garden." [Nat] (252:11) 25 Mr 91, p. 390.

NATON, Leslie
See LESLIE, Naton

4386. NATSUME, Soseki
"Zen Haiku of Winter" (tr. by Soiku Shigematsu). [Talisman] (6) Spr 91, p. 21-23.

4387. NATT, Gregory
"Sleep (After Jimenez)" (in memory of Louise Natt, 1922-84). [Vis] (36) 91, p. 51.

4388. NATT, Rochelle
"I Am Called to Remember." [Pearl] (13) Spr-Sum 91, p. 13.

4389. NAUEN, Elinor
"At the Milliner's." [Talisman] (7) Fall 91, p. 92.
"Pines and Rocks." [Talisman] (7) Fall 91, p. 92.

4390. NAVASKY, Bruno Peter
"Evening Glow" (tr. of Kuroda Saburo). [ParisR] (33:121) Wint 91, p. 209.
"Laundry" (tr. of Kuroda Saburo). [ParisR] (33:121) Wint 91, p. 208-209.
"Three O'clock Autumn Afternoon" (tr. of Kuroda Saburo). [ParisR] (33:121) Wint
    91, p. 210.

4391. NDUKA, Uche
"With the Earth." [LitR] (34:4) Sum 91, p. 534-535.
4392. NEEDELL, Claire
"Color Alone or Collisions." [Talisman] (7) Fall 91, p. 136-139.
4393. NEELON, Ann
"Instructions for Interpreting a Stela" (tr. of Jose Roberto Cea). [MidAR] (12:1) 91,
p. 163.
"San Juan del Rio Coco" (for Esperanza Torrez de Rivera, Nicaragua, July 1987).
[Calyx] (13:3) Wint 91-92, p. 8-9.
"To a Human Fetus in a Jar, Seen in the Offices of Colprosumah, a Union of 27,000
Honduran Teachers." [Calyx] (13:3) Wint 91-92, p. 6-7.
4394. NEGRI, Sharon
"Blood's Precision." [Gypsy] (17) 91, p. 5.
4395. NEGRONI, Maria
"Islandia" (Fragmentos). [Inti] (34/35) Otoño 91-Primavera 92, p. 273-276.
4396. NEHEMIAH, Marcia
"David." [EngJ] (80:3) Mr 91, p. 96.
4397. NEILSON, Melanie
"Civil Noir" (Excerpts). [Aerial] (6/7) 91, p. 44-47.
"Species of Fit (My Red Room Hangs There)." [Aerial] (6/7) 91, p. 41-43.
NEJAT, Murat Nemet
See NEMET-NEJAT, Murat
4398. NEJGEBAUER, Aleksandar
"Banovo Brdo" (tr. of Miroslav Maksimovic). [InterPR] (15:1) Spr 89, p. 15.
"Common Apartment Lights" (tr. of Miroslav Maksimovic). [InterPR] (15:1) Spr 89,
p. 17.
4399. NELMS, Sheryl (Sheryl L.)
"Aunt Emma Collected Teeth." [Kaleid] (23) Sum-Fall 91, p. 32.
"Frogs." [SlipS] (11) 91, p. 74.
"Going Down into Brown." [MidwQ] (32:3) Spr 91, p. 295.
"Head Under Glass." [Pearl] (14) Fall-Wint 91, p. 66.
"Montana Wind." [Plain] (11:3) Spr 91, p. 15.
"Morning Comes." [SoCoast] (11) Wint 91, p. 56.
"My Kitchen." [Pearl] (13) Spr-Sum 91, p. 50.
4400. NELSON, Crawdad
"How We Make Lumber Out of Trees." [Spirit] (11) 91, p. 30-33.
4401. NELSON, Eric
"Grandmother's Poems." [PoetryNW] (32:1) Spr 91, p. 22-23.
"A Mind of Summer." [Poetry] (158:5) Ag 91, p. 259-260.
4402. NELSON, Howard
"Pine Needles, Middle Settlement Lake, Ha-De-Ron-Dah Wilderness Area."
[Blueline] (12) 91, p. 66-67.
4403. NELSON, Jennifer
"Beulah the Maid Asks for Help." [KenR] (NS 13:3) Sum 91, p. 64-65.
"Beulah the Maid in the House of Love." [KenR] (NS 13:3) Sum 91, p. 62-63.
"Me and Marilyn in Beulah's Mind." [KenR] (NS 13:3) Sum 91, p. 63-64.
"Why Beulah?" [KenR] (NS 13:3) Sum 91, p. 65-66.
4404. NELSON, Jo Ann
"Filling." [CharR] (17:1) Spr 91, p. 68.
4405. NELSON, Karen
"Italian Dreams." [PottPort] (13:2) Fall-Wint 91, p. 35.
"Nightmare." [PottPort] (13:2) Fall-Wint 91, p. 32.
"Reluctant Volunteer." [PottPort] (13:2) Fall-Wint 91, p. 33.
"Temporary Insanity." [PottPort] (13:2) Fall-Wint 91, p. 36.
"Waiting." [PottPort] (13:2) Fall-Wint 91, p. 34.
4406. NELSON, Kay
"Waiting." [Crucible] (27) Fall 91, p. 28.
4407. NELSON, Paul
"Anecdote of the Couch." [RiverS] (33) 91, p. 15.
"Knots." [RiverS] (33) 91, p. 16.
"The Museum of Natural History." [Salm] (90/91) Spr-Sum 91, p. 95-97.
"Solstice, 1989." [RiverS] (33) 91, p. 14.
4408. NELSON, Sandra
"A Doll." [Prima] (14/15) 91, p. 27.
"Things Near Seeming Far." [VirQR] (67:2) Spr 91, p. 264-265.
"Traveling South." [PoetryNW] (32:2) Sum 91, p. 3-6.

"Tree." [PennR] (5:1) Spr 91, p. 5.
"Van Gogh at St. Paul's Hospital." [CreamCR] (15:1) Spr 91, p. 60.
4409. NELSON-TAKIGUCHI, Mimi
"First Class." [OnTheBus] (8/9) 91, p. 114.
"Hairstyle." [OnTheBus] (8/9) 91, p. 114.
4410. NEMEROV, Howard
"The Beekeeper Speaks, and Is Silent." [Salm] (92) Fall 91, p. 267-269.
"The End of the Opera." [NewYorker] (67:18) 24 Je 91, p. 38.
"The End of the Opera" (to Mona Van Duyn). [NewL] (58:1) Fall 91, p. 75.
"Soundings." [SouthwR] (76:3) Sum 91, p. 336-338.
"Trying Conclusions." [LaurelR] (25:1) Wint 91, p. 5.
4411. NEMET-NEJAT, Murat
"The rough man entered the lover's garden" (tr. of Pir Sultan Abdal). [Talisman] (6)
Spr 91, p. 97.
4412. NEOLIBORIO
"Mas Allá del Silencio." [Nuez] (3:7) 91, p. 14.
4413. NEPINAK, Douglas
"Clarity." [PraF] (12:1 #54) Spr 91, p. 47.
"Disjointed Lines of Communication." [PraF] (12:1 #54) Spr 91, p. 49.
"Earth." [PraF] (12:1 #54) Spr 91, p. 50-51.
"Lead Us Out of Bondage." [PraF] (12:1 #54) Spr 91, p. 48.
4414. NERUDA, Pablo
"Cortés" (tr. by John Felstiner). [NoDaQ] (59:4) Fall 91, p. 53.
"The Great Urinator" (tr. by John Felstiner). [NoDaQ] (59:4) Fall 91, p. 54.
"They Reach the Gulf of Mexico (1493)" (tr. by John Felstiner). [NoDaQ] (59:4)
Fall 91, p. 51-52.
4415. NERVAL, Gérard de
"Horus" (tr. by William Clark). [WilliamMR] (29) 91, p. 19.
4416. NESHEIM, Steven
"Hookworm." [ArtfulD] (20/21) 91, p. 53.
4417. NESTER, Richard
"Anger." [ChatR] (11:4) Sum 91, p. 34.
"A Military History." [SenR] (21:1) Spr 91, p. 70-72.
"Under the Knife." [HolCrit] (28:4) O 91, p. 15.
4418. NEUBAUER, Suzanne
"Regatta" (A Haiku Sequence). [Elf] (1:1) Spr 91, p. 41.
4419. NEUFELD-RAINE, Heidi
"Her Memory" (tr. of Carmen Rodriguez, w. the author). [CapilR] (2:6/7) Fall 91,
p. 56-59.
4420. NEVAQUAYA, Joe Dale Tate
"The Dream Warrior." [Contact] (10:59/60/61) Spr 91, p. 28.
4421. NEVILLE, Tam Lin
"Reading Yu Hsuan-chi Late at Night." [HopewellR] (1991) 91, p. 18.
"With Anna." [IndR] (14:2) Spr 91, p. 84-87.
4422. NEW, Joan Cockrell
"The Music Room." [Crucible] (27) Fall 91, p. 38.
4423. NEWCOMB, James
"Anthem" (tr. of Yang Lian, w. Li Xijian). [PraS] (65:2) Sum 91, p. 80.
"Girls Drum Corps" (tr. of Liang Xiaobin, w. Li Xijian). [PraS] (65:2) Sum 91, p.
36-37.
"Rose on the Forehead" (tr. of Liang Xiaobin, w. Li Xijian). [PraS] (65:2) Sum 91,
p. 38.
"Shoes at the Edge of the Fields" (tr. of Wang Xiaoni, w. Li Xijian). [PraS] (65:2)
Sum 91, p. 100.
"Smoke from the White House" (tr. of Mang Ke, w. Li Xijian). [PraS] (65:2) Sum
91, p. 56.
"Spring" (tr. of Mang Ke, w. Li Xijian). [PraS] (65:2) Sum 91, p. 56.
"The Wide Road, Free as a Lyric" (tr. of Liang Xiaobin, w. Li Xijian). [PraS] (65:2)
Sum 91, p. 39.
4424. NEWCOMB, P. F.
"Six Ways of Believing." [CapeR] (26:2) Fall 91, p. 26.
4425. NEWLOVE, John
"Biography." [Quarry] (40:1/2) Wint-Spr 91, p. 129.
4426. NEWMAN, Harry
"Absence." [Vis] (36) 91, p. 13.

4427. NEWMAN, Jerry
    "Why Not?" [CapeR] (26:2) Fall 91, p. 36.
4428. NEWMAN, Leslea
    "When We Fight." [JamesWR] (9:1) Fall 91, p. 11.
4429. NEWMAN, Michael
    "City Fragment." [Bogg] (64) 91, p. 46.
4430. NEWMAN, P. B.
    "Diving to Chicago" (For my father). [PoetL] (86:2) Sum 91, p. 44.
    "The Women of Henry James." [RiverC] (11:2) Spr 91, p. 74.
4431. NEWMAN, Richard
    "Children's Game." [ChangingM] (22) Wint-Spr 91, p. 12.
4432. NEWMAN, Robert
    "Mystery." [RiverC] (11:2) Spr 91, p. 59.
4433. NEWMAN, Wade
    "Midtown Adultery." [ManhatPR] (13) [91?], p. 17.
    "Not Every Couple." [ManhatPR] (13) [91?], p. 17.
    "Thales (640?-546 B.C.)" (for Bill and Tracy). [CalQ] (35/36) 91, p. 93.
    "Threshold." [CumbPR] (10:2) Spr 91, p. 19.
    "To a Bum" (Edinburgh, Scotland). [Bogg] (64) 91, p. 68.
4434. NEWMARK-SHPANCER, Brittany
    "Night." [CreamCR] (15:1) Spr 91, p. 74.
NGAWANG, Nyima
    See NYIMA, Ngawang
4435. NHUNG, Tran Thi My
    "A Vietnamese Bidding Farewell to the Remains of an American." [VirQR] (67:3)
        Sum 91, p. 391-392.
4436. Ni DHOMHNAILL, Nuala
    "The Language Question" (tr. by David Young). [Field] (44) Spr 91, p. 56.
4437. NIATUM, Duane
    "After an Exhibit of Jasper Johns' Lithographs." [Archae] (2) Spr 91, p. 13-15.
    "Awe-Shaker." [CharR] (17:1) Spr 91, p. 67.
    "Moonrise at Oak Bay" (for Karen). [CharR] (17:1) Spr 91, p. 66.
    "November Watercolor." [Archae] (2) Spr 91, p. 16-17.
4438. NICASTRO, Kathleen
    "Instrument of Ten Strings" (for O. Mandelstam). [Quarry] (40:4) Fall 91, p. 28-33.
4439. NICCUM, Terri
    "He Has Made My Arms a Parachute." [OnTheBus] (8/9) 91, p. 112-113.
    "Paper Dreams." [OnTheBus] (8/9) 91, p. 110.
    "The Pot Maker's Lover Speaks." [OnTheBus] (8/9) 91, p. 113.
    "This Is the Time We're Going to Be Dying" (for Verena and Ruthie Cady, Siamese
        twins, age seven). [OnTheBus] (8/9) 91, p. 111.
4440. NICHOLAS, Douglas
    "A Dream" (2nd Prize, 5th Annual Contest). [SoCoast] (10) Fall 91, p. 34-35.
    "Praise of Slow Things." [SoCoast] (10) Fall 91, p. 25.
    "Stuyvesant." [SouthernPR] (31:1) Spr 91, p. 11-12.
4441. NICHOLS, Cindy
    "Country of Thistle." [MidAR] (11:1) 91, p. 103-105.
    "Here and There." [MidAR] (11:1) 91, p. 101-102.
4442. NICHOLS, Jeanne M.
    "The 19th Century Maiden Moves into the 20th Century." [Nimrod] (34:2) Spr-Sum
        91, p. 122.
4443. NICHOLS-ORIANS, Judith
    "Blister." [WebR] (15) Spr 91, p. 62.
    "Cuando No Hay Agua." [PraS] (65:1) Spr 91, p. 106.
    "A Husband and Wife." [PraS] (65:1) Spr 91, p. 107.
    "Waiting for the Baby" (Puerto Viejo, Costa Rica). [WebR] (15) Spr 91, p. 63.
4444. NICHOLSON, Olin
    "Can't Get There From Here." [EmeraldCR] (4) 91, p. 53.
    "Ronnie." [EmeraldCR] (3) 91, c1990, p. 45-46.
4445. NICK, Dagmar
    "Duel" (tr. by Jim Barnes). [SycamoreR] (3:1) Wint 91, p. 41.
    "Flugwetter." [SycamoreR] (3:1) Wint 91, p. 42.
    "Flying Weather" (tr. by Jim Barnes). [SycamoreR] (3:1) Wint 91, p. 42.
    "Zweikampf." [SycamoreR] (3:1) Wint 91, p. 40.
4446. NICKELSON, Christopher
    "Mary Elizabeth." [Obs] (6:2) Sum 91, p. 86-87.

"Untitled: I don't get the hidden meaning." [Obs] (6:2) Sum 91, p. 87-89.
4447. NICKERSON, Sheila
"Returning Home from Work: October." [HayF] (8) Spr-Sum 91, p. 82.
4448. NICKLAS, Deborah
"After the Art Show." [ManhatPR] (13) [91?], p. 22.
4449. NICOLETTI, Allan
"(In) Definite Articles." [PoetryNW] (32:2) Sum 91, p. 19.
4450. NIDITCH, B. Z.
"1945." [CrabCR] (7:3) 91, p. 28.
"Anna Akhmatova." [WebR] (15) Spr 91, p. 98.
"At a Critic's Critique." [SpiritSH] (56) Spr-Sum 91, p. 20.
"At Robert Duncan's Wake." [ChangingM] (23) Fall-Wint 91, p. 37.
"Berlin." [DenQ] (25:4) Spr 91, p. 42-46.
"Berlin, 1940-1990." [OxfordM] (7:2) Fall-Wint 91, p. 45.
"Bourgeois." [SpiritSH] (56) Spr-Sum 91, p. 24.
"Braque." [Os] (33) Fall 91, p. 37.
"Budapest." [ChamLR] (8-9) Spr-Fall 91, p. 131.
"Death Squads." [RedBass] (15) 91, p. 54-55.
"A Dream." [SpiritSH] (56) Spr-Sum 91, p. 22.
"The Europeans." [PassN] (12:2) Wint 91, p. 10.
"Goodbye Karl Marx." [SpiritSH] (56) Spr-Sum 91, p. 18-19.
"Gulag, Once Removed." [Os] (33) Fall 91, p. 36.
"Indian Lake." [OxfordM] (7:2) Fall-Wint 91, p. 46.
"The Isolated." [OxfordM] (7:2) Fall-Wint 91, p. 44.
"Liberation." [CrabCR] (7:3) 91, p. 28.
"Martin Robbins" (In Memoriam). [Os] (32) Spr 91, p. 36.
"Not the Last." [SpiritSH] (56) Spr-Sum 91, p. 21.
"On the Charles, Cambridge, 1990." [SpiritSH] (56) Spr-Sum 91, p. 25.
"Political Prisoners." [RedBass] (15) 91, p. 90.
"Robert Penn Warren: In Memoriam (1905-1989)." [HolCrit] (28:2) Ap 91, p. 19.
"Romance About My Motherland" (tr. of Yuli Daniel). [InterPR] (17:2) Fall 91, p. 77.
"Stendahl at Trieste." [SpiritSH] (56) Spr-Sum 91, p. 23.
"Les Temps Modernes." [SmPd] (28:2, #82) Spr 91, p. 8-10.
"This Twentieth Century." [WritersF] (17) Fall 91, p. 165.
"Time of Well Being." [Lactuca] (14) My 91, p. 21.
"Warsaw." [ChamLR] (8-9) Spr-Fall 91, p. 130.
"Wounds." [CrabCR] (7:3) 91, p. 28-29.
4451. NIELSEN, A. L.
"The Day Lady Died." [WashR] (17:1) Je-Jl 91, p. 26.
4452. NIELSEN, Dan
"Crime & Punishment." [WormR] (31:4, #124) 91, p. 104.
"Death & Hunger." [ChironR] (10:3) Aut 91, p. 14.
"The End." [WormR] (31:4, #124) 91, p. 103.
"Infidelity: How He Got the Idea." [ChironR] (10:3) Aut 91, p. 14.
"A Letter to the Pope." [ChironR] (10:3) Aut 91, p. 14.
"Must Have Been Drunk." [ChironR] (10:3) Aut 91, p. 14.
"Rubbing Elbows." [WormR] (31:4, #124) 91, p. 103.
4453. NIELSEN, Daryl
"Watching robins." [BlackBR] (14) Fall-Wint 91, p. 17.
4454. NIEMIEC, Abigail
"Sorrow." [PikeF] (10) Spr 91, p. 19.
4455. NIMMO, Dorothy
"Eighteen: London, 1655." [Stand] (32:4) Aut 91, p. 6-8.
"Twenty-Three: Launceston, 1655." [Stand] (32:4) Aut 91, p. 8.
4456. NIMMO, Kurt
"All the Women in Suburbia." [Lactuca] (14) My 91, p. 54-55.
"Lady Karma." [Lactuca] (14) My 91, p. 55.
4457. NIMMONS, Dick
"Delicate Imperfections." [OnTheBus] (8/9) 91, p. 116-118.
"Notes in My Diary." [OnTheBus] (8/9) 91, p. 118-119.
"Sons at Eighteen." [OnTheBus] (8/9) 91, p. 115-116.
4458. NIMNICHT, Nona
"Woman Brushing her Hair." [Vis] (36) 91, p. 31-32.
4459. NIMS, John Frederick
"Sonnets" (5 poems). [SewanR] (99:2) Spr 91, p. 167-173.

315

NIORD, Chard de
    See DeNIORD, Chard
4460. NISULA, Dasha Culic
    "Drum" (tr. of Vesna Krmpotic). [ColR] (NS 17:2) Fall-Wint 90, p. 102.
    "Female / Male" (tr. of Neda Miranda Blazevic). [ColR] (NS 18:2) Fall-Wint 91, p.
        79.
    "In an Antique Shop" (tr. of Irena Vrkljan). [ColR] (NS 18:2) Fall-Wint 91, p.
        80-81.
    "Later" (tr. of Irena Vrkljan). [ColR] (NS 18:2) Fall-Wint 91, p. 82.
    "To a Poet Who No Longer Writes" (tr. of Irena Vrkljan). [ColR] (NS 18:2)
        Fall-Wint 91, p. 83.
4461. NITCHIE, George W.
    "For Pam Bromberg, on Becoming Full Professor." [Shen] (41:4) Wint 91, p.
        88-89.
4462. NIX, Debe Brunn
    "A Celebration of Life." [EmeraldCR] (3) 91, c1990, p. 39-40.
4463. NIXON, David Michael
    "July 30, 1971, Plagiarism in the Prison Lit Class." [Gypsy] (17) 91, p. 55.
4464. NIXON, John, Jr.
    "La Marquise." [Comm] (118:21) 6 D 91, p. 728.
    "Wit." [Comm] (118:1) 11 Ja 91, p. 20.
4465. NOACK, Sarah
    "To Aka." [Gypsy] (17) 91, p. 45.
4466. NOBLES, Edward
    "Antiques." [DenQ] (26:1) Sum 91, p. 53.
    "Field & Stream." [DenQ] (26:1) Sum 91, p. 54-55.
    "The Green Bottle." [MissR] (19:3) 91, p. 157.
    "Longing." [Colum] (17) Fall 91, p. 199-200.
    "Reader's Digest." [WilliamMR] (29) 91, p. 65.
    "Talk: A Self-Portrait." [WilliamMR] (29) 91, p. 7.
    "Vogue." [Boulevard] (6:2/3, #17/18) Fall 91, p. 161-162.
    "Weaponry." [PoetryE] (32) Fall 91, p. 126.
4467. NOETHE, Sheryl
    "Goodwill Thrift Store, Missoula." [CutB] (35) Wint-Spr 91, back cover.
4468. NOLAN, Pat
    "Every Little Mote" (a renku, w. Maureen Owen). [HangL] (59) 91, p. 45-50.
    "Frankie." [Talisman] (7) Fall 91, p. 94.
    "No Bread Today." [Talisman] (7) Fall 91, p. 94.
4469. NOLAN, Patrick
    "Making Money in the Persian Gulf." [PoetryUSA] (22) Spr 91, p. 18.
    "My Mother's Fingers." [PoetryUSA] (23) Sum 91, p. 26.
4470. NOLAN, Timohty
    "On Photographic Plates by Edweard Muybridge." [PoetryE] (31) Spr 91, p.
        119-122.
4471. NOLEN, Robert S.
    "The Pickup Zone." [EmeraldCR] (3) 91, c1990, p. 108-111.
NOORD, Barbara van
    See Van NOORD, Barbara
4472. NORA, James J.
    "Was It in *Studs Lonigan*?" [Spitball] (37) Sum 91, p. 42.
4473. NORD, Gennie
    "The Stone with a Woman's Mouth." [CreamCR] (14:2) Wint 91, p. 142-143.
4474. NORDBRANDT, Henrik
    "Hooks" (tr. by Alex Taylor). [Vis] (37) 91, p. 11.
    "No Matter Where We go" (tr. by the author and Alex Taylor). [Vis] (37) 91, p. 10.
4475. NORDHAUS, Jean
    "My Life in Hiding" (for RRN, my love. 38 poems). [QRL] (Poetry ser. 10, vol.
        30) 91, 62 p.
    "The White Meal." [WestB] (29) 91, p. 90-91.
4476. NORDSTRÖM, Lars
    "Bluethroat, Sing and Twitter" (Excerpts. Part 2 of the trilogy "My Home Is in My
        Heart," tr. of Nils Aslak Valkeapää, w. Ralph Salisbury). [Writ] (23/24)
        91-92, p. 5-41.
4477. NORMAN, Glen (Glen Thomas)
    "Crybaby." [Plain] (11:3) Spr 91, p. 29.
    "Ex." [Plain] (11:3) Spr 91, p. 13.

"Living in a Poem" (A Plainsongs Award Poem). [Plain] (11:2) Wint 91, p. 4-5.
"Long Was the Waking." [Plain] (12:1) Fall 91, p. 18.
"One Moment, Please." [Plain] (12:1) Fall 91, p. 19.

4478. NORRED, Sharon Noland
"I Thought You Were an Expert Cyclist." [EmeraldCR] (3) 91, c1990, p. 42-43.
"White Squirrel." [EmeraldCR] (4) 91, p. 34.

4479. NORRIS, Kathleen
"Epiphany" (Vladimir Ussachevsky, 1911-1990). [VirQR] (67:1) Wint 91, p. 68-69.
"A.J.'s Passage." [VirQR] (67:1) Wint 91, p. 69-70.
"The Librarian Confronts Theology." [SoDakR] (29:3 part 2) Aut 91, p. 114.
"Prairie Takes the Blue." [SoDakR] (29:1) Spr 91, p. 47-48.

4480. NORRIS, Ken
"The Fish." [Descant] (22:3, #74) Fall 91, p. 23.
"Fragment." [Quarry] (40:1/2) Wint-Spr 91, p. 130.
"The Lineaments of Gratified Desire." [Quarry] (40:1/2) Wint-Spr 91, p. 130.
"Ode to Baseball." [Descant] (22:3, #74) Fall 91, p. 26.
"Ode to My Daughter." [Descant] (22:3, #74) Fall 91, p. 24-25.
"The Wheel" (Selection: 4). [PoetryC] (12:1) D 91, p. 6.

4481. NORTH, Charles
"Detail." [Talisman] (7) Fall 91, p. 105.

4482. NORTHSUN, Nila
"Every Reservation." [SoDakR] (29:3 part 2) Aut 91, p. 66.
"The Wannabees." [PoetryE] (32) Fall 91, p. 25-26.

4483. NORTON, Camille
"My Chinese Dress." [AmerV] (25) Wint 91, p. 31.

4484. NOSTRAND, Jennifer
"The New York Public Library." [ManhatPR] (13) [91?], p. 28.

4485. NOTLEY, Alice
"They Won't Let Me in Without More Man Money." [Shiny] (6) Spr-Sum 91, p. 69.
"What Does She Think?" [Shiny] (6) Spr-Sum 91, p. 70-71.
"You Haven't Saved Me Any Time." [Shiny] (6) Spr-Sum 91, p. 72.

4486. NOVACK-JONES, Claudia
"A Meditation on Chopin" (tr. of Gregory Kapelyan). [LitR] (34:3) Spr 91, p. 369.
"A Meditation on Death" (tr. of Gregory Kapelyan). [LitR] (34:3) Spr 91, p. 370.

4487. NOVAK, Helga M.
"Gray Owl" (tr. by Sammy McClean). [SnailPR] (1:2) Fall 91-Wint 92, p. 12.

4488. NOWAK, Maril
"Confluence." [DustyD] (2:1) Ja 91, p. 27.
"Exhibition." [DustyD] Ap 91, p. 13.

4489. NOWAK, Mark Andrew
"Factors Other Than Frequency" (Excerpt). [Talisman] (7) Fall 91, p. 120-121.
"Factors Other Than Frequency" (Excerpts). [Aerial] (6/7) 91, p. 178-182.

4490. NOWLIN, Linda
"Landscape with a Book Falling in a Sea." [NewRep] (204:19) 13 My 91, p. 36.

NUÑEZ, Víctor Rodríguez
See RODRIGUEZ NUÑEZ, Víctor

4491. NURKSE, D.
"Lateness." [WestB] (29) 91, p. 68.

4492. NWABUEZE, Chim
"Hermetic Visions" (Selection: VII. Christopher Columbus). [Caliban] (10) 91, p. 40.
"Imago." [Caliban] (10) 91, p. 41.

4493. NYE, Naomi Shihab
"Across the Bay." [ChamLR] (8-9) Spr-Fall 91, p. 90-91.
"Blood." [Spirit] (11) 91, p. 76.
"The Grieving Ring" (In Memory of Izzat Shihab I. Al-Zer, D. 1989, West Bank). [Paint] (18:35) Spr 91, p. 50.
"Holy Land." [ChamLR] (8-9) Spr-Fall 91, p. 92-93.
"Sleepless." [Paint] (18:35) Spr 91, p. 51-52.

4494. NYHART, Nina
"Deep Winter." [Field] (45) Fall 91, p. 63-64.
"Two Faces." [Field] (45) Fall 91, p. 65.

4495. NYIMA, Ngawang
"Tao Te Ching" (Chapter 31, tr. of Tzu Lao). [Archae] (2) Spr 91, p. 49.

4496. NYSTROM, Debra
"The Argument." [PraS] (65:4) Wint 91, p. 87.

"At Ocracoke." [VirQR] (67:1) Wint 91, p. 55.
"The Faithless." [VirQR] (67:1) Wint 91, p. 56.
"In Girls' Cabin B." [VirQR] (67:1) Wint 91, p. 56-57.
"Insomnia." [PraS] (65:4) Wint 91, p. 86.
4497. NYSTROM, Karen
"Faith, Like Weakness." [PassN] (12:1) Sum 91, p. 23.
"I Don't Want to Go to Chelsea" (— Elvis Costello). [PassN] (12:1) Sum 91, p. 24.
4498. OAKLEY, Evan
"Noumenon." [Ploughs] (17:4) Wint 91-92, p. 37-39.
4499. OATES, Joyce Carol
"I Stand Before You Naked." [Quarry] (40:1/2) Wint-Spr 91, p. 131-132.
4500. OBEJAS, Achy
"Cat Lives." [BilingR] (16:1) Ja-Ap 91, p. 56-57.
"Llorona." [SinW] (43/44) Sum 91, p. 158-159.
"Technicalities." [BilingR] (16:1) Ja-Ap 91, p. 58.
4501. OBERG, Robert J.
"Hard Love" (For Rhode Island Hospital). [Comm] (118:10) 17 My 91, p. 318.
4502. OBERST, Terry
"Death and Company" (A Plainsongs Award Poem). [Plain] (12:2) Wint 91, p. 21.
4503. O'BRIEN, Geoffrey
"The Lonely Villa." [BrooklynR] (8) 91, p. 16.
"Well Diary" (Honorable Mention). [HarvardA] (125:4) Mr 91, p. 11.
4504. O'BRIEN, Jean
"The Charnel House." [Interim] (10:1) Spr-Sum 91, p. 24.
4505. O'BRIEN, Judith Tate
"Nine O'Clock in the Morning" (Honorable Mention, 1991 Paintbrush Award in
    Poetry). [PaintedHR] (3) Sum 92, p. 32.
4506. O'BRIEN, Laurie
"Appogiatura." [PaintedHR] (3) Sum 92, p. 7.
"A Canticle for the Equinox." [EmeraldCR] (4) 91, p. 46.
"First Burying." [MissR] (19:3) 91, p. 145.
"A Map of My Brother." [PoetL] (86:3) Fall 91, p. 29.
"Nathan Best Hits on Katie as the Junior Classical League Returns on the Bus from a
    Field Trip to New Orleans." [PaintedHR] (2) Spr 91, p. 25.
"On the First Day, Eve Enjoys." [PaintedHR] (2) Spr 91, p. 24.
"A Postmodernist Looks at Literary Realism." [InterPR] (17:2) Fall 91, p. 124.
"Reencounters." [EmeraldCR] (4) 91, p. 46-47.
"Remembering the Cuban Missiles" (October, 1962). [PoetL] (86:3) Fall 91, p. 30.
"Seeing Things in Another Light" (Van Gogh, 1890. First Place, 1991 Paintbrush
    Award in Poetry). [PaintedHR] (3) Sum 92, p. 6-7.
"Thinking About Skinny-Dipping in February." [Parting] (4:2) Wint 91-92, p. 33.
"Visiting Ft. Benning, 1968." [InterPR] (17:2) Fall 91, p. 123.
"Why I Am Not Living in the Passé Composé." [InterPR] (17:2) Fall 91, p. 124.
4507. O'BRIEN, Michael
"Random Release." [LitR] (35:1) Fall 91, p. 118.
"The Stretch." [ContextS] (2:2) 91, p. 29.
4508. O'CALLAGHAN, T. Colm
"A Class Break." [Parting] (4:2) Wint 91-92, p. 36.
4509. OCHOA, Roger
"Brothers." [PikeF] (10) Spr 91, p. 18.
4510. OCHTRUP, Monica
"Mazurka" (Selections from "Pieces from the Long Afternoon). [LakeSR] (25) 91,
    p. 4.
"The Piano Tuner" (Selections from "Pieces from the Long Afternoon). [LakeSR]
    (25) 91, p. 3.
"Under the Grand Piano" (Selections from "Pieces from the Long Afternoon).
    [LakeSR] (25) 91, p. 3.
4511. O'CONNOR, Deirdre
"Cloak of Daggers." [PaintedB] (43) 91, p. 13.
"I've Never Said Anything Animal." [PaintedB] (43) 91, p. 12.
4512. ODAM, Joyce
"Alive." [SwampR] (7/8) Spr-Sum 91, p. 45.
"All That Is Drowned." [Parting] (4:2) Wint 91-92, p. 15.
"Coping." [DustyD] Je 91, p. 8.
"Death Said." [FreeL] (8) Aut 91, p. 10.
"Guests from Winter." [ChamLR] (8-9) Spr-Fall 91, p. 75.

"Heaviness." [Parting] (4:2) Wint 91-92, p. 21.
"Kitchen Territory." [Lactuca] (14) My 91, p. 33.
"On the Shape of My Head." [WormR] (31:1, #121) 91, p. 13.
"The Point of the Story." [FreeL] (8) Aut 91, p. 9.
"Possessiveness." [Parting] (4:2) Wint 91-92, p. 17.
"Snow Children." [Lactuca] (14) My 91, p. 33.
"Spilling." [WormR] (31:1, #121) 91, p. 12.
"Virginia Woolf." [DustyD] Je 91, p. 8.
"Window." [ChamLR] (8-9) Spr-Fall 91, p. 74.

4513. ODIO, Silvia Eugenia
"La Premeditada Existencia de las Cosas." [LindLM] (10:4) O-D 91, p. 9.
"Quiero Estrechar el Espacio en Mis Brazos." [LindLM] (10:4) O-D 91, p. 9.

4514. O'DONNELL, Mary
"Kildare." [LullwaterR] (3:1) Fall 91, p. 12.
"Midland Winter." [LullwaterR] (3:1) Fall 91, p. 73.

4515. OE no CHISATO (ca. 825)
"Looking at the moon" (tr. by Sam Hamill). [ColR] (NS 17:2) Fall-Wint 90, p. 21.

4516. OEHRING, Connie
"Meeting the Bear." [SouthernPR] (31:1) Spr 91, p. 40-41.

4517. OERTING, McKenzie
"A Ditty for Independence Day." [EmeraldCR] (3) 91, c1990, p. 76.

4518. OESTREICHER, Deb
"Ghazal: The Lithium-Eater." [PennR] (5:1) Spr 91, p. 17.

4519. OFFEN, Ron
"God's Haircut" (for Robert Bradley). [PoetC] (22:3) Spr 91, p. 3-5.
"Post Modern Joads." [Pearl] (14) Fall-Wint 91, p. 62.
"Progress." [WritersF] (17) Fall 91, p. 165.

4520. OFFUTT, David
"Momentary Suicides." [DustyD] Ap 91, p. 21.
"This Time Before Out." [FreeL] (8) Aut 91, p. 27.

4521. OFNER, Terry
"Burial Mounds, Poisel's Pasture." [WorldO] (24:2/3) Spr-Sum 90 [c1992], p. 35.
"A Weed." [WorldO] (24:2/3) Spr-Sum 90 [c1992], p. 35.

4522. OGDEN, Daniel
"Closing Words" (tr. of Karl Vennberg). [Vis] (37) 91, p. 52.
"Dreamless Years" (tr. of Karl Vennberg). [Vis] (37) 91, p. 51.
"If You Could See Me" (tr. of Ylva Egghorn). [Vis] (37) 91, p. 51.
"Letters" (tr. of Ylva Egghorn). [Vis] (37) 91, p. 51.
"The Night Is Not Your Enemy" (tr. of Karl Vennberg). [Vis] (37) 91, p. 52.
"Until You Are Caught" (tr. of Tua Forsstrom). [Vis] (37) 91, p. 31.

4523. OGDEN, Hugh
"Building" (for Brent). [Blueline] (12) 91, p. 14-15.
"Color." [LaurelR] (25:1) Wint 91, p. 88-89.
"The Remnant: Harmonsburg." [PaintedHR] (4) Fall 92, p. 5.
"Summer" (for Annette). [Vis] (36) 91, p. 21.

4524. O'GRADY, Jennifer
"One Afternoon." [AntR] (49:3) Sum 91, p. 435.

4525. O'GRADY, Kevin
"Ashtray Skies" (a white sock poem). [PraF] (12:4) Wint 91-92, p. 68-69.
"Bullets and Sperm." [PraF] (12:4) Wint 91-92, p. 66.
"The Medicated Procession to the Ten Dollar Grave" (a white sock poem). [PraF] (12:4) Wint 91-92, p. 67.

4526. O'HARA, Edgar
"Base Tres: Llegada / Despedida." [Inti] (34/35) Otoño 91-Primavera 92, p. 277-280.
"En la Tibieza del Dia." [Inti] (34/35) Otoño 91-Primavera 92, p. 281-282.

4527. O'HARA, Scott
"Poppies: the Annotated 'In Flanders' Fields'." [JamesWR] (8:4) Sum 91, p. 6.

4528. O'HEAR, Michael David
"Sound Polish." [SlipS] (11) 91, p. 59.

4529. OHNESORGE-FICK, Karen
"Did She Put on His Knowledge with His Power" (A poem found in the commentary on Yeats in *The Norton Anthology of Modern Poetry*). [CoalC] (4) S 91, p. 11.

4530. OHNESORGE-FICK, Marlon
"Your Hands and My Hands." [CoalC] (3) My 91, p. 17.

4531. OHRBOM, Mary Elizabeth
"Love Me." [EmeraldCR] (4) 91, p. 24.
OKIMARO, Naga
See NAGA, Okimaro (702)
4532. OKOME, Onookme
"My Heart Said Things." [LitR] (34:4) Sum 91, p. 554.
4533. OLAH, János
"An Old Workshop" (tr. by Nicholas Kolumban). [MassR] (32:4) Wint 91-92, p. 492.
4534. OLDER, Julia
"Beachwalk." [Salm] (90/91) Spr-Sum 91, p. 204-205.
"Walloon Tavern." [Vis] (36) 91, p. 25.
4535. OLDFIELD, Stephen
"John Donne." [NewAW] (8/9) Fall 91, p. 121.
"Pressure Drop." [NewAW] (8/9) Fall 91, p. 122.
"The Sessions." [NewAW] (8/9) Fall 91, p. 119-120.
"Translation." [NewAW] (8/9) Fall 91, p. 120.
"Veracity." [NewAW] (8/9) Fall 91, p. 118.
"Vox." [NewAW] (8/9) Fall 91, p. 119.
"William Strachey: *The True Reportory*." [NewAW] (8/9) Fall 91, p. 120-121.
4536. OLDKNOW, Antony
"At the Threshold" (tr. of Eugenio Montale). [InterPR] (17:1) Spr 91, p. 47.
"Cliff by the Sea." [SoDakR] (29:3 part 2) Aut 91, p. 105-107.
"Epigram" (tr. of Eugenio Montale). [InterPR] (17:1) Spr 91, p. 47.
"Having Reached a Point of Happiness" (tr. of Eugenio Montale). [InterPR] (17:1) Spr 91, p. 54.
"Portovenere" (tr. of Eugenio Montale). [InterPR] (17:1) Spr 91, p. 54.
"Sarcophagi I-IV" (tr. of Eugenio Montale). [InterPR] (17:1) Spr 91, p. 49-52.
"Ship-Owner" (tr. of Eugenio Montale). [InterPR] (17:1) Spr 91, p. 56-57.
"Sistrum" (tr. of Eugenio Montale). [InterPR] (17:1) Spr 91, p. 56.
"Some Sunday Afternoon" (tr. of Francis Jammes). [PoetryE] (32) Fall 91, p. 118.
"Valmorbia" (tr. of Eugenio Montale). [InterPR] (17:1) Spr 91, p. 54, 56.
"Water Trickles" (tr. of Francis Jammes). [CalQ] (32/33) Spr 90, p. 132.
"Wet Clothes Slap" (tr. of Francis Jammes). [CalQ] (32/33) Spr 90, p. 133.
"You'd Be Naked in the Pink" (tr. of Francis Jammes). [CalQ] (32/33) Spr 90, p. 134.
4537. OLDS, Sharon
"Beyond Harm." [Poetry] (158:6) S 91, p. 318.
"The Feelings." [NewYorker] (67:42) 9 D 91, p. 48.
"His Terror." [Poetry] (158:6) S 91, p. 317.
"The Lumens." [NewYorker] (67:17) 17 Je 91, p. 36.
"The Pull." [Poetry] (158:6) S 91, p. 316-317.
"The Swimmer." [Antaeus] (67) Fall 91, p. 122.
"Waste Sonata." [Antaeus] (67) Fall 91, p. 120-121.
4538. O'LEARY, Patrick
"The Black Garden." [Iowa] (21:3) Fall 91, p. 168-169.
"The Square Dance." [Iowa] (21:3) Fall 91, p. 167.
"What We Carry." [Iowa] (21:3) Fall 91, p. 166.
4539. OLES, Carole (Carole Simmons)
"Basil." [BostonR] (16:1) F 91, p. 24.
"The Caryatid Fallen Carrying Her Stone." [KenR] (NS 13:3) Sum 91, p. 94.
"Dry Ice." [BostonR] (16:1) F 91, p. 24.
"Fugit Amor" (After Rodin, "The Gates of Hell"). [Poetry] (157:5) F 91, p. 287.
"In Time, with Holsteins." [SouthernR] (27:1) Ja 91, p. 79-83.
"John Wesley Orman: *In Utero*, on VCR." [LaurelR] (25:1) Wint 91, p. 52.
"Maria Mitchell in the Great Beyond with Marilyn Monroe." [BostonR] (16:1) F 91, p. 24.
"Poem in One Sentence." [CreamCR] (15:1) Spr 91, p. 83.
"She Who Was Once the Helmet-Maker's Beautiful Wife" (after the bronze by Rodin). [KenR] (NS 13:3) Sum 91, p. 95.
"Stonecarver" (for Father). [BostonR] (16:1) F 91, p. 24.
"Visiting My Formerly Runaway Daughter and Her Husband at the Orchard in Vermont." [CreamCR] (15:1) Spr 91, p. 84-87.
4540. OLINKA, Sharon
"Dissolution of Boundaries." [WashR] (17:1) Je-Jl 91, p. 10.

OLIVE, Charmaine Black
    See BLACK-OLIVE, Charmaine
4541. OLIVE, Harry
    "On the Anniversary." [Plain] (11:2) Wint 91, p. 34.
    "Once, Before We Leave." [Plain] (12:2) Wint 91, p. 23.
    "Remembering a Dogwood Afternoon with Pictures." [NewYorkQ] (44) 91, p. 75.
4542. OLIVEIRA, Carlos de
    "Childhood" (tr. by William Jay Smith). [Trans] (25) Spr 91, p. 111.
    "Map" (tr. by William Jay Smith). [Trans] (25) Spr 91, p. 112.
    "Mildew" (tr. by William Jay Smith). [Trans] (25) Spr 91, p. 113.
    "Psalm" (tr. by William Jay Smith). [Trans] (25) Spr 91, p. 113.
4543. OLIVER, Douglas
    "The Innermost Voyager." [NewAW] (8/9) Fall 91, p. 123-122.
    "The Oracle of the Drowned." [NewAW] (8/9) Fall 91, p. 124-125.
4544. OLIVER, Mary
    "Alligator Poem." [ParisR] (33:120) Fall 91, p. 46-47.
    "A Bitterness." [VirQR] (67:3) Sum 91, p. 478.
    "Field Near Linden, Alabama." [SouthernR] (27:1) Ja 91, p. 86-87.
    "Long, Blue Body of Light." [SouthernR] (27:1) Ja 91, p. 84-85.
    "Picking Blueberries: Austerlitz, New York, 1957." [CreamCR] (14:2) Wint 91, p. 224-225.
    "The Pinewoods." [VirQR] (67:3) Sum 91, p. 480-481.
    "Rain." [Poetry] (159:1) O 91, p. 7-11.
    "Rain." [SouthernR] (27:1) Ja 91, p. 85.
    "The Snowshoe Hare." [ParisR] (33:120) Fall 91, p. 48.
    "This Morning Again It Was in the Dusty Pines." [Poetry] (157:4) Ja 91, p. 192-193.
    "The Waterfall" (For May Swenson). [Poetry] (157:4) Ja 91, p. 191-192.
    "When Death Comes." [VirQR] (67:3) Sum 91, p. 481-482.
    "Wings." [VirQR] (67:3) Sum 91, p. 478-479.
4545. OLLER, Walter
    "Mimesis, the Pan-soul, Its Agony." [Timbuktu] (6) Spr 91, p. 22.
    "Verve." [Timbuktu] (6) Spr 91, p. 22.
4546. OLMSTED, Jane
    "Naming Flowers." [Nimrod] (35:1) Fall-Wint 91, p. 99-101.
4547. OLMSTED, Katya
    "Fugue" (tr. of Nina Iskrenko, w. John High). [Talisman] (6) Spr 91, p. 114-115.
4548. OLNEY, Richard (Richard B., Jr.)
    "Daydream." [EmeraldCR] (3) 91, c1990, p. 98.
    "Red MG." [EmeraldCR] (3) 91, c1990, p. 137-138.
4549. OLSEN, Lance
    "Finding." [CreamCR] (15:2) Fall 91, p. 51.
4550. OLSEN, William
    "Brotherhood." [AntR] (49:2) Spr 91, p. 247.
    "Choir Boys, Canterbury." [NoAmR] (276:1) Mr 91, p. 57.
    "Cruising." [KenR] (NS 13:1) Wint 91, p. 146.
    "Fireworks." [Iowa] (21:2) Spr-Sum 91, p. 145-148.
    "Negative Confession." [Iowa] (21:2) Spr-Sum 91, p. 149-150.
4551. OLSON, Jennifer DeAnn
    "Chasing the Storm." [Sidewalks] (1) Aug 91, p. 2.
4552. OLSON, Jim
    "Freshman." [PikeF] (10) Spr 91, p. 19.
4553. OLSON, Mark
    "Ceremonies of Joy." [Northeast] (5:5) Wint 91-92, p. 39-40.
4554. OLSON, Philip
    "Match." [PoetryE] (31) Spr 91, p. 82.
4555. OLSSON, Kurt
    "The Grounds." [PennR] (5:1) Spr 91, p. 13.
4556. OMANSON, Bradley
    "The Way of the Wind in the Summer Fields." [Shen] (41:3) Fall 91, p. 27.
4557. OMI, Prince (ca. 676 A.D.)
    "This world of exile" (tr. by Sam Hamill). [ColR] (NS 17:2) Fall-Wint 90, p. 16.
4558. ONDAATJE, Michael
    "Elimination Dance." [Harp] (282:1693) Je 91, p. 44.
    "The Martinique." [Quarry] (40:1/2) Wint-Spr 91, p. 133-134.

4559. O'NEILL, Alexandre
"Sopronia Insufflavia" (tr. by Edouard Roditi). [Asylum] (6:3/4) 91, p. 60-61.
4560. O'NEILL, Brian
"Joe, Born 1895 near Bean Blossom Creek, Indiana." [Nimrod] (35:1) Fall-Wint 91,
p. 102-107.
"Tectonic of Love." [SouthernR] (27:3) Jl 91, p. 693.
4561. O'NEILL, Elizabeth Stone
"Little Green Heron." [CrabCR] (7:2) Sum 91, p. 20.
4562. O'NEILL, John
"The Elk." [Grain] (19:2) Sum 91, p. 8.
"Horses." [Grain] (19:2) Sum 91, p. 9.
"Migrations." [Grain] (19:2) Sum 91, p. 7.
4563. O'NEILL, William
"My First Time." [NewYorkQ] (44) 91, p. 84.
4564. ONESS, Chad
"At the Seminary Garden" (for John Carpenter). [CutB] (36) Sum 91, p. 89.
"Mickey Finn." [GreenMR] (NS 5:1) Sum-Fall 91, p. 121.
4565. ONO, Lisa
"Dirty Laundry." [PikeF] (10) Spr 91, p. 20.
4566. ONO no KOMACHI (ca. 850)
"The flowers have bloomed" (tr. by Sam Hamill). [ColR] (NS 17:2) Fall-Wint 90, p.
19.
4567. ONWUDINJO, Peter
"The Green Horns." [LitR] (34:4) Sum 91, p. 555.
"Of Griefs Beyond Words." [LitR] (34:4) Sum 91, p. 555.
4568. ONYSHKEVYCH, Larissa Zaleska
"Litany" (tr. of Wira Wowk). [Agni] (33) 91, p. 218-219.
4569. ORAVECZ, Imre
"After a Long Journey" (tr. by Bruce Berlind and Mária Körösy). [HampSPR] Wint
91, p. 64.
"Dust" (tr. by Bruce Berlind, w. Mária Körösy). [GrandS] (10:1, #37) 91, p.
197-198.
"The Hole" (tr. by Bruce Berlind, w. Mária Körösy). [GrandS] (10:1, #37) 91, p.
199.
"I Couldn't Tell You Back Then" (tr. by Bruce Berlind, w. Mária Körösy). [Stand]
(32:4) Aut 91, p. 24.
"I Have a Recurring" (tr. by Bruce Berlind and Mária Körösy). [InterPR] (17:2) Fall
91, p. 32.
"In the Beginning There Was" (tr. by Bruce Berlind, w. Mária Körösy). [ColR] (NS
17:2) Fall-Wint 90, p. 104.
"Nine A.M." (tr. by Bruce Berlind and Mária Körösy). [InterPR] (17:2) Fall 91, p.
33.
"There I Stood" (tr. by Bruce Berlind and Mária Körösy). [InterPR] (17:2) Fall 91,
p. 35.
"When We Resolved" (tr. by Bruce Berlind and Mária Körösy). [InterPR] (17:2)
Fall 91, p. 34.
4570. ORBAN, Ottó
"America" ("Dear Dr. Orbán — a letter from Washington D.C., February 1987, tr.
by Bruce Berlind, w. Mária Körösy). [OnTheBus] (8/9) 91, p. 218.
"And Sometimes It's the Cities" (tr. by Bruce Berlind and Mária Körösy). [Agni]
(34) 91, p. 223.
"Concert" (tr. by Jascka Kessler, w. Mária Körösy). [Vis] (36) 91, p. 19.
"Europe" (tr. by Bruce Berlind and Mária Körösy). [Agni] (34) 91, p. 224.
"In Theodore Roosevelt Park" (New York Columbus Avenue, tr.tr. by Bruce
Berlind, w. Mária Körösy). [OnTheBus] (8/9) 91, p. 219.
"Jotting" (tr. by Jascka Kessler, w. Mária Körösy). [Vis] (36) 91, p. 19.
"The Landscape Unfolding Before Us" (American Automobile Association Road
Atlas, 1987 Edition, tr. by Bruce Berlind, w. Mária Körösy). [ColR] (NS
18:2) Fall-Wint 91, p. 78.
"A Memorable Fancy" (tr. by Jascka Kessler, w. Mária Körösy). [Vis] (36) 91, p.
18.
"Under the Thundering Ceiling" (Hamline University, St. Paul, Minnesota, tr. by
Bruce Berlind, w. Mária Körösy). [OnTheBus] (8/9) 91, p. 219.
4571. ORFALEA, Gregory
"Birds in an Old Vent." [Paint] (18:35) Spr 91, p. 68.
"The Ecstasy." [Paint] (18:35) Spr 91, p. 67.

ORIANS, Judith Nichols
        See NICHOLS-ORIANS, Judith
4572. ORIEL-PETERSEN, Anne
        "Notes on Escher's Metamorphosis." [PlumR] (1) Spr-Sum 91, p. 72.
4573. ORIZONDO, Hugo Alberto
        "Pensamiento." [LindLM] (10:1) Ja-Mr 91, p. 22.
4574. ORLANDO, Paula M.
        "Sestina: Carmella." [PoetryUSA] (23) Sum 91, p. 18.
4575. ORLEN, Steve
        "Florence" (tr. of Esther Jansma). [PassN] (12:2) Wint 91, p. 27.
        "Tucson, Arizona" (tr. of Esther Jansma). [PassN] (12:2) Wint 91, p. 27.
4576. ORLOWSKY, Dzvinia
        "At the National Home." [Agni] (33) 91, p. 141.
        "In Winter." [Agni] (33) 91, p. 144.
        "Luba Doesn't Have the Mouse." [Agni] (33) 91, p. 142-143.
4577. ORMSBY, Eric
        "Garter Snake." [NewYorker] (67:33) 7 O 91, p. 38.
        "Mutanabbi in Exile." [GrandS] (10:2, #38) 91, p. 165-166.
        "Nose." [SouthwR] (76:3) Sum 91, p. 436.
4578. ORMSHAW, Peter
        "Bohunk." [Event] (20:2) Sum 91, p. 104.
        "Preserves." [Event] (20:2) Sum 91, p. 102.
        "Time Marches On." [Event] (20:2) Sum 91, p. 103.
4579. OROZCO, Olga
        "Animal Catechism" (tr. by Mary Crow). [AmerV] (24) Fall 91, p. 68-69.
        "Omen" (tr. by Mary Crow). [ArtfulD] (20/21) 91, p. 9.
        "Vampire Continent" (tr. by Mary Crow). [GrahamHR] (15) Fall 91, p. 104-105.
ORPINEDA, Andrea Wyser
        See WYSER-ORPINEDA, Andrea
4580. ORR, Gregory
        "The Hinge." [AntR] (49:1) Wint 91, p. 90.
        "Piero Cosima's 'Venus and Sleeping Mars'." [AntR] (49:1) Wint 91, p. 91.
        "A Red T-Shirt with 'Poetry' Emblazoned in Block Letters on Its Chest" (for Lux
            and Knott). [MichQR] (30:1) Wint 91, p. 38-39.
4581. ORR, Verlena
        "Reverence." [PoetC] (23:1) Fall 91, p. 31.
        "Revision at the Whaler Bar — 1980." [PoetC] (23:1) Fall 91, p. 29-30.
4582. ORT, Daniel
        "I Met a Fiction at Club Med." [TexasR] (12:1/2) Spr-Sum 91, p. 116.
4583. ORTEGA, Julio
        "Trilce" (Selections: I-X, tr. of César Vallejo, w. Clayton Eshleman). [DenQ] (25:4)
            Spr 91, p. 69-89.
        "Trilce" (Selections: XI-XX, tr. of César Vallejo, w. Clayon Eshleman. Translation
            Chapbook Series, Number 16). [MidAR] (11:2) 91, p. 71-101.
        "Trilce" (Selections: XXXIII, XXXV, XXXVII, tr. of César Vallejo, w. Clayton
            Eshleman). [Antaeus] (67) Fall 91, p. 107-109.
        "Trilce LX-LXIX" (tr. of Cesar Vallejo, w. Clayton Eshleman). [Sulfer] (11:2, #29)
            Fall 91, p. 4-15.
4584. ORTIZ, Simon J.
        "Irish Poets on Saturday and an Indian." [SoDakR] (29:3 part 2) Aut 91, p. 23.
        "This Preparation." [SoDakR] (29:3 part 2) Aut 91, p. 24.
ORTIZ COFER, Judith
        See COFER, Judith Ortiz
4585. ORTOLANI, Al
        "The Delivery Boy Asserts Himself." [EngJ] (80:3) Mr 91, p. 96.
4586. ORY, Carlos Edmundo de
        "And" (tr. by Maria Bennett). [SnailPR] (1:2) Fall 91-Wint 92, p. 9.
        "Permit Me to Speak of Love" (tr. by Maria Bennett). [SnailPR] (1:2) Fall 91-Wint
            92, p. 8.
4587. OSBEY, Brenda Marie
        "Desire and Private Griefs." [Callaloo] (14:3) Sum 91, p. 557-560.
        "Evidence of Conjure." [Callaloo] (14:3) Sum 91, p. 561-563.
        "Sor Juana." [IndR] (14:3) Fall 91, p. 49-56.
        "Stones of Soweto (A Mourning Poem)" (for Moses Nkondo). [AmerV] (25) Wint
            91, p. 82-85.

4588. OSBORN, Andrew
"From a Time of Low Resolution." [GrahamHR] (15) Fall 91, p. 37-38.
4589. OSBORN, Karen
"The Light of Pinwheels." [PoetL] (86:2) Sum 91, p. 38.
4590. OSHEROW, Jacqueline
"To Victor Jara." [WestHR] (45:4) Wint 91, p. 276-277.
OSHIMA, Takayasu
See TAKAYASU, Oshima (ca. 705)
4591. OSING, Gordon
"Dusk" (tr. of Shu Ting, w. Li Xijian). [PraS] (65:2) Sum 91, p. 58.
"To the Oak Tree" (tr. of Shu Ting, w. Li Xijian). [PraS] (65:2) Sum 91, p. 57-58.
4592. OSMAN, Jena
"'Imposition of Agility' (Notes on the Definition of 'Capture')." [Avec] (4:1) 91, p.
43.
"The Parrot: Distinction of Awkward Shape, Allure of Deep Color." [Avec] (4:1) 91,
p. 42-43.
"Sands" (for Ann). [Avec] (4:1) 91, p. 42.
4593. OSMER, James
"Slamdance." [Bogg] (64) 91, p. 68.
4594. OSTASHCHENKO, Julia V.
"Falling" (tr. of Anna Akhmatova). [Kalliope] (13:1) 91, p. 42.
4595. OSTERTAG, Gary
"Cold in Midsummer." [HolCrit] (28:4) O 91, p. 18.
4596. OSTI, Josip
"After the Exhibit About Jews in Yugoslavia We Went to Dinner" (tr. by Ruzha
Cleaveland). [CimR] (96) Jl 91, p. 23.
"Aha" (tr. by Ruzha Cleaveland). [CimR] (96) Jl 91, p. 24.
"'At Nightfall' — Wine Gurgles, Soup Steams, White Salvos Float Up or Down"
(tr. by Ruzha Cleaveland). [CimR] (96) Jl 91, p. 24.
"First We Fed the Pigeons Around Presernan Memorial, Afterwards Fish Under the
Triple Bridge" (tr. by Ruzha Cleaveland). [InterPR] (17:2) Fall 91, p. 78.
"I Kissed Your Brow as We Looked at an Exhibit About Jews on Yugoslavian Soil"
(tr. by Ruzha Cleaveland). [CimR] (96) Jl 91, p. 23.
"We Resurrected the Dead in Family Albums" (tr. by Ruzha Cleaveland). [InterPR]
(17:2) Fall 91, p. 79.
"We Sleep Shoulders into Each Other, So Gazing at the Same View" (tr. by Ruzha
Cleaveland). [InterPR] (17:2) Fall 91, p. 79.
"When Grandpa Disappeared During the War, Grandma Fell in Love with Jesus" (tr.
by Ruzha Cleaveland). [InterPR] (17:2) Fall 91, p. 78.
4597. OSTRIKER, Alicia
"The Orange Cat" (for Vikram Seth). [US1] (24/25) Spr 91, p. 8.
"Watching the Feeder." [MichQR] (30:2) Spr 91, p. 361.
4598. OSTROM, Hans
"Balloonist's Log, Final Entry." [SpoonRQ] (16:1/2) Wint-Spr 91, p. 63.
"She'll Be Driving Six White Horses." [SpoonRQ] (16:1/2) Wint-Spr 91, p. 64.
"Winter Nocturne." [SoDakR] (29:3 part 2) Aut 91, p. 67.
4599. O'SULLIVAN, Sibbie
"Epithalamium." [LaurelR] (25:1) Wint 91, p. 50-51.
4600. OSUNDARE, Niyi
"In-Flight, Lagos-New York." [LitR] (34:4) Sum 91, p. 556.
"Naipaul's Africa" (Another reading of The Crocodiles of Yamoussoukro). [LitR]
(34:4) Sum 91, p. 557-558.
"Waiting Table." [LitR] (34:4) Sum 91, p. 556-557.
4601. OTEY, Harold L.
"How Come?" [Plain] (12:1) Fall 91, p. 8.
4602. OTOMO, Tabito (ca. 730)
"I pin to my sleeve" (tr. by Sam Hamill). [ColR] (NS 17:2) Fall-Wint 90, p. 17.
4603. OTOMO, Yakamochi (ca. 739)
"I see you only" (tr. by Sam Hamill). [ColR] (NS 17:2) Fall-Wint 90, p. 18.
"I'm wearing your robe" (tr. by Sam Hamill). [ColR] (NS 17:2) Fall-Wint 90, p. 18.
"When my wife left home" (tr. by Sam Hamill). [ColR] (NS 17:2) Fall-Wint 90, p.
18.
OTOMO NO YOTSUNA
See YOTSUNA, Otomo No
4604. OTT, Gil
"First Fourth" (from "The Whole Note"). [WashR] (17:4) D 91-Ja 92, p. 16-17.

4605. OTTEN, Charlotte F.
"Winter's Tale." [Interim] (10:2) Fall-Wint 91-92, p. 13.
4606. OUGHTON, Libby
"Woman/Tongue." [Arc] (26) Spr 91, p. 88-89.
4607. OUIMET, Beth
"Evening Shade." [Blueline] (12) 91, p. 28.
4608. OVERMAN, Linda
"I Don't Want to Go on Living." [OnTheBus] (8/9) 91, p. 131-132.
4609. OVERTON, Ron
"19N 026D." [HangL] (58) 91, p. 56.
"The Acting Program Director Holds a Press Conference to Explain the Death of the
Challenger Shuttle and Seven Aboard in a Fiery Cloud of Snow." [Comm]
(118:3) 8 F 91, p. 92.
"Future Considerations." [HangL] (58) 91, p. 58-59.
"The Go For It Lounge." [MinnR] (NS 37) Fall 91, p. 15-16.
"I Am at a Distance" (for my father, April 7, 1900-Jan. 29, 1989). [HangL] (58) 91,
p. 55-56.
4610. OWECHKO, Hala
"What Are Your Plans for Friday Night?" [ChironR] (10:2) Sum 91, p. 40.
4611. OWEN, Hudson
"American Cool." [InterPR] (17:1) Spr 91, p. 107.
"Shadow Boxer." [Mildred] (4:2/5:1) 91, p. 47.
"Top Secret." [InterPR] (17:1) Spr 91, p. 105-107.
4612. OWEN, Jan
"The Candle." [Verse] (8:2) Sum 91, p. 106.
4613. OWEN, Maureen
"Every Little Mote" (a renku, w. Pat Nolan). [HangL] (59) 91, p. 45-50.
"Topography" (for Meenah Abdus-Salaam & her children . . .). [NewAW] (8/9) Fall
91, p. 1-7.
4614. OWENS, Collie
"Trainee Barracks, October, 1968." [ChatR] (11:2) Wint 91, p. 74.
4615. OWENS, Derek
"Motel Room Third Floor." [YellowS] (38) Wint-Spr 91-92, p. 40.
4616. OWENS, Rochelle
"Blood Fir Palms." [Confr] (46/47) Fall 91-Wint 92, p. 250.
"Discourse on Life & Death" (Selections from an ongoing series of poems).
[Contact] (10:59/60/61) Spr 91, p. 58-68.
"Splits in the Ground." [Confr] (46/47) Fall 91-Wint 92, p. 249-250.
4617. OWENS, Scott
"Between the Rails." [BelPoJ] (42:1) Fall 91, p. 4-5.
"Dowry." [Pembroke] (23) 91, p. 36-37.
"The Fallibility of Memory." [GreensboroR] (51) Wint 91-92, p. 80-81.
"Hearing the Dead." [BelPoJ] (42:1) Fall 91, p. 5-6.
"Meetings in Poultry." [ChatR] (11:4) Sum 91, p. 31.
"Subterranean." [Pembroke] (23) 91, p. 38.
4618. OWENS, Suzanne
"God" (from "Ten Days in Russia"). [Ploughs] (17:2/3) Fall 91, p. 51-52.
4619. OYERLY, Karen
"Rising." [Vis] (35) 91, p. 51.
4620. OZICK, Cynthia
"Commuters' Train through Harlem." [Journal] (14:2) Wint 91, p. 48.
"Eine Kleine Nachtmusik." [Journal] (14:2) Wint 91, p. 49.
4621. P.T.O.
"Memo: Van Leer Containers Ltd., Lagos, Nigeria" (found in 1969 by Tom
Holahan, the text as written, the lining revised). [Pig] (17) 91, p. 62.
4622. PABISCH, Peter
"Sioux" (tr. by Gervase Hittle). [SoDakR] (29:3 part 2) Aut 91, p. 92-93.
4623. PACE, Rosalind
"Man's Head in Woman's Hair" (from a woodcut printed in colors, 1896, by Edvard
Munch). [PoetryE] (32) Fall 91, p. 85.
4624. PACERNICK, Gary
"Frost." [CapeR] (26:1) Spr 91, p. 13.
"Who Am I?" [PoetryE] (31) Spr 91, p. 148.
4625. PACK, Robert
"The Bear on the Unicycle." [PraS] (65:1) Spr 91, p. 83-85.
"Bounty." [NewEngR] (14:1) Fall 91, p. 50-51.

"The Cave of Lascaux." [ColR] (NS 18:2) Fall-Wint 91, p. 65-66.
"Drowning." [SenR] (21:1) Spr 91, p. 5-7.
"Empathy." [Shen] (41:1) Spr 91, p. 7-9.
"The Human Eye." [Shen] (41:1) Spr 91, p. 5-7.
"Hunting." [Shen] (41:1) Spr 91, p. 9-11.
"The Troll under the Bridge." [PraS] (65:1) Spr 91, p. 86-88.
"Wild Turkeys in Paradise." [SouthernR] (27:2) Ap 91, p. 349-350.

4626. PACKARD, William
"After the Class." [NewYorkQ] (45) 91, p. 66.
"Chain Poem." [NewYorkQ] (44) 91, p. 91.
"Letter to the Procurator." [NewYorkQ] (46) 91, p. 44.

4627. PACOSZ, Christina
"Copper Basin Hospital" (Copper Basin, Tennessee). [SingHM] (19) 91, p. 98-99.
"For a Small Girl Staring." [Calyx] (13:2) Sum 91, p. 7.

4628. PADDOCK, Nancy
"Litany." [SingHM] (19) 91, p. 38-39.

4629. PADGETT, Ron
"Fantasy for Kite and Oboe." [HangL] (59) 91, p. 50.
"My Old Muse." [HangL] (59) 91, p. 51.
"Ooo and Ahh." [HangL] (59) 91, p. 50.
"The Prose of the Trans-Siberian and of Little Jeanne of France" (tr. of Blaise
    Cendrars). [Sulfur] (11:1, #28) Spr 91, p. 15-29.
"Prose Poem: The morning coffee. I'm not sure why I drink it." [Sulfur] (11:2 #29)
    Fall 91, p. 144.
"Supernatural Overtones" (w. Clark Coolidge, 10 selections). [Shiny] (6) Spr-Sum
    91, p. 27-36.
"Unable to Nap in Kindergarten." [HangL] (59) 91, p. 52.
"Unnatural Sonnets" (tr. of Blaise Cendrars). [Sulfur] (11:1, #28) Spr 91, p. 30-32.

4630. PADGETT, Tom
"Preachers." [HampSPR] Wint 91, p. 36.
"Some Like It Cold." [HampSPR] Wint 91, p. 37.

4631. PADILLA, Heberto
"La Espera" (Spanish tr. of Yevgeny Yevtushenko). [LindLM] (10:4) O-D 91, p. 5.
"Palmer Square." [LindLM] (10:1) Ja-Mr 91, p. 32.
"Puerta de Golpe, Cuba" (tr. by Alastair Reid and Alexander Coleman). [NewYRB]
    (38:13) 18 Jl 91, p. 39.
"The Rose, Its Specter" (*Rilke*, from "A Fountain, A House of Stone," tr. by
    Alastair Reid and Alexander Coleman). [PartR] (58:4) Fall 91, p. 690.

4632. PADILLA, Mario Réne
"Crows Across Tenotihuacan" (para Victoria, luchamos por ver en momentaria luz).
    [Vis] (36) 91, p. 38-41.

4633. PADILLA, Martha
"Expose." [LindLM] (10:4) O-D 91, p. 12.
"La Faz del Terror." [LindLM] (10:4) O-D 91, p. 12.
"Piedra Gastada." [LindLM] (10:4) O-D 91, p. 12.

4634. PAEZ, Osvaldo
"A Ricardo." [PottPort] (13:1) Spr 91, p. 35.
"Ne Me Demandez Pas Pourquoi Je Ne Ris Plus." [PottPort] (13:1) Spr 91, p.
    36-37.

4635. PAGE, Judith
"Houseplants." [ManhatPR] (13) [91?], p. 19.

4636. PAGE, P. K.
"Lily on the Patio" (for Connie Rooke). [Arc] (26) Spr 91, p. 64.

4637. PAGIS, Dan
"The Justice of the Sting" (tr. by Tsipi E. Keller). [Vis] (36) 91, p. 17-18.
"A Western" (tr. by Tsipi Keller). [ColR] (NS 18:1) Spr-Sum 91, p. 88.
"You Arrive" (tr. by Tsipi E. Keller). [Vis] (36) 91, p. 17.

4638. PAGNUCCI, Gianfranco
"Midwest." [LullwaterR] (3:1) Fall 91, p. 11.

PAHLITZSCH, Lori Storie
    See STORIE-PAHLITZSCH, Lori

4639. PAINO, Frankie
"Against Darkness." [MissouriR] (13:3) 91, p. 120-121.
"Bridge." [PoetryE] (31) Spr 91, p. 79-81.
"Counting." [Kalliope] (13:1) 91, p. 15.
"Elegy, 1822." [Iowa] (21:3) Fall 91, p. 148-149.

"For the Nameless Girl in the Photograph." [Iowa] (21:3) Fall 91, p. 146-148.
"Horse Latitudes." [MissouriR] (13:3) 91, p. 118-119.
"Magic." [BlackWR] (17:2) Spr-Sum 91, p. 37-38.
"One Who Hears." [MissouriR] (13:3) 91, p. 116-117.
"Out of Eden." [PoetryNW] (32:2) Sum 91, p. 18-19.
"The Phenomenology of Roundness." [PoetryE] (31) Spr 91, p. 77-78.
"Rehearsals" (2nd Prize, 1st Annual Martha Scott Trimble Poetry Award). [ColR]
    (NS 18:2) Fall-Wint 91, p. 111-112.
4640. PAINO, Gerrie
    "Shadows." [MidAR] (11:2) 91, p. 108-109.
PALACIOS, Odón Betanzos
    See BETANZOS PALACIOS, Odón
4641. PALADINO, Thomas
    "Cézanne's *Pines and Rocks* at Fontainebleau and Other Spaces." [InterPR] (17:2)
        Fall 91, p. 115.
    "The Grounds at Lake Chebacco." [InterPR] (17:1) Spr 91, p. 95-96.
    "Listening on Radio to the Static of Voyager 2." [InterPR] (17:2) Fall 91, p.
        114-115.
    "Morris Louis and One of the Meanings of Space." [ManhatPR] (13) [91?], p. 43.
    "Of Style, Revised." [InterPR] (17:1) Spr 91, p. 93.
    "Our Time of Brief Dominion." [InterPR] (17:1) Spr 91, p. 97.
    "Pines and Rocks II." [InterPR] (17:2) Fall 91, p. 116.
    "Seeing the Paintings of Millet a Second Time." [InterPR] (17:2) Fall 91, p. 116.
    "Some Lines to a Bewildered Soul." [InterPR] (17:1) Spr 91, p. 93.
    "A Son's Maturity" (For My Mother). [InterPR] (17:2) Fall 91, p. 117.
    "Visit to Ireland: A Retrospective." [InterPR] (17:1) Spr 91, p. 94.
4642. PALANA, Jim
    "Fans." [Spitball] (38) Fall 91, p. 2.
4643. PALANDER, John
    "Rêves à Vendre" (Excerpt, tr. of Félix Leclerc). [AntigR] (85/86) Spr-Sum 91, p.
        239.
4644. PALEY, Grace
    "People in My family." [Spirit] (11) 91, p. 25.
4645. PALLEY, Julian
    "Undated" (to Kafka, tr. of Blanca Varela). [OnTheBus] (8/9) 91, p. 229-230.
4646. PALMA, Lisa
    "Bitch." [NewYorkQ] (45) 91, p. 90.
    "Compulsions." [NewYorkQ] (46) 91, p. 88.
    "Quantum Mechanics." [NewYorkQ] (44) 91, p. 83.
PALMA, Marina La
    See LaPALMA, Marina
PALMA, Ray di
    See DiPALMA, Ray
4647. PALMER, Leigh
    "Children Born in the Sixties." [GreensboroR] (51) Wint 91-92, p. 109.
4648. PALMER, Lesley E.
    "Dump." [SmPd] (28:3, #83) Fall 91, p. 25.
4649. PALMER, Michael
    "Deck II" (Excerpts). [Avec] (4:1) 91, p. 6-14.
    "Eighth Sky" (to Max Jacob). [GrandS] (10:3, #39) 91, p. 150-151.
    "Recursus (to Porta)." [DenQ] (25:4) Spr 91, p. 47-49.
    "SB." [GrandS] (10:3, #39) 91, p. 149.
4650. PALMER, Paula
    "Moving into Light." [EmeraldCR] (3) 91, c1990, p. 88-89.
4651. PALMER, Ronald V.
    "East Side Morning." [EvergreenC] (6:2) Sum-Fall 91, p. 51.
4652. PALUMBO, Maria
    "An officer ordered twenty soldiers to mount a truck." [NewYorkQ] (46) 91, p. 60.
4653. PANKEY, Eric
    "The Angel's Departure." [PraS] (65:4) Wint 91, p. 23.
    "The Clairvoyant." [RiverS] (34) 91, p. 72.
    "The Deposition." [KenR] (NS 13:3) Sum 91, p. 142-143.
    "Eschatology." [KenR] (NS 13:3) Sum 91, p. 143.
    "Exordium." [Journal] (15:1) Spr 91, p. 35.
    "Formal Concerns." [KenR] (NS 13:3) Sum 91, p. 142.
    "The Function of Ornament." [Journal] (15:1) Spr 91, p. 34.

"The History of the World." [GettyR] (4:3) Sum 91, p. 497.
"In Memory." [Iowa] (21:3) Fall 91, p. 87.
"The Manner of Fire." [CharR] (17:1) Spr 91, p. 85.
"Milk Glass." [GettyR] (4:3) Sum 91, p. 495.
"The Other Side of the Argument." [GrandS] (10:3, #39) 91, p. 179.
"Palm Sunday." [PraS] (65:4) Wint 91, p. 23-24.
"Serenade." [BlackWR] (18:1) Fall-Wint 91, p. 93.
"Sortilege." [RiverS] (34) 91, p. 71.
"The Structure of Faith." [GrandS] (10:3, #39) 91, p. 78.
"Te Deum Laudamus." [GettyR] (4:3) Sum 91, p. 496.
"Tenebrae." [Iowa] (21:3) Fall 91, p. 88.
"Triptych." [Antaeus] (67) Fall 91, p. 171-172.
"Variations on a Theme." [PraS] (65:4) Wint 91, p. 21-22.
"The Weekend Gardener." [PraS] (65:4) Wint 91, p. 21.
"With Thanks." [Paint] (18:36) Aut 91, p. 21.
4654. PANKOWSKI, Elsie
"Granary." [Farm] (8:2) Fall-Wint 91-92, p. 57.
"The Home Place." [ManhatPR] (13) [91?], p. 25.
4655. PANNU, Raj
"The Factory People." [CapilR] (2:6/7) Fall 91, p. 135.
"White Liberal Motherfuckers" (Especially for Chrystos). [CapilR] (2:6/7) Fall 91,
p. 133-134.
4656. PAOLA, Suzanne
"Black Raspberries." [MichQR] (30:3) Sum 91, p. 459.
"Daphne." [AmerV] (22) Spr 91, p. 21-22.
"Eros in Love." [DenQ] (26:1) Sum 91, p. 56.
"Medicine." [Ploughs] (17:4) Wint 91-92, p. 112-113.
"Significant Flaw." [Ploughs] (17:4) Wint 91-92, p. 111.
4657. PAPE, Greg
"Birds of Detroit." [PoetryE] (31) Spr 91, p. 115-116.
"Blessing at the Citadel." [CutB] (36) Sum 91, p. 14-17.
"Church." [ColR] (NS 18:1) Spr-Sum 91, p. 83.
"Cows." [ColR] (NS 18:1) Spr-Sum 91, p. 84.
"In Line at the Supermarket." [PoetryE] (32) Fall 91, p. 150-151.
"The Minotaur Next Door." [PoetryE] (31) Spr 91, p. 114.
"Morning of the First Birth." [Poetry] (158:3) Je 91, p. 152-153.
"Morning Shadows, Miami Beach." [RiverS] (33) 91, p. 61-62.
"The Night I Left the Earth." [RiverS] (33) 91, p. 63.
"Song for My Son." [PoetryE] (31) Spr 91, p. 113.
"Wijiji" (winner, 1990-91 Richard Hugh Memorial Poetry Award). [CutB] (36) Sum
91, p. 11-13.
4658. PAPELL, Helen
"Street Children Playing." [Mildred] (4:2/5:1) 91, p. 73.
PAPPAS, Rita Signorelli
See SIGNORELLI-PAPPAS, Rita
4659. PAPPAS, Theresa
"In the Blue Cabin." [CarolQ] (43:2) Wint 91, p. 28-29.
4660. PAQUETTE, Kelly
"Street Scene in the Big City." [PikeF] (10) Spr 91, p. 19.
4661. PARADIS, Philip
"Rainbow Trout on the Wall." [HighP] (6:2) Fall 91, p. 73-74.
"Ruffed Grouse, First of the Season." [SpoonRQ] (16:3/4) Sum-Fall 91, p. 89.
"Waxwings." [Pembroke] (23) 91, p. 108.
4662. PARHAM, Robert
"Chaconne." [SouthernHR] (25:2) Spr 91, p. 148.
"Dots." [CapeR] (26:1) Spr 91, p. 24.
"Harbor Floe." [CharR] (17:1) Spr 91, p. 80.
"Kicking Back in Timbuktu." [LullwaterR] (3:1) Fall 91, p. 13.
"The Knot of Good Sense." [PoetL] (86:2) Sum 91, p. 23.
"A Main Man in the Forest." [Poem] (65) My 91, p. 12.
"Noodling." [Pembroke] (23) 91, p. 71.
"The Stendhal Syndrome." [LitR] (35:1) Fall 91, p. 120.
"The World Quite Springs from Habit." [Poem] (65) My 91, p. 11.
4663. PARISH, Barbara
"Finding My Place." [Plain] (11:3) Spr 91, p. 29.

4664. PARISI, Phillip
"Love of Life" (tr. of Alfonso Gatto). [Sequoia] (34:1) Spr 91, p. 29.
"To a Stranger" (tr. of Alfonso Gatto). [Sequoia] (34:1) Spr 91, p. 32-33.
4665. PARK, Mok-Wol
"A Traveler" (in Korean and English, tr. by Brent Duffin and Yang Seung-Tai).
[InterPR] (17:1) Spr 91, p. 21-22.
4666. PARKER, Alan Michael
"After Surgery" (for G.B.). [US1] (24/25) Spr 91, p. 17.
"Blackbird Villanelle." [ParisR] (33:121) Wint 91, p. 192.
"The Geese." [NewRep] (205:22) 25 N 91, p. 40.
"Landscape with Cows." [Boulevard] (5:3/6:1, #15/16) Spr 91, p. 220.
"A Little Something." [NewRep] (205:22) 25 N 91, p. 40.
"Tsankawi." [Antaeus] (67) Fall 91, p. 208.
4667. PARKER, Allene M.
"Emily Paces." [Plain] (12:1) Fall 91, p. 24.
4668. PARKER, Christopher
"Easy to Follow Instructions: Messages for Evolving Democracies." [JINJPo] (13:2)
Aut 91, p. 14-16.
4669. PARKER, Forrest Christian
"Movement." [CapeR] (26:2) Fall 91, p. 30.
4670. PARKER, Jacqueline Dee
"Razor's Edge." [BlackWR] (18:1) Fall-Wint 91, p. 169.
4671. PARKER, Leslie
"A Small White Glance." [HawaiiR] (15:2, #32) Spr 91, p. 153.
4672. PARKER, Lizbeth
"Like Crescent Moons" (10 poems). [Pearl] (13) Spr-Sum 91, p. 23-36.
4673. PARKER, Pam A.
"Anatomy Lessons." [KenR] (NS 13:3) Sum 91, p. 42-43.
4674. PARR, Christopher
"No Time But the Present." [Agni] (34) 91, p. 236-237.
4675. PARRA, Nicanor
"Cartas a una Desconocida." [NewYorkQ] (46) 91, p. 57.
"Notes on an Unknown Woman" (tr. by Joel Zeltzer). [NewYorkQ] (46) 91, p. 57.
4676. PARRIS, Bill
"Bled My Soul." [ChironR] (10:2) Sum 91, p. 44.
4677. PARRIS, Ed
"Bikini and Bomb." [SlipS] (11) 91, p. 7-8.
"On Donahue This Week." [NewYorkQ] (44) 91, p. 88-89.
4678. PARSHCHIKOV, Aleksei
"Blue Vitriol: The Second Deviation of Labor" (tr. by John High, w. Julie Gesin).
[Avec] (4:1) 91, p. 141-142.
4679. PARSONS, Dave
"Second Marriage." [TexasR] (12:1/2) Spr-Sum 91, p. 117-118.
"Sounding." [TexasR] (12:1/2) Spr-Sum 91, p. 119-120.
4680. PARTRIDGE, Dixie
"Absence: Cross-Country by Pullman." [HolCrit] (28:1) F 91, p. 19.
"Aspen Grove." [Comm] (118:2) 25 Ja 91, p. 53.
"Coda" (for Lena on New Year's). [Kaleid] (23) Sum-Fall 91, p. 31.
"Cold: A Returning" (for J.). [Comm] (118:21) 6 D 91, p. 719.
"The Season as Prophecy." [Kaleid] (23) Sum-Fall 91, p. 30.
4681. PASS, John
"Gimpy Rapture" (2 selections). [CapilR] (2:5) Sum 91, p. 22-23.
4682. PASSARELLA, Lee
"A Second Opinion." [Parting] (4:2) Wint 91-92, p. 23.
4683. PASSERA, William E.
"Conversation at the Disco." [Elf] (1:1) Spr 91, p. 42.
4684. PASSEY, Joel C.
"Outreaching the Wild" (for James Dickey). [WeberS] (8:1) Spr 91, p. 95-96.
4685. PASTAN, Linda
"All We Have to Go By." [Poetry] (158:5) Ag 91, p. 258.
"Angels." [Poetry] (158:5) Ag 91, p. 257.
"At Gettysburg." [KenR] (NS 13:1) Wint 91, p. 30.
"Autobiography in Green." [GeoR] (45:1) Spr 91, p. 105-106.
"The Babies." [SnailPR] (1:1) Spr 91, p. 3.
"Balance." [GettyR] (4:2) Spr 91, p. 215.
"Bed." [KenR] (NS 13:1) Wint 91, p. 31.

"The Book." [GeoR] (45:4) Wint 91, p. 658.
"Boredom." [NewEngR] (13:3/4) Spr-Sum 91, p. 218.
"Domestic Animals." [SnailPR] (1:1) Spr 91, p. 2.
"Duet for One Voice." [PraS] (65:4) Wint 91, p. 32-34.
"The English Novel." [GeoR] (45:4) Wint 91, p. 657.
"Guilt." [KenR] (NS 13:1) Wint 91, p. 32.
"In Midair." [PraS] (65:4) Wint 91, p. 19.
"In the Realm of Pure Color" (after Gauguin's "The Loss of Virginity"). [PraS]
      (65:4) Wint 91, p. 20.
"Letters." [NewEngR] (13:3/4) Spr-Sum 91, p. 219.
"Misreading Housman." [GettyR] (4:2) Spr 91, p. 216.
"Remission." [PraS] (65:4) Wint 91, p. 35.
"Topiary Gardens." [GettyR] (4:2) Spr 91, p. 217-218.
4686. PASTERNAK, Boris
      "Highest Sickness" (tr. by Mark Rudman and Bohdan Boychuk). [Pequod] (32) 91,
            p. 45-53.
4687. PATCHEN, Kenneth
      "I Went to the City." [BlackALF] (25:3) Fall 91, p. 607.
4688. PATERSON, Alasdair
      "Brumaire." [NewAW] (8/9) Fall 91, p. 126-128.
4689. PATRICK, Kathleen
      "Long Walk on Standing Rock" (for Willard Male Bear and Arlin Patrick). [Nimrod]
            (35:1) Fall-Wint 91, p. 108-111.
4690. PATRICK, Reneé
      "Untitled: Yesterday." [EmeraldCR] (4) 91, p. 56.
PATRIDGE, Dixie
      See PARTRIDGE, Dixie
4691. PATTAY, Ricq
      "Jars." [CreamCR] (15:2) Fall 91, p. 78.
4692. PATTEN, Karl
      "You and Blue" (for Iko, 8/22). [SouthernPR] (31:2) Fall 91, p. 44.
4693. PATTEN, Tom
      "Spotter." [Farm] (8:1) Spr-Sum 91, p. 69.
4694. PATTERSON, Veronica
      "Rules for Growing Up." [ColR] (NS 18:2) Fall-Wint 91, p. 126.
      "Widow's Journal: The Body Entries." [ColR] (NS 18:2) Fall-Wint 91, p. 127-128.
4695. PATTON, Kris
      "Dilemma." [ChironR] (10:2) Sum 91, p. 40.
4696. PATTON, Lee
      "A Black American in Paris." [MassR] (32:3) Fall 91, p. 466.
      "Emerson's Jacuzzi." [MassR] (32:3) Fall 91, p. 465.
4697. PATURSSON, Roi
      "Longing" (tr. by Leyvoy Joensen). [Vis] (37) 91, p. 20.
      "Poem About the Moon and Earth" (tr. by Leyvoy Joensen). [Vis] (37) 91, p. 20.
4698. PAU-LLOSA, Ricardo
      "Above Havana." [SenR] (21:1) Spr 91, p. 53-54.
      "Aguas Medicinales." [NewEngR] (13:3/4) Spr-Sum 91, p. 270.
      "Baracoa" (for Mercedes Sandoval). [Caliban] (10) 91, p. 16-18.
      "Belen." [Crazy] (41) Wint 91, p. 19-20.
      "Boleros." [MissouriR] (14:1) 91, p. 125.
      "El Capitolio." [Crazy] (41) Wint 91, p. 17-18.
      "Charada China." [Caliban] (10) 91, p. 20-21.
      "The Cloud." [MissouriR] (14:1) 91, p. 126-127.
      "Demons." [MidAR] (12:1) 91, p. 43-44.
      "Dos Ríos." [Sonora] (21) Sum 91, p. 3-4.
      "Dulce." [Agni] (33) 91, p. 103-104.
      "Enfermas de los Nervios." [MidAR] (12:1) 91, p. 45-46.
      "Frutas." [KenR] (NS 13:3) Sum 91, p. 61.
      "Ganaderia." [MichQR] (30:4) Fall 91, p. 650.
      "Indios con Levita." [MissouriR] (14:1) 91, p. 118-119.
      "Mulata." [MissouriR] (14:1) 91, p. 122-124.
      "Ostiones y Cangrejos Moros." [NewEngR] (13:3/4) Spr-Sum 91, p. 269-270.
      "Paredón." [MissouriR] (14:1) 91, p. 120-121.
      "President for Life." [DenQ] (26:1) Sum 91, p. 57-58.
      "Ron." [Caliban] (10) 91, p. 19.
      "Tropicana." [BlackWR] (17:2) Spr-Sum 91, p. 57.

"View of Miami." [MidAR] (12:1) 91, p. 47-48.
4699. PAULIN, Tom
"Painting the Carport." [GrandS] (10:4, #40) 91, p. 166-167.
4700. PAVESE, Cesare
"Creation" (tr. by Fred Moramarco). [OnTheBus] (8/9) 91, p. 220-221.
"Sad Wine" (tr. by Fred Moramarco). [OnTheBus] (8/9) 91, p. 221.
4701. PAVLENKO, Alexei
"On and On" (tr. of Lev Rubenstein, w. Thomas Epstein). [LitR] (34:3) Spr 91, p.
352-360.
4702. PAVLICH, Walter
"The Boy from Paradise." [CharR] (17:1) Spr 91, p. 82-83.
"Buster Keaton and Fatty Arbuckle in California, 1917." [LaurelR] (25:2) Sum 91,
p. 63.
"Buster Keaton and His Seagoing Car." [CinPR] (22) Spr 91, p. 49.
"Buster Keaton During the Shooting of a Low Budget Mexican Movie, 1934."
[CinPR] (22) Spr 91, p. 51.
"Buster Keaton Sees His First Movie." [LaurelR] (25:2) Sum 91, p. 62.
"Cloud Street." [Manoa] (3:1) Spr 91, p. 21.
"The Cross at the Sea." [Manoa] (3:2) Fall 91, p. 151-152.
"Doves in a Piano." [Journal] (14:2) Wint 91, p. 82.
"Fire Crew, 1910." [CharR] (17:1) Spr 91, p. 84.
"A Firefighter Prepares Three Dreams for the Dreamless." [CinPR] (22) Spr 91, p.
48.
"Hand Impression, 1951." [CinPR] (21) Spr 90, p. 42.
"In the Belly of the Ewe." [Manoa] (3:1) Spr 91, p. 20.
"Keaton at the Circus." [LaurelR] (25:2) Sum 91, p. 65.
"Keaton's Autograph." [LaurelR] (25:2) Sum 91, p. 65-66.
"Late August Isolations." [Vis] (35) 91, p. 24.
"Looking at Buster Keaton." [CinPR] (22) Spr 91, p. 50.
"Near the End." [LaurelR] (25:1) Wint 91, p. 109.
"On a Run Near the Water Project." [Poetry] (158:2) My 91, p. 79-80.
"Poem with a Kite." [Manoa] (3:1) Spr 91, p. 22.
"Running Near the End of the World." [Poetry] (158:2) My 91, p. 81-82.
"The Spirit of Blue Ink." [Manoa] (3:2) Fall 91, p. 152.
"Wings to the Resting Place." [Manoa] (3:2) Fall 91, p. 153.
"Womb." [LaurelR] (25:1) Wint 91, p. 108.
"Work." [LaurelR] (25:2) Sum 91, p. 64.
"You Think You're So Funny." [PaintedHR] (1) Ja 91, p. 24.
4703. PAWLOWSKI, Robert
"After Venezuela." [TexasR] (12:1/2) Spr-Sum 91, p. 121.
"Childrens' Poem." [MissR] (19:3) 91, p. 144.
"Eskia Driving Through Zion" (for Zeke). [TexasR] (12:1/2) Spr-Sum 91, p. 122.
"Operation." [MissR] (19:3) 91, p. 143.
4704. PAXMAN, David
"Ghost Sonata." [TarRP] (31:1) Fall 91, p. 36-37.
4705. PAYNE, Gerrye
"Ancestors." [HayF] (8) Spr-Sum 91, p. 75.
"Resurrection." [Vis] (36) 91, p. 18.
4706. PAYNE, Margaret Gatter
"Reclamation." [ChrC] (108:25) 4-11 S 91, p. 812.
4707. P'BITEK, Okot
"From Where Did God Get the Clay for Making Things?" (tr. by Taban Lo Liyong).
[LitR] (34:4) Sum 91, p. 559-566.
4708. PEABODY, Richard
"Aging Guitar Player" (from "Sad Fashions"). [Bogg] (64) 91, p. 7.
"The Forth Stooge" (from "Sad Fashions"). [Bogg] (64) 91, p. 7.
"She Discovers Jazz." [PoetL] (86:3) Fall 91, p. 31.
"Winter Panacea." [PlumR] (1) Spr-Sum 91, p. 37.
4709. PEACOCK, Molly
"Banquet" (Selections: 5 poems). [Ploughs] (17:1) Spr 91, p. 111-115.
"Floral Conversation." [Nat] (252:15) 22 Ap 91, p. 535.
"The Hunt." [NewRep] (205:3/4) 15-22 Jl 91, p. 30.
"Portrayal." [NewRep] (204:22) 3 Je 91, p. 40.
"Surviving Eggs." [US1] (24/25) Spr 91, p. 4.
4710. PEARN, Victor
"Origami Meatballs." [RagMag] (9:2) 91, p. 31.

"Plaza Mayor Madrid 1974." [RagMag] (9:2) 91, p. 32-33.
4711. PEARSON, Marlene
"That Long Thing Between My Father's Legs." [BrooklynR] (8) 91, p. 8-9.
4712. PEARSON, Ted
"Eight Acoustic Masks." [Epoch] (40:3) 91, p. 256-257.
4713. PECK, Claude
"Found Poem at State High-School Wrestling Tourney Time" (grateful
acknowledgment to the Minneapolis Star Tribune sports section). [JamesWR]
(8:4) Sum 91, p. 7.
"Some Lyrics." [JamesWR] (8:4) Sum 91, p. 7.
4714. PECK, Gail J.
"Hunger." [HighP] (6:3) Wint 91, p. 71.
"This Life." [SouthernPR] (31:1) Spr 91, p. 23-24.
4715. PECZENIK, Fannie
"I Wandered for Years" (tr. of Itzhik Manger). [Agni] (33) 91, p. 153.
4716. PEDISICH, Sam J. (Sam Joseph)
"Milwaukee Mama." [EmeraldCR] (3) 91, c1990, p. 139-140.
"O.K. to Be Shell-Shocked." [EmeraldCR] (4) 91, p. 39.
4717. PEDONE, Ann
"The Bird Happened" (Excerpt). [Notus] (9) Fall 91, p. 28-31.
4718. PEELER, Tim
"I Gamble the Cube." [BlackBR] (14) Fall-Wint 91, p. 4.
"Jim Rice, Viewing the Fenway Wall." [Spitball] (38) Fall 91, p. 5.
"The Walls of Comiskey Caving (on CNN). [Spitball] (37) Sum 91, p. 39.
PEENEN, H. J. Van
See Van PEENEN, H. J.
4719. PEFFLEY, Nola A.
"All I Asked." [Pearl] (14) Fall-Wint 91, p. 61.
4720. PEIRCE, Kathleen
"An Apple, an Orange, an Egg." [NorthStoneR] (10) Fall 91-Wint 92, p. 101.
"Buy Something Pretty and Remember Me." [AntR] (49:3) Sum 91, p. 439.
"Delivery" (for Kathleen Lawless Cox." [NorthStoneR] (10) Fall 91-Wint 92, p.
108.
"The Garden in October" (for Joseph). [GeoR] (45:3) Fall 91, p. 504.
"In Miniature." [Boulevard] (6:2/3, #17/18) Fall 91, p. 40.
"Learning to Walk Lightly." [NorthStoneR] (10) Fall 91-Wint 92, p. 106.
"Long June." [NorthStoneR] (10) Fall 91-Wint 92, p. 102-103.
"Near Burning." [Field] (44) Spr 91, p. 12.
"Out of Disappearance Comes." [AmerPoR] (20:4) Jl-Ag 91, p. 27.
"Out of Disappointment Comes." [AmerPoR] (20:4) Jl-Ag 91, p. 27.
"Parts." [Field] (44) Spr 91, p. 13-15.
"The Raptor Center." [Field] (44) Spr 91, p. 16.
"Second-Hand Portrait, 1910." [NorthStoneR] (10) Fall 91-Wint 92, p. 104-105.
"To the Journey Down." [NorthStoneR] (10) Fall 91-Wint 92, p. 107.
4721. PELIAS, Ronald J.
"Cathy with a C." [SmPd] (28:1, #81) Wint 91, p. 21.
4722. PELLETIER, Gus
"A Remembrance, 1913-1914" (for Mary Aird, whose story it is). [Elf] (1:4) Wint
91, p. 26.
4723. PELTO, Valerie
"I Am Here." [PoetryUSA] (22) Spr 91, p. 9.
4724. PENA, Tony
"The Begging Beat." [SlipS] (11) 91, p. 8.
4725. PEÑALOSA, Joaquín Antonio
"Dying in New York Is Prohibited" (tr. by R. H. Morrison). [AntigR] (85/86)
Spr-Sum 91, p. 177.
"Letrilla Que Abjura del Reloj." [AntigR] (85/86) Spr-Sum 91, p. 180.
"Order of the Day" (tr. by R. H. Morrison). [ColR] (NS 18:2) Fall-Wint 91, p. 88.
"Prohibido Morir en Nueva York." [AntigR] (85/86) Spr-Sum 91, p. 176.
"Receta para Hacer una Naranja." [AntigR] (85/86) Spr-Sum 91, p. 178.
"Recipe for Making an Orange" (tr. by R. H. Morrison). [AntigR] (85/86) Spr-Sum
91, p. 179.
"Short Poem Forswearing the Clock" (tr. by R. H. Morrison). [AntigR] (85/86)
Spr-Sum 91, p. 181.
"Teoria de lo Feo." [AntigR] (85/86) Spr-Sum 91, p. 174.

"Theory of the Ugly" (tr. by R. H. Morrison). [AntigR] (85/86) Spr-Sum 91, p. 175.

4726. PENCE, Amy
"Hostages." [WillowS] (28) Sum 91, p. 64-65.
"The Illuminated Blake." [NewAW] (8/9) Fall 91, p. 45.
"When We're Not Talking." [NewAW] (8/9) Fall 91, p. 44.

4727. PENDER, Stephen
"John Keats after His Lost Letter." [Descant] (22:4, #75) Wint 91-92, p. 7.

4728. PENDLETON, Denise
"Painting the Room." [TarRP] (31:1) Fall 91, p. 31.

4729. PENNANT, Edmund
"Chekhov." [NewL] (58:1) Fall 91, p. 66.
"Perspective." [DustyD] (2:1) Ja 91, p. 23.
"Steepletop" (Home of Edna St. Vincent Millay). [NewYorkQ] (45) 91, p. 87.
"Timor Mortis." [NewL] (58:1) Fall 91, p. 67.
"Who Was I to Say?" [DustyD] Ap 91, p. 23.
"The Wildebeest of Carmine Street." [Spirit] (11) 91, p. 109-110.

4730. PENNEY, Scott
"Vachel Lindsay Approaches Heaven." [GreensboroR] (51) Wint 91-92, p. 141.

4731. PENNISI, Linda T.
"Behind My Tongue." [Paint] (18:36) Aut 91, p. 28.

4732. PENNOYER, Victoria
"Migration." [Confr] (46/47) Fall 91-Wint 92, p. 268.

4733. PENNY, Michael
"Pellagra Apostrophizes His Toenail Clippings." [PraF] (12:4) Wint 91-92, p. 56.
"Pellagra, Waterlogged." [PraF] (12:4) Wint 91-92, p. 57-58.

4734. PENNY, Scott
"Gelatin." [TarRP] (31:1) Fall 91, p. 30.

4735. PEPPER, Patric
"This Windy Afternoon." [Elf] (1:3) Fall 91, p. 44.

PERA, George le
See Le PERA, George

4736. PERCHAN, Robert J.
"Housetrap." [ChironR] (10:4) Wint 91, p. 38.

4737. PERCHIK, Simon
"324. You listen for rain." [SmPd] (28:1, #81) Wint 91, p. 10.
"334. Each Halloween and lifting the door." [PartR] (58:4) Fall 91, p. 689-690.
"372. And this plane somehow." [InterPR] (17:2) Fall 91, p. 137.
"#373. All morning I feed the petals." [OhioR] (46) 91, p. [OhioR] (46) 91, p. 74.
"375. You wrote and beginners sense it's there." [InterPR] (17:2) Fall 91, p. 136.
"377. Once in dirt it wants to thaw." [InterPR] (17:2) Fall 91, p. 135.
"#378. This cup half ecstasy, half adrift." [OhioR] (46) 91, p. 75.
"402. Again the sky rubbing against my legs." [Chelsea] (50) 91, p. 27.
"All the huskies are eaten, my knuckles." [BelPoJ] (42:2) Wint 91-92, p. 1.
"And Forgetting Too Comes Easier." [JINJPo] (13:2) Aut 91, p. 26.
"And the dead can't wait, they crouch." [DenQ] (26:2) Fall 91, p. 44-45.
"And the sun too, goes south." [Os] (33) Fall 91, p. 28.
"And though these shelves are cooled the metal never dries." [SoDakR] (29:4) Wint 91, p. 73.
"Another trench :my fist opened." [CapeR] (26:2) Fall 91, p. 5.
"Beach Blanket Spread." [SoDakR] (29:3 part 2) Aut 91, p. 73.
"The Cots, the Stove, the Crew." [CalQ] (31) Fall 88, p. 64.
"The cots, the stove, the crew." [ConnPR] (10:1) 91, p. 21-22.
"Drink and you are surrounded :the sea will never forgive." [SoDakR] (29:4) Wint 91, p. 71-72.
"Escape from what? this hose." [CreamCR] (14:2) Wint 91, p. 130.
"I dig this grave." [NewYorkQ] (45) 91, p. 58.
"It's Spring on the moon, its light." [PoetL] (86:1) Spr 91, p. 20.
"Now that the planes are gone." [Os] (32) Spr 91, p. 16.
"Redeeming the Wings" (22 poems. To James L. Weil, Edward Butscher, Anselm Parlatore, The Newtown Cafe, The Chicken House, and Canio). [DustyD] (Chapbook Series #1) 91, 24 p.
"Step by step :some key." [NewYorkQ] (44) 91, p. 46.
"Then nudging the cold engineblock." [Os] (32) Spr 91, p. 17.
"These iron faucets, one." [Os] (33) Fall 91, p. 29.
"These rusting wires whose hooks." [DustyD] Je 91, p. 29.

"This gravestone :each sail still leans on course." [Turnstile] (3:1) 91, p. 80-81.
"This loaf and one more bone, the crust must sense how its flesh." [SoDakR] (29:4) Wint 91, p. 70.
"This Pen Clinging to My Hand." [NewYorker] (66:48) 14 Ja 91, p. 28.
"This slab once curled up inside." [Interim] (10:1) Spr-Sum 91, p. 37.
"Two syllables :the curve." [Northeast] (5:4) Sum 91, p. 12.
"Untitled: All night and the rain that's lost." [Manoa] (3:2) Fall 91, p. 60.
"Untitled: As frogs first poison the meal." [Manoa] (3:2) Fall 91, p. 59.
"Untitled: Nothing shows. I water this yard." [Manoa] (3:2) Fall 91, p. 58.
"Untitled: Who can we expect — those markers." [ContextS] (2:2) 91, p. 6.
"What a long way — they know." [BlackWR] (17:2) Spr-Sum 91, p. 96.
"Who knows, with his mouth wide." [BlackWR] (17:2) Spr-Sum 91, p. 97.
"With tiny cuts — in daylight yet." [PoetL] (86:1) Spr 91, p. 19.
"Without let up, half soap half jar." [Talisman] (7) Fall 91, p. 31.
"You don't yell across a tree." [Talisman] (7) Fall 91, p. 31.
"You expect the noon-alarm at City Hall." [DustyD] Je 91, p. 32.
"You will whisper the way rivers." [SouthernPR] (31:1) Spr 91, p. 45.
4738. PERCHUK, Jeff
   "My Old Man." [NegC] (11:3) 91, p. 31-33.
4739. PERDIGO, Luisa M.
   "Hoy Tarde." [Nuez] (3:7) 91, p. 14.
4740. PEREIRA, Sam
   "An Entity of Its Word" (for Linda). [AmerPoR] (20:3) My-Je 91, p. 56.
4741. PERELMAN, Bob
   "From the Front." [NewAW] (8/9) Fall 91, p. 14-17.
   "Person." [Sonora] (20) Wint 91, p. 39.
   "Phorism." [Shiny] (6) Spr-Sum 91, p. 37-41.
4742. PERETZ, Maya
   "Venus" (tr. of Halina Poswiatowska). [SnailPR] (1:2) Fall 91-Wint 92, p. 19.
4743. PEREZ FIRMAT, Gustavo
   "De Ultima Hora." [LindLM] (10:1) Ja-Mr 91, p. 32.
4744. PERILLO, Lucia Maria
   "Death Gets a Chair." [Ploughs] (17:4) Wint 91-92, p. 80-81.
   "Turnpike." [Ploughs] (17:4) Wint 91-92, p. 78-79.
4745. PERIMAN, John
   "After flight the wanderer escapes pursuit." [Talisman] (7) Fall 91, p. 29.
   "Lost." [Talisman] (7) Fall 91, p. 30.
4746. PERKINS, James Ashbrook
   "The Sound of My Brush." [US1] (24/25) Spr 91, p. 20.
4747. PERKINS, Joan
   "Bros." [BambooR] (50/51) Spr-Sum 91, p. 38.
4748. PERLBERG, Mark
   "Awake in the Night." [PraS] (65:1) Spr 91, p. 93.
   "The End of the Holidays." [PraS] (65:1) Spr 91, p. 93-94.
4749. PERLMAN, John
   "December First." [Abraxas] (40/41) 91, p. 120-121.
   "Wind." [Abraxas] (40/41) 91, p. 120.
   "Winter Solstice, 1990." [Abraxas] (40/41) 91, p. 121.
4750. PERLMAN, Katy
   "It Is Like the Rain to Make One Look for Signs." [CalQ] (35/36) 91, p. 133.
4751. PERLONGO, Bob
   "Transformation." [Boulevard] (6:2/3, #17/18) Fall 91, p. 168-169.
4752. PERONARD, Kai
   "First Night." [InterPR] (17:1) Spr 91, p. 118.
4753. PERRINE, Laurence
   "The Creation" (Modern Revised Version). [Poetry] (157:6) Mr 91, p. 323.
   "Justice and Mercy Reconciled." [Poetry] (157:6) Mr 91, p. 323.
   "A Question (for Robert Frost)." [Poetry] (157:6) Mr 91, p. 323.
4754. PERRY, Coties
   "A Serious Vision." [Sequoia] (34:1) Spr 91, p. 76-77.
4755. PERRY, Jorica
   "This Is the Island." [PraF] (12:1 #54) Spr 91, p. 34.
4756. PERRY, Marion
   "Poem to Offend Just About Everyone." [MoodySI] (24/25/26) Spr 91, p. 51.
4757. PERRY, Stephen
   "Blue Spruce." [NewYorker] (66:50) 28 Ja 91, p. 34-35.

"Keats' Opium Dream." [DenQ] (26:1) Sum 91, p. 59-60.
"Metaphysical Green." [Journal] (14:2) Wint 91, p. 83-84.
"Satisfaction." [CimR] (96) Jl 91, p. 110-111.
"Small Myth for My Father." [NewYorker] (67:36) 28 O 91, p. 100.
"Tenements of Rose and Ice." [VirQR] (67:2) Spr 91, p. 268-271.

4758. PERSAUD, Sasenarine
"Tiger Swami." [GrahamHR] (14) Spr 91, p. 20-21.

4759. PERSUN, Terry L.
"The Men." [ChironR] (10:4) Wint 91, p. 7.
"The Showers." [ChironR] (10:4) Wint 91, p. 7.
"Thai Women." [ChironR] (10:4) Wint 91, p. 7.
"The Tying Together." [DustyD] (2:1) Ja 91, p. 26.

4760. PESEROFF, Joyce
"Gingerland." [Agni] (34) 91, p. 151-152.

4761. PESSOA, Fernando (Alberto Caeiro, Alvaro de Campos)
"A alma vive enquanto dura a saudade que deixou na terra." [Trans] (25) Spr 91, p. 36-37.
"In This World Where We Forget" (tr. by Keith Bosley). [Trans] (25) Spr 91, p. 17-18.
"The Keeper of Sheep" (Selections: VII, XI, XIII, XXIX, tr. by Edwin Honig and Susan M. Brown). [Trans] (25) Spr 91, p. 14-16.
"A Letter to Fernando Pessoa" (tr. by Richard Zenith). [Trans] (25) Spr 91, p. 57.
"The soul lives as long as the regret it left on earth" (tr. by the author). [Trans] (25) Spr 91, p. 36-37.
"Time's Passage" (Selection: II, tr. by Richard Zenith). [Trans] (25) Spr 91, p. 30-35.

4762. PETERS, Kimberly
"Both of the Same Beginning." [WestB] (28) 91, p. 5.
"Foreplay" (for Lisa). [WestB] (28) 91, p. 6-7.

4763. PETERS, Mark R.
"Epiphany: Addressing the Hunger." [Elf] (1:4) Wint 91, p. 35.

4764. PETERS, Robert
"Bavaria Needs Him." [CoalC] (3) My 91, p. 19.
"Closeup" (from "Serial Killer"). [ConnPR] (10:1) 91, p. 26.
"Enraged Woman." [JamesWR] (8:2) Wint 91, p. 7.
"Hawthorne and the Chimney Swallows." [CoalC] (3) My 91, p. 2.
"Lady Giving Birth." [ChironR] (10:4) Wint 91, p. 3.
"Lover." [ChironR] (10:4) Wint 91, p. 3.
"Potatoes." [CoalC] (3) My 91, p. 2.
"Red Bougainvillea." [ChironR] (10:4) Wint 91, p. 3.
"Shopping Plaza." [Rohwedder] (6) Sum-Fall 91, p. 18.
"Snapshot of God with Sinner." [ChironR] (10:4) Wint 91, p. 3.

PETERSEN, Anne Oriel
See ORIEL-PETERSEN, Anne

4765. PETERSEN, Yvonne
"Passages." [HawaiiR] (15:3, #33) Fall 91, p. 72.

4766. PETERSON, Allan
"Asleep to the Light." [CapeR] (26:1) Spr 91, p. 4.
"Dark and Heartfelt." [ChatR] (11:3) Spr 91, p. 34.
"Palms." [Poem] (65) My 91, p. 55.
"Queens Waving." [ChatR] (11:3) Spr 91, p. 33.
"Something Inside Him." [EmeraldCR] (3) 91, c1990, p. 17-18.
"Something of a Ghost." [Poem] (65) My 91, p. 56.
"Watch Repair." [EmeraldCR] (3) 91, c1990, p. 75-76.

4767. PETERSON, Jim
"A Drawing of the Laughing Jesus." [SnailPR] (1:2) Fall 91-Wint 92, p. 16.
"Something." [GeoR] (45:4) Wint 91, p. 693-694.

4768. PETERSON, John
"Fire in the Arctic." [PoetC] (22:4) Sum 91, p. 8-9.
"Love, ad Nauseam." [PoetC] (22:4) Sum 91, p. 7.
"Notes from the Art Director." [PoetC] (22:4) Sum 91, p. 6.
"To All Gates" (after a sculpture by George Segal). [PoetC] (22:4) Sum 91, p. 3-4.
"The Years She Saved." [PoetC] (22:4) Sum 91, p. 5.

4769. PETERSON, Karen
"She Was Dancing by the Jukebox Like a Rose That Blooms in Gin." [SwampR] (7/8) Spr-Sum 91, p. 33.

4770. PETERSON, Kris
"Death." [PraF] (12:1 #54) Spr 91, p. 86.
"I Was Just Hungry Fuck." [PraF] (12:1 #54) Spr 91, p. 87.
4771. PETERSON, Lesley
"That Which Is Golden." [PraF] (12:1 #54) Spr 91, p. 69.
4772. PETERSON, Susan
"Allhallows Month." [MidwQ] (33:1) Aut 91, p. 74.
"Classified Ads." [Farm] (8:1) Spr-Sum 91, p. 41-43.
"Romance." [Farm] (8:1) Spr-Sum 91, p. 44.
4773. PETIT, James
"Bateaux." [PoetryNW] (32:3) Aut 91, p. 23.
"Willapa Bay." [PoetryNW] (32:3) Aut 91, p. 22-23.
4774. PETÖFI, Sándor
"At the End of September" (tr. by Leslie Gartner). [NewEngR] (13:3/4) Spr-Sum
91, p. 202.
4775. PETOSKEY, Barbara J.
"Kilauea." [HawaiiR] (15:3, #33) Fall 91, p. 37.
"Sketch." [HawaiiR] (15:3, #33) Fall 91, p. 141.
4776. PETRARCH
"Sonnet 75" (tr. by Lee Harlin Bahan). [Hellas] (2:1) Spr 91, p. 73.
4777. PETREMAN, David A.
"Fidel at Home." [CinPR] (21) Spr 90, p. 70.
4778. PETRI, György
"Dark-Side Up" (tr. by Nicholas Kolumban). [SenR] (21:1) Spr 91, p. 19-20.
"In the Horatian Mode" (tr. by Nicholas Kolumban). [SenR] (21:1) Spr 91, p. 18.
"A Spectacle, an Opinion" (For Sz. V., tr. by Nicholas Kolumban). [SenR] (21:1)
Spr 91, p. 21-22.
"You Were Impersonal Like the Others" (for Imre Nagy, tr. by Nicholas Kolumban).
[NoDaQ] (59:1) Wint 91, p. 118.
4779. PETRIE, Loretta
"Cross-Stitched." [BambooR] (50/51) Spr-Sum 91, p. 255.
4780. PETRIE, Paul
"Condolences" (Tennyson after the death of Thackeray). [AmerS] (60:3) Sum 91, p.
439.
"Late Celebration." [SoCaR] (23:2) Spr 91, p. 120.
"The Scavengers." [TexasR] (11:1/2) Spr-Sum 90, p. 50.
4781. PETROUSKE, Rosalie Sanara
"The Geisha Box." [Parting] (4:1) Sum 91, p. 21.
"Mother & Daughter, Dreaming." [Parting] (4:1) Sum 91, p. 1, insert.
"Mother & Daughter, Remembering." [Parting] (4:1) Sum 91, p. 3, insert.
"Someday the Well Runs Dry." [Parting] (4:1) Sum 91, p. 2-3, insert.
4782. PETROV, Aleksandar
"Aubade" (tr. by Richard Burns and the author). [NewOR] (18:2) Sum 91, p. 88.
"Serbia on the Maps" (tr. by Krinka Vidakovic-Petrov). [CimR] (96) Jl 91, p. 25.
PETROV, Krinka Vidakovic
See VIDAKOVIC-PETROV, Krinka
4783. PETROVA, Alexandra
"1,2,3" (tr. by Laura D. Weeks). [LitR] (34:3) Spr 91, p. 380.
"The Hebrew Alphabet" (tr. by Laura D. Weeks). [LitR] (34:3) Spr 91, p. 380-381.
"In Search of the Desired Name" (tr. by Laura D. Weeks). [LitR] (34:3) Spr 91, p.
381.
"X. The air is skidding. On his native city" (tr. by Laura D. Weeks). [LitR] (34:3)
Spr 91, p. 380.
4784. PETRUCCI, Mario
"Smog." [CoalC] (4) S 91, p. 1.
"Venus." [CoalC] (4) S 91, p. 9.
4785. PETRY, Julia Meeker
"Troubled Shoes." [PacificR] (10) 91-92, p. 124.
4786. PETTET, Simon
"The blue monkey." [HangL] (58) 91, p. 60.
"Rosy Smiles Her Cheeks Adorning." [HangL] (58) 91, p. 61-62.
"Runaway thief from the house of Mrs Mary Bradock." [HangL] (58) 91, p. 62.
"Sad to have to remember." [HangL] (58) 91, p. 60.
4787. PETTIT, Michael
"Four Birds of Paradise." [OhioR] (47) 91, p. 84-85.

4788. PFEIFER, Michael
"Fairy Tales." [PoetL] (86:4) Wint 91-92, p. 43.
"Giving Up." [Grain] (19:4) Wint 91, p. 57.
"In the Readiong Room." [Grain] (19:4) Wint 91, p. 58.
"Italian Movie." [NowestR] (29:3) 91, p. 38.
"Murder." [CalQ] (32/33) Spr 90, p. 139.
4789. PFEIFER, Theresa M.
"The Dog Who Knows." [MinnR] (NS 36) Spr 91, p. 19.
PFIEIFER, Michael
See PFEIFER, Michael
4790. PFINGSTON, Roger
"Cicadas" (Spring, 1987, Bloomington, Indiana). [SpoonRQ] (16:3/4) Sum-Fall 91,
p. 21-22.
"Julie's Game." [Northeast] (5:4) Sum 91, p. 18.
4791. PFLUM, Richard
"Poetry Zoo." [HopewellR] (1991) 91, p. 22.
4792. PHENIX, Patricia
"Through My Pane." [Grain] (19:1) Spr 91, p. 93.
"Viginia's Death." [Grain] (19:1) Spr 91, p. 94.
4793. PHILBRICK, Nathaniel
"Autumn Scene on Orange Street." [ManhatPR] (13) [91?], p. 33.
"The Caretaker." [ManhatPR] (13) [91?], p. 33.
4794. PHILBRICK, Stephen
"Men." [BelPoJ] (41:4) Sum 91, p. 35-37.
"Nothing on Paper." [BelPoJ] (41:4) Sum 91, p. 34.
"Secrest 273" (Every purebred sheep is identified by name, of the farm or famer, and
number). [NewYorker] (67:2) 4 Mr 91, p. 38.
4795. PHILIPS, Elizabeth
"The Goldfish Keeper II." [Grain] (19:3) Fall 91, p. 30-31.
"Meditation on *Chuang Tzu*" (for Patrick). [Grain] (19:3) Fall 91, p. 28-29.
"Meditation on the Domestic." [Grain] (19:3) Fall 91, p. 32.
4796. PHILLIBER, James
"Expressions." [PoetryUSA] (23) Sum 91, p. 20.
4797. PHILLIPS, Carl
"Blue." [Callaloo] (14:2) Spr 91, p. 439.
"Death of the Sibyl." [Callaloo] (14:2) Spr 91, p. 440.
"Elegy." [RiverS] (34) 91, p. 41.
"The Glade." [Agni] (33) 91, p. 56.
"Leda, After the Swan." [Agni] (33) 91, p. 54-55.
"On Being Asked to Recall the Annunciation." [Vis] (36) 91, p. 43.
4798. PHILLIPS, David
"Barry McKinnon Says the Imagination Is the Place." [CapilR] (2:5) Sum 91, p.
78-79.
"Cutthroat." [CapilR] (2:5) Sum 91, p. 72.
"Driving North." [CapilR] (2:5) Sum 91, p. 71.
"Foundations." [CapilR] (2:5) Sum 91, p. 73-74.
"A Note." [CapilR] (2:5) Sum 91, p. 75.
"Poem for Barrie (from Sechelt)." [CapilR] (2:5) Sum 91, p. 76-77.
4799. PHILLIPS, Dennis
"Like a Firespout or Listen." [WashR] (17:1) Je-Jl 91, p. 9.
"Objects of Worship." [WashR] (17:1) Je-Jl 91, p. 9.
"The Theme of Roadways" (from "Etudes"). [WashR] (17:1) Je-Jl 91, p. 9.
4800. PHILLIPS, Frances
"Drifts and Shifts." [HangL] (58) 91, p. 63-67.
"Lilies of the Valley." [HangL] (58) 91, p. 68-69.
4801. PHILLIPS, Frank Lamont
"An Apology." [Obs] (6:1) Spr 91, p. 88.
"For Sarah." [Obs] (6:1) Spr 91, p. 88-89.
"Slave Ship." [Obs] (6:1) Spr 91, p. 89.
4802. PHILLIPS, Kathy
"Kuan Yin, Inventor." [BambooR] (50/51) Spr-Sum 91, p. 320-321.
"Speaking to Kuan Yin." [BambooR] (50/51) Spr-Sum 91, p. 318-319.
4803. PHILLIPS, Louis
"Dick Tracy Pursues Little Face Finny to Mount Olympus Where, Together, They
Enter the Garden of the Gods." [SoCoast] (10) Fall 91, p. 52-53.
"Enzymes." [SoCaR] (23:2) Spr 91, p. 104.

"I Ought Not to Be Writing Stories, But Falling in Love" (Chekhov). [WebR] (15)
    Spr 91, p. 96.
"Life Conceived Not Quite As a Soap Opera." [SoCoast] (11) Wint 91, p. 13.
"My Sons Too Funny for Words." [OxfordM] (7:2) Fall-Wint 91, p. 67.
"The Poet by Day, Imitating Captain Marvel, Utters the Magic Word . . . ."
    [SoCoast] (10) Fall 91, p. 51.
"What Is It That We Desire So Much?" [WebR] (15) Spr 91, p. 95.
4804. PHILLIPS, Mary Gaylen
    "For Daddy." [EmeraldCR] (3) 91, c1990, p. 35-36.
4805. PHILLIPS, Michael Lee
    "The brutal inspiration to move boulders." [ManhatPR] (13) [91?], p. 50.
    "Loess." [AntR] (49:4) Fall 91, p. 552.
    "Night at Racetrack, Death Valley." [ManhatPR] (13) [91?], p. 48.
    "Where early tertiary igneous." [ManhatPR] (13) [91?], p. 49.
4806. PHILLIPS, Robert
    "Genius." [Chelsea] (52) 91, p. 90-91.
4807. PHILLIPS, Walt
    "Another Post-Card from Hell." [BlackBR] (13) Spr-Sum 91, p. 34.
    "Down by the Old Mill Stream." [SlipS] (11) 91, p. 79.
    "Following an Intensity." [BlackBR] (14) Fall-Wint 91, p. 14.
    "John Wayne Memorial Airport." [ChironR] (10:3) Aut 91, p. 46.
    "Neo-Mountain Man." [BlackBR] (13) Spr-Sum 91, p. 34.
    "One Recollection from the Silent Generation." [NewYorkQ] (46) 91, p. 61.
    "Simple Folks." [ChironR] (10:4) Wint 91, p. 36.
    "Who Can Explain the Mind?" [Lactuca] (14) My 91, p. 59.
4808. PHILLIS, Randy
    "Dead." [CapeR] (26:2) Fall 91, p. 46.
    "Partners." [CapeR] (26:2) Fall 91, p. 45.
4809. PHILODEMUS
    "V.4. Philaenis, fill the bedroom's oil lamp" (tr. by Joseph S. Salemi). [Trans] (25)
        Spr 91, p. 219.
    "V.13. Charito is past sixty, and yet sill" (tr. by Joseph S. Salemi). [Trans] (25) Spr
        91, p. 219.
    "V.131. Fingers on the lyre, lilting speech" (tr. by Joseph S. Salemi). [Trans] (25)
        Spr 91, p. 220.
    "X.21. Kypris the serene, lover of nuptials" (tr. by Joseph S. Salemi). [Trans] (25)
        Spr 91, p. 220.
    "XI.34. No more white violets, no, nor tuneful songs" (tr. by Joseph S. Salemi).
        [Trans] (25) Spr 91, p. 221.
    "XI.41. Already, from life's book of years" (tr. by Joseph S. Salemi). [Trans] (25)
        Spr 91, p. 221.
4810. PHILPOT, Tracy
    "The Funeral of Homesickness." [NewAW] (8/9) Fall 91, p. 50.
    "How to Live in the Elegy." [RiverS] (35) 91, p. 28-29.
    "News from Czechoslovakia." [MassR] (32:1) Spr 91, p. 36-37.
    "The Rain My Wife." [RiverS] (35) 91, p. 27.
4811. PHIPPS, Wanda
    "May" (tr. of Natalka Bilotserkivets, w. Virlana Tkacz). [Agni] (34) 91, p. 51-54.
4812. PICARD, Meredith
    "Winter Stream." [Plain] (12:1) Fall 91, p. 33.
4813. PICASSO, Pablo
    "To Alice" (10 February XXXVI, tr. by Vanina Deler). [OnTheBus] (8/9) 91, p.
        190-193.
4814. PICAZO, Alicia
    "The War between the Genitals" (tr. of Guillermo Truculento, w. Janet Sunderland).
        [BilingR] (16:1) Ja-Ap 91, p. 65-66.
4815. PICCOLO, Pina
    "Desert Sand." [PoetryUSA] (22) Spr 91, p. 7.
    "Sindbad." [PoetryUSA] (22) Spr 91, p. 13.
4816. PICKARD, Deanna
    "Chicory." [CinPR] (22) Spr 91, p. 68-69.
    "Night Playing." [Nimrod] (35:1) Fall-Wint 91, p. 79.
4817. PICKARD, Tom
    "Energy." [NewAW] (8/9) Fall 91, p. 133-134.
    "Let's Picket-Out This Scab Summer, Sun" (Miners' strike 1984). [NewAW] (8/9)
        Fall 91, p. 132-133.

338

"Nues" (a painting by Djurdje Teodorvic). [NewAW] (8/9) Fall 91, p. 131-132.
"What Maks Makems." [NewAW] (8/9) Fall 91, p. 129-131.

4818. PICKETT, John
"The Foundry." [CalQ] (35/36) 91, p. 121.
"This Is a Tradition That Dies." [CalQ] (35/36) 91, p. 122.
"The Tick." [CalQ] (35/36) 91, p. 123.

4819. PIEKARSKI, Thomas
"The Breathing Chopin." [CreamCR] (14:2) Wint 91, p. 178.
"Deadwood: Wild Bill." [WebR] (15) Spr 91, p. 109.
"End Zone." [WebR] (15) Spr 91, p. 108-109.
"Tracking Rembrandt." [WebR] (15) Spr 91, p. 109.

4820. PIEKOS, Jeannie L.
"Jacob After One Year — Keeping the Faith in 3/4 Time." [LakeSR] (25) 91, p. 5.

4821. PIERCE, Deborah
"Railroad Crossing." [SouthernPR] (31:1) Spr 91, p. 12.

4822. PIERCE, Pamela
"Roberta." [SoDakR] (29:3 part 2) Aut 91, p. 57-58.

4823. PIERCY, Marge
"The 31st of March." [BostonR] (16:1) F 91, p. 15.
"Anxiety Wins a Round." [HeavenB] (9) Wint-Spr 91-92, p. 2.
"Domestic Danger." [SycamoreR] (3:2) Sum 91, p. 37.
"Little Pischna Revisited." [RiverS] (35) 91, p. 15-16.
"March Comes in Cleft Hooves." [RiverS] (35) 91, p. 17.
"Off Season Rental." [Vis] (36) 91, p. 7.
"Woman in the Bushes." [RiverS] (35) 91, p. 18-18.
"Yearning to Repossess the Body." [Vis] (36) 91, p. 6.

4824. PIERMAN, Carol J.
"The Bromide." [ThRiPo] (37/38) 91, p. 62-63.
"Interstate Travel." [ThRiPo] (37/38) 91, p. 58-59.
"Return." [ThRiPo] (37/38) 91, p. 60-61.

PIERO, W. S. di
See Di PIERO, W. S.

4825. PIGGFORD, George
"You Can't Have Gay Back." [JamesWR] (8:4) Sum 91, p. 13.

PIGNO, Antonia Quintana
See QUINTANA PIGNO, Antonia

4826. PILCHER, Barry Edgar
"It's somebody knocking" (from "Mountain Juggling," art by Jocelyn Almond).
[Bogg] (64) 91, p. 66.

4827. PILKINGTON, Ace G.
"Where We Share." [Interim] (10:1) Spr-Sum 91, p. 46.

4828. PILLER, John
"Domestic Violence." [PoetryE] (32) Fall 91, p. 122.

4829. PINE, Ana
"Freedom." [SmPd] (28:1, #81) Wint 91, p. 22.
"Two Hour Delay." [Gypsy] (17) 91, p. 26-27.

4830. PINE, Connie
"Sin." [PoetryUSA] (22) Spr 91, p. 1.

PING, Chou
See CHOU, Ping

PING, Tang Ya
See TANG, Ya Ping

4831. PINO, José Manuel del
"Doré III" (tr. by G. J. Racz). [PoetL] (86:1) Spr 91, p. 32.
"Doré IV" (tr. by G. J. Racz). [PoetL] (86:1) Spr 91, p. 33-34.
"The Moonbeam" (tr. by G. J. Racz). [PoetL] (86:1) Spr 91, p. 31.
"Sexual Ode II" (To the woman pianist with the light-green eyes, tr. by G. J. Racz).
[PoetL] (86:1) Spr 91, p. 35.

4832. PINSKY, Robert
"The City Dark." [Thrpny] (46) Sum 91, p. 35.
"Dictionary of Wilno Streets (1967)" (from "Beginning with My Streets," tr. of
Czeslaw Milosz, w. the author, Robert Hass and Renata Gorczynski). [ParisR]
(33:120) Fall 91, p. 261-263.
"Everywhere I Go, There I Am." [NewYorker] (66:50) 28 Ja 91, p. 30.
"Ginza Samba." [TriQ] (83) Wint 91-92, p. 95-96.
"The Heartmoss." [Ploughs] (17:2/3) Fall 91, p. 33.

4833. PIOMBINO, Nick
"Aftermath: Epilogue to the *Boundary of Blur*" (Excerpts: entries from 9-8-86 to
12-29-87). [Avec] (4:1) 91, p. 110-112.
"Imprint." [OnTheBus] (8/9) 91, p. 133.
"An Odd Reprisal." [Aerial] (6/7) 91, p. 176-177.
4834. PISTOLAS, Androula (Androula Savvas)
"Darling Fright." [Gypsy] (17) 91, p. 68.
"Frying Time." [ChironR] (10:4) Wint 91, p. 10.
4835. PITTS, Lois
"Dawn in February." [Nimrod] (34:2) Spr-Sum 91, p. 109.
4836. PLATER, Lynda
"Heron and Tree." [Stand] (32:2) Spr 91, p. 70.
4837. PLATH, James
"The Barns in Wisconsin." [SpoonRQ] (16:3/4) Sum-Fall 91, p. 71.
"The Boy Who Would Be God." [SpoonRQ] (16:3/4) Sum-Fall 91, p. 70.
4838. PLATT, Donald (Don)
"Counting Vertebrae." [PoetryNW] (32:3) Aut 91, p. 34-35.
"Grief." [Timbuktu] (6) Spr 91, p. 55.
"Heliotrope." [PoetryNW] (32:3) Aut 91, p. 37.
"My Brother Learns to Eat." [PoetryNW] (32:3) Aut 91, p. 36.
4839. PLAYER, William
"Her Mouth." [ChironR] (10:4) Wint 91, p. 38.
"The Moment of Truth." [ChironR] (10:2) Sum 91, p. 44.
"Note Attached to a Package Sent to the Landlord." [ChironR] (10:3) Aut 91, p. 41.
Reprinted in [ChironR] (10:4) Wint 91, p. 36.
4840. PLEASE, Keith
"Sennes Cove." [Sequoia] (34:1) Spr 91, p. 98.
PLESSIS, Rachel Blau du
See DuPLESSIS, Rachel Blau
4841. PLEYNET, Marcelin
"Some Ruins" (tr. by Michael L. Johnson). [WebR] (15) Spr 91, p. 40.
4842. PLUM, Sydney Landon
"Make Love, Not War." [SoDakR] (29:2) Sum 91, p. 50-51.
4843. PLUMLY, Stanley
"Lazarus at Dawn." [Antaeus] (67) Fall 91, p. 112-113.
"Reading with Poets" (for Stanley Kunitz). [Antaeus] (67) Fall 91, p. 110-111.
4844. PLUMMER, Deb
"Fields of Water." [CapeR] (26:1) Spr 91, p. 6.
"The Ring of Single Solutions." [CapeR] (26:1) Spr 91, p. 5.
4845. PLYMELL, Charles
"San Francisco Ward." [Spirit] (11) 91, p. 107-108.
PO, Chu-i
See BAI, Juyi
PO, Chü-yi
See BAI, Juyi
PO, Li
See LI, Po
4846. POBO, Kenneth
"Andrew, Flying Paper Planes." [NorthStoneR] (10) Fall 91-Wint 92, p. 84.
"Angels at the Border." [Interim] (10:1) Spr-Sum 91, p. 3.
"Angels Don't Tell." [ChamLR] (8-9) Spr-Fall 91, p. 53.
"Cicada Promise." [Grain] (19:3) Fall 91, p. 93.
"Jennifer on a Quiet Night." [Farm] (8:2) Fall-Wint 91-92, p. 41.
"Under Our Eaves." [Interim] (10:1) Spr-Sum 91, p. 4.
4847. POINTER, David S.
"Sign Language." [BlackBR] (14) Fall-Wint 91, p. 31.
4848. POLAK, Maralyn Lois
"Animal Rites" (for Gary). [PaintedB] (43) 91, p. 10-11.
4849. POLGAR, Steven
"Farewell" (tr. of Wojciech Gniatczynski). [AmerPoR] (20:2) Mr-Ap 91, p. 30.
"There Is a Goal to Our Peregrinations" (tr. of Wojciech Gniatczynski, w. the
author). [AmerPoR] (20:2) Mr-Ap 91, p. 30.
4850. POLITE, Frank
"The Fabled Quadrant." [OhioR] (46) 91, p. 46-47.
4851. POLITO, Robert
"Animal Mimicry." [Agni] (34) 91, p. 46-50.

"Orphans." [BostonR] (16:3/4) Je-Ag 91, p. 5.
"To My Father." [Ploughs] (17:2/3) Fall 91, p. 151-153.
4852. POLK, Geoffrey
"Grand Canals." [Parting] (4:2) Wint 91-92, p. 31-33.
POLK, Lara Anderson
See ANDERSON-POLK, Lara
4853. POLLENTIER, Nicole
"Queen of the Leaves." [HangL] (58) 91, p. 86.
4854. POMERANTZ, Gary
"Tomorrow, Perhaps." [Nat] (253:7) 9 S 91, p. 279.
4855. PONIEWAZ, Jeff
"Affluence Terrorizes Globe." [NewYorkQ] (45) 91, p. 60.
"Death Envy." [NewYorkQ] (46) 91, p. 47.
4856. PONSOT, Marie
"All Wet." [KenR] (NS 13:3) Sum 91, p. 96-97.
"Ghazals for Djuna Barnes: The Fall Back." [KenR] (NS 13:3) Sum 91, p. 97.
"I Ask Myself a Few Real Historical Questions" (Selections: 2-3). [BostonR] (16:1)
F 91, p. 8.
4857. POOLE, Joan Lauri
"Bradford Pear Trees." [Shen] (41:2) Sum 91, p. 77.
4858. POOLE, Richard
"Father to Son." [CumbPR] (10:2) Spr 91, p. 52-55.
"Nero to His Mirror." [CumbPR] (10:2) Spr 91, p. 50-51.
4859. POOR, Marjorie
"Lies She'd Tell Her Father." [PraF] (12:1 #54) Spr 91, p. 65.
"She dreams a thief in the night." [PraF] (12:1 #54) Spr 91, p. 65.
"She enters her dream." [PraF] (12:1 #54) Spr 91, p. 65.
POP, Marcel Cornis
See CORNIS-POP, Marcel
POP-CORNIS, Marcel
See CORNIS-POP, Marcel
4860. POPE, Deborah
"The Dentist." [SouthernPR] (31:2) Fall 91, p. 11-12.
"Two in the Moon." [ThRiPo] (37/38) 91, p. 41.
4861. POPE, Deidre
"Cold Snap." [Abraxas] (40/41) 91, p. 150.
4862. POPE, Vernal M.
"Not Just Any Woman." [Kalliope] (13:1) 91, p. 71.
4863. POPKIN, Louise B.
"Conversations with My Sandal" (tr. of Mauricio Rosencof, w. Julia H. Ackerman).
[KenR] (NS 13:3) Sum 91, p. 67-73.
4864. POPLE, Ian
"Therapies." [Verse] (8:2) Sum 91, p. 51.
4865. PORRITT, R. (Ruth)
"Cambium" (for my older brother). [Poem] (65) My 91, p. 13-14.
"Currents." [Poem] (65) My 91, p. 16.
"First Anniversary." [Poem] (65) My 91, p. 15.
"Letting Through." [Poem] (65) My 91, p. 17.
"Where Such a Thing As They Heard Comes From." [VirQR] (67:3) Sum 91, p.
486-490.
4866. PORTER, Anne
"Before the Frost." [Comm] (118:19) 8 N 91, p. 641.
"Listening to the Crows." [Comm] (118:22) 20 D 91, p. 751.
"Scott's Elegy." [Comm] (118:19) 8 N 91, p. 641.
"Wild Geese Alighting on a Lake." [Comm] (118:19) 8 N 91, p. 641.
4867. PORTER, Burt
"Arc Welder." [Hellas] (2:1) Spr 91, p. 72.
"Initiation" (two dreams from boyhood). [AntigR] (84) Wint 91, p. 127-128.
4868. PORTER, Caryl
"The Birthday." [Nimrod] (34:2) Spr-Sum 91, p. 131.
"Memory and Metamorphosis." [Nimrod] (34:2) Spr-Sum 91, p. 129-130.
"Wednesday's Child." [Nimrod] (34:2) Spr-Sum 91, p. 132.
4869. PORTER, Helen Fogwill
"Hot Night in July." [TickleAce] (21) Spr-Sum 91, p. 33.
4870. PORTER, Peter
"The Chair of Babel." [Verse] (8:2) Sum 91, p. 27-28.

4871. PORTLEY, Fran
"The Finger Painting." [Parting] (4:2) Wint 91-92, p. 11.
"It's Going to Be a Hard Winter." [Parting] (4:2) Wint 91-92, p. 12.
4872. POSTER, Carol
"Adam Schwartz Considers Original Scripts." [Outbr] (22) 91, p. 25.
4873. POSTMA, Kathlene
"Alice and Max." [HawaiiR] (15:2, #32) Spr 91, p. 2-3.
4874. POSWIATOWSKA, Halina
"Venus" (tr. by Maya Peretz). [SnailPR] (1:2) Fall 91-Wint 92, p. 19.
4875. POTTER, Carol
"Digging to China." [Journal] (14:2) Wint 91, p. 56-57.
"The Hanged Man." [Journal] (15:2) Fall 91, p. 67-68.
"Hey Baby, Baby." [Journal] (15:2) Fall 91, p. 71-72.
"Looks Like Home." [HighP] (6:3) Wint 91, p. 116-118.
"Pay What You Weigh." [Journal] (14:2) Wint 91, p. 54-55.
"The Summer After the Spring When Everything Flowered." [Journal] (15:2) Fall
91, p. 69-70.
"Trouble Rocking Back and Forth in Her Chair." [Journal] (14:2) Wint 91, p. 51-53.
4876. POTTER, Janice
"The Women Who Leapt from Enchanted Mesa." [DustyD] Je 91, p. 41.
4877. POTTER, Roderick
"Test Pattern." [ColEng] (53:3) Mr 91, p. 311.
4878. POTTINGER, Steve
"Global Warming." [Bogg] (64) 91, p. 56.
4879. POTTS, Randall
"Illustration." [AmerPoR] (20:4) Jl-Ag 91, p. 28.
"Point of No Return." [DenQ] (26:2) Fall 91, p. 46.
"Self Portrait." [AmerPoR] (20:4) Jl-Ag 91, p. 28.
4880. POULSEN, Malan
"Soul" (tr. by Leyvoy Joensen). [Vis] (37) 91, p. 22.
4881. POULSEN, Toroddur
"Hologram" (tr. by Cathryn J. Sanderson). [Vis] (37) 91, p. 22.
4882. POUNCY, C. R. P.
"He Wanted to Believe." [ChangingM] (22) Wint-Spr 91, p. 64.
4883. POUND, Omar
"All Growth Is Silent." [Nimrod] (34:2) Spr-Sum 91, p. 106.
"The Godlet of Assam (1871)." [Nimrod] (34:2) Spr-Sum 91, p. 107-108.
"A Winnibago Indian Tale." [AntigR] (84) Wint 91, p. 37.
"The Wise Mr. Butorides." [AntigR] (84) Wint 91, p. 38.
"With a Martial Air." [AntigR] (84) Wint 91, p. 37.
"A Wreath from Egil's Saga." [AntigR] (84) Wint 91, p. 36.
4884. POWELL, Dannye Romine
"Father." [Crucible] (27) Fall 91, p. 22.
"Van Gogh's Bedroom at Arles." [SouthernPR] (31:1) Spr 91, p. 46-47.
"Yard Sale: Charlotte, NC." [RiverS] (35) 91, p. 6-7.
4885. POWELL, Douglas (Douglas A.)
"Box Until Resembling." [Plain] (12:1) Fall 91, p. 30.
"Device Found Accessible." [Plain] (11:3) Spr 91, p. 17.
"Trousers to Play." [Plain] (11:3) Spr 91, p. 33.
4886. POWELL, Gregory
"Denied Stone." [Poem] (66) N 91, p. 67.
"The Last Supper." [Callaloo] (14:3) Sum 91, p. 668-669.
"The Last Supper." [Poem] (66) N 91, p. 62-63.
"Morning Consideration." [Callaloo] (14:3) Sum 91, p. 667.
"Morning Consideration." [Poem] (66) N 91, p. 66.
"Time Watcher." [Poem] (66) N 91, p. 64-65.
4887. POWELL, Jim
"Hektor and Andromache" (from the Illiad, tr. of Homer). [TriQ] (83) Wint 91-92,
p. 156-167.
"To Hermes" (from the Homeric Hymn to Hermes, tr. of Homer). [TriQ] (83) Wint
91-92, p. 168-182.
4888. POWELL, Joseph
"Last Things" (for Joe McManamy, 1907-1988). [PaintedHR] (1) Ja 91, p. 38-39.
"News Stories." [Hellas] (2:1) Spr 91, p. 58.
"River Crossing." [LouisL] (8:1) Spr 91, p. 37.
"The Social View: An Everyday Epic." [Hellas] (2:1) Spr 91, p. 59.

4889. POWELL, Kevin
"Haiku #2." [Obs] (6:2) Sum 91, p. 49.
4890. POWELL, Lynn
"Balm." [US1] (24/25) Spr 91, p. 3.
4891. POWER, Elise
"Montreal, after Costa Rica." [SmPd] (28:2, #82) Spr 91, p. 7.
4892. POWER, Marjorie
"Beginning of Autumn." [WebR] (15) Spr 91, p. 93.
"Homage to Lucille." [MalR] (97) Wint 91, p. 86.
"Retracting a Dear John Letter." [BellR] (14:1) Spr 91, p. 52.
"The Sanctuary." [ChrC] (108:34) 20-27 N 91, p. 1106.
4893. POWERS, Dan (Dan W.)
"Drought." [PaintedB] (43) 91, p. 8-9.
"Drought." [Poem] (65) My 91, p. 37.
"Faith." [Poem] (65) My 91, p. 36.
"October." [RiverC] (11:2) Spr 91, p. 67.
4894. POWERS, Richard L.
"Filler." [LouisL] (8:2) Fall 91, p. 97.
"The Plant." [Pembroke] (23) 91, p. 102-103.
"Stringer Madonna." [Pembroke] (23) 91, p. 101.
"Wildflowers." [LouisL] (8:2) Fall 91, p. 98.
4895. POYNER, Ken
"Lasting Order." [LaurelR] (25:2) Sum 91, p. 31.
"Stability." [WestB] (29) 91, p. 38.
"Working." [PoetL] (86:4) Wint 91-92, p. 30.
4896. POZARZYCKI, Julia Rhodes
"Someone Is Drowning." [PassN] (12:1) Sum 91, p. 6.
4897. PRADO, Adélia
"Love Song" (tr. by Ellen Watson). [NewOR] (18:4) Wint 91, p. 74.
4898. PRADO, Holly
"Perfection." [Pearl] (14) Fall-Wint 91, p. 50.
4899. PRAFKE, Jean
"Housedress." [InterPR] (17:1) Spr 91, p. 101.
"Selling the Farm." [CinPR] (22) Spr 91, p. 24.
4900. PRAISNER, Wanda S.
"College Pool." [US1] (24/25) Spr 91, p. 15.
4901. PRASSINOS, Gisèle
"Death" (tr. by Elizabeth Hahn and Brenda Casey). [Vis] (36) 91, p. 49.
4902. PRATT, Charels W.
"To Canterbury by the Pilgrims' Way." [LitR] (34:2) Wint 91, p. 202.
4903. PRATT, Minnie Bruce
"#35 We Say We Love Each Other" (for Joan, my lover 1/8/83). [SinW] (43/44)
Sum 91, p. 237-238.
4904. PRECIADO, Minerva
"Quince Fuzz." [OnTheBus] (8/9) 91, p. 134.
4905. PREFONTAINE, Joan Wolf
"Hera." [Plain] (12:2) Wint 91, p. 34.
4906. PRELER, Horacio
"Elogio de la Santidad y la Locura." [Nuez] (3:8/9) 91, p. 34.
"Los Méritos de la Creación." [Nuez] (3:8/9) 91, p. 34.
4907. PRELIPCEANU, Nicolae
"The Ironical Poet" (tr. by Adam J. Sorkin and Sergiu Celac). [LitR] (35:1) Fall 91,
p. 35-36.
4908. PRENTICE, Penelope
"I Have Become" (for Rhoda). [MoodySI] (24/25/26) Spr 91, p. 27.
4909. PRESSMAN, Stephanie
"The Healing." [SingHM] (19) 91, p. 120-121.
4910. PREST, Peter
"Revelation." [MalR] (95) Sum 91, p. 83.
4911. PRESTON, Scott
"Exactly Halfway Between Carey and Arco" (for Charlie Potts). [ChironR] (10:3)
Aut 91, p. 10.
"New Shoshone Song" (for Bill Studebaker). [ChironR] (10:3) Aut 91, p. 10.
"Roadlife." [ChironR] (10:3) Aut 91, p. 10.
4912. PRETTO, Daniel
"Addison's Mom." [EmeraldCR] (4) 91, p. 25.

4913. PRICE, Elizabeth
"Sky." [PaintedB] (42) 91, p. 29.
4914. PRICE, Polly
"Hapgood Street." [PikeF] (10) Spr 91, p. 9.
"Life's Expensive." [PikeF] (10) Spr 91, p. 9.
"My City Brother Writes That He Thinks of Buying a Kitten." [PikeF] (10) Spr 91,
p. 15.
4915. PRICE, Reynolds
"First Green." [SewanR] (99:3) Sum 91, p. 400.
"Lights Out." [SewanR] (99:3) Sum 91, p. 400.
"To the Memory of James Boatwright 1933-1988." [SewanR] (99:3) Sum 91, p.
398-399.
4916. PRICE, Ron
"Migrant Call." [ContextS] (2:2) 91, p. 24.
4917. PRINCE, Heather Browne
"Going Where I Touch." [PottPort] (13:1) Spr 91, p. 7.
"Grieving His Wife." [PottPort] (13:1) Spr 91, p. 8.
"Here Is the Smell of Smoke." [PottPort] (13:1) Spr 91, p. 6.
"Loon" (for Margaret). [TickleAce] (21) Spr-Sum 91, p. 61.
"You Ask Me What I Am Afraid Of." [PottPort] (13:1) Spr 91, p. 5.
4918. PRITCHARD, Selwyn
"Being and Time." [SoDakR] (29:4) Wint 91, p. 149.
"Imitations of Art." [SoDakR] (29:4) Wint 91, p. 147.
"In the Woop-woops" (Poatina, Tasmania). [Iowa] (21:1) Wint 91, p. 24.
"On the New Parliament House, Canberra, New Year, 1990." [SoDakR] (29:4) Wint
91, p. 148.
"The Tempest: Rain Stopped Play." [AntigR] (84) Wint 91, p. 17.
"Washing Up." [Iowa] (21:1) Wint 91, p. 26.
"Williamstown Beach." [Iowa] (21:1) Wint 91, p. 24-25.
"Without Barbarians." [Iowa] (21:1) Wint 91, p. 25-26.
4919. PRIVETT, Katharine
"For John Berryman." [Nimrod] (34:2) Spr-Sum 91, p. 89.
"Long Illness." [Nimrod] (34:2) Spr-Sum 91, p. 90.
"Shadows." [Nimrod] (34:2) Spr-Sum 91, p. 87.
"Two" (in memory of the acting couple, Alfred Lunt and Lynn Fontanne). [Nimrod]
(34:2) Spr-Sum 91, p. 88.
4920. PROCOPI, Nickolas
"15926535." [OnTheBus] (8/9) 91, p. 136.
"Lerner Shops." [OnTheBus] (8/9) 91, p. 135.
4921. PROPER, Stan
"Earthy Moorings." [Lactuca] (14) My 91, p. 47.
"Ghosts Shout." [Pearl] (13) Spr-Sum 91, p. 11.
"Gravestones." [Lactuca] (14) My 91, p. 48.
"People's Lives." [Lactuca] (14) My 91, p. 47.
"Waking Paths." [Lactuca] (14) My 91, p. 48.
"When We Walk Meekly Mute." [DustyD] Je 91, p. 20.
4922. PROSER, Maria A.
"Testament: Fragments" (Quechua People's Poetry, tr. of the Spanish of Jesús Lara,
w. James Scully). [NoDaQ] (59:4) Fall 91, p. 78.
"What Cloud Is That Cloud" (Quechua People's Poetry, tr. of the Spanish of Jesús
Lara, w. James Scully). [NoDaQ] (59:4) Fall 91, p. 78-79.
4923. PROSPERE, Susan
"On Thin Ice." [NewYorker] (66:51) 4 F 91, p. 36.
4924. PRUNTY, Wyatt
"Blue Miniatures." [PacificR] (10) 91-92, p. 17-18.
"Memorial Day." [Hellas] (2:1) Spr 91, p. 127.
4925. PRZYSTUPA, Artur
"XXX" (3 poems, tr. by Tomek Kitlinski, Chris Hurford, and Góska A.
Staniewska). [Verse] (8:2) Sum 91, p. 119-120.
PTO
See P.T.O.
4926. PULIDO, Blanca Luz
"Omen" (tr. by Thomas Hoeksema and R. Enriquez). [Paint] (18:36) Aut 91, p. 63.
4927. PULLEY, Nancy
"Last Night, We Talked About Writing Our Wills." [HopewellR] (1991) 91, p. 21.
"Releasing the Years: Iron Mountain Road." [HopewellR] (1991) 91, p. 17.

4928. PULTZ, Constance
"Crack." [SlipS] (11) 91, p. 71.
"Disinherited." [NegC] (11:3) 91, p. 34.
"Movie Buff." [SlipS] (11) 91, p. 71.
4929. PURCELL, Judi
"The Sun and Me." [EmeraldCR] (4) 91, p. 43.
4930. PURDY, Al
"Chac Mool at Chichen Itza." [Quarry] (40:1/2) Wint-Spr 91, p. 148-149.
"Coastal." [Quarry] (40:1/2) Wint-Spr 91, p. 147.
"The Crucifix Across the Mountains." [Quarry] (40:1/2) Wint-Spr 91, p. 144-146.
"The Freezing Music." [Quarry] (40:1/2) Wint-Spr 91, p. 150.
"Leavetaking." [Quarry] (40:1/2) Wint-Spr 91, p. 151.
4931. PURDY, James
"My Greatest Pain." [RedBass] (15) 91, p. 11.
"The Thick Residuum of Night." [RedBass] (15) 91, p. 12.
4932. PURKEY, Bruce
"Eric's Gift." [BellR] (14:2) Fall 91, p. 7.
4933. PURPURA, Lia
"Exorcist" (tr. of Katarzyna Borun-Jagodzinska, w. the author). [Agni] (34) 91, p.
195.
"A Few Years After Nero" (tr. of Katarzyna Borun-Jagodzinska, w. the author).
[Agni] (34) 91, p. 197-198.
"On Manet's 'Olympia'" (tr. of Katarzyna Borun-Jagodzinska, w. the author).
[Agni] (34) 91, p. 196.
4934. PURSIFULL, Carmen (Carmen M.)
"Elsewhere / Wave #10." [HeavenB] (9) Wint-Spr 91-92, p. 52.
"Fairy Tale for a Tired Feminist." [CoalC] (4) S 91, p. 5.
"Spanish Fly." [CoalC] (3) My 91, p. 4.
4935. PYBUS, Rodney
"From the Northern Greek." [Stand] (32:4) Aut 91, p. 70-73.
4936. QABBANI, Nizar
"The Children of Stone" (in Arabic and English, tr. by Naseer H. Aruri). [InterPR]
(17:1) Spr 91, p. 15.
"Children of the Stones" (tr. by Reja-e Busailah). [InterPR] (17:2) Fall 91, p. 83.
"Diaries of a Woman Who Does Not Care" (in Arabic and English, tr. by Naseer H.
Aruri). [InterPR] (17:1) Spr 91, p. 11.
"Honorary Doctorate in Stone Chemistry" (in Arabic and English, tr. by Naseer H.
Aruri). [InterPR] (17:1) Spr 91, p. 13.
"My Friend, I Am Tired of Being an Arab" (in Arabic and English, tr. by Naseer H.
Aruri). [InterPR] (17:1) Spr 91, p. 6-9.
"The Students of Gaza" (Arabic title: "The Angry Ones," tr. by Reja-e Busailah).
[InterPR] (17:2) Fall 91, p. 82-83.
4937. QABULA, Alfred Temba
"The Wheel Is Turning — The Struggle Moves Forward" (Selections: 1-2, 4, 6-7,
11, 13-15, 19-20, 22, 25-26, 29). [Iowa] (21:2) Spr-Sum 91, p. 33-38.
QASTALLI, Ibn Darraj al
See IBN DARRAJ AL-QASTALLI
QI-JIAO, Cai
See CAI, Qi-jiao
QING, Li
See LI, Qing
QIU, Liu Zhan
See LIU, Zhan Qiu
4938. QIU, Xiaolong
"A Modern Chinese Image." [RiverS] (33) 91, p. 13.
"Night Talk" (After the Massacre of June 4, 1989 in Beijing). [RiverS] (33) 91, p.
12.
4939. QUAGLIANO, Tony
"The Ancient Murmurs in the Blood Meadows." [HawaiiR] (16:1, #34) Wint 91-92,
p. 13.
"Medical News on the Night." [ChamLR] (8-9) Spr-Fall 91, p. 44-45.
"On 'Other Strategies'" (for Reuben Tam). [ChamLR] (8-9) Spr-Fall 91, p. 46.
"This Man's Castle." [HawaiiR] (15:3, #33) Fall 91, p. 128.
4940. QUALLS, Suzanne
"Death of a Scholar" (for Joel Fineman). [TriQ] (83) Wint 91-92, p. 93-94.

4941. QUATTLEBAUM, Mary
"Lot's Daughter" (Honorable Mention, 1991 Paintbrush Award in Poetry).
[PaintedHR] (3) Sum 92, p. 33-34.
"Naming." [PaintedHR] (2) Spr 91, p. 26-27.
4942. QUECHUA PEOPLE'S POETRY
"Testament: Fragments" (tr. of the Spanish of Jesús Lara by Maria A. Proser and
James Scully). [NoDaQ] (59:4) Fall 91, p. 78.
"What Cloud Is That Cloud" (tr. of the Spanish of Jesús Lara by Maria A. Proser
and James Scully). [NoDaQ] (59:4) Fall 91, p. 78-79.
4943. QUENEAU, Raymond
"Oak and Dog" (A Novel in Verse, excerpt, tr. by James Sallis). [Pequod] (32) 91,
p. 27-31.
QUESADA, Isa De
See De QUESADA, Isa
4944. QUESTEL, Victor D.
"Downstairs." [GrahamHR] (14) Spr 91, p. 78-79.
"Judgedreadword." [GrahamHR] (14) Spr 91, p. 80-81.
4945. QUETCHENBACH, Bernard
"Fish and Wildlife Area." [BellR] (14:1) Spr 91, p. 54.
4946. QUIG, Steven
"Epic." [BellArk] (7:6) N-D 91, p. 6.
"History." [BellArk] (7:6) N-D 91, p. 11.
4947. QUINLAN, Kathleen M.
"Staying within the Lines." [Kalliope] (13:2) 91, p. 42-43.
4948. QUINN, Bernetta
"Mansion Without Walls." [SoCaR] (24:1) Fall 91, p. 152.
4949. QUINN, Damian
"Absences." [Verse] (8:1) Spr 91, p. 100.
"Baptism." [Verse] (8:1) Spr 91, p. 99.
"Heroes." [Verse] (8:1) Spr 91, p. 99.
"Landscape." [Verse] (8:1) Spr 91, p. 100.
4950. QUINN, John Robert
"The Begonia." [ChrC] (108:20) 26 Je-3 Jl 91, p. 654.
"Dick Alf." [SpiritSH] (56) Spr-Sum 91, p. 47.
"Lines of an Octogenarian." [SpiritSH] (56) Spr-Sum 91, p. 48.
"Old Whittler." [SpiritSH] (56) Spr-Sum 91, p. 47.
"A Winter Day." [Comm] (118:2) 25 Ja 91, p. 53.
4951. QUINTANA PIGNO, Antonia
"Boulevard Dreams." [KenR] (NS 13:4) Fall 91, p. 139-140.
"Cancion de Cuna." [13thMoon] (9:1/2) 91, p. 37.
4952. RAAB, Lawrence
"Bad Dog." [Journal] (14:2) Wint 91, p. 80.
"The Bad Muse." [Journal] (14:2) Wint 91, p. 78-79.
"The Sudden Appearance of a Monster at a Window." [DenQ] (25:3) Wint 91, p.
14-15.
"The Thing That Happened." [PassN] (12:1) Sum 91, p. 8.
"The Weeping Willows at Home." [PassN] (12:1) Sum 91, p. 8.
4953. RABASSA, Gregory
"As in *Trovatore*, I Take Four Steps" (tr. of Pedro Tamen). [Trans] (25) Spr 91, p.
71.
"Delphi, Opus 12" (Selections: 17-18, tr. of Pedro Tamen). [Trans] (25) Spr 91, p.
72.
"Evening Falls and I Arise" (tr. of Pedro Tamen). [Trans] (25) Spr 91, p. 70.
4954. RABBITT, Thomas
"At Cantalupe the Pope." [GettyR] (4:2) Spr 91, p. 334-335.
"Blue Lights." [GettyR] (4:2) Spr 91, p. 330-331.
"Fireflies During the Blackout" (Hyannis, 1942). [GettyR] (4:4) Aut 91, p. 684-685.
"For Thomas Stearns Eliot on the Occasion of His One Hundredth Birthday."
[GettyR] (4:2) Spr 91, p. 332-333.
"What One Eye Sees." [GettyR] (4:4) Aut 91, p. 686-687.
4955. RABINOVITCH, Sacha
"A Misty Start." [CumbPR] (10:2) Spr 91, p. 28.
4956. RABINOWITZ, Anna
"Anatomy Lab" (for W.G.). [NewYorkQ] (44) 91, p. 92.
"The Foreplay of Hermeneutics." [SouthwR] (76:1) Wint 91, p. 96-97.
"Fragile Dialectics." [Sonora] (20) Wint 91, p. 77-78.

"Home" (for my mother, 1902-1983). [SycamoreR] (3:2) Sum 91, p. 35-36.
4957. RABINOWITZ, Jacob
"Psalms" (Selections: 19, 23, 126, 137, tr. of the Bible). [WorldL] (1:1) 91, p. 27-30.
4958. RABY, Elizabeth
"Sensory Deprivation." [JINJPo] (13:2) Aut 91, p. 37.
4959. RACHEL, Naomi
"Reason in Its Dreams." [Arc] (27) Aut 91, p. 53.
"Regularity." [Outbr] (22) 91, p. 59.
"S.A.S.E." [Outbr] (22) 91, p. 57-58.
"Seaside Misanthropist." [Outbr] (22) 91, p. 60.
4960. RACZ, G. J.
"Doré III" (tr. of José Manuel del Pino). [PoetL] (86:1) Spr 91, p. 32.
"Doré IV" (tr. of José Manuel del Pino). [PoetL] (86:1) Spr 91, p. 33-34.
"The Moonbeam" (tr. of José Manuel del Pino). [PoetL] (86:1) Spr 91, p. 31.
"Sexual Ode II" (To the woman pianist with the light-green eyes, tr. of José Manuel del Pino). [PoetL] (86:1) Spr 91, p. 35.
4961. RADAVICH, David
"Reclaiming Eyrarbakki." [InterPR] (17:1) Spr 91, p. 117.
4962. RADER, Judith
"The Blemished Fig." [SpiritSH] (56) Spr-Sum 91, p. 42.
"Cattail in Autumn." [SpiritSH] (56) Spr-Sum 91, p. 41.
"Fanfare for Blue." [SpiritSH] (56) Spr-Sum 91, p. 43.
"Mother Motion." [SpiritSH] (56) Spr-Sum 91, p. 44.
"Shower Vision." [SpiritSH] (56) Spr-Sum 91, p. 40.
4963. RADMALL, Philip
"Portrait of the Poet As an Old Man." [Stand] (33:1) Wint 91, p. 10-13.
"The Skaters." [Stand] (33:1) Wint 91, p. 9-10.
"Stone Gatherer." [Stand] (33:1) Wint 91, p. 9.
4964. RADNER, Rebecca
"The Mind Returning." [BostonR] (16:5) O 91, p. 23.
"To Die in Benares." [CalQ] (31) Fall 88, p. 33.
4965. RADOJEVIC, Vera
"When a Child Dies" (For Nikola, tr. of Duska Vrhovac, w. Richard Burns). [NewOR] (18:2) Sum 91, p. 83.
4966. RAFFIN, Michelle
"Sharp Curves." [OnTheBus] (8/9) 91, p. 137.
4967. RAGAN, Jacie
"Daughter's Vacation." [Parting] (4:1) Sum 91, p. 30.
"Tropical Heat." [Plain] (11:3) Spr 91, p. 33.
4968. RAGAN, James
"The Bats of the Dowager Empress." [GreenMR] (NS 4:2) Wint-Spr 91, p. 84.
4969. RAHIM, Jennifer
"On Entering Airports or Some Uses of Punctuation." [GrahamHR] (14) Spr 91, p. 84-91.
4970. RAHON, Alice
"Cave of Bronze" (tr. by Vanina Deler and Nancy Deffebach). [OnTheBus] (8/9) 91, p. 195.
"Despair" (to Pablo Picasso, tr. by Vanina Deler and Nancy Deffebach). [OnTheBus] (8/9) 91, p. 188.
"Hourglass Lying Down" (tr. by Vanina Deler and Nancy Deffebach). [OnTheBus] (8/9) 91, p. 196.
"Pointed Out Like a Star" (to Ixtaccihuatl, tr. by Vanina Deler and Nancy Deffebach). [OnTheBus] (8/9) 91, p. 194.
"A Woman Who Was Beautiful" (tr. by Vanina Deler and Nancy Deffebach). [OnTheBus] (8/9) 91, p. 174.
RAINE, Heidi Neufeld
See NEUFELD-RAINE, Heidi
4971. RAISER, Lynne
"Leaving Land." [Kalliope] (13:3) 91, p. 51.
"Nice People." [Kalliope] (13:3) 91, p. 50.
4972. RAISOR, Philip
"1945." [CinPR] (22) Spr 91, p. 36.
"Legacy: For a Bed-Wetter Coping." [CinPR] (22) Spr 91, p. 37.
4973. RAIZISS, Sonia
"Redblooded" (tr. of Luciano Erba). [Boulevard] (6:2/3, #17/18) Fall 91, p. 167.

"Sunset at Montluçon" (tr. of Luciano Erba). [Boulevard] (6:2/3, #17/18) Fall 91, p. 166.
4974. RAKOSI, Carl
"Theme." [Conjunc] (16) 91, p. 296.
4975. RALEIGH, Richard
"Piece of Cake." [ChironR] (10:2) Sum 91, p. 43.
4976. RAMIREZ, Orlando
"Your Going." [PacificR] (9) 91, p. 43-44.
4977. RAMIREZ, Vic
"Bouillabaisse." [WorldL] (1:1) 91, p. 21.
"Pathways of a Labyrinth." [WorldL] (1:1) 91, p. 22-23.
4978. RAMKE, Bin
"At Just That Moment the Rains Began." [DenQ] (25:4) Spr 91, p. 51-52.
"Comic." [WestHR] (45:3) Aut 91, p. 201.
"Dickinson on Grace." [WestHR] (45:3) Aut 91, p. 203.
"Further Documentation." [NewRep] (204:10) 11 Mr 91, p. 38.
"A Happy Childhood." [WestHR] (45:3) Aut 91, p. 202.
"Her Theory of Comedy." [PacificR] (9) 91, p. 11-12.
"It Is the Nature of These People to Embrace Each Other, They Know No Other
        Kind But Themselves" (— John Ashbery). [OhioR] (47) 91, p. 9.
"The Laughter of the Crowds Gathered." [ChatR] (11:2) Wint 91, p. 68-69.
"Like Ulysses." [Agni] (33) 91, p. 231-232.
"Melting Pot." [MissR] (19:3) 91, p. 179-181.
"Moral Equivalence." [WestHR] (45:3) Aut 91, p. 200.
"The New Geometry and the Little Blue Heron." [OhioR] (47) 91, p. 7.
"Nostalgia." [DenQ] (25:4) Spr 91, p. 50.
"The Park Is Varnished for April" (— Donald Revell). [OhioR] (47) 91, p. 10.
"A Simple Criminal." [NewRep] (205:20) 11 N 91, p. 34.
"Sun or Moon." [MissR] (19:3) 91, p. 177-178.
"When I Was a Child." [OhioR] (47) 91, p. 8.
4979. RAMKISSOON-CHEN, Rajandaye
"When the Rainflies Took Over." [GrahamHR] (14) Spr 91, p. 69.
4980. RAMNATH, S.
"Woman at the Beach." [ChironR] (10:3) Aut 91, p. 37.
RAMOS, Reinaldo Garcia
    See GARCIA RAMOS, Reinaldo
RAMOS ROSA, António
    See ROSA, António Ramos
4981. RAMSEY, Paul
"Balance Sheet." [WritersF] (17) Fall 91, p. 209.
"Ghost Me a Story of Long Ago or of When." [CharR] (17:1) Spr 91, p. 87.
"Narrative of Theory." [LullwaterR] (3:1) Fall 91, p. 75.
4982. RAMSEY, William
"Desert Fox." [WindO] (54) Sum 91, p. 33.
4983. RANDELL, Elaine
"Kent, 1990." [NewAW] (8/9) Fall 91, p. 135-136.
"'Men Must Live and Create. Live to the Point of Tears.' Camus" (for Polly
        Hartaup). [NewAW] (8/9) Fall 91, p. 135.
"Polaroid." [NewAW] (8/9) Fall 91, p. 136-137.
"Who Takes the Child by the Hand Takes the Mother by the Heart." [NewAW] (8/9)
        Fall 91, p. 137-138.
4984. RANDOLPH, Sarah
"Astronomers." [AmerPoR] (20:1) Ja-F 91, p. 6.
"Bell." [AmerPoR] (20:1) Ja-F 91, p. 6.
"Doorway." [CarolQ] (44:1) Fall 91, p. 50.
"Hope." [CarolQ] (44:1) Fall 91, p. 50.
"Keeping Still." [CarolQ] (44:1) Fall 91, p. 49.
"Reply." [AmerPoR] (20:1) Ja-F 91, p. 6.
"Splitting Apart." [CarolQ] (44:1) Fall 91, p. 49.
"Still Life." [AmerPoR] (20:1) Ja-F 91, p. 6.
"Theory." [AmerPoR] (20:1) Ja-F 91, p. 6.
4985. RANKIN, Paula
"Godmother." [PoetryNW] (32:3) Aut 91, p. 8-9.
"Last Date." [PoetryNW] (32:3) Aut 91, p. 9-10.
"The Mothers." [PoetryNW] (32:2) Sum 91, p. 8-10.

4986. RANKIN, Rush
"The Women of Maine." [ThRiPo] (37/38) 91, p. 38-40.
4987. RANSICK, Christopher
"Trainride Lengthwise California" (Second Place, 1991 Paintbrush Award in
Poetry). [PaintedHR] (3) Sum 92, p. 13-15.
4988. RANSOM, Cherra S.
"Probabilities." [PraF] (12:3 #56) Aut 91, p. 75.
4989. RANSON, Rebecca
"Bad Girls" (for Mendy Knott). [AmerV] (25) Wint 91, p. 56-59.
4990. RANTALA, Kathy
"August." [PoetryUSA] (22) Spr 91, p. 7.
4991. RANZONI, Patricia (Patricia Smith)
"Bouquet." [Kaleid] (22) Wint-Spr 91, p. 30.
"Dystonic Definitions." [Kaleid] (23) Sum-Fall 91, p. 30.
4992. RAPHAEL, Dan
"As If a Resort." [CentralP] (19/20) Spr-Fall 91, p. 215.
"Police Cars." [PoetryUSA] (22) Spr 91, p. 14.
"Saying Goodbye to the Father." [Caliban] (10) 91, p. 61-62.
"Untitled: I take my love for long walks across the work bench." [Caliban] (10) 91,
p. 63.
4993. RAPPLEYE, Chris
"5:30 P.M." [RiverS] (35) 91, p. 76.
"I Consider Running for Sheriff of Cheboygan County, Michigan." [RiverS] (35)
91, p. 77-78.
4994. RASH, Ron
"Blues for Duane Allman." [LullwaterR] (3:1) Fall 91, p. 64.
"Cleaning Out the Fallout Shelter." [TexasR] (11:1/2) Spr-Sum 90, p. 77.
"July, 1947." [Journal] (15:1) Spr 91, p. 57.
"Leaving 35, Resume Safe Speed." [Plain] (11:2) Wint 91, p. 14.
"Rattlesnake." [TexasR] (11:1/2) Spr-Sum 90, p. 76.
"Watching the Lunatics Fish." [SycamoreR] (3:2) Sum 91, p. 45.
4995. RATCLIFFE, Stephen
"How Plants Coil." [Shiny] (6) Spr-Sum 91, p. 78.
"Maybe a Story." [Shiny] (6) Spr-Sum 91, p. 77.
"Poem in Prose" (Excerpts from a sequence based on poems in "Poèmes en prose"
by Stéphane Mallarmé). [Talisman] (6) Spr 91, p. 78-81.
"Present Tense" (Excerpt). [CentralP] (19/20) Spr-Fall 91, p. 217-222.
"Spaces in the Light Said to Be Where One / Comes From" (Selections: 52-53).
[Talisman] (7) Fall 91, p. 118-119.
"Spaces in the Light Said to Be Where One Comes From" (Selections: 45, 49).
[NewAW] (7) Spr 91, p. 34-35.
4996. RATTAN, Cleatus
"Looking Deep." [TexasR] (12:1/2) Spr-Sum 91, p. 123.
"Making the Grade." [TexasR] (12:1/2) Spr-Sum 91, p. 124.
4997. RATTEE, Michael
"A Blind Girl." [LaurelR] (25:1) Wint 91, p. 104.
"Falling Off the Bicycle Forever." [LaurelR] (25:1) Wint 91, p. 105.
4998. RAUSCHENBUSCH, Stephanie
"Two Russian Poets." [NewYorkQ] (46) 91, p. 56.
4999. RAVEL, Edeet
"Midrash on the Song of Songs, 8:1-6." [Descant] (22:3, #74) Fall 91, p. 27-52.
5000. RAVNDAL, Janeal T.
"On Halos." [ChrC] (108:4) 30 Ja 91, p. 100.
5001. RAWKINREC, Iam
"What Goes 'round Reincarnates." [ChironR] (10:3) Aut 91, p. 41.
5002. RAWLEY, Donald
"Baja." [YellowS] (36) Spr 91, p. 28.
"La Pinta Hotel, Ensenada." [YellowS] (36) Spr 91, p. 29.
5003. RAWLINGS, Jane B.
"Interstate 80." [PraS] (65:1) Spr 91, p. 107-108.
"The Last Empress." [US1] (24/25) Spr 91, p. 39.
"Wood." [JINJPo] (13:1) Spr 91, p. 35.
5004. RAWLINS, Susan
"Intervention." [PoetC] (22:3) Spr 91, p. 18-19.
"The Saturday Night Before Christmas." [BelPoJ] (42:1) Fall 91, p. 33.

5005. RAWN, Michael David
"Festival of Lights" (India, 1987). [HopewellR] (1991) 91, p. 13.
5006. RAWORTH, Tom
"What happens in any sovereign body is created." [NewAW] (8/9) Fall 91, p. 139-142.
5007. RAWSON, JoAnna
"Carpenter's Elegy" (Thomas Rawson, 1901-1988). [SpoonRQ] (16:1/2) Wint-Spr 91, p. 65-68.
"Little Night Music." [AntR] (49:4) Fall 91, p. 554-555.
"Unfinished Piece." [AntR] (49:4) Fall 91, p. 556.
5008. RAY, David
"Alzheimer's." [WritersF] (17) Fall 91, p. 58.
"A Blue Iris." [Ascent] (15:3) Spr 91, p. 52.
"The Chippewa Medicine Man." [FreeL] (8) Aut 91, p. 2-3.
"Dreiser." [DenQ] (25:3) Wint 91, p. 16.
"For Jack Conroy, The Sage of Moberly (1899-1989)." [NewL] (57:4) Sum 91, p. 146-149.
"Lessons of the Sixties." [CharR] (17:1) Spr 91, p. 72-75.
"One Winter." [Ascent] (15:3) Spr 91, p. 52.
"Out of the Fifties" (For Tim Pettet). [NewL] (58:1) Fall 91, p. 108-109.
"Pavement Dwellers Lot Is a Happy One" (headline in a New Delhi newspaper). [ColR] (NS 18:1) Spr-Sum 91, p. 67-69.
"The Pool." [WritersF] (17) Fall 91, p. 57.
"Rossetti." [FreeL] (8) Aut 91, p. 4.
"Third World." [CreamCR] (14:2) Wint 91, p. 49-52.
"This Space, Much Maligned." [NewRep] (205:8/9) 19-26 Ag 91, p. 38.
"To William Sydney Porter (1862-1910)." [Mildred] (4:2/5:1) 91, p. 55-56.
"Two for Eschatology." [NewRep] (204:24) 17 Je 91, p. 43.
5009. RAY, Judy
"Beaches." [CreamCR] (14:2) Wint 91, p. 55-56.
5010. RAYMOND, Clarinda Harriss
"In a Station at the MVA" (Honorable Mention, 5th Annual Contest). [SoCoast] (11) Wint 91, p. 19.
5011. REA, Susan
"The Unexpected Weight." [ArtfulD] (20/21) 91, p. 51.
5012. READER, Willie
"After the Baptist Revival." [WebR] (15) Spr 91, p. 97.
"October House." [WebR] (15) Spr 91, p. 98.
5013. REAGAN, James
"The Loss" (tr. of Yevgeny Yevtushenko, w. the author). [Nat] (253:3) 15-22 Jl 91, p. 135.
5014. REAGLER, Robin
"Pop Poem 17." [CimR] (96) Jl 91, p. 108-109.
5015. REBAZA-SORALUZ, Luis
"Boyacá" (for Olinda Morales and Antonio García, tr. by Elizabeth Doonan Kauffman). [PlumR] (1) Spr-Sum 91, p. 68.
5016. RECHNITZ, Emily
"Decorator Show House." [NewYorker] (67:17) 17 Je 91, p. 42.
"Material." [SouthernPR] (31:1) Spr 91, p. 61-63.
5017. RECHTMAN, Janet
"Rumination." [LullwaterR] (3:1) Fall 91, p. 54.
5018. RECIPUTI, Natalie
"About That Island" (for B.C.R.). [BellArk] (7:3) My-Je 91, p. 7.
"Love for Three Oranges, Sweet." [BellArk] (7:5) S-O 91, p. 10.
"Magician's Small Discovery." [BellArk] (7:5) S-O 91, p. 10.
"Rising." [BellArk] (7:5) S-O 91, p. 10.
"The Stealing Moon." [BellArk] (7:5) S-O 91, p. 10.
"Write 'Care of'." [BellArk] (7:5) S-O 91, p. 10.
5019. RECTENWALD, Michael
"The Eros of the Baby Boom Eras." [NewYorkQ] (44) 91, p. 79.
5020. RECTOR, Liam
"My Pony." [WestHR] (45:2) Sum 91, p. 145-146.
"The Night the Lightning Bugs Lit Last in the Field Then Went Their Way." [Agni] (33) 91, p. 110.
"Reified Broker Ponders Options." [Agni] (33) 91, p. 112.
"Your Livid Early Days." [Agni] (33) 91, p. 111.

5021. RED HAWK
"Zero's 2 Choices." [NewYorkQ] (46) 91, p. 39-40.
5022. REDA, Jacques
"Amen." (tr. by Elton Glaser and Janice Fritsch). [Paint] (18:36) Aut 91, p. 61.
5023. REDGROVE, Peter
"Annalee and Her Sister." [PoetryUSA] (22) Spr 91, p. 8.
"Body of Rock." [Stand] (33:1) Wint 91, p. 30.
"Butcher-Alchemist." [PoetryUSA] (22) Spr 91, p. 5.
"Continuous Journal" (Excerpts). [Ploughs] (17:1) Spr 91, p. 116-120.
"Excitare Muros." [ManhatR] (6:1) Fall 91, p. 60.
"Falmouth Clouds." [ManhatR] (6:1) Fall 91, p. 63-64.
"In Parthenon Beatae Mariae et Sanctae Columbae et Agathae." [PoetryUSA] (22)
    Spr 91, p. 8.
"Last Hope." [PoetryUSA] (23) Sum 91, p. 14.
"Moon and Ocean." [ManhatR] (6:1) Fall 91, p. 62.
"Pigmy Thunder." [ManhatR] (6:1) Fall 91, p. 61.
"Son Pèlerinage." [PoetryUSA] (23) Sum 91, p. 15.
"The Town Alters So the Guides Are Useless." [ManhatR] (6:1) Fall 91, p. 58-59.
5024. REDMOND, Mary Anne
"Twirl." [Prima] (14/15) 91, p. 28.
5025. REECE, Spencer
"O We Happy Now." [WindO] (55) Wint 91-92, p. 35-36.
"Old Money." [WindO] (55) Wint 91-92, p. 37-39.
5026. REED, Alison T.
"An Acre of Grass." [OxfordM] (7:2) Fall-Wint 91, p. 42-43.
"Among Other Schoolchildren." [GreenMR] (NS 5:1) Sum-Fall 91, p. 69.
"Outing." [GreenMR] (NS 5:1) Sum-Fall 91, p. 70-71.
"The Party." [GreenMR] (NS 5:1) Sum-Fall 91, p. 66-68.
5027. REED, Frank
"Evenings with Grandmother" (tr. of Jose Sequeira). [InterPR] (17:2) Fall 91, p. 63.
"Hecatomb" (tr. of Jose Sequeira). [InterPR] (17:2) Fall 91, p. 59.
"Los Angeles" (tr. of Jose Sequeira). [InterPR] (17:2) Fall 91, p. 65.
"Lucila's Son" (tr. of Jose Sequeira). [InterPR] (17:2) Fall 91, p. 57.
"Mestizo" (tr. of Jose Sequeira). [InterPR] (17:2) Fall 91, p. 65.
"Yesterday" (tr. of Jose Sequeira). [InterPR] (17:2) Fall 91, p. 61.
5028. REED, John R.
"Being Tended." [PoetryE] (31) Spr 91, p. 123.
"Easy." [PoetryE] (31) Spr 91, p. 124.
"Lawn Ornaments." [MichQR] (30:2) Spr 91, p. 294.
"Recovery Room." [PoetryE] (31) Spr 91, p. 125.
5029. REES, Elizabeth
"Across from a Woman Trying to Read the Origin of Consciousness in the
    Breakdown of the Bicameral Mind on the IRT." [Mildred] (4:2/5:1) 91, p. 64.
"At Bark Bay, Herbster, Wisconsin." [Kalliope] (13:2) 91, p. 39.
"Layman's Psychiatry." [KenR] (NS 13:3) Sum 91, p. 82.
"Multiple Personality." [PartR] (58:4) Fall 91, p. 687-688.
"Unfinished Grief." [KenR] (NS 13:3) Sum 91, p. 83.
5030. REESE, Steven
"Orison." [WestB] (29) 91, p. 34.
"Tent." [WestB] (29) 91, p. 34-35.
5031. REEVE, F. D.
"Autumn Song." [Poetry] (158:6) S 91, p. 339.
"The Blue Heron." [SewanR] (99:4) Fall 91, p. 552.
"The Gardener." [SewanR] (99:4) Fall 91, p. 553.
"Morning-Glories." [FreeL] (7) Spr 91, p. 32.
"Red Square." [Poetry] (158:6) S 91, p. 338.
"The Unbearable Lightness of Love." [SewanR] (99:4) Fall 91, p. 551-552.
5032. REEVES, Ramona
"Kilimanjaro" (A Manhattan Night Club). [SoCoast] (11) Wint 91, p. 53.
5033. REEVES, Sonya
"Black." [GreensboroR] (50) Sum 91, p. 46.
5034. REGENT, Peter
"Desert Song." [Verse] (8:1) Spr 91, p. 101.
5035. REHM, Pam
"Neurology: In Theory." [Caliban] (10) 91, p. 14-15.
"Out of the place and the feeling pole." [Notus] (9) Fall 91, p. 53.

"Vases and Arrangements." [Sulfur] (11:1, #28) Spr 91, p. 170-171.
5036. REIBER, James T.
    "I Enter Myself" (tr. of Robert Sabatier). [CrabCR] (7:3) 91, p. 11.
    "I Learn the World" (tr. of Robert Sabatier). [CrabCR] (7:3) 91, p. 10.
5037. REIBETANZ, John
    "Eyethurl." [Dandel] (18:2) Wint 91, p. 68-69.
    "Rabbit Fever." [Dandel] (18:2) Wint 91, p. 70.
5038. REID, Alastair
    "Un Bel Morir" (tr. of Alvaro Mutis). [NewEngR] (13:3/4) Spr-Sum 91, p. 205.
    "Puerta de Golpe, Cuba" (tr. of Heberto Padilla, w. Alexander Coleman).
        [NewYRB] (38:13) 18 Jl 91, p. 39.
    "The Rose, Its Specter" (*Rilke*, from "A Fountain, A House of Stone," tr. of
        Heberto Padilla, w. Alexander Coleman). [PartR] (58:4) Fall 91, p. 690.
    "A Street in Cordoba" (tr. of Alvaro Mutis). [NewEngR] (13:3/4) Spr-Sum 91, p.
        203-205.
    "The Wanderer's Accounting" (tr. of Alvaro Mutis). [NewEngR] (13:3/4) Spr-Sum
        91, p. 206.
5039. REID, Bethany
    "Apocalypse Approaching." [BellArk] (7:1) Ja-F 91, p. 4.
    "Measurement." [BellR] (14:1) Spr 91, p. 51.
    "The Red-Tail Over the Freeway" (for Eric). [BellArk] (7:5) S-O 91, p. 8.
    "True West." [BellArk] (7:6) N-D 91, p. 9.
5040. REID, Jamie
    "Homage to Lester Young." [WestCL] (25:1) Spr 91, p. 22-32.
5041. REID, Robert Sims
    "My Great Aunt, Who Did Not Speak Italian, Between Chores." [CutB] (36) Sum
        91, p. 73-74.
5042. REIDEL, James
    "Mermaid." [NewYorker] (67:27) 26 Ag 91, p. 58.
    "Miriam" (tr. of Ingeborg Bachmann). [Vis] (35) 91, p. 11.
    "Nebraska, October." [NewYorker] (67:34) 14 O 91, p. 56.
    "Pill Bugs." [NewYorker] (67:8) 15 Ap 91, p. 36.
    "Roman Night Scene" (tr. of Ingeborg Bachmann). [ArtfulD] (20/21) 91, p. 40.
5043. REIDER-COLLINS, Kate
    "Funeral." [Dandel] (18:1) Spr-Sum 91, p. 8.
5044. REIFF, Sandra
    "A Visit from Father Christmas." [BellR] (14:1) Spr 91, p. 24.
5045. REIGO, Ants
    "Closet Song." [Descant] (22:3, #74) Fall 91, p. 54.
    "Hydrodynamics." [Descant] (22:3, #74) Fall 91, p. 57.
    "Onus." [Descant] (22:3, #74) Fall 91, p. 53.
    "Pyrotechnics." [Descant] (22:3, #74) Fall 91, p. 56.
    "Trompe l'Oeil." [Descant] (22:3, #74) Fall 91, p. 55.
5046. REILLY, Evelyn
    "The Very Rich Hours." [NewYorker] (67:31) 23 S 91, p. 30.
5047. REINKE, Steven
    "Afternoon in Amherst." [Descant] (22:3, #74) Fall 91, p. 7.
    "Attempting to Learn the Language of Love." [Descant] (22:3, #74) Fall 91, p. 7.
    "Family Planning." [Descant] (22:3, #74) Fall 91, p. 9.
    "Notes Toward a Story for the Blind." [Descant] (22:3, #74) Fall 91, p. 8.
5048. REINKING, Victor
    "Suns under Arrest" (for Nelson Mandela and Abraham Serfaty, tr. of Abdellatif
        Laâbi, w. Jean-Jacques Malo). [InterPR] (17:2) Fall 91, p. 19-31.
5049. REISNER, Barbara
    "Goodbye" (for Phyllis). [BellR] (14:1) Spr 91, p. 13.
5050. REISS, James
    "Memorial Quilt, Central Park." [Boulevard] (5:3/6:1, #15/16) Spr 91, p. 151-152.
    "On Block Island Sound." [ThRiPo] (37/38) 91, p. 43.
    "Rock Climber." [ThRiPo] (37/38) 91, p. 42.
5051. REITER, David P.
    "Getting Away" (for Bob Pinter). [Arc] (27) Aut 91, p. 29.
    "The Next Father." [CanLit] (130) Aut 91, p. 68-69.
    "Sugar Shacks." [Arc] (27) Aut 91, p. 27-28.
    "The Water Ate Them." [Dandel] (18:1) Spr-Sum 91, p. 25.
5052. REITER, Jendi
    "The Artist of the Beautiful." [HangL] (58) 91, p. 71-72.

"A Lack of Monuments." [HangL] (58) 91, p. 72-73.
"The Miniaturist." [Poetry] (157:4) Ja 91, p. 197-198.
"Tour de Force." [SouthernPR] (31:2) Fall 91, p. 52-54.
5053. REITER, Thomas
"The Death Watch Beetle." [CimR] (94) Ja 91, p. 131-132.
"On Route." [NewEngR] (13:3/4) Spr-Sum 91, p. 341.
5054. REKDAL, Paisley
"Above the Gulf" (paintings by Paul Havas). [BellArk] (7:4) Jl-Ag 91, p. 22.
"In the Weeds." [BellArk] (7:4) Jl-Ag 91, p. 23.
5055. REMBOLD, Kristen Staby
"Winter Solstice." [Nimrod] (35:1) Fall-Wint 91, p. 95.
5056. REMPLE, Margaret
"Night Stories." [BlackWR] (18:1) Fall-Wint 91, p. 173-175.
5057. RENDLEMAN, Danny
"Cheese Lines, Flint, Michigan." [PassN] (12:2) Wint 91, p. 29.
"The Dangers of Voluntary Memory" (for Janice). [PassN] (12:2) Wint 91, p. 29.
5058. RENÉE, Robin
"Sex Verb." [NewYorkQ] (45) 91, p. 67.
5059. RENNERT-CARTER, Roberta
"Self Defense." [OnTheBus] (8/9) 91, p. 138.
5060. REPP, John
"Light Outside." [CinPR] (21) Spr 90, p. 7.
"No-Goat Hill." [GreensboroR] (50) Sum 91, p. 47.
"She Delicately." [Journal] (14:2) Wint 91, p. 69-70.
"Walking in Pittsburgh, Thinking of the Egg Auction and Paul the Putz." [Journal]
(14:2) Wint 91, p. 67-68.
5061. RESS, Lisa
"Inscape." [SpoonRQ] (16:1/2) Wint-Spr 91, p. 34.
"Passage." [SpoonRQ] (16:1/2) Wint-Spr 91, p. 33.
5062. RESSE, Steven
"Castaway." [PoetryNW] (32:2) Sum 91, p. 22-23.
"The Lover, Sentenced." [PoetryNW] (32:2) Sum 91, p. 23.
5063. RETALLACK, Joan
"Not a Cage" (for John Cage). [Aerial] (6/7) 91, p. 138-139.
5064. RETI, Ingrid
"The Dead Leaf." [Elf] (1:3) Fall 91, p. 37.
5065. RETSOV, Samuel
"Anger." [Talisman] (7) Fall 91, p. 40.
"The Burning." [Talisman] (7) Fall 91, p. 40.
"Delacroix, the Orient." [Talisman] (7) Fall 91, p. 39.
5066. REVARD, Carter
"Communing Before Supermarkets." [PoetryE] (32) Fall 91, p. 32-33.
"What the Eagle Fan Says" (For the Voelkers, the Besses, and all of our Dancers."
[PoetryE] (32) Fall 91, p. 34-35.
5067. REVELL, Donald
"And Nothing But." [Sulfur] (11:1, #28) Spr 91, p. 168-169.
"Anniversary of Many Cities." [Sulfur] (11:1, #28) Spr 91, p. 169.
"Another Day." [Conjunc] (17) 91, p. 212.
"City More Than I Suspected." [Verse] (8:1) Spr 91, p. 37.
"Collateral." [Agni] (34) 91, p. 64.
"The Deposed." [RiverS] (34) 91, p. 11.
"Entire." [ThRiPo] (37/38) 91, p. 24.
"Explicit Vita." [Verse] (8:1) Spr 91, p. 36.
"The Hotel Sander." [ThRiPo] (37/38) 91, p. 22-23.
"Jeremiah." [GettyR] (4:1) Wint 91, p. 130.
"The lesson of the Classics." [Sulfur] (11:1, #28) Spr 91, p. 167-168.
"The Massacre of the Innocents." [NewAW] (8/9) Fall 91, p. 38.
"The Other the Wings." [ThRiPo] (37/38) 91, p. 20-21.
"Polygamy." [BlackWR] (18:1) Fall-Wint 91, p. 117-118.
"Sirius." [Antaeus] (67) Fall 91, p. 176-177.
"A Type of Agnes." [Agni] (34) 91, p. 65-66.
REVUELTA, Gutierrez
See GUTIERREZ REVUELTA, Pedro
REVUELTA, Pedro Gutierrez
See GUTIERREZ REVUELTA, Pedro

5068. REYEZ, Ivanov
"Trip." [Gypsy] (17) 91, p. 65.
5069. REYNOLDS, Gordon
"Death Camp." [Gypsy] (17) 91, p. 72.
5070. REYNOLDS, Kate Fox
"On Discovering Your Father Has Alzheimer's" (for Timothy). [PaintedB] (44) 91,
p. 37.
5071. REYNOLDS, Kelly
"Counterweight." [TampaR] (4) 91, p. 23.
5072. REZMERSKI, John
"A Dream of Horses." [NorthStoneR] (10) Fall 91-Wint 92, p. 225.
"Dreaming of Sparklers." [NorthStoneR] (10) Fall 91-Wint 92, p. 226.
"Soul Auction." [NorthStoneR] (10) Fall 91-Wint 92, p. 224.
5073. RHEA, Michelle
"If Wishes Were Feline." [WormR] (31:4, #124) 91, p. 104.
"Kafka Debugs My Life." [WormR] (31:4, #124) 91, p. 104.
5074. RHEAM, Florence Lee
"One Question, Please: A Celebration of Process." [Nimrod] (34:2) Spr-Sum 91, p.
123.
5075. RHENISCH, Harold
"Night Waltz." [CanLit] (130) Aut 91, p. 26-28.
"Rat Hunting with Bart." [Event] (20:3) Fall 91, p. 62-63.
"Self-Counsel Press Guide to Canadian Architecture, Revised Edition." [CanLit]
(130) Aut 91, p. 89-90.
5076. RHINE, David
"Letter from Editors to Editors of University-Connected Literary Journals."
[ChironR] (10:2) Sum 91, p. 39.
5077. RHOADES, Lisa
"Fire Island." [BellR] (14:1) Spr 91, p. 15.
"New Clothes." [BellR] (14:1) Spr 91, p. 14.
5078. RHODENBAUGH, Suzanne
"Multiple Sclerosis, the 13th Year of It." [CinPR] (21) Spr 90, p. 62.
"Sideyard." [CinPR] (21) Spr 90, p. 30.
5079. RHODES, Shane
"In Numerous Thatched Houses." [Bogg] (64) 91, p. 51.
5080. RICCI, Roy
"Baseball Fan (Voyeur)." [NewYorkQ] (45) 91, p. 68.
5081. RICE, Bruce
"A Friend of Virginia Satir" (Agua Caliente). [Event] (20:3) Fall 91, p. 54.
"Museo Arqueologico" (Cuzco, Peru). [Event] (20:3) Fall 91, p. 55.
5082. RICE, Clovita
"A Comet and a Promise" (to Loren Eiseley). [InterPR] (17:2) Fall 91, p. 119-120.
5083. RICE, Oliver
"The Cats That Live in the Roman Forum." [Ascent] (16:1) Fall 91, p. 56-57.
"Of Sense and Sensibility." [AmerS] (60:2) Spr 91, p. 260.
5084. RICE, Paul
"The Right Words" (for M.). [GreensboroR] (50) Sum 91, p. 77-78.
"A Victorian Costume Brooch." [GreensboroR] (50) Sum 91, p. 75-76.
5085. RICE, Robert Z.
"Elkhorn." [Elf] (1:4) Wint 91, p. 34.
"Endings." [Elf] (1:4) Wint 91, p. 33.
5086. RICH, Adrienne
"An Atlas of the Difficult World" (Selections: I-II, IV-VI, VIII-IX). [AmerPoR]
(20:5) S-O 91, p. 15-17.
"Final Notations." [Poetry] (158:6) S 91, p. 313.
"For a Friend in Travail." [Poetry] (158:6) S 91, p. 311-312.
"Through Corralitos Under Rolls of Cloud." [Field] (44) Spr 91, p. 50-51.
"Two Arts." [Poetry] (158:6) S 91, p. 312-313.
5087. RICHARD, Brad
"Facing the Objects." [BlackWR] (17:2) Spr-Sum 91, p. 58.
5088. RICHARDS, G. D.
"Postcard from the Prairie." [MidwQ] (32:2) Wint 91, p. 194.
5089. RICHARDS, K.
"If a Pattern Holds." [NewRena] (8:2, #25) Fall 91, p. 43.
5090. RICHARDS, Marilee
"The Grandmothers Clara and Madge." [Comm] (118:9) 3 My 91, p. 292.

"Wearing the Moon." [Comm] (118:2) 25 Ja 91, p. 53.
5091. RICHARDS, Peter
"Whose Breath We Know." [Caliban] (10) 91, p. 84-85.
5092. RICHARDS, Robert
"Big on the Wall." [NewYorkQ] (46) 91, p. 78-79.
5093. RICHARDS, Robert B.
"The August Constitutional." [PottPort] (13:2) Fall-Wint 91, p. 48-49.
5094. RICHARDSON, Eve
"A Family Not Given to Explanation." [SoCaR] (24:1) Fall 91, p. 134.
5095. RICHARDSON, Fred
"The Fall." [Pearl] (14) Fall-Wint 91, p. 14.
"Gift." [Pearl] (14) Fall-Wint 91, p. 14.
"Iceberg." [Pearl] (14) Fall-Wint 91, p. 14.
5096. RICHARDSON, Steve
"Sleeping in Space." [NegC] (11:3) 91, p. 35.
5097. RICHERT, Mark
"Power." [Blueline] (12) 91, p. 27.
5098. RICHETTI, Peter
"The Drowned Man." [RiverS] (33) 91, p. 56.
"Explanation." [RiverS] (33) 91, p. 57.
5099. RICHEY, V. J.
"The Lion in August." [Writer] (104:9) S 91, p. 21.
5100. RICHIE, Eugene
"Metamorphosis" (tr. of Jaime Manrique). [Ploughs] (17:4) Wint 91-92, p. 110.
5101. RICHMAN, Elliot
"The Face in the Ice." [Confr] (46/47) Fall 91-Wint 92, p. 283.
"The Hummingbird" (For Alexis). [HiramPoR] (50) Spr-Sum 91, p. 20.
"A Lesson in Capitalism." [CoalC] (4) S 91, p. 14.
"The Love Song of a Mandarin Lady from the City of Hue . . . ." [Lactuca] (14) My
91, p. 39-40.
"The Orange Altar." [CoalC] (4) S 91, p. 15.
"Pictures at an Exhibition." [CoalC] (4) S 91, p. 15.
"Schwanenlied." [CoalC] (4) S 91, p. 15.
"The Steel Drivin' Man." [CoalC] (4) S 91, p. 14.
5102. RICHMAN, Jan
"History." [Caliban] (10) 91, p. 45.
5103. RICHMAN, Robert
"Favored Light" (On I. M. Pei's addition to the Louvre). [SouthwR] (76:2) Spr 91,
p. 297-298.
"The Wellhouse." [Nat] (252:10) 18 Mr 91, p. 354.
5104. RICHMOND, Don
"A Housepainter's Guide to Horticulture." [Plain] (12:1) Fall 91, p. 35.
5105. RICHMOND, Steve
"Gagaku." [DogRR] (10:1) Sum 91, p. 12.
"Gagaku." [SlipS] (11) 91, p. 58.
"Gagaku: demons? some don't care for the mere word." [DustyD] Je 91, p. 11.
"Gagaku: fresh poems are pouring out of him again at age 49." [DustyD] Je 91, p.
13.
"Gagaku: he thought more about her than himself." [DustyD] Je 91, p. 12.
"Gagaku: last night a young japanese whore." [Lactuca] (14) My 91, p. 57.
"Gagaku: nothing a young waitress hates worse than an empty house." [Lactuca]
(14) My 91, p. 57.
"Gagaku: the body that must die puzzles th'hell out of me." [DustyD] Je 91, p. 14.
"Gagaku: the last time he lit the candle he burned his finger." [DustyD] Je 91, p. 10.
"Some." [Lactuca] (14) My 91, p. 56.
"Weapon." [DustyD] Je 91, p. 40.
5106. RICHTER, Harvena
"Remembering Harry Roskolenko." [SoDakR] (29:1) Spr 91, p. 161.
"The Self in Variation" (more scenes from meditation). [SoDakR] (29:3 part 2) Aut
91, p. 78-81.
5107. RICHTER, Milan
"Never at the Horse at Two" (tr. by Jascha Kessler). [MassR] (32:3) Fall 91, p. 333.
"Roots in the Air" (tr. by Jascha Kessler, w. the author). [ParisR] (33:119) Sum 91,
p. 140.
"Spoiled Poem" (tr. by Jascha Kessler). [MassR] (32:3) Fall 91, p. 334.

"Spoiled Poem" (tr. by Jascha Kessler, w. the author). [ParisR] (33:119) Sum 91, p. 139.

5108. RICKEL, Boyer
"Night Sweats 2" (for Michael Canter). [Crazy] (40) Spr 91, p. 37.
"Poem to Begin the Second Decade of AIDS." [NoDaQ] (59:1) Wint 91, p. 69-70.

RIDING, Laura
See JACKSON, Laura (Riding)

5109. RIFBJERG, Klaus
"Olof Palme" (tr. by Steven T. Murray). [Vis] (37) 91, p. 12-13.

5110. RIGGS, Dionis Coffin
"Bulldozers Everywhere" (Tervuren, Gelgium [i.e. Belgium], October). [InterPR] (17:1) Spr 91, p. 113.
"Endless Boredom" (tr. of Ahmet Muhip Diranas, w. Ozcan Yalim and William A. Fielder). [InterPR] (17:1) Spr 91, p. 19.
"In the Home for the Elderly" (tr. of Özcan Yalim, w. the author and William A. Fielder). [InterPR] (17:1) Spr 91, p. 20.
"Such Love" (tr. of Attila Ilhan, w. Ozcan Yalim and William A. Fielder). [InterPR] (17:1) Spr 91, p. 17.
"To Live" (tr. of Cahit Külebi, w. Ozcan Yalim and William A. Fielder). [InterPR] (17:1) Spr 91, p. 19.

5111. RIGSBEE, David
"Buried Head." [PraS] (65:1) Spr 91, p. 94-95.
"F-stop." [PraS] (65:1) Spr 91, p. 97-98.
"Mildew." [PraS] (65:1) Spr 91, p. 96.
"Sequential Views" (For Robbert Flick). [CarolQ] (43:3) Spr 91, p. 45-47.
"Your Heart Will Fly Away." [ManhatR] (6:1) Fall 91, p. 73-76.

RIHAKU
See LI, Po

5112. RILEY, Denise
"Autobiography." [NewAW] (8/9) Fall 91, p. 143-144.
"The Dark-to-Light Mover." [NewAW] (8/9) Fall 91, p. 143.
"Do So." [NewAW] (8/9) Fall 91, p. 144.
"Foxes Pound the Earth." [NewAW] (8/9) Fall 91, p. 145.

5113. RILEY, Joanne M.
"I, the Palmist." [Pearl] (13) Spr-Sum 91, p. 10.

5114. RILEY, Michael D.
"Anglers." [TexasR] (11:1/2) Spr-Sum 90, p. 51.
"The Gear Is Gone." [CapeR] (26:2) Fall 91, p. 48.
"Stations." [CapeR] (26:2) Fall 91, p. 49.

5115. RILEY, Peter
"Eaten Zero." [NewAW] (8/9) Fall 91, p. 150-151.
"Night Thoughts / Languedoc 1987 / Thesis on Distance." [NewAW] (8/9) Fall 91, p. 146-148.
"S. Cecilia in Trastevere." [NewAW] (8/9) Fall 91, p. 148.
"S. Maria in Trastevere." [NewAW] (8/9) Fall 91, p. 149.
"S. Pietro in Montorio." [NewAW] (8/9) Fall 91, p. 149-150.

5116. RILKE, Rainer Maria
"Endlessly I gaze at you in wonder, blessed ones, at your composure" (tr. by Stephen Mitchell). [Talisman] (6) Spr 91, p. 103.
"Fragments from Lost Days" (tr. by Edward Snow). [MassR] (32:2) Sum 91, p. 220-221.
"The Guardian Angel" (tr. by Edward Snow). [MassR] (32:2) Sum 91, p. 219.
"Haiku" (tr. by Stephen Mitchell). [Talisman] (6) Spr 91, p. 103.
"Love Song" (tr. by John Rosenwald). [Mildred] (4:2/5:1) 91, p. 129.
"Startle me, Music, with rhythmical fury!" (tr. by Stephen Mitchell). [Talisman] (6) Spr 91, p. 103.
"Walk at Night" (tr. by Franz Wright). [Field] (44) Spr 91, p. 58.

5117. RIMANELLI, Giose
"September" (tr. by Luigi Bonaffini). [Vis] (36) 91, p. 22-23.

RIN, Ishigaki
See ISHIGAKI, Rin

5118. RINALDI, Nicholas
"Cow Feeding on the Grass in the Park in the Front of City Hall." [SoDakR] (29:3 part 2) Aut 91, p. 63.

5119. RIND, Sherry
"Management." [SouthernPR] (31:1) Spr 91, p. 33-34.

5120. RINDEN, Thor
"On Encountering Yoko Ono in Central Park." [FreeL] (8) Aut 91, p. 21.
5121. RINGER, Darby
"An Annunciation." [BellArk] (7:4) Jl-Ag 91, p. 3.
"The Bellevue Muse." [BellArk] (7:5) S-O 91, p. 11.
"The Kelson of Creation Is Love" (— Walt Whitman, "Leaves of Grass"). [BellArk]
(7:3) My-Je 91, p. 3.
"Nota Bene: Nelson Bentley." [BellArk] (7:1) Ja-F 91, p. 5.
"Silence in the Desert" (for my mother). [BellArk] (7:3) My-Je 91, p. 10.
"Summers of My Childhood." [BellArk] (7:5) S-O 91, p. 11.
5122. RINGER, Marinelle
"Feather and Bone." [Vis] (35) 91, p. 25.
5123. RIOS, Alberto
"Half Hour of August." [NewEngR] (13:3/4) Spr-Sum 91, p. 282-285.
"Passing Late in the Day's Afternoon a History." [NewEngR] (13:3/4) Spr-Sum 91,
p. 279-282.
"Teodoro Luna Confesses After Years to His Brother, Anselmo the Priest, Who Is
Required to Understand, But Who Understands Anyway, More Than People
Think." [RiverS] (33) 91, p. 18-19.
"What Is Quiet in the Spelling of Wednesday." [AmerPoR] (20:3) My-Je 91, p. 41.
"The Work of Remembering Saint Louis." [RiverS] (33) 91, p. 20-21.
5124. RIOS, Alexandra
"Carta a la Abuela Paula de la Viña" (In memoriam). [Americas] (19:1) Spr 91, p.
54-55.
"Domingo." [Americas] (19:1) Spr 91, p. 56-57.
"Hole" (For Dr. Rosemary Leake and patient, Tennyson, Harbor, U.C.L.A. Medical
School). [PoetL] (86:4) Wint 91-92, p. 26.
"Winter in June." [Americas] (19:1) Spr 91, p. 58-59.
5125. RISSET, Jacqueline
"M.S. 1544" (tr. by Norma Cole). [Talisman] (6) Spr 91, p. 40-41.
"La Traduition Commence" (Christian Bourgois, Paris, 1978. Selection: "Bite," tr.
by Norma Cole). [Avec] (4:1) 91, p. 78-79.
"Y K 61" (tr. by Norma Cole). [Talisman] (6) Spr 91, p. 41.
5126. RISTOVIC, Aleksander
"I Am There Where You Will Never Be" (tr. by Dragutin Janjetovic). [CimR] (96) Jl
91, p. 26.
"Touches from Everywhere" (tr. by Dragutin Janjetovic). [CimR] (96) Jl 91, p. 27.
5127. RITCHEY, Jana F.
"For Father." [EmeraldCR] (3) 91, c1990, p. 13.
5128. RITCHIE, Elisavietta
"Ito Jakuchu, Artist, B. 1716, in Kyoto." [Ascent] (15:2) Wint 91, p. 33.
"Pastoral Letter" (for William Packard, written Day Five at the Virginia Center for the
Creative Arts). [NewYorkQ] (44) 91, p. 93.
5129. RITSOS, Yannis
"And Recounting Them" (tr. by Edmund Keeley). [Salm] (92) Fall 91, p. 145-146.
"Attenuation" (tr. by Martin McKinsey). [Poetry] (158:4) Jl 91, p. 204.
"Danaë" (tr. by Edmund Keeley). [ColR] (NS 17:2) Fall-Wint 90, p. 98.
"Evening Procession" (tr. by Kimon Friar and Kostas Myrsiades). [SouthernHR]
(25:1) Wint 91, p. 94.
"First Series" (10 selections, tr. by José García and Adamantia Baltatzi).
[OnTheBus] (8/9) 91, p. 222-223.
"Niobe" (tr. by Edmund Keeley). [ColR] (NS 17:2) Fall-Wint 90, p. 100.
"Pro Forma" (tr. by Martin McKinsey). [Poetry] (158:4) Jl 91, p. 204.
"Repetitions" (Selections: 3 poems, tr. by Edmund Keeley). [Colum] (15) 90, p.
50-52.
"Succession" (tr. by Kimon Friar and Kostas Myrsiades). [SouthernHR] (25:1) Wint
91, p. 93.
"Talos" (tr. by Edmund Keeley). [NewRep] (204:3) 21 Ja 91, p. 28.
"Then and Now" (tr. by Edmund Keeley). [ColR] (NS 17:2) Fall-Wint 90, p. 99.
RITSOS, Yannos
See RITSOS, Yannis
5130. RIVARD, David
"And Continuing." [Agni] (34) 91, p. 57-58.
"The Debt." [Agni] (34) 91, p. 55-56.
"Later History" (for Michael McGuire). [AntR] (49:2) Spr 91, p. 254.
"Little Wing." [Ploughs] (17:2/3) Fall 91, p. 127-128.

"Summons." [NoAmR] (276:1) Mr 91, p. 81.
5131. RIVERA, Frank
"Naufragios." [LindLM] (10:1) Ja-Mr 91, p. 21.
RIVERA, Gerardo Torres
See TORRES RIVERA, Gerardo
RIVEREND, Pablo Le
See Le RIVEREND, Pablo
5132. RIVERO, Adhely
"Cartas." [LindLM] (10:2) Ap-Je 91, p. 8.
"Un cemeterio." [LindLM] (10:2) Ap-Je 91, p. 8.
5133. RIVERO, Raúl
"Marta ha venido del rio." [LindLM] (10:3) Jl-S 91, p. 4.
"Mira un momento atrás" (A Luis Rogelio Nogueras, con qiuen tanto tenemos).
    [LindLM] (10:3) Jl-S 91, p. 4.
"Pan y Circo." [LindLM] (10:3) Jl-S 91, p. 4.
5134. RIVERS, Ann
"Roundup." [Pembroke] (23) 91, p. 26.
5135. RIVERS, J. W.
"Captain Fulano." [SpoonRQ] (16:1/2) Wint-Spr 91, p. 55-56.
"Petition from Eulalia, Whose Husband Is Missing." [SpoonRQ] (16:1/2) Wint-Spr
    91, p. 54-55.
5136. RIXEN, Gail
"I Gotta Be Geraldo." [RagMag] (9:2) 91, p. 49.
"My Father's Fields." [RagMag] (9:2) 91, p. 48.
5137. RIZAL, José
"Last Goodbye" (tr. by Naomi Lazard, w. Bettina Escudero and Eduardo
    Bohorquez). [Trans] (25) Spr 91, p. 209-211.
5138. RIZZUTO, Phil F.
"The Bard of Baseball" (compiled from commentary during baseball games). [Harp]
    (283:1697) O 91, p. 30.
5139. ROADRUCK, Shawn S.
"The Kiss." [PacificR] (10) 91-92, p. 87.
"Tree of Knowledge." [PacificR] (10) 91-92, p. 36.
"Warm Is Where This Man Is." [PacificR] (10) 91-92, p. 40.
5140. ROAT, Adrienne
"Foliage." [SouthernPR] (31:2) Fall 91, p. 24-25.
"The Porcelain Doll at Wegman's." [SouthernPR] (31:2) Fall 91, p. 25-27.
5141. ROBAYNA, Andrés Sánchez
"A una Roca" (from "The Rock"). [Talisman] (6) Spr 91, p. 69.
"Palmas sobre la Losa Fría" (from "Palms on the Cold Flagstone"). [Talisman] (6)
    Spr 91, p. 71.
"Palms on the Cold Flagstone" (part I, tr. by Fernando Galván and Manuel Brito).
    [Talisman] (6) Spr 91, p. 71.
"Spout" (part III, tr. by Fernando Galván and Manuel Brito). [Talisman] (6) Spr 91,
    p. 70-71.
"To a Rock" (tr. by Fernando Galván and Manuel Brito). [Talisman] (6) Spr 91, p.
    69.
"Tromba" (from "The Rock"). [Talisman] (6) Spr 91, p. 70.
5142. ROBBINS, Anthony
"Destroyers." [ParisR] (33:121) Wint 91, p. 127-132.
"Picture of Genevieve, Low Sky, and Panic Song." [SouthernR] (27:3) Jl 91, p.
    706.
5143. ROBBINS, Martin
"Dawn Watch." [SewanR] (99:2) Spr 91, p. 186.
"Exercise in Light Snow." [SouthernHR] (25:1) Wint 91, p. 53.
"On My 'Night Guard'." [CimR] (94) Ja 91, p. 110.
"Uncompleted Call." [CimR] (94) Ja 91, p. 111.
5144. ROBBINS, Richard
"Los Bandidos de Olvera Street, 1923." [Interim] (10:2) Fall-Wint 91-92, p. 19.
"The Bulldog Edition of the *Los Angeles Times*." [Interim] (10:2) Fall-Wint 91-92,
    p. 18.
"The Butcher." [CrabCR] (7:2) Sum 91, p. 25.
"Circle Frame at Nine Below." [LaurelR] (25:2) Sum 91, p. 51.
"A Klondiker's Letter Home, 1897." [Pig] (17) 91, p. 62.
"Lake Bottom." [ColR] (NS 18:2) Fall-Wint 91, p. 64.

"Lon Chaney, Jr., at the Supermarket in Capistrano Beach." [PoetryNW] (32:2)
    Sum 91, p. 25.
5145. ROBBINS, Tim
    "Blind Date." [HangL] (58) 91, p. 75.
    "Missing." [HangL] (58) 91, p. 74-75.
    "The Old Man Gives." [HangL] (58) 91, p. 74.
5146. ROBERTS, Andy
    "The Chef." [ChironR] (10:2) Sum 91, p. 40.
    "Welfare." [ChironR] (10:3) Aut 91, p. 40.
5147. ROBERTS, Gildas
    "Quartz Alarm Clock." [TickleAce] (22) Fall-Wint 91, p. 20.
    "Two Herring Gulls." [TickleAce] (22) Fall-Wint 91, p. 21-22.
5148. ROBERTS, Katrina
    "For Your Departure." [AntR] (49:3) Sum 91, p. 426.
5149. ROBERTS, Kim
    "Money." [HawaiiR] (15:2, #32) Spr 91, p. 11.
    "The River in River." [Blueline] (12) 91, p. 30.
5150. ROBERTS, Len
    "The Bank Barn's Tilt." [WorldO] (24:1/2) Fall 89-Wint 89-90, c1991, p. 21.
    "Building the Chicken Coop in Wassergass." [VirQR] (67:2) Spr 91, p. 261-262.
    "Christmas Day Ride to Visit My Brother at the Ithaca Veterans Hospital." [PoetryE]
        (32) Fall 91, p. 128.
    "Christmas Preparations, First Grade, St. Bernard's." [IndR] (14:2) Spr 91, p.
        38-39.
    "Clean-Crazy." [WestB] (29) 91, p. 58-59.
    "A Drop of Blood on the Ground" (tr. of Sándor Csoóri). [LitR] (34:2) Wint 91, p.
        227.
    "Ez a Nap. This Day" (tr. of Sándor Csoóri). [DenQ] (26:2) Fall 91, p. 12-13.
    "I Have to Look Long" (Hosszan kell nezllem, tr. of Sandor Csoori, w. Gabor
        Toro). [Agni] (34) 91, p. 159.
    "In the End" (tr. of Ida Makay, w. Mária Kurdi). [WebR] (15) Spr 91, p. 31.
    "In the Field, Wassergass, Pennsylvania." [Chelsea] (51) 91, p. 106-107.
    "Learning the Planets." [ParisR] (33:121) Wint 91, p. 122-123.
    "Little Lives." [Boulevard] (5:3/6:1, #15/16) Spr 91, p. 123-124.
    "Maple Leaf" (tr. of Sándor Csoóri, w. László Vertes). [NewEngR] (13:3/4)
        Spr-Sum 91, p. 195-196.
    "The Million Branches." [NoAmR] (276:2) Je 91, p. 25.
    "Mine." [WestB] (29) 91, p. 59-60.
    "My Masters" (tr. of Sándor Csoóri). [Trans] (25) Spr 91, p. 195.
    "My Mother Catalogues the Wrongs." [MassR] (32:3) Fall 91, p. 379-380.
    "The Names of the Presidents." [BostonR] (16:2) Ap 91, p. 27.
    "No Walnuts, October, Wassergass." [Chelsea] (51) 91, p. 104-105.
    "On the Way to Quakertown." [VirQR] (67:2) Spr 91, p. 262.
    "Pissing in the Wind." [AntR] (49:3) Sum 91, p. 431.
    "Plaintive Song to the Members of My Generation" (tr. of Istvan Csukas, w. Marta
        Mezey). [TriQ] (81) Spr-Sum 91, p. 183-184.
    "Planting the Blueberry Bush, Wassergass, Pennsylvania." [PennR] (5:1) Spr 91, p.
        23.
    "Questions, to Carriers of the Dead (Kérdések, halottvivokhoz)" (tr. of Sandor
        Csoori, w. Laszlo Vertes). [Plain] (11:3) Spr 91, p. 24.
    "Questions, to Carriers of the Dead" (tr. of Sándor Csoóri, w. László Vértes). [LitR]
        (34:2) Wint 91, p. 226.
    "Santo and Johnny's Guitar Love-Song" (for Nicholas D. Roberts, 1942-1989).
        [WestB] (29) 91, p. 60-61.
    "Summer, with Halo" (tr. of Sándor Csoóri, w. László Vertes). [NewEngR]
        (13:3/4) Spr-Sum 91, p. 196.
    "Three Acres of Raspberries." [Chelsea] (51) 91, p. 108-109.
    "We Sat, So Patient." [Boulevard] (6:2/3, #17/18) Fall 91, p. 134-135.
    "What Do You Envy Me" (tr. of Sandor Csoori). [Vis] (35) 91, p. 32.
    "You, Hungry for the Sun" (tr. of Sándor Csoóri). [Trans] (25) Spr 91, p. 193-194.
    "Zörög Éjjel a Mák. The Poppy Clatters at Night" (tr. of Sándor Csoóri, w. László
        Vértes). [DenQ] (26:2) Fall 91, p. 14.
5151. ROBERTS, Michael Symmons
    "Cardiff Central Station Song." [Verse] (8:2) Sum 91, p. 51.
5152. ROBERTS, Stephen R.
    "Barn Burning." [ChatR] (11:3) Spr 91, p. 93.

"Corner Posts." [Northeast] (5:5) Wint 91-92, p. 3.
"The Cows." [PaintedB] (42) 91, p. 12.
"Hopkins' Expedition — 1812." [HopewellR] (1991) 91, p. 23.
"Lone Survivor." [Farm] (8:2) Fall-Wint 91-92, p. 22.
"Snake of the Wind." [CapeR] (26:1) Spr 91, p. 25.
"Survivor." [Northeast] (5:5) Wint 91-92, p. 4.
5153. ROBERTS, Tony
"Lady Reading at an Open Window." [SoCoast] (11) Wint 91, p. 40-41.
5154. ROBERTSON, Kirk
"Don't care what they all say" (with drawings by Michael Sarich). [SwampR] (7/8)
Spr-Sum 91, p. 59.
"Juggling what's good, what's bad" (with drawings by Michael Sarich). [SwampR]
(7/8) Spr-Sum 91, p. 51.
"The Misfits." [SoDakR] (29:3 part 2) Aut 91, p. 74-75.
"The real heart, the real head" (with drawings by Michael Sarich). [SwampR] (7/8)
Spr-Sum 91, p. 55.
"Touch Fear Pain" (with drawings by Michael Sarich). [SwampR] (7/8) Spr-Sum
91, p. 53. Also, with different drawing, on p. 57.
"Wonder why I think too much expanding explodes" (with drawings by Michael
Sarich). [SwampR] (7/8) Spr-Sum 91, p. 49.
5155. ROBERTSON, Robin
"Affair of Kites." [Quarry] (40:4) Fall 91, p. 59.
"Fledging." [Quarry] (40:4) Fall 91, p. 59.
5156. ROBERTSON, William
"Maps." [CanLit] (130) Aut 91, p. 117.
5157. ROBERTSON-LORANT, Laurie
"The Woman and the Scythe." [AmerV] (22) Spr 91, p. 66.
5158. ROBESON, Richard
"Attempted Treason." [Obs] (6:2) Sum 91, p. 105-106.
"Cassio's Tale." [Obs] (6:2) Sum 91, p. 104-105.
"To a Son, Killed in Battle." [Obs] (6:2) Sum 91, p. 106-107.
5159. ROBIN, Mark
"Dream with Bob and Sheree." [BrooklynR] (8) 91, p. 38.
5160. ROBINER, Linda G.
"Kimono." [GrahamHR] (15) Fall 91, p. 72.
5161. ROBINS, Corinne
"The Monday Funeral." [Boulevard] (5:3/6:1, #15/16) Spr 91, p. 146-147.
"Museum Prescription" (While standing in front of a conceptual artwork consisting
of a list of names). [Confr] (46/47) Fall 91-Wint 92, p. 261-262.
"Two Beneath Yellow Awnings." [Confr] (46/47) Fall 91-Wint 92, p. 261.
"War." [Contact] (10:59/60/61) Spr 91, p. 36-37.
5162. ROBINSON, Bruce
"Dialing and Dolor." [SpoonRQ] (16:3/4) Sum-Fall 91, p. 96.
5163. ROBINSON, Diane
"The Breath in the Pipe." [DogRR] (10:1) Sum 91, p. 45.
"Tarring the Road." [CimR] (97) O 91, p. 60.
ROBINSON, Edward Arlington
See ROBINSON, Edwin Arlington
5164. ROBINSON, Edwin Arlington
"The House on the Hill." [GettyR] (4:4) Aut 91, p. 669-670.
"Mr. Flood's Party." [Shen] (41:4) Wint 91, p. 61-62.
5165. ROBINSON, Elizabeth
"Amaryllis." [NewAW] (8/9) Fall 91, p. 34.
"Apollo." [Talisman] (7) Fall 91, p. 128.
"Because I Have Feet" (for Jim Stipe). [Talisman] (7) Fall 91, p. 127.
"The Blinds." [Notus] (9) Fall 91, p. 44.
"Boston." [NewAW] (8/9) Fall 91, p. 35.
"Dear Friend" (for Mark Desiderio). [Notus] (9) Fall 91, p. 42.
"Dear Friends." [NewAW] (8/9) Fall 91, p. 33.
"East." [Aerial] (6/7) 91, p. 64.
"Morning's Anomia." [Notus] (9) Fall 91, p. 43.
"Prosopagnosia." [Aerial] (6/7) 91, p. 63.
"String." [NewAW] (7) Spr 91, p. 27-29.
5166. ROBINSON, Ian
"Disappearing." [Os] (32) Spr 91, p. 2.
"Garden at Evening." [Os] (32) Spr 91, p. 3.

5167. ROBINSON, Kit
"Speedball." [Aerial] (6/7) 91, p. 77-78.
5168. ROBINSON, Lou
"Moving Objects at a Distance." [Epoch] (40:1) 91, p. 7-8.
"World Wars Might Happen." [Epoch] (40:1) 91, p. 6.
5169. ROBINSON, Sondra Till
"Blue Bread." [SoDakR] (29:3 part 2) Aut 91, p. 43.
ROBYN SARAH
See SARAH, Robyn
5170. ROCA, Juan Manuel
"Song of the Mirror-maker" (tr. by Don Share). [ColR] (NS 18:2) Fall-Wint 91, p.
85.
"Sorceresses" (tr. by Garry Emmons). [Agni] (33) 91, p. 235.
ROCCA, L. Della
See DellaROCCA, L.
ROCCA, Lynda La
See La ROCCA, Lynda
5171. ROCKWELL, Mary Ann
"Adolescent Mourning." [Mildred] (4:2/5:1) 91, p. 98.
5172. ROCKWELL, Thomas (Tom)
"Alternative Interpretations." [MassR] (32:4) Wint 91-92, p. 510-514.
"I knew a woman with a skin disease." [NewYorkQ] (46) 91, p. 51.
"If Two Slovenly Herky-Jerky." [MassR] (32:4) Wint 91-92, p. 515-516.
5173. RODE, Diane (Diane C.)
"The Buzzing of Bees." [Kalliope] (13:2) 91, p. 15.
"The Sound of Silver Clam Shells Clanging." [Mildred] (4:2/5:1) 91, p. 76-77.
"You Could Die That Way." [Mildred] (4:2/5:1) 91, p. 78.
5174. RODEFER, Stephen
"And Reawakement." [Avec] (4:1) 91, p. 25.
"Harkening Still." [Avec] (4:1) 91, p. 23.
"Le Nuit Fattuski." [Avec] (4:1) 91, p. 24.
5175. RODENKO, Paul
"Love" (tr. by Arie Staal). [Vis] (36) 91, p. 25.
5176. RODERICK, John M.
"Summer Ritual." [EngJ] (80:4) Ap 91, p. 97.
5177. RODERICK, Mary Leary
"Navajo Rain." [HawaiiR] (15:3, #33) Fall 91, p. 34.
5178. RODGERS, Gordon
"True Geography I." [TickleAce] (22) Fall-Wint 91, p. 30.
"True Geography II." [TickleAce] (22) Fall-Wint 91, p. 30.
"Wild Note." [TickleAce] (22) Fall-Wint 91, p. 31.
5179. RODIER, Katharine
"Itinerary for Another Woman." [VirQR] (67:4) Aut 91, p. 680-681.
"Man from Oblivion." [VirQR] (67:4) Aut 91, p. 681-682.
5180. RODITI, Edouard
"I. Rumors" (tr. of Alain Bosquet). [Talisman] (6) Spr 91, p. 107.
"II. By night the young mare" (tr. of Alain Bosquet). [Talisman] (6) Spr 91, p. 107.
"III. Every morning I shrink" (tr. of Alain Bosquet). [Talisman] (6) Spr 91, p. 107.
"Meditation on Dante's 'Divine Comedy'." [Talisman] (7) Fall 91, p. 48-49.
"Nero's Warning" (tr. of Constantine Cavafy). [Talisman] (6) Spr 91, p. 132.
"Prose Poems" (I-VI, tr. of Léon-Paul Fargue). [Talisman] (7) Fall 91, p. 60-63.
"Sopronia Insufflavia" (tr. of Alexandre O'Neill). [Asylum] (6:3/4) 91, p. 60-61.
"The Tomb of the Grammarian Lysias" (tr. of Constantine Cavafy). [Talisman] (6)
Spr 91, p. 132.
5181. RODRIGUEZ, Carlos
"Blind in One Ear." [CalQ] (32/33) Spr 90, p. 89-90.
"Recognition." [CalQ] (32/33) Spr 90, p. 90-91.
"Skin Diving." [CalQ] (32/33) Spr 90, p. 91-92.
5182. RODRIGUEZ, Carmen
"Her Memory" (tr. by Heidi Neufeld-Raine, w. the author). [CapilR] (2:6/7) Fall 91,
p. 56-59.
"Su Memoria." [CapilR] (2:6/7) Fall 91, p. 60-63.
5183. RODRIGUEZ, Luis (Luis J.)
"Chota." [ChironR] (10:3) Aut 91, p. 37.
"The Rooster Who Thought It Was a Dog." [PoetryE] (31) Spr 91, p. 88-89.
"Somebody Was Breaking Windows." [PoetryE] (31) Spr 91, p. 90-91.

"String Bean." [Spirit] (11) 91, p. 206-208.
5184. RODRIGUEZ, W. R.
"The Accordion Player." [Spirit] (11) 91, p. 297-298.
5185. RODRIGUEZ, William
"Beyond the Window." [DustyD] Je 91, p. 21.
"Logic." [DustyD] (2:1) Ja 91, p. 1.
"On the Coping." [DustyD] (2:1) Ja 91, p. 21.
"The Spectacle." [DustyD] Ap 91, p. 5.
5186. RODRIGUEZ NUÑEZ, Víctor
"Water-worship" (tr. by Don Share). [Agni] (33) 91, p. 233-234.
5187. RODRIGUEZ ROSSARDI, Orlando
"Y Si Vieras." [LindLM] (10:1) Ja-Mr 91, p. 15.
5188. ROE, Margie McCreless
"God Eats Cafe." [ChrC] (108:22) 24-31 Jl 91, p. 722.
5189. ROEMER, Marjorie
"Dream House." [Kalliope] (13:2) 91, p. 57.
"Evening Comes." [CinPR] (21) Spr 90, p. 31.
5190. ROEPE, Rebecca A.
"Dreams of Our Fathers." [CumbPR] (11:1) Fall 91, p. 19.
5191. ROESKE, Paulette
"Another Woman." [SpoonRQ] (16:3/4) Sum-Fall 91, p. 10.
"Childhood Friend, Thirty Years Later." [LouisL] (8:1) Spr 91, p. 32-33.
"Family Tree." [LouisL] (8:1) Spr 91, p. 33-35.
"The Shock Ward" (St. Anthony's Hospital). [SpoonRQ] (16:3/4) Sum-Fall 91, p. 8-9.
"The Wife Takes a Child." [SpoonRQ] (16:3/4) Sum-Fall 91, p. 11-12.
5192. ROETHKE, Theodore
"Dolor." [Crazy] (41) Wint 91, p. 83.
5193. ROFFMAN, Rosaly DeMaios
"The Subject Is Walking." [SingHM] (19) 91, p. 1-2.
5194. ROGERS, Bertha
"Encounter." [InterPR] (17:2) Fall 91, p. 129.
"Klee's 'Bird Wandering Off'." [InterPR] (17:2) Fall 91, p. 128-129.
"Three by Gauguin." [Lactuca] (14) My 91, p. 11-12.
5195. ROGERS, Bobby Caudle
"New Bill Meyer Stadium" (home of the Knoxville Bluejays, for S. R. B.). [Shen] (41:1) Spr 91, p. 71.
5196. ROGERS, Bruce Holland
"Jolene: Earth." [BellR] (14:2) Fall 91, p. 35.
5197. ROGERS, C. D.
"Middle Aged Miami Cubans." [LindLM] (10:2) Ap-Je 91, p. 13.
5198. ROGERS, Charles
"Moving Toward the Island in My Heart." [ChatR] (11:3) Spr 91, p. 94-95.
5199. ROGERS, Daryl
"255 Lyndhurst Place." [Pearl] (13) Spr-Sum 91, p. 53.
"City Bus." [WormR] (31:4, #124) 91, p. 131.
"Simple Beauty." [WormR] (31:4, #124) 91, p. 131.
"Toot Owls." [NewYorkQ] (46) 91, p. 59.
5200. ROGERS, Del Marie
"Crystal Ball." [TexasR] (12:3/4) Fall-Wint 91, p. 84.
"The Dreaming Man, the Waiting Mother." [ColR] (NS 18:2) Fall-Wint 91, p. 63.
"Easter, San Augustine." [TexasR] (12:3/4) Fall-Wint 91, p. 85.
"King of the Gypsies." [ColR] (NS 18:2) Fall-Wint 91, p. 60.
"Sleeping on the Floor of an Empty House." [ColR] (NS 18:2) Fall-Wint 91, p. 61.
"White Grass" (for Robert Burlingame). [ColR] (NS 18:2) Fall-Wint 91, p. 62.
5201. ROGERS, Lawrence
"Haiku One." [Paint] (18:36) Aut 91, p. 20.
"Sacred Eve" (tr. of Motomaro Senge). [Paint] (18:36) Aut 91, p. 56.
"A Tiny Smile" (tr. of Motomaro Senge). [Paint] (18:36) Aut 91, p. 56.
5202. ROGERS, Pattiann
"Abomination." [PoetryNW] (32:1) Spr 91, p. 6-7.
"Amen." [Poetry] (158:2) My 91, p. 94.
"Apple Disciples." [PraS] (65:1) Spr 91, p. 20-21.
"By Death." [MissouriR] (13:3) 91, p. 95.
"Carrying on the Tradition, or, The Man in the Moon Brings His Daughter for Lessons in Marble Sculpting." [PoetryNW] (32:1) Spr 91, p. 3-4.

"Faith and Certainty: Arctic Circles." [PraS] (65:1) Spr 91, p. 23-24.
"The Fancy of Free Will." [GettyR] (4:4) Aut 91, p. 632-633.
"Fellfield." [MissouriR] (13:3) 91, p. 94.
"Get on Board." [MissouriR] (13:3) 91, p. 88-89.
"God's Only Begotten Duaghter." [PoetryNW] (32:1) Spr 91, p. 4-5.
"Good Heavens." [GettyR] (4:4) Aut 91, p. 636-638.
"Her Repast" (In Memoriam: Narcissus' Twin Sister). [PraS] (65:1) Spr 91, p. 19-20.
"If Dying Means Becoming Pure Spirit." [WestHR] (45:4) Wint 91, p. 302.
"The Insight of Limitations." [NewEngR] (13:3/4) Spr-Sum 91, p. 293-294.
"More Recollection." [MissouriR] (13:3) 91, p. 92-93.
"My Children (An Old God Remembers)." [PraS] (65:1) Spr 91, p. 18-19.
"The Older Kid." [PraS] (65:1) Spr 91, p. 22-23.
"Prairie Garden, Midnight, Moonless." [WestHR] (45:4) Wint 91, p. 303.
"Seeing Cat Things, Human Things, God Things." [NewEngR] (13:3/4) Spr-Sum 91, p. 294-295.
"Seeing the God-Statement." [MissouriR] (13:3) 91, p. 90-91.
"The Seeming of Things." [WestHR] (45:4) Wint 91, p. 300-301.
"Selene's Generosity." [PoetryNW] (32:1) Spr 91, p. 5-6.
"Still Life Abroad." [GettyR] (4:4) Aut 91, p. 634-635.
"Three's Charm." [MissouriR] (13:3) 91, p. 86-87.
"Why Lost Divinity Remains Lost." [NewEngR] (13:3/4) Spr-Sum 91, p. 292-293.

5203. ROGOFF, Jay
"The Future." [PoetryNW] (32:2) Sum 91, p. 14-15.
"Night Games." [Spitball] (36) Spr 91, p. 24-25.
"Rally-Killing." [Spitball] (36) Spr 91, p. 22-23.

5204. ROGOW, Zack
"The Mad Potter of Biloxi." [Pig] (17) 91, p. 65.

5205. ROITMAN, Judith
"This Hand." [Abraxas] (40/41) 91, p. 149.

5206. ROLLINGS, Alane
"All There Is to Find in Another Person's Eyes." [IndR] (14:3) Fall 91, p. 71-72.
"Dirty Dreams and God Smiling." [GeoR] (45:3) Fall 91, p. 537-538.
"To the Infinite Power." [NoDaQ] (59:3) Sum 91, p. 69.
"Turbulence." [NoDaQ] (59:3) Sum 91, p. 66-68.

5207. ROMAN, Victor
"She at Santa Monica Pier." [PoetryUSA] (22) Spr 91, p. 16.

5208. ROMANO, Ellen
"For Alice." [Lactuca] (14) My 91, p. 40.

5209. ROMANO, Rose
"Only the Americans." [SlipS] (11) 91, p. 9.

5210. ROMER, Barbara
"Daughter's Poem." [CimR] (96) Jl 91, p. 120-122.
"Rendezvous." [PraS] (65:3) Fall 91, p. 125-126.

5211. ROMERO, Leo
"During the Growing Season." [SoDakR] (29:3 part 2) Aut 91, p. 40.
"She Was Lovely." [Pembroke] (23) 91, p. 25.
"What Trees Dream About." [Writer] (104:10) O 91, p. 25.
"You Heard Him, You Heard." [Pembroke] (23) 91, p. 24.

5212. ROMOND, Edwin
"Dream Teaching." [EngJ] (80:4) Ap 91, p. 96.

5213. ROMTVEDT, David
"Kiev, The Ukraine, Nuclear Accident." [Elf] (1:2) Sum 91, p. 28-29.
"Sitka, Alaska, Hidden Faces." [Elf] (1:1) Spr 91, p. 25.
"Summer, 1970, Rich and Poor." [HampSPR] Wint 91, p. 51-52.

5214. RONAN, John
"History" (for C. E.). [GreensboroR] (51) Wint 91-92, p. 82.

5215. RONCI, Ray
"Ghislaine's Three Paintings." [NoDaQ] (59:3) Sum 91, p. 173.
"My Mother's Feet." [NoDaQ] (59:3) Sum 91, p. 171-172.

5216. RONK, Martha
"The Inconceivable." [DenQ] (26:1) Sum 91, p. 61.
"Memory of Tomorrow." [Talisman] (7) Fall 91, p. 129.

5217. ROOD, Diane
"Nebraska Sandhills." [Plain] (11:3) Spr 91, p. 28.

5218. ROOPNARAINE, Rupert
    "Suite for Supriya" (Selections: XXII-XXVII). [GrahamHR] (14) Spr 91, p. 28-31.
5219. ROOT, William Pitt
    "Boy at the Black Window" (for Tim Riley). [SwampR] (7/8) Spr-Sum 91, p.
        127-130.
    "Meat-Gatherers." [HighP] (6:1) Spr 91, p. 40-41.
    "On the Death of Albrecht Haushoffer and Discovery of the Moabit Sonnets."
        [PoetryE] (32) Fall 91, p. 147.
    "One for the Climbers at Shawangunk Ridge." [HighP] (6:1) Spr 91, p. 39.
5220. ROPPEL, Katherine
    "Climacteric." [AnthNEW] (3) 91, p. 11.
    "Lady of Perpetual Penance." [HawaiiR] (15:2, #32) Spr 91, p. 52-53.
    "Near Arco, Idaho 1971." [Pearl] (14) Fall-Wint 91, p. 48.
5221. ROQUÉ, Rosa Maria
    "Revision." [Journal] (15:2) Fall 91, p. 62.
    "Rhyme" (for B.K. Roberts). [Journal] (15:2) Fall 91, p. 61.
5222. ROSA, António Ramos
    "The Book of Ignorance" (Excerpts, tr. by Richard Zenith). [Trans] (25) Spr 91, p.
        94-97.
5223. ROSAS, Yolanda
    "Ahf." [Americas] (19:1) Spr 91, p. 62.
    "Hoy No." [Americas] (19:1) Spr 91, p. 64.
    "No Hay Ausencia." [Americas] (19:1) Spr 91, p. 63.
5224. ROSBERG, Rose
    "Badminton with an Orange Shuttlecock." [Hellas] (2:2) Fall 91, p. 265.
    "Double Observation." [Elf] (1:2) Sum 91, p. 30.
    "Like Vishnu." [Nimrod] (34:2) Spr-Sum 91, p. 105.
5225. ROSE, Anthony
    "City Lights." [OnTheBus] (8/9) 91, p. 140.
    "Gravida 11 & the Dinka." [OnTheBus] (8/9) 91, p. 139-140.
5226. ROSE, Brina
    "As Long As We Are Not Alone" (tr. of Israel Emiot, w. Leah Zazuyer). [SenR]
        (21:1) Spr 91, p. 30.
    "Before You Extinguish Me" (tr. of Israel Emiot, w. Leah Zazuyer). [SenR] (21:1)
        Spr 91, p. 26.
    "My God I Believe in You So Much" (tr. of Israel Emiot, w. Leah Zazuyer). [SenR]
        (21:1) Spr 91, p. 27.
    "A Prayer in Nineteen Forty-Three" (for H. Lang, tr. of Israel Emiot, w. Leah
        Zazuyer). [SenR] (21:1) Spr 91, p. 28.
    "Prayer of a Man in Snow" (tr. of Israel Emiot, w. Leah Zazuyer). [SenR] (21:1)
        Spr 91, p. 29.
    "With or Without Me" (tr. of Israel Emiot, w. Leah Zazuyer). [SenR] (21:1) Spr 91,
        p. 31.
5227. ROSE, Dorothy L.
    "Dick and Beth." [ChironR] (10:3) Aut 91, p. 40.
    "Salinas 1939." [ChironR] (10:2) Sum 91, p. 44.
5228. ROSE, Jennifer
    "Father's Day" (1985). [Ploughs] (17:2/3) Fall 91, p. 149-150.
    "Lines Written During an Autumn Invasion." [Agni] (33) 91, p. 102.
    "Mostar Postcard" (Yugoslavia, 1982). [Agni] (33) 91, p. 101.
5229. ROSE, Judith
    "Woodworms, Christ's Tears." [VirQR] (67:2) Spr 91, p. 265-266.
5230. ROSE, Judith Klinger
    "Fredricksburg." [OnTheBus] (8/9) 91, p. 141.
5231. ROSE, Karen
    "Rules for Crappies." [PoetC] (22:2) Wint 91, p. 22-24.
5232. ROSE, Wendy
    "Do You See Her Alone on the Mountain?" [KenR] (NS 13:4) Fall 91, p. 84.
    "Remember Waking Up with Me." [KenR] (NS 13:4) Fall 91, p. 83.
5233. ROSE, Wilga
    "Traveling Light." [Bogg] (64) 91, p. 49.
5234. ROSEDAUGHTER, Stefanie
    "Glory." [BellArk] (7:3) My-Je 91, p. 3.
    "Magic of the Moon." [BellArk] (7:3) My-Je 91, p. 4.
    "Queen Anne Hill." [BellArk] (7:4) Jl-Ag 91, p. 1.
    "Reflections on Time, Late Spring." [BellArk] (7:4) Jl-Ag 91, p. 12.

"Saint Malo." [BellArk] (7:2) Mr-Ap 91, p. 7.
"Two Artists Dance Beneath the Moon." [BellArk] (7:4) Jl-Ag 91, p. 22.
5235. ROSEN, Michael J.
"The Least That Penn Can Do." [PraS] (65:3) Fall 91, p. 102-104.
"Penn Consults the Magic Eight Ball." [PraS] (65:3) Fall 91, p. 98-101.
5236. ROSENBERG, Liz
"Clouds." [MissouriR] (14:3) 91, p. 34.
"The Details." [Nat] (252:8) 4 Mr 91, p. 283.
"Fireworks." [Nat] (252:8) 4 Mr 91, p. 283.
"Intensive Care Unit." [MissouriR] (14:3) 91, p. 38-39.
"The Method." [MissouriR] (14:3) 91, p. 35.
"New Days." [MissouriR] (14:3) 91, p. 32.
"The New Life." [MissouriR] (14:3) 91, p. 40-41.
"The Smallest Gesture." [MissouriR] (14:3) 91, p. 37.
"Terror." [MissouriR] (14:3) 91, p. 36.
"This Peaceful Street." [MissouriR] (14:3) 91, p. 33.
5237. ROSENBERG, Robert
"The Auto Show." [SpoonRQ]'(16:1/2) Wint-Spr 91, p. 15.
"A Letter to My Wife." [SpoonRQ] (16:1/2) Wint-Spr 91, p. 19.
"Life in Boston." [SpoonRQ] (16:1/2) Wint-Spr 91, p. 18.
"Little Pleasant Bay." [SpoonRQ] (16:1/2) Wint-Spr 91, p. 16-17.
5238. ROSENBERG, Tracey S.
"Requiem." [PikeF] (10) Spr 91, p. 19.
5239. ROSENCOF, Mauricio
"Conversations with My Sandal" (tr. by Louise B. Popkin and Julia H. Ackerman).
[KenR] (NS 13:3) Sum 91, p. 67-73.
ROSENIOR, Arthur de Graft
See De GRAFT-ROSENIOR, Arthur
5240. ROSENSTOCK, Gabriel
"Cloud morning sun filtering through" (in Gaelic and English, tr. by the author).
[PoetryUSA] (22) Spr 91, p. 9.
"Mounting you from the rear" (in Gaelic and English, tr. by the author).
[PoetryUSA] (22) Spr 91, p. 9.
"Somewhere the sun beats down" (in Gaelic and English, tr. by the author).
[PoetryUSA] (22) Spr 91, p. 9.
5241. ROSENSTOCK, Pascal
"Going the Whole Way." [PoetryUSA] (23) Sum 91, p. 15.
5242. ROSENTHAL, David H.
"Manhattan Farewell." [Ploughs] (17:1) Spr 91, p. 121-124.
5243. ROSENTHAL, M. L.
"Snow Man" (NYC, December 1990). [Ploughs] (17:2/3) Fall 91, p. 268.
"The World Pub" (Selection: "Led by the Love of God to the Love of Woman").
[Ploughs] (17:1) Spr 91, p. 125-129.
5244. ROSENWALD, John
"Love Song" (tr. of Rainer Maria Rilke). [Mildred] (4:2/5:1) 91, p. 129.
5245. ROSENWASSER, Rena
"All 'A's'." [HangL] (59) 91, p. 54-55.
"Details of Myself." [CentralP] (19/20) Spr-Fall 91, p. 176.
"Paradeisos" (in Greek: stocked with everything good and valuable). [HangL] (59)
91, p. 53.
"Their Lacquered Faces Red and Slippery." [CentralP] (19/20) Spr-Fall 91, p. 177.
5246. ROSENZWEIG, Dan
"The Un-perfect Poem" (draft). [PoetryUSA] (23) Sum 91, p. 26.
5247. ROSENZWEIG, Geri
"The Calf and the Moon." [GreensboroR] (50) Sum 91, p. 58-59.
"Cloisters: New York." [PoetL] (86:2) Sum 91, p. 13-14.
"A Fine Music." [PoetL] (86:2) Sum 91, p. 15.
"Nocturne." [HiramPoR] (50) Spr-Sum 91, p. 21.
5248. ROSENZWEIG, Phyllis
"Urge." [Aerial] (6/7) 91, p. 144-145.
"Vitality (Five X Five)." [Aerial] (6/7) 91, p. 143.
5249. ROSIC, Tiodor
"The Butterfly" (tr. by Vasa D. Mihailovich). [InterPR] (15:1) Spr 89, p. 79.
"The Cage" (tr. by Vasa D. Mihailovich). [InterPR] (15:1) Spr 89, p. 71.
"A Fig" (tr. by Vasa D. Mihailovich). [InterPR] (15:1) Spr 89, p. 75.
"Kavez." [InterPR] (15:1) Spr 89, p. 70.

"Leptir." [InterPR] (15:1) Spr 89, p. 78.
"A Magpie" (tr. by Vasa D. Mihailovich). [InterPR] (15:1) Spr 89, p. 73.
"Smokva." [InterPR] (15:1) Spr 89, p. 74.
"Svraka." [InterPR] (15:1) Spr 89, p. 72.
"Tambura." [InterPR] (15:1) Spr 89, p. 76.
"Tamburitza" (tr. by Vasa D. Mihailovich). [InterPR] (15:1) Spr 89, p. 77.
5250. ROSIER, R. Peter
"Crap Shoot." [ManhatPR] (13) [91?], p. 20.
"Hope." [ManhatPR] (13) [91?], p. 20.
5251. ROSKILL, Mark
"Back to the bunker again" (Response to "Save the Clerihew" appeal). [BostonR]
(16:3/4) Je-Ag 91, p. 33.
"Edward Clerihew Bentley" (Response to "Save the Clerihew" appeal). [BostonR]
(16:5) O 91, p. 24.
5252. ROSNAY, Jean-Pierre
"From Italy Near Naples" (tr. by J. Kates). [MidAR] (11:2) 91, p. 113-114.
"So-So" (tr. by J. Kates). [MidAR] (11:2) 91, p. 112.
5253. ROSS, David
"An Evening's Rain." [TampaR] (4) 91, p. 72.
5254. ROSS, Jean
"The Mendicant Sends a Declaration by Registered Letter." [Pig] (17) 91, p. 59.
5255. ROSS, Linwood M.
"Against the Subway's Rumble" (Poem for Certain Train Station Hustlers). [Obs]
(6:3) Wint 91, p. 98-99.
"Art Groupie in Exile." [ChangingM] (23) Fall-Wint 91, p. 24.
"My Defiant Earthmother." [Obs] (6:3) Wint 91, p. 99-100.
"Night Unfurls." [Obs] (6:3) Wint 91, p. 100-102.
"Poem for My Colored Father." [Obs] (6:3) Wint 91, p. 100.
5256. ROSS, William Warfield
"Siamese." [PoetL] (86:3) Fall 91, p. 32.
ROSSARDI, Orlando Rodriguez
See RODRIGUEZ ROSSARDI, Orlando
5257. ROSSER, J. Allyn
"Still-Life Movie of America." [DenQ] (25:3) Wint 91, p. 17-20.
"The Sum Contradiction of Our Shades." [Poetry] (157:5) F 91, p. 253-256.
5258. ROSSER, Mirth
"Moving." [PraF] (12:1 #54) Spr 91, p. 79.
"Trouble with Mother." [PraF] (12:1 #54) Spr 91, p. 78.
5259. ROSSI, Lee
"Another Autumn Poem" (tr. of Paul Kersten). [OnTheBus] (8/9) 91, p. 208.
"Cala Muerta" (tr. of Paul Kersten). [OnTheBus] (8/9) 91, p. 209.
"Dead Child" (tr. of Paul Kersten). [OnTheBus] (8/9) 91, p. 209-211.
"The Drill." [Pearl] (14) Fall-Wint 91, p. 51.
"Freedom." [PoetryE] (31) Spr 91, p. 106.
"Lament." [Pearl] (14) Fall-Wint 91, p. 51.
"Prayer Between Beatings." [Pearl] (13) Spr-Sum 91, p. 46.
"Rainbow" (tr. of Paul Kersten). [OnTheBus] (8/9) 91, p. 213-214.
"The Rose" (tr. of Paul Kersten). [OnTheBus] (8/9) 91, p. 214-215.
"Skipping Breakfast." [ChironR] (10:4) Wint 91, p. 35.
"With Colored Pencils" (for Ina, tr. of Paul Kersten). [OnTheBus] (8/9) 91, p.
211-212.
"With the Camera" (for Peter, tr. of Paul Kersten). [OnTheBus] (8/9) 91, p.
212-213.
"Woman After 16 Years of Marriage." [Pearl] (14) Fall-Wint 91, p. 51.
5260. ROSSITER, Charles
"Revving the Metaphysical Engine." [HeavenB] (9) Wint-Spr 91-92, p. 62.
"Work Detail, Zen Mountain Monastery." [HeavenB] (9) Wint-Spr 91-92, p. 37.
5261. ROTELLA, Guy
"Recovery." [DenQ] (26:1) Sum 91, p. 62.
5262. ROTH, Susan Harned
"Bath." [Calyx] (13:3) Wint 91-92, p. 56.
"Pressure." [Calyx] (13:3) Wint 91-92, p. 54-55.
5263. ROTH-NATALE, Nanci
"Aunt Mamie's Ritual." [BellArk] (7:4) Jl-Ag 91, p. 3.
"Jason at School." [BellArk] (7:6) N-D 91, p. 11.

5264. ROTHENBERG, Jerome
    "Chinese Scenes." [PoetryUSA] (23) Sum 91, p. 18.
    "Execution: Poem 9" (tr. of Kurt Schwitters). [Sulfur] (11:1, #28) Spr 91, p. 111.
    "A Flower Like a Raven" (tr. of Kurt Schwitters). [Sulfur] (11:1, #28) Spr 91, p.
      113.
    "Four Ballads in Yellow" (tr. of Federico Garcia Lorca). [SnailPR] (1:1) Spr 91, p.
      16-19.
    "From the Back & From the Front to Start" (tr. of Kurt Schwitters). [Sulfur] (11:1,
      #28) Spr 91, p. 112-113.
    "God, Dark, with Palm Trees" (The Lorca Variations XVIII). [PoetryUSA] (22) Spr
      91, p. 11.
    "Ice Clocks" (tr. of Kurt Schwitters). [Sulfur] (11:1, #28) Spr 91, p. 116.
    "The Lorca Variations" (XI & XII). [Sulfer] (11:2, #29) Fall 91, p. 20-22.
    "The Lorca Variations (XV): Wheel of Fortune" (for Diane Wakoski). [SnailPR]
      (1:1) Spr 91, p. 15.
    "Lorca's Newton" (The Lorca Variations XIII, For Michael Palmer). [PoetryUSA]
      (22) Spr 91, p. 6.
    "Murder Machine 43" (tr. of Kurt Schwitters). [Sulfur] (11:1, #28) Spr 91, p.
      114-116.
    "A Poem of Longing" (for Wai-lim Yip). [PoetryUSA] (23) Sum 91, p. 18.
    "She Dolls with Dollies (1944)" (tr. of Kurt Schwitters). [Talisman] (6) Spr 91, p.
      112.
    "Thou" (tr. of Kurt Schwitters). [Sulfur] (11:1, #28) Spr 91, p. 108.
    "Three Crepuscular Poems" (for my sister Conchita, tr. of Federico García Lorca).
      [Talisman] (6) Spr 91, p. 112-113.
    "Two Chinese Plays." [PoetryUSA] (22) Spr 91, p. 4.
5265. ROTHFORK, John
    "Take the Name War Eagle." [SoDakR] (29:3 part 2) Aut 91, p. 51-53.
5266. ROTHMAN, David J.
    "The Bricklayer's Beautiful Daughter." [GettyR] (4:1) Wint 91, p. 95-96.
    "How to Eat" (for L. Y.). [KenR] (NS 13:1) Wint 91, p. 144-145.
    "A Scent of Lilacs." [PoetryNW] (32:3) Aut 91, p. 27-28.
    "The Turn Things Take" (for Stephen and Mary Rose). [PoetL] (86:2) Sum 91, p.
      24.
5267. ROTHWELL, C. Brooke
    "The Morning I Saved Ty Cobb from Drowning / A Dream." [Spitball] (39) Wint 91,
      p. 18.
5268. ROTKIN, Charlotte
    "Psyche's Market." [DustyD] Je 91, p. 33.
5269. ROUBAUD, Jacques
    "It Would Be Best" (tr. by Rita Kieffer). [InterPR] (17:1) Spr 91, p. 71.
    "Le Mieux Serait." [InterPR] (17:1) Spr 91, p. 70.
5270. ROUND, Jeff
    "Turn." [AntigR] (85/86) Spr-Sum 91, p. 215-216.
5271. ROUNDS, Nathaniel S.
    "It Didn't Hurt." [PottPort] (13:2) Fall-Wint 91, p. 43-44.
5272. ROWAN, Phyllis
    "Crow." [PottPort] (13:2) Fall-Wint 91, p. 20.
    "The Door." [PottPort] (13:2) Fall-Wint 91, p. 21.
5273. ROWDER, Jessica
    "Why the Ocean Always Falls Back." [DenQ] (25:4) Spr 91, p. 53.
5274. ROWLEY, Alexandra F.
    "The Game." [HangL] (58) 91, p. 87.
5275. ROY, Lucinda (Lucinda H.)
    "Book Review." [Callaloo] (14:4) Fall 91, p. 776-779.
    "Lorraine." [Obs] (6:3) Wint 91, p. 79.
    "Reciprocity." [Obs] (6:3) Wint 91, p. 79-80.
5276. ROYAL, Richard
    "Forest Fire." [CentralP] (19/20) Spr-Fall 91, p. 287-295.
RU, Wang Jun
    See WANG, Jun Ru
5277. RUBENSTEIN, Lev
    "On and On" (tr. by Alexei Pavlenko and Thomas Epstein). [LitR] (34:3) Spr 91, p.
      352-360.
5278. RUBIA, Geraldine
    "My Mother Once When She Was Tipsy." [TickleAce] (22) Fall-Wint 91, p. 65.

5279. RUBIN, Larry
"Bus Station Waiting Room." [LullwaterR] (2:2) Spr 91, p. 72.
"Taking the Bus to Visit My Sister's Grave." [Sequoia] (34:1) Spr 91, p. 93.
5280. RUBIN, Louis D., Jr.
"I'll Not Go Donw That Street." [SewanR] (99:4) Fall 91, p. 557-558.
"Poet in Eclipse" (For Karl Shapiro). [SewanR] (99:4) Fall 91, p. 554-556.
"Silver Fox" (In memory of Mac Pitt). [SewanR] (99:4) Fall 91, p. 556.
5281. RUBIN, Mark
"The Curse." [Boulevard] (5:3/6:1, #15/16) Spr 91, p. 221-222.
5282. RUBIN, Mordecai
"Agonía Doméstica." [Nuez] (3:7) 91, p. 24.
"Ausente la Esposa un Día" (A Bárbara). [Nuez] (3:8/9) 91, p. 26.
"Cuéntame." [Nuez] (3:8/9) 91, p. 26.
5283. RUCKER, Trish
"Burning Bridges." [TarRP] (31:1) Fall 91, p. 32.
"Fate, Like Jayne Mansfield, Takes a Road Trip." [PoetL] (86:3) Fall 91, p. 33-39.
"Hummingbirds." [WindO] (54) Sum 91, p. 19.
"Naming Things." [SouthernHR] (25:1) Wint 91, p. 53.
"Nancy Drew." [MinnR] (NS 37) Fall 91, p. 44-46.
"The Need for Maps." [PoetryE] (31) Spr 91, p. 97-99.
"On a Bridge Between Two Places." [CarolQ] (43:2) Wint 91, p. 35-36.
"Origins." [Colum] (15) 90, p. 49.
"Party on Hemingway's Birthday." [WindO] (54) Sum 91, p. 17-18.
"Photographing the Ghost." [PoetL] (86:3) Fall 91, p. 40.
"Spirit Images and the Meaning of Dreams." [CarolQ] (43:2) Wint 91, p. 34.
"The Stranger." [ArtfulD] (20/21) 91, p. 54.
"The Summer Tourists." [BrooklynR] (8) 91, p. 5.
"Swallow Creek." [ThRiPo] (37/38) 91, p. 64.
"The Swallows of Capistrano." [ThRiPo] (37/38) 91, p. 65.
"The Tomato." [BellR] (14:2) Fall 91, p. 47.
"Walking Through Glass." [TarRP] (31:1) Fall 91, p. 32.
"Yeats Moves You." [PoetryE] (31) Spr 91, p. 96.
5284. RUCKS, Carol
"New Mexico." [RagMag] (9:2) 91, p. 21.
5285. RUDMAN, Mark
"Above and Below in Mexico (Seen from the Eleventh Story)." [Ploughs] (17:1) Spr
91, p. 136-142.
"Back Stairwell." [ParisR] (33:119) Sum 91, p. 190-191.
"Don't Know Much." [Ploughs] (17:1) Spr 91, p. 135-136.
"Filmography." [DenQ] (25:4) Spr 91, p. 54.
"Highest Sickness" (tr. of Boris Pasternak, w. Bohdan Boychuk). [Pequod] (32)
91, p. 45-53.
"Love in the West, 1965." [PoetryE] (32) Fall 91, p. 115-116.
"Oscillation." [Thrpny] (47) Fall 91, p. 14.
"Uniforms." [Ploughs] (17:2/3) Fall 91, p. 156-158.
"West of Here, East of There." [Ploughs] (17:1) Spr 91, p. 131-135.
"Where the Story Leaves Off." [Thrpny] (44) Wint 91, p. 14.
RUE, Dorie La
See LaRUE, Dorie
5286. RUEFLE, Mary
"Mid-Autumn Festival." [MichQR] (30:2) Spr 91, p. 293.
"Xingang Zhong Lu." [MichQR] (30:2) Spr 91, p. 292.
5287. RUESCHER, Scott
"Big Black Hearses." [Agni] (34) 91, p. 148-150.
"Concord Truce." [Agni] (34) 91, p. 146-147.
"Dear George." [Agni] (34) 91, p. 144-145.
"Game Called Because of Rain." [Spitball] (38) Fall 91, p. 38-39.
5288. RUFFIN, Paul
"Blackberries." [HawaiiR] (15:3, #33) Fall 91, p. 87-88.
"Devilfish." [CalQ] (35/36) 91, p. 42-43.
"His Grandmother Prays for Rain." [SoDakR] (29:2) Sum 91, p. 153-154.
"Prison Class." [MissR] (19:3) 91, p. 165.
5289. RUGGIERI, Helen
"Dread." [Abraxas] (40/41) 91, p. 148.
"Signs All Around." [Abraxas] (40/41) 91, p. 148-149.

5290. RULE, Bernadette
"North from Fergus in Winter." [Bogg] (64) 91, p. 51.
5291. RUMBERG, Mayda
"Dracula-Daughter." [Plain] (11:3) Spr 91, p. 13.
5292. RUMENS, Carol
"An Attempted Burial." [Stand] (32:4) Aut 91, p. 22-23.
5293. RUMI, Jalaloddin
"The Lovers' Tailor's Shop" (tr. by Peter Lamborn Wilson. w. William C. Chittick).
[Talisman] (6) Spr 91, p. 30.
5294. RUMMEL, Mary Kay
"Connemara Song." [SingHM] (19) 91, p. 95-96.
5295. RUNCIMAN, Lex
"Drill." [NewEngR] (13:3/4) Spr-Sum 91, p. 343-344.
"Missouri Air." [NewEngR] (13:3/4) Spr-Sum 91, p. 342-343.
5296. RUNEFELT, Eva
"Astoria" (tr. by David Harry). [Vis] (37) 91, p. 54.
"Love Poem (Rome)" (tr. by David Harry). [Vis] (37) 91, p. 53-54.
5297. RUNGE, Steven
"I Am Reminded of My Father While Repairing a Bicycle." [WilliamMR] (29) 91, p.
47.
5298. RUNKLE, Stephen
"The Olive Workers." [WillowR] Spr 91, p. 9-10.
5299. RUNNING, Thorpe
"Like the Rivers, Clouds, and Roses" (tr. of Edgar Bayley). [ColR] (NS 18:1)
Spr-Sum 91, p. 86-87.
5300. RUNYAN, Tana W.
"Sound, the Memory." [Calyx] (13:3) Wint 91-92, p. 47.
5301. RUNYON, C. D.
"Annunciation of the Odalisque." [Nimrod] (35:1) Fall-Wint 91, p. 112-113.
5302. RUSEL, Jacob
"How Jacob Loved." [BelPoJ] (42:1) Fall 91, p. 6-7.
5303. RUSS, Biff
"Desideratum." [PoetryE] (32) Fall 91, p. 113.
"Ideogram: Father." [PoetryE] (32) Fall 91, p. 112.
"Lunar Eclipse" (for my niece Jennifer). [PoetryE] (32) Fall 91, p. 111.
"Stained Glass Window, Metz." [CreamCR] (15:1) Spr 91, p. 79-80.
5304. RUSSELL, Dorothy
"Summer's End: Scene One." [Nimrod] (34:2) Spr-Sum 91, p. 91.
"Winter Wind." [Nimrod] (34:2) Spr-Sum 91, p. 92.
RUSSELL, Gillian Harding
See HARDING-RUSSELL, Gillian
5305. RUSSELL, Norman
"Everything the Tree Does It Does Carefully." [Mildred] (4:2/5:1) 91, p. 93.
"Gods Came Flying." [MidAR] (11:1) 91, p. 41.
"Nest and Lodge." [MidAR] (11:1) 91, p. 40.
"What to Teach the Children." [MidAR] (11:1) 91, p. 42.
5306. RUSSELL, Peter
"The Triumph." [JINJPo] (13:1) Spr 91, p. 1.
5307. RUSSELL, Thomas
"Auntie Anthem." [GeoR] (45:1) Spr 91, p. 26.
5308. RUSSELL, Timothy
"In Aquio Amino." [Pearl] (13) Spr-Sum 91, p. 17.
"In Locus Delicti." [Pearl] (13) Spr-Sum 91, p. 17.
5309. RUSSO, Gianna
"When My Husband Cleans the Kitchen." [Calyx] (13:2) Sum 91, p. 64-65.
5310. RUSSO, Linda V.
"Finding Things." [Journal] (15:2) Fall 91, p. 82.
"Sister at the Piano." [Journal] (15:2) Fall 91, p. 81.
5311. RUTH, Barbara
"Pelvic Mass Etiology." [SinW] (43/44) Sum 91, p. 285-287.
5312. RUTSALA, Vern
"The Black Map." [Chelsea] (51) 91, p. 88-89.
"Carpentry." [ColR] (NS 18:1) Spr-Sum 91, p. 79-80.
"Flying Free in 'Fifty-Eight." [SewanR] (99:2) Spr 91, p. 187-188.
"The Fruit Cellar." [ThRiPo] (37/38) 91, p. 78.
"Learning Your Lesson." [PoetryE] (32) Fall 91, p. 125.

"Missing It." [Crazy] (41) Wint 91, p. 15.
"The Super 99 Drive-in Chronicle." [ColR] (NS 18:1) Spr-Sum 91, p. 77-78.
5313. RUZESKY, Jay
"Moose Are Not Philosophers." [Grain] (19:4) Wint 91, p. 51.
"My Grandfather Was Offered a Contract with the Dodgers But My Grandfather's
    Father Offered Him the Farm and Said He Couldn't Have Both." [PoetryC]
    (12:1) D 91, p. 17.
"Nouvelle Cuisine Domestic." [Grain] (19:4) Wint 91, p. 52-53.
"Tsunami" (after Jamie S.). [PoetryC] (12:1) D 91, p. 17.
5314. RYALS, Mary Jane
"The Gate." [BellR] (14:1) Spr 91, p. 30-31.
"Spirits." [SlipS] (11) 91, p. 72.
5315. RYAN, Bill
"The Guide." [PennR] (5:1) Spr 91, p. 14.
"The Heron." [PennR] (5:1) Spr 91, p. 13.
5316. RYAN, Gregory A.
"Conversation on Rue Camou" (To Slawomir Mrozek). [LitR] (34:2) Wint 91, p.
    172.
"Quadrille." [HawaiiR] (15:3, #33) Fall 91, p. 127.
5317. RYAN, Kay
"At the Edge of a Philosophy." [ClockR] (7:1/2) 91-92, p. 55.
"Can a Dog Be As Large As an Elephant?" [ClockR] (7:1/2) 91-92, p. 54.
5318. RYAN, Michael
"Pedestrian Pastoral." [Harp] (282:1689) F 91, p. 38.
5319. RYAN, Mina
"Rearranging My Body." [PlumR] (1) Spr-Sum 91, p. 54.
5320. RYAN, Wes
"Slipping by Degrees." [VirQR] (67:1) Wint 91, p. 60-63.
5321. RYDER, Vanessa
"Dorothy on the Rocks, Ogunquit, Maine — 1910." [IndR] (14:3) Fall 91, p. 39.
"The Hill People." [IndR] (14:3) Fall 91, p. 40-41.
5322. RYDSTEDT, Anna
"Summer Body" (tr. by David Harry). [Vis] (37) 91, p. 55.
5323. RYEL, Deborah E.
"Eating the Heart (of it)." [SpoonRQ] (16:1/2) Wint-Spr 91, p. 91-92.
5324. RYMARUK, Ihor
"A Ballad for the Passerby" (in Russian and English, tr. by Andrew Kaspryk).
    [InterPR] (17:2) Fall 91, p. 74-75.
"Untitled: The calm mouth of the letters' breath" (in Russian and English, tr. by
    Andrew Kaspryk). [InterPR] (17:2) Fall 91, p. 68-69.
"Untitled: There are untold numbers. They march" (in Russian and English, tr. by
    Andrew Kaspryk). [InterPR] (17:2) Fall 91, p. 70-73.
5325. S.T.V.C.
"Repeat Prodigal." [OnTheBus] (8/9) 91, p. 150.
5326. SABA, Mark
"A Love Poem" (for JSL). [Mildred] (4:2/5:1) 91, p. 66.
"The Magnolia Branch." [Mildred] (4:2/5:1) 91, p. 67.
5327. SABA, Umberto
"Old Chimney" (tr. by Will Wells). [NewOR] (18:2) Sum 91, p. 17.
"Winter" (tr. by Christopher Millis). [ColR] (NS 17:2) Fall-Wint 90, p. 105.
5328. SABATELLI, Arnold
"Progreso, Mexico, December 1990." [Os] (32) Spr 91, p. 37.
5329. SABATIER, Robert
"I Enter Myself" (tr. by James T. Reiber). [CrabCR] (7:3) 91, p. 11.
"I Learn the World" (tr. by James T. Reiber). [CrabCR] (7:3) 91, p. 10.
SABURO, Kuroda
    See KURODA, Saburo
SACHIKO, Yoshihara
    See YOSHIHARA, Sachiko
5330. SADLER, Janet Longe
"Pietá II." [LaurelR] (25:1) Wint 91, p. 102-103.
5331. SADLER, Norma
"The Letter." [EngJ] (80:3) Mr 91, p. 97.
5332. SADOFF, Ira
"Above the Cinema Verité: August, 1968." [NewEngR] (14:1) Fall 91, p. 65.
"After My Father's Death." [NewEngR] (14:1) Fall 91, p. 66.

"The Bath." [SewanR] (98:4) Fall 90, p. 616-617.
"Elegy: Ecole Strip Mine, Nebraska." [RiverS] (33) 91, p. 49.
"An Exceptional Joy." [OntR] (35) Fall-Wint 91-92, p. 17.
"For Once." [SewanR] (98:4) Fall 90, p. 619.
"I Forgive the Sparrows." [KenR] (NS 13:2) Spr 91, p. 131.
"My Mother's Funeral." [Antaeus] (67) Fall 91, p. 142.
"On the Job." [ParisR] (33:119) Sum 91, p. 189.
"Resurrection." [KenR] (NS 13:2) Spr 91, p. 130.
"The Same Old Story." [SewanR] (98:4) Fall 90, p. 618.
"Selma." [OntR] (35) Fall-Wint 91-92, p. 14-15.
"Shadow." [OntR] (35) Fall-Wint 91-92, p. 16.

5333. SADOW, Stephen A.
"Age" (tr. of Ricardo Feierstein, w. J. Kates). [InterPR] (17:1) Spr 91, p. 63.
"Full Name" (tr. of Ricardo Feierstein, w. J. Kates). [InterPR] (17:1) Spr 91, p. 59.
"Place of Residence" (tr. of Ricardo Feierstein, w. J. Kates). [InterPR] (17:1) Spr
91, p. 61.
"Profession" (tr. of Ricardo Feierstein, w. J. Kates). [InterPR] (17:1) Spr 91, p. 67,
69.
"Sex" (tr. of Ricardo Feierstein, w. J. Kates). [InterPR] (17:1) Spr 91, p. 65.

5334. SAENZ, Benjamin Alire
"Workers." [PoetryE] (31) Spr 91, p. 129-131.

5335. SAFARIK, Allan
"The Double Broiler." [Grain] (19:4) Wint 91, p. 132-133.
"Letter to the Listener." [AntigR] (85/86) Spr-Sum 91, p. 228.
"Mexican Winter." [AntigR] (85/86) Spr-Sum 91, p. 225.
"Perfect Zero." [AntigR] (85/86) Spr-Sum 91, p. 227.
"Sojourn." [AntigR] (85/86) Spr-Sum 91, p. 224.
"Water Company." [AntigR] (85/86) Spr-Sum 91, p. 226.
"Winter Midnight." [Grain] (19:4) Wint 91, p. 134.

5336. SAFFIOTI, Carol Lee
"Lost Shadow Speaks." [BlackBR] (14) Fall-Wint 91, p. 5.

5337. SAFIE, Doris
"Victoria: A Portrait of My Grandmother." [Paint] (18:35) Spr 91, p. 78-79.

5338. SAGAN, Miriam
"Abelard and Heloise." [PoetryE] (31) Spr 91, p. 33-35.
"Full Moon Ceremony" (Excerpt). [Writer] (104:10) O 91, p. 26.
"If I were a child I would write my name in red crayon." [PoetryE] (31) Spr 91, p.
36-37.
"Isabel: Lullaby." [Writer] (104:10) O 91, p. 24.
"Jewel Net." [ChironR] (10:4) Wint 91, p. 12-13.
"Male and Female Mountains." [Agni] (33) 91, p. 53.
"Sacrifice." [Plain] (11:2) Wint 91, p. 36-37.

5339. SAGARIS, Lake
"The Caleuche." [Descant] (22:4, #75) Wint 91-92, p. 134.
"Circus Love" (Selections: 2 poems). [PraF] (12:2 #55) Sum 91, p. 64-65.
"Echoes." [Grain] (19:2) Sum 91, p. 110.
"Four Seasons in a Day: Poems about Newfoundland & Chiloé." [Descant] (22:4,
#75) Wint 91-92, p. 127-128.
"El Imbunche." [Descant] (22:4, #75) Wint 91-92, p. 129-130.
"Isla Grande." [Descant] (22:4, #75) Wint 91-92, p. 136-137.
"Legacy." [Event] (20:2) Sum 91, p. 108-109.
"Voladora." [Descant] (22:4, #75) Wint 91-92, p. 131.
"Why should anyone deposit her life outside her body?" [Descant] (22:4, #75) Wint
91-92, p. 135.

5340. SAGASER, Elizabeth Harris
"Certainty on Naples Road: Watching Him Sleep." [PraS] (65:4) Wint 91, p.
115-116.
"Love Without Poems." [PraS] (65:4) Wint 91, p. 115.
"One of Your Birthdays." [ChiR] (37:2/3) 91, p. 165.

5341. SAHA, Ananda
"Three Poems Toward One." [Archae] (2) Spr 91, p. 24.

5342. SAHAGUN, Carlos
"Chemistry Class" (tr. by Michael L. Johnson). [CharR] (17:1) Spr 91, p. 59-60.
"The Prisoner" (To the Memory of M.H., tr. by Michael L. Johnson). [CharR]
(17:1) Spr 91, p. 57-58.
"Rain at Night" (tr. by Michael L. Johnson). [CharR] (17:1) Spr 91, p. 58-59.

SAID, 'Ali Ahmad
    See ADONIS
5343. SAIJO, Albert
    "Columba Livia with People in Urban Setting." [BambooR] (52) Fall 91, p.
        105-106.
SAINT
    See also ST. (filed as spelled)
5344. SAIZ, Próspero
    "Accompany accompany." [Abraxas] (40/41) 91, p. 111-112.
    "And." [Abraxas] (40/41) 91, p. 109.
    "The Bird of Nothing" (Selections). [Abraxas] (40/41) 91, p. 103-104.
    "The black sun falls from darkest night." [Abraxas] (40/41) 91, p. 102.
    "The blood of sacrifice confounds the indebted poets." [Abraxas] (40/41) 91, p.
        116-117.
    "Hallo poets of the surface." [Abraxas] (40/41) 91, p. 110.
    "Light." [Abraxas] (40/41) 91, p. 105.
    "Night." [Abraxas] (40/41) 91, p. 101.
    "The night sun." [Abraxas] (40/41) 91, p. 108.
    "Shantam." [Abraxas] (40/41) 91, p. 106.
    "Silence of the white spider only." [Abraxas] (40/41) 91, p. 107.
    "The stone casts a shadow." [Abraxas] (40/41) 91, p. 113-114.
    "Sun shines on tonto rim." [Abraxas] (40/41) 91, p. 115.
    "Trilce" (Selections: XV-XXX, XXXII-XXXIV, XLI, XLIV, XLIX, LV, LVII,
        LX, LXIII, LXVI, LXVIII-LXX, LXXII-LXXIII, tr. of César Abraham
        Vallejo). [Abraxas] (40/41) 91, p. 24-99.
5345. SALA, Jerome
    "3/10/90." [Aerial] (6/7) 91, p. 169.
    "1969." [Aerial] (6/7) 91, p. 171.
    "Iblis." [Aerial] (6/7) 91, p. 170.
    "One Night the Mirror People Exploded." [Shiny] (6) Spr-Sum 91, p. 47-48.
    "Riddle." [Shiny] (6) Spr-Sum 91, p. 49.
5346. SALAAM, Kalamu ya
    "Blues Zephyr." [LouisL] (8:1) Spr 91, p. 42.
5347. SALAGA, Jack
    "4th Persona(fication)." [WormR] (31:4, #124) 91, p. 103.
    "30th Persona(fication)." [WormR] (31:4, #124) 91, p. 102.
5348. SALAMONE, Karen
    "Cream of Tomato Soup." [BellArk] (7:6) N-D 91, p. 1.
    "His Choice." [ChironR] (10:2) Sum 91, p. 42.
    "Immigrant." [BellArk] (7:3) My-Je 91, p. 8.
    "Multiplied Already." [BellArk] (7:3) My-Je 91, p. 3.
    "Poplars." [BellArk] (7:6) N-D 91, p. 6.
    "The Sound of Lullaby." [BellArk] (7:4) Jl-Ag 91, p. 12.
    "Starting to Know." [BellArk] (7:2) Mr-Ap 91, p. 3.
    "What May Be Happening." [BellArk] (7:5) S-O 91, p. 1.
5349. SALAMUN, Tomaz
    "The Burning Bush" (tr. by Michael Biggins). [MissR] (19:3) 91, p. 185.
    "I Do Not Want" (tr. by Sonja Kravanja). [OnTheBus] (8/9) 91, p. 225.
    "Litmus" (tr. by Michael Biggins). [CimR] (96) Jl 91, p. 28.
    "Marko" (tr. by Michael Biggins). [Agni] (33) 91, p. 98.
    "My Glass, My Flour" (tr. by Sonja Kravanja). [OnTheBus] (8/9) 91, p. 225-226.
    "Of Fate" (tr. by Michael Biggins). [CimR] (96) Jl 91, p. 29.
    "Our Faith" (tr. by Michael Biggins). [NewL] (58:1) Fall 91, p. 36-37.
    "Paris, 1978" (tr. by Michael Biggins). [Agni] (33) 91, p. 99.
    "Pour un Jeune Chalamoun Qui Se Vend dans la Rue" (tr. by Michael Biggins).
        [Agni] (33) 91, p. 100.
    "The Power of the *Oeuvre*" (tr. by Michael Biggins). [CimR] (96) Jl 91, p. 30.
    "The Right of the Strong" (tr. by Sonja Kravanja). [OnTheBus] (8/9) 91, p. 224.
    "The Sea Lasts" (tr. by Sonja Kravanja). [PraF] (12:3 #56) Aut 91, p. 29.
    "Seed" (tr. by Sonja Kravanja). [OnTheBus] (8/9) 91, p. 224-225.
    "Things" (VII, tr. by Sonja Kravanja). [PraF] (12:3 #56) Aut 91, p. 28.
    "Turtle" (tr. by Sonja Kravanja). [PraF] (12:3 #56) Aut 91, p. 27.
    "Walls" (tr. by Michael Biggins). [NewL] (58:1) Fall 91, p. 35.
5350. SALASIN, Sal
    "The problem with Buddhism is." [NewAW] (7) Spr 91, p. 69.
    "Son, we don't want you to think the." [NewAW] (7) Spr 91, p. 68.

5351. SALEH, Dennis
"Lamentation" (from "The Somniad"). [SouthernPR] (31:1) Spr 91, p. 47-48.
"Osorkon's Lay." [HayF] (9) Fall-Wint 91, p. 62-63.
5352. SALEMI, Joseph S.
"V.4. Philaenis, fill the bedroom's oil lamp" (tr. of Philodemus). [Trans] (25) Spr
91, p. 219.
"V.13. Charito is past sixty, and yet sill" (tr. of Philodemus). [Trans] (25) Spr 91,
p. 219.
"V.131. Fingers on the lyre, lilting speech" (tr. of Philodemus). [Trans] (25) Spr 91,
p. 220.
"X.21. Kypris the serene, lover of nuptials" (tr. of Philodemus). [Trans] (25) Spr
91, p. 220.
"XI.34. No more white violets, no, nor tuneful songs" (tr. of Philodemus). [Trans]
(25) Spr 91, p. 221.
"XI.41. Already, from life's book of years" (tr. of Philodemus). [Trans] (25) Spr
91, p. 221.
5353. SALERNO, Joe
"Snail." [JINJPo] (13:2) Aut 91, p. 9-10.
"Wounded Knee (1890-1990)." [BlackBR] (13) Spr-Sum 91, p. 23.
5354. SALERNO, Mark
"Elegy." [DogRR] (10:2) Fall-Wint 91, p. 16.
"What We Think." [DogRR] (10:2) Fall-Wint 91, p. 17.
5355. SALINAS, Luis Omar
"Poem for Manuel Vizcaino." [MidAR] (12:1) 91, p. 70.
5356. SALISBURY, Ralph
"Bluethroat, Sing and Twitter" (Excerpts. Part 2 of the trilogy "My Home Is in My
Heart," tr. of Nils Aslak Valkeapää, w. Lars Nordström). [Writ] (23/24)
91-92, p. 5-41.
"A Letter from the Tennessee Colony." [SnailPR] (1:1) Spr 91, p. 20.
"Sacajawea, Bird-Woman, Shows Mrs. America an Old Album." [PoetryE] (32) Fall
91, p. 40.
5357. SALKEY, Andrew
"BUSH, George Herbert Walker, patrician of yore" (Response to "Save the
Clerihew" appeal). [BostonR] (16:3/4) Je-Ag 91, p. 33.
5358. SALLIS, James
"Excuses for Rain." [CharR] (17:1) Spr 91, p. 107.
"February." [CharR] (17:1) Spr 91, p. 106.
"A Marriage." [Ascent] (15:3) Spr 91, p. 43.
"The Nature of Things." [CharR] (17:1) Spr 91, p. 108.
"Oak and Dog" (A Novel in Verse, excerpt, tr. of Raymond Queneau). [Pequod]
(32) 91, p. 27-32.
"Persistence." [CharR] (17:1) Spr 91, p. 106.
"The Surrealist, Married." [SoDakR] (29:3 part 2) Aut 91, p. 100.
5359. SALTER, Mary Jo
"Inside the Midget." [NewYorker] (66:53) 18 F 91, p. 34.
"Two Prayers." [NewYorker] (67:12) 13 My 91, p. 42.
5360. SALTMAN, Benjamin
"The Falls, Big Sur 1989." [PikeF] (10) Spr 91, p. 5.
"The Laundry." [MissR] (19:3) 91, p. 172.
5361. SAMARAS, Nicholas
"Cataract." [OntR] (34) Spr-Sum 91, p. 17.
"Conkers." [OntR] (34) Spr-Sum 91, p. 18.
"The Divorce Clerk." [OntR] (34) Spr-Sum 91, p. 16.
"Getreidegasse 23, Salzburg." [AmerS] (60:3) Sum 91, p. 445.
"Thinking of Your Death." [CarolQ] (43:3) Spr 91, p. 30.
"Translation." [Poetry] (157:6) Mr 91, p. 332.
5362. SAMPSON, Gary
"Saudi Amerika." [DustyD] Ap 91, p. 20.
5363. SANCHEZ, Elba
"Baudelia." [Americas] (19:1) Spr 91, p. 50-51.
"China Syndrome." [Americas] (19:1) Spr 91, p. 53.
"Hermana Centroamérica." [Americas] (19:1) Spr 91, p. 48.
"Maíz Luna." [Zyzzyva] (7:2) Sum 91, p. 69.
"Moon's Harvest." [Zyzzyva] (7:2) Sum 91, p. 70.
"Testimonio desde Esquipulas." [Americas] (19:1) Spr 91, p. 47.
"Watsonville" (9 de septiembre de 1985). [Americas] (19:1) Spr 91, p. 49.

"Yo Naturaleza." [Americas] (19:1) Spr 91, p. 52.
5364. SANCHEZ, Grace
"Untitled: Creating a fist." [CapilR] (2:6/7) Fall 91, p. 11.
5365. SANCHEZ, María Teresa
"I Shall Go without Seeing You" (tr. by Eddie Flintoff). [Stand] (32:1) Wint 90-91,
p. 67.
SANCHEZ ROBAYNA, Andrés
See ROBAYNA, Andrés Sánchez
5366. SANDEEN, Ernest
"Soon After Nightfall." [Poetry] (159:3) D 91, p. 141.
5367. SANDERS, Lori
"Sadie Hawkins." [ChironR] (10:4) Wint 91, p. 34.
5368. SANDERS, Mark
"American History." [CharR] (17:1) Spr 91, p. 46-47.
"The Curio Cabinet." [Northeast] (5:5) Wint 91-92, p. 6-7.
"Digging for Fossils." [TexasR] (12:3/4) Fall-Wint 91, p. 86.
"Flatlander." [NoDaQ] (59:4) Fall 91, p. 124-125.
"In Bed." [Plain] (11:3) Spr 91, p. 6.
"Planning the Affair." [AntigR] (84) Wint 91, p. 19.
"A Point." [Plain] (12:1) Fall 91, p. 27.
"The Weather Bureau." [AntigR] (84) Wint 91, p. 18.
5369. SANDERS, Tony
"Unfinished Portrait." [PoetryE] (32) Fall 91, p. 158-161.
5370. SANDERSON, Cathryn J.
"Early Morning Vigil" (tr. of Carl Johan Jensen). [Vis] (37) 91, p. 19.
"Hologram" (tr. of Toroddur Poulsen). [Vis] (37) 91, p. 22.
5371. SANDFORT, Lolly
"Double Exposure." [EmeraldCR] (3) 91, c1990, p. 116.
"On Margaret Walker Alexander's Reading" (at PJC's Black History Week 1988).
[EmeraldCR] (4) 91, p. 7.
5372. SANDOR, Anne Lyn
"At Greenwood Cemetery with My Father." [Plain] (12:2) Wint 91, p. 8-9.
"Old Dog" (for Norton). [Plain] (12:1) Fall 91, p. 23.
5373. SANDSTROEM, Yvonne L.
"Albrecht Dürer's Rhinoceros, 1515" (tr. of Lars Gustafsson). [SouthwR] (76:1)
Wint 91, p. 139-140.
"Elegy on the Density of the World" (tr. of Lars Gustafsson). [SouthwR] (76:1)
Wint 91, p. 138-139.
"For All Those Who Wait for Time to Pass" (tr. of Lars Gustafsson). [NewYorker]
(67:11) 6 My 91, p. 38.
5374. SANDY, Stephen
"Earth Day Story." [Atlantic] (267:2) F 91, p. 69.
"Great Plains Dooryard." [ParisR] (33:121) Wint 91, p. 126.
"Trifid." [Boulevard] (6:2/3, #17/18) Fall 91, p. 136-137.
5375. SANER, Reg
"Dear Reg." [Pig] (17) 91, p. 53.
"Postcards from Italy." [Poetry] (158:4) Jl 91, p. 190-192.
5376. SANFORD, Carol
"Storms." [Plain] (11:3) Spr 91, p. 35.
"Taking Note of the Vernal Equinox." [Plain] (12:1) Fall 91, p. 15.
5377. SANFORD, Christy Sheffield
"Do-It-Yourself Woman Enveloped and De-enveloping." [Pig] (17) 91, p. 63.
5378. SANGER, Richard
"The Low-Down." [Quarry] (40:4) Fall 91, p. 58.
"Parable." [CanLit] (130) Aut 91, p. 116-117.
"The Snowball." [CanLit] (130) Aut 91, p. 116.
"Thanksgiving." [Quarry] (40:4) Fall 91, p. 57.
"Touring the Atrocities." [Quarry] (40:4) Fall 91, p. 55-56.
5379. SANSIRENE, Teresa
"¿A Quien Se Podria Contar?" [LindLM] (10:1) Ja-Mr 91, p. 8.
5380. SANTIAGO-BACA, Jimmy
"Love Poem." [GrandS] (10:2, #38) 91, p. 23-29.
5381. SANTOS, Cecilia
"The Damned." [WorldL] (1:1) 91, p. 24.
"The Ear." [WorldL] (1:1) 91, p. 25.
"The Saved." [WorldL] (1:1) 91, p. 24.

5382. SANTOS, Pablo Delos
"October Moon" (A brief elegy for lost souls). [ChamLR] (8-9) Spr-Fall 91, p. 15.
5383. SANTOS, Sherod
"Where to Begin." [NewYorker] (67:40) 25 N 91, p. 52.
"Zorah." [NewYorker] (67:33) 7 O 91, p. 44.
5384. SAPIA, Yvonne V.
"The Mythology of Hair." [CinPR] (21) Spr 90, p. 44-45.
5385. SAPINKOPF, Lisa
"Athens" (tr. of Vladimir Levchev). [BlackWR] (18:1) Fall-Wint 91, p. 100.
"Beneath Winter's Roof" (tr. of Ekaterina Yosifova). [BlackWR] (18:1) Fall-Wint
91, p. 98.
"Clay and Star" (tr. of Ivan Davidkov, w. Georgi Belev). [CarolQ] (44:1) Fall 91, p.
44.
"Dedham, Seen from Langham" (title of several paintings by John Constable, tr. of
Yves Bonnefoy). [SouthernR] (27:4) O 91, p. 917-923.
"The Forest Comes Down at Night" (tr. of Georgi Belev, w. the author). [ParisR]
(33:121) Wint 91, p. 119.
"Lake" (tr. of Georgi Belev, w. the author). [Agni] (34) 91, p. 179.
"Love" (tr. of Georgi Belev, w. the author). [Agni] (34) 91, p. 180-181.
"Museum" (tr. of Georgi Belev, w. the author). [BostonR] (16:1) F 91, p. 28.
"Solitary Man" (tr. of Boris Hristov). [BlackWR] (18:1) Fall-Wint 91, p. 99.
"A Summer's Night" (tr. of Yves Bonnefoy). [ParisR] (33:119) Sum 91, p.
255-257.
"Tale" (tr. of Georgi Belev, w. the author). [Poetry] (159:1) O 91, p. 21.
"The Task of Hope" (tr. of Yves Bonnefoy). [ParisR] (33:119) Sum 91, p. 258.
"Train" (tr. of Georgi Belev, w. the author). [Poetry] (159:1) O 91, p. 20.
"Villages Like Ghosts" (tr. of Ivan Davidkov, w. Georgi Belev). [CarolQ] (44:1)
Fall 91, p. 43.
5386. SAPPHO
"17 from Sappho: You Burn Me" (tr. by Stephen Berg). [TriQ] (81) Spr-Sum 91, p.
246-249.
"Sappho" (tr. by Sam Hamill). [TriQ] (81) Spr-Sum 91, p. 243-245.
SARA, Ibn
See IBN SARA
5387. SARAH, Robyn
"Trial Footage: The Farm." [PraF] (12:4) Wint 91-92, p. 11-12.
5388. SARGEANT, Charlotte Walton
"Color Chart." [EmeraldCR] (4) 91, p. 66.
"False Analogy." [EmeraldCR] (4) 91, p. 66.
"Ionic Columns." [EmeraldCR] (4) 91, p. 66.
"Journeying." [EmeraldCR] (3) 91, c1990, p. 133-135.
"Something Falls Against." [EmeraldCR] (4) 91, p. 67.
5389. SARGENT, Robert
"The Artists, Aging." [Nimrod] (34:2) Spr-Sum 91, p. 124.
"The Things of the World." [Poetry] (157:4) Ja 91, p. 217.
"A Visit from Philip Larkin." [Pembroke] (23) 91, p. 139.
"William White of Deep Creek, Virginia." [HampSPR] Wint 91, p. 14.
5390. SARRIS, Nikos
"Variations on a Sunbeam" (a 7-poem sequence: selections: I-II, VII, tr. of
Odysseus Elytis, w. Jeffrey Carson). [ConnPR] (10:1) 91, p. .10-13.
5391. SARTORIS, Brenda E.
"Concentration Camp: Summer School at the University of Chicago." [InterPR]
(15:1) Spr 89, p. 108.
"In the Tenth Year." [InterPR] (15:1) Spr 89, p. 107.
5392. SASANOV, Catherine
"Demolitions V." [Colum] (15) 90, p. 201.
"Ex-Votos: El Senor de los Milagros Church, Mexico." [GrahamHR] (15) Fall 91,
p. 39.
"Ex-Votos: Michoacan, Mexico." [GrahamHR] (15) Fall 91, p. 40.
5393. SASSEEN, Sue B.
"Potential." [Plain] (11:2) Wint 91, p. 35.
5394. SATHER, Jane
"Something of a Ghost Story." [FourQ] (5:1) Spr 91, p. 20.
"Speculations on Weldon Kees." [FourQ] (4:2) Fall 90, p. 35.
5395. SATHER, Wera
"A Young Girl in a German Town" (tr. by the author). [Vis] (37) 91, p. 45.

5396. SATRIANO, John
"Night Hearing" (tr. of Cesare Maoli). [InterPR] (17:2) Fall 91, p. 7, 9.
5397. SAUERS, Frank
"Art." [JamesWR] (8:2) Wint 91, p. 7.
SAUNDERS, Clifford Alan
See DWELLER, Cliff
5398. SAVAGE, Catherine
"Beaching." [SoDakR] (29:3 part 2) Aut 91, p. 13-14.
5399. SAVAGE, Sam
"Evening Sun." [SouthernPR] (31:1) Spr 91, p. 18-19. Reprinted, [SouthernPR]
(31:2) Fall 91, p. 60.
"Good-Bye, 1972." [ChatR] (11:2) Wint 91, p. 70-72.
5400. SAVAGE, Tom
"The Brahms Horn Trio." [NewAW] (8/9) Fall 91, p. 32.
5401. SAVAGEAU, Cheryl
"La Belle Dame." [IndR] (14:3) Fall 91, p. 31-32.
"Department of Labor Haiku." [RiverS] (34) 91, p. 49.
"Like a Good Joke: Grandma at Ninety" (for my grandmother, Delia Lafford
Savageau). [IndR] (14:3) Fall 91, p. 33-34.
"The Sound of My Mother Singing" (for my mother, Cecile Meunier Savageau).
[Agni] (34) 91, p. 202-205.
"Why They Do It." [RiverS] (34) 91, p. 48.
5402. SAVARD, Jeannine
"A Carnival Figure of Guatemalan Clay." [AmerPoR] (20:2) Mr-Ap 91, p. 9.
"Indiscretion at Drake's Auction House." [SouthernR] (27:2) Ap 91, p. 320-321.
"To Live Deliberately." [SouthernR] (27:2) Ap 91, p. 319-320.
5403. SAVARESE, Ralph
"The Man Who Cared About His Teeth." [CreamCR] (14:2) Wint 91, p. 145-147.
5404. SAVITT, Lynne
"What's Good for the Goose." [ChironR] (10:4) Wint 91, p. 33.
"What's Good for the Goose." [NewYorkQ] (46) 91, p. 42.
5405. SAVOIE, Terry
"Hairbrush." [Poetry] (159:3) D 91, p. 153.
"School of Missionaries" (Wisconsin, 1961). [Poetry] (159:3) D 91, p. 154.
5406. SAVVAS, Minas
"17 July 1982." [InterPR] (17:2) Fall 91, p. 145.
"Transcience." [InterPR] (17:2) Fall 91, p. 144.
5407. SAWYER-LAUÇANNO, Christopher
"Circumstantial End" (tr. of Paul Eluard). [Talisman] (7) Fall 91, p. 65.
"Construction Set" (for Raymond Roussel, tr. of Paul Eluard). [Talisman] (7) Fall
91, p. 64.
"First in the World" (for Pablo Picasso, tr. of Paul Eluard). [Talisman] (7) Fall 91,
p. 66.
"No Longer Shared" (tr. of Paul Eluard). [Talisman] (7) Fall 91, p. 65.
"Paul Klee" (tr. of Paul Eluard). [Talisman] (7) Fall 91, p. 64.
5408. SAX, Boria
"Roses and Lilacs." [Archae] (1) Fall 90, p. 35.
5409. SCALAPINO, Leslie
"Waking Life" (Selections). [Avec] (4:1) 91, p. 19-22.
5410. SCALF, Sue
"At an Auction, Maybe." [Poem] (66) N 91, p. 17.
"Conjunctions." [Poem] (66) N 91, p. 18.
5411. SCAMMELL, Michael
"Hands" (tr. of Edvard Kocbek, w. Veno Taufer). [NewYRB] (38:17) 24 O 91, p.
61.
"Now" (tr. of Edvard Kocbek, w. Veno Taufer). [NewYRB] (38:17) 24 O 91, p.
61.
"On Freedom of Mind" (tr. of Edvard Kocbek, w. Veno Taufer). [NewYRB]
(38:17) 24 O 91, p. 61.
"Parrots" (tr. of Edvard Kocbek, w. Veno Taufer). [NewYRB] (38:17) 24 O 91, p.
61.
5412. SCAMMELL, William
"The Charterhouse of Nab." [Verse] (8:2) Sum 91, p. 103.
5413. SCANNELL, Vernon
"Access to the Children." [Shen] (41:3) Fall 91, p. 85.
"Owl Faces." [Shen] (41:3) Fall 91, p. 84.

"War Casualty, Mental Ward." [Shen] (41:3) Fall 91, p. 86.
5414. SCATES, Maxine
"Legacy." [Agni] (33) 91, p. 114-117.
"Someone Knew." [PraS] (65:4) Wint 91, p. 124-126.
"Spring." [PraS] (65:4) Wint 91, p. 126-128.
5415. SCHACHTER, Hindy Lauer
"Esau." [InterPR] (17:1) Spr 91, p. 112.
5416. SCHAEFER, Ted
"Heathcliff in London." [NewL] (58:1) Fall 91, p. 73.
5417. SCHAEFFER, Rebecca
"How little we move." [Calyx] (13:2) Sum 91, p. 115.
"I find my source." [Calyx] (13:2) Sum 91, p. 115.
"We all have our homes." [Calyx] (13:2) Sum 91, p. 15.
5418. SCHAEFFER, Susan Fromberg
"Flowers at Night." [SoDakR] (29:3 part 2) Aut 91, p. 54-55.
5419. SCHAFER, John D.
"Arizona." [BilingR] (16:1) Ja-Ap 91, p. 67.
5420. SCHAFFER, Teya
"We Learn." [SinW] (43/44) Sum 91, p. 275.
5421. SCHANOU, Darcie
"Stuck on the Candy Man's Stick." [Plain] (12:1) Fall 91, p. 17.
5422. SCHEDLER, Gilbert
"Memories of Canada." [ChrC] (108:6) 20 F 91, p. 201.
"Pentecost." [ChrC] (108:12) 10 Ap 91, p. 402.
5423. SCHEELE, Roy
"Effects." [SewanR] (99:4) Fall 91, p. 560.
"Grant Wood's Stone City." [SewanR] (99:4) Fall 91, p. 559.
"Relic." [SewanR] (99:4) Fall 91, p. 560-561.
5424. SCHELLING, Andrew
"Dusting her body with ash from the burning ground" (from the "Sattasai," tr. of
Hasa). [Talisman] (6) Spr 91, p. 24.
"Of the blown out lamp" (from the "Sattasai," tr. of Vajradeva). [Talisman] (6) Spr
91, p. 24.
"Pitch black" (from the "Sattasai," tr. of Abhaya). [Talisman] (6) Spr 91, p. 24.
5425. SCHENDEL, Christopher
"Gopher Hunt." [Pearl] (13) Spr-Sum 91, p. 55.
5426. SCHENKER, Donald
"August Thirty-First, Nineteen Eighty-Nine" (for Kerouac). [WormR] (31:1, #121)
91, p. 5-6.
"Do the Trees Fall in the Forest Without Us?" [WormR] (31:1, #121) 91, p. 6-7.
"Dry July" (Selections). [Abraxas] (40/41) 91, p. 146-147.
"Paranoia." [WormR] (31:1, #121) 91, p. 4-5.
"The Schenkers." [WormR] (31:1, #121) 91, p. 7.
5427. SCHERTZER, Mike
"Her Tears Will Feed Us." [Grain] (19:4) Wint 91, p. 27.
"A Letter." [Grain] (19:4) Wint 91, p. 27.
5428. SCHEVILL, James
"The American Fantasies" (Selections: 3 poems). [Ploughs] (17:1) Spr 91, p.
143-145.
"Kafka in Prague." [Talisman] (7) Fall 91, p. 46-47.
5429. SCHIFF, Jeff
"Carrying." [Pembroke] (23) 91, p. 137.
"Hearld the Drink." [Pembroke] (23) 91, p. 138.
"What Bleeds Away?" [RiverC] (11:2) Spr 91, p. 72.
5430. SCHILKE, Gail
"The Malady of Death Meets the State of Desire." [Lactuca] (14) My 91, p. 19-20.
"Stilltrauma." [Lactuca] (14) My 91, p. 20-21.
5431. SCHIMMEL, Harold
"Lowell" (Selections: 6, 9, 86, tr. by Peter Cole). [Talisman] (6) Spr 91, p.
133-134.
5432. SCHMIDT, Jan Zlotnik
"The Barn Key Was There." [Blueline] (12) 91, p. 56.
"A Corot Landscape." [Blueline] (12) 91, p. 57.
5433. SCHMITT, Peter
"Conversation in Camden County." [MassR] (32:3) Fall 91, p. 443-444.
"A Day at the Beach." [MassR] (32:3) Fall 91, p. 442.

"Friends with Numbers." [ParisR] (33:121) Wint 91, p. 206-207.
5434. SCHMITZ, Dennis
"About Night." [AmerPoR] (20:4) Jl-Ag 91, p. 21.
"Chicago Plastics, 1960." [AmerPoR] (20:4) Jl-Ag 91, p. 20.
"Eeyore." [Field] (45) Fall 91, p. 74-75.
"Post-Partem." [AmerPoR] (20:4) Jl-Ag 91, p. 21.
"Rafting." [Field] (45) Fall 91, p. 76-77.
5435. SCHNEBERG, Willa
"Chiropractic School." [SouthernPR] (31:2) Fall 91, p. 10-11.
5436. SCHNEERMAN, Elio
"Poem: Next to the face of nothing." [BrooklynR] (8) 91, p. 54.
5437. SCHNEIDER, Pat
"Silent Retreat." [SingHM] (19) 91, p. 36-37.
"Sound of the Night Train." [NegC] (11:3) 91, p. 37-38.
5438. SCHOBERT, Chuck
"Offering." [ChangingM] (23) Fall-Wint 91, p. 32.
5439. SCHOENBERGER, Nancy
"Lavish City." [SouthwR] (76:3) Sum 91, p. 372.
5440. SCHOENFELD, Ellie
"Debbie." [RagMag] (9:1) 91, p. 9-10.
"In 1986 the Radio Report." [RagMag] (9:1) 91, p. 12.
"Quilting." [RagMag] (9:1) 91, p. 11.
5441. SCHOERKE, Meg
"Master , Master, We Perish." [AmerS] (60:1) Wint 91, p. 52.
5442. SCHOFIELD, Don
"The Yeoman Sings." [Vis] (35) 91, p. 47.
5443. SCHORB, E. M.
"An Antiquary of the Future." [Ascent] (16:1) Fall 91, p. 50.
"Detective Story." [SouthwR] (76:2) Spr 91, p. 296-297.
"The Getaway." [HawaiiR] (15:3, #33) Fall 91, p. 73.
"Lipstick Skies." [CapeR] (26:1) Spr 91, p. 12.
"New Year Near the Hudson." [HawaiiR] (15:3, #33) Fall 91, p. 74.
"Rodin, Balzac, and the Thinker." [Ascent] (16:1) Fall 91, p. 51.
5444. SCHOTT, Penelope Scambly
"Men Can Leave." [Crazy] (41) Wint 91, p. 73-74.
"Yellow Comb." [AmerV] (22) Spr 91, p. 89-90.
"Yellow Comb." [US1] (24/25) Spr 91, p. 9.
5445. SCHRAMM, Darrell G. H.
"A Word of Advice." [LaurelR] (25:1) Wint 91, p. 101.
5446. SCHRAMM, Richard
"Arrangement in Gray." [KenR] (NS 13:3) Sum 91, p. 17.
5447. SCHRAUFNAGEL, Lynda
"Commerce." [WestHR] (45:2) Sum 91, p. 126-127.
"Trial." [WestHR] (45:2) Sum 91, p. 120-121.
5448. SCHREIBER, Jan
"Acoustics" (for Fran). [TexasR] (11:1/2) Spr-Sum 90, p. 26-27.
5449. SCHREIBER, Ron
"As If It Were Spring." [ChironR] (10:3) Aut 91, p. 41.
"Easter Sunday." [ChironR] (10:4) Wint 91, p. 35.
"One Last Springtime" (in memoriam). [ChangingM] (22) Wint-Spr 91, p. 36.
"Waiting for Uri (to Make Up His Mind)." [JamesWR] (8:2) Wint 91, p. 7.
5450. SCHREIER, Lina
"Cock-a-Doodle-Do." [SoCaR] (24:1) Fall 91, p. 117.
5451. SCHREINER, Steven
"Morning" (after Tzara). [MissouriR] (14:1) 91, p. 149.
5452. SCHUG, Lawrence
"Bears." [Plain] (11:2) Wint 91, p. 37.
"A Burst of Blue Neon." [RagMag] (9:2) 91, p. 18.
"A Letter to Jesus from Paul in the Stearns County Jail." [SmPd] (28:3, #83) Fall
91, p. 18.
5453. SCHULER, Robert
"Poem for Jackie McLean." [LakeSR] (25) 91, p. 13.
"Winter Light" (2 selections). [Northeast] (5:5) Wint 91-92, p. 38.
5454. SCHULMAN, Grace
"The Wedding." [Poetry] (158:3) Je 91, p. 125-126.

5455. SCHULTE, Jane
"At Summer Lake." [WillowR] Spr 91, p. 8.
5456. SCHULTZ, Susan M.
"Adonais." [HawaiiR] (15:2, #32) Spr 91, p. 151-152.
"Angel." [DenQ] (26:1) Sum 91, p. 63-64.
"A General History of Virginia." [HawaiiR] (15:3, #33) Fall 91, p. 42-43.
"The Mountains." [HawaiiR] (16:1, #34) Wint 91-92, p. 26-28.
"Never Seen Volcanoes." [DenQ] (26:1) Sum 91, p. 65-66.
5457. SCHULZ, Paula
"The Safety of a Gun." [Prima] (14/15) 91, p. 93.
5458. SCHUTTE, Linda C.
"Fear of Flying." [EmeraldCR] (3) 91, c1990, p. 41-42.
5459. SCHUTTENBERG, E. M.
"Decades." [JlNJPo] (13:1) Spr 91, p. 29.
5460. SCHUTZER, Amy
"Stillbirth." [Sequoia] (34:1) Spr 91, p. 40-41.
5461. SCHWARTZ, Ed
"The Garden of Eden." [CrabCR] (7:3) 91, p. 14.
5462. SCHWARTZ, Hillel
"Between Terms." [MalR] (97) Wint 91, p. 84-85.
"The Carbon Dating of My Cousin Louis." [Salm] (90/91) Spr-Sum 91, p. 88-89.
"Going Off Under." [MalR] (97) Wint 91, p. 82-83.
"Jus Gentian." [HampSPR] Wint 91, p. 39.
"Man and Woman on Staircase." [Vis] (35) 91, p. 14-15.
"Sancta." [Boulevard] (6:2/3, #17/18) Fall 91, p. 41-42.
"Walking with David Down Amsterdam Avenue." [Thrpny] (46) Sum 91, p. 32.
"Walking with Linda and Peter North and West of Troy." [NewEngR] (14:1) Fall
91, p. 120-121.
"Wonders of the World: Wonderland." [LitR] (34:2) Wint 91, p. 196-197.
5463. SCHWARTZ, Leonard
"Fingers of a Glove." [Talisman] (7) Fall 91, p. 107.
"The Garden of the 9th of January" (tr. of Victor Krivulin, w. Ina Bliznetsova).
[LitR] (34:3) Spr 91, p. 387.
"The Idea of Russia" (tr. of Victor Krivulin, w. Ina Bliznetsova). [LitR] (34:3) Spr
91, p. 387.
"Main Line" (tr. of Victor Krivulin, w. Ina Bliznetsova). [LitR] (34:3) Spr 91, p.
389.
"Mountain Ode" (tr. of Olga Sedakova, w. Ina Bliznetsova). [LitR] (34:3) Spr 91, p.
329-332.
"Nadja." [CentralP] (19/20) Spr-Fall 91, p. 251-253.
"The Road Home" (tr. of Victor Krivulin, w. Ina Bliznetsova). [LitR] (34:3) Spr 91,
p. 388.
5464. SCHWARTZ, Lloyd
"Reports of My Death." [Ploughs] (17:2/3) Fall 91, p. 96-99.
5465. SCHWARTZ, Naomi
"Housekeeping." [AmerPoR] (20:2) Mr-Ap 91, p. 17.
5466. SCHWARTZ, Ruth (Ruth L.)
"Homecoming" (For Theo). [YellowS] (37) Fall-Wint 91, p. 41.
"How We Might" (For Rebecca). [Prima] (14/15) 91, p. 92.
"The Man Speaks" (with thanks to Eric Jasmen). [Nimrod] (35:1) Fall-Wint 91, p.
13.
"Mother and Child." [Vis] (35) 91, p. 41.
"Poems of the Body" (The Pablo Neruda Prize for Poetry, First Prize). [Nimrod]
(35:1) Fall-Wint 91, p. 11-12.
"When." [YellowS] (37) Fall-Wint 91, p. 25.
"When You in Your Sturdy and Luminous Body." [Nimrod] (35:1) Fall-Wint 91, p.
14-15.
5467. SCHWARZENBERGER, Richard
"Fine Weather" (tr. of Orhan Veli Kanik, w. Grace Smith). [Agni] (33) 91, p. 97.
"For the Homeland" (tr. of Orhan Veli Kanik, w. Grace Smith). [Agni] (33) 91, p.
94.
"Illusion" (tr. of Orhan Veli Kanik, w. Grace Smith). [Agni] (33) 91, p. 95.
"Stretched Out" (tr. of Orhan Veli Kanik, w. Grace Smith). [Agni] (33) 91, p. 96.
5468. SCHWITTERS, Kurt
"Execution: Poem 9" (tr. by Jerome Rothenberg). [Sulfur] (11:1, #28) Spr 91, p.
111.

"A Flower Like a Raven" (tr. by Jerome Rothenberg). [Sulfur] (11:1, #28) Spr 91,
    p. 113.
"From the Back & From the Front to Start" (tr. by Jerome Rothenberg). [Sulfur]
    (11:1, #28) Spr 91, p. 112-113.
"Green Child: Poem 1" (tr. by Pierre Joris). [Sulfur] (11:1, #28) Spr 91, p.
    109-110.
"Ice Clocks" (tr. by Jerome Rothenberg). [Sulfur] (11:1, #28) Spr 91, p. 116.
"Murder Machine 43" (tr. by Jerome Rothenberg). [Sulfur] (11:1, #28) Spr 91, p.
    114-116.
"She Dolls with Dollies (1944)" (tr. by Jerome Rothenberg). [Talisman] (6) Spr 91,
    p. 112.
"Thou" (tr. by Jerome Rothenberg). [Sulfur] (11:1, #28) Spr 91, p. 108.
5469. SCOFIELD, James
    "April." [BellArk] (7:4) Jl-Ag 91, p. 23.
    "The Columbia River Gorge." [BellArk] (7:3) My-Je 91, p. 1.
    "Easter" (Grays Harbor, 1990). [BellArk] (7:4) Jl-Ag 91, p. 23.
    "Festival." [BellArk] (7:2) Mr-Ap 91, p. 7.
    "Lucielle." [BellArk] (7:1) Ja-F 91, p. 3.
    "Something Overheard." [BellArk] (7:6) N-D 91, p. 10.
5470. SCOPINO, Adriana
    "Abuela." [Nuez] (3:7) 91, p. 15.
5471. SCOTT, Charlie
    "1969." [NewRep] (204:23) 10 Je 91, p. 36.
5472. SCOTT, Diana
    "Poem for Jacqueline Hill." [PoetryUSA] (23) Sum 91, p. 10-11.
5473. SCOTT, Elizabeth
    "Elegy." [EmeraldCR] (3) 91, c1990, p. 125-126.
5474. SCOTT, Georgia
    "LVIII. A Letter to My Mother Among Things" (tr. of Tadeusz Zukowski, w. David
        Malcolm and Zbigniew Joachimiak). [WebR] (15) Spr 91, p. 41.
    "All Souls'" (tr. of Krzysztof Lisowski, w. David Malcolm and Zbigniew
        Joachimiak). [WebR] (15) Spr 91, p. 44-45.
    "Cell: one plank bed" (tr. of Bronislaw Maj, w. David Malcolm and Zbigniew
        Joachimiak). [WebR] (15) Spr 91, p. 45.
    "Dice" (tr. of Zbigniew Joachimiak, w. David Malcolm and the author). [WebR] (15)
        Spr 91, p. 42.
    "It Was Me" (To Bylam Ja, tr. of Krystyna Lars, w. David Malcolm). [Calyx] (13:3)
        Wint 91-92, p. 12-13.
    "Reflection of an Old Woman in a Mirror" (Odbicie Starej w Lustrze, tr. of Anna
        Janko, w. David Malcolm). [Calyx] (13:3) Wint 91-92, p. 11.
    "Untitled: All you sad ones" (tr. of Anna Czekanowicz, w. David Malcolm). [Calyx]
        (13:3) Wint 91-92, p. 10.
    "Whenever the conversation turned to the issue of dignity" (tr. of Andrzej Szuba, w.
        David Malcolm and Zbigniew Joachimiak). [WebR] (15) Spr 91, p. 42.
    "Winter Time" (tr. of Jerzy Suchanek, w. David Malcolm and Zbigniew
        Joachimiak). [WebR] (15) Spr 91, p. 43.
5475. SCOTT, H. A.
    "Opus None." [EmeraldCR] (4) 91, p. 48.
    "Untitled: I was the tambourine." [EmeraldCR] (4) 91, p. 50.
    "Untitled: She was as smooth as glass." [EmeraldCR] (4) 91, p. 49.
    "Untitled: The leaves are falling." [EmeraldCR] (4) 91, p. 48.
5476. SCOTT, Jeffrey
    "The Edge." [EmeraldCR] (4) 91, p. 60.
    "Veg-A-Matic." [EmeraldCR] (3) 91, c1990, p. 44-45.
5477. SCOTT, Mark
    "An Alien World" (for Loretta and Mark). [US1] (24/25) Spr 91, p. 10.
    "The Cave of AIDS" (In memory of Craig William Scott, 1961-1984). [Poetry]
        (158:1) Ap 91, p. 23-24.
5478. SCOTT, Peter Dale
    "Listening to the Candle: A Poem on Impulse" (Selection: IV.ii. For Raquel Scherr
        and Leonard Michaels. IV.iii. For Stephen Greenblatt). [Agni] (34) 91, p.
        293-303.
5479. SCOVILLE, Jane
    "Shades of Yesterday." [BellArk] (7:2) Mr-Ap 91, p. 10.
5480. SCRIBNER, Dana
    "i. Marymary quite con trary." [PraF] (12:1 #54) Spr 91, p. 38.

"iv. Mary mary one two unbuckle her shoe." [PraF] (12:1 #54) Spr 91, p. 39.
"For You." [PraF] (12:1 #54) Spr 91, p. 37.
5481. SCRIMGEOUR, J. D.
"Among the Mountains." [ColR] (NS 18:2) Fall-Wint 91, p. 56-59.
5482. SCRUGGS, Patricia L.
"Always a War." [OnTheBus] (8/9) 91, p. 142.
5483. SCRUTON, James
"Extra Innings." [Spitball] (36) Spr 91, p. 20-21.
"Far South Enough." [Poem] (65) My 91, p. 53.
"Hourglass." [Poem] (65) My 91, p. 54.
5484. SCULLY, James
"Testament: Fragments" (Quechua People's Poetry, tr. of the Spanish of Jesús Lara,
w. Maria A. Proser). [NoDaQ] (59:4) Fall 91, p. 78.
"What Cloud Is That Cloud" (Quechua People's Poetry, tr. of the Spanish of Jesús
Lara, w. Maria A. Proser). [NoDaQ] (59:4) Fall 91, p. 78-79.
5485. SCULLY, Maurice
"5 Freedoms of Movement" (Excerpt). [NewAW] (8/9) Fall 91, p. 152-153.
"Touring the Lattice." [NewAW] (8/9) Fall 91, p. 153-155.
5486. SEA, Gary
"Blessed Is" (tr. of Jesse Thoor). [NewRena] (8:2, #25) Fall 91, p. 135.
"Da Da" (tr. of Jesse Thoor). [NewRena] (8:2, #25) Fall 91, p. 123.
"Drifter's Sonnet" (tr. of Jesse Thoor). [InterPR] (17:2) Fall 91, p. 55.
"Evening Sonnet" (tr. of Jesse Thoor). [NewRena] (8:2, #25) Fall 91, p. 129.
"First Letter of the Servant Abu" (tr. of Jesse Thoor). [InterPR] (17:1) Spr 91, p.
27.
"First Letter of the Servant Abu" (tr. of Jesse Thoor). [NewRena] (8:2, #25) Fall 91,
p. 121.
"The First Sonnet" (tr. of Jesse Thoor). [InterPR] (17:2) Fall 91, p. 47.
"The Laughter" (tr. of Jesse Thoor). [NewRena] (8:2, #25) Fall 91, p. 131.
"Rat Sonnet" (tr. of Jesse Thoor). [InterPR] (17:2) Fall 91, p. 49.
"The Second Voice" (tr. of Jesse Thoor). [NewRena] (8:2, #25) Fall 91, p. 133.
"Sleep Sonnet" (tr. of Jesse Thoor). [NewRena] (8:2, #25) Fall 91, p. 119.
"Sleepsonnet" (tr. of Jesse Thoor). [InterPR] (17:1) Spr 91, p. 29.
"Sonnet in Winter" (tr. of Jesse Thoor). [NewRena] (8:2, #25) Fall 91, p. 113.
"Sonnet of Depressing Thoughts" (tr. of Jesse Thoor). [NewRena] (8:2, #25) Fall
91, p. 111.
"Sonnet of Good Will" (tr. of Jesse Thoor). [InterPR] (17:1) Spr 91, p. 31.
"Sonnet of the Definitive Question" (Subtitle in Earlier Versions: After a Sonnet by
Pottier. Tr. of Jesse Thoor). [NewRena] (8:2, #25) Fall 91, p. 137.
"Sonnet of the Prodigal Son" (tr. of Jesse Thoor). [InterPR] (17:1) Spr 91, p. 35.
"Sonnet of the Prodigal Son" (tr. of Jesse Thoor). [NewRena] (8:2, #25) Fall 91, p.
125.
"Sonnet of the Profound Rest" (tr. of Jesse Thoor). [NewRena] (8:2, #25) Fall 91,
p. 109.
"Speaking of Ominous Decay" (Earlier Title: Sonnet of Repulsive Satiety, tr. of Jesse
Thoor). [NewRena] (8:2, #25) Fall 91, p. 127.
"Temptation's Sonnet" (Earlier Title: The Eleventh Madhouse Sonnet, tr. of Jesse
Thoor). [NewRena] (8:2, #25) Fall 91, p. 117.
"Ticino Nights" (tr. of Jesse Thoor). [InterPR] (17:1) Spr 91, p. 33.
"To a 50-Cent Piece" (tr. of Jesse Thoor). [InterPR] (17:2) Fall 91, p. 53.
"To a Soldier" (tr. of Jesse Thoor). [NewRena] (8:2, #25) Fall 91, p. 115.
"Tramp's Credo" (tr. of Jesse Thoor). [InterPR] (17:2) Fall 91, p. 51.
5487. SEAL, David O.
"Teeth or Stars." [ChrC] (108:27) 2 O 91, p. 882.
5488. SEARS, Peter
"Dumbo Diner." [CimR] (96) Jl 91, p. 112-113.
5489. SEATON, J. P.
"After the Ancients" (tr. of T'ao Ch'ien). [LitR] (35:1) Fall 91, p. 74.
"Drinking Wine XVI" (tr. of T'ao Ch'ien). [LitR] (35:1) Fall 91, p. 73.
"End of the Year" (tr. of Yuan Mei). [LitR] (35:1) Fall 91, p. 71.
"Something to Ridicule" (tr. of Yuan Mei). [LitR] (35:1) Fall 91, p. 71.
5490. SEATON, Maureen
"All Truth Must Conform to Music." [MissouriR] (13:3) 91, p. 124.
"B-52." [Thrpny] (46) Sum 91, p. 17.
"The Church of God in Christ on the Hill." [Ploughs] (17:2/3) Fall 91, p. 53-54.
"Constance, 1958." [Iowa] (21:1) Wint 91, p. 177-178.

"The Cusp." [NewEngR] (13:3/4) Spr-Sum 91, p. 147-148.
"Involved with This Light." [MissouriR] (13:3) 91, p. 122-123.
"Mercedes Contemplates a Dive off Macmillan Wharf" (for Lisbeth). [ColR] (NS 17:2) Fall-Wint 90, p. 51.
"The Miracles." [Iowa] (21:1) Wint 91, p. 176-177.
"An Ordinary Mass." [IndR] (14:3) Fall 91, p. 63-64.
"Poems for an Ex-Prostitute." [NewEngR] (13:3/4) Spr-Sum 91, p. 146-147.
"The Sacrifice." [ColR] (NS 17:2) Fall-Wint 90, p. 50.
"Scandals." [MissouriR] (13:3) 91, p. 126-127.
"Sonnets for a Young Apostate." [ColR] (NS 17:2) Fall-Wint 90, p. 48-49.
"Truce." [ColR] (NS 17:2) Fall-Wint 90, p. 47.
"Waiting for the Body." [Iowa] (21:1) Wint 91, p. 175-176.
"The Woman Too Large for the Chair." [MissouriR] (13:3) 91, p. 125.

5491. SEAVEY, Wallace
"Colby Pond." [AnthNEW] (3) 91, p. 26.

5492. SEDAKOVA, Olga
"Mountain Ode" (tr. by Ina Bliznetsova and Leonard Schwartz). [LitR] (34:3) Spr 91, p. 329-332.

5493. SEED, John
"Cloud formations shift in the evening air." [NewAW] (8/9) Fall 91, p. 158.
"During War, the Timeless Air." [NewAW] (8/9) Fall 91, p. 159.
"Fifty thousand nights and." [NewAW] (8/9) Fall 91, p. 158-159.
"Out of the warm continuous rain." [NewAW] (8/9) Fall 91, p. 157.
"Shadow of the gable-end." [NewAW] (8/9) Fall 91, p. 156.
"Silence inside the empty nouns." [NewAW] (8/9) Fall 91, p. 156.
"Unrealities of human speech." [NewAW] (8/9) Fall 91, p. 157.

5494. SEIBLES, Tim
"Each Letter." [PassN] (12:1) Sum 91, p. 29.
"Sweet Onion Soup." [PassN] (12:1) Sum 91, p. 29.

5495. SEID, Christopher
"An Apology." [PassN] (12:2) Wint 91, p. 28.
"Hero." [BelPoJ] (42:1) Fall 91, p. 1.

5496. SEILER, Barry
"The Bottle, the Rain, the Peasant." [LitR] (34:2) Wint 91, p. 254-255.
"Exercises for the Hands." [JINJPo] (13:1) Spr 91, p. 21.
"The Lake." [Talisman] (7) Fall 91, p. 26.
"Namesake." [JINJPo] (13:1) Spr 91, p. 20.

5497. SEITER, Verona
"To Children of War." [PoetryUSA] (22) Spr 91, p. 14.

5498. SEITZER, Carol
"War Zone." [NewYorkQ] (44) 91, p. 78.

5499. SELAWSKY, John (John T.)
"The Fig Tree." [Poem] (65) My 91, p. 23.
"Flowering Dogwood." [Blueline] (12) 91, p. 45.
"The Frogs." [Poem] (65) My 91, p. 25.
"June." [CapeR] (26:2) Fall 91, p. 4.
"Orpheus." [Blueline] (12) 91, p. 29.
"Snakeskin." [Poem] (65) My 91, p. 24.
"Solstice." [WestB] (29) 91, p. 15.

5500. SELBY, Spencer
"Battle of the Covered Sea." [Talisman] (7) Fall 91, p. 130-131.
"Crossfire." [Avec] (4:1) 91, p. 44-46.
"Outside Chance." [NewAW] (7) Spr 91, p. 41-42.
"Say When." [Avec] (4:1) 91, p. 46-48.
"Trouble Doll." [CentralP] (19/20) Spr-Fall 91, p. 226-231.

5501. SELLERS, Bettie
"The Songs Nobody Sings." [LullwaterR] (2:2) Spr 91, p. 48.

5502. SELLERS, Heather
"Outburst." [GreensboroR] (50) Sum 91, p. 132.
"Row." [GreensboroR] (50) Sum 91, p. 134.
"Under the Jacaranda." [GreensboroR] (50) Sum 91, p. 133.

5503. SELTZER, Alvin J.
"Daisy's Other Life." [Hellas] (2:2) Fall 91, p. 265.

5504. SELTZER, Joanne
"An African Baby Is Named." [SingHM] (19) 91, p. 117-119.

5505. SELTZER, Michael
"Wind Chime." [Elf] (1:4) Wint 91, p. 43.
5506. SEMANSKY, Chris
"Sleeping on Your Side Too Much." [ChatR] (11:3) Spr 91, p. 14.
5507. SEMONES, Charles
"October." [CapeR] (26:2) Fall 91, p. 29.
5508. SEN, Sudeep
"Remembering Hiroshima Tonight" (for Phillis Levin). [PlumR] (1) Spr-Sum 91, p. 31.
"Sun Streaks on Telephone Lines." [PlumR] (1) Spr-Sum 91, p. 32-33.
5509. SENECHAL, Diana
"Instruction" (tr. of Tomas Venclova). [NewYRB] (38:19) 21 N 91, p. 33.
5510. SENGE, Motomaro
"Sacred Eve" (tr. by Lawrence Rogers). [Paint] (18:36) Aut 91, p. 56.
"A Tiny Smile" (tr. by Lawrence Rogers). [Paint] (18:36) Aut 91, p. 56.
5511. SENGHOR, Léopold Sédar
"Camp 1940" (to Abdoulaye Ly, tr. by Melvin Dixon). [AmerPoR] (20:6) N-D 91, p. 6.
"Elegy for the Queen of Sheba" (for two koras and a balaphon, tr. by Melvin Dixon). [AmerPoR] (20:6) N-D 91, p. 8-10.
"The Enlisted Man's Despair" (tr. by Melvin Dixon). [AmerPoR] (20:6) N-D 91, p. 5.
"Governor Eboué" (to Henri and Robert Eboué, tr. by Melvin Dixon). [AmerPoR] (20:6) N-D 91, p. 6.
"Imaginings, or Dreaming of a Young Girl" (tr. by Melvin Dixon). [AmerPoR] (20:6) N-D 91, p. 6.
"In Memoriam" (tr. by Melvin Dixon). [AmerPoR] (20:6) N-D 91, p. 4.
"Man and Beast" (for the three tabalas or war drums, tr. by Melvin Dixon). [AmerPoR] (20:6) N-D 91, p. 8.
"*Mirrors* Still" (tr. by Melvin Dixon). [AmerPoR] (20:6) N-D 91, p. 7.
"My Greeting" (tr. by Melvin Dixon). [AmerPoR] (20:6) N-D 91, p. 5.
"Shadow Song" (tr. by Melvin Dixon). [AmerPoR] (20:6) N-D 91, p. 4-5.
"To Death" (tr. by Melvin Dixon). [AmerPoR] (20:6) N-D 91, p. 4.
"To New York" (for jazz orchestra and trumpet solo, tr. by Melvin Dixon). [AmerPoR] (20:6) N-D 91, p. 7.
"Totem" (tr. by Melvin Dixon). [AmerPoR] (20:6) N-D 91, p. 4.
5512. SENGUPTA, Mallika
"The Blood-Mark" (tr. by Paramita Banerjee and Carolyne Wright). [MichQR] (30:1) Wint 91, p. 210.
5513. SENS, Jean-Marc
"Mardi Gras Beignets." [CapeR] (26:2) Fall 91, p. 25.
SENTIES, Raquel Valle
See VALLE SENTIES, Raquel
5514. SEQUEIRA, Jose
"Ayer." [InterPR] (17:2) Fall 91, p. 60.
"Evenings with Grandmother" (tr. by Frank Reed). [InterPR] (17:2) Fall 91, p. 63.
"Hecatomb" (tr. by Frank Reed). [InterPR] (17:2) Fall 91, p. 59.
"Hecatombe." [InterPR] (17:2) Fall 91, p. 58.
"El Hijo de Lucila." [InterPR] (17:2) Fall 91, p. 56.
"Los Angeles." [InterPR] (17:2) Fall 91, p. 64.
"Los Angeles" (tr. by Frank Reed). [InterPR] (17:2) Fall 91, p. 65.
"Lucila's Son" (tr. by Frank Reed). [InterPR] (17:2) Fall 91, p. 57.
"Mestizo." [InterPR] (17:2) Fall 91, p. 64.
"Mestizo" (tr. by Frank Reed). [InterPR] (17:2) Fall 91, p. 65.
"Las Noches de la Abuela." [InterPR] (17:2) Fall 91, p. 62.
"Yesterday" (tr. by Frank Reed). [InterPR] (17:2) Fall 91, p. 61.
5515. SERPAS, Martha
"Chase." [Colum] (15) 90, p. 39.
"M Is For the Many." [Colum] (15) 90, p. 37-38.
5516. SESHADRI, Vijay
"Elegy." [NewYorker] (67:39) 18 N 91, p. 46.
"Party Girl." [WestHR] (45:4) Wint 91, p. 288-289.
5517. SETTLE, Judith
"Reservoir." [Crucible] (27) Fall 91, p. 27.
SEUNG-TAI, Yang
See YANG, Seung-Tai

5518. SEVILLA, José Manuel
"Desde los Límites del Paraíso" (Dedicado a la Alenjandría de Terenci Moix). [Nuez]
(3:7) 91, p. 12-13.
5519. SEWELL, John
"Like a Cast Line, the Buzz of the Strip Light." [Verse] (8:2) Sum 91, p. 110.
5520. SEXTON, Tom
"Anchorage." [SwampR] (7/8) Spr-Sum 91, p. 61.
"Chitina." [SwampR] (7/8) Spr-Sum 91, p. 64.
"Harvest." [SwampR] (7/8) Spr-Sum 91, p. 69.
"Nikolaevsk." [SwampR] (7/8) Spr-Sum 91, p. 62.
"On Reading Wang Wei." [SwampR] (7/8) Spr-Sum 91, p. 68.
"Paper Birch." [SwampR] (7/8) Spr-Sum 91, p. 70.
"Resolution Park." [SwampR] (7/8) Spr-Sum 91, p. 73.
"Saint Marys." [SwampR] (7/8) Spr-Sum 91, p. 63.
"Springs." [SwampR] (7/8) Spr-Sum 91, p. 71.
"Sweet Spring Grasses." [SwampR] (7/8) Spr-Sum 91, p. 67.
"Trapper Creek" (for Art Davidson). [SwampR] (7/8) Spr-Sum 91, p. 72.
"Waitresses." [SwampR] (7/8) Spr-Sum 91, p. 66.
"Yakutat." [SwampR] (7/8) Spr-Sum 91, p. 65.
5521. SEXTON, Will
"Sonnet." [Pearl] (14) Fall-Wint 91, p. 58.
5522. SHABTAI, Aharon
"Love" (Selections: 20-21, 26, tr. by Peter Cole). [Agni] (33) 91, p. 42-44.
5523. SHADOIAN, Jack
"Accent Grave." [CreamCR] (14:2) Wint 91, p. 167.
"Busy Spying Sleep (Down Under)." [CinPR] (21) Spr 90, p. 49.
"Since You Fell." [RagMag] (9:1) 91, p. 22.
5524. SHAFFER, Eric
"Hawk in October: A Heresy of Recognition." [CalQ] (32/33) Spr 90, p. 86.
5525. SHAH, Sejal
"Grandmother." [HangL] (59) 91, p. 83.
5526. SHAH, Ushma
"Clown." [PikeF] (10) Spr 91, p. 20.
SHAHID ALI, Agha
See ALI, Agha Shahid
5527. SHAKELY, Farhad
"Qamishli" (tr. by the author, w. B. R. Strahan). [Vis] (36) 91, p. 37.
"Separation" (tr. by the author, w. B. R. Strahan). [Vis] (36) 91, p. 37.
5528. SHAKESPEARE, William
"78. So oft have I invok'd thee for my Muse" (Text of 1609 Quarto of Shakespeare's
Sonnets). [Elf] (1:3) Fall 91, p. 27.
"79. Whilst I alone did call upon thy ayde" (Text of 1609 Quarto of Shakespeare's
Sonnets). [Elf] (1:3) Fall 91, p. 28.
"80. O how I faint when I of you do write" (Text of 1609 Quarto of Shakespeare's
Sonnets). [Elf] (1:3) Fall 91, p. 29.
"81. Or I shall live your Epitaph to make" (Text of 1609 Quarto of Shakespeare's
Sonnets). [Elf] (1:4) Wint 91, p. 21.
"82. I grant thou wert not married to my Muse" (Text of 1609 Quarto of
Shakespeare's Sonnets). [Elf] (1:4) Wint 91, p. 22.
5529. SHAKIR, Parveen
"Confusion" (tr. by Farah Hasnat). [Talisman] (6) Spr 91, p. 131.
"Welcome" (tr. by Farah Hasnat). [Vis] (35) 91, p. 42.
SHANG-YIN, Li
See LI, Shang-yin
5530. SHANGÉ, Ntozake
"Even Tho Yr Sampler Broke Down on You." [YellowS] (36) Spr 91, p. 32.
"Intermittent Celebacy." [YellowS] (36) Spr 91, p. 34.
"Loosening Strings or Give Me an 'A'." [YellowS] (38) Wint-Spr 91-92, p. 16-17.
"Serial Monogamy." [YellowS] (36) Spr 91, p. 33.
5531. SHANNON, Ben
"Collections." [HangL] (58) 91, p. 90.
5532. SHANNON, Mike
"Diane, Before the Cheers." [Spitball] (38) Fall 91, p. 48.
5533. SHAPIRO, Alan
"Dawn Chorus." [AmerPoR] (20:2) Mr-Ap 91, p. 7.
"Purgatory." [AmerPoR] (20:2) Mr-Ap 91, p. 8.

"Rock Pool." [AmerPoR] (20:2) Mr-Ap 91, p. 8.
"The Sweepers." [AmerPoR] (20:2) Mr-Ap 91, p. 7.
"Turn." [Thrpny] (44) Wint 91, p. 4.
"The Visitation." [AmerPoR] (20:2) Mr-Ap 91, p. 7.
5534. SHAPIRO, David
"Broken Objects, Discarded Landscape" (For Christopher Sweet). [Boulevard]
(5:3/6:1, #15/16) Spr 91, p. 225.
5535. SHAPIRO, Gregg
"February." [PlumR] (1) Spr-Sum 91, p. 30.
"Gangland." [CinPR] (21) Spr 90, p. 58.
"Out the Window, 5:44 AM." [WillowR] Spr 91, p. 33.
5536. SHAPIRO, Karl
"The Antimacassars of Wallace Stevens." [Chelsea] (52) 91, p. 88.
"The Antimacassars of Wallace Stevens." [NewYorkQ] (46) 91, p. 21.
"Creative Writing." [NewYorkQ] (45) 91, p. 5.
"Fucking." [GrahamHR] (15) Fall 91, p. 9-12.
"Future-Present." [Chelsea] (52) 91, p. 87.
"The Jewish Problem" (For Stanley Burnshaw). [AmerS] (60:2) Spr 91, p.
199-200.
"New York." [Chelsea] (52) 91, p. 89.
"Robert Lowell." [NewYorkQ] (45) 91, p. 44.
5537. SHAPIRO, Michael
"I Wouldn't Call It Poetry, But I Could If I Liked, Without Fear of Physical or
Emotional Trauma." [PaintedHR] (3) Sum 92, p. 31.
SHARAT CHANDRA, G. S.
See CHANDRA, G. S. Sharat
5538. SHARE, Don
"Saviour." [Agni] (33) 91, p. 229-230.
"Song of the Mirror-maker" (tr. of Juan Manuel Roca). [ColR] (NS 18:2) Fall-Wint
91, p. 85.
"Water-worship" (tr. of Víctor Rodríguez Núñez). [Agni] (33) 91, p. 233-234.
5539. SHARER, Donna
"Now You Have Six Years" (For Jamal). [Contact] (10:59/60/61) Spr 91, p. 44-45.
5540. SHARKEY, Lee
"Afterword." [HayF] (9) Fall-Wint 91, p. 76.
5541. SHATTUCK, Cathleen
"Dis ease." [Notus] (9) Fall 91, p. 58-61.
5542. SHAVIT, Dean D.
"In the Dark Hole, Playing Soldier." [PikeF] (10) Spr 91, p. 12.
5543. SHAW, Beverley
"Going Home" (for Brian Moore). [AntigR] (85/86) Spr-Sum 91, p. 7-8.
5544. SHAW, Catherine
"At Work on the Sabbath." [ChrC] (108:8) 6 Mr 91, p. 253.
"The Beer Garden." [Elf] (1:4) Wint 91, p. 32.
"Disney World Sestina." [Kalliope] (13:3) 91, p. 52-53.
"Sociable Ode." [ChrC] (108:19) 12-19 Je 91, p. 624.
5545. SHAW, Robert B.
"At the Bait Store." [Shen] (41:3) Fall 91, p. 83.
"December Vespers." [Shen] (41:3) Fall 91, p. 81.
"The Key." [Shen] (41:3) Fall 91, p. 82.
"Picturesque." [NewYorker] (67:34) 14 O 91, p. 72.
5546. SHAWGO, Lucy
"A Poor Player." [HolCrit] (28:5) D 91, p. 19.
"The River." [TexasR] (11:1/2) Spr-Sum 90, p. 95.
5547. SHCHERBINA, Tatyana
"Eros Poesis" (tr. by J. Kates). [Agni] (34) 91, p. 227-228.
"The Poet and the Tsar" (tr. by J. Kates). [OnTheBus] (8/9) 91, p. 227-228.
"You can threaten" (tr. by J. Kates). [MissR] (19:3) 91, p. 176.
5548. SHEA, Glenn
"Mont St. Michel" (To Graham). [HiramPoR] (50) Spr-Sum 91, p. 22.
5549. SHEA, Marilyn
"Caribou's." [BellArk] (7:3) My-Je 91, p. 8.
"Looking for Clara." [BellArk] (7:4) Jl-Ag 91, p. 12.
5550. SHEARD, Norma Voorhees
"IKON." [US1] (24/25) Spr 91, p. 14.
"The Lover." [US1] (24/25) Spr 91, p. 14.

"Sermons Before Light" (The Pablo Neruda Prize for Poetry, Honorable Mention).
    [Nimrod] (35:1) Fall-Wint 91, p. 35-40.
5551. SHECK, Laurie
    "Mannequins." [MichQR] (30:4) Fall 91, p. 534-635.
    "The Parking Lot at Night." [AntR] (49:1) Wint 91, p. 94.
5552. SHEEHAN, Tom
    "Blue Lightning and a '33 Ford Touring Car." [LouisL] (8:1) Spr 91, p. 40-41.
5553. SHEFFER, Roger
    "Nerstrand Woods" (Woods Near the Sea). [MidAR] (11:2) 91, p. 122.
    "Sodom." [Blueline] (12) 91, p. 13.
    "Waiting for Her." [LaurelR] (25:2) Sum 91, p. 52.
5554. SHEFFER, Susannah
    "Agreeing to It." [BelPoJ] (41:4) Sum 91, p. 20.
    "Fresh Fig." [BelPoJ] (41:4) Sum 91, p. 21.
5555. SHEFFIELD, Derek
    "Following Through the Cold." [BellR] (14:1) Spr 91, p. 6.
SHEKERJIAN, Regina deCormier
    See DeCORMIER-SHEKERJIAN, Regina
5556. SHELDON, Anne
    "Disposal of the Elements." [PaintedHR] (3) Sum 92, p. 19.
5557. SHELDON, Glenn
    "Letters to Reign (Found Poem)." [ChironR] (10:2) Sum 91, p. 17.
    "Musings of Another Pair of Legs in the Cafeteria's Human Caterpillar Crawl."
        [ChironR] (10:2) Sum 91, p. 17.
    "Unused Tears." [ChironR] (10:2) Sum 91, p. 17.
5558. SHELLER, Gayle Hunter
    "Forgiveness Is Survival." [BellArk] (7:2) Mr-Ap 91, p. 1.
    "Love Feast." [BellArk] (7:1) Ja-F 91, p. 3.
    "My Work." [BellArk] (7:1) Ja-F 91, p. 7.
    "On the Wall." [PaintedHR] (1) Ja 91, p. 11.
    "We've Mountains to Climb." [BellArk] (7:1) Ja-F 91, p. 7.
5559. SHELNUTT, Eve
    "Daughters Weighing Their Legacy." [SoDakR] (29:3 part 2) Aut 91, p. 97.
    "Letter from Camaguey, Cuba 1948." [Pig] (17) 91, p. 54.
    "The Living." [ThRiPo] (37/38) 91, p. 85.
    "The Map of Modern Art." [LullwaterR] (2:2) Spr 91, p. 89.
    "Now Late Afternoon." [ThRiPo] (37/38) 91, p. 86.
    "The Stranger." [LullwaterR] (3:1) Fall 91, p. 74.
    "Who Speaks of Hair and Fingers." [LullwaterR] (2:2) Spr 91, p. 9.
5560. SHEPARD, Gail
    "Parting at the Met." [Chelsea] (52) 91, p. 105.
    "Travel in August." [Chelsea] (52) 91, p. 106-107.
5561. SHEPARD, Jeanne
    "Tenderness." [Sidewalks] (1) Aug 91, p. 53.
5562. SHEPARD, Miriam
    "Slutty Flowers." [Poem] (66) N 91, p. 35.
    "Smoke." [Poem] (66) N 91, p. 36.
    "A Story." [Poem] (66) N 91, p. 37.
5563. SHEPARD, Neil
    "The First Golden Age" (1000 B.C.). [LaurelR] (25:1) Wint 91, p. 110-111.
5564. SHEPHERD, Gail
    "Between 20 and 20,000." [BlackWR] (18:1) Fall-Wint 91, p. 54-55.
    "By Available Light." [BlackWR] (18:1) Fall-Wint 91, p. 53.
    "Girls at Confirmation." [Iowa] (21:3) Fall 91, p. 164.
    "In the Silkworm Pavillion, Hirohito 1937." [Iowa] (21:3) Fall 91, p. 165.
    "In Theory." [BlackWR] (18:1) Fall-Wint 91, p. 52.
5565. SHEPHERD, J. Barrie
    "Blackberry Surprise." [ChrC] (108:18) 29 My-5 Je 91, p. 590.
    "Early Advent." [ChrC] (108:34) 20-27 N 91, p. 1104.
    "Extra-Terrestrials." [ChrC] (108:36) 11 D 91, p. 1156.
    "Hellsjaws." [ChrC] (108:7) 27 F 91, p. 230.
    "Of Christmas Past." [ChrC] (108:37) 18-25 D 91, p. 1202.
    "Role Reversal." [ChrC] (108:35) 4 D 91, p. 1134.
    "Un-dividing Wall." [ChrC] (108:13) 17 Ap 91, p. 430.
    "Undertaker." [ChrC] (108:11) 3 Ap 91, p. 366.

5566. SHEPHERD, Reginald
"Crossing Cocytus." [Callaloo] (14:3) Sum 91, p. 608.
"Sun Setting, Almost Saturday." [CapeR] (26:1) Spr 91, p. 31.
"Wide Sargasso Sea." [Callaloo] (14:3) Sum 91, p. 607.
5567. SHEPPARD, David
"Walking Away." [ParisR] (33:118) Spr 91, p. 248-250.
5568. SHEPPERSON, Janet
"The Scratch." [Stand] (33:1) Wint 91, p. 62.
5569. SHER, Diana
"Women in Battle." [Kalliope] (13:2) 91, p. 9.
5570. SHER, Steven
"What Catching the Cricket Means." [HeavenB] (9) Wint-Spr 91-92, p. 23.
5571. SHERMAN, Ari
"Poem Instead of a Letter for Amira." [CalQ] (32/33) Spr 90, p. 68-69.
5572. SHERMAN, Ken
"Fedora: A Child's Song." [Arc] (26) Spr 91, p. 42-43.
5573. SHERMAN, Kenneth
"Sieve." [CanLit] (129) Sum 91, p. 24.
5574. SHERMAN, Nancy
"Unison." [CreamCR] (15:1) Spr 91, p. 70-71.
5575. SHERRILL, Jan-Mitchell
"Obsession." [JamesWR] (8:4) Sum 91, p. 7.
5576. SHERRILL, Vicki
"Cats Legs." [BlackBR] (13) Spr-Sum 91, p. 24.
5577. SHEVIN, David
"Driving Out of Seneca County." [PoetryUSA] (23) Sum 91, p. 13.
5578. SHI, Mei
"Look Again." [GreenMR] (NS 4:2) Wint-Spr 91, p. 101.
SHI-ZHENG, Wang
   See WANG, Shi-Zheng
5579. SHIELDS, Bill
"Ghost Poem." [RagMag] (9:2) 91, p. 19.
"How the Hell Can." [NewYorkQ] (46) 91, p. 73.
"Wife." [NewYorkQ] (44) 91, p. 77.
5580. SHIFFRIN, Nancy
"For My Neverborn." [Spirit] (11) 91, p. 254.
"Penalty." [NewYorkQ] (45) 91, p. 71.
SHIGEHIKO, Yamano
   See YAMANO, Shigehiko
5581. SHIGEMATSU, Soiku
"Zen Haiku of Winter" (tr. of Natsume Soseki). [Talisman] (6) Spr 91, p. 21-23.
5582. SHIKIBU, Izumi
"No idea where you are" (tr. by Jane Hirshfield). [WilliamMR] (29) 91, p. 20.
"Tedium" (tr. by Graeme Wilson). [LitR] (35:1) Fall 91, p. 108.
5583. SHIMABUKURO, Tari
"Searching." [HawaiiR] (15:2, #32) Spr 91, p. 148.
"A Tahitian Woman" (from a Paul Gauguin oil painting). [HawaiiR] (15:2, #32) Spr
91, p. 149.
5584. SHINDER, Jason
"Ars Cinematica." [MichQR] (30:3) Sum 91, p. 486.
"The End." [MichQR] (30:3) Sum 91, p. 487.
"Fred Ott's Sneeze, 1891." [MichQR] (30:3) Sum 91, p. 485.
"On Colorization." [MichQR] (30:3) Sum 91, p. 487.
5585. SHIPLEY, Vivian
"Bye Bye Birdie" (Third Place Winner, Eve of St. Agnes Poery Awards). [NegC]
(11:3) 91, p. 16.
"Gigged." [NegC] (11:3) 91, p. 39.
"Upon Receiving a Letter from My Friend That Left Me Dissatisfied." [Pig] (17) 91,
p. 60.
5586. SHIPPY, Peter Jay
"Me, My Dog, and Our Pornography." [Ploughs] (17:4) Wint 91-92, p. 89.
"Meditation at Dave's Foxhead" (after Robert Hass). [Ploughs] (17:4) Wint 91-92,
p. 88.
5587. SHIRAISHI, Kazuko
"I See an Ant Hill, Gaudi Is There" (tr. by John Solt). [Manoa] (3:2) Fall 91, p.
183-186.

5588. SHIRLEY, Aleda
    "Eurydice." [SouthernPR] (31:2) Fall 91, p. 55-56.
    "Fourth and Magnolia." [KenR] (NS 13:1) Wint 91, p. 142-143.
    "Learning Disabled." [Journal] (14:2) Wint 91, p. 46-47.
    "Monday Morning." [AmerV] (23) Sum 91, p. 73-74.
    "Remarks on Color." [Journal] (14:2) Wint 91, p. 44-45.
    "Running Lights." [AmerPoR] (20:6) N-D 91, p. 24.
    "The Spirit of the Staircase." [AntR] (49:3) Sum 91, p. 436-437.
5589. SHOAF, Diann Blakely
    "Album." [HampSPR] Wint 91, p. 13.
    "Cassandra." [SouthernHR] (25:1) Wint 91, p. 52.
    "The Homeless in America" (Photographic Exhibit at the Parthenon, Centennial
        Park, Nashville). [Ploughs] (17:2/3) Fall 91, p. 266-267.
    "Planning a Family" (for Suzanne Wise-Thorn). [WebR] (15) Spr 91, p. 90.
    "Premiere Danseuse, at Seventy." [WebR] (15) Spr 91, p. 90.
5590. SHOEMAKER, Gretchen
    "Sonnet XC." [SoDakR] (29:3 part 2) Aut 91, p. 8.
5591. SHOLL, Betsy
    "The Coat." [MassR] (32:2) Sum 91, p. 222-224.
    "Dawn." [BelPoJ] (41:3) Spr 91, p. 6-7.
    "Real Faux Pearls." [BelPoJ] (41:3) Spr 91, p. 2-3.
    "A Small Patch of Ice." [BelPoJ] (41:3) Spr 91, p. 4-5.
5592. SHOMER, Enid
    "A: Rain Making." [CinPR] (22) Spr 91, p. 41.
    "At Dawn." [MassR] (32:3) Fall 91, p. 479-480.
    "Bypass" (For A, after surgery). [Kalliope] (13:2) 91, p. 60.
    "Hydrotherapy." [ParisR] (33:118) Spr 91, p. 251-262.
    "In the Desert" (November 7, 1957. At the ranch in Indio after the final tally).
        [CinPR] (22) Spr 91, p. 42.
    "On the Hustings with Rin Tin Tin" (May 27, 1956, the "salute to Jackie" rally).
        [CinPR] (22) Spr 91, p. 40.
    "Reading a Violent Love Poem to the Deaf." [Poetry] (157:4) Ja 91, p. 214-215.
    "The Suit Too Small, the Words." [Poetry] (158:1) Ap 91, p. 3`-6.
5593. SHORB, Michael
    "The Wildlife Graveyard in Taiwan." [MichQR] (30:3) Sum 91, p. 411-412.
5594. SHORE, Jane
    "Workout." [Ploughs] (17:2/3) Fall 91, p. 154-155.
5595. SHORT, Gary
    "Alas." [QW] (33) Sum-Fall 91, p. 184.
    "Among Old Stones and Bare Trees." [QW] (33) Sum-Fall 91, p. 185-186.
    "Boundaries." [QW] (33) Sum-Fall 91, p. 179-180.
    "Evidence." [QW] (33) Sum-Fall 91, p. 183.
    "Gathering." [QW] (33) Sum-Fall 91, p. 181-182.
    "Movement in the Truckee." [PoetL] (86:2) Sum 91, p. 33.
    "Photograph." [WritersF] (17) Fall 91, p. 84.
    "Tidings of a Dead Horse." [QW] (33) Sum-Fall 91, p. 177-178.
    "Watching the Ax Fall." [WritersF] (17) Fall 91, p. 83.
    "What the Body Knows." [HayF] (8) Spr-Sum 91, p. 92.
    "A White Rock." [HayF] (8) Spr-Sum 91, p. 62.
SHPANCER, Brittany Newmark
    See NEWMARK-SHPANCER, Brittany
5596. SHU, Ting
    "Assembly Line" (tr. by Hua Fengmao). [GreenMR] (NS 4:2) Wint-Spr 91, p. 24.
    "Conspirator" (tr. by Zhang Yichun). [GreenMR] (NS 4:2) Wint-Spr 91, p. 25.
    "Dusk" (tr. by Li Xijian and Gordon Osing). [PraS] (65:2) Sum 91, p. 58.
    "Gifts" (tr. by Carolyn Kizer). [WillowS] (27) Wint 91, p. 32.
    "Saying Good-bye to a Friend Going Abroad" (tr. by Ginny MacKenzie and Wei
        Guo). [Agni] (34) 91, p. 218.
    "To the Oak Tree" (tr. by Li Xijian and Gordon Osing). [PraS] (65:2) Sum 91, p.
        57-58.
5597. SHUBINSKY, Valery
    "In Winter" (tr. by Nina Kossman). [LitR] (34:3) Spr 91, p. 382.
    "Spectrum" (tr. by Nina Kossman). [LitR] (34:3) Spr 91, p. 383.
5598. SHULTZ, Robert O'Neal
    "Bible Study." [DustyD] Je 91, p. 3.
    "Unbirthday at the Bejing Brouhaha." [DustyD] Je 91, p. 2.

5599. SHUMAKER, Peggy
"Ira Pratt's Charts of the Stars." [Manoa] (3:1) Spr 91, p. 26.
"Rapt." [CreamCR] (15:2) Fall 91, p. 72-73.
"Short History of One Hour's Desire." [AmerPoR] (20:5) S-O 91, p. 30.
"Three Notes from a Wooden Flute." [AmerPoR] (20:5) S-O 91, p. 30.
"Wet Clay." [Manoa] (3:1) Spr 91, p. 24-25.
5600. SHURBANOV, Alexander
"If" (tr. of Blaga Dimitrova, w. Jascha Kessler). [Vis] (36) 91, p. 16.
5601. SHURIN, Aaron
"The Depositories." [Sulfur] (11:1, #28) Spr 91, p. 131-132.
"An Exhibition." [GrandS] (10:2, #38) 91, p. 55-56.
"Fin de Siecle." [Talisman] (7) Fall 91, p. 22.
"In." [Sulfur] (11:1, #28) Spr 91, p. 132-133.
"Intersection." [NewAW] (7) Spr 91, p. 31.
"Medium Green." [NewAW] (7) Spr 91, p. 30.
"The Wheel." [Conjunc] (17) 91, p. 171-177.
5602. SHUTTLE, Penelope
"Burn, Witch." [ManhatR] (6:1) Fall 91, p. 65-66.
"Despite." [Verse] (8:2) Sum 91, p. 95-96.
"The First Horses." [Verse] (8:2) Sum 91, p. 98.
"Ghost Train." [ManhatR] (6:1) Fall 91, p. 67-68.
"Jesus Is in Love with Russia." [Verse] (8:2) Sum 91, p. 96-97.
"Nuptial Arts." [Verse] (8:2) Sum 91, p. 95.
"Water Baby." [Verse] (8:2) Sum 91, p. 97.
5603. SHWARTZ, Yelena
"How Andrey Bely Nearly Fell Under a Streetcar" (tr. by Thomas Epstein). [LitR]
(34:3) Spr 91, p. 326-327.
"New Jerusalem" (tr. by Thomas Epstein). [LitR] (34:3) Spr 91, p. 325.
"A Parrot at Sea" (tr. by Thomas Epstein). [LitR] (34:3) Spr 91, p. 328.
"Reminiscence of Psalm 137" (For O. Sedakova, tr. by Laura D. Weeks). [LitR]
(34:3) Spr 91, p. 324.
"What This Avenue Is Called" (tr. by Laura D. Weeks). [LitR] (34:3) Spr 91, p.
323.
SHYH-JEN, Fuh
See FUH, Shyh-jen
5604. SICOLI, Dan
"Down Wind." [SlipS] (11) 91, p. 75.
5605. SIDNEY, Joan Seliger
"Naming." [SingHM] (19) 91; p. 100-101.
"Naming" (for Chris Rogers). [NewYorkQ] (45) 91, p. 75.
5606. SIDON, Weslea
"Sweet May Rhyme." [Confr] (46/47) Fall 91-Wint 92, p. 271.
5607. SIEBURTH, Richard
"Inert" (tr. of Michel Leiris). [Sulfur] (11:2 #29) Fall 91, p. 187.
"Last Writings" (tr. of Michel Leiris). [Sulfur] (11:2 #29) Fall 91, p. 184-188.
"A Map of Mnemosyne" (tr. of Friedrich Hölderlin). [Talisman] (6) Spr 91, p.
51-64.
"Trademarks" (tr. of Michel Leiris). [Sulfur] (11:2 #29) Fall 91, p. 184-186.
"Twigs" (tr. of Michel Leiris). [Sulfur] (11:2 #29) Fall 91, p. 187-188.
5608. SIEFKIN, David
"Collection" (tr. of Luuk Gruwez, w. Catharina Kochuyt). [Trans] (25) Spr 91, p.
233-234.
"Street" (tr. of Luuk Gruwez, w. Catharina Kochuyt). [Trans] (25) Spr 91, p. 235.
5609. SIEGEL, Garret
"Undertow." [AnthNEW] (3) 91, p. 16.
5610. SIEGEL, Joan I.
"Doors" (For Marian Clarke). [Comm] (118:8) 19 Ap 91, p. 258.
"Harvester of Rags." [HampSPR] Wint 91, p. 22.
"Our House." [SmPd] (28:1, #81) Wint 91, p. 36.
"Sex." [PoetC] (23:1) Fall 91, p. 20.
"Six." [Interim] (10:2) Fall-Wint 91-92, p. 39-40.
"To a Friend Whose Cat Has Died Unexpectedly." [PoetC] (23:1) Fall 91, p. 21.
"A Walk in the Country at Night." [Interim] (10:2) Fall-Wint 91-92, p. 41.
"Zazen." [HampSPR] Wint 91, p. 22-23.
5611. SIEGEL, Melanie
"Municipal Rites." [DustyD] Ap 91, p. 10.

"Remembrance." [DustyD] Je 91, p. 16.
5612. SIEGFRIED, Serena
"Science Class." [NewYorkQ] (45) 91, p. 70.
5613. SIERSEMA, Laura
"There Skips an Agent." [CreamCR] (15:1) Spr 91, p. 67.
"A Woman's Life." [HampSPR] Wint 91, p. 20.
5614. SIEVERS, Kelly
"Making Room." [WritersF] (17) Fall 91, p. 200.
5615. SIGFUSSON, Hannes
"Lifelong Journey" (tr. by Hallberg Hallmundsson). [Vis] (37) 91, p. 40.
5616. SIGNORELLI-PAPPAS, Rita
"Ariel." [PoetryNW] (32:3) Aut 91, p. 12-13.
"The Artist's Cat." [SoCoast] (11) Wint 91, p. 8-9.
"Beautiful Girl Cafe." [Poetry] (157:5) F 91, p. 283.
"Francesca de Rimini." [InterPR] (17:1) Spr 91, p. 91-92.
"Hunger Artist." [Poetry] (157:5) F 91, p. 284.
"Pia of Tolomei." [CalQ] (31) Fall 88, p. 59.
"She and I." [HolCrit] (28:5) D 91, p. 17.
5617. SIGURDARDOTTIR, Ragna
"IX. Your tongue circles mine" (tr. by the author). [Vis] (37) 91, p. 35.
"XI. I stand still in the dark" (tr. by the author). [Vis] (37) 91, p. 35.
"XII. We were two" (tr. by the author). [Vis] (37) 91, p. 35.
"XV. She sits on the sofa in the twilight" (tr. by the author). [Vis] (36) 91, p. 15.
5618. SIGURDSSON, Olafur Johann
"Winter Past" (tr. by Alan Boucher). [Vis] (37) 91, p. 38.
5619. SILBERG, Richard
"The Prism." [PoetryUSA] (22) Spr 91, p. 10.
5620. SILBERMAN, Steve
"The Mirror." [JamesWR] (8:3) Spr 91, p. 10.
5621. SILÉN, Iván
"La Comerciante." [Nuez] (3:8/9) 91, p. 20.
5622. SILKIN, Jon
"Civil War Grave, Richmond." [Stand] (32:1) Wint 90-91, p. 13.
"Douglas of Sorbie and the Adder." [NewL] (58:1) Fall 91, p. 68=69.
"Galloway's Religious Killings, And the Lonely Language of Gaelic." [NewL]
(58:1) Fall 91, p. 70-71.
"Lens-Breakers." [Stand] (32:1) Wint 90-91, p. 8-9.
"Tangled in War." [NewL] (58:1) Fall 91, p. 72.
"To a Lighthouse." [Stand] (32:1) Wint 90-91, p. 10-12.
"Woman and Bread." [Bogg] (64) 91, p. 3.
5623. SILVA, Sam
"The Hollow Rain of the City." [DogRR] (10:2) Fall-Wint 91, p. 4.
"Letter Home." [DogRR] (10:2) Fall-Wint 91, p. 3-4.
"Postulate of the Worm." [DogRR] (10:2) Fall-Wint 91, p. 5.
5624. SILVERIO, Nicasio
"Interior Barroco." [LindLM] (10:1) Ja-Mr 91, p. 28.
5625. SILVERMAN, Herschel
"Messiah." [JINJPo] (13:1) Spr 91, p. 7-9.
5626. SILVERTHORNE, Marty
"Waiting by the White Bed." [Crucible] (27) Fall 91, p. 26.
5627. SIMAN, John
"Wind and Pure Reason." [NewYorkQ] (44) 91, p. 64.
5628. SIMAR, Sue Ann
"The Harvest." [BlackBR] (13) Spr-Sum 91, p. 5.
"Rich Things and Poor People." [BlackBR] (13) Spr-Sum 91, p. 29.
5629. SIMIC, Charles
"At the Vacancy Sign." [AmerPoR] (20:5) S-O 91, p. 4.
"Beauty." [GrandS] (10:1, #37) 91, p. 179.
"The Bird." [RiverC] (12:1) Fall 91, p. 43.
"A Book Full of Pictures." [MichQR] (30:4) Fall 91, p. 609.
"Clouds Gathering." [GrandS] (10:4, #40) 91, p. 115.
"Dark TV Screen." [MichQR] (30:4) Fall 91, p. 610.
"Demonology." [AmerPoR] (20:5) S-O 91, p. 3.
"Documentary." [Boulevard] (6:2/3, #17/18) Fall 91, p. 39.
"Figure in the Landscape" (for Mark). [Raritan] (10:3) Wint 91, p. 28.
"Funeral Parlor." [Ploughs] (17:2/3) Fall 91, p. 95.

"Hotel Insomnia." [AmerPoR] (20:5) S-O 91, p. 3.
"The Inanimate Object." [Ploughs] (17:4) Wint 91-92, p. 14.
"The Initiate" (Excerpt). [Field] (44) Spr 91, p. 71-72.
"Lost Glove." [NewYorker] (67:41) 2 D 91, p. 40.
"Makers of Labyrinths." [NewYorker] (67:26) 19 Ag 91, p. 28.
"Many Zeros." [AmerPoR] (20:5) S-O 91, p. 3.
"Marina's Epic." [ParisR] (33:120) Fall 91, p. 49-50.
"My Quarrel with the Infinite." [ParisR] (33:120) Fall 91, p. 51.
"New York Poems." [RiverC] (12:1) Fall 91, p. 46-47.
"Obscure Beginnings." [MichQR] (30:4) Fall 91, p. 608.
"Poem: Those happy days when I climbed." [AmerPoR] (20:5) S-O 91, p. 3.
"The Puppet." [RiverC] (12:1) Fall 91, p. 44-45.
"Quick Eats." [Boulevard] (6:2/3, #17/18) Fall 91, p. 37-38.
"Street Scene." [Raritan] (10:3) Wint 91, p. 29.
"The Tiger" (in memory of George Oppen). [Raritan] (10:3) Wint 91, p. 30-31.
"Tragic Architecture." [NewYorker] (67:45) 30 D 91, p. 70.
"True History." [NewYorker] (66:51) 4 F 91, p. 30.
"The White Room." [Field] (44) Spr 91, p. 68-69.
5630. SIMISON, Greg
"Wolverine." [CanLit] (128) Spr 91, p. 119.
5631. SIMKO, Daniel
"From the Bestiary" (to the memory of Samuel Beckett and Thomas Bernhard). [Ploughs] (17:4) Wint 91-92, p. 46-48.
"The Garden of Theophrastus" (to my son, tr. of Peter Huchel). [Ploughs] (17:4) Wint 91-92, p. 17.
"Landscape Beyond Warsaw" (tr. of Peter Huchel). [Ploughs] (17:4) Wint 91-92, p. 15.
"Psalm" (tr. of Peter Huchel). [Ploughs] (17:4) Wint 91-92, p. 18.
"Roads" (tr. of Peter Huchel). [Ploughs] (17:4) Wint 91-92, p. 16.
5632. SIMMERMAN, Jim
"The Glass Park." [Poetry] (157:4) Ja 91, p. 195-196.
"Take a Hike." [Poetry] (157:4) Ja 91, p. 194.
"Take What You Want But Eat What You Take." [DenQ] (26:1) Sum 91, p. 67-69.
5633. SIMMS, Colin
"18.4.85 Northumberland, for B.B." [NewAW] (8/9) Fall 91, p. 161.
"Above Kepwick Hall." [NewAW] (8/9) Fall 91, p. 161.
"For Janet." [NewAW] (8/9) Fall 91, p. 162-163.
"For M.S." [NewAW] (8/9) Fall 91, p. 162.
"Goshawk Takes Breakfast." [NewAW] (8/9) Fall 91, p. 160.
"Magpie." [NewAW] (8/9) Fall 91, p. 160.
5634. SIMON, John Oliver
"Bacchantes (VIII)" (tr. of Elsa Cross). [ArtfulD] (20/21) 91, p. 60.
"Confessions" (tr. of Alba Azucena Torres). [ArtfulD] (20/21) 91, p. 61.
"On the Edge." [OnTheBus] (8/9) 91, p. 143.
"Raison d'Etre" (tr. of Alfonso Chase). [ArtfulD] (20/21) 91, p. 59.
5635. SIMON, Lourdes
"Carta de una Madre Cubana a su Hija 'Semi'." [LindLM] (10:1) Ja-Mr 91, p. 26.
5636. SIMON, Maurya
"Periyar Lake." [GettyR] (4:1) Wint 91, p. 38.
5637. SIMON, Tracy L.
"The Accomplice." [NewYorkQ] (44) 91, p. 94.
5638. SIMONE, Diane
"The Bay." [Confr] (46/47) Fall 91-Wint 92, p. 269.
"But Not Divine." [Confr] (46/47) Fall 91-Wint 92, p. 269-270.
5639. SIMONSUURI, Kirsti
"The Birth of Tragedy" (tr. by the author and Jascha Kessler). [Vis] (37) 91, p. 32.
"The Garlic: An Aetiological Tale" (tr. from the Finnish w. Jascha Kessler). [Hellas] (2:1) Spr 91, p. 50-53.
"Morning, Evening" (tr. by the author and Jascha Kessler). [Vis] (37) 91, p. 31.
"Travelling Light" (tr. by the author and Jascha Kessler). [Vis] (37) 91, p. 32.
5640. SIMPSON, Glen
"Grandmother at the Mall." [PoetryE] (32) Fall 91, p. 41.
"Quartz Creek Gold Camp: Cassiar District." [PoetryE] (32) Fall 91, p. 41.
5641. SIMPSON, Louis
"Entries." [Ploughs] (17:1) Spr 91, p. 146-159.
"Like a Glass of Tea." [ColR] (NS 18:2) Fall-Wint 91, p. 44.

"Society Notes." [CimR] (96) Jl 91, p. 105.
5642. SIMPSON, Lucy
"Ancestors." [NewRena] (8:2, #25) Fall 91, p. 77.
5643. SIMPSON, Mary Scott
"Elemental." [Farm] (8:1) Spr-Sum 91, p. 70.
5644. SIMPSON, Megan
"Letters Following Travel." [BlackWR] (18:1) Fall-Wint 91, p. 35-37.
5645. SIMS, Ann
"Where Your Feet Pass." [Kalliope] (13:3) 91, p. 17.
5646. SIMS, Tony
"Happenings." [SoCoast] (11) Wint 91, p. 54.
5647. SIN, Kyong-rim
"Revisiting a Mountain Town" (in Korean and English, tr. by Brent Duffin and Yang
Seung-Tai). [InterPR] (17:1) Spr 91, p. 23-25.
5648. SINCLAIR, Michael
"Dolls of the World." [RiverS] (33) 91, p. 70.
5649. SINDALL, Susan
"Elephants." [PraS] (65:3) Fall 91, p. 104-105.
"The Stone Gift." [PraS] (65:3) Fall 91, p. 106-107.
"Walking On." [NegC] (11:1) 91, p. 83.
5650. SINGH, Man Mohan
"The Death of Old Man River" (dedicated to the memory of Budha Nala, a
distributory of the Sutlej River, which . . . has now been killed by pollution).
[RiverS] (35) 91, p. 63.
5651. SINK, Susan
"Exposure." [IndR] (14:2) Spr 91, p. 88-89.
5652. SINNETT, Mark
"As It Was." [Quarry] (40:4) Fall 91, p. 34.
"Over Time, Over Space." [Quarry] (40:4) Fall 91, p. 35.
"Poem for the Bastard That Tried to Destroy My Past." [Quarry] (40:4) Fall 91, p.
36-37.
5653. SIRR, Peter
"Death of a Travel Writer" (Selections: I-X). [Ploughs] (17:1) Spr 91, p. 160-167.
5654. SISSON, C. H.
"Et in Arcadia Ego." [Poetry] (158:6) S 91, p. 340.
"The Wind." [Poetry] (158:6) S 91, p. 341.
5655. SISSON, Jonathan
"1939" (A Found Poem, From "Biographical Notes" in *Klee*, by Gualtieri di San
Lazzaro). [NorthStoneR] (10) Fall 91-Wint 92, p. 73.
"Equivalents." [NorthStoneR] (10) Fall 91-Wint 92, p. 77.
"January 1991." [NorthStoneR] (10) Fall 91-Wint 92, p. 72-73.
"The Lychgate." [NorthStoneR] (10) Fall 91-Wint 92, p. 75.
"May Day." [LakeSR] (25) 91, p. 33.
"On First Looking into Chapman's Homer." [NorthStoneR] (10) Fall 91-Wint 92, p.
76.
"The Secret of Art." [NorthStoneR] (10) Fall 91-Wint 92, p. 76.
"Sound Stage." [NorthStoneR] (10) Fall 91-Wint 92, p. 77.
"The Witch's Tower." [NorthStoneR] (10) Fall 91-Wint 92, p. 74.
5656. SJOBERG, Leif
"Great, Marvelous Structures" (tr. of Werner Aspenstrom, w. Stephen Klass). [Vis]
(37) 91, p. 50.
"Icarus and the Lad Graystone" (tr. of Werner Aspenstrom, w. Stephen Klass).
[Vis] (37) 91, p. 49.
"Mining Country IV" (tr. of Werner Aspenstrom, w. Stephen Klass). [Vis] (37) 91,
p. 49.
"The Position (Version II)" (tr. of Werner Aspenstrom, w. Stephen Klass). [Vis]
(37) 91, p. 50.
"Rousseau the Painter's Departure from Life" (tr. of Werner Aspenstrom, w.
Stephen Klass). [Vis] (37) 91, p. 48.
"The Rower" (tr. of Werner Aspenstrom, w. Stephen Klass). [Vis] (37) 91, p. 50.
5657. SJOBERG, Marie D.
"Coffee Cup." [EmeraldCR] (4) 91, p. 65.
5658. SKALICAN, Jack
"Act 1, Scene 1." [Interim] (10:2) Fall-Wint 91-92, p. 12.
5659. SKARSTEDT, Sonja A.
"Under Kihei." [CanLit] (128) Spr 91, p. 75-76.

5660. SKILLMAN, Judith
"Aftermath." [Plain] (11:3) Spr 91, p. 37.
"Anomalies." [NowestR] (29:3) 91, p. 36.
"Barbed Wire." [HayF] (9) Fall-Wint 91, p. 73-74.
"Blue Rock China" (for Barbara Molloy-Olund). [BellR] (14:1) Spr 91, p. 7.
"Brown Grasses." [Plain] (11:2) Wint 91, p. 24.
"Labor's Child." [Colum] (16) Spr 91, p. 129-136.
"Lethargy." [BellR] (14:1) Spr 91, p. 8-9.
"The Matron." [LaurelR] (25:1) Wint 91, p. 70.
"Mother's Doll." [NowestR] (29:3) 91, p. 35.
"Under Zeus." [WillowS] (27) Wint 91, p. 55.
"Vernal Equinox at the Locks." [NowestR] (29:3) 91, p. 37.

5661. SKINNER, Jeffrey
"All Saints." [PoetryE] (31) Spr 91, p. 46.
"Braiding Your Hair." [PoetryE] (31) Spr 91, p. 47.
"Mark, Fore & Strike." [SouthernPR] (31:1) Spr 91, p. 24-26.
"Questionable Weather." [PoetryE] (31) Spr 91, p. 45.

5662. SKINNER, Knute
"The Door." [NewYorkQ] (46) 91, p. 36.
"Incense." [NewYorkQ] (44) 91, p. 48.
"The Interview." [NewYorkQ] (45) 91, p. 59.
"Ralph's Mother." [MalR] (95) Sum 91, p. 30.

5663. SKLAR, Morty
"Forgetting My Life." [WorldL] (1:1) 91, p. 1-2.
"Getting Called In" (for Vicki, teaching in Oshamanbe). [WorldL] (1:1) 91, p. 3-4.
"The Story of My Life." [WorldL] (1:1) 91, p. 5.

5664. SKLOOT, Floyd
"The Album." [AmerS] (60:1) Wint 91, p. 89.
"Between Brothers." [SnailPR] (1:2) Fall 91-Wint 92, p. 2.
"A Clean Poem." [WritersF] (17) Fall 91, p. 82.
"The Everly Brothers." [PraS] (65:3) Fall 91, p. 71-72.
"Miniatures." [WritersF] (17) Fall 91, p. 80.
"The New World Bar and Grill." [CinPR] (22) Spr 91, p. 38-39.
"Rhapsody in Calico (1925)." [SouthernPR] (31:2) Fall 91, p. 23-24.
"Rose & Max." [SilverFR] (20) Spr 91, p. 38-45.
"Sapphire Fandango." [GettyR] (4:4) Aut 91, p. 594-595.
"A Softer Place." [GettyR] (4:4) Aut 91, p. 596.
"Solstice." [Poetry] (159:3) D 91, p. 131.
"Spanish Revival." [WritersF] (17) Fall 91, p. 81.
"Twilight Time" (The Platters, Spring, 1958). [PraS] (65:3) Fall 91, p. 70-71.
"The Velvet Gentleman." [GettyR] (4:4) Aut 91, p. 593.
"Voices of the Sea." [Shen] (41:1) Spr 91, p. 44-45.
"Where Are They Now?" [Journal] (14:2) Wint 91, p. 81.

5665. SKOYLES, John
"The Repairman." [PoetryE] (31) Spr 91, p. 38-39.
"Visit Home." [PoetryE] (31) Spr 91, p. 40-41.

5666. SKRUPSKELIS, Viktoria (Victoria)
"Bells" (tr. of Judita Vaiciunaite, w. Stuart Friebert). [Mildred] (4:2/5:1) 91, p. 19.
"Bouquet of Marigolds" (tr. of Judita Vaiciunaite, w. Stuart Friebert). [Mildred]
(4:2/5:1) 91, p. 18.
"Butterfly" (tr. of Judita Vaiciunaite, w. Stuart Friebert). [Mildred] (4:2/5:1) 91, p.
21.
"City" (tr. of Judita Vaiciunaite, w. Stuart Friebert). [Mildred] (4:2/5:1) 91, p. 19.
"The Drummer" (tr. of Judita Vaiciunaite, w. Stuart Friebert). [Mildred] (4:2/5:1) 91,
p. 20.
"Evening Light" (tr. of Judita Vaiciunaité, w. Stuart Friebert). [Timbuktu] (6) Spr
91, p. 99.
"Girl with Ermine" (tr. of Judita Vaiciunaité, w. Stuart Friebert). [Timbuktu] (6) Spr
91, p. 99.
"Inheritance" (Excerpt, tr. of Judita Vaiciunaite, w. Stuart Friebert). [Os] (32) Spr
91, p. 28.
"Light from an Autumn Night" (tr. of Judita Vaiciunaite, w. Stuart Friebert). [Os]
(32) Spr 91, p. 24.
"The Owl" (tr. of Judita Vaiciunaite, w. Stuart Friebert). [Os] (32) Spr 91, p. 26.
"Pavilion" (tr. of Judita Vaiciunaité, w. Stuart Friebert). [Timbuktu] (6) Spr 91, p.
100.

"The Silence of Cornflowers" (tr. of Judita Vaiciunaite, w. Stuart Friebert).
   [Mildred] (4:2/5:1) 91, p. 18.
"Spectacle" (tr. of Judita Vaiciunaite, w. Stuart Friebert). [Mildred] (4:2/5:1) 91, p.
   20.
"Two Mutes in Love" (tr. of Judita Vaiciunaite, w. Stuart Friebert). [Os] (32) Spr
   91, p. 27.
"When Wild Apple Trees Blossom" (tr. of Judita Vaiciunaite, w. Stuart Friebert).
   [Crazy] (41) Wint 91, p. 16.
"White Octaves" (tr. of Judita Vaiciunaite, w. Stuart Friebert). [Journal] (15:1) Spr
   91, p. 13-14.
5667. SLAPIKAS, Carolyn
   "God look at us." [NewYorkQ] (44) 91, p. 65.
   "This apple." [NewYorkQ] (46) 91, p. 40.
5668. SLATER, Barbara
   "Late Spring." [PraF] (12:1 #54) Spr 91, p. 85.
   "The Morning After." [Grain] (19:2) Sum 91, p. 70.
   "Storm at Sunset." [Grain] (19:2) Sum 91, p. 69.
5669. SLATKIN, Marcia
   "The Last Duck." [ParisR] (33:119) Sum 91, p. 193.
   "The Passion." [ParisR] (33:119) Sum 91, p. 192.
   "Witness: The Amazon." [SycamoreR] (3:2) Sum 91, p. 41-42.
5670. SLATTERY, Michael
   "All Clear." [PoetryUSA] (23) Sum 91, p. 15.
5671. SLAUGHTER, William
   "Professor Xu / Madame Bovary / Sparrow War." [PoetryE] (31) Spr 91, p.
      126-128.
5672. SLAVEN, Fred
   "Letter to Rimbaud" (Selections). [US1] (24/25) Spr 91, p. 34-35.
5673. SLAVENS, Kerry
   "The Observable Universe." [CanLit] (131) Wint 91, p. 156.
5674. SLAVITT, David R.
   "Crossroads." [Boulevard] (6:2/3, #17/18) Fall 91, p. 213-214.
5675. SLAYMAKER, Bob
   "5:00 P.M., Nairobi Town." [NewYorkQ] (44) 91, p. 76.
   "Johnny (The Torso)." [RiverS] (35) 91, p. 81-82.
   "Operation Rescue." [ChangingM] (22) Wint-Spr 91, p. 32.
   "Poem to My Neighbors." [InterPR] (17:1) Spr 91, p. 116.
5676. SLEA, Vanessa (Van)
   "Ashes to Ashes." [Pearl] (14) Fall-Wint 91, p. 66.
   "No Sale." [ChironR] (10:4) Wint 91, p. 34.
5677. SLEGMAN, Ann
   "Uncle." [NewL] (58:1) Fall 91, p. 106.
5678. SLEIGH, Tom
   "In the Park." [Ploughs] (17:2/3) Fall 91, p. 34-36.
   "Lamentation on Ur" (2,000 B.C.). [TriQ] (83) Wint 91-92, p. 105.
   "The Line." [Agni] (33) 91, p. 9-12.
   "Shame." [TriQ] (83) Wint 91-92, p. 101-104.
   "Song." [TriQ] (83) Wint 91-92, p. 106.
5679. SLESINGER, Warren
   "Stair, Star, Step" (Allan C. Slesinger, 1903-1985). [AntR] (49:2) Spr 91, p. 248.
5680. SLICER, Deborah
   "Missoula, Montana." [PoetryNW] (32:4) Wint 91-92, p. 24-25.
   "Pastoral." [PoetryNW] (32:4) Wint 91-92, p. 25.
5681. SLICK, Richard D.
   "Marcy Remembers." [Elf] (1:4) Wint 91, p. 27.
5682. SLOAN, Gerry
   "At the Revenue Office." [ContextS] (2:2) 91, p. 34.
5683. SLONE, G. Tod
   "Danger Lurks in the Corners of Roominghouses." [SlipS] (11) 91, p. 73.
   "Plum Perfect." [SlipS] (11) 91, p. 74.
5684. SLOOP, Rebecca R.
   "Just Another Game." [Crucible] (27) Fall 91, p. 39-41.
5685. SLOWERY, Janet
   "Betsy." [PoetryE] (31) Spr 91, p. 24.
SLUYS, Sharon M. van
   See Van SLUYS, Sharon M.

5686. SMALL, Jonathan
"Aspirant." [GrahamHR] (14) Spr 91, p. 13.
"Metamorphosis." [GrahamHR] (14) Spr 91, p. 11-12.
"White Sheets." [GrahamHR] (14) Spr 91, p. 9-10.
5687. SMALLDON, Jeffrey L.
"Satori." [MoodySI] (24/25/26) Spr 91, p. 48.
5688. SMALLFIELD, Edward
"Black Dog." [PaintedHR] (4) Fall 92, p. 33.
"Running" (for Eve). [PaintedHR] (4) Fall 92, p. 31-32.
5689. SMARR, Janet
"Basium." [Hellas] (2:2) Fall 91, p. 245-246.
5690. SMART, Carolyn
"The Sound of the Birds" (For Bronwen Wallace). [Quarry] (40:1/2) Wint-Spr 91,
p. 159-169.
5691. SMIDDY, Nina
"Untitled: The air in the creaking of saddles." [AmerPoR] (20:5) S-O 91, p. 41.
5692. SMITH, Allen
"Red Sofa." [Crucible] (27) Fall 91, p. 29.
5693. SMITH, Anita Speer
"Old Sister Moon" (Award of Excellence: Poetry). [HopewellR] (1991) 91, p. 23.
5694. SMITH, Anthony
"A Perte de Vus." [Pearl] (14) Fall-Wint 91, p. 64.
"Fantasy Radio Telephone." [Bogg] (64) 91, p. 16.
"Spitting Sawdust, Not Caviar." [Pearl] (14) Fall-Wint 91, p. 64.
5695. SMITH, Arthur
"End of the Line." [NewEngR] (14:1) Fall 91, p. 15-16.
"Every Night as I Prayed God Would Kill You." [GettyR] (4:1) Wint 91, p. 57-58.
"Harmony." [NewEngR] (14:1) Fall 91, p. 13-14.
"Son's Blues." [Nat] (253:1) 1 Jl 91, p. 28.
5696. SMITH, Beatrice
"My Autumn Years." [US1] (24/25) Spr 91, p. 21.
5697. SMITH, Caroline
"Edith XXIV." [Stand] (32:4) Aut 91, p. 68-69.
5698. SMITH, Cathryn
"Yellow Leaves." [CapeR] (26:1) Spr 91, p. 40.
5699. SMITH, Charlene Mary-Cath
"It Ceases to Amuse." [HawaiiR] (15:2, #32) Spr 91, p. 78-79.
5700. SMITH, Charlie
"Animal and Poetic Notions." [PoetryE] (31) Spr 91, p. 29-30.
"Blue Windows." [VirQR] (67:4) Aut 91, p. 671-672.
"The Day Race." [VirQR] (67:4) Aut 91, p. 674-676.
"Jackplay." [PoetryE] (31) Spr 91, p. 27-28.
"Lies to the Dying." [ParisR] (33:119) Sum 91, p. 182-184.
"Little Doors." [NewAW] (8/9) Fall 91, p. 46.
"Maturity." [AmerPoR] (20:2) Mr-Ap 91, p. 47.
"Mercies." [MissR] (19:3) 91, p. 151-153.
"Passing from Hand to Hand." [PoetryE] (31) Spr 91, p. 25-26.
"A Place in the World." [MissR] (19:3) 91, p. 154-156.
"Revision." [Boulevard] (5:3/6:1, #15/16) Spr 91, p. 126.
"The Shaved Dog." [VirQR] (67:4) Aut 91, p. 672-674.
"Some Don't Go South." [NewAW] (8/9) Fall 91, p. 47.
"Still Winter (Spring)." [NewYorker] (67:7) 8 Ap 91, p. 74.
"Sunday Morning." [Sonora] (21) Sum 91, p. 29.
5701. SMITH, Cheryl H.
"Murderess." [OnTheBus] (8/9) 91, p. 144.
5702. SMITH, Claude Clayton
"Hinc Illae Lacrimae." [Pig] (17) 91, p. 112.
5703. SMITH, Copland
"Lady Lazarus." [Abraxas] (40/41) 91, p. 153.
5704. SMITH, D. J.
"Family Reunion." [EmeraldCR] (3) 91, c1990, p. 14.
"Miss Tammy Receives a Caller." [CumbPR] (10:2) Spr 91, p. 17.
5705. SMITH, Dave
"Basement Waltz." [NewYorker] (67:19 [i.e. 67:13]) 20 My 91, p. 44.
"Big Foot, the Minneconjou Sioux" (d. 1890). [SoDakR] (29:3 part 2) Aut 91, p.
90.

"The Dinner Guest." [SewanR] (99:4) Fall 91, p. 562-563.
"Night Pleasures." [NewYorker] (67:9) 22 Ap 91, p. 78.
"On Adoring Matters." [ColEng] (53:3) Mr 91, p. 310.
5706. SMITH, David-Glen
"The Moon Dreams of Cecilia Dreaming of the Moon." [MidAR] (11:2) 91, p.
56-57.
"The Myth of Falling." [EvergreenC] (6:2) Sum-Fall 91, p. 39.
5707. SMITH, David James
"Dark Blossom" (for Stephen). [SlipS] (11) 91, p. 63.
"Eulogy." [HawaiiR] (15:3, #33) Fall 91, p. 140.
"On the Morning of Your New Life" (for Ingrid). [CarolQ] (44:1) Fall 91, p. 46.
5708. SMITH, Francis J.
"Freesia." [ManhatPR] (13) [91?], p. 26.
5709. SMITH, Grace
"Fine Weather" (tr. of Orhan Veli Kanik, w. Richard Schwarzenberger). [Agni] (33)
91, p. 97.
"For the Homeland" (tr. of Orhan Veli Kanik, w. Richard Schwarzenberger). [Agni]
(33) 91, p. 94.
"Illusion" (tr. of Orhan Veli Kanik, w. Richard Schwarzenberger). [Agni] (33) 91,
p. 95.
"Stretched Out" (tr. of Orhan Veli Kanik, w. Richard Schwarzenberger). [Agni] (33)
91, p. 96.
5710. SMITH, Greg
"As They Appear." [BellR] (14:2) Fall 91, p. 16.
5711. SMITH, Hugh
"In the Reeds." [DogRR] (10:1) Sum 91, p. 18.
5712. SMITH, J. D.
"The Hypothetical Landscape." [RiverC] (11:2) Spr 91, p. 22.
"Offering." [RiverC] (11:2) Spr 91, p. 23.
SMITH, James Sutherland
See SUTHERLAND-SMITH, James
5713. SMITH, Jared
"The Sun Finding Your Hands." [ContextS] (2:2) 91, p. 8.
"They Have Not Forgotten." [ContextS] (2:2) 91, p. 8-9.
5714. SMITH, Jennifer E.
"Ancestry." [Obs] (6:3) Wint 91, p. 50-51.
"B-Level Poem." [Obs] (6:3) Wint 91, p. 49-50.
5715. SMITH, Joan Jobe
"Cars Aren't As Smart As Horses." [ChironR] (10:2) Sum 91, p. 3.
"I Never Went to Bed with the Famous Ballplayer." [ChironR] (10:2) Sum 91, p. 3.
"Loss of Consortium." [ChironR] (10:2) Sum 91, p. 3.
"Lucky Strikes Meant Fine Tobacco." [ChironR] (10:2) Sum 91, p. 3.
5716. SMITH, Joe
"Syrtaki." [Vis] (36) 91, p. 26-27.
5717. SMITH, Jonathan
"79th at the Dan Ryan." [Callaloo] (14:4) Fall 91, p. 920.
"Geologic." [Callaloo] (14:4) Fall 91, p. 921.
5718. SMITH, Jordan
"Hunters in the Snow." [Salm] (90/91) Spr-Sum 91, p. 100.
"What It's Not" (for George Drury). [Salm] (92) Fall 91, p. 153-154.
5719. SMITH, Jules
"Brief Encounter." [ChironR] (10:3) Aut 91, p. 11.
"The History of Shaving." [ChironR] (10:3) Aut 91, p. 11.
"On Seeing Surrealist Paintings with My Love." [ChironR] (10:3) Aut 91, p. 11.
5720. SMITH, Keith (Keith B.)
"Allelomorphic Sonata." [RiverC] (11:2) Spr 91, p. 73.
"Japanese Elegy for My Grandmother." [PoetryNW] (32:2) Sum 91, p. 13.
"Moon Duet." [PoetryNW] (32:2) Sum 91, p. 13.
5721. SMITH, Kevin J.
"At the Corner of Smoke & Mirrors." [ChironR] (10:3) Aut 91, p. 14.
"Happy Hour at the Doomed Romance Bar." [SlipS] (11) 91, p. 72.
"Letter from an Old Friend." [ChironR] (10:3) Aut 91, p. 14.
5722. SMITH, Larry
"Postcard from Youngstown — 1921." [Pig] (17) 91, p. 64.

5723. SMITH, Larry E.
"Crappie Fishing." [Outbr] (22) 91, p. 45.
"This House." [WritersF] (17) Fall 91, p. 155.
5724. SMITH, Lawrence R.
"Pocket Museum." [RiverS] (35) 91, p. 2-3.
"Reservice." [RiverS] (35) 91, p. 1.
5725. SMITH, Macklin
"Airstrip at Alexai Point." [BelPoJ] (41:4) Sum 91, p. 7-8.
"A Mystery." [BelPoJ] (41:4) Sum 91, p. 4.
"A Snowy Owl with a Norway Rat." [BelPoJ] (41:4) Sum 91, p. 5-7.
5726. SMITH, Margaret D.
"Alfalfa." [BellR] (14:1) Spr 91, p. 29.
"Garden." [ChrC] (108:18) 29 My-5 Je 91, p. 592.
5727. SMITH, Michael
"Thanksgiving 1990" (A Plainsongs Award Poem). [Plain] (11:3) Spr 91, p. 4.
5728. SMITH, Michael C.
"Homage." [SenR] (21:1) Spr 91, p. 56-57.
5729. SMITH, Pat
"My Uncle's Name Is Jim Crow." [SoDakR] (29:3 part 2) Aut 91, p. 37.
5730. SMITH, R. T.
"Approach." [CreamCR] (14:2) Wint 91, p. 129.
"By the Book." [TexasR] (12:3/4) Fall-Wint 91, p. 87.
"Distaff." [LullwaterR] (2:2) Spr 91, p. 14.
"Emily's Armistice." [Chelsea] (51) 91, p. 68.
"Ghost Dance." [SouthernPR] (31:2) Fall 91, p. 58-59.
"Gristle and Heron." [Poetry] (158:2) My 91, p. 72.
"Gristlewolf." [Poetry] (158:2) My 91, p. 74-75.
"Hunter-Gatherer." [GeoR] (45:4) Wint 91, p. 762-766.
"In Harvest Season" (Sam Ragan Prize, 1991 Literary Contest). [Crucible] (27) Fall
91, p. 4-5.
"Life List." [PoetC] (23:1) Fall 91, p. 12-13.
"Like Lucifer." [TexasR] (12:3/4) Fall-Wint 91, p. 88.
"St. Gristle Nocturne." [Poetry] (158:2) My 91, p. 73.
"The Uses of Enchantment." [PoetC] (23:1) Fall 91, p. 11.
5731. SMITH, Robert Lavett
"A Letter to Meg in New York." [Vis] (36) 91, p. 31.
"Premonitions." [HawaiiR] (16:1, #34) Wint 91-92, p. 20.
"Saint Jerome and the Skull." [HiramPoR] (50) Spr-Sum 91, p. 23.
"The Unfinished Throne." [HawaiiR] (16:1, #34) Wint 91-92, p. 19.
5732. SMITH, Russell
"The Mongoose Letters." [Event] (20:2) Sum 91, p. 45-52.
5733. SMITH, Thomas R.
"The Water Tank." [HighP] (6:3) Wint 91, p. 121.
5734. SMITH, Tom
"Submarine." [BelPoJ] (42:2) Wint 91-92, p. 34-35.
"Weathervane and Butterfly." [BelPoJ] (42:2) Wint 91-92, p. 33-34.
5735. SMITH, Virgil
"Redsox Retreat / Memorial Stadium, Baltimore — 6/28-30/91." [Spitball] (38) Fall
91, p. 37.
5736. SMITH, William Jay
"Childhood" (tr. of Carlos de Oliveira). [Trans] (25) Spr 91, p. 111.
"Map" (tr. of Carlos de Oliveira). [Trans] (25) Spr 91, p. 112.
"Mildew" (tr. of Carlos de Oliveira). [Trans] (25) Spr 91, p. 113.
"Muriel" (from "Toda a Terra," 1976, tr. of Roy Belo). [Trans] (25) Spr 91, p.
76-79.
"Psalm" (tr. of Carlos de Oliveira). [Trans] (25) Spr 91, p. 113.
5737. SMITH, Willie
"Out to Lunch." [PoetryUSA] (23) Sum 91, p. 19.
5738. SMITH-BOWERS, Cathy
"The Compass." [NewEngR] (13:3/4) Spr-Sum 91, p. 137-138.
"The Love." [GeoR] (45:2) Sum 91, p. 261-262.
"Men." [KenR] (NS 13:1) Wint 91, p. 172.
"October." [GeoR] (45:3) Fall 91, p. 552-553.
"One Hundred and Ten Degrees." [SouthernPR] (31:2) Fall 91, p. 61-62.
"Paleolithic." [SouthernPR] (31:2) Fall 91, p. 60-61.
"Third Floor West." [NewEngR] (13:3/4) Spr-Sum 91, p. 138.

5739. SMITHER, Elizabeth
"Lake Thoughts" (for Allen and Jeny). [Verse] (8:2) Sum 91, p. 35.
"Time, When You Write" (For Allen and Jeny). [Verse] (8:2) Sum 91, p. 34.
5740. SMITS, Ronald (Ronald F.)
"The Adderstongue at Watson's Run." [InterPR] (17:1) Spr 91, p. 122.
"Black Rocks." [Journal] (15:2) Fall 91, p. 23.
"Mating." [InterPR] (17:1) Spr 91, p. 121.
"Natural Science." [PoetL] (86:4) Wint 91-92, p. 45.
"Origins." [MidwQ] (33:1) Aut 91, p. 57.
"Tootsie." [PoetC] (23:1) Fall 91, p. 22-23.
"Wolf Creek." [MidwQ] (33:1) Aut 91, p. 56.
"Word Perfect." [CapeR] (26:2) Fall 91, p. 3.
5741. SMOCK, Ann
"Poèmes de Samuel Wood" (Excerpt, tr. of Louis-René Des Forêts). [Talisman] (6)
Spr 91, p. 82-85.
5742. SMOCK, Frederick
"St. Osyth, Abandoned by Her Husband on Their Wedding Night" (martyred 675?).
[Boulevard] (6:2/3, #17/18) Fall 91, p. 170.
5743. SNEEDEN, Ralph G.
"Cow's Neck." [SycamoreR] (3:1) Wint 91, p. 21-22.
5744. SNEFF, Priscilla
"Once More with Spirit." [Timbuktu] (6) Spr 91, p. 103.
5745. SNEYD, Steve
"Gates of Mars" (from "Bad News from the Stars"). [Bogg] (64) 91, p. 6.
"Moving Target Country." [Bogg] (64) 91, p. 19.
"You Owe It to the Profession" (from "Bad News from the Stars"). [Bogg] (64) 91,
p. 6.
5746. SNIVELY, Susan
"Algebra." [Shen] (41:3) Fall 91, p. 47.
"Roof Life." [Shen] (41:3) Fall 91, p. 48-50.
5747. SNODGRASS, W. D.
"Anniversary Verses for My Oldest Wife." [SouthernR] (27:3) Jl 91, p. 502.
"Birds Caught, Birds Flying." [SewanR] (99:2) Spr 91, p. 189-190.
"An Envoi, Post-TURP." [SouthernR] (27:3) Jl 91, p. 504.
"The Girl Outside Your Window." [SouthernR] (27:3) Jl 91, p. 498-500.
"In Flower." [SouthernR] (27:3) Jl 91, p. 500-502.
"Matona, Mia Cara" (tr. of Orlando di Lasso). [Poetry] (157:5) F 91, p. 270-271.
"Old Apple Trees." [SouthernR] (27:3) Jl 91, p. 515-516.
"An Old Flame." [SouthernR] (27:3) Jl 91, p. 503.
"Owls." [SouthernR] (27:3) Jl 91, p. 512.
"Somnambulist Ballad" (tr. of Federico García Lorca). [Poetry] (157:5) F 91, p.
271-273.
"Summer Sequence." [SouthernR] (27:3) Jl 91, p. 491-498.
"Versions." [SewanR] (99:2) Spr 91, p. 191-193.
5748. SNOTHERLY, Mary C.
"The Story of the Plates and other Stories." [Pembroke] (23) 91, p. 75.
"Toward Short Off Mountain" (for John Marion Mull, First Prize, 1991 Literary
Contest). [Crucible] (27) Fall 91, p. 1.
"Visibility Zero" (First Prize, 1991 Literary Contest). [Crucible] (27) Fall 91, p. 2.
5749. SNOW, Carol
"Asides." [Antaeus] (67) Fall 91, p. 178-179.
"Mourner's *Kasen* (Mourner's Series)" (for Kaela Petrov-Levine, 1920-1987).
[Pequod] (32) 91, p. 21-26.
5750. SNOW, Edward
"Fragments from Lost Days" (tr. of R. M. Rilke). [MassR] (32:2) Sum 91, p.
220-221.
"The Guardian Angel" (tr. of R. M. Rilke). [MassR] (32:2) Sum 91, p. 219.
5751. SNOW, Karen
"Poorhouse." [BelPoJ] (42:1) Fall 91, p. 2.
"Transformations — 1934." [BelPoJ] (42:1) Fall 91, p. 3.
5752. SNYDAL, James
"Auden in Oxford Again." [ChironR] (10:4) Wint 91, p. 23.
5753. SNYDER, Bob
"Adventures of Rainy Raincoats." [Epoch] (40:1) 91, p. 16.
"Birdtide." [Epoch] (40:1) 91, p. 17.

398

SNYDER

5754. SNYDER, Emile
"The Archipelago." [Sulfur] (11:1, #28) Spr 91, p. 79-80.
"The Last Image of Grand-Père" (Summer 1939). [OhioR] (47) 91, p. 81.
"A 'Soirée' at Tante Renée's." [OhioR] (47) 91, p. 82-83.
5755. SNYDER, Jennifer
"The Bird Man." [PoetryNW] (32:4) Wint 91-92, p. 33-34.
"Tiny Buddhas." [PoetryNW] (32:4) Wint 91-92, p. 30-33.
5756. SNYDER, Margery
"Comic Dues." [OnTheBus] (8/9) 91, p. 146.
"Vanishing Point." [PoetryUSA] (22) Spr 91, p. 6.
5757. SOBIN, Anthony
"Pregnancy Test." [HawaiiR] (15:2, #32) Spr 91, p. 162-163.
5758. SOBIN, Gustaf
"The Black Stags" (from "Lascaux," tr. of René Char). [Talisman] (6) Spr 91, p. 8.
"Invitation" (tr. of René Char). [Talisman] (6) Spr 91, p. 10.
"One and the Other" (tr. of René Char). [Talisman] (6) Spr 91, p. 8.
"That It Resume" (tr. of René Char). [Talisman] (6) Spr 91, p. 9.
"The Trout" (from "Four Fascinators," tr. of René Char). [Talisman] (6) Spr 91, p. 8.
5759. SOBSEY, Cynthia
"Prozac." [Nimrod] (34:2) Spr-Sum 91, p. 128.
5760. SOCK, Charles
"Sex Addict 2." [JamesWR] (9:1) Fall 91, p. 6.
5761. SOCOLOW, Elizabeth (Elizabeth A.)
"Atlas, or Another Picture of What Keeps the Earth Held Up." [US1] (24/25) Spr 91, p. 22-23.
"Ophelia." [MichQR] (30:1) Wint 91, p. 12-13.
5762. SOIFER, Mark
"Brewster Road." [Parting] (4:1) Sum 91, p. 11.
SOIKU, Shigematsu
See SHIGEMATSU, Soiku
5763. SOITOS, Stephen
"The Kremlin's coffers have nothing left!" (Response to "Save the Clerihew" appeal). [BostonR] (16:5) O 91, p. 24.
"When John Sununu" (Response to "Save the Clerihew" appeal). [BostonR] (16:5) O 91, p. 24.
5764. SOLARI, Rose
"Distances." [PlumR] (1) Spr-Sum 91, p. 55.
5765. SOLDOFSKY, Alan
"Second Growth." [IndR] (14:2) Spr 91, p. 30-31.
5766. SOLENSTEN, John
"Chernobyl." [LakeSR] (25) 91, p. 23.
5767. SOLHEIM, James
"Against Biography." [MissouriR] (14:2) 91, p. 47.
"The Fear-of-Toadstools Lady." [MissouriR] (14:2) 91, p. 42-43.
"On the Logic and Radiation of Our Love." [MissouriR] (14:2) 91, p. 44-46.
"Return of the Fear-of-Toadstools Lady." [MissouriR] (14:2) 91, p. 48-49.
5768. SOLI, Sandra
"Lucy's Poem" (For Lucy, A. Afaremsis). [NegC] (11:1) 91, p. 89-90.
"Tulsa Unrehearsed." [SouthernPR] (31:2) Fall 91, p. 47-49.
5769. SOLJACK, Katie
"Unofficial Visit." [Pearl] (13) Spr-Sum 91, p. 45-46.
5770. SOLLY, Richard
"The General and His Staff." [PoetC] (23:1) Fall 91, p. 35-37.
5771. SOLNICKI, Jill
"An Ant Is Hard to Kill." [AntigR] (84) Wint 91, p. 106.
"The New Moon." [AntigR] (84) Wint 91, p. 107.
"Waving the Flag." [Dandel] (18:1) Spr-Sum 91, p. 33.
5772. SOLOMON, Marvin
"Agee." [WindO] (55) Wint 91-92, p. 45.
"Answering." [Poetry] (158:1) Ap 91, p. 37.
"Barbers." [WindO] (55) Wint 91-92, p. 46.
"Math." [Poetry] (158:1) Ap 91, p. 39.
"One Flu, Over the Cuckoo's Nest." [Interim] (10:2) Fall-Wint 91-92, p. 21.
"People Who Live on the Fringes of Society." [SmPd] (28:2, #82) Spr 91, p. 19-20.
"Remembering and Forgetting." [SmPd] (28:3, #83) Fall 91, p. 23-24.

"Sympathy Note." [Poetry] (158:1) Ap 91, p. 38.
5773. SOLOMON, Sandy
"In the New Country: Cloudy with Sunny Intervals." [SenR] (21:1) Spr 91, p. 60.
"In the New Country: English English, Body English." [SenR] (21:1) Spr 91, p. 61.
5774. SOLOMON, Suzanne A.
"My Love." [NewYorkQ] (46) 91, p. 45-46.
5775. SOLONCHE, J. R.
"Angels." [CumbPR] (11:1) Fall 91, p. 55.
"Jacob and the Angel." [InterPR] (17:2) Fall 91, p. 140-141.
"Prayer for a Friend Who Probably Committed Suicide." [InterPR] (17:2) Fall 91, p.
139-140.
"Winter Letter in Three Sonnets." [CumbPR] (11:1) Fall 91, p. 53-54.
5776. SOLT, John
"I See an Ant Hill, Gaudi Is There" (tr. of Shiraishi Kazuko). [Manoa] (3:2) Fall 91,
p. 183-186.
"Lie" (tr. of Rin Ishigaki). [Manoa] (3:2) Fall 91, p. 32.
"Lover" (tr. of Sachiko Yoshihara). [Manoa] (3:2) Fall 91, p. 31.
5777. SOMERVILLE, Jane
"It Happens." [SoDakR] (29:4) Wint 91, p. 37.
"Stories." [SoDakR] (29:4) Wint 91, p. 35-36.
"The Sweetness of Melodrama." [SoDakR] (29:4) Wint 91, p. 33-34.
5778. SOMLO, Patty
"If She Could Only." [OnTheBus] (8/9) 91, p. 147.
5779. SOMMER, Jason
"In Memoriam Professor Samuel Konefsky." [WebR] (15) Spr 91, p. 8-9.
"Van Gogh's Boots." [WebR] (15) Spr 91, p. 5-7.
5780. SOMMER, Piotr
"A Maple Leaf" (tr. by the author and John Ashbery). [Ploughs] (17:2/3) Fall 91, p.
228.
5781. SONDE, Susan
"Life in the Dead Streets." [NowestR] (29:2) 91, p. 118-119.
"Part of Living Was." [NowestR] (29:2) 91, p. 117.
5782. SONG, Cathy
"At Some Point." [Zyzzyva] (7:3) Fall 91, p. 106-107.
"Christmas Eve." [Poetry] (159:3) D 91, p. 133-134.
"A Conservative View." [MichQR] (30:4) Fall 91, p. 584-586.
"Eat." [Poetry] (159:3) D 91, p. 132.
"Hearts on Ice" (Cambridge, Winter 1982). [Journal] (15:2) Fall 91, p. 79.
"Out of Our Hands" (For Wing Tek Lum). [Poetry] (157:4) Ja 91, p. 199.
"Shrinking the Uterus." [MichQR] (30:4) Fall 91, p. 582-58.
"This Night." [Journal] (15:2) Fall 91, p. 78.
5783. SONIAT, Katherine
"April 7" (for KLH, 1918-1972). [LaurelR] (25:2) Sum 91, p. 53.
"The Blue Book." [MinnR] (NS 37) Fall 91, p. 13-14.
"Brown vs. Board of Education Day." [MinnR] (NS 37) Fall 91, p. 10-11.
"The Butterfly Garden." [Chelsea] (51) 91, p. 74-75.
"Chapel Series" (in memory, for E.M.). [SpiritSH] (56) Spr-Sum 91, p. 2.
"Exact Autumnal Blue." [SpiritSH] (56) Spr-Sum 91, p. 1.
"Fantasia with Love and Death in the Wings." [PraS] (65:3) Fall 91, p. 74-75.
"The Ghost of Sergeant DuBois Speaks of Radical Chic." [MinnR] (NS 36) Spr 91,
p. 17-18.
"Gifts." [AmerS] (60:1) Wint 91, p. 96.
"House of Cards." [Crazy] (41) Wint 91, p. 45-46.
"Last Song." [PraS] (65:3) Fall 91, p. 75-76.
"Mardi Gras Plans, 1699." [RiverS] (35) 91, p. 4-5.
"Offshore." [SpiritSH] (56) Spr-Sum 91, p. 3.
"Oranges and Rum at Noon." [PraS] (65:3) Fall 91, p. 73-74.
"An Outer Display." [ChatR] (11:2) Wint 91, p. 42.
"Polio Summer." [LaurelR] (25:2) Sum 91, p. 53.
"The Priory Garden." [Northeast] (5:4) Sum 91, p. 3.
"Razzy, Dazzy Turns to Jazz, 1900." [GeoR] (45:2) Sum 91, p. 313-314.
"Recovery: For a Child" (for Ashton). [PraS] (65:3) Fall 91, p. 76.
"Sister Madeleine Recalls Tropical White." [Pig] (17) 91, p. 59.
"A Square in Mozambique." [Thrpny] (46) Sum 91, p. 24.
"Taking Possession." [SpiritSH] (56) Spr-Sum 91, p. 4.
"Terrestrial." [GreensboroR] (50) Sum 91, p. 92.

"Terrestrial." [SpiritSH] (56) Spr-Sum 91, p. 3.
"Two Daughters." [Shen] (41:1) Spr 91, p. 88-89.
"Water Translation." [PraS] (65:3) Fall 91, p. 72-73.
"Words the White Man Use." [MinnR] (NS 37) Fall 91, p. 11-12.
5784. SONNENBERG, Ben
"Dis" (for my daughter Emma). [WestHR] (45:3) Aut 91, p. 199.
"Ever and Ever" (for Susan Minot). [WestHR] (45:3) Aut 91, p. 198.
"Kinkajou." [WestHR] (45:3) Aut 91, p. 198.
"Lefkos (Madouri)" (for George Savidis). [WestHR] (45:3) Aut 91, p. 199.
"Proserpina." [WestHR] (45:3) Aut 91, p. 199.
"Trial Goat" (for Lee and Karen Savage). [Nat] (252:21) 3 Je 91, p. 752.
5785. SONNEVI, Goran
"Blue" (tr. by Rika Lesser). [Vis] (37) 91, p. 48.
SORALUZ, Luis Rebaza
See REBAZA-SORALUZ, Luis
5786. SORBY, Angela
"Storm Porch, at Thirteen." [WilliamMR] (29) 91, p. 22.
5787. SORENSEN, Sally Jo
"Her Style." [Poem] (66) N 91, p. 32.
"Mister Varsey." [Poem] (66) N 91, p. 33.
5788. SORESCU, Marin
"About You" (tr. by Adriana Varga and Stuart Friebert). [FourQ] (5:1) Spr 91, p.
58.
"Apparition" (tr. by Adriana Varga and Stuart Friebert). [NoDaQ] (59:1) Wint 91, p.
119-120.
"Beginning's Shudder" (tr. by Adriana Varge and Stuart Friebert). [RiverS] (33) 91,
p. 38.
"Between Sleepers" (Hyena, tr. by Christopher F. Givan). [WebR] (15) Spr 91, p.
28.
"Cabbage Fleas and Crocodiles" (tr. by Adriana Varga and Stuart Friebert). [PassN]
(12:1) Sum 91, p. 27.
"Caravan" (tr. by Adriana Varga and Stuart Friebert). [GrahamHR] (15) Fall 91, p.
95.
"Cognition" (tr. by Gabriela Dragnea and Stuart Friebert). [Aerial] (6/7) 91, p. 82.
"Cunoasterea." [Aerial] (6/7) 91, p. 82.
"Descent" (tr. by Gabriela Dragnea and Stuart Friebert). [PraF] (12:3 #56) Aut 91, p.
52.
"Este Pamint." [RiverS] (33) 91, p. 45.
"Eyelashes" (tr. by Adriana Varga and Stuart Friebert). [GrahamHR] (15) Fall 91, p.
93.
"The Eyes" (tr. by Christopher F. Givan). [WebR] (15) Spr 91, p. 29.
"Fior de Inceput." [RiverS] (33) 91, p. 39.
"Getting Used to Your Name" (tr. by Gabriela Dragnea and Stuart Friebert). [PraS]
(65:3) Fall 91, p. 122.
"The Ground" (tr. by Adam J. Sorkin and Lidia Vianu). [AmerPoR] (20:6) N-D 91,
p. 26.
"Group" (tr. by Adriana Varga and Stuart Friebert). [GrandS] (10:3, #39) 91, p. 51.
"Holy Fire" (tr. by Christopher F. Givan). [WebR] (15) Spr 91, p. 30.
"Horizontal" (tr. by Stuart Friebert). [Field] (44) Spr 91, p. 45.
"I Stopped Right by the Tragic" (tr. by Adriana Varga and Stuart Friebert).
[GrahamHR] (15) Fall 91, p. 94.
"Icarus" (tr. by Adam J. Sorkin and Lidia Vianu). [LitR] (35:1) Fall 91, p. 38.
"Italics Ours" (tr. by Adam J. Sorkin and Lidia Vianu). [LitR] (35:1) Fall 91, p. 37.
"Miracle" (tr. by Gabriela Dragnea and Stuart Friebert). [PraF] (12:3 #56) Aut 91, p.
51.
"My Soul, You're Good at Everything" (tr. by Stuart Friebert). [Field] (44) Spr 91,
p. 46.
"Paianjenul a Ajuns." [RiverS] (33) 91, p. 43.
"The Path" (tr. by Stuart Friebert). [Field] (44) Spr 91, p. 43.
"Peace" (tr. by Adriana Varga and Stuart Friebert). [PraF] (12:3 #56) Aut 91, p. 50.
"Pedestrian" (tr. by Stuart Friebert). [Field] (44) Spr 91, p. 42.
"A Question" (tr. by Adam J. Sorkin and Lidia Vianu). [LitR] (35:1) Fall 91, p. 37.
"Secret Transfusion" (tr. by Adriana Varga and Stuart Friebert). [Os] (32) Spr 91, p.
4.
"Seeing Clearly" (tr. by Stuart Friebert). [Field] (44) Spr 91, p. 44.

"The Spider Arrived" (tr. by Adriana Varge and Stuart Friebert). [RiverS] (33) 91, p. 42.
"Start" (tr. by Stuart Friebert). [CarolQ] (43:3) Spr 91, p. 28-29.
"Studiu." [RiverS] (33) 91, p. 41.
"Study" (tr. by Adriana Varge and Stuart Friebert). [RiverS] (33) 91, p. 40.
"There Is Earth" (tr. by Adriana Varge and Stuart Friebert). [RiverS] (33) 91, p. 44.
"Transfuzie Secreta." [Os] (32) Spr 91, p. 5.
5789. SORKIN, Adam J.
"Breath" (tr. of Daniela Crasnaru, w. Sergiu Celac). [Poetry] (159:1) O 91, p. 28.
"Certainty" (tr. of Ioana Ieronim, w. Sergiu Celac). [LitR] (35:1) Fall 91, p. 34.
"The Ground" (tr. of Marin Sorescu, w. Lidia Vianu). [AmerPoR] (20:6) N-D 91, p. 26.
"Icarus" (tr. of Marin Sorescu, w. Lidia Vianu). [LitR] (35:1) Fall 91, p. 38.
"The Ironical Poet" (tr. of Nicolae Prelipceanu, w. Sergiu Celac). [LitR] (35:1) Fall 91, p. 35-36.
"Italics Ours" (tr. of Marin Sorescu, w. Lidia Vianu). [LitR] (35:1) Fall 91, p. 37.
"Lethal Dose" (tr. of Daniela Crasnaru, w. Sergiu Celac). [Poetry] (159:1) O 91, p. 28.
"Oath of Allegiance" (tr. of Ioana Ieronim, w. Sergiu Celac). [LitR] (35:1) Fall 91, p. 34.
"A Question" (tr. of Marin Sorescu, w. Lidia Vianu). [LitR] (35:1) Fall 91, p. 37.
"So?!" (tr. of Mircea Dinescu, w. Sergiu Celac). [LitR] (35:1) Fall 91, p. 36.
"To Her Highness Our Landlady for a More Just Apportioning of the Body" (tr. of Mircea Dinescu, w. Sergiu Celac). [LitR] (35:1) Fall 91, p. 36.
5790. SORNBERGER, Judith
"Birthstones." [WestB] (29) 91, p. 14-15.
"Field Mouse." [SingHM] (19) 91, p. 109-110.
5791. SORRELL, David
"Another Belief." [PoetL] (86:3) Fall 91, p. 41-42.
5792. SOSEI (monk, ca. 890)
"Poetic justice?" (tr. by Sam Hamill). [ColR] (NS 17:2) Fall-Wint 90, p. 20.
SOSEKI, Natsume
See NATSUME, Soseki
5793. SOSIS, Phil
"The Uninvited Guest." [US1] (24/25) Spr 91, p. 28.
5794. SOTIROV, Vasil
"You Dance Up There" (tr. by William Matthews). [ColR] (NS 18:2) Fall-Wint 91, p. 77.
5795. SOTO, Gary
"The Box Fan." [Poetry] (158:1) Ap 91, p. 7-8.
"Canal." [MichQR] (30:4) Fall 91, p. 631.
"Not Moving." [Poetry] (158:1) Ap 91, p. 8-9.
"Vernon Manor, or Hotelling on the Cheap." [MichQR] (30:4) Fall 91, p. 629-630.
"A Way of Thinking." [ColR] (NS 18:1) Spr-Sum 91, p. 65-66.
"The Wrestler's Heart." [ColR] (NS 18:1) Spr-Sum 91, p. 62-64.
5796. SOULAR, James
"Last Dance of the Chinook A-Go-Go" (for Joe Talan, 228th Avn. Btln., 1st Cav. Div.). [ChironR] (10:1) Spr 91, p. 8.
"Letter to David, Dead These 20 Years." [ChironR] (10:1) Spr 91, p. 9.
"Shadow." [BlackBR] (14) Fall-Wint 91, p. 10-11.
"The Thousand-Yard Stare" (for Mike Lund, medic, veteran). [ChironR] (10:1) Spr 91, p. 8.
5797. SOUSTER, Raymond
"All the Long Way Home" (in memoriam Austin Holmes Souster). [Quarry] (40:1/2) Wint-Spr 91, p. 170-175.
"Men of Ballymena." [Arc] (26) Spr 91, p. 66.
"Winter-Building." [Arc] (26) Spr 91, p. 65.
5798. SOUTH, Karen
"Bone of Wishes." [HampSPR] Wint 91, p. 30.
"Train to New York City." [ManhatPR] (13) [91?], p. 32.
5799. SOUTHGATE, Christopher
"Bad News About a Friend." [SoCoast] (11) Wint 91, p. 17.
5800. SOUTHWICK, Marcia
"The Magic Broom." [NoAmR] (276:3) S 91, p. 48.
"Romance." [SpoonRQ] (16:3/4) Sum-Fall 91, p. 85-86.
"Study Hall." [SpoonRQ] (16:3/4) Sum-Fall 91, p. 87-88.

5801. SOWDER, Michael (Michael D.)
    "Crow." [Poem] (65) My 91, p. 48-49.
    "Learning Names." [SouthernPR] (31:1) Spr 91, p. 65-66.
    "The Man at the Window" (after the film, *Monsieur Hire*). [Poem] (65) My 91, p. 50.

5802. SOYINKA, Wole
    "Doctored Vision." [LitR] (34:4) Sum 91, p. 567-568.

5803. SPACKS, Barry
    "Back in the Widener Reading Room." [ArtfulD] (20/21) 91, p. 78.
    "The Beekeeper." [SouthwR] (76:1) Wint 91, p. 22.
    "The Call." [PoetC] (22:2) Wint 91, p. 21.
    "The Death of Leonardo Vinci." [NoDaQ] (59:1) Wint 91, p. 207.
    "For Maggie, Who Dreams of Houses." [WebR] (15) Spr 91, p. 89.
    "Inventory." [Chelsea] (51) 91, p. 96.
    "Leo" (Freely re-composed from phrases found in Gertrude Stein Raffel's essay "There Once Was a Family Called Stein"). [Interim] (10:1) Spr-Sum 91, p. 45.
    "Lines for a Shakuhatchi Flute." [WebR] (15) Spr 91, p. 89.
    "Pawn." [Chelsea] (51) 91, p. 93.
    "Professors." [WebR] (15) Spr 91, p. 89.
    "A Stranger." [Chelsea] (51) 91, p. 95.
    "Translated from Basho." [WebR] (15) Spr 91, p. 89.
    "The Wordless Body." [Chelsea] (51) 91, p. 94.

5804. SPADY, Susan
    "Underpants." [Calyx] (13:2) Sum 91, p. 10-11.

5805. SPALATIN, Ivana
    "Litany" (For Aphrodite). [Mildred] (4:2/5:1) 91, p. 101-102.

5806. SPANGLE, Douglas
    "August" (Selections: Sections 10, 15). [PaintedHR] (1) Ja 91, p. 22-23.

5807. SPARA, Walter F.
    "Billy Doesn't Know a Hemorrhoid." [EmeraldCR] (4) 91, p. 40.
    "Prophecy of Brooms." [EmeraldCR] (3) 91, c1990, p. 18.

5808. SPAULDING, John
    "In the Woods, 1957." [Iowa] (21:3) Fall 91, p. 194-195.
    "Menu of Head." [Iowa] (21:3) Fall 91, p. 196.
    "Nineteenth-Century Photographs." [Poetry] (158:6) S 91, p. 336-337.
    "Plague Man." [Iowa] (21:3) Fall 91, p. 196.
    "Summer at the Croft." [Iowa] (21:3) Fall 91, p. 194.
    "Waking." [Iowa] (21:3) Fall 91, p. 195.

5809. SPEAKES, Richard
    "Bedtime Story." [RiverC] (12:1) Fall 91, p. 52.
    "Heather, Spring of Her 16th Year." [RiverC] (12:1) Fall 91, p. 50-51.
    "Out Here, Out West." [PassN] (12:1) Sum 91, p. 28.
    "The Past." [RiverC] (12:1) Fall 91, p. 49.
    "Sweet Dreams at the Silver Slipper Tavern." [PassN] (12:1) Sum 91, p. 28.

5810. SPEARS, Heather
    "The Grinding of Teeth." [CanLit] (131) Wint 91, p. 113.

5811. SPECTOR, Al
    "Tileman." [BrooklynR] (8) 91, p. 25.

5812. SPEECE, Merry
    "At Kennonsburg Church." [GreenMR] (NS 5:1) Sum-Fall 91, p. 13.
    "Sweet Face of the Khmer Woman." [GreenMR] (NS 5:1) Sum-Fall 91, p. 11-12.

5813. SPEER, Laurel
    "Alois the Father, Alois Jr. 14, Adolf 7." [PraS] (65:3) Fall 91, p. 22.
    "How Chicky Went Mad and Killed a Monk at Her Father's Funeral." [MassR] (32:3) Fall 91, p. 441.
    "Mock-General." [Kalliope] (13:3) 91, p. 16.
    "My Dear Boy, Under No Circumstance Are You Ever Again to Append." [SenR] (21:1) Spr 91, p. 69.
    "My Father Told Me to Respect Authority." [CoalC] (4) S 91, p. 12.
    "(Throw These English Assholes Out!)" [Bogg] (64) 91, p. 8.
    "Where Is That Unruly Child?" [PraS] (65:3) Fall 91, p. 21.
    "Why Are They Smiling?" [Pearl] (13) Spr-Sum 91, p. 20.

5814. SPELIUS, Carol
    "Change of Life." [Elf] (1:2) Sum 91, p. 42.

5815. SPENCE, Larry D.
    "Crabs eat my sad fish heart." [BlackBR] (14) Fall-Wint 91, p. 8.

5816. SPENCE, Michael
"Below Decks." [SewanR] (99:2) Spr 91, p. 194-195.
"Sand and Blue-Green Algae." [GeoR] (45:2) Sum 91, p. 233-234.
"Why I Couldn't Write a Poem." [BostonR] (16:5) O 91, p. 7.
5817. SPENCER, Linda Moore
"The Sun Will Shift." [PoetryE] (32) Fall 91, p. 129-130.
5818. SPENDER, Stephen
"Four Sketches for Herbert Read." [NorthStoneR] (10) Fall 91-Wint 92, p.
219-220.
"The Generous Days." [NorthStoneR] (10) Fall 91-Wint 92, p. 222-223.
"To W. H. Auden on His Sixtieth Birthday." [NorthStoneR] (10) Fall 91-Wint 92,
p. 221-222.
5819. SPERANZA, Anthony
"The Old Hunter Writes a Letter." [Plain] (11:2) Wint 91, p. 10.
5820. SPHERES, Duane
"Old Beauty." [BellArk] (7:2) Mr-Ap 91, p. 22.
5821. SPICER, Jack
"The dancing ape is whirling round the beds." [PoetryUSA] (23) Sum 91, p. 1.
5822. SPICKERMAN, Frances
"Bullet Track." [CrabCR] (7:2) Sum 91, p. 26.
5823. SPIDEL, Lianne
"Evidence." [Plain] (11:2) Wint 91, p. 27.
"Mayday." [Plain] (11:3) Spr 91, p. 35.
"Mother's Days." [Plain] (12:1) Fall 91, p. 31.
"Wine Tasting." [Kalliope] (13:2) 91, p. 54.
5824. SPIER, Margaret
"What's Required Is." [Plain] (11:3) Spr 91, p. 7.
5825. SPIGLE, Naomi Halperin
"Hyde Park Boulevard: Chicago, 1937" (Honorable Mention, 5th Annual Contest).
[SoCoast] (11) Wint 91, p. 29.
5826. SPILLEBEEN, Willy
"Unanswered" (tr. by Tefke Goldberger). [Vis] (36) 91, p. 24.
5827. SPILLER, Dorothy Trail
"When I Was Seventeen." [PraF] (12:4) Wint 91-92, p. 41.
5828. SPINGARN, Lawrence P.
"Arse Poetica." [Salm] (90/91) Spr-Sum 91, p. 105.
"The Gardens at I Tatti." [Salm] (90/91) Spr-Sum 91, p. 106.
5829. SPIRENG, Matthew J.
"Baron's Death." [WritersF] (17) Fall 91, p. 166.
"Burn Victim." [HiramPoR] (50) Spr-Sum 91, p. 24.
"The Chess Match." [Outbr] (22) 91, p. 27.
"Childhood's Losses." [OxfordM] (7:2) Fall-Wint 91, p. 76.
"Coming Home." [HampSPR] Wint 91, p. 15-16.
"Deformed Chick." [HiramPoR] (50) Spr-Sum 91, p. 24.
"Father's Whiskers." [HampSPR] Wint 91, p. 15.
"Finding Fossils." [Outbr] (22) 91, p. 26.
"Fishing with Father." [Interim] (10:2) Fall-Wint 91-92, p. 14.
"Indian Hill Dig, 1977." [BellR] (14:2) Fall 91, p. 43.
"Missing Fingers." [SpoonRQ] (16:3/4) Sum-Fall 91, p. 76-77.
"Picture Puzzle." [PoetL] (86:2) Sum 91, p. 41.
"September Night." [Plain] (12:2) Wint 91, p. 7.
"Shadows in Time." [OxfordM] (7:2) Fall-Wint 91, p. 75.
"The Skunk." [SpoonRQ] (16:3/4) Sum-Fall 91, p. 78.
"This Attic" (for Lewis Turco). [HolCrit] (28:4) O 91, p. 19.
5830. SPIRO, Barry
"How to Get Good Reception on Your Radio." [ChironR] (10:2) Sum 91, p. 39.
5831. SPIRO, Peter
"The Burial Detail." [CumbPR] (11:1) Fall 91, p. 44-45.
"The Story of Creation Told by St. Louis, the 'Show Me' Saint" (for Miguel
Pinero). [SlipS] (11) 91, p. 76-78.
5832. SPIVACK, Kathleen
"Diamond Jubilee Rose." [ChiR] (37:2/3) 91, p. 46-47.
5833. SPLAKE, T. Kilgore
"Elegy, Edward Abbey." [DustyD] (2:1) Ja 91, p. 16.
"Letter Found in *Dharma Bums*, Strand, New York City." [MoodySI] (24/25/26)
Spr 91, p. 43.

SPLAKE

"Loving." [DustyD] (2:1) Ja 91, p. 24.
"Solstice Finis." [Pearl] (13) Spr-Sum 91, p. 41.
"Untitled Esse." [DustyD] (2:1) Ja 91, p. 20.
"Why Writers Drink." [Pearl] (13) Spr-Sum 91, p. 41.

5834. SPOONER, Michael
"Saturday Matinee, Box Seats." [SpoonRQ] (16:1/2) Wint-Spr 91, p. 40.
"Winter." [SpoonRQ] (16:1/2) Wint-Spr 91, p. 39.

5835. SPRINGER, Christina
"Wishlist" (for my sisters who think process is permanent). [SinW] (43/44) Sum 91,
p. 214-215.

5836. SPRINGER, Ken
"Spirit." [CimR] (96) Jl 91, p. 127-128.

5837. SPROLES, Karyn
"Divorce." [NorthStoneR] (10) Fall 91-Wint 92, p. 16.

5838. SPRUNT, Haines
"For the Album." [Shen] (41:2) Sum 91, p. 107.
"Waxing." [Shen] (41:2) Sum 91, p. 103-106.

5839. SPRYSZAK, Bob
"Freeze the Beat." [SlipS] (11) 91, p. 24.

5840. SQUIER, J. C.
"Untitled: In the Universe." [ChironR] (10:3) Aut 91, p. 48.

5841. SRYGLEY, Carolyn
"Pastel #2, 6/88." [AntR] (49:4) Fall 91, p. 558.

ST. . . .
See also Saint . . .

5842. ST. ANDREWS, B. A.
"The Hammock Report." [SpoonRQ] (16:3/4) Sum-Fall 91, p. 92-93.
"In the School of the Buddha." [ChamLR] (8-9) Spr-Fall 91, p. 150-151.
"The Isenheim Altarpiece." [ChatR] (11:2) Wint 91, p. 34-36.
"Loveland." [ChamLR] (8-9) Spr-Fall 91, p. 152.
"Night Mail." [HawaiiR] (15:2, #32) Spr 91, p. 12.
"Rhythms for Otis Redding." [ChamLR] (8-9) Spr-Fall 91, p. 146-147.
"Sit Down, Socrates." [ChamLR] (8-9) Spr-Fall 91, p. 148-149.
"Topography: The Brain Scan." [ParisR] (33:121) Wint 91, p. 45-47.

5843. ST. CLAIR, Philip
"Accidents." [MinnR] (NS 37) Fall 91, p. 43.
"The Campground of Eternal Peace." [Shen] (41:2) Sum 91, p. 30-31.
"Menace from Space." [Shen] (41:2) Sum 91, p. 31-32.
"Nancy: August 1916" (from Part Five of Vicksburg: a Civil War narrative).
[ContextS] (2:1) 91, p. 15-16.
"Nancy: March 1881" (from Part Five of Vicksburg: a Civil War narrative).
[ContextS] (2:1) 91, p. 14-15.
"Nancy: October 1878" (from Part Five of Vicksburg: a Civil War narrative).
[ContextS] (2:1) 91, p. 13-14.

5844. ST. GEORGE, Elyse Yates
"Daft Molly Metcalf." [Arc] (26) Spr 91, p. 9.

5845. ST. GERMAIN, Sheryl
"Alcoholic." [SpoonRQ] (16:1/2) Wint-Spr 91, p. 104-105.
"August Fire." [Calyx] (13:2) Sum 91, p. 16.
"Deathbed." [MidAR] (11:2) 91, p. 128.
"Mother's Red Beans and Rice." [TriQ] (81) Spr-Sum 91, p. 215-216.
"Ode to Caffeine." [TexasR] (12:1/2) Spr-Sum 91, p. 125.
"Streetlamps for Moons." [CimR] (94) Ja 91, p. 107.
"Too Late, for My Fingers." [CimR] (94) Ja 91, p. 105-106.

5846. ST. JOHN, David
"The Avenue of Limes." [CarolQ] (43:2) Wint 91, p. 37.
"Los Angeles, 1954." [DenQ] (25:3) Wint 91, p. 21-23.
"Lucifer in Starlight." [DenQ] (25:3) Wint 91, p. 24-26.
"My Friend." [AmerPoR] (20:3) My-Je 91, p. 24.
"Tears Before Their Time." [CarolQ] (43:2) Wint 91, p. 38.
"To Pasolini." [Pequod] (32) 91, p. 12-19.

5847. ST-JACQUES, Jacqueline
"Mater Dolorosa." [PraF] (12:1 #54) Spr 91, p. 68.

5848. STAAL, Arie
"Love" (tr. of Paul Rodenko). [Vis] (36) 91, p. 25.

5849. STAFFORD, Darrell
    "Backyard Grill." [SouthernPR] (31:1) Spr 91, p. 9.
    "Deconstruction." [SouthernR] (27:2) Ap 91, p. 303-304.
5850. STAFFORD, William
    "Afterwards." [TarRP] (31:1) Fall 91, p. 20.
    "At the Edge." [PaintedHR] (1) Ja 91, p. 10.
    "At the Grave of My Brother: Bomber Pilot." [MichQR] (30:2) Spr 91, p. 290.
    "Choosing a Dog." [TarRP] (31:1) Fall 91, p. 19.
    "A Denial." [CharR] (17:1) Spr 91, p. 118.
    "A Few Words from the Little Woman." [AmerS] (60:2) Spr 91, p. 198.
    "Fixers." [TarRP] (31:1) Fall 91, p. 21.
    "For our Party Last Night." [Nimrod] (34:2) Spr-Sum 91, p. 4.
    "A Glimpse: Age 5." [SycamoreR] (3:2) Sum 91, p. 23.
    "How I Endured." [Field] (45) Fall 91, p. 86.
    "How to Be Lucky" (for Leslie Norris). [TarRP] (31:1) Fall 91, p. 18.
    "Influential Writers." [WillowS] (27) Wint 91, p. 57.
    "Learning to Adjust." [Nimrod] (34:2) Spr-Sum 91, p. 5.
    "Living Out Here." [SoDakR] (29:3 part 2) Aut 91, p. 56.
    "Me." [PlumR] (1) Spr-Sum 91, p. 22.
    "Men." [CharR] (17:1) Spr 91, p. 119.
    "On the Bookrack at Corner Drugs." [Field] (45) Fall 91, p. 87.
    "One Good Thing." [TarRP] (31:1) Fall 91, p. 18.
    "A Proposition." [WillowS] (27) Wint 91, p. 56.
    "Right to Die." [MichQR] (30:2) Spr 91, p. 291.
    "Slide Show." [CharR] (17:1) Spr 91, p. 117.
    "Toward the End." [Nimrod] (34:2) Spr-Sum 91, p. 7.
    "Tragedy." [AmerS] (60:2) Spr 91, p. 197.
    "Walking in the Morning." [CreamCR] (14:2) Wint 91, p. 9.
    "The Way I Write." [Writer] (104:5) My 91, p. 11.
    "What We Learned in Kansas." [Nimrod] (34:2) Spr-Sum 91, p. 6.
5851. STAHL, Dick
    "Planting Luck." [Farm] (8:1) Spr-Sum 91, p. 95.
5852. STALEY, Harry
    "Early Gothic." [SnailPR] (1:1) Spr 91, p. 23.
    "Flesh in the Pantheon." [SnailPR] (1:1) Spr 91, p. 24.
5853. STALLWORTHY, Jon
    "The Girl from Zlot" (for Jade Drysz). [Ploughs] (17:1) Spr 91, p. 168-176.
5854. STALLWORTHY, Robert
    "Custodial Care." [PottPort] (13:2) Fall-Wint 91, p. 54.
    "Physician Heal Thyself." [PottPort] (13:2) Fall-Wint 91, p. 55-56.
5855. STAMP, Stephen
    "My Grass." [Grain] (19:1) Spr 91, p. 110.
    "Slug Dance." [Grain] (19:1) Spr 91, p. 109.
5856. STANDING, Sue
    "How to Ballroom Dance." [GrahamHR] (15) Fall 91, p. 71.
5857. STANDISH, Lorraine
    "A Plethora of Blackbirds." [EmeraldCR] (3) 91, c1990, p. 60.
5858. STANDLEY, Gerald
    "Agitation" (tr. of Renalto Caldas). [InterPR] (17:1) Spr 91, p. 39.
    "Confession" (tr. of Renalto Caldas). [InterPR] (17:1) Spr 91, p. 41.
    "Dawn in the Backlands" (tr. of Renalto Caldas). [InterPR] (17:1) Spr 91, p. 37.
    "Flower of the Mato" (tr. of Renalto Caldas). [InterPR] (17:1) Spr 91, p. 37.
    "My Little House" (tr. of Renalto Caldas). [InterPR] (17:1) Spr 91, p. 45.
    "The Oath" (tr. of Renalto Caldas). [InterPR] (17:1) Spr 91, p. 43, 45.
5859. STANFORD, Frank
    "Death and Memory." [NewEngR] (13:3/4) Spr-Sum 91, p. 87-88.
    "The Kite." [NewEngR] (13:3/4) Spr-Sum 91, p. 88-89.
    "Sun Go Down." [NewEngR] (13:3/4) Spr-Sum 91, p. 89-90.
5860. STANHOPE, Patrick
    "Jesse James at the Apollo." [WebR] (15) Spr 91, p. 103-105.
    "Letter to Steven." [WebR] (15) Spr 91, p. 106-107.
5861. STANIEWSKA, Góska A.
    "XXX" (3 poems, tr. of Artur Przystupa, w. Chris Hurford and Tomek Kitlinski).
        [Verse] (8:2) Sum 91, p. 119-120.
5862. STANIZZI, John L.
    "Drink." [Spirit] (11) 91, p. 39-40.

5863. STANKO, Mary Rudbeck
"Matter of Fact." [ChironR] (10:2) Sum 91, p. 41.
"Public Face." [Plain] (12:2) Wint 91, p. 32.
"Rhonchus Rogue." [Comm] (118:7) 5 Ap 91, p. 227.
"Thoughts from a Rocking Horse." [Comm] (118:4) 22 F 91, p. 131.
"Transition." [Comm] (118:2) 25 Ja 91, p. 49.
"The Value of Zero." [Comm] (118:7) 5 Ap 91, p. 224.
5864. STANLEY, Jean
"Embryo." [CreamCR] (15:1) Spr 91, p. 72.
5865. STANLEY, Jennifer
"Girl with Gonorrhea." [AmerPoR] (20:4) Jl-Ag 91, p. 45.
"In Answer to My Name-calling Lover." [AmerPoR] (20:4) Jl-Ag 91, p. 45.
5866. STANTON, Joseph
"Ahead." [PoetryE] (31) Spr 91, p. 23.
"Brazilian Cardinals." [BambooR] (52) Fall 91, p. 107-109.
"Bruegel's *The Dark Day*." [ChamLR] (8-9) Spr-Fall 91, p. 80-81.
"Edward Hopper's *Room in Brooklyn*." [ChamLR] (8-9) Spr-Fall 91, p. 78-79.
"A Field Guide to the Wildlife of Suburban O'ahu." [HawaiiR] (15:3, #33) Fall 91,
p. 2-6.
"Golden Plovers." [HawaiiR] (15:3, #33) Fall 91, p. 7-8.
"Stan, the Man." [Spitball] (39) Wint 91, p. 17.
5867. STANTON, Maura
"Mis-Diagnosis." [Poetry] (158:1) Ap 91, p. 29.
"Number Seventeen." [Ploughs] (17:2/3) Fall 91, p. 175-176.
"A Portrait by Bronzino." [AmerPoR] (20:3) My-Je 91, p. 21.
"Train." [AmerPoR] (20:3) My-Je 91, p. 20.
"The Veiled Lady." [AmerPoR] (20:3) My-Je 91, p. 22.
5868. STARBUCK, George
"Cargo Cult of the Solstice at Hadrian's Wall." [Harp] (282:1688) Ja 91, p. 43.
5869. STARGER, Lisa
"Dorothy in Kansas Some Years Later." [Archae] (2) Spr 91, p. 18.
5870. STARKE, Anthony
"I Fear My Own Forgetting." [Chelsea] (52) 91, p. 86.
5871. STARKEY, David
"The Girl in the Box." [CimR] (95) Ap 91, p. 54.
"Historic American Lighthouses: Limited Edition." [OxfordM] (7:2) Fall-Wint 91, p.
18-19.
"Idyll." [CutB] (35) Wint-Spr 91, p. 89.
"Neighbors." [Pearl] (14) Fall-Wint 91, p. 13.
"New Year's Eve" (for John Elrod). [BellArk] (7:6) N-D 91, p. 10.
"Note of Thanks" (After Li Po). [Pearl] (14) Fall-Wint 91, p. 13.
"Star of Bethlehem." [GreensboroR] (51) Wint 91-92, p. 121-122.
"The U.S.A. School of Writing" (After the essay by Elizabeth Bishop). [Plain]
(12:2) Wint 91, p. 31.
"The Vagrant Martha's Benediction Upon Suburbia." [PoetL] (86:3) Fall 91, p. 43.
5872. STARR, Jean
"Litany to the Winds." [PoetryE] (32) Fall 91, p. 7-8.
5873. STAUDT, David
"Night in the Box" (to the crew of USS Lewis B. Puller, 1987-1991).
[GreensboroR] (51) Wint 91-92, p. 92-93.
"Rattlesnake." [GreensboroR] (51) Wint 91-92, p. 91.
5874. STEARNS, Laura
"Signals." [CutB] (36) Sum 91, p. 70-72.
"Sleeping Sickness." [CutB] (36) Sum 91, p. 68-69.
5875. STEDLER, Harding
"Rush of the Forty-Niner." [InterPR] (17:1) Spr 91, p. 111.
5876. STEDMAN, Judy
"Leading the Blind." [NewYorkQ] (46) 91, p. 72.
5877. STEELE, Colin
"Arbitrary Graveyard Blues." [PraF] (12:1 #54) Spr 91, p. 80-81.
5878. STEELE, Julia
"Sugar." [WestCL] (25:2, #5) Fall 91, p. 42-44.
5879. STEELE, Marian
"Chronos." [SoDakR] (29:4) Wint 91, p. 24.
"Sameness." [SoDakR] (29:4) Wint 91, p. 25.

5880. STEELE, Timothy
    "Georgics." [Zyzzyva] (7:1) Spr 91, p. 71.
    "A Shore." [Zyzzyva] (7:1) Spr 91, p. 69.
5881. STEELE, Tony
    "The Sage." [PraF] (12:3 #56) Aut 91, p. 53.
5882. STEFANESCU, Chrisula
    "About the Country We Come From" (tr. of Ana Blandiana, w. Inta Moriss-Wiest).
        [Iowa] (21:2) Spr-Sum 91, p. 41.
    "The Children's Crusade" (tr. of Ana Blandiana, w. Inta Moriss-Wiest). [Iowa]
        (21:2) Spr-Sum 91, p. 41.
    "Everything" (tr. of Ana Blandiana, w. Inta Moriss-Wiest). [Iowa] (21:2) Spr-Sum
        91, p. 42.
    "Humility" (tr. of Ana Blandiana, w. Inta Moriss-Wiest). [Iowa] (21:2) Spr-Sum 91,
        p. 40.
    "Links" (tr. of Ana Blandiana, w. Inta Moriss-Wiest). [Iowa] (21:2) Spr-Sum 91, p.
        40.
    "Magic Spell of Rain" (tr. of Ana Blandiana, w. Inta Moriss-Wiest). [Iowa] (21:2)
        Spr-Sum 91, p. 39.
    "Vanity" (tr. by the author, w. Emily Chalmers). [Iowa] (21:2) Spr-Sum 91, p. 43.
5883. STEFANILE, Felix
    "Elegy 1942" (Fort Devens, Massachusetts). [Sparrow] (58) Jl 91, p. 25-26.
    "If I Were Fire" (tr. of Cecco Angiolieri). [Hellas] (2:1) Spr 91, p. 65.
    "Lotos-Land: Odysseus." [Hellas] (2:1) Spr 91, p. 64.
5884. STEFANILE, Selma
    "Writing Van Gogh" (after reading his letters). [Sparrow] (58) Jl 91, p. 21.
    "Writing Van Gogh 2." [Sparrow] (58) Jl 91, p. 21-22.
    "Writing Van Gogh 3." [Sparrow] (58) Jl 91, p. 22.
5885. STEFFEN, Mary
    "Night Drive." [MidAR] (12:1) 91, p. 113-114.
5886. STEFFENS, Bradley
    "Checker." [Sidewalks] (1) Aug 91, p. 30.
    "Driving Through Yellowstone at Midnight." [BellR] (14:2) Fall 91, p. 33.
    "Sub-Zero Christmas Day." [Sidewalks] (1) Aug 91, p. 30-31.
5887. STEIN, Agnes
    "Elegy" (tr. of Gunter Kunert). [ColR] (NS 18:2) Fall-Wint 91, p. 89.
    "Limited Light" (tr. of Sarah Kirsch). [Verse] (8:2) Sum 91, p. 119.
    "Warmth of Snow" (tr. of Sarah Kirsch). [Verse] (8:2) Sum 91, p. 118.
    "Wind-Lament Rain-Delusion" (tr. of Stephan Doring). [QW] (32) Wint-Spr 91, p.
        96.
5888. STEIN, Alice P.
    "Poetic License." [Pearl] (13) Spr-Sum 91, p. 49.
5889. STEIN, Charles
    "Magic Topics 1" (from "theforestforthetrees"). [Notus] (9) Fall 91, p. 74-78.
5890. STEIN, Dona Luongo
    "Confess." [Journal] (15:2) Fall 91, p. 73-74.
    "Evasions." [Journal] (15:2) Fall 91, p. 75-76.
    "Ivy." [Journal] (15:2) Fall 91, p. 77.
    "Spring Semester." [PraS] (65:4) Wint 91, p. 129-130.
5891. STEIN, Donna Baier
    "Fishing for Octopus in Leonidion." [PoetL] (86:2) Sum 91, p. 25-26.
    "La Secheresse." [CarolQ] (43:2) Wint 91, p. 39-40.
    "Watchman of the Night." [BelPoJ] (41:3) Spr 91, p. 10-11.
5892. STEIN, Hadassah
    "Raking Leaves." [SoDakR] (29:3 part 2) Aut 91, p. 69.
5893. STEIN, Hannah
    "Messenger." [CalQ] (35/36) 91, p. 86.
    "Reading the Reflections Backward." [CalQ] (35/36) 91, p. 87-88.
5894. STEIN, Jill
    "Pregnancy." [US1] (24/25) Spr 91, p. 16-17.
5895. STEIN, Joyce
    "Names." [OnTheBus] (8/9) 91, p. 148.
5896. STEIN, Kevin
    "Allowances." [PoetryNW] (32:1) Spr 91, p. 20-21.
    "A Circus of Want." [PoetryNW] (32:1) Spr 91, p. 21-22.
    "Creatures Who Must Know Better Have Taken Me for a Blossom." [KenR] (NS
        13:2) Spr 91, p. 122-123.

"In Love with a Middle-Aged Woman." [PoetryNW] (32:1) Spr 91, p. 19-20.
"A White Lie of Sorrow and Comfort." [QW] (32) Wint-Spr 91, p. 94-95.
5897. STEIN, Michael
"The Clothesline." [CharR] (17:1) Spr 91, p. 98.
"Leaving the Barber." [CharR] (17:1) Spr 91, p. 99.
5898. STEINGASS, David
"Picnic in the Lake." [NoDaQ] (59:3) Sum 91, p. 109-110.
5899. STEINGESSER, Martin
"The Disappeared." [ManhatPR] (13) [91?], p. 7.
"Fishing." [AmerPoR] (20:4) Jl-Ag 91, p. 19.
5900. STEINGRABER, Sandra
"Courtroom." [SpoonRQ] (16:1/2) Wint-Spr 91, p. 83-84.
"Custody." [SpoonRQ] (16:1/2) Wint-Spr 91, p. 77-79.
"Extent of the Damage." [SpoonRQ] (16:1/2) Wint-Spr 91, p. 75-76.
"Field." [SpoonRQ] (16:1/2) Wint-Spr 91, p. 88-90.
"Funeral Service for Abbie Hoffman." [SpoonRQ] (16:1/2) Wint-Spr 91, p. 85-87.
"Lecture for a Large Auditorium." [SpoonRQ] (16:1/2) Wint-Spr 91, p. 73-74.
"Manual for the Village Health Worker." [SpoonRQ] (16:1/2) Wint-Spr 91, p.
    81-82.
"Water Over Road." [SpoonRQ] (16:1/2) Wint-Spr 91, p. 80.
5901. STEINKE, René
"Kinsey Hall Burns Down." [CreamCR] (15:1) Spr 91, p. 50.
5902. STEINMAN, Lisa M.
"Small Song for a Sick Friend." [PaintedHR] (2) Spr 91, p. 9.
STELBACH, Marjorie
    See STELMACH, Marjorie
5903. STELMACH, Marjorie
"After Her Death." [Ascent] (15:2) Wint 91, p. 34.
"Ahead of All Partings." [SouthernPR] (31:1) Spr 91, p. 17-18.
5904. STEPANCHEV, Stephen
"Cornered on the Corner." [NewYorker] (67:28) 2 S 91, p. 32.
"November." [Poetry] (159:2) N 91, p. 87.
"To Be." [Confr] (46/47) Fall 91-Wint 92, p. 253.
5905. STEPEK, Peter
"Estuary" (First Prize). [HarvardA] (125:4) Mr 91, p. 36-37.
5906. STEPHENS, Jim
"Adventures at the Ridges Sanctuary." [Abraxas] (40/41) 91, p. 145.
"Friend Spirit Cottonwood." [Abraxas] (40/41) 91, p. 144.
5907. STEPHENS, Michael
"Hong's Geese." [OntR] (34) Spr-Sum 91, p. 19-20.
5908. STEPHENSON, Lois
"Biker." [PacificR] (10) 91-92, p. 93-94.
5909. STEPTO, Gabriel
"Angels." [Callaloo] (14:4) Fall 91, p. 908.
"Saint Paul." [Callaloo] (14:4) Fall 91, p. 907.
5910. STEPTOE, Lamont B.
"Ambush." [ChironR] (10:1) Spr 91, p. 6.
"Burning Waters." [ChironR] (10:1) Spr 91, p. 6.
"Mad Minute." [ChironR] (10:1) Spr 91, p. 6.
"No One Stays." [ChironR] (10:1) Spr 91, p. 6.
"Parts." [ChironR] (10:1) Spr 91, p. 6.
"Returning the Missing." [ChironR] (10:1) Spr 91, p. 6.
5911. STERLING, Phillip
"The Voice [Re]Discovers Evolution." [PassN] (12:1) Sum 91, p. 9.
5912. STERN, Gerald
"The Eyes Are Always Brown." [GettyR] (4:4) Aut 91, p. 614-615.
"Her Right Eye Catches the Lavender" (for Judy Rock). [AmerPoR] (20:6) N-D 91,
    p. 60.
"Ukrainian" (for Robin Beeman). [GettyR] (4:4) Aut 91, p. 616.
"What It Is Like." [NewYorker] (67:22) 22 Jl 91, p. 34.
5913. STERN, Joan
"Fragments." [PoetC] (22:2) Wint 91, p. 11-12.
"Skeletons in the Closet" (A Plainsongs Award Poem). [Plain] (11:2) Wint 91, p.
    38.
5914. STERN, Robert
"Oskar Hoffmann in Siena." [AntigR] (85/86) Spr-Sum 91, p. 212-213.

"Santa Margherita." [AntigR] (85/86) Spr-Sum 91, p. 214.
5915. STERNBERG, Ricardo
"A Pelican in the Wilderness." [CanLit] (128) Spr 91, p. 105-106.
5916. STETLER, Charles
"Becoming a Long Beach Boy." [WormR] (31:1, #121) 91, p. 10.
"The Cat on Kilimanjaro." [WormR] (31:1, #121) 91, p. 12.
"Hit in the Head." [WormR] (31:1, #121) 91, p. 11-12.
"A Slide into the Pacific." [WormR] (31:1, #121) 91, p. 11.
5917. STEVENS, A. Wilber
"The Moth." [LaurelR] (25:1) Wint 91, p. 100.
5918. STEVENS, C. J.
"Clear" (tr. of Ellen Warmond). [NewRena] (8:2, #25) Fall 91, p. 67.
"Roentgenology" (tr. of Ellen Warmond). [NewRena] (8:2, #25) Fall 91, p. 63.
"Small Barbarism" (tr. of Ellen Warmond). [NewRena] (8:2, #25) Fall 91, p. 65.
5919. STEVENS, Geoff
"Call of the Wild." [CoalC] (3) My 91, p. 3.
"Outskirts." [CoalC] (4) S 91, p. 13.
5920. STEVENS, J. R.
"Hair Cut." [AntigR] (84) Wint 91, p. 99-100.
"Matinee." [AntigR] (84) Wint 91, p. 101-102.
5921. STEVENS, Jim
"Gravestone Found in a Garage" (Effie A. Holt, Born March 11, 1891, Died July 3,
1894). [SoDakR] (29:2) Sum 91, p. 170-172.
"Narrative." [SoDakR] (29:2) Sum 91, p. 173.
"The Sounds of Summer." [Arc] (27) Aut 91, p. 26.
5922. STEVENS, May
"For My Loves, Lost and Leaving." [Nimrod] (34:2) Spr-Sum 91, p. 3.
5923. STEVENS, Myles
"There's Nothing." [PoetryUSA] (22) Spr 91, p. 22.
5924. STEVENS, Peter
"Among Students." [PoetryC] (12:1) D 91, p. 11.
"Noblesse Oblige" (for Harry Annan and Duke Ellington). [PoetryC] (12:1) D 91, p.
11.
5925. STEVENSON, Richard
"Getting Away from It All." [AntigR] (85/86) Spr-Sum 91, p. 236.
"This Is Just to Say" (in memoriam, Harold D.). [AntigR] (85/86) Spr-Sum 91, p.
237.
5926. STEVER, Edward William
"Chin Up." [ChironR] (10:3) Aut 91, p. 15.
"The Finger." [ChironR] (10:3) Aut 91, p. 15.
"Freudian Field Day." [ChironR] (10:3) Aut 91, p. 15.
"Show and Tell." [ChironR] (10:3) Aut 91, p. 15.
5927. STEVICK, Mark
"Three Times Round." [SmPd] (28:2, #82) Spr 91, p. 32.
5928. STEWARD, D. E.
"Abril." [NoDaQ] (59:4) Fall 91, p. 135-141.
"August." [NoDaQ] (59:2) Spr 91, p. 161-169.
"Juin." [Chelsea] (52) 91, p. 108-115.
"Julio." [CentralP] (19/20) Spr-Fall 91, p. 123-129.
5929. STEWART, Caroline
"The Kennel Club" (after Robert Browning's "Soliloquy in a Spanish Courtyard").
[EmeraldCR] (3) 91, c1990, p. 123-124.
"The Witches of Bovary Park." [EmeraldCR] (3) 91, c1990, p. 123.
5930. STEWART, Dolores
"Gyfu, the Letter G, Rune of Polarity, Partnership, and Gifts." [Chelsea] (52) 91, p.
82-83.
"Peordh, the Letter P, rune of the Dice Cup, Divination, and Finding What Is Lost."
[Chelsea] (52) 91, p. 84.
"Wynn, the Letter W, Rune of Joy and Illumination." [Chelsea] (52) 91, p. 85.
5931. STEWART, Jack
"Bluepoints" (In memory of my father). [Poetry] (158:2) My 91, p. 96.
"Fishing." [Poetry] (158:2) My 91, p. 95.
5932. STEWART, Pamela
"Sunbathing." [AmerPoR] (20:2) Mr-Ap 91, p. 31.
5933. STEWART, Rosalyn
"Seed." [PraF] (12:4) Wint 91-92, p. 75.

5934. STEWART, Susan
"An Edge." [DenQ] (25:4) Spr 91, p. 55-61.
5935. STEWART, W. Gregory
"Litmus." [Rohwedder] (6) Sum-Fall 91, p. 33.
5936. STICKNEY, John
"Found Poems" (2 poems: "You," "The Laws"). [Caliban] (10) 91, p. 64-65.
5937. STIEBER, Christopher
"Sleeping with the Black Dog." [WindO] (54) Sum 91, p. 39.
5938. STILL, Gloria
"The Home Front." [HopewellR] (1991) 91, p. 21.
5939. STILLWELL, Mary Kathryn
"Claw." [Confr] (46/47) Fall 91-Wint 92, p. 263-264.
5940. STOCK, Norman
"From a Lost Notebook 3/89-6/89." [DenQ] (25:4) Spr 91, p. 62-63.
"The Last Straw." [NewYorkQ] (44) 91, p. 51.
"The Lesson of the Poetry Workshop." [NewYorkQ] (46) 91, p. 41.
"Thank You for the Helpful Comments." [NewYorkQ] (45) 91, p. 10.
5941. STOKES, Deborah E.
"Epicurus's Dominion." [Obs] (6:3) Wint 91, p. 88-89.
"Serenade." [Obs] (6:3) Wint 91, p. 88.
5942. STOKESBURY, Leon
"Fall." [KenR] (NS 13:1) Wint 91, p. 70.
5943. STOLHANSKE, Linda
"Sunrise / Sunset." [EmeraldCR] (3) 91, c1990, p. 93.
"Wings." [EmeraldCR] (3) 91, c1990, p. 85-86.
5944. STOLOFF, Carolyn
"Ascending the Cape Memling's Madonna Wears." [Pembroke] (23) 91, p. 107.
"From the Barrens." [ChamLR] (8-9) Spr-Fall 91, p. 95.
"From the Souk in Marrakesh." [ChamLR] (8-9) Spr-Fall 91, p. 94.
"In the Dead Poet's Room." [Contact] (10:59/60/61) Spr 91, p. 46.
"In the Miraculous Chapel" (for Russell Adams, artist, Taos, New Mexico).
    [Pembroke] (23) 91, p. 106.
"On the Subway Platform." [Pembroke] (23) 91, p. 105.
"Opening." [Caliban] (10) 91, p. 107.
"Sea's Edge." [Pembroke] (23) 91, p. 104.
"Whither." [Contact] (10:59/60/61) Spr 91, p. 46.
"Widow Road." [SouthernPR] (31:1) Spr 91, p. 49.
5945. STONE, Alison
"Better Than Sex." [NewYorkQ] (45) 91, p. 69.
"Colors." [SpoonRQ] (16:1/2) Wint-Spr 91, p. 22-23.
"Having My Wisdom Teeth Pulled Without Anesthesia." [SpoonRQ] (16:1/2)
    Wint-Spr 91, p. 24-25.
"The Water Cycle." [CrossCur] (9:4) Ja 91, p. 171.
"The Way It Sometimes Is." [NewYorkQ] (46) 91, p. 50.
5946. STONE, Arlene
"Minos in Taurus (The Minos Who Had No Minus)." [YellowS] (36) Spr 91, p.
    40-41.
5947. STONE, Carole
"The Butcher." [JINJPo] (13:2) Aut 91, p. 18.
"For Raymond Carver." [US1] (24/25) Spr 91, p. 38.
"God Bless America." [JINJPo] (13:2) Aut 91, p. 17.
5948. STONE, Jennifer
"Ethnic Eros." [PoetryUSA] (23) Sum 91, p. 15.
"High Brow — Low Loins." [PoetryUSA] (23) Sum 91, p. 12.
"High Brow — Low Loins." [Sequoia] (34:1) Spr 91, p. 95.
"Hope Chest." [Sequoia] (34:1) Spr 91, p. 96.
5949. STONE, Jessica
"The Journey." [Zyzzyva] (7:1) Spr 91, p. 122-125.
"Range of Vision." [Zyzzyva] (7:1) Spr 91, p. 118-120.
5950. STONE, Joan
"A Letter to Myself to Water." [SoDakR] (29:3 part 2) Aut 91, p. 47.
5951. STONE, Myrna
"Evening at Abbingdon." [Event] (20:3) Fall 91, p. 70-71.
5952. STONE, Ruth
"All Time Is Past Time." [PoetryE] (31) Spr 91, p. 68.
"Other." [PoetryE] (31) Spr 91, p. 69-70.

5953. STONEHOUSE, Cathy
"After the Whale." [PraF] (12:4) Wint 91-92, p. 85.
"Claustrophobia." [Grain] (19:3) Fall 91, p. 123.
"Fertility." [Grain] (19:3) Fall 91, p. 123.
5954. STONEY, Leland
"Prodigy." [SoCoast] (11) Wint 91, p. 28.
5955. STORIE-PAHLITZSCH, Lori
"Sweet Talk & Woman's Work." [LaurelR] (25:2) Sum 91, p. 95-96.
5956. STORTZ, Joan Colgan
"Dead End." [Dandel] (18:1) Spr-Sum 91, p. 35.
5957. STOTTS, Ann
"Sonnet for Georgia O'Keeffe." [WillowR] Spr 91, p. 14.
5958. STOUT, Glenn
"Fenway Lament." [Spitball] (38) Fall 91, p. 16.
"Opening Day." [Spitball] (38) Fall 91, p. 22-23.
"Whiffle Ball." [Spitball] (38) Fall 91, p. 24.
5959. STOUT, Robert Joe
"In the Oldest Part of Naples." [NewRena] (8:2, #25) Fall 91, p. 61.
"Pete." [ChamLR] (8-9) Spr-Fall 91, p. 143.
"The Work Force." [SoDakR] (29:4) Wint 91, p. 23.
5960. STRAHAN, B. R. (Bradley R.)
"Cancion." [ContextS] (2:1) 91, p. 2.
"Qamishli" (tr. of Farhad Shakely, w. the author). [Vis] (36) 91, p. 37.
"Separation" (tr. of Farhad Shakely, w. the author). [Vis] (36) 91, p. 37.
5961. STRAND, Mark
"The Hill." [GettyR] (4:4) Aut 91, p. 678-679.
"The Idea" (for Nolan Miller). [Field] (44) Spr 91, p. 59.
"Orpheus Alone." [AntR] (49:1) Wint 91, p. 102-103.
"Orpheus Alone." [Field] (44) Spr 91, p. 63-64.
"Viajes" (tr. by Miguel Falquez-Certain). [Nuez] (3:8/9) 91, p. 34.
5962. STRANEY, Susan
"Snow Angel." [Elf] (1:4) Wint 91, p. 40.
5963. STRANGE, Sharan
"Barbershop Ritual." [Callaloo] (14:2) Spr 91, p. 342.
"The Crazy Girl." [Agni] (34) 91, p. 61-62.
"Last Supper." [Callaloo] (14:2) Spr 91, p. 343-344.
"Words During War." [Agni] (34) 91, p. 59-60.
"Zodiac: For Julie." [Agni] (34) 91, p. 63.
5964. STRASSER, Judith
"To Peg in Osaka, 10/31/88." [Pig] (17) 91, p. 62.
5965. STRATIDAKIS, Eileen
"Faces." [LullwaterR] (2:2) Spr 91, p. 52.
5966. STRAUS, Austin
"The Poet As a Jewish Mother." [OnTheBus] (8/9) 91, p. 149.
5967. STRAUSS, Gwen
"Annie's Math." [SouthernPR] (31:2) Fall 91, p. 40-42.
"Learning to Grieve." [SouthernPR] (31:2) Fall 91, p. 39-40.
5968. STREHLOW, Loretta
"Insomnia." [Abraxas] (40/41) 91, p. 147.
5969. STRICKER, Meredith
"The Still Place." [Epoch] (40:3) 91, p. 264-272.
5970. STRICKLAND, Donna
"Breathing." [NowestR] (29:3) 91, p. 39.
5971. STRICKLAND, Stephanie
"Milk in Glass Bottles." [KenR] (NS 13:3) Sum 91, p. 44-45.
"Time-Capsule Contents." [Pig] (17) 91, p. 77.
5972. STRINGER, A. E.
"Fast Forward: Nevada." [PaintedB] (42) 91, p. 8.
5973. STROBLOVA, Jana
"Circus" (tr. by Jarmila and Ian Milner). [HampSPR] Wint 91, p. 65.
"The Slaughterhouse" (tr. by Jarmila and Ian Milner). [HampSPR] Wint 91, p. 66.
5974. STROFFOLINO, Chris
"Circle Jerk." [Caliban] (10) 91, p. 108-109.
"Not Never But Not Now." [Sulfur] (11:1, #28) Spr 91, p. 184-186.
5975. STROM, Eva
"I Am Steinkind" (tr. by David Harry). [Vis] (37) 91, p. 55.

5976. STRUTHERS, Ann
"Friends of My Childhood." [NewRena] (8:2, #25) Fall 91, p. 41.
"Grandma's Button Box" (Abstraction on Spectrum). [PoetC] (22:3) Spr 91, p. 34.
"Inviting Marianne Moore to the Des Moines Art Center." [PoetC] (22:3) Spr 91, p. 35-36.
"Mother and Marmee." [AmerS] (60:1) Wint 91, p. 90.
"Squash Blossom." [NewRena] (8:2, #25) Fall 91, p. 42.
5977. STRUTHERS, Betsy
"Lessons on the Subject of Death." [PoetryC] (12:1) D 91, p. 8.
"The Sentence" (for my father). [PoetryC] (12:1) D 91, p. 8.
5978. STRYK, Lucien
"Sadness of Cool Melons" (28 Haiku, tr. of Issa, w. Naboru Fujiwara). [MidAR] (11:2) 91, p. 1-10.
5979. STUART, Dabney
"Appetites: Variations ." [OhioR] (46) 91, p. 78-81.
"Brothers." [NewEngR] (13:3/4) Spr-Sum 91, p. 181-183.
"Don't Throw Me in the Briar Patch." [OhioR] (46) 91, p. 82-83.
"Fig." [ColEng] (53:3) Mr 91, p. 308.
"Forecast." [ColEng] (53:3) Mr 91, p. 309.
"Grief." [Boulevard] (6:2/3, #17/18) Fall 91, p. 93.
"Grubbing Thistle" (Hunua, New Zealand, for Richard Middleton). [TriQ] (81) Spr-Sum 91, p. 181-182.
"Holding My Own." [WillowS] (27) Wint 91, p. 33-34.
"Recess" (Parnell Elementary School playground, Auckland, New Zealand). [Boulevard] (6:2/3, #17/18) Fall 91, p. 92.
"Seesaw" (a birthday poem). [TriQ] (81) Spr-Sum 91, p. 179-180.
5980. STUART, Jane
"Drinking Song" (tr. of Alcaeus). [GrahamHR] (15) Fall 91, p. 88.
"Hebrus" (tr. of Alcaeus). [GrahamHR] (15) Fall 91, p. 87.
5981. STUBBS, Andrew
"Ephemera 3." [AntigR] (85/86) Spr-Sum 91, p. 206.
"Neighbourhoods." [AntigR] (85/86) Spr-Sum 91, p. 205.
STUBBS, John Heath
See HEATH-STUBBS, John
5982. STUDEBAKER, William
"Death Is Steady." [SoDakR] (29:3 part 2) Aut 91, p. 64.
5983. STULL, Richard
"All the Animals in the Cartoon." [NewAW] (7) Spr 91, p. 49.
"Angel in *Vogue*." [Boulevard] (5:3/6:1, #15/16) Spr 91, p. 208-209.
5984. STURGEON, Shawn
"The Cupidity of a Macedonian Sunrise." [WestHR] (45:4) Wint 91, p. 340.
"The Dead Sea of the Heart." [WestHR] (45:4) Wint 91, p. 341.
"Monuments." [WestHR] (45:4) Wint 91, p. 342.
"One in the Bush." [Pearl] (14) Fall-Wint 91, p. 27.
5985. SUAREZ, Carlos
"In Dreams Awaken." [RiverS] (33) 91, p. 78.
5986. SUBACH, Karen
"In the Baths, in Budapest." [Kalliope] (13:1) 91, p. 19-22.
5987. SUBRAMAN, Belinda
"Karnatik Classical: Thyagaraja Krithis." [CoalC] (3) My 91, p. 6.
"Medieval Times." [ChironR] (10:4) Wint 91, p. 37.
"That Which Only a Fool Would Explain." [HeavenB] (9) Wint-Spr 91-92, p. 31.
5988. SUCHANEK, Jerzy
"Winter Time" (tr. by Georgia Scott, David Malcolm and Zbigniew Joachimiak). [WebR] (15) Spr 91, p. 43.
SUEUR, Meridel le
See LeSUEUR, Meridel
5989. SUGANO, Miyoko
"Otosan." [BambooR] (50/51) Spr-Sum 91, p. 36-37.
"Scout Island — Keaukaha Way." [BambooR] (52) Fall 91, p. 110-111.
5990. SUKENICK, Ronald
"Doggy Bag" (A Long Narrative Poem in Prose). [CentralP] (19/20) Spr-Fall 91, p. 100-121.
5991. SULLIVAN, Chuck
"How We Spent Our Summer at Governor's School East of Eden: For Fred." [Pembroke] (23) 91, p. 91-92.

5992. SULLIVAN, Gary
"Clark Coolidge/Gerturde Stein" (with Marta Deike). [Avec] (4:1) 91, p. 135-136.
"Television." [CentralP] (19/20) Spr-Fall 91, p. 89-95.
5993. SULLIVAN, Gerald
"The Guest in 512." [SpiritSH] (56) Spr-Sum 91, p. 34.
"Off the Bearcamp." [SpiritSH] (56) Spr-Sum 91, p. 33.
"Washington and Orange." [SpiritSH] (56) Spr-Sum 91, p. 35.
5994. SULLIVAN, J. M.
"The thrill boys." [TickleAce] (22) Fall-Wint 91, p. 81-82.
5995. SULLIVAN, John
"Chartres Street Toodeloo." [BlackBR] (14) Fall-Wint 91, p. 23.
5996. SULLIVAN, Mary Jane
"The Weight of the Real" (for Richard). [CentralP] (19/20) Spr-Fall 91, p. 281.
5997. SUMMER, David
"Movement." [RagMag] (9:2) 91, p. 11.
"Not the Saint." [RagMag] (9:2) 91, p. 10.
5998. SUMMERFELDT, Vicki
"I Turn Back to Her Holding" (Short Grain Contest Winners: Prose Poem Winners:
Honourable Mention). [Grain] (19:4) Wint 91, p. 81.
5999. SUMNER, David
"After." [WestB] (29) 91, p. 93.
"Aspects of Death." [FourQ] (5:1) Spr 91, p. 43.
"At Your Side." [WritersF] (17) Fall 91, p. 104-105.
"Blood-Red History." [WritersF] (17) Fall 91, p. 104.
"Broken Monuments." [HawaiiR] (15:3, #33) Fall 91, p. 143.
"Evening Ocean." [Parting] (4:2) Wint 91-92, p. 7.
"Filling in the Spaces." [Poem] (66) N 91, p. 2.
"In the Yard Below the Light." [Plain] (12:2) Wint 91, p. 30.
"Key to Lock." [Callaloo] (14:4) Fall 91, p. 922.
"My Arrival." [WindO] (54) Sum 91, p. 36.
"Returned." [FourQ] (5:1) Spr 91, p. 42.
"Rising to Fall." [Poem] (66) N 91, p. 4.
"Separate Battles." [Poem] (66) N 91, p. 1.
"A Shock to the System." [LouisL] (8:2) Fall 91, p. 54.
"Someone Forgotten" (Editors note: "an apparently plagiarized poem" by Neal
Bowers, first published in *Poetry* Sept. 1990 as "Tenth-Year Elegy"). [Poem]
(66) N 91, p. 3.
6000. SUMRALL, Amber Coverdale
"For My Mother at Seventy-One." [Kaleid] (23) Sum-Fall 91, p. 33.
"For My Mother at Seventy-One." [MidAR] (11:1) 91, p. 19.
"The Making of a Saint." [MidAR] (11:1) 91, p. 14-16.
"Pajaro Valley, Early Spring" (for Ed). [MidAR] (11:1) 91, p. 20.
"Tailings." [MidAR] (11:1) 91, p. 17-18.
"Taproot." [Pearl] (14) Fall-Wint 91, p. 29.
"Tassajara." [MidAR] (11:1) 91, p. 21.
"To Give Our Bodies Away" (for R.H.). [Pearl] (14) Fall-Wint 91, p. 28.
6001. SUNDAHL, Daniel James
"Children Playing Statues on the Lawn at Dusk" (For Bob and Margaret). [Prima]
(14/15) 91, p. 58-59.
"Deuteronomy." [Prima] (14/15) 91, p. 64-65.
"Double Sonnet: Dutch Charlie's Grove." [DogRR] (10:1) Sum 91, p. 44.
"The Enigmatic Variations, part i." [InterPR] (17:2) Fall 91, p. 88.
"Envoi to the Journal of John Woolman: the Grave Digger's Speech" (circa 1772).
[TexasR] (12:3/4) Fall-Wint 91, p. 89.
"Gray Marrow." [WritersF] (17) Fall 91, p. 154.
"Hiroshima Maidens: Imaginary Translations from the Japanese." [Prima] (14/15)
91, p. 60-63.
"Ismene in a Traveling Hat" (circa 400 B.C.). [NewYorkQ] (44) 91, p. 70.
"The Morbidities." [InterPR] (17:2) Fall 91, p. 87.
"Old People in the Sun." [TexasR] (12:1/2) Spr-Sum 91, p. 126.
"Rabbinical Legends: I-II." [InterPR] (17:1) Spr 91, p. 82.
"Rubens Peale with a Geranium" (Circa 1910). [Prima] (14/15) 91, p. 66.
"Vigil Strange" (for John Munchoff). [InterPR] (17:1) Spr 91, p. 80-81.
"The White Island." [SouthernPR] (31:2) Fall 91, p. 54-55.
"Winter, You, Transmutation." [TexasR] (12:3/4) Fall-Wint 91, p. 90.

6002. SUNDERLAND, Janet
"The War between the Genitals" (tr. of Guillermo Truculento, w. Alicia Picazo).
[BilingR] (16:1) Ja-Ap 91, p. 65-66.
6003. SUNDLEE, Loren
"The Battery." [Spitball] (36) Spr 91, p. 45.
"The Guest." [DogRR] (10:1) Sum 91, p. 19.
6004. SUNDVALL, Herbert
"Dead Talk." [BellArk] (7:4) Jl-Ag 91, p. 11.
"Flight of Fancy" (after Chagall). [BellArk] (7:4) Jl-Ag 91, p. 22.
SUNG, Ts'ao
See TS'AO, Sung
6005. SUPERVIELLE, Jules
"The Burden of One Day's Work" (tr. by Geoffrey Gardner). [AmerPoR] (20:4)
Jl-Ag 91, p. 37.
"The First Dog" (tr. by Geoffrey Gardner). [AmerPoR] (20:4) Jl-Ag 91, p. 36.
"The First Tree" (tr. by Geoffrey Gardner). [AmerPoR] (20:4) Jl-Ag 91, p. 35.
"Forest" (tr. by Geoffrey Gardner). [AmerPoR] (20:4) Jl-Ag 91, p. 36.
"God Speaks to Man" (tr. by Geoffrey Gardner). [AmerPoR] (20:4) Jl-Ag 91, p. 34.
"God Thinks of Man" (tr. by Geoffrey Gardner). [AmerPoR] (20:4) Jl-Ag 91, p. 34.
"God's Sadness" (tr. by Geoffrey Gardner). [AmerPoR] (20:4) Jl-Ag 91, p. 35.
"Homage to Life" (tr. by Geoffrey Gardner). [AmerPoR] (20:4) Jl-Ag 91, p. 36.
"Horses Without Horsemen" (tr. by Geoffrey Gardner). [AmerPoR] (20:4) Jl-Ag
91, p. 37.
"If There Weren't Any Trees" (tr. by Geoffrey Gardner). [AmerPoR] (20:4) Jl-Ag
91, p. 36.
"The Star" (tr. by Geoffrey Gardner). [AmerPoR] (20:4) Jl-Ag 91, p. 37.
6006. SUPRANER, Robyn
"Final Event." [ManhatPR] (13) [91?], p. 44.
"The Late Maples." [ManhatPR] (13) [91?], p. 44.
"The Sweet Tide Rising." [Confr] (46/47) Fall 91-Wint 92, p. 271.
6007. SURRATT, Jerl O.
"The Luck of the Draw" (For Tim Dlugos, 1950-1990). [WashR] (16:6) Ap-My 91,
p. 6.
6008. SURVANT, Joe
"Logan Co. Soliloquies" (Selections. The Pablo Neruda Prize for Poetry, Honorable
Mention). [Nimrod] (35:1) Fall-Wint 91, p. 41-47.
6009. SUSSMAN, Dorothy Coffin
"Hiroshima." [KenR] (NS 13:2) Spr 91, p. 126.
6010. SUTCLIFFE, Hal
"Grandfather drank to dead Celts." [NewYorkQ] (44) 91, p. 77.
6011. SUTHERLAND-SMITH, James
"Julie's Recovery." [LaurelR] (25:1) Wint 91, p. 66-67.
"Postcard from Alexandria." [LaurelR] (25:1) Wint 91, p. 67-68.
6012. SUTPHEN, Joyce
"Almost Arriving." [NorthStoneR] (10) Fall 91-Wint 92, p. 67.
6013. SUTTER, Barton
"Shoe Shop." [Spirit] (11) 91, p. 35-36.
6014. SUTTON, Dorothy (Dorothy Moseley)
"Eight O'Clock on a January Morning at the A&P in Oxford, Mississippi" (for
William Faulkner, 1897-1962). [NegC] (11:3) 91, p. 40-41.
"Flakey Blake." [NegC] (11:1) 91, p. 97.
"No Man's Land." [AntR] (49:4) Fall 91, p. 560.
6015. SUTTON, Walt
"Hide and Seek." [OnTheBus] (8/9) 91, p. 151-153.
6016. SUZUKI, M.
"Childhood." [BambooR] (50/51) Spr-Sum 91, p. 63-64.
"Connections." [BambooR] (50/51) Spr-Sum 91, p. 66.
"To Move Your Organs." [BambooR] (50/51) Spr-Sum 91, p. 65.
"Who She Was." [BambooR] (50/51) Spr-Sum 91, p. 67.
6017. SVENDSEN, Sharon
"Forty-five." [Hellas] (2:1) Spr 91, p. 55.
"Forty-four." [Hellas] (2:1) Spr 91, p. 54.
"Forty-three." [Hellas] (2:1) Spr 91, p. 54.
6018. SVENONIUS, Elaine
"Poppies for the Twilight, Roses for the Noon." [OnTheBus] (8/9) 91, p. 154.
"Pursue Astonished Love." [OnTheBus] (8/9) 91, p. 154.

6019. SVENVOLD, Mark
"Eternity, a List." [Agni] (33) 91, p. 140.
"Reliquary." [IndR] (14:3) Fall 91, p. 77.
6020. SVOBODA, Terese
"Baiyer River, Papua New Guinea." [VirQR] (67:3) Sum 91, p. 484-485.
"Fairies." [MassR] (32:1) Spr 91, p. 92-93.
"Inventor." [ParisR] (33:118) Spr 91, p. 135-137.
"Left-Handed Woman." [SouthernR] (27:2) Ap 91, p. 306-307.
"Song Pet." [MassR] (32:1) Spr 91, p. 93-94.
"Sudanese Civil Sonnet." [VirQR] (67:3) Sum 91, p. 486.
"To Autumn." [SouthernR] (27:2) Ap 91, p. 305-306.
6021. SWAN, Alison
"Chains." [ContextS] (2:2) 91, p. 33.
6022. SWAN, Diane
"The Magic 8 Ball." [PassN] (12:1) Sum 91, p. 3.
6023. SWAN, Marc
"A View of the Future." [Gypsy] (17) 91, p. 73.
6024. SWANBERG, Christine (Chris)
"After Watching 'Vincent and Theo'" (Fine Arts Cinema, Chicago). [WillowR] Spr
91, p. 12.
"If Dreams Wrote the Story." [Farm] (8:2) Fall-Wint 91-92, p. 76.
"Mushrooms." [Farm] (8:1) Spr-Sum 91, p. 53.
6025. SWANBERG, Ingrid
"Bridge." [Os] (33) Fall 91, p. 6.
"Sub Rosa." [Os] (33) Fall 91, p. 7.
6026. SWANDER, Mary
"Cool and Cloudy." [Boulevard] (5:3/6:1, #15/16) Spr 91, p. 217.
"Frog Gig." [LaurelR] (25:1) Wint 91, p. 30.
"No Wonder." [Boulevard] (5:3/6:1, #15/16) Spr 91, p. 218-219.
"The Tattooed Man Comes for a Massage." [SouthwR] (76:3) Sum 91, p. 373.
6027. SWANGER, David
"Cow Tipping." [CharR] (17:1) Spr 91, p. 115.
"Dinner with Jerry" (for Jerry Vizenor). [CharR] (17:1) Spr 91, p. 116.
"Photograph." [PoetryNW] (32:2) Sum 91, p. 30.
"This Waking Unafraid." [GeoR] (45:1) Spr 91, p. 93.
6028. SWANN, Brian
"Cargo." [PoetC] (22:2) Wint 91, p. 39.
"In the Beginning." [Shen] (41:3) Fall 91, p. 96.
"Insider Trading." [SouthwR] (76:3) Sum 91, p. 391.
"The Present." [Salm] (92) Fall 91, p. 152.
"Reservation." [Shen] (41:3) Fall 91, p. 94.
"Restoration of a Copy of an Imaginary Painting." [ParisR] (33:119) Sum 91, p.
178-179.
"Translation." [SouthwR] (76:3) Sum 91, p. 390.
"Wake." [Shen] (41:3) Fall 91, p. 95.
6029. SWANNELL, Anne
"At the Ice Palace" (from "Mall," a collection of poems about the West Edmonton
mall). [CanLit] (129) Sum 91, p. 25-26.
"The Wedding Dress." [Grain] (19:4) Wint 91, p. 97-101.
6030. SWANSON, Catherine
"Bright Morning on the Ground Floor." [HopewellR] (1991) 91, p. 9.
6031. SWARD, Robert
"Blackbirds Flying Backwards / Villanelle #2." [PoetryUSA] (22) Spr 91, p. 12.
6032. SWAROOP, Sunita
"The Fish Slipped." [OnTheBus] (8/9) 91, p. 155.
"Waiting." [OnTheBus] (8/9) 91, p. 156.
6033. SWARTS, Helene
"The Passover Moon." [ChrC] (108:10) 20-27 Mr 91, p. 330.
6034. SWARTWOUT, Susan
"Songbird: The Arribatamiento." [Farm] (8:2) Fall-Wint 91-92, p. 56.
6035. SWATLING, Susan
"Last Night on Codine." [DustyD] Ap 91, p. 2.
"Under Cover." [DustyD] (2:1) Ja 91, p. 12.
"The War Room." [DustyD] Ap 91, p. 1.
6036. SWEATMAN, Margaret
"Fish." [Dandel] (18:1) Spr-Sum 91, p. 31.

6037. SWEENEY, Chad
"Tin Man." [Contact] (10:59/60/61) Spr 91, p. 43.
"To the Editor." [Contact] (10:59/60/61) Spr 91, p. 43.
6038. SWEENEY, Matthew
"Cacti." [Poetry] (158:3) Je 91, p. 144.
6039. SWEENEY, Teresa
"Singing." [RiverS] (34) 91, p. 16.
6040. SWEET, Brett
"Concurrence of Time." [EngJ] (80:3) Mr 91, p. 74.
6041. SWEET, Nanora
"Mix of Securities." [RiverS] (35) 91, p. 74-75.
6042. SWEET, William
"Under the Linden" (tr. of Steffen Menching). [AntigR] (84) Wint 91, p. 143.
6043. SWENSEN, Cole
"Les Allures Naturelles" (P.O.L. 1991, selections: 8-9, tr. of Pierre Alferi). [Avec]
(4:1) 91, p. 82-84.
"Corriere della Sera" (from "L'Art Poetic," P.O.L. 1988, tr. of Olivier Cadiot).
[Avec] (4:1) 91, p. 65-67.
6044. SWENSON, Karen
"The Bracelet." [PraS] (65:4) Wint 91, p. 130-131.
"Collision." [ColR] (NS 18:1) Spr-Sum 91, p. 37.
"The Landlady in Bangkok." [DenQ] (26:2) Fall 91, p. 47-48.
"The Lovers." [ColR] (NS 18:1) Spr-Sum 91, p. 35.
"The Other Woman Says." [ColR] (NS 18:1) Spr-Sum 91, p. 36.
6045. SWENSON, May
"7 Days on the Sea." [WeberS] (8:1) Spr 91, p. 8-14.
"Kiwi." [WeberS] (8:1) Spr 91, p. 6-7.
"The Many Christs." [WeberS] (8:1) Spr 91, p. 15-17.
"Memory of the Future? Prophecy of the Past?" [NewYorker] (67:6) 1 Ap 91, p. 32.
6046. SWERDLOW, David
"The Last Hill and the Wild Trees" (Chapbook: 7 poems). [OhioR] (47) 91, p.
55-68.
6047. SWETS, R. D.
"The Indian Revenge." [SoDakR] (29:3 part 2) Aut 91, p. 34.
6048. SWIFT, Doug
"History." [WestB] (28) 91, p. 49.
6049. SWIFT, Michael
"The Mask of Richard Wagner." [NewYorkQ] (46) 91, p. 71.
6050. SWIFT, Todd
"An Elegy As Hanna Senesh." [Quarry] (40:4) Fall 91, p. 72.
"The Last Days of Ontario." [Quarry] (40:4) Fall 91, p. 73.
6051. SWIST, Wally
"The Gristmill's Trough" (Excerpts). [Sparrow] (58) Jl 91, p. 17-20.
"Skunk Lingering." [Os] (32) Spr 91, p. 38.
"Three Haiku." [Os] (33) Fall 91, p. 10.
6052. SWOPE, Mike
"Dog." [MinnR] (NS 36) Spr 91, p. 20-21.
6053. SYLVESTER, Sherry
"Class Acts: Shooting Script of a Poor White Experience." [SinW] (43/44) Sum 91,
p. 217-220.
6054. SYNENKO, Anna
"Joshua." [Grain] (19:3) Fall 91, p. 136-138.
6055. SZASZ, Elizabeth
"Vision" (tr. of Agnes Gergely). [Interim] (10:1) Spr-Sum 91, p. 36.
6056. SZEMAN, Sherri
"At the Point Where Lightning Strikes." [CentR] (35:3) Fall 91, p. 533-534.
"Blood Songs." [CentR] (35:1) Wint 91, p. 137-140.
"On the Other Hand." [BlackWR] (17:2) Spr-Sum 91, p. 83-85.
"Those Who Claimed We Hated Them." [CentR] (35:3) Fall 91, p. 531-532.
6057. SZOBOTA, Lissa
"More Student Poems." [EngJ] (80:4) Ap 91, p. 36.
6058. SZÖKE, Donna
"Baking with My Mother." [PraF] (12:2 #55) Sum 91, p. 62.
6059. SZPORLUK, Larissa
"A Cappella." [Poem] (65) My 91, p. 57.
"Attention to Detail." [PoetL] (86:2) Sum 91, p. 18.

"A Closer Look at Form." [RagMag] (9:2) 91, p. 20.
"The Reaching Out of All Good Things." [Poem] (65) My 91, p. 58-59.
"The Time of Year When Fathers Marry Daughters." [ArtfulD] (20/21) 91, p. 87.
6060. SZUBA, Andrzej
"Whenever the conversation turned to the issue of dignity" (tr. by Georgia Scott,
David Malcolm and Zbigniew Joachimiak). [WebR] (15) Spr 91, p. 42.
6061. SZUMIGALSKI, Anne
"The Dove." [PoetryC] (12:1) D 91, p. 5.
"Foxed." [Grain] (19:2) Sum 91, p. 73.
"i^2=-1." [PoetryC] (12:1) D 91, p. 5.
"Island Sequence." [Grain] (19:2) Sum 91, p. 71-73.
"Rapture of the Deep" (Selections: 7 poems). [PraF] (12:3 #56) Aut 91, p. 6-13.
"A Sanctuary." [PoetryC] (12:1) D 91, p. 5.
6062. SZUMOWSKI, Margaret (Margaret C.)
"Nora at Sea: Letter to Torvald." [Vis] (36) 91, p. 30.
"Ruby the Baobab." [SingHM] (19) 91, p. 115-116.
6063. SZYSZKO, Brian
"The Figure 4." [CreamCR] (15:1) Spr 91, p. 73.
TABITO, Otomo
See OTOMO, Tabito (ca. 730)
6064. TACEY, Ralph
"Cully 005." [JamesWR] (8:4) Sum 91, p. 9.
6065. TACK, B. L.
"Fidelis." [OxfordM] (7:2) Fall-Wint 91, p. 74.
"Paradise Enough." [OxfordM] (7:2) Fall-Wint 91, p. 73.
"The Plum Tree Blossoms." [OxfordM] (7:2) Fall-Wint 91, p. 71-72.
TADAFUSA, Fujiwara
See FUJIWARA, Tadafusa (d. 928)
6066. TADIC, Novica
"An Actor" (tr. by Vasa D. Mihailovich). [InterPR] (15:1) Spr 89, p. 57.
"A Blind Man" (tr. by Vasa D. Mihailovich). [InterPR] (15:1) Spr 89, p. 57.
"The Crazy Landlord" (tr. by Vasa D. Mihailovich). [InterPR] (15:1) Spr 89, p. 51.
"The Crazy Tenant" (tr. by Vasa D. Mihailovich). [InterPR] (15:1) Spr 89, p. 53.
"Dice" (tr. by Vasa D. Mihailovich). [InterPR] (15:1) Spr 89, p. 49.
"A Fur-Cap, Pigeons" (tr. by Vasa D. Mihailovich). [InterPR] (15:1) Spr 89, p. 55.
"The Gardener" (tr. by Vasa D. Mihailovich). [InterPR] (15:1) Spr 89, p. 49.
"Gljive." [InterPR] (15:1) Spr 89, p. 54.
"Glumac." [InterPR] (15:1) Spr 89, p. 56.
"Kocka." [InterPR] (15:1) Spr 89, p. 48.
"Luda Stanodavka." [InterPR] (15:1) Spr 89, p. 50.
"Ludi Stanar." [InterPR] (15:1) Spr 89, p. 52.
"Mushrooms" (tr. by Vasa D. Mihailovich). [InterPR] (15:1) Spr 89, p. 55.
"Slepac." [InterPR] (15:1) Spr 89, p. 56.
"Subara, Golubovi." [InterPR] (15:1) Spr 89, p. 54.
"Vrtlar." [InterPR] (15:1) Spr 89, p. 48.
6067. TAFDRUP, Pia
"Always Now" (tr. by Anne Born). [Vis] (37) 91, p. 9.
"Dark Brightness" (tr. by Anne Born). [Vis] (37) 91, p. 8.
"Keep on Driving" (tr. by Anne Born). [Vis] (37) 91, p. 8.
6068. TAGGART, John
"Aria No. 17." [Conjunc] (16) 91, p. 237-239.
"A Number of Times." [BlackWR] (18:1) Fall-Wint 91, p. 20-22.
"Sisyphus" (fragments: 121-127, tr. of Aeschylus). [Talisman] (6) Spr 91, p. 26.
"Star Dust." [BlackWR] (18:1) Fall-Wint 91, p. 17-19.
"The Wool-Carders" (fragments: 84-87, tr. of Aeschylus). [Talisman] (6) Spr 91, p.
25.
6069. TAGLIABUE, John
"Becoming More Nimble and Amused at My New Task." [Elf] (1:3) Fall 91, p. 31.
"Children of Adam and Eve, High Grass, August." [Elf] (1:3) Fall 91, p. 30.
"China Poems." [GreenMR] (NS 4:2) Wint-Spr 91, p. 116.
"Prescience." [Northeast] (5:4) Sum 91, p. 20.
T'AI-PO, Li
See LI, Po
6070. TAKACS, Zsuzsa
"A Vague Feeling Grips Me" (tr. by Nicholas Kolumban). [MassR] (32:4) Wint
91-92, p. 493.

TAKARA, Katherine Waddell
  See WADDELL-TAKARA, Kathryn
TAKARA, Kathryn Waddell
  See WADDELL-TAKARA, Kathryn
6071. TAKAYASU, Oshima (ca. 705)
  "Melancholy days" (tr. by Sam Hamill). [ColR] (NS 17:2) Fall-Wint 90, p. 16.
TAKIGUCHI, Mimi Nelson
  See NELSON-TAKIGUCHI, Mimi
6072. TAKSA, Mark
  "The Man Who Did Tricks in His Vein." [SlipS] (11) 91, p. 81.
  "Private Thoughts at the Celebration." [NewRena] (8:2, #25) Fall 91, p. 101.
  "Sherry and Sofa Novels." [NewRena] (8:2, #25) Fall 91, p. 100.
  "Two Conclusions of a Road." [PacificR] (10) 91-92, p. 142.
6073. TALAL, Marilynn
  "Edgar Degas: 'Family Portrait (or the Bellini Family) 1858-1860'." [NewRep]
    (204:4) 28 Ja 91, p. 32.
  "Fire." [CalQ] (31) Fall 88, p. 32.
6074. TALCOTT, William (Will)
  "Career Guidance." [FreeL] (8) Aut 91, p. 26.
  "Wet Kleenex." [Pearl] (14) Fall-Wint 91, p. 9.
  "What Remains." [CalQ] (32/33) Spr 90, p. 93.
6075. TALL, Deborah
  "Remains." [Antaeus] (67) Fall 91, p. 173-175.
  "We'll Never Change Our Tune." [Agni] (34) 91, p. 244.
6076. TALLEY, James
  "Keeping a Low Profile." [ChironR] (10:2) Sum 91, p. 41.
6077. TALMOR, Avital
  "Refuge." [NewL] (58:1) Fall 91, p. 39.
6078. TAM, Reuben
  "Other Strategies." [ChamLR] (8-9) Spr-Fall 91, p. 47.
TAMEKANE, Kyogoku
  See KYOGOKU, Tamekane (1254-1332)
6079. TAMEN, Pedro
  "As in *Trovatore*, I Take Four Steps" (tr. by Gregory Rabassa). [Trans] (25) Spr 91,
    p. 71.
  "Delphi, Opus 12" (Selections: 17-18, tr. by Gregory Rabassa). [Trans] (25) Spr 91,
    p. 72.
  "Evening Falls and I Arise" (tr. by Gregory Rabassa). [Trans] (25) Spr 91, p. 70.
6080. TAMMARO, Thom
  "Looking for My Father at Remagen Bridge." [Sidewalks] (1) Aug 91, p. 37-38.
  "Nighthawks." [SoDakR] (29:3 part 2) Aut 91, p. 95-96.
  "Remembering the Bull DeLisio." [Sidewalks] (1) Aug 91, p. 36.
TAN, Lin
  See LIN, Tan
6081. TANG, Lan
  "The Ancient Tree and the Villagers" (tr. by Tang Tao, w. Stuart Friebert). [PraS]
    (65:2) Sum 91, p. 35.
  "The Awakening" (tr. by Tang Tao, w. Stuart Friebert). [PraS] (65:2) Sum 91, p.
    29.
  "Hospital in Winter" (tr. by Tang Tao, w. Stuart Friebert). [PraS] (65:2) Sum 91, p.
    32.
  "Nature" (tr. by Tang Tao, w. Stuart Friebert). [PraS] (65:2) Sum 91, p. 32-33.
  "Not This or That" (tr. by Tang Tao, w. Stuart Friebert). [PraS] (65:2) Sum 91, p.
    34.
  "Rainfall" (tr. by Tang Tao, w. Stuart Friebert). [PraS] (65:2) Sum 91, p. 30.
  "Search" (tr. by Tang Tao). [PraS] (65:2) Sum 91, p. 31.
6082. TANG, Tao
  "The Ancient Tree and the Villagers" (tr. of Tang Lan, w. Stuart Friebert). [PraS]
    (65:2) Sum 91, p. 35.
  "The Awakening" (tr. of Tang Lan, w. Stuart Friebert). [PraS] (65:2) Sum 91, p.
    29.
  "Hospital in Winter" (tr. of Tang Lan, w. Stuart Friebert). [PraS] (65:2) Sum 91, p.
    32.
  "Nature" (tr. of Tang Lan, w. Stuart Friebert). [PraS] (65:2) Sum 91, p. 32-33.
  "Not This or That" (tr. of Tang Lan, w. Stuart Friebert). [PraS] (65:2) Sum 91, p.
    34.

"Rainfall" (tr. of Tang Lan, w. Stuart Friebert). [PraS] (65:2) Sum 91, p. 30.
"Search" (tr. of Tang Lan). [PraS] (65:2) Sum 91, p. 31.
6083. TANG, Ya Ping
"Black Desert" (suite, tr. by Tony Barnstone and Newton Liu). [LitR] (34:2) Wint
91, p. 214-215.
"A Black Tunnel" (tr. by Ginny MacKenzie and Wei Guo). [Agni] (34) 91, p. 220.
TANG, Yaping
See TANG, Ya Ping
6084. TANGORRA, Joanne
"Going Home." [CumbPR] (10:2) Spr 91, p. 22-23.
"Unrecorded Entries in Mary Shelley's Journal." [Kalliope] (13:1) 91, p. 67-69.
6085. TANNEN, Deborah
"The Deer Runs Fast Through the Forest" (tr. of Erling Indreeide, w. the author).
[Vis] (37) 91, p. 44.
6086. TANNER, Anita
"From the Window." [CapeR] (26:2) Fall 91, p. 28.
6087. T'AO, Ch'ien
"After the Ancients" (tr. by J. P. Seaton). [LitR] (35:1) Fall 91, p. 74.
"Drinking Poem V" (For I M, tr. by Matthew Flannery). [CrabCR] (7:3) 91, p. 22.
"Drinking Wine XVI" (tr. by J. P. Seaton). [LitR] (35:1) Fall 91, p. 73.
"Home to Garden and Field V" (For RRF, tr. by Matthew Flannery). [CrabCR] (7:3)
91, p. 22.
TAO, Tang
See TANG, Tao
6088. TARCAY, Eileen
"The Fall." [Nimrod] (34:2) Spr-Sum 91, p. 125.
6089. TARDIEU, Jean
"The Absent-Minded Inventor" (tr. by James V. Gill). [CimR] (94) Ja 91, p. 15-16.
"Adversity" (tr. by James V. Gill). [CimR] (94) Ja 91, p. 16.
"The Dangers of Remembrance" (tr. by James V. Gill). [CimR] (94) Ja 91, p. 13.
"The Diary of a Suspicious Man" (Excerpt, tr. by James V. Gill). [CimR] (94) Ja 91,
p. 15.
"Hölderlin's Grave" (tr. by James V. Gill). [CimR] (94) Ja 91, p. 18-19.
"Images of Time" (tr. by James V. Gill). [CimR] (94) Ja 91, p. 17.
"The Inanimate's Dreams" (tr. by James V. Gill). [CimR] (94) Ja 91, p. 14-15.
"The Secret Tribunal" (tr. by James V. Gill). [CimR] (94) Ja 91, p. 13-14.
"Widow in a Violin Coat" (tr. by Robert Brown). [ArtfulD] (20/21) 91, p. 41.
6090. TARDOS, Anne
"Ami Minden." [Conjunc] (16) 91, p. 173-180.
6091. TARN, Nathaniel
"Bartok in Udaipur." [Conjunc] (17) 91, p. 167-170.
6092. TARPLEY, Natasha
"Chicago" (Third Prize). [HarvardA] (125:4) Mr 91, p. 4.
"Feel Free." [Obs] (6:3) Wint 91, p. 82.
"Haircut." [Obs] (6:3) Wint 91, p. 83.
"Parting the Waters or Sinking" (for Till and all of us who have parted the waters).
[Obs] (6:3) Wint 91, p. 83-84.
"Pregnancy." [Obs] (6:3) Wint 91, p. 84.
"To Alabama" (for my grandaddy and my daddy). [Obs] (6:3) Wint 91, p. 81-82.
6093. TATAN'KA IYOTA'KE
"Song for the Elk" (from "The Songs of Tatan'ka Iyota'ke," tr. by Joseph Bruchac).
[MidAR] (11:1) 91, p. 2.
"Tatan'ka Iyota'ke's Vision" (from "The Songs of Tatan'ka Iyota'ke," tr. by Joseph
Bruchac). [MidAR] (11:1) 91, p. 4.
"Tatan'ka Iyota'ke's Warning to His People" (from "The Songs of Tatan'ka
Iyota'ke," tr. by Joseph Bruchac). [MidAR] (11:1) 91, p. 4.
"While Walking Barefoot at Dawn" (from "The Songs of Tatan'ka Iyota'ke," tr. by
Joseph Bruchac). [MidAR] (11:1) 91, p. 2.
6094. TATARUNIS, Paula
"About Face." [CapeR] (26:1) Spr 91, p. 26-27.
6095. TATE, James
"Annual Report." [Ploughs] (17:4) Wint 91-92, p. 24.
"At the Rest Stop." [Ploughs] (17:4) Wint 91-92, p. 25.
"A Bar in Aspen." [MissouriR] (14:1) 91, p. 25.
"The Beach." [MissouriR] (14:1) 91, p. 30.
"The Beachcomber." [Ploughs] (17:4) Wint 91-92, p. 23.

"From an Island." [MissouriR] (14:1) 91, p. 29.
"I Got Blindsided." [Ploughs] (17:4) Wint 91-92, p. 21-22.
"More About Peggy." [MissouriR] (14:1) 91, p. 28.
"The Morning News." [Ploughs] (17:4) Wint 91-92, p. 19-20.
"Pimone, Stranded in the Countryside." [MissouriR] (14:1) 91, p. 26.
"Porch Theory." [MissouriR] (14:1) 91, p. 27.
"Summer, Maine Coast." [MissouriR] (14:1) 91, p. 31.
6096. TAUFER, Veno
"Hands" (tr. of Edvard Kocbek, w. Michael Scammell). [NewYRB] (38:17) 24 O
    91, p. 61.
"Melancholy of the Second Echelon" (In memory of my father, killed in 1943, tr. by
    Michael Biggins). [CimR] (96) Jl 91, p. 31-33.
"Now" (tr. of Edvard Kocbek, w. Michael Scammell). [NewYRB] (38:17) 24 O 91,
    p. 61.
"On Freedom of Mind" (tr. of Edvard Kocbek, w. Michael Scammell). [NewYRB]
    (38:17) 24 O 91, p. 61.
"Parrots" (tr. of Edvard Kocbek, w. Michael Scammell). [NewYRB] (38:17) 24 O
    91, p. 61.
6097. TAUS, Roger
"Mariza." [OnTheBus] (8/9) 91, p. 157-158.
6098. TAUZIN, Neil
"Bus Stop." [CoalC] (3) My 91, p. 1.
"Busted." [CoalC] (3) My 91, p. 10.
6099. TAWNEY, Robin
"Duplex" (for Jo Anne). [ContextS] (2:2) 91, p. 21-22.
6100. TAYLOR, Alex
"Hooks" (tr. of Henrik Nordbrandt). [Vis] (37) 91, p. 11.
"The Last Poem in the World" (tr. of Benny Andersen). [Vis] (37) 91, p. 14.
"No Matter Where We go" (tr. of Henrik Nordbrandt, w. the author). [Vis] (37) 91,
    p. 10.
"Sound of the Bell" (tr. of Jorgen Gustava Brandt, w. the author). [Vis] (37) 91, p.
    10.
6101. TAYLOR, Anique
"The Beautiful Blue Angel Lady's Grown-Up Children." [SingHM] (19) 91, p.
    48-49.
6102. TAYLOR, Bruce
"Foreigner." [CharR] (17:1) Spr 91, p. 88.
6103. TAYLOR, Catherine
"The Key." [Thrpny] (44) Wint 91, p. 22.
6104. TAYLOR, Craig
"The Californian." [InterPR] (15:1) Spr 89, p. 80-83.
"Getting It Right." [InterPR] (15:1) Spr 89, p. 86.
"The Hills Near the Border." [InterPR] (15:1) Spr 89, p. 84.
"Making Sense of It." [InterPR] (15:1) Spr 89, p. 85.
6105. TAYLOR, Eleanor Ross
"Cuts Buttons Off an Old Sweater." [Ploughs] (17:2/3) Fall 91, p. 188.
"Daytime Moon." [NewYorker] (67:28) 2 S 91, p. 98.
"Escaped." [SouthernR] (27:1) Ja 91, p. 106-107.
"Gainesville, March." [SouthernR] (27:1) Ja 91, p. 107.
"The Greenhouse." [SouthernR] (27:1) Ja 91, p. 108.
"Kitchen Fable." [NewYorker] (67:3) 11 Mr 91, p. 34.
"Pain in the House." [SouthernR] (27:1) Ja 91, p. 105-106.
"Shaking the Plum Tree." [CapeR] (26:2) Fall 91, p. 6.
6106. TAYLOR, Henry
"At South Fork Cemetery." [SouthernR] (27:1) Ja 91, p. 136.
"A Pool Table in Key West." [SouthernR] (27:1) Ja 91, p. 136-138.
"Popped Balloon." [SouthernR] (27:1) Ja 91, p. 139.
6107. TAYLOR, Janis
"The Visitation." [PacificR] (10) 91-92, p. 86-87.
6108. TAYLOR, Jon
"Love Affiar." [Bogg] (64) 91, p. 5.
6109. TAYLOR, Jonathan
"Mr. John Heraclitus Smith Tries to Hang on to the Reality of Things during a Visit
    to Swanage." [CumbPR] (10:2) Spr 91, p. 39.
6110. TAYLOR, Judith
"Visions of Paradise." [OnTheBus] (8/9) 91, p. 159-160.

6111. TAYLOR, Kathleen
"And White Man Conquered." [ChironR] (10:2) Sum 91, p. 47.
"Rodney Called It Bullshit." [ChironR] (10:4) Wint 91, p. 39.
6112. TAYLOR, Kent
"Creatures of Habit." [Abraxas] (40/41) 91, p. 136.
"Jamais Vu." [Abraxas] (40/41) 91, p. 137.
"View from a Junk-Food Emporium." [Pearl] (13) Spr-Sum 91, p. 52.
6113. TAYLOR, Marilyn
"Drive All Night." [IndR] (14:3) Fall 91, p. 144-145.
"The Lovers, at Eighty." [IndR] (14:3) Fall 91, p. 143.
"To a Young Diver." [Poetry] (158:3) Je 91, p. 137-138.
6114. TAYLOR, Millie
"Defeathered Snow Birds." [Kalliope] (13:3) 91, p. 10.
6115. TAYLOR, Reta
"A Good Read." [Pearl] (14) Fall-Wint 91, p. 52.
6116. TAYSON, Richard
"The Lovers." [JamesWR] (8:3) Spr 91, p. 1.
"Your Black Skin My Whiteness." [Vis] (36) 91, p. 14.
6117. TEETS, Troy
"Frozen Hemlock" (A Plainsongs Award Poem). [Plain] (12:2) Wint 91, p. 5.
6118. TEICHMANN, Sandra G. (Sandra Gail)
"Gray Bones Poke into a White Bird Cage." [PoetL] (86:2) Sum 91, p. 7.
"Resemblances" (tr. of Graciela Guzmán). [WritersF] (17) Fall 91, p. 129.
"To Sleep Rocking in the Fear of Termination" (tr. of Graciela Guzman). [Vis] (36) 91, p. 33.
6119. TEIKA, Fujiwara No
"In the Mountains" (tr. by Graeme Wilson). [LitR] (35:1) Fall 91, p. 108.
6120. TEILLIER, Jorge
"Bajo del Cielo Nacido Tras la Lluvia." [IndR] (14:3) Fall 91, p. 114-115.
"Carta de Lluvia." [IndR] (14:3) Fall 91, p. 110-111.
"Clinical Landscape" (tr. by Carolyne Wright). [IndR] (14:3) Fall 91, p. 124-125.
"Los Dominios Perdidos" (a Alain-Fournier). [IndR] (14:3) Fall 91, p. 118-119.
"Games" (tr. by Carolyne Wright). [Boulevard] (6:2/3, #17/18) Fall 91, p. 147.
"Games" (tr. by Mary Crow). [ArtfulD] (20/21) 91, p. 8.
"The Land of Night" (tr. by Carolyne Wright). [Boulevard] (6:2/3, #17/18) Fall 91, p. 148.
"Letter of Rain" (tr. by Carolyne Wright). [IndR] (14:3) Fall 91, p. 112-113.
"The Lost Domain" (to Alain-Fournier, tr. by Carolyne Wright). [IndR] (14:3) Fall 91, p. 120-121.
"No Sign of Life" (tr. by Carolyne Wright). [MidAR] (12:1) 91, p. 157-159.
"Paisaje de Clinica" (a Rolando Cardenas). [IndR] (14:3) Fall 91, p. 122-123.
"Sentados Frente al Fuego." [IndR] (14:3) Fall 91, p. 108.
"Sitting in Front of the Fire" (tr. by Carolyne Wright). [IndR] (14:3) Fall 91, p. 109.
"Under the Sky Born After the Rain" (tr. by Carolyne Wright). [IndR] (14:3) Fall 91, p. 116-117.
6121. TEJERA, Nivaria
"Paris." [LindLM] (10:3) Jl-S 91, p. 6.
6122. TEMME, Leonard A.
"A Crown of Sonnets on the Transformation of the Escambia County Court of Records Building and County Jail into the Pensacola Cultural Center" (Selections: 1-3). [EmeraldCR] (4) 91, p. 8-9.
"Untitled: I said that I could never write a poem." [EmeraldCR] (3) 91, c1990, p. 103-104.
"Untitled: She lay still." [EmeraldCR] (3) 91, c1990, p. 88.
6123. TEMPLE, M. K.
"28. Oktober 1918." [WestB] (28) 91, p. 90.
"Family Reunion." [WestB] (28) 91, p. 91.
"Gourds." [DustyD] (2:1) Ja 91, p. 27.
6124. TEMPLE, Rosalee
"Aireyholme Farm." [BellR] (14:2) Fall 91, p. 15.
"The Transit of Venus: Tahiti, 1769." [BellR] (14:2) Fall 91, p. 14.
6125. TENNYSON, Aileen
"A Measure of Light." [Crucible] (27) Fall 91, p. 44.
6126. TERADA, Rei
"On Painting" (After Cavafy). [Poetry] (158:4) Jl 91, p. 205.
"Wordsworth After *The Prelude*." [Poetry] (158:4) Jl 91, p. 205-206.

6127. TERMAN, Philip
　　"From the Heartland." [MidAR] (11:1) 91, p. 99-100.
　　"Promise." [MidwQ] (32:3) Spr 91, p. 296.
　　"What We Pass On." [Poetry] (158:6) S 91, p. 323-325.
　　"Yom Kippur." [Poetry] (158:6) S 91, p. 326.
6128. TERPSTRA, John
　　"I Moved to Burlington in My Sleep." [Quarry] (40:4) Fall 91, p. 23-24.
　　"The Little Towns of Bethlehem." [Quarry] (40:4) Fall 91, p. 21-22.
　　"No Dwelling Place." [Quarry] (40:4) Fall 91, p. 25-27.
6129. TERRANOVA, Elaine
　　"The Choice." [Confr] (46/47) Fall 91-Wint 92, p. 247.
　　"Their House." [NewYorker] (67:16) 10 Je 91, p. 76.
6130. TERRELL, Linda
　　"Summer Nap." [Crucible] (27) Fall 91, p. 34.
6131. TERRELL, William
　　"Carpe Diem." [Hellas] (2:2) Fall 91, p. 264.
6132. TERRIS, Virginia
　　"The Cat's View." [BostonR] (16:2) Ap 91, p. 20.
　　"Identification." [BostonR] (16:2) Ap 91, p. 20.
　　"November Light." [BostonR] (16:2) Ap 91, p. 20.
　　"The Plain Woman." [BostonR] (16:2) Ap 91, p. 20.
　　"Surfacing." [BostonR] (16:2) Ap 91, p. 20.
　　"The Visit." [BostonR] (16:2) Ap 91, p. 20.
6133. TERRY, Chris
　　"Die Wende" (Oct. 3, 1990). [AntigR] (84) Wint 91, p. 121-122.
6134. TETI, Zona
　　"Joan Outside." [MissR] (19:3) 91, p. 164.
　　"Monologue of the Rich Fool." [Stand] (32:1) Wint 90-91, p. 35.
6135. TETU, Randeane
　　"To Sleep — 1963." [Parting] (4:1) Sum 91, p. 9.
6136. THAKURIA, Joseph
　　"Interstate 81." [SoCoast] (11) Wint 91, p. 12.
　　"Siesta." [SoCoast] (11) Wint 91, p. 50.
6137. THALMAN, Mark
　　"Midwinter: Sauvie Island." [Pearl] (13) Spr-Sum 91, p. 12.
6138. THAM, Hilary
　　"Betrayal." [PoetL] (86:4) Wint 91-92, p. 37.
6139. THARAUD, Ross
　　"The Builder." [Parting] (4:2) Wint 91-92, p. 1, insert.
　　"Camp Followers." [Parting] (4:2) Wint 91-92, p. 2, insert.
　　"Trace." [Parting] (4:2) Wint 91-92, p. 3, insert.
6140. THARP, Peggy
　　"A Woman Eats Dirt." [MinnR] (NS 37) Fall 91, p. 29.
6141. THAYLER, Carl
　　"The Buddy Holly Ode." [Abraxas] (40/41) 91, p. 128-131.
6142. THENY, Janet
　　"Madre." [CapilR] (2:6/7) Fall 91, p. 64-65.
6143. THERSON-COFIE, Larweh
　　"Force." [LitR] (34:4) Sum 91, p. 569-570.
6144. THESEN, Sharon
　　"Galiano Baby Grand." [CapilR] (2:5) Sum 91, p. 53.
　　"Pedestrian, Anonymous." [CapilR] (2:5) Sum 91, p. 52.
　　"Song without Words." [CapilR] (2:5) Sum 91, p. 51.
　　"The Watermelon." [CapilR] (2:5) Sum 91, p. 54-55.
6145. THIBODEAUX, Raymond
　　"Paw-Paw in Autumn." [LouisL] (8:1) Spr 91, p. 50-51.
6146. THIEL, Amy
　　"The Swans." [PikeF] (10) Spr 91, p. 19.
6147. THIERRY, Joyce
　　"Rat Killer." [Grain] (19:3) Fall 91, p. 116.
6148. THIERS, Naomi
　　"Good News." [PoetL] (86:4) Wint 91-92, p. 23-24.
　　"Neighborhood Meeting." [PoetL] (86:4) Wint 91-92, p. 21-22.
6149. THIRD, Eleanor L.
　　"The Woods of Childhood." [Stand] (32:2) Spr 91, p. 59-60.

6150. THOMAS, Denise
"About Fidelity." [GettyR] (4:4) Aut 91, p. 646.
"All of Our Husbands Said They Loved Us." [Manoa] (3:2) Fall 91, p. 95.
"Anniversary." [Manoa] (3:2) Fall 91, p. 96.
"Last Night and Any Other." [ColEng] (53:2) F 91, p. 167.
"Leaving It Up to You." [GettyR] (4:4) Aut 91, p. 644-645.
"New Year's Eve." [GettyR] (4:4) Aut 91, p. 647.
"San Antonio, the Missions." [SoDakR] (29:3 part 2) Aut 91, p. 110.
"The Way Home." [HighP] (6:1) Spr 91, p. 70.
"We Imitate Our Government." [Manoa] (3:2) Fall 91, p. 94.
6151. THOMAS, Dianne
"Junior." [Thrpny] (47) Fall 91, p. 20.
6152. THOMAS, Edith Matilda
"Frost Tonight." [SoCaR] (24:1) Fall 91, p. 155.
6153. THOMAS, F. Richard
"Popping in Hot Ghee." [ChironR] (10:4) Wint 91, p. 22.
6154. THOMAS, Harry
"Odysseus to Telemachus" (tr. of Joseph Brodsky). [PartR] (58:4) Fall 91, p.
680-681.
6155. THOMAS, Jeanne J.
"Cool Cement." [Obs] (6:1) Spr 91, p. 42.
"Dialog." [Obs] (6:1) Spr 91, p. 42-43.
6156. THOMAS, Jim
"Black Well" (for Eddie Bauer, one of my students). [CharR] (17:1) Spr 91, p. 81.
6157. THOMAS, Julia
"The Legacy of Wood." [RagMag] (9:1) 91, p. 13-15.
6158. THOMAS, Larry D.
"Dust Storm." [CapeR] (26:2) Fall 91, p. 9.
"For Purity" (for Georgia O'Keeffe). [TexasR] (12:3/4) Fall-Wint 91, p. 91.
"Fresh Fat." [TexasR] (12:3/4) Fall-Wint 91, p. 92.
"Monhegan Island, Maine." [TexasR] (12:3/4) Fall-Wint 91, p. 93.
"Rattlesnake Roundup." [CapeR] (26:2) Fall 91, p. 10.
6159. THOMAS, Lorenzo
"Speed Key." [TampaR] (4) 91, p. 86-87.
6160. THOMAS, Marilyn
"Run, the House!" (in memoriam). [PoetryUSA] (22) Spr 91, p. 13.
6161. THOMAS, Peter
"Heirlooms." [NegC] (11:1) 91, p. 93-95.
6162. THOMAS, Randolph
"Picture of Norwood Street." [GreensboroR] (51) Wint 91-92, p. 32.
6163. THOMAS, Terry
"A Condemnation of Nimble Jack." [Plain] (12:1) Fall 91, p. 7.
"Epitaph." [Plain] (12:2) Wint 91, p. 29.
"I Drew a Woman." [Plain] (11:3) Spr 91, p. 32.
"King Kong and the Big Building." [WritersF] (17) Fall 91, p. 17.
"Moby-Dick." [Plain] (11:3) Spr 91, p. 9.
6164. THOMAS, Vonnie
"The Dark Color of Loneliness." [AnthNEW] (3) 91, p. 27.
6165. THOMPSON, A. M.
"His First Followers." [ChrC] (108:17) 15-22 My 91, p. 551.
6166. THOMPSON, Clive
"Jazz." [Grain] (19:1) Spr 91, p. 120.
6167. THOMPSON, Cole
"Advice." [MidAR] (12:1) 91, p. 115.
6168. THOMPSON, Earle
"She Listens to the Rhythm." [PoetryE] (32) Fall 91, p. 42.
"The Singular Movement." [PoetryE] (32) Fall 91, p. 43.
6169. THOMPSON, Ginny
"Outside the Tide." [Crucible] (27) Fall 91, p. 42.
6170. THOMPSON, Julius E.
"The Devil's Music in Hell" (For Billie Holiday, 1915-1959). [Obs] (6:1) Spr 91, p.
78.
"The Eddie Carthan Case" (Mississippi, 1980s). [Obs] (6:1) Spr 91, p. 79.
"Mrs. Frederick Sullivan of Byhalia, Marshall County, Mississippi — Lynched on
November 25, 1914 (For the Crime of Arson?)." [Obs] (6:1) Spr 91, p. 78-79.

6171. THOMPSON, Lou
"Silver Eagle." [HighP] (6:1) Spr 91, p. 71-72.
6172. THOMPSON, Phyllis H. (Phyllis Hoge)
"First Gunner: Mortar Squad." [Shen] (41:3) Fall 91, p. 45-46.
"Medicine Bag." [Manoa] (3:2) Fall 91, p. 173.
6173. THOMPSON, Ricki
"Michaelmas" (St. Michael's Day — September 29). [Sidewalks] (1) Aug 91, p. 27.
"Not About Vanity." [Sidewalks] (1) Aug 91, p. 27.
6174. THOMPSON, Sue Ellen
"The B-24." [TarRP] (31:1) Fall 91, p. 42-43.
"Quenched." [TarRP] (31:1) Fall 91, p. 43.
"The Stranger." [TarRP] (31:1) Fall 91, p. 44.
6175. THOMPSON, W. B.
"Wren." [CumbPR] (10:2) Spr 91, p. 38.
6176. THOMSON, David
"By Air, the Jumper's Daze." [CimR] (96) Jl 91, p. 118-119.
6177. THOOR, Jesse
"An ein Funfzigpfennigstuck." [InterPR] (17:2) Fall 91, p. 52.
"An einen Soldaten." [NewRena] (8:2, #25) Fall 91, p. 114.
"Blessed Is" (tr. by Gary Sea). [NewRena] (8:2, #25) Fall 91, p. 135.
"Da Da." [NewRena] (8:2, #25) Fall 91, p. 122.
"Da Da" (tr. by Gary Sea). [NewRena] (8:2, #25) Fall 91, p. 123.
"Drifter's Sonnet" (tr. by Gary Sea). [InterPR] (17:2) Fall 91, p. 55.
"Der Erste Brief des Bedienten Abu." [InterPR] (17:1) Spr 91, p. 26.
"Der Erste Brief des Bedienten Abu." [NewRena] (8:2, #25) Fall 91, p. 120.
"Das Erste Sonett." [InterPR] (17:2) Fall 91, p. 46.
"Evening Sonnet" (tr. by Gary Sea). [NewRena] (8:2, #25) Fall 91, p. 129.
"First Letter of the Servant Abu" (tr. by Gary Sea). [InterPR] (17:1) Spr 91, p. 27.
"First Letter of the Servant Abu" (tr. by Gary Sea). [NewRena] (8:2, #25) Fall 91,
p. 121.
"The First Sonnet" (tr. by Gary Sea). [InterPR] (17:2) Fall 91, p. 47.
"Das Gelächter." [NewRena] (8:2, #25) Fall 91, p. 130.
"The Laughter" (tr. by Gary Sea). [NewRena] (8:2, #25) Fall 91, p. 131.
"Lumpencredo." [InterPR] (17:2) Fall 91, p. 50.
"Rat Sonnet" (tr. by Gary Sea). [InterPR] (17:2) Fall 91, p. 49.
"Rattensonett." [InterPR] (17:2) Fall 91, p. 48.
"Rede von der Bedrohlichen Auflösung" (Früherer Titel: Sonett von der Widerlichen
Sattheit). [NewRena] (8:2, #25) Fall 91, p. 126.
"Schlafsonett." [InterPR] (17:1) Spr 91, p. 28.
"Schlafsonett." [NewRena] (8:2, #25) Fall 91, p. 118.
"The Second Voice" (tr. by Gary Sea). [NewRena] (8:2, #25) Fall 91, p. 133.
"Selig Ist." [NewRena] (8:2, #25) Fall 91, p. 134.
"Sleep Sonnet" (tr. by Gary Sea). [NewRena] (8:2, #25) Fall 91, p. 119.
"Sleepsonnet" (tr. by Gary Sea). [InterPR] (17:1) Spr 91, p. 29.
"Sonett am Abend." [NewRena] (8:2, #25) Fall 91, p. 128.
"Sonett im Winter." [NewRena] (8:2, #25) Fall 91, p. 112.
"Sonett vom Guten Willen." [InterPR] (17:1) Spr 91, p. 30.
"Sonett vom Verlorenen Sohn." [InterPR] (17:1) Spr 91, p. 34.
"Sonett vom Verlorenen Sohn." [NewRena] (8:2, #25) Fall 91, p. 124.
"Sonett von der Beziehungslosigkeit." [InterPR] (17:2) Fall 91, p. 54.
"Sonett von der Endgültigen Frage." [NewRena] (8:2, #25) Fall 91, p. 136.
"Sonett von der Grossen Rast." [NewRena] (8:2, #25) Fall 91, p. 108.
"Sonett von der Versuchung" (Früherer Titel: Das Elfte Irrenhaussonett). [NewRena]
(8:2, #25) Fall 91, p. 116.
"Sonnet in Winter" (tr. by Gary Sea). [NewRena] (8:2, #25) Fall 91, p. 113.
"Sonnet of Depressing Thoughts" (tr. by Gary Sea). [NewRena] (8:2, #25) Fall 91,
p. 111.
"Sonnet of Good Will" (tr. by Gary Sea). [InterPR] (17:1) Spr 91, p. 31.
"Sonnet of the Definitive Question" (Subtitle in Earlier Versions: After a Sonnet by
Pottier. Tr. by Gary Sea). [NewRena] (8:2, #25) Fall 91, p. 137.
"Sonnet of the Prodigal Son" (tr. by Gary Sea). [InterPR] (17:1) Spr 91, p. 35.
"Sonnet of the Prodigal Son" (tr. by Gary Sea). [NewRena] (8:2, #25) Fall 91, p.
125.
"Sonnet of the Profound Rest" (tr. by Gary Sea). [NewRena] (8:2, #25) Fall 91, p.
109.
"Sonnett von der Betrüblichen Überlegung." [NewRena] (8:2, #25) Fall 91, p. 110.

425

"Speaking of Ominous Decay" (Earlier Title: Sonnet of Repulsive Satiety, tr. by
 Gary Sea). [NewRena] (8:2, #25) Fall 91, p. 127.
"Temptation's Sonnet" (Earlier Title: The Eleventh Madhouse Sonnet, tr. by Gary
 Sea). [NewRena] (8:2, #25) Fall 91, p. 117.
"Tessiner Nächte." [InterPR] (17:1) Spr 91, p. 32.
"Ticino Nights" (tr. by Gary Sea). [InterPR] (17:1) Spr 91, p. 33.
"To a 50-Cent Piece" (tr. by Gary Sea). [InterPR] (17:2) Fall 91, p. 53.
"To a Soldier" (tr. by Gary Sea). [NewRena] (8:2, #25) Fall 91, p. 115.
"Tramp's Credo" (tr. by Gary Sea). [InterPR] (17:2) Fall 91, p. 51.
"Die Zweite Stimme." [NewRena] (8:2, #25) Fall 91, p. 132.
6178. THORBURN, Alexander
"The Barbershop." [GettyR] (4:3) Sum 91, p. 482-483.
"The Bottling Plant." [GettyR] (4:3) Sum 91, p. 480-481.
"The Cemetery." [NewYorker] (67:12) 13 My 91, p. 38.
6179. THORBURN, Russell
"Angel." [Parting] (4:1) Sum 91, p. 31.
"Gerard Throws a Snowball Outside St. Bonaventure's." [Parting] (4:2) Wint 91-92,
 p. 9-10.
"The German Soldier and the Jew." [Parting] (4:1) Sum 91, p. 7.
"John the Baptist Who Lives in the Suburbs." [Parting] (4:1) Sum 91, p. 5-6
6180. THORN, David
"Dar la Luz." [PoetryC] (12:1) D 91, p. 20.
"The Hummingbird in Our Garden." [PoetryC] (12:1) D 91, p. 20.
6181. THORNDIKE, Jonathan L.
"A Suburban Dream." [BellR] (14:2) Fall 91, p. 46.
6182. THORNTON, Kevin C.
"If Not Shadows of Men." [OxfordM] (7:2) Fall-Wint 91, p. 33.
6183. THORNTON, Russell
"The Visiting Wind." [CanLit] (131) Wint 91, p. 63.
6184. THORPE, Michael
"Birds of Hong Kong." [AntigR] (84) Wint 91, p. 141.
"The Disarming 'Language of the Birds'" (from the Mantiq al Tayr, School of
 Bihzad, Iran, 1483). [AntigR] (84) Wint 91, p. 140.
"Swans Still at Coole." [AntigR] (84) Wint 91, p. 139.
6185. THURSTON, Michael
"Basketball." [CoalC] (3) My 91, p. 13.
6186. TIAN, Xiaofei
"The Accomplices" (tr. of Bei Dao). [PraS] (65:2) Sum 91, p. 101.
"Ars Poetica" (tr. of Bei Dao). [PraS] (65:2) Sum 91, p. 104.
"The Boggle." [PraS] (65:2) Sum 91, p. 75-76.
"Boundaries" (tr. of Bei Dao). [PraS] (65:2) Sum 91, p. 103.
"Chatting About Summer" (tr. of Liu Zhan Qiu). [PraS] (65:2) Sum 91, p. 59.
"Chimes" (tr. of Luo Yihe). [PraS] (65:2) Sum 91, p. 54-55.
"A China Vase on My Birthday." [PraS] (65:2) Sum 91, p. 77.
"Flight" (tr. of Hwang Yunte). [PraS] (65:2) Sum 91, p. 105.
"The Forerunner" (tr. of Luo Yihe). [PraS] (65:2) Sum 91, p. 55.
"The Homing Birds" (tr. of Luo Yihe). [PraS] (65:2) Sum 91, p. 53.
"The Host" (tr. of Bei Dao). [PraS] (65:2) Sum 91, p. 102.
"A Poem Written at Midnight." [PraS] (65:2) Sum 91, p. 74-75.
"Remembering the Past" (tr. of Zhang Xiaojian). [PraS] (65:2) Sum 91, p. 79.
"The Space" (tr. of Bei Dao). [PraS] (65:2) Sum 91, p. 102-103.
"Temptation" (tr. of Bei Dao). [PraS] (65:2) Sum 91, p. 103-104.
"To a Lost Child" (tr. of Zhang Xiaojian). [PraS] (65:2) Sum 91, p. 78.
6187. TIBBETTS, Frederick
"The Penitent Magdalen." [Epoch] (40:1) 91, p. 14.
"A Song from the Reef." [Epoch] (40:1) 91, p. 15.
6188. TICHY, Susan
"Black Cows at Evening." [Ploughs] (17:4) Wint 91-92, p. 42-45.
6189. TIEBER, Linda
"Pumpkin Orange." [NewYorkQ] (44) 91, p. 80.
"She's running up, bare-breasted from the water." [NewYorkQ] (45) 91, p. 53.
"This is nonsense. I wouldn't smile for them." [NewYorkQ] (46) 91, p. 43.
6190. TIEMAN, John Samuel
"On Lines by Wen I-To." [RiverS] (33) 91, p. 72-73.
"Prose Aubade for Michael and Cassandra." [Pig] (17) 91, p. 61.

426

TIERNEY

6191. TIERNEY, Diane
"River Daughter." [BlackWR] (18:1) Fall-Wint 91, p. 24.
"Sundial." [BlackWR] (18:1) Fall-Wint 91, p. 23.
6192. TIERNEY, Karl
"Cafe Hairdo." [JamesWR] (8:4) Sum 91, p. 9.
"Funereal" (In memory of Don Sherrow). [JamesWR] (8:4) Sum 91, p. 9.
6193. TIFF, Holland
"One Year Mother's Day Was." [Kalliope] (13:2) 91, p. 58-59.
6194. TIGER, Madeline
"Le Retour au Pays, Courbet, 1854." [US1] (24/25) Spr 91, p. 20-21.
"Two Kids." [ChironR] (10:2) Sum 91, p. 43.
6195. TIKKANEN, Marta
"Untitled: A sunny and sheltered Mediterranean harbor" (tr. by Thomas and Vera
Vance). [Vis] (37) 91, p. 30.
"Untitled: In slow motion" (tr. by Thomas and Vera Vance). [Vis] (37) 91, p. 29-30.
6196. TILLER, Ruth
"My Soul to Keep." [ChatR] (11:2) Wint 91, p. 38.
6197. TILLINGHAST, David
"I Have Always Known." [GeoR] (45:3) Fall 91, p. 554-555.
6198. TILLINGHAST, Richard
"Anatolian Journey." [NewYorker] (67:19 [i.e. 67:13]) 20 My 91, p. 38.
"House with Children." [Ploughs] (17:2/3) Fall 91, p. 133.
6199. TILTON, Dave
"Caught Looking." [Spitball] (39) Wint 91, p. 40.
TING, Shu
See SHU, Ting
6200. TITTLER, Nancy
"First Fortepiano Sonnet" (tr. of Innokenty Annensky, w. Devon Miller-Duggan).
[SpoonRQ] (16:3/4) Sum-Fall 91, p. 41.
"The Second Fortepiano Sonnet" (tr. of Innokenty Annensky, w. Devon
Miller-Duggan). [SpoonRQ] (16:3/4) Sum-Fall 91, p. 42.
6201. TJEPKES, Michael
"A Braver Voyage." [NorthStoneR] (10) Fall 91-Wint 92, p. 125.
"Friedrich Hölderlin." [NorthStoneR] (10) Fall 91-Wint 92, p. 124.
"Moon Pull" (For Jo Ann). [NorthStoneR] (10) Fall 91-Wint 92, p. 124.
"Perpetual." [NorthStoneR] (10) Fall 91-Wint 92, p. 125.
6202. TKACZ, Virlana
"May" (tr. of Natalka Bilotserkivets, w. Wanda Phipps). [Agni] (34) 91, p. 51-54.
6203. TOBE, Dorothy
"Inheritance." [PoetL] (86:2) Sum 91, p. 21-22.
6204. TOBIN, Daniel
"The Clock." [HampSPR] Wint 91, p. 46.
"If You Cut Your Finger, Bandage the Knife" (after a sculpture by Joseph Beuys).
[Chelsea] (52) 91, p. 99.
"My Uncle's Watch." [GrahamHR] (15) Fall 91, p. 22-23.
"Passages." [Poetry] (159:2) N 91, p. 88-90.
"Trees of Knowledge" (photograph of a dismembered Salvadoran rebel, Carpenter
Center, 1982). [MinnR] (NS 37) Fall 91, p. 17.
6205. TOBIN, Jim
"Suspension." [PassN] (12:2) Wint 91, p. 9.
6206. TODD, Theodora
"Autumnal." [CalQ] (35/36) 91, p. 130.
"The Corpse." [BelPoJ] (41:3) Spr 91, p. 29-30.
"Modern Birth." [BellR] (14:2) Fall 91, p. 48-49.
"The Physician's Lesson." [BelPoJ] (41:3) Spr 91, p. 28-29.
"Spontaneous Combustion." [CalQ] (35/36) 91, p. 131-132.
6207. TOFER', Merle, II
"Poetic Verses" (for gavin dillard). [HawaiiR] (15:2, #32) Spr 91, p. 87.
6208. TOFERO, Cristian
"Father I Am the Coyote." [Writer] (104:12) D 91, p. 25.
6209. TOGEAS, James
"Autumn's Vortex." [NorthStoneR] (10) Fall 91-Wint 92, p. 64.
"Silvio's Exile in the Steppes." [NorthStoneR] (10) Fall 91-Wint 92, p. 65.
"Vampire." [NorthStoneR] (10) Fall 91-Wint 92, p. 65.
6210. TOKUNO, Ken
"Leaving Something Behind" (for Nelson Bentley). [BellArk] (7:1) Ja-F 91, p. 5.

6211. TOLNAI, Ottó
"The Huge, Dead Eye" (tr. by Nicholas Kolumban). [MassR] (32:4) Wint 91-92, p. 491.
"Watching My Own Face" (tr. by Nicholas Kolumban). [MidAR] (11:2) 91, p. 54.
6212. TOLSON, Melvin B.
"To Jack Conroy." [NewL] (57:4) Sum 91, p. 88-89.
6213. TOMKIW, Lydia
"Latest Ton (Knott's et Al.)." [Aerial] (6/7) 91, p. 175.
6214. TOMLINSON, Charles
"The Broom: The New Wife's Tale." [ParisR] (33:121) Wint 91, p. 44.
"Fire." [Poetry] (158:3) Je 91, p. 136.
"Puerto Rico" (Selections: 4 poems). [Ploughs] (17:1) Spr 91, p. 186-190.
"The Stair." [ParisR] (33:121) Wint 91, p. 43.
6215. TOMLINSON, Rawdon
"Breakdown." [WritersF] (17) Fall 91, p. 32-33.
"Indiahoma." [Vis] (35) 91, p. 25.
"Lost." [WritersF] (17) Fall 91, p. 33-34.
"Mother's Roses." [Interim] (10:2) Fall-Wint 91-92, p. 45.
"Original Sin and Forgiveness at Restland." [CumbPR] (11:1) Fall 91, p. 56.
"Signs." [HolCrit] (28:5) D 91, p. 19.
"Visions of a Bone Hunter: Loren Eiseley 1905-1978." [SewanR] (99:2) Spr 91, p. 196-197.
"Winter Wheat." [Interim] (10:2) Fall-Wint 91-92, p. 46.
TOMOKO, Kuribayashi
See KURIBAYASHI, Tomoko
6216. TOMPKINS, Wayne
"One Shot Kills." [PottPort] (13:1) Spr 91, p. 20.
6217. TONETTO, Walter
"A Poetry of War." [CentR] (35:3) Fall 91, p. 539.
"The Shroud of Oman" (for Elizabeth Curry). [CentR] (35:3) Fall 91, p. 540.
6218. TONTIC, Stevan
"Balada O Konju." [InterPR] (15:1) Spr 89, p. 36.
"Black Flour" (tr. by Simha Levi Bogdanovic). [InterPR] (15:1) Spr 89, p. 31.
"Crno Brasno 41." [InterPR] (15:1) Spr 89, p. 30.
"Going Away" (tr. by Simha Levi Bogdanovic). [InterPR] (15:1) Spr 89, p. 33.
"Harbor of Salvation" (tr. by Maja Herman). [InterPR] (15:1) Spr 89, p. 37.
"A Horse Ballad" (tr. by Maja Herman). [InterPR] (15:1) Spr 89, p. 37.
"The House in the Sky" (tr. by Vasa D. Mihailovich). [InterPR] (15:1) Spr 89, p. 35.
"In My Workshop" (tr. by Vasa D. Mihailovich). [InterPR] (15:1) Spr 89, p. 29.
"Kuca U Nebu." [InterPR] (15:1) Spr 89, p. 34.
"Luka Spasa." [InterPR] (15:1) Spr 89, p. 36.
"News" (tr. by Vasa D. Mihailovich). [InterPR] (15:1) Spr 89, p. 31.
"Odlazak." [InterPR] (15:1) Spr 89, p. 32.
"U Mojoj Radionici." [InterPR] (15:1) Spr 89, p. 28.
"Vijesti." [InterPR] (15:1) Spr 89, p. 30.
6219. TOPAL, Carine
"Throwing the Goddess." [OnTheBus] (8/9) 91, p. 161162.
"Written on My Side." [PacificR] (10) 91-92, p. 75.
6220. TORNES, Elizabeth
"Visiting My Second Cousin." [WestHR] (45:2) Sum 91, p. 110.
"Wash" (for Pam Houston). [HighP] (6:3) Wint 91, p. 69-70.
6221. TORO, Gabor
"I Have to Look Long" (Hosszan kell nezllem, tr. of Sandor Csoori, w. Len Roberts). [Agni] (34) 91, p. 159.
6222. TORRE, Stephan
"Thaw." [SouthernPR] (31:2) Fall 91, p. 67-68.
"We Went Out to Make Hay." [Manoa] (3:1) Spr 91, p. 58-65.
6223. TORRES, Alba Azucena
"Confessions" (tr. by John Oliver Simon). [ArtfulD] (20/21) 91, p. 61.
6224. TORRES RIVERA, Gerardo
"Bodas de Perros." [Mester] (20:1) Spr 91, p. 87.
"Cambio de Estación." [Mester] (20:1) Spr 91, p. 88.
"Cosas de Agustín Lara." [Mester] (20:1) Spr 91, p. 85.
"Disco Disco." [Mester] (20:1) Spr 91, p. 86.
"Estado Pos Lacan." [Mester] (20:1) Spr 91, p. 84.

TORRES RIVERA

"Locuciones." [Mester] (20:1) Spr 91, p. 85.
"Mi Mente y la Raya." [Mester] (20:1) Spr 91, p. 83.
"Primer Estado Lacan." [Mester] (20:1) Spr 91, p. 84.
6225. TORRESON, Rodney
"Joe Dimaggio Never Swings a Bat at Old Timers' Games." [Spitball] (39) Wint 91,
p. 41.
"October '62." [WindO] (54) Sum 91, p. 25.
"Tools of Contention." [Spitball] (39) Wint 91, p. 42-43.
6226. TOWLE, Andrew
"Luna Moth." [Poetry] (157:5) F 91, p. 274.
6227. TOWLE, Parker
"Decibels and Candlepower." [CapeR] (26:2) Fall 91, p. 31.
6228. TOWLE, Tony
"Caprice." [Talisman] (7) Fall 91, p. 96-97.
"Rhapsodic Reviews: IV." [Talisman] (7) Fall 91, p. 97.
6229. TOWNLEY, Roderick
"The Changing Table." [NewL] (58:1) Fall.91, p. 77.
6230. TOWNLEY, Wyatt
"What Keeps Us Still." [NewL] (58:1) Fall 91, p. 76.
6231. TOWNSEND, A. C.
"Amy." [CalQ] (35/36) 91, p. 44.
6232. TOWNSEND, Ann
"Date Nut Bread." [ColEng] (53:1) Ja 91, p. 34.
"In the Limbo of Lost Words." [SouthernPR] (31:1) Spr 91, p. 45-46.
"Irish." [TexasR] (11:1/2) Spr-Sum 90, p. 65.
"Realism." [PraS] (65:4) Wint 91, p. 106-107.
6233. TOWNSEND, Melissa
"Strange, Lean Woman." [CentralP] (19/20) Spr-Fall 91, p. 200-202.
6234. TRACY, Robert
"O This Air" (tr. of Osip Mandelstam). [NewYRB] (38:15 [i.e. 38:16]) 10 O 91, p.
8.
"To Cassandra" (tr. of Osip Mandelstam). [NewYRB] (38:15 [i.e. 38:16]) 10 O 91,
p. 8.
6235. TRAIL, B. D.
"California Dreaming or: Shrapnel of Another Sort." [ChironR] (10:1) Spr 91, p. 10.
"Flashback." [NewYorkQ] (44) 91, p. 55.
"Our Lady of the Flies." [ChironR] (10:1) Spr 91, p. 10.
"Vietnam Veteran Against the Wall." [ChironR] (10:1) Spr 91, p. 10.
"War Story." [ChironR] (10:1) Spr 91, p. 10.
6236. TRAINER, Yvonne
"Flag Girl." [PottPort] (13:1) Spr 91, p. 34.
"On Holidays." [PottPort] (13:1) Spr 91, p. 32.
"Sometime in My Early Teens." [PottPort] (13:1) Spr 91, p. 33.
6237. TRAKL, Georg
"De Profundis" (tr. by Bruce Berlind). [Chelsea] (51) 91, p. 58.
"In the East" (tr. by Bruce Berlind). [Chelsea] (51) 91, p. 59.
"Sinking" (To Karl Borromaus Heinrich, tr. by Bruce Berlind). [Chelsea] (51) 91,
p. 57.
"Sleep" (tr. by Bruce Berlind). [Chelsea] (51) 91, p. 61.
"To the Boy Elis" (tr. by Bruce Berlind). [Chelsea] (51) 91, p. 60.
6238. TRAMMELL, Catherine
"A Summer Scene." [EmeraldCR] (3) 91, c1990, p. 57.
TRAN, Thi My Nhung
See NHUNG, Tran Thi My
6239. TRANQUILLA, Ronald
"The Holy Spirit." [WestB] (29) 91, p. 9.
6240. TRANSMISSION, Otto M.
"The angel said 'Flee' to old Lot." [SoCoast] (11) Wint 91, p. 61.
6241. TRANSTRÖMER, Tomas
"After a Visit to the DDR" (November 1990, tr. by Robin Fulton). [Antaeus] (67)
Fall 91, p. 104.
"April and Silence" (tr. by Robin Fulton). [KenR] (NS 13:3) Sum 91, p. 125.
"National Insecurity" (tr. by Robin Fulton). [Antaeus] (67) Fall 91, p. 105.
"A Page of the Night-Book" (tr. by Robin Fulton). [Antaeus] (67) Fall 91, p. 106.
6242. TRANTER, John
"April Surprise." [NewAW] (7) Spr 91, p. 11.

"At the Florida." [Verse] (8:1) Spr 91, p. 80-81.
"Cable Chimp." [NewAW] (7) Spr 91, p. 10.
"Chicken Shack." [NewAW] (7) Spr 91, p. 9.
6243. TRASK, Haunani-Kay
"Missionary Graveyard" (for Bernard Trask 1910-1976). [ChamLR] (8-9) Spr-Fall
91, p. 1-3.
6244. TRAXLER, Patricia
"The Call." [Ploughs] (17:2/3) Fall 91, p. 32.
"The Driver." [LaurelR] (25:2) Sum 91, p. 97-100.
"The Edge." [Agni] (34) 91, p. 92.
"Faith (or Why I Can't Swim)." [Agni] (34) 91, p. 93-96.
6245. TREADWELL, Florence
"Father's Bed." [PraF] (12:4) Wint 91-92, p. 36.
"In Our Daughters' Eyes." [Grain] (19:2) Sum 91, p. 93.
"Noli Me Tangere." [PoetryC] (12:1) D 91, p. 4.
"Possessed." [PraF] (12:4) Wint 91-92, p. 34.
"Rhapsody for a Blue Sweater." [PraF] (12:4) Wint 91-92, p. 35.
6246. TREBY, Ivor C.
"Woman with Camellias." [PoetryE] (32) Fall 91, p. 137-146.
6247. TREEN, Ellen
"My Rewrites." [Kalliope] (13:1) 91, p. 50.
6248. TREFETHEN, Tracy
"Baptism." [HayF] (8) Spr-Sum 91, p. 86.
6249. TREGEBOV, Rhea
"Respite." [PraS] (65:3) Fall 91, p. 126.
"The Top of My Head." [NoAmR] (276:3) S 91, p. 27.
6250. TREHARNE, Mark
"The Spring on the Lance" (tr. of Yves Bichet). [Verse] (8:2) Sum 91, p. 121-122.
6251. TREIBER, Jay
"Mule Thief" (for Dale Hiatt). [TexasR] (11:1/2) Spr-Sum 90, p. 96.
6252. TREITEL, Renata
"Repose of the Green" (tr. of Rosita Copioli). [Paint] (18:36) Aut 91, p. 54.
"White" (tr. of Rosita Copioli). [Paint] (18:36) Aut 91, p. 55.
6253. TREMBLAY, Bill
"A Bend in the Road." [Journal] (15:2) Fall 91, p. 21.
"A Front Range Sky." [OhioR] (46) 91, p. 114.
"An Inmate at Utah State Prison Looks at Mt. Tippenogas." [HighP] (6:1) Spr 91, p.
89-90.
"Learning to Listen." [Journal] (15:2) Fall 91, p. 20.
"Streetlamp." [OhioR] (46) 91, p. 115.
6254. TREMMEL, Robert
"Dairy Buy-Out." [CinPR] (22) Spr 91, p. 22-23.
"Exodus." [MidwQ] (32:2) Wint 91, p. 195.
"The Pro." [TexasR] (12:3/4) Fall-Wint 91, p. 94.
6255. TRENCHARD, John
"An Environment of Silence." [LouisL] (8:2) Fall 91, p. 55.
6256. TRETHEWEY, Eric
"Aubade." [Poetry] (157:6) Mr 91, p. 314.
"Current." [SewanR] (99:2) Spr 91, p. 200-201.
"Fools and Horses." [SewanR] (99:2) Spr 91, p. 198-200.
"Homesteading." [TexasR] (12:3/4) Fall-Wint 91, p. 95-96.
"Leaf." [SpiritSH] (56) Spr-Sum 91, p. 45.
"The Listeners." [Atlantic] (267:4) Ap 91, p. 86.
"Periphery." [ManhatPR] (13) [91?], p. 10.
"Scar." [ParisR] (33:118) Spr 91, p. 259.
"Stillborn." [PoetryE] (31) Spr 91, p. 92.
"Woods Talk." [Poetry] (157:6) Mr 91, p. 313.
6257. TRIBBLE, Jon
"Dazzle" (Ibn al-Haytham, 965-1039, Arab philosopher of optical theory). [Crazy]
(41) Wint 91, p. 59-60.
"First Rites: Devil's Den State Park." [Crazy] (41) Wint 91, p. 57-58.
"Imago Mundi." [Crazy] (41) Wint 91, p. 47-50.
"Of Light and Love." [Crazy] (41) Wint 91, p. 53-56.
"We Are Part of the Body." [Crazy] (41) Wint 91, p. 51-52.
6258. TRIFF, Soren
"Perpetuum Mobile." [LindLM] (10:1) Ja-Mr 91, p. 28.

6259. TRILLIN, Calvin
"Adieu, Mr. R." [Nat] (253:6) 26 Ag-2 S 91, p. 218.
"After Seeing Mario Cuomo Interviewed on Television." [Nat] (253:22) 23 D 91, p. 801.
"The Art of Conversation." [Nat] (253:17) 18 N 91, p. 613.
"Basic Assumption Shaken." [Nat] (253:8) 16 S 91, p. 290.
"Colin Powell Reconsidered." [Nat] (252:20) 27 My 91, p. 689.
"Commencement Speech." [Nat] (252:23) 17 Je 91, p. 801.
"Disharmony Among the President's Men." [Nat] (252:2) 21 91, p. 41.
"Eureka!" [Nat] (252:9) 11 Mr 91, p. 293.
"Father's Day Isw Gone." [Nat] (253:2) 8 Jl 91, p. 41.
"Foreign Policy Question." [Nat] (252:14) 15 Ap 91, p. 473.
"Fragment of Transcript from Negotiations with Saddam Hussein." [Nat] (252:10) 18 Mr 91, p. 329.
"Gates Gets the Job." [Nat] (253:12) 14 O 91, p. 433.
"Gorby's Our Boy." [Nat] (252:6) 18 F 91, p. 185.
"Gray Area." [Nat] (253:21) 16 D 91, p. 765.
"If You Knew What Sununu (Reprise)." [Nat] (252:19) 20 My 91, p. 653.
"The Iowa Derby." [Nat] (253:10) 30 S 91, p. 361.
"Judging Nancy." [Nat] (252:18) 13 My 91, p. 617.
"The Kurds Are Internal." [Nat] (252:17) 6 My 91, p. 581.
"A Native American View of Columbus's Voyage." [Nat] (253:3) 15-22 Jl 91, p. 126.
"On Campaign Rhetoric." [Nat] (253:18) 25 N 91, p. 657.
"On David Duke." [Nat] (253:16) 11 N 91, p. 577.
"On David Duke as Republonazi (Reprise)." [Nat] (253:20) 9 D 91, p. 729.
"On Not Making the Cut." [Nat] (252:21) 3 Je 91, p. 725.
"On the Banking Practices of Members of the House." [Nat] (253:14) 28 O 91, p. 505.
"On the President's Nuclear Initiative." [Nat] (253:13) 21 O 91, p. 469.
"On the Queen's Visit to Alice Frazier's House in Southeast Washington." [Nat] (252:22) 10 Je 91, p. 761.
"On the Return of the Fuller Figure." [Nat] (252:4) 4 F 91, p. 113.
"One Republican National Committee Chairman in Search of a Pronunciation." [Nat] (252:3) 28 Ja 91, p. 77.
"The Picked Up by the Los Angeles Police Department Blues." [Nat] (252:13) 8 Ap 91, p. 437.
"Quotas." [Nat] (252:1) 7-14 Ja 91, p. 5.
"Respite." [Nat] (252:8) 4 Mr 91, p. 257.
"The Results from Pennsylvania." [Nat] (253:19) 2 D 91, p. 693.
"Rust v. Sullivan." [Nat] (252:24) 24 Je 91, p. 835.
"A Senator and a Top Aide Discuss the Issue of Sexual Harassment." [Nat] (253:15) 4 N 91, p. 541.
"A Short Military Biography of Saddam Hussein." [Nat] (252:11) 25Mr 91, p. 365.
"A Short Review of Kitty Kelley's Biography of Nancy Reagan." [Nat] (252:16) 29 Ap 91, p. 545.
"Singing in the Rain." [Nat] (253:5) 12-19 Ag 91, p. 181.
"A Song for Senator Harkin." [Nat] (253:7) 9 S 91, p. 253.
"A Song of Cost-Effectiveness." [Nat] (252:7) 25 F 91, p. 221.
"Spies, Reconsidered." [Nat] (253:9) 23 S 91, p. 340.
"Suggested Cheers for the Broadway Ticker-Tape Victory Parade." [Nat] (252:12) 1 Ap 91, p. 401.
"The Supremes." [Nat] (253:11) 7 O 91, p. 397.
"Thursday Night War." [Nat] (252:5) 11 F 91, p. 149.
"Two Poems (for the Price of One) on Sununu's Replacement." [Nat] (253:23) 30 D 91, p. 837.
"Victory Parades: A Cowboy's Lament." [Nat] (253:1) 1 Jl 91, p. 5.
"We've Got the Gun Nuts on the Run." [Nat] (252:15) 22 Ap 91, p. 510.
"Zachary Taylor, R. (Mostly) I.P." [Nat] (253:4) 29 Jl-5 Ag 91, p. 145.
6260. TRIMMER, Greg
"Public Notice." [ColEng] (53:2) F 91, p. 166.
"Salt." [ColEng] (53:2) F 91, p. 164.
"Transmigration." [GrahamHR] (15) Fall 91, p. 73.
"Trobule." [ColEng] (53:2) F 91, p. 165.
"Wrens As perfection." [ColEng] (53:2) F 91, p. 163.

6261. TRINIDAD, David
"Dead Flowers." [BrooklynR] (8) 91, p. 7.
"The Kiss." [Bomb] (34) Wint 91, p. 84.
"Love Poem." [BrooklynR] (8) 91, p. 6.
"Pee Shy." [JamesWR] (8:3) Spr 91, p. 7.
"A Photograph." [Bomb] (34) Wint 91, p. 84.
"Reruns" (Haiku). [Harp] (283:1695) Ag 91, p. 34.
"Song." [Bomb] (34) Wint 91, p. 84.
"Sunday Evening." [NewAW] (8/9) Fall 91, p. 31.
"The World." [Bomb] (34) Wint 91, p. 84.
6262. TRIPI, Vincent
"Haiku" (3 poems). [PoetryUSA] (22) Spr 91, p. 6.
6263. TRITICA, John
"Duels and Divergences." [Talisman] (7) Fall 91, p. 41-43.
"Improvisations Beginning with Lines from Clark Coolidge" (Selections: 9-10).
[Aerial] (6/7) 91, p. 173-174.
6264. TRITTO, Michael
"Markers." [CumbPR] (11:1) Fall 91, p. 73-74.
"Pictures on the Table." [CumbPR] (11:1) Fall 91, p. 75.
"Ride." [CumbPR] (10:2) Spr 91, p. 26.
6265. TRIVELPIECE, Laurel
"Dreaming of Lions." [Field] (44) Spr 91, p. 36.
"Eden: The Last Exit." [Field] (44) Spr 91, p. 34-35.
"Lights in the Wheat." [CinPR] (21) Spr 90, p. 10.
"Moonstone." [CalQ] (35/36) 91, p. 139.
"The Swans." [MalR] (96) Fall 91, p. 71.
"Wing Space." [Field] (44) Spr 91, p. 37.
6266. TROTTER, Elizabeth (Elizabeth M.)
"Imprinted." [SpoonRQ] (16:3/4) Sum-Fall 91, p. 28.
"Tornadoes, Black Earth, WI, 1984." [CalQ] (35/36) 91, p. 37.
6267. TROUPE, Quincy
"After Hearing a Radio Announcement, a Comment on Some Conditions, 1978."
[Ploughs] (17:4) Wint 91-92, p. 117-118.
"Avalanche" (for K. Curtis Lyle). [Ploughs] (17:4) Wint 91-92, p. 119-121.
"Conjuring Against Alien Spirits" (for Ishmael Reed). [KenR] (NS 13:4) Fall 91, p.
62-63.
"Reflections on Growing Older." [KenR] (NS 13:4) Fall 91, p. 61.
6268. TROWBRIDGE, William
"The Dead." [TarRP] (31:1) Fall 91, p. 46-47.
"Libraries." [SpoonRQ] (16:1/2) Wint-Spr 91, p. 108.
"Lone Wolf — No Club." [SpoonRQ] (16:1/2) Wint-Spr 91, p. 109.
"Missing Person." [GeoR] (45:3) Fall 91, p. 526.
"Monopause." [PoetC] (22:2) Wint 91, p. 30-31.
"Mort the Dork." [PoetC] (22:2) Wint 91, p. 32.
"O Paradise." [GeoR] (45:4) Wint 91, p. 708.
"Snafu." [CharR] (17:1) Spr 91, p. 42.
"What We Could Do." [TarRP] (31:1) Fall 91, p. 45-46.
"Work." [TarRP] (31:1) Fall 91, p. 45.
6269. TRUCULENTO, Guillermo
"La Guerra entre los Genitales." [BilingR] (16:1) Ja-Ap 91, p. 63-64.
"The War between the Genitals" (tr. by Janet Sunderland and Alicia Picazo).
[BilingR] (16:1) Ja-Ap 91, p. 65-66.
6270. TRUDELL, Dennis
"Milk the Cows." [GeoR] (45:4) Wint 91, p. 674.
6271. TRUSKY, Tom
"Why, to This Day, My Father Does Not Like Pineapple." [SoDakR] (29:3 part 2)
Aut 91, p. 38-39.
6272. TRUSSELL, Donna
"After the Lutheran Retreat." [PlumR] (1) Spr-Sum 91, p. 67.
6273. TSALOUMAS, Dimitris
"The Pale Knight." [CentR] (35:3) Fall 91, p. 535.
"The Panoply." [CentR] (35:3) Fall 91, p. 538.
"A Roman General's Letter." [CentR] (35:3) Fall 91, p. 536-537.
"Waiting for War." [CentR] (35:3) Fall 91, p. 535.

6274. TS'AO, Sung
"The War Year" (tr. by C. H. Kwock and Vincent McHugh). [PoetryUSA] (22) Spr
91, p. 21.
6275. TSUJIMOTO, Joseph I.
"The Man in the Straw Hat." [BambooR] (52) Fall 91, p. 132-135.
6276. TSUKAN (priest, ca. 710)
"How does it happen?" (tr. by Sam Hamill). [ColR] (NS 17:2) Fall-Wint 90, p. 17.
TSURAYUKI, Ki no
  See KI no TSURAYUKI (ca. 872-945), x
6277. TSVETAEVA, Marina
"She planted apples" (tr. by Jean Murphy). [WebR] (15) Spr 91, p. 27.
TU, Fu
  See DU, Fu
6278. TUCKER, Martin
"Fragment." [Boulevard] (5:3/6:1, #15/16) Spr 91, p. 216.
"The Lore of Four Oranges" (To William Carlos Williams). [Boulevard] (5:3/6:1,
#15/16) Spr 91, p. 214.
"Miriam and Her Urn." [Boulevard] (5:3/6:1, #15/16) Spr 91, p. 215.
6279. TUCKER, Memye Curtis
"Aus Meinem Leben." [SouthernR] (27:3) Jl 91, p. 707.
6280. TUFTS, Carol
"The Astrophysicists Listen for a Signal." [CapeR] (26:1) Spr 91, p. 45.
6281. TUGGLE, Mike
"Full Moon, Early Summer." [Zyzzyva] (7:1) Spr 91, p. 105.
"What Lures the Foxes Keeps Away the Deer." [Zyzzyva] (7:1) Spr 91, p. 103.
6282. TUGWELL, Judith A.
"Sun in My Second House: A Collection of Poems." [WorldO] (24:1/2) Fall 89-Wint
89-90, c1991, p. 5.
TULIN, Lois Young
  See YOUNG-TULIN, Lois
6283. TULLOSS, Rod
"How to Know Pollen and Spores" (for Wayne Somers & David Herrstrom). [US1]
(24/25) Spr 91, p. 19.
6284. TULLY, John
"So Wise So Young." [NegC] (11:1) 91, p. 22.
6285. TUMBALÉ, Elkion
"Word Enough of This But Not Enough." [DustyD] (2:1) Ja 91, p. 19.
6286. TUMBLESON, Ray
"Nothing Fabulous." [DogRR] (10:1) Sum 91, p. 33.
6287. TURCO, Lewis
"An Amherst Pastoral" (from lines in Emily Dickinson's letters). [NewOR] (18:3)
Fall 91, p. 27.
"Late Elegy for an Old Suicide." [SewanR] (98:4) Fall 90, p. 666-667.
"Quiescophobia: The Fear of Silence." [HampSPR] Wint 91, p. 61.
"Ruth Carr, 1919-1972." [LitR] (34:2) Wint 91, p. 252-253.
6288. TURNAGE, Sheila
"Dream Lives of Crows." [InterPR] (17:2) Fall 91, p. 97-98.
"In October, Maybe, in the Afternoon." [InterPR] (17:2) Fall 91, p. 100.
"Pilgrims' Wake." [InterPR] (17:2) Fall 91, p. 99.
"Snowfall in Georgia." [InterPR] (17:2) Fall 91, p. 98.
6289. TURNBULL, Gael
"Encountered." [NewAW] (8/9) Fall 91, p. 165.
"Gefryn." [NewAW] (8/9) Fall 91, p. 166.
"No Shelter: Utterance." [NewAW] (8/9) Fall 91, p. 165-166.
"The Office Required of Them (1815)." [NewAW] (8/9) Fall 91, p. 164-165.
"Whin: Mostly and Rarely." [NewAW] (8/9) Fall 91, p. 167.
6290. TURNER, Alberta
"Consider the Self." [ColR] (NS 18:1) Spr-Sum 91, p. 51-52.
"Dim." [ArtfulD] (20/21) 91, p. 69.
"Future." [ArtfulD] (20/21) 91, p. 71.
"God-ing." [ArtfulD] (20/21) 91, p. 70.
"Meditation Upon *Ought*." [ThRiPo] (37/38) 91, p. 36.
6291. TURNER, Donna
"Roofing." [MinnR] (NS 37) Fall 91, p. 32-33.
6292. TURNER, Gordon
"Apples / He's the Same." [CanLit] (131) Wint 91, p. 49-50.

6293. TURNER, Jen
    "The Making of a Warm Winter Coat." [BellR] (14:2) Fall 91, p. 6.
6294. TURNER, Judy
    "*Chez*= Porky." [SoCoast] (10) Fall 91, p. 56.
6295. TURNER, Larry
    "Daughters of Righteousness." [SpoonRQ] (16:3/4) Sum-Fall 91, p. 83-84.
6296. TUSSING, Katharine
    "From Buffalo Gal to Coyote." [MoodySI] (24/25/26) Spr 91, p. 50.
TVETAEVA, Marina
    See TSVETAEVA, Marina
6297. TWICHELL, Chase
    "Dirt." [Antaeus] (67) Fall 91, p. 144-145.
6298. TYLER, R. L.
    "Poetry Reading." [NewYorkQ] (45) 91, p. 72.
6299. TYSH, Chris
    "Per pale azure and sable, two hubbies in chief proper." [RiverS] (34) 91, p. 64.
    "We were always having to read the rubato version of things." [RiverS] (34) 91, p. 63.
6300. UELAND, Carol
    "At the window I watch the nocturnal clouds pass" (tr. of Aleksandr Kushner, w. Paul Graves). [AmerPoR] (20:1) Ja-F 91, p. 3.
    "It's longer, harder saying our goodbyes" (tr. of Aleksandr Kushner, w. Paul Graves). [AmerPoR] (20:1) Ja-F 91, p. 4.
    "Mozart's skull, from between two columns of the news" (tr. of Aleksandr Kushner, w. Paul Graves). [AmerPoR] (20:1) Ja-F 91, p. 4.
    "No woman that I'd met before" (tr. of Aleksandr Kushner, w. Paul Graves). [AmerPoR] (20:1) Ja-F 91, p. 4.
    "On this, the near side of the mystery line, a cloud" (tr. of Aleksandr Kushner, w. Paul Graves). [AmerPoR] (20:1) Ja-F 91, p. 4.
    "Tragedy's easy: once onstage, men wreck or slaughter" (tr. of Aleksandr Kushner, w. Paul Graves). [AmerPoR] (20:1) Ja-F 91, p. 4.
    "Vyritsa" (tr. of Aleksandr Kushner, w. Paul Graves). [AmerPoR] (20:1) Ja-F 91, p. 3.
    "Your exit's into frost, and the audience exits" (tr. of Aleksandr Kushner, w. Paul Graves). [AmerPoR] (20:1) Ja-F 91, p. 4.
UEMA, Marck Beggs (Marck L. Beggs)
    See BEGGS-UEMA, Marck (Marck L.)
6301. ULLMAN, Leslie
    "French." [Poetry] (157:4) Ja 91, p. 205-206.
    "Garnet." [HighP] (6:2) Fall 91, p. 94-95.
6302. ULMER, James
    "Atget." [Journal] (14:2) Wint 91, p. 42-43.
    "Gravity and Flight" (For my grandfather). [Boulevard] (5:3/6:1, #15/16) Spr 91, p. 148-149.
    "The Gulf." [NewYorker] (67:19) 1 Jl 91, p. 58.
    "Late Show." [AntR] (49:2) Spr 91, p. 246.
    "Melville." [BlackWR] (17:2) Spr-Sum 91, p. 21-22.
    "Storm Watch." [NoAmR] (276:2) Je 91, p. 8.
    "A World." [Journal] (14:2) Wint 91, p. 41.
6303. UNDERWOOD, Robert
    "Cheryl." [Pearl] (14) Fall-Wint 91, p. 16.
6304. UNGAR, Barbara Louise
    "Ode to the Grace Building." [LitR] (35:1) Fall 91, p. 86-87.
6305. UNGER, Barbara
    "Dream." [Contact] (10:59/60/61) Spr 91, p. 42.
    "Finally, for Sylvia." [DenQ] (26:1) Sum 91, p. 70-71.
    "French Photos." [NewYorkQ] (46) 91, p. 49.
    "Incantation." [Contact] (10:59/60/61) Spr 91, p. 42.
6306. UNGRIA, Ricardo M. de
    "Island." [Manoa] (3:1) Spr 91, p. 160-162.
    "Maya." [RiverS] (33) 91, p. 66-67.
    "Necessary Distances" (For Krip). [Manoa] (3:1) Spr 91, p. 163-165.
6307. UNSINO, Stephen
    "At the Storms' Summons" (tr. of Alexander Blok). [CrabCR] (7:3) 91, p. 6.
    "The Warthog." [PoetL] (86:3) Fall 91, p. 44.
    "Wings" (tr. of Alexander Blok). [CrabCR] (7:3) 91, p. 7.

6308. UNTERECKER, John
  "Guavas" (For Jim Kraus). [CalQ] (31) Fall 88, p. 35.
6309. UPDIKE, John
  "Bindweed." [NewYorker] (67:27) 26 Ag 91, p. 28.
  "Flurry." [OntR] (35) Fall-Wint 91-92, p. 28.
  "Fly." [ParisR] (33:120) Fall 91, p. 41.
  "Light Switches." [ParisR] (33:120) Fall 91, p. 40.
  "Relatives." [RiverC] (11:2) Spr 91, p. 1.
  "Thin Air." [OntR] (35) Fall-Wint 91-92, p. 28.
6310. UPHAM, Sondra
  "Elf Poem." [Elf] (1:4) Wint 91, p. 38.
6311. UPSHAW, Reagan
  "Dashboard Pantheon." [HangL] (58) 91, p. 76.
6312. UPTON, Lee
  "Cuckoo Clock." [SnailPR] (1:1) Spr 91, p. 9.
  "Jam in Midsummer." [SnailPR] (1:1) Spr 91, p. 8.
  "Lobster." [Boulevard] (5:3/6:1, #15/16) Spr 91, p. 125.
  "Nympheum." [TampaR] (4) 91, p. 43.
  "Peripheral Matters." [AntR] (49:4) Fall 91, p. 561.
  "Puppet Play." [Vis] (36) 91, p. 33.
  "Summer's Customers." [OhioR] (47) 91, p. 88-89.
6313. URBAIN, John
  "Found Poem." [NewYorkQ] (45) 91, p. 73.
6314. URDANG, Constance
  "Mexican Afternoons." [Poetry] (158:4) Jl 91, p. 202-203.
  "The Old Wives' Tale." [OntR] (34) Spr-Sum 91, p. 41.
  "The Snowstorm Collector." [NewL] (58:1) Fall 91, p. 40.
  "A Unified Field Theory." [CharR] (17:1) Spr 91, p. 43.
6315. URDANG, Elliott B.
  "Hunger" (tr. of Maria Banus, w. Marguerite Dorian). [MidAR] (11:1) 91, p. 131.
  "Through Bucharest, After the Rain" (tr. of Maria Banus, w. Marguerite Dorian).
      [MidAR] (11:1) 91, p. 130.
6316. URREA, Luis
  "The Sunday Drive" (1965). [Agni] (33) 91, p. 50-52.
6317. USCHUK, Pamela
  "Balancing." [SwampR] (7/8) Spr-Sum 91, p. 141.
  "Eating Salmon." [SwampR] (7/8) Spr-Sum 91, p. 139-140.
  "Ferry Shelling." [Calyx] (13:2) Sum 91, p. 42-43.
  "Hummingbird." [SwampR] (7/8) Spr-Sum 91, p. 143.
  "Snow Goose Migration at Tule Lake" (for Galen Burrell). [SwampR] (7/8)
      Spr-Sum 91, p. 137-138.
  "To Make the Bull Ascend" (for Fox McGrew). [SwampR] (7/8) Spr-Sum 91, p.
      142.
  "Touch Pool." [Calyx] (13:2) Sum 91, p. 44-47.
6318. UU, David
  "Different Rains" (after Steve Reich & for damian lopes). [WestCL] (25:2, #5) Fall
      91, p. 35.
  "The Fishy Seas of Life" (from the Captain's Diary). [WestCL] (25:2, #5) Fall 91,
      p. 34.
  "Kingston Electric System." [WestCL] (25:2, #5) Fall 91, p. 31-32.
  "Names" (Selections: 2 concretes). [WestCL] (25:2, #5) Fall 91, p. 33.
  "Quiet Complaint." [WestCL] (25:2, #5) Fall 91, p. 36.
6319. UYEMATSU, Amy
  "Corn Seed." [Contact] (10:59/60/61) Spr 91, p. 39.
  "Deliberate." [BambooR] (50/51) Spr-Sum 91, p. 133.
  "Florentino Diaz." [BambooR] (52) Fall 91, p. 136-137.
  "Lettuce and Strawberries." [Contact] (10:59/60/61) Spr 91, p. 38.
  "Lexicon." [BambooR] (50/51) Spr-Sum 91, p. 131-132.
  "Mail Order." [Contact] (10:59/60/61) Spr 91, p. 38.
  "The Talking." [Mildred] (4:2/5:1) 91, p. 61-62.
6320. VAETH, Kim
  "A Flock of Doubts Flying Beyond the Given Boundaries." [13thMoon] (9:1/2) 91,
      p. 44-45.
  "Half Moon over High Street." [13thMoon] (9:1/2) 91, p. 38-39.
  "I Tell You I Want Your Naked Kiss." [13thMoon] (9:1/2) 91, p. 41.
  "Inland Beachchair." [13thMoon] (9:1/2) 91, p. 43.

"The Voice of the Painter" (for Sharron Antholt). [13thMoon] (9:1/2) 91, p. 40.
"Wild Strawberries." [AmerV] (24) Fall 91, p. 89-94.
"With You." [13thMoon] (9:1/2) 91, p. 42.

6321. VAICIUNAITÉ, Judita
"Bells" (tr. by Victoria Skrupskelis and Stuart Friebert). [Mildred] (4:2/5:1) 91, p. 19.
"Bouquet of Marigolds" (tr. by Victoria Skrupskelis and Stuart Friebert). [Mildred] (4:2/5:1) 91, p. 18.
"Butterfly" (tr. by Victoria Skrupskelis and Stuart Friebert). [Mildred] (4:2/5:1) 91, p. 21.
"City" (tr. by Victoria Skrupskelis and Stuart Friebert). [Mildred] (4:2/5:1) 91, p. 19.
"The Drummer" (tr. by Victoria Skrupskelis and Stuart Friebert). [Mildred] (4:2/5:1) 91, p. 20.
"Evening Light" (tr. by Victoria Skrupskelis and Stuart Friebert). [Timbuktu] (6) Spr 91, p. 99.
"Girl with Ermine" (tr. by Victoria Skrupskelis and Stuart Friebert). [Timbuktu] (6) Spr 91, p. 99.
"Inheritance" (Excerpt, tr. by Viktoria Skrupskelis and Stuart Friebert). [Os] (32) Spr 91, p. 28.
"Light from an Autumn Night" (tr. by Viktoria Skrupskelis and Stuart Friebert). [Os] (32) Spr 91, p. 24.
"The Owl" (tr. by Viktoria Skrupskelis and Stuart Friebert). [Os] (32) Spr 91, p. 26.
"Pavilion" (tr. by Victoria Skrupskelis and Stuart Friebert). [Timbuktu] (6) Spr 91, p. 100.
"Per gyva balsais ir alsavimu." [Os] (32) Spr 91, p. 25.
"The Silence of Cornflowers" (tr. by Victoria Skrupskelis and Stuart Friebert). [Mildred] (4:2/5:1) 91, p. 18.
"Spectacle" (tr. by Victoria Skrupskelis and Stuart Friebert). [Mildred] (4:2/5:1) 91, p. 20.
"Two Mutes in Love" (tr. by Viktoria Skrupskelis and Stuart Friebert). [Os] (32) Spr 91, p. 27.
"When Wild Apple Trees Blossom" (tr. by Viktoria Skrupskelis and Stuart Friebert). [Crazy] (41) Wint 91, p. 16.
"White Octaves" (tr. by Viktoria Skrupskelis and Stuart Friebert). [Journal] (15:1) Spr 91, p. 13-14.

6322. VAILLANT, G. Emery
"When Martin Luther King Was President." [PacificR] (10) 91-92, p. 15

6323. VAJRADEVA
"Of the blown out lamp" (from the "Sattasai," tr. by Andrew Schelling). [Talisman] (6) Spr 91, p. 24.

6324. VALAORITIS, Nanos
"Orestes" (Excerpt). [PoetryUSA] (23) Sum 91, p. 5.

6325. VALENTINE, Jean
"American River Sky Alcohol Father." [AmerPoR] (20:4) Jl-Ag 91, p. 38.
"Come Ahkmatova" [sic]. [AmerPoR] (20:4) Jl-Ag 91, p. 38.
"In Fear (1)." [AmerPoR] (20:4) Jl-Ag 91, p. 38.
"In Fear (2)." [AmerPoR] (20:4) Jl-Ag 91, p. 38.
"James Wright: In Memory." [Field] (44) Spr 91, p. 57.
"Lindis Pass, Borage" (in memory of Patricia Walsh). [PlumR] (1) Spr-Sum 91, p. 16.
"The Sea of Serenity." [NewYorker] (67:11) 6 My 91, p. 46.
"Second Mother." [AmerPoR] (20:4) Jl-Ag 91, p. 38.
"The Under Voice." [AmerPoR] (20:4) Jl-Ag 91, p. 38.
"Wish-Mother." [AmerPoR] (20:4) Jl-Ag 91, p. 38.

6326. VALENZUELA, Liliana
"De Triques y Chácharas." [Mester] (20:1) Spr 91, p. 89.
"Piel Canela." [Americas] (19:1) Spr 91, p. 66.
"Sinvergüenza." [Americas] (19:1) Spr 91, p. 65-66.

6327. VALERO, Roberto
"No Estaré en Tu Camino." [Nuez] (3:8/9) 91, p. 13.

6328. VALKEAPÄÄ, Nils Aslak
"Bluethroat, Sing and Twitter" (Excerpts. Part 2 of the trilogy "My Home Is in My Heart," tr. by Lars Nordström and Ralph Salisbury). [Writ] (23/24) 91-92, p. 5-41.

6329. VALLE, Carmen
"Esa Que Era Yo." [Nuez] (3:7) 91, p. 11.
"Vigía." [Nuez] (3:7) 91, p. 11.
6330. VALLE, Victor
"If You Wish" (tr. of Carlos Illescas). [OnTheBus] (8/9) 91, p. 207.
"Invocation" (tr. of Carlos Illescas). [OnTheBus] (8/9) 91, p. 206.
"Let's Bite His Hand" (tr. of Carlos Illescas). [OnTheBus] (8/9) 91, p. 207.
6331. VALLE SENTIES, Raquel
"Culpas." [Americas] (19:1) Spr 91, p. 67-68.
"Egoísmo." [Americas] (19:1) Spr 91, p. 69.
6332. VALLEJO, César (César Abraham)
"The Anger That Breaks the Man" (tr. by Daniel Bosch). [Agni] (33) 91, p. 239.
"Paris, October 1936" (tr. by Daniel Bosch). [Agni] (33) 91, p. 240.
"Trilce" (Selections: I-X). [DenQ] (25:4) Spr 91, p. 68-88.
"Trilce" (Selections: I-X, tr. by Clayton Eshleman and Julio Ortega). [DenQ] (25:4)
Spr 91, p. 69-89.
"Trilce" (Selections: XI-XX, tr. by Clayon Eshleman and Julio Ortega. Translation
Chapbook Series, Number 16). [MidAR] (11:2) 91, p. 71-101.
"Trilce" (Selections: XV-XXX, XXXII-XXXIV, XLI, XLIV, XLIX, LV, LVII,
LX, LXIII, LXVI, LXVIII-LXX, LXXII-LXXIII). [Abraxas] (40/41) 91, p.
24-99.
"Trilce" (Selections: XV-XXX, XXXII-XXXIV, XLI, XLIV, XLIX, LV, LVII,
LX, LXIII, LXVI, LXVIII-LXX, LXXII-LXXIII, tr. by Próspero Saíz).
[Abraxas] (40/41) 91, p. 24-99.
"Trilce" (Selections: XXXIII, XXXV, XXXVII, tr. by Clayton Eshleman and Julio
Ortega). [Antaeus] (67) Fall 91, p. 107-109.
"Trilce LX-LXIX" (tr. by Clayton Eshleman and Julio Ortega). [Sulfer] (11:2, #29)
Fall 91, p. 4-15.
"Until the Day of My Return" (tr. by Daniel Bosch). [Agni] (33) 91, p. 241.
6333. VALLONE, Antonio
"Black Angels." [SycamoreR] (3:2) Sum 91, p. 50-51.
Van . . .
See also names beginning with "Van" without the following space, filed below in
their alphabetical positions, e.g., VANDELOECHT.
6334. Van BRUNT, Lloyd (H. L. Van Brunt)
"Breakfast in Iraq." [Caliban] (10) 91, p. 127.
"Breakfast in Iraq." [SoDakR] (29:4) Wint 91, p. 146.
"Verdigris." [SoDakR] (29:4) Wint 91, p. 140-142.
"Weather Report." [SoDakR] (29:4) Wint 91, p. 144-145.
"Windsurfing in Oyster Harbors." [SoDakR] (29:3 part 2) Aut 91, p. 49.
6335. Van de KAMP, Alexandra
"One Well-Used Chair Talks to Another" (A Conversation of Needs). [PoetryNW]
(32:1) Spr 91, p. 31-32.
"A Portrait of Gray." [PoetryNW] (32:1) Spr 91, p. 26-31.
6336. Van DUYN, Mona
"Chagall's 'Les Plumes en Fleur'." [NewRep] (204:18) 6 My 91, p. 36.
"A Dog Lover's Confession." [NewYorker] (67:44) 23 D 91, p. 42.
"For May Swenson." [Poetry] (157:4) Ja 91, p. 189-190.
"Our Block." [SouthernR] (27:2) Ap 91, p. 269-270.
"What the Motorcycle Said." [Shen] (41:4) Wint 91, p. 64-65.
6337. Van HOUTEN, Lois
"The Celebratory Snow." [JINJPo] (13:1) Spr 91, p. 4-5.
"Fantasy for Ruth." [JINJPo] (13:1) Spr 91, p. 6.
6338. Van METER, Frankie
"Before Coffee." [Plain] (12:1) Fall 91, p. 9.
6339. Van NOORD, Barbara
"Biology Lesson." [Poem] (66) N 91, p. 29-31.
"The Collector." [Poem] (66) N 91, p. 28.
"Georgia O'Keeffe, with Bust by Mary Callery, Photo by Eliot Porter." [Nimrod]
(35:1) Fall-Wint 91, p. 96.
"Ginkos." [SpoonRQ] (16:1/2) Wint-Spr 91, p. 96.
"Orion." [Nimrod] (35:1) Fall-Wint 91, p. 97.
"The Plus Tree." [Poem] (66) N 91, p. 27.
6340. Van PEENEN, H. J.
"Blueberries." [PaintedHR] (1) Ja 91, p. 5.
"Graffiti" (Carnarvon Gorge). [BellArk] (7:3) My-Je 91, p. 10.

"A Sheltering Ledge (Green River, Utah)" (Honorable Mention, 1991 Paintbrush
    Award in Poetry). [PaintedHR] (3) Sum 92, p. 12.
"Writing Home" (Capricornia). [BellArk] (7:3) My-Je 91, p. 10.

6341. Van SLUYS, Sharon M.
"The Editor." [Farm] (8:1) Spr-Sum 91, p. 94.

6342. Van WAGONER, Sandra
"Sex, #2." [ChironR] (10:4) Wint 91, p. 34.
"Strut Your Ass." [ChironR] (10:3) Aut 91, p. 40.

6343. Van WERT, William (William F.)
"The Function of Narrative." [PoetL] (86:2) Sum 91, p. 11-12.
"Imagination, Dead Imagination." [Chelsea] (50) 91, p. 59.
"The Malady of Dying" ((f)or Marguerite Duras). [Chelsea] (50) 91, p. 60-61.
"The Male Gaze." [NegC] (11:3) 91, p. 42-43.
"Near-Death." [Chelsea] (50) 91, p. 62-63.
"The Sacrifice." [Chelsea] (50) 91, p. 64-65.
"The Sacrificial Dead." [Chelsea] (50) 91, p. 66.
"The Shallow Dead." [Chelsea] (50) 91, p. 67.

6344. Van WESTLER, Max
"Karl Marx in Hell." [MinnR] (NS 37) Fall 91, p. 7-8.

6345. Van WINCKEL, Nance
"Ascension, Superimposed" (flea market, Richmond, Illinois). [Shen] (41:4) Wint
    91, p. 26.
"Good Timing." [Nat] (252:2) 21 Ja 91, p. 66.
"The Last Time I Saw Them." [Shen] (41:4) Wint 91, p. 27.
"Please Wake Up." [DenQ] (26:2) Fall 91, p. 49-50.
"Pocket History of Poetry." [PoetryNW] (32:1) Spr 91, p. 18.
"Wake No One." [DenQ] (26:2) Fall 91, p. 51-52.

6346. VANCE, Bob
"For the Piping Plover." [BelPoJ] (42:2) Wint 91-92, p. 6-7.

6347. VANCE, Sylvia
"On My Daughter's Twenty-Third Birthday." [Dandel] (18:1) Spr-Sum 91, p.
    19-20.

6348. VANCE, Thomas
"Like Sitting" (tr. of Bo Carpelan, w. Vera Vance). [Vis] (37) 91, p. 28.
"The Storytellers" (tr. of Bo Carpelan, w. Vera Vance). [Vis] (37) 91, p. 28.
"Untitled: A sunny and sheltered Mediterranean harbor" (tr. of Marta Tikkanen, w.
    Vera Vance). [Vis] (37) 91, p. 30.
"Untitled: In slow motion" (tr. of Marta Tikkanen, w. Vera Vance). [Vis] (37) 91, p.
    29-30.

6349. VANCE, Vera
"Like Sitting" (tr. of Bo Carpelan, w. Thomas Vance). [Vis] (37) 91, p. 28.
"The Storytellers" (tr. of Bo Carpelan, w. Thomas Vance). [Vis] (37) 91, p. 28.
"Untitled: A sunny and sheltered Mediterranean harbor" (tr. of Marta Tikkanen, w.
    Thomas Vance). [Vis] (37) 91, p. 30.
"Untitled: In slow motion" (tr. of Marta Tikkanen, w. Thomas Vance). [Vis] (37)
    91, p. 29-30.

6350. VANDELOECHT, Michael
"Jack's Snub-Nosed .38." [SlipS] (11) 91, p. 78.

Vander . . .
    See also names beginning with "Vander" without the following space, filed below in
    their alphabetic positions, e.g. VanderMOLEN.

6351. Vander WAL, Jane Aaron
"Heat." [TickleAce] (22) Fall-Wint 91, p. 43.

6352. VanderMOLEN, Robert
"Late Notes on the Revolution." [ArtfulD] (20/21) 91, p. 131-133.

6353. VANDERSEE, Charles
"Art of the Road." [OhioR] (46) 91, p. 102-113.
"Museum of Letters." [Pig] (17) 91, p. 128.

VanderWAL, Jane Aaron
    See Vander WAL, Jane Aaron

6354. VANEK, Mary
"Blood Enough and Time." [CutB] (36) Sum 91, p. 92.
"Where There Is to Get to" (for R.W.). [CutB] (35) Wint-Spr 91, p. 17.

6355. VARELA, Blanca
"Undated" (to Kafka, tr. by Julian Palley). [OnTheBus] (8/9) 91, p. 229-230.

438

VARELA

VARELA, Maria Elena Cruz
    See CRUZ VARELA, Maria Elena
6356. VARGA, Adriana
    "About You" (tr. of Marin Sorescu, w. Stuart Friebert). [FourQ] (5:1) Spr 91, p. 58.
    "Apparition" (tr. of Marin Sorescu, w. Stuart Friebert). [NoDaQ] (59:1) Wint 91, p.
        119-120.
    "Beginning's Shudder" (tr. of Marin Sorescu, w. Stuart Friebert). [RiverS] (33) 91,
        p. 38.
    "Cabbage Fleas and Crocodiles" (tr. of Marin Sorescu, w. Stuart Friebert). [PassN]
        (12:1) Sum 91, p. 27.
    "Caravan" (tr. of Marin Sorescu, w. Stuart Friebert). [GrahamHR] (15) Fall 91, p.
        95.
    "Eyelashes" (tr. of Marin Sorescu, w. Stuart Friebert). [GrahamHR] (15) Fall 91, p.
        93.
    "I Stopped Right by the Tragic" (tr. of Marin Sorescu, w. Stuart Friebert).
        [GrahamHR] (15) Fall 91, p. 94.
    "Peace" (tr. of Marin Sorescu, w. Stuart Friebert). [PraF] (12:3 #56) Aut 91, p. 50.
    "Secret Transfusion" (tr. of Marin Sorescu, w. Stuart Friebert). [Os] (32) Spr 91, p.
        4.
    "The Spider Arrived" (tr. of Marin Sorescu, w. Stuart Friebert). [RiverS] (33) 91, p.
        42.
    "Study" (tr. of Marin Sorescu, w. Stuart Friebert). [RiverS] (33) 91, p. 40.
    "There Is Earth" (tr. of Marin Sorescu, w. Stuart Friebert). [RiverS] (33) 91, p. 44.
VARGE, Adriana
    See VARGA, Adriana
6357. VARLEY, Jane
    "Before Throwing a Chicken into an Iowa Valley." [Spirit] (11) 91, p. 41.
    "Heartland." [HolCrit] (28:2) Ap 91, p. 16.
    "View from a Small Room in North Idaho" (For Lex). [PoetryNW] (32:1) Spr 91, p.
        12-15.
6358. VARON, Jodi
    "Tai-Hang Mountain Dawn" (tr. of Li He). [Sequoia] (34:1) Spr 91, p. 60.
    "Wild Song" (tr. of Li He). [Sequoia] (34:1) Spr 91, p. 61.
6359. VARON, Miquel Angel
    "Swing Art Planet." [Rohwedder] (6) Sum-Fall 91, p. 28-31.
6360. VASCONCELLOS, Cherry Jean
    "Milly in Denver." [WormR] (31:4, #124) 91, p. 106.
    "Milly's Mom." [WormR] (31:4, #124) 91, p. 106.
    "One Thing about Celibacy." [Pearl] (13) Spr-Sum 91, p. 62.
    "Why I Read War Books." [NewYorkQ] (46) 91, p. 67-69.
6361. VASQUEZ, Robert
    "At the Rainbow" (for Linda, Theresa and Phyllis). [NewEngR] (13:3/4) Spr-Sum
        91, p. 312-313.
    "Dia de los Muertos" (for Malcolm Lowry). [NewEngR] (13:3/4) Spr-Sum 91, p.
        311-312.
    "Pismo, 1959." [NewEngR] (13:3/4) Spr-Sum 91, p. 310-311.
6362. VASSALLO, Philip
    "The Refuge Room." [ChamLR] (8-9) Spr-Fall 91, p. 76-77.
6363. VASSILAKIS, Nico
    "Deep Down Blues." [ChironR] (10:2) Sum 91, p. 40.
    "Qua Poem." [ContextS] (2:2) 91, p. 38-42.
6364. VATES, Judith
    "Two Seasons and a Japanese Lover in New York City" (for Toyo). [BambooR]
        (50/51) Spr-Sum 91, p. 121-122.
6365. VATSEND, Helge
    "Channels" (tr. by Olav Grinde). [Vis] (37) 91, p. 43.
    "The Silence" (tr. by Olav Grinde). [Vis] (37) 91, p. 42.
6366. VAUGHAN, Frances Downing
    "Horizon" (in memory of Reuben Tam). [ChamLR] (8-9) Spr-Fall 91, p. 38.
6367. VAUGHAN, Henry
    "The Night" (Excerpt). [PoetryUSA] (22) Spr 91, p. 23.
6368. VAZIRANI, Reetika
    "Beijing." [AmerV] (25) Wint 91, p. 27.
6369. VEALE, Bobby
    "The Sound the People the Style." [HangL] (58) 91, p. 93.

6370. VEGA, Janine Pommy
"Erotica." [Archae] (1) Fall 90, p. 29-34.
"The Old Way." [Archae] (1) Fall 90, p. 26-28.
"Pisang." [Archae] (1) Fall 90, p. 24-25.
"Yourself." [MoodySI] (24/25/26) Spr 91, p. 53.
VEGA, Yvonne de la
See De la VEGA, Yvonne
6371. VEIGA, Marisella
"Rolling." [MidAR] (12:1) 91, p. 36.
6372. VENCLOVA, Tomas
"Instruction" (tr. by Diana Senechal). [NewYRB] (38:19) 21 N 91, p. 33.
6373. VENEGAS, Sybil
"Goddamn You." [Pearl] (14) Fall-Wint 91, p. 50.
6374. VENEMA, Kathleen
"All that Time I Thought It Be the War That Done It." [PraF] (12:1 #54) Spr 91, p.
76-77.
6375. VENNBERG, Karl
"Closing Words" (tr. by Daniel Ogden). [Vis] (37) 91, p. 52.
"Dreamless Years" (tr. by Daniel Ogden). [Vis] (37) 91, p. 51.
"The Night Is Not Your Enemy" (tr. by Daniel Ogden). [Vis] (37) 91, p. 52.
6376. VENZKE, Philip
"The Onions." [EngJ] (80:2) F 91, p. 96.
6377. VERLAINE, Paul
"Light of the Moon" (tr. by Gregory McNamee). [WebR] (15) Spr 91, p. 40.
6378. VERNON, William J.
"At the Arts-Fund Sponsored Reception." [ChironR] (10:2) Sum 91, p. 7.
"At the Foot of Harrow-on-the-Hill near Churchill's Grade School." [Bogg] (64) 91,
p. 48.
"The Blizzard of '78." [Hellas] (2:1) Spr 91, p. 70.
"The Decadence of Golf." [ChironR] (10:2) Sum 91, p. 7.
"The Two-Year Guarantee." [ChironR] (10:2) Sum 91, p. 7.
6379. VÉRTES, László
"Maple Leaf" (tr. of Sándor Csoóri, w. Len Roberts). [NewEngR] (13:3/4) Spr-Sum
91, p. 195-196.
"Questions, to Carriers of the Dead (Kérdések, halottvivokhoz)" (tr. of Sandor
Csoori, w. Len Roberts). [Plain] (11:3) Spr 91, p. 24.
"Questions, to Carriers of the Dead" (tr. of Sándor Csoóri, w. Len Roberts). [LitR]
(34:2) Wint 91, p. 226.
"Summer, with Halo" (tr. of Sándor Csoóri, w. Len Roberts). [NewEngR] (13:3/4)
Spr-Sum 91, p. 196.
"Zörög Éjjel a Mák. The Poppy Clatters at Night" (tr. of Sándor Csoóri, w. Len
Roberts). [DenQ] (26:2) Fall 91, p. 14.
6380. VERTREACE, Martha (Martha M.)
"Companion." [WillowR] Spr 91, p. 19-20.
"False Geographies." [ContextS] (2:2) 91, p. 12-13.
"Radium." [NoDaQ] (59:1) Wint 91, p. 132-133.
"Skywriting." [Elf] (1:2) Sum 91, p. 22.
"Surface Tension." [Elf] (1:2) Sum 91, p. 23.
6381. VEST, Dale
"The Day the Blender Broke." [NewYorkQ] (46) 91, p. 70.
6382. VIANU, Lidia
"The Ground" (tr. of Marin Sorescu, w. Adam J. Sorkin). [AmerPoR] (20:6) N-D
91, p. 26.
"Icarus" (tr. of Marin Sorescu, w. Adam J. Sorkin). [LitR] (35:1) Fall 91, p. 38.
"Italics Ours" (tr. of Marin Sorescu, w. Adam J. Sorkin). [LitR] (35:1) Fall 91, p.
37.
"A Question" (tr. of Marin Sorescu, w. Adam J. Sorkin). [LitR] (35:1) Fall 91, p.
37.
6383. VICE, Lisa
"Cleo." [Lactuca] (14) My 91, p. 43.
"Joyce." [Lactuca] (14) My 91, p. 43.
"Marvella." [Lactuca] (14) My 91, p. 43.
6384. VICTOR, Ken
"The Kingdom." [TexasR] (12:3/4) Fall-Wint 91, p. 97.
6385. VIDAKOVIC-PETROV, Krinka
"Serbia on the Maps" (tr. of Aleksandar Petrov). [CimR] (96) Jl 91, p. 25.

6386. VIEIRA, John
"Frogs Come Out in Rain." [BambooR] (52) Fall 91, p. 139.
"Minutes of a Poetry Reading at Rocky Point." [BambooR] (52) Fall 91, p. 141.
"Sunrise." [BambooR] (52) Fall 91, p. 138.
"There is no hiding." [BambooR] (52) Fall 91, p. 140.

6387. VIERECK, Peter
"1. [To Ida Coblenz]" (tr. of Stafan George). [Boulevard] (5:3/6:1, #15/16) Spr 91,
p. 172.
"2 [Year]" (tr. of Stafan George). [Boulevard] (5:3/6:1, #15/16) Spr 91, p. 174-175.
"Love Lyrics by Stefan George: Heterosexual and Homosexual" (tr. of Stafan
George). [Boulevard] (5:3/6:1, #15/16) Spr 91, p. 172-175.
"Southern Strand: Bay" (tr. of Stafan George). [Boulevard] (5:3/6:1, #15/16) Spr
91, p. 173.

6388. VIGLINI, Janelle
"The Fruit Trees Lose Their Blossoms." [Talisman] (7) Fall 91, p. 27.

6389. VILLAFLOR, Genevieve
"Cleaning Fish." [Timbuktu] (6) Spr 91, p. 55.

6390. VILLANUEVA-COLLADO, Alfredo
"El Buen Arte." [Nuez] (3:7) 91, p. 26.
"Tres Meditaciones sobre la Cruz de Palo" (A Reinaldo Arenas, 1943-1990). [Nuez]
(3:7) 91, p. 20.

6391. VILLEGAS, Anna Tuttle
"Cattle in Rain." [ChironR] (10:4) Wint 91, p. 9.
"Garden Shed 1989." [ChironR] (10:4) Wint 91, p. 9.
"Proud Flesh." [ChironR] (10:4) Wint 91, p. 9.

6392. VINZ, Mark
"The Barbershop." [PraF] (12:4) Wint 91-92, p. 87.
"Daydreamer." [Sidewalks] (1) Aug 91, p. 3.
"The Deer." [NoDaQ] (59:1) Wint 91, p. 208.
"Dog Days" (for Jim White). [NoDaQ] (59:1) Wint 91, p. 210.
"Dragging Broadway." [Sidewalks] (1) Aug 91, p. 4.
"Driver's Test." [CharR] (17:1) Spr 91, p. 45.
"Hooked." [NorthStoneR] (10) Fall 91-Wint 92, p. 195.
"Leaf Watchers." [NoDaQ] (59:1) Wint 91, p. 208-209.
"North of North." [SoDakR] (29:3 part 2) Aut 91, p. 76.
"Road Stop." [NoDaQ] (59:1) Wint 91, p. 209.
"Saturday Morning." [NorthStoneR] (10) Fall 91-Wint 92, p. 196.
"A Theory of Poetry." [PraF] (12:4) Wint 91-92, p. 88.

6393. VIOLI, Paul
"Boxcar Crossing." [FreeL] (7) Spr 91, p. 20-21.
"The Curious Builder." [Sulfur] (11:2 #29) Fall 91, p. 115-127.
"Police Blotter." [HangL] (59) 91, p. 62-64.

6394. VIRGA, Michael
"Tribute to James Dean." [PoetryUSA] (23) Sum 91, p. 15.

6395. VISHNEVETSKY, Igor
"The Book of Air" (tr. by Nina Kossman). [LitR] (34:3) Spr 91, p. 376-377.
"Evening Song" (tr. by Thomas Epstein). [LitR] (34:3) Spr 91, p. 379.
"Odysseus's Temptation" (tr. by Nina Kossman). [LitR] (34:3) Spr 91, p. 378.
"Perhaps I Did Come Here" (tr. by Thomas Epstein). [LitR] (34:3) Spr 91, p. 378.
"Teach Me to See the Star in the Deadly Pale Water" (tr. by Nina Kossman). [LitR]
(34:3) Spr 91, p. 377.

6396. VIVEROS, Joy
"Steps." [ChironR] (10:3) Aut 91, p. 39.

6397. VLASOPOLOS, Anca
"Bedtime Stories." [Interim] (10:2) Fall-Wint 91-92, p. 37.
"Sophrosyne." [RiverS] (34) 91, p. 15.
"A Time to Weep" (thinking of Robert Hayden, again). [Interim] (10:2) Fall-Wint
91-92, p. 38.

6398. VOEGTLEN, Anne Reynolds
"Assisted." [PoetryNW] (32:3) Aut 91, p. 17.
"Exit Moves." [PoetryNW] (32:3) Aut 91, p. 18.
"Tide of the Seventy-Seven Stars." [BellArk] (7:3) My-Je 91, p. 24.

6399. VOGEL, Constance
"A Cold Climate." [WillowR] Spr 91, p. 21.
"To Reverend Eustis Kew of Knottwood Church." [Elf] (1:1) Spr 91, p. 21.

441

6400. VOGELSANG, Arthur
"The Bee City." [PassN] (12:2) Wint 91, p. 8.
6401. VOIGT, Ellen Bryant
"At the Piano." [Atlantic] (268:4) O 91, p. 104.
"The Box." [Ploughs] (17:2/3) Fall 91, p. 77.
6402. VOLCHEK, Dmitri
"'Armageddon!' Hoarsely Sang the Iron Fence" (tr. by Thomas Epstein). [LitR]
(34:3) Spr 91, p. 384.
"At Last I've Renounced" (tr. by Thomas Epstein). [LitR] (34:3) Spr 91, p. 385.
"Deceased! What Now for Empty Voids" (tr. by Thomas Epstein). [LitR] (34:3) Spr
91, p. 384.
"Hermit in Bathyscape Besotting Robe" (tr. by Thomas Epstein). [LitR] (34:3) Spr
91, p. 386.
"No *Bool* of Holes No *Ubeshchoor* of Awls Only" (tr. by Thomas Epstein). [LitR]
(34:3) Spr 91, p. 386.
"So What? the Logpile of Culture" (tr. by Thomas Epstein). [LitR] (34:3) Spr 91, p.
385.
6403. VOLD, Jan Erik
"In My Opinion" (tr. by Harold P. Hanson). [Vis] (37) 91, p. 44.
"Not All Caresses" (tr. by Harold P. Hanson). [Vis] (37) 91, p. 44.
"Summer-Song" (tr. by Harold P. Hanson). [Vis] (37) 91, p. 43.
6404. VOLDSETH, Beverly
"I Don't Know What Year It Is." [RagMag] (9:1) 91, p. 34.
"Sitting in the Children's Library in an Orange Chair Facing the YA Fiction Shelf."
[Sidewalks] (1) Aug 91, p. 32.
6405. VOLKMAN, Karen
"For Size." [Ascent] (15:3) Spr 91, p. 24.
"Fortune." [Ascent] (15:3) Spr 91, p. 23.
6406. VOLO, Alfonso
"Charlotte Mew." [MoodySI] (24/25/26) Spr 91, p. 48.
6407. Von HOLTEN, Dan
"At Corss Cemetery" (Bureau County, Illinois). [Farm] (8:1) Spr-Sum 91, p. 91.
"Black Hawk." [Farm] (8:1) Spr-Sum 91, p. 93.
"Catherine Smith: The Homestead." [Farm] (8:1) Spr-Sum 91, p. 92.
6408. VOR, Jon ur
"I Am So Big" (tr. by Hallberg Hallmundsson). [Vis] (37) 91, p. 36.
"What Were You Born For?" (tr. by Hallberg Hallmundsson). [Vis] (37) 91, p. 36.
6409. VORKINK, Nancy
"A Bloodless Coup." [InterPR] (17:1) Spr 91, p. 110.
"Song of Kekula." [InterPR] (17:1) Spr 91, p. 109-110.
6410. VOSE, Devon
"Coming Home." [BellArk] (7:3) My-Je 91, p. 11.
"Oliver's Flowers." [BellArk] (7:3) My-Je 91, p. 1.
6411. VOSS, Fred
"Asking For It." [ChironR] (10:3) Aut 91, p. 2.
"A Christian." [ChironR] (10:3) Aut 91, p. 3.
"The Dream." [ChironR] (10:3) Aut 91, p. 2.
"Easy Rider." [ChironR] (10:3) Aut 91, p. 2.
"Joyride." [ChironR] (10:3) Aut 91, p. 2.
"Justice." [Pearl] (13) Spr-Sum 91, p. 60.
"Life and Death." [SlipS] (11) 91, p. 42.
"Rapport." [ChironR] (10:3) Aut 91, p. 3.
"Revenge." [RedBass] (15) 91, p. 96-97.
"Revolution." [ChironR] (10:3) Aut 91, p. 3.
"Success." [ChironR] (10:3) Aut 91, p. 3.
"Symbiosis." [Pearl] (13) Spr-Sum 91, p. 60.
"That's Why Firetrucks Carry Hacksaws Now." [Pearl] (14) Fall-Wint 91, p. 11.
"Tough." [ChironR] (10:3) Aut 91, p. 3.
"Worth Reading About." [Pearl] (14) Fall-Wint 91, p. 11.
6412. VRHOVAC, Duska
"When a Child Dies" (For Nikola, tr. by Richard Burns and Vera Radojevic).
[NewOR] (18:2) Sum 91, p. 83.
VRIES, Rachel Guido de
See DeVRIES, Rachel Guido

6413. VRKLJAN, Irena
"In an Antique Shop" (tr. by Dasha Culic Nisula). [ColR] (NS 18:2) Fall-Wint 91,
p. 80-81.
"Later" (tr. by Dasha Culic Nisula). [ColR] (NS 18:2) Fall-Wint 91, p. 82.
"To a Poet Who No Longer Writes" (tr. by Dasha Culic Nisula). [ColR] (NS 18:2)
Fall-Wint 91, p. 83.
6414. WACKER, Wendy
"Before I Knew My Father." [WillowR] Spr 91, p. 24.
6415. WADDELL-TAKARA, Kathryn
"Bedside Treasures & Trivia." [BambooR] (52) Fall 91, p. 142-143.
"Cows and Alabama Folklore." [HawaiiR] (16:1, #34) Wint 91-92, p. 54-57.
"Guava Song Dream Tune." [ChamLR] (8-9) Spr-Fall 91, p. 11-12.
"Under This Same Sky" (to K.P.). [HawaiiR] (15:3, #33) Fall 91, p. 53.
6416. WADDINGTON, Miriam
"Freedom Games." [Arc] (26) Spr 91, p. 28-29.
"Living with Rumours of War." [Quarry] (40:1/2) Wint-Spr 91, p. 183.
"Places." [Quarry] (40:1/2) Wint-Spr 91, p. 181-182.
6417. WADE, George E.
"God on Reading Karl Barth's *Church Dogmatics*." [ChrC] (108:26) 18-25 S 91, p.
846.
"Manna." [ChrC] (108:29) 16 O 91, p. 938.
6418. WADE, Seth
"Leda Revisited." [SoDakR] (29:3 part 2) Aut 91, p. 11.
6419. WADE, Sidney
"A Seated Demon" (After a Painting by Mehmet Siyah Qalem). [NewYorker] (67:2)
4 Mr 91, p. 32.
6420. WAGNER, Anneliese
"Bunker." [WestB] (28) 91, p. 94-95.
"Gottschalk's Restaurant Window." [SouthwR] (76:3) Sum 91, p. 371.
"Return to Heinsheim: Ancestral House." [PraS] (65:4) Wint 91, p. 111-112.
"White Sheep." [PraS] (65:4) Wint 91, p. 112.
6421. WAGNER, Chuck
"All the Albino Animals." [HopewellR] (1991) 91, p. 9.
6422. WAGNER, John
"The Kallima Butterfly." [Colum] (15) 90, p. 199.
6423. WAGNER, Kathy
"Engine Failure." [PlumR] (1) Spr-Sum 91, p. 12.
6424. WAGNER, Kenneth
"My Friend the Buddhist Priest." [Bogg] (64) 91, p. 14.
6425. WAGNER, Maryfrances
"Eating an Artichoke." [LaurelR] (25:1) Wint 91, p. 107.
6426. WAGNER, Robert
"Destination: San Francisco." [Archae] (2) Spr 91, p. 46.
"Discovery in the West Delta." [Hellas] (2:2) Fall 91, p. 266-267.
"Do You, Robert, Take This." [FreeL] (8) Aut 91, p. 14-15.
"Learning the Opes." [Hellas] (2:2) Fall 91, p. 267.
"Miss Truesdale." [SmPd] (28:1, #81) Wint 91, p. 20.
6427. WAGNER, Shari
"Carp." [HopewellR] (1991) 91, p. 23.
6428. WAGNER, Shelly
"The Limousine." [OnTheBus] (8/9) 91, p. 163-164.
"Rusty." [OnTheBus] (8/9) 91, p. 163.
WAGONER, Sandra van
See Van WAGONER, Sandra
6429. WAH, Fred
"Aghia: An easthope on that boat going three times as fast as can." [WestCL] (25:1)
Spr 91, p. 50.
"April or Maybe March." [WestCL] (25:1) Spr 91, p. 50.
"For hidden behind glass and silent too." [WestCL] (25:1) Spr 91, p. 51.
"I get up in the morning." [WestCL] (25:1) Spr 91, p. 49.
"Map / Fish / Mind." [WestCL] (25:1) Spr 91, p. 51.
"The 'permanent spirit' turns pages." [WestCL] (25:1) Spr 91, p. 52.
"You want to know until I found you." [WestCL] (25:1) Spr 91, p. 51.
6430. WAHLE, F. Keith
"The Study of Aesthetics." [CinPR] (21) Spr 90, p. 63.

6431. WAINWRIGHT, J. A.
"Open House." [CanLit] (129) Sum 91, p. 7.
6432. WAKOSKI, Diane
"Imagining Emily's Early Summer Garden." [RiverS] (35) 91, p. 52-53.
"Moving the Chair." [CreamCR] (15:1) Spr 91, p. 47.
"Satin." [RiverS] (35) 91, p. 54-55.
"The Tall Boy." [CreamCR] (15:1) Spr 91, p. 48-49.
WAL, Jane Aaron Vander
See Vander WAL, Jane Aaron
6433. WALDERS, Davi
"Concert at the Château" (tr. by the author). [PaintedHR] (2) Spr 91, p. 35.
"Le Concert au Château." [PaintedHR] (2) Spr 91, p. 34.
6434. WALDMAN, Anne
"Can't Touch This." [AmerPoR] (20:3) My-Je 91, p. 5-6.
"Fait Accompli." [AmerPoR] (20:3) My-Je 91, p. 8.
"Glasnost." [AmerPoR] (20:3) My-Je 91, p. 7.
"Iovis Ominia Plena" (Excerpt). [PoetryUSA] (23) Sum 91, p. 7.
"Jurassic." [AmerPoR] (20:3) My-Je 91, p. 6-7.
"Night Wing" (for the Painter Yvonne Jacquette whose aerial pastel inspired this
piece). [Talisman] (7) Fall 91, p. 88-89.
"Ode to Speech." [AmerPoR] (20:3) My-Je 91, p. 7.
"Self Other Both Neither." [AmerPoR] (20:3) My-Je 91, p. 3-5.
"Writing." [AmerPoR] (20:3) My-Je 91, p. 8.
6435. WALDMAN, Ken
"The Actress and Her Therapist." [ContextS] (2:2) 91, p. 30.
"December 26, Wales, Alaska." [SwampR] (7/8) Spr-Sum 91, p. 38.
"The Vacuum Lady." [WritersF] (17) Fall 91, p. 60.
"Warning Delilah." [ChironR] (10:4) Wint 91, p. 35.
"The Whiz." [HighP] (6:2) Fall 91, p. 72.
6436. WALDROP, Keith
"The Idle Wheel." [Conjunc] (17) 91, p. 369-370.
"The Palmer Worm." [Conjunc] (17) 91, p. 365-366.
"Potential Random" (Excerpt). [Epoch] (40:3) 91, p. 251-253.
"Transparent Like the Air." [Conjunc] (17) 91, p. 367-368.
6437. WALDROP, Rosmarie
"Lawn of Excluded Middle" (Excerpts). [Epoch] (40:3) 91, p. 258-259.
"Method" (from "The Book of Resemblances III: The Ineffaceable, The
Unperceived," tr. of Edmond Jabès). [ManhatR] (6:1) Fall 91, p. 40-43.
"Of Absent Mind, Of Whiteness" (from "The Book of Resemblances III: The
Ineffaceable, The Unperceived," tr. of Edmond Jabès). [ManhatR] (6:1) Fall
91, p. 34-39.
6438. WALKER, Anne
"Jupiter (Longing)." [Dandel] (18:2) Wint 91, p. 67.
"Not-Family." [Dandel] (18:2) Wint 91, p. 66.
6439. WALKER, Jeanne Murray
"Aunt Joe Learns to Keep Her Balance." [Poetry] (158:4) Jl 91, p. 198.
"Deciding Where to Stop." [Poetry] (158:4) Jl 91, p. 198-199.
"First Baptist Church, Parkers Prairie, 1952." [NowestR] (29:2) 91, p. 25.
"Roadside Stand." [WestB] (29) 91, p. 79.
"Sophie Larson Waits for the First Mail Delivery." [NowestR] (29:2) 91, p. 23-24.
6440. WALKER, Larry
"Unintentional Reasoning." [BellArk] (7:6) N-D 91, p. 2.
"Walking Through Woods." [BellArk] (7:6) N-D 91, p. 11.
6441. WALKER, Leon
"Unfinished." [Plain] (11:3) Spr 91, p. 25.
6442. WALKER, Lynne
"Froggy Goes-A-Hopping." [PoetryUSA] (22) Spr 91, p. 11.
"The Laughing Woman." [SlipS] (11) 91, p. 87-90.
6443. WALKER, Marylisa
"At the Supermarket." [ChironR] (10:4) Wint 91, p. 35.
"I Ask People How They Are." [ChironR] (10:3) Aut 91, p. 40.
6444. WALKER, Ruth
"Mother of My Christmas Cactus" (For Judy Swann — 9/24/16-10/2/90). [CoalC]
(3) My 91, p. 5.
6445. WALKER, Sue
"Communication with a Sixteen Year Old Son." [SoCoast] (11) Wint 91, p. 20.

"Easter and All That Jazz." [SoCoast] (10) Fall 91, p. 14-15.
"Last Testament of Gardner N. Stile, Holman Prison, Altmore, Alabama, August
1989, on the Eve of Execution." [PikeF] (10) Spr 91, p. 3.
"To Polly Brent from Lucinda Lee" (Virginia — October 17, 1767). [SoCoast] (11)
Wint 91, p. 38.
6446. WALKER, Victoria
"Louie Angel." [WestCL] (25:2, #5) Fall 91, p. 8-9.
"Return" (for Victoria & Edvard Almqvist). [WestCL] (25:2, #5) Fall 91, p. 8.
"Starry Night" (for Camille & Adam). [WestCL] (25:2, #5) Fall 91, p. 10.
"The Voice" (for L.). [WestCL] (25:2, #5) Fall 91, p. 7.
"Without I." [WestCL] (25:2, #5) Fall 91, p. 10.
6447. WALL, Barbara
"The Sage." [EmeraldCR] (4) 91, p. 26.
6448. WALLACE, Anthony
"Guitar Lesson." [ChamLR] (8-9) Spr-Fall 91, p. 142.
"Horseshoes." [ChamLR] (8-9) Spr-Fall 91, p. 141.
6449. WALLACE, Bronwen
"Keep That Candle Burning: Poems for Emmylou Harris" (Selections: 5 poems).
[Quarry] (40:1/2) Wint-Spr 91, p. 184-188.
6450. WALLACE, Bruce
"1 The Final Gift." [Plain] (12:1) Fall 91, p. 10.
"2 Laugh, Little Girls, Laugh." [Plain] (12:1) Fall 91, p. 10.
6451. WALLACE, D. M.
"Cecil Brunner Roses." [SilverFR] (20) Spr 91, p. 21.
6452. WALLACE, Helen
"The Surgeon As Patient." [ClockR] (7:1/2) 91-92, p. 68.
6453. WALLACE, Jan
"The Longing for Rain." [PoetryNW] (32:3) Aut 91, p. 21-22.
"Solving for X." [PoetryNW] (32:3) Aut 91, p. 20-21.
6454. WALLACE, Naomi
"Anna's Discourse." [ChiR] (37:2/3) 91, p. 107.
"The Conquistadores." [Iowa] (21:1) Wint 91, p. 28-29.
"The Divided Garden." [MassR] (32:1) Spr 91, p. 96.
"Escape from Paradise, Kentucky." [Thrpny] (44) Wint 91, p. 12.
"An Execution in the Country." [Iowa] (21:1) Wint 91, p. 27.
"The Goat Rattle." [MassR] (32:1) Spr 91, p. 95.
"The Hunger Madrigal." [MassR] (32:1) Spr 91, p. 97.
"In the Looking Glass." [Iowa] (21:1) Wint 91, p. 30.
"The Prisoner." [Iowa] (21:1) Wint 91, p. 28.
"Vallejo in the Mines of Quivilca." [Iowa] (21:1) Wint 91, p. 29.
"Vallejo in the Mines of Quivilca." [Stand] (32:3) Sum 91, p. 37.
6455. WALLACE, Ronald
"Ballade at the Recycling Center." [Shen] (41:4) Wint 91, p. 25.
"Ballade of the Mussels." [Shen] (41:4) Wint 91, p. 24.
"Ballade of the Orangerie." [PoetryNW] (32:1) Spr 91, p. 24.
"Ballade of the Star Warriors." [PoetryNW] (32:1) Spr 91, p. 25.
"Grouse in the Garden." [CinPR] (21) Spr 90, p. 20.
"In the Piano Store." [PoetryNW] (32:4) Wint 91-92, p. 17-18.
"Mother's Day Pantoum." [PoetryNW] (32:4) Wint 91-92, p. 16-17.
"Pastoral." [GeoR] (45:2) Sum 91, p. 357.
"The Resurrection and the Light." [AntR] (49:3) Sum 91, p. 438.
"The Swing." [Poetry] (158:1) Ap 91, p. 1-2.
"Traveling." [LitR] (34:2) Wint 91, p. 258.
6456. WALLACE, T. H. S.
"Dustjacket Puffery." [SewanR] (99:4) Fall 91, p. 605-607.
6457. WALLACE-CRABBE, Chris
"Afternoon in the Central Nervous System." [Poetry] (158:5) Ag 91, p. 279.
"The Soul." [Verse] (8:2) Sum 91, p. 107.
WALLENDORF, George Carl
See WELLENDORF, George Carl
6458. WALLENSTEIN, Barry
"All the Wonderful Things." [Pembroke] (23) 91, p. 33.
"Love Sequence, Summer and Fall" (Selections: 4 poems). [Ploughs] (17:1) Spr 91,
p. 192-195.
"Post Sequence Drift" (Selections: 1, 3). [Ploughs] (17:1) Spr 91, p. 195-196.

6459. WALSH, Alexandra
  "The Waitress." [ManhatPR] (13) [91?], p. 11.
6460. WALSH, Catherine
  "A Form of Consent." [NewAW] (8/9) Fall 91, p. 173-174.
  "Modalities." [NewAW] (8/9) Fall 91, p. 168-169.
  "Nearly Nowhere." [NewAW] (8/9) Fall 91, p. 169.
  "Short Stories" (Extracts). [NewAW] (8/9) Fall 91, p. 170-172.
  "Uaigneach." [NewAW] (8/9) Fall 91, p. 174.
6461. WALSH, Joy
  "Saint Carolyn by the Sea" (Originally appeared as "Introductory Dialogue" in *Mary Magadalen Sings the Mass in Ordinary Time*, Alpha Beat Press, 1989). [MoodySI] (24/25/26) Spr 91, p. 18.
6462. WALSH, Marty
  "Like Heads Offered to Us." [CreamCR] (14:2) Wint 91, p. 163.
6463. WALTER, Judy
  "Marilyn Weissberg Could Draw." [ThRiPo] (37/38) 91, p. 31.
6464. WALTER, Rod
  "Homestead." [Plain] (12:1) Fall 91, p. 19.
6465. WALTERS, LaWanda
  "Cassandra Austen Burns Jane's Letters." [CinPR] (21) Spr 90, p. 64.
  "The True Story" (based on a photograph found near New Orleans: my grandmother and ladies in front of a church). [LaurelR] (25:2) Sum 91, p. 25-27.
6466. WALTNER-TOEWS, David
  "Postcards from Java: The Subtext Yogyakarta, Indonesia, 1986." [NegC] (11:1) 91, p. 17-19.
6467. WALZER, Kevin
  "Confessional." [CinPR] (22) Spr 91, p. 62.
  "Stasis." [CinPR] (22) Spr 91, p. 63.
6468. WAMPLER, Pamela
  "Dreams of a Victorian Bride." [NegC] (11:1) 91, p. 82.
6469. WANEK, Connie
  "Abstract." [Poetry] (158:4) Jl 91, p. 200.
  "Broom." [Poetry] (158:4) Jl 91, p. 200.
  "The Lights of the Valley." [PoetryE] (32) Fall 91, p. 119.
6470. WANER, Shelly
  "The Black Birds." [AmerPoR] (20:6) N-D 91, p. 46.
  "The Boxes." [AmerPoR] (20:6) N-D 91, p. 47.
  "The Gorillas." [AmerPoR] (20:6) N-D 91, p. 46.
  "Television." [AmerPoR] (20:6) N-D 91, p. 47.
6471. WANG, Gia Xin
  "Chinese Painting — Mountains, Water, People and Things" (tr. by Zhang Yichun). [GreenMR] (NS 4:2) Wint-Spr 91, p. 38.
6472. WANG, Jian
  "The Moon in the Mid-Autumn Night" (tr. by Gao Yu-hua). [GreenMR] (NS 4:2) Wint-Spr 91, p. 113.
6473. WANG, Jun Ru
  "Let's Go" (tr. of Baidao). [Vis] (35) 91, p. 5.
6474. WANG, Shi-Zheng
  "Fishing by an Autumn River" (tr. by Gao Yu-hua). [GreenMR] (NS 4:2) Wint-Spr 91, p. 112.
6475. WANG, Wei
  "Deer Fence" (in Chinese and English, tr. by Matthew Flannery, for JE). [SouthernHR] (25:2) Spr 91, p. 136.
  "Hsin-I Village" (in Chinese and English, tr. by Matthew Flannery, for BMW). [SouthernHR] (25:2) Spr 91, p. 124.
  "On the Mountain Lodge" (in Chinese and English, tr. by Fuh Shyh-jen). [Abraxas] (40/41) 91, p. 154-155.
6476. WANG, Xiaoni
  "Shoes at the Edge of the Fields" (tr. by Li Xijian and James Newcomb). [PraS] (65:2) Sum 91, p. 100.
6477. WANG, Yan
  "Reading Aloud" (tr. by Cao Wei). [GreenMR] (NS 4:2) Wint-Spr 91, p. 8.
6478. WANIEK, Marilyn Nelson
  "The Circus of Hunger" (for my father, who claimed it was true). [IndR] (14:3) Fall 91, p. 20-21.
  "Incomplete Renunciation." [KenR] (NS 13:3) Sum 91, p. 130.

"Invisible" (for Jennifer Geller). [IndR] (14:3) Fall 91, p. 22-23.
"Matins (2:30 A.M.)." [KenR] (NS 13:3) Sum 91, p. 131.
"Psalm." [KenR] (NS 13:3) Sum 91, p. 130.
"Vespers." [KenR] (NS 13:3) Sum 91, p. 132.
6479. WARD, Adam
"The Horse's Mouth." [BrooklynR] (8) 91, p. 43.
6480. WARD, Robert J.
"Landscape in White" (tr. of Anghel Dumbraveanu, w. Marcel Cornis-Pop).
[Talisman] (6) Spr 91, p. 138.
"Magic Words for the One Confined in Silence" (tr. of Anghel Dumbraveanu, w.
Marcel Cornis-Pop). [Talisman] (6) Spr 91, p. 138.
6481. WARD, Robert (Robert R.)
"Death." [SlipS] (11) 91, p. 81-84.
"Of This We Have Never Before Spoken." [PaintedHR] (1) Ja 91, p. 16-19.
6482. WARD, Thomas B.
"Town We Take With Us to Forget." [DogRR] (10:1) Sum 91, p. 32-33.
6483. WARD, William J.
"To Grandmother, After a Photograph of Joseph Cornell." [PoetL] (86:2) Sum 91,
p. 29.
6484. WARDEN, Marine Robert
"Two." [FreeL] (8) Aut 91, p. 12.
6485. WARGO, Nanette Elizabeth
"The Bag Lady of St. Peter's." [PikeF] (10) Spr 91, p. 20.
6486. WARING, Cynthia
"The Bodies of Earth." [OnTheBus] (8/9) 91, p. 165.
6487. WARLAND, Betsy
"Subject to Change: A Collaboration" (tr. by Daphne Marlatt). [CapilR] (2:6/7) Fall
91, p. 73-94.
6488. WARMOND, Ellen
"Clear" (tr. by C. J. Stevens). [NewRena] (8:2, #25) Fall 91, p. 67.
"Helder." [NewRena] (8:2, #25) Fall 91, p. 66.
"Kleine Barbarie." [NewRena] (8:2, #25) Fall 91, p. 64.
"Roentgenology" (tr. by C. J. Stevens). [NewRena] (8:2, #25) Fall 91, p. 63.
"Rontgenologie." [NewRena] (8:2, #25) Fall 91, p. 62.
"Small Barbarism" (tr. by C. J. Stevens). [NewRena] (8:2, #25) Fall 91, p. 65.
6489. WARN, Emily
"After Starting a Forest Fire." [RiverS] (35) 91, p. 79-80.
6490. WARNER, Marilyn
"Sweetwater." [BellArk] (7:4) Jl-Ag 91, p. 12.
6491. WARNER, Patrick
"First Kiss." [TickleAce] (21) Spr-Sum 91, p. 31-32.
6492. WARNOCK, Tilly
"Halloween Night, 1952." [PraS] (65:1) Spr 91, p. 90-91.
6493. WARREN, Charlotte Gould
"Reeling in the World." [HawaiiR] (15:3, #33) Fall 91, p. 131-132.
6494. WARREN, J. B.
"Paranoia." [PraF] (12:3 #56) Aut 91, p. 83.
"Paranoia T(w)oo." [PraF] (12:3 #56) Aut 91, p. 84.
"The Sinking Ship" (Adapted from the children's picture book, "Thirteen"). [PraF]
(12:3 #56) Aut 91, p. 82.
6495. WARREN, James E., Jr.
"Once in the Gulf War." [LullwaterR] (3:1) Fall 91, p. 62.
6496. WARREN, Jim
"At the Walt Whitman Rest Stop." [Shen] (41:2) Sum 91, p. 62.
"Compound Bow." [Shen] (41:2) Sum 91, p. 60-61.
6497. WARREN, Rosanna
"Elegist." [Atlantic] (268:4) O 91, p. 61.
"*Le Ventre de Paris:* A Marriage Poem." [GrandS] (10:2, #38) 91, p. 38-39.
"Science Lessons." [Agni] (33) 91, p. 40.
6498. WARREN, Shirley
"All That's Needed." [JINJPo] (13:2) Aut 91, p. 13.
6499. WARWICK, Ioanna-Veronika
"Antigone." [GreenMR] (NS 5:1) Sum-Fall 91, p. 32-33.
"The Arsonist" (In Memoriam Zygmunt "Walter" Janke, army officer, leader of the
Underground, . . .). [CimR] (96) Jl 91, p. 115-117.
"The Baltic." [Plain] (11:2) Wint 91, p. 25.

"Crows." [Ploughs] (17:4) Wint 91-92, p. 40-41.
"Eyeglasses." [CimR] (96) Jl 91, p. 114.
"Patriotism." [Plain] (12:2) Wint 91, p. 28-29.
"Plaques." [OxfordM] (7:2) Fall-Wint 91, p. 10-11.
"The Power of Silence." [OxfordM] (7:2) Fall-Wint 91, p. 9.
"Reminiscence of Angels." [GreenMR] (NS 5:1) Sum-Fall 91, p. 24-25.
"Le Temps Perdu." [OxfordM] (7:2) Fall-Wint 91, p. 14.
"Verloren" (for Robert von Dassanowsky-Harris). [OhioR] (46) 91, p. 38-39.
"Yin-Yang at Mono Lake." [OxfordM] (7:2) Fall-Wint 91, p. 12-13.

6500. WARWICK, Joanna
"Home" (tr. of Stanislaw Baranczak). [OnTheBus] (8/9) 91, p. 202.
"If Porcelain, Then Only the Kind" (tr. of Stanislaw Baranczak). [OnTheBus] (8/9) 91, p. 201.
"If You Must Scream, Do It Quietly" (tr. of Stanislaw Baranczak). [OnTheBus] (8/9) 91, p. 202-203.
"It Was His Own Fault" (tr. of Stanislaw Baranczak). [OnTheBus] (8/9) 91, p. 202.
"Out of Thin Mud and Clay" (tr. of Stanislaw Baranczak). [OnTheBus] (8/9) 91, p. 203.
"We Can't Get It" (tr. of Stanislaw Baranczak). [OnTheBus] (8/9) 91, p. 203.

6501. WAS, Carol
"Sign Language." [NegC] (11:1) 91, p. 60.

6502. WASHBURN, Laura Lee
"The Albino Sword Swallower at a Carnival in Maryland" (after Diane Arbus). [PoetL] (86:4) Wint 91-92, p. 17-18.
"House Like a Man." [CarolQ] (43:3) Spr 91, p. 41-42.

6503. WASSERMAN, E. H.
"Witches." [BelPoJ] (42:1) Fall 91, p. 31.

6504. WASSON, Kirsten
"You." [NewYorkQ] (44) 91, p. 60.

6505. WATADA, Terry
"Kawai-San." [CanLit] (129) Sum 91, p. 102-104.

6506. WATCKINS, Angus M.
"Her Form, Her Smile and Olive Skin." [RagMag] (9:1) 91, p. 16.

6507. WATERHOUSE, Philip A.
"Author, Author." [ChironR] (10:4) Wint 91, p. 38.
"High Tech." [DustyD] (2:1) Ja 91, p. 14.
"Only Been Here a Year Seems Longer." [ChironR] (10:4) Wint 91, p. 33.

6508. WATERMAN, Cary
"The Heart" (for P.M.). [WebR] (15) Spr 91, p. 75.
"Photograph of the Children of Izieu." [WebR] (15) Spr 91, p. 74-75.
"Storm." [WebR] (15) Spr 91, p. 77.
"Sunday Morning: Brussels, 1984." [WebR] (15) Spr 91, p. 76.

6509. WATERS, Michael
"At Homer's Tomb" (Ios). [Chelsea] (50) 91, p. 84-86.
"The Book of Tea" (in memoriam Kakuzo Okakura & for Jeffrey Skinner). [Chelsea] (50) 91, p. 87-89.
"Mosquito Nets." [SouthernPR] (31:2) Fall 91, p. 33-34.
"Portrait." [MissR] (19:3) 91, p. 160-161.
"River Wife." [GettyR] (4:3) Sum 91, p. 402-403.
"Snow Globe." [NoAmR] (276:3) S 91, p. 14.
"Village Dogs." [OhioR] (46) 91, p. 57-58.

6510. WATERS, Tara
"Livid Face." [DustyD] Ap 91, p. 3.

6511. WATERSON, Michael
"Second Coming." [DogRR] (10:2) Fall-Wint 91, p. 23.

6512. WATKINS, Angus M.
"Deluge." [RagMag] (9:1) 91, p. 17.

6513. WATKINS, Klyd
"Front Porch." [Poem] (65) My 91, p. 60-61.
"Jack and the 3." [Poem] (65) My 91, p. 62-65.
"The Teller." [CumbPR] (10:2) Spr 91, p. 29-30.

6514. WATSON, Arthur R.
"The Suite of the Honeymoon Miscarriage." [RiverS] (35) 91, p. 36-40.

6515. WATSON, Craig
"Logistics." [Avec] (4:1) 91, p. 31-33.

6516. WATSON, Edward Douglas
  "Sophomore." [EmeraldCR] (3) 91, c1990, p. 78.
6517. WATSON, Ellen
  "Love Song" (tr. of Adélia Prado). [NewOR] (18:4) Wint 91, p. 74.
6518. WATSON, Kathryn
  "Durango, Colorado." [ArtfulD] (20/21) 91, p. 91.
  "Thinking About My Father." [ArtfulD] (20/21) 91, p. 90.
6519. WATSON, Lawrence
  "Mated for Life." [Interim] (10:2) Fall-Wint 91-92, p. 36.
  "Unable to Tie Knots." [SpoonRQ] (16:3/4) Sum-Fall 91, p. 40.
6520. WATSON, Meg
  "Aromas of Eternity." [ChrC] (108:20) 26 Je-3 Jl 91, p. 652.
6521. WATSON, Patricia L.
  "Mistake." [NegC] (11:1) 91, p. 112-114.
6522. WATSON, Ron
  "Rediscovering the Trail." [ContextS] (2:2) 91, p. 32.
  "Trading for Bootleg Beer at Junior's House." [ContextS] (2:1) 91, p. 7.
6523. WATSON, Stephen
  "Rain in a Dead Man's Footsteps" (tr. from the /Xam, Southern Cape Bushmen).
    [PartR] (58:1) Wint 91, p. 123-124.
6524. WATSON, Thomas Ramey
  "Ulster Sunday." [ChrC] (108:3) 23 Ja 91, p. 68.
6525. WATT, Danny
  "Children." [PikeF] (10) Spr 91, p. 18.
6526. WATTERSON, William Collins
  "Eine Kleine Nachtmusik." [Poetry] (159:3) D 91, p. 139-140.
6527. WATTISON, Meredith
  "From 'Extinct Moon'" (For John Millett. For Antoine de Saint-Exupery). [Vis] (36)
    91, p. 45.
6528. WATTS, Dick
  "God to St. Peter, Upon Learning of the Death of Dr. Seuss." [ChrC] (108:32) 6 N
    91, p. 1030.
6529. WAUGAMAN, Charles A.
  "Obstacles." [CapeR] (26:2) Fall 91, p. 23.
6530. WAX, Phyllis
  "Lunar Lozenge." [Plain] (11:2) Wint 91, p. 14.
6531. WAY, Marilyn Kim
  "How Old Folks See It." [TickleAce] (21) Spr-Sum 91, p. 14.
6532. WAY, Zilla Sherritt
  "Crickets." [Sidewalks] (1) Aug 91, p. 53.
6533. WAYMAN, Tom
  "The Astonishing Weight of the Dead." [MalR] (95) Sum 91, p. 62-63.
  "Cabin News." [NoDaQ] (59:1) Wint 91, p. 173-174.
  "Correcting 120 Essays on Poetry." [PoetryNW] (32:3) Aut 91, p. 32-33.
  "Country Solitude." [PoetryNW] (32:3) Aut 91, p. 31-32.
  "Fire Elegy" (for Bron Wallace). [Hudson] (43:4) Wint 91, p. 622-623.
  "Geting the News." [PraF] (12:4) Wint 91-92, p. 54.
  "The Gift." [Quarry] (40:1/2) Wint-Spr 91, p. 192—193.
  "The Grave of Literary Ambition." [CanLit] (128) Spr 91, p. 62-64.
  "The Heart Is Also a Meadow." [Hudson] (43:4) Wint 91, p. 621-622.
  "The Lie." [ColR] (NS 17:2) Fall-Wint 90, p. 135-136.
  "Nice Guy." [Event] (20:1) Spr 91, p. 70-72.
  "Night Cabin." [Quarry] (40:1/2) Wint-Spr 91, p. 194.
  "The Politics of the House: Appliances." [ColR] (NS 17:2) Fall-Wint 90, p.
    128-129.
  "The Politics of the House: Curtains." [ColR] (NS 17:2) Fall-Wint 90, p. 132-133.
  "The Politics of the House: Cushions." [ColR] (NS 17:2) Fall-Wint 90, p. 130-131.
  "The Politics of the House: Tables." [PraF] (12:4) Wint 91-92, p. 55.
  "Slocan North." [CanLit] (128) Spr 91, p. 64.
  "Solidarity." [PoetryE] (32) Fall 91, p. 81.
  "Thirteenth Month." [MalR] (95) Sum 91, p. 64-65.
  "Very Zen." [ColR] (NS 17:2) Fall-Wint 90, p. 134.
  "The Winlaw Elegies." [NoDaQ] (59:1) Wint 91, p. 175.
  "Woman Who Calls Horses." [MalR] (95) Sum 91, p. 66-67.
6534. WEATHERFORD, Carole Boston
  "Freedom Rang When She Sang." [Obs] (6:3) Wint 91, p. 85-86.

"The Hanging Tree." [GreensboroR] (51) Wint 91-92, p. 33.
"The Tar Baby on the Soapbox." [Callaloo] (14:4) Fall 91, p. 923.
"Weeds 'Round His Memories." [Obs] (6:3) Wint 91, p. 86-87.
6535. WEAVER, Michael S.
"The Artist's Sister (Mania)." [BellR] (14:2) Fall 91, p. 39.
"The 'Big Bopper'." [RiverS] (34) 91, p. 22-23.
"Christmas, 1941." [IndR] (14:2) Spr 91, p. 90-91.
"Pearl Bailey: an Elegy." [KenR] (NS 13:4) Fall 91, p. 6.
"The Spanish Lesson" (for Jay Wright). [KenR] (NS 13:4) Fall 91, p. 7-10.
"Tuna Fish." [RiverS] (34) 91, p. 24-25.
"A Woman from Fredericksburg." [Callaloo] (14:3) Sum 91, p. 609-610.
6536. WEAVER, Roger
"Simplicity." [PaintedHR] (3) Sum 92, p. 30.
6537. WEBB, Charles
"First Elegy" (for Dr. Hall). [Pearl] (13) Spr-Sum 91, p. 12.
"My Tortoise Keith." [HiramPoR] (50) Spr-Sum 91, p. 25.
"A New Man." [Pearl] (14) Fall-Wint 91, p. 17.
"Squid." [CinPR] (22) Spr 91, p. 53.
"Unhappy Men." [SoCoast] (10) Fall 91, p. 22.
"Upsetting Things." [CinPR] (22) Spr 91, p. 52.
"Weeb, the Naturalist." [Pearl] (13) Spr-Sum 91, p. 62.
"The Whole Truth and Nothing But." [Gypsy] (17) 91, p. 28-29.
6538. WEBER, Elizabeth
"Harmonic Convergence." [SwampR] (7/8) Spr-Sum 91, p. 144-145.
6539. WEBER, Mark
"Dad." [ChironR] (10:4) Wint 91, p. 11.
"Fishbowl Analogies." [SlipS] (11) 91, p. 84.
"A God for Every Weekend, and More." [ChironR] (10:4) Wint 91, p. 11.
"The God Ganesha Works at U.S. Post Office Xmas 1990." [Pearl] (14) Fall-Wint
91, p. 12.
"I Won't Be the First Writer the Post Office Has Fired." [Pearl] (14) Fall-Wint 91, p.
12.
"Night." [ChironR] (10:4) Wint 91, p. 11.
"Our New Supervisor." [Pearl] (13) Spr-Sum 91, p. 58.
"Yearly Facts and Figures of the U.S. Mail." [Pearl] (14) Fall-Wint 91, p. 12.
6540. WEBER, R. B.
"Catching Our Breaths." [Confr] (46/47) Fall 91-Wint 92, p. 267.
6541. WEBSTER, Ed
"Over Dresden Town Hall." [CreamCR] (14:2) Wint 91, p. 141.
6542. WEBSTER, Mark
"The Ghosts Have Much to Celebrate." [MichQR] (30:3) Sum 91, p. 457.
6543. WEDDLE, Jeff
"Alchemy of the Page." [DogRR] (10:2) Fall-Wint 91, p. 13.
"Initiation." [MoodySI] (24/25/26) Spr 91, p. 31.
6544. WEDGE, George
"Persian Gulf Piece" (For Brian). [CoalC] (3) My 91, p. 16.
6545. WEE, Rebecca
"Chiroptera." [Ploughs] (17:4) Wint 91-92, p. 70-71.
"First Child." [Ploughs] (17:4) Wint 91-92, p. 72.
6546. WEEKS, Laura D.
"1,2,3" (tr. of Alexandra Petrova). [LitR] (34:3) Spr 91, p. 380.
"X. The air is skidding. On his native city" (tr. of Alexandra Petrova). [LitR] (34:3)
Spr 91, p. 380.
"The Hebrew Alphabet" (tr. of Alexandra Petrova). [LitR] (34:3) Spr 91, p.
380-381.
"In Search of the Desired Name" (tr. of Alexandra Petrova). [LitR] (34:3) Spr 91, p.
381.
"Reminiscence of Psalm 137" (For O. Sedakova, tr. of Yelena Shwartz). [LitR]
(34:3) Spr 91, p. 324.
"What This Avenue Is Called" (tr. of Yelena Shwartz). [LitR] (34:3) Spr 91, p. 323.
6547. WEEKS, Robert Lewis
"Angels." [HampSPR] Wint 91, p. 34.
"The Idea of Fine Souls." [GeoR] (45:3) Fall 91, p. 570-571.
"The Nudist Colony." [HampSPR] Wint 91, p. 33.
"Pink Dress and Ubiquitous Mirror." [Shen] (41:2) Sum 91, p. 64.

WEI, Cao
    See CAO, Wei
WEI, Guo
    See GUO, Wei
WEI, Wang
    See WANG, Wei
6548. WEI, Ying-wu
    "A Farewell to Guang-Ling" (tr. by Gao Yu-hua). [GreenMR] (NS 4:2) Wint-Spr
        91, p. 111.
6549. WEIGEL, Molly
    "Patrimonies" (tr. of Susana Cerdá, w. Ernesto Livon Grosman). [AmerPoR] (20:5)
        S-O 91, p. 37-38.
6550. WEIGL, Bruce
    "5. Enough for you to simply look at me" (tr. of Gitica Jakopin, w. the author).
        [OhioR] (47) 91, p. 13.
    "7. My door groans this summer night" (tr. of Gitica Jakopin, w. the author). [ColR]
        (NS 18:2) Fall-Wint 91, p. 84.
    "13. All the woods smell of pitch" (tr. of Gitica Jakopin, w. the author). [OhioR]
        (47) 91, p. 12.
    "Anna's Grace." [AmerPoR] (20:4) Jl-Ag 91, p. 8.
    "Elegy for the Swans at Grace Pond." [SouthernR] (27:2) Ap 91, p. 250.
    "Her Life Runs Like a Red Silk Flag" (Hanoi, 1990). [SouthernR] (27:2) Ap 91, p.
        251-252.
    "The Here and There" (for Ruth, in memoriam). [AmerPoR] (20:4) Jl-Ag 91, p. 8.
    "The Loop." [NewEngR] (13:3/4) Spr-Sum 91, p. 44.
    "Peacocks" (tr. of Gitica Jakopin, w. the author). [OhioR] (47) 91, p. 11.
    "Ribbon." [AmerPoR] (20:4) Jl-Ag 91, p. 8.
6551. WEIL, James (James L.)
    "Arts of the Book." [Chelsea] (51) 91, p. 99.
    "Brown." [DustyD] (2:1) Ja 91, p. 19.
    "'Dzhon Kits.' Wood Engraving. 1975." [DustyD] (2:1) Ja 91, p. 5.
    "A Figure, Its Failure." [Chelsea] (51) 91, p. 100-101.
    "For Christa McAuliffe and the Rest of Us, Still." [Chelsea] (51) 91, p. 97.
    "Palenque." [NewYorkQ] (46) 91, p. 36.
    "Real Time." [Chelsea] (51) 91, p. 98.
6552. WEINBERG, Viola
    "Like Anyone." [GeoR] (45:4) Wint 91, p. 798.
6553. WEINER, Hannah
    "Guatemala." [NewAW] (7) Spr 91, p. 24-26.
    "Plus Title" (Excerpt, clairvoyantly written). [CentralP] (19/20) Spr-Fall 91, p. 223.
6554. WEINER, Joshua
    "Blind Cats." [Nat] (253:11) 7 O 91, p. 422.
    "Market Day." [Thrpny] (45) Spr 91, p. 39.
    "Overlooking Berkeley." [Nat] (252:18) 13 My 91, p. 640.
    "Tokens" (for Thomas McGrath, 1916-1990). [Nat] (253:8) 16 S 91, p. 315.
6555. WEINER, Rachel Victoria
    "Women Like Us" (Taos Journal). [CapeR] (26:1) Spr 91, p. 23.
6556. WEINERMAN, Chester
    "Brian Dillard, Where Are You?" [AmerPoR] (20:3) My-Je 91, p. 32.
6557. WEINFIELD, Henry
    "The Afternoon of a Faun" (tr. of Stéphane Mallarmée). [Talisman] (6) Spr 91, p.
        75-77.
6558. WEINGARTEN, Roger
    "Dear Mike." [MissouriR] (14:2) 91, p. 162-166.
    "Jungle Gliders." [MissouriR] (14:2) 91, p. 158-159.
    "Objects in Mirror Are Closer Than They Appear." [Crazy] (40) Spr 91, p. 52-54.
    "Rapid Transit, July, 1955." [MissR] (19:3) 91, p. 158-159.
    "Stomping the Beaver Palace." [MissouriR] (14:2) 91, p. 160-161.
6559. WEINMAN, Paul
    "Photomatic." [FreeL] (7) Spr 91, p. 22.
6560. WEINRAUB, Richard
    "Gypsies." [HawaiiR] (15:3, #33) Fall 91, p. 89.
6561. WEINSTEIN, Debra
    "Boots." [JamesWR] (9:1) Fall 91, p. 6.
6562. WEINSTEIN, Muriel Harris
    "Breakfast." [CapeR] (26:2) Fall 91, p. 34-35.

"The Visit." [CapeR] (26:2) Fall 91, p. 32-33.
6563. WEINSTEIN, Raquel
"Madness." [PoetryUSA] (23) Sum 91, p. 24.
6564. WEINTRAUB, Richard
"Continental Men." [ChangingM] (22) Wint-Spr 91, p. 32.
6565. WEISBERG, Barbara
"Invitation." [BrooklynR] (8) 91, p. 39.
6566. WEISS, Irving
"Number Poem: Eleven." [Archae] (1) Fall 90, p. 41.
"Number Poem: Three." [Archae] (1) Fall 90, p. 42.
"Transformations of Water" (from "Sens-Plastique," tr. of Malcolm de Chazal).
[Archae] (1) Fall 90, p. 43-45.
6567. WEISS, Theodore
"Bad Times: Mother." [NewRep] (205:7) 12 Ag 91, p. 30.
"A Foreign Tongue." [ParisR] (33:118) Spr 91, p. 174-177.
"A Matter of Degree." [PartR] (58:4) Fall 91, p. 685-686.
"Occupied." [Poetry] (157:5) F 91, p. 257-258.
"Satisfied." [Poetry] (157:5) F 91, p. 258-259.
"A Summer Drive." [SouthwR] (76:2) Spr 91, p. 207-208.
"When All the Walls Are Down." [Ploughs] (17:1) Spr 91, p. 197-217.
"Writ in Water." [SouthwR] (76:2) Spr 91, p. 208-210.
6568. WEISSLITZ, E. F.
"Fugitives." [WindO] (55) Wint 91-92, p. 3.
"Solipsisms: Constructions." [WindO] (55) Wint 91-92, p. 4-6.
6569. WEITZ, William
"Bermuda Triangle." [WestHR] (45:4) Wint 91, p. 333.
6570. WEITZMAN, Sarah Brown
"Jesus of My Youth." [YellowS] (38) Wint-Spr 91-92, p. 8.
6571. WELBURN, Ron
"A Beauty Song." [Archae] (2) Spr 91, p. 10.
"Owl" (a portrait by Robert St. Brice, Haitian Painter). [Archae] (2) Spr 91, p. 11.
6572. WELCH, Don
"Notes Toward an Absurd Play." [LaurelR] (25:2) Sum 91, p. 94.
"The Old Woman." [LaurelR] (25:2) Sum 91, p. 92.
"Puritans." [LaurelR] (25:2) Sum 91, p. 93.
6573. WELCH, Enid Santiago
"Gray Eyes." [MinnR] (NS 37) Fall 91, p. 9.
6574. WELCH, James
"Surviving." [SoDakR] (29:3 part 2) Aut 91, p. 25.
6575. WELCH, Liliane
"Pâtisserie" (Short Grain Contest Winners: Prose Poem Winners: Third Prize).
[Grain] (19:4) Wint 91, p. 70.
6576. WELCH, Phillip
"Fifth World." [Chelsea] (50) 91, p. 73-74.
6577. WELDON, S. L.
"I'm afraid Daddy." [PottPort] (13:1) Spr 91, p. 57.
"Please." [PottPort] (13:1) Spr 91, p. 58.
6578. WELISH, Marjorie
"For Four Violins." [Conjunc] (16) 91, p. 129-130.
"Hymn to Life to Cliff, VI." [DenQ] (25:4) Spr 91, p. 94-95.
6579. WELLENDORF, George Carl
"The Desolate Beast." [BlackBR] (13) Spr-Sum 91, p. 27.
"The End of Industry." [BlackBR] (13) Spr-Sum 91, p. 39.
"Poem for My Daughter." [SoCoast] (10) Fall 91, p. 13.
"Sleeping Late." [LitR] (34:2) Wint 91, p. 255.
6580. WELLS, Susan
"Dream." [Caliban] (10) 91, p. 148-149.
6581. WELLS, Will
"Old Chimney" (tr. of Umberto Saba). [NewOR] (18:2) Sum 91, p. 17.
"The Shadow Racers." [Hudson] (44:3) Aut 91, p. 431.
WEN, Li
See LI, Wen
6582. WENDELL, Julia
"Dirty Movie." [PassN] (12:2) Wint 91, p. 11.
"The Merely Physical." [IndR] (14:3) Fall 91, p. 75-76.
"Storm Warning." [IndR] (14:3) Fall 91, p. 73-74.

6583. WENDT, Ingrid
"Poem at Forty-Five." [MassR] (32:2) Sum 91, p. 314-315.
"This Is His Story." [PaintedHR] (1) Ja 91, p. 7.
6584. WENTHE, William
"The End of the Century." [Timbuktu] (6) Spr 91, p. 6.
"Hunting in Midtown." [Timbuktu] (6) Spr 91, p. 7.
6585. WENTWORTH, Marjory
"The Last Night." [BelPoJ] (42:1) Fall 91, p. 22-23.
6586. WEREMCZUK, Ray
"Greece, So They Say." [Event] (20:2) Sum 91, p. 106-107.
WERT, William (William F.) van
    See Van WERT, William (William F.)
6587. WERTZ, William F., Jr.
"Thy Soul I See." [PoetryUSA] (22) Spr 91, p. 18.
6588. WESLOWSKI, Dieter
"Blue Dragonfly." [PikeF] (10) Spr 91, p. 3.
"Injunction Against Shadows." [Pembroke] (23) 91, p. 55.
"On Any Given Day." [MalR] (95) Sum 91, p. 99.
"The Owl and the Pussycat." [CrabCR] (7:3) 91, p. 24.
"The Saints." [Pembroke] (23) 91, p. 56.
"This Morning I Find Myself Waiting." [MalR] (95) Sum 91, p. 98.
6589. WESSEL, Peter
"La Isla de la Calma." [NegC] (11:3) 91, p. 44.
6590. WEST, Kathleene
"What I Ask For." [PoetryNW] (32:3) Aut 91, p. 11-12.
6591. WEST, Peg Flandreau
"Gather Round Me." [ChangingM] (23) Fall-Wint 91, p. 9.
6592. WEST, Richard M.
"The Decline of a West." [WormR] (31:1, #121) 91, p. 15-16.
"Deja Vu." [WormR] (31:1, #121) 91, p. 14-15.
"An Ode to Most Women I Have Known." [ChironR] (10:3) Aut 91, p. 16.
"The Old Volvo in Gramercy Park." [ChironR] (10:3) Aut 91, p. 16.
"The Secret Life of Walter Middling." [WormR] (31:1, #121) 91, p. 15.
"Sometimes a Sudden Madness." [WormR] (31:1, #121) 91, p. 14.
6593. WEST, Thomas A., Jr.
"History." [DustyD] Je 91, p. 17.
6594. WEST, Wes
"The Power of Flight." [EngJ] (80:3) Mr 91, p. 75-76.
6595. WESTBURY, Debbie
"Borderlines." [BellArk] (7:3) My-Je 91, p. 2.
6596. WESTERFIELD, Nancy (Nancy G.)
"The Campus in Holy Week." [ChrC] (108:10) 20-27 Mr 91, p. 316.
"The Cemetery Trees." [Poem] (66) N 91, p. 22.
"Christ in the Sand Hills." [NegC] (11:1) 91, p. 9.
"Church Moon." [PoetL] (86:2) Sum 91, p. 31.
"Clockwork." [CapeR] (26:1) Spr 91, p. 10.
"Comparative Anatomy." [FourQ] (5:2) Fall 91, p. 45.
"The Day of the Moons." [PoetL] (86:2) Sum 91, p. 30.
"The Doll Wash." [Grain] (19:1) Spr 91, p. 77.
"The Goddaughter." [Poem] (66) N 91, p. 23.
"Hair." [Plain] (11:2) Wint 91, p. 7.
"My Ex-." [Plain] (11:2) Wint 91, p. 7.
"The Occupations of the Dead." [Grain] (19:1) Spr 91, p. 78.
"Particulates." [Poem] (66) N 91, p. 20.
"Return Me To." [PraS] (65:3) Fall 91, p. 123.
"Roundtrip." [PraS] (65:3) Fall 91, p. 123-124.
"Sledding on Piedmont Street." [NegC] (11:1) 91, p. 10.
"Summer Theater." [NegC] (11:1) 91, p. 11.
"Twelfth-Century Nebraska." [Plain] (11:3) Spr 91, p. 10.
"A Woman Learning to Drive." [Poem] (66) N 91, p. 21.
"The Workbasket." [PraS] (65:3) Fall 91, p. 125.
6597. WESTLER, Max Jay
"The Door to the River." [GreensboroR] (51) Wint 91-92, p. 63.
WESTLER, Max van
    See Van WESTLER, Max

6598. WESTWOOD, Norma
   "Camille Monet in the Garden." [Interim] (10:1) Spr-Sum 91, p. 9.
6599. WEXLER, Evelyn
   "A Bunch of Keys in Budapest" (Honorable Mention, 5th Annual Contest).
      [SoCoast] (11) Wint 91, p. 26-27.
   "The Geisha House: The Black Kimono." [Nimrod] (34:2) Spr-Sum 91, p. 94.
   "The Geisha House: The White Kimono." [Nimrod] (34:2) Spr-Sum 91, p. 95.
   "The Gypsy Camps." [Nimrod] (34:2) Spr-Sum 91, p. 96.
   "Heirlooms." [Nimrod] (34:2) Spr-Sum 91, p. 93.
6600. WEXLER, Irving
   "Never Again." [RedBass] (15) 91, p. 37-38.
6601. WEXLER, Philip
   "Dear Ingvar." [PaintedHR] (2) Spr 91, p. 43.
6602. WEYL, Judith
   "Hopscotch." [Sidewalks] (1) Aug 91, p. 58-60.
6603. WHALEN, Benji
   "Blacking Out." [PaintedHR] (3) Sum 92, p. 16-17.
   "Snow Tires." [PaintedHR] (3) Sum 92, p. 17-18.
6604. WHALEN, Damian
   "Depoe Bay, Oregon, 1976" (For John Blanchette and Michael Sullivan).
      [SycamoreR] (3:2) Sum 91, p. 48-49.
   "Over." [Poem] (65) My 91, p. 68.
   "A Silent Whistle." [Poem] (65) My 91, p. 66.
   "Song." [Poem] (65) My 91, p. 67.
   "Wilderness Cold." [Poem] (65) My 91, p. 69.
6605. WHALEN, John
   "The Beauty of Tactical Surprise." [VirQR] (67:4) Aut 91, p. 682.
   "Big Cadillac of Spring." [RiverS] (35) 91, p. 22.
6606. WHALEN, Tom
   "Easter." [GeoR] (45:1) Spr 91, p. 63.
   "In the Chamber of Presidents." [ContextS] (2:1) 91, p. 17.
6607. WHALLEY, Karen
   "Across From My Father." [BellArk] (7:5) S-O 91, p. 9.
   "Ask My Brother." [BellArk] (7:5) S-O 91, p. 9.
   "The First Night We Spent in the House on Lopez Street." [BellArk] (7:5) S-O 91,
      p. 9.
   "Grieving a Teacher" (for Nelson Bentley). [BellArk] (7:1) Ja-F 91, p. 4.
   "Handing Down." [BellArk] (7:6) N-D 91, p. 11.
   "The Neighbors' Renovation." [BellArk] (7:3) My-Je 91, p. 4.
   "Owl, Visitation." [BellArk] (7:6) N-D 91, p. 6.
   "Seventeenth Spring of My Son." [BellArk] (7:3) My-Je 91, p. 8.
6608. WHARTON, David
   "Quantum Physics." [Stand] (32:1) Wint 90-91, p. 21.
6609. WHEATLEY, Patience
   "A Shout." [Arc] (26) Spr 91, p. 67-68.
6610. WHEELER, A. G.
   "Summer Afternoon, at the Beach." [Lactuca] (14) My 91, p. 12.
6611. WHEELER, Charles B.
   "Terminal Reflections." [LaurelR] (25:1) Wint 91, p. 112-113.
6612. WHEELER, Susan
   "The Belle." [NewAW] (7) Spr 91, p. 3.
   "Farmers, Falling Down." [13thMoon] (9:1/2) 91, p. 46.
   "Pastoral Care." [NewAW] (7) Spr 91, p. 6.
   "The Soul That Was Sister Carrie's." [NewAW] (7) Spr 91, p. 4-5.
6613. WHEELOCK, C. Webster
   "X. I mark the spot. My intersecting limbs." [Hellas] (2:2) Fall 91, p. 269.
   "Dublin Dust." [Hellas] (2:2) Fall 91, p. 268-269.
6614. WHITE, Boyd
   "Above the Reservoir." [AntR] (49:3) Sum 91, p. 423.
   "The Artificial Heart." [Iowa] (21:1) Wint 91, p. 110-111.
   "Bloodworms." [Iowa] (21:1) Wint 91, p. 108-109.
   "Jim Barnett's Pigs." [Iowa] (21:1) Wint 91, p. 107-108.
   "Paper Planes" (for Carolyn and Paul). [Iowa] (21:1) Wint 91, p. 107.
   "Plow." [IndR] (14:2) Spr 91, p. 92.
6615. WHITE, Calvin
   "Chase." [TickleAce] (21) Spr-Sum 91, p. 62-63.

"The Performer." [TickleAce] (21) Spr-Sum 91, p. 64-65.
"Seeing." [AntigR] (85/86) Spr-Sum 91, p. 240.
6616. WHITE, Catherine
"My Singular and Single Heart" (— June Jordan). [PaintedB] (42) 91, p. 14.
6617. WHITE, Claire Nicholas
"Home Coming." [Prima] (14/15) 91, p. 86.
6618. WHITE, Gail
"Byron at Ravenna." [Hellas] (2:2) Fall 91, p. 247.
"Written on the Head of a Pin." [ChrC] (108:16) 8 My 91, p. 518.
6619. WHITE, J. P.
"Evening with a Hungarian Poet" (for O. O.). [OntR] (34) Spr-Sum 91, p. 87.
"In the Mexican Neighborhood." [HighP] (6:1) Spr 91, p. 36-38.
"Leaving Erie." [ColR] (NS 18:1) Spr-Sum 91, p. 117-118.
"Lights on for Safety" (Florida road sign). [OntR] (34) Spr-Sum 91, p. 86.
"The Mole's Dream." [SewanR] (99:4) Fall 91, p. 565.
"The Sea Lion." [OntR] (34) Spr-Sum 91, p. 85.
"The Singer." [HighP] (6:1) Spr 91, p. 33-35.
"Twenty Dollars Short." [HighP] (6:1) Spr 91, p. 30-32.
"Up High in a Bosun Chair." [SewanR] (99:4) Fall 91, p. 564.
6620. WHITE, Julie Herrick
"Entering In." [Plain] (11:2) Wint 91, p. 23.
6621. WHITE, Lawrence L.
"A Poster of Tristan and Isolde." [PlumR] (1) Spr-Sum 91, p. 39-40.
6622. WHITE, Leland C.
"Death Visits Prison." [PoetryUSA] (22) Spr 91, p. 18.
"Late Evening, December 5th." [PoetryUSA] (23) Sum 91, p. 26.
"Spiritual Transfer." [PoetryUSA] (22) Spr 91, p. 19.
6623. WHITE, Michael (Mike)
"Flight" (homage to Vladimir Nabokov). [GettyR] (4:3) Sum 91, p. 451-453.
"Recurrence." [Journal] (14:2) Wint 91, p. 31-32.
"The View" (for a childhood friend). [Journal] (15:2) Fall 91, p. 24-28.
6624. WHITE, Mimi
"Here on Earth" (January, 1985). [SingHM] (19) 91, p. 27-28.
6625. WHITE, Nancy
"Confection." [BlackWR] (18:1) Fall-Wint 91, p. 94.
"The Function of Clouds." [Ploughs] (17:2/3) Fall 91, p. 269.
"Life of a Girl." [MassR] (32:2) Sum 91, p. 295-296.
6626. WHITE, R. H.
"Seasons." [Poem] (66) N 91, p. 34.
6627. WHITE, Sarah
"Sonnet Lesson" (for S.J. Marks). [NegC] (11:1) 91, p. 98.
6628. WHITEHEAD, James
"For John Clellon Holmes." [CutB] (36) Sum 91, p. 93.
"We're Listening to the Features Editor." [CutB] (36) Sum 91, p. 94-96.
6629. WHITEHEAD, Thomas
"Algernon Packingham Phyfe." [SoCoast] (11) Wint 91, p. 61.
"The Dark Red Meat." [HampSPR] Wint 91, p. 35.
"There once was a woman so slovenly." [SoCoast] (11) Wint 91, p. 61.
6630. WHITEHOUSE, Anne
"The Fogg Poems." [Ploughs] (17:1) Spr 91, p. 218-221.
6631. WHITING, Nathan
"Birds Nibble Fossils." [Chelsea] (50) 91, p. 30.
"Flying Sheep Clothe Reality." [HangL] (58) 91, p. 77.
"A Journey by Tricycle." [HangL] (58) 91, p. 78.
"Kinds of Distance." [Mildred] (4:2/5:1) 91, p. 63.
"Multimuon Events." [Chelsea] (50) 91, p. 29.
"Nonrigidity of Earth." [Contact] (10:59/60/61) Spr 91, p. 41.
"Provisional Courage." [HangL] (58) 91, p. 79.
"Rotating Stars." [Chelsea] (50) 91, p. 28.
6632. WHITLOW, Carolyn Beard
"Herndon's." [IndR] (14:2) Spr 91, p. 93-94.
"South County" (In Memorium — for Robert Hayden). [13thMoon] (9:1/2) 91, p.
48-50.
"Supermarket Blues" (for Sterling A. Brown). [13thMoon] (9:1/2) 91, p. 47.
"Three Cent Stamp." [IndR] (14:2) Spr 91, p. 95-98.

6633. WHITMAN, Ruth
"Birth." [PraS] (65:1) Spr 91, p. 111.
"The Drowned Mountain." [BostonR] (16:1) F 91, p. 13.
"Hatshepsut: Before my father came to the throne." [PraS] (65:1) Spr 91, p. 111-112.
"Hatshepsut: I remember my grandmother." [PraS] (65:1) Spr 91, p. 113.
"Hatshepsut: When I was six." [PraS] (65:1) Spr 91, p. 109-110.
"Looking for Hatshepsut." [PraS] (65:1) Spr 91, p. 108-109.
"Politics." [PraS] (65:1) Spr 91, p. 114.
6634. WHITMORE, S. M.
"David's Turtle." [PoetL] (86:3) Fall 91, p. 45.
6635. WHITNEY, Ross R.
"Dear Miss Etheridge — 1871." [BelPoJ] (42:1) Fall 91, p. 15.
6636. WHITNEY, Tamora
"Table Grass." [Plain] (11:2) Wint 91, p. 27.
6637. WHITTEMORE, Reed
"The Gland." [PlumR] (1) Spr-Sum 91, p. 52.
"The Living." [PlumR] (1) Spr-Sum 91, p. 53.
6638. WICKS, Susan
"Poacher." [PoetryE] (31) Spr 91, p. 75.
6639. WIDERKEHR, Richard
"The City." [Vis] (35) 91, p. 27.
6640. WIDNER, Jill
"Geographers." [BambooR] (50/51) Spr-Sum 91, p. 156-157.
"Glassing the Horizon." [BambooR] (50/51) Spr-Sum 91, p. 154-155.
6641. WIDUP, David
"Performance Appraisal." [OnTheBus] (8/9) 91, p. 166.
6642. WIECZOREK, Paula
"Eating the Flesh" (Photograph in "Newsweek"). [RagMag] (9:1) 91, p. 19.
"Graveside Talk with Grandma" (For A.M.N. 1909-1983). [RagMag] (9:1) 91, p. 20.
"Say Her War." [RagMag] (9:1) 91, p. 18.
6643. WIELAND, Liza
"Holding You Up." [Journal] (14:2) Wint 91, p. 76-77.
6644. WIENER, Chet
"Even Wanting." [Epoch] (40:1) 91, p. 9.
"Not Only Like Moonlight." [Epoch] (40:1) 91, p. 12-13.
"Passage." [Epoch] (40:1) 91, p. 10-11.
6645. WIER, Dara
"Automatic Dialog Replacement." [NewEngR] (13:3/4) Spr-Sum 91, p. 319.
"Chameleons Never Lie." [MassR] (32:3) Fall 91, p. 415-416.
"A Handful of Porcupine Quills." [SouthernR] (27:1) Ja 91, p. 141-142.
"Involuntary Compulsory." [NewEngR] (13:3/4) Spr-Sum 91, p. 317.
"Longing." [SouthernR] (27:1) Ja 91, p. 140-141.
"Positive Response to Reasonable Request." [NewEngR] (13:3/4) Spr-Sum 91, p. 318.
"Torn Between Two Lovers." [NewEngR] (13:3/4) Spr-Sum 91, p. 320.
"Winslow Homer's Blues." [SouthernR] (27:1) Ja 91, p. 143-146.
6646. WIKOFF, Katherine Hennessey
"Breughel's 'Return of the Hunters'." [WindO] (55) Wint 91-92, p. 31.
6647. WILBORN, William
"Lines" (Near Concord). [SouthwR] (76:4) Aut 91, p. 564-565.
6648. WILBUR, Frederick
"The Blues on 501." [GreenMR] (NS 5:1) Sum-Fall 91, p. 106-107.
6649. WILBUR, Richard
"Six Years Later" (tr. of Joseph Brodsky). [Shen] (41:4) Wint 91, p. 79-80.
6650. WILCOX, Dan
"Joe Krausman." [ChironR] (10:3) Aut 91, p. 44.
6651. WILCOXEN, Jacqueline
"The Flutist." [PacificR] (10) 91-92, p. 84-85.
6652. WILD, Danelia
"Dark Red." [OnTheBus] (8/9) 91, p. 170.
"First Light." [OnTheBus] (8/9) 91, p. 169.
6653. WILD, Peter
"The Alphabetical Disadvantage." [NoDaQ] (59:1) Wint 91, p. 96.
"Columbus and the American Kazoo." [OhioR] (47) 91, p. 98-99.

"Disciples." [NoDaQ] (59:1) Wint 91, p. 95.
"Elko, Nevada." [ArtfulD] (20/21) 91, p. 123.
"Holly Oak, Delaware." [ArtfulD] (20/21) 91, p. 122.
"Krakatoa." [PoetL] (86:2) Sum 91, p. 6.
"Librarians." [NoDaQ] (59:1) Wint 91, p. 94.
"Musicians." [ChatR] (11:3) Spr 91, p. 75.
"The Old Whiskey Barrel." [MidAR] (11:2) 91, p. 123.
"Real Joggers." [Journal] (14:2) Wint 91, p. 50.
"The Remittance Man." [Elf] (1:3) Fall 91, p. 43.
"Rio Linda, California." [ArtfulD] (20/21) 91, p. 124.
"Solstice." [PoetL] (86:2) Sum 91, p. 5.

6654. WILDE-MENOZZI, Wallis
"Getting to an Interview in Rome." [MalR] (97) Wint 91, p. 13-15.
"Going on My Motorcycle, Cycle, Cycle, Cycle — Yeah" (for Francesco). [MalR]
(97) Wint 91, p. 16-19.
"It's Now." [MissR] (19:3) 91, p. 132.
"White on White." [MissR] (19:3) 91, p. 131.

6655. WILDER, Jesse Bryant
"With Love for Andrea Taflan, August 18, 1990" (Andrea Taflan died in Fagaras,
August 7, age — almost six). [Gypsy] (17) 91, p. 14-15.

6656. WILDFANG, F. B.
"Hitching from Albuquerque to L.A." [NorthStoneR] (10) Fall 91-Wint 92, p. 155.

6657. WILDING, Margo
"N.Y.C. Oct., 1990." [IndR] (14:3) Fall 91, p. 142.

6658. WILKER, Josh
"Hunger." [GreenMR] (NS 4:2) Wint-Spr 91, p. 108-109.

6659. WILKES, Kenneth H.
"Where the Earth Is." [Gypsy] (17) 91, p. 51.

6660. WILKIE, Pamela
"Equal in the eyes of the birds." [Interim] (10:1) Spr-Sum 91, p. 40.
"Hit and Run." [Interim] (10:1) Spr-Sum 91, p. 41.

6661. WILKINS, W. R.
"Color Blind." [Confr] (46/47) Fall 91-Wint 92, p. 275.
"The Reluctance to Accept Reality for What It Is, Whatever It Is." [Pearl] (13)
Spr-Sum 91, p. 15.
"Sanctuary." [Pearl] (13) Spr-Sum 91, p. 15.
"Vacancy." [CimR] (96) Jl 91, p. 125-126.

6662. WILLARD, Carla
"Anacostia Woman in a Red Frame" (through Williams). [PaintedB] (44) 91, p.
28-29.

6663. WILLARD, Nancy
"One for the Road." [Field] (45) Fall 91, p. 88-89.

6664. WILLEY, Lance
"The Hideaway." [PacificR] (10) 91-92, p. 16.
"Space I'm In." [PacificR] (10) 91-92, p. 145.

6665. WILLIAM, N. Sean
"Annunciation." [Os] (33) Fall 91, p. 9.

6666. WILLIAMS, Ann
"All Words About Death Are Pompous." [SpiritSH] (56) Spr-Sum 91, p. 39.
"Imago Dei." [SpiritSH] (56) Spr-Sum 91, p. 37.
"Old Poets." [SpiritSH] (56) Spr-Sum 91, p. 36.
"Passing Through: a Theology of Death." [SpiritSH] (56) Spr-Sum 91, p. 37.
"Remembering Songs and Wayside Stands." [SpiritSH] (56) Spr-Sum 91, p. 36.
"Roadkill." [SpiritSH] (56) Spr-Sum 91, p. 38.

6667. WILLIAMS, C. K.
"Autumn" (Excerpted from "Canvas," tr. of Adam Zagajewksi, w. Renata
Gorczynski and Benjamin Ivry). [ManhatR] (6:1) Fall 91, p. 50.
"The Bells" (for C. K. Williams, Excerpted from "Canvas," tr. of Adam Zagajewksi,
w. Renata Gorczynski and Benjamin Ivry). [ManhatR] (6:1) Fall 91, p. 51.
"Burgundy's Grasslands" (Excerpted from "Canvas," tr. of Adam Zagajewksi, w.
Renata Gorczynski and Benjamin Ivry). [ManhatR] (6:1) Fall 91, p. 46.
"Canvas" (Excerpted from "Canvas," tr. of Adam Zagajewksi, w. Renata
Gorczynski and Benjamin Ivry). [ManhatR] (6:1) Fall 91, p. 53.
"Electric Elegy" (Excerpted from "Canvas," tr. of Adam Zagajewksi, w. Renata
Gorczynski and Benjamin Ivry). [ManhatR] (6:1) Fall 91, p. 47.

"From the Lives of Things" (Excertped from "Canvas," tr. of Adam Zagajewksi, w.
     Renata Gorczynski and Benjamin Ivry). [ManhatR] (6:1) Fall 91, p. 52.
"The Gas Station." [Crazy] (41) Wint 91, p. 88-90.
"Green Linnaeus" (Excertped from "Canvas," tr. of Adam Zagajewksi, w. Renata
     Gorczynski and Benjamin Ivry). [ManhatR] (6:1) Fall 91, p. 48.
"Jealousy: The Mirror." [NewYorker] (67:35) 21 O 91, p. 84.
"The Knot." [Antaeus] (67) Fall 91, p. 114-115.
"On a Side Street" (Excertped from "Canvas," tr. of Adam Zagajewksi, w. Renata
     Gorczynski and Benjamin Ivry). [ManhatR] (6:1) Fall 91, p. 45.
"Room." [Antaeus] (67) Fall 91, p. 116-117.
"She, Through." [TriQ] (83) Wint 91-92, p. 82-92.
"Spider's Song" (Excertped from "Canvas," tr. of Adam Zagajewksi, w. Renata
     Gorczynski and Benjamin Ivry). [ManhatR] (6:1) Fall 91, p. 44.
"Watching Shoah in a Hotel Room in America" (Excertped from "Canvas," tr. of
     Adam Zagajewksi, w. Renata Gorczynski and Benjamin Ivry). [ManhatR]
     (6:1) Fall 91, p. 49.
"When." [NewYorker] (67:10) 29 Ap 91, p. 42.
6668. WILLIAMS, Daniel
     "Shaman Dreams Dark Houses." [MidwQ] (32:3) Spr 91, p. 283-287.
6669. WILLIAMS, David
     "Available Light." [Paint] (18:35) Spr 91, p. 77.
     "Come Down with Me from Lebanon." [KenR] (NS 13:4) Fall 91, p. 192-193.
     "In Exile." [PoetryE] (31) Spr 91, p. 100-101.
     "In Memory." [PoetryE] (31) Spr 91, p. 102-104.
     "Indian School." [HayF] (8) Spr-Sum 91, p. 94.
     "Singer and Song." [Agni] (34) 91, p. 142.
6670. WILLIAMS, Denise
     "Self Hypnosis" (Second Prize, Cincinnati Poetry Review Competition). [CinPR]
     (21) Spr 90, p. 21.
6671. WILLIAMS, Faith
     "The Grasshoppers and the Ants." [PoetL] (86:2) Sum 91, p. 9.
6672. WILLIAMS, Leslita
     "Non-violence." [SinW] (43/44) Sum 91, p. 259-261.
6673. WILLIAMS, Marie Sheppard
     "Sonya." [AmerV] (22) Spr 91, p. 48.
6674. WILLIAMS, Martha V.
     "Grandma's Palette." [ChironR] (10:3) Aut 91, p. 44.
6675. WILLIAMS, Maurine
     "Sand Man." [Bogg] (64) 91, p. 14.
6676. WILLIAMS, Miller
     "Adjusting to the Light." [NoDaQ] (59:3) Sum 91, p. 96.
     "Despairing of Understanding We Fall into Decadence." [NewL] (58:1) Fall 91, p.
     101.
     "Rodin: The Cathedral, On Coming upon It Unprepared." [NewL] (58:1) Fall 91, p.
     103.
     "The Six Moral Virtues: Grace, Style, Class, Humility, Kindness, and Wisdom."
     [NewL] (58:1) Fall 91, p. 102.
6677. WILLIAMS, Ralph T.
     "English Teacher." [ChamLR] (8-9) Spr-Fall 91, p. 85-86.
6678. WILLIAMS, Roger
     "Learning to Believe." [Shen] (41:4) Wint 91, p. 28.
6679. WILLIAMS, Rynn
     "La Fonda." [SpoonRQ] (16:1/2) Wint-Spr 91, p. 102.
     "The Shepherd." [SpoonRQ] (16:1/2) Wint-Spr 91, p. 103.
     "The Word." [SpoonRQ] (16:1/2) Wint-Spr 91, p. 101.
6680. WILLIAMS, Tennessee
     "We Have Not Long to Love." [Poetry] (157:5) F 91, p. 289.
6681. WILLIAMS, Tyrone
     "66% and Rising." [Obs] (6:2) Sum 91, p. 45.
     "Busy Signals." [KenR] (NS 13:4) Fall 91, p. 112-113.
     "Double Helix: In My Father's House There Are Many Mansions." [RiverS] (34) 91,
     p. 87.
     "Election Night." [KenR] (NS 13:4) Fall 91, p. 113.
     "The Last Cow Boy." [RiverS] (34) 91, p. 86.
     "Love: Take Two." [Obs] (6:2) Sum 91, p. 44-45.
     "Tribute." [KenR] (NS 13:4) Fall 91, p. 112.

"White Noise." [Obs] (6:2) Sum 91, p. 44.
"Woman Troubles." [KenR] (NS 13:4) Fall 91, p. 114.
6682. WILLIAMS, Willie
"Mirrors and Memory Do Lie" (for Ruth Richardson). [Obs] (6:3) Wint 91, p. 52-53.
"White Shirts Dyed Brown Can Not Hide Blood Stains" (for Nkenge Zola). [Obs] (6:3) Wint 91, p. 53-54.
6683. WILLIAMS, Zarle K.
"Night Death." [Obs] (6:3) Wint 91, p. 97.
6684. WILLIAMSON, Alan
"Forest Street." [CalQ] (32/33) Spr 90, p. 67-68.
"Unanticipated Mirrors" (in memory of Alfred Satterthwaite). [Ploughs] (17:2/3) Fall 91, p. 246-247.
6685. WILLIAMSON, Greg
"Below the Bridge." [SouthernPR] (31:1) Spr 91, p. 13.
"Drawing Hands." [Poetry] (158:5) Ag 91, p. 271.
"Picnic in the Park." [Poetry] (158:5) Ag 91, p. 270.
6686. WILLIS, Irene
"To Fit Your Need Exactly." [US1] (24/25) Spr 91, p. 34.
6687. WILLIS, Paul
"Passionate Sins." [ChrC] (108:29) 16 O 91, p. 934.
6688. WILLOUGHBY, Jennifer
"Parity." [SnailPR] (1:2) Fall 91-Wint 92, p. 18.
WILLOW, Ana Beautiful
See BEAUTIFUL WILLOW, Ana
6689. WILLOW, Morgan Grayce
"Dressing." [EvergreenC] (6:2) Sum-Fall 91, p. 14-15.
"The Fact of You" (with thanks to K. D. Lang). [EvergreenC] (6:2) Sum-Fall 91, p. 16-17.
6690. WILLS, Ora
"Another Loss." [EmeraldCR] (3) 91, c1990, p. 4-5.
"Edjication." [EmeraldCR] (3) 91, c1990, p. 98-100.
"Florida, Early Fifties." [EmeraldCR] (4) 91, p. 3-4.
"Metamorphosis." [EmeraldCR] (4) 91, p. 4.
"Trashed." [EmeraldCR] (3) 91, c1990, p. 5-6.
"Yaller." [EmeraldCR] (4) 91, p. 5.
6691. WILLSON, John
"The Motorist's Prayer." [SycamoreR] (3:2) Sum 91, p. 43-44.
6692. WILLUMSEN, Maj-Britt
"An apple, red" (tr. by Susanne Jorn). [AmerPoR] (20:1) Ja-F 91, p. 30.
"You meet the city and the human beings" (tr. by Susanne Jorn). [AmerPoR] (20:1) Ja-F 91, p. 30.
"Your room gets carried away" (tr. by Susanne Jorn). [AmerPoR] (20:1) Ja-F 91, p. 30.
6693. WILMARTH, Richard
"Coffee & Tea." [BlackBR] (13) Spr-Sum 91, p. 14-15.
"Full Moon." [BlackBR] (13) Spr-Sum 91, p. 44.
"The International Observer." [BlackBR] (13) Spr-Sum 91, p. 43.
"Sword and Pen." [BlackBR] (13) Spr-Sum 91, p. 42.
"The Taking Up of the Cross." [BlackBR] (13) Spr-Sum 91, p. 44.
6694. WILMER, Clive
"The Temple of Aphrodite" (Honorable Mention, Robert Penn Warren Poetry Prize Competition). [CumbPR] (11:1) Fall 91, p. 65-67.
6695. WILMOT, Bernard
"Miss Mattie Poems" (7 poems). [Mildred] (4:2/5:1) 91, p. 5-9.
6696. WILNER, Eleanor
"Return to Bali." [Calyx] (13:2) Sum 91, p. 39-41.
6697. WILOCH, Thomas
"Little Boxes." [WorldL] (1:1) 91, p. 8.
"The Magnetic Moon." [WorldL] (1:1) 91, p. 9.
"Marionettes." [WorldL] (1:1) 91, p. 7.
"Postcards." [RiverS] (34) 91, p. 38.
"Tiny White Skulls." [WorldL] (1:1) 91, p. 6.
6698. WILSON, Alan R.
"From the Sonneteer's Sky Atlas." [HampSPR] Wint 91, p. 40-45.

6699. WILSON, Bruce
"To Those Who Saw Me Off at Fang Shan" (tr. of Xie Ling-Yun). [PoetL] (86:4)
Wint 91-92, p. 46.
6700. WILSON, Donald S.
"Prologue to Death." [RiverS] (33) 91, p. 71.
6701. WILSON, Graeme
"Civilized Behavior" (tr. of Otomo No Yotsuna). [LitR] (35:1) Fall 91, p. 108.
"In the Mountains" (tr. of Fujiwara No Teika). [LitR] (35:1) Fall 91, p. 108.
"Tedium" (tr. of Lady Izumi Shikibu). [LitR] (35:1) Fall 91, p. 108.
6702. WILSON, Ian Randall
"Dreams of Harleys." [OnTheBus] (8/9) 91, p. 171.
"Four Rejection Slips." [OnTheBus] (8/9) 91, p. 171.
"The Poetry of Anything." [RagMag] (9:2) 91, p. 8-9.
6703. WILSON, Jack Lowther
"The Walker." [TickleAce] (22) Fall-Wint 91, p. 57.
"Wild Horses." [TickleAce] (22) Fall-Wint 91, p. 58.
6704. WILSON, John
"Sense of Mission." [ChironR] (10:4) Wint 91, p. 22.
6705. WILSON, L. E.
"A Madrigal for Bedtime." [Tribe] (1:2) Spr 90, p. 77.
6706. WILSON, Leonore
"Child." [CalQ] (35/36) 91, p. 38-39.
"Little Mother." [CalQ] (35/36) 91, p. 41.
"Road 32" (for Jim). [CalQ] (35/36) 91, p. 39-40.
6707. WILSON, Patrice M.
"Renting a Room in Newark." [JINJPo] (13:1) Spr 91, p. 30.
6708. WILSON, Peter Lamborn
"The Lovers' Tailor's Shop" (tr. of Jalaloddin Rumi, w. William C. Chittick).
[Talisman] (6) Spr 91, p. 30.
6709. WILSON, Rob
"By the Rivers of Hiroshima." [BambooR] (52) Fall 91, p. 144.
"China." [Manoa] (3:1) Spr 91, p. 158.
"New York, New York." [Manoa] (3:1) Spr 91, p. 159.
"Still Life in Amherst." [Manoa] (3:1) Spr 91, p. 158-159.
6710. WILSON, Ronald
"Fall." [Poetry] (158:5) Ag 91, p. 254.
"Greek Torso." [Poetry] (158:4) Jl 91, p. 193.
"An Old Woman Gives Away Her Things." [Poetry] (158:5) Ag 91, p. 254.
6711. WILSON, Steve
"Bucharest, December 1989." [CharR] (17:1) Spr 91, p. 65.
"Elision." [CharR] (17:1) Spr 91, p. 64.
6712. WIMP, Jet
"Before Divorce." [Paint] (18:36) Aut 91, p. 27.
6713. WINANS, A. D.
"For Angie." [ChironR] (10:4) Wint 91, p. 2.
"For Charles Olcott." [ChironR] (10:4) Wint 91, p. 2.
"Happiness Is a Warm Wedding." [Confr] (46/47) Fall 91-Wint 92, p. 254.
"Jim's Donut Shop." [Lactuca] (14) My 91, p. 32.
"Looking Back." [Pearl] (14) Fall-Wint 91, p. 55.
"Memories." [ChironR] (10:4) Wint 91, p. 2.
"The Old Man." [BlackBR] (14) Fall-Wint 91, p. 37.
6714. WINCH, Terence
"Advanced Civilization." [NewRep] (204:21) 27 My 91, p. 40.
"Cathedral." [NewRep] (205:17) 21 O 91, p. 37.
"The Drift of Things." [Shiny] (6) Spr-Sum 91, p. 73-74.
"Gloria Mundi" (for Tim Dlugos). [WashR] (16:6) Ap-My 91, p. 8.
WINCKEL, Nance van
See Van WINCKEL, Nance
6715. WINDER, Barbara
"West of Omaha" (Honorable Mention, 5th Annual Contest). [SoCoast] (11) Wint
91, p. 31.
6716. WINFIELD, William
"Between Two Skies." [MidwQ] (32:4) Sum 91, p. 428.
"Blade." [MidwQ] (32:4) Sum 91, p. 424.
"Cities." [MidwQ] (32:4) Sum 91, p. 423.
"Flame." [MidwQ] (32:4) Sum 91, p. 426.

"Following the Night." [ManhatR] (6:1) Fall 91, p. 72.
"Home." [MidwQ] (32:4) Sum 91, p. 420.
"Prayer." [Abraxas] (40/41) 91, p. 122-123.
"Pulse." [MidwQ] (32:4) Sum 91, p. 427.
"Totem." [Abraxas] (40/41) 91, p. 122.
"Under October." [MidwQ] (32:4) Sum 91, p. 421.
"Verge." [MidwQ] (32:4) Sum 91, p. 419.
"Victims." [MidwQ] (32:4) Sum 91, p. 425.
"Vigil." [MidwQ] (32:4) Sum 91, p. 422.

WING, Tek Lum
    See LUM, Wing Tek

6717. WINSLOW, Ethel (Ethel M.))
    "The Ordinary." [HopewellR] (1991) 91, p. 14.
    "Writing Is Like Someone Leaving" (A Plainsongs Award Poem). [Plain] (12:1) Fall
        91, p. 4.

6718. WINSLOW, Hall
    "The Abbot of Mega Speilion." [Poem] (66) N 91, p. 46.
    "The Age of Seven." [Poem] (66) N 91, p. 44.
    "Astrolabe." [Poem] (66) N 91, p. 45.
    "Green and Dying." [WindO] (54) Sum 91, p. 20.

6719. WINSTON, Andy
    "Okra." [MidAR] (11:2) 91, p. 52.
    "Raiding the Harvest" (Ozark Mountains, 1985). [MidAR] (11:2) 91, p. 50-51.

6720. WINTER, Jonah
    "Homage to William Shakespeare." [AntR] (49:2) Spr 91, p. 244.
    "The Lord's Prayer in American." [AntR] (49:2) Spr 91, p. 245.
    "Stranger." [ChiR] (37:2/3) 91, p. 176.

6721. WINTER, Kathleen
    "Sadness of the Trees." [TickleAce] (22) Fall-Wint 91, p. 42.
    "You Could Have Been a Gypsy." [TickleAce] (22) Fall-Wint 91, p. 40-41.

6722. WINTER-COYLE, Don
    "Batting Rocks." [CinPR] (22) Spr 91, p. 28.
    "Cleaning Up at the Mattawan Burger Chef." [PassN] (12:1) Sum 91, p. 7.
    "Working Late." [HiramPoR] (50) Spr-Sum 91, p. 26.

6723. WINTERS, Anne
    "The Billboard Man." [BostonR] (16:3/4) Je-Ag 91, p. 26.
    "The First Verse." [ParisR] (33:121) Wint 91, p. 133-137.
    "The Hall of Armor." [BostonR] (16:3/4) Je-Ag 91, p. 26.
    "Manhattan Schist." [BostonR] (16:3/4) Je-Ag 91, p. 26.
    "To New York." [BostonR] (16:3/4) Je-Ag 91, p. 26.

6724. WINTERS, Bayla
    "Love and XXXs." [Kalliope] (13:3) 91, p. 8.
    "Seescape." [OnTheBus] (8/9) 91, p. 172.

6725. WINTERS, Yvor
    "The Barnyard." [TriQ] (81) Spr-Sum 91, p. 163-164.
    "A Fragment." [ParisR] (33:121) Wint 91, p. 242.
    "Noon." [ParisR] (33:121) Wint 91, p. 241.
    "To the Holy Spirit" (from a deserted graveyard in the Salinas Valley). [ParisR]
        (33:121) Wint 91, p. 242-243.

6726. WINWOOD, David
    "Meet the Family." [WritersF] (17) Fall 91, p. 156.
    "Spring on the Road." [Verse] (8:2) Sum 91, p. 108.

6727. WITEK, Terri
    "Leaving Well Enough Alone." [Shen] (41:2) Sum 91, p. 88-89.
    "Man, Woman, Boy." [Shen] (41:2) Sum 91, p. 87-88.
    "What Poets Want I." [HampSPR] Wint 91, p. 59-60.

6728. WITHROW, Shelly
    "Rasp." [BlackWR] (18:1) Fall-Wint 91, p. 171-172.

6729. WITT, Harold
    "American Lit: Discovery." [Interim] (10:1) Spr-Sum 91, p. 11.
    "American Lit: Other Voices, Other Rooms." [NewYorkQ] (45) 91, p. 54.
    "American Lit: The City of Trembling Leaves." [Interim] (10:1) Spr-Sum 91, p. 10.
    "American Lit: Witter Bynner." [WritersF] (17) Fall 91, p. 82.
    "Aria da Capo." [CharR] (17:1) Spr 91, p. 53.
    "Babbitt." [CharR] (17:1) Spr 91, p. 56.
    "Bob Metropolous, Safeway Manager." [WormR] (31:1, #121) 91, p. 13.

"The Conservationist." [PoetL] (86:3) Fall 91, p. 46.
"The Death of the Ball Turret Gunner." [CharR] (17:1) Spr 91, p. 54.
"The Education of Henry Admas." [BellArk] (7:1) Ja-F 91, p. 7.
"The Fact." [WormR] (31:1, #121) 91, p. 13-14.
"Greg Taylor, Psychology Major." [Bogg] (64) 91, p. 17.
"Harley." [BellArk] (7:4) Jl-Ag 91, p. 7-8.
"Henry Miller" (from American Lit). [WindO] (55) Wint 91-92, p. 19.
"Hunt." [LitR] (34:2) Wint 91, p. 201.
"Kunitz." [CharR] (17:1) Spr 91, p. 51.
"Lazarus." [CharR] (17:1) Spr 91, p. 55.
"The Man with the Hoe." [CharR] (17:1) Spr 91, p. 51.
"Mrs. Asquith Decides She Shouldn't Read Yeats Before Bedtime." [DustyD] (2:1)
        Ja 91, p. 2.
"Mrs. Asquith Remembers V-E Day." [DustyD] (2:1) Ja 91, p. 2.
"The Naked and the Dead." [CharR] (17:1) Spr 91, p. 56.
"The Natural." [CharR] (17:1) Spr 91, p. 52.
"Nelson Bentley." [BellArk] (7:6) N-D 91, p. 10.
"Of Golden Light." [LitR] (34:2) Wint 91, p. 200.
"Roughing It." [Interim] (10:2) Fall-Wint 91-92, p. 20.
"The Secret Life of Walter Mitty." [CharR] (17:1) Spr 91, p. 52.
"Test." [BellArk] (7:1) Ja-F 91, p. 3.
"A Texas Twang." [CharR] (17:1) Spr 91, p. 53.
"Typos." [CharR] (17:1) Spr 91, p. 54.
"Vermeer." [PoetL] (86:3) Fall 91, p. 47.
"The Waldport Poems." [PoetC] (22:2) Wint 91, p. 13.
"Who's Afraid of Virginia Woolf?" [CharR] (17:1) Spr 91, p. 55.
WITT, Jim de
        See DeWITT, Jim
WITT, Susan Kelly de
        See KELLY-DeWITT, Susan
6730. WITTE, George
        "Alphabet." [SouthwR] (76:2) Spr 91, p. 238.
        "Hey Buddy." [SycamoreR] (3:2) Sum 91, p. 33-34.
        "Madeline." [Confr] (46/47) Fall 91-Wint 92, p. 272-274.
        "An Open Letter." [SouthwR] (76:2) Spr 91, p. 239.
6731. WITTWER, Rodney
        "Candidate." [AntR] (49:2) Spr 91, p. 241.
        "Holiday." [AntR] (49:2) Spr 91, p. 240.
6732. WOERDEHOFF, Valorie
        "Against Strong Wind." [CapeR] (26:2) Fall 91, p. 38.
6733. WOFFORD, Jan Bailey
        "Leaving." [ChiR] (37:2/3) 91, p. 87.
6734. WOHL, Bess
        "Baby." [HangL] (59) 91, p. 85-86.
        "Everything in Plain Language." [HangL] (59) 91, p. 87.
        "The Sink and Swim of One." [HangL] (59) 91, p. 88-89.
6735. WOHLFELD, Valerie
        "Thinking the World Visible." [Poetry] (158:2) My 91, p. 76-77.
        "Trinkets." [Agni] (34) 91, p. 187-188.
6736. WOJAHN, David
        "Eggplants" (After Amy Wilentz). [MissouriR] (14:2) 91, p. 96-99.
        "Hive Keepers." [GettyR] (4:2) Spr 91, p. 237-238.
        "Late Empire." [MissouriR] (14:2) 91, p. 103-105.
        "A Map." [MissouriR] (14:2) 91, p. 100-102.
        "Wartime Photos of My Father." [GettyR] (4:4) Aut 91, p. 665-668.
        "Xerox of a Photograph of Bergen-Belsen" (for Henry Johnson). [Ploughs] (17:2/3)
                Fall 91, p. 90-91.
6737. WOLBRINK, Paul
        "The English Teacher Envisions His Death." [EngJ] (80:4) Ap 91, p. 97.
6738. WOLF, J. Barrett
        "I am not homeless." [BlackBR] (13) Spr-Sum 91, p. 30.
6739. WOLFF, Daniel
        "Design to Do Away with Sadness." [WestHR] (45:2) Sum 91, p. 87-88.
WOLHEE, Choe
        See CHOE, Wolhee

462

WOLIN

6740. WOLIN, Blema
"November Sky." [HawaiiR] (15:2, #32) Spr 91, p. 66.
"Usual Habits." [AntR] (49:3) Sum 91, p. 433.
6741. WOLMAN, Kenneth
"At My Father's Grave, Montefiore Cemetery." [Parting] (4:2) Wint 91-92, p. 16-17.
6742. WOLOCH, Cecilia
"Sacrifice." [Zyzzyva] (7:1) Spr 91, p. 82.
6743. WOLTHERS, Brad
"East Crater Trail #48 (For Ron)." [PaintedHR] (1) Ja 91, p. 13.
"A Short Renga for Li Po." [PaintedHR] (1) Ja 91, p. 12.
"Stonehenge" (a replica near Maryhill, Washington). [PaintedHR] (2) Spr 91, p. 11.
6744. WOLTHERS, Sarah
"Autumn." [PaintedHR] (1) Ja 91, p. 19.
6745. WONG, Denese
"The Healing." [EmeraldCR] (4) 91, p. 61.
6746. WONG, Vincent
"Safeway Is Like a Heart." [PoetryUSA] (22) Spr 91, p. 22.
6747. WONG-MORRISON, Tamara
"Middle Road." [BambooR] (50/51) Spr-Sum 91, p. 76-77.
6748. WOO, David
"Eden." [NewYorker] (67:20) 8 Jl 91, p. 38.
"Fibre Optics." [NewYorker] (67:30) 16 S 91, p. 38.
"Pattern." [NewYorker] (67:4) 18 Mr 91, p. 44.
6749. WOOD, David
"Castrating the Military." [Pearl] (14) Fall-Wint 91, p. 55.
6750. WOOD, Tex
"Midpoint Lover." [Pembroke] (23) 91, p. 154.
"Savior, After Wars & Wives." [Pembroke] (23) 91, p. 153.
"Winter Woman, Music for Bears." [Pembroke] (23) 91, p. 152.
6751. WOOD, Waylon
"Ole Shiloh." [EmeraldCR] (4) 91, p. 22-23.
"Porch." [EmeraldCR] (4) 91, p. 21-22.
6752. WOODARD, Deborah
"Adopting the Moon." [MidwQ] (32:3) Spr 91, p. 297.
"Hell Town." [WillowS] (28) Sum 91, p. 61.
"Kore" (Excerpt). [WillowS] (28) Sum 91, p. 60.
6753. WOODARD, Fredrick
"En la Bodega." [Iowa] (21:1) Wint 91, p. 33-34.
"Nueva York, New York, 1986." [Iowa] (21:1) Wint 91, p. 32-33.
"Only You Took Hold." [Iowa] (21:1) Wint 91, p. 31-32.
"Spaces." [Iowa] (21:1) Wint 91, p. 31.
6754. WOODCOCK, George
"Death Pauses." [Quarry] (40:1/2) Wint-Spr 91, p. 189-190.
"Invocation at Delos." [Quarry] (40:1/2) Wint-Spr 91, p. 191.
6755. WOODRUFF, William
"A Face on a Upstairs Wall in a Half-Demolished Boarding House." [Lactuca] (14) My 91, p. 41-42.
"In the deep silence." [WormR] (31:4, #124) 91, p. 105.
"The Japanese Garden Bridge." [Lactuca] (14) My 91, p. 42.
6756. WOODS, Christopher
"The Well." [Gypsy] (17) 91, p. 66.
6757. WOODS, John
"A Face in the Leaves" (from "Black Marigolds"). [PoetryNW] (32:1) Spr 91, p. 45.
"Falling with Lucifer." [Field] (45) Fall 91, p. 68.
"I Remember How Easily" (from "Black Marigolds"). [Northeast] (5:4) Sum 91, p. 10.
"Milk, Turning." [PoetryNW] (32:1) Spr 91, p. 47.
"Sally and the Holy Ghost." [PoetryNW] (32:1) Spr 91, p. 46-47.
"Tale of Two Guitars." [Field] (45) Fall 91, p. 69-70.
"To Bilhana" (from "Black Marigolds"). [PoetryNW] (32:1) Spr 91, p. 44.
"The Tulip Tree" (from "Black Marigolds"). [PoetryNW] (32:1) Spr 91, p. 45-46.
"Watching Over the Sleeper" (from "Black Marigolds"). [Northeast] (5:4) Sum 91, p. 11.
6758. WOODSUM, D. (Douglas, Doug)
"The Air Between Us." [WebR] (15) Spr 91, p. 94.

"Family Tree." [MassR] (32:3) Fall 91, p. 464.
"Husks Pillaged for Seeds, A Letter to an Editor." [BelPoJ] (42:1) Fall 91, p. 36-37.
"A Late Raspberry Reminds Him of Her." [SouthernR] (27:3) Jl 91, p. 704.
"Sunset at the Community Mental Health Center." [SouthernR] (27:3) Jl 91, p.
    704-705.
6759. WOODWARD, Angus
    "Azalea Street Winter." [BellR] (14:2) Fall 91, p. 42.
6760. WOODWARD, Gerard
    "The Evolution of Flowers." [Verse] (8:2) Sum 91, p. 111.
6761. WOODWARD, Jeffrey
    "Barricaded." [InterPR] (17:2) Fall 91, p. 106.
    "The Eidolon." [InterPR] (17:2) Fall 91, p. 106.
    "Gay Holly, O!" [SoCoast] (10) Fall 91, p. 50.
    "Profile from the Left." [InterPR] (17:2) Fall 91, p. 105.
6762. WOODWARD, Joe L.
    "Muddy Waters." [BrooklynR] (8) 91, p. 52.
6763. WOODWORTH, Marc
    "Ockham" (for William Brynteson). [Salm] (90/91) Spr-Sum 91, p. 86-87.
6764. WOOLF, Geoffrey
    "The Laws of Kosher." [CinPR] (22) Spr 91, p. 65.
    "The Reason for Sighs." [CinPR] (22) Spr 91, p. 64.
6765. WOOLLEN, Ian
    "Stay." [DustyD] Ap 91, p. 12.
    "Surprise!" [DustyD] Ap 91, p. 15.
6766. WOON, Koon
    "Bronze Statue in Rain." [CrabCR] (7:3) 91, p. 23.
    "NB as Gungu Master." [BellArk] (7:1) Ja-F 91, p. 5.
6767. WORLEY, James
    "Grown Old." [ChrC] (108:6) 20 F 91, p. 188.
    "In Lincoln's Pockets" (April 14, 1865). [ChrC] (108:13) 17 Ap 91, p. 433.
    "In That Great Gettin'-up Mornin'." [ChrC] (108:21) 10-17 Jl 91, p. 687.
    "To the Ends of the Earth." [ChrC] (108:25) 4-11 S 91, p. 796.
    "Waking Up to Bach" (BWV 1069). [ChrC] (108:28) 9 O 91, p. 901.
    "Why? What? When?" [ChrC] (108:11) 3 Ap 91, p. 356.
6768. WORLEY, Jeff
    "Adolescence." [HawaiiR] (15:2, #32) Spr 91, p. 13.
    "After the Divorce." [MalR] (94) Spr 91, p. 33.
    "Hide & Seek" (after a line from William Stafford). [SouthernPR] (31:2) Fall 91, p.
        43.
    "Home Early From Work." [HawaiiR] (15:3, #33) Fall 91, p. 116-117.
    "Hunger." [PoetryNW] (32:4) Wint 91-92, p. 35-36.
    "Knife Creek Uprising." [SoDakR] (29:3 part 2) Aut 91, p. 82-83.
    "Late Afternoon with Jonathan." [PoetryNW] (32:2) Sum 91, p. 35-36.
    "Late Summer: A Look at the Garden." [PoetryNW] (32:4) Wint 91-92, p. 34-35.
    "The Literal." [SouthernPR] (31:1) Spr 91, p. 14-15.
    "Long Distance." [MalR] (94) Spr 91, p. 32.
    "News Item, Sandy Hook, Ky." [CinPR] (22) Spr 91, p. 71.
    "Poem for the End of the 20th Century." [ChiR] (37:2/3) 91, p. 163-164.
    "Pulling the Shades." [SouthernPR] (31:1) Spr 91, p. 15-16.
    "They Say" (for Linda). [PoetryNW] (32:2) Sum 91, p. 34-35.
    "What Turns Out to Be Another Cat Poem." [MalR] (94) Spr 91, p. 34.
    "Why Pitchers Should Bat." [NewYorkQ] (44) 91, p. 85.
6769. WORLEY, Stella
    "Three Hours of Magic: Twenty Cents." [AnthNEW] (3) 91, p. 17.
6770. WORMALD, Mark
    "Dispatches: Prague, November 1989" (after Timothy Garton Ash). [PlumR] (1)
        Spr-Sum 91, p. 28-29.
6771. WORMSER, Baron
    "Comics." [ManhatR] (6:1) Fall 91, p. 56.
    "The Golden Age." [ManhatR] (6:1) Fall 91, p. 57.
    "Housing Project." [PoetryE] (31) Spr 91, p. 31.
    "Ode to Human Nature." [ManhatR] (6:1) Fall 91, p. 54-55.
    "Tranquilizers." [PoetryE] (31) Spr 91, p. 32.
6772. WOROZBYT, Theodore, Jr.
    "X. How easily we number." [CinPR] (21) Spr 90, p. 52-53.
    "The Evolution of Sleep." [CutB] (35) Wint-Spr 91, p. 58.

"Memory of My Father." [CreamCR] (15:1) Spr 91, p. 82.
"Mollusk." [Poetry] (158:2) My 91, p. 97-98.
"The Shooters" (for Kirk Kline, 1960-1977). [PoetC] (22:2) Wint 91, p. 16-17.
"Surviving Tongue." [Poetry] (158:3) Je 91, p. 148-149.
"Tools." [SouthernPR] (31:1) Spr 91, p. 66-67.
"Until This." [PoetC] (22:2) Wint 91, p. 14-15.
"Visitors." [Poetry] (158:3) Je 91, p. 149-151.

6773. WORTH, Jan
"Lust As a Hand-Me-Down." [MichQR] (30:1) Wint 91, p. 93-95.

6774. WOS, Joanna H.
"Lost." [WebR] (15) Spr 91, p. 78-80.

6775. WOSTER, Kevin
"Recovery." [SoDakR] (29:3 part 2) Aut 91, p. 112.

6776. WOWK, Wira
"Litany" (tr. by Larissa Zaleska Onyshkevych). [Agni] (33) 91, p. 218-219.

6777. WOZNIAK, Robert
"On the Suicide of a Friend." [BellR] (14:1) Spr 91, p. 11.

6778. WRBICAN, Sue
"Dust Collection." [WestB] (28) 91, p. 40-41.

6779. WREGGITT, Andrew
"Brick." [Dandel] (18:1) Spr-Sum 91, p. 26-27.
"Building the Dock." [CanLit] (130) Aut 91, p. 61.
"Coyote Ring 1." [Event] (20:2) Sum 91, p. 53-54.
"Coyote Ring 2." [Event] (20:2) Sum 91, p. 55-57.
"Coyote Ring 3." [Event] (20:2) Sum 91, p. 58-59.
"Visiting Lillian." [PraF] (12:3 #56) Aut 91, p. 73-74.

6780. WRIGHT, A. J.
"Lake of the Interior." [SnailPR] (1:2) Fall 91-Wint 92, p. 26.
"A Reader Considers the Options." [SnailPR] (1:2) Fall 91-Wint 92, p. 27.

6781. WRIGHT, C. D.
"The Box This Comes In." [KenR] (NS 13:2) Spr 91, p. 139.
"Just Whistle" (Excerpts). [Conjunc] (17) 91, p. 119-126.
"The Provisional Life." [KenR] (NS 13:2) Spr 91, p. 139.

6782. WRIGHT, Carolyne
"Bestial" (tr. of Anuradha Mahapatra, w. Jyotirmoy Datta). [TriQ] (81) Spr-Sum 91,
p. 223-224.
"The Blood-Mark" (tr. of Mallika Sengupta, w. Paramita Banerjee). [MichQR]
(30:1) Wint 91, p. 210.
"Business Woman's Story" (tr. of Anuradha Mahapatra, w. Paramita Banerjee).
[TriQ] (81) Spr-Sum 91, p. 229.
"Clinical Landscape" (tr. of Jorge Teillier). [IndR] (14:3) Fall 91, p. 124-125.
"Games" (tr. of Jorge Teillier). [Boulevard] (6:2/3, #17/18) Fall 91, p. 147.
"Girl Before Her Marriage" (tr. of Anuradha Mahapatra, w. Paramita Banerjee).
[TriQ] (81) Spr-Sum 91, p. 230-231.
"God" (tr. of Anuradha Mahapatra, w. Jyotirmoy Datta). [TriQ] (81) Spr-Sum 91, p.
232-233.
"The Ice Climber (Upper Grindelwald Glacier)" (For Joseph Maier). [Chelsea] (52)
91, p. 100-104.
"The Land of Night" (tr. of Jorge Teillier). [Boulevard] (6:2/3, #17/18) Fall 91, p.
148.
"Letter of Rain" (tr. of Jorge Teillier). [IndR] (14:3) Fall 91, p. 112-113.
"The Lost Domain" (to Alain-Fournier, tr. of Jorge Teillier). [IndR] (14:3) Fall 91,
p. 120-121.
"No Sign of Life" (tr. of Jorge Teillier). [MidAR] (12:1) 91, p. 157-159.
"Sitting in Front of the Fire" (tr. of Jorge Teillier). [IndR] (14:3) Fall 91, p. 109.
"To You, Mother" (tr. of Anuradha Mahapatra, w. Jyotirmoy Datta). [TriQ] (81)
Spr-Sum 91, p. 235-236.
"Under the Sky Born After the Rain" (tr. of Jorge Teillier). [IndR] (14:3) Fall 91, p.
116-117.
"Wasteland Without Chariot Wheels" (tr. of Anuradha Mahapatra, w. Jyotirmoy
Datta). [TriQ] (81) Spr-Sum 91, p. 225-226.
"Woman, Money, Watch, Gun" (for Margaret Hasse). [Ploughs] (17:2/3) Fall 91, p.
205.
"The Year 1984" (tr. of Anuradha Mahapatra, w. Jyotirmoy Datta). [TriQ] (81)
Spr-Sum 91, p. 222.

465

465

WRIGHT

6783. WRIGHT, Charles
"Black and Blue." [Poetry] (157:4) Ja 91, p. 220-221.
"Blaise Pascal Lip-Syncs the Void." [Field] (45) Fall 91, p. 61.
"Chickamauga." [Poetry] (157:4) Ja 91, p. 219.
"Maple on the Hill." [GrandS] (10:2, #38) 91, p. 113-114.
"An Ordinary Afternoon in Charlottesville." [NewYorker] (67:42) 9 D 91, p. 68.
"The Silent Generation." [NewYorker] (67:4) 18 Mr 91, p. 40.
"Sprung Narratives." [SouthernR] (27:1) Ja 91, p. 70-78.
"Still-Life on a Matchbox Lid." [NewYorker] (67:10) 29 Ap 91, p. 64.
"Thinking of David Summers at the Beginning of Winter." [KenR] (NS 13:1) Wint 91, p. 29.
"Winter-Worship." [Field] (45) Fall 91, p. 62.
6784. WRIGHT, D. W.
"First Typhoon." [SouthernPR] (31:1) Spr 91, p. 20-22.
6785. WRIGHT, Franz
"Depiction of Childhood" (After Picasso). [Field] (45) Fall 91, p. 52.
"For Martha." [Agni] (33) 91, p. 67.
"The Late Late Show." [Field] (45) Fall 91, p. 53.
"Midnight Postscript" (for my friend Joseph Kahn, born 1950, drowned 1982). [Ploughs] (17:2/3) Fall 91, p. 89.
"Reunion." [Field] (45) Fall 91, p. 54.
"Rorschach Test." [Agni] (33) 91, p. 68.
"Walk at Night" (tr. of Rainer Maria Rilke). [Field] (44) Spr 91, p. 58.
6786. WRIGHT, G. T.
"For W. H. Auden, February 21, 1989." [NorthStoneR] (10) Fall 91-Wint 92, p. 68.
"Outcries." [NorthStoneR] (10) Fall 91-Wint 92, p. 69.
"Personal." [NorthStoneR] (10) Fall 91-Wint 92, p. 70.
6787. WRIGHT, Howard
"Mother's Day." [Verse] (8:2) Sum 91, p. 109.
"The Snow Toast." [SoCoast] (11) Wint 91, p. 18.
6788. WRIGHT, James
"Confesión a J. Edgar Hoover" (tr. by Gregory McNamee). [Nuez] (3:7) 91, p. 15.
"The Jewell." [SouthernR] (27:2) Ap 91, p. 434.
6789. WRIGHT, John
"Postcard to Claire." [DogRR] (10:2) Fall-Wint 91, p. 39-40.
6790. WRIGHT, Katharine
"The Tour Group." [NorthStoneR] (10) Fall 91-Wint 92, p. 66.
6791. WRIGHT, Kirby
"Just North of Tijuana." [BlackBR] (14) Fall-Wint 91, p. 22.
"Poolside Confessions at the Kahala Hilton." [HawaiiR] (15:2, #32) Spr 91, p. 54-55.
6792. WRIGHT, Nancy M. (Nancy Means)
"Fay Has a Narrow Escape." [GreenMR] (NS 5:1) Sum-Fall 91, p. 137-138.
"Grace Enters Armageddon." [CarolQ] (43:3) Spr 91, p. 43.
6793. WRIGLEY, Robert
"About Language" (for Jordan). [NewEngR] (13:3/4) Spr-Sum 91, p. 361-362.
"Body and Soul." [Shen] (41:2) Sum 91, p. 7-9.
"Cigarettes" (for Sara Vogan). [CutB] (36) Sum 91, p. 41-42.
"Incident on Hangman Creek Road." [CutB] (36) Sum 91, p. 43-44.
"Parents." [GettyR] (4:4) Aut 91, p. 688.
"Poetry." [NewEngR] (13:3/4) Spr-Sum 91, p. 362-363.
"Shrapnel." [Shen] (41:2) Sum 91, p. 5-7.
6794. WRONSKY, Gail
"Earth: Desdemona" (Excerpts). [BostonR] (16:3/4) Je-Ag 91, p. 12.
6795. WYATT, Charles
"Back Yard." [Mildred] (4:2/5:1) 91, p. 89-90.
"Butterflies." [BelPoJ] (41:4) Sum 91, p. 14-15.
"The Fish." [Mildred] (4:2/5:1) 91, p. 91-92.
"Following." [MidwQ] (32:2) Wint 91, p. 196.
"Gar." [CumbPR] (11:1) Fall 91, p. 31-32.
"In the Light That Does Not Fall." [CumbPR] (11:1) Fall 91, p. 33.
"Portrait of Me Playing the Flute." [BelPoJ] (41:4) Sum 91, p. 15.
"Possum." [CumbPR] (11:1) Fall 91, p. 34-35.
"The Raven." [Lactuca] (14) My 91, p. 28.
"Threshing Machine." [Callaloo] (14:2) Spr 91, p. 550-551.

6796. WYATT, Thomas
"The Lover Showeth How He Is Abandoned of Such As He One Time Enjoyed."
[Shen] (41:4) Wint 91, p. 67-68.
6797. WYLAM, John
"Self-Portrait by Somebody Else." [InterPR] (17:2) Fall 91, p. 126.
"The Zen Laundry Poem." [InterPR] (17:2) Fall 91, p. 127.
6798. WYMAN, Andrea
"Canning Peaches." [Plain] (12:1) Fall 91, p. 16-17.
6799. WYNAND, Derk
"At Two in the Morning, Say." [MalR] (95) Sum 91, p. 16-18.
"Float Plane." [MalR] (95) Sum 91, p. 21.
"Good-byes." [MalR] (95) Sum 91, p. 14-15.
"The Inventor of Tarot Cards" (tr. of H. C. Artmann). [Event] (20:2) Sum 91, p.
62-63.
"Long Weekend." [CanLit] (131) Wint 91, p. 168.
"Mowing the Lawn & Putting It Off." [MalR] (95) Sum 91, p. 18-20.
"Small Certainties." [Grain] (19:3) Fall 91, p. 41.
"Teacher and Janitor" (tr. of H. C. Artmann). [Event] (20:2) Sum 91, p. 60-61.
"A Tension in Winter." [Quarry] (40:1/2) Wint-Spr 91, p. 195.
"Three Attitudes." [Grain] (19:3) Fall 91, p. 42-43.
"Too Shy." [Grain] (19:3) Fall 91, p. 48.
"Two Blues." [Arc] (27) Aut 91, p. 51-52.
"Widow." [MalR] (95) Sum 91, p. 13.
6800. WYREBEK, M.
"Bronchoscopy" (for J.C.W.). [TriQ] (81) Spr-Sum 91, p. 206-207.
"Suspension." [TriQ] (81) Spr-Sum 91, p. 205.
"Three O'clock Dose." [TriQ] (81) Spr-Sum 91, p. 208.
6801. WYSER-ORPINEDA, Andrea
"Untitled Poem: 6 million dead the showers dry." [PacificR] (9) 91, p. 82.
6802. WYTTENBERG, Victoria
"The Big Show." [Calyx] (13:2) Sum 91, p. 8-9.
XIANGHUA, Zhang
See ZHANG, Xianghua
XIAOBIN, Liang
See LIANG, Xiaobin
XIAOFEI, Tian
See TIAN, Xiaofei
XIAOJIAN, Zhang
See ZHANG, Xiaojian
XIAOLONG, Qiu
See QIU, Xiaolong
XIAONI, Wang
See WANG, Xiaoni
6803. XIE, Ling-Yun
"To Those Who Saw Me Off at Fang Shan" (tr. by Bruce Wilson). [PoetL] (86:4)
Wint 91-92, p. 46.
XIJIAN, Li
See LI, Xijian
XIN, Wang Gia
See WANG, Gia Xin
6804. XU, Gang
"Cigarette Butts" (tr. by Edward Morin, Dennis Ding, and Fang Dai). [Iowa] (21:2)
Spr-Sum 91, p. 45.
"A Figure Seen from Behind" (tr. by Edward Morin, Dennis Ding, and Fang Dai).
[Iowa] (21:2) Spr-Sum 91, p. 45.
"Red Azalea on the Cliff" (tr. by Edward Morin, Dennis Ding, and Fang Dai).
[Iowa] (21:2) Spr-Sum 91, p. 44.
"Summer" (tr. by Edward Morin, Dennis Ding, and Fang Dai). [Iowa] (21:2)
Spr-Sum 91, p. 46.
YAKAMOCHI, Otomo
See OTOMO, Yakamochi (ca. 739)
6805. YALIM, Özcan
"Endless Boredom" (tr. of Ahmet Muhip Diranas, w. William A. Fielder and Dionis
Coffin Riggs). [InterPR] (17:1) Spr 91, p. 19.
"In the Home for the Elderly" (tr. by the author, William A. Fielder and Dionis
Coffin Riggs). [InterPR] (17:1) Spr 91, p. 20.

"Such Love" (tr. of Attila Ilhan, w. William A. Fielder and Dionis Coffin Riggs).
[InterPR] (17:1) Spr 91, p. 17.
"To Live" (tr. of Cahit Külebi, w. William A. Fielder and Dionis Coffin Riggs).
[InterPR] (17:1) Spr 91, p. 19.
6806. YAMADA, Leona (Leona N.)
"Bulbuls at Dawn." [HawaiiR] (15:3, #33) Fall 91, p. 130.
"Chicken Feet, Sister Stew." [BambooR] (50/51) Spr-Sum 91, p. 264-266.
"Grandpa." [Contact] (10:59/60/61) Spr 91, p. 27.
"Mall." [BambooR] (50/51) Spr-Sum 91, p. 267-268.
"Tsunami." [ChamLR] (8-9) Spr-Fall 91, p. 106.
"Twelve Now, She." [HawaiiR] (15:3, #33) Fall 91, p. 129.
6807. YAMADA-HANFF, Aaron
"When You Paint the World." [PoetryUSA] (22) Spr 91, p. 22.
6808. YAMANAKA, Lois-Ann
"Kid." [BambooR] (52) Fall 91, p. 145-148.
"Name Me Is." [BambooR] (52) Fall 91, p. 149-157.
"Parts." [BambooR] (50/51) Spr-Sum 91, p. 26-33.
"Turtles." [BambooR] (52) Fall 91, p. 158-159.
6809. YAMANO, Shigehiko
"Two Ways of Thinking." [NegC] (11:1) 91, p. 92.
6810. YAMRUS, John
"The Crazy Poet." [Bogg] (64) 91, p. 46.
6811. YANG, Lian
"Anthem" (tr. by Li Xijian and James Newcomb). [PraS] (65:2) Sum 91, p. 80.
6812. YANG, Liu Hong
"Beijing Morning" (tr. by Lenore Mayhew). [PraS] (65:2) Sum 91, p. 69.
"Empty Seat" (tr. by Lenore Mayhew). [PraS] (65:2) Sum 91, p. 71.
"My Way with Kites" (tr. by Lenore Mayhew). [PraS] (65:2) Sum 91, p. 71.
"Seeing the Sea Again" (tr. by Lenore Mayhew). [PraS] (65:2) Sum 91, p. 72.
"Unexpected" (tr. by Lenore Mayhew). [PraS] (65:2) Sum 91, p. 70.
"Unrealized Omen" (tr. by Lenore Mayhew). [PraS] (65:2) Sum 91, p. 73.
6813. YANG, Seung-Tai
"Revisiting a Mountain Town" (tr. of Kyong-rim Sin, w. Brent Duffin). [InterPR]
(17:1) Spr 91, p. 25.
"A Traveler" (tr. of Mok-Wol Park, w. Brent Duffin). [InterPR] (17:1) Spr 91, p.
22.
6814. YANNONE, Sandra
"My Date with Elvis: Cybill Shepherd, 1973." [Ploughs] (17:2/3) Fall 91, p.
177-178.
"Other Women." [QW] (32) Wint-Spr 91, p. 141.
6815. YANOFSKY, Eddy
"Sgraffito." [Dandel] (18:1) Spr-Sum 91, p. 9.
YAPING, Tang
See TANG, Ya Ping
6816. YARMAL, Ann
"O." [BlackBR] (14) Fall-Wint 91, p. 25.
6817. YATCHISIN, George
"A Big Hole in the Prom Boy." [PoetL] (86:4) Wint 91-92, p. 36.
"Circus of the Stars." [PaintedB] (44) 91, p. 31.
"Disappearances." [PaintedB] (44) 91, p. 30.
"The Gorgeous Cement Truck." [PoetL] (86:4) Wint 91-92, p. 35.
"Room for Error." [FourQ] (4:2) Fall 90, p. 35.
6818. YAU, Emily
"Yearning for the Red Leaves of Xiang Shan" (tr. of Li Qing). [PoetryUSA] (22)
Spr 91, p. 20.
6819. YAU, John
"Angel Atrapado VII." [AmerPoR] (20:4) Jl-Ag 91, p. 48.
"Angel Atrapado XI." [Talisman] (7) Fall 91, p. 106.
"Postcard from Georg Trakl" (2 poems). [GrandS] (10:3, #39) 91, p. 210.
"Postcard from Trakl." [ParisR] (33:118) Spr 91, p. 144.
6820. YEATS, Trevor
"This Body Is to Ask." [PoetryUSA] (22) Spr 91, p. 22.
6821. YEATS, William Butler
"Conjunctions." [SouthernR] (27:2) Ap 91, p. 412.
"The Four Ages of Man." [SouthernR] (27:2) Ap 91, p. 411.
"He and She." [SouthernR] (27:2) Ap 91, p. 407.

"Meru." [SouthernR] (27:2) Ap 91, p. 399-400.
"A Needle's Eye." [SouthernR] (27:2) Ap 91, p. 412.
"Ribh at the Tomb of Baile and Aillinn." [SouthernR] (27:2) Ap 91, p. 402-403.
"Ribh Considers Christian Love Insufficient." [SouthernR] (27:2) Ap 91, p. 406.
"Ribh in Ecstasy." [SouthernR] (27:2) Ap 91, p. 405.
"There." [SouthernR] (27:2) Ap 91, p. 405.
6822. YELLMAN, Luke
"Crows Are Bad. Ducks Are Good." [SoCoast] (11) Wint 91, p. 3-5.
6823. YERPE, Dale G.
"The Baby in the Living Room." [NegC] (11:1) 91, p. 106.
6824. YEVTUSHENKO, Yevgeny
"La Espera" (Spanish tr. by Heberto Padilla). [LindLM] (10:4) O-D 91, p. 5.
"The Loss" (tr. by James Reagan and the author). [Nat] (253:3) 15-22 Jl 91, p. 135.
YICHUN, Zhang
    See ZHANG, Yichun
YIHE, Luo
    See LUO, Yihe
YING-WU, Wei
    See WEI, Ying-wu
6825. YINGLING, Karen
"Variation on a Fig." [Hellas] (2:1) Spr 91, p. 56.
YISRAEL, Shulamith Bat
    See BAT-YISRAEL, Shulamith
6826. YO, Yongt'aek
"Daybreak Moon" (tr. by David R. McCann). [ManhatR] (6:1) Fall 91, p. 33.
"Elephant Rock" (tr. by David R. McCann). [ManhatR] (6:1) Fall 91, p. 28.
"Fairy Village" (tr. by David R. McCann). [ManhatR] (6:1) Fall 91, p. 31.
"Flocks of Gulls" (tr. by David R. McCann). [ManhatR] (6:1) Fall 91, p. 27.
"Lily Valley" (tr. by David R. McCann). [ManhatR] (6:1) Fall 91, p. 29.
"Preface to *Ullung Island*" (tr. by David R. McCann). [ManhatR] (6:1) Fall 91, p. 24.
"Ritual of the Sea God" (tr. by David R. McCann). [ManhatR] (6:1) Fall 91, p. 30.
"Trying for Land" (tr. by David R. McCann). [ManhatR] (6:1) Fall 91, p. 25.
"Ullung-Island" (tr. by David R. McCann). [ManhatR] (6:1) Fall 91, p. 32.
"Ullung Sunset" (tr. by David R. McCann). [ManhatR] (6:1) Fall 91, p. 26.
6827. YOGESHVARA
"The Moon, 1" (in Sanskrit and English, tr. by John E. Cort). [Abraxas] (40/41) 91, p. 158-159.
"The Moon, 2" (in Sanskrit and English, tr. by John E. Cort). [Abraxas] (40/41) 91, p. 158-159.
"Sunrise, 1" (in Sanskrit and English, tr. by John E. Cort). [Abraxas] (40/41) 91, p. 156-157.
"Sunrise, 2" (in Sanskrit and English, tr. by John E. Cort). [Abraxas] (40/41) 91, p. 156-157.
YONGT'AEK, Yo
    See YO, Yongt'aek
YOON, Sik Kim
    See KIM, Yoon Sik
6828. YORK, Maggie
"Signatures." [SoCoast] (11) Wint 91, p. 14.
6829. YOSHIHARA, Sachiko
"Lover" (tr. by John Solt). [Manoa] (3:2) Fall 91, p. 31.
6830. YOSHINO, Kenji
"In the Yellow Ruth of Christian Afternoons." [HarvardA] (125:5) My 91, p. 27.
"Quarry." [HarvardA] (125:5) My 91, p. 18.
"A Soul Declining Full." [HarvardA] (125:5) My 91, p. 10-11.
"To the Virtuous Life That Is." [HarvardA] (125:5) My 91, p. 4.
6831. YOSIFOVA, Ekaterina
"Beneath Winter's Roof" (tr. by Lisa Sapinkopf). [BlackWR] (18:1) Fall-Wint 91, p. 98.
6832. YOTS, Michael
"Losing It" (for Christian). [EmeraldCR] (3) 91, c1990, p. 25-26.
"Poem for a Sister Who Died in Infancy." [EmeraldCR] (3) 91, c1990, p. 26-27.
6833. YOTSUNA, Otomo No
"Civilized Behavior" (tr. by Graeme Wilson). [LitR] (35:1) Fall 91, p. 108.

6834. YOUNG, Bernard
    "The New Man." [SoCoast] (10) Fall 91, p. 42-43.
    "Whistling Frank." [SoCoast] (10) Fall 91, p. 44-45.
6835. YOUNG, Bonnie
    "A Verse of Gardens." [PoetC] (22:2) Wint 91, p. 42.
6836. YOUNG, Brian
    "The Full Night Still in the Street Water." [Agni] (34) 91, p. 143.
    "Slade Addamson Visits Tucson, AZ." [HangL] (59) 91, p. 67.
6837. YOUNG, David
    "Duties of a Train Conductor" (tr. of Miroslav Holub, w. Dana Hábová). [GrandS]
        (10:4, #40) 91, p. 191-192.
    "The End of the Week" (tr. of Miroslav Holub, w. Dana Hábová). [Field] (45) Fall
        91, p. 43.
    "The Language Question" (tr. of Nuala Ni Dhomhnaill). [Field] (44) Spr 91, p. 56.
    "To some, winter is arak and blue-eyed punch" (tr. of Osip Mandelstam). [Field]
        (45) Fall 91, p. 22.
    "The Wall in the Corner by the Stairs" (tr. of Miroslav Holub, w. Dana Hábová).
        [Field] (45) Fall 91, p. 41-42.
6838. YOUNG, Dean
    "The First Time & the Time Before That." [Sulfur] (11:2 #29) Fall 91, p. 112-114.
    "The Hive." [OhioR] (47) 91, p. 72-73.
    "Marriage." [NewAW] (8/9) Fall 91, p. 39-40.
    "What Does Us In." [DenQ] (26:2) Fall 91, p. 53-54.
    "The Yeah, Yeah, Yeah Imperative." [PoetryNW] (32:2) Sum 91, p. 11-12.
6839. YOUNG, Gary
    "Boulders roll and chime beneath the current." [MissouriR] (14:1) 91, p. 152.
    "Five Days: Poems." [NewEngR] (14:1) Fall 91, p. 122.
    "Four Days: Earthquake." [KenR] (NS 13:1) Wint 91, p. 129.
    "The fruit trees bloom at once." [DenQ] (25:4) Spr 91, p. 96.
    "If I could take my son to a city off the map, if I were married." [MissouriR] (14:1)
        91, p. 152.
    "Three Days: Autumn." [Journal] (15:1) Spr 91, p. 64.
6840. YOUNG, George
    "Wallace Stevens, Walking." [SwampR] (7/8) Spr-Sum 91, p. 37.
6841. YOUNG, Karl
    "The Square Four Voice Scherzo." [Avec] (4:1) 91, p. 93-98.
6842. YOUNG, Kathryn
    "Mrs. Savage: A Letter." [SpoonRQ] (16:3/4) Sum-Fall 91, p. 7.
    "The Onion." [WindO] (54) Sum 91, p. 26.
6843. YOUNG, Kevin
    "1975." [Callaloo] (14:4) Fall 91, p. 793-794.
    "Eddie Priest's Barbershop & Notary" (Closed Mondays). [Callaloo] (14:4) Fall 91,
        p. 790.
    "Fever" (Honorable Mention). [HarvardA] (125:4) Mr 91, p. 27.
    "How to Make Rain." [Callaloo] (14:2) Spr 91, p. 340.
    "Hundred & Six Degrees" (for A. K.). [Callaloo] (14:4) Fall 91, p. 791-792.
    "Letters from the North Star." [Callaloo] (14:2) Spr 91, p. 341.
6844. YOUNG, Patricia
    "Armageddon." [MalR] (94) Spr 91, p. 64-65.
    "Clover." [MalR] (94) Spr 91, p. 62-63.
    "During Flood Season My Son Remembers." [Grain] (19:3) Fall 91, p. 20-21.
    "Elopement." [Arc] (26) Spr 91, p. 50-51.
    "Following the Garbage Truck." [MalR] (94) Spr 91, p. 70-71.
    "God's Mother." [MalR] (94) Spr 91, p. 68-69.
    "Gurkha: The Word We Loved." [Quarry] (40:1/2) Wint-Spr 91, p. 198-199.
    "Learning the Signs." [MalR] (94) Spr 91, p. 72.
    "The Pie Story" (Short Grain Contest Winners: Prose Poem Winners: Honourable
        Mention). [Grain] (19:4) Wint 91, p. 82.
    "Pregnancy." [Grain] (19:3) Fall 91, p. 19.
    "Saturday Night Dance at the Boy Scout Hall." [MalR] (94) Spr 91, p. 73.
    "Saying No at the End of Summer." [Grain] (19:3) Fall 91, p. 18.
    "School Washroom." [Quarry] (40:1/2) Wint-Spr 91, p. 196.
    "Social Studies Report." [MalR] (94) Spr 91, p. 66-67.
    "The Third Sex." [Quarry] (40:1/2) Wint-Spr 91, p. 197.
    "Three Point Five Nine." [MalR] (94) Spr 91, p. 60-61.

6845. YOUNG, William
"Sacajawea Sculpture, Cannon Beach." [Shen] (41:3) Fall 91, p. 71.
6846. YOUNG BEAR, Ray (Ray A.)
"Now That It Has Passed." [SoDakR] (29:3 part 2) Aut 91, p. 27.
"The Reptile Decree from Paris." [KenR] (NS 13:4) Fall 91, p. 136-138.
6847. YOUNG-TULIN, Lois
"Mental Hospital." [InterPR] (15:1) Spr 89, p. 116.
6848. YOUNGS, Anne Ohman
"7-Day Forecast." [Elf] (1:2) Sum 91, p. 34-38.
"Nasturtiums." [MidwQ] (32:3) Spr 91, p. 298-301.
6849. YOUNT, Lisa
"Desert." [WritersF] (17) Fall 91, p. 208.
6850. YOZA, Princess (ca. 702)
"Now that nights grow cold" (tr. by Sam Hamill). [ColR] (NS 17:2) Fall-Wint 90,
p. 16.
6851. YU, Clara
"Dedicated to the Master of Silent Garden." [SpoonRQ] (16:1/2) Wint-Spr 91, p.
30-31.
"Wang Zhaojun, Circa 30 B.C." (Watercolor by Peng Xiancheng). [SpoonRQ]
(16:1/2) Wint-Spr 91, p. 32.
6852. YU, Jian
"River." [AmerPoR] (20:5) S-O 91, p. 22.
"River" (tr. by Cao Wei). [GreenMR] (NS 4:2) Wint-Spr 91, p. 36.
6853. YU, Tim
"Judgement Day." [RagMag] (9:2) 91, p. 73.
"Walk." [RagMag] (9:2) 91, p. 72.
YU-HUA, Gao
See GAO, Yu-hua
6854. YUAN, Ch'iung-Ch'iung
"The Fish" (tr. by Steven Bradbury). [BambooR] (52) Fall 91, p. 160.
6855. YUAN, Mei
"End of the Year" (tr. by J. P. Seaton). [LitR] (35:1) Fall 91, p. 71.
"Something to Ridicule" (tr. by J. P. Seaton). [LitR] (35:1) Fall 91, p. 71.
6856. YUND, Ted
"Science Class." [NegC] (11:1) 91, p. 107.
6857. YUNG, Chin
"Citrus." [BambooR] (50/51) Spr-Sum 91, p. 93-94.
6858. YUNGKANS, Jonathan
"Five Secrets Redbook Told on Me." [Pearl] (13) Spr-Sum 91, p. 51.
6859. YURKIEVICH, Saúl
"We Are and We Are Not" (tr. by Cola Franzen). [LitR] (34:2) Wint 91, p. 230.
6860. YURKOVSKY, Alexandra
"Tableau: Two Women, Alone." [PoetryUSA] (23) Sum 91, p. 11.
6861. YURMAN, R.
"Visitation." [NewYorkQ] (46) 91, p. 76.
6862. ZABLE, Jeffrey
"The Attempt." [WorldL] (1:1) 91, p. 44.
"The Makings of a Guru." [WorldL] (1:1) 91, p. 43.
"The Rain in Yr Eyes." [WorldL] (1:1) 91, p. 45.
"What's Left." [WorldL] (1:1) 91, p. 44.
6863. ZAGAJEWKSI, Adam
"Autumn" (Excerpted from "Canvas," tr. by Renata Gorczynski, Benjamin Ivry, and
C. K. Williams). [ManhatR] (6:1) Fall 91, p. 50.
"The Bells" (for C. K. Williams, Excerpted from "Canvas," tr. by Renata
Gorczynski, Benjamin Ivry, and C. K. Williams). [ManhatR] (6:1) Fall 91, p.
51.
"Burgundy's Grasslands" (Excerpted from "Canvas," tr. by Renata Gorczynski,
Benjamin Ivry, and C. K. Williams). [ManhatR] (6:1) Fall 91, p. 46.
"Canvas" (Excerpted from "Canvas," tr. by Renata Gorczynski, Benjamin Ivry, and
C. K. Williams). [ManhatR] (6:1) Fall 91, p. 53.
"Electric Elegy" (Excerpted from "Canvas," tr. by Renata Gorczynski, Benjamin
Ivry, and C. K. Williams). [ManhatR] (6:1) Fall 91, p. 47.
"From the Lives of Things" (Excerpted from "Canvas," tr. by Renata Gorczynski,
Benjamin Ivry, and C. K. Williams). [ManhatR] (6:1) Fall 91, p. 52.
"Green Linnaeus" (Excerpted from "Canvas," tr. by Renata Gorczynski, Benjamin
Ivry, and C. K. Williams). [ManhatR] (6:1) Fall 91, p. 48.

"On a Side Street" (Excerpted from "Canvas," tr. by Renata Gorczynski, Benjamin
Ivry, and C. K. Williams). [ManhatR] (6:1) Fall 91, p. 45.
"Spider's Song" (Excerpted from "Canvas," tr. by Renata Gorczynski, Benjamin
Ivry, and C. K. Williams). [ManhatR] (6:1) Fall 91, p. 44.
"Watching *Shoah* in a Hotel Room in America" (Excerpted from "Canvas," tr. by
Renata Gorczynski, Benjamin Ivry, and C. K. Williams). [ManhatR] (6:1) Fall
91, p. 49.
6864. ZAGAJEWSKI, Adam
"Covenant" (tr. by Renata Gorczynski and Benjamin Ivry). [NewYorker] (66:48) 14
Ja 91, p. 34.
6865. ZAHRAD
"Blind" (tr. by the author and Edward Foster). [Talisman] (6) Spr 91, p. 139.
"Untitled: Which of the sailors first noticed the crutches" (tr. by the author and
Edward Foster). [Talisman] (6) Spr 91, p. 139.
6866. ZAKREWSKY, Jackie
"Trishanku." [PoetL] (86:4) Wint 91-92, p. 44.
6867. ZALEWSKI, Zbigniew
"The Dance" (tr. by John M. Gogol). [NorthStoneR] (10) Fall 91-Wint 92, p. 194.
"Expectation" (tr. by John M. Gogol). [NorthStoneR] (10) Fall 91-Wint 92, p. 194.
6868. ZALUSKI, John
"Berdache." [JamesWR] (8:4) Sum 91, p. 9.
ZAMRAK, Ibn
See IBN ZAMRAK
6869. ZANDER, William
"Saliva." [HiramPoR] (50) Spr-Sum 91, p. 27.
6870. ZANICHKOWSKY, Jane
"Seiji Ozawaour" (Response to "Save the Clerihew" appeal). [BostonR] (16:3/4)
Je-Ag 91, p. 33.
6871. ZANZOTTO, Andrea
"Fosfeni" (Selections: 6 poems, tr. by Pasquale Verdicchio). [Sulfur] (11:2 #29) Fall
91, p. 145-158.
6872. ZAPPALA, Robyn
"Air Worthiness." [HayF] (8) Spr-Sum 91, p. 31-32.
"Reminder" (for Emily Campbell). [HayF] (8) Spr-Sum 91, p. 58.
"Then Suddenly It Stops." [HayF] (8) Spr-Sum 91, p. 91.
"Two Women." [BlackWR] (18:1) Fall-Wint 91, p. 168.
6873. ZARIN, Cynthia
"Kalulu." [NewYorker] (67:43) 16 D 91, p. 50.
"Learning German." [NewYorker] (67:35) 21 O 91, p. 42-43.
"Old Landscape, Umbria." [NewYorker] (67:15) 3 Je 91, p. 46-47.
"The Vestal Birches." [NewRep] (205:6) 5 Ag 91, p. 34.
6874. ZARUCCHI, Roy
"Grape Stakes." [Spirit] (11) 91, p. 332.
6875. ZAWADIWSKY, Christina
"Food." [PoetL] (86:4) Wint 91-92, p. 38.
"Freedom." [PoetL] (86:4) Wint 91-92, p. 39.
6876. ZAWINSKI, Andrena
"I Have Found My Way." [Kalliope] (13:1) 91, p. 53.
"Wishbone" (for the anthropologist). [Kalliope] (13:1) 91, p. 52.
6877. ZAZUYER, Leah
"As Long As We Are Not Alone" (tr. of Israel Emiot, w. Brina Rose). [SenR] (21:1)
Spr 91, p. 30.
"Before You Extinguish Me" (tr. of Israel Emiot, w. Brina Rose). [SenR] (21:1) Spr
91, p. 26.
"History Lesson" (Honorable Mention, 5th Annual Contest). [SoCoast] (11) Wint
91, p. 36-37.
"My God I Believe in You So Much" (tr. of Israel Emiot, w. Brina Rose). [SenR]
(21:1) Spr 91, p. 27.
"A Prayer in Nineteen Forty-Three" (for H. Lang, tr. of Israel Emiot, w. Brina
Rose). [SenR] (21:1) Spr 91, p. 28.
"Prayer of a Man in Snow" (tr. of Israel Emiot, w. Brina Rose). [SenR] (21:1) Spr
91, p. 29.
"With or Without Me" (tr. of Israel Emiot, w. Brina Rose). [SenR] (21:1) Spr 91, p.
31.

6878. ZDANYS, Jonas
"Winter Geese" (To the memory of Thomas G. Bergin). [SewanR] (99:1) Wint 91,
p. 37-39.
6879. ZEALAND, Karen
"Before the Princess Was Lost to a Shoe Store." [HangL] (58) 91, p. 80.
"An Odd Experience in the Living Room of My Suburban Ranch." [PoetL] (86:4)
Wint 91-92, p. 7-8.
"Passion at the Chat 'n Chew Diner." [ThRiPo] (37/38) 91, p. 44.
6880. ZEIGER, David
"A Meditation on Lust." [FreeL] (7) Spr 91, p. 8.
"Visiting Ethel." [MinnR] (NS 36) Spr 91, p. 25.
6881. ZEIGER, Gene
"Argument for the Life Fully Lived." [GreenMR] (NS 5:1) Sum-Fall 91, p. 87.
"Before Leaving the City." [Sonora] (21) Sum 91, p. 62-63.
"Blue Dormitory." [SwampR] (7/8) Spr-Sum 91, p. 42-43.
"Compadre." [PlumR] (1) Spr-Sum 91, p. 64.
"Into the World." [MassR] (32:2) Sum 91, p. 283-284.
"Sad." [CimR] (95) Ap 91, p. 61-62.
"Your Letter." [SenR] (21:1) Spr 91, p. 74-75.
6882. ZELTZER, Joel
"Notes on an Unknown Woman" (tr. of Nicanor Parra). [NewYorkQ] (46) 91, p.
57.
"Sea Water Ballad" (tr. of Federico Garcia Lorca). [NewYorkQ] (45) 91, p. 74.
6883. ZENITH, Richard
"And the Floor Were My Heart" (tr. of João Miguel Fernandes Jorge). [Trans] (25)
Spr 91, p. 141.
"Ida Lupino by Carla Bley (13)" (Excerpt, tr. of João Miguel Fernandes Jorge).
[Trans] (25) Spr 91, p. 139.
"A Letter to Fernando Pessoa" (tr. of Fernando Pessoa (Alvaro de Campos)).
[Trans] (25) Spr 91, p. 57.
"Olympus" (tr. of Sophia de Mello Breyner Andresen). [Trans] (25) Spr 91, p. 92.
"[Perhaps You're Not Nearly As Ambiguous]." [Chelsea] (51) 91, p. 102.
"[The Worst Thing Seems to Be the Balance]." [Chelsea] (51) 91, p. 103.
"Time's Passage" (Selection: II, tr. of Fernando Pessoa (Alvaro de Campos)).
[Trans] (25) Spr 91, p. 30-35.
"Twelve Nocturnes of Ceuta (3)" (Excerpt, tr. of João Miguel Fernandes Jorge).
[Trans] (25) Spr 91, p. 140.
"Twilight" (tr. of Fátima Maldonado). [Trans] (25) Spr 91, p. 110.
"When Over the Water" (tr. of Fátima Maldonado). [Trans] (25) Spr 91, p. 109.
"Writing II" (tr. of Sophia de Mello Breyner Andresen). [Trans] (25) Spr 91, p. 93.
6884. ZEPEDA, Rafael
"Pony." [ChironR] (10:3) Aut 91, p. 19.
6885. ZETTLEMOYER, Eric R.
"The Dead Still Bleed." [BlackBR] (14) Fall-Wint 91, p. 30.
6886. ZHANG, Xianghua
"The One I Love Is on a Fire-Burned Island" (Excerpts, tr. by the author).
[PoetryUSA] (22) Spr 91, p. 20.
"Solo Flight" (tr. by the author). [PoetryUSA] (22) Spr 91, p. 20.
6887. ZHANG, Xiaojian
"Remembering the Past" (tr. by Xiaofei Tian). [PraS] (65:2) Sum 91, p. 79.
"To a Lost Child" (tr. by Xiaofei Tian). [PraS] (65:2) Sum 91, p. 78.
6888. ZHANG, Yichun
"Chinese Painting — Mountains, Water, People and Things" (tr. of Wang Gia Xin).
[GreenMR] (NS 4:2) Wint-Spr 91, p. 38.
"Conspirator" (tr. of Shu Ting). [GreenMR] (NS 4:2) Wint-Spr 91, p. 25.
"Filling the Sea" (tr. of Jiang He). [GreenMR] (NS 4:2) Wint-Spr 91, p. 37.
"In This Broad and Bright World" (tr. of Gu Cheng). [GreenMR] (NS 4:2) Wint-Spr
91, p. 105.
"Spring in the Old Country" (tr. of Li Gang). [GreenMR] (NS 4:2) Wint-Spr 91, p.
39.
"The Woman Strange to Me" (tr. of Hang Dong). [GreenMR] (NS 4:2) Wint-Spr 91,
p. 104.
6889. ZHANG, Zhen
"A Desire." [LitR] (34:2) Wint 91, p. 213.
"The New." [LitR] (34:2) Wint 91, p. 213.

ZHEN, Zhang
> *See* ZHANG, Zhen
ZHONG-YAN, Fang
> *See* FANG, Zhong-yan
6890. ZIEROTH, Dale
> "Apprehension: Three Strike Poems" (Selection: "Our Negotiator Speaks to Theirs").
>> [Quarry] (40:1/2) Wint-Spr 91, p. 200.
> "The Function of the Individual." [CanLit] (131) Wint 91, p. 14.
> "Home." [Quarry] (40:1/2) Wint-Spr 91, p. 201.
6891. ZIETZ, Stephen J.
> "For Herrn H++++++ (RIP)." [NegC] (11:1) 91, p. 79.
> "For Herrn P++++++++." [NegC] (11:1) 91, p. 77.
> "For Miss B+++++++++." [NegC] (11:1) 91, p. 73.
> "For Our Local Celebrity Who Seems to Own More Run-Down Apartment Buildings
>> Than Anyone Else in Germany or the Whole World." [NegC] (11:1) 91, p. 75.
> "For That Classy Broad." [NegC] (11:1) 91, p. 69.
> "For the Aryan Race." [NegC] (11:1) 91, p. 71.
> "For the German Nation." [NegC] (11:1) 91, p. 81.
> "For the Stranger in the Bar." [NegC] (11:1) 91, p. 67.
6892. ZIMM, Therese
> "Cleaning House." [SmPd] (28:2, #82) Spr 91, p. 34.
> "January in Wisconsin." [Kalliope] (13:1) 91, p. 57.
> "Last One to Bed." [Kalliope] (13:1) 91, p. 56.
6893. ZIMMER, Paul
> "The Beautiful Ethiopian Navy." [ThRiPo] (37/38) 91, p. 75.
> "Being a Man." [CharR] (17:1) Spr 91, p. 111.
> "Bitter List." [CharR] (17:1) Spr 91, p. 112.
> "But Bird." [GeoR] (45:3) Fall 91, p. 572-573.
> "The Failings." [ThRiPo] (37/38) 91, p. 76-77.
> "The Humbling." [CharR] (17:1) Spr 91, p. 112.
> "Lightning." [CreamCR] (15:2) Fall 91, p. 79.
> "A Romance for the Wild Turkey." [Antaeus] (67) Fall 91, p. 143.
> "The Tenth Circle." [PennR] (5:1) Spr 91, p. 44.
> "Winter." [PennR] (5:1) Spr 91, p. 43.
6894. ZIMMERMAN, Jean
> "The Back of a Love Note." [Paint] (18:36) Aut 91, p. 22.
6895. ZIMMERMAN, Lisa Horton
> "Letter to My Sister." [WebR] (15) Spr 91, p. 92-93.
> "Releasing the Red-Tail Hawk, Earth Day, 1991." [Gypsy] (17) 91, p. 45.
> "Watching the Canine Weight Championships." [WebR] (15) Spr 91, p. 91.
> "When We're Not Watching." [ColR] (NS 18:2) Fall-Wint 91, p. 132.
6896. ZIMMERMAN, Martha C.
> "Nemesis." [EmeraldCR] (3) 91, c1990, p. 74.
6897. ZIMMERMAN, Thomas
> "Iowa Summers Remembered." [Plain] (11:2) Wint 91, p. 18.
6898. ZINNES, Harriet
> "Pietà." [DenQ] (25:4) Spr 91, p. 97-98.
> "The Road Again." [NewL] (58:1) Fall 91, p. 115.
6899. ZIOLKOWSKI, Heidi
> "After Hours." [Pearl] (13) Spr-Sum 91, p. 19.
6900. ZIRLIN, Larry
> "Mary, Not Mommy." [HangL] (59) 91, p. 66-67.
6901. ZIZIK, Joel
> "A Third Kind of Moment." [Poetry] (158:3) Je 91, p. 145.
> "Why You Burn Photographs." [JamesWR] (8:4) Sum 91, p. 3.
> "Work." [JamesWR] (8:2) Wint 91, p. 5.
6902. ZOGHBY, Mary D.
> "Between the Waves: Thirty Years Later." [Paint] (18:35) Spr 91, p. 29-30.
6903. ZOLA, Jim
> "After Sex and Before What Follows." [InterPR] (17:1) Spr 91, p. 119.
> "Architect of Fire." [GreensboroR] (51) Wint 91-92, p. 50.
> "Blues Lesson." [CapeR] (26:1) Spr 91, p. 2.
> "The Boy Who Wandered" (Honorable Mention). [GreensboroR] (51) Wint 91-92,
>> p. 48.
> "Influence." [CapeR] (26:1) Spr 91, p. 1.
> "Puzzle." [InterPR] (17:1) Spr 91, p. 120.

"Rebuilding." [CinPR] (22) Spr 91, p. 47.
"Sirens." [CinPR] (22) Spr 91, p. 46.
"Uncle Ray." [GreensboroR] (51) Wint 91-92, p. 51.
"Upon Waking." [GreensboroR] (51) Wint 91-92, p. 49.
6904. ZOLYNAS, Al
"Love in the Classroom." [Spirit] (11) 91, p. 56-57.
6905. ZONTELLI, Patricia
"Backwards / Forwards." [SpoonRQ] (16:1/2) Wint-Spr 91, p. 20-21.
6906. ZSOLDOS, Imre P.
"Musing Upon" (about the Taiwan poet, Ho Tsai Hsiou-Lien and dedicated to her
husband, Dr. Ho Chio, tr. by the author, edited by Poetry USA). [PoetryUSA]
(22) Spr 91, p. 21.
6907. ZUBANOVIC, Slobodan
"Again the Morning" (tr. by Vasa D. Mihailovich). [InterPR] (15:1) Spr 89, p. 27.
"Bar 'Planik'" (tr. by Vasa D. Mihailovich). [InterPR] (15:1) Spr 89, p. 19.
"Buffet 'Planik'." [InterPR] (15:1) Spr 89, p. 18.
"Destruction" (tr. by Vasa D. Mihailovich). [InterPR] (15:1) Spr 89, p. 19.
"Exact Outcome" (tr. by Vasa D. Mihailovich). [InterPR] (15:1) Spr 89, p. 23.
"Opet Jutro." [InterPR] (15:1) Spr 89, p. 26.
"Poseta Sa Otvorenim Dijalogom." [InterPR] (15:1) Spr 89, p. 20.
"Sta Sam To Govorio." [InterPR] (15:1) Spr 89, p. 24.
"Tacan Ishod." [InterPR] (15:1) Spr 89, p. 22.
"Unistenje." [InterPR] (15:1) Spr 89, p. 18.
"A Visit with an Open Dialogue" (tr. by Vasa D. Mihailovich). [InterPR] (15:1) Spr
89, p. 21.
"What Did I Speak" (tr. by Vasa D. Mihailovich). [InterPR] (15:1) Spr 89, p. 25.
6908. ZUCKER, David
"Margaret Shamsky." [WebR] (15) Spr 91, p. 13-21.
"Slide Show." [NoDaQ] (59:3) Sum 91, p. 137-138.
6909. ZUCKER, Jack
"The Blackbird." [WebR] (15) Spr 91, p. 73.
"Protest for My Uncle" (1914-1954, Communist Party, U.S.A.). [WebR] (15) Spr
91, p. 70-72.
6910. ZUCKERMAN, Marilyn
"Letting Down Roots" (Wellfleet 1982). [Nimrod] (34:2) Spr-Sum 91, p. 126-127.
"Letting Down Roots" (Wellfleet 1982. Corrected reprint from 34:2, p. 126).
[Nimrod] (35:1) Fall-Wint 91, p. 114.
6911. ZUKOWSKI, Tadeusz
"LVIII. A Letter to My Mother Among Things" (tr. by Georgia Scott, David
Malcolm and Zbigniew Joachimiak). [WebR] (15) Spr 91, p. 41.
6912. ZULAUF, Sander
"Separation in Succasunna." [Spirit] (11) 91, p. 149.
6913. ZURLO, Tony
"The Slave Trade." [Plain] (11:3) Spr 91, p. 11.
"Yakubu's Covenant." [Plain] (11:2) Wint 91, p. 15.
6914. ZÜRN, Unica
"And If They Have Not Died" (for H.B., tr. by Pierre Joris). [Sulfer] (11:2, #29)
Fall 91, p. 81.
"Dans l'Attelage d'un Autre Age" (Line from a poem by Henri Michaux, tr. by Pierre
Joris). [Sulfer] (11:2, #29) Fall 91, p. 81.
"In the Dust of This Life" (tr. by Pierre Joris). [Sulfer] (11:2, #29) Fall 91, p. 80.
"The Lonesome Table" (tr. by Pierre Joris). [Sulfer] (11:2, #29) Fall 91, p. 83-84.
"Nine Anagrammatic Poems" (tr. by Pierre Joris). [Sulfer] (11:2, #29) Fall 91, p.
80-84.
"Once Upon a Time a Small" (tr. by Pierre Joris). [Sulfer] (11:2, #29) Fall 91, p.
80-81.
"The Strange Adventures of Mr K" (tr. by Pierre Joris). [Sulfer] (11:2, #29) Fall 91,
p. 82.
"Uncas, the Last of the Mohicans" (tr. by Pierre Joris). [Sulfer] (11:2, #29) Fall 91,
p. 84.
"Will I Meet You Sometime?" (tr. by Pierre Joris). [Sulfer] (11:2, #29) Fall 91, p.
82.
"You'll Find the Secret in a Young City" (tr. by Pierre Joris). [Sulfer] (11:2, #29)
Fall 91, p. 83.
6915. ZWIRN, Gail
"Community College." [Plain] (12:2) Wint 91, p. 33.

6916. ZYCHLINSKA, Rajzel
      "My Son" (tr. by Aaron Kramer). [Vis] (36) 91, p. 49.
6917. ZYDEK, Fredrick (Frederick)
      "Gathering Shells" (for Bonnie and Tom). [CapeR] (26:1) Spr 91, p. 20.
      "Gully." [HolCrit] (28:1) F 91, p. 17.
      "Ignoring Logical Explanations." [Pearl] (14) Fall-Wint 91, p. 58.
      "Leaving the Children Behind." [Pearl] (14) Fall-Wint 91, p. 59.
      "Moon Over Lopez" (for Hal & Millie Gillespie). [HolCrit] (28:2) Ap 91, p. 18.
      "Third Confession." [ChrC] (108:1) 2-9 Ja 91, p. 6.
6918. ZYMBOLY, Melissa
      "Never Rapunzel." [BellArk] (7:1) Ja-F 91, p. 1.

Title Index

Titles are arranged alphanumerically, with numerals filed in numerical order before letters. Each title is followed by one or more author entry numbers, which refer to the numbered entries in the first part of the volume. Entry numbers are preceded by a space colon space (:). Any numeral which preceeds the space colon space (:) is part of the title, not an entry number. Poems with "Untitled" in the title position are entered under "Untitled" followed by the first line of the poem and also directly under the first line. Numbered titles are entered under the number and also under the part following the number.

At the Hy-Vee : 2044.
At the Ice Palace : 6029.
At the Island : 3043.
At the Jungfrau : 2390.
At the Laundromat : 1600.
At the Lifeboat Races : 4354.
At the Melville Room : 3537.
At the Milliner's : 4389.
At the National Home : 4576.
At the North Cemetery : 3557.
At the North Window, Instead of a Lament :
    2169.
At the Piano : 6401.
At the Planning Commission : 4109.
At the Poetry Stacks of the Engineering College
    Library : 3537.
At the Point Where Lightning Strikes : 6056.
At the Polls : 3109.
At the Pond's Edge : 3845, 4251.
At the Rainbow : 6361.
At the Rally to Protest : 2492.
At the Reading (3) : 451.
At the Rest Stop : 6095.
At the Revenue Office : 5682.
At the Rural Writers' Conference : 2752.
At the Sati Temple, Bikaner : 1462.
At the Seams : 155.
At the Seminary Garden : 4564.
At the Sill : 1682.
At the Storms' Summons : 529, 6307.
At the Subway Station : 3126.
At the Supermarket : 6443.
At the Theater in Athens : 1029.
At the Threshold : 4223, 4536.
At the Train Station : 865, 3284.
At the Trenton State Hospital : 807.
At the Vacancy Sign : 5629.
At the Walt Whitman Rest Stop : 6496.
At the window I watch the nocturnal clouds
    pass : 2280, 3343, 6300.
At the Writers' Conference : 404.
At the Zoo : 672.
At Twenty-Eight Thousand Feet : 478.
At Two in the Morning, Say : 6799.
At War: Winter Night, Parliament Hill : 2884.
At Work on the Sabbath : 5544.
At Wovoka's Ghostdance Place : 640.
At Your Side : 5999.
Atget : 6302.
Atheist Conches : 170.
Athens : 3516, 5385.
The Atlantic Pilot's Bride : 1116.
Atlantis : 2309.
An Atlas of the Difficult World : 5086.
Atlas, or Another Picture of What Keeps the
    Earth Held Up : 5761.
The Atmosphere : 2119.
An Atmosphere of Heat : 4220.
Atropos : 182.
Attack : 93.
Attack of the Fifty-foot Woman : 1806.
Attack Virus : 3880.
The Attempt : 6862.

An Attempted Burial : 5292.
Attempted Treason : 5158.
Attempting Magic : 2989.
Attempting to Learn the Language of Love :
    5047.
Attention Shoppers : 2548.
Attention to Detail : 6059.
Attenuation : 4023, 5129.
Attic Martins : 2530.
Attraction : 2227.
Aubade : 233, 770, 2268, 2870, 3562, 4782,
    6256.
Auction : 3346.
The Auction : 3197.
Auden in Oxford Again : 5752.
Audition : 1874.
Audubon's Border Boy : 476.
August : 1800, 2793, 3082, 3319, 4990, 5806,
    5928.
August 5: Three Fathom Harbour to Hockey
    Island : 1016.
August 8, 1986 : 2042.
The August Constitutional : 5093.
August Depression, Winter Dreams : 1874.
August Fire : 5845.
August Full Moon of No Human Concern Iraq
    Invaded Kuwait : 4256.
August Is the Month of Leaving : 4353.
August Letter : 3718.
August Moon in Harlem, NY : 59.
August Orchard at Chico : 3634.
August Thirty-First, Nineteen Eighty-Nine :
    5426.
Aunt Anne Puts the Cat Out for the Last Time :
    1029.
Aunt Em : 4192.
Aunt Emma Collected Teeth : 4399.
Aunt Fannie : 858.
Aunt Ida Pieces a Quilt : 1465.
Aunt Joe Learns to Keep Her Balance : 6439.
Aunt Linda Speaks : 601.
Aunt Mamie's Ritual : 5263.
Aunt Margaret's Garden : 3097.
Aunt Mary Jean : 2818.
Aunt Maude's Pocketbook : 1841.
Aunt Melita Takes Another Captive : 747.
Aunt Millie's Money : 546.
Aunt Sara and the 4-Letter Word : 1056.
Aunt Sara and the Tattoo : 1056.
Auntie Anthem : 5307.
Auntie Ellen : 273.
The Aura of Distant Objects : 2449.
Aurora Borealis : 2272.
Aurora, New York : 3144.
Aus Meinem Leben : 6279.
Ausente la Esposa un Día : 5282.
Auspicious Clouds at the Wilderness Pavilion :
    3537.
Author, Author : 6507.
The Auto Show : 5237.
The Autobiographies of Parallel Children :
    3719.
Autobiography : 130, 5112.

The Couple : 271.
Couplets : 687.
Courage : 2165.
The Courage Not to Talk : 2574.
Courtroom : 5900.
Courtship : 3281.
Couscous : 2305.
Cousin Gifts : 345.
Cousins : 3082.
The Cousins : 2950.
Cousteau in Normandy : 42.
Cove : 867.
Covenant : 2237, 2907, 6864.
Coventry : 1179.
Cover : 287.
Cover Note : 4097.
Cow : 753, 1669.
Cow Feeding on the Grass in the Park in the
    Front of City Hall : 5118.
Cow Monologue : 2402.
Cow Tipping : 6027.
Cowboys and Indians : 2181.
Cows : 1243, 4657.
The Cows : 5152.
Cows and Alabama Folklore : 6415.
Cow's Neck : 5743.
The Cows of Shambat : 3617.
Cowtalk : 45.
Coyote Night : 3657.
Coyote Ring 1 : 6779.
Coyote Ring 2 : 6779.
Coyote Ring 3 : 6779.
Crabs eat my sad fish heart : 5815.
Crack : 4928.
The Cracked Planet : 311.
Crackers : 995.
Cracking a Few Hundred Million Years : 112.
Cracking Eggs : 810.
Cradle : 3614.
Crane and Chancellorsville : 3610.
Cranes on the Platte at Sunset : 1505.
Craniology : 816.
Crank : 2163.
Crap Shoot : 5250.
Crappie Fishing : 5723.
The Crash : 2735.
Crazy Billy : 2326.
The Crazy Girl : 5963.
The Crazy Landlord : 4120, 6066.
The Crazy Poet : 6810.
The Crazy Quilt of Spoons : 858.
The Crazy Tenant : 4120, 6066.
La Creacion : 830.
Cream of Tomato Soup : 5348.
Creating a fist : 5364.
Creation : 4260, 4700.
The Creation : 4753.
Creation Myth : 2817.
Creative Writing : 5536.
Creativity : 2056.
Creatures of Habit : 6112.
Creatures Who Must Know Better Have Taken
    Me for a Blossom : 5896.

Credibility Gap : 3003.
Creeks in Berkeley : 2605.
The Crib Biter : 2326.
The Cricket in the City : 1547.
Crickets : 6532.
Crime : 3728.
Crime & Punishment : 4452.
Crimes Attempted in Daylight : 3856.
Crimson Cavity : 4332.
Cripple Creek Aforismos : 2750.
The Crippled Godwit : 539.
Crisis Clinic : 3266.
Critic : 3728.
Critical Habitat : 1055.
A Critique of Pure Reason : 2747.
Crno Brasno 41 : 6218.
The Croaker and Other Fish Who Try to Speak :
    4026.
The Crone Sings to the Bear : 3242.
The Cross at the Sea : 4702.
Cross Country Clouds : 2783.
Cross-Stitched : 4779.
Crossfire : 1917, 5500.
Crossing : 3563.
Crossing Cocytus : 5566.
Crossing Kansas in the Dark, 1977 : 3019.
Crossing open fields : 2445, 4374.
The Crossing Over : 519.
Crossing Ross-Shire : 1849.
Crossing the Appenines : 1064.
Crossing the Bosphorus : 3787.
crossing the bridge over the Mosel River : 643.
Crossing the Sea : 1578, 3468.
Crossing the Table : 527.
Crossings : 4171.
Crossroads : 4143, 5674.
Crow : 5272, 5801.
Crow String : 4272.
A Crown of Sonnets on the Transformation of
    the Escambia County Court of Records
    Building and County Jail into the
    Pensacola Cultural Center : 6122.
Crows : 4116, 6499.
Crows Across Tenotihuacan : 4632.
Crows Are Bad. Ducks Are Good : 6822.
The Crucifix Across the Mountains : 4930.
Cruising : 4550.
Cruising State : 740.
The Crumbling Infrastructure : 1457.
Crunching Numbers : 3230.
The Crusts : 2671.
Crybaby : 4477.
The Crying : 2685.
Crystal Ball : 5200.
Crystal Collecting : 309.
Cuando No Hay Agua : 4443.
Cuauhtemoc Calendar, and Cubism : 2821.
Cuckoo Clock : 6312.
Cuéntame : 5282.
Cully 005 : 6064.
Culpas : 6331.
Cultivation : 1243.
Cultural History : 3987.

Despairing of Understanding We Fall into
    Decadence : 6676.
Desperate Pioneers, the Toes : 3914.
Despite : 5602.
Destello : 602.
Destination: San Francisco : 6426.
Destinations : 4040.
Destroyers : 5142.
Destroying Old Loveletters : 3144.
Destruction : 4120, 6907.
Det Var en Gammel Natt : 2922.
Detail : 4481.
The Details : 5236.
The Details Get Lost : 1935, 3315.
Details of Myself : 5245.
Details of the Frozen Man : 1671.
The Detective Gone Bad : 2021.
Detective Story : 5443.
Determinate Flaws : 1067.
Determinism : 271.
Deuteronomy : 6001.
Deuteronomy, a little torque of extruded plastic
    : 135.
Device Found Accessible : 4885.
Devilfish : 5288.
The Devil's Music in Hell : 6170.
The Devoted Dead : 934.
D.H. Lawrence Writes to Katherine Mansfield :
    512.
Dia de los Muertos : 6361.
Diagnosis, Prognosis, Psychosis : 1289.
Dial a Date : 3565.
Dialectica del Amor : 61.
Dialectics of Love : 61.
Dialing and Dolor : 5162.
Dialog : 6155.
Diamond : 4105.
Diamond Jubilee Rose : 5832.
Diamonds : 472.
Diana : 359.
Diane, Before the Cheers : 5532.
Diaries of a Woman Who Does Not Care : 204,
    4936.
The Diary of a Suspicious Man : 2127, 6089.
A Diary of Dying : 3567.
Diary of the Departed : 2692.
A Diary of Water : 576.
Diasporas : 1580.
Dice : 2983, 3767, 4120, 5474, 6066.
Dick Alf : 4950.
Dick and Beth : 5227.
Dick Tracy Pursues Little Face Finny to Mount
    Olympus Where, Together, They Enter the
    Garden of the Gods : 4803.
Dickinson on Grace : 4978.
Dicks in the Desert : 1677.
Dictionary of Wilno Streets (1967) : 2237,
    2541, 4174, 4832.
Did She Put on His Knowledge with His Power
    : 4529.
A Didactic Poem : 2972.
Dies Irae : 238.
Diet of Worms : 1595.

The Difference : 2260.
The Difference Between Self-Abuse & Self-
    Destruction : 3426.
The Difference Three Makes: A Narrative :
    3831.
A Different Life : 2645.
Different Rains : 6318.
The Difficult Colour : 2172.
The Difficult Life of Ideas : 3672.
The Difficulty of Walking Through Walls :
    4200.
Digger Pays Off the Mortgage : 1309.
Digging for Fossils : 5368.
Digging to China : 4875.
Dignity : 948.
Dilemma : 4695.
Dim : 6290.
The Dim Light of Waking : 3971.
Dim Sum : 110.
Dimensions : 2913.
Diminished : 679.
The Din of Ringers : 1401.
Diner : 383.
Diner, Evening : 2011.
Dinner : 2031.
Dinner at Patsy's : 253.
The Dinner Guest : 5705.
Dinner Hour : 2865.
Dinner with Jerry : 6027.
Diogenes : 3663.
Diptera : 2182.
Directional : 2401.
Directions for Obtaining Knowledge of All
    Dark Things : 1538.
Directions for Surprise : 2096.
Directive : 1958.
Directive to the Old Ones : 2440.
Dirge : 2793.
Dirt : 6297.
Dirt Road : 2427.
Dirty Cups : 3819.
Dirty Dreams and God Smiling : 5206.
Dirty Laundry : 4565.
Dirty Movie : 6582.
Dis : 5784.
Dis ease : 5541.
Disappearances : 6817.
The Disappeared : 583, 5899.
Disappearing : 5166.
Disappearing Mountain : 4043.
The Disarming 'Language of the Birds' : 6184.
Disc Jocky Poem : 542.
Disciples : 6653.
Disciplines : 196.
Disco Disco : 6224.
Discourse on Life & Death : 4616.
Discovering America : 3855.
Discovering America! : 2447.
Discovering Columbus : 1059.
Discovery : 663.
Discovery in the West Delta : 6426.
Disease Without a Name : 2994.
Disenchantment : 959.

Early Gothic : 5852.
Early Morning — Ucross, Wyoming : 740.
Early Morning Vigil : 2969, 5370.
An Early Mystery : 1086.
Early November : 2134.
Early plum blossoms : 1860.
Early to Bed : 1935.
Earth : 1568, 4204, 4413.
Earth Crossers : 2566.
Earth Day Story : 5374.
Earth: Desdemona : 6794.
Earth to Earth : 3944.
Earthly Garments : 1247.
Earthly Things : 672.
Earthquake : 1115.
Earthquake under the Ocean : 1264.
EARTH's Answer : 2656.
Earthworms : 630.
Earthy Moorings : 4921.
Earworm : 3743.
East : 5165.
East Berlin Woods : 729.
East Crater Trail #48 (For Ron) : 6743.
East Side Morning : 4651.
East Texas June, 1939 : 3900.
Easter : 5469, 6606.
Easter and All That Jazz : 6445.
Easter at Cassis : 3992.
Easter Eggs : 3556.
Easter Evening : 200, 4223.
Easter, San Augustine : 5200.
Easter Sunday : 5449.
Eastering : 2747.
Eastern Massasauga Rattlesnake : 653.
Eastpoint : 359.
Easy : 1848, 5028.
Easy Rider : 6411.
Easy to Follow Instructions: Messages for
      Evolving Democracies : 4668.
Eat : 5782.
Eaten Zero : 5115.
Eating a Pomegranate in the Bath : 1222.
Eating an Artichoke : 6425.
Eating Salmon : 6317.
Eating Strawberries in the Necropolis : 2837.
Eating the Flesh : 6642.
Eating the Heart (of it) : 5323.
Eating the Kennedys : 3089.
Eating the Shadow : 2279.
Eating You : 2785.
Ebony : 1998.
Ecce Homo : 625.
Echoes : 5339.
Eclipse : 3541.
Eclogue : 1219.
École Normale Supérieure : 2117.
An Ecstasy : 1153.
The Ecstasy : 4571.
Ed Dying : 4216.
Edad : 1766.
Eddie : 3282.
The Eddie Carthan Case : 6170.
Eddie Priest's Barbershop & Notary : 6843.

Eden : 6748.
Eden in Winter : 1651.
Eden: The Last Exit : 6265.
Edgar Degas: 'Family Portrait (or the Bellini
      Family) 1858-1860' : 6073.
Edge : 520.
An Edge : 5934.
The Edge : 5476, 6244.
The Edge of Dreams : 2788.
The Edible World : 687.
Edith XXIV : 5697.
Edith Dyer Climbs Pike's Peak, July 3, 1930 :
      1166.
The Editor : 6341.
Edjication : 6690.
Education : 28.
The Education of Henry Admas : 6729.
L'Educazione Intellettuale : 4223.
Edward Clerihew Bentley : 5251.
Edward Hopper's *Room in Brooklyn* : 5866.
Edward Hopper's U.S.A. : 2504.
Eeyore : 5434.
Effect of : 3304.
Effects : 2299, 5423.
An Effigy of You : 2499.
Egg Crate Creation Poem : 1543.
Egg Harbor : 2217.
The Egg Lady : 2609.
Eggplant : 2024, 2860, 4117.
Eggplants : 6736.
Eggstone Goddess Image, Glastonbury Abbey :
      1156.
Ego Scriptor : 659.
Egoísmo : 6331.
An Egotistical Sublime : 677.
Egypt in Flaubert's Time : 1823.
Egyptian Woman : 1579, 1950, 2158.
The Eidolon : 6761.
Eight Acoustic Masks : 4712.
Eight long legs : 385.
Eight O'Clock on a January Morning at the
      A&P in Oxford, Mississippi : 6014.
Eight Years Old Listening to Classical Music
      and Because I Believed in God When I
      Was Young : 3508.
Eighteen: London, 1655 : 4455.
Eighth Sky : 4649.
'Eighty-Nine : 1037.
Eisenhower : 3392.
Either Way : 563.
Election Night : 6681.
Election Year : 3683.
Electric Elegy : 2237, 2907, 6667, 6863.
Electric Pearls : 4047.
Elegia Molisana : 1284.
Elegies 1-10 : 3621.
Elegist : 6497.
Elegy : 16, 480, 582, 1368, 1809, 3334, 4111,
      4797, 5354, 5473, 5516, 5887.
An Elegy : 399.
Elegy, 1822 : 4639.
Elegy 1942 : 5883.
An Elegy As Hanna Senesh : 6050.

The Friendship of Dogs : 3202.
Friendship with the Virign : 2443.
Frieze Advancing : 2399.
The Frigate Bird : 2855.
The Frightful Gila Monster : 3589.
The Frigid Wind : 778.
Fringe on the Coat, Coat on the Fringe : 1073.
The Frisbee of My Clavicle : 1955.
Frisco, 1899 : 880.
The Frivolousness of Intention : 711.
Frog Gig : 6026.
Frog Prince : 1548.
Froggy Goes-A-Hopping : 6442.
Frogs : 3322, 4399.
The Frogs : 5499.
Frogs and Wasps : 1045.
Frogs Come Out in Rain : 6386.
From a Buick Electra : 3720.
From a Cousin After Many Years : 2420.
From a History of Music : 1974.
From a Lost Notebook 3/89-6/89 : 5940.
From a Madhouse at Arles : 2299.
From a Paper Boat : 2108.
From a Small Town : 3376.
From a Terrible Fire an Escaped Flame : 3287,
    4120.
From a Time of Low Resolution : 4588.
From an Ancient Monastic Customary: Rules
    for Novices : 162, 225.
From an Island : 6095.
From an Old Notebook : 3193.
From Another Desert : 83.
From Blakesware: Mary Lamb : 476.
From Buffalo Gal to Coyote : 6296.
From Chagall's *Lovers in Venice* : 2050.
From 'Extinct Moon' : 6527.
From Fat to Happy : 845.
From Goya's Room : 155.
From Italy Near Naples : 3087, 5252.
From Lawn Mowers I Have Known : 1912.
from now on, i will call you : 643.
From Purgatory Mary Flannery Reflects on
    Peacocks : 3129.
From Taos to Santa Fe : 390.
From the Back & From the Front to Start :
    5264, 5468.
From the Barrens : 5944.
From the Bedroom Window : 1874.
From the Bestiary : 5631.
From the Cloister : 919.
From the Dark Room : 1642.
From *The Death of a Badman*, a New Dime
    Novel by Percy Gilmore, 1876 : 1166.
From the Diaries of Emily Winthrop : 2802.
From the Diary of Courtesan Yang : 3426.
From the Front : 4741.
From the Heartland : 6127.
From the Lives of Things : 2237, 2907, 6667,
    6863.
From the Northern Greek : 4935.
From the Notes : 2605.
From the Old Sewage Plant on Columbia Point
    : 1504.

From the Sierra Trail Calendar, 1983 : 1166.
From the Sonneteer's Sky Atlas : 6698.
From the Souk in Marrakesh : 5944.
From the Window : 6086.
From Twilight to Twilight : 170.
From What I've Heard about Alaska : 1956.
From Where Did God Get the Clay for Making
    Things? : 3617, 4707.
Front Porch : 6513.
A Front Range Sky : 6253.
The Frontier of Hindsight : 536.
Frontispiece : 208.
Frost : 3920, 4624.
Frost Tonight : 6152.
Frozen Hemlock : 6117.
Frugal : 4191.
The Fruit Cellar : 5312.
The fruit trees bloom at once : 6839.
The Fruit Trees Lose Their Blossoms : 6388.
Fruited by Function : 1648.
Frutas : 4698.
Frying Time : 4834.
Fucking : 5536.
Fucking Genius : 503.
Las Fuerzas de Indio : 4377.
Fugit Amor : 4539.
Fugitives : 3856, 6568.
Fugue : 2661, 2896, 4547.
Fugue of Death : 943.
Fulfillment : 4097.
Full Body Erection : 2217.
Full Moon : 6693.
Full Moon Ceremony : 5338.
Full Moon, Early Summer : 6281.
The Full Moon Heron : 3180.
Full Name : 1766, 3087, 5333.
The Full Night Still in the Street Water : 6836.
Fulô do Mato : 820.
The Function of Clouds : 6625.
The Function of Narrative : 6343.
The Function of Ornament : 4653.
The Function of the Individual : 6890.
Funeral : 5043.
Funeral Home : 760, 3984.
Funeral of a Portuguese Milker : 3966.
The Funeral of Homesickness : 4810.
Funeral Parlor : 5629.
Funeral Service for Abbie Hoffman : 5900.
Funereal : 6192.
A Fur-Cap, Pigeons : 4120, 6066.
Furnishings : 3779.
Further Documentation : 4978.
Fuselage Installation : 2636.
A Fusing of Diverse Waters : 1112.
Future : 6290.
Future? : 1243, 2153.
The Future : 113, 271, 717, 2218, 2393, 2429,
    5203.
Future Considerations : 4609.
Future Physicians' Club Field Trip, 1964 :
    2900.
Future Prehistory of Chile : 1243, 3567.
Future-Present : 5536.

Future Realism : 2934.

G.I. Joe : 138.

G17024 : 1090.

Gadding About : 1928.

Gagaku : 5105.

Gagaku: demons? some don't care for the mere word : 5105.

Gagaku: fresh poems are pouring out of him again at age 49 : 5105.

Gagaku: he thought more about her than himself : 5105.

Gagaku: last night a young japanese whore : 5105.

Gagaku: nothing a young waitress hates worse than an empty house : 5105.

Gagaku: the body that must die puzzles th'hell out of me : 5105.

Gagaku: the last time he lit the candle he burned his finger : 5105.

Gainesville, March : 6105.

Galiano Baby Grand : 6144.

The Gallery : 1154.

Gallery of Rivers : 567.

Galloway's Religious Killings, And the Lonely Language of Gaelic : 5622.

Game : 1143.

The Game : 1086, 1219, 5274.

Game 6, World Series, Bottom of the 10th, 2 Outs : 3814.

Game Called Because of Rain : 5287.

The Game of War : 617.

The Gamekeeper : 566, 1284.

Games : 1243, 6120, 6120, 6782.

Ganaderia : 4698.

Ganesh : 1791.

Gangland : 5535.

Gannet : 3694.

Gar : 6795.

Garbage : 2471.

Garbage Day : 580.

Garden : 3017, 3146, 5726.

The Garden : 672, 3207, 3420, 4385.

Garden at Evening : 5166.

The Garden at the Edge of the World : 611.

The Garden in October : 4720.

The Garden of Eden : 5461.

The Garden of the 9th of January : 526, 3308, 5463.

The Garden of the Living and the Dead : 2705.

The Garden of Theophrastus : 2816, 5631.

Garden Shed 1989 : 6391.

Garden Sundial : 2745.

The Garden Walk : 457.

The Gardener : 715, 4120, 5031, 6066.

Gardening : 1701.

Gardens : 3000.

The Gardens at I Tatti : 5828.

The Garlic: An Aetiological Tale : 3159, 5639.

Garnet : 6301.

Garter Snake : 4577.

The Gas Station : 6667.

Gasparillo Remembered : 2219.

The Gate : 5314.

The Gatekeepers : 331.

Gates Gets the Job : 6259.

Gates of Mars : 5745.

Gateway to Manhattan : 2835.

Gather : 506.

Gather Round Me : 6591.

Gathering : 5595.

The Gathering : 2921.

A Gathering of Men : 720.

Gathering Shells : 6917.

El Gato Barcino : 176.

Gauguin's Chair : 2388.

Gay Holly, O! : 6761.

Le geai ébouriffe au bord de la forêt l'encre : 3845.

The Gear Is Gone : 5114.

Geechie Women : 2996.

The Geese : 4666.

Gefryn : 6289.

The Geisha Box : 4781.

The Geisha House: The Black Kimono : 6599.

The Geisha House: The White Kimono : 6599.

Das Gelächter : 6177.

Gelatin : 4734.

Geldings Restored : 2881.

Gemini in the Forest : 2227.

Gender Specific : 287.

Gene Pool : 4375.

Genealogy Program : 1433.

The General and His Staff : 5770.

General and Nofret Rahotep : 3304.

The General Arena : 2156.

General Emotions : 2660.

A General History of Virginia : 5456.

The General on the Eve of His Military Parade : 1166.

The General's Briefing : 4146.

Generation : 3044.

Generic Love Poem : 4260.

The Generosity of Souls : 210.

The Generous Days : 5818.

Genesis : 2632.

Genesis Revised : 1751.

Genin — Darkness Visible : 1555.

Genius : 4806.

Genius of Fog at Ecola Creek Mouth : 4050.

The Gentle Man : 1575.

A Gentle One : 2657.

Genuflecting : 4291.

Geoffrey Chaucer Recants on His Death Bed : 1166.

Geographers : 6640.

The Geographic Center : 3333.

Geography : 1612.

Geography of a Body : 1635.

The Geography of Leaving : 1263.

Geologic : 5717.

Geophagy : 1364.

George Keats Sets Sail for America, 1818 : 1166.

George Rogers Clark (1752-1818) : 3011.

George Washington Bridge, Lower Level, Clear Day : 1098.

Grandma and Buddha : 3552.
Grandma Wulz : 3111.
Grandma's Button Box : 5976.
Grandma's Palette : 6674.
Grandmother : 1571, 1783, 5525.
Grandmother at the Mall : 5640.
The Grandmothers Clara and Madge : 5090.
Grandmother's Dance : 3464.
Grandmother's Poems : 4401.
Grandmother's Tree : 1802.
Grandpa : 1866, 6806.
The Grandsire Bells : 476.
Grandson's Rage : 61.
Grant Wood's Stone City : 5423.
Grape Stakes : 6874.
Graphics : 1067.
Grappling with the Cosmos : 2409.
Grasp : 2535.
Grass : 2091, 2592, 2922.
The Grasshoppers and the Ants : 6671.
Grateful : 3921.
Grating Parmesan : 1239.
Gratitude : 3099.
Grave-Digger : 1720.
The Grave of Literary Ambition : 6533.
The Gravedigger's Nightmare : 22.
A Gravedigger's Soliloquy : 1457.
The Graves of the Old French Settlement Near
     Hamburg : 858.
Graveside Talk with Grandma : 6642.
Gravestone Found in a Garage : 5921.
Gravestones : 4921.
Graveyard Shift : 88.
Graveyard Working : 2275.
Gravida 11 & the Dinka : 5225.
Gravities : 4356.
Gravity : 2338.
Gravity and Flight : 6302.
Gravity As a Consequence of Shape : 1824.
Gray Area : 6259.
Gray Bones Poke into a White Bird Cage :
     6118.
Gray Eyes : 6573.
Gray Marrow : 6001.
Gray Morning : 2553.
Gray Owl : 3935, 4487.
Grease : 1008.
Great Art, Great Criticism : 4050.
Great Brown Prince : 41.
The Great Dark : 902.
The Great Day of the Dead : 1322, 3026.
The Great Depression : 2557.
The Great Divide : 2156.
The Great Leap Forward: Cost Assessment,
     April, '82 : 3323.
Great, Marvelous Structures : 211, 3222, 5656.
The Great Mother : 2501.
Great Plains Dooryard : 5374.
Great-Uncles : 4099.
The Great Urinator : 1777, 4414.
The Great War: A Memory : 2114.
GreatBrownPrince : 41.
Greece, So They Say : 6586.

Greek : 2839, 2845.
A Greek Star : 1285.
The Greek Statuette : 1771.
Greek Torso : 6710.
Green : 1037, 2968, 3024, 3427, 3499.
Green Age : 263.
Green and Dying : 6718.
Green and Sharp : 2076.
Green Belt : 229.
The Green Bottle : 4466.
Green Chair on a Fire Escape in Autumn :
     1024.
Green Child: Poem 1 : 3039, 5468.
The Green Horns : 4567.
Green Is the Color of Blind Horses : 3063.
Green Kindness : 3997.
Green Light : 2922.
Green Linnaeus : 2237, 2907, 6667, 6863.
The Green Notebook : 1159.
Green River : 4272.
Green Wine : 1243, 1285.
The Greenhouse : 6105.
Greenhouses and Gardens : 3483.
The Greening of the Fire Escape : 384.
Greeting to a Paper Star Cutter : 2811, 3015.
Greg Taylor, Psychology Major : 6729.
Gregory : 3839.
Gregory of Bath on the Silk Road — a Frag-
     ment : 2974.
Gretel : 746, 1225.
Gretel II : 1225.
Gretel III : 1225.
Greuor Farm, North Wales : 150.
The Grey Breath : 3450.
Grid : 2615, 2953.
Grief : 4838, 5979.
Grieving a Teacher : 6607.
Grieving His Wife : 4917.
The Grieving Ring : 4493.
Griffin : 2526.
The Grinding of Teeth : 5810.
The Grip : 1540.
Gristle and Heron : 5730.
Gristlewolf : 5730.
The Gristmill's Trough : 6051.
Grizzlies : 1701.
Grocery Shopping, St. Petersburg, Florida :
     805.
The Ground : 5788, 5789, 6382.
Ground Round : 1752.
Grounded Angels : 59.
The Groundfall Pear : 2689.
The Grounds : 4555.
The Grounds at Lake Chebacco : 4641.
Group : 5788.
Grouse in the Garden : 6455.
The Groves : 1970.
Growing the Season : 3666.
Growing Up : 245.
Grown Old : 6767.
Grubbing Thistle : 5979.
Grudge Match : 4261.
Les Grues : 4010.

History Lesson : 26, 1637, 3866, 6877.
History Lessons : 3269.
A History of Aesthetics : 2419.
The History of Armenia : 279.
The History of Facial Expressions : 1034.
A History of Sears Roebuck : 2419.
The History of Shaving : 5719.
A History of Small Life on a Windy Planet :
　　1118.
The History of the World : 4653.
The History of Women in Space : 944.
Hit and Run : 6660.
Hit in the Head : 5916.
Hitching from Albuquerque to L.A. : 6656.
The Hive : 6838.
Hive Keepers : 6736.
L'Hiver : 402.
Hmong People at the Holloween Play : 307.
Hoagie : 1309.
Hoarfrost. The branches : 4322.
Hokusai in the Light of Print : 4256.
Hold on a moment : 2445, 4124.
Hölderlin's Grave : 2127, 6089.
Holding My Own : 5979.
Holding Patterns : 3236.
Holding You Up : 6643.
Holdup : 1454.
Hole : 5124.
The Hole : 444, 3280, 4569.
Holiday : 212, 297, 6731.
Holiday in Yuma : 2941.
Holidays Suck : 926.
Holland Avenue : 4377.
The Hollow Rain of the City : 5623.
Holly Oak, Delaware : 6653.
Hollyhocks on the Alley : 2052.
Hollywood Boulevard: Christmas Eve : 3156.
Hollywood Legend : 1830.
Hologram : 4881, 5370.
Holy Cross Hospital : 1409.
Holy Fire : 2150, 5788.
Holy Land : 4493.
The Holy Spirit : 6239.
Holy Thursday : 891, 1656.
Holy Water : 4148.
Holyrood Beach : 3142.
Homage : 1729, 2039, 4188, 5728.
Homage to Benvenuto Cellini : 940.
Homage to Gerolamo Marcello : 680.
Homage to Goya : 1084, 2369.
Homage to Lester Young : 5040.
Homage to Life : 2032, 6005.
Homage to Lucille : 4892.
Homage to Our Lady of the Strays : 1034.
Homage to the Corn : 1034.
Homage to the Square : 2216.
Homage to the Undertaker : 1034.
Homage to Velasquez : 1084, 2369.
Homage to William Shakespeare : 6720.
Homan's Etchings : 2605.
Home : 142, 279, 299, 3226, 3527, 4956, 6500,
　　6716, 6890.
A Home : 2384.

Home Again : 3398.
The Home Again of Noname Beginning : 1232.
Home Coming : 6617.
Home Early From Work : 6768.
Home Fires : 1118.
Home from Work : 1710.
The Home Front : 5938.
Home Galaxy — in August : 1444.
Home Ground : 3101.
Home, Home on the Harangue : 170.
Home Life : 4310.
Home Movie : 801.
Home Movies : 4287.
Home of the Brethren : 2085.
Home Ownership : 682.
The Home Place : 858, 4654.
Home Stay : 1805.
Home to Garden and Field V : 1843, 6087.
The Home Town Boys Mark Their Calendars :
　　4072.
Homecoming : 695, 5466.
Homecoming, With Cat : 2098.
Homeless : 4253.
The Homeless in America : 5589.
A Homeless Woman's Civic Center Plaza
　　Prayer : 2797.
Homeplace : 2767.
Homesick : 660, 1532.
Homesick for Spring : 3363.
Homestead : 6464.
Homesteading : 6256.
Hometown : 1495, 3693.
The Homing Birds : 3681, 6186.
Honey : 3004, 4272.
Hong's Geese : 5907.
Honking Horns : 1705.
Honorary Doctorate in Stone Chemistry : 204,
　　4936.
Hood : 3962.
The Hood : 4341.
Hooked : 6392.
Hooks : 4474, 6100.
Hookworm : 4416.
Hoop Dance : 914.
Hopalong Cassidy : 3856.
Hope : 261, 4984, 5250.
Hope Chest : 5948.
Hope in the Air : 444, 2869, 3280.
The Hopi Potter Nampeyo : 4228.
Hopkins' Expedition — 1812 : 5152.
Hopscotch : 6602.
Horizon : 6366.
Horizontal : 1935, 5788.
Horoscope : 1100.
Horror Film : 3940.
Horror Vacui : 3393.
A Horse Ballad : 2633, 6218.
Horse Hair Mattress : 3832.
The Horse in the Cellar : 2192.
The Horse Is Pounding Her Heart Out Below
　　the Silver Sky : 3539.
Horse Latitudes : 4639.
Horse of My Body : 1628.

Iblis : 5345.
Icarus : 3146, 5788, 5789, 6382.
Icarus and the Lad Graystone : 211, 3222, 5656.
Icarus on Stone Mountain : 2520.
Ice : 1309.
Ice Boats : 4063.
Ice Carver : 3147.
The Ice Climber (Upper Grindelwald Glacier) :
    6782.
Ice Clocks : 5264, 5468.
The Ice-Cream Return : 1283.
Ice Cream Won't Freeze Without Rock Salt :
    180.
Ice Fog : 3998.
Ice Seed : 2012.
Ice Storm : 1093.
Iceberg : 3482, 5095.
The Icelandic Consul : 1101, 2703.
Ici : 421, 482.
Icon : 601.
Icy Mountains, South Seas : 636, 4120.
I'd Rather Have a Running Vehicle Than
    Therapy : 1923.
Ida Lupino by Carla Bley (13) : 3038, 6883.
Idalou Spencer, My Eighth-Grade Teacher, Is
    Found Dead in the Middle of Summer :
    1807.
The Idea : 1232, 5961.
The Idea of Fine Souls : 6547.
The Idea of Russia : 526, 3308, 5463.
The Idea of the Holy : 996.
The Idea of What's Here : 478.
The Idea Who Dreamed Plato : 695.
Ideas : 4202.
Identification : 6132.
Identifying the Fire : 2950.
Identities : 967, 2319, 2715.
Ideogram: Father : 5303.
Ides of March : 4085.
The Idiot Box : 3043.
Idiot / M : 3405.
The Idle Wheel : 6436.
Idyll : 5871.
Idyll Worship : 314.
If : 1446, 3159, 4383, 5600.
If a Pattern Holds : 5089.
If All of Us Worry : 2492.
If Dreams Wrote the Story : 6024.
If Dying Means Becoming Pure Spirit : 5202.
If He'd Listen : 1166.
If I Could Play the Cello : 3695.
If I could suffocate within myself right now,
    I'm sure I would : 2222.
If I could take my son to a city off the map, if I
    were married : 6839.
If I Hadn't Met You : 2643.
If I Hold This Pen : 3698.
If I Were a Chef, I'd Say : 2574.
If I were a child I would write my name in red
    crayon : 5338.
If I Were a Swan : 2912.
If I Were Fire : 156, 5883.
If It Isn't Something It's the Fucking Phone :
    3093.

If It Were Human, the Ear Would Look Like a
    Banker : 3914.
If Not in the Field Then Where : 3110.
If Not Shadows of Men : 6182.
If One Should Be Thought a Freak Because Of :
    1232.
If Porcelain, Then Only the Kind : 299, 6500.
If pressed to compare : 2445, 3801.
If She Could Only : 5778.
If the Last Words I Speak Are 'Piet Mondrian' :
    2182.
If the Truth Hurts, Wear It : 4092.
If There Is a Hell, It Is the Threat of Hell :
    3539.
If There Weren't Any Trees : 2032, 6005.
If This Quilt of Names Were Made of Fire :
    130.
If Those Bodies Are Only Objects : 1232.
If Two Slovenly Herky-Jerky : 5172.
If We Should Meet : 3212.
If Wishes Were Feline : 5073.
If You Are a Poet : 1408, 1664.
If You Can't Stand the Heat : 4064.
If You Could See Me : 1618, 4522.
If You Cut Your Finger, Bandage the Knife :
    6204.
If You Knew What Sununu (Reprise) : 6259.
If You Must Scream, Do It Quietly : 299, 6500.
If You Wish : 2867, 6330.
If You're an Indian, Why Don't You Write
    Nature Poetry? : 79.
Ignoring Logical Explanations : 6917.
IKON : 5550.
Iliad (Book III, lines 310-78) : 2766, 4075.
I'll Have It to Go : 751.
I'll Make a Good Wife : 3869.
I'll Not Go Donw That Street : 5280.
I'll Take You There When Spring Returns :
    4251.
Illinois Primer : 601.
The Illuminated Blake : 4726.
Illusion : 3070, 5467, 5709.
Illusion from a Quilt by Louise Williams :
    4050.
Illustration : 4879.
I'm afraid Daddy : 6577.
I'm Always Coming Across the South : 4028.
I'm Confessin' That I Love You : 1647.
I'm Dating : 1068.
I'm Falling Out of Love With You : 1018.
I'm Flattered : 751.
I'm glad I'm at Green Bank, where I map
    neutral : 391.
I'm Going Where the Women Point : 452.
I'm in a lion's trench, plunged in a fort : 2301,
    3781.
I'm leaving you for another man : 3029.
I'm Married and My Daddy's Rich Too : 1161.
I'm not sure : 445.
I'm Sorry : 2698.
I'm Talking Fast to My Sister on How to
    Sharpen an Axe : 130.
I'm wearing your robe : 2445, 4603.

Jacuzzi : 1219.
Jade : 3870.
Jade Plant : 3175.
Jael : 3224.
A Jaguar for Jack : 2177.
Jailhouse Games : 2787.
Jaipur to Delhi : 1257.
Jakarta Airport : 1257.
Jam in Midsummer : 6312.
A Jamaican Airman Foresees His Death : 1287.
Jamais Vu : 6112.
James Dean's Jacket : 3141.
James Gutmann Greets Mark Van Doren :
      3313.
James Madison Chandler, 1962 : 965.
James Wright: In Memory : 6325.
James Wright, Richard Hugo, the Vanishing
      Forests of the Pacific Northwest : 3993.
Jamy : 1723.
Jan : 3531.
January : 3565.
January 1, 1965 : 536.
January 13, 1991 : 4083.
January 22, 1990 : 4114.
January 1991 : 5655.
January 1991 at Langley/Porter Psychiatric
      Institute : 3095.
January in Wisconsin : 6892.
January of '36 : 1582.
January Rain : 4069.
January Thaw : 1780, 3140.
Japanese Carp in the Pond: Maui : 1380.
Japanese Elegy for My Grandmother : 5720.
The Japanese Garden Bridge : 6755.
Japanese Spring : 2466.
The Jape of the Mock : 1314.
Jardin du Luxembourg : 3891.
Jars : 4691.
The Jar's Story : 1161.
Jason and Medeia : 173, 2295.
Jason at School : 5263.
Jaws : 1667.
Jazz : 3675, 6166.
Jazz in the Garden : 575.
(J.D.) : 1460.
Jealousy : 46.
Jealousy and the Things You Are Not : 2311.
Jealousy: The Mirror : 6667.
Jean Giono's *Blue Boy* : 2572.
Jefferson's Arch : 2740.
Jennifer on a Quiet Night : 4846.
Jeremiah : 5067.
Jericho : 3791.
Jerome : 3728.
Jerry : 2434.
Jesse James at the Apollo : 5860.
Jessehelms : 3652.
Jessie : 2687.
Jesus in Madrid : 2081.
Jesus in Muncie : 2717.
Jesus Is in Love with Russia : 5602.
Jesus of My Youth : 6570.
Jeu de Paume: Paris : 2786.

Jewel Net : 5338.
Jeweler's Hammer : 500.
The Jewell : 6788.
The Jewels : 361, 3989.
The Jewish Problem : 5536.
A Jewish Woman's Poem: Not in Your Mu-
      seum Anymore : 50.
Jiggers : 728.
Jillian *am Klavier* : 3645.
Jim Barnett's Pigs : 6614.
Jim Rice, Viewing the Fenway Wall : 4718.
Jimmy : 833.
Jim's Donut Shop : 6713.
Jingsheng Does Not Regret His Crime : 1236.
J.J. Muscles : 1814.
Joachim of Fiore : 3630.
Joan Armatrading : 2427.
Joan Outside : 6134.
Joanne's Birthday Breakfast : 2441.
The Job : 3437.
Job and His Accusers : 3483.
Job's Daughters : 1809.
Joe, Born 1895 near Bean Blossom Creek,
      Indiana : 4560.
Joe Dimaggio Never Swings a Bat at Old
      Timers' Games : 6225.
Joe Krausman : 6650.
The John Ball Park Zoo : 4338.
John Berryman's Bridge : 336.
John Bryan in Clifton Gorge : 2161.
John Donne : 4535.
John / Henry : 1976.
John Hollander : 586.
John Keats after His Lost Letter : 4727.
John, that passionate man, in his action tower :
      1173.
John the Baptist Day : 668.
John the Baptist Who Lives in the Suburbs :
      6179.
John Wayne Memorial Airport : 4807.
John Wesley Orman: *In Utero*, on VCR : 4539.
Johnny (The Torso) : 5675.
Jolene: Earth : 5196.
Jon Olson : 3692.
Jonah and the Whale : 4184.
Jones / Baraka : 121.
Joshua : 6054.
Jotting : 3159, 3280, 4570.
The Journal : 2683.
Journal 7/22/90: The Feminist Writers Work-
      shop : 3350.
Journal Entries : 2623.
Journey : 384, 1399.
The Journey : 5949.
A Journey by Tricycle : 6631.
Journey to Orchard House : 3873.
A Journey Woman's Travel Log : 686.
Journeying : 5388.
Journeys : 2876.
Jóvenes Poetas : 185.
Joy Kogawa at La Quena : 466.
Joyce : 6383.
Joyce on the French Coast Waiting for the Dark
      : 4288.

Mayday : 5823.
The Maze : 2876.
Mazurka : 4510.
Me : 5850.
Me and Evelyn : 2708.
Me and Marilyn in Beulah's Mind : 4403.
Me and Paul Newman : 666.
Me Aproximo a la Realidad Subterranea : 3856.
Me, My Dog, and Our Pornography : 5586.
Meander : 3034.
Means and Ends : 4382.
Means of Flight : 3293.
A Measure of Light : 6125.
Measurement : 5039.
Meat : 3269.
Meat-Gatherers : 5219.
Medals: A Processional of Rooms : 567.
Medea Has Forgotten How to Cry : 590, 3293.
Medea to Jason : 2679.
Medical News on the Night : 4939.
Medical Report (Ashau Valley, 1969) : 2155.
The Medicated Procession to the Ten Dollar
	Grave : 4525.
Medicine : 4656.
Medicine Bag : 6172.
A Medicine Song : 2620.
Medicine Stone : 1200.
Medieval Times : 5987.
Meditation #1 : 4256.
Meditation #3, and When Asked : 4256.
Meditation #4 : 4256.
Meditation #8, the Emotions : 4256.
Meditation at Dave's Foxhead : 5586.
Meditation from a Beer Joint : 2963.
Meditation on a Skull Carved in Crystal : 2410.
Meditation on Ambition at Triple Creek —
	Ucross, Wyoming : 740.
A Meditation on Bob Kaufman : 298.
A Meditation on Chopin : 3072, 4486.
Meditation on Chuang Tzu : 4795.
Meditation on Dante's 'Divine Comedy' : 5180.
A Meditation on Death : 3072, 4486.
A Meditation on Lust : 6880.
Meditation on Nietzche's Death Mask : 2020.
Meditation on the Domestic : 4795.
Meditation on the Three Forms of Tongue
	Protrusion : 1034.
Meditation Upon Ought : 6290.
Meditations of Mr. Cogito on Redemption :
	876, 878, 2631.
Meditations on Marie : 2400.
Medium Green : 5601.
Medusa's Dread Locks : 700.
Meet : 3652.
Meet the Family : 6726.
Meeting : 3867.
Meeting My Birthmother : 1709.
Meeting the Bear : 4516.
Meeting with Mary Magdalene : 724.
Meetings in Poultry : 4617.
Mehinaku Indian : 438.
Meine Muse : 559.
Melancholy days : 2445, 6071.

Melancholy of the Second Echelon : 480, 6096.
Melancholy Waltz : 3262.
Melanie Soffa : 1942.
The Meld, or Eclat of Your Pillow-Talk : 1232.
Melinda: Dawn : 116.
Melody : 775, 1392.
Melted Crayons : 1147.
Melting Pot : 4978.
Melville : 6302.
Melville and His 'Battle-Pieces' : 3610.
Memento Mori : 182, 1904.
Memento Mori: Pajamas He Fell Away from Us
	In : 4050.
Memo : 2877.
Memo: Van Leer Containers Ltd., Lagos,
	Nigeria : 2732, 4621.
Memoir of the Magician's Girl : 2739.
A Memorable Fancy : 3159, 3280, 4570.
Memorial Day : 2773, 4924.
Memorial Quilt, Central Park : 5050.
Memorial Weekend, Sargent's Beach : 3220.
Memories : 60, 6713.
Memories Are Made Of : 3304.
Memories at Times Are Solid Things : 2170.
Memories of Canada : 5422.
Memories of Marie : 654, 4245.
Memory #28 : 1598.
Memory and Imagination : 233.
Memory and Metamorphosis : 4868.
The Memory of Fingers : 2595.
Memory of My Father : 6772.
Memory of the Future? Prophecy of the Past? :
	6045.
Memory of the Hand : 2221.
Memory of the Oregon Trail : 1128.
Memory of Tomorrow : 5216.
Men : 4794, 5738, 5850.
The Men : 4759.
Men at My Father's Funeral : 3885.
Men begin to resemble the idealogical [sic] con-
	structs : 135.
Men Can Leave : 5444.
Men Holding Eggs : 2828.
Men Like That Are Great : 3565.
'Men Must Live and Create. Live to the Point
	of Tears.' Camus : 4983.
Men of Ballymena : 5797.
The Men of Mars : 2494.
Men Waiting in a Gynecologist's Office : 819.
Menace from Space : 5843.
Mènage : 3793.
The Mendicant Sends a Declaration by Regis-
	tered Letter : 5254.
Mending Socks : 2818.
Mengele's Bones : 3748.
Menjacnica : 3764.
Mennonite Funeral on the Olentangy : 3019.
Men's Slow-Pitch : 1477.
Mental Hospital : 6847.
A Mention of Some Lucky Pay-Offs : 751.
Menu of Head : 5808.
Mercedes Contemplates a Dive off Macmillan
	Wharf : 5490.

Minha Casinha : 820.
Miniatures : 5664.
The Miniaturist : 5052.
Minigolf Love, Corsica : 1309.
Minimal Audio Plays : 3286.
Mining Country IV : 211, 3222, 5656.
The Mink : 2392.
The Minks : 1409.
A Minnesota Norseman Asks for a Viking
    Funeral : 3144.
Minnow : 2912.
Minor Earthquake : 695.
The Minor Manchu's Daughter : 2245.
The Minor Poet : 2921.
Minos in Taurus (The Minos Who Had No
    Minus) : 5946.
The Minotaur Next Door : 4657.
The Minotaur Sutra : 1871.
Minuet in G : 4071.
Minutes of a Poetry Reading at Rocky Point :
    6386.
Mira un momento atrás : 5133.
Miracle : 1528, 1935, 5788.
The Miracles : 5490.
Mirage : 711.
El Mirage : 1013.
Miranda Cries, Father's Raping Me and
    Blaming It on Caliban : 2256.
Miriam : 252, 5042.
Miriam and Her Urn : 6278.
The Mirror : 1496, 4002, 5620.
Mirror in the Men's Room : 2255.
Mirror, Mirror : 2830.
Mirror Talk : 1567.
Mirrors and Memory Do Lie : 6682.
Mirrors Still : 1465, 5511.
Mis-Diagnosis : 5867.
Mis Tias se Despiden : 176.
Miscarriage : 3278.
The Misconstrued : 439.
Misdemeanors : 79.
Misericordia : 1925.
The Misfits : 5154.
Misreading Housman : 4685.
Miss Calculation Learns the Facts : 505.
Miss Intensity Meets the Holy Ghost : 4348.
Miss Mattie Poems : 6695.
Miss Tammy Receives a Caller : 5704.
Miss Truesdale : 6426.
Miss Vermilion : 1641.
Miss Zhou's Essay Concerning Solitude : 1631.
Missing : 5145.
Missing Fingers : 5829.
Missing It : 5312.
The Missing Man : 2130.
Missing Mom : 4326.
Missing Person : 6268.
Missing the Moon : 2725.
Missing the Mulberries, Missing the Black Caps
    : 3565.
Mission Boulevard : 1111.
Missionary Graveyard : 6243.
Mississippi Gothic : 3689.

Missoula, Montana : 5680.
Missouri : 271.
Missouri Air : 5295.
Missouri Summer : 1262.
Mist and Fire : 90.
Mistake : 6521.
Mistakes : 3857.
Mister Hanusevich : 2541, 4174.
Mister Varsey : 5787.
Misty Sky : 361, 2399.
A Misty Start : 4955.
Mix of Securities : 6041.
Mládí : 1809.
Mnemosyne : 1787, 2736.
Mobil Station : 1981.
Mobley : 3164.
Moby II : 3238.
Moby-Dick : 6163.
Mock-General : 5813.
Mocking Bird Again : 3588.
Modalities : 6460.
Models : 3227, 4383.
Modern African Stories 1 : 53.
Modern Birth : 6206.
A Modern Chinese Image : 4938.
Modern History : 1951.
Modern Life : 2299.
Modern Love : 1400.
Modern Poetry : 3141.
Modern Western Romance : 4323.
Mohawk Land Dispute: Red Sanctuary : 2347.
Mole : 4256.
The Mole Beatitudes : 13.
Molecule Daisies : 3880.
The Mole's Dream : 6619.
Molisan Elegy : 566, 1284.
Mollusk : 6772.
Molly : 3146.
The Moment Before the Song Begins : 1858.
The Moment of Green : 4097.
The Moment of Truth : 4839.
A Moment with Apples : 501.
Momentary Suicides : 4520.
Mom's Thunderbird : 1234.
Mon Semblable, Mon Frère : 1199.
The Monarch of Meritocracy : 2681.
Monastery : 2338.
The Monastery : 1365.
The Monday Funeral : 5161.
Monday Morning : 5588.
Mondays on this Island : 1795.
Monet's Beard : 1818.
Monet's Venice : 1768.
Money : 5149.
The Money I Am Worth Is Singing : 4352.
Money's Worth : 1647.
The Mongoose Letters : 5732.
Monhegan Island, Maine : 6158.
Monkey Fur : 4288.
Monkey on the Ceiling : 965.
Monologue of the Rich Fool : 6134.
Monopause : 6268.
Monsters : 3787.

National Insecurity : 1974, 6241.
A Native American View of Columbus's
   Voyage : 6259.
Nativity : 4306.
The Natural : 6729.
Natural History : 3120.
Natural Science : 5740.
Natural Selection : 3856.
Nature : 1935, 4188, 6081, 6082.
The Nature of Things : 5358.
Nature on Television : 1533.
Naufragios : 5131.
Naughty : 3961.
The Navajo Hear about a U.F.O. : 392.
Navajo Rain : 5177.
The Navigators : 145, 3527.
NB as Gungu Master : 6766.
Ne Me Demandez Pas Pourquoi Je Ne Ris Plus
   : 4634.
Neanderthal : 2747.
Near : 564.
Near Arco, Idaho 1971 : 5220.
Near Burning : 4720.
Near Charles Olson's Home in Worcester : 538.
Near-Death : 6343.
Near Eldorado : 3907.
Near Ephesus : 2594.
Near Ice-out : 1029.
Near Macpherson National Cemetery : 1851.
Near McNeil Point : 3830.
Near Pigeon Key : 2788.
Near Rapid City : 1444.
Near the atomic plant : 72.
Near the Danube : 3267.
Near the End : 4702.
Near the End of the Twentieth Century,
   Brighton Beach : 4115.
Near the Hospital : 1594.
Near the Mediterranean : 2493.
Near the Supposed Gravesite of Loyalist
   Officers : 1900.
Near the Top : 316.
Nearbeer & Riots : 1928.
Nearly Nowhere : 6460.
Nearly Working : 2836.
Nebraska, It Was Nebraska and I Remember
   What Day of the Week It Was : 2286.
Nebraska, October : 5042.
Nebraska Sandhills : 5217.
Necessary Distances : 6306.
Necessity, Certainty, Questions to Ask : 3854.
A Neckeverse : 276.
The Need for Maps : 5283.
Needle's Eye : 1044.
A Needle's Eye : 6821.
Needy Relatives : 3914.
Nefertiti in Berlin : 3944.
Negative Confession : 4550.
Negotiable Demands : 3238.
Neighbor : 1376, 3173.
The Neighborhood : 273, 3974.
Neighborhood Meeting : 6148.
The Neighborhood Speaks : 675.

Neighbors : 2073, 5871.
The Neighbors : 3300.
Neighbors Near the Fence : 3711.
The Neighbors' Renovation : 6607.
Neighbour : 3126.
Neighbourhoods : 5981.
Neighbours : 3482.
Neil's View : 2181.
Neither Father Nor Lover : 1976.
Nelson at Lake Sammamish, 1970 : 1294.
Nelson Bentley : 232, 6729.
Nelson Bentley, Poet: 1918-1990 : 2879.
Nemesis : 6896.
Neo-Mountain Man : 4807.
The Neo-Natal Intensive Care Unit : 2786.
A Neoteric, the Nemesis : 3622.
Nero to His Mirror : 4858.
Nero's Last Word : 1166.
Nero's Warning : 932, 5180.
Nerstrand Woods : 5553.
Nerve : 2407.
Nerve Gas : 697.
The Nest : 4212.
Nest and Lodge : 5305.
Net Murder at Sea : 3699.
Neurology: In Theory : 5035.
Never Again : 6600.
Never at the Horse at Two : 3159, 5107.
Never Go on a Picnic with an Artist : 1754.
Never Rapunzel : 6918.
Never Say Die : 3109.
Never Seen Volcanoes : 5456.
The New : 6889.
New Adirondacks : 118.
New Age Rebel : 1445.
New Bill Meyer Stadium : 5195.
New Birth : 925.
New Clothes : 5077.
New Creature : 1758.
New Days : 5236.
The New Dress : 747.
New England Nights : 338.
New England Primer : 3313.
A New Exile Talks of His Country : 287.
The New Geometry and the Little Blue Heron :
   4978.
New Grass : 1092.
New Haven, 1969 : 4239.
The New Intimacy : 1258.
New Jerusalem : 1683, 5603.
New Lady : 3685.
The New Laws of Contracts : 3025.
New Leaf : 1330.
The New Life : 5236.
A New Man : 6537.
The New Man : 6834.
New Mexico : 5284.
New Mexico Style : 2227.
New Moon : 2388.
The New Moon : 5771.
New Music : 3690.
New New Poetics : 2427.
New Orleans : 2932.

Sister Mary Appassionata to the Eighth Grade Boys and Girls on the First Degree of Lust: *Visus*, Sight : 1034.
Sister Mary Lucinda : 1421.
Sisters : 322, 1044, 2183, 2644.
Sisters — Manele Beach : 322.
Sistrum : 4223, 4536.
Sisyphus : 44, 6068.
Sit : 2730.
Sit Down Meals : 1177.
Sit Down, Socrates : 5842.
Sitka, Alaska, Hidden Faces : 5213.
Sittin'-Log Blues : 1658.
Sitting in a Field on a Windy Day : 2317.
Sitting in Front of the Fire : 6120, 6782.
Sitting in the Children's Library in an Orange Chair Facing the YA Fiction Shelf : 6404.
Sitting Outside, at the Cabin, Nightfall : 1150.
Situation : 2292.
Situation Ethics : 920.
The Situation Room : 1839.
Situations Theoretical and Contemporary : 3496.
Six : 5610.
Six Goodbyes : 3266.
The Six Moral Virtues: Grace, Style, Class, Humility, Kindness, and Wisdom : 6676.
Six of One : 2399.
Six Sonnets for Leigh : 3124.
Six Ways of Believing : 4424.
Six Years Later : 680, 6649.
Sixteenth Century, Brush and Ink: A Hermit on a Riverbank : 2190.
The Sixth Grade Reader : 2446.
Sixth Sense : 1359.
Size : 460.
Skagit Flats : 232.
Skamonkas Kisos / Corn Moon : 729.
Skater : 2926.
The Skaters : 4963.
Skating : 1953.
Skeletons : 879, 2714.
Skeletons in the Closet : 5913.
Sketch : 2490, 4775.
Sketch for an Elegy : 1554.
Sketches of Mysore City : 3033.
Sketches of Spain : 3624.
Skill of the Heart : 240.
Skin : 1848, 2069, 2724.
Skin Diving : 5181.
Skin of Glass : 1303.
Skink : 3949.
Skinny-Dipping : 751.
Skipping Breakfast : 5259.
Skipping School : 762.
Skirt : 2427.
The Skunk : 1184, 5829.
Skunk Cabbage : 2106.
Skunk Hour : 3662.
Skunk Lingering : 6051.
Sky : 287, 4913.
Sky e Me, Eagle : 980.
Sky Lab : 2091, 2592, 2922.

Skylights : 2005.
Skywriters over Tokyo : 206.
Skywriting : 2685, 6380.
Slade Addamson Visits Tucson, AZ : 6836.
Slag : 4272.
Slam, Dunk, & Hook : 3269.
Slamdance : 4593.
Slant Acres : 4272.
Slash Art : 4030.
Slate Juncos : 2455.
Slattery's, in Ballsbridge : 459.
The Slaughterhouse : 4172, 4173, 5973.
Slave Ship : 4801.
Slave Ships : 3938.
The Slave Trade : 6913.
Sledding on Piedmont Street : 6596.
Sleep : 444, 1043, 1097, 6237.
Sleep (After Jimenez) : 4387.
The Sleep of Beasts : 1153.
Sleep Returning : 507.
Sleep Sonnet : 5486, 6177.
The Sleepers : 1429.
Sleeping Alone, Sleeping Together : 4260.
Sleeping Gypsy : 4239.
Sleeping in Space : 5096.
Sleeping Late : 6579.
Sleeping on the Floor of an Empty House : 5200.
Sleeping on Your Side Too Much : 5506.
Sleeping Room Only : 1764.
Sleeping Sickness : 5874.
Sleeping Together : 124, 3530.
Sleeping with the Black Dog : 5937.
Sleepless : 4493.
Sleepsonnet : 5486, 6177.
Sleepwalk : 3104.
Sleepwalker : 3321.
The Sleepwalker's Ballad : 2992.
Sleepy's Entrance : 2399.
Sleight of Hand : 1606.
Slender Pines in Smoky Light : 174.
Slepac : 6066.
A Slice of Palestine : 781.
Slicing Ginger : 501.
A Slide into the Pacific : 5916.
Slide Show : 5850, 6908.
Sliding Home : 2326.
A Slight Chill : 4112.
Slipping by Degrees : 5320.
Slocan North : 6533.
Sloughter : 4272.
Slow Dancing by Blue Neon : 3693.
Slow Down Construction : 665, 976, 1655, 1845, 4093.
Slow Freight : 3069.
Slow Movement in G : 397.
Slow River : 2960.
Slow Runner : 3166.
Slow Train : 4143.
Slow Work : 3885.
Slug Dance : 5855.
Slutty Flowers : 5562.
Small Barbarism : 5918, 6488.

Startled by the 'l's : 2900.
Starvation in the Sudan : 3609.
Stasis : 6467.
State of the Art : 3790.
The State of Things : 4019.
State Schools in the 1970's : 3783.
State Visit : 3517.
Stations : 1575, 4312, 5114.
A Statistician to His Love : 2212.
The Statue : 776.
Statues : 4319.
Stay : 6765.
Staying Home from Work : 3230.
Staying in One Place : 2543.
Staying within the Lines : 4947.
Steadfastness : 225.
The Stealing Moon : 5018.
Stealing Peaches : 3220.
Stealth : 1, 666.
Steel : 729.
The Steel Drivin' Man : 5101.
Steepletop : 4729.
Stellar Vision : 3004.
Stendahl at Trieste : 4450.
The Stendhal Syndrome : 4662.
A Step : 399.
Step by step :some key : 4737.
Steps : 6396.
Stereotypes : 1482.
Sterling Diner : 791.
Stigmata : 1268.
Still I Hope : 142, 3527.
Still Life : 1350, 1759, 4984.
Still Life, 1933 : 1128.
Still Life Abroad : 5202.
Still Life in Amherst : 6709.
Still Life in Grays and Blues : 491.
Still-Life Movie of America : 5257.
Still-Life on a Matchbox Lid : 6783.
Still Life with Jacket : 271.
Still Life with Lemons : 567.
Still Life with Women : 3354.
Still on Purity : 142, 3527.
The Still Place : 5969.
Still Praying : 814, 1742, 4277.
Still Winter (Spring) : 5700.
Stillbirth : 5460.
Stillborn : 6256.
Stillshot : 2245.
Stilltrauma : 5430.
Stillwater Canticles : 695.
Stinging Nettles : 2231.
Stockbridge, Massachusetts : 1131.
Stocks and Bonds : 1102.
Stoking the Fire : 1342.
Stomping the Beaver Palace : 6558.
Stone : 4351.
Stone & Carver : 2942.
The stone casts a shadow : 5344.
Stone Forest : 267.
Stone Gatherer : 4963.
The Stone Gift : 5649.
A Stone of the First Water : 2853.

Stone Rose: a Letter from the Eocene : 3951.
The Stone Sea : 2775.
Stone Soup : 1659.
Stone Tip the Flight of the Arrow : 2048.
Stone Village : 4097.
The Stone with a Woman's Mouth : 4473.
Stonecarver : 4539.
The Stonecutter : 1372.
Stonehenge : 6743.
Stones : 3397, 3651, 3722.
The Stones : 3089.
The Stones and the Stars I Have Often : 1232.
Stones of My Flesh : 506.
Stones of Soweto (A Mourning Poem) : 4587.
Stony Brook on Long Island : 601, 2959.
Stooge : 2309.
Stopping by Woods to Find My Golf Ball : 692.
Stopping on Two Photographs in the University
    of Nevada at Reno Athletic Hall of Fame
    Catalog : 3931.
Stopping to Buy Bread on the Way to the
    Cemetery : 1998.
Stopping to Dance : 1931.
Le Storie Letterarie : 4223.
The Storied Year : 2319.
Stories : 5777.
Stories from the Body : 1560.
Storm : 285, 751, 1957, 2827, 3192, 6508.
The Storm : 2360.
Storm at Sunset : 5668.
The Storm Flag : 2538.
Storm in the Briar Patch : 174.
'The Storm Is Passing Over,' She Sang : 3945.
Storm Porch, at Thirteen : 5786.
Storm Warning : 6582.
Storm Watch : 6302.
Storms : 5376.
Storms We Can't Name : 3648.
Story : 369, 2621, 2864.
A Story : 5562.
The Story : 421, 3236.
The Story As Told by Ice : 1008.
Story from a Greek Island : 2020.
The Story Goes On : 996.
The Story of a Soul : 3807.
The Story of Breathing : 1850.
The Story of Creation Told by St. Louis, the
    'Show Me' Saint : 5831.
The Story of Keys : 2021.
The Story of Mist : 1587.
The Story of My Life : 5663.
The Story of My Name : 2214.
The Story of the Plates and other Stories : 5748.
The Storyteller : 672.
The Storytellers : 875, 6348, 6349.
Straight Outta Truth : 2119.
Straight-Pins : 3892.
The Strange Adventures of Mr K : 3039, 6914.
Strange Country : 3997.
Strange Days : 3458.
Strange, Lean Woman : 6233.
A Strange Menagerie of Golden Monsters :
    1455.

The World : 6261.
The World According to Bird : 3272.
The world 'as got me snouted jist a treat : 1402.
The World Before the Story of Jonah : 42.
The World Famous Davenport Brothers : 111.
The World in My Mother's Hair : 2163.
The World Is a Still Life : 601, 3756.
The World Pub : 5243.
The World Quite Springs from Habit : 4662.
World Sadness : 4349.
The World They Went Into : 3120.
World War 2 : 3565.
The World War One Movies : 751.
World Wars Might Happen : 5168.
World Without End : 860, 2453.
Worlds : 1310.
Worm Becomes Bird : 154.
Worship in the United States : 2093.
[The Worst Thing Seems to Be the Balance] :
    6883.
Worth Reading About : 6411.
Would You Know a Snook, or a Large-eyed
    Whiff, from a Goggle-eyed Scad, Should
    the Necessity Arise? I Thought So : 2190.
The Wound : 2851.
The Wound-Dresser : 3762.
Wounded Doll : 2569.
Wounded Knee (1890-1990) : 5353.
Wounds : 4450.
The Wounds of Life and the Glass Heart of
    Love : 278.
Wounds of War : 2653.
Wrapped : 1118.
Wrapping the Body : 3750.
The Wrath of Medea : 440.
A Wreath from Egil's Saga : 4883.
A Wreck : 707.
Wrecking Yard : 1513.
Wrecks : 3890.
Wren : 6175.
The Wrens Are Back : 1226.
Wrens As perfection : 6260.
The Wrestler's Heart : 5795.
Wrestling with the Angel : 3302.
The Wristwatch : 3431.
Writ in Water : 6567.
Write 'Care of' : 5018.
The Writer : 825.
The Writers Ancestral Sense of Place : 4143.
The Writer's Carousel : 4143.
Writers' Colony : 1239.
Writing : 4188, 4290, 6434.
Writing Back : 606.
Writing Down the Holes : 3397.
Writing Home : 6340.
Writing II : 145, 6883.
Writing Is Like Someone Leaving : 6717.
Writing Italian Christmas at 'The Foreigner's
    Desk' : 1848.
Writing Off : 2800.
Writing on Silence : 3928.
Writing the Day : 1267.
Writing Van Gogh : 5884.

Writing Van Gogh 2 : 5884.
Writing Van Gogh 3 : 5884.
The Writing Workshop : 2937.
Written on My Side : 6219.
Written on the Head of a Pin : 6618.
The Wrong Coat Home : 1092.
Wynn, the Letter W, Rune of Joy and Illumina-
    tion : 5930.
X : 4358.
X-Ray : 2508.
Xanía, 1983 : 1024.
Xenia : 280, 1529, 2602.
Xenia I : 200, 4223.
Xerox of a Photograph of Bergen-Belsen :
    6736.
Xian #3 : 267.
Xian #4 : 267.
Xingang Zhong Lu : 5286.
XXX : 2845, 3215, 4925, 5861.
Y K 61 : 1101, 5125.
Y Si Vieras : 5187.
Yacht Brokers : 632.
Yahrzeit : 4208.
Yakubu's Covenant : 6913.
Yakutat : 5520.
Yaller : 6690.
Yankee Doodle Dharma : 922.
The Yanks : 3267.
The Yard : 271.
Yard Sailing in San Francisco : 3160.
Yard Sale: Charlotte, NC : 4884.
Yasamak : 3332.
The Yeah, Yeah, Yeah Imperative : 6838.
[Year] : 2082, 6387.
The Year 1984 : 1321, 3746, 6782.
The Year Drops Anchor, Tihany : 444, 2869,
    3280.
Yearly Facts and Figures of the U.S. Mail :
    6539.
Yearning for the Red Leaves of Xiang Shan :
    3550, 6818.
Yearning to Repossess the Body : 4823.
Years : 3043.
The Years : 3581.
The Years She Saved : 4768.
Yeast : 2156.
Yeats Moves You : 5283.
Yellow : 653.
Yellow Blue Tibia : 276.
Yellow Comb : 5444.
Yellow Leaves : 5698.
The Yellow Sky Mentions Tornadoes : 4343.
Yellow Slips into White : 3071.
The Yellow Star That Goes with Me : 2296.
Yemanja : 241.
The Yeoman Sings : 5442.
Yes : 1511.
Yes I'd : 2498.
Yes, We Have No Nirvanas : 3537.
Yes, Well : 1875.
Yes, Yes, I Offered Him a Cigarette : 459.
Yesterday : 4690, 5027, 5514.
Yesterday I Scattered Lime : 2838.